THE OXFORD HAND

CW01648094

MEDITATION

Meditation techniques, including mindfulness, have become popular wellbeing practices. The scientific study of their effects has recently turned 50 years old. But how much do we know about them? What were they developed for and by whom? How similar or different are they? How effective can they be in changing our thoughts, feelings, behaviour, and biology? What are their social, spiritual, and ethical implications?

The Oxford Handbook of Meditation is the most comprehensive volume published on meditation, written in accessible language by world-leading experts on the science and history of these techniques. It covers the development of meditation across the world and the varieties of its practices and experiences. It includes approaches from various disciplines, including psychology, neuroscience, history, anthropology, religious studies, and sociology, and it explores its potential for therapeutic and social change, as well as unusual effects.

Edited by practitioner-researchers, this book is an essential guide for all interested in meditation, including teachers, clinicians, therapists, researchers, or anyone who would like to better understand this topic.

Miguel Farias is the founder of the Brain, Belief, & Behaviour Lab at Coventry University, a former Lecturer at the University of Oxford, and a regular speaker at science festivals. He received the William Bier award from the American Psychological Association for his work on the psychology of spiritual practices and beliefs.

David Brazier is president of the International Zen Therapy Institute, author of a dozen books and many chapters and articles on Buddhism, psychology, and culture. He holds professional qualifications in psychotherapy, social work, and management, and is an authority on Buddhist psychology. He lectures on Buddhism and Buddhist psychology in Europe, Asia, and North & South America and supervises educational programs in English and Spanish.

Mansur Lalljee is an Emeritus Fellow of Jesus College, University of Oxford. He has published on a wide range of psychological issues concerning social relationships including the psychology of respect; the psychology of explanation; religion; social and political attitudes; and interpersonal communication. He has been invited to talk on these issues at conferences and in universities around the world.

OXFORD LIBRARY OF PSYCHOLOGY

The Oxford Handbook of Adult Cognitive Disorders
Edited by Michael L. Alosco and Robert A. Stern

The Oxford Handbook of Eating Disorders, 2e
Edited by W. Stewart Agras and Athena Robinson

The Oxford Handbook of Group and Organizational Learning
Edited by Linda Argote and John M. Levine

The Oxford Handbook of Cyberpsychology
Edited by Alison Attrill-Smith, Chris Fullwood, Melanie Keep, Daria J. Kuss

The Oxford Handbook of Personality Assessment
Edited by James N. Butcher

The Oxford Handbook of Workplace Discrimination
Edited by Adrienne J. Colella and Eden B. King

The Oxford Handbook of Personality and Social Psychology, 2e
Edited by Kay Deaux and Mark Snyder

The Oxford Handbook of Infant, Toddler, and Preschool Mental Health Assessment, 2e
Edited by Rebecca DelCarmen-Wiggins and Alice S. Carter

The Oxford Handbook of Evolutionary Psychology
Edited by Robin Dunbar and Louise Barrett

The Oxford Handbook of Spontaneous Thought: Mind-Wandering, Creativity, and Dreaming
Edited by Kieran C.R. Fox and Kalina Christoff

The Oxford Handbook of Voice Perception
Edited by Sascha Frühholz and Pascal Belin

The Oxford Handbook of Hope
Edited by Matthew W. Gallagher and Shane J. Lopez

The Oxford Handbook of Psycholinguistics, 2e
Edited by Gareth Gaskell

The Oxford Handbook of Positive Emotion and Psychopathology
Edited by June Gruber

The Oxford Handbook of Music Psychology
Edited by Susan Hallam, Ian Cross, and Michael Thaut

The Oxford Handbook of Social Psychology and Social Justice
Edited by Phillip L. Hammack

The Oxford Handbook of Stress and Mental Health
Edited by Kate L. Harkness and Elizabeth P. Hayden

The Oxford Handbook of Moral Development: An Interdisciplinary Perspective
Edited by Lene Arnett Jensen

The Oxford Handbook of Internet Psychology
Edited by Adam Joinson, Katelyn McKenna, Tom Postmes, and Ulf-Dietrich Reips

The Oxford Handbook of Job Loss and Job Search
Edited by Ute-Christine Klehe and Edwin van Hooft

The Oxford Handbook of Parenting and Moral Development
Edited by Deborah J. Laible, Gustavo Carlo, Laura M. Padilla Walker

The Oxford Handbook of Stigma, Discrimination, and Health
Edited by Brenda Major, John F. Dovidio, and Bruce G. Link

The Oxford Handbook of Deaf Studies in Learning and Cognition
Edited by Marc Marschark and Harry Knoors

The Oxford Handbook of 4E Cognition
Edited by Albert Newen, Leon De Bruin, and Shaun Gallagher

The Oxford Handbook of Attention
Edited by Anna C. Nobre and Sabine Kastner

The Oxford Handbook of Clinical Child and Adolescent Psychology
Edited by Thomas H. Ollendick, Susan W. White, and Bradley A. White

The Oxford Handbook of Group Creativity and Innovation
Edited by Paul B. Paulus and Bernard A. Nijstad

The Oxford Handbook of Organizational Citizenship Behavior
Edited by Philip M. Podsakoff, Scott B. MacKenzie, and Nathan P. Podsakoff

The Oxford Handbook of Digital Technologies and Mental Health
Edited by Marc N. Potenza, Kyle Faust, David Faust

The Oxford Handbook of Sexual and Gender Minority Mental Health
Edited by Esther D. Rothblum

The Oxford Handbook of Psychological Situations
Edited by John F. Rauthmann, Ryne Sherman, David C. Funder

The Oxford Handbook of Human Motivation, 2e
Edited by Richard Ryan

The Oxford Handbook of Integrative Health Science
Edited by Carol D. Ryff and Robert F. Krueger

The Oxford Handbook of Positive Psychology, 3e
Edited by C.R. Snyder, Shane J. Lopez, Lisa M. Edwards, Susana C. Marques

The Oxford Handbook of Dialectical Behaviour Therapy
Edited by Michaela A. Swales

The Oxford Handbook of Music and the Brain
Edited by Michael H. Thaut and Donald A. Hodges

The Oxford Handbook of Expertise
Edited by Paul Ward, Jan Maarten Schraagen, Julie Gore, and Emilie M. Roth

The Oxford Handbook of Singing
Edited by Graham F. Welch, David M. Howard, and John Nix

The Oxford Handbook of Evolutionary Psychology and Behavioral Endocrinology
Edited by Lisa L. M. Welling and Todd K. Shackelford

The Oxford Handbook of Autism and Co-Occurring Psychiatric Conditions
Edited by Susan W. White, Brenna B. Maddox, Carla A. Mazefsky

The Oxford Handbook of Adolescent Substance Abuse
Edited by Robert A. Zucker and Sandra A. Brown

THE OXFORD HANDBOOK OF

MEDITATION

Edited by

MIGUEL FARIAS,
DAVID BRAZIER,
AND MANSUR LALLJEE

OXFORD
UNIVERSITY PRESS

OXFORD
UNIVERSITY PRESS

Great Clarendon Street, Oxford, OX2 6DP,
United Kingdom

Oxford University Press is a department of the University of Oxford.
It furthers the University's objective of excellence in research, scholarship, and education by publishing worldwide. Oxford is a registered trade mark of Oxford University Press in the UK and in certain other countries

© Chapters 1–24 and 26–43 © Oxford University Press 2021
Chapter 25 © Pew Research Center 2021

The moral rights of the authors have been asserted

First published 2021
First published in paperback 2025

All rights reserved. No part of this publication may be reproduced, stored in a retrieval system, or transmitted, in any form or by any means, without the prior permission in writing of Oxford University Press, or as expressly permitted by law, by licence or under terms agreed with the appropriate reprographics rights organization. Enquiries concerning reproduction outside the scope of the above should be sent to the Rights Department, Oxford University Press, at the address above

You must not circulate this work in any other form
and you must impose this same condition on any acquirer

Published in the United States of America by Oxford University Press
198 Madison Avenue, New York, NY 10016, United States of America

British Library Cataloguing in Publication Data
Data available

Library of Congress Cataloging in Publication Data
Data available

ISBN 978-0-19-880864-0 (Hbk.)
ISBN 978-0-19-898556-3 (Pbk.)

Links to third party websites are provided by Oxford in good faith and for information only. Oxford disclaims any responsibility for the materials contained in any third party website referenced in this work.

Advisory Board

JARED LINDAHL
WILLOUGHBY BRITTON
GAVIN FLOOD
RONALD PURSER

Acknowledgments

The planning and making of this Oxford Handbook have been a considerable journey. We are especially indebted to those at Oxford University Press who have walked it with us from the beginning: Charlotte Holloway and Martin Baum. The copyediting team was equally extraordinary, and we are very grateful to S. Manikandan and Katherine Ulrich. Thank you also to Elizabeth Morales for designing the Meditation Tree.

We have been heavy-handed editors with our benevolent group of authors. Our Advisory Board substantially assisted us in this task with their detailed comments: Jared Lindahl, Willoughby Britton, Gavin Flood, and Ronald Purser.

None of this would have been possible without the long stream of women and men who have created and passed on the variety and wisdom of meditation practices.

Table of Contents

List of Contributors

Juhn Y. Ahn is Associate Professor of Buddhist and Korean Studies at the University of Michigan. He is the author of *Buddhas and Ancestors: Religion and Wealth in Fourteenth-Century Korea* (University of Washington Press, 2018). Ahn's research focuses on the history of Chan/Zen Buddhism and also the history of wealth, weather, and the monastic economy in fourteenth- and fifteenth-century Korea.

Katherine M. Auty is a Senior Research Associate in the Prisons Research Centre, Institute of Criminology, University of Cambridge. Katherine received her PhD in forensic psychiatry from Barts and The London School of Medicine and Dentistry in 2013. Her research interests include prison yoga and meditation programs, and their relationship to prisoner well-being.

Manu Bazzano is a psychotherapist, psychotherapy supervisor, and internationally recognized lecturer and author. He tutors philosophy, psychotherapy, and creative writing at the University of Cambridge. His latest books are *Nietzsche and Psychotherapy* (Routledge, 2019) and *Re-Visioning Existential Therapy: Counter-traditional Perspectives* (Routledge, 2020). In 2004 he was ordained in the Soto and Rinzai tradition of Zen Buddhism.

David Brazier is President of the International Zen Therapy Institute and author of a dozen books and many chapters, monographs, and articles on Buddhism, psychology, and culture. He lectures on Buddhism and Buddhist psychology in Europe, Asia, and North & South America and supervises educational programs in English and Spanish. He has practiced meditation for over fifty years.

Inti A. Brazil is an Associate Professor at the Donders Institute for Brain, Cognition and Behaviour. His research is primarily focused on the cognitive and neural mechanisms driving behavioral change in offender populations. He has been involved in research related to the usefulness of interventions, such as yoga and meditation, in facilitating change of behavior in both general and incarcerated populations.

Willoughby B. Britton is an Assistant Professor of Psychiatry and Human Behavior and the Co-director of the Clinical and Affective Neuroscience Laboratory at Brown University Medical School. Her research investigates the neurophysiological and psychological effects of contemplative practices in both clinical and non-clinical samples and settings, with a focus on moderators of outcome, practice-specific effects, and adverse effects.

Candy Gunther Brown is Professor of Religious Studies at Indiana University and the author or editor of six books, most recently *Debating Yoga and Mindfulness in Public Schools: Reforming Secular Education or Reestablishing Religion?* (University of North Carolina Press, 2019). Dr. Brown has served as an expert witness in four legal challenges to school meditation and yoga—testifying for both parents and school districts.

Ivana Buric is a Marie Skłodowska-Curie Fellow at the University of Amsterdam. Her research focuses on examining mind-body interventions with approaches from different disciplines, including psychology, molecular biology, and cognitive neuroscience.

B. Rael Cahn is Assistant Professor of Psychiatry and Director of the USC Center for Mindfulness Science at the University of Southern California. Dr. Cahn is a neuroscientist and psychiatrist focusing on researching the neurophysiologic bases and clinical impact of meditative practices, psychedelic psychotherapy, and other integrative psychiatric approaches.

Etzel Cardeña holds the endowed Thosen Chair at the Department of Psychology, Lund University, Sweden, where he directs CERCAP, Center for Research on Consciousness and Anomalous Psychology. He has more than 350 publications and is the senior editor of *Varieties of Anomalous Experience*, the two volumes of *Altered Consciousness: Mutidisciplinary Perspectives*, and *Parapsychology: A Handbook for the 21st Century*, among other books.

Douglas E. Christie is Professor of the Theological Studies Department at Loyola Marymount University in Los Angeles. He is the author of *The Word in The Desert: Scripture and the Quest for Holiness in Early Christian Monasticism* (Oxford), *The Blue Sapphire of the Mind: Note for a Contemplative Ecology* (Oxford) and is the founding editor of *Spiritus: A Journal of Christian Spirituality* (Johns Hopkins). He has been awarded fellowships from the Luce Foundation, the Lilly Foundation, and the National Endowment for the Humanities. From 2013–2015 he served as Co-director of the Casa de la Mateada study abroad program in Córdoba, Argentina, a faith-based program rooted in the Jesuit vision of education for solidarity. He lives in Los Angeles.

David J. Cooper, a researcher in the Department of Psychiatry and Human Behavior at Brown University, has worked on the Varieties of Contemplative Experience Project since 2014. Cooper received an M.A. in Religious Studies from the University of California, Santa Barbara, where he focused on Buddhist traditions. His research interests include narrative and social dimensions of religious experience, particularly those relating to the sense of self and to the body.

Patricia Lynn Dobkin is an Associate Professor in the Department of Medicine at McGill University in Montreal, Canada. She is a clinical psychologist specialized in mind-body medicine and is a certified Mindfulness-Based Stress Reduction (MBSR) teacher. Her two books on mindful medical practice showcase how the MBSR program has been adapted for health care professionals.

Dusana Dorjee is Associate Professor of Psychology in Education at the University of York in the UK. Dr. Dorjee is a cognitive neuroscientist and psychologist investigating the core neurocognitive and psychophysiological mechanisms of meditation from a developmental perspective, mostly in the context of education.

Miguel Farias is the founding director of the Brain, Belief, and Behaviour Lab and an Associate Professor and at the Centre for Trust, Peace, and Social Relations, in Coventry University. Previously he was a lecturer in Experimental Psychology at Oxford University. His book with C. Wikholm, *The Buddha Pill: Can Meditation Change You?* (2015), has been translated into various languages.

Nathan Fisher is a PhD student in Religious Studies and Cognitive Science at the University of California, Santa Barbara. He was formerly the research coordinator of the Varieties of Contemplative Experience Project at the Clinical and Affective Neuroscience Laboratory at Brown University, and his current research interests include Abrahamic contemplative traditions and dynamical approaches to cognitive and clinical science.

Gavin Flood FBA is Professor of Hindu Studies and Comparative Religion at Oxford University. He has worked on Hindu Tantric traditions and has research interests in comparative religion and hermeneutical phenomenology. Among his books are *Religion and the Philosophy of Life* (2019) and *The Truth Within: A History of Inwardness in Christianity, Buddhism, and Hinduism* (2013).

Kieran C. R. Fox is a neuroscientist in the Department of Neurology and Neurological Sciences at Stanford University. Dr. Fox's research focuses on the neural basis of higher human capacities, including meditation, mind-wandering, creativity, and consciousness. He is currently an MD candidate at Stanford's School of Medicine.

Jessica Frazier is a University Research Lecturer in Theology and Religion at Oxford University and a Fellow of the Oxford Centre for Hindu Studies. Her work explores key philosophical themes across cultures, from Indian concepts of "Being" to 20th-century Phenomenology. She is the founding editor of the *Journal of Hindu Studies* and an occasional contributor to BBC programs. Her books include *Hindu Worldviews: Theories of Self, Ritual and Reality* (Bloomsbury, 2017), and *Categorisation in Indian Philosophy* (Ashgate, 2014).

Ann Gleig is an Associate Professor of Religion and Cultural Studies at the University of Central Florida. She is author of *American Dharma: Buddhism Beyond Modernity* (Yale University Press, 2019) and co-author with Lola Williamson of *Homegrown Gurus: From Hinduism in America to American Hinduism* (SUNY Press, 2013).

Madhav Goyal is an Assistant Professor at Johns Hopkins School of Medicine. He is an internal medicine physician whose research focuses on the effects of meditation on health, pain, and chronic symptoms.

Conrad Hackett is Associate Director of Research and Senior Demographer at Pew Research Center. At Maryland Population Research Center, he is a visiting research professor. He studies global religious change and the demographic characteristics of religious groups.

Georgios T. Halkias is Associate Professor of Buddhist Studies at the University of Hong Kong. His research focuses on Tibetan Pure Land Buddhism, Indo-Tibetan Vajrayāna traditions, Himalayan Studies, and Buddhism and Hellenism in India and Central Asia. He is the co-editor-in-chief of the *Oxford Encyclopedia of Buddhism*.

Cyril Hovorun is Professor of Ecclesiology, International Relations, and Ecumenism at the Stockholm School of Theology/Sankt Ignatios College in Sweden. He has published books and articles covering the fields of patristics, ecclesiology, ecumenism, and public theology.

Richard King is Emeritus Professor of Buddhist and Asian Studies at the University of Kent. He has published numerous books and articles on Hindu and Buddhist philosophy, postcolonial theory and the study of India, theories of religion, and spirituality and capitalism. His books include: *Early Advaita Vedānta and Buddhism* (1995), *Orientalism and Religion* (1999); *Selling Spirituality* (2005), and *Religion/Theory/Critique* (2017, Ed.).

Laurence J. Kirmayer is James McGill Professor and Director of the Division of Social and Transcultural Psychiatry, McGill University, Canada. He is editor-in-chief of the journal *Transcultural Psychiatry* and directs the Culture and Mental Health Research Unit at the Jewish General Hospital in Montreal, where he studies cultural contexts of illness and healing. He is a Fellow of the Canadian Academy of Health Sciences and the Royal Society of Canada.

Louis Komjathy 康思奇 is an independent scholar-educator and translator. He researches and has published extensively in contemplative studies, Daoist studies, and religious studies, with specific interests in contemplative practice, embodiment, and mystical experience. He is founding co-chair of the Daoist Studies Unit (2004–2010) and the Contemplative Studies Unit (2010–2016) in the American Academy of Religion. In addition to over thirty academic articles and book chapters, he has published nine books to date, including *Taming the Wild Horse: An Annotated Translation and Study of the Daoist Horse Taming Pictures* and *Introducing Contemplative Studies.* He lives on the Northshore of Chicago, Illinois.

Scott Kugle serves as Professor in the Department of Middle Eastern and South Asian Studies at Emory University in Atlanta, USA. His fields of expertise include Sufism, Islamic society in South Asia, and issues of gender and sexuality. He is the author of seven books, including *Sufis and Saints' Bodies: Corporeality and Sacred Power in Islam* and *Sufi Meditation and Contemplation: Timeless Wisdom from Mughal India.* He conducts research in India and Pakistan, on Sufi ethics and sacred music, while his research languages are Arabic, Urdu, and Persian.

Martin Laird, OSA, is Professor of Early Christian Studies at Villanova University, USA. Laird has written a host of books and articles on early Christian thought and

Christian contemplative life, including *Into the Silent Land*; *A Sunlit Absence*; and *An Ocean of Light*. He lectures widely throughout the United States, the United Kingdom, and Ireland.

Mansur Lalljee is an Emeritus Fellow of Jesus College, University of Oxford. He has published work on a wide range of psychological issues including the psychology of respect; the psychology of explanation; religion; social and political attitudes; and interpersonal communication. He has been an editor of the *European Journal of Social Psychology* and the Chair of the Social Psychology Section of the British Psychological Society.

David Lewis is an independent researcher of Western and Eastern philosophical and psychological traditions at The Center for Trauma and Contemplative Practice, and a long-time Buddhist practitioner under the tutelage of the late Gelek Rimpoche and others. He is a retired computer scientist, mathematician, and software professional, and served in that capacity on the faculty at Brown University, Cornell University, and Ithaca College.

Jared R. Lindahl is Visiting Assistant Professor in the Department of Religious Studies at Brown University. At Brown, he is also affiliated with Contemplative Studies and is co-director of the Clinical and Affective Neuroscience Lab. His work on the Varieties of Contemplative Experience Research Project is emblematic of his broader interest in bringing an interdisciplinary perspective to bear on the range of contemplative practices and resultant experiences.

Tim Lomas is a Senior Lecturer in positive psychology at the University of East London. Since 2013, Tim has published numerous papers and books relating to well-being, involving topics that include linguistics, mindfulness, Buddhism, gender, art, and cross-cultural enquiry. His current main area of research involves creating a lexicography of untranslatable words relating to well-being (www.drtimlomas.com/lexicography).

Kaveh Monshat is a consultant psychiatrist, psychotherapist, researcher, and a mindfulness and non-violent communication teacher. He completed his doctorate and held an academic post at the University of Melbourne, Australia.

Ayesha Nathoo is a Senior Honorary Research Fellow at the University of Exeter where she recently completed a Wellcome Research Fellowship for the project "Cultivating Relaxation in Twentieth-Century Britain." She is a cultural historian of modern medicine, and her current research focuses on holistic healthcare, healing, and the development of mind-body medicine. She has previously held Research Fellowships at Clare Hall, University of Cambridge, and at the Science Museum, London.

Doug Oman is a Professor at UC Berkeley's School of Public Health, having taught there since 2001. His research investigates spirituality/religion and health and includes two randomized trials of spiritual meditation. He directs a training program on spirituality and public health and edited *Why Religion and Spirituality Matter for Public Health: Evidence, Implications, and Resources* (Springer, 2018).

David W. Orme-Johnson is Professor Emeritus of Psychology at Maharishi International University, where he was a founding faculty member in 1972, serving as chair of the psychology department and director of its doctoral program. Orme-Johnson has over 100 publications on the effects of the Transcendental Meditation and other meditation techniques, having pioneered in meditation's effects on stress reduction, prison rehabilitation, health, neurophysiological effects, and cognitive abilities.

Michal Pagis is Associate Professor of Sociology at Bar-Ilan University, Israel. She is the author of *Inward: Vipassana Meditation and the Embodiment of the Self* (Chicago, 2019). She studies transformations of self and identity in contemporary culture and has published on meditation, life-coaching, spirituality, and the intersection of religion and popular psychology.

Tomer Persico is the Scholar in Residence for the Shalom Hartman Institute in the San Francisco Bay Area, and the Koret Visiting Assistant Professor of Jewish and Israel Studies at UC Berkeley. His fields of study are contemporary spirituality, Jewish renewal, Jewish religious extremism, and forms of secularization and religiosity.

Ronald E. Purser is Professor of Management at San Francisco State University. His recent writings critically examine Buddhism's encounter with modernity and capitalism, particularly in corporate settings. He is the author of eight books, including *McMindfulness: How Mindfulness Became the New Capitalist Spirituality.* His study of Buddhism began forty years ago at the Tibetan Nyingma Institute in Berkeley, California.

Masoumeh Rahmani is a Lecturer in Religious Studies at Victoria University of Wellington, New Zealand. She previously held a Research Associate position in the Brain, Belief and Behaviour lab at Coventry University. Rahmani received her PhD from University of Otago in 2017. Her research interests include religious change, meditation movements, and Asian religions in non-Asian contexts.

Harold D. Roth is Professor of Religious Studies and East Asian Studies and the Director of the Contemplative Studies program at Brown University. Roth is a scholar of classical Chinese philosophy and religion where he has focused on the contemplative foundations of classical Daoism. He is also a pioneer in the new field of Contemplative Studies.

Heather L Rusch is a Research Fellow in the National Institutes of Health (NIH) and Karolinska Institute collaborative doctoral program in Clinical Neuroscience. She earned her MS in Neuroscience at Columbia University and completed her clinical training at the New York State Psychiatric Institute. Ms. Rusch specializes in post-traumatic stress disorder (PTSD). Her research aims to inform new insights into pathogenic markers and targeted therapeutics for individuals challenged with PTSD.

Peter Sedlmeier is Professor of Psychology at the Chemnitz University of Technology, Germany. He has held positions at the Universities of Konstanz, Salzburg, Chicago, and

Paderborn before, and has spent several sabbaticals at Pondicherry University, India. His current areas of interest include the psychology of meditation, music psychology, time processing, and computer modeling of cognitive and statistical processes.

Deane H. Shapiro, Jr. has served as a Professor of Psychology, emeritus, Department of Psychiatry and Human Behavior, University of California, Irvine, School of Medicine, Dean of Academic Affairs at the Pacific Graduate School of Psychology, and on the Clinical Faculty, Stanford School of Medicine. He has devoted his professional career to seeking to understand how individuals can gain, maintain, and regain a positive sense of control in their lives—mentally, emotionally, interpersonally, and in their views of the nature of the universe. His research involved developing a theory of human control, a psychological test to measure a person's control profile (the SCI), and a specific therapeutic approach (Control Therapy) to match the most effective strategies to a person's particular control profile. His interest in control took him to Zen and Chan monasteries in Japan and Taiwan to explore meditation; the jungles of Bali to study stress management and trance dances; and the mystical hills of Safed, Israel, where the main obstacle to a good night's sleep is purported to be the fluttering sound of angels' wings.

Sarah Shaw is the Khyentse Foundation Reader in Buddhist Studies, University of South Wales, UK. She is a fellow of the Oxford Centre for Buddhist Studies and a member of the faculty of Oriental Studies, University of Oxford. She has written a number of books on meditation, mindfulness, and early Buddhist text, chant, and narrative. She is a longstanding practitioner and teacher with the Samatha Trust, UK.

Carlos Henrique do Carmo Silva is an independent scholar and Emeritus Associate Professor of Philosophy at the Catholic University of Lisbon. He has also held lecturing appointments at the University of Lisbon and the University of Évora. He has authored over one hundred articles and chapters on various topics, including ancient philosophy, Christian mysticism, Eastern philosophy, and consciousness studies.

Kunchapudi Srinivas† was Professor of Philosophy at Pondicherry University, India. He held a PhD from Jawaharlal Nehru University and was an expert in both Eastern and Western philosophy. His areas of research included epistemology, Indian and Western, philosophy of science, symbolic logic, and the philosophical foundations of meditation.

Caroline Starkey is Associate Professor of Religion and Society at the University of Leeds. Her research focuses on religion in contemporary Britain, particularly in relation to minority religions and gender. Her monograph, *Women in British Buddhism: Connection, Commitment, Community*, was published by Routledge in 2020.

Valerie van Mulukom is an Associate Professor at Coventry University. She is a cognitive scientist whose research focuses on imagination, memory, and belief, using methodologies from experimental and social psychology, and embodied and cognitive neuroscience. She is an editor of the *Journal for the Cognitive Science of Religion*.

Brian Victoria is a Senior Research Fellow at the Oxford Centre for Buddhist Studies and a fully ordained priest in the Sōtō Zen sect of Buddhism. He is the author of a trilogy on the role Zen Buddhism played within Japanese totalitarianism including *Zen at War*, *Zen War Stories*, and *Zen Terror in Prewar Japan: Portrait of an Assassin*.

Bjarne Wernicke-Olesen is a Research Lecturer at the Oxford Centre for Hindu Studies and a tutor in Hinduism, Buddhism, and Sanskrit at the Faculty of Theology and Religion, University of Oxford. He is the director of the Śākta Traditions Research Programme at the Oxford Centre for Hindu Studies, and his research focuses on goddess traditions, yoga, and asceticism in South Asia.

Nobuyoshi Yamabe is Professor of Asian Philosophy at Waseda University. His academic interests include Yogācāra Buddhism (in particular, the theory of *ālayavijñāna* in the context of mind-body correlation) and Buddhist meditation and visualization in Central Asia.

Caifang Zhu is the Founding Director of Beijing Counseling and Meditation Center. He is an Associate Director and Research Fellow at Hebei Research Institute of Chan Buddhism in China. He is also the Deputy Secretary and board member of the International Transpersonal Association. While studying at Harvard Divinity School he was a teaching fellow with the East Asian Studies Program (2002–2004) and chaired the Harvard Buddhist Community (2003–2004).

PART I

OVERVIEW

CHAPTER 1

INTRODUCTION

Understanding and Studying Meditation

MIGUEL FARIAS, DAVID BRAZIER, & MANSUR LALLJEE

Meditation Today

The *Oxford Handbook of Meditation* responds to the interest in contemplative methods that has grown in recent decades and has spread beyond the religious and spiritual disciplines into medicine, psychology, and popular culture. Originally developed by and for religious women and men who lived within monastic contexts or at the margins of society, some of these practices underwent significant adaptations to allow practically anyone, from any background, to use them. From being regarded as odd and marginal, what used to be derided as navel gazing or New Age fad has become a prescription for survival in an increasingly stressful and complex modern environment.

This increased popular interest has underlined the importance of questions about the origins, aims, and effects of meditation. How much is known about its varieties? What were they developed for and by whom? How similar or different are they? How effective can they be in changing our minds and bodies? What are their social and ethical implications? To answer these and other questions, we have put together this Handbook with contributions from leading experts.

Our aim is to pitch this volume at a level that is rigorous academically while still easily understandable to all interested in exploring or learning more about meditation, whether the interest be personal, professional, or spiritual. To this end we have encouraged contributors to use less jargon and technical language than they might otherwise have been inclined. It is, however, inevitable that a book of this kind includes a range of technical terms and, where this is so, we have tried to see that as far as possible they are described in a way accessible to the general reader. This is such a broad field that even specialists in one tradition or method are general readers when they approach one of the other areas.

It is relatively easy to fall into the trap of imagining that the meditation that one practices, or the tradition that one is versed in, is sufficiently representative of the whole field. Simply by reading through Part II, Meditation Across the Word's Traditions, many readers are likely to find themselves astonished by the rich tapestry of practices, the ferment of ideas, and the varied contexts in which these practices were developed. But there are other surprises throughout the volume, not only concerning the varieties of meditation (Part III), or the novel findings across thematic approaches, from biology to anthropology (Part IV), but also the individual and social applications of meditation (Part V). Part VI, the last part of the Handbook, is dedicated to debates and controversies, some of which have been acknowledged for centuries, such as using meditation to gain special powers or experiencing challenging and adverse effects. These are potentially sensitive topics, but their discussion is now timely given meditation's popularization and widespread therapeutic use. As editors, we hope that you will find in this volume many revelations, along with opportunities to deepen your understanding and experience of meditation.

The Meaning of Meditation

We must start by acknowledging that the original meaning and boundaries of meditation are blurry. If we consider spiritual practices like prayer or chanting, there is some overlap with meditation, particularly when this involves concentrating on the repetition of religious syllables or names, or excerpts from sacred writings. The popular use of the term meditation today tells us that this is different from other religious practices because it implies a reduction in reflective thought or even in mental activity. This is a common conception which runs counter to the original meaning of the word: the Latin roots of meditation (*meditatio*) suggest that this is a mental activity of "thinking over" or "thinking carefully," also linked to the act of "measuring" (Latin *mete*) (Cassell's Latin Dictionary, 1927). The books of "meditations" by Marcus Aurelius (2016) or Descartes (1950) are examples of how this term was employed throughout the centuries as serious and sustained reflection. To meditate, therefore, implied an activity of quiet reflection aimed at arriving at a serious conclusion. So it might have made sense to say that one is meditating the consequences of a certain course of action, such as, say, whether to marry a certain person, but very rarely now do we find meditation used in the sense of a deep reflection (Oxford English Dictionary, 2010–).

Today to meditate means to practice a particular kind of concentrative exercise. The related term "contemplation" has been used in the Christian tradition in a way that resembles more closely how we think of meditation today—contemplative prayer has been described as a practice of deep silence and special openness to God that is differentiated from vocal prayer and meditation, both of which involve more sensorial, imaginative, and affective elements (Catechism of the Catholic Church, 2016, Part 4, section 1, chapter 3). This contemplative exercise, which involves achieving mental silence, has similarities with terms from other spiritual traditions; think, for example, of Patañjali's *Yoga Sūtras* (Aranya, 1963/1983), one of the first recorded meditation manuals (third century CE), where he describes Yoga as a practice which leads to the cessation of mental fluctuations (*yogaś cittavṛtti nirodhaḥ*), through a sustained exercise of attention (see chapter on Hinduism and Meditation: Tantra). Or consider the practices of classical Daoism in the *Zhuangzi* (compiled from the third century BCE onward), where the technique of "inner cultivation" involved the focus of attention on one thing, often the breath, for a sustained period of time, with the aim of gradually emptying out everyday thoughts, perceptions, and emotions, in order to develop a special awareness (see chapter on Classical Daoist Meditation: From 400–100 BCE).

There are various obvious commonalities between these different traditions of contemplation, yoga, and inner cultivation. First, they all seem to involve actions of attention, particularly of sustained concentration, with the aim of moving away from the usual flux of thoughts, sensations, and feelings. Second, they all aim to arrive at a transformed state of consciousness categorically different from the everyday self. Third, quite often they involve particular postures such as sitting or kneeling. These are relatively consensual aspects that a modern audience would easily recognize as characteristic of meditation. Beyond this, though, meditation branches out in different ways: there are innumerous combinations and particularities of meditation techniques, different states of consciousness, and its ambitioned aims are equally plural, including the liberation from the cycle of death and rebirth, union with the divine, salvation of the soul, physical immortality, harmony, well-being, and the development of supernatural powers.

The Varieties of Meditation

This section will review the varieties of meditation techniques by going through the various Eastern and Western religious traditions, as well as the modern therapeutic practices with their particular focus on achieving well-being. We must begin by stressing that, when studying the plurality of meditation techniques and their effects, it is vital to avoid oversimplification. Very easily one can slip into characterizations that attempt a kind of synthesis that may be misleading. Take, for example, this statement, part of the introduction of an article published in the journal *Science*:

> Many philosophical and religious traditions teach that happiness is to be found by living in the moment, and practitioners are trained to resist mind wandering and to "be here now." (Killingsworth & Gilbert, 2010, p. 932)

The history of religions shows that the opposite of this statement is closer to the truth: world religions are generally suspicious of the idea of living in the moment, or of a *Carpe Diem* (seize the day) mentality, and most meditation exercises are a clear example of that suspicion. Meditation practices tend to be effortful; they take time to master and to reap effects; and they are often embedded in other-worldly ideas that urge the practitioner to think beyond the present world and moment. Such misconceptions may be hard to resist, as we intuitively try to interpret the past based on the present. In the present day, the tendency is to understand meditation as a technique that helps the individual to function better in this world, as a kind of self-enhancement method. This is characteristic of therapeutic types of meditation developed throughout the twentieth century. Yet the historical development of meditation is clearly rooted in something altogether different: the purpose of meditating is not to become more accomplished or resilient, but to transcend the world and the everyday self. The aim of meditation was more often to eclipse the everyday self, with its myriad passions and frustrations, than to foster self-enhancement.

There are exceptions to this, of course, but even in Buddhism, which in the West is increasingly associated with "living in the moment," this motto is not a usual Buddhist prescription for a successful spiritual life. This may come as a surprise to many readers interested in mindfulness meditation, which is a good example of how a rich, plural tradition of meditation has come to be particularly identified with a single technique. This has not happened overnight: it was over a hundred years ago that two Burmese monks from the Theravada Buddhist tradition started adapting one meditation practice for the general population; soon the Buddhist context was replaced by a more secular garb that eased its popularization in the West (see the chapters Theravada Buddhism and Meditation and Meditation and the Modern Encounter Between Asia and the West). By the time mindfulness meditation was adapted into a form of therapy by Kabat-Zinn (2011), as a technique of paying attention to the present moment in a non-judgmental way, it had already undergone various mutations throughout the twentieth century. Even the original term for mindfulness, from the Pali *sati* and the Sanskrit *smṛti*, which means "memory," has been retranslated by a Western Buddhist monk as "bare attention" (Nyanaponika, 1954), with the purpose of presenting this as a scientific method for shaping the mind.

None of this means that meditation techniques turned into therapies, such as mindfulness or Transcendental Meditation, are of less value than those developed within the context of spiritual traditions. In many ways, these therapeutic meditation techniques are substantially different from the ones that inspired them. We also owe to these therapeutic meditation practices the development of a mainstream science of meditation that uses an array of methods from the medical, psychological, biological, and brain sciences. We must nonetheless note that when meditation techniques and their aims go through substantial mutations, this creates tensions and debates. We have attempted to cover many of such controversies in this volume, both those that have recently developed with the popularization and "scientification" of these techniques, as well as much older discussions about the use of meditation for obtaining particular powers (see Part VI on Debates and Controversies in Meditation).

The meditation science movement has recently turned fifty years old, and it is fascinating to learn about the ambitious and varied scope of studies on its efficacy, ranging from its effects on heart rate to changes in personality traits (see chapter on Studying the Effects of Meditation: The First Fifty Years). The studies before 1970 are rare and usually focused on expert meditators and yogis, instead of attempting to develop meditation as a therapeutic method accessible to everyone. The notable exception to this, rarely mentioned by meditation academics and teachers, is the case of muscular relaxation techniques. These started becoming fashionable in the late nineteenth century and involved various concentration and visualization methods. Although influenced by Eastern traditions as well as Western esoteric spirituality, progressive muscular relaxation became popular as a therapeutic method with the publication of Jacobson's book *You Must Relax: A Practical Method of Reducing the Strains of Modern Living* (1934), a technique that is still taught and practiced by many psychotherapists today. This fascinating episode allows us to have a clearer understanding of how the adaptation of meditation practices as an antidote to our stressful lives has been fermenting in the West for a while (see chapter on Relaxation and Meditation).

Below we have sketched a Meditation Tree to provide an illustration of the variety of techniques across traditions, bearing in mind that the figure is only indicative of the richness developed by each tradition (see Figure 1.1). The left-hand side represents the Western-based traditions, and this follows a chronological order, with Judaism emerging earlier than Christianity and Islam. For the Eastern traditions, we have placed Buddhism after Hinduism, given the Indian origins of Buddhism. But Daoism, with its origins in China, may be older than Buddhism (the legendary Laozi perhaps lived in the sixth century BCE). At the top of the tree, we have the more recent therapeutic techniques, with their focus on muscular relaxation, on the flow of awareness (mindfulness-based therapies), or on the repetition of a mantra (Transcendental Meditation). We describe each of the Meditation Tree practices in the following paragraphs, noting the chapters where one can find a more complete account of their contexts, histories, and effects on the mind and body.

In Hinduism, we have well-known practices such as yoga, which, stripped down to its essence, is a technique of concentration on a single point (*ekāgratā*), often involving breath control and physical postures, that aims to reveal the true nature of the self as *brahman* (God or ultimate reality), or to identify with a more personalized god, such as Śiva (see chapter on Hinduism and Meditation: Yoga). There are various descriptions of the effects of this meditation technique that leave little doubt about its expected transformation of consciousness:

> When [someone], having made his mind (*manas*) completely motionless, without dissolution or distraction, goes to a state without mind, that is the highest place. The mind has to remain suppressed until it is destroyed in the heart. This is knowledge, this is liberation; the rest, on the other hand, is bookish proliferation. The bliss, purified by concentration, which arises when the spotless mind (*cetas*) has been made to enter into the self, cannot be described with words.
>
> (From the *Maitrāyaṇīya Upaniṣad*, 6:34; Buitenen, 1962, p. 105)

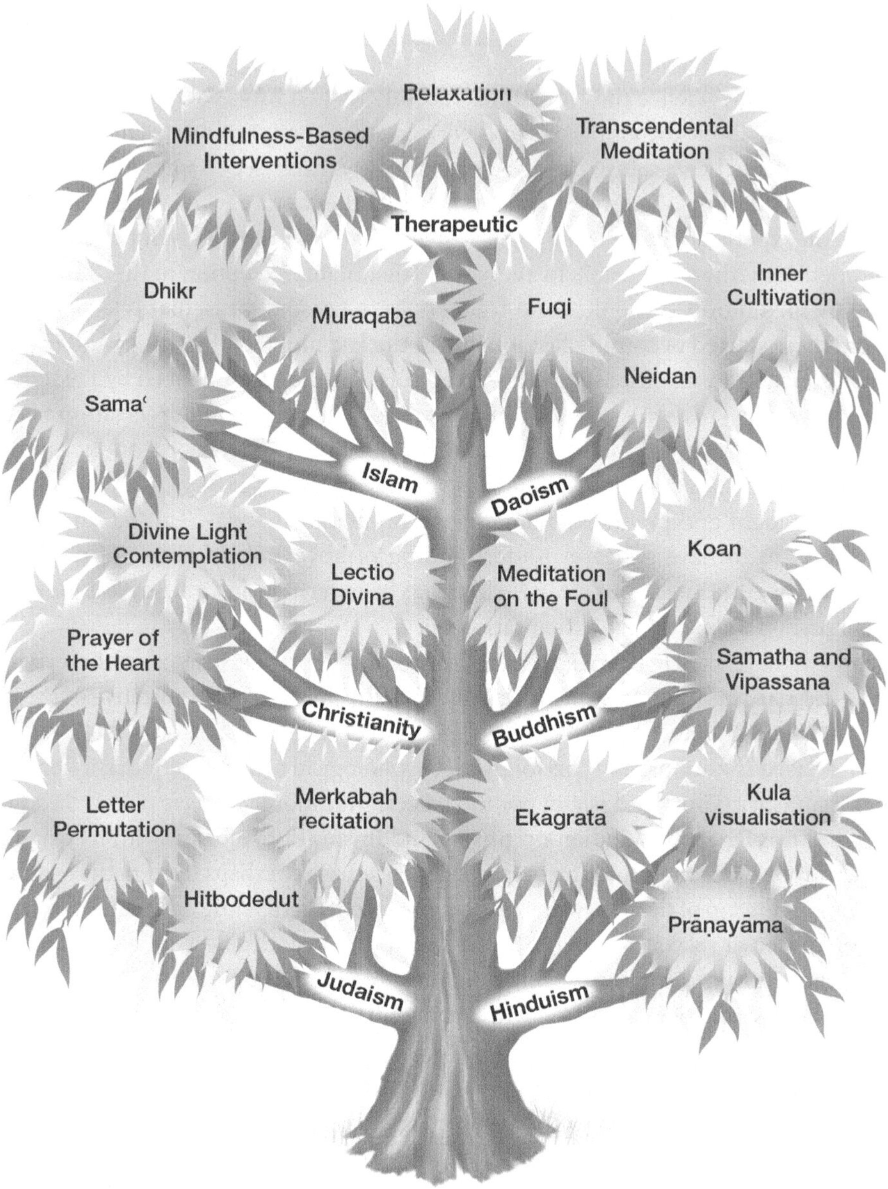

FIGURE 1.1 Meditation Tree with examples of practices from various Eastern (right side) and Western (left side) traditions, and the modern therapeutic techniques (middle top). Hinduism: *Ekāgratā* (concentration on a single point), *Prāṇayāma* (breath control), *Kula* visualization (focusing on the chakras). Buddhism: Meditation on the Foul (visualizing a decomposing corpse), *Samatha* (calm-abiding meditation) and Vipassana (direct-insight meditation), Koan (reflecting on paradoxical statements). Daoism: Inner Cultivation (apophatic meditation), *Fuqi* (ingestion of qi energy), *Neidan* (internal alchemy). Judaism: Letter Permutation (technique of combining Hebrew letters), *Merkabah* recitation (reciting angelic names), *Hitbodedut* (focusing on intense religious emotions). Christianity: Prayer of the Heart (continuous repetition of a short prayer); *Divine Light* contemplation (meditating on God's light), *Lectio Divina* (varied techniques focused on sacred scriptures). Islam: *Dhikr* (repetition of key phrases focused on God), *Muraqaba* (contemplation of the "inner" heart), *Samaʿ* (meditation on religious music). Therapeutic: Relaxation (focusing on contraction and relaxation of muscles), Transcendental Meditation (mantra recitation), Mindfulness-Based Therapies (focusing on flow of awareness).

In contrast, we find other techniques, like those developed in Tantra schools, which emphasize the use of detailed visualizations and mantra recitation. In the West, a well-known image for this type of meditation is the representation of the human body with an internal axis of energy circles (*cakras*, commonly known as chakras), starting at the root of the spine and ending at the crown of the head. In the *Kula visualization* practice, one progressively opens these energy centers to flood the body with a special nectar that grants the meditator physical immortality (see chapter on Hinduism and Meditation: Tantra).

Mixed meditation practices are common in other traditions. In Daoism, *ingestion* meditation (*fuqi*) aims to bring various energies (*qi*) into the body, by using visualization, chanting, and the swallowing of saliva. By contrast, the earlier *inner cultivation* Daoist methods, which aimed to attain unity with the Dao, used techniques that focused one's attention on the breath and progressively emptied the mind and cut off sensorial perception:

> Unify your attention
> Don't listen with your ears, listen with your mind;
> Don't listen with your mind, listen with your breathing
> Listening stops at the ears; the mind stops at what it can objectify
> As for your breathing, it becomes empty and waits to respond to things.
> The Way gathers in emptiness.
> (From the *Zhuangzi* 3; Graham, 1981. See chapter on Classical Daoist Meditation: From 400–100 BCE).

The later Daoist development of *neidan* (literally, "inner pill") is known as a form of internal alchemy, where various techniques are used to transform the *qi* energy until one becomes identified with the Void (Dao). One of these techniques employed detailed visualization of the *qi* circulating through body points, usually mapped onto energy meridians, and ending in the navel region (see chapter on Daoist Meditation: From 100 CE to the Present).

Another technique found in many traditions involves not only mental visualization but the contemplation of an object. The focus may be on a painted image or a statue, but can also take more unusual formats, such as the "contemplation of the foul," that is, a decomposing corpse, as found in Buddhism. In Tibetan Buddhism, the meditation practice known as as *chöd* (meaning "cutting or severance") may combine looking at a corpse while using rhythmic instruments and visualizing one's own body being chopped into pieces and offered to demons and gods. The purpose of this practice was to sever attachment to the physical body and attain freedom from the fear of death (see chapter on Buddhist Meditation in Tibet: Exoteric and Esoteric Orientations).

Other types of contemplation are more minimalist and aim to cut through directly to the vision of God. Within Eastern Christianity seeing the Light of God is both an experience of spiritual insight and a contemplation exercise:

> [The elder] asks: "What did you see, my child?"
>
> — : "A light, my father, a sweet sweet light; and my mind does not know how to describe it to you… At once the space of my cell vanished and the world disappeared. I was left alone with this light… There was ineffable joy, which is still in me, and great love and desire, so that streams of tears flowed out of me, as you see now."
>
> (*Ethical* 5 in Alfeyev, 2000, p. 22; see chapter on Eastern Christianity and Meditation)

To reach this stage of contemplation, though, it was a pre-requirement to engage in other meditative exercises to purify one's heart. A preferential practice, which also occurs in Western Christianity, is the recitation of the Jesus Prayer— "Lord Jesus Christ, Son of God, have mercy on us sinners"—though shorter versions are often used, such as "Lord, have mercy." This can be said verbally, murmured, or mentally, and practiced seated and in combination with focused breathing, but ideally it becomes a ceaseless repeated meditation throughout everyday life (see chapter on Western Christianity and Meditation).

Using meditation in order to achieve a vision of God, or of supernatural angelic beings, can be found in many traditions. In Judaism, by the thirteenth century we find descriptions of various techniques used for this aim, which included an original meditation method of "letter permutation" that consists of mentally combining Hebrew letters taken from biblical verses: "to turn them over and roll them quickly until your heart is warm with the rolling. And when you feel that your heart is very warm… you are ready to accept the [divine] affluence" (Abulafia, 2001, p. 67). This technique was followed by rhythmic recitation of the letters using particular breathing patterns and accompanied by the slow swinging of the head (see chapter on Judaism and Meditation).

Overall, the Jewish meditative tradition places a particular emphasis on the Hebrew alphabet and language in order to attain closeness with God. A *Merkabah* technique (third to seventh centuries CE) included learning the names of angels who guard the heavens, as one journeyed upward, but this was preceded by a period of fasting, sexual abstinence, and meditative techniques such as the repeated recitation of divine names. *Hitbodedut*, an eighteenth-century Hasidic practice, used an array of emotional techniques, such as expressing sorrow, longing, and actual weeping, while talking to God, in order to abandon one's ordinary self and commune with the divine.

The Islamic tradition likewise emphasizes communion with God as the goal of meditation practice. One fundamental meditation exercise, *dhikr*, uses the repetition of key phrases invoking God, particularly its testament of faith: *La ilaha illa ʾllah* ("There is no god but God"). There are different forms of doing this, either vocally or mentally, and with various levels of complexity by adding breathing patterns or particular bodily postures. Take the example of these *dhikr* instructions from an eighteenth-century Sufi master from Delhi:

> One should sit cross-legged with the back straight, the eyes closed, and the hands resting on the thighs. One then uses the big toe and the next toe of the right foot to

> firmly grip the sciatic nerve (*rag-i kimas*) that runs behind the left knee. Putting pressure on this will produce enough warmth in the heart to generate purity (*tasfiya*)... This will reduce the temptations and pollutions that plague the heart. Taking up this position, one should perform the meditation with single-minded heart and with assertive voice, either saying the words aloud or keeping silent as is suitable to one's situation and disposition. (Kugle, 2012, p. 59)

One other Islamic practice includes meditating on religious music (*sama*ʿ). Various types of *sama*ʿ have been developed, such as qawwali music from South Asia, where singing is usually accompanied with intense percussion. A more contemplative technique, the *muraqaba*, is a meditation strictly focused on the "inner" heart (*sirr*): this is understood as the unique point that connects the physical to the divine world, and is, in itself, an organ of awareness (see chapter on Islam and Meditation).

These are only some examples of meditation techniques across traditions. We have picked these ones to illustrate the breadth of concentration methods employed, often in combination with breathing exercises or postures, or music and images, which can be practiced silently or vocally. A more detailed description, along with that of other practices and their history, can be found in the respective chapters in Part II.

So far, we have focused on the description of the practices without offering much of the underlying context. Various debates have inevitably arisen throughout the centuries about the uses and aims of meditation. In the remaining part of this section, we would like to touch upon three points of friction or controversy.

First, we have already alluded in the previous section (The Meaning of Meditation) that meditation in our times has become almost synonymous with the idea of non-analytical or non-rational contemplation. However, religious traditions emphasize the study of sacred texts as a necessary requirement, generally above that of meditation practices, in order to achieve spiritual transformation. And the use of more analytical techniques can also be found in meditation, whether through the use of startling or paradoxical statements, such as the koan in the Chan and Zen traditions (see chapter on Chan Buddhism and Meditation), or in the multi-layered technique of *lectio divina*, which purposed to engage all rational, affective, and imaginative faculties, moving from the study of scripture into communion with God (see chapter on Western Christianity and Meditation).

A second point concerns the reflections about the experiences resulting from meditation, often embedded in intricate religious arguments. For example, the "Divine Light" contemplation became the subject of a major controversy in the Eastern Christian religious tradition: was this a true vision of God's light, or something from one's deeper mind—or even a delusion? These reflections gave rise to particular literatures on what could go wrong with one's meditation practice, in the sense that it either prevented one's spiritual development or led to psychological problems (see chapter on Meditation Sickness). It is important to note that meditation techniques were part of a wider structure of ideas and, in this sense, one cannot read descriptions of meditation practices as if they were modern self-help manuals; they are always embedded in a rich fabric of ideas that were used to examine and validate the meditation experiences and guide the spiritual development of the practitioner.

A final point concerns a more academic discussion about the commonalities and differences between the processes and results of these techniques. The question about results is often framed like this: Can we speak of these varied techniques as many different paths leading to the same experience or outcome? As editors, we have exercised prudence on this matter and firmly avoided adopting or denying a single final state of meditation experience. We leave it to the reader to decide after reading this volume.

As to the commonalities between the processes of meditation, it is not too hard to find similarities between techniques across traditions. For example, practices similar to the Theravada Buddhist techniques of *samatha* (tranquility) and Vipassana (insight) can be found elsewhere—the early Christian "watchfulness" approximates Vipassana; and *samatha* as a form of intense, focused meditation, is found across all major religious traditions. But there are also plenty of culture-specific aspects and idiosyncrasies, either in the performing of the technique or the frame in which it is embedded, which guide the meditation experience. Thus, while not denying various commonalities, which are justified given our shared bio-psychological structure, as well as by the historical influences of meditators who learned from other traditions, we simply do not have the evidence to ascertain that these exercises all do or do not work in the same way. If anything, the current evidence suggests that various meditation techniques stimulate different brain regions (see chapters on Meditation and the Brain and Psychophysiology of Meditation) and that different individuals may react in contrasting ways to meditation techniques (see chapter on Individual Differences in Meditation Outcomes).

Major Achievements in the Study of Meditation: Overview of Handbook Contents

The various sections of this Handbook address major achievements in our understanding of meditation across many fields, from history to anthropology to neuroscience. Part I surveys the field in two major ways: by examining how meditation techniques have been adapted in the East-West encounter (chapter by Richard King) and how psychological science has played a key role in the study of its effects for the past 50 years (chapter by Doug Oman). This overview hints at the contrast between modern applications and the religious origins of meditation, a dynamic tension that runs through this volume in different ways. These adaptations were started by religious traditions over one hundred years ago, and the current popularization of meditation has not only branched into the therapeutic and self-help world, but there is a feedback into the religious traditions that started these techniques. In this expanding growth process many questions arise about the origins and purpose of these techniques, as well as its ethics, meaning and consequences.

Some of these questions are dealt with in Part II, which surveys the history and development of meditation techniques across the world's major religious traditions: Hinduism: Yoga (Wernicke-Olesen) and Tantra (Flood); Judaism (Persico); Christianity: Eastern (Hovorun) and Western (Laird); Islam (Kugle); Buddhism: Theravada (Shaw), Tibetan (Halkias), and Chan (Zhu); and Daoism (Roth; Komjathy). These chapters convey both the richness and tensions of the various religious schools of meditation, stretching back for hundreds of years. These traditions are not static: some practices have gone through changes and innovations, while others have been mostly forgotten. The scholarship underlying these chapters includes updated information on relevant meditation texts that were recently discovered, which has deepened our understanding of the development and practice of meditation.

Many readers, even those familiar with the scientific study of these techniques or the history of one tradition, are likely to find themselves fascinated by the kaleidoscope of meditation techniques. Some are simple but, more often, the preparations are complex and long, or the practices are combined so one ends up with sequences of concentration, visualization, recitation, and breathing exercises. We tend to think, by contrast, that simplicity is the mark of modern meditation and that this is something that can be taught in an eight-week course, or even accessed without prior expertise via a phone app. The religious disciplines from which these techniques derive were often the converse, involving many years of dedication and discipline from adepts who were not trying to survive, thrive, and prosper within the stressful modern world, but were actively renouncing and escaping from such worldly involvement. At the same time, the reader will probably also be surprised to find the plurality of motivations to engage with meditation, and how more utilitarian aims are as old as meditation techniques. For example, in the classical Daoist text, *Zhuangzi*, we find a criticism of those who practice meditation techniques with the sole aim of prolonging their longevity, instead of seeking deeper self-transformation:

> To huff and puff, exhale and inhale, blow out the old (breath) and take in the new, do the (gymnastic positions of the) "Bear Stride" and the "Bird Stretch," and to be interested in nothing more than longevity, these are the methods of those who practise the "guiding and pulling" exercises, those who nourish the body and who try to attain the longevity of Ancestor Peng. . . . But to attain longevity without guiding and pulling, to forget everything and yet possess everything, to be serenely without limit yet have many wonderful things follow you, this is the Way of Heaven and Earth, the Potency of the Sage." (*Zhuangzi* 15; Graham, 1981)

There are some unanswered questions and areas that are not covered in detail in this section, or elsewhere in the Handbook. For example, while death is a subject of meditation practices, we don't have a chapter specifically covering meditation on death or meditations for the dying. Likewise, although meditation stimulates various altered states of consciousness, which are described throughout the Handbook, there is no single chapter focusing on these in a more structured way.

As to unanswered questions, an obvious one for which there is no easy answer is: how old are meditation techniques? The oldest recorded traditions are from Hinduism (*Atharvaveda*, c. 1000 BCE; see chapter by Wernicke-Olesen), which includes allusions to mantra recitation, and Daoism (*Zhuangzi*, from third century BCE; see chapter by Roth), with descriptions of the focused attention and breathing practices of inner cultivation. It is unclear, though, how much earlier the meditative oral tradition is, as well as the continuity and differences with older shamanic practices. One possibility is that meditation simply continues earlier shamanic practices, which aim to stimulate ecstatic states of consciousness; another possibility, though, is that the development of meditation is relatively recent in human religious history, and it happened alongside the major religious traditions with their emphasis on self-examination and finding meaning in one's life. When early in the preparation of this Handbook we consulted with specialists on the religious practices of indigenous cultures, they concurred that meditation was a non-existent or uncommon practice in these contexts. Likewise, in his description of shamanic practices, Eliade (1966, p. 417) considers these to be substantively different from meditative techniques like yoga: "But let us emphasise once again the structural difference that distinguishes classic Yoga from shamanism. Although the latter is not without certain techniques of concentration...its final goal is always ecstasy and the soul's ecstatic journey through the various cosmic regions, whereas Yoga pursues enstasis, final concentration of the spirit and 'escape' from the cosmos."

What is unclear in this explanation, though, is whether the different goals entail different processes of meditation. It is not entirely clear that it does, and there may be more continuity between shamanistic and religious meditative practices than we presently are aware of. This is a fascinating, neglected topic, and we hope that future research will shed light into it.

Part III of the Handbook extends the previous section in various ways. It looks at the development of therapeutic meditation practices throughout the twentieth century (chapter by Nathoo), it looks more deeply at the uses of visualization techniques in Buddhist meditation (chapter by Yamabe), it explores similarities and differences among techniques and consciousness states from the Hindu Yoga and Christian traditions (chapter by Carmo Silva), and it analyzes how meditation brings about alterations to the self in rather creative, sometimes unexpected, ways (chapter by Frazier).

In Part IV we have included thematic approaches to the study of meditation, ranging from biology and neuroscience to psychology, sociology, and anthropology. These chapters portray the explosion of interest in meditation from a range of specialists, and they provide fascinating information, though not always what we would expect. It is clear that there are major gaps in our knowledge of meditation, regarding its effects on our mind and bodies, but also on who uses it and how. For example, demographic surveys with national representation samples are rare, but one undertaken in the USA tells us that the religious group that reports to use meditation most often is not Buddhist or Hindu but that of Jehovah's Witnesses (see chapter by Hackett).

This shows that meditation has different meanings: for this group, meditation is a form of reflecting on God's qualities. Another finding that some will find surprising is that Asians or Asian-Americans are less likely to meditate than Whites (36 percent), Latinos (49 percent), or Blacks (52 percent). This mirrors the use of meditation in Eastern cultures, which has historically been the practice of a minority, mostly of monks and nuns, while most of the religious population engages with prayer and devotional rites.

Other chapters highlight how meditation has become either a key component of religious Buddhist life in the West (Starkey), or how Christianity has revived ancient contemplative practices (Christie). In addition, there are chapters with the updated evidence on brain (Fox & Cahn), psychophysiological (Dorjee), and psychological (Lomas; Buric, Brazil, & van Mulukom) correlates and effects of meditation, which describe what we know and what we yet don't. We also include a more speculative chapter on the psychology of meditation in Yoga and early Buddhism (Sedlmeier & Srinivas), and we end this subsection with a chapter reviewing the role of meditation in improving control and self-regulation, written by a pioneer in the psychological study of meditation (Shapiro).

Concerning more social dimensions, we cover the growing interest in studying meditation from a sociological perspective (Pagis), the popular Vipassana meditation retreats, which are probably less secular than they appear (Rahmani), and where meditation might be heading as a post-modern movement (Bazzano).

The first section of Part V covers modern applications of meditation, whether as form of physical or mental health therapy. In this respect, by far the most-well-researched meditation types are those based on mindfulness (Goyal & Rusch) and Transcendental Meditation (Orme-Johnson). In addition, we have chapters that reflect on how religious meditation can be used therapeutically (Brazier) and how a meditation framework may allow for a different understanding of mental illness (Dobkin & Monshat). The focus of the remaining chapters of Part V is on broader applications of meditation, specifically on prison (Auty), education (Brown), and as part of social-political movements and protests (Gleig). The work presented in these chapters is more contentious than that of the previous therapeutic section, in part because they deal with wider applications that involve either children or vulnerable populations, but also because there has been, thus far, less research on these topics.

Part VI, the final one of this volume, covers debates and controversies in meditation. It is unusual to give prominence to such topics in a thematic Handbook but, as one reads through these chapters, it becomes clear that these matters are intrinsic to the meditation traditions and have been discussed for centuries. We start by reviewing the growing literature on the adverse effects of meditation and how to understand and deal with these in a way which is more centered on the person and relies less on systems of mental health diagnosis (Lindahl, Britton, Cooper, & Kirmayer). This is followed by a review of similar challenging experiences in the Jewish, Christian, and Islamic meditative traditions (Fisher), and by a detailed account of how the Buddhist tradition has addressed these difficulties, which are sometimes understood as "meditation sickness" (Ahn), for over fifteen hundred years.

These chapters portray meditation in a much less tamed format than is usual: its dynamics and outcomes can be very different from what is reported in a self-help book or in a therapeutic intervention guide. Yet, if we think about it carefully, this untamed character is hardly unexpected if one considers the potential of these techniques for deep self-transformation. Not only that, the occurrence of such adverse events gives us a glimpse of how limited our understanding of the human mind still is. If our minds were simply a muscle that we exercised, we would be able to quite accurately predict strained or sore outcomes. But we can't predict or control these difficult meditation experiences in the same way as we can understand an overworked muscle. Perhaps this untamed side of meditation, which escapes our attempts to make of it a fully controlled well-being tool, might pave the way for a more complex understanding of the human mind.

If the chapters in this part of the volume somewhat disrupt the one-sided, benevolent view of meditation that has become common in the West, given its association with well-being, the chapter by Brian Victoria adds a wider lens to this disruption, by its depiction of how Zen spiritual ideas and meditation techniques were used by the Japanese military during World War II. It is timely to bring this evidence to the surface, as it meets ongoing debates about the use of meditation techniques stripped of their ethical basis, and of the potential extent of their application—such as by military taking part in armed conflict.

The final chapters tackle two different matters: the problems that arise when using a modern cognitive psychological and neuroscience language to explain the workings of ancient meditation techniques (Purser & Lewis), and the claims of extraordinary abilities and paranormal powers arising from meditation practice that are often mentioned in ancient meditation texts (Cardeña).

To conclude, the field is evidently vast. We have attempted to give an indication of major boughs and roots of the tree, but we have not traced every root, branch, and twig. We were also constrained by the state of the research on meditation; while much effort has gone into studying its psychobiological effects, there is considerably less work on its broader, interpersonal, and societal implications, for instance as an educational or peacemaking tool. Nonetheless, the reader will surely find here dimensions she or he has not formerly been aware of and will be stimulated to continue with further investigation, thought, and study whether the interest be personal, professional, spiritual, or historical.

References

Abulafia, A. (2001). *Hayyei ha-"olam ha-ba"* [Hebrew] (Amnon Gross, Ed.). Jerusalem: Barazani.

Alfeyev, H. (2000). *St. Symeon the new theologian and Orthodox tradition*. Oxford: Oxford University Press.

Aranya, Swami H. (1983). *Yoga philosophy of Patañjali* (P. N. Mukerji, Trans.). Albany: State University of New York Press. (Original work published 1963).

Aurelius, Marcus (2016). *Meditations* (R. Hard & C. Gill, Eds.). Oxford: Oxford University Press.

Buitenen, J.A.B. van (1962). *The Maitrāyaṇīya Upaniṣad: A critical essay, with text, translation, and commentary*. Gravenhage: Mouton.

Cassell's Latin dictionary: Latin-English and English-Latin. (1927). New York: Funk & Wagnalls.

Catechism of the Catholic Church. (2016). London: Catholic Truth Society.

Descartes, R. (1950). *Méditations.* Paris: Larousse.

Eliade, M. (1966). Shamanism: Archaic techniques of ecstasy. London: Routledge & Kegan Paul

Graham, A. C. (1981). *Chuang Tzu: The inner chapters.* London: Allen and Unwin.

Jacobson, E. (1934). *You must relax: A practical method of reducing the strains of modern living.* New York: McGraw-Hill.

Kabat-Zinn, J. (2011). Some reflections on the origins of MBSR, skillful means, and the trouble with maps. *Contemporary Buddhism 12*, 281–306.

Killingsworth, M. A., & Gilbert D. T (2010). A wandering mind is an unhappy mind. *Science 330*, 932.

Kugle, S. (2012). *Sufi meditation and contemplation: Timeless wisdom from Mughal India.* New Lebanon, NY: Suluk Press.

Nyanaponika, T. (1954). *The heart of Buddhist meditation (Satipaṭṭhāna): A handbook of mental training based on the Buddha's way of mindfulness, with an anthology of relevant texts translated from the Pali and Sanskrit.* York Beach: Samuel Weiser

Oxford English dictionary: The definitive record of the English language. (2010–). Oxford: Oxford University Press.

CHAPTER 2

MEDITATION AND THE MODERN ENCOUNTER BETWEEN ASIA AND THE WEST

RICHARD E. KING

What is Meditation?

Meditation remains an under-theorized concept. Everybody thinks that they know what it means, but that very certainty obscures and elides the complexity of the practices, worldviews, and traditions to which the term can be related. For instance, the English word "meditation" carries a certain ambiguity in its use. The term is sometimes used as a synonym for sustained mental reflection or contemplation (as in phrases such as "I will meditate upon that question further"). However, in contemporary popular discourse "meditation" more frequently denotes practices aimed at a pacification of mental activity—a calming of the mind. This latter usage, I would suggest, has become the dominant connotation of the English term "meditation" in modern Western culture. The ambiguity associated with the term can be summed up in the following question: "Does meditation involve deep reflection and processes of mental analysis or does it denote, by contrast, a disciplined pacification of such cognitive processes?" This semantic tension however is not peculiar to the West and reflects the fact that the technologies of the mind that we classify under the general rubric of "meditation" are in fact multiform and diverse (King, 2016).

The precise nature of such mind-transforming practices and their outcomes also generated much discussion within Asian traditions themselves and, again, is reflective of discussion of a wide range of psychosomatic techniques for altering one's state of mind or perception of reality. The classical Buddhist traditions, for instance, distinguish between *samatha* (Sanskrit: *śamatha*) practices, which are said to induce emotional tranquility, cognitive quiescence, and a deepening concentration of the mind, and *vipassanā* (Sanskrit: *vipaśyanā*) practices, which are claimed to increase levels of mental acuity and attention to the activities of mind and body. In the classical Buddhist sources these constitute two of the essential steps of the Buddhist Eightfold Path and are generally treated as co-dependent in one way or another. One set of techniques focuses upon cessation (*nirodha*) and the second on insight (Bronkhorst, 2000). This distinction can be found more widely in Asian meditative traditions, not only in Brahmanical discussions of yoga in texts such as the *Bhagavad Gītā* (Malinar, 2012) but also in the classical *ur*-text of the "Hindu" yoga tradition, the *Yoga Sūtras* (YS) of Patañjali. Therein, the stated goal of meditative practice is to achieve a state of mental equipoise (*samādhi*) characterized by the cessation (*nirodha*) of all mental fluctuations (*citta-vṛtti*, YS 1.2). Although this sounds like it refers to a pacification of cognitive activity, Patañjali states that it is nevertheless a truth-bearing state of "great insight" (*prajñā*, YS 1.48). As I have argued elsewhere,

> The cessation of the fluctuations of consciousness does not lead to the attainment of a blank state of mind, but instead results in a reflexive and stable awareness of the witness-consciousness in its own form. Moreover, *samādhi* is not merely a mental state, since it affects the entire mind-body complex of the yogin. This is even more clearly the case in the Hatha Yoga tradition where the body is a vehicle of liberation and is transformed in the process. (King, 1999b, p. 192)

The distinction between these techniques and their stated goal generated a complicated series of debates with Asian intellectual circles about the precise nature of what we call meditation, whether it was conducive to "sudden" or "gradual" transformations in perspective, and what the precise relationship might be between insight and insentience (Sharf 2014a, 2014b).

Meditation practices and traditions have been particularly associated with Asian traditions and the "Mystic East" but sometimes to the detriment of our understanding of other dimensions of such traditions, which give context and a more rounded view of those practices. The exclusive association between a highly psychologized notion of meditational practice and Asian traditions has not only divested them from a broader structural understanding of ritual repetition and performance within those traditions but also enabled the translation of them into supposedly "free floating" and adaptable spiritualities amenable to customization and detraditionalization for the spiritual consumer in capitalist societies.

The Western Encounter with Asia

Mutual exchange and influence between Asia and the West has been much more widespread than has hitherto been acknowledged (Hobson, 2004).[1] Dominant histories of

[1] We know for instance that there were contacts and established trade links between ancient Mesopotamia and the Indian subcontinent as early as 2400 BCE. Similarly, scholars such as Thomas

Western civilization, however, have tended to underplay such early examples of "globalization" across trade routes, offering instead accounts of the rise of the West that have tended to treat it as a largely self-contained and self generating agent of history. Such one-sided and Eurocentric accounts have increasingly come under attack as evidence mounts of the cultural, philosophical and mercantile interchange between "East" and "West" that helped forge Western and Asian cultural identities as well as stimulate technological and cultural innovations in both contexts. Similarly, sporadic cultural awareness of Asian traditions of meditative practice in the West go back to classical (McEvilley, 2002) and medieval periods (Ristuccia, 2013) but grew exponentially as a result of European colonial expansion from the seventeenth-century onward. This colonial context had a profound impact upon Western conceptions not only of Asia but also of the nature of meditation itself (King, 1999a). By the mid-nineteenth century, Asian religious traditions came to be particularly associated in the West with the practice of meditation, and for good reason, though often this association has been at the expense of a richer understanding of how meditation is situated in relation to a diversity of practices.

Although sometimes submerged and given less emphasis than other practices such as prayer, credal formulae, and so on, there are of course meditative techniques present within Western traditions as well. This can be seen in various forms of what have come to be called the Jewish (see chapter 7) and Christian mystical traditions (chapters 8, 49) as well as in Western occultism and esotericism (chapter 15). Indeed, for some contemporary Westerners, encounter with "eastern meditation" has revivified their experience and encounter with their own contemplative traditions. In a lecture delivered in Calcutta in 1968 shortly before his death, the American Catholic theologian and writer Thomas Merton described himself as a "pilgrim to Asia" remarking that:

> I think that we have now reached a stage of (long-overdue) religious maturity at which it may be possible for someone to remain perfectly faithful to a Christian and Western monastic commitment and yet to learn, in depth, from, say, a Hindu or Buddhist discipline or experience. Some of us need to do this in order to improve the quality of our own monastic life. (Burton & Laughlin, 1973, p. 313)

More recently, Christian theologian Paul Knitter (2009) has offered a similar reprise, arguing that his encounter with Buddhist meditation and philosophy has deepened and enriched his own Christian faith and practice.

Encounter with Asian traditions however has also precipitated a negative reaction toward their meditative practices, usually in the form of cultural criticism of the negative influence of "Eastern" ideas and practices on the West, an approach that resonates with an earlier history of Christian missionary antipathy toward the "Mystic East."

McEvilley (2002) have argued for a fundamental reappraisal of the level of Indo-Greek philosophical cross-fertilization in the ancient and classical periods. Although contact ebbed and flowed over the millennia, the incursions of Alexander the Great into the Indian subcontinent in 326 BCE and the Buddhist missions sent out to the western frontiers by King Ashoka (ruled 273–232 BCE) represent two clear historical examples of East-West interactions.

Historically for instance the Roman Catholic position has tended to be expressed by the maxim "*Extra Ecclesiam nulla salus*" ("Outside the church, there is no salvation"). Within the Eastern Orthodox tradition, there has always been an important emphasis upon meditation, especially among movements like Hesychasm but also a suspicion of oriental incursions. In 1977, Harvard theologian Harvey Cox expressed his doubts about the "New Orientalism" in contemporary Western society, arguing that Asian meditation practices, when transplanted from their original cultural, religious, and institutional moorings, were potentially psychologically damaging and dangerous.

> The problem is, however, that in a culture like ours, already steeped in the philosophy of "You do your thing and I'll do mine," the lofty Buddhist idea of nonattachment can hardly escape distortion. Westerners will not be able to practice the Oriental posture of nonattachment until they move beyond attachments but also beyond an "I" which does "my thing." Real nonattachment will become possible only when self slips away too. But this is something most Westerners either cannot or will not concede. (Cox, 1977, p. 84)

Popular novels such as Robert Pirsig's *Zen and the Art of Motorcycle Maintenance*, although generally positive about "Eastern wisdom," also encouraged the idea that Asian experiences of enlightenment might lead to a loss of a sense of self or to madness. Most strikingly, R. C. Zaehner, Spalding Professor of Comparative Religion and Ethics at the University of Oxford from 1952 to 1974, suggested, rather controversially, that the cultural consequence of importing Hindu texts like the *Bhagavad Gītā* into Western culture was Charles Manson, the famous mass murderer and cult figure (Zaehner, 1974, pp. 47–72). Less extreme, but symptomatic of a similar cultural anxiety, Colin Campbell has argued that the late twentieth century can be characterized by a significant "Easternization of the West."[2] Similarly, Slovenian cultural critic Slavoj Žižek has argued in a number of works that the greatest threat to Western civilization is the importation of eastern New Age ideas. This has become central to his atheistic defense of the Christian culture and identity of Europe and The West (see for instance Žižek, 2001).

Coloniality and the Translation of Asian Meditation Traditions

Languages are unequal. For instance, although Sanskrit for millennia was the dominant language of South Asia, in the modern period, because of the colonial hegemony of the Europeans, and in particular Britain and its colonies in the "New World," modern discourse has been dominated by Anglophone mediation. Thus, when we translate a

[2] For discussion and critique of Campbell's thesis see Hamilton (2002), A. Dawson (2006) and Steve Bruce (2017).

term from Sanskrit into English in the modern period we must also pay attention to the *politics of translation*, that is, to the imbalance of power and influence between the original and the recipient/host language. For instance, when terms like "*dharma*" are translated in terms of the western concept of "religion," they become transposed into a series of assumptions that transform our understanding of the original term as it operated in its own specific linguistic, cultural, and historical context. Drawing attention to this process of interpellation and transformation allows us to resist an otherwise unnoticed transition into the dominant language and interpretive frameworks of the culture of reception.

In what follows I will focus attention not upon the translation of specific words and terms from Asian languages into Western ones but rather upon *the politics of macro-translation*, that is a consideration of the normative tropes and registers that have framed the reception of Asian meditative traditions, texts and practices into a Western-dominated vision of modernity.

I would suggest, following the productive insights of structuralist writers like Lévi-Strauss, that every civilization or "macro-tradition" develops a series of over-arching and dominant binaries that frame the conditions of possibility for thought. These oscillate and combine to produce what the French philosopher Michel Foucault calls an *episteme*. These categorical binaries function as points of discursive tension within specific cultures, traditions, and groups and generate debates, controversies, contestations, and attempted reconciliations. The encounter between Europe and Asia has been peculiarly affected by the prevailing cultural tensions emerging from the Reformation and the European Enlightenment.

Any new cultural form which entered the European mindset in the last two centuries will have been caught in a translational binary generated by the emergence of a dichotomy within European thought not only between "mind" and "body" but also between the concepts of "science" and "religion." As Peter Harrison (2006) has demonstrated, what we call science and what we call religion emerged out of a process of mutual self-definition that began in the early modern period and continues to this day. This binary was further energized by the discursive separation of religion and the secular which emerged as a distinctive "semantic pattern" by the mid-nineteenth century (Hölscher, 2013). The two, often thought to be engaged in a fundamental struggle for authority within Western societies according to one dominant narrative of "modernity," became mutually constituted mirrors of each other and conditioned the reception of Asian meditation into a modern Western context. As Kocku von Stuckrad (2015, pp. 179–181) has argued,

> It is in discursive re-entanglements of religious and cultural negotiations of meaning that European societies generate the conceptual borders between the religious and the non-religious and between religion and science...Talking of discourse strands, which can be entangled in manifold ways, enables us to see how binary constructions emerge in concrete historical settings, how they are supplemented with other discourse strands, and how they change their meaning and constellation

> over time. Similar to what Bruno Latour calls "networks" (Latour, 1993, p. 3), these discourses do not have a fixed center around which they are organized; they are a moving target of scholarly analysis, creating new centers in shifting alliances, dispositives and discursive configurations.

The colonial encounter between Europe and Asia precipitated a new lexicon and discursive context for the articulation of Asian traditions and involved interpellating them into European language games based upon the idea of "religion" and its perceived clash with the rising authority of the "natural sciences." Asian meditative traditions have been interpolated into Western cultural contexts through a process of conceptual filtration, dominated by this binary. This is not to say that one cannot find instances that can be read as a contestation between something called "science" and something called "religion" in Asian civilizations but, rather, that to focus on those and to frame the distinction in that way is to translate them into a Western-defined binary. Once we recognize this we are in a position to understand the different ways in which "Asian meditation" has been understood and interpreted in the West.

This conceptual framework, which strongly differentiates religion from science, generated a range of largely Western-driven questions about Asian practices and philosophies that framed the reception, understanding, and interpretation of Asian traditions of meditation in the modern period. Is the practice of meditation or yoga a religious practice?[3] Is meditation more of a spiritual than a religious practice? Is meditation compatible with science? Can meditation be approached from a purely therapeutic/health-oriented and secular perspective? Is Buddhism even a religion or is it more accurately to be rendered as a sort of Asian-derived, introspective "science of the mind."[4] It is not that these are inappropriate or even unproductive questions to ask. Far from it. Rather, the point is that they are generated out of a specific cultural experience—the recent historical memory of the West—and therefore reflect cognitive assumptions largely derivative of those experiences.

As Argentinian philosopher Anibal Quijano (2000) has suggested, what white Euro-Americans experience as "modernity" is, for much of the rest of the world, simultaneously an experience of coloniality. Quijano argues that, because "modernity" and coloniality are essentially two sides of the same coin, they should both be recognized as mutually constitutive of each other. Thus, Eurocentric narratives which focus upon Europe in terms of its self-determination and autonomy occlude the impact of the colonial encounter with the non-European as crucial in the formation of modern European identity. Similarly, the lived experience of "modernity" for members of

[3] See for instance Malnak v Yogi (1979), which found that Transcendental Meditation (TM) was a religion and the 2015 legal controversy in Encinitas, California, over whether the teaching of yoga in schools was a religious practice and therefore a potential "gateway" to conversion to Hinduism. For a useful discussion of the framing of yoga as explicitly religious see Andrea Jain (2015), chapter 6.

[4] For a contemporary example of an attempt to render Buddhist meditation as a scientific technology, rather than a specifically religious practice, see Alan Wallace (2003). For a critical perspective on attempts to align Buddhist meditation with the claims of science see Donald Lopez Jr. (2008).

colonized societies has been and continues to be framed by the expansionist visions and cultural hegemony of European peoples and their conceptual frameworks.

This is no more apparent than in the context of Asian societies. We should note then that the modern conceptual distinction between a realm of life known as "the religious" from another called "the secular" has not been a feature of non-Western civilizations before the advent of European colonial expansion and the eventual spread of Western(ized) conceptions of the world and of history. It does not map well onto non-European civilizations without severe distortion of their own local histories and indigenous categories (King, 1999a; Fitzgerald, 2000, 2007). At an epistemological level, the story of the normalization of Western conceptions of the world is an important chapter in the larger story of the birth of the modern world and the transformation of non-Western civilizations that this influence represents.

Although the category of "religion" has a long and varied history in the West it has been fundamentally molded by two overarching and universalist worldviews—firstly Western Christianity (which predisposes us to think of "religion" as a phenomena characterized by faith, belief, adherence to a creed, and to one of a number of variant forms of mono/poly/pantheisms) and more recently the European "Enlightenment" leading to the birth of secular humanism and the modern nation-state (an *episteme* that causes us to think that "religion" is somehow associated with violence, intolerance, fundamentalism, and division). Careful attention to the history of non-Western civilizations demonstrates that these assumptions are not only problematic but also distort our attempts to understand non-Western experiences of the world in the pre-modern period.

Through European colonialism and broader Western influence across Asia, the Americas, and Africa, European assumptions about "the religious" were gradually universalized. "Religion" effectively became naturalized as a feature of "universal history." The category could be re-defined and re-shaped to a degree from one context to the next (indeed recognition of a variety of members of the genus "Religion" required this), but the concept became established as a normative category to such an extent that it becomes increasingly difficult to question the category as a "naturally" occurring feature of all cultures. Today, we simply assume that all cultures have one or more "religions" and never ask why this "common-sense" appears so obvious to us, when it would not have appeared so self-evident to many before the advent of European colonialism. This largely unquestioned ideology (though contested in a variety of ways, including ongoing attempts to re-shape the category to fit non-European contexts) became the lynchpin first of a Christian missionizing vision of the world ("we must convert the heathens to the truth of the gospel") and then of a similarly missionizing secularist modernism ("we must bring our 'enlightened' and secular view of the world to liberate the masses from their superstitious and mystifying worldviews"). In this way, the diverse histories and civilizations of the "rest of the world" become reduced to a series of footnotes to the West.

In the late colonial era, Western writers created a lexicon of new categories to classify the newly discovered "religions" of Asia. By the 1830s terms such as "Hinduism,"

"Buddhism," and "Taoism" gained currency as ways of classifying these ancient traditions. These terms circulated across colonial networks and became popular in the context of an emerging geo-political system which reflected the dominant role of Western nations and which framed much of what counts as "international relations" as an attempt to globalize the Westphalian model of the secular nation-state. In this way,

> The "religion vs. secular" division of society came to function as the dominant template through which colonized and semi-colonized Asian countries sought entrance to "modernity"—that is to gain recognition as civilized and sovereign nation states in a context of military, economic and political encroachment into their regions by western powers. Thus, in the late nineteenth and early twentieth centuries we see the rise of a variety of new "reformist" and "modernizing" agendas in various Asian countries, exemplified by the Meiji regime in Japan (1868–1912), the establishment of the Republic of China (1912–1949) and trends such as the late nineteenth-century "Bengali Renaissance" in India, which sought, in their own ways, to respond to a western-driven conception of modernity. These "reformist" trends sought to organize and reform indigenous traditions and polities in response to such demands. (King, 2011, pp. 45–46)

Asian traditions, practices, interpretations, and the institutions with which they are associated were transformed by the colonial encounter with the West, which energized reformist trends within those traditions. The transmission of Asian forms of meditation to the West in the twentieth century can be seen as manifesting in two distinct yet related ways, mapping onto Western distinctions between "mind" and "body." As Kate Crosby (2005) has argued, framed by the mind-body distinction of Western thought, Buddhist "meditation" came to be seen in the West as an intellectualist, primarily mental exercise in contrast to Hindu "yoga," which took on more physicalist aspects, emphasizing the importance of postural forms (*āsana*). This dichotomy, driven by the Cartesian dichotomy between mind and body, is however highly misleading as bodily-oriented practices remain central to Buddhist practices and what we tend to call yoga denotes a multitude of approaches from the intellectualist *Jñāna Yoga* of Swāmi Vivekānanda (1863–1902) to the many forms of contemporary practice that take their inspiration from Hatha Yoga ("The Yoga of Force").

The initial importation of yoga into the Western world was largely inspired by the writings of Swāmi Vivekānanda, who offered an account of yoga that represented it simultaneously as a "science of the mind" and as Hinduism's distinctively spiritual contribution to human civilization. However, the form of yoga that became popularized in the West grew out of the complicated fusion of a highly masculinized and gymnastic cult of muscularity centered upon Indian fitness and wrestling traditions merged with practices and philosophies associated with Hatha Yoga that emerged particularly in Mysore in the period between the first and second world wars (Sjoman, 1999; Singleton, 2010; Goldberg, 2016). Key figures here were the Indian bodybuilder K. V. Iyer (1894–1986) and yoga teachers such as Sri Yogendra (1897–1989), Swami Kuvalayananda (1883–1986), Yogacharya Sundaram (1901–1994), T. Krishnamacharya (1888–1989),

Swami Sivananda (1887–1963), and B. K. S. Iyengar (1918–2014). Collectively, this group established a modern tradition of yoga that sought to link meditative practice with bodily health and fitness aimed at muscular dexterity and strength. This was to be cultivated via the practice and achievement of a range of postures (*āsana*), which were then claimed to be crucial to cultivating a spiritual achievement of meditative concentration (*samādhi*). The form of modern postural yoga that emerged from the crucible of Mysore became increasingly promoted on a national level across India in the 1920s and 1930s as a means of disciplining an entire generation of young Indian males and inculcating within them a sense of national pride in India, Hinduism, and the ancient traditions of yoga, which, in this way, became a powerful cultural symbol, following Vivekānanda's interventions, of the spiritual "essence" of Hinduism and one of India's contribution to human civilization.

As we shall see, these two strands established the parameters of the translation of Asian meditational teachings and practices into the Western world in the twentieth and early twenty-first centuries. In this way, Asian meditative systems became translated and incorporated into Western cultures via the emerging concepts of spirituality; the fields of psychology and psychotherapy; and institutions, groups, and discourses that focus upon meditation as an aid to bodily health, fitness, and general well-being.

The "Religious" Nature of Asian Meditation

The dominant mediating term or conceptual "entry-point" by which Westerners have encountered and classified Asian forms of meditation has been through the idea of religion. A considerable academic literature has now emerged tracking the emergence of the modern Western category of religion and the impact of its application in non-Western, colonized societies in the last few centuries. Since the Treaties of Westphalia in 1648 established a curtailment of the power of ecclesiastical institutions in matters of state governance among the emerging Northern European states, the normative approach to "religion," especially in Northern Europe and North America, conceived it as a realm to be clearly differentiated from the public exercise of state-craft. In other words, religion came to be classified as existing within the private realm. This model, the basis for the modern liberal nation-state, became enshrined in the French Revolution and in the United States Constitution and Bill of Rights, and became a central assumption associated with emerging ideas of civil liberty and the discourse of human rights. As William T. Cavanaugh (2017, p. 592) notes,

> The point is not that the concept of "religion" was simply absent in the sixteenth and seventeenth centuries, but that the distinction between religion and social or political factors was in the process of development as new forms of power—what

> would become known as the "state"—were developing. The modern idea of religion as a realm of human activity inherently separate from politics and other "secular" matters depended upon a new configuration of Christian societies in which many legislative and jurisdictional powers and claims to power—as well as claims to devotion and allegiance of the people—were passing from the church to the new sovereign state. The secular/religious binary helped facilitate this shift.

Under the model established by the Westphalian treaties (which were instrumental in establishing the legal framework for the emergence of the modern secular nation-state) "religion" is seen as private and contrasted not only with politics, but also with philosophy and the sciences, which came to be viewed as preeminently public and subject to the contestations of reasoned argument and experimentation. When viewed from a binary standpoint such as this, the practice of Asian forms of meditation has usually resulted in them being classified as religious and thus excluded from the realm of science. Consequently, to engage meditation in a scientific manner has generally required a cognitive disassociation from their purportedly religious implications, which usually means distinguishing such practices from their cultural, communal, and institutional roots. As we shall see, this is where the concept of spirituality has proven particularly effective in the late twentieth century precisely because of the way in which it elides the binary between the religious and the secular and therefore opens up engagement with meditation practices by scientific and professional healthcare communities. Throughout much of the twentieth century, however, once framed as a private, introspective practice, much of the Western engagement with Asian meditative traditions has been filtered through the notion of the "Mystical East" (King 1999a).

"The Mystic East" and the Psychologization of Asian Meditation

Framed by the idea of religion and its fundamentally private nature, the central category in the translation and reception of Asian meditative systems from the late nineteenth century has been via the category of mysticism. The representation of Asian contemplative traditions as "forms of mysticism" or "Eastern spirituality" has been a powerful trope in Western culture throughout the twentieth century. These traditions have been endlessly compared and contrasted by numerous twentieth-century theologians, scholars of mysticism, and proponents of inter-faith dialogue, most famously by Swāmi Vivekānanda, Sarvepalli Radhakrishnan, Rudolf Otto, William James, D. T. Suzuki, and Alan Watts. They have also been the focus of a plethora of popular literature on "spirituality" in the West since the 1960s. There is no sign of this abating.

Famously, William James (1842–1910), in his highly-influential work *The Varieties of Religious Experience* (1901), discussed meditation and yoga in terms of a psychological analysis of these systems, based upon the assumption that their central preoccupation was the cultivation of extraordinary states of consciousness or what subsequently came to be known as "Altered States of Consciousness." This characterization of Asian meditative traditions continues to dominate modern accounts.

James, of course, was one of the pioneering figures in the establishment of the academic subject of psychology. Indeed, as he once remarked: "the first lecture in psychology that I ever heard was the first I ever gave" (King, 2005). The twentieth century has been dominated by the rise of psychological accounts of human experience; from figures like James, to Freud and Jung, popularizing a psychological understanding of the human self. Asian meditation systems, because of their preoccupation with the analysis, modulation, and transformation of consciousness, have been easily translated into a modern psychologized language.

There are however a number of problems with the representation of ancient meditative traditions as forms of mysticism in the modern psychologized sense of the term. First, one needs to acknowledge that Asian meditative systems, philosophies, and practices reflect considerable variety in terms of the traditions, practices, and worldviews to which they relate. Although traditional Asian meditative practices and traditions clearly involved the sustained application of "psychosomatic" techniques aimed at the transformation of one's perspective upon reality, it is not clear that the emphasis that is placed upon different "levels of attainment" within such literature is accurately represented if interpreted through modern (i.e., post-Enlightenment) notions of "private experience."

Until comparatively recently, meditative practice has largely been the preserve of the elite virtuosi of Asian traditions such as Buddhism, Daoism and Hindu forms of yoga. The work of scholars such as Robert Buswell Jr. (1992) have also demonstrated through extensive fieldwork experience that everyday Buddhist monastic life provides a rich tapestry of practices that challenge Western stereotypes about the centrality of meditative practice to Buddhist monastic life. Moreover, what counts as meditation in these contexts can vary quite considerably. Kate Crosby (2005, p. 272) has argued that in pre-modern South East Asian Buddhism the characteristic division between devotion and "meditation" is rarely seen as a polarity and that devotion remains a practice "advocated for the religious specialist, the monk or layperson undertaking the more rigorous path of meditation aimed at Buddhahood." Similarly, Robert Sharf (1995) has called into question the tendency to approach Buddhist monastic literature "as if they present a phenomenological analysis of the experiences of seasoned meditators" and argues that "the actual practice of what we would call meditation rarely played a major role in Buddhist monastic life" (1995, pp. 232, 241). For Sharf, traditional references to mental training or cultivation (*bhåvanå*) should be seen not as descriptions of a set of mystical practices aimed at producing extraordinary and private states of consciousness, but rather as liturgical and propadeutical inducements. What we call meditation "consisted largely of the recitation of Pāli texts pertaining to meditation…chanting verses enumerating the qualities of the Buddha, reciting formulaic lists of the thirty-two parts of the body, and so on." (1995, p. 242). Moreover, Sharf argues, the modern "rhetoric of experience" functions as a largely vacuous intellectual category, which is popular precisely because it can be deployed from a variety of different ideological positions; this has been the case when classifying Asian traditions such as Buddhism as institutionalized modes of "mysticism" or "spirituality" with a "trans-cultural, trans-historical reality" that can be abstracted from the institutional and culturally specific dimensions of their original practice. On the other hand, Janet Gyatso (1999) has argued that Sharf underplays the discussion of unmediated meditative experiences in Asian accounts and that he also overstates the lack of discussion of personal experience, especially in the case of Tibetan Buddhist writers.

It is important to note that there are many highly technical and systematic discussions of "consciousness" and the mind within classical Asian philosophical thought but that we should be careful not to read such texts as if they were psychological treatises in the modern sense. Traditional Buddhist discussions of mental training (*bhāvanā*), for instance, are not so much concerned with the cultivation of "altered states of consciousness" as they are driven by the goal of developing analytical insight (*prajñā*), emotional equanimity (*upeksā*) and calm (*śamatha*). Even *śamatha* techniques, focusing on the cultivation of a sense of calmness, are not as focused on the attainment of a transient or altered state of consciousness as one might think from their delineation of various stages on the path. As Sharf argues, much of the discussion devoted to *jhāna*s (states of meditative absorption) represents a rather ancient and formulaic presentation of stages rather than a phenomenological account of actual experiences. Moreover, the primary goal of such practices is said to be the cultivation of a persistent state of mental and emotional stability throughout one's life. Similarly, in traditional Buddhist accounts of the eight (occasionally nine) *jhāna*s, the higher levels of attainment correspond to planes of existence within traditional Buddhist cosmology into which one can be reborn and should not simply be read as referring to transient psychological states in the modern sense. Repeated cultivation of these states were seen as opportunities to "visit" such realms and fine-tune one's consciousness for a future, more favorable, rebirth. This reflected the aim for many traditional practitioners of being reborn in one of these realms in a future life. To put this another way, traditional Buddhist contemplative literature reflects a traditional cosmological dimension that tends to be ignored by modern psychologized interpretations. The modern psychological interpretation of classic Buddhist accounts is not the abstraction of Buddhist meditative experience into some universalized, neutral, and culture-free framework, but the reinterpretation of classical understandings according to a modern interpretive framework with its own metaphysical assumptions about reality and the nature of the human.

We should also note that much Asian contemplative literature assumes that it is "everyday" experiences, rather than the rarefied states with which they are concerned, that are more appropriately characterized by fluctuation and "alteration." States of meditative-concentration (*samādhi*) represent increasingly focused and stabilized patterns of consciousness. The goal, as stated by the *Yoga Sūtras of Patañjali*, is the eradication of transient mental states rather than their cultivation (YS1.2) through the eventual realization of one's status as a stabilized witness-consciousness established in an isolated state of liberation (*kaivalya*). To interpret classical Asian contemplative literatures as if they only provide accounts of mystical experiences ignores the ritual, didactic, propadeutical, and soteriological functions that they perform within their respective traditions. As Robert Sharf (1995, p. 238) notes, Buddhist meditative manuals like Buddhaghosa's *Visuddhimagga* (Theravāda) are "first and foremost scholarly compendiums, compiled by monks of formidable learning who were attempting to systematize and schematize the confused and often conflicting descriptions of practices and stages scattered throughout the canon." Such works are often expressing polemical arguments or didactic points with a decidedly liturgical dimension.

The twentieth-century psychologized translations of Asian contemplative literature have provided the means for constructing highly reified and ahistorical representations of the "world religions." This approach simultaneously divests such traditions, practices, and literature of their cultural and philosophical specificity and renders them amenable to both perennialist claims for the existence of a transhistorical set of practices known as mysticism and also secular approaches that seek to "strip back" and divest meditative practices of their ancient metaphysical, cultural, and "Oriental" associations. In this way, Asian contemplative technologies become divorced from the liturgical, doctrinal, ethical, and cosmological context in which they operated.

Psychologically inflected approaches also tend to ignore the social, political, and institutional history of Asian meditative traditions. It is clear, for instance, that before the Samnyasi Rebellion against the East India Company of the late eighteenth century and the suppression of their networks by the British Raj, Indian renouncers and ascetics were often heavily involved in the social, economic, and political activities of Indian communities, acting as traders, money-lenders, and military mercenaries (van der Veer, 1988; Pinch, 1996). One might also think of the role of Buddhist secret White Lotus societies in the Ming revolution in China or the Daoist-inspired Yellow Turban Revolution (184–204 CE) which contributed to the fall of the Han dynasty (206 BCE–220 CE). This history, however, does not sit well with prevailing Western assumptions about other-worldly mystics or with the "spiritualizing" agenda of reformist figures like Vivekānanda. The study of Asian meditative traditions and institutions needs to take account of this history if it is to avoid an account based on ideal forms and Orientalist stereotypes.

The partiality of psychologized accounts of meditation enabled the occlusion of the social, institutional, and cosmological/metaphysical context in which traditional meditative traditions and practices have operated. It only became possible to represent Asian traditions in this stereotypical and homogeneous fashion because of the unprecedented transformation of Asian societies and polities brought about by European colonization and the "modernization" agenda that emerged from this encounter (see Braun, 2013; Schedneck, 2015; Cassanita, 2018).

It is important to challenge an uncritical reading of ancient Asian traditions and literature in terms of modern psychological constructions of "religious experience." While there is much in pre-modern Asian contemplative literature discussing states of meditative awareness, undue emphasis upon this in contemporary accounts of these traditions has often been at the expense of an appreciation of their institutional, ritual, and cosmological dimensions (Sharf, 1995; King, 1999a, 2005). Through a complex process of cultural mediations a largely ahistorical and homogeneous category has been constructed—"Eastern spirituality" or "Eastern meditation"—which has also contributed to the homogenization and commodification of such traditions in a modern consumerist and capitalist context.

Asian traditions, therefore, entered the Western mindset framed by an Orientalist stereotype, which tended to portray "the East" as the mirror opposite of Western modernity. "The West" was often seen as masculine, dominant, rational and scientific whereas "the East" was, by nature, seen as more feminine (or feminized), subjugated, irrational, superstitious and mystical. That this is a classic case of projection should not be difficult to see. Throughout most of the twentieth century, discussion about "Eastern religions" and meditation were framed by their association with the mystical, these stereotypes, and the reaction to them. By the late twentieth century the emphasis upon "mysticism" began to subside, being replaced by the rising discourse of "spirituality."

The psychological framing of yoga and meditation maps all too easily onto modern Western notions of an atomistic and autonomous individual (Carrette, 2007). However, the psychological interpretive frame within which discussions of "mysticism" and "spirituality" unfolded has also tended to confuse philosophical claims about the nature of reality in classical Asian literature with a post-Enlightenment intellectual framework, where such accounts are read as referring to extraordinary and transitory experiences of a private, individual, and extraordinary nature (King, 1999a, ch. 1 and 8). This shift is rendered largely invisible precisely because of the centrality of psychological accounts of the human being to contemporary assumptions about modernity and human existence, but it is important to note that its normativity masks an act of appropriation and a translation of such traditions in relation to a modern *dispositif* (to adapt a term from Foucault), grounded in the hegemony of the "psy disciplines" as the key entrance point for understanding modern subjectivity (Rose, 1998).

The rise of the discourse of the various "*psy* disciplines" has been crucial in the cultural mediation and translation of Asian contemplative traditions into the interpretive framework of Euro-American models of modernity. One consequence of this, building upon earlier colonial mediations of Asian traditions, has been the emphasis that has been placed upon a preoccupation with "mystical experiences" as peculiarly constitutive of Asian religious traditions. This has rendered such traditions amenable to appropriation by a modern psychological discourse of "spirituality" and by various New Age "self-religions" (Heelas, 1996) in the latter half of the twentieth century. These contemporary cultural forms build upon earlier characterizations of India as "the home of spirituality" (Vivekānanda et al.), and interest in such movements by Occultists,[5] Theosophists, Transcendentalists, and figures such as William James, but only really took root in Euro-American mainstream culture in the 1960s. The emphasis on individual

[5] For a particularly insightful discussion of the often-overlooked, occultist dimensions of the reception of Asian meditational traditions in the West see Payne (2012).

self-expression and interiorization that characterized this phase in the transculturation of yoga in the West also provided the platform for the more recent commodification of such traditions in a global marketplace of corporate business activity (Lau, 2000; Carrette & King, 2005). Although the selective appropriation of Indian contemplative traditions within "New Age" circles already exemplifies a significant transformation of such traditions, the emergence of explicitly capitalist forms of religiosity did not develop significantly until the 1980s and 1990s, where one finds an explosion of popular literature on "eastern spirituality" within business, professional, and educational spheres and staff development courses designed to alleviate stress in the workplace. Much of this phenomenon reflects a further stage in the "de-traditionalization" and commodification of yoga systems and practices and amounts to what one might call a corporatization of Asian religions (see Carrette & King, 2005). In this way we can talk, broadly speaking, of three phases in the modern encounter between Asian traditions of meditation and the West. The first phase (pre-1960) involved assimilation by various Occultist and eastern-oriented movements in the Western world. The second phase (1960s–1990s) involved the assimilation of Asian meditation as alternative forms of spirituality in the counter-cultural movements of the late twentieth century. By the end of that century, however, the third phase of assimilation establishes itself through the appropriation, commodification, and reinterpretation of Asian meditative techniques in ways that facilitates everyday life and consumer activity in an age of global capitalism. This final phase involves the domestication or normalization of meditation as an everyday feature of modern secular life.

Asian Meditation and Science

Avoiding the Scylla of interpreting Asian meditational practices and traditions in terms of the concepts of "religion" and "mysticism" has generated a tendency in some circles to rush toward the Charybdis of emphasizing their essential compatibility with science. This trend, as we have seen, goes back to the colonial period and the rise of reformist perspectives within the various Asian traditions. There are three fundamental ways in which Asian meditation has been interpolated into existing discourses of medical science: first, through an emphasis on bodily health, fitness, and well-being; second, as a form of or aid to psychotherapeutic practice and stress reduction; and third, via cognitive scientific and neurological research on the effects of meditation on the brain.

Yoga and Bodily Health

The first avenue by which practices and traditions of Asian meditation have been incorporated into a scientific discourse in Western societies has been through claims about its efficacy as a means of maintaining bodily health and fitness. Here, we have sometimes seen an interesting bifurcation of (Hindu) yoga from (Buddhist) meditation, with discourses about the former often focusing upon posture, fitness, and physical health benefits, and the latter treated, as discussed in our next section, as a means of maintaining mental health. As I have suggested this division replicates the Cartesian dualism between mind and body that still resonates in modern Western culture and also reflects the different translational trajectories of an ethnically-framed notion of "Hindu yoga" from a heavily abstracted, psychologized, and trans-historical representation of "Buddhist meditation."

As mentioned earlier, in India "Yoga" became fused with an emphasis on muscularity, fitness, and the culture of the gymnasium. Already upheld as a national symbol of India and as a spiritual "science" by Vivekānanda from the end of the nineteenth century, by the 1930s yoga had become nationalized, partially "de-traditionalized," and its introspective and individualistic dimensions increasingly emphasized at the expense of its soteriological underpinnings. With regard to the seminal role played by Sri Yogendra in this process, Elliott Goldberg (2016, p. 73) notes that,

> By stripping hatha yoga of its traditional ideology, methodology, and community in the early 20th century, he helped make possible (but, needless to say, didn't envision) the development of embodied yogic meditation—the integration of meditation into one's conditioning *asana* practice—in the late 20th century.

Figures such as the Indian bodybuilder Venkatesha Iyer (1898–1980) facilitated the combination of muscle cult and Hatha Yoga practice by juxtaposing pictures of bodybuilding poses and yoga postures in works such as *Perfect Physique—A Proem in My System* (Iyer, 1936; see also Goldberg, 2016, pp. 149–150). This association, cemented by figures such as the yoga teacher Tirumalai Krishnamacharya (1888–1989), promoted widespread instruction in a modern posturally-oriented form of yoga practice as a crucial remedy for the perceived crisis of Indian masculinity that had been generated by colonial rule. It was through the dissemination of yoga training and practice across India that Indian men could regain their cultural and individual self-confidence and authority and overcome colonially inspired stereotypes about Indian effeminacy (King, 1999a, pp. 113–116; Sinha, 1995). The hyper-masculine nature of this form of yoga became rather ironically transposed and transformed in the West when, under the influence of writers such as the American journalist Louise Morgan (1903–1983; see Goldberg, 2016, ch. 22), yoga was first introduced to middle-class women as a potent elixir of youth, vitality, and feminine fitness (Strauss, 2005, pp. 79–80) and merged with contemporary interests in gymnastics, posture and dance as quintessentially "feminine" fitness pursuits (Singleton, 2010, ch. 7).

Mindfulness Meditation and the Pursuit of Mental Health

While yoga in the modern Western world tended to take a physicalist and largely Hindu-inflected route in the late twentieth century, meditation, especially in its Buddhist forms, has increasingly been represented as focused upon the mind, mirroring the Cartesian dualism of Western culture. Responding to the classificatory binaries of European/Western society, which were generating a lively and sometimes fractious ideological dispute between Darwinian science and traditional forms of Christian belief during the Victorian period, a range of Buddhist modernists from Anagārika Dharmapāla (1864–1933) in Ceylon to Japan's Shaku Sōen (1860–1919)—the first Zen master to teach in the United States—began to argue that Buddhist teachings and meditational practices were not primarily "religious" or "dogmatic" like Christianity but were essentially philosophical, scientific, and humanistic in nature (Almond, 1998; Lopez, 2008, McMahan, 2008). Once "re-classified" in this fashion, a process began whereby Buddhist meditation could be shorn of itsx specifically Asian cultural accretions, its institutional and social roots, and its highly ritualized forms and re-presented to the world as a technology of introspection—a "science of the mind." As Donald Lopez Jr. notes:

> Whether to counter the missionary's charge that Buddhism was superstition and idolatry, or to counter the colonialist's claim that the Asian was prone to fanciful flights of the mind and meaningless rituals of body, science proved the ideal weapon for the Buddhists. It was not Christianity but Buddhism, in fact, that was the scientific religion, the religion best suited for modernity, not just in Asia but throughout the world. Buddhism was the opposite of Christianity. Christianity has a creator God and Buddhism has no God; Christianity has faith, Buddhism has reason; Christianity has dogma, Buddhism has philosophy; Christianity (at least a certain kind) has public ritual, Buddhism has private reflection; Christianity has sin, Buddhism has karma; Christianity has prayer, Buddhism has meditation; Christ is divine, the Buddha is human . . . Some even went so far as to declare that Buddhism was not a religion at all, but was itself a science, a science of the mind.
>
> (Lopez, 2012, p. 11)

The emergent Buddhist modernisms of Asia during this period, responding to the agenda and binaries of European intellectual thought, provided the intellectual foundations for the subsequent emergence of the Mindfulness-Based Stress Reduction (MBSR) program of Jon Kabat-Zinn (1990) and its variants that have become so popular today. This of course would have been impossible without the earlier contribution of figures such as Swāmi Vivekānanda and Dharmapāla, as well as mid-twentieth-century figures such as D. T. Suzuki (1870–1966) who sought to distill the "universal" message of "eastern spirituality" from its specifically *Asian* cultural and religious underpinnings, thereby facilitating the migration and translation of classical Buddhist discussions of mental training into a modern psychologized discourse of "experience" (Sharf, 1995; King, 1999a; Carrette & King, 2005). As I have attempted to demonstrate, this process of translation and transformation is not a value-neutral de-contextualization of Asian meditational practices but rather their *re-contextualization* in terms of a new cultural, political, and symbolic order (Sharf, 1995; King, 1999a).

One particular candidate for this transformation has been the rise of mindfulness-based meditation techniques in the contemporary era and their popularity, in the form of a mostly secularized therapeutic context, as a form of stress reduction. Although traditional Buddhist accounts speak of the cultivation of right mindfulness (*sati*) and right concentration (*samādhi*) as important, and mutually reinforcing, steps on the Buddhist eightfold path, the notion of "pure mindfulness" or "insight-only" meditation, like the formation of modern postural yoga in India in the 1920s and 1930s, is a relatively recent development emerging out of the colonial context of Burmese Buddhism in the early twentieth century.

The contemporary global spread of modern "mindfulness" practices has been driven by the impact of figures such as the Vietnamese Zen teacher Thich Nhat Hanh (b. 1926) and the 14th Dalai Lama (b. 1935) but also, quite crucially, by the twentieth-century revival of Theravāda meditation in South East Asia and the meditational teachings of the Burmese monk Ledi Sayadaw (1846–1923) and his student Mahāsī Sayādaw (1904–1982). Concerned about the perceived decline of Buddhism under British colonial rule, a new form of Buddhist meditation—called "pure insight" (*suddha-vipassanā*) or "mindfulness-only"—was developed in Burma that could be taught in a simplified form to the laity (Braun, 2013). In this way, for the first time, a new distinctive form of Buddhist meditation was developed and taught to the Burmese masses in a way that directly parallels the Indian example with regard to the spread of modern postural yoga during the same period. This Burmese Buddhist method, interspersed with influences from Japanese and Korean Zen, Hindu Advaita Vedānta, and the teachings of contemporary spiritual teachers such as Jiddu Krishnamurti (1895–1986) and Ramana Maharishi (1879–1950) produced a fertile ground for the emergence of what is now known as mindfulness in the Western world. Carried forward by a generation of North American acolytes such as Jack Kornfield, Joseph Goldstein, Sharon Salzberg, and Jon Kabat-Zinn, who furthered the integration of Asian meditative practice with Western psychology, these practices were exported to the Western world and are now widely adopted as techniques for stress reduction and general health and well-being in healthcare systems across the Western world. It is somewhat ironic that Buddhist meditation, traditionally understood as a means of increasing awareness of the impermanent (*anitya*), stressful, and unsatisfactory nature of existence (*duḥkha*), now finds itself being deployed in the contemporary period as a therapeutic technique for overcoming stress.

Asian Meditation and "Brain Science"

In the last three decades, energized by the modernist characterization of Asian (especially Buddhist) meditation as a "science of the mind," there has been a steady growth of interest among neurologists and cognitive scientists in the effects of sustained meditation practice on brain states. Early studies by cognitive neuroscientists focused on the practice of Transcendental Meditation as taught by Maharishi Mahesh Yogi and demonstrated a recognizable decrease in respiration, heart rate, metabolism, and oxygen consumption as well as a shift from alpha to slower theta waves, with additional faster beta-waves emerging from deep meditative states of concentration. Subsequent research has taken many forms but has also been energized by a series of conferences between the 14th Dalai Lama, French writer and Buddhist monk Matthieu Ricard (b. 1946), and various cognitive psychologists and neuroscientists (most notably Francisco Varela, 1946–2001) leading to the establishment of organizations such as the Mind and Life Institute to explore the integration of scientific research with "contemplative practice and wisdom traditions." This work is still in its relative infancy but, as Donald Lopez (2008, p. 207) remarks, introduces "a welcome empirical element to the discourse." Nevertheless, there are a number of philosophical limitations in much of the neurological research on brain states and meditation. First, contemporary neurological approaches generally lack a full appreciation of the context and role of meditative practices within the history of Asian traditions and the rich and varied philosophical debates about their meaning and significance. Similarly, the social, ethical, ritual, and cosmological dimensions of Asian meditational practices are ignored. Modern neurological studies of brain states, framed as they are within a discourse of scientific objectivity and neutrality, offers little in the way of an appreciation of the cultural location and embedded assumptions of their own approach to the subject-matter (see Carrette, 2007). In this way, prevailing assumptions about the materialistic nature of reality, the primacy of brain over mind, and metaphysical and methodological assumptions about the individuality of human consciousness continue to frame most of the work within the field and remain largely unquestioned. As Evan Thompson (2017, pp. 55–56) suggests, the assumptions at work within mainstream cognitive science in its study of meditation also tend to reinforce certain prevailing cultural assumptions:

> Mindfulness does not exist inside the brain; it exists in the social world of human life. Furthermore, what counts as being mindful depends on the social context and the culture... The idea that mindfulness is in the head feeds the current mindfulness mania. It reinforces selfish individualism—all you really need to deal with is your own mind, not the larger social setting. You can practice mindfulness in the privacy of your own office cubicle. The idea that mindfulness is a private practice reinforces consumerism by making mindfulness into a commodity that an individual can acquire.

Conclusion: "Spirituality" and the Secular Adaptation of Asian Meditation

There have been and continue to be many interesting and creative intersections and cross-fertilizations occurring on the interface of modern psychotherapy, medical science, and Asian meditational practice, not least because it is primarily through the medium of psychotherapy, psychology, and health and well-being discourses that Asian meditational practices and teachings have been imported to the West, once those practices have been cognitively disassociated from their apparently "religious" moorings. One reason for the rise in popularity of the discourse of spirituality in the late twentieth and early twenty-first centuries has been the utility of the concept of the spiritual as a means of overriding the "secular versus religion" binary in modern societies where secularization has been especially influential. Meditation, when understood in this fashion as a portable "technology of the self," becomes available to those with no institutional religious affiliation or sensibility, as well as to those of a specific religious affiliation (such as liberal Christians) precisely because it has become detached from traditional Asian cosmological world views and social identities and presented as an empirical science of the mind. The concept of spirituality created the mediating cultural space for "non-religious" and (secular) scientific engagement with Asian forms of meditation by creating a bridge between the religious and the non-religious. In this way, meditation became sufficiently dis-embedded from specifically Asian "religious" or metaphysical frameworks for modern scientists to approach its study as a distinct and accessible set of psycho-physical practices.

It is important to remember however that Asian meditation practices in their original cultural contexts were largely the province of the virtuosi rather than the masses, prior to the modern period. Meditational practices did not constitute a form of psychotherapy or healthcare, though they were often claimed to have beneficial therapeutic consequences for the practitioner; nor were they an ancient form of psychotherapy, though they may have provided insights about the inner workings of the human mind and body. Most significantly, the underlying worldviews of modern Western psychology and traditional Asian meditational systems differ both in their framing of the transformation of consciousness and in the wider existential, soteriological, and cosmological significance of their practice.

References

Almond, P. (1988). *The British discovery of Buddhism*. Cambridge: Cambridge University Press.

Altglas, V. (2014) *From Yoga to Kabbalah: Religious exoticism and the logics of bricolage*. New York: Oxford University Press.

Braun, E. (2013). *The birth of insight: Meditation, modern Buddhism, and the Burmese Monk Ledi Sayadaw*. Chicago: University of Chicago Press.

Bronkhorst, J. (2000). *The two traditions of meditation in ancient India* (2nd ed.). Delhi: Motilal Banarsidass.

Bruce, S. (2017). *Secular beats spiritual: The westernization of the easternization of the west*. Oxford: Oxford University Press.

Burton, N., & Laughlin, J. (1973). *The Asian journal of Thomas Merton*. New York: New Directions Books.

Buswell, R., Jr. (1992). *The Zen monastic experience: Buddhist practice in contemporary Korea*. Princeton, NJ: Princeton University Press.

Carrette, J., & King, R. (2005). *Selling spirituality: The silent takeover of religion*. Routledge.

Carrette, J. R. (2007). *Religion and critical psychology: Religious experience in the knowledge economy*. London: Routledge.
Cassanita, J. L. (2018). *Remembering the present: Mindfulness in Buddhist Asia*. Ithaca, NY: Cornell University Press.
Cavanaugh, W. T. (2017). Religion/nation/globalization: Religion and violence. In Richard King (Ed.), *Religion, theory, critique: Classic and contemporary approaches and methodologies* (pp. 589–599). New York: Columbia University Press.
Cox, H. (1977). *Turning East: The Promise and Peril of the New Orientalism*. New York: Simon and Schuster. doi:10.2307/3710219
Crosby, K. (2005).'Devotion to the Buddha in Theravāda and its role in meditation,' in John Brockington and Anna King (eds.). The Intimate Other: love divine in Indic religions, New Delhi: Orient Longman: 244–277.
Crosby, K. (2013). *Traditional Theravada meditation and its modern-era suppression*. Hong Kong: The Buddha Dharma Centre of Hong Kong.
Dawson, A. (2006). East is east except when it's west: The easternisation thesis and the western habitus. *Journal of Religion and Society 8*, 1–13.
Fitzgerald. T. (2000). The ideology of religious studies, Oxford: Oxford University Press.
Fitzgerald, T. (2007). Discourse on civility and barbarity, Oxford: Oxford University Press.
Goldberg, E. (2016). *The path of modern yoga: The history of an embodied spiritual practice*. Rochester, VT: Inner Traditions.
Gyatso, J. (1999). Healing burns with fire: The facilitations of experience in Tibetan Buddhism. *Journal of the American Academy of Religion 67*(1), 113–147.
Hamilton, M. (2002). The easternisation thesis: Critical reflections. *Religion 32*, 243–258.
Harrison, P. (2006). "Science" and "religion": Constructing the boundaries. *Journal of Religion 86*(1), 81–106.
Heelas, P. (1996). The new age movement. The celebration of the self and the sacralization of modernity, Oxford: Blackwells.
Hobson, J. M. (2004). *The eastern origins of western civilization*. Cambridge: Cambridge University Press.
Hölscher, L. (2013). The religious and the secular: Semantic reconfigurations of the religious field in Germany from the eighteenth to the twentieth century. In M. Eggert and L. Hölscher (Eds.), *Religion and secularity: Transformations and transfers of religious discourses in Europe and Asia* (pp. 9–33). Leiden: Brill.
Iyer, K. V. (1936). *Perfect physique—A proem to my system*. Bangalore City, India: Bangalore Press.
Jain, A. (2015). *Selling yoga: From counterculture to pop culture*. Oxford: Oxford University Press.
Kabat-Zinn, J. (1990). Full catastrophe living: Using the wisdom of your body and mind to face stress, pain and illness. New York, NY: Delacorte.
King, R. (1999a). *Orientalism and religion: Postcolonial theory, India and "the Mystic East."* Routledge.
King, R. (1999b). *Indian philosophy: An introduction to Hindu and Buddhist thought*. Edinburgh: Edinburgh University Press.
King, R. (2005). Asian traditions and mysticism: The legacy of William James in the study of religions. In J. Carrette (Ed.), *William James and the Varieties of Religious Experience. A Centenary Celebration*. London: Routledge.
King, R. (2011). Imagining religions in India: Colonialism and the mapping of South Asian history and culture. In M. Dressler and A-P. S. Mandair (Eds.), *Secularism and religion-making*. New York: Oxford University Press.

King, R. (2016). "Paying attention" in a digital economy: Reflections on the role of analysis and judgement within contemporary discourses of mindfulness and comparisons with classical Buddhist accounts of *sati*. In R. E. Purser, D. Forbes, & A. Burke, *Handbook of mindfulness: culture, context and social engagement*. Switzerland: Springer.

Knitter, P. (2009). *Without Buddha I could not be a Christian*. Oxford: One World.

Von Stuckrad, K. (2014) *The Scientification of Religion: An Historical Study of Discursive Change*. doi:10.1515/9781614513490.178

Latour, B. (1993). We have never been modern, Cambridge: Harvard University Press.

Lau, K. J. (2000). *New Age capitalism: Making money east of Eden*. University of Pennsylvania Press.

Lopez, D., Jr. (2008). *Buddhism and science: A guide for the perplexed*. Chicago: University of Chicago Press.

Lopez, D., Jr. (2012). *The scientific Buddha: His short and happy life*. New Haven, CT: Yale University Press.

Malinar, A. (2012). Yoga practices in the Bhagavadgita. In D. G. White (Ed.), *Yoga in Practice* (pp. 58–72). Princeton, NJ: Princeton University Press.

McEvilley, T. (2002). *The shape of ancient thought*. New York: Allworth Press.

McMahan, D. (2008), The making of Buddhist modernism, New York and Oxford: Oxford University Press.

Payne, R. K. (2012). Buddhism and the powers of the mind. In David McMahan (Ed.), *Buddhism in the modern world* (pp. 233–255). New York: Routledge.

Pinch, W. R. (1996). *Peasants and monks in British India*. Berkeley: University of California Press.

Quijano, A. (2000). Coloniality of power, Eurocentrism, and Latin America. *Nepantla: Views from South 1*(3), 533–580.

Ristuccia, N. J. (2013). Eastern religions and the west: The making of an image. *History of Religions* 53(2), 170–204.

Rose, N. (1998). *Inventing our selves, psychology, power and personhood*. Cambridge: Cambridge University Press.

Schedneck, B. (2015). *Thailand's international meditation centers: Tourism and the global commodification of religious practices*. Abingdon: Routledge.

Sharf, R. (1995). Buddhist modernism and the rhetoric of meditative experience. *Numen* 42(3), 228–283.

Sharf, R. (2014a). Mindfulness and mindlessness in early Chan. *Philosophy East and West* 64(4), 933–964.

Sharf, R. (2014b). Is nirvāṇa the same as insentience? Chinese struggles with an Indian Buddhist ideal. In J. Kieschnick & M. Shara (Eds.), *India in the Chinese imagination: Myth, religion, and thought* (pp. 141–170). Philadelphia: University of Pennsylvania Press.

Singleton, M. (2010). *Yoga body. The origins of modern postural practice*. Oxford: Oxford University Press.

Sinha, M. (1995). *Colonial masculinity: The "manly Englishman" and the "effeminate Bengali" in the late nineteenth century*. Manchester: Manchester University Press.

Sjoman, N. E. (1999). *The yoga tradition of the Mysore palace* (2nd ed.). New Delhi: Abhinav Publications.

Strauss, S. (2005). *Positioning yoga: Balancing acts across cultures*. Oxford & New York: Berg.

Thompson, E. (2017). Looping effects and the cognitive science of mindfulness meditation. In D. L. McMahan and E. Braun (Eds.), *Meditation, Buddhism and science*. New York: Oxford University Press.

Van der Veer, P. (1988). *Gods on earth: The management of religious experience and identity in a North Indian pilgrimage centre*. Athlone Press, Continuum.

Wallace, A. (2003). *Buddhism and science: Breaking new ground*. New York: Columbia University Press.

Zaehner, R. C (1974). *Our Savage God: The perverse use of eastern thought*. New York: Sheed & Ward.

Žižek, S. (2001). *On Belief*. London: Routledge.

CHAPTER 3

STUDYING THE EFFECTS OF MEDITATION

The First Fifty Years

DOUG OMAN

The Development of Meditation

Art is long, life is short [*Ars longa, vita brevis*]

—Hippocrates

This chapter offers a condensed overview of the main currents of modern empirical research on meditation, which began in earnest in approximately 1970. A full understanding of modern meditation research requires taking into account the historical context, conceptual richness, and complexity of meditative traditions. We first recall key features of the traditional approaches to meditative practices that launched and have informed modern scientific research on meditation. Next, we examine major post-1970 trends, turning points, findings, and challenges in empirical meditation research. We also sketch recent ethical and cross-cultural controversies, describing potentially helpful emerging lines of research. We close by revisiting the status of research on alternative states of consciousness.

Modern scientific meditation research has been shaped in numerous ways by spiritually rooted premodern meditative traditions that began to coalesce as long ago as early Indian civilization, perhaps supported by newly evolved genetically supported human capacities (Crangle, 1994; Rossano, 2007). Over time, meditative traditions gradually emerged in all major world religions and are known today by names such as Kabbalah, Hesychasm, Sufism, Astanga Yoga, and Vipassana. Such meditation traditions have been a source of meditative techniques, meditation teachers, descriptions of meditation-induced states of consciousness, and theories about how meditation transforms consciousness.

Both the processes and content of meditative activities can potentially be important, according to many influential pre-modern understandings of meditation (e.g., Patanjali's *Yoga Sūtras*; Oman & Bormann, 2018). Many influential meditation researchers who began their careers in the 1960s or 1970s, such as Roger Walsh, Deane Shapiro, David Orme-Johnson, Richard Davidson, and Jon Kabat-Zinn, learned meditation through meditative traditions, and their writing and thinking has been informed by what has often amounted to multi-year or lifelong participant observation in such traditions. Several meditative traditions—primarily Asian-based—have also been sources of what scholars have called *meditation adepts*—people proficient at using meditation for sustaining unusual states of consciousness or demonstrating extraordinary capacities, such as exercising volitional control over heart rate or other normally involuntary bodily processes.

The empirical study of meditation thus began not with a blank conceptual slate, but with a rich and varied, but unsystematized array of culturally and religiously derived inputs, both practical and conceptual. In the 1970s, as the new field sought order and coherence, multiple cross-cultural reviews sought to identify parallel themes or "common denominators" across major traditional systems worldwide (Goleman, 1977; Naranjo and Ornstein, 1972, p. 5). Three decades later, positive psychologists identified numerous examples of what they called "coherent resemblance" across culturally diverse conceptions of character strengths and virtues (Peterson and Seligman, 2004, p. 35). Similarly, these early meditation reviews, quoted several times in the next section, identified several conceptual and practical parallels among meditative traditions that remain useful for framing cross-culturally resonant understandings of meditation.

Nature and Purpose of Meditation

Although no consensus definition exists, in its first decades, most or all modern meditation research investigated practices that combine three cardinal features. First, meditation generally involves *sitting*. That is, meditation is an activity that is usually done in a seated posture, with little or no physical movement. Such an understanding of meditation is consistent with contemporary Western popular cultural representations of meditation as a seated activity. And sitting is, indeed, an integral feature of meditation systems ranging from Zen ("Zazen" literally means seated meditation), Transcendental Meditation (TM), and sitting components of Buddhist Vipassana and of Mindfulness Based Stress Reduction (MBSR), to methods described in Patanjali's *Yoga Sūtras* and the *Bhagavad Gītā*, as well as practices such as Hesychasm in Eastern Orthodox Christianity, and modern forms of Christian Centering Prayer (Johnson, 2010).

Second, meditation is part of an effort not only to regulate attention but also to *train attention*. Four decades ago, Goleman's (1977) survey of diverse worldwide systems of meditation-based spiritual practice concluded that "the need for the meditator to retrain his attention, whether through concentration or mindfulness, is the single invariant ingredient in the recipe for altering consciousness of every meditation system" (p. 111). Similarly, for Rao (2017, p. 132), "the core commonality, the invariant condition among all systems of meditation past and present, undoubtedly has to do with attention."

Third, seated meditation is typically done during a *dedicated time period*, often in seclusion or with other people who are meditating. For example, TM and MBSR teach people to meditate seated between twenty and forty minutes per day. Often meditators are encouraged to engage in meditation regularly, usually as a daily routine.

For clarity, this chapter will whenever possible reserve the phrase *sitting meditation* and the noun *meditation* for practices that combine all three of these cardinal features. In contrast, practices that serve attention-training functions but that involve physical movement or are done throughout the day can be termed *non-seated practices*, which we discuss mainly as ancillary practices done in conjunction with meditation. Our nomenclature is thus largely aligned with that of Sedlmeier et al. (2012) as well as that of Rao (2017, pp. 125–126), who noted that "much confusion" has been generated by scientific discourse in which "the meaning of meditation is significantly stretched beyond its conventional meaning to include any kind of practice that could conceivably lead to a quiet focused mind." Research on motion-oriented practices such as Tai Chi or yoga posture-exercises (*āsanas*), for example, are beyond the scope of this chapter.

Goals of Meditation

It is important to remember that the traditional overarching *goals* of meditation have been spiritual, aiming to transform the meditator's consciousness and will, to align them with the eternal realities and sacred truths of life, however such truths have been understood in each tradition. These spiritual goals of traditional meditation were well understood by many of the early empirical meditation researchers and are an inescapable if sometimes overlooked facet of meditation as a cultural phenomenon and as a complex practice meriting multi-disciplinary empirical investigation.

A great deal of early meditation research explored how seated meditation might induce an *altered state of consciousness* (ASC). Such investigative aims made sense because virtually all traditional meditative systems, ranging from Zen to Hesychasm, have identified discrete altered states of consciousness that may be attained during a meditation session and are "set off from other states... mutually exclusive of the normal... waking, sleeping, and dreaming" (Goleman, 1977, p. 116). Properly cultivated, such meditation-facilitated ASCs are viewed as spiritually helpful. Yet meditative states experienced in-session are ultimately intended and expected to facilitate the transformation of all of daily living—that is, meditation "paths all propose the same basic formula... the diffusion of the effects of meditation into the meditator's waking, dreaming, and sleep states" (Goleman, 1977, p. 117).

Most commonly, this diffusion is supported by what for convenience—and because this chapter is focused on meditation—we call *ancillary practices*, which traditions view as able to aid and synergize with seated meditation in fostering altered states of consciousness and other beneficial effects. Categories of ancillary practices include non-seated practices, in-session preparatory practices, and adherence to *ancillary beliefs*. For example, the Buddhist Noble Eightfold Path enjoins eight practices ranging from "right concentration" and "right speech" to "right livelihood" and "right view." With regard to ancillary beliefs, in varying ways, virtually all meditative traditions (but not necessarily all modernized clinical forms of meditation) have taught that meditators should assimilate what might be called meditative or spiritual schemas, or *meditative/spiritual framing resources* that support viewing meditative experiences as well as everyday events through a spiritual lens.

Finally, every traditional meditative system has taught the existence of at least one "awakened state" that results when meditatively generated ASCs have been cultivated and some of their features integrated into all departments of daily living. Acquisition of such an awakened state "appends new functions on the normal states [such as waking and dreaming], changing their character... this kind of transformation of awareness is an altered *trait* of consciousness, an enduring change transforming the meditator's every moment.... Virtually every system of meditation recognizes the awakened state as the ultimate goal of meditation" (Goleman, 1977, p. 116, emphasis added). Yet each tradition labels its awakened state with a different name (including Sahaj Samadhi, Devekut, Purity of Heart, Baqa, Jivamukti, Cosmic Consciousness, Turiyatita, Siddha, Boddhisattva, Mujodo no taigeu ["no-mind"], and Arhantship, from a tabulation in Goleman, 1977, p. 117), leaving unresolved the significant and debated question of their degree of mutual resemblance across traditions.

Expanding Research and Fluctuating Goals

The earliest empirical meditation research did not engage with the diverse forms or spiritual goals of traditional methods of meditation. Instead, the handful of meditation studies published prior to 1970 focused primarily on physiologic indicators such as blood pressure and brain wave measures (e.g., Bagchi and Wegner, 1957). Many of these early studies examined advanced Indian yogis or Japanese Zen practitioners, and they provided some of the earliest evidence that meditative states may have distinct physiologic correlates.

But the late 1960s brought an explosion of Western popular interest in meditation, opening up new possibilities for study design and sample recruitment, thereby launching the main currents of modern meditation research. A steady stream of empirical research began to appear in 1970 and greatly accelerated from the mid-1990s, as shown in Figure 3.1.

By 2015, well over a thousand refereed empirical meditation research reports had been published as journal articles. To date, meditation research reports have appeared most often in the professional literatures of psychology, psychiatry, or neuroscience,

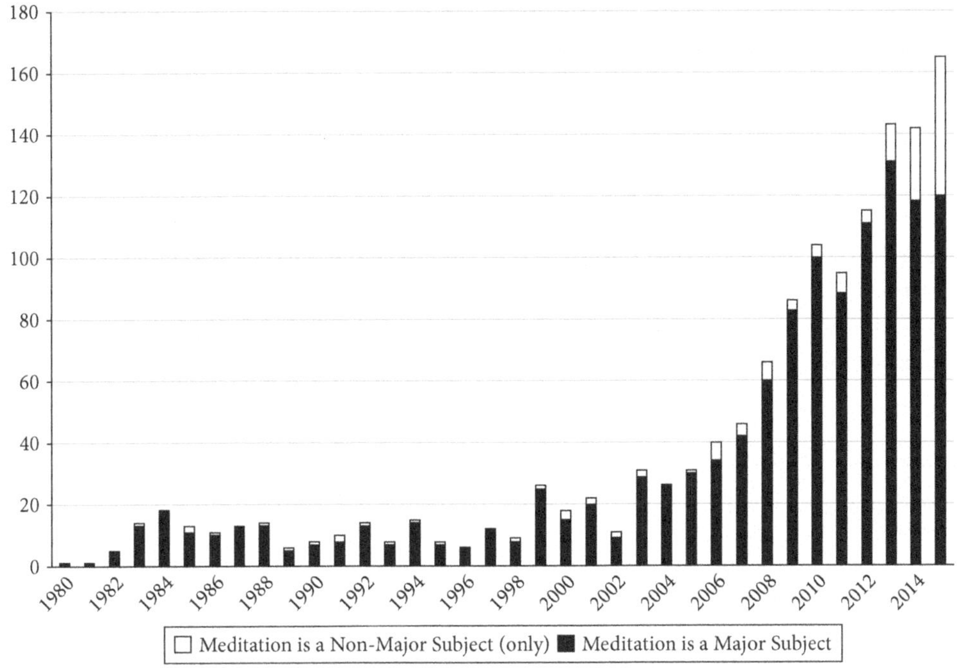

FIGURE 3.1 Publications Per Year on Subject "Meditation" Indexed in PsycINFO.

Note: Restricted to Peer reviewed, Methodology = Empirical study, Publication type = Journal article (searches conducted 12 June 2019). The chart begins in 1980 because only five earlier items were indexed in the PsychINFO database, which, although not exhaustive, was preferred because it permitted restriction to refereed empirical studies.

but have also appeared in interdisciplinary journals such as *Science*, *PLoS One*, and *PNAS*, and in journals for other medical fields, gerontology, counseling, nursing, and occasionally ethnic studies, education, religious studies, social work, and criminology. These empirical investigations have aimed to address a wide range of questions on the varieties, effects, aids, correlates, dynamics, and motivational sources of meditative practices. As we shall see, various research paradigms have come and gone, and interest in the spiritual sources and applications of meditation has fluctuated but never entirely abated, and in significant ways is now being rediscovered, even as clinical interest has become pervasive.

Table 3.1 presents a timeline that reflects many of the major themes, contending forces, and key events commonly emphasized in earlier histories of meditative research. Apart from Taylor's (1999) introduction to Murphy, Donovan, and Taylor's (1999) review and bibliography, very few attempts have been made, as we do here, to write chapter- or book-length histories of meditation research in its entirety, although numerous more circumscribed histories are available, such as a history of TM research (Farias & Wikholm, 2015, chapter 3), and other histories embedded in reviews or bibliographies (see also Ospina et al., [2007]). Notable recent events have also been added.

New scientific research fields employ simplified procedures and conceptions because they initially *need* such simplification to make their empirical task tractable. If so, then several dominant trends in meditation research appear to have provided gifts of temporary simplification that the field has needed–simplified views of ancillary practices, or of mediating processes that generate observed benefits, or the relevance or irrelevance of altered states of consciousness and of pre-existing spiritual diversity. Then, after a period of simplification, researchers have re-engaged with the temporarily marginalized facets of meditation, and re-aligned their models with the breadth of the phenomenon under study. In approximately chronological order, the following subsections explicate many key events from Table 3.1, and several cycles of simplification and movement toward re-alignment.

Table 3.1 Timeline of Major Events in Empirical Research on Meditation

Year	Event
1950s–60s	Earliest published empirical studies of meditation (e.g., Bagchi & Wegner, 1957)
1970	First TM study is published (in *Science*, by Wallace, 1970)
1973	Early (perhaps first) randomized trial of meditation (Vahia et al., 1973)
1975	Benson's (1975) *Relaxation Response*
1977	Goleman's (1977) *Meditative Mind*
1982	Kabat-Zinn's (1982) first published study
1984	Shapiro and Walsh's (1984) *Meditation: Classic and Contemporary Perspectives*
1991	First meta-analysis of meditation (Alexander, Rainforth, & Gelderloos, 1991)
1991	Mind and Life Institute founded with Dalai Lama's support
1995	NIH Technology Assessment Statement concludes relaxation and meditation are effective ways of reducing chronic pain (Taylor, 1999)
2000	First functional neuroimaging study of meditation (Lazar et al., 2000)
2002	Manifesto of Indian Psychology (Cornelissen, 2002)
2012	First meta-analysis of mindfulness meditation (Baer, 2003)
2005	First randomized trial of "spiritual" versus "secular" foci for sitting meditation (Wachholtz & Pargament, 2005)
2006	Lack of inclusiveness and "assimilative integration" critiqued in *American Psychologist* (Walsh & Shapiro, 2006)
2010	First issue of journal *Mindfulness* (Singh, 2010)
2011	*Contemporary Buddhism* special issue on mindfulness and science
2012	First comparative preference study (Burke, 2012)
2013	Mindfulness identified as top trend in psychology (Norcross et al., 2013)
~2013	Term "McMindfulness" gains usage
2015	Release of "Mindful Nation UK," a report by the British Parliament's Mindfulness All-Party Parliamentary Group

Early Ferment and the TM Paradigm

R. K. Wallace's (1970) study of Transcendental Meditation, published in the prominent journal *Science*, was a watershed event that in many ways launched the main currents of modern meditation research. Investigating a sample of fifteen college students, Wallace documented clear changes in oxygen consumption, heart rate, skin resistance, and brain wave frequencies as measured by electroencephalogram (EEG), leading him to argue that the meditators were experiencing a potentially clinically beneficial state of consciousness that "seems to be distinct from commonly encountered states of consciousness, such as wakefulness, sleep, and dreaming" (p. 1754). Importantly, Wallace observed that prior investigators had "difficulty in obtaining expert practitioners," and argued that TM could address this difficulty by supplying "a large number of subjects [who] were readily available [and] had received consistent and uniform instruction through an organization that specializes in teaching this technique" (p. 1752).

Wallace's paper, the first published study of TM, shows in microcosm many of the themes that were to emerge in TM research over the following decades. Already in the late 1960s, since at least 1967 when the Beatles went to India to spend time with the TM leader Maharishi Mahesh Yogi, TM had been the most prominent and widely practiced form of meditation in the West. In the mid-1970s, more than a thousand people were newly learning TM each day, and TM became nearly synonymous with meditation for much of the public and mass media. The TM organization began conducting a large number of scientific studies, and by the 1990s had conducted hundreds of empirical studies, many published in refereed journals (Farias & Wikholm, 2015; Taylor, 1999). Like Wallace's paper, many of these studies emphasized the clinical relevance of their findings, which linked the practice of TM to favorable outcomes such as reduced blood pressure, reduced substance abuse, and increased resistance to stress. In TM's six-volume collection of its first five-hundred-plus research studies, the published papers were indexed under headings such as health, metabolic changes, physiologic efficiency and stability, athletic performance, intelligence, education, development of personality, rehabilitation, and productivity and quality of life (Orme-Johnson et al., 1977–1990).

Methodologically, the first two decades of TM research were both innovative and limited. TM studies helped expand research designs beyond purely lab-based approaches. The TM research utilized longitudinal as well as cross-sectional designs, and sometimes employed control groups that were randomized or matched for demographic characteristics. However, the intervention itself was never fully explained (the TM organization treated it as proprietary), and it remained in significant ways an enigmatic "black box," impeding study of the psychological processes through which it induced change. Nor were attempts to understand change processes aided by the claims in many TM research papers that the intervention produced change in ordinary populations by inducing a "fourth state of consciousness"—a claim viewed with skepticism by those most familiar with traditional Indian concepts of a fourth state as comprising an ineffable, "unthinkable," and "ungraspable" direct experience of the true self (*ātman*), considered to be "extremely rare" (Rao & Paranjpe, 2016, pp. 42, 241).

By the mid-1970s, TM had produced a substantial body of empirical work and had published studies on a wide range of outcomes, documenting what appeared to be favorable causative influences from meditation on mental and physical health. However, in 1977 the TM organization launched the TM-Siddhi program, which purported to yield a highly extraordinary outcome: the ability to levitate. Little empirical research emerged from the TM-Siddhi program, and it represented a turning point, not entirely positive, in how the TM organization was perceived. Regardless of such events, and though its public profile has diminished, the TM organization has continued to publish an enormous number of research studies. As Farias and Wikholm (2015) put it, "without TM paving the way with its hundreds of studies and its ability to spread the practice of meditation throughout social groups, it is highly unlikely that we'd now be experiencing a new wave of interest that focuses on other forms of meditation" (p. 74).

Herbert Benson's Relaxation Response

An important offshoot of TM research was the work of Herbert Benson, a young cardiologist and hypertension researcher at Harvard Medical School in the late 1960s who began investigating TM when TM practitioners requested that he study them. To describe a key purported effect of meditation, Benson soon coined the term *relaxation response*, conceptualized as the opposite of the well-known physiologic "stress response."

Benson's first meditation studies focused on TM and were collaborations with R. K. Wallace, also by then at Harvard. Benson soon began wondering whether equal benefit could come from a simplified method of meditation that dispensed with the ideological dimensions of TM. He therefore developed his own method—never given a formal name—in which a person meditates on the word "one" instead of the mantra supplied by TM. Benson's studies revealed similar benefits from this simplified method, and he published a trade book, *The Relaxation Response* (1975), that described his results and helped bring additional public attention to meditation.

But meditation's benefits only accrue to those who actually meditate, and Benson discovered that some of his patients were more motivated to meditate when they meditated on a phrase they found spiritually meaningful, rather than the generic word "one." In these clinical observations, Benson was rediscovering the effects of ancillary beliefs, and a decade after his first book, Benson published *Beyond the Relaxation Response* (Benson & Proctor, 1984), another trade book that offered a nonsectarian framework that encouraged readers to use meditation in ways that synergized with their own belief systems. Later clinical work by Benson, also publicized in trade books, suggested additional ancillary practices, such as fellowship and altruism, for facilitating the integration of beneficial meditative states, into the remainder of daily living. In addition, Benson coined the term *remembered wellness* as a positive framing of expectancy-related processes catalyzed by placebos, thereby offering a helpful framing of a potentially important ancillary process connected to meditation-related belief systems (Benson & Friedman, 1996) (See also Handbook chapter on Relaxation).

Benson's work contributed greatly to a growing perception in Western culture that meditation could offer many benefits, and that its benefits were not the monopoly of any single method. Benson also scientifically documented that some advanced meditators—in this case Tibetan monks—could demonstrate extraordinary self-regulatory powers, such as the ability to raise their bodily temperature more than 10 degrees Farenheit above normal (Benson & Proctor, 1984). Benson's systematic research, however, remained focused largely on physiologic processes, and offered little documentation of how various forms of meditation and ancillary practices might synergize.

Rich and Diverse Early Ferment

Although TM remained the most prominent mode of meditation both in research and in popular culture, many other methods of meditation were studied in the 1970s and early 1980s. This grew naturally from the fact that spiritual seeking was common during this period among young well-educated Westerners, many of whom entered into academic careers and eventually studied forms of meditation most familiar to them—not only TM, but also Zen, Ananda Marga, Vipassana, and other methods.

This diversity of methods appeared at a scholarly and scientific level in the first major broadly focused book on meditation research, *Meditation: Classic and Contemporary Perspectives*, edited by psychologist Deane Shapiro and psychiatrist Roger Walsh, who through their careers have remained consistent voices for integrative and non-reductionist understandings of meditation. Containing sixty chapters, Shapiro and Walsh's (1984) volume encompassed more than a dozen original contributions plus more than three dozen republished refereed journal articles, reporting research findings on meditation methods that ranged from TM and Zen to Tantric Yoga and Mindfulness. In one of the editors' opening chapters, Shapiro affirmed a view, widespread at the time and persisting today, that much can be learned about meditation by "looking at the classical texts [that] provide phenomenological reports of the experience of advanced meditation" (p. 16; see Sharf [1995] for a critique arguing that classical texts possess little value as sources of phenomenological reports.). This view was reflected not only in the volume's title and in various citations to classical texts scattered across many chapters, but also in a chapter by Goleman (1984) wholly dedicated to the Buddhist *Visuddhimagga*, and another chapter by Daniel Brown that focused on texts of the Tibetan Mahāmudrā tradition, offering many potentially testable hypotheses.

More generally, the volume illustrates how the empirically oriented meditation literature of this period grappled with a wide range of issues and questions, some of which later drew ever-expanding research attention, whereas others became transformed, marginalized, or were rediscovered. Numerous chapters focused on physiological correlates or clinical outcomes from meditation, topics that soon generated large literatures. Other chapters reported investigations of "altered states of consciousness," and one probed *adverse* effects from meditation, topics that were later often neglected (for contemporary discussions, see chapters by Lindhal, Britton, and Cooper; and Fisher, this volume). Ancillary practices were occasionally mentioned—for example, Shapiro and Zifferblatt's chapter (republished from 1976) noted that Zen includes "informal meditation," and suggested "coupling it with.... focused breathing" (p. 527), and Goleman's (1984, pp. 320, 322) chapter acknowledged the importance in Buddhism of practices such as *sila* ("virtue or moral purity") and "right livelihood." But ancillary practices received little if any *empirical* attention in the volume or in the wider meditation research literature; Walsh's (1984) overview chapter acknowledged "other forms of training given simultaneously" (p. 29) as a category of potential independent variable, but offered no further elaboration.

A Plethora of Outcomes

Findings from the early research were both tantalizing and inconclusive. Already by the early 1980s, research had linked meditation to a wide range of physiological and psychological variables. Papers collected in the volume by Shapiro and Walsh (1984) show the breadth of this early research as well as some of its limitations. For example, three reviews of physiologic correlates linked various forms of meditation—especially Yoga, TM, and Zen—to assessments brain activation with the EEG, as well as depth and rate of breathing, oxygen consumption, heart rate, blood pressure, and skin conductance. Findings linked many methods of meditation to states of lowered arousal, but details across meditation methods and measurement techniques varied. Furthermore, a few advanced meditators demonstrated the contrary phenomenon of *higher* levels of arousal during meditation. Such diverse findings precluded uniform generalizations (see Vaitl et al., 2005). These early reviews also evaluated a then-prominent hypothesis suggesting that many benefits from meditation might occur because of heightened activity in the meditators' right brain hemispheres, thought to be the seat of meditation-related capacities such as holistic thinking. Again, a complex picture emerged, suggesting that the role of activation in early stages of meditation differed between specific meditative methods, and that the right hemisphere fails to play a disproportionate role in more advanced stages of meditation. In sum, these early reviews revealed some recurring patterns of physiological correlates, but offered few uniform conclusions about all forms of meditation.

Psychological and especially psychotherapeutic effects from meditation also drew considerable attention in the 1970s and early 1980s. Shapiro and Walsh's volume republished two reviews that reported apparent beneficial effects that included significantly diminished anxiety, reduced substance abuse, reductions in pathological behavior, and improved psychological adjustment. Other findings encompassed what might now be called adult development and/or positive psychology outcomes, such as salutary effects on capacity for intimate contact, spontaneity, self-regard, and inner directedness. Still further findings included reduced rates of hypertension. Nor were the contemporaneous reviews in Shapiro and Walsh's volume uncritical—they noted various methodological weaknesses, including lack of controls for sitting quietly or for expectancy effects, and inadequate description of procedures, especially about the intervention and clinician interactions that may affect study participants' perceptions of how they are *expected* to respond (so-called "demand" characteristics).

Over time, as published research kept expanding, meta-analysis gradually emerged as a common method to make sense of large and sometimes disparate bodies of findings. Table 3.2 presents examples of the wide range of meditation-related research questions that have now been meta-analyzed, usually on the basis of a substantial body of published studies (see table's final columns). Yet no meta-analysis, however sophisticated, guarantees a conclusion that accounts for all strengths and limitations of study designs. Consequently, despite an outpouring of published meta-analyses, answers have remained contested to many enduring questions of interest. For example, Table 3.2 lists two different meta-analyses, both published in 2018, that arrived at opposite conclusions on whether extant scientific evidence shows that meditation fosters prosociality (Kreplin, Farias, & Brazil, 2018, say no; Luberto et al., 2018, say yes).

Mindfulness Catches the Zeitgeist

Among the many methods of religiously derived meditation investigated during the early ferment of meditation research was the Buddhist-derived "mindfulness" meditation, first studied empirically by Deatherage (1975). A limitation of studying mindfulness meditation was that in contrast to Yoga and Zen, comparatively few advanced adepts were available. However, like Benson's method, mindfulness possessed certain features that made its usage by professionals comparatively easy and convenient, particularly its use of non-theistic language. A further possible advantage, frequently invoked but seldom analyzed in depth, was that the meditative process—"observing" the working of one's own mind—could be presented as akin to scientific research with its connotations of progress and rationality: As Deatherage (1975) put it, "Buddhist psychology . . . makes each individual a scientist, carefully observing his own mental processes" (p. 133).

The science-like, non-metaphysical framing of mindfulness meditation was appealing to researchers, as well as clinicians, who were unsure whether TM might conflict with the religious beliefs of their patients. And when empirical studies of mindfulness meditation accumulated, it soon became evident that mindfulness meditation could generate an evidence base for clinical benefit that was similar to the evidence generated for TM.

One early adaptation of mindfulness meditation was the Mindfulness-Based Stress Reduction program, developed by Jon Kabat-Zinn, which soon gained much attention from researchers and clinicians. Typically formulated as an eight-week,

Table 3.2 Questions Addressed in Empirical Meditation Research, Selected Meta-Analytic Highlights

	Meta-Analyzed Question	N	K
I.	Physiological		
	How does meditation (TM) affect systolic and diastolic blood pressure? (Bai et al., 2015)	996	11 RCTs
	How does meditation (mindfulness) affect telomerase? (Schutte & Malouff, 2014)	190	4 RCTs
II. a.	Psychological: Comprehensive		
	How is meditation (many types) associated with psychological outcomes? (Sedlmeier et al., 2012)	8161	125 Refereed
b.	Psychological: Clinical		
	How does meditation (many types) affect psychological stress outcomes: anxiety, depression, pain, positive mood, attention, substance use, eating habits, sleep, and weight? (Goyal et al., 2014)	3515	47 RCTs
	How does meditation (mindfulness) affect depression and anxiety? (Chen et al., 2012)	869	11 RCTs
	How does meditation (TM) affect anxiety? (Orme-Johnson & Barnes, 2014)	1295	16 RCTs
	How does meditation (mindfulness, other) affect PTSD symptoms? (Gallegos, Crean, Pigeon, & Heffner, 2017)	999	15[a] RCTs
	How does meditation (mindfulness) affect prisoners' psychological well-being and behavioral functioning? (Auty, Cope, & Liebling, 2017)	1544	12[b] Intervs.
c.	Psychological: Positive/Developmental		
	How does meditation (loving kindness) affect mental and social health and well-being? (Galante, Galante, Bekkers, & Gallacher, 2014)	1747	22 RCTs
	How does meditation (mindfulness) in non-clinical settings affect psychological outcomes: well-being, stress, attention, intelligence, positive and negative emotions, emotion regulation, personality traits, self-concept, self-attributed mindfulness, self-realization? (Eberth & Sedlmeier, 2012)	1616	38 CTs
	How does meditation (many types) affect well-being, burnout and job satisfaction of (i) informal caregivers and (ii) health professionals? (Dharmawardene, Givens, Wachholtz, Makowski, & Tija, 2016)	274 + 173	7 RCTs + 4 RCTs
	How does meditation (loving kindness) affect daily positive emotions? (Zeng, Chiu, Wang, Oei, & Leung, 2015)	1163	10 RCTs
	How does meditation (many types) affect empathy, compassion, and prosocial behavior? (Luberto et al., 2018)	1714	26 RCTs
	How does meditation (many types) affect empathy, compassion, and prosocial behavior? (Kreplin et al., 2018)	1078	16 RCTs

III.	Substance Abuse		
	How does meditation (TM) affect use of substances that include alcohol, nicotine, and other drugs? (Alexander, Robinson, & Rainforth, 1994)	4524	19 studies
	How does meditation (mindfulness) affect smoking cessation? (Maglione et al., 2017)	1192	10 RCTs
IV.	Chronic Pain and Insomnia		
	How does meditation (mindfulness) affect chronic pain? (Hilton et al., 2017)	2561	30 RCTs
	How does meditation (mindfulness) affect insomnia? (Gong et al., 2016)	330	6 RCTs
V.	Neural Activation (Neuroimaging)		
	How does meditation affect brain structure? (Fox et al., 2014)	997[c]	21
	What brain areas are functionally activated or deactivated through different types of meditation (focused attention, mantra recitation, open monitoring, compassion)? (Fox et al., 2016b)	527	31 Exps.
	What brain areas are (i) functionally activated or (ii) structurally altered through meditation (many types)? (Boccia, Piccardi, & Guariglia, 2015)	642 + 1652	37 + 63 Exps.
VI.	Psycho-spiritual Growth		
	How does meditation (mindfulness, other) affect posttraumatic growth? (Shiyko, Hallinan, & Naito, 2017)	990	10[d] Intervs.
	How does meditation (TM, other) affect self-actualization? (Alexander et al., 1991)	1181	42 Effects

CTs=Controlled Trials; Exps.=experiments; Intervs.=interventions; k=number of studies, effects, or experiments; N=total number of study participants; RCTs=Randomized Controlled Trials; TM=Transcendental Meditation

[a] Totals do not include four additional studies analyzed by Gallegos et al. (2017) that did not include a meditation component.

[b] Totals to not include a thirteenth yoga-only study analyzed by Auty et al (2017).

[c] We computed 507 meditators plus 490 controls, equaling 997 total study participants, but Fox et al. (2014, p. 54) note that "the difficulty in recruiting highly experienced practitioners has resulted in repeated use of the same subjects in several studies," and estimate only about 300 distinct meditators across studies.

[d] Totals do not include an 11th study analyzed by Shiyko et al. (2017) that did not include a meditation component.

two-hour-per-week intervention, MBSR combined elements of Buddhist-inspired mindfulness meditation with Hindu-derived Hatha Yoga postures (*āsanas*). Each of these ingredients was presented as free from esoteric beliefs, and MBSR programs gradually spread to clinics across the United States, even as a growing body of research demonstrated favorable treatment effects for conditions ranging from chronic pain to psoriasis. The MBSR program and its accompanying research were guided by Kabat-Zinn's carefully framed but somewhat selective definition of mindfulness as "paying attention in a particular way: on purpose, in the present moment, and nonjudgmentally" (1994, p. 4; see Kabat-Zinn, 2003 for his view on the relation between MBSR and Buddhism), an approach that was rapidly embraced by the research community as if it were an old friend (Robertson, 2010).

Importantly, Kabat-Zinn's MBSR approach clearly articulated several types of ancillary practices that were intended to aid a person in integrating the benefits of seated meditation throughout the day. First, MBSR taught what Kabat-Zinn called "informal practices" for re-centering one's mind at times of stress at any time and in any location, such as by bringing the mind back to the breath (akin to the suggestion of Shapiro & Zifferblatt, 1976). A second category of MBSR ancillary practice involved cultivating "mindfulness qualities" such as patience and non-judgment.

Soon following MBSR were several similar healthcare interventions that collectively have become known as mindfulness-based interventions (MBIs) (de Souza et al., 2015). A sitting meditation component was included not only in MBSR, but also in other MBIs such as Mindfulness-Based Cognitive Therapy (MBCT) for treating depression relapse, and Mindfulness-Based Eating Awareness Training (MB-EAT) for treating eating disorders. The burgeoning MBI literature did not possess a uniform definition of mindfulness, but commonly employed definitions closely aligned with that quoted earlier from Kabat-Zinn (1994, p. 4).

This expansion did not mean that the "mindfulness" framing of meditation was universally embraced in all its details. Rosch (2007, p. 262), for example, penetratingly pointed out that many so-called mindfulness interventions "could as much be called wisdom-based as mindfulness-based. Mindfulness would seem to play two roles: as a part of the therapy itself and as an umbrella justification ('empirical') for the inclusion of other aspects of wisdom that may be beyond our present cultural assumptions." Later, Rosch (2015) documented ways that the role in MBSR of mindfulness itself is somewhat surprisingly problematic.

Such criticisms notwithstanding, an exploding interest in mindfulness led to the establishment in 2010 of the journal *Mindfulness* (ISSN 1868-8527), which had a 2017 impact factor of 3.024, placing it in the top quartile (29th) out of 127 journals in the clinical psychology category. In 2013, a Delphi poll of experts predicted that "mindfulness" would show the greatest increase in the next decade out of thirty-one psychotherapy orientations (Norcross, Pfund, & Prochaska, 2013).

The explosion of research was complemented by an upsurge in popular interest in mindfulness, indicating that mindfulness had in some way resonated with both the popular and professional zeitgeist. The February 3, 2014, cover story of *TIME Magazine*, for example, was entitled "The Mindful Revolution: The Science of Finding Focus in a Stressed-Out, Multitasking Culture."

Reframing Purpose: A Mid-Level Goal for a Middle Path

One important consequence of increased attention to mindfulness was that it offered new ways to frame meditative states of mind and the goals of meditation. The most influential previous approaches had emphasized either spiritual or clinical goals of meditation: TM researchers had long asserted that TM meditators entered a "fourth state of consciousness" as described in Hindu scriptures, whereas Benson and other clinicians had emphasized relaxation as an outcome. Kabat-Zinn and other mindfulness researchers did not deny the potential for altered states of consciousness. Instead, they emphasized cultivating a specific mental quality or factor, "mindfulness," that was one of the practices in the Noble Eightfold Path, as well as one of the Buddhist Seven Factors of Enlightenment, along with concentration, tranquility, equanimity, investigation, energy, and joy. From the standpoint of Buddhist traditions, such relabeling shifted attention from ultimate spiritual goals (such as enlightenment/nirvana) to a proximate spiritual goal ("mindfulness"), that was often claimed to facilitate secular goals (e.g., personal well-being).

Conversely, from the standpoint of clinical intervention, the new framing shifted attention from relaxation to a construct, "mindfulness," that soon was professionally embraced as a resilience factor. Like other scientific paradigm shifts, this new framework simultaneously obscured some lines of investigation and opened up important new vistas for exploration.

A Monsoon of Measures

Until 2002, almost all empirical investigations that focused on mindfulness also included a major focus on meditation, as shown in Figure 3.2. However, this situation rapidly changed after 2003, when Brown and Ryan (2003) published the first self-report mindfulness scale, the fifteen-item *Mindful Attention Awareness Scale* (MAAS), which was intended to measure "trait mindfulness" (p. 837). Brown and Ryan's lengthy paper reported five studies that revealed positive correlations of MAAS scores with other measures of psychological awareness, well-being, positive emotional states, and self-regulated behavior. Among cancer patients who received an MBSR-like meditation intervention, increases in MAAS over time were related to declines in stress and mood disturbance. The MAAS scores were also found to be higher in a sample of Zen meditators than in a demographically matched community sample. As a measure of "trait mindfulness," the MAAS could be administered to anyone, whether or not they were meditating.

Thus, meditation research suddenly possessed an easy-to-use tool for assessing something tantalizingly close to a *meditative state* that had been diffused throughout the day. Yet the MAAS also possessed a variety of limitations. Nobody claimed that the MAAS was a perfect measure of transformational effects from mindfulness meditation. Mindfulness was only one of the Seven Factors of Enlightenment—why should it draw all the attention? Nor had Brown and Ryan attempted to theorize the utility of the MAAS for assessing effects from concentrative or non-Buddhist methods of meditation.

Nonetheless, for the first time, the MAAS allowed meditation research to conveniently deploy face-valid assessments of attentional effects from meditation. As shown in Figure 3.2, a torrent of research soon followed, as if a dam had burst. Prior to 2003, very few empirical studies indexed in the psychology literature had a major focus on mindfulness. But soon thereafter, the number of such studies began growing exponentially. Yet even in 2003, as well as in every year thereafter, only a small fraction of studies of mindfulness also possessed meditation as a major focus. Since 2007, research articles on meditation have been roughly equally divided between studies focused on mindfulness meditation, and studies presumably focused on other methods of meditation (see Figure 3.2). But each of these literatures is now dwarfed by the outpouring of studies of mindfulness *apart* from meditation, which by 2010 exceeded both meditation categories combined, and by 2015 did so by a factor of more than three.

This torrent of research was driven by numerous self-report instruments that soon joined the MAAS in attempting to assess mindfulness. Most aimed to assess trait mindfulness or mindfulness skills (Bergomi, Tschacher, & Kupper, 2013). Many of these measures were multidimensional, reflecting diverse conceptions about the precise nature of mindfulness, not always well-grounded from the perspectives of Buddhist traditions. Several assessment dimensions have emphasized attentional factors, but others have focused on ostensible facets of mindfulness such as self-acceptance, curiosity, and skill at describing one's feelings.

Some investigators began to hypothesize that gains in mindfulness might be an underlying process that *mediates* (explains) some or all of the observed effects of meditating. For example, if meditating causes gains in mindfulness, and mindfulness in turn causes reduced stress, then mindfulness would be said to mediate the effects of meditation on stress. Researchers say that *statistical mediation* exists when data about the main relevant variables support the possibility of such causal mediation. Intriguingly, some of the new measures of mindfulness were found to fully or partially statistically mediate effects of meditation interventions on mental health outcomes (e.g., Shapiro, Oman, Thoresen, Plante, & Flinders, 2008). One recent systematic review identified twelve randomized trials that collectively used four distinct measures to test for mediation by mindfulness, with such measures often showing mediation independent of other measured variables (Gu, Strauss, Bond, & Cavanagh, 2015).

Now that researchers were finally investigating mediating factors, researchers did not restrict themselves to mindfulness. For example, Fresco et al. (2007) developed a measure of "decentering" (viewing one's thoughts and feelings in a detached manner), conceptualized as a potential mediator of effects from mindfulness-based interventions.

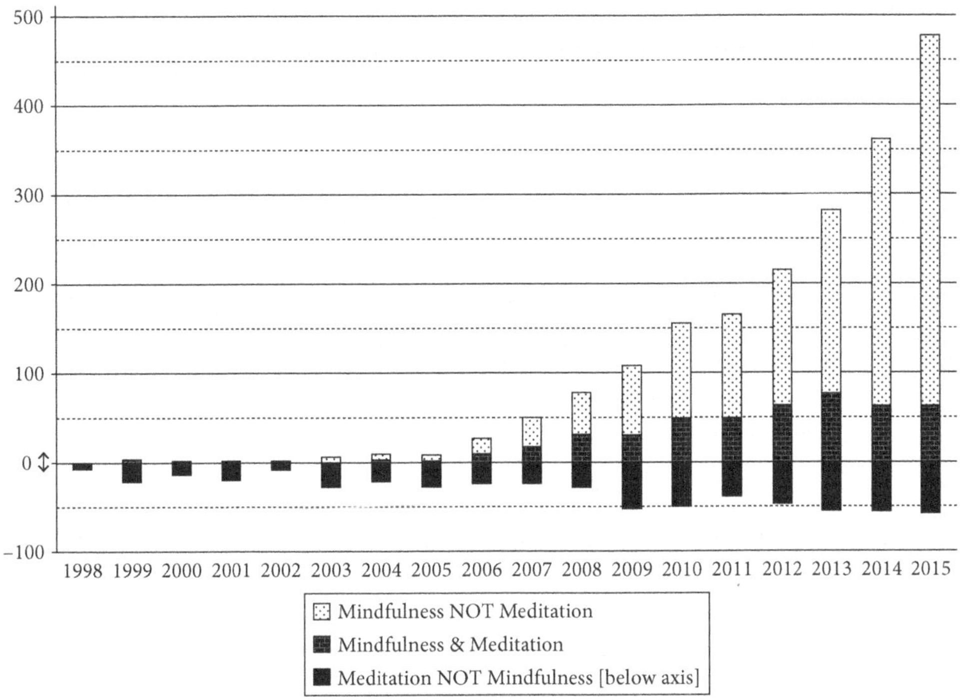

FIGURE 3.2 Publications with Major Subject "Meditation" and/or "Mindfulness," Per Year, Indexed in PsycINFO.

Note: Restricted to Peer reviewed, Methodology = Empirical study, Publication type = Journal article (searches conducted 12 June 2019).

Others developed measures of altered states during and after meditation (Reavley & Pallant, 2009).

In a noteworthy parallel development during roughly this same time period, Lazar and colleagues (2000), and thereafter other neuroimaging researchers, began applying newly developed functional Magnetic Resonance Imaging (fMRI) and other sophisticated techniques to measure brain activity during meditation. Their work inaugurated a complex technical field that is discussed elsewhere in this volume (see chapter in this volume by Fox and Cahn on Meditation and the Brain).

Studies of Mediating Factors and Their Skeptics

With novel plausible measurement instruments in hand, researchers began to investigate attention-related factors that might mediate effects of meditation. Mindfulness meditation has been most commonly studied, although mediators of concentrative forms of meditation have also been investigated (e.g., Shapiro et al., 2008). Gu and colleagues (2015) meta-analyzed twenty studies of MBSR and MBCT, identifying evidence that their effects were mediated by cognitive and emotional reactivity, mindfulness, rumination, and worry (see also van der Velden et al., 2015). One study also reported that effects of MBSR on cognitive skills were mediated by enhanced concentration (i.e., reduced mind wandering, Mrazek, Franklin, Phillips, Baird, & Schooler, 2013).

While such findings were promising, some observers pointed out that even in randomized trials, statistical mediation need not imply causation. As Rosch (2007) had observed, MBSR and other MBIs included many "wisdom-based" components, deemed by tradition to exert a range of transformative effects. Only "mindfulness" was typically measured, but multiple dimensions of change were plausibly correlated with it, and could potentially be equally or more causative—wouldn't assigning causative primacy to mindfulness be a non-scientific inferential leap? Thus, for example, Mikulas (2007, p. 20) noted that "many mindfulness-based programs are actually cultivating both concentration and mindfulness, but all results are attributed to mindfulness."

Rediscovering Ancillary Practices

Even as researchers were reframing the purpose of meditation and developing measures, they were also rediscovering ancillary practices as conjoint practices with seated meditation, a phenomenon that had long been hidden in plain sight. Whereas TM research had placed virtually all emphasis on seated meditation and the ostensible fourth state it produced, MBSR was transparent and explicit about the need for informal practices and mindfulness qualities. This shift realigned meditation research with emphases on sets of conjoint practices evident in traditional systems of meditation such as the Buddhist Noble Eightfold Path (*ariyo aṭṭhaṅgiko maggo*) and Patanjali's Eight-Limbed Yoga (*astanga yoga*), with the latter's mandate to cultivate virtues and adhere to ethical rules (*yamas* and *niyamas*). More broadly, this shift realigned meditation research with traditional religious conceptions of meditation that typically emphasize the conjoint cultivation of character strengths and virtues (e.g., Peterson & Seligman, 2004), along with adherence to major tenets of the host tradition (e.g., in Eastern Christian Hesychasm meditation, adherence to the religious community's "sacramental and liturgical life," Coniaris in Johnson, 2010, p. 49). No cross-culturally canonical list or periodic table of ancillary practice categories and their functions has emerged, although various recurring themes can be identified (e.g., Oman, 2010; Walsh, 1999).

Having rediscovered ancillary practices, researchers could also theorize and study their roles in cultivating and diffusing meditative states of mind and fostering positive health. One of the first to do so had been meditation researcher Johnathan C. Smith, who developed a "cognitive behavioral" theory of relaxation that emphasized the role of cognitive structures in maintaining meditative states (Smith, 1988; Smith, Amutio, Anderson, & Aria, 1996). Yet Smith was somewhat ahead of his time.

Only with the increased popularity of mindfulness in the early 2000s did larger numbers of empirical studies of ancillary practices begin to appear. For example, in MBSR research, concomitant in-session practices such as body-scan and yoga postures were studied by Carmody and Baer (2008), who found that formal MBSR practices, including seated meditation, body scan, and yoga movements, were all linked to reductions in symptoms and improvements in mindfulness (see also Sauer-Zavala, Walsh, Eisenlohr-Moul, & Lykins, 2013).

Several published studies have also examined so-called informal practices, such as focusing on the breath on occasions throughout the day. Many reported null relations between informal practices and well-being outcomes, perhaps due to confounding by reverse causality—that is, those participants with the largest numbers of life-stressors would have the most occasions to employ informal practices (e.g., Carmody & Baer, 2008; Crane et al., 2014; Hawley et al., 2014). However, other studies did report that adherence to informal practices was significantly predictive of reduced perceived stress (Shapiro et al., 2008), reduced anxiety and improved quality of life (Morgan, Graham, Hayes-Skelton, Orsillo, & Roemer, 2014), or enhanced observer-rated positive behavior change (Griffiths et al., 2018), suggesting the need for more research. At least one meditation study has quantitatively examined adherence to a generalized life practice, utilization throughout the day of focused or "one-pointed" attention, reporting that it was more powerful than mindful awareness in predicting stress reductions (Shapiro et al., 2008). More broadly, a qualitative interview study of healthcare professionals uncovered fifteen distinct patterns by which participants experienced meditation and seven ancillary practices as causally fostering efficacy at work (Oman, Richards, Hedberg, & Thoresen, 2008).

Perhaps understudied are character strengths, which have been investigated most often as a meditation outcome rather than an ancillary practice, although Niemiec, Rashid, and Spinella (2012) formulated several hypotheses for how character strengths should synergize with mindfulness meditation. Also understudied are the effects of ancillary beliefs, although Benson and Proctor (1984) had long ago argued that such beliefs, when harnessed, can enhance adherence to a practice of meditation, and more recently, Wachholtz and Pargament (2005, p. 380) suggested that differential effects from meditating on a spiritual versus a secular focus phrase might be explained by the activation of such cognitive frames—by a participant being "more likely to interpret everyday occurrences through a spiritual lens" (see also Oman & Bormann, 2018, on cognitive framing implications of focus objects).

Viewing seated meditation as operating synergistically in concert with other conjoint practices represents an important re-alignment with earlier traditional understandings of meditation. But the shift from so-called "single-component" or "summative component" conceptions of meditation interventions to an "interactive component" conception also imposes a burden (Melendez-Torres, Bonell, & Thomas, 2015, p. 3; West, Aiken, & Todd, 1993, p. 575): Scientists who seek to disentangle and understand the effects of any individual intervention component, such as seated meditation itself, must employ greater statistical power (hence larger samples) and utilize more nuanced theoretical models about how components interact. One potential source of such guiding theories, of course, is the meditative traditions themselves.

Buddhists Wonder: What Is This So-Called "Mindfulness"?

Ironically, even as research expanded and interest in mindfulness and Buddhist-inspired forms of meditation was welcomed, many observers pointed out that what the scientific research literature was calling "mindfulness"—sometimes called "psychological mindfulness"—was quite different from the mindfulness of traditional Buddhist conceptions. Buddhist authors increasingly began to trace sources and note the implications of this discrepancy. Mikulas (2011, p. 5), for example, noted that "a decade ago, a North American group interested in developing integrative therapies discovered mindfulness... But rather than turn to the Buddhist literature, they chose to ask each other what they meant and understood about mindfulness." Largely unanalyzed by scholarship or empirical research has been how the modern cultural reception of mindfulness has been conditioned by the West's cultural inheritance from ancient Greece, where philosophy represented a "way of life" similar to a spiritual path, and "the theme of the value of the present instant plays a fundamental role in all the philosophical schools" (Hadot & Davidson, 1995, pp. 69, 104). Robertson (2010) argues that "when we read about Buddhism being a 'here and now' [*hic et nunc*] philosophy we are unwittingly viewing it through the lens of an ancient turn of phrase which we only understand because our dimly-recollected European philosophical heritage made such extensive use of this concept" (p. 153), raising questions about how much of popular and "psychological mindfulness" may represent metaphorical Greek wine wrapped in Buddhist wineskins, rather than anything distinctly Buddhist (see also Rosch, 2015).

Two often-noted discrepancies with tradition have been the overwhelming emphases that psychological mindfulness places on (i) present-moment awareness and (ii) nonjudgment. For example, Alan Wallace (2006), a scholar and experienced personal translator for the Dalai Lama, noted that the original term for mindfulness (*sati* in Pali and *smṛti* in Sanskrit) primarily referred to *memory* and recollection. Wallace observed that the "modern understanding departs significantly from the Buddha's own account of *sati*, and from those of the most authoritative commentators in the Theravada and Indian Mahayana traditions" (p. 62). The broader traditional view is illustrated in the Buddhist *Samyutta Nikāya* 48:9, which records the Buddha asking:

> What, monks, is the faculty of mindfulness? Here, the noble disciple is mindful, possessing supreme mindfulness and alertness, one who remembers and recollects what was done and said long ago. This is called the faculty of mindfulness.
>
> (translated in Bodhi, 2011, p. 23)

Similarly, Wallace (2006, p. 61) pointed out that "rather than refraining from labeling or categorizing experiences in a nonjudgmental fashion, in the earliest, most authoritative accounts, *sati* is said to distinguish between wholesome and unwholesome, beneficial and unbeneficial tendencies. The contrast between the ancient and modern accounts is striking." According to Rupert Gethin, president of the Pali Text Society, "ancient Buddhist texts understand the presence of mindfulness as in effect reminding us of who we are and what our values are" (quoted in Oman, 2015, p. 40). Such concerns have been corroborated and refined in detailed analyses of classical Buddhist sources (e.g., Dreyfus, 2011; Levman, 2017; see also Bodhi, 2011; Oman, 2015).

To address such rising waves of concern, Williams and Kabat-Zinn (2011, p. 4) edited a special issue of *Contemporary Buddhism*, aiming to "spark ongoing dialogue and conversation across disciplines" and asking many questions, including "What are the potential negative effects of the confluence of these different epistemologies at this point in time?" Reassuringly, many contributing scholars expressed appreciation that disseminating even a diluted or truncated version of Buddhist-derived practices could be good if it provided clinical or educational benefit.

But much alarm was also building, even among non-Buddhists, about the increasingly pervasive and seemingly relentless commercialization of mindfulness. Critical articles began to regularly appear in both scholarly journals and major popular media—for example, the *New Yorker* published an article on "the long marriage of mindfulness and money" (Goldberg, 2015). Before long, the term "McMindfulness" emerged to criticize the fruit of this marriage, perceived as a "denatured" and "stripped down, secularized technique," a form of "technical spirituality... extracted from [its] soteriological context, instrumentalized, and applied as tools for improving efficiency . . ." (Purser & Milillo, 2015, p. 15; see also chapter by Purser & Lewis, this volume).

Green Shoots: Inching Toward Inclusiveness, Breadth, and Depth

By many metrics, the first decade of the twenty-first century was a period of unprecedented success and mainstreaming for meditation research, as shown in the rapidly growing research base and widespread popular and professional interest in "mindfulness," commonly seen as related to meditation. But Buddhists and social justice critics were not the only groups troubled by how this success was manifesting. In the pages of the *American Psychologist*, long-standing meditation researcher Roger Walsh pointed out that this success had been accompanied and perhaps accomplished by a deep if not profound *recontextualization* of meditation, as reflected in research reports and as presented in methods taught by Benson, Kabat-Zinn, and others:

> [Meditation] research findings have been interpreted almost exclusively within Western psychological frameworks, ignoring meditation's complementary psychological and philosophical perspectives. This has been widely described as a necessary "decontextualization," but it is actually far more. It is also a major recontextualization

> and revisioning of the practices within an exclusively Western psychological and philosophical framework. In anthropological terms, this is the trap of adopting a purely etic (outsider) perspective rather than both etic and emic (insider or native) perspectives. (Walsh & Shapiro, 2006, pp. 227–228)

This pervasive externalized recontextualization has elicited increasing criticism. Some have pointed out that over-reliance on secularly recontextualized meditation fails to support clinicians in proactively respecting their patients' diverse religious and cultural (emic) perspectives, as enjoined by the ethics codes of psychology, medicine, and other health professions. For example, do religiously committed patients receive less benefit from secularly recontextualized meditation than they would from learning methods of meditation derived from or better adapted to their own tradition? Would such patients benefit from greater transparency about religious sources, or opportunities to discuss whether the method taught is compatible with their religion? (Brown, 2017; Oman, 2012; Palitsky & Kaplan, 2019). The dominant approach, some suggested, can foster an "ironic *unmindfulnes*" of meditation-related cultural diversity issues (Oman, 2015, p. 36). Walsh and Shapiro (2006, p. 228), quoting Marsella (1998, p. 1286), concluded that

> [What has emerged] is an assimilative integration that feeds the global "colonization of the mind" by Western psychology that "undermines the growth and credibility of other psychologies"...As such, it overlooks much of the richness and uniqueness of the meditative disciplines and the valuable complementary perspectives they offer.

This assimilative integration can be contrasted, they suggest, with several more *inclusive* potential stages and forms of integration, such as "pluralism and accommodation" (involving mutual enrichment), "integrative" (systematic mutual enrichment), and "integral" (a comprehensive holistic framework).

"The beginnings... are already visible" of these enhanced forms of integration, Walsh and Shapiro (2006, p. 228) noted. To spotlight such green shoots—potentially integrative new initiatives—the following subsections examine recent history of research on (i) diverse traditions of religious/spiritual meditation, (ii) accommodating diversity in research and practice, and (iii) relations of meditation with spirituality.

Studying Alternative Meditation Traditions

Even as mindfulness has gained some types of dominance, other alternative approaches to meditation research have continued. As shown earlier in Figure 3.2, approximately half of all meditation research continues to investigate methods other than mindfulness. Furthermore, as Taylor (1999) noted two decades ago in his earlier history, much meditation research continues to be produced in India, although "only a fraction of this makes its way into the Western scientific and medical literature" (p. 25)—a situation that appears to have continued.

Yet, while much of the Indian meditation research literature appears to have emphasized physiological outcomes, Indian psychological interest is growing. In 2002, 160 psychologists in India gathered in Pondicherry to sign a *Manifesto* that launched what has become known as the Indian Psychology Movement. Offering several policy recommendations, the *Manifesto* affirmed that "classical Indian thought is rich in psychological content... sophisticated in its methods and valuable in its applied aspects" (Cornelissen, 2002, p. 168). Signatories and their colleagues have now prepared a report for government and published a series of volumes pursuing this agenda, often with considerable attention to research on meditation (e.g., Rao, 2017; see also Oman, Duggal, & Misra, 2018).

A considerably smaller number of twenty-first-century studies have also investigated methods of meditation in Abrahamic religions. Several studies have now been published on Christian Centering Prayer (e.g., Asbill, 2016; Fox, Gutierrez, Haas, & Durnford, 2016a), and some on other types of Christian contemplative prayer (Newberg et al., 2003). And as noted in a later subsection, some research has begun comparing unadapted versus religiously adapted meditation-based mindfulness programs (Ford & Garzon, 2017; Huennekens, 2018; Palitsky & Kaplan, 2019). But empirical studies of Jewish and Islamic (e.g., Sufi) methods of meditation or closely analogous practices remain extremely rare. One Indonesian study reported calming effects from *zikr sirri* (silent repetition of God's name), as measured by heart rate variability (Wahab & Rahman, 2015).

Remembering and Accommodating Diversity

Despite the globally diverse wellsprings of meditation practice, much of the recent mindfulness-oriented meditation literature has been what Oman (2015) called ironically *unmindful* of diversity issues. A systematic review by DeLuca et al. (2018, p. 117) uncovered twenty-four US-based MMBI studies that involved "minority inclusion in sample composition, cultural adaptations of interventions, and/or planned comparisons of outcomes for different ethnoracial groups" (p. 117). Unfortunately, only three used a "culturally adapted intervention," highlighting an overall "dearth of diversity focus in MBI research," although the authors noted that elsewhere in the world, detailed diversity information relevant to cultural adaptation had been provided in MBI studies in China, Taiwan, Thailand, and Sri Lanka.

Importantly, multiple lines of US-derived evidence confirm the common-sense proposition that different people prefer—and plausibly may benefit most highly from—different methods of meditation, and that half or fewer may prefer mindfulness meditation (Burke, 2012; Burke, Lam, Stussman, & Yang, 2017). Such findings suggest a need for additional systematic research to guide improved individual, cultural, and religious tailoring of meditation interventions.

In particular, a recent six-year study of college students in San Francisco found that less than one-third preferred mindfulness meditation, with a majority preferring mantra-focused or other methods (Burke, 2012). Such findings are consistent with national surveys, which indicate that each month, an estimated 7.0 million US adults engage in some form of "spiritual meditation," nearly twice the number estimated to engage each month in mindfulness meditation (3.6 million; Burke et al., 2017, p. 1).

Although preferences do not inherently correspond with what is optimal spiritually or psychologically, investigation of the sources and consequences of individual preferences has also begun. Anderson and Farb (2018) examined patterns of individual partiality to different types of attentional anchors in meditation (phrase, image, or breath), finding that motivation predicted diverse anchor preferences among undergraduates (N=82). They argued that "offering alternate anchors is a tangible next-step that could be integrated into existing interventions" (p. 7) as an aid to establishing adherence to an ongoing daily practice. This addresses an age-old question of what technique is best suited to whom.

Furthermore, a pioneering quasi-experiment by Burke (2012) revealed that study participant *age* was associated with preferences for some specific methods such as Zen (older students) or mindfulness (younger students). Perhaps this is because different methods each "have their moment of cultural relevance" (p. 241) amid "the transitory popularity of any [specific] method" (p. 240). Burke argued that "a proper fit between the individual and the method may help to increase comfort with the method, perceived self-efficacy, and consequently, maintenance of practice over time" (p. 240).

Determining optimal approaches for accommodating diversity may not be easy. Different scholars have emphasized different ethical issues (e.g., Brown, 2017; Palitsky & Kaplan, 2019). Some speculate that optimally balancing other legitimate concerns with respect for diversity might ultimately require organizations such as colleges to teach not only diverse methods of meditation, but also to employ multiple alternative meditation course structures. For example, colleges have taught meditation through various single-class structures that include dedicated single method courses (e.g., on MBSR, Patanjali, or a Sufi method), sampler courses that briefly introduce diverse methods, and courses that outsource in-depth instruction to community-based organizations. Oman (2016) speculates that optimal balancing requires teaching multiple *structures*.

Remembering Spiritual Sources

Efforts to recover the richer context of meditation mentioned by Walsh and Shapiro (2006) often attend to spiritual and/or religious components of meditation. A small but growing and suggestive empirical research literature now examines relations of spirituality and/or religion with meditation, as noted in a review by Kristeller and Jordan (2018).

Effects from spiritual components of meditation were strikingly demonstrated in a randomized trial by Wachholtz and Pargament (2005), subsequently replicated multiple times (see Wachholtz, Malone, & Pargament, 2017), that reported lower rates of migraine headaches among participants who used a spiritual focus of meditation, versus participants using a secular focus of meditation. Perhaps consistent with such findings, multiple studies have also reported that religiously adapted forms of mindfulness have been more effective for some outcomes than unadapted mindfulness interventions (e.g., for enhancing compliance and reducing stress and depression, by Ford & Garzon, 2017; for enhancing state mindfulness decentering and closeness to God, by Huennekens, 2018).

A second line of investigation has revealed that even secular forms of meditation may foster increased spirituality. At least three studies have reported that MBSR or similarly secularized meditation programs can foster gains in measures of implicit or explicit spirituality (Crescentini, Urgesi, Campanella, Eleopra, & Fabbro, 2014; see Kristeller & Jordan, 2018). Yet not all benefits appear equal between different methods. For example, Oman et al. (2007) reported that both MBSR and meditation on memorized spiritual texts can reduce negative religious coping and negative God-images, but that only meditating on spiritual texts increased several measures of learning from spiritual exemplars (see also Oman & Bormann, 2018). Similarly, a recent study of Buddhist meditators in the United Kingdom reported that for most, "meditation and Buddhism were not initially linked. The majority first tried meditation—as an activity not necessarily connected to Buddhism—before subsequently engaging with Buddhism" (Lomas, Cartwright, Edginton, & Ridge, 2015, p. 201). Such findings raise questions about the degree to which long-term health benefits from meditation may be mediated by spiritual/religious engagement (Oman, 2015). One study also reported evidence suggesting that mental health gains from MBSR were partially mediated by spirituality (Greeson et al., 2011).

Exploring meditation's links and synergies with spiritual/religious factors is arguably a natural and promising direction for additional research. Independently of meditation research, spirituality and religion are the focus of a rapidly growing empirical research literature, comprising thousands of empirical studies and dozens of meta-analyses, that link these factors to many of the same clinical outcomes that have brought attention to meditation (Koenig, King, & Carson, 2012; Oman, 2018). Importantly, the history of science supports the possibility that diverse Buddhist and non-Buddhist spiritual meditation traditions might supply helpful theories and insights: Syntheses that integrate scientific and religious ideas "can be found in each of the centuries since the rise of modern science and in each of the sciences" (Barbour, 2000, p. 5; regarding science/religion integration, see also Mind & Life Institute, 2018; Oman & Singh, 2018; Walsh & Shapiro, 2006).

Awakened States: Beacon, Puzzle, or Myth?

Fifty years have now elapsed since Wallace's (1970) assertion in *Science* that his findings "seem to distinguish the state produced by transcendental meditation from commonly encountered states of consciousness" (p. 1751). Although Wallace's claim was initially influential, empirical support ultimately proved lacking for the contention that meditation novices can reliably enter sharply distinguishable states of consciousness (e.g., Vaitl et al., 2005). Nonetheless, understanding meditatively induced altered states of consciousness retains long-term importance, holding relevance to inclusive forms of integration (Walsh & Shapiro, 2006).

While the modern scientific understanding of such states has progressed, it remains very incomplete. The field appears to have arrived at a challenging and puzzling crossroad that calls for expanded and perhaps transformed interdisciplinary collaboration, and that merits detailed exposition here.

On the side of progress, empirical researchers have collected and analyzed a great deal of scientific data about primarily Western lay (non-monastic) meditators who have ranged in experience from novice through total lifetime practice that substantially exceeds the 10,000-hour threshold deemed necessary for expertise in many fields. Such studies have begun revealing interpretable relations between method, length of practice, and patterns of neural activation and other outcomes of interest (Fox et al., 2014; Fox et al., 2016b; see chapter by Fox and Cahn on Meditation and the Brain).

But from traditional perspectives, lengthy lifetime practice is not *sufficient* for ensuring attainment of either the more advanced meditative states, or an "awakened" state that reflects altered consciousness *traits*. Although all major traditions affirm that meditative and contemplative practices can play important or necessary roles in preparing for such states, they also assert that additional factors must be present. Scientifically, some of these factors might be called "fortuitous determinants," and in many spiritual traditions they are called grace (*kṛpā* in Sanskrit). Consequently, the so-called "expert meditators" with over 10,000 hours lifetime meditation that serve as subjects in many recent research studies need not be understood, on that basis alone, as supplying information about the most advanced meditative states recognized in tradition (Sedlmeier et al., 2012). Irrespective of the terms they may use, generally such studies tell us about long-term meditators, not about highly advanced or "awakened" meditators (e.g., Wahbeh, Sagher, Back, Pundhir, & Travis, 2018). Yet it is especially the so-called awakened meditators that are viewed as beacons of spiritual renewal in many traditions (e.g., see Underhill, 1911, on "vitality," pp. 429, 431; Woods, 1980, p. 5, on how "a society renews its spiritual vigor.").

It's not that researchers have lacked diligence in recruitment. Awakened states are traditionally viewed as quite rare (see, e.g., Goleman, 1977, p. xxiv; Goleman, 1984, p. 322; Rao & Paranjpe, 2016, p. 241). Such alleged rarity represents a major roadblock to business-as-usual Western-style empirical research. One of the few sustained considerations of the implications of this rarity is offered by Nagel (1999), who identified several resulting research problems. He argued that the rarest types of advanced meditative states may be essentially unresearchable due to lack of participants. Even when a few scattered participants can be found, internal validity of quantitative studies would still be undermined by lack of statistical power, and the employment of ad hoc recruitment methods could compromise the bases for generalization (external validity). Yet Nagel concluded hopefully, suggesting that "a low number of participants would not prohibit the development of a descriptive science of [advanced meditative states of consciousness] made possible by the application of human science research methods [such as] phenomenology, qualitative interview, and case study" (p. 17).

The ostensible extreme rarity and elusiveness of advanced states raises the possibility that they might be dismissed in their entirety as fictitious, perhaps merely a premodern myth. But such interpretations fail to explain the case report literature on experienced traditional meditators, which has long documented a range of remarkable capacities and states. In addition to Benson and Proctor's (1984) studies of Tibetan monks noted earlier, other case reports have documented abilities such as generating extremely high or low heart rates at will, and various other feats (Norris, 1986). Although these individuals may or may not have become established in any traditionally recognized "awakened" state, they seem to demonstrate that extraordinary meditation-related states exist.

From an inclusive integration perspective (Walsh & Shapiro, 2006), it would be of special interest to generate, test, and refine approaches that join non-reductionist and perhaps methodologically agnostic (Porpora, 2006) human science perspectives with traditional mappings of higher and awakened states in diverse traditions. Sources for such mappings range from the Buddhist *Visuddhimagga* to figures such as John of the Cross, who distinguished between a "night of sense" (a purgation of mind) and a considerably more advanced "night of the spirit" (e.g., see Underhill, 1911, p. 353). Equally relevant are collaborative efforts between scholars/scientists and the rare individuals who may plausibly provide first-person reports of advanced meditative experiences (e.g., Ekman & Dalai Lama, 2008).

Further progress would seem to require interdisciplinary collaboration, perhaps drawing together fields ranging from the humanities to social sciences, neurosciences, and biomedical and health sciences. This next half-century will reveal whether meditation research rises to the challenge of a far-reaching and methodologically instructive multidisciplinary synthesis, lapses into new forms of what critics call assimilative integration, or exhibits a patchwork blend of these and other possibilities.

Conclusion

We have examined the history of meditation research, seeing how it has progressed through periods of physiological measurement and early ferment, reformulation and expansion of physiological and questionnaire-based empirical measurement, and small beginnings toward greater inclusiveness and integration. It seems clear that popular interest in meditation as well as scientific interest in meditation research are both here to stay. Forecasting their future trajectories, however, is much more difficult. After another half-century, will corporatized and secularized forms of meditation aimed at productivity and social adjustment be predominant, displacing traditional meditation paths for self-realization and spiritual transformation? Or, conversely, will there emerge a thriving global cross-cultural alliance of diverse integrated contemplative sciences of meditation, each integrating the best scientific knowledge with the best traditional wisdom and most sagacious culturally grounded practical application? Or will the coming decades witness an unstable and fluctuating co-existence of these and additional possibilities? However the next half-century unfolds, even as the founding generation of modern meditation researchers gradually passes from the scene, it also seems evident that we have much more to learn about meditation—more than can easily fit into a single lifespan. To paraphrase Hippocrates ("Art is long, life is short"), one lifetime may be short compared to the length of time required for understanding the depths of the art of meditation and its possibilities, limitations, and necessary accompaniments. In the meantime, we hope that this brief and condensed history, and the *Handbook* that contains it, will be of use to meditation researchers and others seeking to understand meditation and maximize this ancient art's positive contribution to our collective human future.

References

Alexander, C. N., Rainforth, M. V., & Gelderloos, P. (1991). Transcendental meditation, self-actualization, and psychological health: A conceptual overview and statistical meta-analysis. *Journal of Social Behavior & Personality* 6(5), 189–248.

Alexander, C. N., Robinson, P., & Rainforth, M. (1994). Treating and preventing alcohol, nicotine, and drug abuse through transcendental meditation: A review and statistical meta-analysis. *Alcoholism Treatment Quarterly* 11(1–2), 13–87.

Anderson, T., & Farb, N. A. S. (2018). Personalising practice using preferences for meditation anchor modality. *Frontiers in Psychology* 9, Article 2521.

Asbill, L. M. (2016). *Spiritually oriented interventions: Comparing mindfulness and centering prayer as interventions for anxiety reduction* (PhD dissertation). Biola University.

Auty, K. M., Cope, A., & Liebling, A. (2017). A systematic review and meta-analysis of yoga and mindfulness meditation in prison. *International Journal of Offender Therapy and Comparative Criminology* 61(6), 689–710.

Baer, R. A. (2003). Mindfulness training as a clinical intervention: A conceptual and empirical review. *Clinical Psychology: Science & Practice* 10(2), 125–143.

Bagchi, B. K., & Wegner, M. A. (1957). Electrophysiological correlates of some yogi exercises. *Electroencephalography and clinical neurophysiology* 7(Supp.), 132–149.

Bai, Z., Chang, J., Chen, C., Li, P., Yang, K., & Chi, I. (2015). Investigating the effect of transcendental meditation on blood pressure: A systematic review and meta-analysis. *Journal of Human Hypertension* 29(11), 653–662.

Barbour, I. G. (2000). *When science meets religion*. San Francisco: HarperSanFrancisco.

Benson, H. (1975). *The relaxation response*. New York: William Morrow.

Benson, H., & Friedman, R. (1996). Harnessing the power of the placebo effect and renaming it "remembered wellness." *Annual Review of Medicine* 47(12), 193–199.

Benson, H., & Proctor, W. (1984). *Beyond the relaxation response*. New York: Times Books.

Bergomi, C., Tschacher, W., & Kupper, Z. (2013). The assessment of mindfulness with self-report measures: Existing scales and open issues. *Mindfulness* 4(3), 191–202.

Boccia, M., Piccardi, L., & Guariglia, P. (2015). The meditative mind: A comprehensive meta-analysis of MRI studies. *BioMed Research International 2015*, Article 419808.

Bodhi, Bhikkhu (2011). What does mindfulness really mean? A canonical perspective. *Contemporary Buddhism 12*(1), 19–39.

Brown, C. G. (2017). Ethics, transparency, and diversity in mindfulness programs. In L. M. Monteiro, J. F. Compson, & F. Musten (Eds.), *Practitioner's guide to ethics and mindfulness-based interventions* (pp. 45–85). Cham, Switzerland: Springer International.

Brown, K. W., & R. M. Ryan (2003). The benefits of being present: Mindfulness and its role in psychological well-being. *Journal of Personality and Social Psychology 84*(4), 822–848.

Burke, A. (2012). Comparing individual preferences for four meditation techniques: Zen, vipassana (mindfulness), qigong, and mantra. *Explore: The Journal of Science and Healing 8*(4), 237–242.

Burke, A., Lam, C. N., Stussman, B., & Yang, H. (2017). Prevalence and patterns of use of mantra, mindfulness and spiritual meditation among adults in the United States. *BMC Complementary and Alternative Medicine 17*, Article 316.

Carmody, J., & Baer, R. A. (2008). Relationships between mindfulness practice and levels of mindfulness, medical and psychological symptoms and well-being in a mindfulness-based stress reduction program. *Journal of Behavioral Medicine 31*(1), 23–33.

Chen, K. W., Berger, C. C., Manheimer, E., Forde, D., Magidson, J., Dachman, L., & Lejuez, C. W. (2012). Meditative therapies for reducing anxiety: A systematic review and meta-analysis of randomized controlled trials. *Depression and Anxiety 29*(7), 545–562.

Cornelissen, M. (2002). Pondicherry Manifesto of Indian Psychology. *Psychological Studies 47*(1–3), 168–169.

Crane, C., Crane, R. S., Eames, C., Fennell, M. J. V., Silverton, S., Williams, J. M. G., & Barnhofer, T. (2014). The effects of amount of home meditation practice in mindfulness based cognitive therapy on hazard of relapse to depression in the staying well after depression trial. *Behaviour Research and Therapy 63*, 17–24.

Crangle, E. F. (1994). *The origin and development of early Indian contemplative practices.* Wiesbaden, Germany, Harrassowitz Verlag.

Crescentini, C., Urgesi, C., Campanella, F., Eleopra, R., & Fabbro, F. (2014). Effects of an 8-week meditation program on the implicit and explicit attitudes toward religious/spiritual self-representations. *Consciousness and Cognition 30*, 266–280.

de Souza, I. C. W., de Barros, V. V., Gomide, H. P., Mendes Miranda, T. C., de Paula Menezes, V., Kozasa, E. H., & Noto, A. R. (2015). Mindfulness-based interventions for the treatment of smoking: A systematic literature review. *Journal of Alternative and Complementary Medicine 21*(3), 129–140.

Deatherage, G. (1975). The clinical use of "mindfulness" meditation techniques in short-term psychotherapy. *Journal of Transpersonal Psychology 7*(2), 133–143.

DeLuca, S. M., Kelman, A. R., & Waelde, L. C. (2018). A systematic review of ethnoracial representation and cultural adaptation of mindfulness- and meditation-based interventions. *Psychological Studies 63*(2), 117–129.

Dharmawardene, M., Givens, J., Wachholtz, A., Makowski, S., & Tjia, J. (2016). A systematic review and meta-analysis of meditative interventions for informal caregivers and health professionals. *BMJ Supportive & Palliative Care 6*(2), 160–169.

Dreyfus, G. (2011). Is mindfulness present-centred and non-judgmental? A discussion of the cognitive dimensions of mindfulness. *Contemporary Buddhism 12*(1), 41–54.

Eberth, J., & Sedlmeier, P. (2012). The effects of mindfulness meditation: A meta-analysis. *Mindfulness* 3(3), 174–189.

Ekman, P., & Dalai Lama, H.H. XIVth (2008). *Emotional awareness: Overcoming the obstacles to psychological balance and compassion: A conversation between the Dalai Lama and Paul Ekman*. New York: Times Books.

Farias, M., & Wikholm, C. (2015). *The Buddha pill: Can meditation change you?* London: Watkins Publishing.

Ford, K., & Garzon, F. (2017). Research note: A randomized investigation of evangelical Christian accommodative mindfulness. *Spirituality in Clinical Practice* 4(2), 92–99.

Fox, J., Gutierrez, D., Haas, J., & Durnford, S. (2016a). Centering prayer's effects on psycho-spiritual outcomes: A pilot outcome study. *Mental Health, Religion & Culture* 19(4), 379–392.

Fox, K. C. R., Dixon, M. L., Nijeboer, S., Girn, M., Floman, J. L., Lifshitz, M., . . . Christoff, K. (2016b). Functional neuroanatomy of meditation: A review and meta-analysis of 78 functional neuroimaging investigations. *Neuroscience & Biobehavioral Reviews* 65(Supplement C), 208–228.

Fox, K. C. R., Nijeboer, S., Dixon, M. L., Floman, J. L., Ellamil, M., Rumak, S. P., . . . Christoff, K. (2014). Is meditation associated with altered brain structure? A systematic review and meta-analysis of morphometric neuroimaging in meditation practitioners. *Neuroscience & Biobehavioral Reviews* 43, 48–73.

Fresco, D. M., Moore, M. T., van Dulmen, M. H. M., Segal, Z. V., Ma, S. H., Teasdale, J. D., & Williams, J. M. G. (2007). Initial psychometric properties of the experiences questionnaire: Validation of a self-report measure of decentering. *Behavior Therapy* 38(3), 234–246.

Galante, J., Galante, I., Bekkers, M.-J., & Gallacher, J. (2014). Effect of kindness-based meditation on health and well-being: A systematic review and meta-analysis. *Journal of Consulting and Clinical Psychology* 82(6), 1101–1114.

Gallegos, A. M., Crean, H. F., Pigeon, W. R., & Heffner, K. L. (2017). Meditation and yoga for posttraumatic stress disorder: A meta-analytic review of randomized controlled trials. *Clinical Psychology Review* 58(Supplement C), 115–124.

Goldberg, M. (2015). The long marriage of mindfulness and money. *The New Yorker*. April 18, 2015. https://www.newyorker.com/business/currency/the-long-marriage-of-mindfulness-and-money

Goleman, D. (1977). *The varieties of the meditative experience*. New York: Irvington Publishers.

Goleman, D. (1984). The Buddha on meditation and states of consciousness. In D. E. Shapiro & R. Walsh (Eds.), *Meditation, classic and contemporary perspectives* (pp. 317–360). New York: Aldine.

Gong, H., Ni, C.-X., Liu, Y.-Z., Zhang, Y., Su, W.-J., Lian, Y.-J., . . . Jiang, C.-L. (2016). Mindfulness meditation for insomnia: A meta-analysis of randomized controlled trials. *Journal of Psychosomatic Research* 89(Supplement C), 1–6.

Goyal, M., Singh, S., Sibinga, E. M. S., Gould, N. F., Rowland-Seymour, A., Sharma, R., . . . Haythornthwaite, J. A. (2014). Meditation programs for psychological stress and well-being: A systematic review and meta-analysis. *JAMA Internal Medicine* 174(3), 357–368.

Greeson, J. M., Webber, D. M., Smoski, M. J., Brantley, J. G., Ekblad, A. G., Suarez, E. C., & Wolever, R. Q. (2011). Changes in spirituality partly explain health-related quality of life outcomes after Mindfulness-Based Stress Reduction. *Journal of Behavioral Medicine* 34(6), 508–518.

Griffiths, R. R., Johnson, M. W., Richards, W. A., Richards, B. D., Jesse, R., MacLean, K. A., . . . Klinedinst, M. A. (2018). Psilocybin-occasioned mystical-type experience in combination with meditation and other spiritual practices produces enduring positive changes in psychological functioning and in trait measures of prosocial attitudes and behaviors. *Journal of Psychopharmacology* 32(1), 49–69.

Gu, J., Strauss, C., Bond, R., & Cavanagh, K. (2015). How do mindfulness-based cognitive therapy and mindfulness-based stress reduction improve mental health and wellbeing? A systematic review and meta-analysis of mediation studies. *Clinical Psychology Review* 37, 1–12.

Hadot, P., & Davidson, A. I. (1995). *Philosophy as a way of life: Spiritual exercises from Socrates to Foucault.* Malden, MA: Blackwell.

Hawley, L. L., Schwartz, D., Bieling, P. J., Irving, J., Corcoran, K., Farb, N. A. S.,... Segal, Z. V. (2014). Mindfulness practice, rumination and clinical outcome in mindfulness-based treatment. *Cognitive Therapy and Research* 38(1), 1–9.

Hilton, L., Hempel, S., Ewing, B. A., Apaydin, E., Xenakis, L., Newberry, S.,... Maglione, M. A. (2017). Mindfulness meditation for chronic pain: Systematic review and meta-analysis. *Annals of Behavioral Medicine* 51(2), 199–213.

Huennekens, A. O. (2018). *Comparing the effectiveness of Christian and secular Mindfulness-Based Stress Reduction: A randomized controlled trial* (PhD dissertation). University of South Alabama.

Johnson, C. D. L. (2010). *Globalization of Hesychasm and the Jesus prayer: Contesting contemplation.* New York: Continuum.

Kabat-Zinn, J. (1982). An outpatient program in behavioral medicine for chronic pain patients based on the practice of mindfulness meditation: Theoretical considerations and preliminary results. *General Hospital Psychiatry* 4(1), 33–47.

Kabat-Zinn, J. (1994). *Wherever you go, there you are: Mindfulness meditation in everyday life.* New York, Hyperion.

Kabat-Zinn, J. (2003). Mindfulness-based interventions in context: Past, present, and future. *Clinical Psychology: Science & Practice* 10(2), 144–156.

Koenig, H. G., King, D. E., & Carson, V. B. (2012). *Handbook of religion and health.* Oxford; New York: Oxford University Press.

Kreplin, U., Farias, M., & Brazil, I. A. (2018). The limited prosocial effects of meditation: A systematic review and meta-analysis. *Scientific Reports* 8(1), 2403.

Kristeller, J. L., & Jordan, K. D. (2018). Spirituality and meditative practice: Research opportunities and challenges. *Psychological Studies* 63(22), 130–139.

Lazar, S. W., Bush, G., Gollub, R. L., Fricchione, G. L., Khalsa, G., & Benson, H. (2000). Functional brain mapping of the relaxation response and meditation. *Neuroreport: For Rapid Communication of Neuroscience Research* 11(7), 1581–1585.

Levman, B. (2017). Putting *smṛti* back into *sati* (putting remembrance back into mindfulness). *Journal of the Oxford Centre for Buddhist Studies,* 13, 121–149.

Lomas, T., Cartwright, T., Edginton, T., & Ridge, D. (2015). A qualitative analysis of experiential challenges associated with meditation practice. *Mindfulness,* 6(4), 848–860.

Luberto, C. M., Shinday, N., Song, R., Philpotts, L. L., Park, E. R., Fricchione, G. L., & Yeh, G. Y. (2018). A systematic review and meta-analysis of the effects of meditation on empathy, compassion, and prosocial behaviors. *Mindfulness* 9(3), 708–724.

Maglione, M. A., Maher, A. R., Ewing, B., Colaiaco, B., Newberry, S., Kandrack, R.,... Hempel, S. (2017). Efficacy of mindfulness meditation for smoking cessation: A systematic review and meta-analysis. *Addictive Behaviors* 69(Supplement C), 27–34.

Marsella, A. J. (1998). Toward a "global-community psychology": Meeting the needs of a changing world. *American Psychologist* 53(12), 1282–1291.

Melendez-Torres, G. J., Bonell, C., & Thomas, J. (2015). Emergent approaches to the meta-analysis of multiple heterogeneous complex interventions. *BMC Medical Research Methodology 15*, Article 47.

Mikulas, W. (2011). Mindfulness: Significant common confusions. *Mindfulness 2*(1), 1–7.

Mikulas, W. L. (2007). Buddhism & Western psychology: Fundamentals of integration. *Journal of Consciousness Studies 14*(4), 4–49.

Mind & Life Institute. (2018). *Mission.* Mind & Life Institute. Available: https://www.mindandlife.org/mission/.

Morgan, L. P. K., Graham, J. R., Hayes-Skelton, S. A., Orsillo, S. M., & Roemer, L. (2014). Relationships between amount of post-intervention mindfulness practice and follow-up outcome variables in an acceptance-based behavior therapy for generalized anxiety disorder: The importance of informal practice. *Journal of Contextual Behavioral Science 3*(3), 173–178.

Mrazek, M. D., Franklin, M. S., Phillips, D. T., Baird, B., & Schooler, J. W. (2013). Mindfulness training improves working memory capacity and GRE performance while reducing mind wandering. *Psychological Science 24*(5), 776–781.

Murphy, M., Donovan, S., & Taylor, E. (1999). *The physical and psychological effects of meditation: A review of contemporary research with a comprehensive bibliography, 1931–1996.* Sausalito, CA: Institute of Noetic Sciences.

Nagel, M. (1999). Researching advanced meditative states: Problems of subject selection. *Journal of Transpersonal Psychology 31*(1), 11–21.

Naranjo, C., & Ornstein, R. E. (1972). *On the psychology of meditation.* New York: Viking.

Newberg, A., Pourdehnad, M., Alavi, A., & D'Aquili, E. G. (2003). Cerebral blood flow during meditative prayer: Preliminary findings and methodological issues. *Perceptual and Motor Skills 97*(2), 625–630.

Niemiec, R., Rashid, T., & Spinella, M. (2012). Strong mindfulness: Integrating mindfulness and character strengths. *Journal of Mental Health Counseling 34*(3), 240–253.

Norcross, J. C., Pfund, R. A., & Prochaska, J. O. (2013). Psychotherapy in 2022: A Delphi poll on its future. *Professional Psychology: Research and Practice 44*(5), 363–370.

Norris, P. (1986). Biofeedback, voluntary control, and human potential. *Biofeedback and Self-regulation 11*(1), 1–20.

Oman, D. (2010). Similarity in diversity? Four shared functions of integrative contemplative practice systems. In T. G. Plante (Ed.), *Contemplative practices in action: Spirituality, meditation, and health* (pp. 7–16). Santa Barbara, CA: Praeger.

Oman, D. (2012). Shall the twain meet? Buddhist meditation, science, and diversity. *PsycCRITIQUES* 57(Release 30), Article 2.

Oman, D. (2015). Cultivating compassion through holistic mindfulness: Evidence for effective intervention. In T. G. Plante (Ed.), *The psychology of compassion and cruelty: Understanding the emotional, spiritual, and religious influences* (pp. 35–57). Santa Barbara, CA: Praeger.

Oman, D. (2016). International collaboration for living with the richness of spiritual diversity. *Journal of the Indian Academy of Applied Psychology 42*(2), 373–378.

Oman, D. (Ed.). (2018). *Why religion and spirituality matter for public health: Evidence, implications, and resources.* Cham, Switzerland: Springer International https://doi.org/10.1007/978-3-319-73966-3

Oman, D., & Bormann, J. E. (2018). Eknath Easwaran's mantram and passage meditation as applied Indian psychology: Psycho-spiritual and health effects. *Psychological Studies 63*(2), 94–108.

Oman, D., Duggal, C., & Misra, G. (2018). Introduction to the special issue: Spirituality and psychology, emerging perspectives. *Psychological Studies* 63(2), 89–93.

Oman, D., Richards, T. A., Hedberg, J., & Thoresen, C. E. (2008). Passage meditation improves caregiving self-efficacy among health professionals: A randomized trial and qualitative assessment. *Journal of Health Psychology* 13(8), 1119–1135.

Oman, D., Shapiro, S. L., Thoresen, C. E., Flinders, T., Driskill, J. D., & Plante, T. G. (2007). Learning from spiritual models and meditation: A randomized evaluation of a college course. *Pastoral Psychology* 55(4), 473–493.

Oman, D., & Singh, N. N. (2018). Combining Indian and Western spiritual psychology: Applications to health and social renewal. *Psychological Studies* 63(2), 172–180.

Orme-Johnson, D. W., & Barnes, V. A. (2014). Effects of the transcendental meditation technique on trait anxiety: A meta-analysis of randomized controlled trials. *Journal of Alternative and Complementary Medicine* 20(5), 330–341.

Orme-Johnson, D. W., Farrow, J. T., Chalmers, R. A., Clements, G., Schenkluhn, H., Weinless, M., . . . Dillbeck, M. C. (eds.). (1977–1990). *Scientific research on Maharishi's Transcendental Meditation and TM-Siddhi program, Vols. 1–6.*

Ospina, M. B., Bond, K., Karkhaneh, M., Tjosvold, L., Vandermeer, B., Liang, Y., . . . Klassen, T. P. (2007). Meditation practices for health: State of the research (Evidence Report/ Technology Assessment no. 155). University of Alberta Evidence-Based Practice Center.

Palitsky, R., & Kaplan, D. M. (2019). The role of religion for mindfulness-based interventions: Implications for dissemination and implementation. *Mindfulness.* https://doi.org/10.1007/ s12671-019-01253-0

Peterson, C., & Seligman, M. E. P. (2004). *Character strengths and virtues: A handbook and classification.* Washington, DC/New York: American Psychological Association/Oxford University Press.

Porpora, D. V. (2006). Methodological atheism, methodological agnosticism and religious experience. *Journal for the Theory of Social Behaviour* 36(1), 57–75.

Purser, R. E., & Milillo, J. (2015). Mindfulness revisited: A Buddhist-based conceptualization. *Journal of Management Inquiry* 24(1), 3–24.

Rao, K. R. (2017). *Foundations of yoga psychology.* Singapore: Springer Nature.

Rao, K. R., & Paranjpe, A. C. (2016). *Psychology in the Indian tradition.* New Delhi: Springer.

Reavley, N., & Pallant, J. F. (2009). Development of a scale to assess the meditation experience. *Personality and Individual Differences* 47(6), 547–552.

Robertson, D. (2010). *The philosophy of cognitive-behavioural therapy (CBT): Stoic philosophy as rational and cognitive psychotherapy.* London: Karnac Books.

Rosch, E. (2007). More than mindfulness: When you have a tiger by the tail, let it eat you. *Psychological Inquiry* 18(4), 258–264.

Rosch, E. (2015). The emperor's clothes: A look behind the Western mindfulness mystique. In: B. D. Ostafin, M. D. Robinson, & B. P. Meier (Eds.), *Handbook of mindfulness and self-regulation* (pp. 271–292). New York: Springer.

Rossano, M. J. (2007). Did meditating make us human? *Cambridge Archaeological Journal* 17(1), 47–58.

Sauer-Zavala, S. E., Walsh, E. C., Eisenlohr-Moul, T. A., & Lykins, E. L. B. (2013). Comparing mindfulness-based intervention strategies: Differential effects of sitting meditation, body scan, and mindful yoga. *Mindfulness* 4(4), 383–388.

Schutte, N. S., & Malouff, J. M. (2014). A meta-analytic review of the effects of mindfulness meditation on telomerase activity. *Psychoneuroendocrinology* 42, 45–48.

Sedlmeier, P., Eberth, J., Schwarz, M., Zimmermann, D., Haarig, F., Jaeger, S., & Kunze, S. (2012). The psychological effects of meditation: A meta-analysis. *Psychological Bulletin 138*(6), 1139–1171.
Shapiro, D. H., & Walsh, R. N. (eds.) (1984). *Meditation: Classic and contemporary perspectives.* New York: Aldine.
Shapiro, D. H., & Zifferblatt, S. M. (1976). Zen meditation and behavior self-control: Similarities, differences, and clinical applications. *American Psychologist 31*(7), 519–532.
Shapiro, S. L., Oman, D., Thoresen, C. E., Plante, T. G., & Flinders, T. (2008). Cultivating mindfulness: Effects on well-being. *Journal of Clinical Psychology 64*(7), 840–862.
Sharf, R. H. (1995). Buddhist modernism and the rhetoric of meditative experience. *Numen 42*(3), 228–283.
Shiyko, M. P., Hallinan, S., & Naito, T. (2017). Effects of mindfulness training on posttraumatic growth: A systematic review and meta-analysis. *Mindfulness 8*(4), 848–858.
Singh, N. N. (2010). Mindfulness: A finger pointing to the moon. *Mindfulness 1*(1), 1–3.
Smith, J. C. (1988). Steps toward a cognitive-behavioral model of relaxation. *Biofeedback & Self Regulation 13*(4), 307–329.
Smith, J. C., Amutio, A., Anderson, J. P., & Aria, L. A. (1996). Relaxation: Mapping an uncharted world. *Biofeedback & Self Regulation 21*(1), 63–90.
Taylor, E. (1999). Introduction. In M. Murphy, S. Donovan, & E. Taylor (Eds.), *The physical and psychological effects of meditation: A review of contemporary research with a comprehensive bibliography, 1931–1996* (pp. 1–32). 2nd ed. Sausalito, CA: Institute of Noetic Sciences.
Underhill, E. (1911). *Mysticism: A study in the nature and development of man's spiritual consciousness.* New York: E.P. Dutton.
Vahia, N. S., Jeste, D. V., Kapoor, S. N., Ardhapurkar, I., & Nath, R. S. (1973). Further experience with the therapy based upon concepts of Patanjali in the treatment of psychiatric disorders. *Indian Journal of Psychiatry 15*(1), 32–37.
Vaitl, D., Birbaumer, N., Gruzelier, J., Jamieson, G. A., Kotchoubey, B., Kubler, A., . . . Weiss, T. (2005). Psychobiology of altered states of consciousness. *Psychological Bulletin 131*(1), 98–127.
van der Velden, A. M., Kuyken, W., Wattar, U., Crane, C., Pallesen, K. J., Dahlgaard, J., . . . Piet, J. (2015). A systematic review of mechanisms of change in mindfulness-based cognitive therapy in the treatment of recurrent major depressive disorder. *Clinical Psychology Review 37*, 26–39.
Wachholtz, A. B., Malone, C. D., & Pargament, K. I. (2017). Effect of different meditation types on migraine headache medication use. *Behavioral Medicine 43*(1), 1–8.
Wachholtz, A. B., & Pargament, K. I. (2005). Is spirituality a critical ingredient of meditation? Comparing the effects of spiritual meditation, secular meditation, and relaxation on spiritual, psychological, cardiac, and pain outcomes. *Journal of Behavioral Medicine 28*(4), 369–384.
Wahab, M. N. A., & Rahman, A. A. (2015). A study of the effect of dzikr on the psychology of students with disciplinary problems using heart rate variability (HRV). *International Journal in Management & Social Science 3*(3), 52–58.
Wahbeh, H., Sagher, A., Back, W., Pundhir, P., & Travis, F. (2018). A systematic review of transcendent states across meditation and contemplative traditions. *Explore: The Journal of Science and Healing 14*(1), 19–35.
Wallace, B. A. (2006). *The attention revolution: Unlocking the power of the focused mind.* Boston: Wisdom Publications.

Wallace, R. K. (1970). Physiological effects of transcendental meditation. *Science 167*(3926), 1751–1754.

Walsh, R. (1984). An evolutionary model of meditation research. In D. E. Shapiro & R. Walsh (Eds.), *Meditation: Classic and contemporary perspectives* (pp. 24–31). New York: Aldine.

Walsh, R., & Shapiro, S. L. (2006). The meeting of meditative disciplines and western psychology: A mutually enriching dialogue. *American Psychologist 61*(3), 227–239.

Walsh, R. N. (1999). *Essential spirituality: The 7 central practices to awaken heart and mind.* New York: Wiley.

West, S. G., Aiken, L. S., & Todd, M. (1993). Probing the effects of individual components in multiple component prevention programs. *American Journal of Community Psychology 21*(5), 571.

Williams, J. M. G., & Kabat-Zinn, J. (2011). Mindfulness: Diverse perspectives on its meaning, origins, and multiple applications at the intersection of science and dharma. *Contemporary Buddhism 12*(1), 1–18.

Woods, R. (1980). Introduction. In R. Woods (Ed.), *Understanding mysticism* (pp. 1–15). Garden City, NY: Doubleday.

Zeng, X., Chiu, C. P. K., Wang, R., Oei, T. P. S., & Leung, F. Y. K. (2015). The effect of loving-kindness meditation on positive emotions: A meta-analytic review. *Frontiers in Psychology 6*, Article 1693.

PART II

MEDITATION ACROSS THE WORLD'S TRADITIONS

CHAPTER 4

HINDUISM AND MEDITATION

Tantra

GAVIN FLOOD

Introduction

DURING the early Middle Ages (approximately seventh–tenth centuries CE) a new tradition arose within Hinduism commonly called Tantra or Tantrism. This tradition, or to be more precise range of traditions, developed initially within Śaivism, the religion focused on the deity Śiva, and due to its success rapidly spread to other religions, including Jainism and above all Buddhism, where it underwent a transformation into the Vajrayāna, the "Diamond Vehicle." From its roots in the Gupta period—the earliest textual material can be dated to the fourth century CE—it became the dominant form of religion in South Asia to around the thirteenth century. Tantric traditions continued in an attenuated way through to modernity and came to be exported to the West, especially in the 1960s through the Hindu diaspora and the movement of gurus to Europe and America to satisfy the spiritual longings of a disaffected youth. In the following I present an account of the purpose of meditation in the tantric traditions along with the methods of practice as presented in the textual sources that have come down to us, rather than accounting for tantric meditation in a contemporary context. The main texts I will be referring to are from the tantric traditions of Śiva, called the Mantra Mārga ("path of mantras") that developed from as early as the fifth century CE and flourished from the tenth to thirteenth centuries. The Mantra Mārga comprised two main traditions, the normative Śaiva Siddhānta and non-Siddhānta groups. It is these that are particularly important for understanding tantric meditation (see Figure 4.1). In particular the texts I will refer to are the *Netra-tantra*, the *Mālinīvijayottara-tantra*, and the *Vijñānabhairava-tantra*. These were all composed between the seventh to tenth centuries. I will also refer to the tantric tradition of Viṣṇu called the Pañcarātra, particularly one of its key scriptures,

FIGURE 4.1 Tantric figure. Tantrika painting. Cakras in the body. Indian depiction of the *cakra* and *nadi* in the Śaiva tradition. Color painting of a cross-legged meditator showing cakras and kuṇḍaliṇī.
Wellcome Collection, under the terms of the Creative Commons Attribution License (CC BY 4.0)

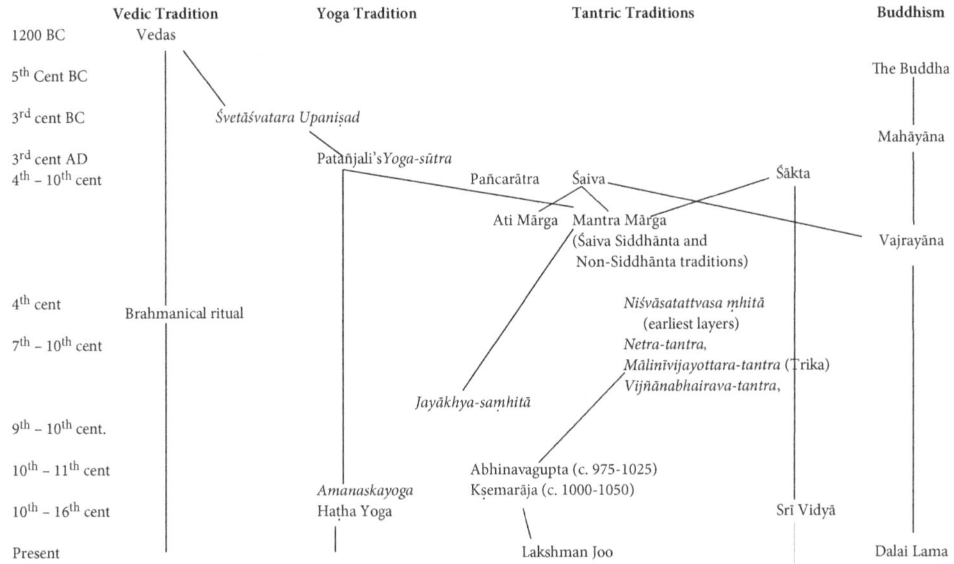

FIGURE 4.2 Chronology of texts and traditions mentioned in the chapter.

the *Jayākhya-saṃhitā* composed before the tenth century. For a diagrammatic representation of these texts I refer the reader to Figure 4.2.

The Goals of Meditation

Meditation in Tantrism is central to the process of attaining the highest human good of liberating the soul from its entrapment in the cycle of reincarnation and also in the process of gaining lesser goods, such as the satisfaction of desire. Both the spiritual goal of liberation (*mokṣa*), common to most Indic religions, and the worldly goal of attaining magical power (*siddhi*) and pleasure (*bhoga*) in this and higher worlds were regarded as compatible, and both were achieved through meditation.

Liberation was understood differently by different traditions. For the normative, dominant tantric tradition, the Śaiva Siddhānta, it was not a complete extinction of the individual self but rather the achievement of equality with Śiva (*śivatulya*), the condition of being the same as Śiva although numerically distinct and not performing the functions of creation, maintenance, and destruction of the universe (Goodall, 2004, 2.123–124). For other traditions, the non-Saiddhāntika, liberation was understood non-dualistically as union with Śiva or recognition (*pratyabhijñā*) of one's identity with that reality. Each tantric tradition regarded itself as transcending the goal of the earlier and mapping a hierarchy of liberation onto the hierarchical levels of the cosmos (Watson, 2013, pp. 15–63). For example, in the non-dualist Śaivism of Kashmir, the philosopher Kṣemarāja (c. CE 1000–1075) ranks the various systems of philosophy along the vertical axis of cosmological levels, with his own system at the top, the Śaiva Siddhānta below this, and other orthodox and heterodox philosophies arranged below that, with Buddhism at the level of *buddhi*, higher mind (*Pratyabhijñāhṛdaya* 8). We find the same kind of mapping in the Śaiva Siddhānta too (Watson, 2013). The Śaiva Siddhānta maintained that liberation could be achieved at death (*videhamukti*) by following its ritual system, whereas the non-Saiddhāntika traditions believed that liberation could be attained in this very life (*jīvanmukti*) through a program of radical practice. Although the conception of liberation varies along with the ranking of its attainment by different systems, the process of meditation is common and assumes certain fundamental principles shared by all yoga or meditation schools, particularly that the uncontrolled mind causes suffering and that the mind can be controlled and thereby transformed through concentration. But beyond this generality, the tantric traditions developed their own particular use of terminology, and the relationship of these traditions to other kinds of yoga is historically complex.

Patañjali's classic definition in the *Yoga Sūtras* (1.2) is that "yoga is the cessation of mental fluctuation" (*yogaścittavṛttinirodhaḥ*) (Aranya, 1983, p. 6). Through focusing on a single point (*ekāgratā*), the wandering mind or mental fluctuation can be calmed and one-pointed concentration achieved. This one-pointed focus leads into a condition of absorbed consciousness (*samādhi*) in which the practitioners or yogis are no longer aware of their ambient surroundings but is absorbed in the object of meditation. This state of absorption or trance is attested in tantric texts (see Figure 4.2). The *Mālinīvijayottaratantra*, for example, speaks of the yogi becoming absorbed through contemplating the object of meditation and achieving identification with it, upon attaining which the mind is without the support of an object and the yogis become completely unaware of their surroundings: he becomes like a log or clod of earth (Vasudeva, 2004, pp. 435–446). In *samādhi* the mind is inactive and the body goes into a state of quiescence, neither sleeping nor waking, neither breathing nor not breathing (*Amanaskayoga*, cited by Birch, 2013). This *samādhi* is a prerequisite for liberation and is sometimes identified with liberation itself (Birch, 2013). Patañjali's system of eight ancillaries of yoga is often assumed by tantric texts and in one text, the *Netra-tantra* as we will see, is reinterpreted in the light of the text's metaphysics. Another common tantric system is not the eightfold yoga, but sixfold yoga (*ṣaḍaṅga-yoga*) that again highlights concentration as the transforming power of the mind (Vasudeva, 2004, pp. 367–436). Indeed, the term *yoga* can often simply be translated as "meditation." Through concentration the world of experience for the yogi is changed: with a change of consciousness comes a change of world, and while this can mean that our mental state conditions our experience of the world, it also means a more radical shift that propels the yogi into other worlds of experience in the cosmical hierarchy. Thus, along the vertical axis of the universe different worlds (*bhuvana*) are arranged that the yogis can enter due to their absorbed state of concentration (Goodall, 2004, chapter 5). Even toward the end of life the advanced yogis can propel their consciousness into another world or gain enlightenment in a process that has been referred to as yogic suicide (*utkrānti*) (Vasudeva, 2004, pp. 437–445). In the end, of course, the highest good is entry into the state of final release.

So far all this is standard fare in Yoga traditions. Indeed, Yoga and Tantra significantly overlap. The mind is transformed through concentration on a single point and the yogi can enter into higher worlds through such concentration. What is distinctive about tantric meditation is rather the techniques that emphasize visual contemplation along with meditation on mantra and inner sound. Apart from the word *yoga*, one of the main terms for meditation that we find in tantric texts is *dhyāna*. This is the same word that is used in Buddhism to denote eight levels of meditational experience, the four *dhyānas* of form and the four formless ones (Flood, 2013, pp. 172–174), but comes to have the specific connotation in Tantrism as visualization of a deity and/or of the body. The term is also used in its verbal form such as the very common *dhyāyet*, the third person singular optative, meaning "one should visualize" or "meditate." Other verbs used as synonyms in the optative are *cintayet* (one should meditate or cause to think about) and *vikalpayet* (one should imagine) (Flood, 2013, p. 178). Such visualization is accompanied by the repetition of mantra, the sound-form of the god, which is an aid to concentration and absorption of the practitioner in the object of meditation. Usually *vikalpa* is used negatively as "imagination" and therefore a fluctuation of the mind that the yogi seeks to prevent, but the faculty of imagination can be used positively for the purpose of meditation and focusing the mind. The most general and common term for meditation is *bhāvanā*, which Vasudeva translates as "contemplative insight" (Vasudeva, 2004, p. 221). There are degrees of intensity here, and contemplative insight leads to one-pointed absorption (*samādhi*) in the object of contemplation. The tantric traditions assume a model of the mind that consciousness takes on the form of its objects (Vasudeva, 2004, p. 222), so meditation on a pure object, such as mantra or deity, transforms the mind into the purity of its object. The term *dhāraṇā* can also be translated as "meditation" and is used in the sense of visual contemplation or introspection (Vasudeva, 2004, p. 148), as well as denoting a more general range of practices, as in the *Vijñānabhairava-tantra*.

Another distinctive aspect of tantric meditation is initiation (*dīkṣā*). To practice meditation and to be given a mantra by the guru, the practitioner needs to be initiated by a teacher into a particular system. In the Śaiva Siddhānta this was formalized into a common or shared initiation (*samaya-dīkṣā*) that gave the initiate permission to read particular texts, followed by the liberating initiation (*nirvāṇa-dīkṣā*) that guaranteed liberation at death or within a few restricted reincarnations (Brunner, 1977, pp. iii–xiii; xxx–xliii). Following initiation, the practitioner desiring pleasure and magical powers (*bubhukṣu*) could undergo a further consecration and become a *sādhaka*, or a practitioner desiring only liberation (*mumukṣu*) could become an *ācārya*, a teacher in the tradition (Brunner, 1975). To qualify for initiation the practitioner needed to be high caste, whereas this was not always a requirement in other tantric sects, although for the more extreme Goddess-orientated tradition of the Kula, signs of possession such as trembling were an expected prerequisite (Sanderson, 1986).

Meditation is not isolated from other practices and, indeed, a whole way of life. There is a spectrum of uses from external ritual, both for liberation and magical purposes, that involves some visual contemplation, to forms of meditation that are purely internal and do not require any external ritual. These kinds of meditation disparage external rites as being useless in the pursuit of liberation. Generally, this spectrum from external ritual to purely internal meditation maps on to the tantric traditions from the Śaiva Siddhānta whose main concern was ritual action in the belief that such action will remove the residues of past action (karma) from the soul, to tantric sects such as the Krama for whom meditation was an internal process in which cognition rather than action frees the spirit. Alongside this are magical practices in extreme tantric sects that also used some visual contemplation in their rites (on these see Goodall and Isaacson, 2016, pp. 26–34).

The Tantric Traditions

Tantric meditation develops from earlier Brahmanical religion where the Upaniṣads bear witness to meditation practice, such as the *Śvetāśvatara Upaniṣad* (2.8–14) that describes an upright meditation posture and breath control (Olivelle, 1998, p. 419). It is also influenced by early yoga, possibly from a source prior to Patañjali (Vasudeva, 2004, p. 430). Meditation is part of a range of practices in tantric traditions, by which I mean those religions that regarded the tantras as revelation from a divine source. These traditions comprising the Śaiva Siddhānta and non-Saiddhāntika religions are classified as belonging to the path of mantras (*mantra-mārga*) and distinguished themselves from the ascetic, higher, or outer path (*ati-mārga*) as well as from orthodox Smārta or Puranic worship of Śiva (Sanderson, 1988). In contrast to the higher path for ascetics only, the path of mantras was for householders. The Śaiva Siddhānta formed the normative ritual system comprising daily and occasional rites along with rites for a desired end, which became pan-Indian by around the eleventh century. Daily ritual observance at the three junctures of the day (dawn, midday, and dusk) involved bathing, the purification of the body (*bhūtaśuddhi*) through its symbolic destruction in the imagination, the creation of a divine body (*divya-deha*) by imposing mantras, inner or mental worship (*mānasa-yāga*) followed by external worship (*bahya-yāga*), making offerings to an icon of the god or the *liṅga*, the symbol of Śiva (Flood, 2006, pp. 106–107). The physical or gross body is symbolically destroyed and a divine body created because only a god can worship a god in Tantrism, a belief possibly rooted in the idea that the universe is an emanation of an absolute reality and so implicitly all manifestation is in essence divine. Here visualization plays an integral role in ritual practice, especially in mental worship during which the practitioner would visualize the deity located at the crown of the head and coming down into the body to be seated on a throne in the heart where he would be offered mental flowers and incense. This basic ritual structure was shared by all tantric traditions, not only those of Śiva but of Viṣṇu too where the Pañcarātra tradition (the tantric worship of Viṣṇu) simply replaces Śiva with one of the forms of Viṣṇu, particularly Nārāyaṇa.

This normative system of ritual was complemented by other practices by non-Saiddhāntika groups. Among these the Trika tradition, so called because of its worship of three goddesses Parā, Parāparā, and Aparā on a trident visualized as pervading the body (Sanderson, 1990), demanded ritual sex, at least annually, to reflect the union of Śiva and the Goddess. Such practices became an aesthetic version of more extreme tantric rites of ritualized sex as transgression of orthodox norms and the production of sexual fluids for offering to ferocious deities of their cult (White, 2003) as we find in Tantras such as the *Brahmayāmala* or *Picumata* (Kiss, 2015, pp. 257–283). Visualization that enabled the identification of the practitioner with the deity was integral to these ritual practices. There was also a tradition of pure gnosis that rejected ritual as efficacious in attaining liberation. It is not action that liberates but the gnosis of identity with pure consciousness that is achieved by meditation. This contrasts with the orthodox Advaita Vedānta tradition of Śaṅkara, for whom meditation was classified as action and action cannot lead to gnosis. But even in the tantric traditions, enlightenment does not automatically follow from meditation, but meditation calms the mind and creates the conditions for its arising. What follows presents a more detailed treatment of this spectrum.

Meditation as Visual Contemplation

The central component of tantric meditation is visualization or visual contemplation. Visual contemplation is the creation of a world in the practitioner's imagination that is regarded not as illusory but as a more intense reality than that of everyday transaction. Visual contemplation is pervasive in tantric traditions from Śaiva Siddhānta daily ritual to non-Saiddhāntika visualization of deities in various tantric pantheons to achieve power or protection. Chapter 18 of the Nepalese recension of the *Netra-tantra*, for example, describes magical rites for destroying enemies by sending demonic beings against them, while affording protection through the visualization of the deity Mahābhairava, who has a huge beard, a monstrous shape, a gaping mouth filled with fangs, and so on (NTb 18.14–29). But visualization is particularly important when it comes to the body and the identification of the practitioner with the deity.

One of the clearest accounts of the tantric ritual process and identification of the body with the cosmos is found in a Pañcarātra scripture, the *Jayākhya-saṃhitā* (JS). Here the practitioner performs the purification of the body by visualizing the body as a hierarchical structure mapped onto the cosmos. Thus the elements earth, water, fire, air, and ether are imagined as pervading different areas, the earth from feet to knees, water from knees to thighs, fire from thighs to navel, air from navel to throat, and ether from throat to the crown of the head, known as the aperture of God (*brahmarandhra*). For example, for visualizing the earth element the text reads:

> [The practitioner] should visualize a yellow square [representing] the earth, marked with sign of thunder and connected with the five, sound and so on [i.e., the subtle elements of sound, touch, form, taste, and smell]. It is filled with trees and mountains, adorned with oceans, islands, good rivers, and walled towns. He should visualize

> [that earth] entering his own body from the outside with an inhaled breath, and uttering the mantra he should imagine it as calmed, pervading in due order from the knees to the soles of the feet by means of the retained breath, O Brahmin. Then [the earth] is gradually dissolved in its own mantra form, and this mantra king [dissolved] into the energy of smell. After that he should emit the energy of smell with the exhaled breath. (JS 10.26–30ab)

Here the process is described clearly. The practitioner imagines a yellow square representing the earth element in front of him, inscribed with a thunderbolt emblem and other visual details. He breathes it in while repeating its mantra, holds his breath while it pervades from knees to feet in imagination, where it dissolves into its mantra, this mantra itself dissolves into the subtle element of smell, then he exhales "smell" that merges into the next element of water, visualized in front of him as a white half-moon shape. The same process continues with each of the elements represented by different symbols. The mantra of the earth is *OṂ ŚLĀṂ PṚTHIVYAI HUṂ PHAṬ*, comprising mostly meaningless sounds called "seed syllables" (*bīja*, so called because they give rise to ritual language) apart from the word "earth" (*pṛthivi*), that is replaced by the different elements respectively in the dative case until the process is complete with the symbolic destruction of all.

One of the notable things about this text is the elaborate detail of the visualization. It is not simply a yellow square, but the visualized earth element contains all manner of phenomena experienced on the earth—trees, mountains, towns, and rivers—all constructed in his inner mind's eye. This degree of detail was to disappear in later yoga traditions that became more stripped down of what they regarded as unnecessary accretion (Birch, 2011).

The repetition of mantras is crucial to visual contemplation. There can be meditation simply on mantra that is pan-Indian and not restricted to the tantric tradition. Orthodox Brahmins repeat mantras on ritual occasions and gurus teach mantra repetition as part of the common parlance of meditation. But tantric meditation differs here firstly in having distinctly tantric mantras in contrast to Vedic ones and in its emphasis on the mantra as the deity, or more precisely the sound-form of the god (Padoux, 2011; Goodall and Isaacson, 2016, pp. 4–17). Gods have a body that is visualized in meditation but also a body manifested as sound. In repeating the mantra yogis raise their minds to the level of the mantra. If the cosmos is a vibration (*spanda*) of consciousness, as the non-Saiddhāntika traditions maintain, then deities are different levels of vibration within it. Through repeating the mantra in meditation the practitioner is raising oneself to the level of the mantra's resonance. Mostly these mantras are meaningless seed syllables such as *HUṂ, PHAṬ, KLĪṂ, KRĪṂ*, and so on, such as the "eye" or *netra* mantra, *OṂ JUṂ SAḤ*, of the *Netra-tantra*, which is the sound form of the God Amṛteśa or Mṛtyunjaya. Often these seed syllables are interspersed with the name of the deity as we saw in the JS.

Finally all the elements are dissolved in the body and the practitioner imagines one's soul leaving the body through the crown of the head (*brahmarandhra*) where he beholds Nārāyaṇa effulgent, standing in a circle of light, a standard identification of the god with the sun (JS 10.49–57). The soul or individual consciousness (*caitanya*) has transcended the limitation of the physical body in imagination, but the process is not yet complete. He then visualizes the body being burned by the deity Kālāgni, the fire of time, from the feet upward into a pile of ashes that are then swept away by a flood of milky water arising through the repetition of mantras (JS 10.72–77). Having purified the body in this way through its symbolic destruction, which daily recapitulates in the microcosm of the practitioner the macrocosm of the cosmic destruction of the universe at the end of many aeons, the practitioner creates a new divine body through touching different parts of the body and repeating mantras (*nyāsa*). Again, this is a complex process involving placing the deities of the Pañcarātra pantheon on the body. Beginning with the right hand, Nārāyaṇa is placed on the thumb with mantras (*OṂ KṢAIṂ KṢIḤ NAMAḤ, NĀRAYĀṆA VIŚVĀTMANE HRĪṂ SVAHĀ*) followed by the mantras or sound bodies of the goddesses Lakṣmī, Kīrti, Jayā, and Māyā on the fingers (JS 11.10–17; see Rastelli, 1999, pp. 241–244). Once the hands are covered with mantras, the process continues to cover the whole body—head, eyes, ears, mouth, shoulders, hands (again), buttocks, heart, back, navel, hips, knees, and feet—and finally the seven-syllable mantra of Nārāyaṇa is applied to the whole body (JS 11.35cd–36). This completes the process and the meditator is identified with the supreme God Viṣṇu-Nārāyaṇa, possessing the six qualities (*guṇas*) of knowledge, majesty, power, strength, energy, and splendor (JS 11.39cd–40). This visualization process has identified the practitioner with God and he repeats "I am the Lord Viṣṇu, I am Nārāyaṇa Hari, and I am Vāsudeva" (JS 11.41). Although the Pañcarātra is metaphysically dualistic with the soul ontologically distinct from God, for ritual and meditation this is not the case and, as with all tantric traditions, we have the identification of the practitioner with the deity. The ordinary, everyday self or "indexical-I" (the first-person pronoun as an index of the self) is identified with the greater subjectivity of God: the indexical-I is expanded to a cosmic subjectivity through the process of visualization.

With the physical body destroyed in the meditator's imagination and a divine body created, he can then worship the deity firstly within himself. He visualizes a throne in the heart and Nārāyaṇa brought down into it from his location at the crown of the head, to be seated on the throne and worshiped there in his four-armed form. The construction of the throne in the heart is itself a complex process built up from within the body. From the genitals to the navel four regions are imagined beginning with the earth, then the fire of time (Kālāgni) who had previously burned the body, the god Ananta, and the Earth Goddess at the navel. From there the practitioner visualizes a milky ocean out from which springs a lotus that grows up to the heart where it opens. The eight petals of the lotus are identified with the directions, with the four Vedas, and with different theriomorphic deities who support the throne built up upon them (JS 12.1–15). With the creation of the throne, Nārāyaṇa is seated upon it and worshiped in the imagination. After this the practitioner opens his eyes and performs external worship to an icon of the deity before him (JS chapter 13).

I have offered some detail to illustrate the complexity of tantric visualization systems. There is a spectrum of practice involved, from purely mental operations in visualizing processes within the body, to ritual actions with the hands, and finally external worship of the deity. Furthermore the ritual and meditative process is not always consonant with the metaphysical tenets of the system, as with the JS whose theology maintains a distinction between God and self but whose daily ritual process involves their identification.

The basic ritual structure outlined here involving a lot of visualization is shared by all tantric traditions. Indeed, the JS is influenced by the Śaiva tradition but is perhaps the clearest and most systematic exemplar of the identification of the body with the cosmos and of the practitioner with God. One of the notable features is the visualization of the body as comprising a vertical axis along which different cosmological levels are plotted and the supreme deity, located at the crown of the head, is brought down into the heart. This vertical axis is developed in other systems that we might say are more focused on meditation without the emphasis on external ritual. As we saw in the JS, the visualization of the body is of a subtle body, with the physical body being symbolically destroyed. This vertical axis of this subtle body is the basis for the later yogic emphasis on Kuṇḍalinī yoga that finds its origin in these earlier tantric traditions and the idea of subtle energy or breath (*prāṇa*) circulating through the body. An important text that displays the structure of the subtle body is the *Netra-tantra*.

This text, which was popular in the Kashmir valley, may go back between 700 and 850 (Sanderson, 2004, pp. 274–294; Padoux, 2002; Brunner, 1974). It was used as a text of the royal court for the protection of the king and his family (NT 6.35; Sanderson, 2004) and integrates a panoply of deity visualization systems within it. One structure is particularly interesting, three chapters on what the text calls the gross (*sthula-*), subtle (*sūkṣma-*), and supreme meditation (*para-dhyāna*). The gross meditation is focused on rites of protection from demonic forces or appeasement (*śanti*) and prosperity (*puṣṭi*), these rites involves meditation along with procedures such as the construction of ritual diagrams on which the name of the person to be protected is written, and the subtle meditation involves visualizing the body and awakening powers within it. The supreme meditation is a reinterpretation of Patañjali's eight ancillaries of yoga along more purely meditative lines. But I will here focus on the subtle meditation to illustrate the importance of the subtle body in these systems. The subtle meditation is especially interesting because it contains two techniques or systems of meditation on the subtle body. In his commentary on the text, the Kashmir Śaiva philosopher Kṣemarāja (c. CE 1000–1075) calls these the Tantra system (*tantraprakrīyā*) and the Kula system (*kulaprakrīyā*), the former being for the normative non-dualist Śaivism and the latter being for elite esoteric Goddess worship.

The purpose of the subtle meditation is liberation or more specifically the state of immortality. Indeed, the text worships Śiva in his form as the Conqueror of Death, Mṛtyunjaya, or Lord of Immortality, Amṛteśa. Through a process of breath control, the yogi awakens a power within oneself that originates at the organ of generation and rises up through the subtle body, piercing blockages or "knots" along its vertical axis. These knots are also called circles (*cakra*) and centers (*ādhāra*). The structure of the subtle body comprises three vertical channels connected at the base (in later tradition, the two channels either side of the central channel begin at the nostrils). The central channel traverses from the "root," perhaps located at the perineum, to the crown of the head, as we had in the JS. This vertical structure is the support (*ādhāra*) of the soul and contains six circles (*cakra*), twelve "knots" (*granthi*), and other cosmological features such as the three luminous abodes, sun, fire, and moon. This subtle body is permeated by seventy-two thousand or more channels, although the central channel is the most important and is the one to which the others are connected. These channels are impure and filled with disease, so the immediate purpose of the subtle meditation is to purify them and rise above them (NT 7.1–4).

The text first describes the Goddess-oriented practice of the Kula system of visualization (NT 7.1–16). Here the power that the yogi awakens, his "own vibration," rises up through these channels as "the needle of sound," piercing the blockages along its axis, he penetrates to the supreme abode of Śiva at the crown of the head. Having become equal to the all-pervading Śiva through this process, the yogi becomes a divine body (*divya-deha*) bereft of all disease (NT 7.5; 7.12). Resting for a moment in that supreme state and meditating upon the elixir of immortality obtained, the yogi should then force the nectar that dwells at the crown of the head down into the rest of the body so that it flows through all the channels (NT 7.13). The nectar of immortality fills the entire body and is retained within the body, envisaged as the body pervaded by the subtle sound. This practice leads to the end of old age and death (NT 7.13).

What is striking here is that the purpose of this meditation is indeed immortality, the ending of old age and death, that the text seems to mean literally. The model of the person presented is slightly different from the purely vertical ascent model, for here having penetrated into the supreme abode at the crown of the head, the yogi releases the nectar of immortality that dwells there so that it flows through the body, rejuvenating it. This technique of flooding the body (*plāvana*), that Wernicke-Olesen calls a 'Śākta Anthropology,' is particular to the Śākta or Goddess tradition, that is contrasted with an earlier system in which immortality is achieved when semen (*bindu*) is thought to be stored and retained at the crown of the head (Wernicke-Olesen and Einarsen, 2018, p. 10; Mallinson, 2015, pp. 109–140). The Kula system is more physicalist than the normative tantric system in its emphasis on flooding the body with nectar and attaining physical immortality.

The second method of the normative system or *tantraprakrīyā* assumes a similar hierarchy of levels along the vertical axis of the body. The yogi establishes his consciousness in the vibration at the root center (in the area of the perineum) and through his will drives it up the central channel (NT 7.19–20). This power pierces the knots as it rises upward. These knots are also identified with regions of the cosmos governed by different gods, so through penetrating the channel the yogi is also penetrating up through the levels of the cosmos, which the text lists as being ruled by the gods Brahmā, Viṣṇu, Rudra, Īśvara, and Sadāśiva (NT 7.23). When consciousness reaches the crown of the head the yogi becomes the all-pervading, supreme Śiva. As in the previous meditation, he draws down the consciousness back to his heart and the nectar of immortality spreads through the body (NT 7.47–48). There is yet another, higher level where there is an ocean of nectar and the yogi there can finally become one with Śiva and he should realize this in his own experience (NT 7.49–50).

In this chapter of the NT meditation is focused on the body imagined as a subtle form, pervaded by channels invisible to the naked eye and knots along a central pathway up which consciousness or energy is transferred by the yogi in an act of will in order to be united with the all-pervading Śiva at the crown of the head. This is a precursor to the later idea of the Goddess Kuṇḍalinī who moves up the central channel, the *suṣumna*, piercing the *cakras*. This idea became pan-Indian, entering popularity in the West initially through the translation of an eighteenth-century text, the "Description of the Six Centers" (*Ṣaḍcakranirupaṇa*), Arthur Avalon's *The Serpent Power* (1974), and has become widely known through Indian gurus coming to America and Europe, such as Rajneesh and Muktananda (Rawlinson 1999). This six-center version of the system has its origin in the eleventh-century *Kubjikāmata-tantra* (Goudriaan & Schoterman, 1988; White, 1996, p. 73), a Goddess or Śākta text belonging to what is known as the Western Kaula transmission (Dyczkowski, 1988). Kubjikā is the Goddess in the form of an old crone, bent over, whose name is connected to Kuṇḍalinī, the coiled one, the power of the Goddess envisioned as a snake resting in the root center until awakened through meditation and breath control (Silburn, 1988, pp. 25–35). Once aroused she moves up through the central channel, piercing the six centers from the root, through the genital center, to the navel, heart, throat, between the eyes to finally merge with the thousand-petalled lotus at the crown of the head. This system of six centers with the thousand-petalled lotus, sometimes included as a seventh, entered the Haṭha Yoga tradition and became widely popular. Although this system became reified and the cakras even identified with organs in the body during the nineteenth century in some Indian medical books (Wujastyk, 2002), the subtle-body meditation remained much more fluid in earlier texts, where it is clear that it is not to be taken in a literal sense, but is a system of meditation for the purpose of gaining enlightenment, or flooding the body with nectar to realize immortality.

One more variation on this basic theme of visualizing the body as a vertical axis should be given as an important practice of the tantric householder in Kashmir during the medieval period (the same time as the NT and the JS). The famous philosopher Abhinavagupta (c. CE 975–1050) is an exponent of the Trika tradition mentioned above. Having performed the symbolic destruction of the body in a similar way to the process described in the JS, the daily meditation here involved visualizing a trident maṇḍala along the axis of the body with three Goddesses—Parā, Parāparā and Aparā—on its prongs. I refer the reader to Sanderson's exposition of this process, but in brief the meditator imagines the trident extending beyond the crown of the head and its central axis overcoded with levels of the cosmos, such as the *tattvas*, from various tantric systems. The meditator identifies himself with the Goddess Parā, who ascends up the trident to the central prong, and there he imagines himself merging into a fourth Goddess, Kālasaṃkarṣiṇī, who is the source of the other three Goddesses—who are her emanations and indeed the very ground of being and consciousness (Sanderson, 1986, p. 164; 1990). In this meditation the practitioner recognizes himself as identical with pure consciousness, which is the source of his meditation and indeed the source of all appearances (*ābhāsa*).

One of the key ideas behind such forms of meditation is that the hierarchical structure of the universe is reflected in the vertical structure of the human body. The microcosm reflects the macrocosm and what happens within the self is connected to the wider cosmos. This pattern of the overlap between what we would now call psychology and cosmology is a feature of early Indian traditions, both Buddhist and Hindu, that we see exemplified in the Sāṃkhya system of levels or *tattva*s, which are simultaneously cosmic levels and psychological functions (such as intellect [*buddhi*], ego [*ahaṃkāra*], and mind [*manas*]). Although this is a common idea, it does not entail a necessarily shared metaphysics, thus the Sāṃkhya is dualistic—maintaining an eternal distinction between matter and self, a metaphysics that goes into the Śaiva Siddhānta—whereas the Trika system is non-dualistic, maintaining the identity of self and God, while sharing the same hierarchical cosmology. There are also different values at play here. Although the goal of Tantrism is liberation from the cycle of reincarnation, it also puts great emphasis on magical power and pleasure in higher worlds. And, as we have seen, a further value of physical immortality and transcending old age and death, enters the frame; an idea that was to gain traction in later Haṭha Yoga and the quest for longevity (Birch, 2011).

Meditation Without Visualization

Other tantric forms of meditation disparaged the complexity of such systems of meditation on the subtle body, emphasizing, rather, awareness of oneself as the light of consciousness and the mind itself as meditation. Here meditation is not absorption but awareness. This pure awareness of consciousness as a flow is a feature of some tantric sources: meditation can be understood as a stream of thought (*cintā*) in the *Mālinīvijayottara-tantra*, where the mind is "engaged in contemplative realization of its ultimate state" (Vasudeva, 2004, p. 430). Indeed, even the NT itself presents the supreme meditation that transcends the subtle. This supreme meditation is the immediate identification of the yogi with the absolute reality of Śiva, without the need for any mediating structure. Through this identification the yogi becomes ageless and deathless (NT 8.3ab). The eternal reality is transcendent and ineffable; it is "what speech cannot say, what cannot be seen by the eye, what cannot be heard by the ears, what cannot be smelled by the nose, and what cannot be tasted by the tongue, what cannot be felt by the sense of touch, what cannot be thought by the mind, freed from all color and taste, it is yet joined to all color and taste, immeasurable, beyond the senses" (NT 8.3ab–5). In their meditation yogis become united with that reality and so gain immortality. This realization entails the destruction of greed and delusion, the abandoning of intoxication and jealousy, and conceit and arrogance (NT 8.7). All that is needed is a moment's insight ("in the blink of an eye") and that reality is realized; henceforth the yogi will not be born again.

The NT describes the supreme meditation, which is a reinterpretation of the classical eight-part yoga of Patañjali. The text simply uses these eight as an opportunity to state its goal: the reality beyond the senses. Thus self-control (*yama*) is really the cessation of wandering in the world of becoming; restraint (*niyama*) is meditation on the supreme reality; posture (*āsana*) is fixing consciousness in the middle breath between inhalation and exhalation. Breath control (*prāṇayāma*) is the stilling of the mind. Withdrawal into the self (*pratyahāra*) is cutting the bond of becoming through entering into the supreme place; and meditation (*dhyāna*) means focusing on the unchanging Lord and thereby having one's own consciousness as the object of meditation. Keeping the mind there is the holding concentration (*dhāraṇā*), and absorption (*samādhi*) is awareness of one's equality with all beings in the world, which is awareness of one's identity with God (NT 8.10–18). Knowing that "I am Śiva, I am without second" (NT 8.18) is knowledge of one's true essence and all-pervading consciousness. Knowing this reality, the yogi cheats time and becomes a conqueror of death (NT 8.21); that is, the yogi becomes identified with the deity Mṛtyunjaya or Amṛteśa, the central focus of the NT.

This supreme meditation is therefore one in which the goal itself is the method. Thus, having God as an object of meditation is actually having one's consciousness as that object, and this pure meditation is purely reflexive. What is needed is a sudden awakening to the truth of the identification of individual or limited consciousness with unlimited consciousness that is one's essence and the heart of the universe itself. Once this is realized the yogi is freed from the terror of the cycle of becoming (NT 8. 26).

A remarkable text called the *Vijñānabhairava-tantra* (VB), a text of the Mantra Mārga composed probably in the eighth century, contains the visualization of the subtle body and the release of Kuṇḍalinī energy (VB 25–31), but also contains various meditations (*dhāraṇa*) that do not involve visualization. Indeed, it even says that visualization of a deity with body, eyes, mouth, and so on is not really meditation (*dhyāna*) but, rather, meditation is the mind abiding in itself without any image or support (VB 128, 146). The text describes how the yogi should be seated comfortably on a soft bed or cushion (VB 78–79) and a variety of meditation techniques. One practice is sitting with the eyes closed, focusing on the inside of the skull, from which practice the yogi will discern the supreme object of meditation (VB 34), that is, the supreme reality of pure consciousness. Again, meditating on the body as empty (VB 46–48), or with eyes partly open on the space inside a pot (VB 59), or gazing upon an empty landscape (VB 60), or well (VB 115), or space containing rays from the sun (VB 76), or meditating on the body as the entire universe, but without imagination (*nirvikalpa*), the yogi realizes the awakening of supreme consciousness (VB 63). The text even describes meditation on the "unstruck," inner sound of the absolute; the yogi who is steeped in the sound that is uninterrupted (*abhagna*) and heard only with the inner ear goes to the supreme absolute (VS 38). This is a practice attested in later Haṭha Yoga texts and also in the Sant tradition where meditation on inner sound is one of the central practices that leads to God and liberation, after one is initiated by the guru (Juergensmeyer, 1991, pp. 88–109).

The idea of an objectless or pure meditation is consonant with a non-dualist metaphysics. If there is only one reality in the universe, the reality of Śiva who is pure consciousness and light, where can the mind go that is not that reality, asks the VB rhetorically (VB 116). Abhinavagupta develops this theme in his analysis of spiritual methods. The source revelation of the Trika tradition, the esoteric Śaivism that forms the basis of Abhinavagupta's theology, is the *Mālinīvijayottara-tantra* (Hanneder, 1998, Vasudeva, 2004). This text presents three "immersions" (*samāveśa*) or ways of realizing and becoming Śiva: the divine immersion (*śāmbhava*), the power immersion (*śākta*), and the individual immersion (*āṇava*). In his *Essence of the Tantras* (*Tantrasāra*) Abhinavagupta identifies these with the three human faculties of willing, thinking, and acting (TS, p. 6). That is, human transformation occurs through using these faculties to transcend the everyday pattern of becoming to gain access to the ground of being which is pure consciousness. The semantic range of "will" (*icchā*) includes desire or urge, and this first method refers to the upsurge of drive and emotion to shatter thought construction (*vikalpa*) and with that shattering to realize non-dual awareness. This can happen in emotional extremes such as seeing one's beloved unexpectedly or even in situations of pain where thought construction is shattered. The second method uses thought itself by holding on to a pure thought, such as "I am God," which gradually purifies in stages (*krama*) all other thoughts until the pure thought is existentially realized. The third individual way uses actions to realize the goal. Such actions include mantra repetition, ritual, and meditation. Here meditation in the sense of visualization is relegated to a low level in the hierarchy of practice, although all the methods lead to the same goal of identity with God (*samāveśa*).

Now Abhinavagupta introduces a fourth method, his own innovation, that he calls the "non-method" (*anupāya*). This is the spontaneous realization of one's identity with pure consciousness. It is called a non-method because the goal of non-dualism is already realized, for there is only that reality; humans have to open their eyes to it. This idea generates a language of non-dualism that is apophatic, and Abhinavagupta raises a series of rhetorical questions such as: if there is no covering over pure consciousness, how can there be the cessation of a covering; if there is no distinct goal how can there be the attainment of a goal (TS, p. 8)? Consciousness is one, undivided by methods or a distinction between subject and object. This realization is a form of meditation without an object, or rather with only itself as its object: a pure reflexivity as we saw with the highest meditation in the NT and also in the meditations of the VB. Whereas with the other methods, meditation is a means to an end, a ladder that can be kicked away once the goal is reached, here meditation is pure awareness itself, the identification with absolute consciousness beyond duality.

Meditation and Tantric Philosophy

This last sense of meditation, meditation without a formal object or reflection on consciousness itself, relates to the predominant kind of philosophy of traditions of Tantra outside of the dualist Śaiva Siddhānta. This philosophy of recognition (*pratyabhijñā*) of oneself as absolute consciousness, expounded by Abhinavagupta and his tradition, came to center stage in Kashmir and traveled to the south of India where it influenced tantric worship of the Goddess, the tradition called the Śrī Vidyā. The practice of this philosophy would probably remain that of the virtuosi, but the philosophy came to be more widely accepted. Yet the values implicit in such a practice and worldview undermine the orthodox Brahmanical view of society. Whereas orthodox Brahmanism wished to maintain caste restrictions and uphold a hierarchical and patriarchal social order of adherence to caste and station in life (*varṇāśramadharma*), the non-dualist tantric practitioners undermined that social order through the idea that all are equal in pure consciousness and in the desire to develop power, often through transgression of social norms (Sanderson, 1986).

We might even say that there is an implicit politics of meditation here in that meditation designed to realize one's non-difference from God is potentially undermining of Brahmanical social order, which is strictly hierarchical. There is little evidence that such meditation in itself had much impact, but there were groups of people intent on realizing non-dual awareness who were evidently perceived as a problem by orthodox Brahmanism. The Nyāya philosopher Jayanta Bhaṭṭa (ninth century), for example, writes a play lampooning such groups, *Much Ado About Religion* (Dezso, 2005), and warns against their deleterious effect on society (Flood, 2006, pp. 48–49). Traditions that maintained a metaphysical non-dualism were critical of ritualistic practices as being blind alleys in terms of realizing the truth of reality and thereby finding liberation.

A related distinction is between world-affirming and world-negating values. Hindu society had codified a distinction between the world affirmation of the householder who upholds worldly values of duty (*dharma*), wealth or prosperity (*artha*), and desire (*kāma*), in contrast to the world-negating value of the renouncer who seeks only liberation (*mokṣa*) (see Dumont, 1970, pp. 267–286). On the one hand, the high-caste householder maintains strict ritual purity and makes distinctions between social groups while, on the other, the renouncer has gone beyond social distinctions in the quest for the world-transcending goal of liberation. The reality is more complex, of course, in that the renouncers also lived in social groups of celibate men and sometimes women, but the principle remains concerning the two realms of value. The tantric traditions complicate this further through maintaining that the householder can be liberated and that power can be gained through the disruption of orthodox social values. Transgression became a reality on the extreme of the Tantric spectrum although modified for the Tantric householder as Abhinavagupta advocates (Sanderson 1995). Tantric meditation can therefore be in the service of a religion that adheres to Brahmanical orthodoxy, namely the Śaiva Siddhānta, or it can be in the service of non-dualist tradition that disrupts and challenges orthodoxy, as with the Trika of Kashmir.

In more general terms, we might say that one of the implications of tantric meditation is that the householder can practice it, not only the renouncer. This is to bring a vision of the cosmos into the life of daily transaction (*vyavahārika*) that sees the world not entirely as a trap or prison of the soul in its possibly endless journey of reincarnation, but the world as an expression of the power (*śakti*) of God (Śiva) or an absolute reality conceptualized as the Goddess in the esoteric heart of tantric traditions. Meditation itself is value free, but the techniques used have different implications within different worldviews.

Conclusions

In sum, tantric meditation principally involves visualization and is practiced as part of a ritual or on its own to achieve the goals of liberation and pleasure in other worlds or power in this world. This is the case in the mainstream tantric tradition of the Śaiva Siddhānta and the non-Saiddhāntika groups such as the Trika and the tradition of the NT. Visualization is central to the daily practice of tantric Vaiṣṇavism or Pañcarātra and also for Buddhism, where deity yoga becomes an important practice of the Vajrayāna or tantric Buddhism that developed in Tibet. Tantric meditation means on the one hand pure awareness and on the other visual contemplation, especially of the body as a vertical axis containing channels and centers of power. This is the subtle body that forms the structure of the soul when it leaves the physical body. But we also have the idea of immortality in the physical body that meditation can attain. These ideas of immortality and the subtle-body meditation find their way into mainstream and non-initiatory yoga that anyone can perform. This Haṭha Yoga tradition became pan-Indian and has now spread to the West along with the Buddhist version of Kuṇḍalinī as Caṇḍālī and four centers from the navel, up which she climbs. Tantric practice in the West has adopted ritualized sex that contains an element of meditation although it is not clear that the purpose is any longer the traditional goals of freedom from the cycle of reincarnation and power. Tantric meditation takes a high degree of concentration, and the transformation of the mind thereby achieved has physiological correlates in brain state. Tantric meditation along with the mantra repetition it entails seems to bypass linguistic consciousness to reach areas of the brain that are deeper than the neo-cortex (Timalsina, 2015), but whether this is any different to other kinds of meditation, such as Theravāda *samatha* or *vipassanā*, remains to be seen.

Although many tantric traditions have been lost, some continue to exist in South Asia both in continuity with the past and as modern revitalizations. In the Tamil-speaking south, the Śrī Vidyā tradition focused on the beautiful Goddess Tripurasundarī has become absorbed into orthodox Brahmanical practice, and in Kerala tantric Hinduism is normative, a Tantri being an orthodox Brahmin priest who performs rites in the temple. These traditions have remained much the same through the centuries. Traditions that are more focused on meditation rather than simply external rites are also still in existence. Such traditions can be found, for example, in Nepal. The tantric traditions in Kashmir have mostly gone, although in modified form they have been transplanted to the West. The Kashmir Śaiva guru Lakshman Joo (1907–1991) was instrumental in teaching Westerners tantric meditation but was the last traditional teacher. Swami Muktananda (1908–1992) also taught tantric meditation and his Siddha Yoga tradition attracted Western followers, as did the guru Bhagawan Shree Rajneesh (1931–1990). These traditions have also gained a large following in India. Tantric Buddhist meditation still thrives in Tibetan Buddhism that has likewise found a large following in the West, especially the tradition of the Dalai Lama. There are Hindu tantric traditions still in existence in South East Asia, especially on Bali, which have preserved older forms of the religion.

Abbreviations

JS	*Jayākhya-saṃhitā*
NAK	National Archives Kathmandu
NGMPP	Nepal-German Manuscript Preservation Project
NT	*Netra-tantra*
TS	*Tantrasāra* of Abhinavagupta
VB	*Vijñānabhairava*

References

Primary Sources

Jayākhya saṃhitā. (1957). Edited by E. Krishnamacharya. Baroda: Baroda Oriental Institute.

Netra-tantra: (a) *Netra tantra with uddyota by Kṣemarāja.* (1925 and 1927). (Vols. 1–2). Edited by M. S. Kaul. Srinagar: Kashmir Series of Texts and Studies, nos 46 and 61.

(b) *Amṛteśatantra.* (AD 1220 [= Saṃvat 320]). NAK MS 1–285, NGMPP Reel No. B 25/5. Palm leaf; Nepalese variant of proto-Bengali script.

(c) NAK 5–4866. (no date). NGMPP Reel No. A 171/12.

Pratyabhijñāhṛdaya by Kṣemarāja. Ed. J.C. Chatterji (Srinagar, Kashmir Series of Texts and Studies no. 3, 1911). English translation by Jaideva Singh, *Pratyabhijñāhṛdaya* (Delhi: MLBD, 1980).

Vijñānabhairava-tantra: (a) *The Vijñānabhairava: With commentary called Kaumadi by Ānanda Bhaṭṭa.* (1918). Edited by M. Śāstri. Śrīnagara: Kashmir Series of Texts and Studies.

(b) Singh, J. (Trans.). (1979). *Vijñānabhairava or divine consciousness.* Delhi: MLBD.

Secondary Sources and Translations

Aranya, Swami H. (1983). *Yoga philosophy of Patañjali* (P.Â N. Mukerji, Trans.). Albany: State University of New York Press. (Original work published 1963).

Avalon, A. (1974). *The serpent power.* New York: Dover. (Original work published 1918).

Birch, J. (2011). The meaning of haṭha in early Haṭhayoga. *Journal of the American Oriental Society, 131*(4), 527–554.

Birch, J. (2013). *The Amanaska: King of All Yogas. A Critical Edition and Annotated Translation with a Monographic Introduction.* DPhil Dissertation. Oxford: University of Oxford Library.

Brunner, H. (1977). Introduction. In *Somaśambhupaddhati* (Vol. 3). Pondichéry: Institute Français de Pondichéry.

Brunner, H. (1975). Le Sādhaka, personne oublié de l'Inde du Sud. *Journal Asiatique*, *263*, 411–443.

Brunner, H. (1974). Un tantra du nord: Le "Netra Tantra." *Bulletin l'École-Français d'Extrême-Orient*, *61*, 125–197.

Dezso, C. (2005). *Much ado about religion by Jayanta Bhatta*. New York: Clay Sanskrit Library.

Dumont, L. (1970). *Homo hierarchicus: The caste system and its implications*. Chicago: University of Chicago Press.

Dyczkowski, M.Â S.Â G. (1988). *The canon of the Śaivāgama and the Kubjikā tantras of the western Kaula tradition*. Albany: State University of New York Press.

Flood, G. (2006). *The tantric body*. London: I B Tauris.

Flood, G. (2013). *The truth within: A history of inwardness in Christianity, Hinduism, and Buddhism*. Oxford: Oxford University Press.

Goodall, D. (Ed. and Trans.) (2004). *Parākhyatantra, a scripture of the Śaiva Siddhānta: A critical edition and annotated translation*. Pondichéry: Institute Français de Pondichéry.

Goodall, D., & Isaacson, H. (2016). On the shared "ritual syntax" of the early tantric traditions. In D. Goodall and H. Isaacson (Eds.), *Tantric studies: Fruits of a Franco-German project on early Tantra*. Pondichéry: Institute Français de Pondichéry.

Goudriaan, T. & Schoterman, J.Â A. (Eds.). (1988). *The Kubjikāmatantra: Kulālikāmnāya version*. Leiden: Brill.

Hanneder, J. (Ed. & Trans.). (1998). *Abhinavagupta's philosophy of revelation, an edition and annotated translation*. Groningen: Egbert Forsten.

Juergensmeyer, M. (1991). *Radhasoami reality: The logic of a modern faith*. Princeton: Princeton University Press.

Kiss, C. (Ed. & Trans.). (2015). *Brahmayāmalatantra or Picumata*. Vol. 2: *The religious observances and sexual rituals of the tantric practitioner: Chapters 3, 21, and 45, a critical edition and annotated translation*. Pondichéry: Institute Français de Pondichéry.

Mallinson, J. (2015). Śāktism and Haṭha Yoga. In B.Â W. Olesen (Ed.), *Goddess traditions in tantric Hinduism: History, practice and doctrine* (pp. 109–140). London: Routledge.

Olivelle, P. (1998). *The early Upaniṣads*. Oxford: Oxford University Press.

Padoux, A. (2002). Corps et cosmos, L'image du corps du yogin tantrique. In V. Bouillier & G. Tarabout (Eds.), *Images du corps dans le monde hindou* (pp. 163–187). Paris: CNRS.

Padoux, A. (2011). *Tantric mantras*. London: Routledge.

Rastelli, M. (1999). *Philosophisch-theologische Grundanschauungen der Jayākhyasaṃhitā*. Wien: Österreichen Akadamie der Wissenschaften.

Rawlinson, A. (1999). *Book of Enlightened Masters: Western Teachers and Eastern Traditions*. New York: Open Court.

Sanderson, A. (1986). Maṇḍala and āgamic identity in the Trika of Kashmir. In A. Padoux (Ed.), *Mantras et diagrammes rituelles dans l'hindouisme* (pp. 169–214). Paris: CNRS.

Sanderson, A. (1995). *Meaning in tantric ritual*, Essais sur le ritual III. Louvain-Paris: Bibliotèque de l'école des hautes etudes, section des sciences religieuses.

Sanderson, A. (2004). Religion and the state: Śaiva officiants in the territory of the king's chaplain. *Indo-Iranian Journal*, *47*, 229–300.

Sanderson, A. (1988). Śaivism and the tantric traditions. In S. Sutherland, L. Houlden, P. Clarke, & F. Hardy (Eds.), *The world's religions* (pp. 660–704). London: Routledge.

Sanderson, A. (1990). The visualization of the deities of the Trika. In A. Padoux (Ed.), *L'image divine* (pp. 169–214). Paris: Éditions du CNRS.

Silburn, L. (1988). *Kuṇḍalinī: the energy from the depths*. Albany: State University of New York Press.

Timalsina, S. (2015). *Tantric visual culture: A cognitive approach*. London: Routledge.

Vasudeva, S. (2004). *The Yoga of the Mālinīvijayottaratantra, chapters 1–4, 7, 11–17*. Pondichéry: Institute Français de Pondichéry.

Watson, A. & Goodall, D. (2013). *An Enquiry into the Nature of Liberation: Bhatta Ramakantha's Paramoksanirasakarikavrtti, a commentary of Sadyojyotih's Refutation of Twenty Conceptions of the Liberated State*. Pondichery: Institut Français d'Indologie.

Wernicke-Olesen, B. (Ed.). (2015).*Goddess traditions in tantric Hinduism: History, practice and doctrine*. London: Routledge.

Wernicke-Olesen, B., & Einarsen, S. L. (2018). Übungswissen in Yoga, Tantra und Asketismus des frühen indischen Mittelalters. In A.-B. Renger & A. Stellmacher (Eds.), *Übungswissen in Religion und Philosophie: Production, Weitergabe, Wandel* (pp. 241–257). Berlin: Lit Verlag.

White, D. (1996). *The Alchemical Body: Siddha Traditions in Medieval India*. Chicago: Chicago University Press.

White, D. (2003). *The kiss of the yogini: Tantric sex and its South Asian contexts* Chicago: University of Chicago Press.

Wujastyk, D. (2002). Interpréter l'image du corps humain dans l'Inde pré-moderne. In V. Bouillier & G. Tarabout (Eds.), *Images du corps dans le monde hindou* (pp. 71–100). Paris: CNRS.

CHAPTER 5

HINDUISM AND MEDITATION

Yoga

BJARNE WERNICKE-OLESEN

Introduction

AROUND the time of the Buddha in the middle of the first millennium BCE we see the rise of new ascetic movements and traditions in northern India. These were often quite radical and diverse renouncer traditions including Buddhists and Jains and lesser-known traditions such as materialists and skeptics. These movements of wandering ascetics or "strivers" (*śramaṇa*) initiated a highly formative period in Indian religious history marking the transition from the Vedic religion (ca. 1700–500 BCE) to classical Hinduism (ca. 200–1100 CE). This period also coincided with the so-called "axial age" of religious transition in different world civilizations as pointed out by Hermann Kulke (1986), Robert Bellah (2011, pp. 481–566) and Gavin Flood (2019, pp. 131–173). One of the key features of this age of criticism and reflexivity was the development of a "theoretic culture" (Donald, 1991) defined by a capacity to examine one's own assumptions (Eisenstadt, 1986) and indeed for "questioning all human activity and conferring upon it a new meaning" in the words of Karl Jaspers (1953, p. 1). It is in this period of ascetic reformism that we find the first systematic developments of yoga and meditation as well as classical formulations of key concepts and values in Indian religions, such as the notions of karma and rebirth, the notion of an inner truth, and liberation as the goal of human existence (*mokṣa*, *nirvāṇa*).

Although yoga, meditation, and asceticism are usually understood as very different and even distinct forms of practices in contemporary Westernized yoga discourse, they have in fact been intimately linked throughout Indian history. Yoga has often been identified with meditative techniques such as *dhyāna* (a cognate with Chinese *chan* and Japanese *zen*) and also with the more extreme ascetic practices generating *tapas* or "inner heat." Some of our oldest textual sources reflecting this discourse of the ascetic reformism are known as the early Upaniṣads (ca. 700–100 BCE). According to our knowledge most early renouncer traditions participated in this discourse, whether confirming (*astika*) or rejecting (*nāstika*) the sacred status of the Vedas, sharing many of the fundamental concepts and values including notions of yoga and meditation. Thus, from an early time onward, yoga and meditation did not belong to any particular system of thought (Bronkhorst, 1981, p. 317) but were adapted by a number of competing traditions and philosophies, such as Buddhism and Jainism, and somewhat later by the Brahmanical Sanskritic religion as is evident in famous works like the *Bhagavad Gītā* (ca. 200 BCE) and the *Yoga Sūtra* of Patañjali or *Pātañjalayogaśāstra* (ca. 325–425 CE). Due to this Brahmanical adaptation, yoga and meditation, and to some extent asceticism itself, were made to conform with more worldly activities of the householder and the Brahmanical system of caste and life stages (*varṇāśramadharma*). In this way yoga and meditation became gradually incorporated into the mainstream of Indian religious life and were successfully exported to the Western world almost two millennia later.

In the following I shall present a tentative historical view of the roots and developments of yoga and meditation, along with an account of the methods and purposes of what might be called traditional and classical yoga as presented in some of the most important textual sources that have come down to us. Although the classical yoga presented here has had a long and influential history in the Indian subcontinent and is now part and parcel of a global religious history, this presentation will limit itself to the classical formative phase of yoga and meditation in relation to what has become known as Hinduism. Furthermore, it should be noted that yoga and meditation in this period often differ quite significantly from the later visualizing meditation of tantric yoga (*dhyāna*, *bhāvanā*, and *dhāraṇā*), which is dealt with in the chapter on Tantra by G. Flood in this volume.

Origins of Yoga

Although the history of yoga in Hinduism is long and ancient, we are left with little more than speculation regarding an ancient yogic culture preceding the period of ascetic reformism in India. There is, unfortunately, no real evidence for a systematic yoga practice in the Indus Valley civilization (ca. 2500–1750 BCE) or in Vedic culture related to psycho-physiological techniques—and the word "yoga" itself has a very different meaning in the Vedic corpus of texts than what it subsequently came to denote (White, 2012, p. 3; Mallinson & Singleton, 2017, p. xii). However, we do find a few remarkable passages in the *Ṛgveda* (ca. 1500–1200 BCE) and *Atharvaveda* (ca. 1000 BCE) describing mystical and long-haired ascetics who walk around naked or wearing dirty rags and who live on the fringes of society. The description of their appearances and practices are striking and indeed suggestive of the much later tantric traditions, including bodily postures, breathing techniques, visionary meditation, sexualized ritual, and the acquisition of supernatural powers. The latter being specific yogic powers (*siddhis*), such as the ability to read other peoples' minds, fly outside the body, and so on. These powers or "extraordinary capacities attained through meditation and concentration" (Jacobsen, 2012a) are produced as "side-effects" in the classical yoga of Patañjali (*Pātañjalayogaśāstra* [PYŚ] 3), but are directly aimed for by the accomplished yogis or *siddhas* in later tantric traditions belonging to the Śaiva Mantramārga and the Śākta Kulamārga (Sanderson, 2014; Olesen, 2016, p. 5; Wernicke-Olesen & Einarsen, 2018). Thus, in the tenth book of the *Ṛgveda Saṃhitā* (10.136) we find the famous hymn dedicated to the ecstatic state of the long-haired ascetics or Keśins and their remarkable yogic powers:

> Long-hair holds fire, holds the drug, holds sky and earth. Long-hair reveals everything, so that everyone can see the sun. Long-hair declares the light.
>
> These ascetics, swathed in wind, put dirty red rags on. When gods enter them, they ride with the rush of the wind.
>
> "Crazy with asceticism, we have mounted the wind. Our bodies are all you mere mortals can see."
>
> He sails through the air, looking down on all shapes below. The ascetic is friend to this god and that god, devoted to what is well done.
>
> The stallion of the wind, friend of gales, lashed on by gods— the ascetic lives in the two seas, on the east and on the west.
>
> He moves with the motion of heavenly girls and youths, of wild beasts. Long-hair, reading their minds, is their sweet, their most exciting friend.
>
> The wind has churned it up; Kunaṃnamā prepared it for him. Long-hair drinks from the cup, sharing the drug with Rudra. (O'Flaherty, 1981, pp. 137–138)

We have here in the *Ṛgveda* an indication of what might be termed a yogic counter-narrative to the Vedic narrative of sacrifice, Brahmin priests, and poets (*ṛṣis*) as suggested by Karel Werner (1994) and Daniel Raveh (2012, p. 6). It is clear that the long-haired ascetic or Keśin is a contrasting model of the human, which is without relevance to Vedic ritual and placed outside the Vedic Brahmanical world. Like the Buddha, the Keśin is also called a *muṇi* or "silent one" and may be seen as a precursor to the Upaniṣadic yogi (O'Flaherty, 1981, p. 137), as well as a precursor to the yogi of Patañjali's *Yoga Sūtra* (Raveh, 2012, p. 7). Nevertheless, he differs from both in his ecstatic state of visionary meditation similar to later tantric traditions, but in this case induced by what seems to be a psychoactive drug or "poison" (*viṣa*), related to but different from the Vedic *soma*. According to some translators of this hymn (e.g., Jamison & Brereton, 2014, p. 1622) the drug is prepared for the ascetic by the goddess Kunaṃnamā, who is only mentioned once in the *Ṛgveda*, again suggestive of a non-Vedic origin. Furthermore, the ascetic drinks the "poison" in the company of the god Rudra, a precursor to Śiva, the god of asceticism and ecstasy in later Hinduism, who is denied the right to participate in the Vedic ritual sacrifice according to a famous myth in the *Śiva Purāṇa* (2.16–43), thus placing him outside the Vedic Brahmanical world. In this hymn from the *Ṛgveda*, we therefore have one of the first expressions of a key theme in yoga: the characteristic psycho-physiological experimentation with human consciousness shared by both classical yoga and later tantric traditions.

In the Vedas we also find mention of bands of warrior like ascetics, who were "bound by the vow" or Vrātyas, living on the fringes of Vedic society like the Keśins and migrating east to Magadha, the hotspot for wandering ascetics and later *śramaṇa* movements (Bronkhorst, 2007). The Vrātyas may be taken as a classical example of the often-close link between asceticism and martialism, where the outer martialism is internalized in the form of inner *áskēsis* or "training," in an attempt to conquer and transcend the body and its senses (Lorenzen, 2006, pp. 37–63; Pinch, 2006; Sloterdijk, 2009). Indeed, even the Buddha and his disciples were from a warrior background (*kṣatriya*). The religion of the Vrātyas was recorded and assimilated in the fifteenth book or *Vrātyakaṇḍa* of the *Atharvaveda* (ca. 1000 BCE) (Chand 1982, 627–654). Here we find forms of practice that again point toward later yogic techniques of bodily postures (*āsana*), breath-control (*prāṇāyāma*), and the chanting of mantras (*mantrajapa*). The Vrātyas were described as fierce-looking wandering ascetics dressed in black rags, with a white and black ram skin over their shoulders, and wearing a turban (Eliade, 1969, pp. 103–105; Heesterman 1962, pp. 1–37). They did not practice the Vedic rites of passage (*saṃskāra*), but had their own ritual system of which we know very little. However, it is mentioned that the priest (*hotṛ*) of the Vrātyas would chant mantras at the summer solstice in relation to a "great vow" (*mahāvrata*) with reference to the three breaths—inhalation (*prāṇa*), breath-retention (*vyāna*), and exhalation (*apāna*)—accompanied by what may be termed "transgressive rites" of obscene dialogue and ritual sex between a bard (*māgadha*) and a prostitue (*puṃścalī*) (AV 15.2, 15.14–18).

In addition, the Brāhmaṇas bear witness to different kinds of ascetic practices or heat-generating austerities (*tapas*), such as chastity, fasting, and not cutting the hair, nails and beard (Oldenberg, 1894, pp. 427–430) as well as indications of later yogic techniques. Thus, in the *Jaiminīya Upaniṣad Brāhmaṇa* (ca. 800–600 BCE) we find a description of the chanting of a Vedic mantra in combination with yogic breath-control (JUB 3.5.4–5; Mallinson & Singleton, 2017, p. 266).

From our textual evidence it becomes increasingly clear that the development and purpose of yoga and meditation should be understood in the context of ascetic practices (*tapas*), and in the context of the somewhat later systematic discourse of ascetic reformism, which seems to have emerged outside the Brahmanical world, but was gradually assimilated into it. This development is reflected in the Upaniṣads (ca. 700–100 BCE), being the latest part of the Vedic corpus of texts (*vedānta*). It seems evident that the asceticism found in the Upaniṣads is directly related to the Vedic ritual system, but at the same time it is clearly representative of a reformation and discontinuity of Vedic Brahmanical religion most likely due to non-Vedic influences as indicated in the Ṛgvedic hymn of the Keśins. Indeed, the question of the continuity and discontinuity of yoga and meditation with Vedic religion remains a highly debated topic. Our understanding of this development is sometimes obscured by the fact that later Brahmanical traditions have incorporated Vedic motifs that have been adapted and reinterpreted in the context of yogic practices, sometimes adding to the authority of these practices (e.g., in the *Mahābhārata*).

Unfortunately, these instances of Vedic references found in later yoga literature cannot be taken as points of departure for conclusions about systematic yoga practice in the

Vedas. Nevertheless, they often form the basis for retroactive projections that are not historically valid. An important example of the historical reinterpretation of a Vedic motif is the word "yoga" itself and its reference to a war chariot (*ratha*). In the *Ṛgveda* we find the word in its original Indo-European sense of a "yoke" that one placed on a bullock or on a horse to yoke (*yukta*) it to a plow or a war chariot respectively (Monier-Williams, 1899, s.v. *yoga*). Through metonymy the word "yoga" came to denote the war chariot itself and by dying a heroic death on the battlefield one could become metaphorically "yoked" to a heavenly war chariot (*yoga-yukta*), which in a flash of light would take one through the sun and onward to the highest heaven of gods and heroes. The Vedic gods (*deva*s) and Vedic poet-priests (*ṛṣi*s) were also yoked to their chariots and traveled across heaven or in their minds "on a vision quest across the universe" (White, 2012, p. 4). This Vedic understanding of the word "yoga" is still evident in the *Mahābhārata* (third century BCE to third century CE), where dying heroes travel in their "yoga" or divine chariot through the sun to the highest heaven. However, we also find the original Vedic sense of yoga as a "yoke" or as a chariot reinterpreted as a metaphor for the soteriological method in later works, for example in the *Kaṭha Upaniṣad* and in the *Mokṣadharma* section of the *Mahābhārata* (White, 2009, pp. 60–67; Fitzgerald, 2009, 2012).

Although there is no conclusive evidence for a systematic yoga practice in the Vedas, some principles and key themes are indeed identifiable in Vedic religion that are of relevance for our understanding of Indian religions in general and the further development of yoga and meditation. As Robert Bellah has stated with particular reference to the history of religions in India: "Nothing is ever lost" (Bellah, 2011, p. 489). One fundamental concern in Vedic religion was with "cosmical homology" as Mircea Eliade has famously termed the phenomenon (Eliade, 1937), which was referred to as "connections" or "causes" (*bandhu*, *nidāna*) in the Brāhmaṇas. The hierarchical cosmological structure of the universe was identified with the mesocosmic structure of society and with the microcosm of the human body.

All three cosmological levels were mediated by the Vedic sacrificial ritual. In particular, the identification between the universe, the body, and the sacrifice became of key importance in the Upaniṣads and in later yoga traditions. Another key theme was ritual and mystical experience, which we find expressed in Vedic ritualism par excellence, namely the *śrauta* ritual, the offering of things into the fire (*agnihotra*), and the *soma* ritual, the pressing and consumption of the milk from the *soma* plant inducing ecstatic and mystical experiences recorded in the Vedic hymns (Witzel, 2005).

In the collections of texts known as the Brāhmaṇas and the Āraṇyakas, we find a development of the speculations regarding the Vedic sacrifice and its cosmic homologies and their significance. These speculations are continued in the Upaniṣads, but often in a more radical sense. Already in the Brāhmaṇas we see how the focus is shifted from the Vedic gods to the sacrificial ritualism itself, that is to say that the Brahmin priests who conducted the rituals became more important in a sense than the Vedic gods, who subsequently lost their power. In the Upaniṣads the Brahmins, as well as the sacrificial ritualism, lose significance. The Vedic *śrauta* ritual centered on *agni* (fire) and *soma* is internalized and spiritualized, whereby parts of the ritual are identified with the physical body. Focus is shifted from outer action to inner meditation. Thus in the fifth chapter of the *Chāndogya Upaniṣad* (ca. 700–500 BCE) the Vedic fire sacrifice (*agnihotra*) is internalized and related to breath (*prāṇa*), becoming the inner true fire sacrifice (*prāṇāgnihotra*). The mouth is the offertorial fire (*āhavanīya*) into which food oblations are offered to the five breaths, namely, the out-breath, inter-breath, in-breath, link-breath, and up-breath, conceived of as five deities (CU 5.19–24; Olivelle, 1999, p. 51). The breaths are further homologized with fires and breath itself is linked to the mind (CU 6.8.2). This way of internalizing the Vedic fire sacrifice became a point of departure for the development of esoteric anatomy and yoga traditions, as well as the gnostic soteriology of the Upaniṣads, which were central to the traditions of the ascetic reformism.

The development leading from the early Vedic *saṃhitās* to the asceticism and yoga of the Upaniṣads and the famous *ātman-brahman* identification of the inner self with the absolute is a matter of complicated debate. It is, however, often reducible to a question of continuity or discontinuity with Vedic religion and culture. Thus, the development can be viewed as a continuous and logical process rooted in Vedic ritualism and culminating in the internalization of the Vedic sacrifice as suggested by Jan C. Heesterman (1985), Madeleine Biardeau (1989), and others. Alternatively, one may focus on the discontinuity and the rootedness of ascetic phenomena in developments outside the Vedic world, as Louis Dumont (1980) and Johannes Bronkhorst (1993) have suggested, that is, in what has been identified as "Greater Magadha" in modern-day Allahabad (Bronkhorst, 2007). However, such developments in the history of religions are usually highly complex, and we may perhaps have to accept the fact that the development leading to the asceticism and yoga of the Upaniṣads constitute a "mixture of things," namely, the result of a complex process of assimilation and transformation of both elements within Vedic religion and from the outside, as suggested by Gavin Flood (1996, p. 90) and Patrick Olivelle (2005, p. 273). Furthermore, one should keep in mind that these texts "provide only a tiny window into this period, and that too only throws light on what their priestly authors thought it important to record" (Olivelle, 2005, p. 273).

The Ascetic Reform Movements and the Upaniṣads

Ascetic movements flourished in the late Vedic period forming an intermezzo between Vedic religion and later classical Hinduism. The period may be seen as a fascinating time of religious creativity and experimentation in its own right, beginning from around the sixth or fifth century BCE with the earliest Upaniṣads and lasting several centuries. It has been termed the ascetic reformism by Axel Michaels (2004, p. 36), India's axial age by Hermann Kulke (1986), and the formative period of Indian religions by Patrick Olivelle (2005, p. 273). While one should remember that this kind of periodization is always analytically determined and decided by our theoretical underpinnings and empirical interests, it is useful in emphasizing an important breakthrough or "shift" (Flood 2019, p. 131) in the history of religions, which may otherwise run the risk of being trivialized in more particular and specialized studies. It should therefore be safe to say that in the elite culture of the time a decisive change was taking place, which can be related to the emergence of a new ascetic discourse claiming a relative independence from earlier dominating discourses.

What led to this development in the time of the Magadha Empire (560–345 BCE) continues to be a matter of debate. A classical explanation is that in the middle of the first millennium BCE we find an increase in the population density in the Ganges Valley resulting in migration and urbanization (Michaels, 2004, pp. 36–38). With this development followed a specialization of the professions as indicated in the Pali Canon of early Buddhism. As a result individualism arose, as suggested by the sociologist Émile Durkheim, causing a kind of rootlessness and *Weltschmerz* termed "anomie" (Durkheim, 1897) and *duḥkha* "suffering" or *āpad* "crisis" by contemporary Indians (Michaels, 2004, p. 37). This seems to have increased the interest in individualized and liberation-oriented religions represented by the *śramaṇa* movements at the time. Indeed, "suffering" (*duḥkha*) became the axiom constituting the religious discourse of the ascetic reformism as expressed in the Four Noble Truths of suffering (or rather: "four realities for the noble," P. *cattāri ariyasaccāni*) ascribed to the historical Buddha (SN 56.11). Furthermore, the sociologist Max Weber linked the origins of Buddhism to the growing urbanization and emphasized the middle class (*vaiśya*s and *kṣatriya*s) as the Buddha's main audience (Weber, 1978).

Characteristic of this period of ascetic reformism in India was that young men in the householder stage (*gṛhastha*) started to abandon their families and religious duties on a large scale and left their villages and cities to live alone in the forest as wandering ascetics (*śramaṇa*) (Figure 5.1). The prototypical narrative of such a wandering ascetic is the legend of the historical Buddha, who started out as the prince Siddhārtha Gautama, forsaking his beautiful wife, newborn son, and his whole kingdom to wander off as a naked yogi and ascetic into the forest to practice severe austerities (*tapas*) and meditation (*dhyāna*). Here the forest or "wilderness" (*vana*, *āraṇya*) may be taken in its metaphorical sense as the anti-structure to Vedic society and the village, an unknown space of liminality, transformation, and insight as pointed out by Olivelle and others (Olivelle, 2005, p. 276; Raveh, 2012, p. 7). The yogi would wander alone into the forest, but in contrast to the Judeo-Christian desert the forest would not be empty, but a place inhabited by holy men (*sādhu*s), animals, and supernatural beings with whom to consult in the search for new and alternative knowledge (Raveh, 2012, p. 7).

Key concepts and values of the ascetic reformism and yoga are anticipated in the Brāhmaṇas (1000–700 BCE), but are more fully developed in the secret (*rahasya*) teachings of the Upaniṣads (700–100 BCE). As is the case in Buddhism and Jainism, empirical existence in the Upaniṣads is characterized by suffering (*duḥkha*) and at the risk of great oversimplification, the discourse may be summarized in its main elements as follows: All humans are bound by their actions (karma) in an endless cycle of rebirths

FIGURE 5.1 Buddha as a *śramaṇa* ascetic and yogi practicing severe austerities (*tapas*) and meditation (*dhyāna*, *samādhi*) before his awakening (*bodhi*) and rejection of the extremities of the ascetic path, Gandhara, 2nd–3rd century CE, Lahore Museum, Pakistan.

Source: The Image Bank Unreleased/Getty Images

(*saṃsāra*) due to their desire (*kāma*) and ignorance (*avidyā*) about the identity between the impersonal self (*ātman*) and the absolute reality (*brahman*) leading to a life in illusion (*māyā*). However, the esoteric knowledge (*jñāna*) of the *ātman-brahman* correlation can lead to liberation (*mokṣa*, *nirvāṇa*) via a moral and meditative discipline known as yoga. Thus, yoga is a practical solution to an epistemological problem leading to liberation. It is the ascetic discipline par excellence for controlling the mind, body, breath, and senses and experiencing the highest states of consciousness (*samādhi*) through meditation (*dhyāna*) leading to transformative experiences. The discipline, when not confined to any particular religious system, as Gavin Flood (2004) has pointed out, is mainly a method or technique aimed at the transformation of consciousness through concentration on a single point (*ekāgratā*). The continuous practice of concentration releases the practitioner of mental restrictions, fluctuations, and moral impurities, such as the three *kleśa*s or "afflictions" known from classical Buddhism and Patañjali's *Yoga Sūtra*: delusion (*moha*), attraction (*raga*, *kāma*), and aversion (*dveśa*). An emphasis on this kind of transformative inner experience through meditation became a key theme in Indian religions from the time of the ascetic reform movements and onward. Furthermore, this transformation was fundamentally linked to the discovery of the true nature of the self or "the truth within" (Flood, 2013). Thus, what might be one of the earliest textual references to meditation is found in the seventh-century-BCE *Bṛhadāraṇyaka Upaniṣad* centered upon the discovery of the true nature of the self as *brahman* (BU 4.4.23):

> A man who knows this, therefore, becomes calm, composed, cool, patient, and collected. He sees the self (*ātman*) in just himself (*ātman*) and all things as the self. Evil does not pass across him, and he passes across all evil. He is not burnt by evil; he burns up all evil. He becomes a Brahmin—free from evil, free from stain, free from doubt. He is the world of *brahman*. (Olivelle, 1998, p. 127)

In addition, we find in the *Bṛhadāraṇyaka Upaniṣad* a direct formulation of how this basic insight formed an impetus for the ascetic reform movements at the time (BU 4.4.22):

> It is he [the *ātman*] that Brahmins seek to know by means of Vedic recitation, sacrifice, gift-giving, austerity, and fasting. It is he, on knowing whom a man becomes a sage. It is when they desire him as their world that wandering ascetics undertake the ascetic life of wandering. It was when they knew this that men of old did not desire offspring, reasoning: "Ours is this self, and it is our world. What then is the use of offspring for us?" So they gave up the desire for sons, the desire for wealth, and the desire for worlds, and undertook the mendicant life. (Olivelle, 1998, p. 125)

Subsequently, in the *Kaṭha Upaniṣad* (ca. third century BCE) we find one of the earliest systematic accounts of yoga drawing on the well-known Vedic motif of the war chariot reinterpreted in a soteriological perspective. The account is embedded in the story of the encounter between the young ascetic Naciketas and Yama, the god of death. Yama presents Naciketas with an analogue between human life and the task of riding a war chariot, summarizing a number of key concepts in yoga (KU 3.3–6):

> [3] Know the self [*ātman*] as a rider in a chariot,
> and the body [*śarīra*], as simply the chariot.
> Know the intellect [*buddhi*] as the charioteer,
> and the mind [*manas*], as simply the reins.
> [4] The senses [*indriya*], they say, are the horses,
> and sense objects [*viṣaya*] are the paths around them;
> He who is linked to the body (*ātman*), senses, and mind,
> the wise proclaim as the one who enjoys.
> [5] When a man lacks understanding,
> and his mind is never controlled;
> His senses do not obey him,
> as bad horses, a charioteer.
> [6] But when a man has understanding,

and his mind is ever controlled [*yukta*];
His senses do obey him,
as bad horses, a charioteer.

(Olivelle, 1998, p. 389)

It is further stated that if the mind and the senses are not restrained or "yoked" by the intellect (*buddhi*), then one is reborn (KU 3.7). However, if one is able to control the senses, including the mind, then one reaches the final step and is not reborn again (KU 3.8). This final step is identified with the Sāṃkhya term *puruṣa* or "indwelling person" in the third chapter of the *Kaṭha Upaniṣad*, while in the discourse on the self and *brahman* this state of consciousness is identified as *yoga* (KU 6.10–11):

[10] When the five perceptions [*jñānāni*] are stilled,
together with the mind,
And not even reason bestirs itself;
they call it the highest state.
[11] When senses are firmly reined in,
that is Yoga, so people think.
From distractions a man is then free,
for Yoga is the coming-into-being,
as well as the ceasing-to-be.

(Olivelle, 1998, p. 401)

These verses may be our first detailed information about meditation in ancient India (Bronkhorst, 1993, p. 46). Thus it should be noted that the term yoga, from an early time onward, may indicate both a method of liberation and a particular state of consciousness. Furthermore, in the *Kaṭha Upaniṣad* we find a range of constitutive elements for later yoga traditions and for what might be termed a yogic anthropology or model of the human. At the center stands a non-dualistic conception of the immortal self (*ātman*) as identical with the absolute *brahman* (KU 5.8). In addition, we find a notion of a subtle body where a "person the size of a thumb in the body (*ātman*), always resides within the hearts of men" (KU 4.12). The body is said to be "a fort with eleven gates" (KU 5.1) and containing 101 "veins of the heart" or channels (*nadī*) with the most important channel running up to the crown of the head (KU 6.16), indicative of later esoteric anatomy. We also find the use of mantras such as the syllable *OṂ* being the acoustic-phonetic expression of the supreme *brahman* (KU 2.15). Finally, the anthropological categories (senses, mind, intellect, person, etc.) of the dualistic Sāṃkhya philosophy are presented in hierarchical order (KU 3.10–11; 6.7–8) forming a soteriological model that became highly influential in later classical yoga, as we find it expressed in the *Pātañjalayogaśāstra* (ca. 325 CE).

In later Upaniṣads a remarkable theological shift takes place from impersonal monism to a personalized theism, when the self (*ātman*) is identified with the supreme reality in the form of a personal god (*Hochgott*), such as Śiva or Viṣṇu-Kṛṣṇa. This may occur for the first time in the *Śvetāśvatara Upaniṣad*, where the self (again designated with the Sāṃkhya term *puruṣa*) is identified with the god Śiva and the notion of loving devotion (*bhakti*) is introduced (ŚU 6.23; Oberlies, 1988). However, the dating of this

Upaniṣad reminds us once again that the relative chronology and subsequent dating of ancient Indian texts are "as stable as a house of cards" (Olivelle, 1998, p. 12). In the case of the *Śvetāśvatara Upaniṣad* the dating ranges from the fifth century BCE (Flood, 1996, p. 153) through the first century BCE (Oberlies, 1995, p. 68; Olivelle, 1998, p. 13) to the sixth century CE (Mallinson & Singleton, 2017, p. xxxix). Thus, if Oberlies (1995) and others are right in their later dating, the entry of theism and devotionalism into Indian religious thinking would have taken place in the *Bhagavad Gītā* rather than in the *Śvetāśvatara Upaniṣad*, as was already claimed by R.C. Zaehner in 1969. Here it is important to point out, that the identification of the self with a personal god or goddess, under the influence of the Sāṃkhya-Yoga philosophy, becomes a point of departure for later theistic traditions of India. These traditions or network of traditions were mainly articulated in the Purāṇas in the latter half of the first millennium CE, and are today known as Vaiṣṇavism, Śaivism and Śāktism. They are often referred to as the three major Hindu religions (Biardeau, 1989; Stietencron, 1997). As we shall see, the understanding of yoga as devotion to a personal god also becomes increasingly important in later theistic traditions of India, especially from the 16th century onwards.

In the *Śvetāśvatara Upaniṣad* we also find the Vedic motif of the war chariot used again as a metaphor for the heroic yogi as a charioteer keeping his mind under control as he would with a chariot yoked to unruly horses (ŚU 2.8–9):

> [8] Having made the body straight with its three parts upright and used the mind to insert the senses into the heart, the wise man may cross all terrifying rivers by means of the raft of Brahman.
>
> [9] With his actions controlled, the wise man should press the breaths in [the body]. When the breath is expended, he should exhale through one nostril. He should restrain the mind vigilantly, as if it were a chariot yoked to badly behaved horses.
>
> (Mallinson & Singleton, 2017, p. 60)

Here we should notice the withdrawal (*pratyāhāra*) of the senses as being a central precondition for the practice of yoga—"just as a tortoise draws its limbs into itself, so does the yogi withdraw his senses into himself" as it is famously stated in the thirteenth-century-CE *Vivekamārtaṇḍa* (Mallinson & Singleton, 2017, p. 297). Furthermore, the close link between sense-withdrawal, breath-control, and mind-control in the *Śvetāśvatara Upaniṣad* should be mentioned, pointing toward later classifications of six or eight yoga-auxiliaries or limbs (*aṅga*) such as *aṣṭāṅgayoga*. Finally, the *Śvetāśvatara Upaniṣad* may be seen as an early and significant expression of how asceticism flourished within what Gavin Flood has termed cosmological religion in India (Flood, 2004, p. 2); for instance, the cosmological elements (*mahābhūta*) are homologized with the human body, which in turn can be purified through asceticism and cured in the "fire of yoga" (ŚU 2.12):

> When earth, water, fire, air, and ether have arisen together, and the body made up of these five becomes equipped with the attribute of yoga, that man, obtaining a body tempered by the fire of yoga, will no longer experience sickness, old age, or suffering.
>
> (Olivelle, 1998, p. 419)

The Transition to Classical Yoga

Although the Upaniṣads are preoccupied with the cultivation of esoteric knowledge or gnosis (*jñāna*) as a path to liberation (*jñānamārga*), there are many references to techniques aimed at a practical realization of the truth within, as we have seen, that can be subsumed under the broad category of yoga. However, when the word yoga is used in a traditional sense and without qualifications, the main reference is to the practice of meditation (*dhyāna*) as described and systematized in the later classical yoga of Patañjali (ca. 325 CE). A yogi is one who practices such meditational yoga (Bryant, 2009, p. xxii; Larson & Bhattacharya, 2008).

At the same time it is clear that the Upaniṣads and the yoga system of Patañjali, as well as Buddhism and Jainism and philosophical schools such as Sāṃkhya, draw on a common reservoir or "ascetic soup" of related yogic ideas, practices, and terminology, which had not yet been systematized and separated into different schools. As pointed out by James Mallinson and the Haṭha Yoga Project, it appears that not only the meditative practices (*dhyāna*) and breathing techniques (*prāṇāyāma*) of the *Pātañjalayogaśāstra*, but also the bodily postures (*āsana*) and yogic seals (*mudrā*) of later Hatha Yoga (ca. 1000 CE) are rooted in the ascetic austerities (*tapas*) of the *śramaṇa* movements (Mallinson & Singleton, 2017, p. xv). Indeed, in India's great epic the *Mahābhārata* (third century BCE to third century CE) yoga and *tapas* are often used as synonyms and in the *Pātañjalayogaśāstra tapas* is seen as a necessary preliminary for yoga practice, while *prāṇāyāma* is identified as a form of *tapas* in the *Mānavadharmaśāstra* or "Laws of Manu" (Mallinson & Singleton, 2017, p. xiv). Thus, although yoga, meditation, and asceticism are usually separated in modern yoga discourse, it becomes increasingly clear that they have been intimately linked throughout Indian religious history (Figure 5.2).

FIGURE 5.2 Rāmānandī ascetics practicing *tapas* (*dhuni tap*) with five fires (*pañcāgni*), Ujjain, India, 2016.

Source: © Image courtesy of Prema Goet

The *Mahābhārata* (including the *Bhagavad Gītā* as its sixth book) contains interesting but somewhat overlooked material on the transition and development of yoga and meditation from the time of the Upaniṣads until the later systematic yoga philosophies as represented by the *Pātañjalayogaśāstra*. We find in the *Mahābhārata*, and other works from the centuries following the period of ascetic reformism, expressions of an identifiable set of basic yogic ideas, techniques, and meditational practices that seem to have been widespread in the first centuries BCE and onward. The *Mokṣadharma* section of the twelfth book of the *Mahābhārata* especially contains references to yoga practice and Sāṃkhya philosophy and may represent our oldest known systematization of yoga and meditation practice. Furthermore, it is notable that the *Mahābhārata* contains 884 references to yoga, but only two references to *āsana* (Bryant, 2009, p. xxx).

Likewise the *Pātañjalayogaśāstra* and the *Bhagavad Gītā* show a minimal interest in *āsanas*, devoting less than ten verses to the subject, indicating that the understanding of yoga as primarily a system of bodily postures is indeed a modern Western phenomenon (Singleton, 2010). Instead we have in the *Mahābhārata* the first direct mentioning of *dhyānayoga* ("yoga by means of meditation," MBh 12.188.1–22) and a number of references to practices that are relatable to the classical yoga of Patañjali. Among these is a specific definition by the Vedic sage Vasiṣṭha of meditation as "the most powerful method of yoga" (MBh 12.294.6–9):

> Vasiṣṭha said: [6] Now I shall tell you what you are asking about. Hear from me in secret how yoga should be performed, O great king. [7] Of the different ways in which yoga should be performed, meditation is the most powerful. And people who know the Vedas say that meditation is of two kinds: [8] focus of the mind [*ekāgratā*] and breath-control [*prāṇāyāma*]. Breath-control has attributes (*saguṇa*) and [focus] of the mind is without attributes (*nirguṇa*). [9] At three times, urination, defecation and eating, O king, one should not practise yoga. One should practise it intently the rest of the time. (Mallinson & Singleton, 2017, p. 306)

The focus of the mind, "one-pointedness" (*ekāgratā*) or "fixation" (*dhāraṇā*) leading to a transformation of consciousness, is a method that is central to traditional yoga. It is closely linked to sense-withdrawal (*pratyāhāra*) and breath-control (*prāṇāyāma*) as seen in the *Śvetāśvatara Upaniṣad* and in the six yoga-auxiliaries (*ṣaḍaṅga*) of the *Maitrāyaṇīya Upaniṣad* and the extended eight yoga-auxiliaries or eight limbs (*aṣṭāṅga*) of the *Pātañjalayogaśāstra* (MU 6.18; PYŚ 2.29). Like the *Mahābhārata*, the *Maitrāyaṇīya Upaniṣad* (probably from the first centuries BCE) represents a transition from the Upaniṣads to later systematic and philosophical yoga traditions. The *Maitrāyaṇīya Upaniṣad* is much more specific in its description of yoga, meditation, and Sāṃkhya philosophy than earlier Upaniṣads, and a yogic method is fixed in a list of six limbs (MU 6.18): (1) breath-control (*prāṇāyāma*), (2) withdrawal of the senses (*pratyāhāra*), (3) meditation (*dhyāna*), (4) fixation of the mind (*dhāraṇā*), (5) inquiry or insight (*tarka*), and (6) absorbed consciousness (*samādhi*). A few verses in the *Maitrāyaṇīya Upaniṣad* describe meditation in some detail (MU 6.34):

> When [someone], having made his mind (*manas*) completely motionless, without dissolution or distraction, goes to a state without mind, that is the highest place [7]. The mind has to remain suppressed until it is destroyed in the heart. This is knowledge, this is liberation; the rest, on the other hand, is bookish proliferation [8]. The bliss, purified by concentration, which arises when the spotless mind (*cetas*) has been made to enter into the self, cannot be described with words. It is in that state (*tadā*) itself experienced by the inner organ [9]. (Buitenen, 1962, p. 105)

In comparison we find in the *Pātañjalayogaśāstra* the well-known set of eight limbs or yoga-auxiliaries (PYŚ 2.29): (1) ethical rules (*yama*), (2) ethical observances (*niyama*), (3) bodily postures (*āsana*), (4) breath-control (*prāṇāyāma*), (5) withdrawal of the senses (*pratyāhāra*), (6) fixation of the mind (*dhāraṇā*), (7) meditation (*dhyāna*), and (8) absorbed consciousness (*samādhi*). More or less similar lists of eight auxiliaries are found in other traditions, such as the Noble Eightfold Path of classical Buddhism (SS 23), the Eightfold Path in the Ayurvedic *Carakasaṃhitā* (CS 4.1.148–151), and the Eightfold Path of *dharma* in the *Mahābhārata* (MBh 3.2.71–77), as well as similar paths in later purāṇic and tantric traditions (cf. Mallinson & Singleton, 2017, pp. 7–11). It is thus generally accepted in yoga scholarship that the system of eight auxiliaries (*aṣṭāṅgayoga*) existed as an independent tradition before being incorporated into the *Pātañjalayogaśāstra* and other traditions (White, 2014, p. 47; Birch, 2014). This also implies that *aṣṭāṅgayoga* has had a life of its own and a different reception history than that of the non-sectarian *Pātañjalayogaśāstra*. Accordingly, *aṣṭāṅgayoga* has been adopted and incorporated into various traditions belonging to Śaivism, Vaiṣṇavism, and Jainism independently of the Sāṃkhya philosophy and terminology known from the *Pātañjalayogaśāstra* (Birch, 2014, p. 417).

At the risk of oversimplification, we may here try to sum up a basic set of identifiable yogic ideas and techniques at the heart of traditional meditational practices as we find them in many six- and eightfold systems: The control of the senses and the subsequent withdrawal of the senses from the outer world of phenomenal objects (like a charioteer controls unruly horses and a tortoise draws its limbs into itself) is the point of departure and *conditio sine qua non* for inner meditative practices and indeed for inner control. The withdrawal of the senses (*pratyāhāra*) therefore marks the transition from outer practices to inner (*antaraṅga*) practices. Furthermore, the control of the senses (*pratyāhāra*) is closely linked to the control of breath (*prāṇāyāma*) and the control of mind understood as a fixation (*dhāraṇa*) or concentration (*ekāgratā*) of the mind on a single point. In other words, one has to still the body, the senses, and the mind with bodily postures (*āsana*), withdrawal of the senses (*pratyāhāra*), breath-control (*prāṇāyāma*), and by focusing the mind (*dhāraṇā*) on a single point (*ekāgratā*) in order to practice meditation (*dhyāna*) and achieve the highest state of absorbed consciousness (*samādhi*). The goal is thus *samādhi*, a transformative inner experience par excellence, which may lead to the attainment of yogic powers (*siddhi*s) or final liberation (*mukti*, *mokṣa*, *nirvāṇa*, or *kaivalya*) (Figure 5.3).

This basic set of yogic meditational techniques in combination with the "ascetic soup" of India's axial age ideas, practices, and terminology found its first systematic and

FIGURE 5.3 A Rāmānandī ascetic practicing breath retention (*prāṇāyāma*) during *tapas* (*dhuni tap*), Allahabad, India, 2019.

Source: © Image courtesy of Prema Goet

philosophical crystallization in the work of Patañjali in the fourth century CE. Like the *Bhagavad Gītā*, the work represents an adaptation of yoga and meditation and, to some extent, of asceticism by the Brahmanical Sanskritic religion. Although with an emphasis on Sāṃkhya philosophy, the work is a mixture of things, including material from Buddhism and a wide array of other *śramaṇa* movements rooted in the ascetic reformism (Singleton, 2008, p. 79). As we are reminded by Knut Jacobsen, Sāṃkhya itself refers to a plurality of traditions (Jacobsen, 2011, pp. 79–80). The Sāṃkhya metaphysic and terminology are very ancient, have been highly influential like yoga itself, and are found in both early and late Upaniṣads (e.g., in the *Śvetāśvatara Upaniṣad*), although it did not find a developed systematic formulation before Īśvarakṛṣṇa's *Sāṃkhyakārikā* in the second century CE. All in all, Patañjali is working with the well-known terminology of the time with a clear Buddhist influence, such as "suffering" (*duḥkha*), the "cessation" of suffering (*nirodha*), and "liberation" (*nirvāṇa*) or "isolation" (*kaivalya*), the latter being a Sāṃkhya term. Furthermore, Sāṃkhya and Yoga were classed together as a pair in later lists of India's six orthodox philosophical systems (*ṣaḍdarśana*), and indeed they seem to go hand in hand to such a degree that it has been questioned if they have ever been separate (Liberman, 2008, p. 105). Thus, we may have to accept David White's conclusion, that the historical relationship between Saṃkhya and Yoga is at bottom a "chicken and egg question" (White, 2014, p. 23).

As we have seen, yoga is an attempt at a practical solution to the problem of suffering, which we find at the very basis of Sāṃkhya, yoga, and Buddhism and, indeed, at the basis of the ascetic reformism itself. Thus, while the goal of liberation is the same, the methods differ. In a striking passage in the *Mahābhārata*, Bhīṣma explains the relationship between Sāṃkhya and Yoga to Yudhiṣṭhira in the following way (MBh 12.289.7):

> Both the followers of Sāṃkhya and those of Yoga praise their own way as the best... The followers of Yoga rely on experiential methods [*pratyakṣahetavaḥ*], and those of Sāṃkhya on scriptural interpretation [*śāstraviniścayāḥ*]. I consider both these views true. Followed according to their instructions, both lead to the ultimate goal. (Bryant, 2009, p. xxviii)

This relationship is mirrored in the later historical developments of Yoga and Sāṃkhya, where "Yoga philosophy became the field of practical philosophical analysis and meditative experimentation, while the Sāṅkhya system emphasized the theoretical analysis of cosmic evolution" in the words of Barbara Stoler Miller (1998, p. 12). Like most Upaniṣads, the Sāṃkhya tradition(s) seemed preoccupied with the cultivation of esoteric knowledge or gnosis (*jñāna*) concerning cosmology and the nature of the self as a path to liberation (*jñānamārga*), while Patañjali proposed the view that it is the systematic practice of meditation in combination with this knowledge that will end suffering and lead to liberation.

Sāṃkhya basically means "enumeration" of the cosmological evolution and its twenty-five *tattva*s or elementary principles. It is based on the notion of an atheistic dualism of spirit (*puruṣa*) and matter (*prakṛti*) and on a triad of qualities (*guṇa*s) related to matter (*sattva*, *rajas*, and *tamas*). There is no personal creator god and the cosmogonical process of the universe was accidentally started by an imbalance in the three *guṇa*s, that is, the closeness of the male *puruṣa* to the female *prakṛti*. From the unmanifested original matter (*mūla-prakṛti*) the world suddenly evolved with all its beings and humans dominated by the quality of *sattva* or "lightness" (i.e., individual souls [*puruṣa*] caught in matter [*prakṛti*]). In the human "person" the interplay between the *guṇa*s brought forth the intellect (*buddhi*). From the intellect, egotism (*asmitā*, *ahaṃkāra*) evolved; and from the intellect, the mind (*manas*) arose, with its five senses and their objects, and thereupon the five organs of action and movement. A dominance of the dark *tamas* brought forth the five subtle (*sūkṣma*) elements and the five gross (*sthūla*) elements.

According to Sāṃkhya the tragedy of the human condition and the reason for suffering and distress (*duḥkha*) is to be found in the mistaken identification with forms of *prakṛti* producing attachment. The liberating insight is to be found in the realization of the separation and isolation (*kaivalya*) of *puruṣa* and *prakṛti*. They never mixed, just came close. The identification of *puruṣa* with *ātman*, "the self," is therefore obvious and the two words are often used as synonyms in later theistic Upaniṣads (Jacobsen, 1995,

p. 214). The way to liberation is therefore to reverse the evolution of material nature or *prakṛti*. Due to this involution a reabsorption is triggered when the *puruṣa* is again separated from *prakṛti* and the balance between the *guṇas* is restored. The individual soul is thereby set free, isolated and liberated (*kaivalya*). Thus, yoga is the practical philosophy and method facilitating this process of cosmic involution by embodying the condition of *sattva* in an attempt to reach the original state of consciousness without attributes (*nirguṇa puruṣa*) before creation took place (Olesen, 2014, pp. 82–86). *Puruṣa* itself in the words of Axel Michaels is "completely unchanging, eternal, omnipresent, pure spiritual light; in short, pure consciousness, sufficient unto itself, but not consciousness of something; its individuations, also called *puruṣa*, are the "parts" of the individual soul capable of salvation" (Michaels, 2004, p. 264). As Knut Jacobsen points out, Sāṃkhya, Yoga, Jainism, Mīmāṃsā, Nyāya and other philosophical systems operate with a "plurality of selves" (*puruṣa-bahutva*), while Advaita Vedānta makes out the exception by only recognizing *brahman* (Jacobsen, 1995, p. 215).

At the same time, *puruṣa* remains a single *tattva*. The plurality of selves are not individual souls and do not transmigrate, but are only distinguishable from one another by a kind of soul cover or "subtle body" (*sūkṣmaśarīra*) disguising an original unity (Michaels, 2004, p. 265). Indeed, this system of Sāṃkhya categories and the three *guṇas* have permeated Hindu traditions in manifold ways with regard to rules of purity, food, social structure, cosmology, anthropology, and soteriology, especially in its more basic forms as a kind of unsystematized "proto-Sāṃkhya" reaching back to the time of the Upaniṣads.

Classical Yoga and the *Pātañjalayogaśāstra*

Along with the *Bhagavad Gītā*, the *Yoga Sūtra* of Patañjali or the *Pātañjalayogaśāstra* (including the commentary ascribed to Vyāsa) may be one of the most famous Sanskrit works on yoga theory and practice today. Around the fourth century CE Patañjali compiled and unified various fragments and textual traditions on yoga and meditation reaching back to the first centuries BCE within a structured framework of Sāṃkhya metaphysics. In 196 *sūtras* or short aphorisms, written in a language resembling Buddhist Hybrid Sanskrit, the author not only compiled but actively contributed to the formulation of a systematic philosophy of yoga based on the most important material available at the time of composition.[1] It describes the practice of meditation as a method aimed at liberation from transmigration (*saṃsāra*) and suffering (*duḥkha*) drawing on a

[1] Translations of *sūtras* from the *Pātañjalayogaśāstra* (PYŚ) are my own unless otherwise noted. Following the arguments of Maas (2013, p. 58), and the colophons of most manuscripts, I refer to the Yoga Sūtra and its commentary (*bhāṣya*) as a single work with the title *Pātañjalayogaśāstra*.

Sāṃkhya philosophical discourse. It is divided into four chapters on meditation (*samādhi*), practice (*sādhana*), yogic powers (*vibhūti*), and liberation (*kaivalya*).

In accordance with the *sūtra* genre the work is highly dense and technical in style and close to unreadable without the help of a commentary or "skeleton key" (White, 2014, p. 10), especially the commentary (*bhāṣya*) attributed to the Vedic sage Vyāsa who is also claimed to have written the entire *Mahābhārata*. It is striking that this commentary ascribed to Vyāsa is syntactically almost inseparable from the main text, which has led to the assumption that the commentary may indeed have been written by Patañjali himself. This is, however, not unusual, and we find this to be the case with other famous commentaries, for example the Buddhist philosopher Nāgārjuna commenting on his own work in the *Pratītyasamutpādahṛdayavyākhyāna* (Jamieson, 2000). Thus Philip Maas has pointed out that there are no old manuscripts where the *sūtra* text and commentary are separate, but that it is highly likely that Patañjali collected the *sūtras* from different traditions and wrote the commentary himself, being a scholar rather than a practitioner (Maas, 2013, p. 58). Furthermore, Maas has shown that the colophons of old manuscripts read *Pātañjalayogaśāstra* or *Pātañjala-Yoga-Śāstra Sāṃkhya-Pravacana* ("the authoritative exposition of yoga that originates with Patañjali, the mandatory Sāṃkhya teaching") rather than *Yogasūtra* (Maas, 2013, p. 58).

If we accept this argument by Maas, the text as a whole may be dated to some time between 325 and 425 CE and should be referred to as the *Pātañjalayogaśāstra* rather than the *Yoga Sūtra* (as is the case in this article). However, it should be noted that a very different and contradicting view has been proposed by the French scholar Michel Angot (2008), who stated that the first three chapters of Patañjali's *Yoga Sūtra* were primarily of a Buddhist orientation and originated in the first century CE. The commentator Vyāsa (if he ever existed) then added a fourth chapter and adapted the work to the (Hindu) Brahmanical Sanskritic tradition through his commentary as late as the sixth or seventh century CE (Angot, 2008). Whatever may have been the case, it seems safe to say that the *Pātañjalayogaśāstra* (including the commentary) became the locus classicus of the classical formative phase of yoga and meditation in the first millennium CE, and set the standards for a systematic and consistent yoga nomenclature for the following centuries that would be adopted by Hindu, Jain, and Buddhist traditions alike. Although David White (2014) and Knut Jacobsen (2011, p. 76) have argued that the work was never really important, and most likely unknown to most yogis and serious practitioners of physical yoga in India, James Mallinson has reminded us that the *Pātañjalayogaśāstra* nevertheless remained one of the most important and popular intellectual works on yoga philosophy among learned scholars and was included in the influential twelfth-century *Sarvasiddhāntasaṃgraha* compendium and other lists of India's philosophical systems (e.g., Mallinson, 2016, p. 124n3; Halbfass, 1990, p. 351). On the other hand, it is interesting to note that the main interest of modern yoga practitioners has been in its practical aspect and description of the eight yoga-auxiliaries (PYŚ 2.29–3.9), while this part has never received much attention in the commentarial tradition or in academic works (Feuerstein, 1989, p. 17).

Turning to the work itself, we find some of the most specific and influential definitions of traditional meditation and yoga as well as a highly technical terminology. Thus,

Patañjali's classic definition of yoga in the opening verse of the *Pātañjalayogaśāstra* reads that "yoga is the cessation of the activities of the mind" (PYŚ 1.2: *yogaś citta-vṛtti-nirodhaḥ*), indicating that yoga in this context is understood as the resulting state of mind (i.e., non-cognitive *samādhi*) rather than a method. The activities or fluctuations (*vṛtti*) of the mind are further defined as those mental functions that restrict consciousness: "proper cognition, wrong cognition, [referenceless] verbal imagination, sleep and memory" (PYŚ 1.6: *pramāṇa-viparyaya-vikalpa-nidrā-smṛtayaḥ*). These mental activities can be either afflictive (*kliṣṭa*) and cause involvement with the world (PYŚ 2.3–9) or be non-afflictive (*akliṣṭa*) and contribute to the yogic endeavor (PYŚ 1.17, 1.42, 1.44). As we have seen, the method to contain and conquer these mental activities is simply designated *aṣṭāṅga* or "eight limbs" (PYŚ 2.29–3.9). In the *Pātañjalayogaśāstra* the earlier mentioned meditative practices of fixation of the mind (*dhāraṇā*), meditation (*dhyāna*), and absorption (*samādhi*) are classed together as three successive inner practices (*antaraṅga*), and subsequently termed *saṃyama* or "[inner] control" (PYŚ 3.4). *Dhāraṇā* is defined as "the locking of the mind on a [single] place" (PYŚ 3.1: *deśa-bandhaś cittasya dhāraṇā*), but the "place" of focus is not defined.

The commentary, however, lists a number of suitable external objects and body parts including *cakra*s and the light in the head (*hṛdayapuṇḍarīka*). Through focusing on such a place or point (*ekāgratā*) the wandering mind can be calmed and a deep concentration can be achieved. Meditation is defined as a "one-directedness of consciousness in that [i.e., in the course of *dhāraṇā*]" (PYŚ 3.2: *tatra pratyaya-ekatānatā dhyānam*), which may be understood as a continuous flow of one-pointed consciousness, or simply concentration following from the practice of fixing the mind on a single object. The resulting *samādhi* is "that [*dhyāna*] having the appearance of the object only, as if empty of its own essense" (PYŚ 3.3: *tad eva artha-mātra-nirbhāsaṃ svarūpa-śūnyam-iva samādhiḥ*). The mind is thus absorbed in the object of meditation and emptied of any other cognitive content. Interestingly, this type of *samādhi* with a particular focus or support (*saṃprajñāta samādhi*) is further divided into four specific levels of elevated consciousness or absorption: "Due to it taking on the appearance of attention [to gross objects], pondering [on subtle objects], bliss and egoism, it is cognitive [*samādhi*]" (PYŚ 1.17: *vitarka-vicāra-ānanda-asmitā-rūpa-anugamāt saṃprajñātaḥ*). These four levels or types of cognitive absorption (*saṃprajñāta samādhi*) are thus included within the object-centered *samādhi* category (PYŚ 1.46: *sa-bīja*).

There is also a corresponding and more advanced state of consciousness without object (*asaṃprajñāta samādhi*), namely the "other [*samādhi*] achieved through the initial repetitive practice of cessation of the activities of the mind leaving only the *saṃskāra*s [karmic impressions]" (PYŚ 1.18: *virāma-pratyaya-abhyāsa-pūrvaḥ saṃskāra-śeṣo 'nyaḥ*). Finally, "when there is cessation even of this [*saṃskāra*], there is cessation of all [mental activities] being *samādhi* without an object" (PYŚ 1.51: *tasya-api nirodhe sarva-nirodhān nirbījaḥ samādhiḥ*). This deepest state of concentration and objectless absorption has been variously interpreted in a Western context as trance, enstasy, or mystical experience (*unio mystica*) and, likewise, we find no consensus in classical India as to the nature of non-cognitive *samādhi*. While Johannes Bronkhorst claims that yogic absorption results in a mystic state (Bronkhorst 2012; 2017), Gerald Larson (2012, p. 78) has suggested that there may be nothing mysterious at all about the realization obtained in yoga and although the final stage of yoga transcends ordinary consciousness and language, this is not necessarily achieved via a mystical experience, but rather through "a logical series of meditative practices and hyperconscious thought experiments" in the words of Barbara Stoler Miller (1998, p. ix). Nevertheless, whether the final stage of non-cognitive *samādhi* is understood as a mystical experience or not, it should be safe to speak of a transformative experience and to conclude with James Mallinson that "the category of *samādhi* provides an invaluable prism through which to consider the farthest reaches of the yogic endeavour" (Mallinson & Singleton, 2017, p. 323).

In addition to the non-cognitive *samādhi*, we do however find the mentioning of an alternative method for obtaining *samādhi* in the *Pātañjalayogaśāstra* 1.23: "Or [*samādhi*] through dedication to god" (*īśvara-praṇidhānād vā*). Thus, although Sāṃkhya philosophy is often said to be atheistic, the *Pātañjalayogaśāstra* may be said to be an inherently theistic text (Bryant, 2009, p. xxiv). As the twelfth-century term *seśvara-sāṃkhya* ("Sāṃkhya-with-*īśvara*") would indicate, this may in fact be the only difference between *Pātañjala* yoga and Sāṃkhya (White, 2014, p. 22). However, the matter is somewhat more complicated as Knut Jacobsen has pointed out (Jacobsen, 2012b, p. 326). Sāṃkhya does reject a personal theistic god but does not reject the Indian pantheon. Likewise it is uncertain what the exact reference is of *īśvara* ("Lord") in the *Pātañjalayogaśāstra* (1.23–28), other than a *puruṣa* untouched by the afflictions (*kleśa*) who is identified with the sacred syllable *OṂ* (*praṇava*). *Īśvara* in the *Pātañjalayogaśāstra* is therefore not a typical purāṇic or theistic god, but may first and foremost be an alternative tool for meditation and an aid in obtaining liberation (Jacobsen, 2012b, p. 326). However, we do find examples of this alternative *samādhi* through dedication to a personal theistic god in other traditions, most famously in the *Bhagavad Gītā*'s sixth chapter on *dhyānayoga* as a form of devotional (*bhakti*) yoga. In the following verses the theistic god himself, i.e. Kṛṣṇa, provides the instructions for meditation leading to liberation (*nirvāṇa*) by fixing the mind on a personal god or *īśvara* (BhG 6.11–15):

> [6.11] In a clean place establishing
> A steady seat for himself,
> That is neither too high nor too low,
> Covered with a cloth, a skin, and kuśa-grass,
> [6.12] There fixing the thought-organ on a single object,
> Restraining the activity of his mind and senses,
> Sitting on the seat, let him practice
> Discipline unto self-purification.
> [6.13] Even body, head, and neck
> Holding motionless, (keeping himself) steady,
> Gazing at the tip of his own nose,
> And not looking in any direction,
> [6.14] With tranquil soul, rid of fear,
> Abiding in the vow of chastity,

Controlling the mind, his thoughts on Me,
Let him sit disciplined, absorbed in Me.
[6.15] Thus ever disciplining himself,
The man of discipline, with controlled mind,
To peace that culminates in *nirvāṇa*,
And rests in Me, attains.

(Edgerton, 1944, p. 63)

Indeed, from the time of the *Bhagavad Gītā* and the theistic Purāṇas onward this understanding of yoga as devotion to a personal god rather than "cessation of the activities of the mind" (PYŚ 1.2) became increasingly influential at the expense of the *īśvara* of the *Pātañjalayogaśāstra*. According to David White the Sāṃkhya-Yoga system of Patañjali had been completely forgotten within Indian philosophy around the sixteenth century CE, not least due to the strong influence of Vedānta and its identification of the universal self with a personal god: "And so it was that by the sixteenth century, devotional Hinduism... had collapsed nearly every philosophical system into its perfect theological crystal. In a complete reversal of Patanjali's and Vyasa's original positions, the Ishvara of the Yoga Sutra had come to be equated with the Krishna of the Bhagavad Gita" (White, 2014, pp. 49–50).

Conclusion

Yoga, meditation, and asceticism are closely linked and rooted in the ascetic reformism of India's axial age. Traditional yoga addresses the main concerns of ascetic reformism and is a practical method to solve the problem of suffering and attain liberation from the cycle of rebirth. Yoga primarily refers to the practice of meditation as described and systematized in the later classical yoga of Patañjali, where yoga is a synonym for non-cognitive *samādhi*, the highest state of consciousness or absorption. As indicated in the Upaniṣads and pinpointed in the yoga-auxiliaries, meditation consists in stilling the body, the senses, and the mind through a withdrawal of the senses, breath-control, and fixing the mind on a single point (including god or *īśvara*) as a way to reach *samādhi*. These techniques were combined with Sāṃkhya philosophy and other ideas and terminology (especially Buddhist) from the ascetic reformism discourse and systematized into a whole by Patañjali in the *Pātañjalayogaśāstra* in the fourth century CE. While Patañjali's work has been influential with regard to yoga terminology and Indian philosophy, its accumulation of complexity with regard to Sāṃkhya philosophy has never been of real interest to yoga practitioners before recently. Furthermore, its practical dimension, that is, the yoga-auxiliaries or *aṣṭāṅga*, which may represent an independent tradition, remains the most interesting part for contemporary practitioners. However, the work does not pay much attention to the practice of *āsana*s or bodily postures apart from sitting still and erect (PYŚ 2.46) and even encourages disgust or aversion with

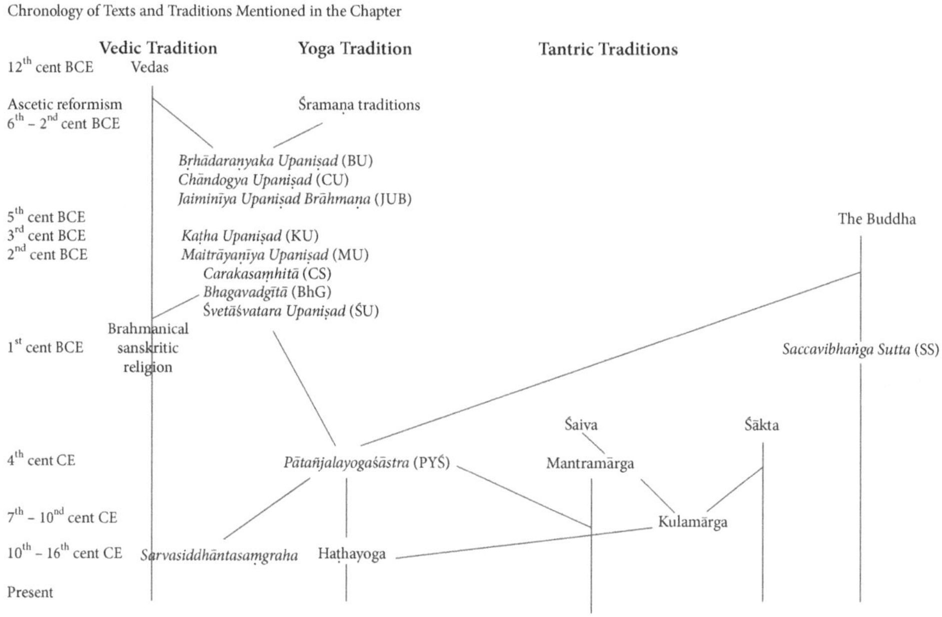

FIGURE 5.4 Chronology of Texts and Traditions Mentioned in the Chapter

respect to one's own body and contact with others (PYŚ 2.40). Thus, traditional and classical yoga is clearly rooted in asceticism and implies a disinterest in the outer world and one's own body. Instead it concentrates on human consciousness and a practical realisation of the truth within, i.e. a transformative experience through experiential techniques of the self. These non-cognitive and pre-verbal meditational experiences (e.g. "the bliss, purified by concentration") transcends language and ordinary consciousness and "cannot be described with words" (MU 6.34), but may nevertheless be dressed in a doctrine such as Buddha's *dharma* or Patañjali's Sāṃkhya-Yoga (Figure 5.4).

Abbreviations

AV	*Atharvaveda*
BhG	*Bhagavad Gītā*
BU	*Bṛhadāraṇyaka Upaniṣad*
CU	*Chāndogya Upaniṣad*
CS	*Carakasaṃhitā*
JUB	*Jaiminīya Upaniṣad Brāhmaṇa*
KU	*Kaṭha Upaniṣad*
MBh	*Mahābhārata*
MU	*Maitrāyaṇīya Upaniṣad*
P	Pali
PYŚ	*Pātañjalayogaśāstra*

RV *Ṛgveda*
ŚP *Śiva Purāṇa*
ŚU *Śvetāśvatara Upaniṣad*
SN *Saṃyutta Nikāya*
SS *Saccavibhaṅga Sutta*

References

Primary Source

Pātañjalayogaśāstra (Yoga Sūtra with bhāṣya by Patañjali). (1904). Ed. Kāśinātha Śāstrī Āgāśe: Vācaspatimiśraviracitaṭīkāsaṃvalitavyāsabhāṣyasametāni Pātañjalayogasūtrāṇi, tathā bhoj adevaviracitarājamārtaṇḍābhidhavṛttisametāni pātañjalayogasūtrāṇi. sūtrapāṭhasūtravarṇ ānukramasūcībhyāṃ ca sanāthīkṛtāni (...), *Ānandāśrama Sanskrit Series*, 47. Pune: Ānandāśramamudraṇālaye.

Secondary Sources and Translations

Angot, M. (2008). *Le yoga-sūtra de Patañjali. Le yoga-bhāṣya de Vyāsa avec des extraits du yoga-vārttika de Vijñāna-Bhikṣu*. Paris: Le Belles Lettres.

Bellah, R. N. (2011). *Religion in human evolution: From the Paleolithic to the axial age*. Cambridge, MA: Harvard University Press.

Biardeau, M. (1989). *Hinduism: The anthropology of a civilization*. New Delhi: Oxford University Press.

Birch, J. (2014). Rājayoga: The reincarnations of the king of all yogas. *International Journal of Hindu Studies 17*(3), 401–444.

Bronkhorst, J. (1981). Yoga and Seśvara Sāṃkhya. *Journal of Indian Philosophy* 9, 309–320.

Bronkhorst, J. (1993). *The two traditions of meditation in ancient India*. Delhi: Motilal Banarsidass.

Bronkhorst, J. (2007). *Greater Magadha: Studies in the culture of early India*. Leiden: Brill.

Bronkhorst, J. (2012). *Absorption. Human nature and Buddhist liberation*. Paris: UniversityMedia.

Bronkhorst, J. (2017). Can religion be explained? The role of absorption in various religious phenomena, *Method and Theory in the Study of religion*, 29, 1-30.

Bryant, E. F. (Trans.) (2009). *The yoga sūtras of Patañjali*. New York: North Point Press.

Buitenen, J. A. B. van. (Ed. & Trans.) (1962). *The Maitrāyaṇīya Upaniṣad: A critical essay, with text, translation, and commentary*. Gravenhage: Mouton.

Chand, D. (Trans.) (1982). *The Atharvaveda: Sanskrit text with English translation*. New Delhi: Munshiram Manoharlal.

Donald, M. (1991). *Origins of the modern mind: Three stages in the evolution of culture and cognition*. Cambridge, MA: Harvard University Press.

Dumont, L. (1980). *Homo hierarchicus: The caste system and its implications*. Chicago and London: University of Chicago Press.

Durkheim, É. (1897). *Le suicide: Étude de sociologie*. Paris: Les Presses Universitaires de France.

Edgerton, F. (Trans.) (1944). *Bhagavad Gītā*. London: Oxford University Press.

Eisenstadt, S. N. (1986). Introduction: The axial age breakthroughs—their characteristics and origins. In S. N. Eisenstadt (Ed.), *The origins and diversity of the axial age*. Albany: State University of New York Press.

Eliade, M. (1937). Cosmical homology and yoga. *Journal of the Indian Society of Oriental Arts* 5, 188–203.
Eliade, M. (1969). *Yoga: Immortality and freedom*. Princeton, NJ: Princeton University Press. (Original work published 1958).
Feer, L. (Ed. & Trans.). (2008). *The Saṃyutta-nikāya of the Sutta-piṭaka: Pt. 5. Mahāvagga*. Pali Text Society Text Series 97. Oxford: Pali Text Society.
Feuerstein, G. (Trans.) (1989). *The yoga-sūtra of Patañjali: A new translation and commentary*. Rochester, VT: Inner Traditions India.
Fitzgerald, J. L. (2009). The Sāṃkhya-Yoga "manifesto" at MBh 12.289–290. In J. Brockington (Ed.), *Battles, bards, Brahmans: Papers from the Epics section of the 13th World Sanskrit Conference, Edinburgh, 10th–14th July 2006* (pp. 185–212). Delhi: Motilal Banarsidass.
Fitzgerald, J. L. (2012). A prescription for yoga and power in the Mahābhārata. In D. G. White (Ed.), *Yoga in practice* (pp. 43–57). Princeton, NJ: Princeton University Press.
Flood, G. (1996). *An introduction to Hinduism*. Cambridge: Cambridge University Press.
Flood, G. (2004). *The ascetic self: Subjectivity, memory and tradition*. Cambridge: Cambridge University Press.
Flood, G. (2013). *The truth within: A history of inwardness in Christianity, Hinduism, and Buddhism*. Oxford: Oxford University Press.
Flood, G. (2019). *Religion and the philosophy of life*. Oxford: Oxford University Press.
Halbfass, W. (1990). *India and Europe: An essay in understanding*. Delhi: Motilal Banarsidass.
Heesterman, J. C. (1962). Vrātya and sacrifice. *Indo-Iranian Journal* 6(1), 1–37.
Heesterman, J. C. (1985). *The inner conflict of tradition: An essay in Indian ritual, kingship, and society*. Chicago: University of Chicago Press.
Jacobsen, K. A. (1995). The anthropocentric bias in Eliade's interpretation of the Samkhya and the Samkhya-Yoga systems of religious thought. *Religion* 25(3), 213–225.
Jacobsen, K. A. (2011). Samkhya-Yoga traditions. In J. Frazier (Ed.), *The Continuum companion to Hindu Studies* (pp. 74–83). London: Continuum International Publishing Group.
Jacobsen, K. A. (Ed.). (2012a). *Yoga powers: Extraordinary capacities attained through meditation and concentration*. Leiden: Brill.
Jacobsen, K. A. (2012b). Songs to the highest god (*īśvara*) of Sāṃkhya-Yoga. In D. G. White (Ed.), *Yoga in practice* (pp. 325–336). Princeton, NJ: Princeton University Press.
Jamieson, R. C. (2000). *A study of Nāgārjuna's twenty verses on the great vehicle (Mahāyānaviṃśikā) and his verses on the heart of dependent origination (Pratītyasamutpadahṛdayakārikā) with the interpretation of the heart of dependent origination (Pratītyasamutpādahṛdayavyākhyāna)*. Toronto Studies in Religion 15. Oxford: Peter Lang.
Jamison, S. W. & Brereton, J. P. (Trans.). (2014). *The Rigveda: The earliest religious poetry of India* (3 vols.). South Asia Research. Oxford: Oxford University Press.
Jaspers, K. (1953). *The origin and goal of history*. London: Routledge & Kegan Paul. (Original work published 1949).
Kulke, H. (1986). The historical background of India's axial age. In S. N. Eisenstadt (Ed.), *The origins and diversity of axial age civilizations* (pp. 374–392). Albany: State University of New York Press.
Larson, G., & Bhattacharya, R. S. (Eds.). (2008). *Encyclopedia of Indian philosophies: Vol. 12. Yoga: India's philosophy of meditation*. Delhi: Motilal Banarsidass.
Larson, G. J. (2012). Pātañjala yoga in practice, In D. G. White (Ed.), *Yoga in practice*. Princeton: Princeton University Press.

Liberman, K. (2008). The reflexivity of the authenticity of Haṭha Yoga. In B. Diken & C. B. Laustsen (Eds.), *Yoga in the modern world: Contemporary perspectives* (pp. 100–116). New York: Routledge.

Lorenzen, D. (2006). *Who invented Hinduism? Essays on religion in history*. New Delhi: Yoda Press.

Maas, P. (2013). A concise historiography of classical yoga philosophy. In E. Franco (Ed.), *Periodization and historiography of Indian philosophy* (pp. 53–90). Vienna: Sammlung de Nobili, Institut für Südasien-, Tibet- und Buddhismuskunde der Universität Wien.

Mallinson, J. (2016). Śāktism and Haṭhayoga. In B. W. Olesen, *Goddess traditions in tantric Hinduism: History, practice and doctrine* (pp. 109–140). London: Routledge.

Mallinson, J., & Singleton, M. (Trans. & Ed.) (2017). *Roots of yoga: Translated and Edited with an introduction by James Mallinson and Mark Singleton*. London: Penguin Classics.

Michaels, A. (2004). *Hinduism: Past and present* (B. Harshav, Trans.). Princeton, NJ: Princeton University Press.

Miller, B. S. (Trans.) (1998). *Yoga: Discipline of freedom*. New York: Bantam Books.

Monier-Williams, M. (1899). *A Sanskrit-English dictionary: Etymologically and philologically arranged with special reference to cognate Indo-European languages*. Oxford: Oxford University Press.

Oberlies, T. (1988). Die Śvetāśvatara-Upaniṣad: Eine Studie ihrer Gotteslehre. *Wiener Zeitschrift für die Kunde Südasiens/Vienna Journal of South Asian Studies* 32, 35–62.

Oberlies, T. (Ed. & Trans.) (1995). Die Śvetāśvatara-Upaniṣad: Einleitung-Edition und Übersetzung von Adhyāya I. *Wiener Zeitschrift für die Kunde Südasiens/Vienna Journal of South Asian Studies* 39, 61–102.

O'Flaherty, W. D. (Trans.) (1981). *The Rig Veda: An anthology. One hundred and eight hymns, selected, translated and annotated*. London: Penguin Books.

Oldenberg, H. (1894). *Die Religion des Veda*. Berlin: Verlag von Wilhelm Hertz.

Olesen, B. W. (2014). *Gudernes Sprog. Klassisk sanskrit på dansk. II: Tekster*. Højbjerg: Forlaget Univers.

Olesen, B. W. (Ed.). (2016). *Goddess traditions in tantric Hinduism*. London: Routledge.

Olivelle, P. (Trans.) (1992). *The Saṃnyāsa Upaniṣads: Hindu scriptures on asceticism and renunciation*. Oxford: Oxford University Press.

Olivelle, P. (Ed. & Trans.) (1998). *The early Upaniṣads: Annotated text and translation*. New York: Oxford University Press.

Olivelle, P. (1999). Young Śvetaketu: A literary study of an Upaniṣadic story. *Journal of the American Oriental Society* 119, 46f.

Olivelle, P. (2005). The renouncer tradition. In G. Flood (Ed.), *The Blackwell companion to Hinduism*. Oxford: Blackwell Publishing.

Pinch, W. R. (2006). *Warrior ascetics and Indian empires*. Cambridge: Cambridge University Press.

Rastogi, N. (1992). The yogic disciplines in the monistic Śaiva tantric traditions of Kashmir: Threefold, fourfold, and six-limbed. In T. Goudriaan (Ed.), *Ritual and speculation in early Tantrism: Studies in honor of André Padoux* (pp. 247–280). New York: State University of New York Press.

Raveh, D. (2012). *Exploring the yogasūtra: Philosophy and translation*. London: Continuum.

Sanderson, A. (2014). The Śaiva literature. *Journal of Indological Studies (Kyoto) 24 &* 25(2012–2013), 1–113.

Singleton, M. (2008). The classical reveries of modern yoga: Patañjali and the construcive orientalism. In B. Diken & C. B. Laustsen, *Yoga in the modern world: Contemporary perspectives* (pp. 77–99). New York: Routledge.

Singleton, M. (2010). *Yoga body: The origins of modern posture practice.* New York: Oxford University Press.

Sloterdijk, P. (2009). *Du mußt dein Leben ändern: Über Anthropotechnik.* Frankfurt am Main: Suhrkamp.

Stietencron, H. von. (1997). Hinduism: On the proper use of a deceptive term. In G.-D. Sontheimer & H. Kulke (Eds.), *Hinduism reconsidered* (pp. 32–53). New Delhi: Manohar.

Weber, M. (1978). *Gesammelte Aufsätze zur Religionssoziologie II: Die Wirtschaftsethik der Weltreligionen—Hinduismus und Buddhismus.* Tübingen: J.C.B. Mohr (Paul Siebeck). (Original work published 1921).

Werner, K. (1994). The longhaired sage of RV 10,136: A shaman, a mystic or a yogi? In K. Werner (Ed.), *The yogi and the mystic: Studies in Indian and comparative mysticism* (pp. 33–53). Durham Indological Series 1. London: Curzon Press.

Wernicke-Olesen, B. (2014). *Gudernes sprog. Klassisk Sanskrit på dansk. II Tekster.* Højbjerg: Forlaget Univers.

Wernicke-Olesen, B. & Einarsen, S. L. (2018). Übungswissen im Yoga, Tantra und Asketismus des frühen indischen Mittelalters. In A.-B. Renger & A. Stellmacher (Eds.), *Übungswissen in Religion und Philosophie: Produktion, Weitergabe, Wandel* (pp. 241–257). Berlin: Lit Verlag.

White, D. G. (2009). *Sinister yogis.* Chicago: University of Chicago Press.

White, D. G. (Ed.). (2012). *Yoga in practice.* Princeton, NJ: Princeton University Press.

White, D. G. (2014). *The yoga sutra of Patanjali: A biography.* Princeton, NJ: Princeton University Press.

Witzel, M. (2005). Vedas and Upaniṣads. In G. Flood (Ed.), *The Blackwell companion to Hinduism* (pp. 68–101). Oxford: Blackwell Publishing.

Wujastyk, D. (2012). The path to liberation through yogic mindfulness in early Āyurveda. In D. G. White (Ed.), *Yoga in practice* (pp. 31–42). Princeton, NJ: Princeton University Press.

CHAPTER 6

JUDAISM AND MEDITATION

TOMER PERSICO

Introduction

Judaism, at its base, is not a personal ethical path, but a communal commitment to a sacred covenant, made between a particular people and a particular God. As such it did not aim, at least in the first two millennia of its existence, to develop the individual to spiritual perfection, but rather to establish a collective that would follow the divine law. It is hardly surprising, therefore, that meditative techniques were always peripheral to the main current of this faith community and its sacred cannon.

Though this is generally still the case, important changes have taken place since the eighteenth century, and at present the practice of meditation, and no less so the active search for meditation techniques, has become widespread. This in turn has underlined the inherent tension between the search for inner transformation and devotion to strict compliance with heteronomous custom.

In this chapter I will offer a short survey of the meditative techniques that were developed in the Jewish tradition. I will proceed chronologically from the Bible to contemporary developments, noting only the major, more influential manifestations of Jewish meditation. Subsequently I will consider the sociological and cultural shifts that have led to perceived changes in principal traits of the meditative techniques that have developed within this tradition. I will also note how these same cultural shifts pose a considerable challenge to the Halakhic tradition today, that is, to the traditional observance of Jewish religious law. Understanding these will allow us to better grasp the particular place meditation is given in the Jewish tradition.

Definition of Meditation

I define meditation in a very broad sense, as *an intentional action initiated in order to bring personal mental transformation of a therapeutic or soteriological character.* As such, meditative techniques are diverse ways of regulating body and mind, ranging through the physical, the ethical, and the psychological. Thus fasting, textual recitation, deliberate hyper-ventilation, concentration, or premeditated emotional exuberance, if aimed toward the above ends, are all forms of meditation. What is common to all these exercises is the attempt to undermine the habitual patterns of consciousness, while challenging the mundane perception of the world, one's sense of self, and the relationship between self and world.

As will be obvious, Jewish meditative techniques are not, as it were, variations on a theme, or different branches expanding from the same trunk. There is no one meditative stem in the Jewish tradition, such as you will find, for example, in Buddhism. This is due to the marginal place meditation had within the Jewish world. When taken up it was by unique individuals setting their own course, often with no knowledge of their predecessors and usually being inspired by non-Jewish practices in their surroundings. That being said, we can find common elements among the varied Jewish techniques, such as the central place allotted to the Hebrew language; a practical, world-affirming, and world-benefiting direction; and of course the constant desire to achieve intimate contact with the monotheistic Godhead.

Meditation in the Bible

When looking for meditative techniques in the Hebrew Bible (the "Old Testament") most modern commentators, whether rabbis or New Age enthusiasts, point to the prophets. Envisioning these as mystics, they look for the "mystical path" that led to their prophetic manifestations. Alas, even a superficial reading of the prophets' chronicles shows that their revelations come to them as a great surprise, and that often they initially tried to reject their divine mission. These are hardly the responses one would expect from a person initiating contact with the divine. Indeed, there is no textual evidence for meditative techniques used by the classical prophets.

Offering mainly historical narrative and judicial codices, the Bible is hardly a manual for mysticism. Even so, looking for clear cases of meditation in the Bible, one is able to find two techniques, both given a minor place by the biblical editors. These are the use of music and the use of self-laceration.

The first is to be found in 1 Samuel 10. The prophet Samuel sends the newly anointed king, Saul, to receive the spirit of God (*Ruaḥ Elohim*) and be "changed into a different person" (here and below I will use the NIV translation). This is achieved by joining "a procession of prophets coming down from the high place with lyres, timbrels, pipes and harps being played before them, and they will be prophesying."

The "high place," *bama* in Hebrew, is a local sacrificial site, and the prophesying is apparently achieved by using music. We know of similar use of music as a meditative technique from a wide range of ancient cultures and practices, such as shamanic séances or Greek chorus singing (Lewis, 2003; Seaford, 2013). Of course, the group are not prophets in the same sense that the classic prophets, and for that matter Samuel, are, and prophesying here is not speaking the words of God to the people, but entering into ecstatic trance (Uffenheimer, 1973). Such sort of prophecy was always collective and frequently connected with battle in the name of God. These groups of prophets would charge ecstatically into battle, under the spell of the divine spirit and aiming to advance God's glory (Ibid.). As such the soteriological goals of this meditation are communal more than individual, underlining the collective nature of ancient Judaism (and somewhat stretching my definition of meditation).

It is also on the brink of a religious battle that we find the other biblical meditative technique. Here it is the prophets of the god Baal, challenged by the prophet Elijah to burn a sacrificial bull by calling upon their god to conjure fire, who lacerate themselves in order to prophesize:

> And they cried aloud, and cut themselves after their manner with knives and lancets, till the blood gushed out upon them... and they prophesied until the time of the offering of the evening sacrifice. (1 Kings 18)

Here again, there are parallels for this practice in other cultures. A clear example would be the Maya use of bloodletting to achieve communion with their gods (McKillop, 2004). Apparently intentional drawing of blood from one's body induces, under proper conditions, a state of trance. The prophets of Baal indeed prophesied following their self-abrasion, but the requested fire did not appear, and Elijah, with the help of others, proceeded to slaughter them.

Meditation in the Late Antiquity

Post-biblical Judaism witnesses a significant increase in personal efforts to achieve soteriological transformation. As a result of a process of individualization, whose main expression is the development of Christianity as a personal and universal religion, Judaism displayed the appearance of private mystical journeys achieved through personal meditative practice. As a result, during the early centuries CE we first encounter a complete Jewish mystical tradition, offering meditative instructions. These developments are joined by a new soteriological model adopted all through the area at the time (alongside but counter to the Apocalyptic genre), which places salvation not at the end of time, but at the top of space. From Plotinus to the Gnostic sects, the idea that that the soul must ascend in order to be redeemed became generally accepted.

Out of these processes rose what today we call the Hekhalot and Merkabah literature. This body of texts was written approximately between the third and seventh centuries, and offers, among cosmological, cosmogonic, and magical teachings, the chronicles of the heavenly ascents and journeys of pseudepigraphically placed known Jewish sages. The sages travel up a series of seven heavens (*Hekhalot*, literally "halls"), only to reach the divine *Merkabah* ("assembly"), which is the form constructed by the Divine Persona, sitting on His throne, hovered over on all sides by superior angels. The goal of these ascents is the divine vision. Seeing the Divine Persona is followed by ecstatic glossolalia and usually also by the receipt of secret knowledge, which is to be taken down through a peaceful descent and used for the benefit of all (Pedaya, 2002; Idel, 2005).

The ascent to the divine vision is impossible without the knowledge of the names of all the angels that guard the seven heavens—eight to each entrance. The Merkabah voyager travels to the center and peak of the heavenly structure by displaying the correct name-bearing "seal" to each angel. Naturalistic analysis may assume that these mystics enter a state of trance, in the context of which mythical maps are translated into inner psychic space (Garb, 2011).

But how does the journey begin? In order to make the first ascent to the upper realms, the Merkabah voyager needs to recite a specific divine name. As preparation for this practice he (those engaging in such practices were assumed by the texts to be men) must abstain from sexual intercourse and partially fast for forty days. Following that he must sit on the ground and place his head between his knees (Schafer, 1981, passages 681–684). Then, according to the instructions, "his mouth should exclaim names and his fingers count up until one hundred and eleven . . . not to add and not to draw from the names or else he will die" (Schafer, 1981, passage 681). Another passage instructs reciting one hundred and twelve times and gives out the name that is to be recited: *Totrosoai Zortak Totrival Tophager Ashroyliai Ashroiilii* (Schafer, 1981, passage 204–205).

Thus, in order to enter the trance-induced journey to the heavens we are prescribed a mnemonic and mantra-like practice, involving memorizing and reciting difficult divine names an exact number of times, and later following an ascending path by producing specific names in correct sequence. This practice, which demands significant powers of concentration and memory, consumes the Merkabah voyager's consciousness and induces a state of trance, in which a mythical map of the heavenly realms, which had been memorized before, is internalized and mentally constructed, and a journey through the Hekhalot and up to the divine throne is experienced.

Meditation in Kabbalah

At the beginning of the thirteenth century, Europe was becoming more literate, city-oriented, and increasingly exposed to Hellenistic philosophy. Coming into the fore in West Europe at that time, Kabbalah (along with Maimonidean rationalism, Ashkenazi Hasidism, and Ibn Ezra's astrology) was one answer the Jewish tradition gave to the rising questions of an age (Idel, 2002). The need for systematic explanations drew complex maps of the world, which, through commentary on the canon and varied interpretations of Halakha and customs, offered the erudite elite an analytic understanding of the cosmos. Kabbalah, accordingly, held two principal "secrets": (1) the structure and dynamics of the divine worlds, and (2) the specific connections between the different Halakhic commandments and the rectification (the unification of the fractured divine emanations) of those worlds. Such rectification was the goal to which the Kabbalist's religious efforts were dedicated. Kabbalah is thus an esoteric lore meant to position the Jewish individual (and collective) both metaphysically and normatively.

The place of mystical techniques and experience within this lore is debated. It is clear that some Kabbalists experienced visions and communion with the divine, and it is clear that they used different methods—such as crying, guided imagination, oneiric (dream) questions, concentration, recitation of verses—in order to achieve these (Idel, 1988a). What is hard to decipher is the exact practices the Kabbalists employed, as what we know depends on cursory comments, and there is hardly anything resembling meditation instructions in the early texts.

An extreme exception to this rule is Rabbi Abraham Abulafia (1240–ca. 1291), who already in his lifetime developed a different strand of Kabbalah and offered the most elaborate and systematic meditation technique in the Jewish tradition until the twentieth century. I will describe his method in brief and then refer to another technique, as well as the general meditative attitude, both found in what was to be the definitive interpretation of Kabbalah, sixteenth-century Lurianic Kabbalah.

As opposed to most thirteenth-to-fourteenth-century Kabbalah, often called "Theosophic" and dealing with the structure and amelioration of the upper worlds, Abulafia's method, which he himself refers to as "Prophetic Kabbalah," focuses on the individual and promises to bring the Kabbalist into direct connection with the divine. Abulafia saw himself as a follower of the famed Maimonides. The latter's *Guide to the Perplexed* offers a distinct meditative method, using concentration on Halakhic ritual and prayer to connect the mind to the Aristotelian "Agent Intellect," which Maimonides viewed as an emanation of the divine, and ending in "prophecy" (Persico, 2016). Abulafia combined the *Guide to the Perplexed* with *Sefer Yetzirah*, a text from the first centuries CE emphasizing the magical use of the Hebrew alphabet, and introduced a two-stage technique, which first demands hastened play with letters of divine names, and then utilizes rhythmic pronunciation of these divine names, punctuated by recurring deep breathing and slow movements of the head, in order to achieve, again, "prophecy."

He presents his technique fully in two of his books, *Hayyei ha-'Olam ha-Ba'*, and *Or Ha'sekhel*. I will outline the technique instructed in the first. The other is very similar, but uses the tetragrammaton as its chosen divine name. In *Hayyei ha-'Olam ha-Ba'*, Abulafia instructs the would-be prophet to use the "72 letter name." This divine name is created by the juxtaposition of three successive biblical verses—Exodus 14, 19–21—each with exactly 72 Hebrew letters. According to Abulafia one is to write different combinations of the name's letters, "to turn them over and roll them quickly until you heart is warm with the rolling. And when you feel that your heart is very warm... you are ready to accept the [divine] affluence" (Abulafia, 2001, p. 67). Figure 6.1 shows examples of Abulafian "circles," containing explanations on the use of divine names in meditative practice.

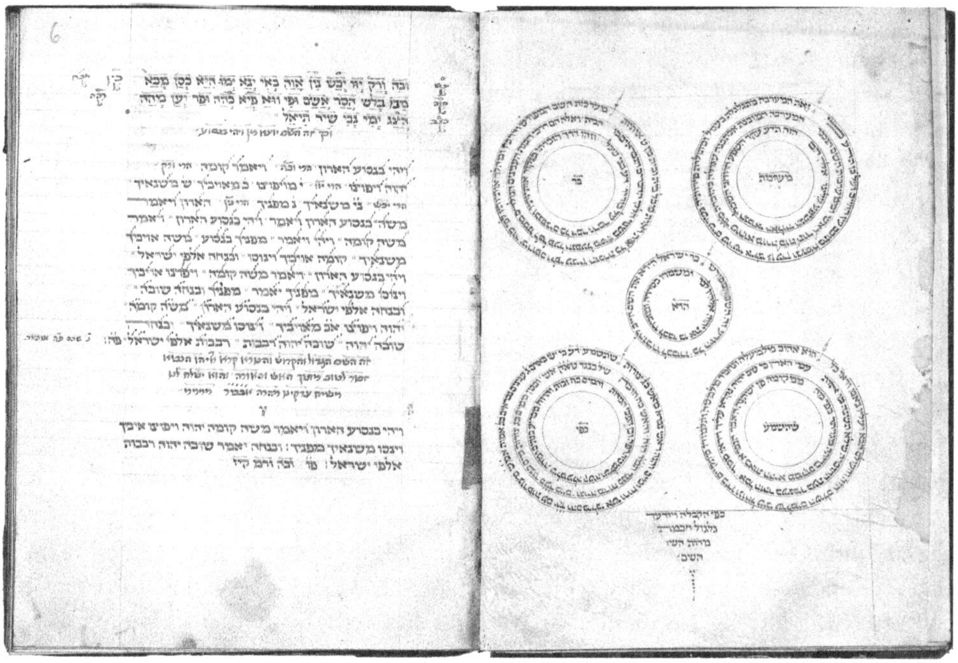

FIGURE 6.1 Meditation circles and explanations on the use of divine names from Abulafia's book, Hayye Ha'Olam Ha'Ba.

After physical and emotional arousal the practitioner begins the second stage, in which one recites traditional combinations of the letters of the said divine name. Each letter is pronounced though one whole breath, while moving the head, slowly, in the direction set by the particular phonetic punctuation given to it in the Hebrew language. Between the letters one may breathe three long breaths. This is done under fervent concentration and should open the practitioner to the effects of divine affluence. The desired result is a vision of an image that is the angel Metatron, communion with which is the knowledge of the Agent Intellect, and thus prophecy according to Abulafia.

Abulafia's Kabbalah was outspokenly different from the mainstream, and a formal ban was issued concerning him and his teaching. Nonetheless, his work had great influence in the following generations, and parts of his meditative system can be found in later mainstream Kabbalist texts, such as R. Haim Vital's *Shaarei Kedusha*. Vital, Rabbi Isaac Luria's (Ha'Ari) most prominent student and promoter, expounded his master's teaching and laid the ground for the formulation of Lurianic Kabbalah, which till today functions as the infrastructure for any further development of Kabbalah.

Sixteenth-century Lurianic Kabbalah offered quite a few meditative practices, all of which were part of an intricate, multilayered, extraordinarily complex system of esoteric lore and practice. The Lurianic Kabbalist envisaged himself as an intrinsic part of the divine machine, encompassing the whole cosmos and functioning though the elaborate inter-relations of sexualized celestial forces placed within a mythical narrative of love, loss, and reunification. As the Kabbalist is an analogous microcosm to the divine macrocosm, every act of the Kabbalist on earth affects this system, and as such was to be performed with correct intention, concentration, and precision. This form of mythical consciousness (Cassirer, 1971; Pedaya, 2005) led to a life of extreme religious tension, in itself heightening awareness and serving to ritualize daily actions and transform them into meditative practices.

The transformation of daily actions into meditative practice was completed by special mental exercises called *Yichudim* and *Kavvanot*. These included the visualization and mental combination of divine names, corresponding to celestial forces. The Kabbalist, while performing a Halakhic action (typically in prayer), would imagine and concentrate on divine names. These were analogous to the divine powers, which the exact action the Kabbalist took was supposed to affect (Fine, 1987). Mentally combining these names would aid in rectifying the relationship between said powers, that is, unifying them. This in turn, again by the magical principal of correspondences between macro- and microcosm, would also modify and advance the Kabbalist's soul.

Over and above this daily, indeed hourly, ardor, there were specific meditative techniques. One of these, which will be brought here for illustrative purposes, was the recitation of verses from the *Mishnah*. This method was known among Kabbalists of sixteenth-century Safed (northern Israel), with Vital developing it and describing it most clearly. According to Vital one should be alone, wear a *talith* (prayer shawl), close the eyes, and "leave materiality as if your soul left the body and rose to the heavens." Then one should recite a specific verse from the *Mishnah* very quickly, while intending to "join your soul with the soul of the sage who mentioned that verse." In due course the soul of the sage enters the Kabbalist's soul, and "while you recite the verse he will talk in your mouth, and greet you. And everything you will then think to ask him he will answer you, talk through your mouth while your ear is listening. And not you but he will talk from yourself" (Vital, 2005, p. 154).

Here we find the use of mantra-like recitation in order to summon an angelic being, or, in naturalistic terms, in order to enter a state of trance and experience automatic speech. The practical application of this meditation—learning answers to questions asked—is a prevailing characteristic of Jewish mysticism, which customarily is not satisfied with the experiential dimension alone, but wishes to acquire knowledge or power at the end of the spiritual journey (Idel, 2000).

Hasidism

Hasidism opens a new age in the Jewish mystical and meditative tradition. As the embodiment of the first modern religious awakening in Judaism it proclaimed no less than a religious revolution. By regarding the individual as a modern subject, God as immanent, and personal emotional experience as a direct connection with the divine, Hasidism offered a new way to imagine and express the Jewish relationship with the divine, and it continues to be an almost inescapable inspiration for any contemporary Jewish attempt at spiritual revival.

Coming to the fore in Eastern Europe at the second half of the eighteenth century, Hasidism internalized the elaborate Kabbalistic celestial structures. Emphasizing inner, not upper rectification, it demoted the huge Kabbalistic body of complex esoteric lore, underlined individual internal experience and transformation, and dramatically democratized the mystical journey. No longer an endeavor restricted to the learned elite, the direct contact with the divine could now be potentially realized by anyone, while simplicity, lack of intellectual sophistication and unpretentiousness might actually be an advantage. Following a Romantic-like ethos, Hasidism favored sincerity, intention, and experience over knowledge, precision, and ritual. It situated these as the elements from which its meditative path was constructed and offered a radical refashioning of Jewish mysticism.

It might be said that Hasidism popularized the religious ethos of Abraham Abulafia, in which every individual is invited to take a personal spiritual journey. On the other hand, relegating Lurianic lore to the periphery came with the loss of its specific, systemized meditative exercises. Accentuating the emotional realm through a Romantic prism also did not encourage adopting or developing systemized techniques, and so Hasidism, at least until it's third generation, offers no detailed meditative method.

What it does offer is a new attitude toward the body and its emotive capacities. For Hasidism, sense impressions, feelings and emotional experience are perceived as elements of divine presence (Seeman, 2008). The divine, as it were, cascades down and manifests in the flesh of the Hasid as emotions, especially during prayer. This "light," "abundance," "brain-stuff," or "sperm" enters the Hasid and is perceived as divine embodiment. It is thus through both stimulating the emotions and being in close attention to them that Hasidic meditation usually proceeds, and although any action is suitable as a basis for this practice, it is usually executed in prayer.

A seminal example for this can be found in the Ba'al Shem Tov's famous letter to his brother-in-law, R. Abraham Gershon of Kitov. Rabbi Israel Ben Eliezer, the Ba'al Shem Tov, is considered the founder of the Hasidic movement. Born circa 1700 and active until his death in 1760, the Ba'al Shem Tov can be typologically labeled as a shaman. He treated ailments using divine names, expelled demons, and wandered in what is today west Ukraine, gathering a circle of followers whom he taught by words and action. He wrote almost nothing, the letter to his brother-in-law being a rare exception. In this text he gives very concise instructions for Hasidic meditation:

> In prayer and study and every act of speaking, whatever comes from your lips, intend to unite there, because in every letter and letter there are worlds and souls and divine essence and they rise and connect and unite with one another, and then the letters connect and unite and become a word and unite in true unification in God, and include your soul with them in every way mentioned, and all the worlds unite as one and rise and there is great joy and bliss to no end.
>
> (Ba'al Shem Tov, 2008, p. 40)

The Ba'al Shem Tov directs his brother-in-law to concentrate on whatever he is saying, not only on the semantic level, but on the audio level (Idel, 2000, p. 102). The underlying assumption is that divine essence is in the letters and their respective sounds, and that combining letters into words unites the divine in them. This approach is linked to Hasidism's theology of immanence. The depreciation of the importance of metaphysics follows the decrease in the status of the removed, transcendental God. Mainstream Jewish tradition always believed in the possibility of communication, even dialogue, with the divine, but in Lurianic Kabbalah, as mentioned above, the divine is no longer a remote persona to be engaged discursively with, but a succession of levels of divine imminence, of which the Kabbalist is an organic part, acting in, through, and on It. Hasidism further increases the divine's presence in the material world and in persons, internalizing the divine drama and designating an extremely positive value to feelings and emotions.

Thus R. Jacob Joseph of Polonne, one of the Ba'al Shem Tov's prominent followers, writes that "[t]he main meaning of the [divine] names' *Kavvanot* mentioned in the Lurianic path is not the literal one [*Ke'peshuto*], but rather to cling [*Le'davek*] himself there" (Jacob Joseph, 1973, p. 141). Clinging, or *Devequt*, was a central Hasidic ideal, meaning communion, and indeed union, with the divine, through concentration, awareness, and intimacy with the Hasid's actions and with the feelings aroused from these actions. *Devequt* substitutes the intricate and complex Lurianic combinations of divine names, thus, in effect, displacing the metaphysical world as the focal field of the practitioner and replacing it with inner intentionality and experience. The practice of *Devequt* generates an experience of pleasure or bliss, which, as it is construed as divine presence, is interpreted as contact with the divine. In different Hasidic courts *Devequt* will imply inner transformation. This transformation is often understood as a progressive shedding of dimensions of the self, a process that is considered as a precondition for intimate contact, if not union, with the divine. Thus the Magid of Mezeritch, the other prominent follower of the Ba'al Shem Tov, writes (Dov Baer, 2008, pp. 121–122):

> In prayer he must put all his strength in the words, and proceed from letter to letter until he forgets about the physical body, imagining the letters join and connect to each other, and that is a great pleasure. Imagine, if it's a great pleasure in physicality, how much more so in spirituality, and that is the world of *Yetzira* [lit., formation]. Then he will proceed to the letters of thought, and will not voice what he is saying, and thus he enters the world of *Beriah* [lit., creation]. And then he proceeds to the quality of *Ayin* [lit., nothingness], and that is the world of *Azilut* [lit., emanation], the level of *Chokhmah* [lit., wisdom].

The "worlds" mentioned are Lurianic metaphysical categories referring to upper spiritual realms. Here the ascent through them is done by descending inwardly, relinquishing levels of personality (body, senses, and finally self), though, interestingly, not pleasure, at least not initially. Putting "all his strength" in prayer means concentrating on the words, as mentioned above. This alone will raise the practitioner from the lowest, basic level, *Asiya* (lit., work), to the level of *Yetzira*. Omitting sound, and, arguably, concentrating further, thus disconnecting from the senses, brings the inner journey to *Beriah*. Finally, though further concentration, the practitioner achieves complete self-annulment in the level of *Azilut*, which also corresponds, according to Kabbalistic maps, to the emanation of the first divine entity after the godhead, *Chokhmah*. Metaphysical worlds are thus turned into psychological states, and a mystical path that would once connect the Kabbalist to the upper realms is now perceived as a gradual interior exfoliation of self-stuff. This ends with the dissolution of the self, perceived as the connection with the highest divine level humanly approachable. As the Magid's prominent adherent and founder of the Chabad (Lubavitch) Hasidic court writes: "[In divine worship] the most important thing is achieving the level of *Ayin* [lit., nothingness], when he is included in the Infinite, blessed be He, and annuls himself to all reality totally"(Shneur Zalman, 1981, p. 61). Such explicit reports of absolute annulment of the self are not common. More often the pinnacle of the meditative path will be described through images of contact or unification with the divine. Moreover, for some Hasidic masters this end point is devoid of characteristics; for others the practitioner still experiences pleasure, or rather bliss, perhaps analogous to the bliss reported by yogis or Buddhist meditators in states of internal absorption (Austin, 2006; Brown, 1986).

The first generations of the Hasidic movement gave no clearer meditative instructions. There is almost an inverse relation between the emphatic calls for a personal, mystical connection with the divine and the elaborated methods textually recorded. Though definitely Kabbalistically erudite, the Hasidic masters' methods were mostly simple, mediated by neither complex esoteric lore nor systematic practices. This changed in the third generation of the movement (meaning the pupils of the pupils of the Ba'al Shem Tov) and beyond, though not in a dramatic way. The Chabad Hasidic court, a prominent branch of the tree of Hasidism, is an exception, as it presented, since beginning of the nineteenth century, a systemized mystical path and meditative method, to an extent returning to characteristics of Lurianic Kabbalah (Persico, 2016). In the following we will nevertheless focus on Bratslav Hasidism, as the method it presented remains a central inspiration for contemporary Jewish meditation, and comparison of its origin with its current manifestations will allow us to further grasp the shifts in emphasis and direction within the Jewish Meditative tradition.

Bratslav Hasidism

Rabbi Nachman of Bratslav (1772–1810), great-grandson of the Ba'al Shem Tov, was a brilliant exponent of Hasidism. In his short life he managed to create a unique Hasidic court, which would continue leaderless after his death, often ridiculed and harassed, until experiencing a tremendous sociological and cultural revival since the 1990s. Rabbi

Nachman's teachings are of an engaging, existentialist tone, broadening, rather than settling, theological complexities. Our concern will be his contribution to the Jewish meditative tradition, which is embodied in the practice of *Hitbodedut*. The term itself has had a long history in the Jewish mystical tradition, but contrary to the usual use of it, denoting mental concentration (Idel, 1988b), R. Nachman often uses it in its basic and literal meaning, which simply means going into seclusion. This practice, which R. Nachman ordered his followers to devote a daily hour to, comprises usually of the Hasids verbally laying their souls bare before God. Ideally however, Bratslav *Hitbodedut* is meant to offer a framework for intense meditative practice, with an end goal of unifying the practitioner with the divine.

Discourse 52 of R. Nachman's most important monograph, *Likutey Moharan*, is one of the main sequences in which R. Nachman explains *Hitbodedut* as a meditative practice and a mystical path (Nachman, 1997, p. 119):

> To acquire that, to be included in his Root (*lehikalel be'shorsho*), that is to go back and be included in the unity of God blessed be He, which is Imperative Reality (*mechuyav ha'Metziut*). That cannot be accomplished by any means other than annulment (*bitul*). That he nullifies himself completely. Until he is included in the unity of God blessed be He. And there is no way to accomplish annulment, but through *Hitbodedut*. Because by going into *Hitbodedut* and laying out a talk between him and his Maker, through that he achieves annulment of all the lusts and bad traits, till he achieves nullification of all his corporality (*gashmiyuto*), and to be included in his Root.... and he should turn his heart and mind (*libo ve'da'ato*) from all matters of this world, and nullify all, till he achieves true annulment.... And later still something remains of him etc., and later that too shall be annulled, until nothing remains of him. And when he achieves true nullification, then his spirit (*nafsho*) is included in his Root, that is in Him blessed be He, which is Imperative Reality. Then the entire world is included with his spirit in his Root, that is Imperative Reality, because everything depends on Him, as we said, and then all the world is made by Him as if it is Imperative Reality.

According to these instructions, *Hitbodedut*, culminating in *unio mystica*, is a multileveled process. First, it cleanses one from bad traits and lusts. This includes, as the final and ultimate point, sexual lust (in the above text R. Nachman refers to sexual lust with the adverb "etc.," a common convention in the Jewish mystical tradition). Sexual passion is the primal passion according to R. Nachman, and nullifying it nullifies the self (Mark, 2011), enabling the practitioner to unite with his Root, that is, with the divine. Finally, the whole world is raised to the level of "as if... Imperative Reality," meaning, arguably, seen as God by the practitioner. This therefore is the supreme accomplishment of *Hitbodedut*.

But how is this done? The text above mentions "turn[ing] his heart and mind from all matters of this world," so obviously a degree of mental seclusion is required, but what else? Here, as is characteristic of Hasidism, emotional experience plays a crucial role.

In the second volume of *Likutey Moharan* (i.e., *tinyana*), discourse 99, R. Nachman underscores the emotional extent that his followers should reach in *Hitbodedut* (Nachman, 1997, p. 83):

> That the primary element of *Hitbodedut* and the talk between him and his Maker in wholeness is that he lays before God blessed be He his words so thoroughly, that he will be very close to abdicating his soul, perish the thought (*Khas Ve'Shalom*), until he almost dies, perish the thought, until his soul is tied to his body only by a thread because of all his real sorrow and longing and craving to God blessed be He.

According to R. Nachman the monologue before God is supposed to bring the Hasid to an ecstatic emotional fervor. Longing for the divine is manifested as an overwhelming outflowing of emotion, so much so that the practitioner is close to complete mental, perhaps also physical, breakdown. This annuls the passions, and finally nullifies the self, leading to the goal as expressed above. *Likutey Moharan tinyana*, part 95 (p. 82), makes a similar point: "On the matter of *Hitbodedut* and the talk between him and his Maker and the saying of psalms and supplications and requests, it is very good when able to say them with a whole heart, so that he will be allowed to cry before the Lord blessed be He." The meditative path R. Nachman lays out is therefore ecstatic: in order to reach self-annulment and *unio mystica* it is imperative that our mind will not be occupied by daily matters, and then will be filled with sorrow, longing, and weeping anguish, with the divine as the object of craving. This brings the practitioner to an annulment of the self and oneness with the divine.

Obviously, most followers of R. Nachman did not practice *Hitbodedut* this way, and the path laid out here is meant for the more accomplished individuals. This remains, however, the end-goal of *Hitbodedut*, marking it as another significant step in the Jewish meditative tradition. As we shall see, it will play a role in later Jewish meditative practices.

The Rabbi of Piaseczno

The twentieth century initiates a new era in the history of Jewish meditative techniques. Both before and after World War Two—a defining event in Jewish history—Jewish spiritual leaders offer practices that are in principal ways different from any before. Introspective meditation, demanding awareness (not concentration), was introduced, and the focus was generally turned from the mental manipulation of divine names, or the concentration on the words of prayer, to reflective investigation of consciousness.

One should not get the impression that the whole field of Jewish meditation changed—Jewish meditative circles were always characterized by a high level of diversity, and still are—but a new paradigm was adopted, one that not only places the inner realms, as in the Hasidic movement, at the center of the meditative path, but lays special stress on mindfully analyzing them. Following the move away from metaphysics that began with Hasidism, Kabbalistic lore was further sidelined, as was also the intentional vector leading up and away from the practitioner. Hasidism's emphasis on the imminent presence of the divine was now the simple, matter-of-fact presupposition, and the remote and personal dimensions of God, once distinctive attributes of the Jewish religious tradition, were almost totally abandoned within these circles. We shall witness these developments in the teachings of two modern Neo-Hasidic writers, one from the beginning of the twentieth century, and one from the beginning of the twenty-first.

Most meditation practiced today in the Jewish world can be attributed to the ideational and social circles of Neo-Hasidism. Defining Neo-Hasidism as the deliberate and conscious attempt to draw inspiration, tools, and cultural capital from early Hasidic texts and practices in order to bring about a contemporary spiritual revival (Persico, 2014), we can trace the phenomenon to the beginning of the twentieth century. At that time two divergent streams of Neo-Hasidism may be discerned. The first, related to the work of Martin Buber (1878–1965), was antinomian, using the Hasidic emphasis on inner work as legitimation for dispensing with the Halakha. The second, which can be labeled Orthodox Neo-Hasidism, tried to rejuvenate traditional Judaism by infusing it with Hasidic spirit. To this second strand of Neo-Hasidism belongs Kalonymus Kalman Shapira, the Rabbi of Piaseczno, whose meditative system will now be briefly expounded.

Shapira, born in 1889 in a small town near Warsaw, was the descendent of a distinguished line of Hasidic masters. During the 1920s, witnessing the breakdown of traditional Jewish society around him due to secularization, and disappointed with the state Hasidism was in, he wished to revitalize observant Judaism through "true Hasidism," founding groups of "holy friends" who would study and engage in spiritual exercises together. He wrote several instruction manuals for the formation of such groups, most of which were not published during his life, but hidden in the Warsaw Ghetto. He was murdered by the Nazis in Trawniki concentration camp in 1943.

Shapira's works present a dramatic development in the history of Jewish meditative techniques, offering a complete, elaborate system of meditation based on guided imagination and mindful awareness, and revealing profound analysis of the workings of the human mind. As the *summum bonum* of his spiritual path Shapira places the realization of prophecy, though for him this does not manifest as a vision, followed by a mission, from God, but as an internal experience that transforms the senses of the individual, allowing one to perceive the divine presence on earth. The path itself is divided into two stages: the first involves the arousal of emotional excitement in the Hasid's body; the second comprises the inner investigation of said arousal, which is enhanced and followed by mindful awareness.

"Hasidism," teaches Shapira, "is the path of prophecy, and the precondition for the gift from above is an unveiled spirit [*nefesh*]" (Shapira, 2001, p. 15). In order for the spirit to bear itself in front of its owner, its contents need to be clearly perceived. For that, they need to be highlighted. Excitement fleshes out the contents of the spirit, while at the same time weakening the stream of discursive thought, which is obstructing the view to the spirit. This is therefore the first step of Shapira's meditative path. "Excitement is the beginning of the revelation of the spirit," writes Shapira (Ibid.), and he duly suggests a method of generating excitement. Here again we find the perception of excitement as the presence of the divine. Indeed, as Don Seeman incisively notes (Seeman, 2008, pp. 477–478), Shapira takes for true the then-popular anti-Semitic stereotype of Jews as effeminate and emotional—but sees it as a boon: "The sons of Israel tend by their nature to nervousness...as at their root they are sons of prophets" (Shapira, 2001, p. 22). Prophets are nervous people, it seems, and being nervous helps one achieve prophesy.

Shapira holds that excitement is generated by guided imagination, that is the intentional imagination of exciting content (oneself in the Exodus from Egypt, in the Temple in Jerusalem, etc.). The excitement generated is "the light of holiness," which allows the purging of confusing thoughts and the discovery of the inner worlds. This discovery is done through mindful awareness of the excited body and psyche, which in turn strengthens the ability to be mindfully aware: "this is our goal and the goal of our group: to enhance the consciousness, to draw it forward and to widen it and to strengthen it, and not only is this a revelation of the consciousness but it is a revelation of the spirit" (Shapira, 1973, p. 36). Note that in order to write about consciousness Shapira uses the word *Machshava*, "thought" in Hebrew, as in his time Hebrew did not yet have a direct translation (see Persico, 2016, pp. 173–176).

The revelation of the spirit is a crucial step on the path to the revelation of God. Widening and strengthening consciousness allows one to detach from discursive thought. Much like practices that can be found in contemporary versions of Buddhist Vipassanā meditation, Shapira instructs his followers to "observe with your awareness the wild fooling around" of thought, until the thoughts "grow weaker up to a point where you really have, as if with a broom, cleaned your brain" (Shapira, 2001, p. 129; "brain" here means "mind," another word missing, till this day, from the Hebrew language). And it is with a clean mind that one has the vision of God: "if man would make still and stop for an hour his entire stream of thoughts and wishes, the portion of God would be revealed to him without any cover" (Shapira, 2011, p. 27). This is the goal of the Shapira's meditative path. He emphasizes that he is not talking about any vision of heavenly spheres, nor cutting off the senses so as not to see the world. "He will see the world, but will see the sacredness of God on it" (Shapira, 1973, p. 26).

Shapira writes about an inner transformation that drops the scales from one's eyes and allows the practitioner to see the presence of God in the world. A "new sense" awakes in such a person, which enables the seeing "on all the world only lights and sacredness" (Shapira, 1973, p. 32; Shapira, 1957, p. 108). That is a degree of Prophecy, writes Shapira, and the highest achievement humans can realize. In naturalistic terms, Shapira's system aims at the weakening of the sense of self by the manipulation of consciousness through mindful awareness. This quiets down the "stream of thoughts and wishes" and dilutes the apparent boundary between subjective and objective realms, causing an experience that can be interpreted as seeing the presence of the divine in material reality (Persico, 2016, pp. 35–42). Shapira's meditative path is wholly internal, presenting an extreme point of departure from the generation-long quest in the Jewish mystical tradition of ascending above, in mind if not in actual body.

Rabbi Israel Isaac Besancon

The contemporary Neo-Hasidic field in Israel is in large part the playing ground of multiple offshoots of the Bratslav court. Since the 1990s the decedents of Rabbi Nachman have witnessed an impressive bourgeoning, with the Hasidic movement welcoming tens of thousands of Ba'al Teshuva (BT) Jews, that is, Jews who are "returning" from a secular lifestyle and adopting a religiously observant one. Indeed, the original, Haredi (Ultra-Orthodox) part of the court, for generations a small, at-times-scorned group, is now experiencing unprecedented adoration, and at the same time becoming a small minority in the versatile kaleidoscope that is contemporary Bratslav. Following their origin, once-secular individuals bring with them the dispositions and preferences of contemporary Western culture. In order to suit their needs, and no less so in order to attract many more, the Hasidic movement offers new forms of worship, among them, and expressively stated, is "Jewish Meditation," which is the title given to *Hitbodedut*.

Contemporary Bratslav meditation uses the traditional daily *Hitbodedut* practice as its foundation, but as we shall shortly see, changes it according to current tastes and sensitivities. This meditation is offered in the context of varied popularizations of Rabbi Nachman's teachings, taught by charismatic rabbis, often more spiritual teachers then halakhic instructors. One of these is Rabbi Israel Isaac Besancon (b. 1944), a French-born BT himself, who today heads a community in Tel Aviv. Besancon has written more than ten books; one of them, *Hitbodedut: To Talk With God*, is devoted to the practice.

For Besancon *Hitbodedut* is "a secret" Rabbi Nachman had disclosed, and the key to "private redemption" (Besancon, 2001, pp. 3–4). Unlike Rabbi Nachman, however, Besancon's *Hitbodedut* does not employ an ecstatic emotional outburst in order to nullify the self, but calm and composure so as to investigate it. As he writes:

> In its essence, the goal of Hitbodedut is to disconnect our consciousness, even partly, from all the stimulations that pull it in different and scattered directions, in order to connect it back to its spiritual Root. This temporary disconnection from the noisy surroundings brings calm, mental stability, that help us establish a personal relationships with our Maker, to learn to be assisted by Him, blessed be He, and to win a measure of *Devequt*—which promises us supreme spiritual happiness.
>
> (Besancon, 2001, p. 5)

Besancon keeps the connection of the soul with its Root, though this is done not by ecstatic annulment of the passions and self, but by disconnection from the senses. Following the mental stability that arises from such disconnection, we acquire a measure of *Devequt*, a common Hasidic term denoting conscious and felt intimate connection with the divine. The practitioner becomes supremely happy, and that through assistance from God. Besancon elaborates on this further:

> As far as we will be able to persist in these [*Hitbodedut*] meetings, after a few times we will talk to God blessed be He in our language, we will be able, sometimes, to feel His presence. In the light of this splendor we shall be able with ease to look inside as well, to our real, inner self. Without make-up or fear our ego will be revealed to us under the generous supervision of the divine Being. In this way the secrets of our soul will be disclosed to our eyes, slowly, and we will be surprised to discover in it hidden glamour, which was waiting to be unveiled. At the same time, the spiritual light will shine on the complicated net of our feelings, and expose the sources of wrong patterns of thought and behavior, that we were not aware existed.
>
> (Besancon, 2001, p. 6)

Besancon's interpretation of *Hitbodedut* is clearly different than Rabbi Nachman's. It emphasizes introspection, self-analysis, and the discovery of inner treasures. Most importantly, the divine here is not an end-goal to be reached, but a tool to be used on the way: God's light and supervision allows one to unveil one's soul, to observe and correct wrong "patterns of thought and behavior" and to find concealed light. While for Rabbi Nachman the practice of *Hitbodedut* involved a craze of lamentation ending with *unio mystica*, in Besancon's *Hitbodedut* we find an inner-directed psychological process of therapeutic self-improvement, ending with internal illumination and happiness. Besancon's language is clearly correlative to that of contemporary mindfulness meditation, and is probably influenced by it. It is interesting to consider why Besancon decided to change Rabbi Nachman's meditative instructions. We must ask what social need or purpose is served by changing Rabbi Nachman's *Hitbodedut* from a dialogical, upward-ascending relationship with the divine to an introspective, wellness-procuring quest aided by the divine.

The Jewish Meditative Subjective Turn

As noted above, the twentieth century saw a significant change in the general character of Jewish meditative techniques. Mindfulness is introduced, and in many circles replaces concentration as a basic building block of the practice. The techniques also become much more introverted, and the intentional direction aims within, and not above, toward the heavens. Calm and composure, in general, replace ecstasy, and the methods further depart from the traditional rituals and laws that once served as a platform for meditation. The type of mystical experience aimed at also changes, and the direction that began with Hasidism, namely manipulation of the sense of self, is accentuated (Persico, 2016).

These developments should be understood as a direct consequence of the transformation of Jewish society, whether in Israel, the United States, or Europe, from traditional to modern. Excluding enclaves of radical Ultra-Orthodoxy, as modern subjects, members of Jewish communities find sources of meaning, authority, and identity in autonomous, internal realms of thought and feeling. As such these communities are of course no different from the general Western society, which over the last few hundred years has gone through what different social theorists call a "subjective turn." This term signifies a growing engrossment with inner, psychological life, finding within ourselves not only hitherto unnoticed levels and depths, but attributing these with meaning and authority that had up to this era been reserved to heteronomous traditions and norms (Taylor, 1989). A life lived in such a way undermines the authority of social roles and structures extraneous to the self, and turns inside for answers, meaning, and validity: in reason, emotions, or subjective experience. In the field of religion, the phenomenon created is what we call "spirituality," often identified with the New Age cultic milieu (Heelas & Woodhead, 2005).

As Steven Cohen and Arnold Eisen write (Cohen & Eisen, 2000, p. 2),

> Today's Jews, like their peers in other religious traditions, have turned inward in the search for meaning. They have moved away from the organizations, institutions, and causes that used to anchor identity and shape behavior.... The principal authority for contemporary American Jews, in the absence of compelling religious norms and communal loyalties, has become the sovereign self.

"American Jews" here stand for Jews who are part of Western contemporary culture, the same culture that introduced the logic that in the field of religion produces contemporary spirituality. What is in fact happening is a massive shift in the character of religion, which is turning from a communal social system into an individual ethical path. Although there were always individuals who took off on personal spiritual quests, this religious vector has become at this time unprecedented in its popularity and in the almost exclusive legitimation it claims. For many, individualistic, therapeutic, self-directed spirituality is considered the only authentic form of religion, while organized religion is sometimes presented not only as inferior, but as a veritable obstacle to "true" spirituality. These developments increase the demand for personal spiritual techniques, and thus boost the demand for inner-directed meditation. The public search for "Jewish Meditation" is thus at an all times high. Pointedly, the meditation practices contemporary Jewish spiritual seekers want are, as mentioned, quite different than those traditionally practiced.

The late modern and contemporary era introduces, therefore, a novel and challenging direction in the history of the Jewish meditative tradition. Never before have Jewish meditative practices been so popular, and never before have they been so focused on the self, and specifically on its internal life. Emphasizing the individual's inner life comes with stressing the need for inner transformation and makes subjective experience the measure for religious significance, even pertinence. It thus relocates the center of religious drama from the community to the individual, and from the covenant between the People of Israel with God to the experience of the subject with the divine—which she or he finds internally.

Quite obviously, this internalization of religious significance and authority is at odds with the predominant direction the Jewish religious tradition has historically emphasized, underlying community, ritual, and heteronomous authority. A Jewish spiritual path whose inner logic demands the autonomy of the individual and which seeks religious experience as a goal and a mark of authenticity is virtually antithetical to the inner logic of traditional Judaism, understanding itself, as mentioned, as a communal commitment to a sacred covenant. Today even in Orthodox circles we will find individuals that decide to relinquish parts of the Jewish law on the basis of intuition, feelings, or the wish to further their individual spiritual path. Ritual, law, and custom stands at a point of tension with individual psychological states and impulses.

Tension is not univocally a negative thing. It may be quite fruitful. It may also be destructive. The way different parts of the Jewish world respond to this challenge will decide whether they see it as just another obstacle to be weathered through, or as a chance for development, through an inner transformative act comparable to that which its individual meditators wish to achieve.

References

Primary Sources

Abulafia, A. (2001). *Hayyei ha-'olam ha-ba'* [Hebrew]. (Amnon Gross, Ed.). Jerusalem: Barazani.

Ba'al Shem Tov. (2008). *Igeret aliyat ha'neshama* [Hebrew]. Tel Aviv: Yedioth Sefarim.

Besancon, I. I. (2001). *Hitbodedut: To talk with God* [Hebrew]. Tel Aviv: Shir Chadash.

Dov Baer of Mezeritch. (2008). *Magid devarav l'Yaakov* [Hebrew]. Tel Aviv: Yedioth Sefarim.

Jacob Joseph of Polonne. (1973). *Toldot Yaakov Yosef* [Hebrew]. Jerusalem: Agudat Beit Wielopole.

Nachman of Bratslav. (1997). *Likutey moharan* [Hebrew]. Jerusalem: Torat Ha'nezach.

Shapira, K. K. (1957). *Chovat ha'talmidim* [Hebrew]. Tel Aviv: Yahalom.

Shapira, K. K. (1973). *Benei machshava tova* [Hebrew]. Tel Aviv: Vaad Hasidei Piaseczno.

Shapira, K. K. (2001). *Hachsharat ha'avrechim* [Hebrew]. Jerusalem: Feldheim Publishers.

Shapira, K. K. (2011). *Derech ha'melech* [Hebrew]. Jerusalem: Feldheim Publishers.

Shneur Zalman of Liadi. (1981). *Ma'amarei admor ha'zaken ha'ketzarim* [Hebrew]. Brooklyn: Otzar Hasidim.

Vital, H. (2005). *Shaarei kedusha* [Hebrew]. ed. Amnon Gross. Jerusalem: Barazani.

Secondary Sources

Austin, J. H. (2006). *Zen-brain reflections: Reviewing recent developments in meditation and states of consciousness*. Cambridge, MA: MIT Press.

Brown, D. P. (1986). The stages of meditation in cross-cultural perspective. In K. Wilber, J. Engler, & D. P. Brown (Eds.), *Transformations of consciousness: Conventional and contemplative perspectives on development* (pp. 219–283). Boston: Shambala.

Cassirer, E. (1971). *The philosophy of symbolic forms: Vol. 2. Mythical thought*. (R. Manheim, Trans.). New Haven, CT: Yale University Press.

Cohen, S. M., & Eisen, A. M. (2000). *The Jew within: Self, family and community in America.* Bloomington: Indiana University Press.
Fine, L. (1987). The contemplative practice of Yichudim in Lurianic Kabbalah. In A. Green (Ed.), *Jewish spirituality: From the sixteenth century revival to the present* (pp. 65–98). New York: Crossroad.
Garb, J. (2011). *Shamanic trance in modern Kabbalah.* Chicago: University of Chicago Press.
Heelas, P., & Woodhead, L. (2005). *The spiritual revolution: Why religion is giving way to spirituality.* Malden: Wiley.
Idel, M. (1988a). *Kabbalah: New perspectives.* New Haven, CT: Yale University Press.
Idel, M. (1988b). Hitbodedut as concentration in Jewish philosophy. *Jerusalem Studies in Jewish Thought 7*, 39–60.
Idel, M. (2000). *Hasidism: Between ecstasy and magic* [Hebrew]. Jerusalem: Schoken.
Idel, M. (2002). *Absorbing perfections: Kabbalah and interpretation.* New Haven, CT: Yale University Press.
Idel, M. (2005). *Ascensions on high in Jewish mysticism: Pillars, lines, ladders.* Budapest: Central European University Press.
Lewis, I. M. (2003). *Ecstatic religion: A study of shamanism and spirit possession.* London: Routledge.
Mark, Z. (2011). *Revelation and rectification in the revealed and hidden writings of R. Nachman of Breslav.* Jerusalem: Magnes.
McKillop, H. (2004). *The ancient Maya: New perspectives.* Santa Barbara: ABC-CLIO.
Pedaya, H. (2002). *Vision and speech: Models of revelatory experience in Jewish mysticism* [Hebrew]. Culver City, CA: Cherub Press.
Pedaya, H. (2005). The mystical experience and the religious world in Hasidism [Hebrew]. *Da'at* 55, 73–108.
Persico, T. (2014). Neo-Hasidic revival: Expressivist uses of traditional lore. *Modern Judaism* 34(3), 278–308.
Persico, T. (2016). *The Jewish meditative tradition* [Hebrew]. Tel Aviv: Tel Aviv University Press.
Schafer, P. (1981). *Synopse zur Hekhalot Literatur.* Tubingen: J.C.B. Mohr (Paul Siebeck).
Seaford, R. (2013). The politics of the mystic chorus. In J. Billings, F. Budelmann, F. Macintosh (Eds.), *Choruses, ancient and modern.* Oxford: Oxford University Press.
Seeman, D. (2008). Ritual efficacy, Hasidic mysticism, and 'useless suffering' in the Warsaw Ghetto. *Harvard Theological Review 101*(3–4), 465–505.
Taylor, C. (1989). *Sources of the self: The making of the modern identity.* Cambridge, MA: Harvard University Press.
Uffenheimer, B. (1973). *Ancient prophecy in Israel* [Hebrew]. Jerusalem: The Magnes Press.

CHAPTER 7

WESTERN CHRISTIANITY AND MEDITATION

MARTIN LAIRD

Introduction

This chapter examines key components of the tradition of Christian meditation, its "practice of contemplation," from the fourth through fourteenth centuries. Beginning with Jesus' regularly going to pray in solitude, and especially his temptation in the desert, it examines five signal authors or traditions that best express key features of Christian contemplative practice: Evagrius Ponticus, the Jesus Prayer tradition, John Cassian, Guigo II on *lectio divina*, and the anonymous English author of *The Cloud of Unknowing*. For reasons of space this chapter ends its investigations with the fourteenth century text, *The Cloud of Unknowing*. Therefore it will not examine the contributions of, among many others, the mediaeval German lineage, especially Meister Eckhart, the late medieval Flemish master, Jan van Ruuysbroec or the Carmelite and Ignatian traditions. These authors are studied in magisterial fashion by Bernard McGinn (2005, 2012, 2017). However, the foundations for the most important teachings regarding the concrete *practice* of contemplation are found in the authors and texts that are the subject of this chapter. Their contributions were fundamental to later developments and remain so today.

Contemplation trains the mind. Interior silence is the ideal condition for overcoming the illusion of separation from God. Training the mind involves disciplines of concentration and expanding awareness that gradually declutter the mind and reveal the silent ground of our being in God. The authors we shall meet understood that the mind is anything but silent. Its wild thoughts and unrealistic expectations of life and love maintain the sense of being separate from God and others. To give the attention something to concentrate on and gently repeat gradually quietens the wondering, roving mind. A sign of a quiet mind is an increasing inner sense of vast, uncluttered awareness and an ever more expansive love of God and neighbor. Training the mind also involves spiritual battle. The prayer word and the cultivation of silent contemplation are strengthened by such warfare, and thus the mind is strengthened and its energy moved from fragmentation to the focused inner silence of togetherness with God. Each of the authors we will examine works with these themes.

Learning to deal with distracting thoughts is a primary focus of the practice of contemplation. Whether the distractions are mild, silly, deeply afflictive, or even deceptively pious they hold captive our attention with the result that we remain profoundly ignorant of the seat of our deepest identity, our very life, that is, as St. Paul says, "hidden with Christ in God" (Col 3:3). Similarly, St. Augustine says, "Unquiet people recoil from the Holy Spirit. They love quarrelling. They love argument. In their restlessness they do not allow the silence of the Lord's Sabbath to enter their lives. Against such restlessness we are offered a kind of Sabbath of the heart. As if God were saying 'Stop being so restless, quieten the uproar in your minds. Let go of the idle fantasies that fly around in your head.' God is saying, 'Be still and see that I am God' (Ps 46)" (Augustine of Hippo, 1992, p. 244).

Jesus: Prayer in Solitude

Christian contemplation finds its originating inspiration in Jesus' own prayer life and teachings. While we can safely presume that Jesus participated in the liturgical prayer that characterized the Jewish community in early first-century Israel, the most consistent New Testament account we have of Jesus' personal prayer life consistently emphasizes his solitary prayer. Jesus frequently goes off to an *erēmos*—a solitary or deserted place—to pray. Luke's Gospel reveals two important examples. Jesus returns to Galilee to take up his ministry of teaching, healing, and the calling of followers. "The report about him spread all the more, and great crowds assembled to listen to him and to be cured of their ailments, but he would withdraw to deserted places to pray" (Lk 5:15–16). Luke places Jesus' withdrawal into solitude between two healing stories, the healing of a leper (Lk 5:12–14) and the healing of a paralytic (Lk 5:17–26), and these healing stories are themselves bracketed by accounts of Jesus forming a community as he calls people to follow him (Lk 5:1–11). In the second of these call-stories Jesus' mountain solitude leads to his calling the twelve apostles. "In those days he departed to the mountain to pray, and he spent the night in prayer to God. When day came, he called his disciples to himself, and from them he chose Twelve, whom he also named apostles" (Lk 6:12–13). This culminates in Jesus' teachings on happiness, famously known as The Beatitudes (Lk 6:20–23). Other teachings follow. A pattern emerges in these Gospel stories of calling, healing, and compassion, which always take precedence over the Law (e.g., Lk 5:29–39; Lk 6:6–11), following on from solitary prayer.

Matthew's Gospel reveals the same pattern. After hearing of the beheading of John the Baptist, Jesus "withdrew in a boat to a deserted place by himself. The crowds heard of this and followed him. When he disembarked and saw the vast crowd, his heart was moved with pity for them, and he cured their sick" (Mt 14:13–15). As evening approaches the disciples urge Jesus to dismiss the crowds so that they can go to the villages to buy food. But "Jesus said to them, 'There is no need for them to go away; give them some food yourselves'" (Mt 14:16). From this follows the miracle of the multiplication of loaves and fishes. Immediately after this Jesus dismisses the crowds and instructs the disciples to get into the boat and precede him to the other side of the lake. As soon as the disciples depart Jesus returns to solitude: "After doing so, he went up on the mountain by himself to pray. When it was evening he was there alone" (Mt 14:23).

Once again we see Jesus' solitary prayer leading to an act of compassion, in this case the calming of fear. The sea suddenly grows stormy and the apostles' boat is being tossed about. Jesus "came toward them, walking on the sea" (Mt 14:25). Taking him to be a ghost, the disciples are terrified. In order to calm their fears Jesus says, "Take courage, it is I; do not be afraid." Peter steps out of the boat to walk across the water toward Jesus, but he becomes frightened and begins to sink. "Lord," he cried, "save me!" Immediately Jesus stretched out his hand and caught him (Mt 14:31). When they got into the boat the winds immediately die down. "Those who were in the boat did him homage, saying, 'Truly, you are the Son of God'" (Mt 14:33). The boat made shore at Gennesaret, and word of Jesus' presence spread throughout the countryside. "People brought to him all who were sick and begged him that they might touch only the tassel of his cloak, and as many as touched it were healed" (Mt 14:35–36). As before, at the center of Jesus' compassion for others is an account of his solitary prayer.

The same happens in Mark's Gospel. "Rising very early before dawn, he left and went off to a deserted place, where he prayed" (Mk 1:35). Knowing that Jesus would be praying in solitude, Simon and his companions go looking for him and having found him say, "Everyone is looking for you. He told them, 'Let us go on to the nearby villages that I may preach there also. For this purpose have I come.' So he went into their synagogues, preaching and driving out demons throughout the whole of Galilee" (Mk 1:35–39). Yet again we see Jesus going off to pray in solitude at the very center of the calling of the disciples and the compassion for and healing of many.

These examples undergird the basic pattern of the more explicitly contemplative practices that have come down to us. Key features of this pattern include solitude, community, compassion and, as we shall soon see, vigilance (or watchfulness). However, while Jesus practices periods of regular reclusion, he is not reclusive. Christian solitude expresses solidarity. Solitude joins things up. The Gospels place Jesus' periods of solitary communion with the Father—"Abba"—in the midst of building a community of followers. This includes not only his calling the apostles to follow him but also his miracles of healing and acts of compassion. Healing meant not only the healing of an affliction such as leprosy, but also the reintegration of the person back into community. Solitary prayer, healing, and the reintegration of others into community form a whole.

What did Jesus himself realize in his frequent sojourns in solitude? Neither Matthew, Mark, nor Luke actually say. Perhaps John's Gospel provides a clue. "The Father and I are one" (Jn 10:30). "Whoever has seen me has seen the Father" (Jn 14:9). Jesus' solitary prayer is the event of overcoming the illusion of separation from God.

Jesus' Teaching on How to Pray

Jesus is not only an example of prayer but also a teacher of prayer. How does Jesus teach us to pray? While The Lord's Prayer (Mt 6:9–13), commonly called the Our Father by Christians, has pride of place, Jesus also teaches us to pray in a manner far more similar to his own communing with the Father in silence and solitude: "When you pray, do not be like the hypocrites, who love to stand and pray in the synagogues and on street corners so that others may see them. Amen, I say to you, they have received their reward. But when you pray, go to your inner room, close the door, and pray to your Father in secret. And your Father who sees in secret will repay you. In praying, do not babble like the pagans, who think that they will be heard because of their many words. Do not be like them. Your Father knows what you need before you ask him" (Mt 6:5–8). Jesus emphasizes solitude and the intimacy of silent communion with God. Moreover, Jesus' teaching is a challenge to what he took to be fundamentally flawed in the religious leadership of his day: praying as a way of drawing attention to oneself; praying so as to be seen to be praying as some of the Pharisees were doing.

Another New Testament passage of signal importance is the account of Jesus' temptation in the desert (Mt 4:1–10). The devil tempts Jesus with different forms of power: power over the natural world (turning stones into bread), power over the spiritual world (the angels will come to Jesus' aid), and political power over all the kingdoms of the world if Jesus but worships the devil (Fig. 7.1).

The prolific early monastic writer, Evagrius Ponticus (344/5–399), points out that in each case Jesus *refrained* from engaging in dialogue with the devil by quoting passages from Scripture. In his book, *Talking Back*, Evagrius observes that Jesus "passed on to us what he did when tempted by Satan. In a moment of struggle, when the demons attack we must answer them with a verse from Holy Scripture" (Evagrius Ponticus, 2009, p. 4). Thus, when we try to pray in silence and are beset by an afflictive thought, let us quietly replace that thought with an appropriate phrase from Scripture quietly repeated. Thus, our mind is stilled instead of being drawn into obsessive inner chatter that results from being embattled with afflictive thoughts, images, and feelings.

Evagrius Ponticus: On Watchfulness

Evagrius Ponticus was born in Ibora, near the Black Sea (Palladius, 2015, pp. 94–98). The son of a bishop who served the rural areas, he was well connected to prominent church leaders of the day. Through a series of great successes and humiliating failures, Evagrius eventually found his way to a group of Egyptian monks in Nitria.

Among the most important and enduring of Evagrius's contributions to the Christian contemplative tradition both East and West is his teaching on inner watchfulness or vigilance that serves to declutter our minds and prepare us for "pure prayer," beyond all thoughts, images or words.

FIGURE 7.1 *The Temptation of Christ on the Mountain*, Duccio di Buoninsegna, 1308–1311.
Purchased by The Frick Collection in New York in 1927.

Fourth-century desert psychology employs the use of "demons." The demons' primary role is to keep us from praying, and their primary artillery consists of *logismos*. Their target is the human *pathos*. For Evagrius, *logismos* means an afflictive or distracting thought that steals our attention from its focus on God when we are trying to pray in silence. *Pathos* means passion in the negative sense of deeply ingrained, compulsive tendencies in the mind that cling to a thought (See chapter on "Eastern Christianity and Meditation"). The untrained mind's tendency to cling causes us to obsess to the point of inner confusion about what is fantasy and what is reality. The demons are astute strategists in this regard and are keenly aware of the psychological vulnerabilities each person has. The demons launch, so to speak, a thought or thoughts (they can team up) at a passion or passions. If the passions have not been trained by stillness, they will latch onto and cling to the thought. When this happens, an anxious inner commentary on the thought (or feeling) immediately ensues, often rather vivid. In *The Praktikos*, written for beginners in their contemplative training, Evagrius famously indicates eight of these mental patterns of anxious obsession, eight areas of life where the mind is especially vulnerable to clinging: gluttony, impurity, avarice, sadness, anger, vainglory, and pride (Evagrius, 1972, pp. 16–20).

Evagrius states plainly in *The Praktikos* that the chief role of the demons, with their artillery of thoughts, is "causing us to cease to pray so that we might not stand in the presence of God, not dare to raise our hands in supplication to one against whom we have had such frightful thoughts" (Evagrius, 1972, chap. 46, p. 29). Far from dismissing thoughts that afflict us at the time of prayer, Evagrius wants us to get to know all about them. He writes, "We must take care to recognize the different types of demons and take note of the circumstances of their coming" (Evagrius, 1972, chap. 43, p. 28). Vigilance is not a means of avoidance but of examining and warding off their malign influence. "We ought to consider which of the demons [thoughts] are less frequent in their assaults, which are the more vexatious, which are the ones which yield the field more readily and which are the more resistant" (Evagrius, 1972, chap. 43, p. 28). These of course will vary from person to person, but the advice remains the same: the monk must know the patterns of these afflictive thoughts. What sets them off? Which are more difficult to cope with, which are not especially challenging? The reason we must know everything about these thoughts is so that "we are in a position to address effective words against them, that is to say, those words which correctly characterize the one present" (Evagrius, 1972, p. 28).

In chapter 50, Evagrius continues his teaching on cultivating inner vigilance. He says that if there is anyone "who wishes to take the measure of some of the more fierce demons so as to gain experience in his monastic art, then let him keep careful watch over his thoughts" (Evagrius, 1972, p. 29). He wants us to direct our attention right at the thought(s) and know everything we can about them. Evagrius is aware that these afflictive thoughts can team up. For example, we can envy the financial success of another, especially with a view toward how we think this might affect our own reputations. In this case avarice and vainglory have teamed up. How often do they come, and how long do they remain? What triggers them? Evagrius is keenly aware that we each have different minds and hence different struggles. What thought is especially defeating for one person might be easier to cope with for another, or for yet another not be an issue at all, or only rarely. Crucial to Evagrius's teaching is that we are aware of what is going on *as it is going on* before we add any commentary, and not just upon reflection. Evagrius's contemplative training uses inner conflict to strengthen, deepen, and declutter awareness.

How does Evagrius's training in watchfulness or vigilance contribute to his teaching on prayer? In his *Chapters on Prayer* he defines prayer with desert simplicity in chapter 35: "Prayer is an ascent of the spirit to God" (Evagrius, 1972, p. 60). The spiritual motif of "ascent" is common in ancient texts. But in order to "ascend" something else must be taking place at the same time: a letting go of thoughts. Without letting go, there will be no ascent. Hence, "Prayer is the letting go of concepts" (Evagrius, 1972, p. 66; translation altered slightly). This form of imageless prayer would have been impossible before inner vigilance had been mastered. But now, being habitually free of the narrative grip of thoughts (and considerably less inner noise) we are free to let them go and simply be silent. Evagrius's emphasis on letting go of thoughts or images extends also to holy thoughts or images: "Beware of the traps your adversaries lay for you. For suddenly it may happen when you are praying purely, free from all disturbance, that some unusual or strange form appears so as to lead you into the presumptuous thought that God is actually situated there as in a place. This is calculated to persuade you...that God is something quantitative. But God is without quantity and without all outward form" (Evagrius, 1972, p. 66).

The Jesus Prayer

The Jesus Prayer is primarily associated with Eastern Christianity but is widely practiced by contemporary Western Christians as well (Johnson, 2010, p. 52). The key feature is quiet, consistent repetition of some form of the Jesus Prayer during set periods of prayer, typically in solitude, but also while walking or doing manual labor or during any activity when the discursive mind is not needed. The *Catechism of the Catholic Church* says: 'This simple invocation of faith developed in the tradition of prayer under many forms in East and West. The most usual formulation, transmitted by the spiritual writers of the Sinai, Syria and Mt. Athos, is the invocation, "Lord Jesus Christ, Son of God, have mercy on us sinners" (*Catechism*, 1994, no. 2667).

The Jesus Prayer is simple and simplifying. It leads to real virtue. "The invocation of the holy name of Jesus is the simplest way of praying always. When the holy name is repeated often by a humbly attentive heart, the prayer is not lost by heaping up empty phrases (Cf Mt 6:7), but holds fast to the Word and brings forth fruit with patience (Cf Mt 6: 7)" (Catechism, 1994, no. 2667).The historical origins of the Jesus Prayer are not easy to trace. There is (disputed) evidence that it existed from the fourth-century Egyptian desert and that it was taught to Evagrius by his teacher, Macarius. Evagrius asks Macarius, "Father, give me a word to live by." Macarius responds: "Secure the anchor rope to the rock and by the grace of God the ship will ride the devilish waves of this beguiling sea.... The ship is your heart; keep guard over it. The rope is your mind; secure it to our Lord Jesus Christ, who is the rock who has power over all the waves...because it is not difficult, is it, to say with each breath, 'Our Lord Jesus, have mercy on me: I bless thee, my Lord Jesus, help me'" (Guillaumont, 1974, p. 67.)

The oldest undisputed documentation of the use of the Jesus prayer is provided by St. Diodochos of Photiki (ca. 400–ca. 486) in his treatise "On Spiritual Knowledge and Discernment." He writes, "We should give [the intellect] nothing but the prayer, 'Lord Jesus'... Let the intellect continually concentrate on these words within its inner shrine with such intensity that it is not turned aside to any mental images" (Palmer, Sherrard, & Ware, 1979, p. 270). In Greek "Lord Jesus" is in the vocative case, which indicates direct address. We are not to cultivate any images, so this is apophatic or imageless prayer.

From early in its history there is consistent teaching of combining one's breathing with the Jesus Prayer to help silence the inner chatter of the mind (Laird, 2007). In the seventh century, St. John Climacus (579–649) writes in his influential book, *Ladder of Divine Ascent*: "Let the remembrance of Jesus be with your every breath. Then indeed you will know the value of silence" (John Climacus, 1998, p. 270, translation altered slightly). A number of teachers recommend a seated posture to stabilize the body in prayer. Egyptian monks sat on "small stools, known as *embrimia*, woven from papyrus stalks" (Harmless, 2004, p. 175). St. Gregory of Sinai (ca. 1265–1346) recommends "a seat about nine inches high" (Palmer, Sherrad, & Ware, 1979, p. 264). A prayer bench or stool has the advantage of creating a solid, tripod posture allowing for greater physical stability and enabling one to remain comfortably still. Physical stillness facilitates interior stillness. These days, in the West, the prayer bench is placed above the Achilles tendon, and one sits back on it with the result that the knees are then below the hips. Thus, the thoracic cavity opens to facilitate abdominal breathing, which we know cultivates inner calm.

Down the centuries the phrasing of the Jesus Prayer has changed and lengthened. The essential element is simply to say the holy name, "Jesus" as a profound act of faith.

John Cassian

More than any monastic figure, John Cassian (ca. 360–ca. 434) brought the wisdom of Egyptian monasticism to the Christian West. Cassian taught the practice of contemplation by suggesting the use of a *versiculum*, a prayer word or phrase drawn from Scripture. In his *Conferences*, especially Conference 10, he quotes verbatim the teachings he and his friend Germanus received ten years earlier from a monk called Isaac. Germanus seeks guidance from Isaac on the problem of the wandering, roving mind during prayer, for it is "forever wandering and is tossed in all directions like a drunk. If by chance—and not because of any effort of its own—it comes into direct encounter with something spiritual, it is powerless to hold on to it firmly and for a long time. One thought follows upon another, arriving, coming into being, ending and going away—all without the mind noticing" (Cassian, 1985, p. 131). Isaac responds:

> To keep the thought of God always in your mind you must cling totally to this formula of piety: O God, come to my assistance; Lord, make haste to help me (Ps 69:2).
>
> It is not without good reason that this verse has been chosen from the whole of Scripture as a device. It carries within it all the feelings of which human nature is capable. It can be adapted to every condition and can be usefully deployed against every temptation. It carries within it a cry of help to God in the face of every danger. It expresses the humility of a pious confession.... It conveys a sense of our frailty, the assurance of being heard, the confidence in help that is always and everywhere present. Someone forever calling out to his protector is indeed very sure of having him close by, this is the voice filled with the ardor of love and of charity. This is the terrified cry of someone who sees the snares of the enemy, the cry of someone besieged day and night and exclaiming that he cannot escape unless his protector comes to the rescue. (Cassian, 1985, pp. 132–133; translation altered slightly)

Cassian says our mind must "cling totally" to the prayer word. More than just serving as an anchor to return to when we become distracted, Cassian emphasises the importance and power of concentration. As we "cling totally" concentration deepens. Total clinging to the prayer word permits no thoughts to come between the mind and the prayer word. Concentration takes us deeper into the tremendous expanse of inner silence. Moreover, the prayer word itself is holistic. Due to its concentrating power, it gathers or centers "all the feelings of which human nature is capable." In this way the silence of a concentrated mind becomes the consummation of all other human sentiments. But most intriguingly Cassian says that intrinsic to the prayer word itself is a silent "cry of help." We are aware of our "frailty." It maintains our "confidence in help that is always and everywhere present." By this Cassian reminds us that we do not become isolated and convinced that it is up to us alone to accomplish this unassisted. The practice reminds us of our frailty and hence our need for trust and confidence in God's grace at every turn.

Such contemplation is never a means of avoiding struggle. We are involved in spiritual warfare on the contemplative path, and the prayer word serves as our battle gear in the midst of all manner of trials. "This short verse is an indomitable wall for all those struggling against the onslaught of demons. It is an impenetrable breastplate and sturdiest of shields. Whatever the disgust, the anguish, or the gloom in our thoughts, this verse keeps us from despairing of our salvation since it reveals to us the One to whom we call, the One who sees our struggles and who is never far from those who pray to Him." (Cassian, 1985, p. 133). Most tellingly Cassian reassures us that we will be protected from any despair we meet and that the prayer word becomes a vehicle of God's loving presence. For the prayer word "reveals to us the One to whom we call." (Cassian, 1985, p. 133).

To conclude this section on Cassian's *Conferences*, we must emphasize that the practice of contemplation eventually leads to union with God. Isaac is quoted as saying: "[God] will be all that we think about, all our living, all that we talk about, our very breath. And that the union of Father and Son, of Son and Father, will fill our senses and our minds. As God loves us with a love that is true and pure, a love that never breaks, we too will be joined to him in a never-ending unshakeable love, and it will be such a union that our breathing and our thinking and our talking will be God. And we will come at last to that objective which the Lord prayed to be fulfilled in us: 'That they may all be one as we are one, as I am in them and you in me so that they are utterly one' (Jn 17:22–23)."

Lectio Divina

For Christians of Late Antiquity through the late Middle Ages, the Bible was more than just the gathered writings of what came to be called the Old and New Testaments. It was itself seen as a *living* manifestation of God. Therefore, to *engage in* the art of reading Scripture was to be *engaged by* this very Mystery, incarnate in the history of ancient

Israel and in the person of Jesus the Christ. To engage in the exegesis of Scripture was more than just interpreting the many and varied historical memories preserved in the Bible. Exegesis was a spiritual practice. Scriptural exegesis was itself to embark upon a journey of inner transformation leading to loving communion with God in the silence of the text. The reading of Scripture is, therefore, a divine reading, a *lectio divina*.

As a contemplative practice *lectio divina* enjoyed a great flourishing in medieval monasticism and was also practiced by the laity throughout the Middle Ages (Alford, 1995). It remains a widely known practice to the present day. Its pre-monastic beginnings can be traced back at least to Origen of Alexandria (ca. 185–ca. 253) (Crouzel, 1961), among the most important early Christian theologians (Crouzel, 1989). In *On First Principles*, Origen says that we must place ourselves *within* the text of Scripture and inscribe its inner meaning upon the soul. Like much of the ancient and medieval worlds, Origen presumes a threefold structure of the human person: body, soul, and spirit. "Just as the human being consists of body and soul and spirit, in the same way so also does Scripture, arranged by God to be given for the salvation of human beings" (Origen, 2018, pp. 497–499). To these three correspond three stages of the spiritual life: beginners are nourished by the literal story line of the text; the proficient are nourished by Scripture's moral teaching; and the perfect enjoy the hidden mysteries of Wisdom itself.

For Origen, Scripture (both Old and New Testaments) reveals the vastness of God in which the soul can meander, explore, and encounter the immense garden of the Word. Thus the Cistercian monk Guerric d'Igny (1070/80–1157) wrote: "Therefore, you who walk in the gardens of Scripture, take care not to fly through them inattentively. Rather examine each thing, and like hardworking bees gathering honey from the flowers, gather the spirit in the words of Scripture. 'For my spirit,' says Jesus, 'is sweeter than honey and my inheritance is better than honey, and the honeycomb.' In my opinion the one who enters the garden of the Lord becomes oneself a garden. Therefore, the Bridegroom will praise the bride saying, 'You are an enclosed garden, my sister, my bride'" (Song 4:12) (my translation; Guerric d'Igny, 1973, p. 522). Through the patient, engaged and vigilant practice of reading Scripture, Christians discover themselves only in the discovery of God.

The Ladder of Monks

The Carthusian monk Guigo II (d. 1188) must be credited with providing the most accessible medieval text on the practice of *lectio divina*. *The Ladder of Monks*, an allusion to Jacob's ladder (Gen 28:12), is as useful today as it was when Guigo composed it in the mid-twelfth century.[1] Guigo's teaching takes the form of a letter to his friend Gervase. It

[1] The image of Jacob's ladder in Gen 28 is the inspiration for other treatises on the spiritual life as well, the most famous of which is by St. John Climacus, 1998.

gives precise instructions on the practice of *lectio divina* and indicates some of the chief trials that one may expect to encounter.

According to Guigo II the goal of *lectio divina* is to lead the reader to the perpetual peace of contemplation. Here "[God's chosen enjoy the sweetness of divine contemplation, not drop by drop, not now and then, but in an unceasing flow of delight which no one shall take away, an unchanging peace, the peace of God Himself" (Guigo II, 1979, p. 86, translation altered slightly).

Guigo II presents four stages in spiritual exercise: reading, meditation, prayer, and contemplation. "These make up a ladder for monks by which they are lifted up from earth to heaven. (Guigo II, 1979, pp. 67–68)." Note that instead of the monk climbing each rung, the monk is "lifted up." Being lifted up indicates the inflow of grace and the consequent expansion of awareness as one moves first from reading, then to meditation, then to prayer, and finally to contemplation. This expansion of awareness is characterized by a dynamic flow from reason to non-discursive awareness, beyond the grasp of concepts and images.

On the first rung, reading involves "the careful study of Scripture, concentrating all one's powers on it" (Guigo II, 1979, p. 68). Normally one takes a short passage of Scripture, say for example one of the versions of the story of the healing of the man born blind (Mt 9:27–30, Mk 8:22–25, or Jn 9:1–7). A passage could likewise be from the Old Testament. By reading one grasps the story line or "the outside of" the text. Although reading "seeks for the sweetness of a blessed life (Guigo II, 1979, p. 68)," to truly taste it one must go deeper

The second rung, meditation, entails greater egoic release and, hence, a deeper resting in the text. Like reading, meditation is a discursive activity, but with increased powers of concentration, one reads with deeper reflection. This meditation is the "busy application of the mind to seek, with the help of one's reason, for knowledge of hidden truth"(Guigo II, 1979, p. 68). Whereas the stage of reading desires the sweetness of "a blessed life," meditation begins to perceive it. "Reading, as it were, puts food whole into the mouth, meditation chews on it and breaks it up" (Guigo II, 1979, p. 69). The image of scripture as food suggests how the stages are intrinsically linked. Placing food in one's mouth is necessary but by itself insufficient. Only by chewing food with a view to swallowing it will the food be digested and metabolized. Guigo II later identifies the food as a grape. The grape of Scripture is placed in the mouth with a view to being chewed.

On the third and fourth rungs, "Prayer extracts its flavour, contemplation is the sweetness itself, which gladdens and refreshes" (Guigo II, 1979, p. 69). Guigo neatly sums up the stages for us neatly: "Reading works on the outside, meditation on the pith: prayer asks for what we long for, contemplation gives us delight in the sweetness which we have found" (Guigo II, 1979, p. 69). *Lectio divina* is a matter of engaging the text and being drawn ever more deeply into it by means of release and rest, resulting in what is true spiritual nourishment, namely union to God.

Guigo now goes into greater description of these stages by likening the process of a grape becoming wine. His use of the metaphors of a grape becoming wine and bread being broken and shared to describe the transformation process of *lectio divina* is no mere literary flourish. Rather he attempts to unite the personal in the heart of the communal. The personal journey to divine union that is the goal of *lectio divina* is not a separate sort of union from that experienced in the central celebration of the Christian community: bread broken and wine outpoured in the celebration of the Eucharist.

Trials and Training

Guigo II concludes his treatise by addressing spiritual trials that those practicing *lectio divina* will undoubtedly face. While these trials seem to threaten defeat, they, in fact, serve to further the training and deepening spirituality of the monk.

The mind tends to cling, especially to spiritual experiences, seeking a continuous sense of divine presence and consolation. The problem of clinging is based on a profound ignorance. The mind tries to grasp as its own possession what is in fact always present, a sheer gift, that Christians call grace. In order to train the monk to assume a stable posture of interior receptivity instead of one of grasping and conquest, Guigo employs a metaphor from the Song of Songs, which is replete with imagery of the Spouse appearing and disappearing so as to train and deepen the bride's desire for her Spouse (the Word). The Spouse appears to withdraw, and the monk, now called the bride, experiences the Spouse's presence as absence. The apparent departure of the Spouse is good for the monk. Guigo II says that the monk who experiences too much consolation is put at risk—"consolation" is term used to refer to various positive feelings such as joy, love, and elation. "He comes for your consolation, He goes away to put you on your guard, for fear that too much consolation should puff you up, and that you having the Spouse always with you, should begin to despise your brethren, and to attribute this consolation not to His grace but to your own natural powers" (Guigo II, 1979, p. 77). Guigo is aware that divine consolation can be appropriated selfishly with the result that the monk looks down upon others with condescension and pride for apparently not being as spiritually advanced as he. Likewise, the monk can misconstrue what is essentially a sheer gift as something he has attained by his own striving. Worse, he can think he possesses a sense of consolation "as though by lawful title" (Guigo II, 1979, p. 77). All these manifestations of ego-driven, delusional thinking are healed by the balm of the Spouse's apparent absence. The sweetness of divine presence is replaced for a while by the bitterness of perceived absence.

This experience of presence as absence also creates in the monk a greater capacity for longing. Guigo writes, "that being desired He may be sought more eagerly, that having been sought for He may at last be found with greater thankfulness" (Guigo II, 1979, p. 77). The monk's grasping presumption is transformed into deeper receptivity and gratitude. "So, therefore, lest we should consider this present exile our true home, this pledge our whole reward, the Spouse comes and withdraws by turn, now bringing us consolation, now exchanging all this for weakness. For a short time He allows us to taste how sweet He is, and before our taste is satisfied He withdraws; and it is in this way, by flying above us with wings outspread, that He encourages us to fly, and says in effect: See now,

FIGURE 7.2 *Our Lady Holding the Bible*, detail from *Virgin Mary Annunciation*, Fra Angelico, 1431–1433. Panel, tempera, Detroit Institute of Art. Bequest of Eleanor Clay Ford.

you have had a little taste of how sweet and delightful I am, but if you wish to have your fill of this sweetness, hasten after me" (Guigo II, 1979, pp. 77–78).

Throughout, Guigo remains ever reassuring. He encourages the monk, "But do not fear, bride of the Spouse, do not despair, do not think yourself despised, if for a little while He turns His face away from you. These things all work together for your good, and you profit from His coming and from His withdrawal" (Guigo II, 1979, 77). Even though it feels as though God is absent, God is yet present, however hidden: "but yet He stays, for He directs us, He gives us grace, He joins us to Himself" (Guigo II, 1979, 76).

The Cloud of Unknowing

The Cloud of Unknowing is a work of signal importance. While the author wrote or translated several other works in Middle English, it is *The Cloud of Unknowing* that remains his most widely read and translated work. We know virtually nothing about the anonymous author, but there is broad scholarly consensus that he was a Carthusian monk who wrote in the last decades of the fourteenth century. The regional dialect of his Middle English prose is that of the northeast Midlands (McGinn, 2012, p. 397).

The title of the book is a biblical metaphor drawn from Moses' journey to the summit of Mount Sinai, the mountain of God. There "Moses approached the darkness where God dwelled" (Ex 20:21). The author of the *Cloud* likens the contemplative path to Moses' journey up Mount Sinai to encounter God. This becomes a symbol of the spiritual journey, where we, like Moses, ascend an interior mountain, and enter "the darkness where God dwelled," and become one with God through love.

The *Cloud*'s author teaches the practice of contemplation in a fairly straightforward manner. In the final two paragraphs of chapter 7, he presents basic instructions. He wishes us to have our intention directed to God alone. He suggests the use of a prayer word: "If you want to have this intention wrapped and enfolded in one word, so that you can hold on to it better, take only a short word of one syllable; . . . for the shorter it is, the better it agrees with the work of the spirit. A word of this kind is the word GOD or the word LOVE. Choose whatever you wish, or another as you please, whichever you prefer of one syllable, and fasten this word to your heart, so that it never parts from it, whatever happens" (*The Cloud of Unknowing*, chap. 7; Spearing, 2001, p. 29). Notice he does not insist that a prayer word be used at all. But if our attention is too fidgety, the use of a prayer word will help. He is obviously aware that when one begins the practice one does not typically experience undulating peace but a deluge of thoughts, just as Evagrius and countless others knew from their own experience of trying to sit in silence. A distinctive feature is that he says that it must be of one syllable, preferably "God" or "Love," providing an anchor for the wondering, roving mind. His insistence that a prayer word of one syllable "better agrees with the work of the spirit" is idiosyncratic to the author himself as he addresses an English-speaking audience (*Cloud*, chap. 7; Spearing, 2001, p. 29).

Far more important than the syllable count of the prayer word is his more nuanced teaching of how to use it. "This word is to be your shield and spear, whether you ride in peace or in war" (*Cloud*, chap. 7; Spearing, 2001, p. 29). Here the author clothes his teaching in the metaphor of a knight kitted out properly with shield and spear—a culturally familiar image to a fourteenth-century audience—as though to say the practice of contemplation involves one in spiritual warfare. Having captured the readers' attention with this image, he introduces his teaching: the quiet repetition of the prayer word that gradually integrates awareness into it, strengthening our powers of concentration. This assists our entering the cloud of unknowing where no thought or image can enter and deals with distractions, whether they be afflictive, mundane, or pious.

"With this word you are to beat on the cloud and the darkness above you [the summit of Mount Sinai]" (*Cloud*, chap. 7; Spearing, 2001, p. 29). "With this word you are to hammer down every kind of thought beneath the cloud of forgetting" (*Cloud*, chap. 7; Spearing, 2001, p. 29). He also warns us against thinking about the meaning of the prayer word. "And if, in its great learning, it offers to expound that word and tell you its attributes, say that you wish to have it quite whole, and not analysed or explained" (*Cloud*, chap. 7; Spearing, 2001, p. 29). Not a few get caught up in thinking about the meaning of the prayer word: "How good God is" or "How unfailing God's love is." This means that they are caught up in thoughts, albeit pious thoughts. But God is not a thought and cannot be captured by any thought or image.

If no thought or image can enter the cloud of unknowing, the ineffable mystery where God dwells, how do we become one with God? He answers this by identifying two different faculties that each human possesses: a faculty of knowledge and a faculty of love.

> Only see: all rational beings, angels and men, have in them, each individually, two principle faculties, one a faculty of knowledge; and the second a faculty of love; and God, their maker, is forever beyond the reach of the first of these, the intellectual faculty; but by means of the second, the faculty of loving, [God] can be fully grasped by each individual being, to such an extent that each single loving soul may, by the virtue of love, embrace within itself [God] who is fully sufficient (and beyond comparison more than fully) to fill all the souls and angels that can ever exist. And this is the unending marvelous miracle of love...
>
> (*Cloud*, chap. 4; Spearing, 2001, p. 23)

What the author presents in chapter 7 is for beginners in the practice of contemplation. In chapter 32, however, he addresses a clearly more mature audience who no longer use the prayer word as weaponry. Thoughts are still present, but we are able to see more deeply into their nature: thoughts are impermanent and transparent and so have lost their narrative grip. We no longer think we are the changing weather round Mount Sinai because we have ceased from clinging to our preference as to whether the sun is shining or fierce storms rage within. And when we cease to cling, the narrative grip of distractions opens its palms. Thoughts remain, but we can see through or past them: "look over their shoulders, as it were, searching for something else—and that something is God" (*Cloud*, chap. 32; Spearing, 2001, p. 55). The tables have been turned: thoughts that once derailed our practice now help steady our gaze.

The practice of contemplation is good for both body and soul. The author of the *Cloud* says, "The work of contemplation will have a favourable effect on the body as well as the soul of anyone who practices it, and make him agreeable to everyone, man or woman, who sees him [or her]; so that the appearance of the most ill-favoured man or woman living on earth, if they could by grace be enabled to engage in this work, would be suddenly transformed into graciousness" (*Cloud*, chap. 54; Spearing, 2001, p. 78).

The author of the *Cloud* sees the practice of contemplation as a vehicle of integration that brings Christian living to a fully embodied spiritual maturation and as the perfect expression of humility. Furthermore, contemplation removes the threat of the other by revealing that we share a grounding union. We are already one. Finally, the practice of contemplation contributes to the well-being not simply of all people but of the entire universe, for in the medieval world it was inconceivable to separate person from cosmos.

The essence of contemplation is humility. The *Cloud*'s author distinguishes two types of humility: imperfect and perfect. By "perfect" we should understand "complete," not flawless. He writes, "Humility in itself is nothing but a true knowledge and feeling of oneself as one is; for certainly anyone who could truly see and feel himself as he is would be truly humble" (*Cloud*, chap. 13; Spearing, 2001, p. 37). Imperfect humility is to do with "humanity's impurity, wretchedness and weakness, into which we have fallen by sin, and which we must always feel to some degree while we live on earth, however holy we may be" (*Cloud*, chap. 3; Spearing, 2001, p. 37). It is knowledge of our own faults, failings, and sins. However, this humility is imperfect, incomplete: necessary but insufficient. He writes, "Yes, and without this self-knowledge it is impossible for a sinner to achieve the perfect virtue of humility, or to keep it when he has achieved it" (*Cloud*, chap. 14; Spearing, 2001, p. 38). What then is perfect humility? "... I hope to tell you and show you how this spiritual exercise excels all other exercises.... [It] subtly and completely contains within it the perfect virtue of humility" (*Cloud*, chap. 14; Spearing, 2001, p. 38). For the author of *The Cloud of Unknowing* the humblest thing a person can do is to sit in silence and practice contemplation.

The practice of contemplation removes the threat of otherness. After he has explained contemplation as perfect humility, he moves on to teach in chapter 24 how this practice also fulfills one of Jesus' most challenging teachings, "But I say to you love your enemies, and pray for those who persecute you" (Mt 5:44). He writes, "And it appears from experience... [that] "a perfect worker in contemplation has no regard to any specific person for his own sake, whether kin or stranger, friend or foe; for all seem kin to him, and none seems a stranger. All seem his friends, and none seem his enemies, so that for him all those who torment him and cause him distress on earth are his particular friends, and he feels moved to desire as much good for them as he would for the closest friend he has" (*Cloud*, chap. 24; Spearing, 2001, p. 49). He is speaking from a deeply liberating depth of contemplative realization where no thoughts reach whether afflictive or holy; "for while engaged in contemplation a perfect worker cannot allow thoughts, even of the holiest being that God ever made, to enter his mind" (*Cloud*, chap. 24; Spearing, 2001, p. 49).

In deep contemplation the self is unselfed with the result that the ego that maintains the sense of separation from God and others falls away. We encounter others not as objects but as subjects. We encounter others interiorly as our very selves. When this begins to happen on a more or less regular basis, "subject permanence" becomes established and allows us to realize that the ground of each one of us is God (Laird, 2019). There is no separate self to do the hating and no separate object to scorn or lynch. This is the full flowering of the human as God intended and the greatest contribution to peace among peoples.

The author of the *Cloud* writes, "All people living on earth are marvelously helped by this work [the practice of contemplation] in ways you do not know" (*Cloud*, chap. 2; Spearing, 2001, p. 22). For Christians the belief that we, though different, are yet one body is among the fundamental teachings of the New Testament. In his Letter to the Romans, St. Paul provides one of the most authoritative teachings of this. "For as in one body we have many parts, and all the parts do not have the same function, so we, though many, are one body in Christ and individually parts of one another" (Rom 12:4–5; see also 1 Cor 12:12). What is noteworthy is that the *Cloud*'s author sees the practice of contemplation as vital not only to the unity of all but also to maintaining that unity. The practice of contemplation contributes to everybody's well-being. He goes on to indicate its effects throughout the cosmos (a dynamic, interconnected cosmos that characterized the world of medieval Christians). The effects of this practice affect the heavens, purgatory, and the demonic realms: "This is the work of the soul that pleases God most. All the saints and angels rejoice in this work, and hasten to help it with all their might. All the devils are driven crazy when we do this, and try to frustrate it in all ways they can. All people living on earth are marvelously helped by this work, in ways you do not know. Yes, the very souls in purgatory are relieved of their pain by the power of this work. You yourself are cleansed and made virtuous by this work more than by any other" (*Cloud*, chap. 3; Spearing, 2001, p. 22). While contemplation is deeply personal it is far from private, for it affects all beings.

Conclusion

This chapter examined key characteristics of some Christian practices of contemplation during the fourth to fourteenth centuries, practices that remain of central importance even today. They underscore the importance of training the mind by cultivating interior skills of awareness, posture, and breath. Physical stillness supports inner stillness.

Scripture played a significant role in each of the texts we examined. This was evident not only in the use of a *versiculum* (the prayer phrase or prayer word) that is drawn or adapted from Scripture, but also in the contemplative practice of *lectio divina*.

Training the mind to be silent is a crucial aspect of contemplative practice. The wandering, roving mind is vulnerable to all manner of distracting thoughts whether they be devilishly afflictive or sweetly pious. We are attracted to silence but as soon as we try to be interiorly silent, we are caught up in a spiritual battle. Evagrius and Cassian taught us how to withdraw our attention from the barrage of stories going on in our heads and to shift attention to awareness itself; for that in us which is aware of the afflictive thought(s) is free of them. Otherwise we could not see them. Over time this becomes second nature, and we live increasingly in freedom and calm as we meet whatever each day brings. The Jesus Prayer tradition summarizes and consummates all these concerns.

Guigo II's *Ladder of Monks* represents a contemplative practice that predates him: *lectio divina*. His treatise makes explicit what preceding centuries likewise held. Scripture is a living manifestation of divine presence. To read Scripture slowly, taking in a mere word or phrases or just a few sentences, is to embark on a fourfold journey where abiding union with God is realized. Just as in the previous authors, the spiritual battle is essential to the process of making the mind a monk.

The anonymous author of *The Cloud of Unknowing* emphasizes especially that the mystery we call God cannot be grasped by any thought or image but can be thoroughly known by love. With the assistance of a prayer word, all thoughts and images that come into the mind during prayer are let go of. We put them under "the cloud of forgetting."

Perhaps more than any other author we examined, the *Cloud*'s author draws out the ethical implications of this practice. The practice of contemplation is the humblest thing a person can do. It leads to the realization that we are all and always have been connected on a deep level, and as a result the otherness of our fellow humans is no longer experienced as a threat. Finally, by this humble practice of contemplation we contribute something of vital importance to the world. "All people living on earth are marvelously helped by this work, in ways you do not know" (*Cloud*, chap. 3; Spearing, 2001, p. 22).

References

Alford, J. A. (1995). Rolle's "English psalter" and "lectio divina." *Bulletin of the John Rylands Library* 77(3), 47–60.

Augustine of Hippo. (1992). Sermon 8, on the third commandment. In E. Hill (Trans.), *The works of St. Augustine* (Vol. III/1). Brooklyn, NY: New City Press.

Augustine of Hippo. (1998). *Confessions* (H. Chadwick, Trans.). Oxford: Oxford University Press.

Cassian, John (1985). *Conferences* (C. Luibhied, Trans.). New York: Paulist Press.

Catechism of the Catholic Church (1994). London: Geoffrey Chapman.

Crouzel, H. (1961). Origène, précurseur du monachisme. In *Théologie de la vie monastique* (pp. 15–38). Paris: Aubier.

Crouzel, H. (1989). *Origen: The life and thought of the first great theologian* (A. S. Worral, Trans.). New York: HarperCollins.

Evagrius Ponticus. (1972). *The Praktikos and chapters on prayer* (J. E. Bamberger, Trans.). Kalamazoo, MI: Cistercian Publications.

Evagrius Ponticus. (2009). *Talking back: A monastic handbook for combating demons* (D. Brakke, Trans.). Collegeville, MN: Liturgical Press.

Guerric d'Igny (1973). *Sermons: Sources Chrétiennes 202* (Vol. 2, D. Placide, Trans., J. Morson & H. Costello, Crit. Ed., pp. 516–573). Paris: Les Éditions du Cerf.

Guigo II. (1979). *The ladder of monks and twelve meditations* (E. Colledge & J. Walsh, Trans.). Kalamzoo, MI, Cistercian Publications.

Guillaumont, A. (1974). The Jesus Prayer among the monks of Egypt. *The Eastern Churches Review* 6, 66–71.

Harmless, W. (2004). *Desert Christians: An introduction to the literature of early monasticism.* New York: Oxford University Press.

Hausherr, I. (1978). *The name of Jesus.* Kalamazoo, MI: Cistercian Publications.

John Climacus. (1998). *The ladder of divine ascent* (C. Luibheid & N. Russel, Trans.). New York: Paulist Press.

Johnson, C. D. L. (2010). *The globalization of hesychasm and the Jesus Prayer: Contesting contemplation.* London: Continuum.

Laird, M. (2007, Summer). Continually breathe Jesus Christ: Stillness and watchfulness in *The Philokalia. Communio* 34, 243–263.

Laird, M. (2019). *An ocean of light: Contemplation, transformation, and liberation.* Oxford: Oxford University Press.

McGinn, B. (2005). *The harvest of mysticism in medieval Germany.* New York: Herder and Herder.

McGinn, B. (2012). *The varieties of vernacular mysticism, 1350–1550*. New York: Herder and Herder.

McGinn, B. (2017). *Mysticism in the golden age of Spain, 1500–1650*. New York: Herder and Herder.

Origen. (2018). *On first principles* (J. Behr, Ed. & Trans.). Oxford: Oxford University Press.

Palladius of Aspuna. (2015). Chapter 38. In J. Wortley (Trans.), *The Lausiac history* (pp. 94–98). Athens, OH: Cistercian Publications.

Palmer, G., Sherrard, P., & Ware, K. (Trans.) (1979). *Philokalia* (Vol. 1). London: Faber and Faber.

Spearing, A. C. (Trans.). (2001). *The cloud of unknowing and other works*. London: Penguin.

Stewart, C. (1998). *Cassian the monk*. New York: Oxford University Press.

CHAPTER 8

EASTERN CHRISTIANITY AND MEDITATION

CYRIL HOVORUN

INTRODUCTION

EASTERN **Orthodox** Christianity features both prayer and meditation. Prayer addresses the personality of God. Moreover, because the Christian God is a Trinity, prayer can address all three persons of God: the Father, the Son, and the Holy Spirit. Because they are personal beings, even if bodiless, prayer is possible to them, according to Orthodox Christianity. Prayer, thus, is primarily an interpersonal communication: between sinful human personalities, who live in this world, and holy personalities, who live beyond this world.

Meditation in Eastern **Orthodox** Christianity is also personal. However, the personal reflection on the object of meditation is in the third or first person, unlike prayer, which is a communication in second person. Meditation can be interpreted as a reflection on prayer. Unlike prayer, meditation can be directed at one's own personality—the self. In such case it is a dialogue with the self, as in the following *kontakion* of the *Great Canon of Saint Andrew of Crete*:

> My soul, my soul, arise, why do you sleep?
> The end draws near, and you shall be confounded:
> Therefore rise up, that Christ God may spare you,
> He who is everywhere, and filling all things.
>
> (St. Andrew of Crete, 2013, p. 172)

The purpose of meditation directed at the self is to cleanse oneself from sinful intentions—the passions (*τὰ πάθη* [*ta pathe*]). Unlike prayer, which does not seek to change its object—the personalities of God or saints—the goal of meditation is to change its object, that is, the self of the meditator. Eastern Christians believe that this change of self, which they also render as a purification of the heart, helps them make their prayer "stronger" and "better heard by God"—they use these words to describe a closer connectedness between the person who prays and God. Prayer, in return, helps the self to transfigure into a better person. The two acts, which engage the individual—prayer and meditation—help each other accomplish their goals: to improve one's connectedness with God and to improve one's self correspondingly. Moreover, they are insufficient on their own: prayer without meditation and meditation without prayer do not function properly.

Combined, prayer and meditation lead an individual to salvation from sins and, ultimately, to *theosis*—divinization, which is the endmost purpose of human existence according to the Orthodox tradition. In this tradition, divinization means a quality of human existence, which becomes similar to God's being. It comes as a result of the appropriation of the divine properties in human nature.

In the Eastern Christian literature, there is not a word which translates as "meditation," in the way we use it today. There are, however, various concepts and practices that could be described as meditative. In this chapter we will consider four of these practices: the contemplation of sins, the contemplation of the Divine Light, the Jesus prayer, and hesychasm. They are intrinsically connected with one another: reflection on one's sins leads one to seeing God as uncreated Light. Ceaseless repetition of the prayer "Lord Jesus Christ, Son of God, have mercy on me, a sinner" (also known as the Jesus prayer) facilitates this passage and leads a person to internal calm (*hesychia*).

We will begin with Origen (ca. 185–ca. 254), a prolific author from Alexandria. In his time in Egypt, the monastic movement emerged, which soon spread to Palestine and Syria, and later to other parts of the Roman empire, including the western empire, and beyond. Cells of hermits and monastic communities became laboratories of prayer and meditative practices. The wisdom they produced was articulated in many forms. Among the earliest were the *Apophthegmata Patrum*—a collection of stories and quotes by the fathers and mothers of the desert. Evagrius Ponticus (345–399) summarized meditative experiments as being a taxonomy of spiritual life. For this purpose, he employed philosophical and ethical categories from Platonism, Aristotelianism, and Stoicism. The so-called Cappadocian Fathers: Basil of Caesarea (330–379), Gregory of Nazianzus (329–390), and Gregory of Nyssa (335–394) employed the same categories to explain the Trinitarian dogma and the Incarnation of God. Their theology reflected their spiritual experience, which they also explicated in the forms of monastic rules, spiritual poetry, and allegorical exegesis of the scriptures. Genres of ascetical literature evolved and multiplied. Now they included treatises, extended letters, florilegia, and mélanges of different genres—corpuses. One of them is the so-called "Macarian corpus." This is a collection of spiritual writings, including epistles and homilies. The corpus is ascribed to a certain person, who is sometimes identified as Macarius and sometimes as Symeon. We will identify him as pseudo-Macarius. These writings with disputable authorship reflected mostly the Syriac tradition in the fourth century. A monk named John was also from Syria (ca. 579–ca. 649). However, most of his life he lived as a hermit and then as an abbot at Mount Sinai, at the western edge of the Syriac world. He composed a letter, which became one of the most famous spiritual treatises of all times. Its initial title was "Spiritual Tablets"—evoking the tablets given to Moses at Sinai. Eventually another title prevailed: "The Ladder." This title reflected the structure of the book, which in thirty chapters describes the steps of spiritual ascent of a monk to God. Approximately in the same period of time, on the eastern edge of the Syriac world, another ascetic writer flourished, whose name was Isaac. He was born in what is modern Qatar and was for a short while a bishop in Nineveh. Most of his life, however, he spent as an ascetic. Maximus the Confessor (ca. 580–662) was an insightful theologian and spiritual writer. He reunited theories and practices of asceticism and meditation with theology—something that other spiritual writers tended to neglect. All these authors flourished in the period of Late Antiquity.

The Middle Ages in the Christian East produced a corpus of spiritual literature with distinct themes and theological approaches. It put more emphasis on subjective experiences and techniques of prayer and meditation. One of the most prominent medieval writers was Symeon the New Theologian (ca. 949–1022). He expounded his visions and meditations in numerous hymns. At the core of his experience was the Divine Light. This experience became central for the monasticism that developed on the Mount Athos—a peninsula in what is now the north-eastern part of Greece. It flourished in the period of the decline of the Byzantine empire and produced what we now call hesychasm. This is a tradition of ceaseless prayer with complete silence (in Greek *ἡσυχία* [*hesykhia*]) of mind and the reunion of mind with heart. A spokesman for this tradition, who later became archbishop of Salonica, Gregory Palamas (1296–1359), conceptualized it in his theology, which became known as Palamism. In some sense, it was a theology of meditation.

This tradition and theology never ceased in the Christian East, even under the circumstances of Ottoman rule from the fifteenth through the nineteenth centuries. During the Ottoman period, it was in decline. It resurged in the eighteenth century as the movement of Kollyvades—Athonite monks who practiced and disseminated hesychasm in the context of a society that remained under the Muslim rule and was already touched by modernization and secularization. This movement produced a book titled *Philokalia*. It is a compilation of ancient ascetical texts on prayer, meditation, and spiritual perfection. *Philokalia* significantly widened the initial audience of these texts, who were mostly monks, to everyone who pursued spiritual life, including lay people living in cities and villages. In line with the Philokalic movement, modern spiritual authors continued instructing lay people how to follow the path of ancient ascetics. Among them can be named Lev Gillet (1893–1980), who wrote spiritual books under the name of "A monk of the Eastern Church"; and Archimandrite Sophrony Sakharov (1896–1993), a founder of the Monastery of Saint John the Baptist in England.

The Contemplation of Sins and Repentance

Theology in the Christian East developed around a soteriological framework that had at its heart one question: "What did God do for our salvation?" Only matters relevant to this question were regarded as theologically meaningful. Practices of meditation were included as part of this soteriological framework, for they dealt with the related question: "What do human beings need to do to appropriate salvation, which has been provided by God?"

Within this soteriological framework, meditation is linked intimately to theology. As early as the third century, Origen equated theology (*θεολογία* [*theologia*]) with contemplation (*θεωρία* [*theoria*]). A century later Evagrius of Pontus made this connection more explicit: "If you are a theologian, you will pray truly. And if you pray truly, you are a theologian" (*Chapters on Prayer*, 61, in Bingaman & Nassif, 2012, p. 119). A connection between theology, prayer, and meditation is possible because theology, as a human word about God, requires both communication with God through prayer and meditative reflection on the revelation received.

The beginning of the human response to God is repentance. Repentance in Greek is *μετάνοια* [*metanoia*], which can be translated as a "change of mindset." The word suggests both intellectual and contemplative dimensions of repentance. In antiquity, intellect, *νοῦς* [*nous*], also included will (see Dihle, 1982, pp. 20–67). Repentance, thus, also requires volitional effort. A person makes this effort after realizing their sins. Gregory Palamas described the chain of repentance as follows:

> The awareness of common transgressions leads to self-accusation; this in turn results in sorrow for sinfulness, which Paul called godly sorrow. This godly sorrow naturally is followed by a broken-hearted confession and supplication before God and the promise of avoidance of evil from then on; and this is repentance.
> (*Logos* 28 in Athanasopoulos, 2015, p. 3)

The "awareness of common transgressions" is a meditative process. This process is paradoxical. Following common sense, the more a person repents, the fewer sins they should contemplate. However, according to the Eastern Christian spiritual writings, the opposite is true: the more one advances in one's spiritual journey, the sharper becomes the vision of one's sins. Thus, saints are those who sincerely believe that they are the most sinful people in the world. *Apophthegmata Patrum* quotes the Coptic monk Matoes in this regard: "The nearer a man draws to God, the more he sees himself a sinner" (in Ward, 1984, p. 143).

Meditating on sins can also be misleading. This occurs when one confuses what is sinful with human nature itself, wrongly perceiving this nature as being inherently damaged or corrupt down to its roots. Such a vision of human nature is almost inevitably associated with a dualistic worldview, where things and beings are seen as either black or white. Some movements, such as the Montanists, Manichaeans, and Messalians adopted this bleak outlook, which is not accepted by the mainstream Eastern or Western Christianity.

For Eastern Christians, contemplation is not a passive condition but an active process. It requires what is called "synergy" (*συνέργεια* [*synergeia*]) or the co-working of human beings with God. The contribution to this relationship is not an equal one, as God contributes much more than we humans. Nevertheless, *active* human participation in the relationship is crucial. The synergetic character of the relationship between God and humankind manifests itself most particularly in the transition from the stage of contemplating one's own sins to the stage of contemplating God. This transition requires extraordinary efforts from those who seek God. The eagerness and persistence that a person needs to demonstrate at this stage is described in the following autobiographical sketch by Symeon the New Theologian:

> I never turned back . . .
> I did not slow down my running
> But with all my strength,
> With all my power
> I searched for Him Whom I did not see.
> I looked around the roads
> And behind the fences, to discover where He might appear.
> I was filled with tears
> And I asked everyone
> Who had ever seen Him:
> The prophets, Apostles, and Fathers.
> I asked them to tell me
> Where they had ever seen Him.
> And when He spoke with me,
> I started running with all my strength
> And I saw Him totally,
> And He united Himself entirely with me.
>
> (Hymn 29, in Alfeyev, 2000, p. 54).

This kind of meditation requires a high level of intellectual awareness and effort as one turns the mind to focus on one's sins. It is thus not surprising that Eastern **Orthodox** Christianity developed systematic theories of what sins are, as well as of their opposing forces—virtues. One of the earliest authors who produced a taxonomy of sins based on his ascetic experience of the desert was Evagrius Ponticus. He suggested that sins are connected with each other through a causal train: pride, vanity, sloth, anger, sorrow, greed, lust, and gluttony (*Practicus* 6, in Guillaumont, 1971; see Tilby, 2013). John Cassian, who spent time with Evagrius in Egypt, brought his taxonomy of sins to the west but replaced the category of "sin" with that of "thought" (*λογισμός* [*logismos*])—the notion was that "thoughts" are entities capable of infecting human minds. The stages of the spread of a "spiritual infection" in the human soul are similar to how viruses infect the body, except that the human soul cannot be infected without consent.

At the initial stage, a sinful thought approaches one's mind from outside. This stage is called "assault" (*προσβολή* [*prosbolé*]) and, according to Evagrius, its source can be a demon or another person. The ascetic writers underlined that this is the easiest stage at which to get rid of sin, because it is still unattached to the human mind. They advise to watch out for approaching thoughts and drive them away as quickly as possible. If thoughts are not repelled in time, a "conjunction" (*συνδυασμός* [*syndyasmos*]) can develop between mind and *logismos*, which then is much harder to destroy. At this stage, a passion begins growing in one's soul. It advances to the stage of "compliance" (συγκατάθεσις [*synkatathesis*]), when the human will complies with *logismos*. A "struggle" (πάλη [*pale*]) may follow, as the soul attempts to free itself from the bad thought, but now that the mind and the will have embraced it, it becomes much harder to win the battle. The sinful thought gradually becomes an acquired "property" (ἕξις [*eksis*]) of the soul, which "surrenders" (αἰχμαλωσία [*aekhmalosia*]) to sin (see Зарин, 1907, pp. 248–258).

Meditation on sins leads one to realize the distinction between sins and passions (see Зарин 1907, pp. 211–219). Sin is a deed, while passion (πάθος [*pathos*]) is an intention to do something wrong. Passions generate sins. Even when a person does not commit sins, they can be in captivity to passions (ἐμπαθῆς [*empathés*]). The Eastern Orthodox ascetic tradition pays particular attention to eradicating passions rather than plucking out sins.

A person who manages to eradicate passions from one's soul becomes dispassionate (ἀπαθής [*apathés*]). The condition of dispassion (ἀπάθεια [*apatheia*]) is the purpose of one's spiritual battle. Origen (ca. 185–ca. 254) urged to achieve a state of "purification" and "nakedness" from passions (see *Fragmenta in Psalmos 1–150* [Dub.], Psalms 64:3 and 118:95, in Pitra). In this state, as pseudo-Macarius clarified, the soul becomes "incapable of falling away, dispassionate and unshakeable" (*Homily* 45.7, in Alfeyev, 2000, 251). To illustrate this state of dispassion or *apatheia*, we find in the *Apophthegmata* a story about Abba Serapion, who went to a prostitute and spent a night in her room reciting the Psalter (Ward, 1984, pp. 220–221).

An individual, thus, begins their spiritual journey with the realization of their own passionate condition. Then they fight the passions and reach a state of dispassion. John Climacus described this process as that of climbing a ladder. The ladder has three sections: (1) breaking with the world, (2) fighting passions and pursuing virtues, and 3) union with God (I follow the systematisation of the "ladder" by Chryssavgis, 2004, pp. 28–29). See Box 8.1 for how John wrote about the thirty steps of the ladder that lead one to the love of God.

Some of the steps of spiritual ascent can be facilitated by meditation directly. For example, meditating on one's sins helps to get rid of judging other peoples. Judging others is regarded one of the most dangerous sins. Jesus directly warned about it: "Judge not, that you be not judged. For with the judgment you pronounce you will be judged, and with the measure you use it will be measured to you." (Matt 7:1–2 English Standard Version). Judging others, therefore, directly invokes judgement from God. Meditating on one's own sins allows one to tackle this passion, because when one judges oneself, one finds it much harder to judge others. The *Apophthegmata* tells the following story:

> There was at that time a meeting at Scetis about a brother who had sinned. The Fathers spoke, but Abba Pior kept silence. Later, he got up and went out; he took a sack, filled it with sand and carried it on his shoulder. He put a little sand also into a small bag which he carried in front of him. When the Fathers asked him what this meant he said, "In this sack which contains much sand, are my sins which are many; I have put them behind me so as not to be troubled about them and so as not to

Box 8.1 The Thirty Steps of the ladder that lead one to the love of God.

Data from Chryssavgis, 2004, pp. 28–29.

Stage 1: Break with the world

Step 1: renunciation
Step 2: detachment
Step 3: exile

Stage 2: Virtues and passions

Fundamental virtues

Step 4: obedience
Step 5: repentance
Step 6: remembrance of death
Step 7: joyful sorrow

The struggle against the passions

(a) Passions that are predominantly non-physical

Step 8: anger
Step 9: malice
Step 10: slander
Step 11: talkativeness
Step 12: falsehood
Step 13: despondency

(b) Passions that are predominantly physical and material

Step 14: gluttony
Step 15: lust
Steps 16–17: avarice

(c) Passions that are predominantly non-physical and spiritual

Steps 18–20: insensitivity
Step 21: fear
Step 22: vainglory
Step 23: pride (including blasphemy)

Higher virtues of the "active life"

Step 24: simplicity
Step 25: prayer
Step 26: discernment

Stage 3: Union with God

Step 27: stillness
Step 28: prayer
Step 29: dispassion
Step 30: love

> weep; and see here are the little sins of my brother which are in front of me and I spend my time judging them. This is not right, I ought rather to carry my sins in front of me and concern myself with them, begging God to forgive me for them." The Fathers stood up and said, "Truly, this is the way of salvation."
>
> (In Ward, 1984, pp. 199–200)

As one climbs the stairs of the spiritual ladder, one can increasingly see not only the darkness of sins, but also the brightness of virtues. Spiritual writers advise to never abandon meditation on one's sins. However, as a person advances spiritually, virtues appear increasingly as a focus of meditation. Evagrius, for instance, considered meditation on the good things coming from God an important spiritual exercise (*Rerum monachalium rationes* 9 in Migne, vol. 40, col. 1261). He believed this type of meditation enriched prayer (Casiday, 2013, p. 139). The key difference between meditating on one's sins and virtues is that when focusing on one's sins these are regarded as coming from one's own faults, while when focusing on virtues these stem directly from God. Thus, contemplation on the virtues is understood as a doorway to seeing God—*θεοπτία* [*theoptia*].

Contemplation of the Divine Light

God can be contemplated by spiritual sight. An early Christian writer Theophilus, who lived in the second century in Antioch, described the eyes of the soul in his apology to Autolycus:

> But if you should say, "Show me thy God," I may reply to you, "Show me your man and I will show you my God." You must show me that the eyes of your soul can see and that the ears of your heart can hear. For just as those who see with bodily eyes contemplate the affairs of life on earth and distinguish things that differ . . . just so, the ears of the heart and the eyes of the soul are potentially capable of beholding God. For God is seen by those who are capable of seeing him, once they have the eyes of the soul opened. (*Ad Autolycum* 1.2, in Grant, 1970, p. 4)

For pseudo-Macarius, the entire soul turns into a spiritual eye and an organ of meditation by the contemplation of God: "The soul that is counted worthy to participate in the spirit of the Lord's light and illumined by the beauty of His unspeakable glory . . . becomes all light, all face, all eye" (*Homily* i.2, in Alfeyev, 2000, p. 22).

The Eastern Fathers and Mothers developed a language to describe their experience of seeing God, in which the central concept is "light" (*φῶς* [*fōs*]). Indeed, most descriptions of meditation on God feature the experience of light at their core. Symeon the New Theologian, more than any other spiritual writer, wrote about the experience of the Divine Light:

> If there exists someone who has explained this to him before, since he has already come to know God, he comes to that person and tells him: "I have seen!" [The elder]

> asks: "What did you see, my child?" — "A light, my father, a sweet sweet light; and my mind does not know how to describe it to you . . . At once the space of my cell vanished and the world disappeared. I was left alone with this light... There was ineffable joy, which is still in me, and great love and desire, so that streams of tears flowed out of me, as you see now." And he answers and tells him: "It is He, my child."
> (*Ethical* 5, in Alfeyev, 2000, p. 22)

After one enjoys seeing the Light, its disappearance is experienced as pain. This pain causes an individual to seek the Light with greater eagerness:

> I have frequently seen light, sometimes within me... and sometimes it appeared externally, from afar, or even it was completely hidden, and by its hiddenness caused me unbearable pain, because I thought I would never see again. But when I again lamented and wept... it appeared like the sun which penetrates through the thickness of the clouds and gradually shows itself as a gently glowing sphere.
> (*First Thanksgiving* 172–180, in Alfeyev, 2000, p. 233)

The Divine Light became a subject of theological debates in the late Byzantine period. The two protagonists of the debates were Gregory Palamas (1296–1359) and Barlaam (ca. 1290–1348), a Greek monk from Italy and a scholar in classical philosophy. They disagreed on explaining what monks contemplated as Light. For Barlaam, it was at best an illumination coming from the human mind. In the worst case, it was a delusion. Gregory Palamas insisted that the Light that monks saw was a true revelation from God. Moreover, it was the revelation *of* God. The argument between Barlaam and Gregory was effectively about the outcomes of meditation: were they an illusion or revelation? At one point, this discussion became public, and was addressed by councils held in Constantinople: the councils in June and August 1341 scrutinized the teaching of Barlaam and found it wrong. Barlaam was condemned and had to go back to Italy.

The theological disagreements during the fourteenth century (also known as the Palamite controversies) on what this Light is had far-reaching theological and epistemological implications. In particular, they posed the question, how can God be both accessible and inaccessible? The medieval Eastern theologians built on the thought of the theologians from Late Antiquity, such as Gregory of Nazianzus, who differentiated two modes of existence of God: God himself and what surrounds him: "Only the intellect (*νοῦς* [*nūs*]) might roughly depict Him, however, in some obscure and mediocre manner, and not in His nature, but in what is around Him" (Discourse 38, in Alfeyev, 2000, p. 157). Gregory Palamas one thousand years later identified "what is around" God as the Divine Light. It is also "deifying grace," "energy" (*Physical and Theological Chapters* 68–69, in Lossky, 1983, p. 157), "power and universal operation of the Trinity" (*Theophanes*, in Lossky, 1983, p. 157). In result, on the one hand, God has essence, which remains inaccessible for humans to see or experience. On the other hand, God radiates "energy," which human beings can contemplate as Light. Therefore, meditation on God can produce not just an idea about God, but also leads to actually touch God, or rather, to being touched by God. Gregory insisted that God is fully present in his uncreated Light.

While the existence of God directed at the world was called Light (φῶς [*fōs*]), his existence in himself was called "darkness" (γνόφος [*gnofos*], σκότος [*skotos*]) (Meyendorff, 1974, p. 84). This darkness has to be interpreted not in the sense of something evil, but as something inaccessible for human thought or experience. God, therefore, is both light and darkness. Gregory of Nyssa explained this duality of experience by referring to two biblical stories about Moses. Moses, on the one hand, could see the light of the burning bush. This was an allegory for the revelation of the accessible God. On the other hand, when Moses ascended to Mount Sinai to receive commandments, he entered darkness. This was that aspect of God that is inaccessible for any meditation (see Malherbe and Ferguson, 1978, pp. 94–97).

Barlaam argued that a person can only think of God and believe in him, but not experience God. From Barlaam's perspective, it was possible to meditate on God, but this was a purely intellectual exercise, which cannot engage God directly. In other words, meditation may help one to know more *about* God, but not to know God "face to face."

The initial target of Barlaam's polemics was not Gregory Palamas, but Western theologians. Barlaam could not stand the idea, which by his time had developed within Western scholastic theology, that God is fully accessible to human experience. This idea was clearly articulated by Thomas Aquinas. In his *Summa Theologiae*, while addressing the question, "How God is known by us?" Thomas demonstrates that it is wrong to suggest that "no created intellect can see the essence of God":

> As the ultimate beatitude of man consists in the use of his highest function, which is the operation of his intellect; if we suppose that the created intellect could never see God, it would either never attain to beatitude, or its beatitude would consist in something else beside God; which is opposed to faith. For the ultimate perfection of the rational creature is to be found in that which is the principle of its being; since a thing is perfect so far as it attains to its principle. Further the same opinion is also against reason. For there resides in every man a natural desire to know the cause of any effect which he sees; and thence arises wonder in men. But if the intellect of the rational creature could not reach so far as to the first cause of things, the natural desire would remain void. Hence it must be absolutely granted that the blessed see the essence of God. (*Summa* I, 12.1, in Thomas, 2007, p. 49)

Barlaam strongly rebuked this idea. He insisted that it is impossible to contemplate God, who remains transcendent to human knowledge: "Thomas and everyone who reasons as he does thinks that there is nothing inaccessible to the human mind; that we believe that this opinion comes from a soul of demoniacal and evil pride; for most divine things transcend human knowledge" (in Meyendorff, 1974, p. 84).

While Thomas and Barlaam had opposite views, Gregory Palamas suggested a middle way, by arguing that God is both accessible and inaccessible for human knowledge and experience. (It is unlikely that Palamas read Thomas or was aware of his positions [see Pacella, 2015, p. 200.]) This is possible because of the distinction between the essence and the energy or Light of God. This proposal of Palamas, nevertheless, was opposed by

FIGURE 8.1 *Pantokrator* or *Spas v Silakh*, end of 15th century, by unknown painter, Cyril-Belozero monastery in Russia. The dark halo surrounding Christ on this type of icons means the "darkness" of God's inaccessibility.

both Barlaam and Western scholastics. In 1336 Pope Benedict XII promulgated the constitution *Benedictus Deus*, where he confirmed the theological points of Thomas regarding *theoptia*:

> After the passion and death of our Lord Jesus Christ, they (the elect) will see and do see the divine essence in an intuitive and face to face vision, without any created intermediary which would interpose itself as an object of vision, the divine essence appearing to them immediately, without a veil (*nude*), clearly and openly; so that in this vision they might enjoy the divine essence itself. (in Farrell, 1997, p. 451)

Benedict not only endorsed Thomas, but also rebuked the Easterners. He did so in 1341, when a group of Armenians asked for union with the church of Rome. Benedict commissioned Richard Radulph, the archbishop of Armagh and primate of Ireland, to study the Armenian doctrine. The archbishop composed a theological treatise, *De quaestionibus Armenorum*, where he attacked the Armenians and even more the Greeks for holding allegedly heretical views regarding the impossibility of seeing the essence of God. Persistent attacks on the "Greek doctrine" continued in the following centuries, and so this matter has become one more that divides Eastern and Western Christianity regarding the ways and outcomes of the meditations on God.

Incarnation of God

Meditation on the Divine Light in the Christian East inevitably refers to the incarnation of God in the person of Jesus Christ. As Symeon the New Theologian puts it: "the Word which became flesh lives in us as light" (*Ethical* 10.448–465, in Alfeyev, 2000, p. 59). This makes the Eastern Christian meditation fundamentally Christocentric—focused on the person of Jesus Christ.

This Christocentric character of meditation reaches a peak in the event of the transfiguration (*μεταμόρφωσις* [*metamorfosis*]), the moment in the Gospels when Jesus took Peter, James, and John to Mount Tabor, where he appeared to them shining "like the sun" and talking to Moses and Elijah (Matt 17:2–9 ESV). This event comprises all the above-mentioned aspects of the Christian meditation: climbing the spiritual ladder and the contemplation of Light. The event of the transfiguration demonstrated what those who meditate on God might see. For Gregory Palamas, the transfigured Jesus became a manifestation of the divine character of the Light that is shown to monks. Gregory insisted that at Mount Tabor Jesus appeared to his disciples,

> not revealing his essence—for it is invisible and appears nowhere, even though it is present everywhere. He is not experienced in his essence, he does not reveal it, nor does he bestow it—it would be blasphemy to think it—but in a most mysterious manner, he shines upon them the radiance of his proper nature and grants them to participate in it. (*Antirrhetic against Akindynos* 4.14.36, in Mantzaridis, 1996, p. 213)

Just as the incarnation of God in Jesus made salvation available for every human being, the transfiguration of Jesus on Mount Tabor demonstrated that all Christians can contemplate the divine Light and become transfigured like Jesus. The transfiguration of a Christian is the result of a process of "deification" or *theosis* (*θέωσις*) (see Russell, 2009). *Theosis* means to become similar to God and it is the most complete participation in the life of God. Eastern theologians stressed, however, that it is participation, but not dissolution in or turning into God.

The transfiguration of the human nature through the process of *theosis* does not mean that this nature becomes ontologically different from what it was—it still remains human. What changes is not human nature as such, but its properties, as an individual adopts properties that are similar to God's. This can be called *communicatio idiomatum*—communication of properties, where a person obtains divine properties yet keeps human ones. The incarnation of God made *theosis* possible in principle, while meditation and other spiritual exercises help a person to become "god-like" according to his or her appropriated *idiomata*. Symeon the New Theologian described the theological underpinnings of deification in verses:

> The Word remained immutable in His divinity,
> And yet He became man by assumption of the flesh;
> In the same manner He kept me man, immutable in flesh and soul,
> And yet He made me entirely god,
> When He assumed my condemned flesh
> And clothed me in His divinity,
> For when I was baptized in Christ, I put on Christ...
> How is he not god by grace and adoption
> Who has put on the Son of God
> In assurance, knowledge and contemplation...?
> God totally became man,
> And so you should think in the Orthodox way
> That I become totally god by communion with God,
> In assurance and knowledge, and not by substance, but by participation.
>
> (*Hymn* 50, in Alfeyev, 2000, p. 263)

Theosis requires considerable ascetic effort and persistence in meditation, but one also needs to participate in the Eucharist, which can be understood both as an object of contemplation and of ritual ingestion (see Зарин, 1907, p. ii).

According to Symeon, the Eucharist shines with the very light of God, and thus becomes an object of meditation. It appears to those who contemplate it as light. When the Russian saint Sergius of Radonezh (1314/1322–1392), as written by his disciple Epiphanius, celebrated the liturgy, the chalice was filled with light:

> When the saint celebrated [the liturgy], one could see a fire moving on the prothesis, covering the altar and surrounding the holy table from all sides. And when the saint wanted to take communion, the divine fire curled up like a shroud and entered the holy chalice. So the holy monk took communion. (in Тихонравов, 1892, pp. 141–142)

The Jesus Prayer

The most common form of meditative practice in Eastern **Orthodox** Christianity is the "Jesus prayer." According to the Synodical Tome produced by the Palamites in the fourteenth century, this prayer consists of repeating: "Lord Jesus Christ, Son of God, have mercy on me" (*Synodical Tome* 1.47, in Migne, vol. 151, col. 689). There also is a slightly longer version: "Lord Jesus Christ, Son of God, have mercy on me a sinner," and a shorter one: "Lord, have mercy," or simply "Lord Jesus Christ." This prayer can be said in full voice, whispered, or silently. It can be repeated under all circumstances, but there are some physical and mental practices that facilitate it.

The usual position to say the Jesus prayer is to sit on a low chair, with knees a bit higher than hips. The body should lean a bit forward keeping the head down. Eyes may be directed at the navel area. Usually the right hand holds a prayer rope. With one's fingers, a person draws a knot on it with each prayer. While saying the first half of the prayer, a person inhales, and exhales for the second half. There are indications that some of these techniques have been known since the times of John Climacus (see Gillet, 1987, pp. 23–52).

This prayer technique became a part of the Palamite controversies in the fourteenth century. Barlaam considered it a magic ritual that attempts to force God to appear to those practicing the Jesus prayer. He characterized them as "navel worshipers" because, as he caricatured it, they stared at their navel, breathing in and out, and eventually saw light coming from their bellies. But other monks rebuked his mockery. Gregory Palamas, for instance, stressed that the technique of prayer does not secure the result—seeing God. It is up to God to reveal himself to the person who prays. Techniques such as the Jesus prayer are only meant to help prepare the soul to receive the revelation of the Light (see Mantzaridis, 1996, p. 211).

Some modern scholars have identified parallels between the psychosomatic techniques of the Jesus prayer and meditative techniques in Sufism. The Sufi practice of *dhikr* features the same elements in the practices of invocation of the name of God. For Kallistos Ware, these similarities cannot reconcile the theologies behind the meditative practices. He suggests that mutual influence of practices might have occurred between Christians and Muslim Sufis. Bearers of these traditions had chances to exchange techniques, as for instance, when Gregory Palamas spent a year in captivity among the Turks (see Ware, 1992, pp. 6–35).

Hesychasm

Techniques of prayer have the power to teach one to make prayer a habit. At a certain stage prayer can become ceaseless and effortless. A person then repeats it with the lips or in the mind, sometimes even when sleeping. The prayer becomes a "state of mind" as described by Evagrius (*Skemmata* 29–30, *On Prayer* 53, in Casiday 2013, pp. 138–139). In the East, Christians believe that this state is a fulfilment of Paul's words: "Rejoice always, pray without ceasing, give thanks in all circumstances; for this is the will of God in Christ Jesus for you" (1 Thess 5:16–18 ESV).

The favorite Eastern word for this state of mind is *hesychia* (ἡσυχία), the Greek word for silence or calmness. This represents a peace of the mind and a quietness of the soul that are free from passions. In this state, the mind is neither disturbed by *logismoi* (thoughts) or by passions. This state, according to Gregory Palamas, gives a person "stability of mind and of the surrounding world, abandonment of things below, initiation to things above, concentration of thoughts on that which is good. *Hesychia* is indeed an action, leading to true contemplation, or the vision of God" (*Homily* 53.33, in Mantzaridis, 1996, p. 210).

The *hesychast* movement, which Gregory Palamas led in the fourteenth century, has its roots in Christian Antiquity. Some monastic movements like that of Messalianism emphasized ceaseless prayer, for which reason its followers were also called "euchites"—those who pray. "Euchites" also insisted that they can see God. In these points, they were similar to the later Eastern hesychasts. The difference between them, however, was that ceaseless prayer made the sacraments of the church, primarily the Eucharist, needless for the former, but not for the latter.

During the Middle Ages, there was a transformation of the hesychast movement: from being popular mostly among low-key illiterate monks, it turned into an elitist movement with many followers from the most educated people of the time. In the modern era, there were attempts to bring it back to the grass-roots level and to popularize it beyond monastic communities.

The protagonists of this popularization of hesychasm were monks, who associated themselves with the so-called Kollyvadic movement, which emerged in the second half of the eighteenth century at Mount Athos. Its most important text is the *Philokalia*, a compilation of texts relevant to asceticism, prayer, and meditation from the third through the fifteenth centuries. As Lev Gillet has put it, it is a "Summa of the Jesus Prayer" (Gillet, 1987, p. 67). The *Philokalia*, through its multiple editions and translations to modern languages, made the elitist spiritual practices of the past available to everyone. As a result, the Jesus prayer and other meditative practices, which had been elaborated in monastic circles, have become widely spread in our days.

The invocation of Jesus's name became a subject of controversy in the beginning of the twentieth century. This controversy initially divided the Russian monastic community on Mount Athos. The monks disagreed on the interpretation of the invocation of Jesus's name: does this mean participation in the divinity or is it just like invoking any name? For one group of monks, the name of Jesus was divine, the manifestation of God himself. Their adversaries, though, regarded this as heresy. They reduced this view *ad absurdum* as implying a fourth hypostasis in the Trinity (in addition to the accepted hypostases of the Father, the Son, and the Holy Spirit). The "worshipers of the name" rebuked this accusation. In return they accused their opponents, whom they called "*imyabortsy*" (имяборцы)—"the fighters against the name,"—of rejecting God by rejecting the divine character of the name of Jesus. Among the protagonists of the "worshipers" were the monks Hilarion Domrachyov (ca. 1845–1916) and Antoniy Bulatovich (1870–1919). Among the leaders of the opposite group were two hierarchs: Metropolitan Antoniy Khrapovitskiy (1863–1936) and Archbishop Nikon Rozhdestvenskiy (1851–1919). Their reservations against worshiping Jesus's name were supported by the synods of the churches of Constantinople and Russia. Eventually the Russian government had to intervene in the controversy, which became violent, and the "worshipers" were forcefully removed from Mount Athos by the Russian navy.

The epicenter of the controversy regarding Jesus's name moved to Russia. In the beginning, the "worshipers of Jesus's name" were rejected by both the Russian synod and the court. Soon, however, they reconciled with the court, but not with the synod. In the court, Tsar Nicholas II (1868–1918) and the influential Gregory Rasputin (1869–1916) turned from adversaries to supporters of the "worshipers." The court did not survive the Russian revolutions of 1917, but the synod did. The church under the Bolshevik regime continued suspecting the "worshipers of the name" of being not quite Orthodox. Such was the attitude that the newly elected Russian patriarch Tikhon Bellavin (1865–1925) adopted. Soon, however, Tikhon reconciled himself with the "worshipers of the name." After the death of Tikhon in 1925, the Russian church in the Soviet Union divided into those who conformed with the regime and those who did not. The conformists were either radical or moderate. The "Alive church" completely and willingly embraced the new Soviet regime and was favored by the regime in return. A group under the leadership of Metropolitan Sergiy Stragorodskiy (1867–1944) hesitantly supported the regime under the threat of arrest and execution. This group survived the persecutions under Joseph Stalin and constituted a basis for the modern Russian Orthodox Church. The non-conformists also included both radicals and moderates. Among the moderates were those Russian hierarchs who refused to commemorate the name of Metropolitan Sergiy, who in their judgement went too far in compromising with the Communists. They did not, however, break communion with the church that Sergiy led. The more radical non-conformists broke the communion and turned into an underground or "catacomb" church, as they preferred to call themselves. The latter group incorporated the largest part of the "worshipers of the name." Among the intellectual leaders of this group were Michael Novosyolov (1864–1938) and Aleksey Losev (1893–1988), who elaborated on theories and practices of meditation and prayer in line with the medieval hesychasts. When Losev was arrested by the Soviet security services, he testified to them about an assumed political program of the "worshipers of the name":

> The Soviet authorities and Socialism are regarded by the worshipers of the name as a manifestation of the triumph of the antichrist, as the work of Satan who revolted against God. The political ideal of the worshipers is an unlimited monarchy, which completely supports the Orthodox church and relies on it... A radically negative attitude of the worshipers of the name to the Soviet regime made them positively consider the military fight against the regime, with the purpose to overthrow it.
>
> (in Лурье, 2014, p. 261)

Thus, meditative practices of Eastern **Orthodox** Christianity sometimes translated into political programs and influenced the formation of ecclesial groups. After the collapse of the Soviet Union and the liberation of the Russian Orthodox Church, these practices were reintroduced into the church. They also revived in other churches, such as in Greece, Romania, and Serbia. The so-called Neopalamite movement, which largely relies on these practices, became a theological mainstream of modern times (see Louth, 2015, pp. 178–179). Eastern Christian practices of meditation are not confined in the Eastern Christian milieu anymore. They have become popular among Christians of other confessions. In this regard, they have turned ecumenical.

Conclusion

Eastern **Orthodox** Christianity has developed a wide variety of theories and practices of meditation. Among the features of Eastern Christian meditation is an active engagement with the personal God, who reveals himself in Jesus Christ. The Jesus prayer—the amalgam of the Eastern meditative spirituality—pursues personal connection with God. It includes both bodily and spiritual engagement. Eastern Christian meditation can focus both on vices and virtues, on the good things coming from God, and on God himself. The latter is particularly important. Seeing God as Light, and divinization (*theosis*) as a result of this vision, have become not only an important goal and theological concept in Eastern Christianity, but also its identity.

References

Alfeyev, H. (2000). *St. Symeon the new theologian and Orthodox tradition*. Oxford: Oxford University Press.

Andrew of Crete, St. (2013). *The Great Canon of Saint Andrew of Crete and The Life of Saint Mary of Egypt*. Abbess Thekla and Mother Katherine from the Monastery of the Assumption of the Mother of God near Whitby (Eds. and Trans.). n.p.: Finnan Books.

Athanasopoulos, C. (Ed.). (2015). *Triune God: Incomprehensible but knowable—the philosophical and theological significance of St Gregory Palamas for contemporary philosophy and theology*. Newcastle upon Tyne: Cambridge Scholars Publishing.

Bingaman, B., & Nassif, B. (Eds.). (2012). *The Philokalia: A classic text of Orthodox spirituality*. New York: Oxford University Press.

Casiday, A. (2013). *Reconstructing the theology of Evagrius Ponticus: Beyond heresy*. Cambridge: Cambridge University Press.

Chryssavgis, J. (2004). *John Climacus: From the Egyptian desert to the Sinaite mountain*. Aldershot: Ashgate.

Dihle, A. (1982). *The Theory of Will in Classical Antiquity*. Berkeley, CA: University of California Press.

Farrell, J. (1997). *God, history, and dialectic: the theological foundations of the two Europes and their cultural consequences*. Tulsa, OK: Seven Councils Press.

Gillet, L. (1987). *The Jesus prayer*. Crestwood, NY: St. Vladimir's Seminary Press.

Grant, R. (Ed.). (1970). *Theophilus of Antioch. Ad Autolycum*. Oxford: Claredon Press.

Guillaumont, C., & Guillaumont, A. (1971). *Traité pratique, ou, Le moine*. Sources chrétiennes 170–171. Paris: Éditions du Cerf.

Louth, A. (2015) *Modern Orthodox Thinkers: From the Philokalia to the Present Day*. Downers Grove, IL: IVP Academic.

Lossky, V. (1983). *Vision of God*. Crestwood, NY: St Vladimir's Seminary Press.

Malherbe, A., & Ferguson, E. (Eds.). (1978). *Gregory of Nyssa: the Life of Moses*. New York: Paulist Press.

Pacella, M. (2015). Aquinas and Palamas. In C. Athanasopoulos (Ed.), *Triune God: Incomprehensible but knowable—the philosophical and theological significance of St Gregory Palamas for contemporary philosophy and theology*. Newcastle upon Tyne: Cambridge Scholars Publishing.

Pitra, J.B. (1883 & 1884). *Analecta sacra spicilegio Solesmensi parata*. Vols. 2 and 3. Paris: Tusculum.

Mantzaridis, G. (1996). Spiritual Life in Palamism. In Raitt, J. (Ed.). (1996). *Christian Spirituality: High Middle Ages and Reformation*. Vol. 2. New York: Crossroad.

Meyendorff, J. (1974). *St. Gregory Palamas and Orthodox spirituality*. Crestwood, NY: St. Vladimir's Seminary Press.

Migne, J.P. (Ed.). (1857–866). *Patrologiae Cursus Completus: Series Graeca*. Vols 1-167. Paris: Imprimerie Catholique.

Russell, N. (2009). *Fellow workers with God: Orthodox thinking on theosis*. Crestwood, NY: St. Vladimir's Seminary Press.

Thomas Aquinas. (2007). *Summa Theologica*. Vol. 1, part 1. New York: Cosimo Classics.

Tilby, A. (2013). *The seven deadly sins: Their origin in the spiritual teaching of Evagrius the Hermit*. New York: SPCK.

Ware, K. (1992). Praying with the Body: The Hesychast Method and Non-Christian Parallels. *Sobornost: Incorporating Eastern Churches Review* 14/2: 6–35.

Ward, B. (Ed.). (1984). *The sayings of the Desert Fathers: The alphabetical collection*. Kalamazoo, MI: Cistercian.

Зарин, С. (1907). *Аскетизм по православно-христианскому учению* [S. Zarin. *Asceticism according to the Orthodox Christian teaching*]. Vol. 1, book 2. Saint Petersburg: V.F.Kirschbaum.

Лурье, Г. (2014). *Жития радикальных святых* [G. Lourie, *Vitae of the radical saints*]. Moscow: Eksmo.

Тихонравов, Н. (1892). *Древние жития преподобного Сергия Радонежского* [N. Tikhonravov. *Ancient vitae of Saint Sergiy of Radonezh*]. Moscow.

CHAPTER 9

ISLAM AND MEDITATION

SCOTT KUGLE

Introduction

Many consider Islam to be a religion uniquely oriented toward worldly action. From late medieval times, Western travelers noted that Muslims seem unduly obsessed with exacting ritual, from the punctual call to prayer to ostentatious washing to dietary scruples. From the eighteenth century, Orientalist scholars systematized these observations into the theory that Islam is the quintessential "Semitic" religion, which is dry, legalistic, and formulaic. By the late nineteenth century, colonizing Europeans considered Muslims to be dangerously fanatic since they acknowledge no easy division between "church and state." These stereotypes are deeply rooted in Western culture (Ernst, 2003, pp. 1–36). They persist into the present, with journalistic media and films warping our view of Muslims by spotlighting the terrorist, the protestor, or the political victim. If one trusts Western portrayals, it would seem that Muslims can barely sit still let alone concentrate on meditation.

However, these portrayals are illusory. They encode the fear and prejudice that Westerners hold against Muslims, who have often been their closest religious neighbors and fiercest competitors. When we set these portrayals aside, we find that meditation has been an integral part of the Islamic tradition since its inception; it continues to be central, though some Muslims value it more than others, with the Sufis among them specializing in meditation techniques. There is no single word that corresponds to "meditation" in Arabic and other languages used by Muslims (I will also consider terms from Persian and Urdu) but rather many words, just as there is no single term for "prayer" but rather a plethora of terms. This chapter will provide a brief introduction to the variety of meditation techniques developed by Muslims, explain them through description and contrast, and emphasize their deep connection to the ritual and scriptural basis of the religion.

This chapter combines emic and etic insights to give a comprehensive view of the broad spectrum of meditative techniques in Islam. It provides short examples of each type of meditation practice from the very rich and varied literature of medieval Arabic and Persian. Previous scholarship about meditation in Islam has drawn examples from the Naqshbandi, Kubrawi, and Shadhili Sufi Orders. In contrast, this chapter mostly draws from the practices and literature of the Chishti and Shattari Sufi Orders, which became popular in South Asia (India, Pakistan, and Bangladesh). I gratefully acknowledge and bow to those who have written on this topic before—many of whom are named in the bibliographical references—and I dedicate this chapter to Dr. Mir Valiuddin.[1]

Inner Jihad

There is much discussion today about the nature of jihad or the Islamic struggle to overcome an enemy. Is it defensive or offensive warfare? Do Muslims instigate attacks or only respond to unjust assaults? Which weapons and what strategies are allowed in fighting? Yet these debates forget a famous story that tells how some early Muslims returned to Medina from battle, full of pride in their successful fight against the pagan Arabs. In response to their hubris, the Prophet welcomed them back with these words—"We have returned from the lesser Jihad to the greater Jihad." His stunned followers inquired, "Prophet of God, what do you mean by the lesser Jihad?" He replied, "That is to struggle with swords against an enemy who oppresses you." They responded, "But what struggle could be greater than this?" Muhammad answered them, "To struggle against the enemy who resides here..." as he held his hands up on either side of his chest, "that is the greater Jihad." (Ernst, 2003, pp. 117–118; Neale, 2017, pp. 3–7). The greater jihad is an inner struggle against the enemy of torpor, distraction, and egoistic illusion that infests the breast of each person, veiling her or his heart from the presence of the divine. The Prophet Muhammad was calling for an inner jihad: one that does not need a sword beyond your breath, one that you can engage in at home to conquer your own impulses, one that forces you to turn your every daily routine into an act of worship. This inner struggle is the essence of Islamic meditation practices.

This story of the Prophet's teaching explains many verses of the Qur'an, which allude to the greater jihad. *O you who believe, stay aware of God and strive to draw close to God through skillful means and struggle hard for God's sake, so that you may succeed* (Qur'an, Surat al-Ma'ida 5:35).[2] The success (*falah*) that the Qur'an urges is leaving worldly ambitions and entering into the bliss of paradise by dying to one's ego and living in the awareness of God. The skillful means (*wasila*) by which to draw near to God and stay aware of

[1] Mir Valiuddin (d. 1975) was a professor of philosophy at Osmania University in Hyderabad and a Sufi of the Qadiri Order, who authored several books on Islamic meditation; his books in English include *Qur'anic Sufism*, published in 1959; and *Contemplative Disciplines in Islam* (1980), which is quoted extensively in this article.

[2] All verses from Qur'an are translated in *italics* by the author; transliteration of words from Arabic has been rendered without complex diacritics, with only the addition of special markers for the letters *'ain* and *hamza'*. For an introduction to Qur'an as scripture, see Esack, 2002.

God is meditation, and that is the hard struggle (*jihad*) for God's sake. For this reason, one Muslim writer entitled his book about meditation practice: "The Key to Salvation and the Lamp of Souls" (*Miftah al-Falah wa Misbah al-Arwah*) in eloquent rhyming Arabic cadence. The inner jihad must be directed toward one's own chest, as the Prophet himself pointed out, because the enemy is one's own ego. It is susceptible to the whispering of temptation and delusion. The Qur'an urges believers to seek shelter from this most stealthy of enemies: *Say 'I seek refuge with the lord of humanity…from the harm of the creeping tempter that whispers in the breasts of humanity* (Qur'an, Surat al-Nas 114:1, 4–5). The creeping whisperer (*khannas*) is that aspect of Satan (*shaitan*) that is internal to us, which veils the heart with ignorance and misleads the ego into negligence, torpor, and vile deeds (Lawrence, 1992, pp. 164–165).

The Prophet Muhammad overpowered these forces of delusion and cleared them from his heart. In the Qur'an, God asks the Prophet, *Haven't we opened wide your breast? and removed from you the burden that weighed upon you? And raised high your remembrance? For surely every difficulty will clear, every difficulty will clear. So when you are free, stand upright and to your Lord draw near* (Qur'an, Surat al-Inshirah 94:1–8). God asked him rhetorically to recall that God *raised high your remembrance.* This is a clue, that remembrance (*dhikr*) is the skillful means to overcome the ego. The Prophet waged the inner jihad against his ego and his success allowed him to draw so near that he became the bearer of revelation and founder of a new religion. Likewise, all Muslims who follow him must make the same struggle: though they cannot bear revelation as he did, they can follow his admonition to "Die before you die," which means make your egoism die before you are made to die in body (Schimmel, 1975, p. 135).[3] How to turn inward and travel to the frontlines and confront the ego? There are no road signs to follow, no weapons to grasp, and the enemy appears to be one's very self. Sufi Muslims are often pictured wrapped in cloaks—symbolizing detachment from outward perception and social engagement—and engaged in meditation to turn the gaze inward to combat the ego (Figure. 9.1).

Dhikr: Meditation of Remembrance

Human beings forget their true nature in relation to God and the cosmos, and thus are called to engage in remembrance to overcome egoism and arrogance. Ritual remembrance is the central practice of meditation in Islam, and it is called *dhikr* (in Arabic, or *zikr* in Persian and Urdu). Sometimes translated into English as "invocation" or "remembrance," this practice involves repetition and internalization of the testament of faith, or phrases glorifying God and seeking forgiveness, or the various names of God. These words are extracted from the Qur'anic discourse, and as such are sacralized by

[3] Some scholars assert that this report (*hadith*) is not authentically attributed to the Prophet Muhammad, yet admit that its meaning is true to his teaching and to the Qur'anic message—see Brown, 2011.

FIGURE 9.1 Portrait of a dervish, sixteenth century. The Persian calligraphy above and below the portrait reads: "Why am I then obliged to Heaven that it has given me a soul? For it has created within me a source of sorrows from which that soul suffers."

Source: Cora Timken Burnett Collection of Persian Miniatures and Other Persian Art Objects, Bequest of Cora Timken Burnett, 1956. MET Museum, Accession Number 57.51.27.

having been part of God's revealed speech before being spoken by the practitioner. The words are recited either vocally or internally, in rhythm with the breath and heartbeat, sometimes framed by bodily posture and movement or sometimes externalized through sung melody, accentuated percussion, or instrumental music.

Sufi orders have elaborated many different styles of performing *dhikr*, both as individual practice and communal ritual. The most basic practice involves the repetition and internalization of the testament of faith: "No god but God" or *La ilaha illa ʾllah*. Skillful statement of these words is the very foundation of all *dhikr* practices. These four words have many benefits: they are easy to learn, having inherent alliteration and rhythmic cadence, and are taken from God's own reminder in the Qurʾan—*Indeed I alone am God, there is no God but I, so worship me and establish the prayer for my remembrance* (Qurʾan, Surat Ta Ha 20:14). Indeed, the best way to remember God is to forget oneself, and these words are an effective means to do that because they are originally God's own words; to say them is not to assert oneself but rather to efface oneself in the memory of God's original speech. For this reason, the Prophet Muhammad taught, "The best thing that I and the Prophets before me have brought is *La ilaha illa ʾllah*" (Iskandari, 1996, p. 119).

From an orthodox point of view, this phrase is the very bedrock of Islamic dogma: saying it in public with sincerity and freewill makes one a Muslim. This phrase's words echo in each call to five times daily formal prayer or *salat* (in Arabic, also called *namaz* in Persian and Urdu). They are pronounced verbally in each cycle (*rakʿa*) of the prayer ritual, as one kneels while extending the right forefinger in an affirmation of faith. Yet how can one say them with not just the tongue or the mind, but also with the heart? For that, the ritual of remembrance uses these words as a mnemonic device, to strip away the ego and recover original memories of the soul's harmonious presence with God (or even dissolution in God's oneness). The Qurʾan tells of a time before time when God asked the souls of all humanity before their embodiment, *Am I not your Lord?* and they bore witness by answering *Indeed, you are*! (Surat al-Aʿraf 7:172). This is an event called the "primordial covenant" (*mithaq*), the memory of which one tries to recover through meditation of remembrance.

That is a very idealistic portrait of *dhikr* practice, but how does it actually look and sound? The best way to know is to attend a Sufi gathering, for Sufi masters have always insisted one must learn *dhikr* directly from an initiated master for it to be effective. Despite that caution, Sufi masters have composed guidebooks for doing it, some of them with great precision (Kugle, 2014; see also Ernst, 1999). The following is a description of how to do *dhikr* with the phrase "No god but God," penned by the Chishti master Shaikh Kaleemullah Shahjahanabadi in early eighteenth-century Delhi:

> One should sit cross-legged with the back straight, the eyes closed, and the hands resting on the thighs. One then uses the big toe and the next toe of the right foot to firmly grip the sciatic nerve (*rag-i kimas*) that runs behind the left knee. Putting pressure on this will produce enough warmth in the heart to generate purity (*tasfiya*). This warmth will melt and remove the fat that surrounds and constricts

> the heart, which is known as the dwelling place of the tempter (*khunnus*). This will reduce the temptations and pollutions that plague the heart. Taking up this position, one should perform the meditation with single-minded heart and with assertive voice, either saying the words aloud or keeping silent as is suitable to one's situation and disposition. (Kugle, 2012, p. 59)

According to this practice, the words "No god but God" should be said in a four-beat pattern. There are many internal conditions to performing this meditation practice.

For instance, while practicing it one must imagine the face or form of one's spiritual guide (*tasawwur al-shaikh*). This is not associating anyone with God, but rather acknowledging the source of the *dhikr* practice—it has come from one's own guide, who was initiated into the practice by his guide (*murshid* or *shaikh*, or *pir* in Persian and Urdu) in a chain of guides leading back to the companions of the Prophet (primarily ʿAli ibn Abi Talib and Abu Bakr al-Siddiq), who himself taught them how to perform it.[4] ʿAli said to Muhammad, "O Prophet, show me the way which is the most direct of all the ways to God and which is excellent in God's eyes and which is easiest for God's servants!" The Prophet replied, "Keep repeating *dhikr* secretly." The Prophet then taught him how to recite *La ilaha illa ʾllah* and had him repeat it to show that he understood its use in *dhikr* (Valiuddin, 1980, p. 75). Later, this technique was taught to saints (*awliya*) who followed ʿAli (d. 661 in Kufa, Iraq).

Imagining the face of one's own spiritual guide is a form of giving thanks and acknowledging the origins of the practice. His form acts as a *barzakh* or "medium," an intermediary space between the ego and God.[5] Holding that form in one's imagination is an effective way to concentrate one's attention and ward off distracting thoughts that interfere with doing *dhikr*: one relinquishes one's whole humanity in all its weakness and negligence to one's spiritual guide, so that what is left is the soul's dependency on the pure spirit that animates one and connects one to God. Through this strategy, one can find the strength of resolve to focus on doing *dhikr* with a whole heart. Sufis call this process *fanaʾ fiʾl-shaikh* or "effacement of the ego in the person of the spiritual guide."

Shaikh Kaleemullah explains that there are two other conditions. One must "draw out" (*madd*) or prolong the first syllable "a" in *La ilaha* or "no god." And one must "intensify" (*shadd*) or accentuate the first syllable "i" when saying *illa ʾllah* or "but God." One raises the words from below while pronouncing *la ilaha* by facing down toward the left knee and then raising the head up toward the right shoulder. Then one pauses for a

[4] Reports in the *hadith* collection *Sahih Bukhari* refer to how the Prophet taught *dhikr* to Fatima (his daughter) and ʿAli (her husband). Other reports explain how the Prophet taught some of his poorer companions to do *dhikr* (traditional stories relate the names of his best friend, Abu Bakr, who gave away all his wealth, along with Salman Farsi and Bilil Habshi, who were freed slaves of Persian and African origin, and Owais Qarani, who was a Yemeni who loved the Prophet from afar and learned this practice through dream-connections with him).

[5] Valiuddin (1980, p. 76), cites a couplet from Shaikh Kaleemullah's *Alms Bowl* about how the *barzakh* or intermediary state is a reference to the image of the shaikh, a "similitudinary form," that is held in the imagination as a focus on meditation.

moment holding the breath, before pronouncing *illa ʾllah* or "but God" from above down onto the heart with great force.

> To understand the meaning of the above-mentioned method of meditation, one should know that there are four kinds of thoughts. There are tempting thoughts (*shaitani*) which cause feelings of pride, anger, enmity, envy and other destructive emotions. Then there are egoistic thoughts (*nafsani*) which cause feeling of craving for food, sexual pleasure, accumulation of wealth, love of display and other such selfish emotions. Then there are angelic thoughts (*malaki*) which cause devotion, worship and other such acts which accrue spiritual reward. Finally, there are divine thoughts (*rahmani*) which cause virtues like sincerity, love, longing and other positive emotions. So when one performs this meditation and begins facing the left knee, this is to negate tempting thoughts since the left is the abode of the tempter. Saying this, one moves to face the right knee to negate the lusts of the ego, which reside in the right lower body, for the ego and Satan mutually oppose each other and the ego is tempted to stray. The right shoulder is the abode of angelic thoughts, for the angelic scribe who writes all good deeds is there and called "the recorder of the right" (*katib-i yamini* as cited in Qurʾan, Surat al-Infitar 82:10–11). Finally, the area of the heart is the abode of divine thoughts. To try to hold all these concepts in mind at one time causes hesitation and confusion, so therefore they are taught within the simple process of performing this meditation (in four beats) which encompasses all these regions and spiritual realities. (Kugle, 2012, pp. 59–60)

The complexity of this meditation practice might confuse the beginner, for its external actions are harmonized with internal spaces and their psycho-spiritual forces. Therefore, Shaikh Kaleemullah says, it is best to just teach it as a practice with simple words and motions. As the practitioner becomes accustomed to its external movements, then the internal correspondences can be learned, for a steadily deepening practice.

The baroque elaboration of such *dhikr* practices might alarm certain Muslims of a legalistic or literalist mindset. This is, after all, a practice that not all Muslims choose to do. It looks more complicated than formal ritual prayer, and when done as a group it can be rather loud and heated, for giving up the ego is not an easy job. There will surely be exhaustion before completion and excess before success. For this reason, some jurists and scholars (especially in modern times when Salafi and Wahhabi movements have gained a wide following) are suspicious of *dhikr* practices such as those described by Shaikh Kaleemullah. Some even claim that Sufism, the devotional movement that developed *dhikr* practice, is an innovation and is not authentically part of Islam (Sirriyeh, 1999).

What these critics forget is that the Qurʾan itself enjoins believers to do *dhikr*, and that simple forms of this practice are inscribed in the basic ritual of formal prayer (*salat*).[6] The Qurʾan commands, *Recite what has been revealed to you in the message and establish*

[6] At the end of formal prayer, one is enjoined to do a small *dhikr* of silently reciting one-hundred words of remembrance: "Glory be to God" thirty-three times, "Praise be to God" thirty-three times, and "God is Greater" thirty-four times.

the prayer, for prayer keeps immorality and sin at bay, yet remembrance of God is greater still (Qur'an, Surat al-ʿAnkabut 29:45). It is not enough to do formal observances (like prayer, fasting, pilgrimage, and alms) if these only feed one's ego. Rather the Qur'an enjoins people to heal the wound that they bear in their breast, and that is the ego that inflicts the heart with spiritual disease. *O humankind, there has come to you instruction from your Lord, and healing for what is in the breast, and guidance, and mercy for those who believe* (Qur'an, Surat Yunus 10:57). This instruction for healing the breast is the guidance on how to do *dhikr*, to bring the heart tranquility. *The hearts of those who believe are calmed by the remembrance of God, for surely God's remembrance is calming for hearts* (Qur'an, Surat al-Raʿd 13:28). Those who practice remembrance constantly, in all phases of life and all moments of the day—well beyond the limits of formal prayer and other rituals—are called "the people with understanding hearts" (*ulu'l-albab*). Of them, the Qur'an says, *Those who keep the remembrance of God while standing, sitting, and lying down* (Qur'an, Surat Al ʿImran 3:191). The only way that one can keep this remembrance going, while working or even sleeping, is to yoke the words to the breath itself, and habituate oneself to remembering God in one's very breathing (D'Silva, 2020). The goal of performing words of remembrance is to internalize their meaning and inscribe them onto the tablet of the heart with the pen of the breath.

When Muslims speak of emptying the self through such meditation practices, they hold a complex notion of "self." In fact, one of the major gifts that Sufis have given to Islam is a deep reflection on the Qur'an to describe the hidden architecture of the self. In Arabic, the "self" (*nafs*) refers not merely to one's sense of ego autonomy but rather to a shifting entity called the soul, an effervescent vibration that occurs when the God blows the divine spirit (*ruh*) into the material body (*jism*). Inasmuch as the soul is an expression of the spirit, it is eternal, apparently pre-existing its bodily dwelling and predicted to persist after the body's death in another state entirely (described by the Qur'an through metaphors of terror and judgment, resurrection and transformation, reward or punishment, ecstatic bliss or painful misery). The Qur'an affirms that its message is true by swearing upon *the soul and the One who engendered it, and inspires it with its iniquity or its awareness—those who purify it succeed and those who corrupt it fail miserably* (Qur'an, Surat al-Shams 91:8–10). The word for soul (*nafs*) is related to the breath (*nafas*) just as the word for divine spirit (*ruh*) is related to the word for wind (*riyah*).[7] Inquisitive Muslims have long speculated about the nature of the soul: whether it is a substance or an entity and how it correlates to the body that can be sensed. One particularly eloquent Sufi, Jalal al-Din Rumi (d. 1273 in Qonya, Turkey) describes it through the poetic metaphor of a flag (Rumi, 2004, p. 40).

> We are just like lions men paint on their flag
> who only charge when wind should make it sag
> Our charge is visible, while wind is not

[7] The derivation of these terms of soul and spirit are similar to Hebrew (*nephesh* and *ruach*) and Greek (*psyche* and *pneuma*), the latter two terms related to the blowing of wind.

May that which is invisible be sought!
This wind, our very being, blows from You
You brought to life our whole existence too.

In Book Four of his epic Sufi poem, Rumi specifies that the human body is like the lion-emblazoned flag: it flaps in the breeze making the lion appear to run, leap and attack just like our body moves by our thoughts (Rumi, 2017, p. 182). It could be a gentle easterly wind that causes kind and compassionate actions, or it could be a severe westerly wind that causes harsh and discordant actions. The harsh westerly wind is like thoughts that are driven by the ego (*nafsani*), while the gentle easterly wind is like thoughts impelled by spiritual forces (*ruhani*). The person who watches an image on a cloth that moves by the force of another and mistakes it for an actual lion is an idiot. Yet we all begin as idiots!

Nafs: Self-Delusion in the Architecture of the Soul

Unlike the speculation of philosophers and medical doctors in the Islamic tradition, the Sufi masters observed that the soul is not a fixed entity. It shifts in nature depending upon the experiential nexus between body, mind, perception, intention, and action in the world. This circle of causation and effect gives rise to one's sense of ego. The ego misunderstands the "self" to be the body-in-this-world, giving rise to all kinds of distraction, agitation, anxiety, fear, and craving. Depending upon whether the ego dominates the soul or not, the soul could be in different states ranging from torpid and darkened to subtle and luminous. Reflecting upon the Qur'an, Sufis extracted four names to describe these states. The lowest state is that of the "soul that commands harmful behavior" (*al-nafs al-ʿammara biʾl-suʾ* cited in Qur'an, Surat Yusuf 12:53). In this lowest stage, the soul is overpowered by the ego and its destructive enmeshing in the pain-or-pleasure whirlwind of sensory and social phenomena.

With a combination of ascetic discipline, religious knowledge, and moral restraint, the soul can ascend to a higher level. This median level is that of the "soul that calls to blame" (*al-nafs al-lawwama* cited in Qur'an, Surat al-Qiyama 75:2). In this level, the soul struggles with the ego, sensing that its own attitudes are harmful, its actions are mean-spirited, and its routines are self-destructive. In this state, the soul finds itself blameworthy for its condition and also rightly blames the ego for dominating it and dragging it into harmful actions; in this state, the soul hopes for release, searches for skillful means to escape egoism's snare, and forms an intention to improve. This state is characterized by a growing perception of a split, a discontinuity between the shallow ego of the routine self-in-the-world and the deep soul of extraordinary self-dependent-upon-spirit.

With a combination of worshipful devotion, intuitive insight, spiritual guidance, and strenuous struggle, the soul ascends to a higher level. This is the level of the "soul that is tranquil" (*al-nafs al-mutmaʾina* cited in Qurʾan, Surat al-Fajr 89:27). At this level, the soul has tamed the ego and refused to be limited by its intemperate demands. In this state, the soul is purified of corrupting influences; it looks down upon the ego as a pitiful yet dangerous thing and has found skillful means to contain and quiet the ego. The soul cannot kill or suppress the ego, since the ego itself is an epiphenomenon of the soul's own existence in the embodied world. Yet the soul can perceive that the ego is just a shadow cast by the light of the spirit as it shines on the soul, granting it life, power, knowledge, and all manner of aptitudes.

The soul, like an aspiring tree, reaches up toward the light of the spirit, knowing that its energy comes from there, even as it casts a shadow on the ground of this phenomenal world and keeps its roots firmly in the soil of the body. The Chishti Sufi master and scholar, Muhammad Husaini Gisudiraz (d. 1422 in Gulbarga, India) compared the human soul to a tree:

> Love is the seed from which grows a tree, through which existence is known and it is called "the body." This tree grows from five roots, which are called intellect, imagination, spirit, knowledge and life. These roots are also called "the divine reality" (*haqiqa*). From the tree based upon these five roots grow five branches. Corresponding to the root intellect grows the branch called seeing, from the root imagination grows the branch called hearing, from the root spirit grows the branch called speaking, from the root knowledge grows the branch called understanding, and from the root life grows the branch called doing. From these five branches extend five leaves. From the branch seeing extends the leaf called greed, from the branch hearing extends the leaf called hatred, from the branch speaking grows the leaf called anger, from the branch understanding grows the leaf called pride, and from the branch doing grows the leaf called jealousy. These five leaves are also called "the self" or soul (*nafs*) and they constitute the heart, which must be trained by religion (*shariʿa*)... You have considered this tree's roots, branches and leaves, so ponder now its flower and fruits! Through the obscuring foliage it blossoms with five flowers: worship, renunciation, recitation, contentment and generosity. These altogether are called "the spiritual path" (*tariqa*). My dear, the fruits that ripen from these are also five: kindness, love, compassion, blessedness and aspiration. These five fruits are united in love, and in fact they are nothing but love. They are altogether called "mystical insight" (*marʿifa*). Now listen carefully... the seed that is hidden in the center of these fruits is called "unity" (*wahda*). This whole tree was in the beginning a seed and at the end of its perfection is the same seed. The whole circle of its being is called love (*ʿishq*) and love is God, through whom all that is comes into being. In this way, you should understand that the One through whom you manifest in this phenomenal world of being and becoming is the eternal and everlasting One.
>
> (Husaini, n.d., pp. 187–189; see also Valiuddin, 1967; Hussaini, 1983)

The soul that knows its reality—from root to branch to leaves to flowers to fruits to seed—enters into a tranquil state when it realizes its essential unity with God through love. It is unperturbed by temporary pains, undisturbed by fleeting pleasures, unmoved by tempting thoughts. With a combination of high aspiration, single-pointed concentration, compassionate interaction with others, and firm endurance, the soul can persist in this state finding new qualities of purity. Meditation, whether as *dhikr* or in other forms, is the key to moving the soul higher from one stage to another.

Sufis have reflected deeply on the psychology of the self, the meaning of the Qur'an, and the practice of self-emptying meditation. They refuse to reify the "self" as many modern psychologists do, and also resist identifying the soul with the "mind" as many new-age spiritual seekers do. Some elitist Sufis who verged toward Neoplatonism occasionally identify the ascension of the soul toward the pure spirit as the merging of the ego with the "universal intellect" (*'aql kulli*), but this is certainly not a reification of the mind as some modern neurobiologists identify it. Rather, Sufis understand that the "self," which take shape in the struggle between the ego and the soul, is affected by many forces that run like currents through its energy.

These forces give rise to different types of "thoughts" (*khatarat*). There are satanic forces (*shaitani*), egoistic forces (*nafsani*), spiritual forces (*ruhani*), and divine forces (*rahmani*), as discussed by Shaikh Kaleemullah in relation to parts of the body that act as their channels (see previous section). Thoughts caused by satanic forces prompt "destructive emotions" in the self—in the words of Shaikh Kaleemullah—emotions such as pride, anger, hatred, envy. Satanic forces emerge from below and invade the region of the heart, trying to pierce its defenses and overpower it. Egoistic forces prompt "selfish emotions" like craving for bodily pleasures, fear of injury, lust for power, greed for wealth, and arrogance in reputation. Egoistic forces veil the heart from its true nature and weaken its natural defenses, making it susceptible to satanic influence. Angelic forces cause aspiring motivation, good intention, and conscientious remembering, which strengthen the heart's resolve and fortify its light to ward off the previous two kinds of influences. Finally, divine force comes from within, causing "positive emotions" such as sincerity, love, longing, and compassion. These emerge from within the heart, because the presence of God is already there in its innermost secret kernel. That is difficult to perceive only because of veils of fatty darkness that cover the heart when the ego gets the upper hand.

The heart is not seen as merely the blood-pumping muscle in the chest. It is an organ with spiritual senses, the metaphorical core of the person, the seat of the soul where the spirit and body are conjoined. In a Sufi view of the human being, the "self" is not an entity but rather a stage where this drama plays out around the heart, with the soul either dragged down toward phenomenal materiality or raised up toward spiritual subtlety until it can dissolve in the presence of God.

Asma': Meditation on God's Names

In this drama, Sufi masters see themselves as doctors, administering meditation practices like *dhikr* to treat spiritual atherosclerosis. In relation to common people and Sufi followers, they are doctors, healing the sickness of others, which is ego, while avoiding that sickness themselves. In relation to the Prophet Muhammad, they are sages, for they are linked to him by a chain of charismatic initiation (*silsila*), through which they receive these meditation practices to dispense to others. When Muhammad was asked to explain the nature of the Qur'an, the revelation urged him—*Say, "It is guidance and healing for those who believe"* (Qur'an, Surat al-Dukhan 41:44). How can there be healing without doctors?

Just as doctors must know a variety of medicines to treat all possible maladies, so Sufi masters have elaborated many kinds of *dhikr* for the limitless permutations of egoism. They turn to the Qur'an as the central resource for developing meditative practices. The Qur'an presents itself as full of potential cures: *We reveal of the Qur'an that in which there is healing and mercy for those who believe* (Qur'an, Surat al-Isra' 17:82). The most valuable elements revealed in it are the names of God (*asma' allah al-husna*), traditionally numbered at ninety-nine (Ernst, 2011; see also Lawrence, 2006, chap. 8). *Call upon God or call upon the merciful One, call upon whatever you like of the most beautiful names that belong to God* (Qur'an, Surat al-Isra' 17:110). In the starkly monotheistic world of Islam, there is allowance for a bewildering plurality of God's names. The many names of God do not violate the absolute oneness of God--*God, there is no god but that One, to whom belong the most beautiful names* (Qur'an, Surat Ta Ha 20:8). God's names, which sometimes appear contradictory, display particular qualities such that each name has a distinct purpose and role.

The Qur'an waxes hymnic when recounting the luminous names of God: *That One is God, there is no god but that One, the knower of the hidden and the apparent—that is the merciful One, the compassionate One. That One is God, there is no god but that One, the possessor, the holy, the peaceable, the believer, the securer, the mighty, the overwhelming, the lordly One. Glory be to God despite all that they ascribe as partners. That One is God, the creator, the originator, the shaper—to God belong the most beautiful names by which all things in the heavens and the earth glorify that One, the mighty, the wise* (Qur'an, Surat al-Hashr 59:22–24). The names indicate relationships: on the one hand, they indicate the One named—God—and, in that sense, they are unified; yet on the other hand, the diverse attributes of God point to qualities in us and our phenomenal world, and in that sense they are pluralized. In this relating function, they reveal that the transcendent God is also immanent with us. The names serve as secret connectors from the unknowably singular God to our embodied and ever-changing life situations. They are the perfect elements from which to devise *dhikr* practices of meditation, to move from a state of dispersal and distraction to a state of integration and concentration.

Take for example one of the most famous and beloved verses of the Qur'an—the Throne Verse, which is often recited for protection. That long verse begins with the phrase: *God, there is no god but that One, the living One, the One everlasting* (Qur'an, Surat al-Baqara 2:255). Praise of God immediately splits into glorification of two different names—the living (*hayy*) and the everlasting (*qayyum*). This pair of names are often used in *dhikr*. They illustrate the delicate interplay of transcendence and immanence inherent in God's names. God is the living One, and we understand that quality in comparison with ourselves since we are alive—our life is derived from and similar to that of God who is the living One. Yet God is also the everlasting One, and we understand that quality in distinction from ourselves since we are finite and perishing—our duration in this life is miniscule, almost non-existent, as distinct from the transcendent One who is everlasting with no beginning and no ending. Remembering God through the ritual repetition of these words, which are two of the names of God, can generate deep insights. The names must not be merely read as in a sentence read from this page or spoken as when one recites the verse from the Qur'an. Rather the names must be recollected through rhythmic repetition, so that their effect can work deep into one's consciousness and, in fact, displace one's self-consciousness. This is how the names work in *dhikr* meditation (Iskandari, 1996).[8]

These two names frame a third name, that of Allah. Allah itself is a name of God, meaning simply "the God" that effaces all others (as opposed to "a god" from among many possible deities). Muslim theologians call Allah the "essential name" of God (*ism al-dhat* or *ism mufrad*) because it indicates God singularly. Some meditation teachers consider it to be more concentrated and powerful than other names of God, because it is linked to God directly without reference to any other quality or attribute (Iskandari, 2018; see also for a modern take on the Islamic use of "Allah," Lawrence, 2015, chap. 1, 3). Shaikh Kaleemullah instructed people in how to do meditation using only this name, Allah, repeated continuously and without gap or pause, such that it ceases to be a pronounced name or a distinct word but rather becomes an undulating flow of vibrating sound. This method, he explained, is called the babbling meditation (*dhikr-i laqlaqa*) (Kugle, 2012, p. 83). Another method of meditation he teaches uses the name Allah to observe the breath.

> This meditation of "observing the breath" (*pas-i anfas*) is sometimes taught such that one only recites the name Allah. The method of doing this is to recite the name Allah while extending the final letter "h" with a long "u" so that it takes on the sound of "*hu*."[9] While inhaling, one recites *Alla-* and when exhaling, one recites *-hu*. Doing this does not employ the voice; rather one lets the breath expresses the language of the heart... One does this with each breath exhaled and inhaled while keeping one's concentration upon the navel as it is drawn in and extended out during breathing. After one does this meditation continuously and extensively, the meditation continues with one's breathing even if one is asleep or awake. (Kugle, 2012, p. 88)

I have cited Shaikh Kaleemullah often, though he is just one of many Sufi masters who have written about the practice of meditation in the Islamic tradition. His book on med-

[8] Abu Hamid Ghazali wrote a book about the names, *al-Maqsad al-Asna fi Sharh Asma' Allah al-Husna* (for a translation, see Ghazali, 1992). For a modern interpretation of the psychic significance of the names in meditation practice, see Meyer, Hyde, Kahn, & Muqaddam, 2011.

[9] In Arabic grammar, this is called pronouncing with *ashba'*, which extends the vowel sound (which is not an inherent part of the word) and pronounces it audibly; saying God's name as *Alla-hu* gives it the implied meaning of "God is."

itation, *Kashkul* or *The Alms Bowl*, is a relatively late summation and clarification of a rich tradition, and I cite it because he teaches meditation in a way that readers of varied backgrounds can understand.

In eighteenth-century India, Shaikh Kaleemullah was teaching much the same wisdom as Sufi masters before him. Most early Sufis who wrote books included a section on *dhikr*, but one of the first to write a full book dedicated to it was Shaikh Ibn ʿAtaʾillah al-Iskandari of the Shadhili Sufi Order (d. 1309 in Cairo, Egypt). His book, *The Key to Salvation*, speaks more to the theory behind *dhikr* than to its actual practice. He emphasizes that remembrance of God is not merely a ritual practice, for anything that reminds one of God's presence can become a means for remembrance. The central principle is to spark awareness and dispel negligence:

> Remembrance of God is liberation from ignorance and forgetfulness through the permanent presence of the heart with the true One (*haqq*)... It is alike whether it is God who is remembered, or one of God's attributes, or one of God's commandments, or one of God's deeds... Remembering God may take the form of a supplication to God, or the remembrance of God's messengers, prophets, saints or of anyone related to or close to God in some way, or because of some deed like reciting the Qurʾan, mentioning God's name, poetry, singing, a conversation or a story.
>
> (Iskandari, 1996, p. 45)

Ibn ʿAtaʾillah al-Iskandari cites many different objects of remembrance beyond God and God's names. Let us follow his lead and explain other types of meditation practice based upon benediction, supplication, recitation, contemplation, or cantillation in song.

Salawat: Invoking Benediction and Peace

Most writings about meditation in Islam—whether by Muslims or outside observers—focus on *dhikr*. Yet there are other forms of devotional practice in Islam that can be considered meditative if not exactly "meditation." Many consider sitting in silence to be the definitive form of meditation, but this definition excludes most forms of Islamic meditation. If we widen the definition to any ritual practice designed to focus concentration, intensify awareness, and shift mental faculties away from routine egoistic thoughts, then the practice of *salawat* (in Arabic, also called *durud* in Persian, Urdu, and Bengali) can also be considered meditative.

Salawat means "benediction" or offering peace and blessing upon beloved people such as prophets and spiritual guides. In Islamic communities of all kinds, this practice focuses especially upon the Prophet Muhammad and his close family members. Offering *salawat* is probably the most "orthodox" kind of meditative practice, because it is integral to formal prayer (*salat*); the two terms even share a verbal root.[10] After each cycle of formal prayer (*rakʿa*) one intones silently while kneeling, "Sincere greetings to God, and may benedictions and wholesome peace be upon you, O Prophet, with God's compassion and blessings. May peace be upon us and upon all the righteous servants of God." Then after completing all the cycles of a formal prayer, one recites silently while kneeling, "Dear God, send benedictions to Muhammad and the family of Muhammad as you sent benedictions to Abraham and the family of Abraham. Dear God, send blessings upon Muhammad and the family of Muhammad as you sent blessing upon Abraham and the family of Abraham. In all the worlds, you are praiseworthy and mighty." This is the ritual root of offering *salawat*.

Offering benedictions, peace, and blessings on the Prophet is not merely part of formal prayer. It flows out beyond the limits of the ritual into daily life. Many Muslims add small phrases of benediction after every mention of the Prophet Muhammad, in conversing and writing, to show their admiration and love for him. The Qurʾan enjoins this practice, testifying that *God and God's angels send blessings upon the Prophet—O you who believe, send him blessings and benedictions* (Qurʾan, Surat al-Ahzab 33:56). Many Muslims are content to hear this as a command and obey by sprinkling their discourse with pauses to bless the Prophet at his every mention. However, some Muslims have probed deeper to discover why sending benedictions and peace to him is enjoined, and how that might be cultivated as a meditative practice.

The Qurʾan hints that remembrance (*dhikr*) and the blessing of benediction (*salawat*) are related: *O you who believe, keep the remembrance of God with continuous recollection, and glorify God morning and evening. God is the One who sends benediction upon you, as do God's angels, to bring from you from the depths of darkness into the light, for God is a compassionate One to the believers* (Qurʾan, Surat al-Ahzab 33:41–43). God and God's angels send blessings and benediction to each of us, but most especially to the Prophet and those linked to him (as to the prophets who came before him, such as Abraham). When we send benedictions, peace, and blessings to the Prophet, his family, and those like him, we establish an inner spiritual connection to him through which divine qualities like light, compassion, and knowledge can flow.

In most Sufi gatherings, *dhikr* meditation begins or ends with *salawat*, either recited or sung, often in a repetitive pattern. This is a way of acknowledging that *dhikr* came to us from the Prophet's teaching. It is also a way of establishing a channel of blessings through his name and persona, so that *dhikr* practice might be beneficial and not merely rote. Without him there is no religion, no knowledge of God, no path to performing good works, and no practice of meditation. In his book on meditation, Shaikh Ibn ʿAtaʾillah explains that the Prophet "is the intermediary between God and us, our guide to God and our means of knowing God through gnosis (*maʿrifa*). Attachment to the intermediary precedes attachment to the One who sent him." (Iskandari, 1996, p. 95). So

[10] The verbal root *s-l-w* means "to connect with" and connotes the basic meaning of "to worship" or to give oneself over to that which is adored and thereby elicit a state of grace through connection with a divine source.

fundamental is this insight—that the Prophet's person is the foundation of any Islamic meditation practice—that the first caliph, Abu Bakr al-Siddiqi (d. 634 in Medina), used to teach that the beginner in meditation should simply call down blessings and peace upon the Prophet, without any other kind of invocation or remembrance practice. This is because one's connection with God is primarily through one's Prophet.

The Prophet Muhammad taught that "Benediction upon me is a light" and "The hearts of believers are made pure and cleansed of rust through benediction upon me" (Iskandari, 1996, p 95). The heart is the locus of sincerity, so it must be purified and cleared of all selfish concern and objects that are other-than-God. Benediction upon the Prophet and blessing him are a means to focus the heart and resolve it in sincerity, so that its love for the Prophet becomes a channel for it to love the One who sent the Prophet. As quoted earlier, the Qur'an asks Muhammad, *have we not raised your remembrance*? (Qur'an, Surat al-Inshirah 94:4). This means that God should not be remembered without also mentioning the Prophet, sending him benedictions, and calling down blessings and peace upon him.

It is primarily Sufis who elaborated the pious practice of calling benedictions upon the Prophet. This is because they believe that the Prophet Muhammad is still present in the world even after his bodily death.[11] Therefore, invoking benedictions upon him is not merely a pious demonstration of love or expression of fidelity to his community; rather it is a practical way of attaching oneself to him through inner channels of blessing in hopes of keeping one's heart pure and one's mind illuminated. Sufis have invested much energy in finding the right words to invoke benedictions on the Prophet and his family, ranging from the profoundly simple to the philosophically complex. Compare the invocation attributed to the founder of the Chishti Sufi Order, Khwaja Muʿin al-Din Chishti (d. 1236 in Ajmer, India)—"O God, grant peace and benedictions upon our leader Muhammad in whatever ways you love and with whatever means you are content"—with that of the later Chishti master, Shaikh Kaleemullah—"O God, grant blessings and peace upon our beloved Muhammad, the most primal emanation from you and most comprehensive appearance of your greatest name, as much as are the manifestations of your essence beyond dualities and as varied as are the forms of being derived from your qualities, and upon his family members be blessings just the same."

Perhaps the richest and most baroque elaboration on *salawat* is a composition by Shaikh Muhammad ibn Sulaiman al-Jazuli (d. 1465 in Marrakesh, Morocco) a master from the Shadhili Sufi Order. He wrote a book entitled *Dala'il al-Khairat* or "Demonstrations of Benevolence," a series of benedictions of great complexity—one for each day of the week—which Muslims all over the world in many orders now utilize.[12]

[11] Sufis generally believe that just as Muhammad was present before his bodily birth (as the radiance of divine light through which creation came into being and which is reflected in all the prophets before him) so he continues to be present after his bodily death (as merciful helper conveying supplications and petitions, as guide through dreams and visions, and as intercessor during judgment day).

[12] The book's title, *Dala'il al-Khairat* or "Demonstrations of Benevolence," is actually the pluralization of one of the praise names of the Prophet Muhammad, namely *Dalil al-Khairat* or "Demonstration of Benevolence," for Muhammad is the proof that benevolent action yields enduring merit. The very title

In its great flood of words, the author and reciters reconceive time and space in a struggle to imagine infinity within singularity. The words conceive of the Prophet as blessed for all time—including pre-infinity and post-infinity, from before time began and until time ceases—in ways and extents that implement means of counting and multiplying blessings. As an example, take this one passage from the invocation for Fridays:

> O God, I request... that you grant benedictions upon your prophet, Muhammad, to the extent that you created him before the skies were raised up and the earth was laid down, before the mountains were anchored and the seas were spread, before the springs and the rivers were set flowing, before the sun was radiant and the moon was reflective and the stars were illumined. You were then as you are now and no one knows how you are except yourself, you singly without any partner... Grant benedictions upon Muhammad through the expanse of your heavens and grant benedictions upon Muhammad through the breadth of your earth. Grant benedictions upon Muhammad by the vastness of your throne and grant benedictions upon Muhammad by all contained in your throne's shadow. Grant benedictions upon Muhammad to the extent of all that has been inscribed by your pen upon your cosmic tablet. Grant benedictions upon Muhammad to the limit of all you create within the seven spheres of the heavens and grant benedictions upon Muhammad to the number of creations you engender within them until the day of resurrection a thousand times over for each day. (Jazuli, 1996, n.p.)

This gives just a sample of the almost two hundred pages of invocations; reciting these invocations generates the dizzying effect of perceiving the whole cosmos as if it were contained in the person of the Prophet or that the essence of the Prophet was the very foundation of being for all that exists. Sufis call this effect *fana' fi'l-rasul* or "effacement of the ego in the persona of the Prophet."

Wird: Reciting Litanies to Personalize Scripture

Salawat grew from a simple practice that is integral to the formal prayer to become a very complex independent meditative practice. Similarly, reciting a *wird* or litany has evolved to become an intricate literary composition used for meditative devotion. Again, this practice evolved among Sufi communities but now has become more widespread.

Formal prayer involves many elements, including *dhikr* and *salawat*, yet the primary element in prayer is reciting from scripture, from the Qur'an. Each cycle of prayer requires one to recite the short Opening Chapter (Surat al-Fatiha) of the Qur'an twice,

hints that the meditative practice of invoking blessings upon Muhammad yields a profound connection to his transformative persona, long after his death in the body.

along with two other passages that one can choose for oneself. Interspersed between these scriptural recitations are ample moments for personal supplication (*duʿa*). Supplication is a form of prayer that is open-ended and personal. Its words are not fixed or formulaic. The supplicant can give thanks, ask for aid, specify obstacles, complain about problems, beseech forgiveness, request favors, or express awe as she or he sees fit, in words of the supplicant's own choosing. Of course, there are formulaic expressions for these needs which one finds used commonly in supplication, which have become hallowed because they were transmitted as the Prophet's own expressions in personal supplication or were used by great saints of the Sufi communities.

The *duʿa* is the most personal part of formal prayer, and it changes from moment to moment and day by day, depending upon what one is confronting. At times of crisis and anxiety, the *duʿa* might expand into an extended monologue. This is called *munajat* or intimate conversation with God, and it can be an effective vessel for the outpouring of grief or overflowing of hope. Over the centuries, Sufi masters have recorded models of *munajat* that become less about their own personal state and more about expressing intimacy and total dependence upon God. These *munajat* have become means for meditative introspection, and they can be moving poetic or aphoristic expressions useful for spiritual seekers to train their own hearts. The most famous example is probably the *Munajat* of Khwaja ʿAbdullah Ansari (d. 1089 in Herat, Afghanistan), a pithy and moving string of Persian couplets that chart the soul's discourse with God, an exchange which vacillates between hope and fear, yearning and awe (Danner & Thackston, 1978, pp. 167–239). Such literary devotional works were crafted into "wisdom literature" (*hikam*) for others to ruminate over and by which their meditative journeys could be guided.

Over time, these intricate literary works were incorporated into Islamic devotional communities in the form of the *wird* or "litany" (the same term is used in Persian and Urdu, though in Arabic, *hizb* is also used). The term *wird* literally means "arriving at a place of nourishment," just as flocks of sheep arrive at a watering place to drink. These are structured literary pieces to be recited on a regular basis. Often, they are composed by saints who gave their name to distinct Sufi orders, and recitation of a *wird* is normally a marker of allegiance to a particular Sufi path. The *wird* is a collection of verses or phrases from the Qurʾan that are strung together with short passages of *dhikr* or *duʿa* to achieve particular spiritual benefits, such as protection from harm, acquiring virtues, overcoming obstacles, or attaining spiritual states. Perhaps the most famous *wird* today is the one by Shaikh Abuʾl-Hasan al-Shadhili (d. 1258 in Humaithara, Egypt), entitled *Hizb al-Bahr* or "The Litany of the Sea" (Douglas, 1993, pp. 74–78). Its author is the founder of the Shadhili Sufi order that spread from North Africa to as far as Indonesia and, in the twentieth century, into Europe.

> O God, the elevated One, the great One, the forbearing One, the knowing One! You are my lord and your knowledge of me suffices me. What a fine lord is my lord and how sufficient is my sufficiency! You give aid to whomever you will for you are the mighty One, the compassionate One. We ask that you grant us protection in our

> movements and our stillness, in our words and our intentions and our thoughts, from misguided opinions, doubts and delusion that cover the hearts from perceiving the unseen reality. For *the believers are tested with trials and quake with a terrible trembling. When the hypocrites and those in whose hearts is disease may say, "God and God's messenger have only warned in vain!"* (Qurʾan, Surat al-Ahzab 33:11–12) then steady us and grant us aid! Make subservient to us this sea as you made the sea subservient to Moses (Qurʾan, Surat al-Shuʿaraʾ 26:60–66), upon whom be peace, and made the fire subservient to Abraham (Qurʾan, Surat al-Anbiyaʾ 21:68–70), upon whom be peace, and made the mountain and iron subservient to David (Qurʾan, Surat Sad 38:18), upon whom be peace, and made the wind and the demons and the jinn subservient to Solomon (Qurʾan, Surat Sad 38:36), upon whom be peace. Make subservient to us every sea that is yours on the earth and in the heavens and the cosmos and the angelic realm, the sea of this world and the sea of the hereafter. Make subservient to us everything, o God, *in whose hand is dominion over all things* (Qurʾan, Surat al-Jathiya 45:11–12).

This is only the first passage from the *Hizb al-Bahr*, which should be recited under certain ritual conditions, with particular movements of the hands at specified moments along with repetition of certain phrases or personal intention. One can observe the inclusion of the names of God as in *dhikr*, supplication as in *duʿa*, and the weaving together of verses, phrases, or images from the Qurʾan.

Those who recite such a *wird* regularly commit it to memory, so that it becomes less a reading and more a vehicle for meditative concentration and purifying one's intention. The *Hizb al-Bahr* spread among Sufis of the Shadhili order in North Africa and Egypt, but soon became widely respected and adopted by other Sufi orders as well; now with the internet and global communication, Muslims of any kind adopt it and other such devotional practices, whether or not they belong to a Sufi order (Figure. 9.2). However, it must be stressed that all the litanies and meditation practices this chapter offers as examples are to be used with the direction of a spiritual guide who has training in how to use them; in the age of internet this rule is often quoted but seldom followed.

Dhikr biʾl-Jahr: Meditation through the Tongue

Meditative practices discussed thus far involve speech. They are examples of meditation through the tongue; whether the words are spoken aloud (*dhikr biʾl-jahr*) or spoken silently (*dhikr khafi*), they involve directing the mind through words to achieve certain states of heart. Many of them also involve bodily motion of the hands or the head or, as some groups do *dhikr* as a communal practice, the whole body in motion. Because many readers may assume that "real meditation" involves stillness and silence, this reliance on speech in the Islamic tradition may require a deeper explanation.

FIGURE 9.2 The names of God embedded in the *wird* of Sayyid ʿAli Hamadani (d. 1314) entitled *Awrad-e Fathiya* or "Litanies of Divine Opening." The whole litany is painted on calligraphic modelled and richly painted papier-mâché that tiles the walls of the Khanqah-e Muʿalla, built in 1395 in Srinagar, Kashmir (known locally as Khanqah-e Moula or Khanqah Shah-e Hamdan), a mosque that houses relics of this leader of the Kubrawi Sufi Order who spread Islam in Kashmir and is built around spot where he meditated beside the Jhelum River.

Source: Scott Kugle.

The purpose of using speech in meditative practices is twofold. First, we are accustomed to expressing intentions and ideas in words that are realized in speech acts. This is the primary way that we exercise our subjectivity, so the best way for us to grasp the self and refashion it is to use speech. Second, the most powerful resource that Muslims have is the Qurʾan, which is itself divine speech. Reciting verses of Qurʾan is the primary mode of worship for all Muslims (literally offering the speech of God back to God, as a way of embodying the message). Therefore, spoken words, especially those from Qurʾan, are very powerful tools. It is said that an elderly man once asked the Prophet Muhammad, "O Messenger of God, the ways of doing good are many but I cannot perform them all, so tell me something which I can follow but do not make it too long for me, lest I forget!" The Prophet answered him, "Your tongue should not cease to be moist with the remembrance of God" (Iskandari, 1996, p. 60; see also Valiuddin, 1980, p. 34).

In *dhikr* and other meditative practice, however, the outer objective of speaking—communicating to achieve an effect in the outer world—is abandoned in favor of a more internal goal. The intent is to turn words inward in order to alter one's own consciousness. Through words spoken with the tongue one can address the heart, and through the inner heart one can alter one's consciousness which will transform the entire being. Abu Hamid al-Ghazali (d. 1111 in Tus, Iran) expressed this idea by saying that remembrance (*dhikr*, here translated as "invocation") has three coverings over the kernel: "Invocation is an inner reality in which the One invoked takes possession of the heart while the one invoking is effaced and vanishes. But it has three coverings, one closer to the kernel than the others. The kernel as such is beyond the three coverings, yet the virtue of the coverings lies in their being the way to the kernel" (Valiuddin, 1980, p. 47). Ibn ʿAtaʾillah al-Iskandari explains this somewhat cryptic saying:

> The uppermost covering is remembrance with the tongue only. The invoker unceasingly invokes with his tongue, striving for the presence of the heart simultaneously, since the heart must consent to be present in the invocation... [When the heart, the second covering, joins the tongue in invocation] its own invocation would take hold and invocation of the tongue would become weaker; then body and soul would become filled with light; and the heart would be purified of other-than-God... When remembrance permeates the heart and diffuses throughout the body, then every member of the body invokes God commensurate with its spiritual state.
>
> (Valiuddin, 1980, pp. 47–48)

The coverings are the tongue (*lisan*), the heart (*qalb*), the body as a whole (*qālib*); the kernel (*lubb*) is the hidden core of the heart, which is the secret (*sirr*) seat of the self, which must become emptied if the presence of God is to reside there in intimacy and inspiration and enlightenment. *Dhikr* permeates these various layers, providing nourishment to the inner heart and thereby affecting the whole body. Ibn ʿAtaʾillah al-Iskandari explains, "Sustenance of the outer person comes from the movements of the body; sustenance of the inner person comes from the movements of the heart; spiritual sustenance of one's most interior being is through tranquility; and sustenance of the intellect is through extinction of one's consciousness of tranquility, so that the servant is tranquil for God and with God.... As God most high has said, *Those who believe and whose hearts have rest in remembrance of God, for surely in the remembrance of God do hearts find rest*" (Iskandari, 1996, p. 51, quoting Surat al-Raʿd 13:28).

From this perspective, it does not matter whether the remembrance is performed with words pronounced aloud (*jahri*) or imagined silently (*khafi*). Words recited aloud have the benefit of engaging the senses and pulling them away from worldly entanglements by binding them into the meaning of the words recited. Spoken words also serve as a foundation for group cohesion, as when many people gather to perform *dhikr* together; the sound of unified voices has a very fortifying effect on the heart and gives it courage and renewed aspiration where individually it might falter. The Prophet said, "When you pass by the verdant meadows of paradise, graze in them." When asked what he meant by the meadows of paradise, he explained that they are "the circles of those invoking God" (Iskandari, 1996, p. 58). This report establishes that the Prophet advocated his people to gather to invoke God's names and qualities, and this gathering is called a "circle" because those gathered for this activity are joined like points forming a circle united in one intention and one voice.

This report also indicates that even one person doing *dhikr* is a "circle" because the angels gather around her or him, as alluded to in hadith reports (Iskandari, 1996, pp. 541–557). The Prophet Muhammad is relayed to have said, "God says, 'I am with the thought of my servant and am with him when he remembers me. If he remembers me in his heart, I too remember him in my heart. If he remembers me in an assembly, I too recollect him in an assembly that is better than his assembly" (Valiuddin, 1980, p. 35; see also Iskandari, 1996, pp. 54–57). The better assembly implies that those who invoke God's names and qualities are encircled by angels who join in their remembrance. Those who invoke God are in God's presence, alluded to by the word "paradise" (*jannat*), which means intimacy with God to the extent that they are absent from their own selfish concerns. Those who invoke God gain nourishment and sustenance of the spirit, as alluded to with the verb "graze," which means to eat leisurely and without search and struggle, the way gazelles graze on the grasses of a verdant meadow.

Those who gather in circles to do *dhikr* usually recite words aloud, sometimes to melody and rhythm. Such meditators often appreciate the beauty of the voice and its musicality. For them, to have the senses engrossed in the word's voiced beauty (*jamal*) helps the meaning of the *dhikr* to reach the heart. Other meditators eschew pronouncing the words with the voice. By conceiving the words mentally and not vocally, they sharpen their focus and incite the heart to grasp more deeply their meaning; this way, they spur the heart to follow the path of the words' indication toward the reality to which they point. For them, voicing the words would create a sensory distraction from internalizing the meaning, and so they pronounce the words mentally, perhaps with a movement of the tongue but with no voice. Such meditators tend to shy away from musicality and the aspiration for beauty, tending toward asceticism and the apprehension of divine might (*jalal*).

Whether the words are voiced or silent, meditation through recitation relies upon techniques of repetition for interiorization of the meaning of words. If done in groups or vocally, one relies on listening to a leader to know when repetition is sufficient; if done individually or silently, one relies on a string of beads (called *tasbih*, often ninety-nine in number) to keep count through tactile motion of the fingers. Silently or vocally, meditation through words is an effective means of engaging the tongue to connect to the heart. Through it, the heart can be contacted and awareness of the heart deepened. Then the hard work of purifying the heart's intent can begin. Surveying the variety of Islamic meditation techniques, the insightful twentieth-century scholar Mir Valiuddin noted that they all have one goal: "Cleansing of the heart means detachment from everything that is other than God, emptying the heart of the love of the world and dispelling all evil thoughts from it. This is the outcome of recollection of God. When the effulgence of [God's] remembrance enters into the heart, it becomes devoid of the griefs and sorrows of the world, and is filled with the love of God alone. The light of [God's] remembrance turns the heart into a radiant lamp" (Valiuddin, 1980, p. 31).

With the image of a lamp, Mir Valiuddin alludes to the Light Verse from the Qurʾan: *God is the light of the heavens and the earth* . . . and the metaphor for understanding God's light is imagined as a niche in a solid wall, while in the niche stands a lamp, and within the lamp is a glass, and inside the glass is olive oil so pure it radiates light without being lit by fire (Qur'an, Surat al-Nur 24:35). As Abu Hamid al-Ghazali interpreted it, the solid wall is like the human body and its niche is like the breast. The lamp is like the heart, and its glass is like the kernel or the spiritual core of the heart. The oil is like the presence of God that illumines the mind with faith and enlightens the imagination with inspiration (Gairdner, 2010; see also Valiuddin, 1980, p. 140).

The body, heart, soul, and spirit are a continuum rather than a contradiction, when they are properly purified and harmonized. Reciting with the tongue and voice is not to deny the deeper resonance of words through their rarified meaning. Yet there are Islamic techniques of meditation that employ silence, and these we can call "contemplation" rather than meditation.

Muraqaba: Contemplation through Mental Focus

Meditation or *dhikr* is often contrasted with thought or *fikr*. The two words rhyme in Arabic, and the Qur'an urges the human being to deeply engage both, to recollect in remembrance and to ponder in reflection. But thought cannot attain to God—rationality cannot define the divine as an object of conception. However, thought as "reflection" may attempt to draw close to God by displacing routine rationality; that kind of reflective thought is contemplation.

Contemplation in the Islamic tradition is known as *muraqaba*. The term is an abstract noun derived from "to be on the watch"—it means engaging in single-pointed thought in order to guard the heart's awareness from any object other-than-God (Valiuddin, 1980, p. 93). The locus of contemplation is the *sirr*, the secret inner kernel of the heart, the pivot point connecting the material phenomenal world to the spiritual eternal realm of divinity. The *sirr* is the connection between the heart (conceived as within an individual body) and the spirit (conceived as beyond an individual body yet permeating the body and giving it life, awareness, and power). Thus, the *sirr* within the heart is an organ of awareness, knowledge, and vision. *Muraqaba* is focusing one's mental faculty on the *sirr*, eliminating all distracting thoughts that obstruct it, and employing skillful means to clarify its apprehension of the truth. "This concentration should be with all the power of mind, thought and imagination, so that that which is not perceived or felt may be intuited and known clearly" (Valiuddin, 1980, pp. 95–96).

The basic idea is to begin with one's own mental faculties, attaching one's thought to divine objects in such a way that ideation becomes imaginalization and then realization: that is, the subject-object relationship becomes ultimately reversed. Usually, the ego imagines itself to be the subject, the one who actively thinks, conceives, and knows an object. However, when the thinking process is directly toward an object created by God (*makhluq*), toward God's actions (such as continuous creation, *takhliq*), toward God's qualities (such as God as "the creating One" *khaliq*), then the egoistic subject/object dichotomy is reversed. God is recognized as the real subject, the unmoved mover, the primal cause, or the necessary existent. God is the subject and the ego of the one contemplating becomes a mere object—it knows only inasmuch as it reflects the quality of knowing, which is ultimately the character of God, who knows all things individually (*ʿalim*) and knows in an absolute sense generally (*ʿallam*).

Therefore, contemplation is not an assertion of the ego through thought, as in rational calculation. Rather, contemplation is clearing away rational calculation in order for the mind to reflect upon divine realities, until the mind simply reflects divine realities. It is a kind of negative assertion (*nafi* in Arabic) that guards over the thought process and prevents it from straying toward egoistic notions. Mir Valiuddin sums up contemplation beautifully: "It is preventing the heart from thinking of anything whatsoever, keeping it free from all vain thoughts, while sitting or reclining in public or private, and disengaging it from cogitating on the past or the future. While engaged in contemplation, if the thought of even prayer or worship comes, it should be negated at once, because this will bring contemplation from a higher to a lower level" (Valiuddin, 1980, p. 97).

Some Sufi orders have concentrated special effort on practicing contemplation. The Naqshbandi Order is characterized by silent *dhikr* and contemplation.[13] It originated in Central Asia (present-day Uzbekistan) but spread to South Asia, Turkey, China, and beyond; one practitioner-scholar, the late Arthur Buehler, has written a fine article on contemplation practices in the Naqshbandi Order, based on evidence from twentieth-century Hyderabad in India (Buehler, 2015; see also Buehler, 2016). In Central Asia, Naqshbandi Sufis competed with other Sufi groups who had varying *dhikr* practices, from silent and still to musical and raucous (Bashir, 2013). In South Asia, the Naqshbandis competed hotly with the Chishtis, who favored both vocal *dhikr* and music. However, the Chishti master cited above, Shaikh Kaleemullah, also had initiation in the Naqshbandi Order as a strategy to quell such competition between orders; he described many contemplative practices, some indigenous to the Chishtis and some adopted from the Naqshbandis.

In South Asia, the Shattari Order held that contemplation on God could bring very quick union with God. This Order has roots in Central Asia and evolved from the Kubrawi Sufi Order, whose focus on contemplation has been well documented by Jamal Elias (Elias, 2013; see also Zargar, 2013).[14] The Kubrawis specialized in contemplation involving complex visualizations of subtle energy centers in the body (*lataʾif*) associated with particular colors and prophets. Their system of spiritual anatomy is analogous to

[13] The Naqshbandi Order was "founded" by Bahaʾ al-Din Naqshband (d. 1389 in Bukhara); "founders" of Sufi orders do not originate them, but rather systematize the practices they inherited from earlier generations and lend that system their own name as a principle of organization.

[14] The Kubrawi Order was "founded" by Najm al-Din Kubra (d. 1221 in Urgench near Khiva in Uzbekistan); see also Zargar, 2013, which documents Kubrawi conceptions of meditation and contemplation, and notes how they used the term Shattari (or *shuttari*) for those crafty meditators who realize the goal most quickly.

the yogic system of *chakras*, and it was elaborated upon in various ways by later orders like the Chishti, Naqshbandi, and Shattari Orders (Dahnhardt, 2002). The Shattari Order moved from Central Asia to India in the fifteenth century where it promoted very intense exercises of visualization and concentration, which brought its members into close association with yogic and tantric practitioners.[15] One Shattari master, Bahaʾ al-Din Husaini Shattari (d. 1515 in Daulatabad, India) wrote a book called *Risala Shattariyya*, which includes analogies to yogic positions, mental exercises, and breath control. His biographer, the Sufi scholar ʿAbd al-Haqq Muhaddith Dihlawi, notes the importance of *muraqaba* to him:

> The reason why this practice has been named *muraqaba* is because it is extracted from the root *raqib*, meaning protector who "keeps one under surveillance." This means that while people are engaged in *muraqaba*, they are divinely protected from lust, satanic interferences, physical demands, and an unstable heart. Thus, they are peacefully focused on God. Then it is said, "*Fikr* is more excellent than *dhikr*." This is so because *fikr* [thinking] is a secret devotion which is concealed from all. *Muraqaba* means [thinking in such a way as] to safeguard the heart and focus on God and remove everything besides God from the heart.
>
> (Dihlawi, 2011, v. 2, p. 351)

As a Naqshbandi, ʿAbd al-Haqq asserts that contemplation is better than vocal meditation or ritual prayer because it is concealed from others, not because it leads to union with God; thus, one can meditate even while working in society, rather than secluding oneself or being estranged from society. Even as he records the biography of Bahaʾ al-Din, he does not really sympathize with the Shattari use of contemplation. He does not want his readers to take the comparison to yoga too far and blur the boundaries between religions.

ʿAbd al-Haqq Muhaddith Dihlawi gives examples of how to do *muraqaba* based on visualizing and internalizing phrases from the Qurʾan. They are based on verses that depict God in an immanent way: verses such as *Wherever you turn your face there is the face of God*, or *God encompasses all things*, or *God is closer to you than the artery in your neck*, or *God is with you wherever you may be* (Qurʾan, Surat al-Baqara 2:115; Surat al-Nisaʾ 4:126; Surat Qaf 50:16; & Surat al-Hadid 57:4). The rational mind can conceive of God as transcendent because it operates by division, exclusion, and separation. However, only the reflective or contemplative mind can understand God as immanent because it operates by union, inclusion, and fusion. Muslim theologians assert that God is transcendent because they rely on a limited use of the mind through rationality, yet they ignore key verses of the Qurʾan that contradict their conception. This is the root of many quarrels between Muslim theologians and Sufis.

Sufis understand that all things which have being are essentially empty since they emerge from non-being; they are sustained by God, the only real being, as ephemeral

[15] The Shattari Order was "founded" by Shah ʿAbdullah Shattar who emigrated from Central Asia and settled in India (d. 1485 in Mandu, Madhya Pradesh).

subjects that are conditioned by temporality, spatiality, and adhesion of diverse elements and are therefore subject to passing away, disintegration, and decomposition. Their being is only borrowed from the One true being, which is God the creator, sustainer, and caller to account. Inasmuch as we look to ourselves, imagining that our ego awareness and our will can sustain us by its volition, then we experience anxiety, agitation, craving, suffering, fear, and torment. Inasmuch as we look to the One that creates us, attributing our being to dependence and reliance upon the One true being, then we experience calm, resignation, rest, tranquility, contentment, hope, love, and ecstatic bliss. Rational thought and calculated effort cannot engineer the release of awareness from the ego. Only meditation (*dhikr*) coupled with discipline (*riyadat*) can achieve this. Then, intuitive knowledge (*maʿrifa*) replaces egoistic thought as the basis for one's awareness and action in the world, and increasingly contemplation (*muraqaba*) balances our routine reliance on rational thought (*ʿaql*). If outward acts of worship do not foster intuitive knowledge and only reinforce egoistic thought, they are not conductive to real salvation.

I have suggested that all methods of meditation mentioned above (*salawat*, *munajat*, *wird*, *wazifa*, and *dhikr* both silent and chanted) are rooted in the act of formal prayer (*salat*), but what about contemplation? Its roots are also in formal prayer but in a more hidden way. When formal prayer is done with deep concentration, the practitioner sometimes gets engrossed in awe and bewilderment, loosing count of how many bowings or prostrations have been done. For many Muslims, this is a moment of consternation, and the prayer must be repeated to make sure one "gets it right." But for others, these moments of losing self-consciousness in the act of doing are to be savored. These pauses, when time stands still and calculating thought ceases, are the root of contemplation that occur in formal prayer. For this reason, the Prophet Muhammad is reported to have prayed in supplication, "Dear God, increase my bewilderment in you!" (Sells, 1994, pp. 101–103). Both meditation and contemplation are essential complements to acts of ritual worship and serve as the means to keep them sincere and pure (Figure. 9.3).

Samaʿ: Meditation through Music

While contemplation is silent and purely introspective, there are other meditative techniques that are melodious and extroverted. As noted above, many Sufi communities do *dhikr* aloud, and often chant with melody and rhythm. The rhythm could be provided simply by the cadence of the words and swaying of the body, or it could be externalized through drumming (use of a simple frame-drum or *daff* is traditional in many groups, because it was the common instrument in the Prophet Muhammad's early community). When musical elements of *dhikr* are emphasized over chanting, then the ritual takes on a different character: it is called *samaʿ* or meditation through listening to music.

Using music as a means of meditation is an innovation in the Islamic tradition that was unknown in the early community. The Prophet Muhammad's community used music for work songs, wedding celebrations, eulogizing praise for the Prophet, and the call to

FIGURE 9.3 "Hermit in Prayer" holding a string of beads in his right hand while lifting his left in a gesture of supplication; painting from Iran (Isfahan, from late sixteenth/early seventeenth century).

Source: Photo © RMN-Grand Palais (musée du Louvre)/Jean-Gilles Berizzi.

prayer, but they did not use music in worship; the melodious quality of Qur'an recitation is not considered to be "music" but rather cantillation or *tilawat* (Faruqi, 1985). In the early Islamic community, music was associated with pagan rituals, concubine singers, or luxurious wine parties and was thus labeled immoral. But as Muslims created a vast inter-regional empire by 750 CE, they inherited courtly music of many styles, from Greek, Persian, and Andalusian to South Asian. By the eighth century, Sufis were using this refined courtly music for setting devotional poems, redirecting images of passionate love to the quest for God's presence (During, 1999). At that point, music became a form a meditation.

The musical aspect of meditation can be classified into different kinds. There are musical forms that all participants in a group *dhikr* can perform together without special skills; an example of this is *ilahis* or hymns that various Turkish Sufi groups sing in chorus (Gill, 2017, pp. 71–72).[16] Evolving from these, there are musical forms that feature skilled singers who lead the group, which follows by singing a refrain in unison; an example of this is in Andalusian-style *dhikr* (now cultivated by Sufi groups in North Africa) with Sufi poems sung in highly ornate melody and verses interspersed with communal singing of *dhikr* formulas.[17] There are musical forms that are more artistic and require professional skill, which often involve instrumental accompaniment. In such forms, those meditating do not sing or play; rather, the meditation consists of listening intently and cultivating an emotional response to the words and images rendered in music. An example of this is qawwali, the South Asian style of *sama*ʿ in which hereditary families of musicians sing Persian poems (and now poems in Urdu, Punjabi, and other vernacular languages) rendered with intense percussion and instrumental support (Qureshi, 1986; Ernst & Lawrence, 2002).[18] There is an elaborate ritual etiquette to listening, and qawwali sessions could extend all night, sometimes inducing trace states in listeners. An Arab comparison would be the Egyptian *munshid* tradition, featuring a primary singer backed up by an instrumental ensemble that also functions as a chorus (Waugh, 1989).[19]

Musical meditation is further elaborated by adding the element of motion or dance. Some forms of musical *dhikr* require participants to stand in lines facing each other or in interlocking circles and move with the rhythm of the *dhikr*. The movement could involve gentle swaying and stepping, or accelerate into raising and lowering of the head or the full torso to induce intense breathing patterns. Where more intricate motion is involved, specialized skills are required for a few elite participants while the audience watches. An example of this is the Mevlevi ritual of whirling, in which formal Ottoman court music is adapted by professional musicians for a Sufi audience; meditators include both the

[16] For a classical rendition of *ilahi* hymns, listen to the CD recording by Aydogdu & Cevikoglu, 2002.

[17] Listen for instance to the CD recording from Morocco by Ensemble Ibn Arabi, 2003; and from Egypt by El Halbawy, 1999.

[18] A wide selection of audio recordings with good translations of lyrics can be found in *Jashn-e-Khusrau*, 2013.

[19] Listen also to the recording of al-Tuni, 2000.

listening audience (as in qawwali) but also individuals who whirl to the beat of the music, adding an element of highly stylized choreographed motion to the music (Friedlander & Uzel, 1992).[20] Intensive training is required before one is allowed to engage in whirling meditation. In contemporary Turkey, this kind of *samaʿ* has become a tourist attraction due to its visual appeal, and the ritual meaning is often diluted. Similar popularization has happened with qawwali vocal music; as its aesthetic beauty got co-opted by globalized "world music" its ritual importance is often effaced or commercialized. Meditative techniques that involve highly skilled artistic production are vulnerable to this kind of distortion or appropriation.

Conclusion

This chapter provides an overview of diverse meditative practices in Islam. It argues that these practices are integral to the Islamic tradition and expand on core elements that are part of the basic prayer ritual (*salat*). It was primarily Sufi Muslims who advocated them, bringing them out of prayer and exploring their potential as independent practices (Fig. 9.4). These are resources for Muslims who feel the urge to introspect, uncover the delusion of the ego, purify the heart, and ultimately elevate the soul. Not all Muslims feel this urge, and thus the basic rituals of Islam do not require them. Yet they are present in the basic ritual as seeds are present in the ground, waiting only for the right conditions in which to sprout.

In Islam, there is no single term that corresponds to "meditation." Rather, there are many terms describing various types practices, with *dhikr* coming closest to what English speakers think of as meditation. *Dhikr* consists of repeating sacred words or names of God, either with the voice or without, to induce the remembrance of God's presence with us, as it was originally in our nature (*fitra*) as souls engendered by the everlasting spirit, but which we continuously forget due to our egoistic negligence and distraction by the phenomenal world. Focusing on God's presence without words, through visualization or other more abstract thought, is called *muraqaba* or contemplation. More embodied practices that focus on divine beauty use music or motion as meditative tools, and these musical forms known as *samaʿ* are considered distant from formal Islamic worship. Other worship practices have meditative use, such as *duʿa* or supplication, *salawat* or benediction, and *wird* or reciting litanies. These practices are rooted in the formal worship and make use of the Qurʾan's divine speech to combat the ego and purify the soul. All these meditative practices have the single aim of waging the "greater jihad" against selfishness and egoistic delusion.

[20] Listen to the recording by Tekbilek, 1994.

FIGURE 9.4 "Qalandari Derwish" or antinomian Sufi, popular in South and Central Asia, who often use drumming, singing, and ecstatic dance as means of meditation (shown with staff and begging bowl, above which is written the caption "O Prophet from the Hashimite Clan, we beseech your aid"); from the Deccan (south central India, from early seventeenth century).

Source: Portrait of a Sufi, first quarter of seventeenth century. MET Museum. Bequest of Cora Timken Burnett, 1956. Accession number 57.51.30.

References

Aydogdu, T., & Cevikoglu, T. (2002). *Sufi music from Turkey* [CD]. Germany: ARC Music.

Bashir, S. (2013). Movement and stillness: The practice of dhikr in 14th century Central Asia. In H. Eifring (Ed.), *Meditation in Judaism, Christianity and Islam: Cultural Histories* (pp. 201–211). London: Bloomsbury.

Brown, J. (2011). *Muhammad: A very short introduction*. Oxford: Oxford University Press.

Buehler, A. (2015). Sufi contemplation: ʿAbdullah Shah's *Suluk-i Mujaddadiyya*. In L. Komjathy (Ed.), *Contemplative literature: A comparative sourcebook on meditation and contemplative prayer* (pp. 307–358). Albany: State University of New York Press.

Buehler, A. (2016). *Recognizing Sufism: Contemplation in the Islamic tradition*. London: I.B. Taurus.

Dahnhardt, T. (2002). *Continuity and change in Indian Sufism: A Naqshbandi-Mujaddidi branch in the Hindu environment*. Delhi: DK Printworld.

Danner, V., & Thackston, W. (Trans.). (1978). *Ibn Ata'illah's book of wisdom and Khwaja Abdullah Ansari's intimate conversations*. New York: Paulist Press.
Dihlawi, ʿAbd al-Haqq Muhaddith. (2011). *Akhbar al-Akhyar fi Asrar al-Abrar* (ʿAbd al-Hadi al-Qadiri Radawi, Trans.). *Information of the righteous concerning the state of the pious*. Durban: Sufi Pages on behalf of Imam Ahmad Raza Academy.
Douglas, E. (Trans.). (1993). *The mystical teachings of al-Shadhili including his life, prayers, letters, and followers, by Ibn al-Sabbagh*. Albany: State University of New York Press.
D'Silva, P. (2020). Bodies in translation: Esoteric conceptions of the Muslim body in early-modern South Asia. In G. Pati, & K. Zubko (Eds.), *Transformational embodiment in Asian religions* (pp. 168–186). New York: Routledge.
During, J. (1999). What is Sufi music? In L. Lewisohn (Ed.), *The heritage of Sufism: Vol.2. The legacy of medieval Persian Sufism (1150–1500)* (pp. 277–288). Oxford: Oneworld.
El Halbawy, Cheikh M., et al. (1999). *La Chadhiliyya: Sufi chants from Cairo* [CD]. Paris: Institute Du Monde Arabe.
Elias, J. (2013). Sufi dhikr between meditation and prayer. In H. Eifring (Ed.), *Meditation in Judaism, Christianity and Islam: Cultural histories* (pp. 190–200). London: Bloomsbury.
Ensemble Ibn Arabi. (2003). *Chants Soufi Arabo-Andalous* [CD]. N.p.: LongDistance.
Ernst, C. (1999). Chishti meditation practices of the later Mughal period. In L. Lewisohn & D. Morgan (Eds.), *The heritage of Sufism: Vol. 3. Late Classical Persianate Sufism (1501–1750)* (pp. 344–357). Oxford: Oneworld.
Ernst, C. (2003). *Following Muhammad: Rethinking Islam in the contemporary world*. Chapel Hill: University of North Carolina Press.
Ernst, C. (2011). *Sufism: An introduction to the mystical tradition of Islam*. Boston: Shambhala.
Ernst, C., & Lawrence, B. (2002). *Sufi martyrs of love: The Chishti Order in South Asia and beyond*. New York: Palgrave.
Esack, F. (2002). *The Qur'an: A short introduction*. Oxford: Oneworld.
Faruqi, L. I. (1985). Music, musicians and Muslim law. *Asian Music* 10(2), 3–36.
Friedlander, S., & Uzel, N. (1992). *The whirling dervishes: Being an account of the Sufi order known as the Mevlevis*. Albany: State University of New York Press.
Gairdner, W. H. T. (Trans.). (2010). *A niche for lights: Al-Ghazali's Mishkat al-Anwar*. New York: Cosimo.
Ghazali, A. H. (1992). *Al-Ghazali: The ninety-nine beautiful names of Allah* (D. Burrell & N. Daher, Trans.). Cambridge, UK: Islamic Text Society.
Gill, D. (2017). *Melancholic modalities: Affect, Islam and Turkish classical musicians*. New York: Oxford University Press.
Husaini, Muhammad Gisudaraz (n.d.). *Yazdeh Rasa'il* [Eleven treatises] (Qazi Ahmed ʿAbd al-Samad, Trans. [Urdu]). Lahore: Sirat Foudation.
Hussaini, S. S. K. (1983). *Sayyid Muhammad Husaini Gisudiraz on Sufism*. Delhi: Idarah-i Adabiyat-i Dilli.
Iskandari, Ibn ʿAta'illah. (1996). *Miftah al-Falah fi Misbah al-Arwah. Key to salvation and the lamp of souls: A Sufi manual of invocation* (M. A. Koury-Danner, Trans.). Cambridge, UK: Islamic Texts Society.
Iskandari, Ibn ʿAta'illah. (2018). *Al-Qasd al-Mujarrad fi Maʿrifat al-Ism al-Mufrad. The pure intention on knowledge of the unique name* (K. Williams, Trans.). Cambridge, UK: Islamic Texts Society.
Jashn-e-Khusrau: A Collection [book with CDs]. (2013). Delhi: Roli Books.

Jazuli, Muhammad ibn Sulaiman (1996). *Dala'il al-Khairat*. Cairo: Tijara Nabawiyya.
Kugle, S. (2012). *Sufi meditation and contemplation: Timeless wisdom from Mughal India*. New Lebanon, NY: Suluk Press.
Kugle, S. (2014). Sufi meditation manuals from the Mughal era. In D. Giordani (Ed.), *Faith and practice in South Asian Sufism*. Rome: Oriente Moderno.
Lawrence, B. (Trans.). (1992). *Morals for the heart: Conversations of Nizam al-Din Awliya recorded by Amir Hasan Sijzi*. Mahwah, NJ: Paulist Press.
Lawrence, B. (2006). *Qur'an: A biography*. London: Atlantic Books.
Lawrence, B. (2015). *Who is Allah?* Chapel Hill: University of North Carolina Press.
Meyer, W. A., with Hyde, B., Kahn, S. & Muqaddam, F. (2011). *Physicians of the heart: A Sufi view of the ninety-nine names of Allah*. LaVergne, TN: Ingram International.
Neale, H. (2017). *Jihad in premodern Sufi writings*. New York: Palgrave Macmillan.
Qureshi, R. B. (1986). *Sufi music of India and Pakistan: Sound, context and meaning*. New York: Cambridge University Press.
Rumi, Jalal al-Din. (2004). *The Masnavi: Book one* (J. Mojaddedi, Trans.). New York: Oxford University Press.
Rumi, Jalal al-Din. (2017). *The Masnavi: Book four* (J. Mojaddedi, Trans.). New York: Oxford University Press.
Schimmel, A. (1975). *Mystical dimensions of Islam*. Chapel Hill: University of North Carolina Press.
Sells, M. (1994). *Mystical languages of unsaying*. Chicago: University of Chicago Press.
Sirriyeh, E. (1999). *Sufis and anti-Sufis: The defense, rethinking and rejection of Sufism in the modern world*. London: Curzon Press.
Tekbilek, O. F. (1994). *Whirling* [CD]. Tucson, AZ: Celestial Harmonies.
al-Tuni, Sheikh A. (2000). *Sultan of all Munshidin* [CD]. N.p.: Long Distance.
Valiuddin, Mir (1959). *Qur'anic Sufism*. Delhi: Motilal Banarsidas.
Valiuddin, M. (1967). *Khwaja Banda Nawaz ka tasawwuf*. Delhi: Nadwatul Musannifeen.
Valiuddin, M. (1980). *Contemplative disciplines in Sufism*. London: East-West Publications.
Waugh, E. (1989). *The Munshidin of Egypt: Their world and their song*. Columbus: University of South Carolina Press.
Zargar, C. A. (2013). The ten principles: Theoretical implications of volitional death in Najm al-Din Kubra's *Al-Usul al-Ashara* (study and translation). *The Muslim World 103*(1), 107–130.

CHAPTER 10

THERAVADA BUDDHISM AND MEDITATION

SARAH SHAW

INTRODUCTION

THIS chapter describes some texts and practices associated with what is known as Southern, or Pali, Buddhism, often termed Theravada. Meditation is core to the teachings and life story of Gotama Buddha, and a particularly central element in Buddhism's travel to other regions. Practices, techniques, theoretical explication, narratives, and manuals are diverse in many Buddhisms; this is particularly the case in Southern Buddhism, where research is revealing a far more complex and variegated system of meditation teachings and practice than had hitherto been supposed. This chapter explores the background and context to this diversity.

Adaptation was key from early times: during the Buddha's lifetime, teachings, monks, nuns, and artifacts associated with his teachings started to travel. While eventually much of the teachings became more actively promoted, it would not be correct to say that at this early stage Buddhism was a "missionary" religion; rather, Buddhist orders made teachings on meditation, ethics, and theory available in the regions to which they traveled (Skilling, 2009; Dixon, 2015). Over time evolutionary changes in some doctrines, practices, and ritual grew from this dissemination. This chapter considers South and Southeast Asian Buddhism, as practiced in the regions now termed Cambodia, Thailand, Laos, Burma/Myanmar, and Sri Lanka.

Buddhism came to these regions from an early period, though dates are contested (Harvey, 2013, pp. 196–202). At certain stages, in areas so closely connected by riverine and maritime routes, the Buddhisms practiced acquired some self-conscious homogeneity, and all are to a greater or lesser degree unified by a single text group: the Pali Canon and commentaries. Although possibly not our oldest collection of Buddhist texts, the canon constitutes the oldest complete version that includes:

- a code of behavior for monks and nuns (Vinaya)
- a group of teachings that are said to have arisen from specific occasions in Gotama Buddha's lifetime, the Sutta collection
- the collection of texts that explain the "higher" teaching of the Abhidhamma, a series of treatises delineating the movement of consciousness and matter as they arise in each moment, particularly in advanced meditation states.

The relationship between Pali text and language with practice and theory in this region is complex, subject to local variation; but most adhere to some form of Påli formulation (Skilling, 2009).

The term "Theravada," literally meaning "the way of the elders" is recent, scarcely found in any literature before the twentieth century (Gethin, 2012); as Skilling notes, "there is no evidence so far that in the premodern period Theravada had any application outside the sangha" (Skilling, 2012, p. xxi). While certainly applicable to some degree now, only in the twentieth century did it describe teachings and meditative customs that had often evolved closely in conjunction with local devotional practices, art, technologies, and mythologies. Various autonomous hubs, however, studded throughout ports, towns, and centers in South and Southeast Asia, followed, at least from the twelfth century onward, broadly similar Pāli text bases and Vinaya (Gethin, 2012; Skilling, 2012). These regions sustained often highly localized areas of religious interest and doctrine, but there was a free flow of artifacts, monastic rules, teaching, and meditation methods between them. This chapter terms these aligned, though often distinct, traditions of this region "Southern Buddhisms," in contrast to the Northern Buddhisms of Tibet and Mongolia, and the Eastern Buddhisms of China, Japan, Korea, and, to a certain extent, Vietnam (see other chapters on Tibetan Buddhism and Chan Buddhism).

The Life of the Buddha and Meditation

The paradigm taken in Southern Buddhist countries for the Middle Way, and the place of meditation practice within that, is the textual life-story of Gotama. After renouncing the pleasures of his palace, Gotama practiced two meditations. These meditations, focusing on nothingness and on neither identification nor non-identification, were later incorporated into the Buddha's overall system. He saw at that time, however, that they did not lead to awakening on their own (M 26; M 36).

After a period of extreme mortification, he took food, and remembered the meditation he discovered as a child. This state is known as the first *jhāna* and, later, became the basis of the Buddha's own meditative system. It is a unification of the mind (*ekaggatā*, literally "gone to oneness"), that produces great happiness and joy, along with other factors including applied and sustained thought. Gotama asked himself if this, rather than self-mortification, might offer the way to liberation.

Table 10.1 The Buddhist *jhānas*

First *jhāna*	Accompanied by thinking, exploring, joy, happiness, and one-pointedness	Experienced by the Buddha spontaneously as a child—recollected by him before the awakening and used as the basis of the practice of all of these meditations on the night of the awakening
Second *jhāna*	Accompanied by joy, happiness, and one-pointedness	Said to be accompanied by "internal peace" as various thinking processes are suspended
Third *jhāna*	Accompanied by happiness and one-pointedness	Associated with an increase of mindfulness and clarity
Fourth *jhāna*	Accompanied by one-pointedness	This *jhāna* is particularly associated with the equanimity that arises after the emotional purification of the first three *jhānas*. All these first four *jhānas* were practised before the awakening
1st formless sphere (*arūpa*): 5th *jhāna*	Sphere of infinite space	
2nd formless sphere (*arūpa*): 6th jhāna	Sphere of infinite consciousness	
3rd formless sphere (*arūpa*): 7th *jhāna*	Sphere of no-thingness	Practiced by Gotama before the awakening and subsequently integrated into his system as a *jhāna*
4th formless sphere (*arūpa*): 8th *jhāna*	Sphere of neither identification nor non-identification	Practiced by Gotama before the awakening, and subsequently integrated into his system as a *jhāna*

On the night of the awakening, Gotama made this state his starting point for the cultivation of all four *jhānas*: the first, we have described, and three more, where the mind is trained to attain a state of profound equanimity and balance, in the fourth *jhāna* (see Table 10.1). It is not clear whether these states preceded Gotama's practice; he did, though, systematize them after the awakening as a fourfold *jhāna* system. This possibly represents his primary contribution to Indian meditative method.

Developing the recollection of his own past lives, and the observation of the rise and fall of other beings according to their *kamma* (more commonly referred to as *karma*), on the night of his awakening his practice moved to insight, and the eradication of all defilements (M 36). After that he taught an apparently syncretic as well as innovatory meditation system, including, for instance, the meditations he had practiced before the awakening, later termed the third and fourth formless spheres.

As the Buddha's life-story indicates, from the outset, teachings concerned with meditation are central to consideration of Buddhist practice, the Eightfold Path, and the Middle Way. Early texts are steeped in discussion of meditation, and some clearly represent ways in which a number of systems, such as the formless states and the practices on the elements, have been integrated or adapted into the new movement (Wynne, 2007, pp. 8–44). Many texts recommend repeatedly the practice of *jhāna*. They also usually include a number of other practices and work on the purification of views; it is, however, difficult to find a text which *only* describes meditation, and most include other elements too. In the *Mahāsakuliyadi Sutta*, the Buddha validates a number of diverse meditation practices, some probably derived from other systems. The Buddha was a creative syncretist and says they are all viable, if conducted with appropriate balances. The Eightfold Path and the pattern of *sīla*, *samādhi*, *paññā* or ethics, meditation and wisdom respectively, provide the underlying ordering system (M 77).

The Four Noble Truths, teachings ascribed to Buddha in the *Dhammacakkapavattana Sutta*, are differentiated from one another by four different verbs: the first is to be understood, the second to be abandoned, the third to be realized, and the fourth to be practiced or cultivated (*bhāvanā*) (S V 420–424). An eightfold path involving all elements of the teaching is needed and meditation is one aspect of a broader range of activities "to be cultivated." The Eightfold Path involves:

- right view and right resolve, sometimes classed as its "wisdom" (*paññā*) section
- right speech, action, and livelihood, as its morality (*sīla*) section
- right effort, mindfulness, and concentration (*samādhi*), as its meditative element.

This comprehensiveness needs to be borne in mind while considering the specifics of any one meditative school. Broadly speaking, there is a distinction made between meditative schools that are based on arousing calm (*samatha*), with an emphasis on right concentration, and those based on insight (*vipassanā*), with an emphasis on wisdom (*paññā*). Calm schools encourage the practice of *jhāna*, the awake, deep meditative state the Buddha cultivated before moving on to insight. One could say they develop a way of being—a steady and unwavering emotional basis—before practicing insight. Insight schools, which have flourished since the early twentieth century, encourage insight from the outset: one could say they develop means of transforming how we see, and how we form views, on the route to wisdom. It is an eightfold path, however: in practice, most schools encourage elements both of calm and insight from the outset. The difference between the two styles will be discussed later in this chapter.

It is not yet possible to build up a complete picture of how meditation practice worked in monastic and lay life before the last two hundred years. There are few biographical records, and customs of privacy with regard to meditation make this exercise difficult. Unlike some other Buddhisms, the Southern Buddhists have no tradition of liberation narrative—an account of the means by which awakening was obtained—as found in Tibet, or the lineage accounts in Chan/Zen/Seon traditions of Eastern Buddhism (Shaw, 2010). Meditation is a private matter, and, as one monk pointed out to me, one could be in the next room to another monk for years and never find out his practice (Shaw, 2006, p. 11). In traditional contexts, it is often discussed only with a teacher or "good friend," and is considered deeply personal. But we are finding important indications as to how practices were conducted, and what they were likely to have been, from around the eighteenth century, and possibly before that period (Crosby, 2013; 2020). François Bizot's research on Cambodia and parts of Thailand revealed widespread *samatha* practices associated with ritual, mantra, and visualization, linked to the breath (Bizot, 1976, 1980, 1992, 1993; Crosby, 2000). These offer a strong emotional element, as the breath, or other chosen object of meditation, is treated with great respect, and there are associated bodily exercises, mantras, and visualizations to support the meditation. There is a great emphasis on finding joy, peacefulness, and happiness as a preliminary to further investigation of the mind, and insight.

Recently, Kate Crosby, Andrew Skilton, and Phibul Choompolpaisal have been conducting research on South and Southeast Asian manuscripts, manuals, and papers that have corroborated personal accounts, testimonies, and reports of traditional rural practices throughout the region (Crosby, 2000, 2013; Choompolpaisal & Skilton, 2014, 2015). The term loosely applied to these practices is *Borān Kamaṭṭhāna*, or ancient approaches to practice.

For the twentieth and twenty-first century we have fuller information, as more first-hand accounts and commentaries emerge, particularly in the form of free distribution booklets and pamphlets, a notable and significantly successful feature of modern Southern Buddhist meditation teaching. Autobiographies of senior monks have become widespread, and the internet has now made many of these widely available (e.g., Boowa, 1976). It should be borne in mind that for many South and Southeast Asians meditation remains a private undertaking, involving trust and confidentiality in interactions with the meditation guide. Teachings are sometimes still esoteric, or only given and discussed at a time when the meditator is felt to be ready for them (Cousins, 1997a; Shaw, 2006, pp. 24–26; Harvey, 2013, pp. 318–321). Despite these qualifications, meditation is taught now, and has been for centuries, with various schools and traditions that support it.

The Teacher or "Good Friend"

One feature common to most schools is the stated need for an experienced teacher, or good friend (*kalyāṇamitta*), who can guide the meditator through the necessary stages and recognize the signs when the practitioner is ready to develop further, or perhaps needs to relax effort, or include an additional supplementary practice (Ud 44–47; Nidd I 360). "Meditation requires personal guidance, as it is a subtle skill which cannot properly be conveyed by standardized written teachings" (Harvey, 2013, p. 319). The Buddha saw the "good friend" or teacher in the practice as the single most important outside factor in aiding the development of meditation and the purification of the heart (A I 14).

Such guidance is usually considered the principal element that ensures and safeguards meditation teaching: without individual discussion and care, the meditation is at best mildly ineffective and, at worst, too much so, in the sense that a major element can go unbalanced and not be corrected (Gethin, 1998, pp. 178–179; Shaw, 2006, pp. 10–12). Clearly one cannot prevent problems completely in any setting, whether on a meditation course or not, but modern Buddhist practice and traditional teaching of injunctions concerning frequent consultation with a guide are helpfully straightforward. One text, for instance, cites the times one should consult with a teacher (A III 316). One characteristic that differentiates the Buddha from other teachers of his time is a careful flexibility in choosing, teaching, and, if necessary, changing people's meditation practices according to their needs.

The accommodation of diversity, both of object of meditation (*kammaṭṭhāna*), and of individual proclivities and weaknesses, is perhaps the single most obvious, yet often overlooked, feature of the way early texts say the Buddha taught meditation (Shaw, 2006, pp. 194–198). What suits one person at one stage may be different for another person or for the same person at a different time. It is a graduated path requiring care, "maps," and an experienced guide (Vajiriñāṇa, 1975, p. 97; Khantipālo, 1980; Shaw 2016).

Often it is common-sense and friendly "down-to-earth" advice that are all that are needed. Reputable meditation courses offer the chance, and indeed usually insist upon the need for, regular consultation and monitoring of one's daily practice, alongside careful advice for continuing the practice after retreats or courses end, during the important return to family and friends. This is stressed within the teachings of an eightfold path, which includes attention to both personal development and generosity and ethics within the world. Clearly mistakes can never be ruled out—commentarial stories, for instance, relate how even Sāriputta misjudged a meditator's capability and had to take the practitioner to the Buddha, but he knew when he needed to take advice and acted accordingly. Continual monitoring and discussion are assumed throughout these early stories (DhpA III 424–429; Shaw, 2014, pp. 174–196).

Buddhaghosa's meditation manual says that ideally one should learn from someone of high attainment. He then moves the scale down through increasingly lower attainments, depending on availability of teachers, and finishes with the comment that if one does not have an experienced guide, then "one who is conscientious," or careful of risks, "will guard it" (Vism III 64; see also Ehara et al, 1977, p. 100). Within Southern Buddhist temples and centers this need for guidance is taken as given and tends to operate even on courses where the contact might be less formal, but careful.

Preliminaries to Meditation

Another feature common to most schools, certainly in Southeast and South Asia, is the need for preliminaries to meditation. These basic practices are considered to give an alignment to the meditator and protect him or her in the undertaking of meditation itself. "Taking refuge," in the Triple Gem, is a crucial aspect of meditation practice (*bhāvanā*), intended to set one's orientation, help deal with the balance between student and teacher, and arouse confidence in one's own resources. Thus the chanting and understanding of the traditional refuges—the three repeated mindfulnesses (*anussatis*) of the Buddha, his teaching (*dhamma*), and his community (*saṅgha*)—and of the five precepts are omnipresent throughout South and Southeast Asia. These are believed to free the practitioner from some of the "teacher-student" difficulties that can arise in meditation teaching. The three refuges say that I "go" or I "understand" (*gacchāmi*) the refuge (*saranaṃ*) of the Buddha, the one who knows, the teaching (*dhamma*) and the community (*saṅgha*) and give five guidelines, or "rules of training" (*sikkhāpadaṃ*) to help one in daily life: not to kill, not to steal, not to indulge in harmful or excessive sexual behavior, not to lie, and not to allow intoxication with drink or drugs to take over the mind. The five precepts are felt by many South and Southeast Asian Buddhists to offer almost magical protection. Underestimated sometimes, such protection is usually considered essential for the safe cultivation of both the lower and the higher stages of meditation practice (Viradhamma, 2017, pp. 82–87).

Viradhamma notes: "All the schools of Buddhism concur that Buddhism is a 'doing'—that it's a cultivation or a craft." (Viradhamma, 2017, p. 80). Meditation is something to be integrated into daily life: the morality (*sīla*) elements of right speech, action, and livelihood, and taking refuge, are felt to help this. It is an ongoing challenge in the Western adoption of Buddhist practice to find the confident groundedness, cheerfulness, and intuitive sense of the "Middle Way" that such practices are intended to arouse as necessary precursors to successful exploration of the mind and mental states. Within the tradition they are not considered "trappings," but as important *bhāvanā*, helping to ensure that the meditator stands his or her own ground, senses themselves what will bring their mind to health (*kusala-citta*), and make good-humored individual contact with the Triple Gem of Buddha, *dhamma*, and the larger community (Harvey, 2013, pp. 237–249; Shaw, 2006, pp. 109–123). Many who are not from a Buddhist background do not necessarily feel they want to do these at the outset, but they are designed to give support and confidence in one's own ability and capacity to derive benefit from the practice itself.

Samatha and *Vipassanā*

Within meditation practice itself, there are two main strands of meditative cultivation, *samatha* and *vipassanā*. *Samatha*, "calm," is concerned with how we *are* in ourselves and *vipassanā*, "insight," is concerned with how we *perceive* and experience the world around and within us. They are complementary. A sense of complementary but distinct functions is necessary to understand the basis of both the practice of insight and calm (Cousins, 1984; Chah, 2007).

The teacher Boonman Poonyathiro, in July 2016, at a *samatha* meditation course at the Samatha Centre, Greenstreete, Llangunllo, Wales, compared the effect of the two kinds of meditation to cleaning a tank: calm practice and the cultivation of loving-kindness, compassion, sympathetic joy, and equanimity are like a flow of clean water passing through to remove the bulk of the dirt; but you also need some careful scrubbing to get rid of the ingrained stains, which is the work of insight. If you miss out the scrubbing of the sides, the tank is not completely clean, but if it is not refreshed and sluiced by clean water, the tank does not get washed through either. However, the sequencing of and relative emphasis between these two activities varies from school to school.

Both calm and insight are needed for awakening. There are many traditions of meditation practice, and they tend towards the cultivation of one of these, though not usually to the exclusion of the other. An early text describes four means to liberation (A II 157):

- The first is through the development of *jhāna* and stages of calm, which then leads to liberating insight.
- The second is through a preliminary insight, which is then deepened into a state of *jhāna* for liberation.
- The third is the two, calm and insight, "yoked together," so they work in unison.
- The fourth is elliptically described as "*dhamma* excitement," a kind of investigation leading to insight, and then concentration. This is sometimes associated with modern insight schools.

The difference of emphasis between *samatha* and *vipassanā*, in both technique and theory, has ancient roots and was described in early texts, vividly and aptly, as the difference between a "wet" approach to meditation and a "dry" one (Cousins, 1984, 1996). Loosely speaking the "wet" approach of *samatha* is intuitive and feeling based. It works on purifying craving, the emotional release and purification of the four "form" *jhāna*s, and then turns the mind to insight, or to the four formless meditations, which act as antidotes to any problems arising from attachment to form *jhāna*s. Form and formless *jhāna*s will be described below. These practices in turn ensure that formless meditation is grounded and based in the emotional steadiness and balance provided by the earlier *jhāna*s. These are features that were presumably absent when Gotama tried them without this basis.

The "dry" approach feels, literally, more "dry," and is less intent on the development of feeling. Rather, it works on how the meditator "sees." It explores the link between name and form and mental formations (*saṅkhāra*s). Insight breaks down the power of labeling and thus undermines "I making" and attachment. Encouragement of letting go means that there is less need for the cultivation of feeling. Again, both schools need elements of the other throughout, though the way that a particular school employs its counterpart may be very carefully chosen and context-specific.

When learning and perhaps researching the techniques and contexts involved in crafts like singing, music, gymnastics, or even knitting, one takes as a given that different rules, protections, and safeguards need to be learnt to ensure that the crafts are learned with due care and attention. The same can broadly be said about the practice of meditation, and various traditions need different associated safeguards and balances (Gethin, 1998, pp. 79–84; Harvey, 2013, pp. 319–321). The differing emphases in the two strands of meditation give them different qualities and ways of working. It is usually strongly recommended that practitioners adopt one, with its own balances and correctives for individual temperament and experience, rather than try to mix them without guidance. For instance, walking practices in each school will be designed to complement the sitting practice. Some insight schools might stress labeling each stage of lifting, moving, lowering, and pressing the foot (Dhammasāmi, 1999, pp. 33–35). A *samatha* school, however, might encourage a sense of feeling and the physical sensation of walking on the ground. Boonman Poonyathiro teaches walking practices linked to those on loving-kindness and the breath (Samatha Centre, Greenstreete, Llangunllo, Wales, August 2012). Wide attention is an aspect of both schools, but such instructions vary according to the needs of the practitioner and time (Sumedho, 1987, pp. 39–40).

Each school has its own mix of ways that insight and calm are taught. Mixing them in a "buffet" kind of way does not work, as over the years methods develop to balance out a particular practice in specific ways: so an insight school will not encourage the development of deeper stages of calm, which a calm school would do in a systematic way.

Samatha

The primary intention of *samatha* is to arouse calm and well-being in and for itself as well as as a preliminary. *Samatha* includes the four form *jhāna*s and the four formless *jhāna*s. The terms "form" and "formless" refer principally to the nature of the object of meditation. There is also a state that is described in post-canonical literature as access concentration (*upacāra-samādhi*), as well as a ninth *jhāna*, *nirodha-samāpatti* (see Table 10.1), which is a method based on right concentration in the Eightfold Path.

The objects leading to these states are extensive, and not necessarily classifiable, but forty are described in the meditation manual that has been quite influential in Southern Buddhism, Buddhaghosa's *Visuddhimagga*. These fall into seven groups as follows:

1. The ten *kasiṇa*s. This technical term, associated with the word for "whole," usually refers to a disc or a confined space, of a particular color or element, such as water, or earth, which is taken as the object of the meditation. Sometimes natural objects, such as free-flowing water or a field of earth, are used as the preliminary object.
2. Ten "foul" meditations, usually practiced only in monastic settings.
3. Ten "repeated mindfulnesses" (*anussati*), on the Buddha, the *dhamma*, the *saṅgha*, virtue, generosity, *deva*s, body, death, the breath, and peace. These are significant both for laity and monastics. As with the taking of refuge described above, they are reflections designed to encourage peacefulness and a sense of stability—they are areas that we can be mindful of, repeatedly, to arouse calm.
4. Four divine abidings, of loving-kindness, sympathetic joy, compassion, and equanimity. These are considered important, as underlying all our dealings with the mind and with others.

5. Four formless spheres.
6. Meditations on the repulsiveness of food, conducted only under special circumstances, with a teacher.
7. The four elements.

These objects for sitting meditation are assigned according to temperament (*carita*) and experience (see Nidd I 360; Vism III 74–103; Shaw, 2006, pp. 8–12; Vajirañāṇa, 1975, p. 98, 103–112; and Ehara, 1977, pp. 54–62). Some lead to *jhāna*s; others are considered essential for happiness and balance in daily practice (Vism III 106–107; Ehara, 1977, pp. 63–64). Some, such as the "foul," are only assigned under specialized conditions, with close supervision and teacher contact (S V 320; Vin III 68; Khantipālo, 1980; Vajirañāṇa, 1975, pp. 166–167; Shaw, 2006, pp. 101–108). There is not really a hierarchy within these practices. Some, such as the divine abidings, are needed by most people, others only by some.

The difference between *samatha* and *vipassanā* is more of function than of "either/or," as evinced by the meaning of the two words. *Samatha* derives from the word for "even," *sama* (like the English word "same"). It is a method for changing the state of one's being and establishing calm. It is linked to active cultivation of the meditations and the divine abidings, and the promotion of a sense of well-being and unification (*ekaggatā*). According to the usual pattern, this unified mind is gradually purified through the first four *jhāna*s, until the *khandha* of feeling is purified and there is no attachment to pleasant feeling, or, importantly, unpleasant feeling. As Harvey puts it, in *jhāna*, there is "a perspective from which the limitations and lack of subtlety of normal conscious experience can be directly seen. It also produces valuable changes in a person, such as a deepening of morality" (Harvey, 2013, p. 333).

Jhāna, as it is described and practiced traditionally, always involves the strong development of mindfulness and wisdom (Cousins, 1984; Shaw, 2014, pp. 139–156). From a base of stability, the mind can be applied to formless meditations. These are advanced practices cultivated only after the first four *jhāna*s. They are meditations on the sphere of infinite space, the sphere of infinite consciousness, the sphere of no-thingness, and the sphere of neither identification nor non-identification. The last two were practiced by the Buddha before his awakening and integrated into his teaching after his awakening, though only on the basis of the preceding *jhāna*s, which are, in his system, needed first for a balanced path. In these, the relationship between the subject and object is both dissolved and explored, leading to investigation of the nature of consciousness itself.

The four formless meditations are not considered finally salvific, but as useful specialist practices correcting any attachment to the great joy and peace of the "form" meditations, which in turn can be practiced again to ensure a basis of emotional stability and tranquility, before the development of insight. The importance of the first *jhāna*, in particular, in establishing this basis is demonstrated in the *Mahāsaccaka Sutta*, a possibly later canonical text, indicative that the tradition from early times emphasized this state (M 36).

For *samatha* practitioners, the interrelatedness of the "play of *jhānas*" (*jhānakīḷa*), and freedom of movement within them, is felt to be as important as the cultivation of any one in particular, so that the mind moves freely, back and forth between "forms" and "formlessness." Calm, or "evenness," applies to the effects on the mind of being able to allow emotional expression and release through *jhāna*, but also to the loosening of attachment to any particular state or manifestation of joy or peace, ensuring it is not mistaken for the full attainment of the path. The lists of the deliverances (*vimokkhā*) and the spheres of transcendence (*abhibhāyatanāni*), also found scattered frequently throughout the canon, relate to various masteries of *samatha* practice and reinforce this sense of "evenness" and interplay between meditative states (D 11; D 33; M 77; Shaw, 2006, pp. 92–99; Vajirañāṇa, 1975, pp. 57–75.).

Many *samatha* schools employ a breathing mindfulness practice. This will develop and encourage a fine training and ever more mindful appreciation of the breath. Sometimes, control is exercised over length of breath, to facilitate the movement between *jhānas* and, crucially, a safe return to the "normal" breath and one's daily life (Buddhadāsa, 1998; Bluck, 2008, pp. 49–64; Shaw, 2012). When mindfulness and concentration come into balance, a visual mental image (*nimitta*) arises. When this becomes steady, with the help of guidance from the teacher, the practitioner feels unified, and the mind becomes steady too. So it may then be used to develop the *jhānas* and support further emotional strength and resilience. This form of practice is associated with the arousal of a particular kind of good-humored contentment, essential for the development of a rounded equanimity, that allows the mind to explore insight or develop formless meditation (Cousins, 1997b).

Vipassanā

Vipassanā schools stress the element of insight and "seeing things as they are." The word means, literally, "seeing in many directions." It is directly associated with right view and the right application of mind, under the wisdom elements of the Eightfold Path. The term "right view" (*sammādiṭṭhi*) suggests a "seeing" that is not colored by partiality, views, or dislikes. Schools that term themselves *vipassanā* place primary emphasis on this wisdom and adopt somewhat different methods, each reflecting a different emphasis. They aim to address how the mind "sees" and names objects, thus purifying the mind of views and opinions that cloud the vision. They try and address ways we build constructions, or fabrications, in the mind that prevent clear vision and more direct experience.

Two texts are particularly favored by such schools.

- The *Satipaṭṭhāna-Sutta*, which avoids the close dwelling on the nature of the *jhānas* often found in other texts. In this text, the word *jhāna* is never mentioned, though it should be stressed it is implied, and the text includes many *samatha* practices.

- The *Rathavinita-Sutta*, which delineates seven stages of purification through insight. It is frequently taken as a model for stages of insight meditation (Gethin, 1998, pp. 187–194; Ñānarāma, 1997). This latter text formed the underlying structural model for the great Southern Buddhist commentary on meditation practice, Buddhaghosa's *Path of Purification* (*Visuddhimagga*).

A *vipassanā* school, in contrast to *samatha*, may give instructions to ignore all images and arouse "letting go," observing their rise and fall, and sometimes resting attention on a particular area of the body, such as the abdomen. By allowing attention to settle there it is possible to observe and investigate the rise and fall of physical, mental, and emotional phenomena. For most *vipassanā* practices it is important not to allow the attention to dwell on feeling but rather to focus in an analytical manner, with mindfulness of sense impressions and ideas and emotions as they arise, thus keeping a wide span of attention. This is an illustration; there are other techniques associated with the various schools in their various forms. To take one example, the methods of U Ba Khin (1899–1971) use the labelling of every movement and action in one's life as a means of freeing the mind from "fabrications" that it constructs about events in the world.

Some insight schools take the fourth option of the "means to liberation" and, minimizing the importance of *samatha*, follow what they regard as the way of the "dry insight-worker" (*sukkhavipassaka*), who practices insight and purifies him- or herself of the "defilements" of insight. These defilements are various "traps" the insight meditator can fall into, such as views, particular beliefs about the world, or stages of joy and happiness, believing them to be the final liberation. The meditator then finally moves to concentration. This is possibly the method practiced and advocated by Ajahn Mun (1913–2011) in the famously rigorous forest tradition. Despite undertaking *samatha* practices previously, he describes avoiding one-pointedness, or stages of deep meditation, in order to arouse a highly focused insight (Boowa, 1976, pp. 2–6). Burmese methods of "bare insight," perhaps of that kind, also avoid teaching stages of meditation, preferring to go straight to insight (Nyanaponika, 1972, pp. 102–107; Ñānarāma, 1997). More usually, they suggest the second option—the practice of *vipassanā* leading then to *samatha*.

Vipassanā within *Samatha*

Some *samatha* schools use the breath as a meditation object, which not only conduces to calm and *jhāna*, but also serves as a less prominent, but still important insight element. Other *samatha* schools additionally teach some insight, partly through the development of the formless states, particularly needed for a path that builds great strength, stability, and purpose, and partly through the inclusion of exercises, perhaps after the main practice, that allow the three signs of impermanence (*anicca*), disease (*dukkha*), and non-self (*anattā*) to be seen. The three signs can then be applied specifically to the states just experienced, so that those states do not themselves become objects of attachment: it is easy to become fixed on one happy state, but this too needs to be seen as impermanent.

This corresponds with the first and the third options of the four ways to awakening, discussed earlier. With the first, the *jhāna*s are cultivated, then insight. With the third, the two are "yoked together," so calm leads naturally to insight into the impermanance, unsatisfactoriness, and non-self nature of the breath and even of the *jhāna* that has just been experienced. Such insight then facilitates cultivation of the higher *jhāna*s (Cousins, 1973, 1984).

Samatha within *Vipassanā*

Insight schools cultivate liberating wisdom for awakening and for the eradication of the defilements. However, such insight is not possible without the divine abidings (*brahmavihāra*s, described in the section on *samatha* above), and the development of calm (Shaw, 2014, pp. 139–148). Historically this has usually been taken to mean the practice of *jhāna*. Most *vipassanā* schools, such as those of the Burmese movements, place considerable emphasis on the divine abidings from the outset (Dhammasāmi, 1999, pp. 9–19).

As with most Southern Buddhist meditations, *vipassanā* practitioners undertake the preliminary refuges in the Triple Gem, and the undertakings for morality. They usually pursue such meditations routinely, as well as other calm recollections, said to arouse peace and happiness in daily life and in sitting practice, known as "repeated mindfulnesses." Many of these recollections are chanted, and hence, where chanting itself is seen as a form of calming meditation practice, *vipassanā* practitioners in such contexts undertake a great deal of calm practice to accompany their work on insight.

Just as *samatha* schools inevitably need some insight, so insight schools need to cultivate calm since awakening is not possible without unification (*ekaggatā*), the fifth *jhāna* factor, as well as the *samatha* practice of the four divine abidings, which have been stressed as an accompaniment for meditative practice since early times (Sumedho, 1987, pp. 35–38; Dhammasāmi, 1999, pp. 9–19; Aronson, 2008).

One Pāli text compares the mind to a city. Good mindfulness, the function of the doorman or watchman at the gates, is always necessary. Wisdom, or insight, is the ramparts, needed to protect the city and people inside. The fuel for fire, food to eat, spices, and medicines that the people require are the specific meditations (A IV 106–113; Shaw, 2014, pp. 51–57). This important distinction goes to the heart of the difference of purpose of the two strands of meditative practice: one looks and watches, and ensures that the "view" is clear, from a safe vantage point; the other provides necessary sustenance and provisions to maintain health and well-being.

Complementary Practices

The principle of the Middle Way can be seen in many aspects of daily practice, that are considered just as important as the meditation itself. In all Southern Buddhist traditions it is emphasized not to consider sitting meditation as somehow divorced from other events in the day.

Venerable Anālayo recently explored a famous simile employed by the Buddha about acrobats, who need one another to be able to operate (S V 169; Anālayo, 2017, pp. 13–16). The Buddha compares one acrobat to the cultivation of the four foundations of mindfulness, a practice one needs for oneself, and the other, balanced with him, to the patience, harmlessness, and loving-kindness involved in dealings with others. So protection of others is poised, in dependence, with protection of oneself. This sense of balancing slightly different qualities, in this case one's own mindfulness development with the necessary basis in calm, attention to others, and morality, is crucial to understanding how most of the different meditation traditions work; each tends to have its own ways of doing this, suited to its own style—an idiosyncratic balance of practices with a careful equipoise of supporting factors.

Thus most modern schools of Southern Buddhist meditation, in varying degrees, have many concomitant practices designed to keep them on track. In order to ensure that each person's practice is individually apt and deals with all areas of their lives, meditation is taught as being closely linked to other things to be cultivated by the practitioner (Sumedho, 1993; Dhammasāmi, 1999, pp. 94–102). Varied aspects of conduct in daily life, being careful that one is not forming rigid views and opinions, behaving ethically (*sīla)* and practising generosity are almost always taught in close connection to meditation, both in text and in modern praxis (Shaw, 2006, pp. 194–198; see Starkey, this volume).

In Southern Buddhist Abhidhamma, intuitive ethical behavior, flexibility, and a stated close association between ethics, skillful consciousness (*citta*), and happiness and peace of mind are an integral part of the formulation of the principles operating in the practice of mindfulness (DhS 9–17; Shaw, 2006, pp. 109–134; Dhammasāmi, 2000, pp. 54–55). This then can be continued in daily life: the *Mettā Sutta*, perhaps the most famous Pāli text of all, describes the happiness of the practice of loving kindness (*mettā*) toward all beings as a "mindfulness" (Sn 25–26).

Eifring notes the need to focus "on the meditative practice and the complexity of its relation to the cultural webs surrounding it," if issues are to be addressed "that are easily ignored in contemporary or religious studies" (Eifring, 2015, p. 4). Little attention has been paid historically by scholars of Southern Buddhism to the background range of activities considered essential for the healthy development of meditation practice.

Chanting, accompanied sometimes by prostrations, offerings, mantras, and circumambulations, is considered a practice in itself, allowing energies to flow through all points within the body, while cultivating strong collective as well as individual mindfulness and focus. These practices have historically been dismissed as "mere" devotions and are largely unresearched. But devotional practices are regarded as important preliminaries, preparing the body and mind for meditation. The physical, emotional, and attentive qualities aroused by chanting, both as a solitary and collective exercise, also ensure it is seen as a form of meditation practice (*bhāvanā*) in itself (Harvey, 1993; Piyadassi, 1999; Tanabe, 2004; Shaw, 2009, pp. 92–110).

In South and Southeast Asia a number of lay groups are dedicated to different forms of chant practice collectively, employing exercises intended to balance the faculties, to allow purification of the heart through the practice of faith, and to arouse mindfulness of one's own body and those of others. "Pitching" the chant at the right shared tempo, volume, and note supports this (Shaw, 2009, pp. 92–110; Shaw, 2014, pp. 130–139). The acts of listening to, learning, and reciting texts, whether devotional or not, have always been perceived as a form of *bhāvanā* (Boowa, 1973, p. 92; Gethin, 1992; Blackburn, 2001).

Varied posture is also one aspect of this sense of balance: most meditation teachings involve walking practices (*caṅkamāna*) (Shaw, 2006, pp. 15–18). Although not delineated in detail in early texts, areas for walking and associated practices are frequently described in early Pāli literature, where changes of posture during the day are also recommended (A III 29; A IV 84–88). Most meditation retreats will also have two long walks a day for practitioners. Monks used to go on the alms round to "beg" for food in ancient times, and many still do. This offers good physical exercise as part of the meditating monk's day. So, in addition, in both traditions of practice, what Anālayo terms "cumulative" as well as "sequential" practices are usually encouraged: the practice of *sīla*, restraint of the senses, and attentive alertness in all dealings tend to be taught in all schools (Anālayo, 2017, p. 8). Such wide-ranging *bhāvanā* is stressed in most reputable Buddhist schools of meditation (eg. Buddhadāsa, 1998, p. 127).

The Early Importance of *Samatha*

Regions vary within South and Southeast Asia in their attitude to meditation, and such diversity has probably always been a feature of how meditation is seen and undertaken. It has been generally recognized, however, that the normative mix of practices in most Southeast Asian countries was largely *samatha* based, and taught both to monastic and laity in some areas, with *vipassanā* as a later element after these had become well established (Cousins, 1984; Gethin, 1998, pp. 174–187). This is the usual way of early texts, where, in those instances recorded of the Buddha giving meditation advice to followers, there is often a strong emphasis on *sīla* (moral conduct) before the development of various *samatha* practices, including frequently the divine abidings, and then finally, an apt piece of *vipassanā*, or insight practice, particularly geared to the predisposition of the person involved (Shaw, 2006, pp. 194–198).

There are many examples. Meghiya, an aspirant meditator who mistakenly tries to "go it alone" without taking advice, when he realizes that he does need guidance, is given several meditation practices designed to complement one another (Ud 34–37). The Buddha's son, Rāhula, is taught *samatha* in one *sutta*, and then, later, the insight practices that allow him to obtain liberation (M 147; M 62). The *Sāmaññaphala Sutta*, the great text on meditation, starts with *sīla*, daily life mindfulness, and then meditation, and, finally, insight (D.2).

When one explores the narratives, meditational allegories, and manuals of Southeast Buddhism, an organic relationship appears established between the practice of *samatha*, leading almost inevitably to the cultivation of insight. The forest tradition of northeast Thailand has been exceptionally rich in twentieth-century *samatha* teachers, who have had international followings, as well as insight teachers (Chah, 2007; Tiyavanich, 1997). A number of meditation manuals now being researched suggest a great variety of stories, methods, and practices associated with the development of calm, loosely termed the *Borān Kammaṭṭhāna* (Choompolpaisal & Skilton, 2014, 2015; Crosby 2020, 21–26).

Their methods and theory are steeped in and frequently cite and deploy Abhidhamma, Sutta, and commentarial sources (Crosby, 2013, pp. 51–55; Crosby 2020). Since the reign of King Mongkut (1804–1865) and various reforms, however, attempts have been made to undermine such meditation manuals and techniques as being "unorthodox." But, to take an example, practices on the four elements described in one of the *Borān Kamaṭṭhāna* works correctly invoke the *Mahārahulovada Sutta* as a canonical counterpart to its own (Choompolpaisal & Skilton, 2014, 2015). The close relationship between canon, commentary, practice, and technique cannot be seen simply in terms of "orthodoxy" or "orthopraxy." In such texts, chant, mantra, visual images, allegories, stories, and methods all weave together, with Pāli terms, syllables and stories contributing to a living transformatory language, descriptive both of the body of the texts, and, within the esoteric teachings, of the body of the practitioner (Crosby, 2013, pp. 82–87). As the language thought by Southeast Asians to have been that of the Buddha, its syllables were felt to be imbued with transformatory power, and the sacred syllables the means by which transformation can be effected. So some of the stories, allegories, and techniques of the *Borān Kamaṭṭhāna* integrate Abhidhammic understanding into the visualization techniques, such as the mantra *Saṃ Vi Dha Pu Ka Ya Pa*, the seven syllables that open each of the books of the Abhidhamma, visualized within the body (Bizot, 1976; Crosby, 2013, pp. 46–51).

The practice of *jhāna* and these associated texts are concerned with building a body of the practice, through the feeling base. That this is part of the *jhāna* process is implied and stated in many different ways. Evidence of the influence of Abhidhamma and Pāli theory can be seen in *samatha* teachings: the *Borān Kamaṭṭhāna* discusses the "limbs" of *jhāna* (the five factors) and the six pairs—the second element in the *Amatākaravaṇṇanā*—applying to both body and mind (Bodhi, 2000, II:1901, n.61; Shaw, 2006, pp. 33–34; Anālayo, 2017, pp. 55–57; Crosby, 2013, pp. 46–51). The pericopes for the *jhāna*s themselves, found in the *Sāmaññaphala Sutta,* strikingly emphasize the importance of the body both as the base and the experiencer of these peaceful states (D 2; Shaw, 2006, pp. 62–65). So often overlooked, these are clearly intended to communicate a sense that some "body" of the realm of the form *jhāna* is still there, and indeed is needed as the mind develops the strength and support needed to attain ever more subtle *jhāna*s.

The practice of *sīla*, *jhāna*, divine abidings, and insight, as we have seen, work together, in specially arranged ways, whereby, like medicines, they are given in careful relationship to one another. The whole is described in what could be termed a *samatha* understanding, whereby intuition and the heart work on the interplay between the body and the mind. One early text says, "Hearing *dhamma* at the right time; discussing *dhamma* at the right time; *samatha* at the right time, and *vipassanā* at the right time" (A II 141). This sense of an organic season for each form of practice permeates many modern Buddhist discourses, and some modern teachers communicate this sense of the process: Pyosobhon Bhikkhu, for instance, takes the four seasons to show impermanence as something both natural, and in the end, restorative as well as decaying, thus protecting against some of the more reductive understandings of the workings of impermanence present in more "hardline" Buddhist teaching (Piyabhoson, 2001).

Lay people also learnt *samatha* practices (Crosby, 2013). Bizot records this to be the case in Cambodia, and, with Becchetti and Lagirarde, has translated much of the material, such as the *Saddavimala* (Bizot & Lagirarde, 1996; see also Bizot, 1976, 1980, 1992, 1993; Becchetti, 1994). In the late nineteenth century, however, the pattern started to change. In Burma, this took the form of the traditional *samatha*/*vipassanā* axis; in other regions of Southeast Asia, until recently, it was more commonly articulated as a tension between the *Borān Kamaṭṭhāna* methods and *vipassanā* (Crosby, 2013, pp. 51–52). Within these regions, *samatha* practice is still conducted, but is less publicly emphasized and taught. The lay/monastic Wat Pak Nam movement, which uses visualization of the *nimitta* in connection with the breath, has been a key player, however. Ajahn Lee Dhammadhāro (1907–1961) taught a classical pattern of *jhāna* leading to formless meditation, disseminated in many teachings still widely available (Dhammadhāro, 1990). The meditation teachings of Buddhadāsa, though in many ways "reform," sustained a strong breathing mindfulness *samādhi* practice, taking the sixteen stages of the *ānāpāṇasati* practice described in the canon through its traditional stages from the establishment of calm through, in the last tetrad, to the arousal of insight by means of the breath (Buddhadāsa, 1998). Outside Southeast Asia, the Samatha Trust/Foundation teaches traditional Thai *Borān Kammaṭṭhāna* methods of breathing mindfulness concentration, to *jhāna* and formless meditation, under the tutelage of Boonman Poonyathiro (Bluck, 2008, pp. 49–64; Poonyathiro, 2003). The many monastic centers founded by Southeast and South Asian diaspora communities also sometimes teach *samatha*.

The Growth of Insight Meditation Schools

Other dynamics have come into play over the last two hundred years, as the history of Southern Buddhist meditation has been shaped, and to a certain extent created, by the emergence of a wave of interest in the practice of *vipassanā*. The origins of this movement are unclear; it developed, however, from Burmese meditators and commentators in the late nineteenth century (Houtman, 1990; Cousins, 1996).

It has its basis in early Buddhist texts, in particular Buddhaghosa's commentaries. Although the *Visuddhimagga* works on the assumption that the practitioner would develop *jhāna* and formless attainments first, on the lines of the *Rathavinita Sutta* (M 24), the new movement of those "who take insight as their vehicle" developed practices, which some claimed could bypass any *samatha* basis. Some few suggest that only *upacāra-samādhi*, not *jhāna*, is necessary for liberation, and develop insight for everyone from the outset. This last position is contested by most meditators and scholars, such as Soma Thera (Ehara, 1977, pp. 353–362).

Other scholars also argue that insight was the Buddha's contribution to meditative practice in India, and that the other *jhāna* practices and *brahmavihāras* were pre-existent, an understanding often communicated in the academic teaching of Buddhism in the West and East. Recently, however, many have challenged this, and, with Wynne, suggest that it is more likely that the *jhānas* represent the Buddha's systematic development of early Indian meditation (Wynne, 2007, pp. 122–124.).

Since the early nineteenth century, government and sangha movements, particularly in Burma/Myanmar and cosmopolitan areas of Thailand, wished to render and describe the Buddhist tradition as scientific, and in line with Western models this fostered a new perspective on meditation. The impact of those interested in meditation coming to the regions, the arrival of scientific, medical, and physiological methodology from the West, and a growing international interest in the Buddhist understanding of the relationship between mind and matter, have fostered this emphasis. As Crosby demonstrates, this process started well in the nineteenth century (Crosby, 2013, 2020).

After ongoing reform movements in Burma aimed at rationalizing systems throughout the regions, a number of centers and monasteries devoted to *vipassanā* were established; works designed for Anglophone and European readers also became available. They have done a great deal to promote the practice of meditation at an international level. The popularity of some insight methods has meant that many Westerners, often with a secular interest, are attracted to a tradition that is "without trappings" and might, perhaps, represent a "pure" form of Buddhism without local practices and mythologies.

Conclusion: *Vipassanā* and the Mindfulness Movement

The success of the insight movements may be seen in their great popularity internationally, particularly in the United States, Australia, New Zealand, and India. They are also becoming increasingly promoted throughout Southeast and South Asia. Some features that the schools share are a strong emphasis on the *Satipaṭṭhāna Sutta* (Nyanaponika, 1972), though it is not exclusively a *vipassanā* text. The practices focus upon four foundations: mindfulness of body, feelings, *citta* (mind or heart), and *dhammas*—events as they occur in the world. Attention is directed to physical sensations in particular, and then feelings, mental states, and, in the relationship between all of these, to events occurring in the world. Stress is placed on the rise and fall of all events, and the way that no abiding self can be perceived within this flow, so that analysis and observation can be applied to seeing all mental and physical events as impermanent and non-static.

Some Burmese figures associated with the early days of this movement are Ledi Sayādaw (1846–1923), Mahāsī Sayādaw (1904–1982), a disciple of U Nārada, known also as Mingun Jetawun Sayādaw (1868–1955), and U Ba Khin (Houtman, 1990; Cousins, 1996; Ledi, 2007; Kyaw, 2012). Their practices all emphasized meditation, taught in a number of international, often urban, centers disseminating their methods. The Mahāsī Sayādaw movement was promoted particularly in the 1950s in Burma, with government support for intensive meditation centers, and has been extremely influential internationally. It is linked to a technique that involves labeling and classifying all experience, stabilized by a practice involving observing the rise and fall of the abdomen as one breathes in and out, a concentration device that is felt to aid the observation and analysis of events in the body, feelings, and mind. The slant is strongly insight-based:

> The method of developing this wisdom is to observe matter and mind, which are the two elements existing in a body, to know them in their true form.... it can successfully deal with both matter and mind. It makes use of one's own mind for analytical purpose by fixing bare attention on the activities of matter and mind as they occur in the body. By continually repeating this form of exercise the necessary concentration can be gained and when the concentration is keen enough, the ceaseless course of arising and passing away of matter and mind will be vividly perceptible.
>
> (Tan, 2011, p. 21)

In this process calm is also required since such close analysis requires a particular kind of concentration, suggesting the best remedy in a crisis is the practice of *samatha* or *vipassanā* together (Tan, 2011, pp. 7–9). The techniques are linked to a particularly strong classificatory emphasis.

Another central figure was U Ba Khin, a layman who taught in the methods of two leading Burmese monastic teachers, Ledi Sayādaw and Webu Sayādaw. In 1952 he opened the International Meditation Centre in Rangoon, with strong government support, soon gaining an international following. A "power house of dynamic energy" (Coleman, 2000, p. 42), he taught while sustaining a high-powered, full-time government post. He did not fulfill his ambition to teach internationally, but many of his pupils did, notably S. N. Goenka (1924–2013), whose teachings have been particularly popular in India and the United States (Kornfield, 1988, pp. 241–244).

Goenka has established centers and teaching groups throughout the world, teaching techniques that emphasize the rise and fall of the breath as the means of discriminating between name, or mind (*nāma*), and form (*rūpa*). There is usually some loving-kindness practice included. John Coleman, an ex-CIA agent, one of U Ba Khin's pupils, vividly describes the method in his autobiography, *The Quiet Mind*. The method uses the point of contact of the breath on the nose, a stage in the breathing practices taught by Buddhaghosa known as the "touching" (*phusanā*). Here, however, the technique is not directed to the development of *jhāna*, as it is described in that work and practiced by *samatha* schools, but to cultivating a steady point of stability in daily life, which arouses then the possibility of observing the impermanence of phenomena. With particular emphasis on the sense of touch, a perspective is obtained from which clusters of events can be seen arising and falling within the body and the mind, which are simply observed, with "bare attention," until a sense of peacefulness is found (Coleman, 2000).

Vipassanā methods are especially undertaken in their homeland, Myanmar/Burma, and most of the major meditation centers teach highly diverse variations. So Monguk temples teach meditation based on the stages of the dependent origination cycle. Others associate the practice of the seventh book of the Abhidhamma, the *Paṭṭhāna*, much beloved in *Borān Kamaṭṭhāna* texts, with meditation (Kyaw, 2012; Crosby, 2013, pp. 99–102). The Pa-Auk center, Moulmein, however, teaches the four *jhāna*s and then the application of these to insight.

Insight methods are extensively practiced in many areas of Southeast Asia, such as Bangkok and Chiang Mai, where there is a strong middle-class support base, and in temples throughout Sri Lanka. They have also proved popular in the West. Their appeal to the cognitive, rather than the overtly emotional, has often meant they are perceived as in some way more scientific. There are many *vipassanā* centers in the United States, Australia, New Zealand, Europe, and Singapore.

Ajahn Chah (1918–1992), a pupil of Ajahn Mun, and proficient in both *samatha* and *vipassanā* meditation, was the inspiration behind the Forest Sangha, an order of monks and nuns guided by his teachings. This group of often Western monastics teach largely insight-based methods, associated with a particularly humorous and down-to-earth "take" on daily mindfulness, observation of the precepts, generosity, and the practice of the divine abidings; there is less emphasis on *jhāna*. Groups have a strong lay base of meditators.

Modern diaspora movements that teach all methods described above have, in varying degrees, spread internationally; most retain strong links with "parent" teachers and teachings (Bluck, 2008; Shaw, 2010; Starkey & Tomalin, 2016). Lay practice is a marked feature, as, apparently, in early times (M I 491; Bluck, 2008; Shaw, 2006, pp. 12–15).

Final Word

Clearly one chooses the method where one feels at home. The picture in South and Southeast Asia is varied, subject to change, and has many manifestations. This chapter gives only a brief description of the various schools teaching Southern Buddhist meditation today. A still-living tradition, its adaptive and flexible quality may be seen in the variety of physical methods and techniques associated with, and influenced by, slightly different orientations and goals. All, however, come under the heading of "meditation." But to counteract simplistic and partial understandings of the rich trainings in meditation of these regions, and to avoid their name and technical vocabulary being subject to misrepresentation, we need to ensure that our heading includes also the word *bhāvanā*, or practice. This umbrella term is applied to the ways not only that meditation is undertaken, but also to how it is balanced, grounded, and kept on track. Attention is directed not only to one's own meditative development, but also to happy and ethical interaction with others around. The Middle Way is applied in all areas of life. The ways such protections of and balances to meditation are transmitted, alongside basic techniques, will be significant for the integration and long-term acceptance of Buddhist meditative methods in an international context.

References

Primary Sources

All editions are from the Pali Text Society; unless otherwise noted, citations are to volume and page of Pali Text Society editions.

A *Aṅguttaranikāya*
D *Dīghanikāya* (cited by the number of *sutta* [e.g., D 11])
DhpA Commentary to the *Dhammapada*
DhS *Dhammasaṅgani*
M *Majjhimanikāya* (cited by the number of *sutta* [e.g., M 33])
Nidd *Mahāniddesa*
S *Saṃyuttanikāya*
Sn *Suttanipāta*
Ud *Udāna*
Vism *Visuddhimagga* (cited by chapter and paragraph in Ñāṇamoli, 1976)

Secondary Sources and Translations

Anālayo, Bhikkhu. (2017). *Early Buddhist meditation studies* (Vol. 1). Barre, MA: Barre Center for Buddhist Studies, CreateSpace Independent Publishing Platform.

Aronson, H. B. (2008). *Love and sympathy in Theravāda Buddhism* (2nd ed.). New Delhi: Motilal Banarsidass.

Becchetti, C. (1994). Une ancienne traon de manuscrits au Cambodge. In F. Bizot (Ed.), *Recherches nouvelles sur le Cambodge* (pp. 47–62). Paris: L'École française d'Extrême-Orient.

Bizot, F. (1976). *Le figuier à cinq branches. Recherches sur le bouddhisme khmer* (Vol. 2). Publications de l'École française d'Extrême-Orient 107. Paris: L'École française d'Extrême-Orient.

Bizot, F. (1980). La grotte de la naissance, *Recherches sur le bouddhisme khmer* (Vol. 2). *Bulletin de l'École française d'Extrême-Orient 67*, 222–273.

Bizot, F. (1992). *Le Chemin de Lankā. Textes bouddhiques du Cambodge* (Vol. 1). Paris: L'École française d'Extrême-Orient.

Bizot, F. (1993). *Le Bouddhisme des Thais*. Bangkok: Editions des Cahiers de France.

Bizot, F., & Lagirarde, F. (1996). *Saddavimala; la pureté par les mots*. Paris: L'École française d'Extrême-Orient.

Blackburn, A. M. (2001). *Buddhist learning and textual practice in eighteenth-century Lankan monastic culture*. Princeton, NJ: Princeton University Press.

Bluck, R. (2008). *British Buddhism: Teaching, practice and development*. London: Routledge.

Bodhi, Bhikkhu. (2000). *Connected discourses of the Buddha* (2 vols). Somerville, MA/London: Wisdom/Pali Text Society.

Boowa, Mahā Ṇyaṇasampanno. (1973). *Forest dhamma: A selection of talks on Buddhist practice*. (Bhikkhu Paññāvaddho, Trans.). Bangkok: Sathirakoses–Nagapradipa Foundation.

Boowa, Mahā Ṇyaṇasampanno. (1976). *The Venerable Phra Acharn Mun Bhuridatta Thera: Meditation master*. Bangkok: Mahamakut Rajaviyalaya Press.

Buddhadāsa, Bhikkhu. (1976). *Ānāpānasati (Mindfulness of breathing)*. (Bhikkhu Nāgasena, Trans.). Bangkok: Buddha Dharma Education Association. Retrieved from http://www.buddhanet.net/pdf_file/anapanasati.pdf

Buddhadāsa, Bhikkhu. (1998). *Mindfulness with breathing: A manual for serious beginners*. Somerville, MA: Wisdom. Also available as Buddhadāsa 1976.

Chah, Ajahn. (2007). Dhamma talk on meditation. Ubon Ratchathani: Wat Nong Pah Pong, Retrieved from https://www.ajahnchah.org/book/On_Meditation1.php (updated June 2008).

Choompolpaisal, P., & Skilton, A. (2014). The Old Meditation (*boran kammatthan*), a pre-reform Theravāda meditation system, from Wat Ratchasittharam: The pīti section of the kammatthan matchima baeb lamdap. *Aséanie* 33, 83–116.

Choompolpaisal, P., & Skilton, A. (2015). The Ancient Theravāda meditation system, *Borān Kammaṭṭhāna*: Ānāpānasati in Kammatthan Majjima Baeb Lamdub. *Buddhist Studies Review* 32(2), 207–229.

Coleman, J. E. (2000). *The quiet mind* (2nd ed.). Onolaska, WA: Pariyatti Press. Retrieved from https://store.pariyatti.org/Quiet-Mind-The_p_1383.html

Cousins, L. S. (1973). Buddhist *jhāna*. *Religion* 3, 115–131.

Cousins, L. S. (1984). *Samatha-yāna* and *Vipassanā-yāna*. In D. Dhammapala et al. (Eds.), *Buddhist studies in honour of Hammalava Saddhatissa* (pp. 56–68). Nugegoda, Sri Lanka: Hammalava Saddhatissa Felicitation Volume Committee.

Cousins, L. S. (1996). The origins of insight meditation. In T. Skourpski (Ed.), *The Buddhist Forum 4* (pp. 35–38). London: London School of Oriental Studies.

Cousins, L. S. (1997a). Aspects of esoteric southern Buddhism. In P. Connolly and S. Hamilton (Eds.), *Indian insights: Buddhism, Brahmanism, and bhakti* (pp. 185–208). London: Luzac Oriental.

Cousins, L. S. (1997b). Buddhism. In J. R. Hinnells (Ed.), *A new handbook of living religions* (pp. 369–444). Oxford: Blackwell.

Crosby, K. (2000). Tantric Theravāda: A bibliographic essay on the writings of Francois Bizot and others on the Yogāvacara tradition. *Contemporary Buddhism 1*(2), 141–198.

Crosby, K. (2013). *Traditional Theravada meditation and its modern-era suppression*. Hong Kong: The Buddha Dharma Centre of Hong Kong.

Crosby, K. (2020). *Esoteric Theravada*. Boulder, Colorado: Shambhala.

Dhammadhāro, Ajaan Lee. (1990). *Keeping the breath in mind & lessons in samadhi* (3rd ed.). (Ṭhānissaro Bhikkhu [G. DeGraff], Trans.). Rayong, Thailand: Buddha Dharma Education

Association. Retrieved from www.buddhanet.net/pdf_file/breathmind.pdf. (Original work published 1979).

Dhammasāmi, K. (1999). *Mindfulness meditation made easy.* Penang: Inner Path.

Dhammasāmi, K. (2000). *Different aspects of mindfulness.* Penang: Inward Path.

Dixon, G. (2015). Assertion and restraint in dhamma transmission in early Pāli sources. *Buddhist Studies Review* 32(1), 99–141.

Ehara, N. R. M, & Soma Thera. (1977). *The path of freedom: The Vimuttimagga of the Arahat Upatissa.* (Kheminda Thera, Trans.). Kandy, Ceylon: Buddhist Publication Society.

Eifring, H. (Ed.). (2015). *Meditation and culture: The interplay of practice and context.* London: Bloomsbury.

Gethin, R. (1992). The *Mātikās*: Memorization, mindfulness and the list. In J. Gyatso (Ed.), *In the mirror of memory: Reflections on mindfulness and remembrance in Indian and Tibetan Buddhism* (pp. 149–172). Albany: State University of New York Press.

Gethin, R. (1998). *The foundations of Buddhism.* Oxford: Oxford University Press.

Gethin, R. (2012). Was Buddhaghosa a Theravādin? Buddhist identity in the Pali commentaries and chronicles. In P. Skilling, J. A.Carbine, C. Cicuzza and S. Pakdeekham (Eds.), *How Theravada is Theravada? Exploring Buddhist identities* (pp. 1–63). Chiang Mai: Silkworm Books.

Harvey, P. (1993). The dynamics of paritta chanting in Southern Buddhism. In K. Werner (Ed.), *Love divine: Studies in bhakti and devotional mysticism* (pp. 53–84). Durham Indological Series 3. London: Curzon Press.

Harvey, P. (2013). *Introduction to Buddhism* (2nd ed.). Cambridge: Cambridge University Press.

Houtman, G. (1990). *Traditions of Buddhist practice in Burma* (Doctoral dissertation). School of Oriental and African Studies, University of London.

Khantipālo, Bhikkhu. (1980). *Bag of bones: A miscellany on the body.* The Wheel Publication, nos. 271/2. Kandy, Sri Lanka: Buddhist Publication Society.

Kornfield, J. (1988). U Ba Khin. In *Living Buddhist masters* (pp. 241–244). Kandy, Sri Lanka: Buddhist Publication Society.

Kyaw, P. P. (2012). The *Paṭṭhāna* (Conditional Relations) and Buddhist meditation: Application of the teachings in the *Paṭṭhāna* in insight (*vipassanā*) meditation practice. Conference Proceedings of the 2nd International Association of Buddhist University Conference: Buddhist Philosophy & Praxis. Retrieved from http://www.undv.org/vesak2012/iabudoc/07PyiPhyoKyawFINAL.pdf

Ledi Sayadaw. (2007). *Ānāpāna-Dīpanī (The light of breathing).* Yangon, Myanmar: Promotion and Propagation of Ledi-Dīpanī Organization.

Ñāṇamoli, Bhikkhu. (1976). *The path of purification* (2 vols.). Berkeley: Shambala.

Ñānarāma, Mahāthera. (1997). *The seven contemplations of insight: A treatise on insight meditation.* Kandy, Sri Lanka: Buddhist Publication Society.

Nyanaponika, Thera. (1972). *The heart of Buddhist meditation: A handbook of mental training based on the Buddha's way of mindfulness.* Kandy, Sri Lanka: Buddhist Publication Society.

Piyadassi, Bhikkhu. (1999). *The book of protection: Paritta.* Kandy, Sri Lanka: Buddhist Publication Society. Retrieved from www.accesstoinsight.org/lib/authors/piyadass/protection.html

Piyasobhon, Bhikkhu. (2001). *Buddhism at home.* Bangkok: Rama IX Golden Jubilee Temple.

Poonyathiro, Boonman. (2003). *From one to nine.* Bangkok.

Shaw, S. (2006). *Buddhist meditation: An anthology of texts.* London: Routledge.

Shaw, S. (2009). *Introduction to Buddhist meditation.* London: Routledge.

Shaw, S. (2010). Perceptions of Buddhist meditation in Britain at the beginning of the twenty-first century. Paper given at the World Buddhist Federation conference in celebration of the Saṅgharājā's ninety-sixth birthday, Bangkok, October 2009. *JIABU (Journal of the International Association of Buddhist Studies)* 2, 1–27.

Shaw, S. (2012). Breathing mindfulness: Text (*Ānāpānasati-Sutta*), commentaries and modern contexts. *Buddhist Philosophy and Praxis Conference, Conference Volume* (Mahachulalongkornrajavidyalaya University, Bangkok, Thailand).

Shaw, S. (2014). *The spirit of Buddhist meditation.* New Haven, CT: Yale University Press.

Shaw, S. (2016). Meditation teaching and suitability: The depiction of temperament in Pāli canonical text and commentarial narrative. In H. Eifring (Ed.), *Asian traditions of meditation* (pp. 122–144). Honolulu: University of Hawai'i Press.

Skilling, P. (2009). Redaction, recitation, and writing: Transmission of the Buddha's teachings in India in the early period. In S. C. Berkwitz et al. (Eds.), *Buddhist manuscript cultures: Knowledge, ritual, and art* (pp. 53–75). London: Routledge.

Skilling, P. (2012). Introduction. In P. Skilling, J. A. Carbine, C. Cicuzza, & S. Pakdeekham (Eds.), *How Theravada is Theravada? Exploring Buddhist identities* (pp. xiii–xxx). Chiang Mai: Silkworm Books.

Starkey, C., & Tomalin, E. (2016). Building Buddhism in England: The flourishing of a minority faith heritage. *Contemporary Buddhism 17*, 326–356.

Sumedho, Ajahn. (1987). *Mindfulness: The path to the deathless.* Hemel Hempstead: Amaravati Buddhist Publications.

Sumedho, Ajahn. (1993) Meditation in daily life: Just sitting is not enough. Audio Dhamma Talks. Amaravati Buddhist Monastery. Retrieved from http://www.amaravati.org/audio/meditation-in-daily-life-just-sitting-is-not-enough/

Tan, Uncle. (2011). *A collection of Mahāsī Sayādaw's discourses on meditation* (2nd ed.). Yangon: Buddhasāsana Nugaha Organization.

Tanabe, G. T. (2004). Chanting. In R. Buswell, Jr. (Ed.), *Encyclopedia of Buddhism* (Vol 1, pp. 137–139). New York: Macmillan.

Tiyavanich, K. (1997). *Forest recollections: Wandering monks in twentieth-century Thailand.* Honolulu: University of Hawai'i Press.

Vajirañāṇa, Mahāthera. (1975). *Buddhist meditation in theory and practice: A general exposition according to the Pali Canon of the Theravada School* (2nd ed.). Kuala Lumpur: Buddhist Missionary Society.

Viradhamma, Ven. (2017). *The contemplatives' craft: Internalizing the teachings of the Buddha.* Perth, Ontario: Tisarana Buddhist Monastery. Retrieved from https://forestsangha.org/teachings/books/the-contemplative-s-craft?language=English

Wynne, A. (2007). *The origins of Buddhist meditation.* London: Routledge.

CHAPTER 11

CHAN BUDDHISM AND MEDITATION

CAIFANG ZHU

Introduction

It is generally agreed that Buddhism was introduced into China around the first century AD. Subsequently eight major schools or sects of Mahāyāna Buddhism and two schools of Theravada Buddhism came into being in China. The Mahāyāna schools are Sān lùn (Mādhyamika based), Tiān tái (*Lotus Sūtra* based), Hūa yán (*Avataṃsaka Sūtra* based), Wéi shí (Yogācāra), Lǜ zōng (Vinaya based), Chan/Zen, Jìng tǔ (Pure Land), and Mì Zōng (Esoteric school). The Theravada are Jǜshe (*Abhidharmakośaśāstra*), and Chēng shí (Satyasiddhi).

It took about five centuries for the so-called sinification of Indian Buddhism to ripen. This was marked by the establishment of the Chan School which then reached its highest development in the Tang dynasty (618–907) (Chen, 1964; Robinson & Johnson, 2004).

Chan is the short form of *chán nà*, the Chinese transliteration of the Sanskrit word *dhyāna* (meditation). The practice of *dhyāna* in Indian Buddhism is characterized by individual progressive deepening and purifying practice, conducted in formal sitting postures. In Chan, however, it is sudden awakening (*dùn wù*) to the nature of mind and the functioning of such an awakened mind in interpersonal encounters and daily performances that is emphasized (McRae, 2003; Suzuki, 1953).

Scholars attribute such a spirit to the integration of Buddhism with indigenous Daoism (Ma, 1997; Yinshun, 1992). Chan Buddhism was also widely adopted by Confucian followers in the Song and Ming dynasties, resulting in the development of an approach called Neo-Confucianism (Chan, 1963; Fung, 1948). In similar fashion, Daoism then also absorbed some teachings of Buddhism to yield a new denomination called Quanzhen (Complete Perfection) Daoism (Zhu, 2009).

The development of classical Chan Buddhism can be divided into three periods: the Pure Chan Period (*chǔn chán shí daì*), the Opportune-Moment Encounter Period (*chán jī shí daì*), and the Overly Ripe Period (*làn shú shí daì*) (Sheng-yen, 1988). This chapter will focus on the main teachings and practices of the Pure Period, the Opportune-Moment Encounter Period, and contemporary development instead of the Overly Ripe Period in classical Chan Buddhism. Bodhidharma, Dào Xìn, and Huì Néng are chosen to represent the Pure Chan Period. For the Opportune-Moment Encounter Period, the Lín jì (J. Rinzai), Cáo dòng (J. Sōtō) and Yǖn mén schools will be presented. Finally, we will consider Shēng-huó Chan as advocated by master Jìng Hùi as representative of Chan in contemporary China.

The Pure Chan Period

Bodhidharma (?–528) is generally recognized as the first patriarch of Chan Buddhism in China. The period from Bodhidharma until the sixth patriarch Huì Néng (638–713) is known as the Pure Chan Period. It was an era when formal meditation practices predominated and koans were rarely used.

Bodhidharma arrived in China from the south of India. *The Biography of Bodhidharma* in Chinese was written by Tán Lín, allegedly one of his less prominent disciples, the most important being Hùi Kě. Tán Lín also authored a text known as *Two Entrances*, which Bodhidharma is believed to have taught to his disciples Hùi Kě, Dào Yù, and Dào Fù. In *The Continued Records of Eminent Monks* (*xù gāo sēng zhùan*), completed in 667, Dào Xüān (596–667) included the *Bodhidharma Biography* and the *Two Entrances.*

Two Entrances and Four Practices

The two entrances are the Entrance by Principle (*lǐ rù*) and the Entrance by Practices (*xíng rù*). The Entrance by Principle means that one enters the stream of Buddhism by understanding the essential teachings of the Buddha: the Three Dharma Seals, the Four Noble Truths, the Eightfold Path, and so on.

The Entrance by Practices Bodhidharma taught as fourfold:

1. the practice of non-requital of injury (*bào yuàn xíng*);
2. the practice of following circumstances (*suí yuán xíng*);
3. the practice of pursuing nothing (*wú suǒ qiú xíng*) while knowing everything co-arises;
4. the practice of according with the dharma (*chēng fǎ xíng*). (Dào Xüān, n.d.)

Facing the Wall

Bodhidharma is also known for teaching wall meditation 壁觀, the practice of sitting meditation facing a wall. In the *Two Entrances*, it is written:

> If one rejects the false and reverts to the real and in a concentrated state abides in wall-gazing, then self and other, common man and sage, are identical; firmly abiding without shifting, in no way following after the written teachings—this is mysteriously tallying with principle.
>
> (Broughton, 1999, pp. 66–67)

The Laṅkāvatāra Sūtra Period

Bodhidharma transmitted his robe together with the *Laṅkāvatāra Sūtra* to Hùi Kě (487–593) as his dharma heir, saying, "As I observe that there are no other sutras in China but this, take it for your guidance and you will naturally save the world."

The robe Bodhidharma had worn was revered as holy by later successors and practitioners in the way the Holy Grail was venerated by Christians. The Buddhist doctrine that Bodhidharma taught to his disciples was that of the *Laṅkāvatāra Sūtra*. It was not literally the case that there were no other sutras in China but Bodhidharma's statement indicates that he considered the *Laṅkāvatāra* to be the supreme teaching. Bodhidharma probably brought the sutra to China with him from India.

The *Laṅkāvatāra* is a compendium of Mahāyāna Buddhist teaching explaining such fundamental concepts "as Śūnyatā (emptiness), Anutpāda (being unborn), Anābhoga (being effortless), Cittamatra (mind-only), etc." (Suzuki, 1999, p. 43). It covers a wide range of topics and must have formed the basis of Bodhidharma's didactic teaching. The sutra is, however, a lengthy book, and the language is not easy. There was, therefore, a difficulty in making the teaching accessible.

Hùi Kě, the second patriarch, in turn, transmitted Bodhidharma's lineage of Chan to Sēng-càn (n.d.–606). There is little recorded literature about Sēng-càn, but he succeeded in making the essence of the *Laṅkāvatāra* clear by writing the famous Chan verse known as *Trust in Mind* (*xìn xīn míng*). The first four lines, probably the most remembered, read:

zhì dào wú nán 至道無難 Arriving at the Dao is without difficulty
wéi xián jiǎn zé 惟嫌揀擇。Only avoid picking and choosing
dàn mò zēng ài 但莫憎愛，Just refrain from hating and loving
dòng rán míng bai 洞然明白 Such is illumination

(Sengcan, n.d.)

Dào Xìn

Dào Xìn (580–651) was the fourth patriarch of Chan Buddhism. His major contribution was to transform the wandering tradition of his predecessors to a settled monastic community practice. He picked Double Peak Mountain (*shuāng fēng shān*) in present Hubei province as the site of his community for collective practice. He dwelled there for thirty years or so until he passed away. As many as five hundred monks and nuns practised in this first-ever monastic community in the history of Chan Buddhism. Subsequently, other monasteries were built and statues carved and erected for worship. This marked a milestone achievement and progress for Chan Buddhism. In the monastery, meditation, sutra reading and chanting, worshiping by invoking Buddha's names, and other rituals were all integrated into the daily practice.

Threefold Teaching

Dào Xìn's teaching can be summarized in three points:

1. integrating Chan meditation with the observation of monastic rules;
2. the addition of *Prajñāpāramitā* in his teaching, while continuing to revere the *Laṅkāvatāra Sūtra*;
3. The identification of invoking Buddha with being Buddha. (Yinshun, 1992)

Dào Xìn added study of the *Saptaśatikaprajñāpāramitā Sūtra*, the *Perfection of Wisdom in Seven Hundred Lines*. The characteristic feature of the *Laṅkāvatāra Sūtra* is the teaching of *tathāgatagarbha* (the embryo of Buddha nature), whereas the *Perfection of Wisdom in Seven Hundred Lines* features the wisdom of emptiness, deriving from the Buddhist tenet that everything results from dependent co-origination and that nothing is independent.

The identification of invoking Buddha with being Buddha is Dào Xìn's form of what is known as "one-practice *samādhi*" (*yī xíng sān mèi*), or single-mode *samādhi* (Faure, 1986). Dào Xìn took his one-practice *samādhi* from the invocation of Buddha in the *Perfection of Wisdom in Seven Hundred Lines*. Its central point is that "The mind that invokes the Buddha is Buddha, whereas discriminative thoughts bring one back to the mundane person" (Yinshun, 1992, p. 51).

A comprehensive summary of Dào Xìn's teaching is recorded in a text known as *The Expedient Way to Practice the Essentials of Identifying with Dao and Pacifying the Mind* (*rù dào ān xīn yào fāng biàn fǎ mén*), hereafter the *Expedient Way*.

The Expedient Way

I will outline the main teachings of meditation recorded in the *Expedient Way* (taken from the *Record of the Master and Disciples of the Laṅkāvatāra Sūtra(léng jiā shī zī jì)*; (T85, 2837).

The *Expedient Way* is about 4,300 Chinese characters long. There are no marked divisions or structure in the original text, but the one-practice *samādhi*, which is an advanced practice, is narrated right at the beginning, while practices for beginners are mentioned toward the end of the text. To honor the original order of the text, I will discuss the one-practice *samādhi* first, followed by *shouyi buyi*, "staying with oneness unmoved," and then end with the practices for beginners.

One-Practice *Samādhi*

Dào Xìn quoted Buddha's teaching in the *Perfection of Wisdom in Seven Hundred Lines* as saying: "The Dharma realm is oneness and one perceives the Dharma realm as such. This is called one-practice *samādhi*" (*fǎ jiè yī xiàng xì fǎ jiè shì míng yī xíng sān mèi*). To enter one-practice *samādhi* Dào Xìn taught:

> One needs to be free from activities and let go of random thoughts. One sits upright facing the direction of Buddha, invoking the name of the Buddha without perceiving the face of the Buddha. The invocation should be continuous with no intruding thoughts at all. In the midst of chanting, one can see Buddhas in the past, present and future.... People who enter such a one-practice *samādhi* don't see myriad Buddhadharma realms as different. For these people, either raising the foot or putting the foot down, they are always in the Dharma realm with their body and mind harmonized. Whatever they do, their behaviors are manifestations of awakening.

Dào Xìn thus teaches that "to invoke Buddha is to invoke the mind. Seeking mind is seeking Buddha. Why is this? Because consciousness is formless and so is Buddha. If you know this truth, you have pacified your mind." Thus, the one-practice *samādhi* as taught by Dào Xìn was to single-mindedly chant the name of Buddha. At a practical level this is no different from the main practice of the Pure Land school. In Pure Land one chants with the intention of being reborn in the Pure Land (*jìng tǔ*) of Amitābha (*Mí tuó*). For Dào Xìn, "pure land" meant the manifestation or revelation of the non-discriminative mind. In other words, Chan takes it that the Pure Land is a state of mind, whereas the Pure Land school takes the idea of a Pure Land more literally as a domain where one will be in the presence of Buddha. There has been much controversy about whether these two are the same or different. However, later, Yǒng-míng Yán-shòu (904–975) instituted the "dual practice" (*shuāng xiū*) of the two schools together, and this integration continues to be a strong influence on the Chinese practice of Buddhism to this day.

Shǒu-yī bù-yí

Dào Xìn describes shǒu-yī bù-yí as follows:

> Shǒu-yī bù-yí is paying attention to one object with the pure and empty eye, day and night, concentrating without moving. When the mind wanders away, the practitioner needs to call it back immediately just as when the bird wants to fly away, one pulls it back with a cord tied to the bird's foot. With such practice of watching all day long, the mind will quit discriminating and naturally be steady and concentrated.

Although Dào Xìn did not use the term, this method of meditation practice is quite reminiscent of *śamatha*, as contrasted with Vipassana, in the early Buddhist practice (Zhu, 2005) of the Theravda tradition.

Practice for Ordinary People

After teaching the advanced meditation method and arts, Dào Xìn says:

> The profound part of the method should not be taught usually. This is not because I want to reserve it and not share it, but because I suspect ordinary people won't believe it and that will result in the evil karma of slandering the Dharma. So, we must choose the right people to teach this part and should refrain from teaching and transmitting it to unworthy people. Caution, please! Caution, please!

Thus, toward the end of the *Expedient Way* he shifts gear to explain how to teach beginning practitioners:

> Beginners in the practice of sitting meditation for observing the mind need to find a solitary place, sit upright, unfasten the belt and tight clothes, and relax the body. They may massage the abdomen seven or eight times to let the obstructed qi (energy) release completely, so that they will attain to a clear, tranquil, and serene state of mind-body harmony. When the mind is pacified, the subtle energy cools down and runs on a concentrated smooth track, a mystical path, leading to the ground of luminosity and purity. When practitioners observe carefully and experience emptiness and purity inside and out, they experience the cessation of the activities of the mind and the mind-source. As the cessation of mind activities comes, the divine mind manifests. Although the mind-source is formless, its spiritual presence is apparent and never gone. It is called the Buddha nature. Those who see Buddha nature are free from birth and death. Those people are known as the other worldly people.

Reading through this quotation, one notices that although Dào Xìn begins the passage by addressing beginners, he then addresses the methods of concentration (*śamatha*) and observation (Vipassana), which suggests that the practitioners following these instructions would move beyond the beginners' stage.

Huì Néng

Although Chan Buddhism is generally credited with the idea of a "transmission outside the scriptures," the *Laṅkāvatāra Sūtra* was always considered a key text, from Bodhidharma all the way through to Hóng-rěn (601–674), the fifth patriarch. That is why they are all included in the *Record of Masters and Disciples of the Laṅkāvatāra Sūtra*. Huì Néng (638–713) is not in the *Record*, though, probably because he was still alive when Jingjue completed the record in 708.

Huì Néng stands out among the patriarchs as he revolutionized the interpretation of the concept and practice of seated meditation (*zuò chán*) and *samādhi* (*sān mèi*). Another important change Huì Néng made was to break with the tradition of transmitting the Chan lineage to only one legitimate heir. He transmitted to more than a dozen heirs. Perhaps for these reasons, Huì Néng, the sixth patriarch, is revered as the real founder of Chan Buddhism (Suzuki, 1934; Jinghui, 2014).

Huì Néng's biography is entitled *The Platform Sutra of the Sixth Patriarch* (Liù Zǔ Tán Jīng), and it covers topics such as conduct (*śīla*), meditation (*dhyāna*), and wisdom (*prajñā*). The *Platform Sutra* underwent various redactions. Although traditionally attributed to Fǎ Hǎi, a close disciple of Huì Néng, there is disagreement among scholars on its origin and development (Hu, 2007). The Dunhuang versions are the oldest texts available. Two copies dated to between 830 and 860 have been found in the Mogao Caves in Dunhuang. Both are thought to be based on an edition from about 780 CE. In 1056, the Chinese scholar-monk Qì Sōng produced a larger edition, entitled *Precious Record of the Dharma of the Sixth Patriarch* (Liù Zǔ Fǎ Bǎo Jì), and in 1291, Zōng Bǎo produced the ten-chapter edition that became part of the Ming-dynasty Chinese Buddhist canon.

The Platform Sutra

In the following I will try to outline the major content of the *Platform Sutra* based on the ten-chapter edition (translations by Wong Mou-Lam in Huì Néng, 1969, unless otherwise indicated).

Chapter One: Personal History

The first chapter contains the story of the contest for the succession of Hóng-rěn, the fifth patriarch. It has become a household story and an important part of the traditional narrative of Chan Buddhism. According to the story, Huì Néng won this contest but had to flee the monastery to avoid the catastrophic rivalry from disciples of a fellow practitioner. The contest was between Shén-xiù, the head monk, who was expected to succeed Hóng-rěn at the time, and Huì Néng who then was an unknown, but very sharp, lay practitioner in the monastery. Whoever wanted to be Hóng-rěn's heir should present a verse to show his understanding of Chan.

Shén-xiù's verse reads:
The body is the bodhi tree;
The mind is like a bright mirror's stand.
Be always diligent in wiping the mirror;
Do not let it collect any dust.
Huì Néng's verse in response reads:
Bodhi is fundamentally without any tree;
The bright mirror is not a stand either.
Originally there is not a single thing;
Where could any dust be collected?

According to the traditional interpretation by Gūi-fēng Zǒng mì, a sixth-generation successor of Huì Néng, the two verses represent respectively the gradual and the sudden approach in Chan Buddhism. John McRae (2003), however, argues that Shén-xiù's verse does not refer to gradual or progressive endeavor, but to a *constant* practice of cleaning the mirror, the endless personal manifestation of the bodhisattva ideal. McRae believes Huì Néng's verse does not stand alone but forms a pair with Shenxiu's verse.

Chapter Two: Prajñā

When our mind works freely without any hindrance and is at liberty to "come" or to "go," we attain the *samādhi* of *prajñā*, or liberation. Such a state is called being without deliberate thought. This is not the same as suppressing thought. Suppressing thought is an erroneous view, sometimes called being "Dharma ridden."

Chapter Three: Questions

Huì Néng answers questions from the lay audience. He discusses the famous story of Bodhidharma telling Emperor Wu of the Liang dynasty that his good deeds would bring him no merit. Huì Néng explains this by distinguishing between "merit" and "blessings." Good deeds bring worldly blessings by karma. Merit, however, Huì Néng says, means insight into the essence of mind. He says that the emperor failed to understand this and Bodhidharma departed.

Next, he discusses the Pure Land of the West, asserting the greater importance of one's inner state compared to one's physical location, such as a monastery. Huì Néng then concludes that practicing as a lay person is preferable to following the forms of monastic renunciation without doing the inner practice.

Chapter Four: Meditation and Wisdom

In this sermon, meditation (*dìng*) and wisdom (*huì*) are spoken of as being united like a lamp and its light. The lamp is the substance, and the light is its function. Similarly, meditation is the substance, and wisdom is the function. They cannot be separated. One does not come before the other. At times of wisdom, meditation exists in that wisdom; at times of meditation, wisdom exists in that meditation.

He defines the one-practice *samādhi* (*yī xíng sān mèi*) as maintaining a straightforward mind in all circumstances.

Chapter Five: Seated Meditation

This chapter details the "purity of our fundamental nature." Huì Néng holds that if your mind becomes attached to purity, you will only generate a false purity. He also revolutionized the understanding of the concept of seated or sitting meditation (*zuò chán*). "Sitting is having no judgments arising in mind when facing all circumstances, good or bad; meditating is seeing the innate nature of the mind unmoved."

Chapter Seven: Temperament and Circumstance

Toward the end of this chapter there is a competing set of verses. A monk quotes Chan Master Wo Lun as saying:

Wo Lun has ways and means,
to insulate the mind from all thoughts.
When circumstances don't react on the mind,
the bodhi tree will grow steadily.

Huì Néng argues that believing in this teaching will not set the practitioner free, but rather bind him more tightly. He responds to this wrong teaching with the following verse:

Huì Néng has no ways and means
To insulate the mind from all thoughts.
Circumstances often react on my mind,
And I wonder how the bodhi tree can grow? (Huì Néng, 1969, p. 82)

Huì Néng's verse emphasizes the dynamic and functional wisdom from the awakened mind rather than the quiescence through concentrative meditation. This approach of preferring wisdom and function to discipline and quiescence is at the heart of Chan Buddhism.

Chapter Eight: Immediate and Gradual (Encounter Stories and Dialogues)

Those who followed Shén-xiù developed the "gradual approach" in Northern China, while the followers of Huì Néng favored a "sudden approach" in Southern China. Debating the sudden approach versus the gradual approach, Huì Néng addressed his assembly as follows:

> So far as the Dharma is concerned, there can be only one school. (If a distinction exists) it exists in the fact that the founder of one school is a northern man, while the other is a southerner. While there is only one Dharma, some disciples realize it more quickly than others. The reason why the names "Sudden" and "Gradual" are given is that some disciples are superior to others in mental dispositions. So far as Dharma is concerned, the distinction of "Sudden" and "Gradual" does not exist.

Another example from the Northern school speaks of Shén-xiù's teaching on *śīla* (disciplinary rules), *dhyāna* (meditation), and *prajñā* (wisdom):

To refrain from all evil actions is śīla,
to practise whatever is good is prajña,
and to purify one's own mind is dhyāna.
In order to challenge this, Huì Néng wrote:
To free the mind from all impurity is the śīla of the Essence of Mind.
To free the mind from all ignorance is the wisdom of the Essence of Mind.
To free the mind from all disturbance is the dhyāna of the Essence of Mind.
That which neither increases nor decreases is the Diamond.
"Coming" and "going" are different phases of *samādhi*. (Huì Néng, 1969, pp. 83–86)

Chapter Nine: The Imperial Summons

This chapter describes the request of the Imperial Court for Huì Néng to visit the emperor. However, following his predecessors such as Hóng-rěn and Dào Xìn, Huì Néng declined the request.

Chapter Ten: Last Words

At the end of his life, Huì Néng gathers his ten leading disciples together and tells them to go forth and spread the Dharma, each in a different direction. He tells them how to teach by staying true to the self-nature and meeting all propositions with a balancing opposite. He also warns: "Those who grasp at emptiness slander the sutras by maintaining that written words have no use. Since they maintain they have no need of written words, they should not speak, because written words are merely the marks of spoken language. They maintain that the direct way cannot be established by written words, and yet these two words, 'not established' are themselves written.... Do not slander the sutras for if you do, your offense will create countless obstacles for you."

The Opportune-Moment Encounter Period

After Huì Néng, Chan gradually evolved into what is known as the five houses or five lineages: Wéi yǎng, Lín jì (J. Rinzai), Cáo dòng (J. Sōtō), Yún mén, and Fǎ yǎn. From Huì Néng onward, Chan meditation is no longer confined to a formal sitting practice. It is practised in every possible way in daily life. Interpersonal exchanges or encounters at the opportune moment become especially important: a style of practice that produces numerous wonderful and remarkable koans (Cleary & Cleary, 2005; Cleary, 1990; Heine & Wright, 2000).

In this period, we see exchanges or encounters, verbal or non-verbal, between Chan adepts or between masters and disciples. Chan Buddhists resort to symbolic and physical expressions, including various non-verbal expressions, hitting, and shouting, allegedly to awaken the deluded mind, although they also use affectionate speech. This unique Chan behavioral pattern "sets it up for an unconventional path as contrasted with the normal path of Buddhism" (Sheng-yen, 2006, p.104).

Among the five houses, Lín jì, Cáo dòng, and Yún mén have become much more influential than the other two. Each of the five houses has its own principles for embodying and interpreting the highest truths Buddha taught. I will sketch the distinctive characteristics of Lín jì, Cáo dòng, and Yún mén below.

The Lín jì House

The style of Linji Chan is usually compared to that of a powerful general, while the genre of Caodong is akin to that of a gentle citizen (Zhengguo, 2007). In the Linji teaching we find the four ways of interaction (*sì liào jiǎn*), and the four guest-host relationships (*sì bīn zhǔ*).

The four ways of interaction are the ways in which Master Lín Jì (?–867) interacted with his disciples or visitors in a Chan encounter. They are:

1. breaking the student's attachment to the ego rather than the object;
2. breaking the student's attachment to the object rather than the ego;
3. breaking the student's attachment to both the ego and object;
4. breaking neither if the student is not attached to either.

The expediency of using one or a combination of means merely depends on the condition or outlook of the student and the circumstances of the encounter.

The Linji lineage puts much emphasis upon encounters where a questioner approaches a master. Lín Jì typified the outcomes of such encounters using the terminology of host and guest. The four outcomes are:

1. "guest sees host" (*bīn kàn zhǔ*): the student sees more than the master;
2. "host sees guest" (*zhǔ kàn bīn*): the master is able to penetrate the mind of the visiting guest, but the guest is still stuck;
3. "host sees host" (*zhǔ kàn zhǔ*): a host seeing another host, meaning the two in a Chan encounter understand each other and are on the same wavelength;
4. "guest sees guest" (*bīn kàn bīn*): a guest meeting with another guest, meaning an encounter of two practitioners, neither of whom "have the eye" to see the true nature of the mind (Xingyun, 1970–1980, p. 6506; Yuho, 1991).

Foulk (2000) has argued that social hierarchical structures pre-determine the master's victory over the student in koan encounters. While it is true that there is master-disciple hierarchy, nevertheless students also stand a chance to be an equal to the master, or even turn the situation around and assume the leading role. Examples of this kind abound in Chan literature (Cleary & Cleary, 2005; Puji, 1984). For instance, in *The Recorded Sayings of Chan Master* Zhào-zhōu (*zhào zhōu chán shī yǔ lù*), there are a good number of cases where Zhào-zhōu Cōng-shěn often had the best of his teacherNán-qúan (Green, 2001). Similarly, Lín Jì, after being hit three times, ended up hitting his master Huángbó Xīyùn as well as master Dayu (CBETA, n.d.; Waston, 1993).

The Caodong House

The Caodong lineage was established by Dòng-shān Liáng-jiè (807–869) and Cáo-shān Běn-jì (?–901), who were contemporary with Lín-jì. The later development of the Caodong House, called Silent Illumination (*mò zhào chán*), attracted enormous attention. It is epitomized by Hongzhi Zhengjue (1091–1157) who authored *The Book of*

Serenity (*cóng róng lù*) with Wàn-sōng Xíng-xiù, which features one hundred koans and commentaries from the practice of the Caodong lineage. It is primarily the teaching from the silent illumination tradition of the Caodong House that Dōgen (1200–1253) took from China to Japan.

In volume eight of *The Extended Record of Chan Master Hongzhi* (*hóng zhì chán shī guǎng lù*), we find "The Inscription of Silent Illumination" (*mò zhào míng*). This gives us a brief account of what silent illumination practice is like. The Inscription consists of seventy-two four-character lines or thirty-six stanzas full of terminology, metaphors, and allusions that are challenging to average readers, even inside Chan Buddhism.

The inscription begins:

In silence language is forgotten, but things appear as they are.
Mirroring the experience feels vast, experiencing this feels luminous.
Luminosity alone illumines and in illumination wonder comes:
The moon, stars and galaxy, the snow pines and cloud peaks.
...
The wonders are stored in the silent realm and their merits are forgotten in illumination.
Why is the wondrous experience saved? Just to keep the awakening to break through the unconscious.
The way of silent illumination is the root of leaving the subtle cloud and confusion.

(Hongzhi Zhenjue, n.d.)

Sheng-yen provides a three-stage depiction of the practice of silent illumination:

1. The first stage centers on the practice of "just sitting"—attentively minding the body, poised in the posture of seated meditation.
2. The second stage entails an expansion of one's field of awareness from the body to the external environment. Distinctions between the body and one's surroundings dissolve, so that one sits with bald awareness of this larger, expanded field in the same way that one previously attended to the seated body.
3. In the third stage subtle reifications of self and object disappear, and everything is present except oneself. There are no thoughts of self, no dualistic oppositions between self and external environment, and no discrimination or self-grasping thoughts. Hear something, and it is as though nothing is heard. See something, and it is as though nothing is seen. Yet the mind is perfectly clear and unclouded (Sheng-yen & Stevenson, 2001, pp. 152–153).

Sheng-yen says this clarity of the mind "is not the clarity experienced by ordinary people, which is contaminated by discriminatory attachment. This is the clarity of things as perceived by *prajñā* wisdom—as they are, in and of themselves" (Sheng-yen & Stevenson, 2001, p. 158). The third-stage experience of silent illumination is not "a pessimistic, nihilistic nothingness" because there is clarity, vividness, and knowing that accompany the experience. It is "the fullest and most direct expression of the unmediated realization of Buddha-nature espoused in the Chan school" (Sheng-yen & Stevenson, 2001, p. 143).

Finally, he says that the three-stage outline is not a hard and fast formula of progression for the practice of silent illumination. Responses may differ considerably from one practitioner to another. He also points out that the practice is generally suitable for a time set aside specifically at home or during a retreat. It is not suitable for practice in the workplace or during social occasions.

Sheng-yen also summarizes a few pitfalls found in the practice of silent illumination. One of them is to grasp a mistaken concept of illumination. He clarifies that "illumination" is not to be shining like a sun, moon, or even a light. Rather it simply means "to be aware" with luminosity. Another common mistake Sheng-yen singles out is that practitioners may "fall into a condition of blankness or stupor, where the mind does not reflect or register anything." Sheng-yen calls this a "lazy and hazy state of blankness," "a dull and dissipated state" (Sheng-yen & Stevenson, 2001, p. 150) different from sheer drowsiness or sleep. He compares such a state to "standing on the seashore on a gray, rainy day, not seeing anything anywhere" (Sheng-yen & Stevenson, 2001, p. 151). He also believes that such a phenomenon may also result from trying too hard to suppress thoughts, perceptions, and sensations. The most serious pitfall he mentions is that of overestimating one's attainment, which can easily occur as it is technically difficult to know whether the meditator's mind is really silent and motionless while open and luminous at the same time.

Kàn Huà Chán

The two main forms of meditation in Chan and Zen today are silent illumination and *kàn huà* practice. They stand in striking contrast to one another. *Kàn huà* was pioneered by Dà-huì Zōng-gǎo (1089–1163) in the Linji House, and is practiced by watching (*kàn*) or meditating on a *huà tóu*. A *huà tóu* is the head or crux of a Chan saying (Sheng-yen & Stevenson, 2001) or the theme of a speech or critical phrase from a koan (Buswell, 1986). One of the most famous *huà tóu* expressions is *wú* (J. *mu*), literally meaning "no." It is from a very well-known koan where Chan Master Zhào-zhōu said, "*Wú*," in response to the query "Does a dog have Buddha nature?"

When watching the *huà tóu wú*, the meditator does nothing but keep contemplating the expression *wú*, which is the short form of "the dog having no Buddha nature," an expression or a theme not easily comprehensible. There are two ways to practice it: a gentle way and a forceful way. The gentle way is suitable for beginners with an untamed or coarse mind, while the forceful is believed suitable for experienced practitioners or those with a stable and calm mind. The forceful approach "should be taught selectively, and above all, used under strictly controlled conditions" (Sheng-yen & Stevenson, 2001, p. 135) because it may lead to madness or psychological disorders if not handled or supervised properly.

In the course of continuous concentration on *wú* the practitioner develops the *yí qíng* or "feeling of doubt." The *yí qíng* becomes greater as the meditation goes on and intensifies until the *yí qíng* reaches its peak and results in enlightenment. Contemporary neurocognitive psychologists have shown an interest in this practice, but have not yet successfully uncovered the mechanism underlying it (Austin, 2006; Varela, Thompson, & Rosch, 1991).

An important distinction in this type of practice is that between "live words" (*huó jù*) and "dead words" (*sǐ jù*). In the practice of Kàn Huà Chán, "live words" or live themes are tasteless or meaningless semantically, whereas "dead words" or dead themes are intellectually meaningful. In the case of "Does the dog have Buddha nature?" concentrating on its possible meaning is known as working with "dead words" because intellectually a meaningful mental exercise is unlikely to lead you to the non-discriminative state of mind, or enlightenment. It is concentration on the seemingly meaningless or tasteless word (*wu* in this case) that is more likely to lead to enlightenment (Buswell,1986; Minghai, 2015; Zhengguo, 2007). This practice is traditionally known as a meditation on the mystery of transcending life and death.

Kàn Huà Chán spread to Korea and Japan and became as popular there as in China. Chinul (1158–1210), the Korean Buddhist monk, believed that "in matters of spiritual technique, speed of consummation, and the purity of view, the 'shortcut' *hwadu* approach is clearly superior to the sudden awakening/gradual cultivation approach advocated by Tsung-mi" (Buswell, 1986, p. 219). Today in Korea, Kàn Huà Chán continues to be "the primary technique employed in meditation halls, and virtually all masters advocate its use for students at all levels of spiritual development" (Buswell, 1986, p. 218).

The Yún mén (864–949) House

In the Song dynasty, *Yún mén* was the most popular among the five houses (Ma, 1997). Yunmen is similar to Linji in following the "heroic" or "general's" style (Sanxingtang, 2007). To understand Yunmen koans, it is important to know the three principle phrases or sentences of Chan master Yún-mén Wén-yǎn (*yún mén sān jù*):

1. the phrase that encloses heaven and earth (*hán gài qián kūn jù*)—universal;
2. the phrase that follows the wave (*suí bō zhú liú jù*)—skillfully adjusting to and guiding the inquirer's situation;
3. the phrase that cuts off myriad streams (*jié duàn zhòng liú jù*)—blocking all discriminative activities of the inquirer's mind.

Yuán-wù Kè-qín, the great compiler and commentator of *The Blue Cliff Record* (*bìyán lù*), reminds readers: "As soon as you make a principle, you fall into a pit. The three phrases are inherent in every one phrase of Yunmen. Since the source inspiration of his family is like this, when Yunmen utters a phrase, it must be returned to the source. Anything but this will always be phony" (Cleary & Cleary, 2005, p. 40). Like the Linji and Caodong principles or formulae, we see Yunmen use the three phrases as the expedient means or *upāya* to interact with students or fellow practitioners of Chan Buddhism.

The Existence of General Principles

Despite the fact that Chan, especially in the Opportune-Moment Encounter Period, is highly unconventional and perplexing, there are principles such as Linji's *sì liào jiǎn* and Yumen's three phrases suggestive of a general inner logic behind these irrational words and behaviors. Reading through many of the koans in *The Blue Cliff Record* and *The Book of Serenity*, one may agree that "it is the opportune moment that holds the secret key to an encounter dialogue and the interpretation of it as a text. The opportune moment of responding swiftly and skillfully and yet always grounding one in the openness and flow of the mind highlights the inner logic of the behavior of adept Chan Buddhists." (Zhu, 2011, p. 390).

Contemporary Development

Shēng-huó Chán, or Everyday Chan, is the updated development of Chan Buddhism in China today. Reverend Jìng-huì (1933–2013), the proponent of Shenghuo Chan, was a dharma heir to Xū-yún (1840–1959), translated literally as Empty Cloud, a quintessential Chan master in modern China, who received transmissions from all of the five houses. While grounded in the tradition of Chan, Jìng-huì was also an enthusiastic follower of the master Tài-xū (1890–1947), another charismatic Buddhist monk important in the history of modern Chinese Buddhism. Tài-xū's advocacy of humanistic Buddhism had a lasting impact on Jìng-huì, who started to promote Shenghuo Chan in 1992 as a further development of humanistic Buddhism in mainland China.

Shēng-huó Chán teaches "practicing Chan in the midst of life while living a life in the midst of practicing Chan" (Jinghui, 2014, p. 187; 2013, p. 329; 2005, p. 138, 168). From this central idea, over twenty years, Jìng-huì formulated a framework of theory and practice that caters to contemporary people, both lay and monastic.

Jìng-huì's teaching has four basic tenets:

1. Apply your faith to your life;
2. Make your practice here and now;
3. Let Buddhadharma be integrated in worldly affairs;
4. Let the individual merge in the community (Jinghui, 2013, pp. 182–184; 2005, pp. 103–107).

Under the framework of these four tenets, he then technically fleshed out the practice with four steps:

1. Radiate an enlightened heart (*fā pú tí xīn*);
2. Establish a wisdom view (*shù bō rě jiàn*);

3. Cultivate observation of the breath (*xiu xī dào guān*);
4. Enter the Chan of everyday life (*rù shēng huó chàn*) (Jinghui, 2014).

He presents the first two steps as establishing the "right view" and the second two as applying the practice, thus following the format of the Eightfold Path.

This stands out from the traditional practice of Chan Buddhism, as it presents an integration of breathing practices popular in the Theravada tradition with the practice of Chan in everyday life. Nonetheless, it is a genre of Chan that emphasizes functionality—active expression—over quiescence, which has been a fundamental Chan principle since the time of Huì Néng.

In meditation practice, Jìng-huì proposes that, first, one needs to go through a certain period of intensive training, such as formal sitting- meditation retreats. Then one may apply the practice to everyday life. Counting the breath (*shǔ xī*) and following the breath (*suí xī*) are two methods he uses, especially in teaching beginners, or people that resonate with the methods. For more experienced or intermediate-level practitioners, he shares the practices of "concentration (*zhuān zhù*), serenity (*qīng míng*) and being meticulous (*mián mì*)" (Jinghui, 2011, p. 15). For more advanced practitioners he teaches that in daily life one needs to be "grounded in mindfulness and observe every thought and behavior in the moment. This is Shēng-huó Chán" (Jinghui, 2014, p. 186).

While addressing the ultimate concern, his teaching is:

> No matter [if] one is dying or living, one needs to be able to ground oneself in the present moment and use intuition. Thus one faces whatever calmly and one sees life and death as a unity. Only by grounding oneself moment by moment in such a nirvana state of present karma can one really transcend the samsara of life and death. This is the solution Chan Buddhism or Shenghuo Chan offers to the ultimate concern.
>
> (Jinghui, 2013, p. 308)

His elaboration of Chan Buddhism in modern language is also comprehensive and succinct:

Seek satisfaction in working with responsibility,
Seek peace of mind in fulfilling one's duty,
Seek happiness in devotion,
Seek progress without an attachment to the self,
Present the opportune moment in everyday life. (Minghai, 2017, p. 58)

For two decades, Jìng-huì served as an associate chair of the Chinese Buddhist Association (CBA), and was the chief editor of its flagship journal *The Voice of Dharma*. Jìng-huì was the abbot of Bailin Chan Monastery (*bǎi-lín chán sì*) for many years, the monastery where Zhào-zhōu Cōng-shěn had lived and preached. From there, in 1992, he launched the Shēng-huó Chán summer camp for college and university students, which still takes place once per year.

The Shēng-huó Chán advocacy has won much recognition in the Buddhist community of practice and scholarship in China today (Huang, 2015, 2012, 2011; Minghai, 2015) and has also spread internationally with centers in Germany, Switzerland, Hungary, and other countries. Jinghui passed away on April 20, 2013, after spending his last ten years as the abbot in the Fourth Patriarch Monastery where Dào Xìn lived and preached in Huangmei, Hubei province.

Conclusion

This chapter has summarized the development of Chan Buddhism. I considered three main periods, the Pure Chan Period, the Opportune-Moment Encounter Period, and the Contemporary Period. In describing the representative figures of each period, I have tried to present a balance of the essential Chan ideas and of the practices based upon them. Bodhidharma, Dào Xìn, and Huì Néng were selected to represent the Pure Chan Period where formal sitting meditation was much appreciated. Huì Néng marked a turning point, though, as he received traditional training from his master Hóng-rěn, but started a major reform. With Huì Néng we witness what is regarded as a complete sinification of Indian Buddhism in general and Indian *dhyāna* or meditation in particular. This sinification boils down to the reinterpretation of sitting meditation, which is no longer bound by the sitting posture. Instead, Chan from Huì Néng onward tends to value meditation in the midst of functional daily performances rather than quiescence in a retreat.

Following Huì Néng we have the Opportune-Moment Encounter Period, which includes Linji, Caodong, and Yunmen houses. Each of the three exemplifies the practice of Chan meditation in the dynamic relation of the encounter between master and disciple or in the midst of the practitioner's active daily life.

The Contemporary Period is epitomized by Jinghui's advocacy of Shenghuo Chan. In meditation practice, Shenghuo Chan integrates the training of mindful breathing, popular in early Buddhism, with the Chinese genre that features mindful practice—grounding in the present moment in the midst of everyday life. The broad conception of Shenghuo Chan attempts to make Chan practice more accessible to contemporary people in China and beyond.

With the renaissance of traditional Chinese culture, Chan Buddhism has witnessed a great development in China over the past three decades. In the meantime, the open-door policy and modernization has brought a diversification of values and lifestyles. The introduction of the secularized mindfulness movement, psychotherapy, and transpersonal psychology has posed challenges to the further development of Chan. In the future, Chan Buddhism may need to pay more attention to issues such as gender equality and to skills to help with the practical psychological and spiritual issues of its followers. It may not only need to aim at spiritual liberation but also to function as a therapy for the vast number of stressed lay practitioners (Brazier, 1995; Zhu, 2015a, 2015b).

References

Austin, J. H. (2006). *Zen-brain reflections*. Cambridge, MA: MIT Press.

Brazier, D. (1995). *Zen therapy: Transcending the sorrows of the human mind*. New York: John Wiley & Sons.

Broughton, J. L. (1999). *The Bodhidharma anthology: The earliest records of Zen*. Berkeley, CA: University of California Press.

Buswell, R. E. (1986). Chinul's systemization of Chinese meditative techniques in Korean Son Buddhism. In Peter N. Gregory (Ed.), *Traditions of meditation in Chinese Buddhism* (pp. 199–242). Honolulu: University of Hawai'i Press.

Chan, W-T. (1963). *A source of Chinese philosophy*. Princeton, NJ: Princeton University Press.

Chen, K. (1964). *Buddhism in China: A historical survey*. Princeton, NJ: Princeton University Press.

Chinese Buddhist Electronic Text Association. (n.d.). *The jingde record of the lamp transmission* 景德傳燈錄. Retrieved from Chinese Buddhist Electronic Text Association. http://www.cbeta.org/result/normal/T51/2076

Cleary, T. (Trans.). (1990). *Book of serenity*. Hudson, NY: Lindisfarne Press.

Cleary, T. & Cleary, J. C. (Trans.). (2005). *The blue cliff record* 碧岩錄. Boston: Shambhala.

Dào Xüān 道宣. (n.d.). *The continued records of eminent monks* 續高僧傳. Retrieved from Chinese Buddhist Electronic Text Association, http://tripitaka.cbeta.org/T50n2060 (Original work published 667 CE).

Faure, B. (1986). The concept of one-practice samadhi in early Chan. In Peter N. Gregory (ed.), *Traditions of meditation in Chinese Buddhism*. Honolulu: University of Hawai'i Press.

Foulk, T. G. (2000). The form and function of koan literature: A historical overview. In Steven Heine & Dale S. Wright (Eds.), *The koan: Text and contexts in Zen Buddhism* (pp. 15–45). Oxford: Oxford University Press.

Fung, Y.-L. 馮友蘭. (1948). *A short history of Chinese philosophy*. London: Free Press.

Green, J. (Trans.). (2001). The Recorded Sayings of Zen Master Joshu. Boston: Shambhala.

Heine, S. & Wright, D. S. (eds). (2000). *The koan: Texts and contexts in Zen Buddhism*. Oxford: Oxford University Press.

Hongzhi Zhenjue 宏智正覺. (n.d.). *The extended record of Chan Master Hongzhi* 宏智禪師廣錄. Retrieved from Chinese Buddhist Electronic Text Association, http://tripitaka.cbeta.org/T48n2001

Hu, S. (2007). *Essays on Chan Buddhism by Hu Shi* 胡適說禪. China: Tuanjie Press.

Huang, X. N. (Ed.). (2011). *Essays on Shenghuo Chan*生活禅研究. China: Zhongzhou Guji Publisher.

Huang, X.N. (ed.). (2012). Essays on Shenghuo Chan (Vols. 2a–b) 生活禅研究2(上、下). China: Zhongzhou Guji Publisher.

Huang, X. N. 黄夏年 (Ed.). (2015). *Essays on Shenghuo Chan* (Vol. 3) 生活禅研究(3). China: Daxiang Press.

Huì Néng 慧能. (1969). *The sutra of Huì Néng*壇經 (W. Mou-Lam, Trans.). In A.F. Price and Wong Mou-Lam (trans.), *The Diamond Sutra, and, the sutra of Huì Néng*. Berkeley, CA: Shambala Publications.

Jinghui 淨慧. (2005). *Chinese Buddhism and Shenghuo Chan*中國佛教與生活禪. Beijing: Religion and Culture Press.

Jinghui 淨慧. (2011). *Staying with oneness unmoved* 守一不移. China: Zhaozhou Bailin Chan Monastery.

Jinghui 淨慧. (2013). *Introduction to Chan* 禪宗入門. Shanghai: East China Normal University.

Jinghui 淨慧. (2014). *Key to Shenghuo Chan* (2nd ed). 生活禪鑰 增訂版. Beijing: Life, Reading and New Knowledge Press.

Jingjue 淨覺. (n.d). *The record of the master and the disciples of Laṅkāvatāra Sūtra* 楞伽師資記. Retrieved from Chinese Electronic Text Association, http://tripitaka.cbeta.org/T85n2837_001(Original work published 708 CE).

Ma, T. 馬天祥. (1997). *The development history of Chan Buddhism in China* 中國 禪宗發展史. Changsha, China: Hunan Education Press.

McRae, J. (2003). *Seeing through Zen*. Berkeley: University of California Press.

Minghai 明海. (2017).A collection of humanistic Buddhists and their thoughts: Jinghui人间佛教思想文库：净慧卷.Beijing:Religion and Culture Press.

Minghai 明海. (Ed.). (2015). *Proceedings of the fourth Three-Chan Conference (Part 2): Studies of Reverend Jinghui and Shenghuo Chan* 第四届三禅论坛研讨会论文集(2)：净慧长老和生活禅研究. Beijing: Religion and Culture Press.

Puji 普濟. (1984). *Wu Deng Huiyuan* (3 vols.) 五燈會元, 上中下. Beijing: Zhonghua Publishing House.

Robinson, R. & Johnson, W. (2004). *Buddhist religions: A historical introduction* (5th ed.). New York: Wadsworth Publishing Company.

Sanxingtang 三省堂 (Ed). (2007). *Chan Records of the Five Schools and Seven Houses*禪宗五宗七家語錄. Shijiazhuang, China: Hebei Research Institute of Chan Buddhism.

Sengcan 僧璨. (n.d.). *Inscription on trust of mind*信心銘. Retrieved from Chinese Buddhist Electronic Text Association, http://tripitaka.cbeta.org/T48n2010 (Original work published ca. late 6th–early 7th cen. CE).

Sheng-yen 聖嚴. (1988). Chan as in Chinese Chan Buddhism 中國禪宗的禪. In Zhang Wenda & Zhang Li (Eds.), *Chan Buddhism: History and culture* 宗:歷史與文化. Harbin, China: Heilongjiang Education Press.

Sheng-yen 聖嚴, with Stevenson, D. (2001). *Hoofprint of the ox*. Oxford: Oxford University Press.

Sheng-yen 聖嚴. (2006). *Spinning the flower and smiling at it* 拈花微笑. Shanghai, China: Shanghai Sanlian Shudian.

Suzuki, D. (1999). *Studies in the Lankavatara Sutra*. Delhi: Motilal Banarsidess.

Suzuki, D. T. (1934). *Essays in Zen Buddhism*. Kyoto: Eastern Buddhist Society.

Suzuki, D. T. (1953). Zen: A reply to Hu Shih. *Philosophy East and West* 3(1), 3–25.

Varela, F., Thompson, E., & Rosch, E. (1991). *The embodied mind*. Cambridge, MA: MIT Press.

Waston, B. (1993). *The Zen teachings of Master Lin-Chi*. New York: Columbia University Press.

Xingyun 星雲 (Ed.). (1970–1980). *The Great Dictionary of Buddha Light*佛光大辭 典 (Vols. 2 and 7). Taiwan: Fo Guan Shan Foundation for Buddhist Culture and Education.

Yinshun印順. (1992). *The history of Chinese Chan Buddhism*中國禪宗史. Shanghai, China: Shanghai Bookstore Press.

Yuho, Y. (1991). *The Japanese-English Zen Buddhist dictionary*. Tokyo: Sankibo Buddhist Bookstore.

Zhengguo 正果. (2007). *The essentials of Chan Buddhism*禪宗大意. Beijing: Renmin University of China Press.

Zhu, C. (2005). From Vipassana in Theravada to guan xin in Chinese Tian Tai and Chan Buddhism: A comparative study of Buddhist meditation techniques. *Contemporary Buddhism (UK)*, 6(1), 53–64

Zhu, C. 朱彩方(2009). Analytical psychology and Daoist inner alchemy: A response to C. G. Jung's "Commentary on 'The secret of the golden flower.'" *Journal of Analytical Psychology* [London] 54(4), 493–512.

Zhu, C. 朱彩方(2011). The hermeneutics of Chan Buddhism: Reading koans from *The blue cliff record*. *Asian Philosophy 21*(4), 373–393.
Zhu, C. 朱彩方. (2015a). Extending the practice of Shenghuo Chan 生活禪發微. In Minghai (Ed.), *Proceedings of the fourth Three-Chan Conference (Part 2): Studies of Reverend Jinghui and Shenghuo Chan*. Beijing: Religion and Culture Press.
Zhu, C. 朱彩方. (2015b). A general survey on Reverend Jinghui's thoughts of Buddhism and praxis of Shenghuo Chan. In Huang X. 黄夏年 (Ed.), *Research on Shenghuo Chan: Proceedings of the third Hebei Cultural Forum of Chan Buddhism*. Zhengzhou: Daxiang Press.

Glossary

ān xīn 安心
mind at peace, settled faith
Bǎi-lín chán sì 柏林禪寺
Bailin Chan Monastery (lit., Cedarwood Chan Monastery)
bào yuàn 報怨
avenge
Bìyán Lù 碧巖錄
The Blue Cliff Record, a collection of huà tóu
bīn kàn bīn 賓看賓
"guest sees guest": a discussion between two who are both deluded
bīn kàn zhǔ 賓看主
"guest sees host": an encounter where the student sees more clearly than the supposed master
bō rě 般若
wisdom (Skt. *prajñā*)
bù yí 不移
steadfast, unmoving
Cáo dòng zōng 曹洞宗
one of the five schools of Chan (J. Sōtō Shu)
Cáo-shān Běn-jì 曹山本寂
(?–901) Chan master, a disciple of Dòng-shān (J. Sōzan Honjaku)
chán 禪
the meditation school of Chinese Buddhism (J. Zen)
chán shī 禪師
Chan master
chán jī 禪機
Chan moment
chēng 稱
match, fit
zhuàn 傳
impart, pass on
Cóng Róng Lù 從容錄

The Book of Serenity (or Easy-Going Record)
Dà-huì Zōng-gǎo 大慧宗杲
(1089–1163; J. Daie Sōkō) Chan monk who introduced the study of *huà tóu*
Dào Xìn 道信
(580–651) fourth Chan patriarch in China
Dào Xuān 道宣
(596–667) patriarch of Vinaya School, author of *Continued Biographies of Eminent Monks*
dìng 定
meditation
Dòng-shān Liáng-jiè 洞山良階
(807–869) founded the Cáo dòng school of Chan (J. Tōzan Ryōkai)
dùn wù 頓悟
sudden realization
fǎ 法
Dharma
Fǎ hǎi 法海
supposed author of the first version of the *Platform Sutra*
fa jiè yī xiàng 法界一相
Dharma realm
fǎ jiè yī 法界一
the Dharma realm is oneness
fǎ jiè yī xiàng xì yuán fǎ jiè shì míng yī xíng sān mèi 法界一相,系緣法界,是名一行三昧
“The Dharma realm is oneness and one perceives the Dharma realm as such. This is called one-practice samādhi,” a famous saying of Dào Xìn.
fā pú tí xīn 發菩提心
radiate an enlightened heart, send forth the bodhi mind
Fǎ yǎn zōng 法眼宗
one of the five schools of Chan
fāng biàn 方便
convenient, facilitate
gāo sēng 高僧
eminent monk
Guī-fēng Zōng-mì 圭峰宗密
fifth patriarch of the Huayan school as well as a patriarch of the Heze school of Southern Chan Buddhism.
hán gài qián kūn jù 函蓋乾坤句
the phrase that encompasses heaven and earth
Hóng-rěn 弘忍
(601–674) fifth Chan patriarch in China
hóng zhì 宏智
great wisdom
hóng zhì chán shī guǎng lù 宏智禪師廣錄

The Extended Record of Chan Master Hóng-zhì
Hóng-zhì Zhèng-jué 宏智正覺
(1091–1157) scholar monk, author of *The Book of Serenity* and other works
huà tóu 話頭
a story or question used as a subject for meditation (J. *kōan*); the thread of an argument which is also the meaning of the Sanskrit *sūtra*
Huángbò Xīyùn 黄檗希運
(d. 850) Chan master, teacher of Lín-jì (J. Ōbaku Kiun)
huó jù 活句
live words
Huì Kè 慧可
disciple of Bodhidharma and second Chan patriarch in China
Huì Néng 慧能
(638–713) sixth patriarch of Chinese Chan
jì 記
record, chronicle
jié duàn zhòng liú jù 截斷眾流句
the phrase that cuts off myriad streams
jīng 經
sutra
Jìng-huì 净慧
(1933–2013) founder of Shēng-huó Chán, disciple of Xū-yún
jìng tǔ 淨土
Pure Land, the realm of Amitābha Buddha
kàn huà chán 看話禪
meditation upon a story or question (J. *kōan zen*)
làn shú 爛熟
over ripe, well cooked
léng jiā 楞伽
Lanka, short for *Laṅkāvatāra Sūtra*
lǐ 理
principle, order
Lín-jì Yì-xuán 臨濟義玄
(d. 866) founder of the Lín jì school of Chan (J. Rinzai Gigen)
Lín jì zōng 臨濟宗
one of the five schools of Chan (J. Rinzai Shu)
liù zǔ 六祖
sixth patriarch, i.e., Huì-Néng
Liù Zǔ Fǎ Bǎo Jì 六組法寶記
Precious Record of the Dharma of the Sixth Patriarch
Liù Zǔ Tán Jīng 六祖壇經
The Platform Sutra of the Sixth Patriarch

mén 門
gate
Mí tuó 彌陀
Amitābha
mián mì 綿密
detailed, meticulous
míng 銘
inscription
mò zhào chán 默照禪
silent illumination (literally, silent shining Chan); the form of meditation in Caodong and Sōtō.
Mò Zhào Míng 默照銘
"The Inscription of Silent Illumination"
Nán-quán 南泉
(c. 749–c. 835; J. Nansen) Chan master, originally a hermit, who later had many disciples
pú tí 菩提
enlightenment (Skt. *bodhi*)
Qì-sōng 契嵩
scholar monk
qián kūn 乾坤
heaven and earth, the universe
qīng míng 清明
serene, clear and bright, sober and calm
rù 入
entrance, enter
rù dào 入道
to enter the Dao
rù Shēng-huó Chàn 入生活禪
enter the Chan of everyday life
sān mèi 三昧
samādhi
Shén-xiù 神秀
(607–706) leading disciple of Hóng-rěn
Sēng-càn 僧璨
(n.d.–606) disciple of Huì Kè, third Chan patriarch in China
shēng huó 生活
normal life
Shēng-huó Chán 生活禪
Everyday Chan
shī zī 師資
master and disciple
shí daì 時代

period
shǒu yī 守一
guarding the one
shù bō rě jiàn 樹般若見
establish a wisdom view, see with the eye of *prajñā*
shǔ xī 數息
counting the breath
Shuāng Fēng Shān 雙峰山
Double Peak Mountain
shuāng xiū 雙修
dual practice, meaning the practice of Chan and Pure Land together.
sì liào jiǎn 四料簡
four ways of interaction. A form used in the Lín jì school.
sì bīn zhǔ 四賓主
four guest-host (relations). A form used in the Lín jì school.
sǐ jù 死句
dead words
suí bō zhú liú jù 隨波逐流句
the phrase that follows the wave
suí xī 隨息
following the breath
suí yuán 隨緣
follow along, accommodate to circumstance
suǒ qiú 所求
seek, demand
Tài-xū 太虛
(1890–1947) Buddhist modernist who advocated the reform and renewal of Chinese Buddhism
tán 壇
altar or platform
Tán Lín 曇林
disciple of Bodhidharma
Wàn-sōng Xíng-xiù 萬松行秀
(1166–1246) Influential Caodong monk during the Mongol invasion of China
Wéi yǎng zōng 潙仰宗
one of the five schools of Chan
wú 無
nothing, not
xù 續
continue
xìn xīn 信心
faith, trusting the heart/mind
Xìn Xīn Míng 信心銘

famous Chan poem that begins *zhì dào wú nán* 至道無難 Arriving at the Dao is without difficulty / *wéi xián jiǎn zé* 惟嫌揀擇。Only avoid picking and choosing / *dàn mò zēng ài* 但莫憎愛Just refrain from hating and loving / *dòng rán míng bai* 洞然明白 Such is illumination
xíng 行
practice, walk, go
xiū xī dào guān 修息道觀
cultivate observation of the breath, see the Dao in every breath
Xū-yún 虛雲
(1840–1959) most famous Chan master of modern times
yào 要
important, essential
yī 一
one, oneness
yí qíng 疑情
the feeling of doubt
yī xíng sān mèi 一行三昧
single-practice *samādhi*
Yǒng-míng Yán-shòu 永明延壽
(904–975) Buddhist master famous for synthesizing and unifying the approaches of different schools
Yuán-wù Kè-qín 圓悟克勤
(1063–1135; J. Engo Kokugon) Chan monk who compiled the *Blue Cliff Record*
Yún-mén sān jù 雲門三句
the three phrases of Yunmen
Yún-mén Wén-yǎn 雲門文偃
(862 or 864–949) founder of the Yún mén zōng (J. Ummon Bun'en)
Yún mén zōng 雲門宗
one of the five schools of Chan
Zhào-zhōu Cōng-shěn 趙州從諗
(778–897; J. Jōshū Jūshin)Chan master noted for his dialogues, many of which became koans
Zhào zhōu chán shī yǔ lù 趙州禪師語錄
The Recorded Sayings of Chan Master Zhào-zhōu
zhǔ kàn bīn 主看賓
"host sees guest": an encounter where the master sees clearly but the student remains stuck in his dilemma
zhǔ kàn zhǔ 主看主
"host sees host": an encounter where equals meet, both clearly seeing the Dharma
zhuān zhù 專注
concentration, single-mindedness
chún chán 純禪
Pure Chan

zōng 宗
school, sect
Zōng bǎo 宗寶
scholar monk
zuò chán 坐禪
sitting meditation (J. *zazen*)

CHAPTER 12

BUDDHIST MEDITATION IN TIBET

Exoteric and Esoteric Orientations

GEORGIOS T. HALKIAS

Introduction: Buddhist Schools and Their Meditation Lineages

Tibetan contemplative texts and their accompanying commentarial literature encompass a staggering number of scriptures marked by indigenous pre-Buddhist elements, foreign influences, and innovating developments that span over a millennium. The majority of scriptures were translated from Buddhist Sanskrit texts procured from India, Nepal, and Central Asia with just a few Tibetan translations from Chinese despite a notable presence of Chinese scholars and monks at Samyé and in Lhasa (Halkias, 2004, 2014). A good number of the earliest translations are preserved in the Tibetan Buddhist canon divided into the "words of the Buddha," the Kangyur (*bka' 'gyur*; all terms in parentheses are Tibetan rendered according to the Wylie system of transliteration unless otherwise indicated) and the "commentaries on the teachings of the Buddha," the Tengyur (*bstan 'gyur*). This is by far the largest canonical collection of Tibetan Buddhist doctrines and practices. Other, but no less important collections, are the *Collected Tantras of the Nyingma School* (*rnying ma rgyud 'bum*) and the *Collected Works* (*gsung 'bum*) of scholars-cum-adepts (*mkhas grub*; Sanskrit [Skt.] *paṇḍita-siddha*) from all four Tibetan schools of Buddhism.

A common way of introducing Tibetan meditation practices is in terms of Tibet's main Buddhist schools: the Nyingma or Ancient School and the New Schools, the Kagyü, Sakya, and Geluk. What distinguishes these schools from each other is their adherence to specific tantric masters and lineages, while they share for the most part exoteric contents and texts of the sutra variety. Esoteric teachings are part of Vajrayāna, the vehicle of the *vajra* (*rdo rje*), also known as the vehicle of the "Secret Mantra," no doubt because of the frequent use of ritual speech in the form of secret utterances or mantras applied as essential aids in tantric practice. The *vajra* is commonly used as a tantric ritual object and translates as "diamond" and "thunderbolt," two words that refer to the indestructability and immutability of the awakened state. For the sake of simplicity, and as it is understood by the tradition, the terms "Vajrayāna," "tantra," and "esoteric Buddhism" are used interchangeably. While tantric meditations feature in other Indian religious systems, most notably Śaivism, in Tibetan Buddhism their aim accords with the ideals of Mahāyāna and is meant for those practitioners who are cognitively capable of overcoming dualistic divisions and incorporating all experiences in the path of practice.

The Ancient School of Tibetan Buddhism

The Nyingma purports to be the oldest school of Tibetan Buddhism because its inception goes back to the turbulent times of Tibet's royal conversion to Buddhism (Kapstein, 2000, pp. 51–65). Its founder, the semi-legendary Indian tantric yogi Padmasambhava from Uḍḍiyāna (Figure. 12.1), Swat valley in present-day Pakistan, was allegedly invited by the Tibetan Emperor Trisong Detsen (r. 755–ca. 797/8) to subdue forces hostile to the spread of Buddhism and assist in the establishment of Tibet's first Buddhist monastery at Samyé. He is best known for his astonishing facility to conceal precious meditation instructions in physical locations and in the mind-streams of his Tibetan disciples with the mandate that they are to be revealed and propagated by their reincarnations in future times when they would be of benefit to people. Many contemplative teachings are said to have been hidden across Tibet by his consort and chief disciple Lady Karchen or Yeshe Tsogyal, the first Tibetan woman to have attained enlightenment following the instructions of her tantric master.

The redaction of hidden texts, the so-called "treasures," refer for the most part to earth *terma* (*sa gter*), scriptures extracted from the earth (rocks, caves, pillars, etc.), and mind-*terma* (*dgongs gter*), derived from the mind-streams of chosen adepts known as *tertöns* (treasure revealers). The discovery of Buddhist texts and ritual objects from the eleventh century onward is an ongoing processs and includes another class of revealed scriptures, the pure-vision treasures (*dag snang gter*). Such teachings were retrieved by advanced meditators through a variety of extraordinary communicative means like beatific visions, disembodied utterances, texts appearing in the sky, and so on (Halkias, 2013, pp. 165–169).

The lineages of extracted and revealed scriptures are represented, to a large extent, in the *Treasury of Precious Treasures*, the *Rinchen Terdzö* (*Rin chen gter mdzod*)—a voluminous collection containing tantric rituals, Dzogchen meditations, as well as some of the most important liturgical cycles of the tradition, like the *One Hundred Peaceful and Wrathful Deities* or *Karling Shitro* (*Kar ling Zhi khro*), the *Eight Transmitted Precepts* or

FIGURE 12.1 Statue of Padmasambhava, Mongolian representation. Erdene Zuu Monastery. Photo by author.

Drupa Kagyé (*Sgrub pa bka' brgyad*), the cycles of the wrathful Vajrakīlaya (*Rdo rje phur ba*), and others (Dudjom Rinpoche, 1991). In addition to the compilation of treasures, the old tantras of the Mahāyoga, Anuyoga, and Atiyoga class are included in the *Collected Tantras of the Nyingma School*. Among them, the single most influential text of the school is the *Tantra of the Secret Essence*, the *Guhyagarbha* (*Gsang ba'i snying po*), the main tantra of the Mahāyoga class that has inspired over the centuries a large number of commentaries.

The New Schools of Tibetan Buddhism

From the eleventh century onward a new wave of Indian tantric lineages and texts entered Tibet, contributing to the formation of the New Tibetan Buddhist Schools (*gsar ma*). Many of these relied on the unconventional teachings of the Indian *mahāsiddhas* (lit. "great adepts"), wandering tantric yogis who commonly practiced in seclusion and in unorthodox places such as charnel grounds and attained the supreme *siddhi* (Skt.

mahāsiddhi) of enlightenment. Despite the later domestication of their teachings by Buddhist monastics, they taught an antinomian path to liberation that characterizes the tantric teachings as a whole. This great variety of contemplative methods was also indebted to commentarial treatises and esoteric manuals written by expert meditators, as well as instructive spiritual poetry (*nyams mgur*; Skt. *dohā*) sung by adepts in praise of the qualities of the awakened state. The spiritual songs of the Tibetan ascetic Milarepa (ca.1052–1135), the so-called whispered transmission of meditation instructions, is an early example of the *dohā* tradition or rhyming couplets. It goes back to the seventh century CE when North Indian Buddhism saw "the emergence of a poetic form of religious expression . . . extolling the beauty and simplicity of tantric spiritual experience and social practice" (Schaeffer, 2005, p. 5).

Many tantric teachings are shared by the New Schools, like the *Wheel of Time Tantra*, the *Kālacakra* (*Dus kyi 'khor lo*) with its emphasis on Six Yogas (*sbyor drug*) (Wallace, 2001). These distinct esoteric meditations commonly involve: the "withdrawal" of the senses from consciousness; meditative concentration (*bsam gtan*; Skt. *dhyāna*) on the empty-form appearances; breath control utilizing the subtle energies of the body; retention of the subtle energies in the central channel; recollection during which time the objects of cognition and cognition become one; and lastly, meditative absorption (*ting nge 'dzin*; Skt. *samādhi*) for realizing one's physical body as an empty form (Hatchell, 2014, pp. 32–41).

The most important source for the specific teachings that characterize the school of the Kagyü (*bka' brgyud*) and its many sub-schools is the Indian *mahāsiddha* Tilopa (988–1069) and his successor Nāropā (ca. 956–1040). Distinct practices of this school include the highest teachings of Mahāmudrā, and tantric cycles associated with the *Cakrasaṃvara Tantra* (Gray, 2007) and the *Six Dharmas of Nāropā*. Tantras like the *Hevajra* (Snellgrove, 2012/1959), which is traditionally attributed to *mahāsiddha* Virūpa, are held in high esteem by the Sakya School (*sa skya*) along with the contemplative system of the Lamdre (*lam 'bras*), the "Path and Fruit" rooted in the tantric view that the result, or fruit, is contained in the path of spiritual practice. Lastly, the Geluk (*dge lugs*) is the youngest major school that came to dominate the religious and political life of Tibet. Its founder, Tsongkhapa Losang Drakpa (1357–1419) was an eclectic scholar-adept inspired by the Old Kadampa, an earlier non-extant school formed by the Tibetan disciples of the Indian master Atiśa Dīpaṃkara Śrījñāna (982–1054). The central teachings of this school are attributed to Tsongkhapa known for his systematic treatise on the gradual stages of the path, the *Lamrim Chenmo* (*Lam rim chen mo*) and for articulating and defending the superiority of the philosophical view of the "Consequentialists," the Prāsaṅgika-Madhyamaka, which along with the Svātantrika-Madhyamaka refer to two dominant philosophical systems upheld by Buddhapālita and Bhāvaviveka respectively. Among his tantric teachings, the *Clear Exposition of the Five Stages of Guhyasamāja* (*Gsang 'dus rim lnga gsal sgron*) is an illustrious commentary on the *Tantra of the Secret Assembly*, the *Guhyasamāja Tantra* (*Gsang ba 'dus pa rgyud*) that remains to this day a seminal text for yoga, ritual, and meditation in the Geluk School (Fremantle, 1971).

Gradual versus Non-gradual Paths to Enlightenment

An introduction to Tibet's contemplative orientations would be incomplete without mentioning a reported eighth-century intrareligious conflict that had a profound and lasting effect both on the philosophical tenet system and the way meditation has been practiced in Tibet. Tibetan histories recount a public confrontation between two factions at Samyé that gave rise to a series of doctrinal debates under the scrutiny of emperor-judge Tri Songdetsen. Chinese and Tibetan sources disagree as to which school left victorious from the public debate, and some contemporary scholars have even questioned the historicity of the event (Guenther, 1989, p. vii). Whichever may have been the truth of the situation, the views advanced by the Indian faction had significant implications for the ways meditation has been conceptualized in Tibetan religious history.

The Chinese school of Heshang Mahāyāna, led by a Chan master from Dunhuang, the Chinese monk (Ch. *heshang*) Moheyan, had a substantial following of Chinese monks and according to some generous estimates as many as 5,000 Tibetan followers (Demiéville, 1952, p. 25). Moheyan advocated a non-gradual, instantaneous path to enlightenment (*cig car ba*) that does not depend on the gradual cultivation of contemplative practices (*rim gyis pa*). In philosophical opposition to Moheyan, Śāntarakṣita's chief disciple Kamalaśīla (ca.740–795) argued for a gradual model of spiritual progression (*lam rim*) that relied on the methods of *śamatha* (calm-abiding) and *vipaśyanā* (direct-insight) outlined in his *Stages of Meditation* (*Sgom rim*; Skt. *Bhāvanākrama*). His model became the prevailing way of training in the trilogy of the view of emptiness (*lta ba*), meditation in *śamatha* and *vipaśyanā* (*sgom pa*), and maintaining ethical conduct in one's activities (*spyod pa*). Even though Chan Buddhism appears to have lost Tri Songdetsen's public support, we cannot assume that it ceased to be practiced altogether. The discovery of forty-two Tibetan Chan scriptures from Dunhuang attest to the continuation of Chinese non-gradual meditative systems (Schaik, 2014).

MEDITATION: DEFINITION AND AIMS

Since the earliest days of Buddhism, contemplative practices have been regarded necessary for attaining liberation from samsara—a compulsive cycle of embodied becomings through endless births, deaths, and rebirths. While there is no single term in Buddhist literature that precisely corresponds to what is generally referred to in English as "meditation," when this is conveyed in Buddhist contexts it is understood to encompass a wide range of methods depending upon different schools, texts, and interpretations of different aspects of the teachings. The Tibetan term *gom* (*sgom*) translates the Sanskrit word *bhāvanā*, but *gom* is not confined to the conventional "seated posture" and "quieting of mind" that we often associate with meditation in the West. In fact, this term encompasses a far-reaching semantic range relating to "habituation," "contemplation," "spiritual development," "reflection," "cultivation," "creative imagination," "freedom from thought," "attention," and so forth. Understood broadly, the aim of meditation is to utilize a variety of "skillful means" (Skt. *upāya-kauśalya*) for the purpose of integrating the Buddhist teachings into one's daily experience and world-view. To complicate matters further, for the teachings of Dzogchen (Great Completion/Perfection) and the fourth stage Mahāmudrā (Great Seal), the highest form of meditation is "non-meditation" (*sgom med*). This refers to an advanced practice of abiding in a state of lucid and uninterrupted awareness without holding onto distinctions and divisions between objects of observation and the activity of meditation (*sgom bya sgom byed med*).

Nowadays there is much misleading emphasis on the practice of mindfulness stripped of its Buddhist framework as the quintessential contemplative technique in secular settings. In Tibetan contexts, there are Four Applications of Mindfulness (*dran pa nyer bzhag bzhi*), namely, being aware of one's body, feelings, mental states, and the Buddhist doctrines. Mindfulness (*dran pa*) is only one of the five powers (*stobs*) or aids of liberation (*thar pa cha mthun*, the others being faith [*dad pa*]; effort [*brtson 'grus*]; concentration [*ting nge 'dzin*]; and wisdom [*shes rab*]) and is by no means a pivotal Buddhist practice. Tsultrim Gyamtso (1988, p. 13) explains that meditation without "listening and reflecting is blind," and reflection "without meditation is like having eyesight and no legs." The threefold training entails reading or "listening" (*thos*) to the Buddhist teachings on liberation, "reflecting and contemplating" (*bsam*) on their relevance to our life, and integrating them in our daily "actions" (*spyod pa*).

Arguably, an empirical understanding of how the mind operates is the main focus of all Buddhist teachings and contemplative practices. There are myriad techniques and methods for examining how mental states arise and how to transform deluded thought-habits and negative proclivities through a moral course of action, reflection, and contemplative practice. Mind pervades all of our experiences, and therefore any of our physical, verbal, and mental activities can be taken on as "objects of training" (*sgom bya*). Hence, one can meditate while walking, talking, standing, sitting, or lying down as long as one does not get distracted by the five hindrances (*sgrib pa lnga*) to contemplative life: sensual-desire and craving; malice and ill-will; sloth and torpor; restlessness and worry; and skeptical doubt.

Emic Divisions of Meditation

All Tibetan meditations can be theoretically divided into sūtra and tantra, exoteric and esoteric respectively, even if this division is blurred at times in scriptures and practices that combine both approaches. This differentiation is crucial and operative in the Tibetan tradition for allocating texts in the Tibetan Buddhist canon and for maintaining a hierarchical arrangement in which esoteric teachings are placed higher than the exoteric on the grounds that the former possesses the most expedient means for completing one's training. While meditations of an exoteric assortment draw from sermons said to have been delivered by Buddha Śākyamuni to his bodhisattva disciples, tantric teachings are intended for those initiates who have taken vows or pledges (*dam tshig*; Skt. *samaya*) to uphold certain conduct and maintain the secrecy of their practices. A qualified guru or lama (*bla ma*) is necessary for granting the requisite initiations/empowerments (*dbang*) in the mandala of a specific Buddhist deity, providing detailed explanations on how to practice (*khrid*), and ensuring the continuity of the oral transmission (*rlung*). This is not to say that a teacher is not important for the transmission of exoteric teachings. However, in Vajrayāna the lama is of pivotal importance, being the one to bestow the vase, secret, wisdom, and word initiations (*dbang bzhi*) required for advanced tantric practice.

There is an important difference on how the sutra and tantra views the question of practice. In the former, the path of training (*lam*) leads progressively to the culmination of the goal, the fruit (*'bras bu*), but for tantra the path is indistinguishable from the fruit, because according to the esoteric view cause and result are not discreet and independent events separated in time. Arguably, there is another irreconcilable difference between the two. The origins of the sutras go back to the times the Buddhist doctrine was flourishing in India, whereas the esoteric teachings are said to have been transmitted in beginningless time in the Akaniṣṭha heaven, the field of reality where all Buddhas attain enlightenment. Whichever way one wishes to approach the distinction between exoteric and esoteric orientations, Tibetan scholars from all schools insist on an eventual synthesis between the two and advise that one ought to first gain mastery in the exoteric doctrines and practices before embarking on the esoteric paths of Vajrayāna.

Exoteric Orientations

Mahāyāna or Bodhisattvayāna, the vehicle (Skt. *yāna*) of bodhisattvas, stresses the bodhisattva's aspiration to attain complete awakening (Skt. *bodhi*) and fulfil one's spiritual purpose (*rang don*) and that of leading others to the same realization (*gzhan don*). The mind of awakening (*byang chub kyi sems*; Skt. *bodhicitta*) is the raison d'être for all Tibetan contemplative practices and is cultivated by nurturing sublime qualities, the "four divine abidings" (*tshangs pa'i gnas bzhi*; Skt. *brahmavihāras*): loving-kindness (*byams pa*), compassion (*snying rje*), contentment (*dga' ba*), and equanimity (*btang snyoms*). Śāntideva's treatise, the *Bodhicaryāvatāra* (*The Bodhisattva's Way of Life*), has been the most widely read and cited text in the whole of the Tibetan tradition and a primary source in Tibetan Buddhist literature for the cultivation of *bodhicitta* and the Six Perfections (Wallace and Wallace, 1997).

The second formative aim of Mahāyāna is the realization that all *dharmas* (phenomena) have the nature of emptiness (*stong pa nyid*; Skt. *śūnyatā*). Through the Mahāyāna practices supporting these two aims, one is said to traverse Five Paths (*lam lnga*) of training that lead to enlightenment: the *Path of Accumulation* (*tshogs lam*) where one makes special effort to accumulate merit and generate the altruistic mind of enlightenment (Skt. *bodhicitta*); the *Path of Preparation* or *Application* (*sbyor lam*) where one unifies the practices of *śamatha* and *vipaśyanā* and takes the illusory activities of the mind as an object of observation; the *Path of Seeing* (*mthong lam*) emptiness, or reality as-it-is with experiential freedom from verbal expectations and conceptual fabrications; the *Path of Meditation* (*sgom lam*) where one discards what is to be discarded and attains what is to be attained; and lastly, the *Path of No More Learning* (*mi slob pa'i lam*) where one overcomes all obstructions to liberation and there is nothing more to learn or attain.

The Mind of Awakening

The altruistic intention to attain enlightenment for the benefit of leading others to the same state has been extolled by the Indian Buddhist teachers like Śāntideva, Kamalaśīla and Atiśa Dīpaṃkara. Indian scholastic treatises divide the altruistic mind set on awakening into "relative" and "absolute." Relative *bodhicitta* is divided into the "*bodhicitta* of intention" and the "*bodhicitta* of application." A common method for nurturing "relative *bodhicitta*" (*kun rdzob sems skyed*) is the meditation of *tonglen* (*gtong leng*), literally "sending and receiving," that synchronizes the outward and inward movement of breath with an unselfish intention. With each exhalation one imagines sending out loving kindness toward all beings (and especially one's enemies), and with each inhalation one envisions receiving their suffering and alleviating their pain.

Mind training exercises or *lojong* (*blo sbyong*) are used for the cultivation of the "*bodhicitta* of intention" (*smon pa sems skyed*). They commonly include: "seeing others as equal to oneself" (*bdag gzhan mnyam pa*), "exchanging oneself with others" (*bdag gzhan brje ba*), and "taking others as more important than oneself" (*bdag las gzhan gces pa*). For the *bodhicitta* of application (*'jug pa sems skyed*) one trains in the development of Six Perfections (*pha rol tu phyin pa*; Skt. *pāramitā*), namely, generosity (*sbyin pa*), moral discipline (*tshul khrims*), patience (*bzod pa*), perseverance (*brton 'grus*), meditative concentration (*bsam gtan*) and wisdom (*shes rab*). The first five perfections fit briefly under the heading of the "accumulation of merit" (Skt. *puṇyasaṃbhāra*) that leads to temporal contentment and higher rebirths. The "accumulation of wisdom" (Skt. *jñānasaṃbhāra*) refers to the sixth, the recognition of an awareness beyond concepts, or *prajñā*. This leads to the realization of absolute *bodhicitta* (*don dam sems skyed*), a term that is synonymous to the final level of spiritual attainment in Mahāyāna, the *Path of No More Learning*.

The View of Emptiness

Having established *bodhicitta*, the proper intention for spiritual practice, the next objective is to cultivate an accurate way of seeing reality (*lta ba*; Skt. *dṛṣṭi*) according to the philosophical tenets of the Middle View (*dbu ma'i lta ba*). During the *Path of Seeing*, one attains the correct view that there are no unchanging, unconditioned, and substantial entities in our world (*bdag med*; Skt. *anattā*, or non-self). Non-self is understood to be of two types, the "non-self of persons" (*gang zag gi bdag med*) and the "non-self of phenomena" (*chos kyi bdag med*). This simply means that neither our manufactured ideas of a fixed personhood nor our reified experiences of the world correspond to inherently existing entities. All material and immaterial phenomena are impermanent and without an intrinsic reality (*rang dngos*; Skt. *svabhāva*) since their origination and cessation is contingent upon specific causes and conditions. Failing to recognize the emptiness of phenomena, grasping after illusory substantial entities, and longing for permanence or annihilation, leads to discontent and suffering or *duhkha* one of the basic teachings of the Buddha outlined in his sermon of the Four Noble Truths; i.e., the truth of suffering (*sdug bsngal bden pa*), the truth of the origin of suffering (*kun 'byang bden pa*); the truth of the cessation of suffering (*'gog bden pa*), and the truth of the path (*lam bden pa*).

The view of emptiness or *śūnyatā* is at the heart of Mahāyāna soteriology and Vajrayāna practice. Emptiness is a technical term in Buddhism that describes the lack of independently existing, permanent, and uncaused entities in the world. In terms of training, a deeper understanding develops through contemplation and analysis of the teachings on causality and dependent origination. Meditation on emptiness (*stong nyid sgom*) refers to training in wisdom, the last of the Six Perfections. The question of how to approach the topic of emptiness depends on the interpretations upheld by different philosophical orientations in India and Tibet (Hopkins 1983).The Tibetan School of Jonang for example is known for its controversial view of extrinsic or other-emptiness (*gzhan stong*), according to which ultimate reality, one's buddha-nature (Skt. *tathāgatgarbha*) or "innate potential for enlightenment" is empty of the conventional, superficial, and false, but not empty of its own absolute non-dual nature. Philosophically opposed by the Geluk School that sides with the Consequentialist-Madhyamaka position of self-emptiness (*rang stong*), the Jonang survived strict persecution and suppression for political reasons at the hands of the Fifth Dalai Lama Ngawang Lobsang Gyatso, but endured as a distinct school to this day, albeit greatly reduced in number.

The Training: Calm Abiding and Direct Insight

Śamatha (calm-abiding; *zhi gnas*) and *vipaśyanā* (direct-insight; *lhag mthong*) are two meditation techniques common to all Buddhist traditions. *Śamatha* is also known as "stabilizing meditation" (*'jog sgom*) since it entails training in one-pointed concentration on an "object of observation" (*dmigs pa*) ranging from the concrete to the abstract; that is, from an external physical object like an image, to the inhalation and exhalation of breath, or an internal object such as a concept or one's own thoughts (Lati Rinbochay et al., 1983, pp. 52–91). The role of Tibetan religious art has been paramount in providing an astounding variety of symbolic supports for contemplation, while visions occurring during meditation have been responsible for shaping much of the religious imagery in Tibet. Examples of symbolic supports include Buddhist statues, two- or three-dimensional mandalas, and painted scrolls (*thangka*) depicting a number of male and female Buddhist deities.

The practitioner of *śamatha* commonly follows the Sevenfold Posture of Vairocana (*rnam snang chos bdun*) as described in Kamalaśīla's second text of the tripartite *Stages of Meditation* (Adam, 2002, p. 195). Having selected a comfortable and quiet place, one sits with (1) legs crossed in the full-lotus or half-lotus posture of Vairocana; (2) eyes neither too wide nor too tightly closed, gazing past the tip of the nose; (3) hands resting on the lap or knees; (4) spine kept straight, leaning neither forward nor backward; (5) shoulders relaxed and made to rest evenly; (6) head not tilted forward, backward, or to the sides so that the nose and navel are aligned; and (7) lips in the usual position with the tongue touching the upper palate so that the inhalation and exhalation flows effortlessly and gently without undue noise or agitation. With persistent training, the disciplined meditator who has mastered *śamatha* overcomes laxity, dullness, and excitement and is able to remain in meditation without effort, unmoved by external and internal distractions. She attains mental and physical pliancy and experiences recurring states of bliss, clarity, and nonthought.

In Indo-Tibetan contexts, *śamatha* is held as a precondition for the attainment of *vipaśyanā*. *Vipaśyanā* is defined as the technique through which one gains a heightened awareness that ascertains with clarity, precision, and sustained attention what transpires within and outside the body. (*Vipaśyanā* in this context seems to differ from what is understood by the same term in early Buddhism, on which see Zahler, 2009, p. 305). The emphasis here is on "a superior seeing . . . leading to a higher insight into the ultimate nature of things," a "higher vision" and "the function of allowing an enhanced comprehension of usually inaccessible grounds of experience." *Vipaśyanā* thus refers to a " 'transcendental,' 'extraordinary,' and 'penetrative insight,' and a 'clear seeing of the patterns of mind and its world' " (Rosenthal, 1981, p. 131).

There are several *vipaśyanā* methods practiced across Tibetan schools, including a rich variety of analytical meditations whose aim is to use reasoning, inference, and/or deduction to arrive at a deep-seated conviction of the fundamental insights of Buddhism. For example, according to Khenchen Thrangu's (1993, pp. 84–92) commentary on the eighth chapter of Jamgön Kongtrul's *Treasury of Knowledge*, there are three main categories of *vipaśyanā* meditations that are analytical in nature: the *vipaśyanā* of the *four essences*, the *vipaśyanā* of the *three doorways*, and the *vipaśyanā* of the *six investigations*. As before, one assumes the Sevenfold Posture and observes the nature of one's thoughts without altering, blocking, or fixating on their contents. Through regular practice one is able to differentiate between the arising and ceasing of mental events and eventually gains experiential certainty in the insubstantial and impermanent nature of phenomena. The union of *śamatha* and *vipaśyanā* is described as genuine *samādhi* (*ting nge 'dzin*), a state of profound realization where the meditative and post-meditative sessions blend into each other and one develops a thorough understanding of the empty nature of all feelings, sensations, beliefs, and mental states. Therefore, by integrating *bodhicitta* with the view of emptiness, applying oneself to the cultivation of the Six

Perfections, and training in the unification of *śamatha* and *vipaśyanā*, one completes the bodhisattva's stages according to the exoteric path and attains complete awakening.

Esoteric Orientations

The word tantra (*rgyud*) translates also as "thread" and denotes the uninterrupted continuity of awakening, a state that is simultaneously held as the starting point (the base), the course of training (the path), and the outcome (the fruit) of all Vajrayāna instructions. In other words, from a tantric perspective the whole world is perceived as a pure and divine mansion and every sentient being therein a god or goddess endowed with ultimate value. As a term for a collection of methods, it includes a variety of esoteric techniques whose aim is to induce a rapid cognitive-cum-emotive transformation or redirection of our delusional patterns and negative habits through the employment of visualizations, sounds, symbols, and rituals.

The New Schools (Kagyü, Sakya, and Geluk) divide their esoteric literature in four classes laid out in sequential order from the lowest to the highest based on their respective initiatory rites (*dbang*; Skt. *abhiṣeka*): Action Tantra (*kriyā*), Conduct Tantra (*caryā*), Yoga Tantra (*yoga*), and the Highest Yoga Tantra (*anuttarayoga*). The Highest Yoga tantras are further subdivided into the so-called "father tantras" that place emphasis on the aspects of method (e.g., *Guhyasamāja Tantra*), and the "mother tantras" that emphasize the aspects of wisdom (e.g., *Cakrasaṃvara Tantra*, *Hevajra Tantra*; (for a meaningful survey of the different tantras and related rituals, see Snellgrove, 2002, pp. 117–294). The Nyingma School follows for the most part the first three categories but concludes with a different set of three, Mahāyoga, Anuyoga, and Atiyoga, or Dzogchen, in a successive scheme of nine vehicles that subsume all of the Buddha's teachings.

It is deemed necessary before engaging in tantric meditations of the various classes that one gains familiarity with the outer preliminary practices that belong to the category of analytical meditations (*dpyad sgom*). These include a methodical examination of seminal Buddhist topics, such as the impermanent nature of phenomena and their interdependent mode of arising and ceasing, the truth of dissatisfaction/suffering (Skt. *duḥkha*) permeating all conditioned phenomena, the law of karma vis-à-vis the cultivation of morality, the defects of samsara and the merits of renunciation, and the lasting benefits of liberation from samsara. Having ascertained the soteriological value of these Buddhist insights, one then trains in the "inner preliminary practices" (*sngon 'gro*) whose purpose is to purify obscurations and judgements associated with body, speech, and mind, and induce a lasting transformation at the physical, emotional, and cognitive level of our being.

The inner preliminaries or foundational practices normally include: (1) extensive full-body-length prostrations to the objects of Buddhist refuge—an antidote to pride and the impetus for setting the right aspiration for Buddhist application; (2) visualization of Buddha Vajrasattva and the recitation of his hundred-syllable mantra for the purpose of overcoming unresolved issues and healing past traumas; (3) offering a symbolic representation of the contents of the universe, the mandala (Figure. 12.2), for enhancing personal virtue, promoting a meritorious mind-set, and cultivating universal generosity; and (4) the supplication of the guru for attaining confidence in the expressions of our own enlightened awareness. The practice of "guru-yoga" (*bla ma'i rnal sbyor*) is crucial

FIGURE 12.2 The *maṇḍala*, an offering of a symbolic representation of the contents of the universe. Eastern Tibet. Photo by author

in tantric practice. It is through indivisible trust in a qualified guide that one gains confidence in the empowerments, transmissions, and instructions of tantric training and comes to a profound recognition of one's own awakened nature reflected in the teacher.

The Five Buddha Families

The symbolism of the Five Buddhas (Skt. *pañcatathāgata*) of the Five Enlightened Families (*rigs lnga*) is emblematic of the internal logic of the tantras whose principle aim is to help us break free from routine conceptuality and an ordinary perception of ourselves and the world and to come to experiential terms with our dynamic potential for awakening. Just as it is said that all forms of interaction are characterized by the Five Buddhas (Figure. 12.3), all of the tantric deities in the Vajrayāna pantheon are subsumed under one of these *tathāgatas:* Vairocana, Akṣobhya, Ratnasambhava, Amitābha, and Amoghasiddhi. In a correlative system of concrete and abstract correspondences, each Buddha is assigned a spatial coordinate (center and four directions) in a geometric mandala, a consort, a bodhisattva, an aggregate, a color, an element, a poison, an animal throne, a specific time of day, season, organ, seed syllable, mudra (hand gesture), and so forth (see Table 12.1).

FIGURE 12.3 Statues of the Five Buddhas. Ta Dzong Museum, Bhutan. Photo by author.

Table 12.1 Diagram of the Five Buddha Families and their Main Correspondences

BUDDHA FAMILY	BUDDHA	VAJRA	RATNA	PADMA	KARMA
Wisdom-Buddha	Vairocana	Akṣobhya (or Vajrasattva)	Ratnasambhava	Amitābha	Amoghasiddhi
Consort	Dhātviśvarī	Māmakī	Locanā	Pāṇḍarāvasinī	Samayatārā
Bodhisattva	Samantabhadra	Vajrapāṇi	Ratnapāṇi	Avalokiteśvara	Viśvapāṇi
Wisdom	all-pervasive	mirror-like	equalizing	discerning	all-accomplishing
Skandha	form or matter	consciousness	feeling	perception	mental formations
Kleśa	ignorance	anger	pride	desire	jealousy
Color	White	blue	yellow	red	green
Element	Space	water	earth	fire	air
Direction	centre	east	south	west	north
Symbol	eight-spoked wheel	vajra	jewel	lotus	double vajra
Initiation	fifth initiation	first initiation	second initiation	third initiation	fourth initiation
Animal	lion or dragon	elephant	horse	peacock	*garuḍa*
Seed syllable	*oṃ*	*hūṃ*	*traḥ*	*hrīḥ*	*āḥ*
Season	none	winter	autumn	summer	spring
Sense	sight	touch	sound	smell	taste
Temperature	neutral	cool	warm	hot	cold
Mudrā	*dharmacakra*	*bhūmisparśa*	*varada*	*dhyāna*	*abhaya*
Cakra	crown	heart	navel	throat	sexual center
Organ	heart	kidneys	spleen	liver	lungs

BUDDHA FAMILY	BUDDHA	VAJRA	RATNA	PADMA	KARMA
Time	no time	dawn	midday	sunset	evening
Wind	pervading	life-supporting	downward-voiding	upward-moving	equally-abiding
Nectar	excrement	urine	blood	semen	marrow or flesh
Finger	thumb	forefinger	middle finger	ring finger	little finger
Sense offerings	mirror	silk cloth	lute or cymbals	incense or conch	fruit
Ornament	bracelets & anklets	crown jewel	necklace	earrings	girdle
Bardo visions	first day	second day	third day	fourth day	fifth day

The scheme of the Five Buddhas represents five fundamental displays of awakening that operate in the unenlightened mind as five distortions or confused emotions. The transformation of our compulsive cognitive-cum-emotive patterns into their purified counterparts entails working creatively with a relational collection of symbols, signs, and signifiers represented by the Five Buddha Families. In short, these transformative techniques enable us to disassociate from habitual ways of self-grasping and to transmute our five "delusional states or poisons" (*nyon mongs*; Skt. *kleśas*) into five inherent patterns of awakening. Experience turns into symbolic activity whereby ignorance and mental dullness is transformed into an all-pervasive awareness symbolized by Vairocana; anger and aggression into a non-dual awareness or mirror-like wisdom personified by Akṣobhya; self-inflated importance and pride into an equalizing awareness that discerns the sameness of all phenomena represented by Ratnasambhava; passion and desire into a wisdom that differentiates truth from delusion exemplified by Amitābha; and jealousy and covetousness into an all-accomplishing awareness symbolized by Amoghasiddhi.

Deity Yoga

Divided in two consecutive stages (*rim gnyis*), "deity yoga" (*lha'i rnal 'byor*) constitutes the quintessence of all tantric meditations prescribed in the tantras of the Old and New Schools. It is considered the most expedient and effective means to attain realization through an experiential process of re-creating oneself and one's world. During the Generation or Creation Stage (*bskyed rim*) one mentally transforms into the form-body of a Buddhist deity (*yi dam*)—manifesting in a peaceful or wrathful male or female form arising out of emptiness, as prescribed in tantric *sādhanas* (*sgrub thabs*) or means of accomplishment. Most deity-yoga *sādhanas* include the creative placement of three relational beings integrated in a single visualization: (1) the pledge-being (*dam tshig sems pa*), oneself generated in the semblance of a Buddhist deity prescribed in the *sādhana*; (2) the awareness-being (*ye shes sems pa*) invited to dwell at the heart of the pledge-being that it resembles; (3) and the contemplation-being (*ting nge 'dzin sems pa*) imagined at the heart of the awareness-being in the form of a seed syllable or symbolic implement. At the end of each meditation session the entire mental operation of constructing the mandala of the deity is made to dissolve into one's own awareness, from which it has never departed. The self-generation of oneself in the form of a Buddha is a distinctive feature of the tantras and it is not found in the exoteric teachings of the sutras.

The second phase of deity yoga is the Completion or Perfection Stage Yoga (*rdzogs rim*). It is described in terms of its "causal aspects" (*rgyu'i rdzogs rim*) that serve as causal factors for the experience of bliss during the dissolution of subtle winds in the central channel and in terms of its "resultant aspects" (*'bras bu'i rdzogs rim*), which experientially manifest in the indivisibility of appearances and emptiness (*snang stong*). The causal features employ a sophisticated subtle-body (*phra ba'i lus*) system that relies on an interiorized body made out of refined channels or pathways (*rtsa*; Skt. *nāḍī*), energy currents (*rlung*; Skt. *prāṇa* or *vāyu*) responsible for the movement of body and consciousness, and seminal nuclei (*thig le*; Skt. *bindu* or *tilaka*) located within the conduits supported by the winds.

During the conceptual stage of the Completion Stage one engages in concrete imagery of the subtle body and the withdrawal of the winds or currents (*rlung*) into the central channel (*rtsa dbu ma*; Skt. *avadhūti*) that runs parallel to the spine. The physical body is said to be permeated by 72,000 subtle channels forming pathways for energy currents. For the most part three passages are used during "wind-meditation" (*rlung sgom*): the central channel and two parallel conduits to its left (*rkyang ma*) and right (*ro ma*). Internal yogic meditations have both therapeutic and soteriological applications, and detailed descriptions of the subtle body are also found in Tibetan medical literature (For a comprehensive study of the subtle body in Tibetan Buddhism, see Rangjung Dorje, 2014).

The Generation Stage of deity yoga involves a transformative reconceptualization, during which one ascertains the illusory nature of ego-centred attachments to self and external objects and, in this way, purifies conventional perception, fixation toward existence, and a false sense of pride. By working creatively with the dynamic patterns of mental and emotional misperception of self and phenomena that characterizes samsara, the practitioner engages in Completion Stage practices, confronting the fear of loss and de-individuation in the process of dying.

Meditations on Death

Unlike the non-conceptual Completion Stage where one's self is absorbed in reality without effort, the conceptual Completion Stage focuses on the manipulation of subtle currents toward the central channel, directing them to dissolve into the heart center. This technique is said to bring about psychosomatic conditions similar to those occurring during the process of death. The aim of such tantric meditations of the highest class is to transform birth, death, and the intermediate state between the two, the *bardo* (*bar do*; Skt. *antarabhāva*), into a recognition of the continuity of the awakened state. The dissolution of winds into the indestructible drop residing in the heart center gives rise to the most subtle of all states of consciousness, the mind of "clear light" (*'od gsal*). At the time of ordinary death the gross winds involuntarily dissolve into the right and left channels and in turn disperse into the central channel, inducing the manifestation of subtle awareness. The meditator familiarizes oneself with particular signs and experiences as they mimic the death process in eight consecutive dissolutions (Lati Rinbochay & Hopkins, 1979). However, unlike the actual dying process that leads to the intermediate state, the adept arises in an illusory body made of subtle wind and progresses toward the attainment of complete awakening.

Meditations on death can be performed by oneself and on behalf of the deceased; they fulfil several aims, such as increasing one's renunciation of worldly concerns, coming to accept the process of dying, providing safe passage in the *bardo*, facilitating transference to a buddha-field (*zhing khams*; Skt. *buddhakṣetra*) or Pure Land, and ultimately, from a higher tantric perspective, lead to enlightenment. The so-called *Tibetan Book of the Dead*, whose actual title is *Liberation through Hearing in the Intermediate State* (*Bar do thos grol*), provides detailed instructions to guide the dead through the peaceful and agitated experiences of the transitional state after death, the *bardo*, while offering various opportunities for liberation in the identification with the most subtle level of consciousness, the mind of clear light (Gyurme Dorje, 2006).

There are a number of practices whose aim is to circumvent the *bardo* by allowing the deceased to take rebirth directly in a Pure Land (Halkias, 2013) such as Sukhāvatī, Buddha Amitābha's buddha-field. It is believed that upon rebirth in Sukhāvatī the conditions are conducive for making swift progress toward liberation. The tantric yoga of *phowa* (*'pho ba*) or "transference of consciousness" entails the separation of coarse and subtle bodies in the ejection of one's consciousness from the upper fontanel (the aperture of Brahma) into a buddha-field of one's choice. *Phowa* belongs to the *Six Dharmas of Nāropā* taught by the *mahāsiddha* Nāropā to his Tibetan disciple Marpa (1012–1097). These should not be confused with the *Six Yogas* (*sbyor drug*), which contain instructions for Completion Stage practices found in root tantras, such as the *Kālacakra*, *Hevajra*, *Guhyasamāja*, *Cakrasaṃvara*, and *Vajrabhairava* tantras among others (For a commentary on the *Six Dharmas* by Tsongkhapa, see Mullin (2005); see also parallels with the *Six Dharmas of Niguma* preserved by the Shangpa Kagyü lineage, Harding, 2010).The other five *dharmas* or yogas also included in some major Indian Buddhist tantras feature: the yoga of inner heat or *tummo* (*gtum mo*) using visualizations, breath-control, and physical yoga exercises (*'khrul khor*) for the purpose of gaining mastery over subtle body-mind processes (For a detailed study of different physical yoga postures and their relation to subtle-body meditations see Baker, 2017); the attainment of a pure illusory body, the *gyulü* (*sgyu lus*) prescribed in Completion Stage practices; lucid awareness, manipulation and transformation of dream states during "dream meditations" or *milam* (*rmi lam*); identification with the "mind's luminosity" or *ösel* (*'od gsal*) during clear-light practices; and *bardo* teachings related to the recognition of the intermediate state between death and rebirth.

The Practice of Severance

Last but not least, mention should be made of an important syncretistic and synesthetic contemplative system originating with the famous Tibetan female adept Machik Labdrön (1055–1153). Some elements of the *chöd* (*gcod*), "cutting or severance" meditation can be traced back to Labdrön's Indian teacher Padampa Sangye and his lineage, which is known as the "pacification of suffering" (*sdug bsngal zhi byed*). *Chöd* fits nicely with the wandering lifestyle of a yogi and, for this reason, it did not develop in "monastic institutions with successions of lineage holders like the other major traditions" (Harding, 2016, p. xv). It is usually performed in groups or alone in desolate and frightening places like charnel grounds, empty caves, cemeteries, or temple ruins with the aid of liturgical songs and ritual instruments such as bells, drums, and thighbone trumpets.

The meditators follow a coordinated series of mental and physical exercises visualizing their body chopped into pieces and offered as a symbolic feast to gods and demons alike. The purpose of this meditation is to sever fixation and attachment to the physical body, cut through doubt and deep-rooted fears of death, and confront our "demonic propensities" by recognizing them as projections of our dualistic mind (For an informative study on the practice of severance, see Sheehy, 2005).

Mahāmudrā and Dzogchen

The principal aim of the so-called formless or non-conceptual contemplative systems is to recognize and abide in a "pure awareness" or *rigpa* (*rig pa*), beyond the ordinary dualistic mind dividing the world into subjects (*byed po*), objects (*byed pa*), and actions (*bya ba*). For this reason, in both Mahāmudrā and Dzogchen it is customary for the master to give instructions that point out the nature of mind (*ngo 'phrod*) as opposed to ordinary mind (*sems*). The attainment of an unmediated experience of awakening, free from dichotomizing perceptions, intellectual speculation, and contrived effort, is also the goal of the non-conceptual Completion Stage practices of the highest yoga tantras where self-clinging is severed at its root.

Mahāmudrā has a long history in Tibet with original contributions by the Kagyü School but also from scholars of other schools and lineages (For a collection of Mahāmudrā writings in the Kagyü Schools, see Roberts, 2011). The term Mahāmudrā (*phyag rgya chen po*) occurs in Indian sūtras and tantras where it denotes a variety of practices ranging from a hand gesture (Skt. *mudrā*) used in esoteric rituals and visualizations, a symbolic or actual consort employed in sexual union (*sbyor ba*), a lineage of tantric teachings traceable to the Indian *mahāsiddhas* Saraha, Nāgārjuna, Tilopa, Nāropā, and Maitrīpa, and a style of non-dual meditation focusing on the recognition and identification with the nature of mind (Jackson, 2016). Sexual yoga practices requiring a "physical seal" or consort (*las kyi phyag rgya*; Skt. *karmamūdra*) are also included under Completion Stage practices, but for monastics bound to celibacy these are restricted to an imagined or visualized sexual partner, a so-called "awareness seal" (*ye shes gyi phyag rgya*; Skt. *jñānamudrā*).

Familiarity with formless meditation is not a beginner's practice, for it aims toward the contemplation of the fundamental nature of mind, the *tathāgatagarbha* or "buddha-nature" taken as the base (*gzhi*), path (*lam*), and result (*'bras bu*) of meditation. At the level of path, in Mahāmudrā one progresses through Four Yogas (*rnal 'byor bzhi*). As explained by Khenchen Thrangu (2004, pp. 157–158), in the first "yoga of one-pointedness" one sees the true nature of mind with clarity and is able to rest in that state. In the second "yoga of simplicity" one experiences freedom from conceptual elaboration. During the third "yoga of one taste" one attains freedom from dualistic thinking, namely, likes and dislikes, beautiful and ugly, good and bad, and so on. And lastly, during the "yoga of non-meditation," following the exhaustion of habitual patterns one abides effortlessly in the nature of mind. Through the application of these Four Yogas one attains experiential confidence in a lucid, immutable, and all-encompassing primordial awareness that lies beyond existence and non-existence. Simply abiding in awareness without clinging to anything at all, without following or rejecting whatever comes to the field of cognition, is the practice of non-meditation (*mi sgom*).

Dzogchen (*rdzogs chen*, contraction of *rdzogs pa chen po*), or the Great Completion teachings, also blend tantric instructions with non-dual style of discourses. Arguably, they predate the teachings of Mahāmudrā and for this reason there are no references by Nyingma scholars to this system. There have been later attempts by Kagyü adepts like Karma Chakmé (1613–1678) to bring the highest contemplative traditions together in a synthetic structure (Karma Chakmé, 2000), and it is not surprising to find Tibetan masters trained in both systems. For the Nyingma and Bön Schools, Dzogchen is seen as the culmination of all contemplative paths laid out in the sutras and tantras. Even if no Indian Dzogchen texts have been discovered to date, the Nyingma maintain that these unique teachings go back to a series of foreign teachers, starting with Garab Dorje and leading to Padmasambhava, Vimalamitra, and the Tibetan translator Vairocana who introduced them to Tibet during the times of the Tibetan empire (Karmay, 2007). While the Bön are often considered to be the indigenous religious tradition of Tibet, they seem to have formed as a self-conscious movement in response to the formation of Buddhist Schools in the eleventh century. They have their own Dzogchen lineages, the most important being the oral lineage of Zhang zhung (*zhang zhung snyan rgyud*) (Tenzin Namdak, 2006).

The Nyingma Dzogchen lineages were not systematized until the fourteenth century by Longchen Rabjam (1308–1363), and several centuries later by the visionary Jikmé Lingpa (1730–1798), two very important figures of the Nyingma School whose works constitute the height of Dzogchen discourse, exegesis and practice.

The *khordé rushen* (*'khor 'das ru shan*), differentiating between samsara and nirvana, are part of the Dzogchen preliminary practices for preparing the meditator to recognize the "intrinsic nature of mind" (*sems nyid*) or *rigpa*. The actual teachings of Dzogchen are divided into three sets of instructions whose aim is to resolve beyond any doubt this intrinsic nature. The first is the Mind Series (*sems sde*) that includes most of the early Dzogchen literature and provides step-by-step instructions on how to recognize the nature of mind. The little-known Space Series (*klong sde*) focuses on the simultaneous experience of the Four Signs (*brda bzhi*) of *rigpa*, namely clarity, non-thought, bliss, and indivisibility. And lastly, the Pith Instructions Series (*man ngag sde*) presuppose one's familiarity with *rigpa*, focusing on maintaining the indivisibility of awareness and emptiness (For an overview of the systematization of Dzogchen literature from early to modern times, see van Schaik, 2016).

The Pith Instructional Series is divided into *trekchö* meditations, "cutting through primordial purity" (*ka dag khregs chod*), and *tögal* (*'od gsal thod rgal*), "direct crossing to luminosity" and attaining "spontaneous presence" (*lhun grub thod rgal*). In *trekchö*, the practitioner cuts through all compulsive mentation and attains certainty in the nature of his own primordial awareness, devoid of dualistic fixations and intellectual fabrications. This practice forms the basis for the second set of instructions known as *tögal*, where the practitioner works directly with visionary experiences arising either in retreat conditions of complete darkness (*mun mtshams*) or by utilizing light and open space during sky-gazing practices. Training in *tögal* is said to yield Four Visions (*snang ba bzhi*): vision of direct perception of reality (*chos nyid mngon sum gi snang ba*); vision of ever-increasing meditative experience (*nyams gong 'phel ba'i snang ba*); vision of the culmination of awareness (*rig pa tshad phebs kyi snang ba*); and the vision of the cessation of clinging to reality (*chos nyid du 'dzing pa zad pa'i snang ba*). The end of the Fourth Vision is said to lead to the dissolution of one's physical experience of identity into particles of light. Known as the rainbow body (*'ja' lus*), this is a unique achievement of the Dzogchen tradition that occurs when *rigpa* integrates into space and manifests as a vision of a body of light.

Contemplative Rituals and Ritualized Meditations

Ritual experts are commonly divided into celibate nuns and monks who wear the maroon robes, the "red sangha" (*dge 'dun mar po*), and the lay community of male and female tantrists or *ngakpa* (m. *sngags pa*/f. *sngags ma*; Skt. *māntrin*), the "white sangha" (*dge 'dun dkar po*). They perform for soteriological and various worldly aims a bewildering assortment of rites for every occasion and there is no doubt that for many professional ritualists the performance of rituals are merely a routine execution of ceremonial motions and recitations of texts to satisfy the needs of monastic institutions and sponsoring patrons. Nevertheless, rituals gain their effectiveness from the meditations that accompany them and whose outward expression they are. This has led Bentor (1996, p. 290) to aptly remark that "almost all forms of Tibetan meditation are highly ritualized and therefore fall in this category as well. Western scholarship, however, has not yet adequately reflected this Tibetan preoccupation with ritual." Thus our overview of Tibetan meditations would not be complete if it failed to address that the efficacy for a good number of exoteric and esoteric "rituals" (*cho ga*) depends on the meditative efforts of the performer, and at the same time, rituals may constitute unique forms of contemplation that lead to the mental transformation of the actors involved.

Many tantric rituals and liturgies require that the ritual specialist is able to perform the union of Generation and Completion Stages or, at the very least, is able to meditate on emptiness when performing all kinds of *sādhanas*, that is, for longevity (*tshe sgrub*), the propitiation of *dharma* protectors (*chos skyong*), and when granting initiations (*dbang*). Meditations often accompany the use of ritual instruments, like a *vajra* (Figure. 12.4), a bell, a *kīla*, and a two-headed drum, the *ḍāmaru*, as well as an assort-

FIGURE 12.4 A vajra. Swayambhunath Stupa, Nepal. Photo by author.

ment of musical instruments used during liturgies like horns, cymbals, and drums. Meditations are also meant to accompany the construction of sand mandalas (*dkyil 'khor*), the preparation of ritual cakes (*torma* [*gtor ma*]) and medicine (*sman sgrub*), *homa* rituals (*sbyin sreg*), tantric feasts (*tshogs 'khor*; Skt. *gaṇacakra*), rites of ransom (*glud*) and for clearing obstacles (*zlog pa*), cremations (*ro sreg*), petition offerings (*gsol mchod*), consecration of sites (*gnas chen byin 'bebs*), and divinations using a rosary (*phreng mo*), to mention some of the more common rituals performed by specialists.

To these we may add some contemplative ritualized activities involving physical movement, like circumambulating sacred sites such as mountains and lakes, and structures like stupas, statues, and temples, turning prayer wheels, performing masked dances (*'cham*) that presuppose facility in tantric visualization, and carrying out external yogic practices focusing on the channels and winds (*rtsa rlung 'khrul 'khor*) that involve "acrobatic movements combined with expanded respiration and associated visualizations" (Baker, 2017, p. 62). Last but not least, we may consider the category of trance mediums (*sku rten pa*) or *lha pa* who act as vessels for spirits to descend into their bodies (*bab*), like Nechung, the famous state-oracle of Tibet that facilitates the entering of the protector known as Pehar Gyalpo, as forms of expert trance-styled meditations.

Concluding Remarks

The cases we have discussed cover some of the most important types and common varieties of Tibetan exoteric and esoteric meditations practiced by monastics and lay tantrists for the purpose of attaining temporal happiness, spiritual realization, and ultimately awakening. Meditations performed daily by practitioners of Tibetan Buddhism vary according to the teachings they have received, their knowledge and understanding, and their stage of training. Though it is true that for a good number of lay Tibetans the "recitation of mantras" (*sngags bzla ba*), like the widespread six-syllabled mantra of Avalokiteśvara, *OṂ MAṆI PADME HŪṂ* (Figure. 12.5), constitutes the main form of practice, group or solitary meditation retreats are set in place for those intent on deepening their spiritual training and attaining enlightenment in this lifetime. Many Tibetan monasteries maintain isolated meditation retreat sites and hermitages for

FIGURE 12.5 The six-syllabled mantra of Avalokiteśvara, *OṂ MAṆI PADME HŪṂ*. Mahābodhi, Bodhgaya, Photo by author.

the use of members of the monastic community and for advanced lay practitioners. The most usual length for a long-term retreat is three years, three months, and three days (*lo gsum phyogs gsum*), and it is not uncommon for some meditators to spend extended lengths of time in intensive daily practice, observing four formal sitting meditation sessions (*thun bzhi*; roughly from around 4–7 A.M, 8–11 A.M, 2–5 P.M., and 7–10 P.M.), and some even devoting their entire life in retreat (*tshe mtshams*).

References

Adam, M. T. (2002). *Meditation and the concept of insight in Kamalaśīla's Bhāvanākramas* (Doctoral dissertation). Montreal: McGill University.

Baker, I. (2017). Yoga and physical culture in Vajrayāna Buddhism and Dzogchen, with special reference to Tertön Pema Lingpa's "Secret key to the winds and channels." In Dasho Karma Ura et al. (Eds.), *Mandala of 21st century perspectives: Proceedings of the international conference on tradition and innovation in Vajrayana Buddhism* (pp. 54–101). Thimphu: The Centre for Bhutan Studies.

Bentor, Y. (1996). Literature on consecration (Rab gnas). In J. I. Cabezon & R. Jackson (Eds.), *Tibetan literature studies in genre* (pp. 290–311). Ithaca, NY: Snow Lion.

Demiéville, (1952). *Le concile de Lhasa: Une controverse sur le quiétisme entre bouddhistes de l'Inde et de la Chine au VIIIe siècle de l'ère chrétienne.* Paris: Impr. Nationale de France.

Dudjom Rinpoche. (1991). *The Nyingma school of Tibetan Buddhism: Its fundamentals and history* (Gyurme Dorje with M. Kapstein, Trans.) Boston: Wisdom Publications.

Dzogchen Ponlop. (2003). *Awakening: The heart of Mahamudra and Dzogchen.* Boston: Shambhala.

Fremantle, F. (1971). *A critical study of the Guhyasamāja Tantra* (Doctoral dissertation). London: School of Oriental and African Studies.

Gray, D. (2007). *The Cakrasamvara Tantra (The discourse of Śrī Heruka): A study and annotated translation.* New York: American Institute of Buddhist Studies at Columbia University.

Guenther, H. (1989). *Tibetan Buddhism in Western perspective.* Berkeley, CA: Dharma Publishing.

Gyurme Dorje. (2006). *The Tibetan book of the dead.* New York: Viking Penguin.

Halkias, G. (2004). Tibetan Buddhism registered: Imperial archives from the palace-temple of 'Phang-thang. *Eastern Buddhist* 36 (1–2), 46–105.

Halkias, G. (2013). *Luminous bliss: A religious history of Pure Land literature in Tibet.* Pure Land Buddhist Studies Series. Honolulu: University of Hawai'i Press.

Halkias, G. (2014). Translating the foreign into the local: The cultural production and canonization of Buddhist texts in imperial Tibet. In L. W.-c. Wong & U. S.-p. Kwan (Eds.), *Translation and global Asia: Relocating cultural production network* (pp. 143–168). Hong Kong: The Chinese University of Hong Kong, Research Centre for Translation.

Harding, S. (2010). *Niguma: Lady of illusion.* Ithaca, NY: Snow Lion.

Harding, S. (2016). *Chöd: The sacred teachings on severance.* Boulder, CO: Snow Lion.

Hatchell, C. (2014). *Naked seeing: The great perfection, the wheel of time, and visionary Buddhism in renaissance Tibet.* Oxford: Oxford University Press.

Hopkins, J. (1983). *Meditation on emptiness.* London: Wisdom Publications.

Jackson, R. (2016). *Mahāmudrā in India and Tibet.* In *Oxford Research Encyclopedia of Buddhism.* Oxford: Oxford University Press. Online access,15/10/2017.

Kapstein, M. T. (2000). *The Tibetan assimilation of Buddhism: Conversion, contestation, and memory.* Oxford: Oxford University Press.

Karma Chakmé. (2000). *Naked awareness: Practical instructions on the union of Mahāmudrā and Dzogchen.* Ithaca, NY: Snow Lion.

Karmay, S. (2007). *The great perfection (rdzogs chen): A philosophical and meditative teaching of Tibetan Buddhism.* Leiden: Brill.

Khenchen Thrangu.(1993). *The practice of tranquility and insight: A guide to Tibetan Buddhist meditation.* Boston: Shambhala.

Khenchen Thrangu. (2004). *An ocean of the ultimate meaning: Teachings on Mahamudra.* Boston: Shambhala.

Lati Rinbochay & Hopkins, J. (1979). *Death, intermediate state and rebirth in Tibetan Buddhism.* Ithaca, NY: Snow Lion.

Lati Rinbochay, Denam Lochö Rinbochay, Zahler, L., & Hopkins, J. (1983). *Meditative states in Tibetan Buddhism: The concentrations and formless absorptions.* London: Wisdom Publications.

Mullin, G. H. (2005). *The six yogas of Naropa: Tsongkapa's commentary entitled a Book of Three Inspirations, a treatise on the stages of training in the profound path of Naro's six dharmas.* Ithaca, NY: Snow Lion.

Rangjung Dorje. (2014). *The profound inner principles: with Jamgön Knogtrul Lodrö Taye's commentary illuminating "the profound principles."* (E. M. Callahan, Trans.). Boston: Snow Lion.

Roberts, P. A. (2011). *Mahāmudrā and related instructions: Core teachings of the Kagyü schools.* Library of Tibetan Classics 5. Boston: Wisdom Publications.

Rosenthal, J. M. (1981). *An introduction to the theory and practice of Tibetan Buddhist psychology* (Doctoral dissertation). Honolulu: University of Hawaii.

Schaeffer, K. (2005). *Dreaming the great Brahmin: Tibetan traditions of the Buddhist poet-saint Saraha.* Oxford: Oxford University Press.

Sheehy, M. R. (2005). Severing the source of fear: Contemplative dynamics of the Tibetan Buddhist Gcod tradition. *Contemporary Buddhism 6*(1), 37–51.

Snellgrove, D. (2002). *Indo-Tibetan Buddhism.* Boston: Shambhala.

Snellgrove, D. (2012/1959). *The Hevajra Tantra: A critical study.* Bangkok, Thailand: Orchid Press.

Tenzin Namdak, L. (2006). *Bonpo Dzogchen teachings.* Kathmandu, Nepal: Vajra Publications.

Tsultrim Gyamtso. (1988). *Progressive stages of meditation on emptiness.* (S. Hookam, Trans.). Oxford: Longchen Foundation.

van Schaik, S. (2014). *The Tibetan Chan manuscripts.* Papers on Central Asia 41. Bloomington: The Sinor Research Institute for Inner Studies.

van Schaik, S. (2016). Dzogchen. In *Oxford research encyclopedia of Buddhism.* Oxford: Oxford University Press. Online access, 15/10/2017.

Wallace, V. (2001). *The inner Kālacakratantra: A Buddhist view of the Tantric individual.* Oxford: Oxford University Press.

Wallace, V., & Wallace, A. (Trans.) (1997). *A guide to the bodhisattva way of life.* Ithaca: Snow Lion.

Zahler, L. (2009). *Study and practice of meditation: Tibetan interpretations of the concentrations and formless absorptions.* Ithaca, NY: Snow Lion.

CHAPTER 13

CLASSICAL DAOIST MEDITATION, 400–100 BCE

HAROLD D. ROTH

DAOISM, also spelled Taoism,[1] is the indigenous religious tradition that has, along with its counterpart and sometimes rival, Confucianism, shaped Chinese life for almost two and a half millennia. It is grounded in a comprehensive cosmology that places the Dao ("Way") as its central power or force and is based upon a related set of philosophical ideas that center on a practice of a meditation that involves contextualizing the self within a greater whole through developing attentional focus and mental tranquility. In the broadest sense, a Daoist attitude toward life can be seen in the open minded acceptance of the Way as this deeper power or force in the universe that forms the basis for a life of selfless simplicity and a profound embracing of a flowing cognition that accepts change as a natural process in life and seeks to accord with it. This attitude of accepting and yielding offsets and complements the more rigid, rule-bound, moral, and duty-conscious and purposeful character often ascribed to Confucianism (Mote, 1971; Maspero, 1981; Robinet, 1997; Schipper, 2000; Miller 2005; Littlejohn 2009; Komjathy, 2013, 2014).

The origins of classical Daoism are shrouded in mystery. Tradition claims they go back to the time of legendary sage Laozi ("Old Master") in the sixth century BCE. While there is scant viable historical evidence for this myth, it probably points to early origins of a distinctive practice of breathing meditation and a distinctive cosmology that derived from early hermit teachers in the eastern Yangzi River basin of central China in what was then the state of Chu and in the Shandong peninsula in the state of Qi. Early

[1] This chapter uses Pinyin Romanization for Mandarin pronunciations of Chinese characters. Dao, Daoism, and Daoist derive from this system, while Tao, Taoism, and Taoist, which are still pronounced with a "d" sound, derive from the older Wade-Giles system. Unless otherwise indicated, all translations are author's own.

teachings were probably transmitted orally in rhymed verse and formed a genre of early Daoist wisdom poetry that was later written down in collections such as "Inward Training" (*Neiye*) from the *Guanzi* (Book of Master Guan) (Rickett, 1985, 1998; Roth, 1994, 1999a and b) and the *Laozi* (Book of the Old Masters) (Lau, 1982; Mair, 1990; Henricks, 1989, 2005). For several centuries these teachings were transmitted from teachers to students, some of whom ended up as advisors to the kings of Chinese states. Some of these teacher-advisors found their way into stories included within the later narrative genre that transmitted classical Daoist teachings in such works as the *Zhuangzi* (Book of Master Zhuang) (Graham, 1981; Mair, 1994) and certain sections of the *Lüshi chunqiu* (Spring and Autumn Annals of Master Lü) (Knoblock & Riegel, 2001). It was in this role that these teachers began to develop political ideas that applied these teachings on cosmology and meditation to the problems of governing and which, as the Warring States epoch was drawing to a close, led some of these teachers, now in possession of written texts as well as techniques, to begin to form a self-identifying tradition that placed the historical figure of Laozi as its founder and his reputed work, *Laozi*, as its canon (Graham 1990b). Arising circa 240 BCE, this tradition survived the turmoil of the Qin unification and its fall to the Han and formed the principal challenge to the other main surviving tradition, the Confucians, as the Han dynasty moved into its first century (Roth, 1991b; Robinet, 1997). The intellectual pinnacle of this classical Daoist tradition is the great compendium, *Huainanzi* (Book of the Huainan Masters) presented at the Imperial court in 139 BCE by its sponsor, Liu An, second king of Huainan (Major, Queen, Meyer, & Roth (Trans.), 2010). This event, and the subsequent fall of Liu's court in 122 BCE due to intrigues that centered on the Han centralization of power, mark the end of the formative or "classical" period in the Daoist tradition, the period that set the foundations for the institutionalized Daoist religion to follow some three centuries later.

Recent Revisions of Scholarship on Daoism

The history of classical Daoism has not always been understood in this way. Previous generations of scholars, relying on a literati tradition going back to the third century CE, have divided the Daoist tradition into two distinct parts: an earlier, "philosophical" tradition found mainly in the abstract and mystical interpretations of two of the foundational works of the tradition: (1) the *Laozi*, which ancient mythology claims to have been written by the sixth-century-BCE scholar who schooled the historical Confucius in how to perform his own central practice: ritual; and (2) the *Zhuangzi*, particularly its first seven chapters, ascribed to a historical person named Zhuang Zhou who lived at the close of the fourth century BCE. This is often contrasted with "religious" Daoism, in all its manifold forms, a superstitious religion of peasants that arose toward the end of the second century CE in the form of two millennial rebellions against the

Han Empire: that of the Tianshi (Celestial Masters) movement in Sichuan and that of the Taiping (Great Peace) movement, also known as the Yellow Turbans, located in Shandong.

When these rebellions were quelled through vast military expenditures that helped facilitate the collapse of the Han Empire, the religious institutions they formed remained intact and constituted the basis for the organized Daoist church. Yet somehow this religion of the Dao continued to claim these two "philosophers" as the founders, despite apparently developing beliefs and practices including the worship of Laozi as a deity and attempts to transcend death rather than adapt to it as a natural transformation (Littlejohn, 2009; Komjathy, 2013, 2014). Commenting on these major discrepancies, renowned Sinologist A. C. Graham (1990c, p. xi) once put it: "the Christian churches never departed quite as far from the gospel as this."

We now know that this overly simplistic picture of these two contrasting forms of Daoism is nothing more than a long-treasured myth. There is no reliable information that the historical figure of Laozi ever existed (Graham, 1990b). Indeed, while earlier versions of the text that was later given this title may have existed (see, e.g., the parallels to about one third of the complete work found at Guodian in a tomb sealed ca. 310 BCE), the complete eighty-one-"chapter" version that has come down to us cannot date from much earlier than the middle of the third century BCE, when it begins to be extensively referenced (Allan and Williams, 2000). Indeed it was at this time, and perhaps in as specific a place as the court of the Qin king who later unified China as its first emperor, that an extant legend of an Old Master (literally, *Lao zi*) who taught the rites to Confucius proved a convenient tale to be used by early practitioners of the Dao, who were building their own tradition to rival that of the Confucians (Graham 1990b). We further know that the text of the *Zhuangzi* was compiled over perhaps two centuries starting circa 320 BCE, and that while handed down within a lineage of teachers and students, has contributions from four distinctive authorial voices (Graham 1990a; Roth, 1991a; Liu, 2004). Other early texts claimed as part of this ancient tradition of so-called "philosophical Daoism," the *Liezi* (Book of Master Lie) and the *Wenzi* (Book of Master Wen), are now well known to be historical forgeries from the third or fourth centuries CE that used a modicum of original textual material (Graham, 1961; Le Blanc, 2000; Littlejohn and Dippman, 2011). We now also know that there are a series of other important texts that contain some of the central concepts and practices that constituted a tradition of "classical" Daoism that is first given this designation by the Han dynastic bibliographer Sima Tan circa 120 BCE as part of his famous essay "On the Six Intellectual Traditions" in chapter 130 of his famous work, *The Historical Records* (Queen and Roth, 1999).

Classical Daoism

During the past four decades a flurry of archaeological excavations in China at such important sites as Mawangdui near Changsha, Zhangjiashan in Hunan, and Guodian in Hubei have produced important textual discoveries that have led to a major re-evaluation of the classical Chinese intellectual traditions, particularly that of Daoism. These discoveries and their analyses have forced scholars to work with a wider range of early Chinese philosophical and religious texts than were heretofore found relevant. When they did, many concluded that some of these texts were part of an early tradition of practice, thought, and literature that was later associated with the label "Daoism." These texts include not only the foundational works *Laozi* and *Zhuangzi*, but also a set of others that have been often overlooked: the four so-called "Techniques of the Mind" (*Xinshu*) works within the *Guanzi* (Baxter, 1998), four chapters in the eclectic compendium, *Lüshi chunqiu*, the important excavated work found at Mawangdui, the "Silk Manuscripts of Huang-Lao" (*Huang Lao boshu*) (Peerenboom, 1992; Yates, 1997), and the Han-dynasty philosophical compendium, *Huainanzi*. Analyzing these works has led to the discovery of a distinctive series of common intellectual categories, philosophical concerns, and literary genres that provide solid evidence of this distinctive tradition of thought and practice. Since the label "Daoism" (literally "the lineages of the Way," *Daojia*) was retrospectively applied to this tradition as it came to a close in the late second century BCE, some scholars prefer to use a different name for it: the "inner cultivation" tradition, based on its oldest extant work, *Inward Training* (*Neiye*), the oldest of the "Techniques of the Mind" works within the seventy-six-text compendium, the *Guanzi* (Roth, 1991b; 1994, 1999a and b).

The distinctive ideas of inner cultivation begin and end with the Way or Dao as the ultimate source of the cosmos and Potency (*De*) as its manifestation in terms of concrete phenomena and experience; non-action or "effortless action" (*wuwei*) as the definitive movement of the Way, and formlessness (*wuxing*) as its spatial mode are both essential as well. There is also a common self-cultivation vocabulary that includes such results as stillness and silence (*jimo*), tranquility (*jing*), emptiness (*xu*), and a variety of apophatic, self-negating techniques and qualities of mind that lead to a direct apprehension of the Way (Roth, 1996; 1997a; 1999a, 1999b).

It is these distinctive ideas and practices that formed the basis for the famous identification of the distinctive *jia*—often misleadingly translated as "schools," but better rendered as intellectual "lineages" or "traditions"—of the pre-Han period by Sima Tan (d. 110 BCE). In writing his "Analysis of the Six Intellectual Lineages," he focused on the particular techniques that each one practiced: ritual for the Confucians, economy in state expenditures for the Mohists, rectification of state hierarchies for the Legalists, and philosophical syncretism and apophatic self-cultivation for the Daoists. Some recent scholarship has been critical of assuming these retrospective descriptions should be taken at face value (Sivin, 1978; Queen, 2001; Csíkszentmihályi and Nylan 2003). While contextualizing these categories has merit, the evidence that they were based upon distinct lineages of thought and practice is substantial. Indeed, the unique constellations of ideas associated with inner cultivation meditation in the early texts of the tradition and that Sima Tan later labeled as "Daoist" support the existence of a social organization and literary tradition (both oral and written) that accompanied and transmitted these practices. Without them it would be difficult to satisfactorily explain how the distinctive set of core ideas common to these inner cultivation works came to exist. It is these core ideas and practices that formed the foundation for the entire Daoist tradition. Thus this inner cultivation tradition richly deserves the title of "classical Daoism." (Queen and Roth, 1999; Komjathy, 2013, 2014; Roth, 2015).

The Cosmology of Classical Daoism and Its Meditative Foundation

The distinctive cosmology of classical Daoism is first and foremost a tradition based on a related series of contemplative practices that were most commonly undertaken in a sitting or kneeling posture and probably done for relatively long periods of time (when compared to similar techniques practiced for health and longevity). The insights into the nature of the mind and the cosmos that were attained through these practices were transmitted in the form of collections of rhymed verse (like "Inward Training" and *Laozi*) and later through didactic narratives and short essays (like *Zhuangzi*, the Huang-Lao silk manuscripts, and *Huainanzi*). These insights eventually coalesced into a distinctive worldview centered on the key ideas of the Way (*Dao*) and its Potency (*De*), and eventually, by the time of the *Huainanzi*, produced a sophisticated cosmology in which all things and events were accounted for in a universe of constant change (Komjathy, 2013, 2014; Roth, 2015).

In this sophisticated cosmology that the *Huainanzi* authors presented as a comprehensive system into which all phenomena in the world could be incorporated, the classical Daoist ideas of the Way and its Potency are primary forces that infuse the cosmos and that enable it to spontaneously function in a harmonious matter. They are made manifest through the *li* (natural patterns or laws), which provide the structures through which all things develop according to their innate natures (*xing*), through which they act in the world, and through which they interact with one another. Because of these patterns and natures, all things in the world have natural and spontaneous reactions (*qing*) to the other things and the environments they encounter. All these structures and patterns occur in a cosmos that is infused with *qi*, a vital energy/matter that resonates according to its particular category: earth, fire, metal, wood, and water. These five categories or "phases" represent not just the phenomena for which they are labels but, rather, types of vital energy that have unique characteristics. For example, earth *qi* is dense and unmoving; water *qi* is wet and flowing; fire *qi* is hot and rising. The comprehensive cosmology of the *Huainanzi* also found roles for the values of the Confucian tradition in maintaining the social order and governing the interactions among human beings, for the Mohists in maintaining frugality in government expenditures, for the Bureaucratic thinkers (often called "Legalists") in establishing and maintaining a government bureaucracy. But all were subsumed within a cosmos infused by the Way and its Potency and governed by the natural patterns and inborn natures of things. In essence what they presented was an all-encompassing normative natural order that itself was a source of sacrality and divinity. This cosmic vision provided a foundation for the texts of the second-century-CE "early Daoist" institutionalized religion, such as the *Taiping jing* (Classic of Great Peace) and for the overarching ideal held by the millenarian movements that established these religious institutions of a harmonious imperial state totally in touch with the Dao, governed by Daoist adepts, and establishing a rule of "Great Peace" (*taiping*). These all grew directly—although not exclusively—out of classical Daoism.

The specific types of contemplative or meditative practices that were transmitted in classical Daoism involve, first and foremost, the apophatic emptying of the normal contents of the conscious mind through concentrating on the breath and various objects of internal visualization. Specific techniques for moving meditation were also known as well, although they are most often found in the context of health and longevity practices, such as we find in the famous painting of the various positions of the "Guiding and Pulling Diagrams" (*Daoyin tu*) that was found at Mawangdui (Harper, 1995, 1998). The classical Daoist inner cultivation tradition referred to its practices as *yang shen* or *yang xing*—("nourishing the inner spirit" or "nourishing innate nature"). While it shared concepts and some practices with the medical health and longevity practices (often referred to as *yang sheng* or *yang xing*—"nourishing vitality" or "nourishing the body"), they practiced them much more assiduously, and they were careful to differentiate themselves from these people whom they considered as "health freaks." For example, In *Zhuangzi* 15 we read:

> To huff and puff, exhale and inhale, blow out the old (breath) and take in the new, do the (gymnastic positions of the) "Bear Stride" and the "Bird Stretch," and to be interested in nothing more than longevity, these are the methods of those who practice the "guiding and pulling" exercises, those who nourish the body and who try to attain the longevity of Ancestor Peng.... But to attain longevity without guiding and pulling, to forget everything and yet possess everything, to be serenely without limit yet have many wonderful things follow you, this is the Way of Heaven and Earth, the Potency of the Sage. Thus it is said that serenity and indifference, stillness and silence, emptiness and nothingness, and Non-Action, these are the even level of Heaven and Earth, the substance of the Way and Potency. Therefore the sage finds rest in them and thereby attains balance and ease. (*Zhuangzi* 15; Graham, 1981, p. 265)

Here we see as well one of the preeminent dimensions of apophatic practice, that of cultivating the related psychological states of serenity, equilibrium, stillness and silence, and nothingness. Simply put, the basic practice of inner cultivation is to unify or focus attention on one thing, often the inhalation and exhalation of the breath for a sustained period of time. Through this one comes to gradually empty out the thoughts, perceptions, and emotions that normally occupy the mind and develop an awareness of the presence of the Way that resides at the ground of human consciousness. We can analyze these apophatic practices into a number of basic categories.

Classical Daoist Techniques of Apophatic Meditation

Proper Posture

An aligned sitting position for body and limbs is frequently recommended. The most famous example of this is the renowned passage in *Zhuangzi* 6 in which the leading disciple of Confucius, Yan Hui, teachers the Master about how to attain the experience of "merging with Great Pervader" (*tong yu datong*) through the practice he calls "sitting and forgetting" (*zuowang*). Yan Hui describe this as:

> I let organs and members drop away, dismiss eyesight and hearing, part from the body and expel knowledge, and merge with Great Pervader (=the Dao). This is what I mean by "just sit and forget". (*Zhuangzi* 6; Graham, 1981, p. 92)

To let "organs and members drop away" (*duo zhi ti*) means to lose visceral awareness of the emotions and desires, which, for the early Daoists, have "physiological" bases in the various organs; to "dismiss eyesight and hearing" (*chu cong ming*) means to deliberately cut off sense perception. To "part from the body and expel knowledge" (*li xing qu zhi*) means to lose bodily awareness and remove all thoughts from consciousness. All of these are apophatic techniques found in the important sources of this tradition. Notice that the ultimate result of these apophatic practices, to "merge with Great Pervader" implies that, as a result of these practices, Yan Hui has become united with the Dao. In many ways this passage contains a succinct statement of inner cultivation practice and its principal goal (Roth, 2000, 2018).

Other important passages detailing posture are found in *Guanzi*'s "Inward Training," in the notions of "aligning the body" (*zheng xing*) in verse XI, aligning the four limbs (*zheng siti*) in verses VIII, XIV, and XIX, and keeping the body calm and unmoving (*xingan er busi*) in verse XXIV (Roth, 1999a and b).

Breath Cultivation

Cultivating the breath or vital energy (*qi*) is a foundational practice in all the major sources of classical Daoist inner cultivation. It is often spoken of as concentrating or refining the breath (*zhuan qi*), as in this locus classicus from *Laozi* X, but is given a fuller expression in the "Inward Training" verse XIX that is found in other early sources:

***Laozi* 10**
Amidst the psychic turmoil (of daily living) (lit. While carrying on your head your perplexed bodily soul)

Can you embrace the One and not let go?
In concentrating your breath can you become as supple
As a babe?
Can you wash clean your mysterious mirror
And leave no blemish?
Can you love the people and govern the state
Without resorting to action? (Lau, 1982, ch. 10)

"Inward Training" XIX
By concentrating your vital breath as if numinous
The myriad things will all be contained within you.
Can you concentrate? Can you unify?
Can you not resort to divining by tortoise or milfoil
Yet know bad and good fortune?
Can you stop? Can you cease?
Can you not seek it in others
Yet attain it within yourself?...
When the four limbs are aligned
And the blood and vital breath are tranquil,
Unify your awareness, concentrate your mind,
Then your eyes and ears will not be overstimulated.
And even the far-off will seem close at hand.... (Roth, 1999b, p. 92)

In classical Daoism, breath cultivation is essential to all forms of higher cognition and to the attainment of the way. "Inward Training" contains a variety of phrases dealing with similar aspects of concentrating on one's breathing. In verse V we read of the importance of having "patterned breathing" (*qi li*); in verse VIII having guided breathing (*qi dao*); in verse XXIV we read about relaxing and expanding the vital breath (*kuan qi er guang*). The famous "fasting of the mind" narrative in *Zhuangzi* 4 gives the following advice involving breathing:

Unify your attention
Don't listen with your ears, listen with your mind;
Don't listen with your mind, listen with your breathing
Listening stops at the ears; the mind stops at what it can objectify
As for your breathing, it becomes empty and waits to respond to things.
The Way gathers in emptiness.
Emptiness is attained through the fasting of the mind... (Graham, 1981, pp. 68–69, modified)

Zhuangzi 6 also contrasts the deep breathing ("from their heels") of the genuine (*zhenren*) with that of the common people, who breathe from their throats. All the passages affirm the importance of concentrated breathing in the inner cultivation tradition.

These passages also affirm that another dimension of breath cultivation is to unify or focus one's attention. This is first found in "Inward Training" XIX: "Can you concentrate? Can you unify?" (*Neng zhuan hu? Neng yi hu*; Roth, 1999b, p. 82). In "Inward Training"

XXIV we find advice to "guard the One and discard myriad disturbances" (*shou yi er qi wange*; Roth, 1999b, p. 92). This is the oldest extant example of the hallowed contemplative technique of "guarding the One" that became so important in later Daoist and Buddhist meditative practice. *Laozi* 5 contains the related concept of "guarding the center" (*shou zhong*). These are phrases that speak of meditative techniques of developing acute attentional focus on one mental object.

Apophatic Psychological Techniques

In addition to proper posture and concentration of breath and attention, these inner cultivation texts also present a wide variety of techniques that have the effect of emptying out the normal contents of consciousness and hence approaching the Dao by apophatic means. Principal among these is the very frequent admonition in "Inward Training" to restrict or eliminate desires (*jing yu, jie yu*) (e.g., verses XXV and XXVI) that occurs in similar form in the *Laozi* as "to minimize or be without desires" (*gua yu, wu yu*) (chapters 1, 19, 37, 57). The *Zhuangzi*, the *Guanzi* 13("Techniques of the Mind"), and the *Lüshi chunqiu* also contain nearly identical phrases. Other related apophatic techniques include restricting or eliminating emotions, a staple of "Inward Training" (see verses III, VII, XX, XXI) as in verse XXV: "When you are anxious or sad, pleased or angry, the Way has no place to settle within you." Discussion of the deleterious effects of the emotions are absent from the *Laozi*, but present in *Zhuangzi* 5 in the well-known dialogue between Zhuangzi and his Logician foil, Huishi, about how sages (*shengren*) do not have the essential responses of human beings (*ren zhi qing*): "these people inwardly do not wound their being by likes and dislikes but they constantly go by the spontaneous and do not add anything to the process of life . . . " (Graham, 1981, p. 82).

Restricting or eliminating thought and knowledge is also commended in inner cultivation texts. This is prevalent in "Inward Training" (e.g., verses V, VIII, XX, XXIII): ". . . Whenever your states of mind have excessive knowledge, you have lost your vitality . . . " (Roth, 1999b, verse VIII, p. 60). It occurs as well in more general phrases in *Laozi* such as "exterminate sageliness, discard wisdom" (*jue sheng, qi zhi*) then the people will benefit a hundred fold" (chapter 19) and, in contrast in chapter 48, between the daily increase in knowledge during the pursuit of learning and the daily decrease in knowledge during the pursuit of the Way. Finally, in *Zhuangzi*, we find the phrase "part from the body and expel knowledge" in the "sitting and forgetting" passage already discussed. The admonition against sageliness and wisdom from *Laozi* 19 is repeated in chapters 10 and 11 of *Zhuangzi* and several other related references such as "excessive knowledge is ruinous" (*duozhi wei bai*) from Guang Chengzi's teaching in chapter 11 and the advice to "discard knowledge and precedent" (*qu zhi yu gu*) in chapter 15.

Finally, inner cultivation texts recommend in some cases restricting or completely eliminating sense-perception. "Inward Training" recommends avoiding the overstimulation of the senses in verses XIII, XIX, XXVI. The *Laozi* chapters 52 and 56 give the advice to "block the openings and shut the doors [of the senses]" (*sai qi dui cai qi men*), and chapter 12 warns against the deleterious effects of the five colors, tones, and tastes. *Zhuangzi* 6 has Confucius singing the praises of those perfected people who "roam beyond the boundaries of the world" to his disciple Zigong, and describes them as having "left behind hearing and seeing" (*yi qi ermu*) and later in the famous "sitting and forgetting dialogue" has Yanhui teach Confucius about an inner cultivation practice to "dismiss eyesight and hearing" (*chu cong ming*).

Taken together these passages recommend an apophatic regimen that develops concentration by focusing on the breathing, and stripping away the common cognitive activities of daily life, something that must, of practical necessity, be done when not engaged in these activities, hence while sitting unmoved in one position. There are a wide variety of metaphorical descriptions of these apophatic regimens. These include the idea that following the Way involves "daily relinquishing" (*risun*) in *Laozi* 48, *Zhuangzi*'s famous phrases of the "fasting of the mind" (*xinzhai*) in chapter 4, and "sitting and forgetting" (*zuowang*) in chapter 6. Both *Zhuangzi* 23 and *Lüshi chunqiu* 25.3 talk of "casting off the fetters of the mind" (*jie xin miu*). Another common phrase with a few close variations, "to discard wisdom and precedent" (*qu zhigu*), is found in these texts. Finally, who can forget the beautifully evocative parallel metaphors for these apophatic mental processes as "diligently cleaning out abode of the vital essence" (*jingqu jingshe*) from "Inward Training" XIII; "sweeping clean the abode of the spirit" (*saoqu shenshe*) in verse III of the *Guanzi*'s "Techniques of the Mind" Part 1 and "washing clean the Profound Mirror" (*diqu xuanjian*) from *Laozi* 10. This metaphor is echoed in *Zhuangzi* 5: "None of us finds our mirror in flowing water, we find it in still water... If your mirror is clear, dust will not settle. If dust settles then your mirror is not clear" (Graham, 1981, p. 77).

Resultant States

The direct results of following these apophatic psychological practices are remarkably similar across many early texts of the inner cultivation tradition, thus indicating a consistency of actual methods and some sharing of ideas and texts. It is useful to borrow an important contrast from personality psychologists and talk about these results in terms of "states," which pertain to the inner experience of individual practitioners and tend to be transient, and in terms of "traits," which pertain to more stable character qualities developed in interactions in the phenomenal world (Cahn & Polich, 2006, an excellent overview of neuroscientific research on meditation).

Probably the two most common resultant states of inner cultivation practices are "tranquility" (*jing*), the mental and physical experience of complete calm and stillness, and "emptiness" (*xu*), the mental condition of having no thoughts, feelings, and perceptions yet still being intensely aware. These are both prioritized in such well-known passages as this from *Laozi* 16: "attaining emptiness is the ultimate result; focusing on tranquility is its central practice" (*zhi xu ji, shou jing du*). Tranquility is prized in "Inward Training" in verses XI, XVI XIX. XXII, XXV and in these lines from verse XXVI:

> When the mind can hold on to tranquility
> The Way will become naturally stable. (Roth, 1999b, p. 96)

Tranquility is quite common to the *Zhuangzi*, although the specific term is absent from the "Inner Chapters." There are, however, a number of close synonyms for tranquility that do occur in this section of *Zhuangzi* and in other inner cultivation texts that differentiate subtle dimensions of it, including "calmness" (*an*), "equanimity" (*qi*), balance (*ping*), repose (*ning*), "stillness" and "silence" (*jimo*).

Emptiness as a specific term is absent from "Inward Training," although it is certainly implied as the result of many of its apophatic practices. It is fairly common in both *Laozi* and *Zhuangzi*. In the latter we find assertions such as this famous one from chapter 4: "... The Way coalesces in emptiness (*Dao ji xu*); Emptiness is attained through the fasting of the mind." (Graham, 1981, p. 68, modified)

In chapter 15 we read these ideas linking emptiness with various aspects of tranquility:

> Thus it is said that serenity and detachment (*tiandan*), stillness and silence (*jimo*), emptiness and nothingness, and Non-Action, these are the even level of Heaven and Earth, the substance of the Way and Potency. Therefore the sage finds rest in them and thereby attains balance and ease. (Graham, 1981, p. 265, modified)

Thus states of tranquility and emptiness are both closely associated with a direct experience of the Way, perhaps the penultimate result of apophatic inner cultivation practices. There are a number of striking metaphors for this experience of unification of individual consciousness with the Way; three use the concept of merging to express it. Chapter 56 of *Laozi* contains advice on apophatic practice (e.g., "block the openings and shut the doors [of the senses]") and identifies the ultimate result as "Profound Merging" (*xuantong*). *Zhuangzi* 6 parallels *Laozi* 56; therein Yanhui teaches Confucius about the apophatic practice of "sitting and forgetting," the penultimate result of which is "merging with Great Pervader" (*tong yu datong*). Chapter 2 also engages this metaphor for the Way, stating that the Way "pervades and unifies" (*Dao tong weiyi*) phenomena as different from one another as a stalk from a pillar, a leper from the beauty Xishi.

Other early inner cultivation sources contain similar descriptions of the direct experience of the Way. *Lüshi chunqiu* 3.4 links this experience directly to emptiness and speaks of "attaining the One"; *Lüshi chunqiu* 25.3 and its parallel passage in *Zhuangzi* 23 talk of attaining emptiness as the penultimate result of correct sitting and attaining tranquility. *Guanzi*'s "Techniques of the Mind" also describes apophatic practices that lead to "attaining the empty Way" (*de xu Dao*). "Inward Training" verse V speaks of using tranquility to "halt the Way" (*zhi Dao*): "When the mind is tranquil and the Vital

Table 13.1

VERB	OBJECT
hold fast to (*zhi bao*) embrace (*bao*) guard or focus on (*shou*)	the One, the Center, the Way

Breath is regular, the Way can thereby be halted." Finally, there are a series of similar locutions in "Inward Training" (IX, XXIV) and *Laozi* (5, 10, 14, 22, 32, 52) that evoke this experience of the merging of individual consciousness with the Way through the following pattern (Roth 1997a; 1999a and b, 2015; 2018) (Table 13.1):

The conceptualizations of the Way in these various sources are quite consistent. As the major force or power that underlies the cosmos, it is responsible for the spontaneous self and relational generation of all its animate and inanimate constituents. It is this activity that leads to some famous metaphors for the Way in the *Laozi* (e.g., ch. 1, 20, 52) and *Zhuangzi* (e.g., ch. 5, 7, 13), such as the "mother" (*mu*) and the Ancestor (*zong*). Because it can only be directly experienced but never completely understood as an object of perception or thought, its qualities can only be evoked. Verse VI of "Inward Training" accurately captures the concept of the Way for all the major pre-Han inner cultivation sources:

> As for the Way:
> It is what the mouth cannot speak of,
> The eyes cannot look at,
> And the ears cannot listen to.
> It is that by which we cultivate the mind and align the physical form.
> When people lose it they die;
> When people gain it they flourish.
> When endeavors lose it they fail;
> When they gain it they succeed.
> The Way never has a root or trunk,
> It never has leaves or flowers.
> The myriad things are generated by it;
> The myriad things are completed by it.
> We designate it "the Way." (Roth, 1999b, p. 56)

It is important to also note that these profound states of experience of the Way are quite often linked with preserving the spirit internally or becoming spirit-like (*shen/rushen*) in "Inward Training" (e.g., verses IX, XII, XIII), "Techniques of the Mind," the *Lüshi chunqiu* 3.4 and the *Huang Lao boshu* (*Jingfa* 6). They are further associated with a highly refined and concentrated form of vital energy called the Vital Essence (*jing*) in "Inward Training" verses V, XIX and these latter three sources.

Resultant Traits

As the direct result of the experience of these various dimensions of union with the Way—which are internal experiences attained in isolation from all interactions with the phenomenal world—adepts develop a series of what are best thought of as traits, more or less continuing alterations in their cognitive and performative abilities that were highly prized by rulers and their literati subjects alike for obvious reasons.

Perhaps the most famous of these is the idea that one can take no deliberate and willful action from the standpoint of one's separate and individual self, and yet nothing is left undone (*wuwei er wu buwei*). This works because adepts have so embraced and embodied the Way, that their actions are the actions that are perfectly harmonious expressions of the Way itself in a given situation. One of the most famous phrases in the *Laozi*, we find this implicit in all of the other early sources of inner cultivation and repeated verbatim in many others, including the "Outer and Miscellaneous Chapters" of the *Zhuangzi* and *Lüshi chunqiu* 25.3, and the *Huainanzi*. A very similar idea to efficacious non-action is the concept of being able to respond spontaneously and harmoniously to whatever situation arises. We find this discussed in several sources but none as directly as this passage from "Techniques of the Mind I" in *Guanzi* 13:

...Exemplary persons *(junzi)* are not enticed by likes
Nor oppressed by dislikes.
Calm and tranquil, they act without effort,
And they discard wisdom and precedent.
Their responses are not contrived.
Their movements are not chosen.
The mistake lies in intervening directly oneself.
The fault lies in altering and transforming things.
Therefore the ruler who has the Way:
At rest seems to be without knowledge,
In response to things seems to fit together with them.
This is the Way of tranquility and adaptation. (my translation; *Guanzi* [*SBCK* ed.], 13/2a/2–3)

The internal commentary to this passage includes mention of the important concept of resonance (*ganying*), a cosmic principle that Exemplary Persons are able to manifest in their interactions:

...Their responses are not contrived,
Their movements are not chosen.

This says that they are adaptable (*yin*). To be adaptable is to relinquish the self and take other things as standards. To respond only when stimulated (*gan erhou ying*) is not something you contrive to do. To move according to inherent patterns (*li*) is not something you [deliberately] choose to do... (my translation; *Guanzi* [*SBCK* ed.], 13/4a/7-10)

These traits of immediate and uncontrived responsiveness describe well one of the ideas for which the *Laozi* is famous: spontaneity (*ziran*). A quality of the Way, the phenomenal world, and the Cultivated Sage in chapters 17, 23, 25, 51, it refers to their natural, instantaneous and non-reflective responses.

In a fundamental fashion, this almost magical ability to spontaneously accomplish all without seeming to exert any deliberate action is frequently associated with great Potency (*De*), an idea some have linked to charisma. Potency is a kind of aura of spontaneous efficacy that develops in a person through repeated experiences of tranquility, emptiness, and merging with the Way and is visible for all to see. We find it in all the early sources of inner cultivation theory, often in conjunction with apophatic techniques. For example in "Inward Training" verse XI:

> When your body is not aligned
> Potency will not come.
> When you are not tranquil within
> Your mind will not be in order.
> Align your body, summon your Potency
> Then it will come cascading on its own. (Roth, 1999b, p. 66)

Greatly improved cognitive abilities are also found among the significant traits that result from apophatic practice. In "Inward Training" verse XVI we read:

> If people can be aligned and tranquil
> Their skin will be ample and smooth
> Their hearing and vision will be acute,
> Their muscles will be elastic and the bones strong...
> They will mirror things with great purity
> And will see things with great clarity.
> Diligently attend and do not waver,
> And you will everyday renew your Inner Power. (Roth, 1999b, p. 76)

Perceptual acuity and general cognitive accuracy are two main results of apophatic practice. Notice the phrase "mirror things with great purity" (*jianyu daqing*), which utilizes the metaphor of the mirror found in *Laozi* 10 and *Zhuangzi* 4, indicating a special kind of unerring cognition of the world. It is the kind of instantaneous knowledge of the world that we find in the "Normative Models" (*Jingfa*) text of the *Huang Lao boshu* as the direct result of being aligned, tranquil, even, serene, pure, and numinous: "Seeing and knowing are never deluded" (*jianzhi buhuo*). There are also physical traits that adepts develop in "Inward Training," which are reminiscent of the qualities suppleness (*rou*) and pliancy (*ruo*) that sages possess in *Laozi* chapters 3, 36, 55, and 76.

Each of the main inner cultivation tradition sources details additional cognitive abilities and personality traits that derive from apophatic practices. "Inward Training" says such practices create mental stability and psychic order (*dingxin* in verse VIII; *zhixin* in verse X). The *Laozi* speaks of becoming impartial (*gong*) in chapters 16 and 42 and selfless (*wusi*), in chapters 7, 19; and simple and whole (*su pu*) in chapters 19 and 38. These qualities are a direct result of experiencing a reduction or elimination of desires, one of the preferred meditational techniques of inner cultivation.

The *Zhuangzi* details a number of different "technical" skills that derive from inner cultivation practice. In chapter 3 Cook Ding is an "ox-carver" who trusts the numinous within, does not look with his eyes, and realizes the limits of perception as he relies on the patterns of Heaven to guide him through the interstices of the ox. In chapter 19, the bellstand carver must first make his mind tranquil until he eventually reaches a point where he forgets he has four limbs and a body. Then he can go into the forest to choose a tree to carve. Indeed, the *Zhuangzi* collection is, in many ways, devoted to the cultivation of perhaps the most comprehensive of all these character traits, one that encompasses all of the others discussed to this point: a mode of cognition called *yinshi*. The late A. C. Graham translates this in a very literal fashion: "the that's it which goes by circumstance"; but in essence, the concept is really that of flowing, totally changing and transforming to whatever the situation is. It is exemplified in many of the narratives of the *Zhuangzi*, for example: the "free and easy wandering" of chapter 1; the monkey keeper handing out nuts in chapter 2; Cook Ding in chapter 3; Cripple Shu in chapter 4; Wang Tai in chapter 5; Master Lai in chapter 6; Huzi in chapter 7. All of them respond without egotism, without selfishness, without insisting on any one fixed point of view: that is how they survive and flourish. This kind of indifference to fortune or misfortune and creative spontaneous responsiveness to all situations is characteristic of people "in whom Potency is at its utmost" (*Zhuangzi* 9) (Roth, 2000; 2018).

So the basic contours of inner cultivation are this: apophatic practices of sitting still and concentrating on—and paying attention to—one's breathing lead to gradual reductions in desires, emotions, thoughts, and perceptions. States of experience result from these reductions that make one feel tranquil, calm, serene, states in which one's consciousness becomes emptied of its usual contents, states in which one feels unified with the Way. These states lead to a series of beneficial cognitive changes and the development of new traits such as acute perception, accurate cognition, selflessness and impartiality, the ability to spontaneously be in harmony with one's surroundings no matter what the situation, and the ability to be flexible and adjust to whatever changes may come one's way. Table 13.2 summarizes these practices and results:

Conclusions: From Meditation to Political Philosophy

One of the primary areas of change and transformation within classical Daoism involves the application of its practices to the fundamental concern of the late Warring States Chinese thinkers: rulership. While the oldest extant texts of classical Daoism—*Guanzi*'s "Inward Training" and the first seven "Inner Chapters" of the *Zhuangzi*—almost completely eschew political advice in favor of cosmology and inner cultivation practice, the tradition gradually over time develops a political philosophy aimed at convincing rulers to follow their meditative techniques and apply them in a personal fashion to gov-

Table 13.2 A Summary of Inner Cultivation Ideas

Cultivation Practices	*Posture:*	*Apophatic Techniques*:
	Aligning the body; 正形, 正四體	Restricting desires, 寡 欲, 節欲, 無 欲,
	keeping it still: 形安而不移	Restricting thoughts, 出 聰 明, 屈 知, 棄 知, 去 知
		Restricting perceptions: 塞 其 兌 閉 其 門; 遺 其 耳 目; 墮 支 體 離 形, 出 聰 明,
	Breathing	
	Concentrate專氣,	*Apophatic Metaphors*:
	Order氣理,	Mind fasting心齋,
	Guide氣導,	Sitting+Forgetting坐忘,
	Attention	Casting off mental fetters解 心 繆.
	Focus on 1守一, Focus on ctr.守中	Sweeping clean numinous lodge 掃除神舍,
		Cleaning off the Profound Mirror滌 去玄鑑
		The Way of Stillness+Adapting靜 因 之 道
Resultant States	Tranquility靜	Detachment 淡
	Emptiness虛	Refined/concentrated精
	Calmness安	Spirit-like 神
	Equanimity齊	Hold fast to the One 執 一
	Repose寧	Attain Empty Way 得虛道
	Stillness 寂	Halting the Way 止道
	Silence漠	Guarding/Returning to the Ancestor 守/反 宗
	Serenity恬	
Resultant Traits	Non action無 為	Suppleness 弱
	All done無 不 為Potency 德	Pliancy 柔
	Resonance 感 應	Psychol order定心, 治心
	Spontaneity 自然	Selflessness無私
	Perceptual acuity鑑於大清	Impartiality公
		Simplicity 素
	Instant+accurate knowledge: 見知不惑	Wholeness僕
		Psychol Skill 心 術
		Flowing cognition因是

erning. These ideas presumably developed as Daoist thinkers joined local courts to serve as philosophical advisors to their rulers, a process that probably began with the famous Jixia Academy in the state of Qi in the Shandong peninsula circa 340 BCE.

One of the earliest sources of such advice is the *Laozi* (e.g., ch. 37, 46), which begins to address how some of the traits derived from inner cultivation practice are beneficial for rulership. For one, they give sage rulers a distinct lack of attachment to themselves and their own desires that leads to making better decisions in governing (e.g., ch. 22, 49). Later texts, such as *Guanzi*'s "Techniques of the Mind" and *Zhuangzi* 13 and 33, demonstrate thinking aimed at applying the techniques, states, and traits of inner cultivation to governing. They developed catch-phrases for these applications: for example, "the Way of tranquility and adaptation (*jingyin zhi Dao*) in the *Guanzi*, "tranquil and sagely, active and kingly" (*jing er sheng, dong er wang*) and "internally a sage, externally a king" (*neisheng waiwang*) in *Zhuangzi* 13 and 33. This trend continues into the *Huainanzi*, which develops this unlikely mix of apophatic inner cultivation practices and results and political thought into a sophisticated new synthesis.

The *Huainanzi* presents a sustained argument for a political philosophy in which the king is both ruler and adept. Because he has cultivated himself to develop the traits of a sage, he is able to function with cognitive acuity. Grounded in the Way that infuses the cosmos and all phenomena within it, he is able to respond spontaneously and harmoniously to whatever situation arises. Because he has both this experiential ability and the contents of the twenty-one essays of the text of the *Huainanzi*, which presumes to comprehensively present the fundamental patterns, natures, laws, and taxonomies of all things in the cosmos, the Daoist sage-king sets up his government to parallel these macrocosmic forces. Human society is an integral part of what Joseph Needham once called "an organismic cosmos," with everything cooperating with one another and with the whole, guided by the one power or force that infuses both the whole and all of its parts, the Way. It is, as Needham aptly called it, "an ordered harmony of wills without an Ordainer" (Needham, 1956, p. 287). Within the human realm, the Daoist sage-ruler parallels the mode of activity of the Way, setting his bureaucracy with a formal and structured hierarchy that parallels what is writ large in the cosmos and governing spontaneously through taking no action. A passage in *Zhuangzi* 14 contains perhaps the most characteristic metaphor for this classical Daoist model of sage rulership. In it, the Yellow Emperor, the most common interlocutor and imperial student in a wide variety of classical Daoist works, conducts the performance of a grand symphonic piece called the "Pond of Totality," in which, as ruler of both the human world and cosmos, he directs the regular patterned movements of all parts as a vast harmonic whole. One may see in this passage and the entire symbolism of classical Daoist sage-rulership, pretentions to the creation of a political order grounded in cosmic authority that are very likely contributors to the bravado that created the two great second-century millenarian rebellions, the Way of Great Peace and the Celestial Masters, that led to the eventual formation of the institutionalized Daoist religion (Roth, 2014).

Glossary

an	安
chu cong ming	出聰明
Dao ji xu	道集虛
Dao tong weiyi	道通為一
Daojia	道家
Daoyin tu	導引圖
de	德
de xu Dao	得虛道
dingxin	定心
diqu xuanjian	滌去玄鑑
duo zhi ti	墮支體

duozhi wei bai	多知為敗
gan erhou ying	感而后應
ganying	感應
gong	公
Guanzi	管子
gua yu	寡欲
Huainanzi	淮南子
Huang Lao boshu	黃老帛書
jia	家
jianyu daqing	鑑於大清
jianzhi buhuo	見知不惑
jie xin miu	解心繆 or 謬
jie yu	節欲
jimo	寂漠
jing	精
jing	靜
jing er sheng, dong er wang	靜而聖, 動而王
Jingfa	經法
jingqu jingshe	敬除精舍
jingyin zhi Dao	靜因之道
jing yu	靜欲
jue sheng, qi zhi	絕聖棄知
junzi	君子
kuan qi er guang	寬氣而廣
Laozi	老子
li	理
Liezi	列子
li xing qu zhi	離形屈知
Lüshi chunqiu	呂士春秋
mu	母
neisheng waiwang	內聖外王
Neiye	內業
Neng zhuan hu? Neng yi hu	能專乎能一乎
ning	寧
ping	平
qi	氣
qi	齊
qi dao	氣導
qi li	氣理
qing	情
qu zhi yu gu	去知與故
qu zhigu	除智故
ren zhi qing	人之情

risun	日損
rou	弱
ruo	柔
sai qi dui cai qi men	塞其兌閉其門
saoqu shenshe	掃除神舍
shen/rushen	神/如神
shengren	聖人
shou yi er qi wange	守一而棄萬苛
shou zhong	守中
Sima Tan	司馬談
su pu	素僕
Taiping	太平
Taiping jing	太平經
tiandan	恬淡
Tianshi	天師
tong yu datong	同於大通
Wenzi	文子
wusi	無私
wuwei er wu buwei	無為而無不為
wuwei	無為
wuxing	無形
wuyu	無欲
xing	性
xing an er busi	形安而不移
Xinshu	心術
xinzhai	心齋
xu	虛
xuantong	玄同
yang xing	養形
yang shen	養神
yang sheng	養生
yang xing	養性
yi qi ermu	遺其耳目
yin	因
yinshi	因是.
zheng siti	正四體
zheng xing	正形
zhenren	真人
zhi Dao	止道
zhi xu ji, shou jing du	致虛極, 守靜督
zhixin	治心
Zhuangzi	莊子

zhuan qi	專氣
ziran	自然
zong	宗
zuowang	坐忘

References

Allan, S., & Williams, C. (Eds.). (2000). *The Guodian Laozi: Proceedings of the international conference, Dartmouth College, May, 1998*. Early China Special Monograph Series 5. Institute for East Asian Studies, University of California, Berkeley.

Baxter, W. H. (1998). Situating the language of the *Lao Tzu*: The probable date of the *Tao Te Ching*. In M. LaFargue & L. Kohn (Eds.), *Lao-Tzu and the Tao-Te-Ching*, (pp. 231–254). Albany: State University of New York Press.

Cahn, R., & Polich, J. (2006). Meditation states and traits: EEG, ERP, and neuroimaging studies. *Psychological Bulletin 132*(2), 180–211.

Csíkszentmihályi, M., & Nylan, M. (2003). Constructing lineages and inventing traditions through exemplary figures in early China. *T'oung Pao 89*, 59–99.

Graham, A. C. (1961). The date and composition of the Liehtzyy. *Asia Major* [second series] *8*(2), 139–199.

Graham, A. C. (1981). *Chuang Tzu: The inner chapters*. London: Allen and Unwin.

Graham, A. C. (1989). *Disputers of the Tao*. Chicago: Open Court Press.

Graham, A. C. (1990a). How much of *Chuang Tzu* did Chuang Tzu write? In *Studies in Chinese philosophy and philosophical literature* (pp. 283–321). Albany: State University of New York Press.

Graham, A. C. (1990b). The origins of the legend of Lao Tan. In *Studies in Chinese philosophy and philosophical literature* (pp. 111–124). Albany: State University of New York Press.

Graham, A. C. (1990c). *The book of Lieh Tzu*. Morningside Edition. New York: Columbia University Press.

Harper, D. J. (1995). The bellows analogy in *Laozi* V and Warring States macrobiotic hygiene. *Early China 20*, 381–392.

Harper, D. J. (1998). *Early Chinese medical literature: The Mawangdui medical manuscripts*. London: Kegan Paul International.

Henricks, R. (1989). *Lao-Tzu: Te Tao Ching: A new translation based on the recently discovered Ma-wang-tui texts*. New York: Ballantine.

Henricks, R. (2005). *Lao Tzu's Tao Te Ching: A translation of the startling new documents found at Guodian*. New York: Columbia University Press.

Knoblock, J., & Riegel, J. (2001). *The annals of master Lü Buwei*. Stanford: Stanford University Press.

Komjathy, L. (2013). *The Daoist tradition: An introduction*. London: Bloomsbury.

Komjathy, L. (2014). *Daoism: A guide for the perplexed*. London: Bloomsbury.

Komjathy, L. (ed.). (2015). *Contemplative literature*. Albany: State University of New York Press.

LaFargue, M. (1992). *The Tao of the Tao Te Ching*. Albany: State University of New York.

LaFargue, M. (1994). *Tao and method: A reasoned approach to the Tao Te Ching*. Albany: State University of New York Press.

Lau, D. C. (Trans.). (1982). *Chinese classics: Tao Te Ching*. Hong Kong: Chinese University Press.

Le Blanc, C. (2000). *Le Wen zi: á la lumiére de l'histoire et de l'archéologie*. Montreal: Presses de l'Université de Montréal.

Littlejohn, R. (2009) *Daoism: An Introduction*. London: I.B.Taurus.

Littlejohn, R., & Dippmann, J. W. (2011). *Riding the wind with Liezi: New perspectives on the Daoist classic*. Albany: State University of New York Press.

Liu, X. (2004). *Classifying the Zhuangzi chapters*. Michigan Monographs in Chinese Studies. Ann Arbor: University of Michigan Press.

Mair, V. H. (Trans.). (1990). *Tao Te Ching: The classic book of integrity and the way*. New York: Bantam Books.

Mair, V. (1994). *Wandering on the way: Early Taoist tales and parables from Chuang Tzu*. New York: Bantam Books

Major, J. S., Queen, S., Meyer, A. S., & Roth, H. D. (Trans.). (2010). *The Huainanzi: A guide to the theory and practice of government in early Han China, by Liu An* 劉安, *King of Huainan*. New York: Columbia University Press.

Maspero, H. (1981). *Taoism and Chinese religion*. (Frank Kierman, Trans.). Amherst: University of Massachusetts Press.

Miller, J. (2005). *Daoism: A short introduction*. Oxford: Oneworld.

Mote, F.W. (1971). *Intellectual Foundations of China*. 2nd. ed, 1989. New York: McGraw-Hill

Needham, J. (1956). *Science and civilization in China* (Vol. 2). Cambridge: Cambridge University Press.

Peerenboom, R. P. (1992). *Law and morality in ancient China: The silk manuscripts of Huang-Lao*. Albany: State University of New York Press.

Queen, S. A. (2001). Inventories of the past: Re-thinking the "school" affiliation of the Huainanzi. *Asia Major* [third series] *14*(1), 51–72.

Queen, S., & Roth, H. D. (Trans.). (1999). On the six lineages of thought, by Sima Tan. In I. Bloom & W. T. deBary (Eds.), *Sources of Chinese tradition* (2nd ed., Vol. 1, pp. 278–282). New York: Columbia University Press.

Rickett, A. (1985, 1998). *Guanzi: Political, economic, and philosophical essays from early China* (2 vols.). Princeton, NJ: Princeton University Press.

Robinet, I. (1997). *Taoism: Growth of a religion* (P. Brooks, Trans.). Palo Alto, CA: Stanford University Press.

Roth, H. D. (1991a). Who compiled the *Chuang Tzu*? In H. Rosemont, Jr. (Ed.), *Chinese texts and philosophical contexts: Essays dedicated to Angus C. Graham* (pp. 79–128). Chicago: Open Court.

Roth, H. D. (1991b). Psychology and self-cultivation in early Taoistic thought. *Harvard Journal of Asiatic Studies 51*(2), 599–650.

Roth, H. D. (1994). Redaction criticism and the early history of Taoism. *Early China 19*, 1–46.

Roth, H. D. (1996). The inner cultivation tradition of early Taoism. In S. F. Teiser (Ed.), *Religions of China in practice* (pp. 123–148). Princeton, NJ: Princeton University Press.

Roth, H. D. (1997). Evidence for stages of meditation in early Taoism. *Bulletin of the School of Oriental and African Studies 60*(2), 295–314.

Roth, H. D. (1999a). *Lao Tzu* in the context of early Taoist mystical practice. In P. J. Ivanhoe & M. Csíkszentmihályi (Eds.), *Essays on the religious and philosophical aspects of the Laozi*. Albany: State University of New York Press.

Roth, H. D. (1999b). *Original Tao: Inward training and the foundations of Taoist mysticism*. New York: Columbia University Press.

Roth, H. D. (2000). Bimodal mystical experience in the Qiwulun of *Chuang Tzu*. *Journal of Chinese Religions 28*, 1–20.

Roth, H. D. (2014). Daoist inner cultivation thought and the textual structure of the *Huainanzi*. In Sarah Queen and Michael Puett (Eds.), *The Huainanzi and textual production in early China* (pp. 40–82). Leiden: Brill.

Roth, H. D. (2015). Daoist apophatic meditation: Selections from the classical Daoist textual corpus. In Komjathy (Ed.), *Contemplative Literature* (pp. 89–143). Albany: State University of New York Press.

Roth, H. D. (2018). Cognitive attunement in the *Zhuangzi*. In Roger Ames and Carine Defoort (Eds.), *Having a word with Angus Graham at twenty-five years into his Immortality* (pp. 49–78). Honolulu, HI: University of Hawaii Press.

Sibu Congkan SBCK. (1919–1936). *The four branches of literature collection*. Shanghai: The Commercial Press.

Schipper, K. (2000). *The Taoist body*. (K. C. Duval, Trans.). Berkeley: University of California Press.

Sivin, N. (1978). On the word 'Taoist' as a source of perplexity. *History of Religions* 17(3/4), 303–330.

Yates, R. D. S. (1997). *Five lost classics: Tao, Huanglao, and Yin-yang in Han China*. New York: Ballantine Books.

CHAPTER 14

DAOIST MEDITATION

From 100 CE to the Present

LOUIS KOMJATHY

Note to Reader

This chapter uses Pinyin Romanization for Mandarin pronunciations of Chinese characters. Dao, Daoism, and Daoist derive from this system, while Tao, Taoism, and Taoist, which are still pronounced with a "d" sound, derive from the older Wade-Giles system. Daoist texts are cited according to Komjathy, 2002, with DZ referring to the received *Daozang* (*Tao-tsang*; Daoist Canon) and ZW referring to the *Zangwai daoshu* (Daoist Books Outside the Canon). Catalogue numbers for the *Daozang* parallel those of Kristofer Schipper and his colleagues. Unless otherwise indicated, all translations are my own.

Introduction

Considered as a whole, the diversity and complexity of Daoist (Taoist) meditation methods rival any fully developed contemplative system or religious tradition, such as those found in Buddhism, Christianity, or Hinduism. Although one of the least understood and least engaged of the major "world religions," Daoism (Taoism) represents a sophisticated soteriological system in which meditation has occupied and continues to occupy a central place. In fact, meditation and ritual are the two major forms of Daoist religious practice. The present chapter provides a general overview of the five major types of meditation, namely, apophatic meditation, ingestion, visualization, inner observation, and internal alchemy. Particular attention is given to historical background, associated movements and textual corpuses, as well as technical specifics. As apophatic meditation emerged within the context of the inner cultivation lineages of classical Daoism, and receives its own chapter in the present volume, this chapter devotes primary attention on the other four practices.

The Tradition of the Dao

The Daoist tradition consists of various adherents, communities, movements, and lineages committed to cultivating and realizing the Dao (Tao; Way), which is the sacred or ultimate concern of Daoists. As an emerging tradition, it began with the inner cultivation lineages of classical Daoism, which is the earliest Daoist religious community, in the Warring States period (480–222 BCE) and Early Han dynasty (202 BCE–9 CE), developed with the earliest distinct movements of organized Daoism in the Later Han dynasty (25–220 CE), and became systematized as a fully organized and integrated religious institution during the Period of Disunion (221–581) and Tang (618–907) and Song (960–1279) dynasties. The latter periods also involved increasing recognition of Daoism as a vital partner in Chinese culture, society, and politics. Broadly understood, Daoists are adherents of Daoism, the tradition of the Dao. Emphasis is placed on attuning oneself with and living through the Dao. For Daoists, the Dao has four primary characteristics: (1) source of everything (*yuan*); (2) unnamable mystery (*xuan*); (3) all-pervading sacred presence (*qi*); and (4) universe as transformative process (*hua*). Daoism does not have a founder, central text, or centralized authority (see Komjathy, 2013b, 2014a). Thus, the purpose of Daoist meditation centers on "realizing the Dao" (*dedao*), although the approach and characteristics vary depending on the specific system. As a more complete expression of Daoist views, one might further consider Daoist meditation in a larger sense of cultivation, embodiment, and transmission.

The Daoist tradition may be engaged through what I refer to as the "seven periods" and "four divisions" (see Komjathy, 2013b, 2014a), as depicted in figure 14.1.

The seven periods roughly correspond to major watersheds for Daoism in Chinese dynastic and post-dynastic history: (1) Warring States (480–222 BCE), Qin (221–206 BCE), and Early Han (202 BCE–9 CE); (2) Later Han (25–220 CE); (3) Period of Disunion (220–589) and Sui (581–618); (4) Tang (618–907), Song (Northern: 960–1127; Southern: 1127–1279), and Yuan (1260–1368); (5) Ming (1368–1644) and Qing (1644–1911); and (6) Republican (1912–49; 1949–present) and early Communist (1949–1978). I in turn divide the modern period into "early modern Daoism" (1912–1978) and "late modern Daoism" (1978–present), with the latter including contemporary expressions and developments.

Each of these periods saw the emergence of specific communities and movements. Briefly stated, classical Daoism encompasses the diverse communities and "schools" of the inner cultivation lineages as well as Huang-Lao dao (Way of the Yellow Emperor and Laozi). Major movements associated with early Daoism include Taiping (Great Peace) and Tianshi (Celestial Masters). Early medieval Daoism consisted of such important movements as Taiqing (Great Clarity), Shangqing (Highest Clarity), and Lingbao

Period	Division
1. Classical Daoism	Classical Daoism
2. Early Daoism	Early Organized Daoism
3. Early Medieval Daoism	
4. Late Medieval Daoism	Later Organized Daoism
5. Late Imperial Daoism	
6. Early Modern Daoism	Modern Daoism
7. Late Modern Daoism	

FIGURE 14.1 Seven Periods and Four Divisions of the Daoist Tradition

© Louis Komjathy, 2013, *The Daoist tradition: An introduction*, Bloomsbury Academic, an imprint of Bloomsbury Publishing Plc.

(Numinous Treasure). Late medieval Daoism consisted of a variety of internal alchemy movements, including Quanzhen (Ch'üan-chen; Complete Perfection) and so-called Nanzong (Southern School), as well as new deity cults and ritual movements. Late imperial and modern Daoism was dominated by Zhengyi (Cheng-i; Orthodox Unity; a.k.a. Tianshi) and Complete Perfection, though it also saw the emergence of major lineages of the latter as well as new lineages of internal alchemy. The constituents of global Daoism are a highly complex topic. Briefly stated, from a tradition-based and institutional perspective, global Daoism remains primarily an Orthodox Unity/Complete Perfection tradition. Orthodox Unity Daoism is largely a householder community consisting of married priests (male and female) and family lineages and primarily located in south and southeast China as well as Taiwan. Complete Perfection, including its Longmen (Dragon Gate) lineage, is primarily a monastic community consisting of celibate clergy and monastics (male and female) living in temples and monasteries throughout mainland China, Hong Kong, and Taiwan. There are also dynamic (and problematic) recent developments, including mediumistic cult influences, obscure family lineages, and diverse organizations.

For simplicity's sake, we might further speak of four basic divisions of Daoism: (1) classical Daoism; (2) early organized Daoism; (3) later organized Daoism; (4) modern Daoism. The rationale for this grouping is to distinguish historical developments, types of community, and distinctive models of practice. It draws our attention to the ways in which the inner cultivation lineages of classical Daoism differ from the householder, ascetic, and eremitic communities of early organized Daoism, as the Later Han dynasty witnessed the emergence of Daoism as an organized religious tradition with enduring institutions. Early organized Daoism may be distinguished from later organized Daoism based on the ascendance of a monastic model in the latter and the emergence of new models of practice, especially internal alchemy. Modern Daoism corresponds to the end of dynastic rule in China and the increasing influence of Western values and political ideologies. In its more contemporary form, it directs our attention toward Daoism as a global religious tradition with worldwide distribution and international adherence.

Here it should be mentioned that Daoism is the object of various Western fabrications, fictions, and fantasies, which are rooted in colonialist, missionary, and Orientalist legacies. The most epidemic of these is the inaccurate and outdated distinction between so-called "philosophical Daoism" and so-called "religious Daoism," the usage of which should be taken *ipso facto* as a misunderstanding concerning Daoism. As herein employed, "classical Daoism" replaces so-called "philosophical Daoism," while "organized Daoism" replaces so-called "religious Daoism." This revisionist framework allows individuals to engage the tradition in a more neutral and receptive, a more integrated and sophisticated manner. Readers should also note remnants of the old interpretive framework in the present volume, given that one chapter covers the fourth century BCE–second century CE, while this chapter covers the following two thousand years of history. That is, while Buddhism and Christianity are framed in terms of sub-traditions, and while Hinduism is examined through types of practice, Daoism is divided according to historical periodization that may obscure as much as reveal. However, this volume also evidences the influence of revisionist scholarship: It recognizes that meditation was a central dimension of the inner cultivation lineages of classical Daoism.

For present purposes, meditation has been a major form of Daoist religious practice from the beginning of the tradition and throughout its history. As discussed in the next section, there are diverse forms of Daoist meditation, which emerged during different periods, are associated with specific movements, and are documented in distinct textual corpuses.

Types of Daoist Meditation and Textual Corpuses

Before examining Daoist meditation in depth, it is important to recognize that "meditation," often referred to as *dazuo* ("engage in sitting") in Chinese, is a particular type of practice, and that practice, including meditation, cannot be reduced to technique. In my way of thinking, "praxis," used as an overarching technical and theoretical term, includes specific views, methods, experiences, and goals. That is, an integrated and sophisticated understanding of meditation must consider informing worldviews, including anthropology (personhood), psychology (consciousness), soteriology (ultimate purpose), and theology (ultimate reality), as well as associated experiences. These are interrelated and, in fact, inseparable as enacted, experiential, and lived activity in the world. Understood from a more comprehensive perspective, meditation usually is located in a larger religious and/or soteriological system. The latter includes aesthetics, community, material culture, place, posture, and so forth (see Komjathy, 2015, 2018, forthcoming).

We may begin by recognizing that there are at least five major types of Daoist meditation, with each emerging during a specific period of Daoist history and often associated with particular Daoist movements. They include apophatic or quietistic meditation, ingestion (*fuqi*), visualization (*cunxiang*), inner observation (*neiguan*), and internal alchemy (*neidan*). "Apophatic meditation" approximates a variety of Daoist technical terms, including *shouyi* (guarding the One), *xinzhai* (fasting the heart-mind), *zuowang* (sitting-in-forgetfulness), and *jingzuo* (quiet sitting) in later periods. (*Shouyi* eventually became a generic name for Daoist meditation and may, in turn, refer to a variety of methods, even visualization [see Kohn, 1989a; Komjathy, 2013b].) Associated with the inner cultivation lineages of classical Daoism, that is, the earliest Daoist religious community during the Warring States period (480–222 BCE) to the Early Han dynasty (202 BCE–9 CE), apophatic meditation emphasizes emptying and stilling the heart-mind and attaining mystical union with the Dao. It is primarily contentless, non-conceptual, and non-dualistic. Ingestion and visualization practices first appeared in the context of early and early medieval Daoism, from the Later Han dynasty (25–220 CE) to the Period of Disunion (220–589 CE). Ingestion generally involves bringing various energies (*qi* [*ch'i*]), such as solar, lunar, and astral effulgences (*jing*), into the body. Visualization involves imagining (actualizing?) the body in multiple ways, such as the five yin-organs (*zang*) as orbs of light or residences of deities. These practices are particularly associated with the Highest Clarity movement, although there are earlier precedents such as in the Great Clarity movement and *Huangting jing* (Scripture on the Yellow Court; DZ 331; DZ 332). Inner observation is a Daoist adaptation of Buddhist "insight meditation" (Pali: *vipassanā*; Skt.: *vipaśyanā*), which generally involves maintaining non-discriminating awareness of all phenomena. This practice became especially prominent in the Tang dynasty (618–907 CE) and integrated into the Daoist monastic and ordination system. Finally, internal alchemy emerged in fully systematized expressions in the later Tang and early Song dynasty (960–1279 CE). From that point forward, it became the primary form of Daoist meditation, although apophatic meditation remained foundational and central. Internal alchemy utilizes complex, often sequential stage-based techniques with the goal of complete psychosomatic transformation, or "immortality" in Daoist terms. It is especially associated with the so-called Southern School and Complete Perfection movements, including their various lineages.

These movements and associated meditation practices are expressed in specific Daoist textual corpuses. Here it should be mentioned that there is no central Daoist text. Daoist literature is best understood through movement- and lineage-specific textual corpuses and the *Daozang* (*Tao-tsang*; Daoist Canon). The latter, first compiled during the early medieval period, but with the received version dating to the late imperial period (1445/1607), is the primary Daoist textual collection and consists of about 1,500 texts (see Komjathy, 2002; Schipper & Verellen, 2004). Only a small portion of these texts address meditation and even a smaller percentage are "meditation manuals," that is, works that provide technical instruction (see Komjathy, 2015). These various texts are often anonymous and of unclear provenance. With respect to textual corpuses related to meditation, the *Laozi* (*Lao-tzu*; Book of Venerable Masters), also known as the *Daode jing* (*Tao-te ching*; Scripture on the Dao and Inner Power), and *Zhuangzi* (*Chuang-tzu*; Book of Master Zhuang) are the two central texts of classical Daoism, although Harold Roth and others include additional texts such as the "Xinshu" (Techniques of the Heart-mind) chapters of *the Guanzi* (*Kuan-tzu*; Book of Master Guan) (see Roth's chapter, this volume). References in the *Guanzi* and throughout the classical Daoist textual corpus to *xin*, which refers to both the physical heart and mind in a more abstract sense, are significant because the term becomes pivotal in Daoist "contemplative psychology" more generally; the heart-mind is considered the center of human personhood, the locus of intellectual and emotional activity, and the storehouse of spirit. In a habituated and agitated state ("ordinary mind") it leads to spiritual disorientation, while in a realized and stabilized state ("original mind") it leads to attunement with the Dao. The latter is related to "innate nature" (*xing*), one's original and inherent connection to the Dao. The *Scripture on the Dao and Inner Power* and the *Book of Master Zhuang* have, in turn, been highly influential in the later Daoist tradition (and beyond), with many Daoists reading them as providing guidance on meditation. For example, the passage on "sitting-in-forgetfulness" in chapter six of the *Book of Master Zhuang* became the basis for the eighth-century *Zuowang lun* (Discourse on Sitting-in-Forgetfulness; DZ 1036) (see Kohn, 1987, 2010). In terms of early organized Daoism, the Highest Clarity textual corpus, which incorporates technical terminology and methods from other contemporaneous and currently obscure religious communities, provides detailed information on ingestion, visualization, and what might be referred to as proto-*neidan*. Some representative works include the possibly third-century *Huangting jing* (Scripture on the Yellow Court; DZ 331; DZ 332) and fourth-century *Dadong zhenjing* (Perfect Scripture of Great Profundity; DZ 6) (see Robinet, 1989a, 1993), although the history of the former is complex and may be of "non–Highest Clarity" provenance. Inner observation developed under the influence of Buddhist insight meditation in later organized Daoism, specifically during the Tang dynasty. This technique is not associated with a particular Daoist movement, as Daoism became organized and systematized within the Tang Daoist monastic system, which also received imperial patronage (see Kohn, 2003). However, some key texts include the anonymous eighth-century *Dingguan jing* (Scripture on Concentration and Observation; DZ 400) and anonymous eighth-century *Neiguan jing* (Scripture on Inner Observation; DZ 641) (see Kohn, 1987, 1989b). These works are closely associated with what I have labeled the "Clarity-and-Stillness literature," of which the anonymous eighth-century *Qingjing jing* (Scripture on Clarity and Stillness; DZ 620) is most influential (see Komjathy, 2008a, 2013a, 2013b). As the name suggests, the latter text, which evidences strong influence from classical Daoism, emphasizes the cultivation of "clarity and stillness" (*qingjing*) through dedicated and prolonged Daoist meditation. That is, *qingjing* is both a practice and a meditative state/trait. Finally, internal alchemy became systematized during the late Tang and early Song dynasty. While the other types of Daoist meditation, especially quiet sitting, continued to exist and to be practiced independently, internal alchemy became more prominent from this point forward. Fully developed internal alchemy systems often incorporate all of the other techniques, namely, apophatic meditation, ingestion, visualization, and inner observation. The earliest "lineage" and textual corpus is known as "Zhong-Lü," which refers to the legendary immortals Zhongli Quan (second century CE?) and his supposed disciple Lü Dongbin (b. 798?). These texts are usually in the form of dialogic exchange and discourse records, with the anonymous tenth-century *Chuandao ji* (Anthology of Transmitting the Dao; DZ 263, j. 14–16; DZ 1309) being especially influential. In its latter expression, internal alchemy is associated with Complete Perfection and the so-called Southern School. Both textual corpuses are vast and complex (see Boltz, 1987; Schipper & Verellen, 2004; Komjathy, 2007, 2013a). Moreover, the authors often employ cryptic and esoteric poetry, which makes reconstructing the actual practices difficult (see Komjathy, 2007, 2013a). In any case, a representative and highly influential text of the Southern School is the eleventh-century *Wuzhen pian* (Chapters on Awakening to Perfection; DZ 263, j. 26–30; DZ 1017, j. 18) by Zhang Boduan (d. 1082). Like similar texts, this work was often read with accompanying Daoist commentaries in the later Daoist tradition. There are two additional developments that deserve note. First, during the later Song and Yuan dynasties, individuals began composing illustrated manuals of *neidan* practice (see Needham et al., 1983; Despeux, 1994; Baryosher-Chemouny, 1996), including ones that address what I have labeled the "Daoist alchemical body" (see Komjathy, 2008b, 2009, 2011). Second, the imperial period witnessed a gradual simplification and popularization of internal alchemy, represented in such texts as the late eighteenth-century *Huiming jing* (Scripture on Wisdom and Life-Destiny; ZW 131) by Liu Huayang (1735–1799) and the nineteenth-century stele *Neijing tu* (Diagram of Internal Pathways) commissioned by Liu Chengyin (d. 1894) (see Komjathy, 2008b, 2009, 2015). This process culminated in the modern Qigong (Ch'i-kung) movement (see Komjathy, 2006; Palmer, 2007), some practices of which incorporate elements from Daoist internal alchemy.

As Harold Roth addresses classical Daoist apophatic meditation in the **previous chapter**, here I concentrate on the later periods and movements of Daoist history, with particular attention to the technical specifics of the other four forms of meditation.

Technical Specifics

While the present chapter concentrates on the historical and technical specifics of Daoist meditation, with particular attention to methods, a few words are in order about the other dimensions. Generally speaking, Daoists have engaged in meditation as a solitary practice, although there are some communal forms (see Komjathy, 2013a, 2014b). Daoist meditation has been and is undertaken in caves, hermitages, monasteries, and temples, including private meditation rooms and occasionally meditation halls. Mountains have been and remain especially preferred practice locales (see Schipper, 1993; Komjathy, 2013b, 2014a). At these places, Daoist aesthetics and material culture mirrored traditional Chinese culture, with some parallels with that of pre-modern Japan. One major difference involved the presence of specifically Daoist art, themes, and symbolism. For example, a traditional monastic cell on Qingcheng shan (Azure Wall Mountain; Guanxian, Sichuan), which preserves the layout and possessions of a former famous monastic resident, contains an altar, small bed, desk, meditation mat and cushion, as well as scroll-mounted rubbings of the *Neijing tu* (Diagram of Internal Pathways) and *Xiuzhen tu* (Diagram for Cultivating Perfection) (author's field observations; see also Komjathy, 2013a). These scrolls derive from two highly influential late nineteenth-century steles housed at Baiyun guan (White Cloud Temple; Beijing); they depict the "Daoist alchemical body" and contain instructions on Daoist internal alchemy (*neidan*) (see Komjathy, 2008b, 2009, 2011). Considering embodiment, every type of meditation, whether Daoist or not, utilizes specific postures. That is, even in systems that primarily emphasize "consciousness" or "mind," practice is always *embodied*. As I have previously suggested, specific practices, communities, and traditions become embodied, both literally and symbolically, through specific practices (see Komjathy, 2015, 2018). In addition, it may be that aesthetics, community, posture, place, and the like are determinative in the efficacy of a given practice. In the case of Daoism, as far as current research goes it appears that the earliest posture involved sitting on heels in a manner paralleling the later and now widely disseminated Japanese *seiza* position. This is supported by archaeological materials (see Roth, 2015). Following the introduction of Buddhism during the Later Han dynasty, during the first to second century CE, Daoists increasingly adopted the full- and half-lotus posture (*jiafu zuo*; "sitting cross-legged"). This finds evidence in illustrations, art, and other forms of material culture. One lingering question involves the history and usage of furniture and other paraphernalia in Chinese culture. For example, some depictions show figures using small benches to increase the level of comfort while sitting on the heels. While Daoist meditation usually involves various seated postures, there are also standing, walking, and even sleeping practices.

Ingestion

Moving into the technical specifics of Daoist meditation, ingestion and visualization are closely connected. As mentioned, these forms emerged in early organized Daoism and are especially associated with the Highest Clarity movement, wherein they became incorporated into a larger soteriological system aimed at rarefication and self-divinization. They also became integrated into later Daoist *neidan* systems. Here it should be mentioned that ingestion methods also are part of Yangsheng (lit., nourishing life) practice, which usually refers to health and longevity techniques, and may be categorized as a form of "Daoist dietetics" (see Komjathy, 2013b, 2014a). In any case, ingestion, with the associated Chinese terms more literally meaning something like "eating *qi*," involves the absorption of seasonal and locality influences as well as astral effulgences. That is, it involves gathering terrestrial and celestial energies and

FIGURE 14.2 Ingesting Solar Effulgences

Source: *Yuyi jielin tu*, DZ 435

incorporating them into one's own body as energetic system. Some of the most well-known methods involve ingesting the energies of the five directions and of the sun, moon, and stars (figure 14.2).

Like visualization, Daoist ingestion methods usually utilize traditional Chinese cosmology, specifically the various Five Phase (*wuxing*) associations, namely, Wood/east/green/liver, Fire/south/red/heart, Earth/center/yellow/spleen, Metal/west/white/lungs, and Water/north/black (purple)/kidneys. They also tend to be time-specific. One key characteristic is the central importance of light (see Robinet, 1989a, 1993). This is so much the case that one might understand the practice as "nourishing on light" or "living on light."

A representative example is the technique known as "Method of Mist Absorption," which involves ingesting the so-called "five sprouts" (*wuya*). The method is early on described in various Highest Clarity and Numinous Treasure texts and was supposedly transmitted to the Highest Clarity medium Yang Xi (330–386) by Wei Huacun (251–334) (Robinet, 1989a, p. 165). According to the standard practice, one absorbs the *qi* of the five directions and locates the *qi* in the corresponding yin-organ. The method begins with swallowing saliva while chanting invocations to the original *qi* of the directions. At dawn, one faces the associated direction, usually beginning with the east, and visualizes the *qi* of that direction in its corresponding colors. A general mist in the beginning, it gradually forms into an orb of light. It then becomes more concentrated, during which it decreases in size and approaches the adept's body. Eventually the size of a pill, the sprout is swallowed and directed to its corresponding yin-organ. According to the late seventh-century *Fuqi jingyi lun* (Discourse on the Essential Meaning of Absorbing Qi; DZ 277; DZ 830; DZ 1032, j. 57) by Sima Chengzhen (647–735), the Twelfth Patriarch of Highest Clarity, there are five associated invocations.

The first and second lines of the invocations refer to the esoteric names of the corresponding external sprout (directional *qi*) and internal yin-organ (liver, heart, spleen, lungs, kidneys). The final lines are also esoteric names for corporeal locations and substances (root of upper teeth, root of lower teeth, root of molars, saliva inside the lips, saliva on the tongue). After chanting each invocation, one stimulates the salivary glands by rubbing various parts of the mouth with the tongue and swallows the saliva three times for each sprout.

As Isabelle Robinet (1989a, p. 166) has pointed out, the sprouts originally are the "germinal essences of the clouds" or "mist." They represent the yin principle of heaven—that is, yin within yang. They manifest in human saliva, again a yin element in the upper, yang part of the body ("heaven"). They help to nourish and strengthen the five yin-organs. They are tender, comparable to fresh sprouts of plants, and assemble at dawn in the celestial capital, from where they spread all over the universe until the sun begins to shine. Turning like the wheels of a carriage, they ascend to the gates of the nine heavens, from where they continue to the medium level of the world—to the Five Marchmounts ruled over by the Five Thearchs of the five directions—and finally descend into the individual adept. They thus pass through the three major levels of the cosmos, namely, heaven, earth, and humanity.

VISUALIZATION

Moving into visualization, Daoist methods are diverse and complex, often involving what might be understood as the "cosmicization" of the human body. They thus employ Daoist microcosmic/macrocosmic views of personhood. Some Daoist visualization techniques parallel ingestion practices by focusing on various Five Phase constituents (e.g., Five Marchmounts, Five Thearchs) as well as the sun, moon, and stars. Other forms of visualization center on esoteric Daoist pantheons, including inner body-gods associated with various corporeal locations. The latter are frequently described as a somatic landscape, which consists of mountains (spine and head), rivers (meridians), water (*qi* and body fluids), forests (liver), and so forth (see Needham et al., 1983; Schipper, 1993; Komjathy, 2008b, 2009, 2011).

A representative Daoist visualization focuses on the constellations, including the associated "gods" (divine presences) and astral effulgences. In the *Jinque dijun sanyuan zhenyi jing* (Scripture on the Perfect Ones of the Three Primes by Lord Golden Tower; DZ 253; cf. DZ 1314; trl. Andersen 1980), part of the original fourth-century Highest

FIGURE 14.3 Visualizing the Northern Dipper

Source: *Jinque dijun wudou sanyi tujue*, DZ 765, 16b

Clarity revelations, aspiring adepts are instructed to visualize the Northern Dipper (Big Dipper; Ursa Major) according to the method of "guarding the One" (*shouyi*), also referred to as "guarding the Three Ones" (*shou sanyi*), as shown in figure 14.3.

Within this method, the Daoist adept visualizes the Northern Dipper, associated with "fate" (*ming*) in the Daoist tradition, above his or her head. The seven visible stars are identified as follows (from bowl to handle): (1) Yangming (Yang Brightness); (2) Yinjing (Yin Essence); (3) Zhenren (Perfect One); (4) Xuanming (Mysterious Darkness); (5) Danyuan (Cinnabar Prime); (6) Beiji (North Culmen); and (7) Tianguan (Celestial Pass). The two lower stars of the dipper bowl rest in close proximity to the top of the head, while the handle extends forward so that the seventh star, called Celestial Pass, rests in front of the mouth. At the beginning of spring, one faces east; that is, one enters a posture of cosmological alignment based on the Five Phases (Wood/spring/east). One in turn visualizes the Three Ones, also known as the Three Primes or Three Purities (*sanqing*), in the dipper bowl. They ascend together to the fourth star, Mysterious Darkness, move to the seventh star, Celestial Pass, and wait there facing toward the adept's mouth. The adept then visualizes each one in sequence (upper, middle, lower) entering their respective corporeal locations (Niwan [center of head], Scarlet Palace [heart], Cinnabar Field [navel region]). In this way the Three Heavens and their corresponding gods become located in the Daoist adherent's very own body. The text, in turn, advises the Daoist aspirant to follow the same instructions for the commencements of the other seasons: *lixia* (Summer Begins; approx. May 5) facing south; *liqiu* (Autumn Begins; approx. August 8) facing west; and *lidong* (Winter Begins; approx. November 11) facing north. The corresponding time seems to be the same, namely, 11pm to 1am. There are thus seasonal, cosmological, and theological dimensions of the practice.

Inner Observation

A third major type of Daoist meditation is inner observation. As mentioned, this approach and practice emerged and developed during the late medieval period, specifically in the context of later organized Daoism and the Tang-dynasty monastic system. Inner observation is a Daoist adaptation of Buddhist insight meditation (Pali: *vipassanā*; Skt.: *vipaśyanā*; Chn.: *guan*). The latter is sometimes referred to as "mindfulness," although that term technically corresponds to the Pali *sati* (Chn.: *nian*). The relationship between calming meditation (Pali: *samatha*; Chn.: *zhi*) and insight meditation in late medieval Buddhism is complex (see Gregory, 1986; Donner & Stevenson, 1993). In considering the complex interactions, and potential cross-pollination, between Buddhism and Daoism, it is important to recognize that Daoist meditation methods resembling *samatha* far predate the introduction and Sinification of Buddhism (second–sixth centuries CE); Daoist emptiness- and stillness-based meditation is first documented in the texts of the inner cultivation lineages of classical Daoism (fourth–second centuries BCE). For present purposes, the influence of Buddhist *vipassanā* on Daoist *neiguan* is most relevant. Although the former is complex, it often involves non-discriminating awareness of all phenomena and realization of the three (Buddhist) characteristics of existence, namely, suffering, impermanence, and no-self (no-soul). The practice is documented in such seminal Southern ("Theravāda") Buddhist texts as the *Ānāpānasati Sutta* (Discourse on Mindfulness of Breathing; Majjhima Nikaya [MN] 118) and *Satipaṭṭhāna Sutta* (Discourse on the Foundations of Mindfulness; Majjhima Nikaya 10). These discuss the "Four Foundations of Mindfulness," namely, body (including breathing), feelings, mind, and *dhammas* (phenomena) (see, e.g., Shaw, 2015). In any case, as the name suggests, Daoist inner *observation* involves increasing attentiveness and awareness. While some late medieval approaches focus on the body as internal landscape, the foundational Daoist practice combines classical Daoist views with Buddhist-influenced notions of mind and existence (see Kohn, 1987, 1989b). This is clearly articulated in the influential, anonymous eighth-century *Neiguan jing* (Scripture on Inner Observation; DZ 641). By recognizing the emptiness of each and every phenomenon, whether physical or psychological, one enters a state of meditative absorption. This is mystical union with the Dao.

Internal Alchemy

Internal alchemy is another major type of Daoist meditation. "Internal alchemy" translates the Chinese term *neidan*, which literally means "inner pill" or "inner cinnabar." *Dan* technically refers to cinnabar (mercuric sulfide; HgS), which was a key ingredient of elixirs and alchemical formulas in early medieval Daoism. As internal alchemy developed during the late medieval period, it incorporated much of the language of external alchemy (*waidan*) as well as earlier esoteric terminology such as that found in the *Yijing* (Classic of Changes) and the previously mentioned *Scripture on the Yellow Court* (see Needham et al., 1983; Baldrian-Hussein, 1984; Robinet, 1989b; Pregadio & Skar, 2000; Komjathy, 2007, 2013a). Although the particular corporeal locations sometimes vary according to community, lineage, and text, common examples include Celestial Pond (mouth), Crimson Dragon (tongue), Jade Pillow (occiput), Mount Kunlun (head), Ocean of Qi (lower abdomen/navel region), Sweet Dew (saliva), and Yellow Court (spleen). Scholars in Daoist Studies adopted and continue to employ the language of Western alchemy because the transformation emphasized in *neidan* is analogous to the refinement and transmutation of base materials into their refined or divine counter-parts. Alchemical language, like "refining" and "smelting," also pervades the texts. That is, like transmuting base metals into gold, *neidan* involves refining the mundane self into a refined being capable of transcending death ("immortality"). The latter is often referred to as the "body-beyond-the-body," "immortal embryo," and/or "*yang*-spirit." Daoist internal alchemy, in turn, incorporates the other four types of meditation (apophatic meditation, ingestion, visualization, and inner observation) into a more comprehensive and integrated, stage-based system. Interestingly, there is intra-Daoist debate about the relevance and necessity of ingestion, sometimes seen as a form of quasi-external alchemy, in internal alchemy practice. As mentioned, the earliest *neidan* texts are either esoteric poetry or discourse records. It is only in the subsequent period, namely, the late Song and Yuan dynasties, that one finds illustrated manuals with detailed technical instructions.

Daoist internal alchemy utilizes a distinctive view of human personhood, which again draws from earlier Daoist training regimens. A standardized framework of "subtle anatomy and physiology" emphasizes the Three Fields (navel, heart, head) and the associated Three Treasures (vital essence, *qi*, and spirit). The Three Fields are often referred to as "elixir fields" (*dantian*), although the latter without qualification usually correspond to the navel region. Internal alchemy systems also utilize the organ-meridian system derived from classical Chinese medicine. This is an interconnected network of energy channels through the body. The standard system includes the twelve primary organ meridians and the "Eight Extraordinary Vessels." The latter, especially the Governing Vessel (perineum to crown-point [then upper-lip]) and Conception Vessel (perineum to lower-lip), are particularly emphasized in *neidan*. Daoist internal alchemy tends to emphasize sequential training utilizing specific methods, which must be practiced in order until completion; if one's practice is interrupted, one often is instructed to return to the beginning. In a condensed version, *neidan* involves three primary stages: (1) transforming vital essence into *qi*; (2) transforming *qi* into spirit; and (3) returning spirit to the Void (Dao). That is, a process of rarefication and self-divinization is involved.

It would require a much lengthier contribution in order to summarize a fully developed system of internal alchemy. Here I will simply provide two fairly representative examples, with details on one associated method. According to the mid- to late thirteenth-century illustrated *Dadan zhizhi* (Direct Pointers to the Great Elixir; DZ 244; see Komjathy, 2013a), a text attributed to the Third Patriarch of Complete Perfection Qiu Chuji (1148–1227), there are nine stages of alchemical transformation:

1. Coupling the Dragon and Tiger and Inverting the Five Phases
2. Firing Times of the Celestial Cycle and Inverting the Five Phases
3. Reversion of the Three Fields and Flying the Gold Essence behind the Elbow
4. Reversion of the Three Fields and the Reverted Elixir of the Gold *Ye*-Fluids
5. Five Qi Meeting the Origin and Refining Form into Greater Yang
6. Union of Spirit and Qi and the Consummation of the Three Fields
7. Five Qi Meeting the Origin and Refining Spirit to Enter the Summit
8. Initiating the Fire through Inner Observation and Refining Spirit to Merge with the Dao
9. Casting off the Husk to Ascend to Immortality and Transcending the Mundane to Enter the Sacred

In contrast, the late eighteenth-century *Huiming jing* (Scripture on Wisdom and Life-Destiny; ZW 131; see Komjathy, 2015) by Liu Huayang (1735–1799), a Chan Buddhist monk with connections to the Dragon Gate lineage of Complete Perfection and its later Wu-Liu sub-lineage, identifies eight stages in a Buddho-Daoist syncretism:

1. Sealing the Body
2. Activating the Dharma Wheel
3. Connecting the Governing and Conception Vessels
4. Coalescing the Immortal Embryo
5. Sending Out the Transcendent Spirit
6. Manifesting the Transformation Body
7. Entering Silence
8. Disappearing into Emptiness

Among these various transformative techniques, the Microcosmic Orbit (*xiao zhoutian*), also translated as the Celestial Cycle and referred to as the Dharma Wheel (*falun*) and Waterwheel (*heche*), is centrally important. In the standard practice, one circulates *qi* up the Governing Vessel (centerline of the spine) and down the Conception Vessel (centerline of the front torso), as illustrated in figure 14.4.

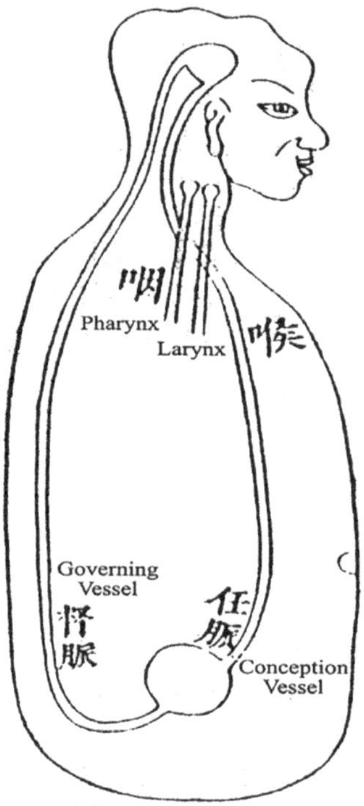

FIGURE 14.4 Diagram of Connecting the Governing and Conception Vessels
Source: *Huiming jing*, ZW 131, 5.880

Sometimes this involves moving point by point, beginning with the perineum or coccyx, moving up the spine to the occiput, continuing to the crown-point, and eventually ending at the navel region. In some systems, the spine is mapped in more esoteric ways, such as using the stars of the Northern Dipper, the Three Passes and a series of mountain ridges, or the Three Carts (see Komjathy, 2007, 2009, 2011, 2013a). In any case, the method activates a single energetic circuit in the body, and, from at least one perspective, unites all of the other meridians. This is because the Governing Vessel contains the *qi* of the yang-organ meridians, while the Conception Vessel contains the *qi* of the yin-organ meridians. As both alchemical systems indicate, the ultimate goal is the *creation* of a pure *yang*-spirit capable of transcending physical death, entering the Daoist immortal realms, and uniting with the Dao.

In terms of the modern and contemporary periods, Daoists continue to practice each of the five types of meditation, either independently or in combination. This largely depends on personal affinities as well as individual teachers and specific communities and lineages. The mostly widely practiced and disseminated methods are apophatic meditation and internal alchemy. Usually integrating the other four types, modern *neidan* systems tend to be relatively simplified versions indebted to late imperial Daoism. They often begin and end with quiet sitting. As mentioned, some *neidan* techniques have also been incorporated into contemporary Qigong. In any case, modern Daoists tend to meditate in the evening, usually just before going to sleep. The double-hour of *zi* (11pm–1am) is highly significant, as it corresponds to the winter solstice (yang [spiritual clarity] emerging from yin [stillness]). Based on my participant-observation ethnographic study of contemporary Complete Perfection Daoist monasticism and global Daoism, Daoists often sit in modified "Burmese" posture using the *ziwu* mudra (see Komjathy, 2013b). They usually meditate in isolation sitting in front of a personal altar for between 30–45 minutes, although the duration may increase dramatically in a state of meditative absorption. In fact, the possibility of complete forgetfulness is well illustrated in a famous Daoist folkloric tale. An aspiring Daoist adept hears that there is an advanced practitioner and realized teacher living in a remote hermitage. The aspirant resolves to seek out the teacher and become his disciple. Upon arriving at the hut, he knocks on the door, but no one answers. Smelling a fire and tea brewing, he decides to wait, believing that the teacher is out walking or gathering firewood and will soon return. However, an hour passes, and there is still no sign of activity. The adept wonders if something is wrong, so he opens the door. Thereupon he sees the teacher in deep meditation. He slowly and quietly shuts the door, resolving to return in a few hours. Again reaching the hermitage, he knocks on the door. Still there is no answer. The adept opens the door, only to discover the Daoist still meditating. The fire has burned out on its own and the tea is cold. The adept then simply sits down and begins meditating.

Living in Attunement with the Way

A more complete account of the various forms of Daoist meditation would have to address not only the informing views, but also the associated experiences and goals. As we have seen, Daoist meditation generally involves some type of rarefication or transformation, a movement from mundane being to realized being. Sometimes this involves simply sitting in silence and returning to one's innate nature, while at other times it centers on ingesting external energies or visualizing subtle or divine presences in the body. In other cases, one explores the hidden, somatic landscape or activates the body's subtle networks while undertaking a larger process of refinement and transmutation. In my way of thinking, the ultimate goal of Daoist meditation involves the formation of a new being, a type of transformed identity in which one literally embodies and circulates something else. From a Daoist perspective, this is not just *qi*, "vital breath" or "energy," in a general sense, but a particular type of *qi*. While the *qi* in question often includes geographical, solar, lunar, and stellar energies, Daoists often refer to the latter as "numinous *qi*" (*lingqi*) or the "*qi* of the Dao" (*daoqi*). It is a subtle or sacred presence that circulates through the body and that becomes embodied in one's life. Viewed comparatively and cross-culturally, such Daoist practices make radical claims about human potential and actualization. They point toward a type of identity that is transpersonal and non-dualistic, toward a way of life that is enacted and participatory. Here Daoist practitioners become infused with the numinous presence of the Dao. Daoist meditation techniques thus map out a path for living in attunement with the Dao, the Way that encompasses all other ways. Such is Daoist contemplative-being-in-the-world.

Glossary

Baiyun guan
白雲觀
Chuandao ji
傳道集
cunxiang
存想
Dadan zhizhi
大丹直指
Dadong zhenjing
大洞真經
dan
丹
dantian
丹田
Dao
道
Daode jing
道德經
Daozang
道藏
dazuo
打坐
dedao
得道
ding
定
Dingguan jing
定觀經
falun
法輪
fuqi
服氣
Fuqi jingyi lun
服氣精義論

guan
觀
Guanzi
管子
heche
河車
hua
化
Huang-Lao
黃老
Huangting jing
黃庭經
Huiming jing
慧命經
jiafu zuo
跏趺坐
jing (effulgences)
景
jing (stillness)
靜
jingzuo
靜坐
Jinque dijun
金闕帝君
Jinque dijun sanyuan zhenyi jing
金闕帝君三元真一經
Jinque dijun wudou sanyi tujue
金闕帝君五斗三一圖訣
Laojun
老君
Laozi
老子
Lingbao
靈寶
Liu Chengyin
劉誠印
Liu Huayang
劉華陽
Longmen
龍門
Lü Dongbin
呂洞賓
ming

命
Nanzong
南宗
neidan
內丹
neiguan
內觀
Neiguan jing
內觀經
Neijing tu
內經圖
nian
念
qi
氣
Qingcheng shan
青城山
qingjing
清靜
Qingjing jing
清靜經
Qigong
氣功
Qiu Chuji
丘處機
Quanzhen
全真
sanqing
三清
seiza
正座
Shangqing
上清
shou sanyi
守三一
shouyi
守一
Sima Chengzhen
司馬承禎
Taiping
太平
Taiqing
太清

Tianshi
天師
waidan
外丹
wuxing
五行
wuya
五芽
Wuzhen pian
悟真篇
xiao zhoutian
小周天
xin
心
xing
性
"Xinshu"
心術
xinzhai
心齋
Xiuzhen tu
修真圖
xuan
玄
Yangsheng
養生
yuan
元
Yuyi jielin tu
鬱儀結璘圖
zang
臟
Zhang Boduan
長伯端
Zhengyi
正一
zhi
止
Zhong-Lü
鐘呂
Zhongli Quan
鐘離權

Zhuangzi
莊子
zuowang
坐忘
Zuowang lun
坐忘論

References

Andersen, P. (1980). *The method of holding the three ones: A Taoist manual of the fourth century A.D.* London: Curzon.

Baldrian-Hussein, F. (1984). *Procédés secrets du Joyau magique—Traité d'alchimie taoïste du XI siècle.* Paris: Les Deux Océans.

Baryosher-Chemouny, M. (1996). *La quete de l'immortalité en Chine: Alchimie et payasage intérieur sous les Song.* Paris: Editions Dervy.

Boltz, J. (1987). *A survey of Taoist literature: Tenth to seventeenth centuries.* Berkeley: University of California, Institute of East Asian Studies.

Despeux, C. (1994). *Taoïsme et corps humain. Le Xiuzhen tu.* Paris: Guy Trédaniel.

Donner, N. & Stevenson, D. (1993). *The great calming and contemplation: A study and annotated translation of the first chapter of Chih-i's Mo-ho chih-kuan.* Honolulu: University of Hawaii Press.

Gregory, P. (Ed.). (1986). *Traditions of meditation in Chinese Buddhism.* Honolulu: University of Hawaii Press.

Kohn, L. (1987). *Seven steps to the Tao: Sima Chengzhen's Zuowang lun.* St. Augustin: Steyler Verlag.

Kohn, L. (1989a). Guarding the One: Concentrative meditation in Taoism. In L. Kohn (Ed.), *Taoist meditation and longevity techniques* (pp. 125–158). Ann Arbor: University of Michigan, Center for Chinese Studies.

Kohn, L. (1989b). Taoist insight practice: The Tang practice of *neiguan*. In L. Kohn (Ed.), *Taoist meditation and longevity techniques* (pp. 193–224). Ann Arbor: University of Michigan, Center for Chinese Studies.

Kohn, L. (2003). *Monastic life in medieval Daoism.* Honolulu: University of Hawaii Press.

Kohn, L. (2010). *Sitting in oblivion: The heart of Daoist meditation.* Dunedin, FL: Three Pines Press.

Komjathy, L. (2002). *Title index to Daoist collections.* Cambridge, MA: Three Pines Press.

Komjathy, L. (2006). Qigong in America. In L. Kohn (Ed.), *Daoist body cultivation* (pp. 203–235). Cambridge, MA: Three Pines Press.

Komjathy, L. (2007). *Cultivating perfection: Mysticism and self-transformation in early Quanzhen Daoism.* Leiden: Brill.

Komjathy, L. (2008a). *Handbooks for Daoist practice.* 10 vols. Hong Kong: Yuen Yuen Institute. (Original work published 2003).

Komjathy, L. (2008b). Mapping the Daoist body: part I: The *Neijing tu* in history. *Journal of Daoist Studies* 1, 67–92.

Komjathy, L. (2009). Mapping the Daoist body: part II: The text of the *Neijing tu*. *Journal of Daoist Studies* 2, 64–108.

Komjathy, L. (2011). The Daoist mystical body. In T. Cottai & J. McDaniel (Eds.), *Perceiving the divine through the human body: Mystical sensuality* (pp. 67–103). New York: Palgrave Macmillan.

Komjathy, L. (2013a). *The way of complete perfection: A Quanzhen Daoist Anthology*. Albany: State University of New York Press.

Komjathy, L. (2013b). *The Daoist tradition: An introduction*. London & New York: Bloomsbury Academic.

Komjathy, L. (2014a). *Daoism: A guide for the perplexed*. London & New York: Bloomsbury Academic.

Komjathy, L. (2014b). Daoist clepsydra-meditation: Late medieval Quanzhen monasticism and communal meditation. In H. Eifring (Ed.), *Hindu, Buddhist and Daoist meditation* (pp. 185–214). Oslo, Norway: Hermes Academic Publishing.

Komjathy, L. (Ed.). (2015). *Contemplative literature: A comparative sourcebook on meditation and contemplative prayer*. Albany: State University of New York Press.

Komjathy, L. (2018). *Introducing contemplative studies*. Hoboken, NJ & West Sussex, UK: Wiley-Blackwell.

Komjathy, L. (Forthcoming). Praxis. In T. Knepper & G. Kopf (Eds.), *Global-critical philosophy of religion*. New York: Springer Publishing Company.

Needham, J., et al. (1983). *Science and civilisation in China*. Vol. V: *Chemistry and chemical technology*. Part 5: *Spagyrical discovery and invention: Physiological alchemy*. Cambridge: Cambridge University Press.

Palmer, D. (2007). *Qigong fever: Body, science, and utopia in China*. New York: Columbia University Press.

Pregadio, F., & Skar, L. (2000). Inner alchemy (*neidan*). In L. Kohn (Ed.), *Daoism handbook* (pp. 464–497). Leiden: Brill.

Robinet, I. (1989a). Visualization and ecstatic flight in Shangqing Taoism. In L. Kohn (Ed.), *Taoist meditation and longevity techniques* (pp. 159–191). Ann Arbor: Center for Chinese Studies, University of Michigan.

Robinet, I. (1989b). Original contributions of *neidan* to Taoism and Chinese thought. In L. Kohn (Ed.), *Taoist meditation and longevity techniques* (pp. 297–330). Ann Arbor: Center for Chinese Studies, University of Michigan.

Robinet, I. (1993). *Taoist meditation: The Mao-shan tradition of great purity*. (J. Pas and N. Girardot, Trans.). Albany: State University of New York Press.

Roth, H. (2015). Daoist apophatic meditation: Selections from the classical Daoist textual corpus. In L. Komjathy (Ed.), *Contemplative literature* (pp. 89–143). Albany: State University of New York Press.

Schipper, K. (1993). *The Taoist body*. (K. C. Duval, Trans.). Berkeley: University of California Press.

Schipper, K., & Verellen, F. (Eds.). (2004). *The Taoist canon: A historical guide*. Chicago: University of Chicago Press.

Shaw, S. (2015). Southern Buddhist meditation: The *Ānāpānasati Sutta*. In L. Komjathy (Ed.), *Contemplative Literature* (pp. 265–306). Albany: State University of New York Press.

PART III

VARIETIES OF MEDITATIVE PRACTICES AND EXPERIENCES

CHAPTER 15

RELAXATION AND MEDITATION

AYESHA NATHOO

Introduction

The relationship between meditation and relaxation is contentious. As pioneer of modern mindfulness meditation Jon Kabat-Zinn asserted in his best-selling book *Coming to Our Senses*: "[mindfulness] meditation is not relaxation spelled differently. Perhaps I should say that again...Meditation is not relaxation spelled differently" (Kabat-Zinn, 2005, p. 58). However, arguing that "meditation is not relaxation" (or indeed that it is) implies a common and static understanding of these terms. As this chapter will demonstrate, relaxation and meditation have been fluid constructs, denoting a diverse set of techniques and ideologies that have variously tessellated, overlapped, and disconnected.

Contemporary mindfulness meditation practitioners often acknowledge relaxation as a common, pleasant, but unintentional "by-product" of meditation, albeit one that shares little or no emphasis on the supposed fundamental objectives of meditation such as "the cultivation of inquiry or insight" (Shapiro, 2009, p. 602). But this distinction and relationship between relaxation and meditation is ambiguous: As the Vietnamese Zen Buddhist monk and peace activist Thich Nhat Hanh recently declared in his popular book *How to Relax*: "You need insight in order to relax" (Hanh, 2015, p. 41).

Among contemporary Western populations, meditation and relaxation are most commonly connected through their functioning as therapeutic and, in particular, "stress management" techniques. In a large part this association builds on Harvard cardiologist Herbert Benson's seminal work outlined in *The Relaxation Response* (Benson, 1975). Here he proposed common underlying physiological changes resulting from a diversity of relaxation and meditation techniques, including progressive relaxation, Autogenic Training (AT), yoga, and Transcendental Meditation (TM). However, as I will demonstrate, prior to Benson's work, relaxation and meditation were terms that were used interchangeably by some, and keenly differentiated by others, as interest in and demand for these practices grew among twentieth-century health-seeking populations.

This chapter does not intend to provide a comprehensive overview or assessment of the commonalities and differences between the myriad relaxation and meditation methods practiced today, nor to determine the merits or drawbacks of specific techniques, their proposed psychophysiological effects, or the neurobiological pathways by which they operate. Instead, with a focus on the Anglo-American context, I will present a cultural-historical account of how and why notions of relaxation and meditation became variously entangled and differentiated in the course of the twentieth century. I will demonstrate the extent to which contemporary secularized meditation methods, including TM and mindfulness, connect to and build upon prior therapeutic relaxation ideologies, strategies, and structures. This is a generally overlooked historical aspect of meditation, as practiced by modern Western populations, that tends to focus either on the "authentic" interpretations of ancient teachings or on the biographies of individual pioneers and popularizers of contemporary meditative practices.

In European and North American contexts, meditation and relaxation methods have been most keenly developed and sought for their therapeutic potential: to address specific physical and mental health concerns, to manage the strains of everyday living, and to enhance well-being. The WHO's definition of health—as "a state of complete physical, mental, and social well-being and not merely the absence of disease or infirmity"—and the more recent designation of mental health, as "a state of well-being in which every individual realizes his or her own potential, can cope with the normal stresses of life, can work productively and fruitfully, and is able to make a contribution to her or his community," provide telling insights into the aspirations of modern populations and the uptake of strategies adopted to achieve sound health (WHO, 2001, 2006). This is particularly the case for Western ageing populations, striving to be "better than well," whilst individuals and healthcare systems become overburdened by escalating incidence of chronic physical and mental ill-health. Although the WHO definitions of health are universally declared, they are culturally and historically embedded, and tend to reflect the values and concerns of the most influential members. Likewise, popular relaxation and meditation practices in the West have been largely reformulated for a relatively narrow demographic—predominantly white, middle-class city dwellers—seeking to further culturally specific socio-economic and therapeutic agendas. From early twentieth-century formulations of therapeutic relaxation to the late twentieth-century development of the "mindfulness movement," this chapter will demonstrate the ways in which relaxation and meditation have been interwoven into the tapestry of modern healthy living.

Relaxation and Meditation: Constructing the Therapeutic Potential

Relaxation methods were taken up by Western populations through parallel developments in the late nineteenth and early twentieth centuries, notably "Autogenic Training" and neuromuscular relaxation techniques, as well as practices influenced by New Thought. The breathing, movement, and relaxation teachings of the New Thought-inspired Boston writer, Annie Payson Call (1853–1940), developed a particularly wide following among middle-class women, as "nerve training" and different gymnastic and health movements propagated in America and Europe into the early decades of the twentieth century. Call's relaxation techniques were influenced by a number of traditions, including Transcendentalism, Swedenborgism, mesmerism, and the psycho-physical culture of Delsartism (Capps, 2009; Andrick, 2012). Together with other "suggestive therapeutics" linked to New Thought healing movements, affirmations, visualizations, and concentration methods were rendered to further spiritual and corporeal health. Philosopher and physician William James, who fundamentally shaped the nascent discipline of psychology, paid homage to such strategies in his lecture "The Gospel of Relaxation" (James, 1899).[1] According to James, relaxation was central to a fulfilling spiritual life. He personally endorsed Call, and her publications *Power Through Repose* (1891) and *As a Matter of Course* (1895), and supported her systems of both muscular and "moral relaxation"—which he described as "dropping things from the mind, and not 'caring' " (Saumaa, 2017, p. 74).

Many early Anglo-American relaxation advocates and disciples of Western esotericism, including Call, were influenced by Indian religious worldviews and practices (Albanese, 2007). Nonetheless, what was created was a distinctly modern, Westernized set of ideologies and techniques that in the most part bore little resemblance to premodern Indian contexts and traditions. While often promoted as encapsulating authentic age-old "Eastern wisdom," the "spiritual relaxation" techniques and comparable methods that are still routinely incorporated into today's modern yoga-meditation-relaxation practice derive in a large part from this late-nineteenth century hybridization (Singleton, 2005, 2007; Harrington, 2008).

Meanwhile, in Europe, a technique that gained considerable currency from the 1930s was "Autogenic Training" (AT), devised by the German neurologist Johannes Heinrich Schultz (1884–1970). Although Schultz did not himself characterize it specifically as a relaxation technique (but rather a self-hypnotic procedure), AT has subsequently been understood and applied as an archetypal relaxation method. Influenced by yoga and

[1] James borrowed the phrase "The Gospel of Relaxation" from the title of an earlier speech by Herbert Spencer. See Sutton (2012) for an analysis of how James's multiple experiences as a patient of various "mind-cure" healers significantly informed his philosophical worldview.

Japanese methods of Zen meditation, the therapeutic effects of hypnosis and autosuggestion, psychoanalytical frameworks and the psychosomatic research of psychiatrist Oscar Vogt (1870–1959), Schultz devised a therapeutic technique involving "passive concentration" combined with verbal formulae and mental images to induce a state of relaxation (Kanji, 1997; Linden, 2007). These formulae suggested bodily sensations that subjects undergoing hypnosis had commonly self-reported, for example warmth and heaviness in the extremities and coolness of the forehead. "Passive concentration" involved concentration on inner sensations rather than environmental stimuli; not forcing but allowing sensations to happen in an accepting way, without judgement, preference, or criticism; observing rather than manipulating. Schultz claimed this technique gained therapeutic effects comparable to hypnosis but by being self-induced (autogenic meaning self-generated), it did away with the need for a hypnotist.[2] Schultz published his method and its associated clinical applications in the early 1930s (Schultz, 1932), gaining attention in Germany and continental Europe, especially among psychotherapists. However, it was not until Schultz's teachings were elaborated, systematized and made available in English by the physician Wolfgang Luthe (1922–1985), that AT disseminated more widely in America and Britain (Schultz & Luthe, 1959; Luthe, 1963).

Contemporaneous to Schultz's advancement of AT was the pioneering development of neuromuscular relaxation therapy by the Chicago physician Edmund Jacobson (1888–1983). There was personal animosity between the two men, stemming from Schultz's overt anti-Semitism, but they also clashed intellectually in their characterization of relaxation.[3] Jacobson's seminal texts, *Progressive Relaxation: A Physiological and Clinical Investigation of Muscular States and Their Significance in Psychology and Medical Practice* (1929), technically written for a specialist biomedical audience, and his widely popular *You Must Relax: A Practical Method of Reducing the Strains of Modern Living* (1934) are foundational to modern understandings and applications of relaxation therapy. Jacobson contended that it was impossible to be both tense and relaxed in body or mind at the same time. Neuromuscular tension, he asserted, was responsible for a host of physical and mental ailments—ranging from high blood pressure to anxiety—which could be prevented and alleviated by methodically releasing this tension. He devised his method of progressive relaxation to achieve these ends, training patients to systematically finely recognize and release their muscular tension. Cultivating this proprioceptive skill was key, and Jacobson's method involved regular training by a physician for months in addition to one or two hours of daily home practice. Subsequent practitioners advocated modified and shortened versions of his technique, but the efficacy of Jacobson's original method was reliant on this long, thorough training (Lehrer, 1982).

Jacobson endeavored to redefine what was understood by "relaxation," away from the popular connotations of recreation, laziness, or even rest, instead to denote "tension

[2] For a comprehensive history of hypnotism, see Gauld (1992).

[3] Schultz worked for the fascist German Medical Society for Psychotherapy, run by the cousin of the Nazi military leader Hermann Goering.

control." In a period during which the "rest cure" for neurasthenia and hysteria was still widely prescribed, and industrial "rest pauses" were being introduced to increase worker efficacy, Jacobson argued that one could be resting (or indeed sleeping) without reaping the benefits of relaxation due to residual muscular-skeletal tension.[4] Jacobson's neuromuscular relaxation, or "scientific relaxation" as he also termed it, was demonstrable through the use of laboratory equipment, which made tension both visible and measurable. He built his own neuro-voltmeter or electromyography (EMG) equipment, capable of detecting miniscule changes in the electrical activity of muscles that signified tension (Kroker, 2003). Although this was a precursor to later biofeedback technology, Jacobson did not encourage reliance on any device that would detract from the body's own sensitivity to tension. The equipment was used to objectively display the workings of his method on controlling states of tension.

For Jacobson, his method was a scientific enterprise, and he was keen to differentiate it from the esoteric work of Annie Payson Call and other "followers of certain cults." While recognizing that Call helped people to "cultivate poise and to use relaxing exercises" and was "in certain practical respects highly commendable," Jacobson lamented that this "follower of Swedenborg" did not have interests that were "scientific" (Jacobson, 1934, pp. 44–45). Similarly, Jacobson keenly separated his method from positive thinking and autosuggestive methods, especially "Coué and pseudo-religious cults which teach the sufferer to say 'All is well,' whatever the conditions."[5] By contrast, he declared, "during treatment by relaxation…The purpose is not to palliate the unavoidable hardships of life but to recognize them clearly and to live through them successfully…the aim is to reduce excess emotion so that adjustment can be made to the source of grief or anxiety with such calm that health and efficiency are not seriously affected" (Jacobson, 1934, pp. 123–124).

Jacobson's emphasis on health, success, and efficiency betray a historically and culturally embedded set of concerns directed at "high tension living," fatigue and nervousness, characteristic of an individualistic, competitive, modern, urban way of life. Although the condition of "neurasthenia," commonly known as "Americanitis," typified by exhaustion, was a diagnostic label falling out of fashion in the interwar period, the associated symptoms and concerns remained widespread (Gijswijt-Hofstra & Porter, 2001; Schuster, 2011). Relaxation was designed as a therapeutic aid to such conditions that Jacobson believed to derive from excessive chronic tension. Bettering individual health and increasing efficiency, two primary goals of his relaxation method, have had a significant influence on the development and use of later comparable methods put to use in neoliberal economies. In this respect, perhaps more significant than his systematic method of progressive relaxation, only achievable through lying down for long periods, was Jacobson's delineation of "differential relaxation," applicable to everyday living.

[4] The "rest cure" was originally devised by neurologist Silas Weir Mitchell in the 1870s–1880s, involving weeks of bed rest, feeding on a fatty, milk-based diet, and isolation from friends and family.

[5] Jacobson here is referring to the French pharmacist Emilé Coué (1857–1926), who introduced a popular method of autosuggestion involving the repetition of the phrase: "every day in every way I am getting better and better."

Differential relaxation involved efficient activity, using the minimum amount of energy or effort (and hence holding the least amount of tension) required for the task at hand. Jacobson noted common occurrences of excess tension in daily life including individuals who "gesticulate unnecessarily, speak rapidly or with a shrill pitch, shift or turn about excessively." Conversely, he took heed of the "speaker with a trained voice [who] does not tire even after prolonged effort if he keeps his throat differentially relaxed" or the "clever acrobat [who] produces an impression of grace and of ease by relaxing such muscles as he does not require" (Jacobson, 1934, pp. 106–107).

Indeed, the performing arts and speech therapy widely adopted forms of relaxation training. In 1920s Britain, Frances Archer (wife of playwright William Archer), who had learnt therapeutic relaxation methods directly from Annie Payson Call in Boston, started a "nerve-training colony" specifically for actors (Caton & Archer, 1936). Combining Archer's teachings with Jacobson's, speech therapists M. A. Richardson and E. J. Boom established relaxation classes in the 1930s and popularized relaxation therapies through their book *Relaxation in Everyday Life* (1938). They advised on treatments for conditions such as stammering, insomnia, ulcers, asthma, and hypertension that became prototypical conditions within the developing field of "psychosomatic medicine" (Browne, 2000). While Jacobson focused primarily on therapeutic gain, and helping productive, efficient individuals to better prosper, Boome and Richardson (1938) also identified the potential wider societal benefits of relaxation. Suggesting relaxation training for teachers, nurses, and parents, they envisaged a means by which to positively affect wider environments and cultures of care whereby relaxed modes of being would not only support individuals but osmotically impact on students, patients, and households.

In sum, in the early decades of the twentieth century, "relaxation" was given a new set of meanings that diverged from prior vernacular connotations implying recreation or laziness. Instead, relaxation became a cultivated set of skills, holding great therapeutic potential, which could be incorporated into high-tension everyday living. Therapeutic relaxation denoted a diverse collection of techniques with various spiritual and secular scientific ideological underpinnings. Neuromuscular relaxation, AT, and New Thought–inspired methods such as Call's were key branches that influenced the mid-century development and amalgamation of modern yoga, relaxation, and meditation methods. As the next section will discuss, these techniques particularly appealed to specific therapeutic communities and demographics.

Women, Modern Yoga, and Therapeutic Relaxation

During the mid-twentieth century, middle-class women became key consumers of relaxation instruction, in part continuing in the tradition of earlier health and fitness movements. In Britain, women's interest in relaxation training was largely connected to the interwar work of obstetrician Grantly Dick-Read, who introduced relaxation exercises as a means to prepare for and experience a "natural childbirth" (Dick-Read, 1933; Nathoo, 2016). Working within a socio-political context pervaded by eugenic concerns regarding the fitness of the population, Dick-Read postulated that the relatively low reproduction rates of middle-class women were due to their fear of the pain of childbirth (Moscucci, 2003). This fear caused excessive tension, which in turn caused undue pain. Breathing exercises and muscular relaxation techniques, he proposed, were a means of breaking this fear-tension-pain cycle. Although ostracized by his professional colleagues, popular support for Dick-Read's work led to the establishment of the National Childbirth Trust (NCT; originally the Natural Childbirth Association) in 1954 (Kitzinger, 1990). The development of the field of obstetric physiotherapy, together with the work of the NCT, helped routinize relaxation training within antenatal care. In part stemming from its application during childbirth, to counteract pain and tension, relaxation training was further developed for pain management more generally, and for treating anxiety.

Physiotherapists and antenatal teachers, who had previously taught relaxation within the narrow context of childbirth, extended their teachings to wider audiences through a variety of teaching resources. These included books, pamphlets, cassettes, magazines, and newspaper articles, as well as radio and television programs and classes (Nathoo, 2020). Relaxation methods were increasingly promoted and sought for the prevention and treatment of supposed tension-related ailments, such as migraines and insomnia, and as a possible alternative to taking pharmaceutical drugs such as the minor tranquillizers that were widely prescribed to women, in particular, from the mid-1950s. Many attendees of early relaxation classes were middle-class housewives, keen to better manage their responsibilities as mothers and wives and to improve their own states of health and well-being.

As Newcombe (2007) has detailed, demand for yoga teaching was also largely generated by a similar section of society for comparable reasons. Popular writings of modern yoga practitioners demonstrate well one of the central ways in which popular understandings of meditation and relaxation were brought together. In the late 1940s, one early yoga advocate, Desmond Dunne, who started the first yoga school in England and later moved to the United States, characterized the most important element of yoga as "deep relaxation," achieved through adopting the position and practice of *śavāsana*—or "Death Pose"—that brought "deep, soothing rest" to "the ancients." Nonetheless, in *Deep Relaxation: The Yogism Technique Based on Relaxation of the Voluntary Muscles* he contended, "little is revealed about Savasana in the old Sanskrit texts beyond the fact that the Yogis abstracted their minds from their bodies and passed into a deep, trance-like sleep" (Dunne, ca. 1950, p. 16). His method, therefore, was derived from inferring actions and intentions from the yogic postures, studying animals relaxing in their "natural state," in addition to personal experience and current scientific research on muscular tension. Although Jacobson is not acknowledged, there is clear resonance with his work, as well as influences from visualization and auto-suggestive techniques.

Dunne advocated his method of "Deep Relaxation" as an antidote to "High Tension"—the "most lethal threat to human life... [that] accounts for more deaths than all the diseases treated by our hospitals, or all the devilish inventions of our perverted age" (the latter, alluding to the atomic bomb). Relaxation was delineated as a key to a long life and happiness, a "cure for a great many ailments" and a "preventative against all manner of sickness of mind, body and estate. For even our worldly success is influenced by our ability to relax deeply." In addition, he espoused the argument that mid-twentieth-century living was detrimentally characterized by a "fear of silence... solitude... and contemplative thought," and presented Deep Relaxation as a means to stop avoiding and instead embrace such essential human states (Dunne, ca. 1950, p. 51).

Dunne published widely on both sides of the Atlantic from the 1950s, including *Yoga Made Easy* in 1961, specifically for an American readership, which advertised on its sleeve: "In this book, the ancient Asian discipline of yoga is adapted to the American way of life—to let you benefit from nature's own way of maintaining physical and mental health." The book presented a chapter on Deep Relaxation as the "first step toward serenity and health" and Meditation as the "final step toward true self mastery." Here the two practices are differentiated but intimately connected, and Dunne states that "without relaxation neither Deep Concentration nor Meditation are at all possible." The methods and applications prescribed by Dunne formed part of the growing genre of "self-help" publications by authors and practitioners writing for Western audiences in the postwar decades, many of which linked together and helped formulate popular understandings of yoga, meditation, and relaxation. As one mid-century popular relaxation book, *A New Way to Relax*, outlined: "Relaxation... means far more than supple muscles and freedom from fatigue. It means the ability to bend with the storm... A person who learns how to relax completely—or meditate, as the Eastern teachers call it—acquires the capacity of freeing himself from fears and useless brooding over bad experiences" (Roon, 1951, p. 252). Similar sentiments were shared, for example, in Tony Crisp's *Yoga and Relaxation*, where he described relaxation as something to be "realised" and used the terms relaxation, meditation and yoga synonymously: "After practising these methods of relaxation or Yoga... certain principles will be seen... Relaxation is the absence of personal effort. Yoga is conscious union with the unconditional" (Crisp, 1970, p. 59).

The therapeutic employment of ostensibly ancient Oriental wisdom also resulted in part from the contributions of Westernized Indian practitioners who reformulated their native traditions to appeal to modern Western audiences. In 1960s Britain, for example, "Yoga-Relaxation" consultant Professor Gopal S. Puri promoted his philosophies and practices through classes, demonstrations, talks, and publications including: *Yoga-Relaxation-Meditation: A Western-Trained Biologist Takes a New Look at an Age Old Eastern Science*. Alongside photographs of him meeting the pope and other dignitaries, and endorsements for his cause: "to obtain 'Peace on Earth and Goodwill to all men,'" this booklet provided explanations and descriptions of the methods and aims of yoga. "Pratihara relaxation" was one such example, referring to the "withdrawal of energy and consciousness from organs of the body," resulting in "the magnetisation of the local part and eventually the whole nervous system giving immense relief from tension" (Puri, 1974, p. 32). Manifestly drawing on mesmerism, auto-suggestion, and modern neuromuscular relaxation techniques, Puri's teachings were framed as reconciling "ancient forms of wisdom" with the cultural authority of modern science.

Similarly, Bombay-born Yogini Sunita, a trained Indian classical dancer, concert pianist, and a former student of the Tibetan yogi known as Narainswami, initiated a local following in Birmingham for her teachings of "Pranayama Yoga" (Newcombe, 2014). Sunita's central teachings included bodily Deep Relaxation, as well as the "slip second" mental relaxation exercise involving "learning to live for the present moment" and detaching the mind "from your family...from your friends...and from your work." As Sunita philosophized: "The past and future, faced continually, are really the 'present'.... There is nothing, but *nothing*, to compare with living for the present moment, with all its pangs, and even the height and depth of emotion" (Sunita, 1971, p. 14). She established The Yoga Relaxation Centre for Great Britain in 1962 and published *Pranayama Yoga: The Art of Relaxation* in 1965, which went through several additional reprints after her untimely death in 1970. Promoted as "more than a textbook...a guide to a new way of life," Sunita prefaced *Pranayama Yoga* by explaining: "this particular form of Yoga is non-religious, non-political and non-competitive... [and] gives the ability to face the ruthless demands of the Rat Race, without fatigue in mind or body" (Sunita, 1971, p. 7). In line with other secular relaxation practices, here yoga was utilized for its therapeutic potential and to help people succeed in, without necessarily needing to change, their life contexts and the demands placed upon them.

The Science of Stress and Coping with Modern Life

As is well documented, yoga and meditation practices became an integral part of the 1960s and 1970s New Age movement and were absorbed into various countercultural modes of operation, embracing alternative ways of living that to varying degrees aimed to challenge or "drop out" of capitalist modes of operation (Heelas, 1996). Nonetheless, a significant proportion of people who sought to learn these techniques did not identify with countercultural currents but took an instrumentalist approach to these methods in order to individually manage and indeed prosper within the status quo. Neoliberal agendas in the Thatcher-Reagan era compounded but did not instigate this trend, which had been espoused by therapeutic relaxation practitioners since the early decades of the twentieth century. Jacobson, for example, advocated his technique as a means to reap the benefits of modern civilization "without burning the candle at both ends" (Jacobson, 1934, p. 8). And popular texts such as *Relax and Be Successful* (1951) and *The Art of Relaxed Living* (1955), by relaxation practitioner James Hewitt, promoted relaxation to counter nervous exhaustion, to increase energy and happiness, and to promote "success."

The rhetoric of relaxation was thereby routinely adopted by Western yoga and meditation popularizers. The reasons for this included relaxation's deepening position and connotations as an established, secular, and increasingly medically and scientifically supported set of practices, familiar to and deemed suitable for mainstream Western publics. New psychological models pertaining to an individual's means and methods of "coping," alongside the influential research relating to the science of "stress," driven by endocrinologist Hans Seyle (1907–1982), gave fresh terminology, scientific legitimation, and popular support for these practices (Jackson, 2013). Under this paradigm, stressful environments were not in and of themselves problematic, as they could be modulated by the way in which an individual coped with, responded to, or adapted to external stressors. Relaxation was variously presented as a safe and effective method for developing calmer, happier, more efficient, and fruitful ways of living within perpetually stress-inducing environments.

For such reasons, interest in relaxation and meditation teachings steadily increased among working men and women. As a means of addressing growing incidence of chronic diseases afflicting Western populations, public health measures started to focus on campaigns for "healthy lifestyles" and the individual's responsibility to reduce their own "risk factors." As with relaxation, physical and mental health was constructed as being achievable through a certain way of living. In line with the much publicized work on the links between personality types and incidence of heart disease, "Type A" personalities—typified by competitive, middle-aged male executives operating under intense and constant pressure—were deemed to be a population particularly at risk of heart attacks.[6] The links between hypertension, heart disease and "stress" remained contentious among the biomedical community throughout the twentieth century, but certainly in the popular imaginary, by the 1970s chronic stress was considered to be a "risk factor," considerably detrimental to health and well-being. As had been claimed by practitioners from the early twentieth century, relaxation methods were put forward as a way to slow down, reduce tension, and live happier, healthier, and indeed longer lives.

By the early 1970s, relaxation classes for both men and women were part of the social fabric in Britain, offered through organizations such as Stress Watch and the charity Relaxation for Living (Nathoo, 2016). These "physical relaxation" courses involved weekly lessons, which included movement exercises, educative material on physiology and the body's stress response, group discussions sharing personal experiences and reflections, as well as instruction in deep and differential relaxation methods. Regular home practice, aided by audio recordings, was a requisite for reaping therapeutic benefits. Corporations also started to include taught relaxation methods, including Autogenic Training, deployed, for example, by Marks and Spencer and the National Coal Board. Also operational by the early 1970s were organizations specifically combining relaxation and meditation teaching. In Britain, these included the Relaxation Society, which offered literature, lectures, and classes in relaxation and meditation held in a London church for tired-out city workers (Harding, 1990, 2003); and the Institute of

[6] Although chronic-disease epidemiologist Michael Marmot's seminal Whitehall studies of British civil servants (Marmot et al., 1978) demonstrated that from the 1950s individuals of lower socio-economic status were the demographic most at risk of heart disease, the association of "Type A" male executives (Friedman & Rosenman, 1974) being the most "coronary-prone" population persisted into the 1980s.

Applied Meditation which ran rural residential and city courses for adults and children that included teaching "self-awareness" and applying relaxation to everyday life (van Someren, 1974).

Due to this common rhetorical fusion between relaxation, yoga, and meditation, some relaxation practitioners, especially those who more narrowly followed in the Western neuromuscular relaxation tradition of Edmund Jacobson, sought to distinguish relaxation from techniques associated with "meditation, hypnotic suggestion, or difficult postures" (Madders, 1973, p. 8). As physiotherapist Laura Mitchell, who developed her own method of "physiological relaxation" in the early 1960s, assured readers of her popular book *Simple Relaxation*:

> You will not be asked to think fanciful thoughts like floating in space. No self-hypnosis is involved. You will not be asked to do strange things like 'dwelling on your solar plexus' or 'feeling your warm blood coursing through your arms'. This is not another form of meditation... You will not be asked to perform any gymnastic exercises or use visualization or distraction methods. This is not another Yoga book nor another massage book. (Mitchell, 1977, pp. 4–5)

As the next section will discuss, alongside and impacting these developments within the field of relaxation and yoga came a parallel wave of interest in Transcendental Meditation (TM)—the mantra-based meditative technique imported to the West by Maharishi Mahesh Yogi (1918–2008). Harvard cardiologist Herbert Benson's scientific investigations, initially focused on advanced TM practitioners and later extrapolated to a range of other techniques, provided a common understanding of the physiological effects of relaxation, yoga, and meditative practices and their utility to modern Western populations. Nonetheless, albeit ambivalently, by the 1970s meditation and relaxation were already practically and culturally interwoven. Benson's work, therefore, served to conjoin them further.

Transcendental Meditation, Scientific Investigation, and the "Relaxation Response"

Maharishi Mahesh Yogi, an Indian physical sciences graduate who had spent fourteen years in a Himalayan monastic community under the guidance of Swami Brahmananda Saraswati (1869–1953), arrived in the USA in 1959. Initially under the rubric of the "Spiritual Regeneration Movement," Maharishi started to extend his Hindu-rooted spiritual teachings to American and European populations. De-emphasizing the specific religious framework from which it derived, and extracting the meditative technique from other devotional aspects, was key to developing a transcultural, secularized interest in his teachings. By the end of the 1960s, his system had adopted a new official label: "The Science of Creative Intelligence," making it more cognitively compatible with a Western worldview, grounded in science, with practical, this-worldly applications. The method had a claim to perennial, universal wisdom, but one with relevant, wide-reaching, modern applications (Weber, 2014).

Maharishi described TM as "turning the attention inwards towards the subtler levels of a thought until the mind transcends the experience of the subtlest state of the thought and arrives at the source of the thought" (Maharishi Yogi, 1969). What this practically amounted to was sitting with eyes closed for a 15–20-minute period twice a day, mentally repeating a personally assigned word or phrase. Potential TM practitioners could not learn how to do this just from a book but were required to attend a course for a fee, where practical instruction and support would be shared by a teacher who was qualified directly by Maharishi. Following this initiation, it was a simple technique to practice, with limited time investment purportedly yielding significant gains even for the newly inducted.

At first buoyed by and limited to youth culture and the countercultural movement, TM achieved global fame after being endorsed by members of the Beatles, the Beach Boys, and other celebrities in the late 1960s and early 1970s, sweeping it into the cultural mainstream. By the mid-1970s, the theory and practice of TM was run as a credit course within prestigious universities such as Stanford, and taken up within prisons, schools, and workplaces. In Britain, the Civil Aviation Authority and the Police Federation both invested in its use.[7] And as with 1970s yoga and neuromuscular relaxation classes, "ordinary housewives" made up a large proportion of initiates (Newcombe, 2008, p. 160). Transcendental Meditation considerably extended its reach not only through tapping into and offering solutions to a range of medical and social issues, but also through heavily marketing efforts from within the organization that elicited widespread media attention (Johnston, 1980).[8] In 1974, *New Scientist* announced "The birth of Creative Intelligence" (Halperin, 1974) and the next year Maharishi featured on the front cover of *Time* magazine (October 13, 1975) under the caption: "Meditation: The Answer to all Your Problems?"

As public and professional interest in meditation practices continued to grow, a few critical rumblings could also be heard. "Should we be playing with techniques to allow people to survive in society? Or should we look further and try to find out why such techniques are necessary?" asked a professor of medicine, Ivor Mills, at a well-attended

[7] This was discussed on a BBC 2 *Horizon* television program, "Meditation and the Mind" (August 4, 1975).

[8] Maharishi fostered an organized, media-savvy set of transnational advocates and institutions that made the most of new technologies such as domestic television to publicize the cause; TM even built its own television studio. TM organizations included The Students International Meditation Society (SIMS), originally established in Germany and spreading internationally with over a thousand student campus centers by 1970. In 1974 the movement established the Maharishi International University (later the Maharishi University of Management) in Iowa, and in 1975 the Maharishi European Research University in Switzerland.

academic meeting held with Maharishi at the University of Cambridge (Halperin, 1974). Others criticized the neat assimilation of meditative techniques within individualistic, capitalist agendas. An article in *The Atlantic Monthly*, "The Meditation Game," for example, attacked TM as the "McDonald's of the meditation business... a relatively low fixed price, a standard item, and an increasing number of franchises or outlets.... Like McDonald's TM suggests 'you deserve a break today'... [and] has processed about half a million Americans" (Smith, 1975).

Although still supported by hundreds of thousands of practitioners today, TM's heyday is long gone. In 1977 a federal judge halted the teaching of TM within public schools after a group of New Jersey parents and clergy won a court case on the grounds that TM was "religious in nature." As Humes (2005) has argued, this period marked TM's "fall from grace," with public uptake decreasing thereafter.[9] A lasting legacy of TM, however, was the significant increase in scientific investigation into meditation that it generated, in particular the exploration of neurophysiological and behavioral changes that resulted from its systematic practice. As discussed, relaxation practices had been therapeutically framed and scientifically explored since the early twentieth century, but TM helped place therapeutic meditation firmly on the map. As a large, organized movement involving a relatively standardized practice, TM was especially amenable to scientific inquiry. Notably, researchers affiliated to the two Maharishi universities, established in the United States and Europe, strategically and proactively grounded TM in the language and authority of science to lend the movement legitimacy and demonstrate TM's therapeutic, social, and economic utility.[10] Other research, in particular by Benson, served to significantly raise the profile and therapeutic potential of meditative practices more generally, and to further fuse together popular and scientific notions of meditation and relaxation.

In the late 1960s, John Allison in Britain, and Keith Wallace and Herbert Benson in the United States, were independently conducting physiological research into TM practitioners. On learning of each other's work, Wallace, a recent PhD graduate from the University of California, and Benson, an associate professor of cardiology at Harvard, started to collaborate in the early 1970s. Allison, a medical doctor and TM proponent, had tried for some years to have his physiological studies published in a scientific journal, eventually outlining his findings in a letter to the editor of *The Lancet*,

[9] This period also coincided with the introduction of the "TM-Sidhi" program, which required hours of meditation a day in order to achieve a state of "Yogic Flying," and claimed to be able to cumulatively bring down crime rates and achieve world peace (the so-called "Maharishi Effect"). Among other factors, such as factions forming within the organization, these aims and methods served to further reduce TM's credibility and popular uptake (Humes, 2009).

[10] By the mid-1970s over a hundred scientific research papers had been conducted (Orme-Johnson & Farrow, 1977). Early research looked into TM's link to "self-actualization" and personality change, its effect on productivity at work, neuroticism, and intelligence, as well as on drug abuse and hypertension. See Humes (2011) for more on the relationship between the TM Organization and its strategic employment of scientific research and authority.

"Respiratory changes during Transcendental Meditation" (Allison, 1970).[11] He wrote of "profound changes in physiological events [accompanying] this simple mental activity" and pointed to further work planned to "establish the basis of the freshness of mind and body and the release of tension which result from this practice."

That same year Wallace published some of his PhD findings on "The Physiological Effects of Transcendental Meditation" in *Science* (Wallace, 1970). While his PhD thesis highlighted that "participation in meditation may be considered as a possible contribution to general health, as well as a spiritual odyssey," the *Science* article narrowed in on the medico-scientific results and applications. Among other findings, the article reported on specific changes in electroencephalograph (EEG) recordings that were distinguishable from sleeping and hypnotic states. It also reported the "significant and reproducible decrease in oxygen consumption and metabolic rate" of TM practitioners, the latter indicated by raised skin resistance and decreased heart rate. Wallace highlighted the numerous applications within clinical medicine, including relieving physical and mental tension.[12]

Although a number of ad hoc physiological investigations had been previously conducted on advanced meditators from a range of traditions (Murphy, Donovan, & Taylor, 1997), Wallace commended TM for being particularly conducive to scientific study, partly because it allowed access to large samples of people who had received relatively uniform instruction.[13] With the encouragement of Maharishi, young TM meditators were proactive in their wish to be investigative subjects, and have their personal observations of bodily changes verified and quantified by laboratory science. Wallace had access to forthcoming members of the TM-specific Students' International Meditation Society (SIMS), whose headquarters were nearby his university campus in Los Angeles. Benson recalls young TM practitioners approaching him for scientific study and his initial reluctance to be associated with an obscure subject matter that might tarnish his professional reputation (Benson, 2000, p. 7). Nonetheless, with a specialist interest in hypertension he started to investigate changes in blood pressure during TM practice, inadvertently also finding that many TM practitioners claimed to have stopped abusing drugs. Countercultural exploration of recreational drugs, including hallucinogens and amphetamines, for many of these committed TM practitioners seemed to have been replaced wholesale by their meditative experiences. In a letter to the editor in the *New England Journal of Medicine*, "Yoga for Drug Abuse,"

[11] Allison had featured alongside John Lennon and George Harrison on the popular BBC talk show, The Frost Programme, hosted by broadcaster David Frost in 1967. These Beatles members had first appeared on The Frost Programme in September 1967 with Maharishi, and given the overwhelmingly positive audience response, they were invited back again in October 1967 to further debate TM with a panel that included John Allison.

[12] Writing soon after the 1969 moon-landing, he also speculated on other potential uses such as "in space travel and in certain diseases where extended periods of low oxygen consumption that are simultaneous with responsive mental activity would be very useful"; Wallace (1970, p. 1754).

[13] Wallace also claimed that subjects' meditation was little interrupted by the investigatory process, an opinion not shared by Allison, who had specifically noted that "the investigation was undoubtedly a disturbing factor in these experiments" (Allison 1970, p. 834).

Benson urged further exploration of TM, which he described as a "yoga-like practice" (Benson, 1969).

Benson and Wallace's research in the late 1960s and early 1970s coincided with the growth of the field of "biofeedback" (also termed "applied psychophysiology" and "instrumental conditioning") whereby subjects were taught to make changes affecting the typically involuntary and unconscious autonomic nervous system. Early research by biofeedback pioneers, for example that showed learned changes to brain wave patterns (signifying altered states of consciousness), skin temperature, and cardiac function, generated much clinical and popular excitement (Brown, 1975).[14] Biofeedback demonstrated the intimate connection between mind and body and the ability for self-regulation, and was taken up in diverse areas from transpersonal, humanistic, and behavioral psychology to rehabilitation work, psychosomatic research, and relaxation training.[15] In the mid-1960s, Benson himself had successfully experimented with conditioning monkeys to consciously alter their blood pressure. His later work with TM practitioners gave him the opportunity to work with human subjects and investigate a wider range of physiological functions.

Together with Wallace, Benson further explored the numerous and varied potential applications of TM and its overall physiological effects that produced what they termed a "wakeful hypometabolic state" (Benson & Wallace, 1972). This was an integrated bodily response brought about by meditation, which was consistent with a state of decreased sympathetic nervous-system activity. Unlike with biofeedback training, TM practitioners made no conscious attempt to produce specific physiological changes, but Wallace and Benson's findings suggested that TM practice nonetheless duly resulted in this unified response. By 1974, Benson had started to use the term the "relaxation response" to describe these physiological correlates and parted with Wallace and other TM supporters in his delineation of the relaxation response as not being particular to TM, but in fact achievable through a whole host of methods. According to Benson, progressive relaxation, Autogenic Training, yoga, Zen meditation, as well as repetitive prayer, for example, all produced the same underlying set of physiological responses. As with the hypometabolic state, he described the relaxation response as being opposite to the body's "fight or flight" response, or "defense alarm." This was first outlined by Harvard physiologist Walter Cannon in the 1920s and informed much of the subsequent

[14] The term "biofeedback" was coined at a conference in 1969. Researchers Joe Kamiya, Elmer and Alyce Green, and Barbara Brown were key innovators and popularizers of the field. Science writers Gay Luce and Erik Peper's 1971 article in the *New York Times Magazine*, "Mind Over Body, Mind Over Mind," which received the American Psychological Association award for scientific reporting, was also central to alerting academic and public spheres to the new developments in biofeedback (Peper & Shaffer, 2010).

[15] As portable, less expensive machines became more readily available (such as the Galvanic Skin Response [GSR] "relaxometer"), biofeedback became widely used as a teaching aid within relaxation training. The technology was also put to use in developing lie detectors, ostensibly demonstrating bodily changes such as increased sweat levels, associated with high-tension states. See Bunn (2012) for the history of the lie detector.

scientific research into acute and chronic "stress."[16] Whereas the "fight or flight" response was characterized by an increase in blood pressure, rate of breathing, muscle blood flow, metabolism, and heart rate, the relaxation response was diametrically different. Benson described it as an innate physiological response, and one that could be evoked through various means as long as four essential elements were incorporated: (1) a quiet environment; (2) repetition of a mental device; (3) the adoption of a passive attitude (which he deemed the most important element); and (4) a comfortable position. To this end, he outlined his own "noncultish," secularized psychophysiologic method in his book *The Relaxation Response* (1975), whereby he suggested for step (2) to repeat internally the word "one" on each outbreath, although he contended that any word or phrase would be sufficient. Many TM practitioners of course disagreed that the precise sound or phrase was not relevant, given how crucial that was within Maharishi's method, and researchers have continued to debate whether and to what extent all the techniques and traditions outlined by Benson do in fact evoke neurophysiologically equivalent responses.[17]

Benson's work from the 1970s onward was no doubt foundational to raising the public and scientific profile of meditation and relaxation strategies and the preventative and therapeutic possibilities implicated by "mind-body" medicine, particularly for conditions caused or exacerbated by "stress."[18] The year it was published, *The Relaxation Response* topped the *New York Times* best-seller list, and it has since sold in its millions internationally. Scientific interest in relaxation and meditation practices as viable alternatives to pharmaceuticals, such as hypertensive drugs and tranquillizers, increased dramatically from the late 1970s. Leading British investigator into relaxation, meditation, and biofeedback therapies, Chandra Patel, concluded in 1981: "relaxation-based behavioural methods might be offered as a first-line treatment to patients with mild hypertension" (Patel, Marmot, & Terry, 1981). This statement was echoed in a report by the National Institutes of Health in the United States soon after.[19]

Benson's research had not only bolstered such investigation, but also further encouraged the merging of relaxation and meditation nomenclature and understandings. Physician Malcolm Carruthers, for example, who was largely responsible for establishing Autogenic Training in the UK, characterized the technique in 1979 as both a "pleasant

[16] As Benson noted, the Relaxation Response was comparable to the "trophotropic" mechanisms of the parasympathetic nervous system promoting rest and reconstitution of energy, outlined by the Swiss physiologist and Nobel laureate W. R. Hess (1881–1973) in the 1950s. Hess had also spoken of the trophotropic system constituting a mechanism for protection against overstress.

[17] See for example Boals (1978), Lehrer et al. (1983 and 1994), Lehrer (1996), and Orme-Johnson and Walton (1998).

[18] Benson has tirelessly advocated "self-help" meditative and relaxation techniques as providing the "third leg of the stool" for biomedicine and modern health-seeking populations, in addition to pharmaceuticals and surgery. See Harrington (2008) for a comprehensive history of "mind-body medicine" including how Benson is positioned within this genre. See Komjathy (2015) for a detailed discussion of Benson's work, including his more recent studies on the role of prayer in healing.

[19] The NIH report recommended the use of relaxation, along with salt restriction and weight loss as the first therapy for mild hypertension, before resorting to drug treatments.

relaxation technique" and a form of meditation: "If meditation can be defined as 'direction of attention towards an object', AT can be regarded as a Western form of meditation" (Carruthers, 1979). Referring to the widespread prescription of hypertensive drugs, he called instead for "meditation, not medication."

Meanwhile, other relaxation advocates were quick to reinforce the close links between the aims, methods and outcomes of relaxation and meditative practices. In his popular book *Relaxation East and West: A Manual of Poised Living*, James Hewitt, for example, reflected that his earlier works had omitted:

> the presentation of meditation as a method of deep relaxation... [and]... discussion of what might be called relaxation's wider dimensions... Relaxation followed right through offers a way—even a 'Way' in the Eastern sense of a mystical 'path'—to expansion of consciousness, to greater freedom from conditioning, to spiritual unfoldment and experiential wisdom. (Hewitt, 1982, p. 7)

Therefore, when mindfulness meditation was reformulated from its Buddhist context to appeal to American healthcare consumers in the late 1970s, popular demand for scientifically endorsed, therapeutic relaxation and meditation strategies had already been established. Just as Benson, and Jacobson fifty years before him, had done for therapeutic relaxation, dressing mindfulness in the language of science was key to furthering its acceptance among the biomedical community and encouraging its popular uptake. To this end, as the next section will further address, linking mindfulness meditation to the language of relaxation and stress was strategically important.

The Mindful Moment

Molecular biologist Jon Kabat-Zinn is most commonly acknowledged as the originator of today's "mindfulness movement," largely stemming from his development of what became the Mindfulness-Based Stress Reduction (MBSR) program. Kabat-Zinn recalls that the idea to extract a component of Buddhist meditative practice and turn it into a biomedical intervention for Western clinical populations came to him in a "vision" in late 1970s Massachusetts while on a silent meditation retreat (Kabat-Zinn, 2011a, p. 287). He first came into contact with Zen Buddhist teachings as a graduate student at MIT in the 1960s, and in the ensuing years he also trained in Theravadin Buddhist traditions and yoga practice.[20] The "modern Buddhism" (McMahan, 2008) that Kabat-Zinn was introduced to was a reformulation of Buddhist thought and practice, largely derived from intercultural exchange during the late nineteenth and early twentieth-century colonial era (see chapter by King, this volume). Here, meditation became the most

[20] Kabat-Zinn studied with influential Asian Buddhists teachers, including Thich Nhat Hanh and Seung Sahn, and trained at the Insight Meditation Society in Barre, Massachusetts, alongside the Society's founding members Jack Kornfield, Joseph Goldstein, and Sharon Salzburg (Wilson, 2014, p. 35).

salient feature, foregrounding individual experiences and worldly applications while deemphasizing traditional Buddhist doctrines and rituals.[21] In the postwar period there were increasing attempts to relate Buddhist practices and theory to Western psychology, together with growing support for humanistic psychotherapy that held central the "non-judgmental acceptance of people and symptoms" (Dryden and Still, 2006). This was highly compatible with Kabat-Zinn's delineation of mindfulness as "moment to moment non-judgmental awareness." While maintaining that on his retreat vision he saw "in a flash" how the model could be put in place and spread into clinics country-wide and globally, Kabat-Zinn also acknowledges that MBSR did not grow out of a vacuum. Although the influences from psychology and modern Buddhism that helped to bring mindfulness meditation into Western therapeutic culture are commonly acknowledged, the longer socio-cultural history of relaxation therapy has been largely overlooked. Moreover, as previously mentioned, in recent writings Kabat-Zinn has specifically and strongly uncoupled relaxation from mindfulness both practically and ideologically, asserting: "Meditation is not relaxation spelled differently" (Kabat-Zinn, 2005, p. 58).

But a deeper look at the origins of MBSR elucidates its close links with therapeutic relaxation practice. The original program that Kabat-Zinn set up at the University of Massachusetts Medical School, Worcester, in 1979, was in fact called the Stress Reduction and Relaxation Program (SR&RP). It was established for outpatients with a range of intractable problems who were referred from the pain and orthopedic clinics and primary care. The ten-week (later reduced to eight-week) SR&RP course closely resembled the contents of established relaxation courses, which included psycho-educational material and recordings for home practice as well as technical instruction.[22] Early journal publications, recording promising results obtained through mindfulness practice for chronic pain and psoriasis, also demonstrate the close associations made between (mindfulness) meditation and relaxation techniques in the first decade of SR&RP (Kabat-Zinn, 1982, 1988).

In the specialist journal *General Hospital Psychiatry* in 1982, Kabat-Zinn outlined the key elements of the course, which included: "didactic material presented on the relationship of stress to illness, the consequences of suppression of the Flight or Fight response, and the Relaxation Response as a balance to autonomic arousal." Kabat-Zinn also noted "expectation of relief" as being an integral part of the program: "Meditation was presented with the suggestion that the techniques are powerful and that regular practice can bring relief from pain in many cases." His 1982 article outlined for the medical readership the two major classes of meditation practice: concentration methods (such as TM), involving "the restriction of attention to a single point or object," and mindfulness or awareness meditation (terms used here interchangeably), that "emphasizes the detached observation, from one moment to the next, of a constantly

[21] See also Jan Nattier's outlining of "Elite Buddhism" in America, constituting a majority white, upper-middle-class set of converts whose practice emphasizes meditation and who form a group quite distinct from ethnic Asians born into a Buddhist cultural heritage (Nattier, 1997).

[22] See Stanley and Longden (2016) for a detailed discourse and conversation analysis of MBSR courses.

changing field of objects" (Kabat-Zinn, 1982, p. 34). While noting how awareness and concentration methods "differ radically in the way in which attention is utilized," he acknowledged that "the practice of mindfulness meditation presupposes concentration to maintain steady attention" and that his SR&RP program utilized a "spectrum of meditation techniques." Reverberating with some of the central claims of Benson (who was acknowledged for providing critical comments on the paper), Kabat-Zinn emphasized that the "approach underscores that there is no one right way to meditate or to relax and that any method is only a tool" (Kabat-Zinn, 1982, p. 37). Media attention garnered by the SR&RP in the 1980s also largely framed it as a form of therapeutic relaxation: For example the *New York Times* article, "Relaxation: Surprising Benefits Detected" (Goleman, 1986), focused on Benson and Kabat-Zinn and the health benefits of their respective training methods.

As Kabat-Zinn's SR&RP was only for outpatients who could attend the course, he also created an hour-long audio-visual recording to "teach hospitalized patients how to meditate" and to "provide a resource for the individual patient to participate more directly in his or her own healing." This "televised outreach program," created in 1982 for inpatients and distributed to hundreds of hospitals in the United States and Canada, was called *The World of Relaxation* (Kabat-Zinn, 2013, pp. 210–213). As Kabat-Zinn acknowledged, "naming is very important in how things are understood and either accepted or not" (Kabat-Zinn, 2011a, p. 288), and he explained "we call what we do stress reduction because everybody can relate to that" (Kabat-Zinn, 2011b, p. 36). The inclusion of "relaxation" at first would no doubt also have been chosen carefully, in line with the "great effort" made from the start "to avoid the risk of mindfulness being seen as Buddhist, 'New Age', 'Eastern Mysticism' or just plain 'flakey'" and instead to present it as "commonsensical, evidence-based, and ordinary, and ultimately a legitimate element of mainstream medical care" (Kabat-Zinn, 2011a, p. 282).

In the late 1980s the SR&RP became the Stress Reduction Clinic, to emphasize that "it was a clinical service... in the Department of Medicine," and only in the early 1990s was it renamed MBSR, as Kabat-Zinn explained, "to differentiate the approach from many programmes that also used the term stress reduction or stress management but that had no dharma foundation whatsoever" (Kabat-Zinn, 2011a, p. 289).[23] It is interesting to recall that starting with Edmund Jacobson, a similar process of differentiation had been made at various points by "scientific relaxation" advocates, keen to disassociate their methods from the popular, self-help therapeutic marketplace.

Kabat-Zinn's move away from the terminology of relaxation, toward a more singular focus on mindfulness as an awareness-based model, might be understood in the context of long-standing debates among Buddhist scholars and practitioners regarding the relationship between, and the relative value of, the cultivation of *samatha*

[23] Due to wider institutional reorganization, in the late 1990s, it became the Center for Mindfulness in Medicine, Health Care, and Society, a medical school–affiliated center for private, paying patients. For an institutional history of the Stress Reduction Clinic at the University of Massachusetts Medical School, see More (2012).

(concentration, calmness, and stability) and *vipassana* (insight) through meditative practice (Kirmayer, 2015, p. 448).[24] Although Kabat-Zinn's teachings drew on a range of yogic and Buddhist traditions, the discursive shift in the framing of mindfulness meditation would have been shaped by his close affiliation to the Insight Meditation Society in Massachusetts (founded in 1975) and the growing influence and uptake of specific cultural adaptations of insight meditation practices in the United States. As Fronsdale (1998, p. 166) describes, a distinguishing feature of a key approach to *vipassana* meditation, systematized and propagated by the Burmese monk Mahasi Sayadaw (1904–1982), was its "dispensing with the traditional preliminary practice of fixed concentration or tranquilization."

Decoupling mindfulness from relaxation might also be attributable to the changing set of meanings, associations, and methods of relaxation, which varied in relevance to the developing discourse of mindfulness. Vernacular usages and connotations of the term "relaxation" persisted (such as being akin to languidness), that were unconstructive for neuromuscular relaxation and mindfulness practitioners alike, and within therapeutic contexts, Jacobson's original progressive relaxation methods were considerably shortened and adapted for modern, time-pressed populations. As Kabat-Zinn reflected:

> This emphasis on nonattachment to outcome is a radical departure from most clinical interventions. Yet it can be found at the heart of Jacobson's pioneering work (1938), which emphasized learning to recognize and trust the direct proprioceptive experience of the landscape of sensation within tension rather than striving to achieve a more desirable state, such as relaxation. It was only when his method was condensed... that the nonstriving, slow, mindful element was, ironically, abandoned—probably unwittingly—in favour of time efficiency and, with it, the primacy of the experiencing of the sensations themselves, without judgment or editing. (Kabat-Zinn, 2003, p. 148)

The practical, scientific, and methodological links between relaxation and mindfulness were therefore gradually deemphasized as mindfulness established a cultural and clinical path of its own. In 1993 an entire television episode of Bill Moyers's award-winning series "Healing and the Mind" was devoted to Kabat-Zinn and MBSR, significantly boosting its public profile. Since the late 1990s, scientific study and popular uptake of mindfulness has grown exponentially. Dryden and Still (2006) partly account for this due to the "manualization" of MBSR allowing well-controlled and replicable outcomes of an "evidence-based" practice, published in professional journals, endorsed by a powerful academic institution, and led by an energetic and charismatic leader. Comparing the popular success of mindfulness to the relative decline of TM, Wilson (2014, p. 80) also acknowledges that while TM was often mediated by stereotypes of "oriental monks"

[24] See Gombrich (1996) for a seminal discussion on insight and concentration practices within the Pali canon and Shankman (2008) for a thorough exploration of *samādhi* and *samatha* within Buddhist meditation.

applied to the brown-skinned, bearded Maharishi, "Jon Kabat-Zinn, the face of MBSR, is a clean-shaven white American doctor with short hair . . . who delivers his teachings in business attire."

For a diverse set of reasons, including the development of Mindfulness-Based Cognitive Therapy (MBCT) in Britain (Segal, Williams, & Teasdale, 2002), mindfulness has become the therapeutic meditation method to dominate Anglo-American clinical and popular landscapes. The "mindfulness movement" or indeed the "mindful revolution" as the front cover of *Time* magazine declared in 2014 (Pickert, 2014), has brought this practice into all aspects of contemporary Western living, from schools, prisons, and workplaces, to self-help literature, yoga and meditation, parenting and antenatal classes, pain and stress management, and psychotherapy (Wilson, 2014).

With this meteoric rise has also come a vocal backlash, including its denotation as "McMindfulness," concerns over its unmitigated therapeutic suitability, and conversely its overall restricted target audience differentiated through race, class, and gender.[25] Echoes of the past ring loud. The woman pictured on the 2014 cover of *Time* magazine—white, young, middle-class, and conventionally attractive—is to an extent a twenty-first century iteration of a typical attendee of an inter-war health and fitness class, a postwar NCT antenatal class, a 1960s yoga class, or a 1970s TM initiation. Mindfulness, described on the *Time* cover as "the science of finding focus in a stressed-out, multitasking culture," could have been describing Edmund Jacobson's progressive relaxation, or equally Autogenic Training, or indeed Benson's own relaxation response technique.

Conclusions

This chapter has foregrounded the twentieth-century history of therapeutic relaxation strategies, demonstrating their influence on contemporary, secular meditation practices, which are largely sought after and framed in terms of their therapeutic potential. From the early decades of the twentieth century, Western populations started to employ relaxation methods to help treat and prevent physical and mental illness and to better manage the strains of everyday living with greater efficiency and ease. And by the 1960s, a diversity of relaxation, yoga, and meditation teachings shared a set of aims and applications and appealed to common demographics, ranging from middle-class housewives to business executives to adherents of the counterculture.

Following the proliferation of public, corporate and clinical interest in Transcendental Meditation, and Herbert Benson's seminal publication of *The Relaxation Response* in 1975, applications and understandings of meditation and relaxation became further conjoined. As this chapter has demonstrated, many strategies used to support and promote TM—such as grounding it in the language and cultural authority of science

[25] See the edited volume by Purser, Forbes, and Burke (2016) for a thorough study of current critiques of mindfulness and a "critical inquiry into the meaning of mindfulness today."

and promoting it as a simple and effective non-pharmaceutical alternative for managing the strains of modern living—echoed much earlier initiatives of therapeutic relaxation practitioners. When Kabat-Zinn developed the SR&RP at the University of Massachusetts in the late 1970s, he tactically drew on the pedagogical methods, scientific literature, and popular understandings and expectations of established therapeutic relaxation practices, in order to bring mindfulness into mainstream popular and clinical settings.

Mindfulness has since been criticized for selectively extracting and decontextualizing this element of meditative practice from its wider Buddhist ethical framework, theological basis, and cultural origins. However, as this chapter has demonstrated, it can also be seen as part of a more recent tradition of secular, therapeutic relaxation initiatives. Although there are common threads that methodically and experientially connect certain meditation and relaxation techniques, this chapter has not been concerned with the degree to which meditation and relaxation can be seen as equivalent practices. Instead, it has demonstrated how twentieth-century relaxation practices have significantly contributed to the cultural conduciveness to modern meditation methods and the uses to which they are put. Understanding secularized, therapeutic meditation as part of the longer history of therapeutic relaxation practice elucidates the common cultural drivers that have led to their clinical innovation and popular uptake, their critiques, and their enduring potential.

Acknowledgements

This work was supported by the Wellcome Trust through a Research Fellowship in Medical Humanities [grant number 104411/Z/14/Z].

References

Albanese, C. L. (2007) *A republic of mind and spirit: A cultural history of American metaphysical religion*. New Haven, CT: Yale University Press.

Allison, J. (1970). Respiratory changes during transcendental meditation. *Lancet 1*(7651), 833–834.

Andrick, J. M. (2012). Delsartean hypnosis for girls' bodies and minds: Annie Payson Call and the Lasell Seminary nerve training controversy. *History of Psychology 15*(2), 124–144.

Benson, H. (1969). Yoga for drug abuse. *New England Journal of Medicine 281*(20), 1133.

Benson, H. (1975). *The relaxation response*. New York: Morrow.

Benson, H. (2000). *The relaxation response: 25th anniversary edition*. New York: HarperTorch.

Benson, H., & Wallace, R. K. (1972). The physiology of meditation. *Scientific American 226*, 84–90.

Boals, G. F. (1978). Towards a cognitive reconceptualisation of meditation. *Journal of Transpersonal Psychology 10*, 143–182.

Boome, E. J., & Richardson, M. A. (1938). *Relaxation in everyday life*. London: Methuen.

Brown, B. B. (1975). *New mind, new body: Bio-feedback: New directions for the mind*. London: Hodder & Stoughton.

Browne, T. 2000. The rise and fall of American psychosomatic medicine. Retrieved from http://www.human-nature.com/free-associations/riseandfall.html.

Bunn, G. C. (2012). *The truth machine: A social history of the lie detector*. Baltimore, MD: Johns Hopkins University Press.
Call, A. P. (1891). *Power through repose*. London: Sampson Low & Co.
Call, A. P. (1895). *As a matter of course*. London: Sampson Low & Co.
Capps, D. (2009). Relaxed bodies, emancipated minds, and dominant calm. *Journal of Religion and Health 48*(3), 368–380.
Carruthers, M. (1979). Autogenic training. *Journal of Psychosomatic Research 23*(6), 437–440.
Caton, A. R., & Archer, F. E. (1936). *Activity and rest: The life and work of Mrs. William Archer*. London: P. Allan.
Crisp, T. (1970). *Yoga and relaxation*. London; Glasgow: Collins.
Dick-Read, G. (1933). *Natural childbirth*. London: William Heinemann.
Dryden, W., & Still, A. (2006). Historical aspects of mindfulness and self-acceptance in psychotherapy. *Journal of Rational-Emotive & Cognitive-Behaviour Therapy 24*(1), 3–28.
Dunne, D. (ca. 1950). *Deep relaxation: The yogism technique based on relaxation of the voluntary muscles*. Surbiton, Surrey: School of Yoga.
Dunne, D. (1961). *Yoga made easy*. Englewood Cliffs, NJ: Prentice-Hall.
Friedman, M., & Rosenman, R. H. (1974). *Type A behavior and your heart*. New York: Alfred Knopf.
Fronsdal, G. (1998). Insight meditation in the United States: Life, liberty, and the pursuit of happiness. In C. S. Prebish & K. K. Tanaka (Eds.), *The faces of Buddhism in America* (pp. 163–182). Berkeley: University of California Press.
Gauld, A. (1992). *A history of hypnotism*. Cambridge: Cambridge University Press.
Gijswijt-Hofstra, M., & Porter, R. (2001). *Cultures of neurasthenia from Beard to the First World War*. Amsterdam: Rodopi.
Goleman, D. (1986, May 13). Relaxation: Surprising benefits detected. *New York Times*.
Gombrich, R. F. (1996). *How Buddhism began: The conditioned genesis of the early teachings*. London: Athlone.
Halperin, S. (1974). The birth of creative intelligence. *New Scientist 62*(899), 459.
Hanh, T. N. (2015). *How to relax*. Berkeley, CA: Parallax Press.
Harding, G. (1990). *Lying down in church: Stress in the city*. Worthing, UK: Churchman.
Harding, G. (2003). *The path to well-being: A Christian perspective*. Alresford, UK: John Hunt Publishing Ltd.
Harrington, A. (2008). *The cure within: A history of mind-body medicine*. New York: W.W. Norton.
Heelas, P. (1996). *The New Age movement: The celebration of the self and the sacralization of modernity*. Oxford: Blackwell.
Hewitt, J. (1951). *Relax and be successful*. London: Thorsons.
Hewitt, J. (1955). *The art of relaxed living. Health, happiness and success in an age of stress*. London: Thorsons.
Hewitt, J. (1982). *Relaxation East and West: A manual of poised living*. London: Rider.
Humes, C. A. (2005). Maharishi Mahesh Yogi: Beyond the TM technique. In T. A. Forsthoefel & C. A. Humes (Eds.), *Gurus in America* (pp. 55–80). Albany: State University of New York Press.
Humes, C. A. (2009). Schisms within Hindu guru groups: The Transcendental Meditation movement in North America. In: J. R. Lewis & S. M. Lewis (Eds.), *Sacred schisms: How religions divide* (pp. 287–305). Cambridge: Cambridge University Press.
Humes, C. A. (2011). The Transcendental Meditation organization and its encounter with science. In J. R. Lewis & O. Hammer (Eds.), *Handbook of Religion and the Authority of Science* (pp. 345–370). Leiden; Boston: Brill.

Jackson, M. (2013). *The age of stress: Science and the search for stability*. Oxford: Oxford University Press.

Jacobson, E. (1929). *Progressive relaxation: A physiological and clinical investigation of muscular states and their significance in psychology and medical practice*. Chicago, IL: University of Chicago Press.

Jacobson, E. (1934). *You must relax: A practical method of reducing the strains of modern living*. New York: McGraw-Hill.

James, W. (1899). The gospel of relaxation. *Scribner's Magazine XXV* (April), 499–507. (Based on a lecture first delivered in 1896).

Johnston, H. (1980). The marketed social movement: A case study of the rapid growth of TM. *The Pacific Sociological Review* 23(3), 333–354.

Kabat-Zinn, J. (1982). An outpatient program in behavioral medicine for chronic pain patients based on the practice of mindfulness meditation: Theoretical considerations and preliminary results. *General Hospital Psychiatry* 4(1), 33–47.

Kabat-Zinn, J. (2003). Mindfulness-based interventions in context: Past, present, and future. *Clinical Psychology: Science and Practice* 10(2), 144–156.

Kabat-Zinn, J. (2005). *Coming to our senses: Healing ourselves and the world through mindfulness*. London: Piatkus.

Kabat-Zinn, J. (2011a). Some reflections on the origins of MBSR, skillful means, and the trouble with maps. *Contemporary Buddhism* 12(1), 281–306.

Kabat-Zinn, J. (2011b). Some clinical applications of mindfulness meditation in medicine and psychiatry: The case of mindfulness-based stress reduction (MBSR). In J. Kabat-Zinn & R. Davidson (Eds.), *The mind's own physician: A scientific dialogue with the Dalai Lama on the healing power of meditation* (pp. 35–47). Oakland, CA: New Harbinger Publications.

Kabat-Zinn, J. (2013). *Full catastrophe living: How to cope with stress, pain and illness using mindfulness meditation*. London: Piatkus.

Kanji, N. (1997). Autogenic training. *Complementary Therapies in Medicine* 5(3), 162–167.

Kirmayer, L. J. (2015). Mindfulness in cultural context. *Transcultural Psychiatry* 52(4), 447–469.

Kitzinger, J. (1990) Strategies of the early childbirth movement: A case-study of the National Childbirth Trust. In J. Garcia, R. Kilpatrick & M. Richards (eds.), *The politics of maternity care: Services for childbearing women in twentieth-century Britain* (pp. 61–91). New York: Oxford University Press.

Komjathy, L. (2015). Therapeutic meditation: Herbert Benson's the Relaxation Response. In L. Komjathy (Ed.), *Contemplative literature: A comparative sourcebook on meditation and contemplative prayer* (pp. 593–644). Albany: State University of New York Press.

Kroker, K. (2003). The progress of introspection in America, 1896–1938. *Studies in History and Philosophy of Biological and Biomedical Sciences* 34(1), 77–108.

Lehrer, P. M. (1982). How to relax and how not to relax: A Re-evaluation of the work of Edmund Jacobson—I. *Behavior Research and Therapy* 20(5), 417–428.

Lehrer, P. M. (1996). Varieties of relaxation methods and their unique effects. *International Journal of Stress Management* 3(1), 1–15.

Lehrer, P. M., Carr, R., Sargunaraj, D., & Woolfolk, R. L. (1994). Stress management techniques: Are they all equivalent, or do they have specific effects? *Biofeedback and Self-Regulation* 19(4), 353–401.

Lehrer, P. M., Woolfolk, R. L., Rooney, A. J., McCann, B., & Carrington, P. (1983). Progressive relaxation and meditation. A study of psychophysiological and therapeutic differences between two techniques. *Behavior Research & Therapy* 21(6), 651–662.

Linden, W. (2007). The autogenic training method of J. H. Schultz. In R. L. Woolfolk, P. Lehrer, & W. E. Sime (Eds.), *Principles and practice of stress management* (pp. 151–174). 3rd ed. New York: The Guilford Press.

Luthe, W. (1963). Autogenic training: Method, research and application in medicine. *American Journal of Psychotherapy 17*, 174–195.

Madders, J. (1973). *Relax: The relief of tension through muscle control.* London: BBC.

Maharishi Mahesh Yogi. (1969). *Maharishi Mahesh Yogi on the Bhagavad-Gita: A new translation and commentary with Sanskrit text.* Harmondsworth, UK: Penguin Books.

Marmot, M., Adelstein, A., Robinson, N., & Rose, G. A. (1978). Changing social-class distribution of heart disease. *British Medical Journal 2*(6145), 1109–1112.

McMahan, D. L. (2008). *The making of Buddhist modernism.* Oxford: Oxford University Press.

Mitchell, L. (1977). *Simple relaxation: The physiological method for easing tension.* London: John Murray.

More, E. S. (2012). *A history of the University of Massachusetts Medical School: Integrating primary care and biomedical research.* Worcester, MA: Lamar Soutter Library, University of Massachusetts Medical School.

Moscucci, O. (2003). Holistic obstetrics: The origins of "natural childbirth" in Britain. *Postgraduate Medical Journal 79*(929), 168–173.

Murphy, M., Donovan, S., & Taylor, E. (1997). *The physical and psychological effects of meditation: A review of contemporary research with a comprehensive bibliography, 1931–1996.* Sausalito, CA: Institute of Noetic Sciences.

Nathoo, A. (2016). Initiating therapeutic relaxation in Britain: A twentieth-century strategy for health and wellbeing. *Palgrave Communications* 2(16043). doi:10.1057/palcomms.2016.43.

Nathoo, A. (2020). Your life in your hands: Teaching relaxed living in postwar Britain In M. Jackson & M. Moore (Eds.), *Balancing the Self: Medicine, politics and the regulation of health in the twentieth century* (pp. 158–189). Manchester: Manchester University Press.

Nattier, J. (1997). Buddhism comes to Main Street. *Wilson Quarterly 21*(2), 72–80.

Newcombe, S. (2007). Stretching for health and well-being: Yoga and women in Britain, 1960–1980. *Asian Medicine* 3(1): 37–63.

Newcombe, S. (2008). *A social history of yoga and ayurveda in Britain* (Doctoral dissertation). University of Cambridge.

Newcombe, S. (2014). The institutionalization of the yoga tradition: "Gurus" B. K. S. Iyengar and Yogini Sunita in Britain. In M. Singleton & E. Goldberg (Eds.), *Gurus of modern yoga* (pp. 147–167). New York: Oxford University Press.

Orme-Johnson, D., & Walton, K. (1998). All approaches to preventing or reversing effects of stress are not the same. *American Journal of Health Promotion 12*(5), 297–299.

Orme-Johnson, D. W., & Farrow, J. T. (Eds). (1977). *Scientific research on the Transcendental Meditation program: Collected papers.* Rheinweiler, W. Germany: MERU Press.

Patel, C., Marmot, M. G., & Terry, D. J. (1981). Controlled trial of biofeedback-aided behavioural methods in reducing mild hypertension. *British Medical Journal (Clinical Research Edition) 282*(6281), 2005–2008.

Peper, E., & Shaffer, F. (2010). Biofeedback history: An alternative view. *Biofeedback 38*(4), 142–147.

Pickert, K. (2014). The mindful revolution. *Time* (3 February), 34–38.

Puri, G. (1974). *Yoga-relaxation-meditation: A Western-trained biologist takes a new look at an age old Eastern science.* Liverpool: Self-published.

Purser, R. E., Forbes, D., & Burke, A. (eds) (2016). *Constructing the mindful subject: Reformulating experience through affective–discursive practice in mindfulness-based stress reduction*. Cham, Switzerland: Springer.

Roon, K. (1951). *The new way to relax*. Kingswood: World's Work.

Saumaa, H. (2017). Annie Payson Call's training in release and somatic imagination. *Dance Research Journal 49*(1), 70–86.

Schultz, J. H. (1932). *Das Autogene Training-Konzentrative Selbstentspannung*. Leipzig, Germany: Thieme.

Schultz, J. H., & Luthe, W. (1959). *Autogenic training: A psychophysiologic approach in psychotherapy*. New York: Grune & Stratton.

Schuster, D. G. (2011). *Neurasthenic nation: America's search for health, happiness, and comfort, 1869–1920*. New Brunswick, NJ: Rutgers University.

Segal, Z. V., Williams, J. M. G., & Teasdale, J. D. (2002). *Mindfulness-based cognitive therapy for depression: A new approach to preventing relapse*. New York: Guilford Press.

Shankman, R (2008) *The experience of samādhi: An in-depth exploration of Buddhist meditation*. Boston, MA; London: Shambhala.

Shapiro, S. L. (2009). Meditation and positive psychology. In S. J. Lopez & C. R. Snyder (Eds.). *The Oxford handbook of positive psychology* (pp. 601–610). 2nd ed. New York: Oxford University Press.

Singleton, M. (2005). Salvation through relaxation: Proprioceptive therapy and its relationship to yoga. *Journal of Contemporary Religion 20*(3), 289–304.

Singleton, M. (2007). Suggestive therapeutics: New thought's relationship to modern yoga. *Asian Medicine 3*(1): 64–84.

Smith, A. (1975). The meditation game. *Atlantic Monthly 236*(4), 33–45.

Someren, L. van (1974). *Biofeedback Newsletter 7*. Cambridge: Aleph One Ltd.

Stanley, S., & Longden, C. (2016). Constructing the mindful subject: Reformulating experience through affective–discursive practice in mindfulness-based stress reduction. In R. E. Purser, D. Forbes, & A. Burke (Eds.). *Handbook of Mindfulness* (pp. 305–322). Cham, Switzerland: Springer.

Sutton, E. (2012). Interpreting "mind-cure": William James and "the chief task of the science of human nature." *Journal of the History of the Behavioral Sciences 48*(2), 115–133.

Sunita, Y. (1971). *Pranayama yoga: The art of relaxation*. 3rd ed. Walsall, West Midlands: The Lotus and The Rose Private Trust.

Wallace, R. K. (1970). Physiological effects of Transcendental Meditation. *Science 167*(3926), 1751–1754.

Weber, J. (2014). *Transcendental Meditation in America: How a New Age movement remade a small town in Iowa*. Iowa City: University of Iowa Press.

WHO. (2001). Strengthening mental health promotion. World Health Organization (fact sheet no. 220). Geneva.

WHO. (2006). Constitution of the World Health Organization [Online]. Retrieved from www.who.int/governance/eb/who_constitution_en.pdf.

Wilson, J. A. (2014). *Mindful America: The mutual transformation of Buddhist meditation and American culture*. New York: Oxford University Press.

CHAPTER 16

CONCENTRATION AND VISUALIZATION TECHNIQUES IN BUDDHIST MEDITATION

NOBUYOSHI YAMABE

Introduction: Early Applications of Mindfulness

According to the common tradition, the founder of Buddhism, Śākyamuni Buddha (ca. fifth century BCE), attained awakening while in meditation under the Bodhi tree. Thus, from the earliest stages of Buddhism, meditation played a central role. My own specialty is in meditation and visualization in Chinese Central Asia (Xinjiang), as recorded in Sanskrit and Chinese meditation texts (from around the fifth century or later). However, the meditation and visualization in Central Asia is a development of the meditative practice found in early Buddhist scriptures (Pāli [P.], *sutta*; Sanskrit [Skt.], *sūtra*).[1] A wide variety of meditative methods are found already in early scriptures, but here I will focus on *satipaṭṭhāna* (P., "application of mindfulness,"[2] corresponding to Skt., *smṛtyupasthāna*) as one of the starting points for later development.

[1] I thank Miguel Farias and David Brazier for their editorial assistance and Bhikkhu Anālayo and Else Anders for their comments on earlier drafts of this chapter. I regret that due to lack of time and my limited capacity, the final version could not fully reflect their suggestions, although I did incorporate many of them. Last but not least, I thank Robert Kritzer for checking the English of the final version.

These scriptures are compiled into five *nikāyas* in Theravāda Buddhism prevalent in South and Southeast Asia and four *āgamas* in the traditions transmitted to Central and East Asia. (Since Buddhism has largely disappeared from its motherland, India, here "South Asia" primarily refers to Sri Lanka.)

[2] Although I prefer this translation, it is also often translated as "the foundations (or bases) of mindfulness."

Important early sources of *satipaṭṭhāna* meditation include the *Satipaṭṭhāna Sutta* ("Sutta on the Application of Mindfulness"; English translations in Horner, 1954/2004, pp. 70–82; Ñāṇamoli & Bodhi, 1995, pp. 145–155; Anālayo, 2003, pp. 3–13; 2013, pp. 253–269) of the *Majjhima Nikāya* ("Collection of Middle-Length Suttas" 1:55–63 [No. 10]), and the *Kāyagatāsati Sutta* ("Sutta on Mindfulness of the Body"; English translations in Horner, 1959/2004, pp. 129–138; Ñāṇamoli & Bodhi, 1995, pp. 949–958) of the *Majjhima Nikāya* (2:88–99 [No. 119]). There is also a longer version, the *Mahāsatipaṭṭhāna Sutta* ("Large Sutta on the Application of Mindfulness"; English translations in Rhys Davids, 1910/2000, pp. 327–346; Nyanaponika, 1962/1983, pp. 115–135; Walshe, 1987/1995, pp. 335–350) of the *Dīgha Nikāya* ("Collection of Long Suttas" 2:290–315 [No.22]), which seems to be an enlargement of the *Satipaṭṭhāna Sutta* with an intrusion of commentarial exegesis into the discussion of the Four Noble Truths (see Anālayo, 2014, pp. 91–100).[3]

Satipaṭṭhāna consists of the following four basic items: mindfulness of the body, feelings (various kinds of pleasant, unpleasant, and neutral sensations), mental states (for example, with or without lust, hatred, and delusion; great or small; surpassable or unsurpassable; concentrated or distracted; liberated or fettered), and doctrinal elements (five hindrances, five aggregates, twelve sense bases, seven factors of awakening, four noble truths). With respect to the fourfold mindfulness, here I would like to focus on the first item, the mindfulness of the body, because of its importance for later developments. Therefore, I now outline the structure of mindfulness of the body according to the *Kāyagatāsati Sutta*, a scripture specifically devoted to this topic (see also Table 15.1 below).

(1) When a monk practices mindfulness of the body, first he sits cross-legged with his backbone erect in a wilderness, under a tree, or in an empty house.[4] He tries to be clearly aware of his own breathing. Namely, he clearly recognizes whether his inhalation and exhalation are long or short. Then he breathes feeling his whole body, and he also breathes calming his bodily activity.

(2) The next step is to be aware of all bodily postures: walking, standing, sitting, and lying down. The point seems to be to retain awareness at all times—not only while sitting but also in the other postures.[5]

[3] It has been pointed out that a more accurate translation of Pāli *ariya-sacca* is "true realities for the spiritually ennobled" (Harvey, 1990/2013, pp. 20–52). In this chapter I use the widely used English translation, "Noble Truths," merely for the sake of conciseness and convenience.

[4] This line about the physical settings of meditation does not appear in the version found in the *Madhyama-āgama* extant in Chinese (Taishō No. 26 [81]). See Anālayo, 2013, p. 47. Here I follow the Pali text. Quotations from all Pāli texts in this chapter (except the *Visuddhimagga*) are from the Pāli Text Society editions. Quotations of all Chinese Buddhist texts are from the Taishō Buddhist Canon (*Taishō shinshū daizōkyō* 大正新脩大藏經, abbreviated as "T", Takakusu & Watanabe, 1924–1932). The numbers ("No.") correspond to the catalog number of this canon. In the *Kāyagatāsati Sutta*, the subject is a monk (*bhikkhu*). Therefore, I use male pronouns to reflect the wording of the original *sutta*.

[5] Schmithausen (1976/2016) argues that this was the original element of the mindfulness of the body. Anālayo (2013, pp. 48–50) points out that the mindful breathing was incorporated into the scheme of the fourfold mindfulness from the *Ānāpānasati Sutta*.

(3) The next step is application of mindfulness to various daily activities, namely, walking forward and backward; looking at and observing things; bending and stretching [one's body]; holding a monastic robe and bowl; eating, drinking, chewing and tasting; and excreting and urinating. The point here is that he should perform monastic activities with clear comprehension.[6]

(4) Then, he investigates various anatomical elements of his own body, like hair, body hair, nails, teeth, skin, muscle, tendon, bones, marrow, kidneys, heart, liver, pleura, spleen, lungs, intestine, bowls, the contents of the stomach, excrement, bile, phlegm, pus, blood, sweat, fat, tears, grease, saliva, mucus, the fluid that lubricates the joints, and urine. The purpose of this meditation would be to free himself from attachment to his own body.

(5) Next, he investigates the material elements that constitute the body: earth, water, fire, and wind. According to another Pali scripture, the *Dhātuvibhanga Sutta* (*Majjhima Nikāya* 3:240–242 [No. 140], a partial critical edition in Stuart, 2015, 2:222–301; English translations in Horner, 1959/2004, pp. 287–289; Ñāṇamoli & Bodhi, 1995, pp. 1089–1091; see also Greene, 2012, p. 140; Yamabe, 2006, pp. 326–327), the point of this kind of meditation is the realization that no self can be found in any of these elements.

(6) Finally, he observes various stages of decomposition of a corpse in a charnel ground, namely: the corpse having turned blue and bloated, oozing matter as it festers; the corpse being devoured by various animals; a skeleton with flesh and blood and joined together by tendons; then the skeleton without flesh but smeared with blood and joined together by tendons; the skeleton from which muscle and blood are gone but is joined together by tendons; then the skeleton disconnected and scattered all over; then mere rotten and powdered bones. Thus, he realizes that his own body has the same nature and is not exempt from the same destiny. (See Figure 15.1 for a depiction of this type of practice.)

Subsequently, experiences in the four stages of meditation are described. In the first stage, one's body is filled with pleasure and comfort that have arisen from detachment. In the second stage, one's body is filled with pleasure and comfort that have arisen from concentration. In the third stage, pleasure ceases but one experiences comfort in one's body. In the fourth stage, both pleasure and comfort cease—one's mind is filled only with purified equanimity.

This sequence includes many ways of regarding the body. First of all, one must be seated in a proper bodily posture (cross-legged and backbone erect).[7] In addition, regarding the long and short breaths mentioned in the section on mindful breathing, a doctrinal text of the Sarvāstivāda school, the *Abhidharma-mahāvibhāṣā* ("Extensive

[6] Anālayo points out that the preceding mindfulness of the bodily postures also concerns monastic begging. See Anālayo, 2017, p. 39.

[7] This statement is missing in the corresponding portion of the Chinese version (see n. 9) but is a stock phrase frequently seen in the Chinese Āgamas as well.

Commentary on Abhidharma," extant in Chinese, ca. third century [?], hereafter *Mahāvibhāṣā*), states that when the practitioner starts practicing, his breathing is short, but when the practice advances, breathing becomes longer (T27:136a24–25). Thus, it follows that meditative practice affects not only the mind but also breathing.

Furthermore, the practitioner is not merely mindful of inhalation and exhalation but also feels the whole body. According to the *Mahāvibhāṣā*, this is because when one becomes proficient in this practice, breathing goes in and out of the pores all over the body (T29:136a27–b1).

Finally, the practitioner calms down his bodily activity. Interpretation of "bodily activity" (*kāyasaṅkhāra*) in the Pali tradition is not uniform.[8] The most comprehensive and well-known meditation text in Pali, the *Visuddhimagga* ("The Path for Purification," fifth century CE), explains "bodily activity" in the following way: After one runs, comes down from a mountain, or puts down a great burden from one's head, one's breath becomes agitated, but after one rests, it becomes tranquil and subtle. In the same way, when the body and mind are agitated, the breath is also agitated, but when the body and mind are under control, the breath also becomes calm (p. 227, §177 [in summary]; Ñāṇamoli, 1975/1999, pp. 267–268; Anālayo, 2003, p. 132). One might further refer to the *Mahāvibhāṣā*, which states that if a person carries a heavy burden and travels a difficult path, the breath becomes fast, but if that person later reaches a level path, his breath becomes calm (T27:136a25–27). These explanations seem to show only that the body (and mind) influence the breath, and not vice versa. However, since this *Visuddhimagga* passage is an interpretation of the scriptural line, "calming down bodily activity, I shall breath out/in," the other direction (i.e., respiration influencing the body) must naturally be implied. (The Japanese translation by Mizuno Kōgen [2004, pp. 90–91] interprets the passage this way). In this regard, another passage from the *Mahāvibhāṣā* says that just as good or bad food benefits or harm the body, well-regulated or ill-regulated breathing benefits or harm the body (T27:134a15–18). This passage suggests that calm breathing calms bodily activity. It seems to me that in this context, the "bodily activity" calmed down by mindful breathing does not to refer to external acts but to internal conditions (agitation and tranquility) of the body.

The importance of the physical aspect is also conspicuous in the four stages of meditation. In each of the four stages positive sensations induced by meditative practice (including the pure equanimity and mindfulness attained in the fourth stage) suffuse the whole body. This may be related to the aforementioned experience of breathing that

[8] It is interpreted as "breathing" or "bodily acts in general" in Pali sources. For example, the *Cūḷavedalla Sutta* (*Majjhima Nikāya* 1:301 [No. 44]; English translation in Horner, 1954/2004, p. 363) says that *kāyasaṅkhāra* means "inhalation and exhalation." On the other hand, in the *Aṅguttara Nikāya* (2:231 [No. 232]; English translation in Woodward, 1933/2001, p. 238), *kāyasaṅkhāra* seems to refer to "bodily acts in general" (i.e., bodily karma). See Anālayo, 2003, pp. 131–132. Here, the first interpretation appears possible, because, as we have seen, breathing becomes calmer and subtler as one's meditation progresses. However, the context is a discussion of breathing. If, when the text says, "calming down the bodily activity, I shall breath in/out," the author meant "breathing" by "bodily activity," it seems unnatural to me that the author did not say so more explicitly. "Bodily acts in general" is more unlikely, since the practitioner is now in seated meditation, most of the external movements are not taking place in the first place.

comes in and goes out of the pores of the entire body (found in the *Mahāvibhāṣā*). Here again, breathing somehow affects the whole body. As Anālayo (2017, pp. 43–63) has pointed out, the image of the body is not only negative (with regard to its impurities) but also positive in the context of Buddhist meditation.

This practice of mindfulness of the body seems to be largely divided into two parts. The first ([1]–[3]) discusses mindful breathing and mindfulness in daily activities. The second ([4]–[6]), which is different from the first, is observation of various elements of a living body and meditation on the decomposition of a dead body.[9]

In the first part, the point is that the practitioner should have a clear comprehension of what he is doing right now. In that sense, this is not "meditation" in its original sense in English ("thought, reflection"); rather the point seems to be to dispel discursive thoughts,[10] which hinder clear awareness of what is going on right now. Here also, the practitioner thinks to himself, "I shall breathe out feeling my whole body," and so forth. Thus, I do not claim that this is completely free from thinking like the non-conceptual yogic perception discussed in later Buddhist epistemological traditions (see, for example, Hattori, 1968, p. 27). The practitioner clearly has some thought, but this is not analytical or reflective thought. The emphasis seems to be rather on being clearly aware of what he is doing here and now. One should also note here that this does not involve any particular visual image.

By contrast, in the second half of the mindfulness of the body, many of the objects of the fourth and the fifth items (anatomical parts and the four elements) are things within the body, which are not perceivable. Though one can feel some of them (like the heat in the body), they are mostly objects of analytical thinking or visual imagination.[11] The object of the sixth item is a decomposing corpse, which itself is an external object that one can see. The practitioner, however, subsequently thinks that his own body also has the same nature and is not free from the same destiny. This clearly is a reflective thought (see n. 9).

Thus, the observations in the second half involve reflective mental activities and, accordingly, are closer to the original English concept of "meditation." It is also noteworthy that at least the object of the last item (a decomposing body) is clearly visual.

[9] For the first and the second items, the verb is *pajānāti*, "he knows" (which, in this context, would mean, "to be clearly aware of"), and in the third item, it is *sampajānakārī hoti*, "with clear comprehension he does [something]." On the other hand, for the fourth and fifth items, the verb is *paccavekkhati*, "he analyzes." For the sixth item, it is *passeyya*, "as if he were to see [the decaying corpse]." See Anālayo, 2017, pp. 48–49. Note that throughout the *Kāyagatāsati Sutta*, the subject is a monk (*bhikkhu*) which is the reason why the pronoun "he" is used throughout.

[10] *Aṅguttara Nikāya* 4:35[8] (No. 9.3); *Śrāvakabhūmi*, Taishō Daigaku Sōgō Bukkyō Kenkyujo Shōmonji Kenkyūkai, 2007, pp. 50–52; *Abhidharmakośabhāṣya*, 333.9–14; *Zuochan sanmei jing*, Yamabe & Sueki, 2009, pp. xiii–xviii, 18–33.

[11] Most of the anatomical parts and the four elements are not visible from the outside, but the practitioner is compared respectively to a person inspecting various kinds of grains in a bag and a butcher dissecting a cow. (The simile of a butcher is quoted later in this chapter). Though these similes do not expressly state that somebody is "seeing" something, I think the context suggests visual observation. Thus, these internal elements could have been seen as visual images in meditative practices.

FIGURE 16.1 A monk visualizing a skull, from Qizil Cave 212 ("Seafarers' Cave"). Source: Meditierender Mönch, Seefahrerhöhle (Kizil Höhle 212). 56.6 × 27.2 cm. Inv. Nr. III 8401 c. © Staatliche Museen zu Berlin, Museum für Asiatische Kunst/Jürgen Liepe.

This meditation on a decomposing body seems to have been the starting point for the later development of visualization.

Therefore, the first half is "mindfulness proper," so to speak, and the second half involves more reflective thought and, at least to some extent, visual images. In the later Sarvāstivāda tradition (*Dharmaskandha*, T26:496a23–24 [No. 1537]; *Pañcavastuka*, T28:989c17–9 [No. 1555]; *Mahāvibhāṣā*, T27:662c8–10 [No. 1545], *Abhidharmakośabhāṣya*, Pradhan 1967, 337.9–14, etc.), mindful breathing (*ānāpāna-smṛti*) and meditation on impurity (*aśubhā*) came to be regarded as two cardinal methods of Buddhist practice. These two methods were already incorporated into the "mindfulness of the body" in early Buddhist scriptures (see n. 10).

The Subsequent Development of Mindfulness

Later, meditation manuals that were more sytematized were compiled based on the early scriptures. In the Theravada tradition, the best-known meditation text is the *Visuddhimagga* by Buddhaghosa (fifth century), mentioned previously. In the traditions transmitted through the northern routes (from Northwest India via Central to East Asia), many meditation texts are known, including the *Yogācārabhūmi* ("Stages of Yoga Practitioners") of Saṅgharakṣa (ca. second century, translated into Chinese as the *Dao di jing* [No. 607] in the second century and the *Xiuxingdao di jing* [No. 606] in the third century) and the *Yogācārabhūmi of Dharmatrāta* (translated into Chinese as the *Damoduoluo chan jing* in the fifth century; for these texts, see Demiéville, 1954; Yamabe, 1999a). In addition, in theoretical treatises ("Abhidharma") of the Sarvāstivāda tradition, like the *Mahāvibhāṣā* (ca. third century[?]; extant in Chinese) and the *Abhidharmakośabhāṣya* ("Commentary on the Compendium of Abhidharma") of Vasubandhu (ca. fifth century; extant in Sanskrit, Tibetan, and Chinese), and even in literary texts, like Aśvaghoṣa's *Saundarananda* ("Nanda the Fair," ca. second century), we can find fairly detailed discussions of meditation (see Yamabe, 2003). A practico-philosophical tradition called "Yogācāra" also built its own system of practice based on the preceding literature. The earliest and most voluminous work of this tradition, the *Yogācārabhūmi* ("Stages of Yoga Practitioners" attributed to Maitreya or Asaṅga, ca. fourth century),[12] especially one of its oldest portions, the *Śrāvakabhūmi* ("The Stage of Auditors"), draws heavily on some of these earlier texts (see Deleanu, 2006). In all of these texts, mindful breathing is treated as one of the cardinal methods of practice.

[12] This text shares the title with the aforementioned two texts (Saṅgharakṣa's *Yogācārabhūmi* and Dharmatrāta's *Yogācārabhūmi*), but they are separate texts, though Saṅgharakṣa's *Yogācārabhūmi* seems to have been one of the sources of the voluminous *Yogācārabhūmi* attributed to Maitreya or Asaṅga. See Yamabe, 2013. For the chronology of these texts, see Deleanu, 2006, pp. 195–196.

Mindful breathing was also a central meditation method at the earliest stage of Chinese Buddhism. One of the first Buddhist texts to be translated into Chinese was the *Da anban shouyi jing* ("Large Sūtra on Mindful Breathing" [No. 602]). It was translated by An Shigao (ca. 117–80 CE), a Parthian who came to China around 148CE. This text is closely related to the *Anāpānasmṛti* chapter of Saṅgharakṣa's *Yogācārabhūmi*. As the title clearly shows, the subject of this sutra is mindful breathing.[13]

In the fifth century, Kumārajīva (350?–409?), a renowned Mahāyāna master from Kucha, just after his arrival at Chang'an (present-day Xian), compiled the *Zuochan sanmei jing* ("Sūtra on the Concentration of Sitting Meditation" [No. 614], hereafter, "*Sitting Meditation Sūtra*") largely based on Indian sources.[14] In this text also, mindful breathing is explained in great detail. According to its explanation, one can eliminate six kinds of discursive thoughts by practicing mindful breathing (Yamabe & Sueki, 2009, pp. 18–33, 82).

Mindful breathing was also a key method for Zhiyi (538–597), the de-facto founder of the Tiantai tradition. His *Liu miaofamen* ("Six Excellent Meditative Methods" [No. 1917]), for example, teaches six stages of mindful breathing (counting the breath [*gaṇanā*], following the breath [*anugama*], fixing one's mind at one point [*sthāpanā*], observing [*upalakṣaṇā*], turning [*vivartana*], and purifying [*pariśuddhi*]). These stages are mentioned in Indian sources on mindful breathing, and Zhiyi's teaching thus reflects the Indian tradition of mindful breathing (see, e.g., *Abhidharmakośabhāṣya* 339.16–340.11). Zhiyi's system of fourfold concentration, namely, while sitting, walking, half sitting and half walking, and neither sitting nor walking (i.e., daily activities without fixed postures), taught in his *Mohe zhiguan* ("Great Calming and Contemplation," T46:11a–15b [No. 1911]) is also reminiscent of "mindfulness of the body" as described in the *nikāya* texts. The point is that one should cultivate concentration not only in static, but also in active situations. Although Zhiyi's direct sources are primarily Mahāyāna sutras, it would be fair to say that he inherits the spirit of the earlier texts.

Mindfulness is also important in the Chan/Zen tradition, although it is not always mentioned explicitly (Nyanaponika, 1962/1983, p. 14; Dumoulin, 1991). Here I would like to focus on Dōgen (1200–1253), who introduced the Sōtō (Chinese, Caodong) tradition to Japan. He greatly emphasized the importance of both practicing seated meditation and undertaking daily activities in full awareness. In this respect, in spite of the difference in location, time, and lineage, the Theravāda method of *satipaṭṭhāna* and Dogen's Zen practice share the same spirit in that both of them emphasize the importance of seated meditation in full awareness and its application to other monastic activities. In Table 15.1, passages in the left column are taken from the *Kāyagatāsati Sutta*. Those in the right column are from Dōgen's writings.

[13] In the version found in the Taishō Canon, the sutra and commentaries are mixed together. Thus, this is a very problematic text to read. Recently, a manuscript of a sutra entitled *Anban shouyi jing* 安般守意經 was found in Kongōji 金剛寺temple, which is not identical to the *Da anban shouyi jing* 大安般守意經but is closely related to it. This manuscript will advance the study of this problematic text. See Deleanu, 2003.

[14] See Yamabe & Sueki, 2009, xiii–xviii. Although this text is entitled as "sūtra," it is clearly a compilation of passages taken from texts written by masters after Śākyamuni Buddha.

Table 16.1. Comparison of the *Kāyagatāsati Sutta* and Dōgen's Writings

Kāyagatāsati Sutta (*Majjhima Nikāya* 3:89–90)	Dōgen
(1) Here, monks, a monk staying in the wilderness, at the foot of a tree, or in an empty house, sits down *cross-legged*, keeps his *body erect* and his *mindfulness present*.	Therefore, the Buddha taught his disciples the method of sitting in *cross-legged* posture and with *the body erect*. For what reason? If the body is erect, the mind can be easily straightened. If one sits with one's body erect, one's mind is not lazy. The mind is regulated, and the *mindfulness becomes present*. (*Shōbōgenzō zanmaiō zanmai*, Ōkubo, 1969/1989, p. 540)
(2) He *breathes in mindfully* and he *breathes out mindfully*.	Once you have settled your posture and have *regulated your breathing*, when a thought occurs, *be aware of* it; as soon as you are aware of it, it will vanish. (*Fukan zazengi*, Ōkubo, 1970/1989, p. 4; Bielefeldt, 1988, p. 181 [modified])
(3) Breathing in long, he knows "*I breathe in long*"; breathing out long, he knows "*I breathe out long*"; breathing in short, he knows "*I breathe in short*"; breathing out short, he knows "*I breathe out short*." "Feeling the whole body, I shall breathe in," thus he trains himself. "Feeling the whole body, I shall breath out," thus he trains himself. "*Calming the bodily activity, I shall breathe in*," thus he trains himself; "*Calming the bodily activity, I shall breathe out*," thus he trains himself.	Mahāyāna also has the method of regulating breath. Namely, one knows, "*This breath is long. This breath is short*"; this is the Mahāyāna method of breath regulation. Breath reaches the lower abdomen and then goes out from the lower abdomen. Though [the breaths] coming in and going out are different, both rely on the lower abdomen. [If one practices this way,] one can easily realize impermanence and regulate the mind. (*Eihei kōroku*, fasc. 5, Ōkubo, 1970/1989, p. 96)
	If you grasp the point of this [practice], *the four elements [of the body] will naturally become light and at ease*, the spirit will be fresh and sharp, *the right mindfulness will be clear*; the flavor of the dharma will benefit the spirit, and you will be calm, pure, and happy. (*Fukan zazengi*, Ōkubo, 1970/1989, p. 4; Bielefeldt, 1988, p. 182 [modified])
(4) In addition, monks, when walking, a monk knows "I am *walking*"; when standing, he knows "I am *standing*"; when sitting, he knows "I am *sitting*"; when lying down, he knows "I am *lying down*"; or however his body is employed, he knows it.	When you arise from sitting, *move slowly* and arise calmly; do not be hasty or rough. *At all times protect and maintain the power of concentration.* (*Fukan zazengi*, Bielefeldt, 1988, p. 183 [modified])
(5) In *wearing his robes* and carrying his outer robe and *bowl*, he does so with clear comprehension.	Always watch to make sure that the robe is arranged neatly. When you want to *put on the robe*, first [show respect] to it [by] doing *gasshō* [*añjali*, putting the hands together] and then put it on. (*Bendōhō*, Ōkubo, 1970/1989, p. 317; Leighton & Okumura, 1996, p. 71 [modified])

(Continued)

Table 16.1. (Continued)

Kāyagatāsati Sutta (*Majjhima Nikāya* 3:89–90)	Dōgen
	Buddhist *bowls* are the body and mind of the Buddhas and patriarchs. (*Shōbōgenzō hō*, Honzan ed., p. 637)
(6) In *eating*, drinking, chewing and tasting, he does so with clear comprehension.	Just let the Dharma be the same as *eating*, and let eating be the same as the Dharma. (*Fushukuhanpō*, Ōkubo, 1970/1989, p. 348; Leighton & Okumura, 1996, p. 83 [modified])
(7) In *excretion*, he does so with clear comprehension.	You *should not be slack* [when you] *wash [hands, etc.] after using toilets*. Śāriputra has once subdued non-Buddhist practitioners with this method. (*Shōbōgenzō senjō*, 1969/1989, p. 468)

The expressions and ideas do not correspond exactly in every detail, but from his own express statement, it is clear that Dōgen was aware of the historical link between the traditional practice of mindful breathing and his own method. Table 15.1 shows that even though Dōgen was a Mahāyāna Buddhist, he definitely inherited the spirit of the early Buddhist practice of mindfulness. Dōgen's great emphasis on the importance of mindful daily activities also resonates with the spirit of *satipaṭṭhāna*.

Since Dōgen's method is highly influential even now, the tradition of the mindfulness of the body retains its influence not only in Theravāda Buddhist countries but also in Japan and elsewhere where Dogen's teachings are still followed.

Development of Visualization

Now let us come back to the second part of the mindfulness of the body. In this portion, the practitioner meditates on his internal organs and the four elements as well as the decomposition process of a corpse.

In the *Kāyagatāsati Sutta*, observation of and meditation on the decomposition of a dead body are described in the following way (*Majjhima Nikāya* 3:91):

> Further, monks, as if a monk were to see a body abandoned in a charnel-ground, one day, two days, or three days after the death, swollen, blue, and festering, he thinks about the body [of his own] as follows: "This body also has indeed such a nature, such existence, and not free from such [destiny]."

These are vivid visual images, and this can (though not necessarily) involve observation of a dead body (see Anālayo, 2003, pp. 152–153 and n. 149). One would not call it a full-fledged "visualization" because a concrete method of mentally constructing these images is not provided. These visual images are clearly intended to remove attachment to one's own body. The message is straightforward, and there is nothing esoteric or symbolic in these descriptions.

Later texts show significant development on both points. First, in later meditation manuals, the method of grasping and holding on to visual images of the decomposing corpse in one's mind came to be described in greater detail. Second, many symbolic visual images became associated with visualization (or meditation in general). As for the first point, see, for example, the following account of the observation of a corpse from the *Visuddhimagga* (pp. 151–152, §§50–51):[15]

> The *yogin* should grasp the image in that [dead] body well by means of the aforementioned [manner] of grasping images. Having made his[16] mindfulness steadfast, he should contemplate [the image]. Doing this way again and again, he should contemplate and determine it well. Standing or sitting in a place not too far from or too close to the body, *he should open his eyes, look at [the body], and grasp the image. He should open [his eyes] and look at [the body, thinking] "A disagreeable swollen [image], a disagreeable swollen [image]" one hundred times or one thousand times, [then] shut [his eyes] and contemplate [it].*
>
> Doing so again and again, the image to be grasped becomes well-grasped. When does that become well-grasped? *If [the image] appears in a similar way when one is looking at [it] with one's eyes open or when one is contemplating [it] with eyes closed,* then it is called "well-grasped."

Here, the practitioner grasps and retains an image in his mind that can be seen and meditated on even when his eyes are closed. In other words, the practitioner is consciously forming a visual image in his mind. This can be called "visualization." It is notable that this type of "grasping image" method is also seen in the same context in a nearly contemporary Sanskrit meditation text of the Yogācāra tradition, the *Śrāvakabhūmi* (Taishō Daigaku Shōmonji Kenkyūkai, 2018, 126–128):

> Go to a charnel ground and so forth and *grasp an image from a blue [corpse] up to [the image] of bones or skeletons.* If not from a charnel ground, grasp an image from a charnel ground in a *painting* or *made of wood, stone, or mud.* Having grasped [it], come back to the place of residence. Having come back, being in the wilderness, at the root of a tree, or in an empty house, sit on a couch, seat, or a bed of grass. Having crossed the legs and having washed the feet, having put the body erect, making the

[15] I have referred to an English translation by Ñāṇamoli (1975/1999, p. 180). This and the following passages are discussed more in detail in Yamabe (2009).

[16] In this passage, the subject is a masculine *yogin*. Therefore, following the original text, I use a masculine pronoun.

> mindfulness present in front, sitting, first tie the mindfulness to the one-pointedness and the non-distraction of mind...[17]

Therefore, this kind of method was used in both Pali and Sanskrit Buddhist meditation texts. (There is a very similar passage in the *Mahāvibhāṣā* [T27:205b14–19]). A noteworthy point in this quotation is that the use of paintings or statues is mentioned clearly for the purpose of visualization (discussed in Schmithausen, 1982, p. 63; 2007, p. 226). Perhaps by the time the *Śrāvakabhūmi* was composed, dead bodies were no longer very commonly seen near Buddhist monasteries. In any case, the use of a human-made visual aid at the first step of practice is significant because this method is also used in the visualization of a Buddha or bodhisattva discussed later in this article.

The use of human-made visual aids is not mentioned in this context in the *Visuddhimagga*. If one looks at the section of the same text on a practice called *kasiṇa*,[18] which is meditation on the elements of earth, water, fire, wind, blue, yellow, red, white, ether, and light, one finds an external object (which is also called *kasiṇa*) used as a visual aid for creating images (pp. 100–102, §§22–31, excerpted; an English translation is found in Ñānamoli 1975/1999, 122–125):

> One who is grasping the earth *kasiṇa* grasps the image either in crafted or natural earth.... A portable or fixed [*kasiṇa*] should be crafted.... During the preparatory practice, one should stretch the [portable *kasiṇa*] on the ground and look at it .... As if seeing the image of [one's own] face on the surface of a mirror, one should open one's eyes in a balanced way and practice grasping the image....
>
> One should contemplate the image, sometimes with [eyes] open, sometimes with [eyes] shut. As long as a grasped image does not arise, one should practice according to this method, for a hundred times, a thousand times, or even more.
>
> *To a person practicing this way, when he shuts [the eyes] and is contemplating [the image, the image] appears as when [the eyes] are open.* Then it is said that a grasped image has arisen. Once [the image] arises, one should not be seated in that place. *One should enter his own residence and practice there seated* .... Then, if the tender concentration disappears due to some hindrance, one should put on sandals, take a walking stick, and go to that place. [One should then] *take the image*, come back, be seated comfortably and practice...
>
> For the person who is thus doing [practice], the obstructions gradually are suppressed, and the defilements are subdued. His mind is concentrated by the *upacāra-samādhi* ("simulacra *samādhi*"), and the "corresponding image" arises.

Thus, using an external object as a visual aid and impressing its images on one's mind seems to have been a fairly well-established visualization method by the fifth century.

[17] See Yamabe, 2009, pp. 53–54 and n. 12.

[18] In full, *kasiṇāyatana*, corresponding to Sanskrit *kṛtsnāyatana*, "the sphere of totality."

Mystification of Visualization

Another important line of development takes place when Buddhist visualization comes to involve more mysterious and enigmatic images.[19] In this regard, the most noteworthy text is the so-called *Yogalehrbuch*, an anonymous Sanskrit meditation text found in Central Asia (for the details of this text, see Schlingloff 1964/2006; Yamabe, 1999b, 2006).

In the *Kāyagatāsati Sutta*, one finds the following simile in the investigation of the four material elements (*Majjhima Nikāya* 3:91.3–9):[20]

> In this body, there are elements of earth, water, fire, and wind. Just as if, monks, a skillful *cow-butcher* or his apprentice were to be seated at a crossroad after slaughtering a cow and dividing its portions. Likewise, monks, a monk analyzes his own body into elements however it is placed or disposed, as follows: "In this body, there are elements of earth, water, fire, and wind."

Here, a butcher slaughtering a cow is mentioned. This, however, is just a simile and not a visionary image. On the other hand, in the *Yogalehrbuch*, we find the following, fairly unusual scene (Schlingloff, 1964/2006, 160V1–4[21]):

> Here in order to conform to the examination of the six elements, a *cow-butcher* holding a sword appears to him. He slaughters a cow and examines part by part the six parts on its skin. Then a sword comes out from the navel of the *yogin* and puts the body of the *yogin* on his [own] skin in six parts part by part. The right... [represents] the element of the earth because it is more solid. The left... [represents] the element of water because it is weaker. The right arm [represents] the element of wind because it is more solid. The left [arm represents] the element of fire because.... For the same reason, [the element of fire] of the people who lie on their left side declines quicker.[22] The center of the cheek [represents] the element of the space because it is hollow. The whole mouth [represents] the element of consciousness because it evolves...

Here, a vision of a butcher appears to the meditator, slaughters a cow, and divides its body in front of him.[23] Then the meditator imagines his own body slaughtered and

[19] These sorts of images are typically seen in Tantric/Esoteric Buddhism, which is the last phase of Indian Buddhism. In my opinion, some of the images seen in the meditation texts discussed in this chapter foreshadow those found in later Tantric Buddhism.

[20] I have referred to and partly made use of the corresponding portions of the English translations of the *Mahāsatipaṭṭhāna Sutta* by Nyanaponika (1962/1999, p. 120) and of the *Satipaṭṭhāna Sutta* by Anālayo (2003, p. 6).

[21] This number refers to the folio number, recto (=Vorderseite), and the line numbers. This text is usually referred to in this way.

[22] According to Buddhist monastic rules, monks are supposed to lie on the right side of the body.

[23] This refers to the male *yogin* mentioned in the original text.

divided in a similar fashion. The atmosphere here is very different from the straightforward images of the *Kāyagatāsati Sutta*.

It is noteworthy that the "mystification" of meditation even influenced the practice of mindful inhalation and exhalation (*ānāpānasati*). As discussed above, this has been a very basic method of meditation since the days of early Buddhism to this day. As we have seen in Table 15.1, items (2)–(3) above, the instructions on mindful breathing found in the *Kāyagatāsati Sutta* are very concrete and straightforward. There is nothing mysterious about it. However, if one looks at the *Yogalehrbuch* once again, we find the following rather amazing description of the same method (Schlingloff, 1964/2006, 127V1–3):

> Furthermore, a crystal world and a crystal body appear to [the meditator] *practicing inhalation and exhalation. Then (a jewel tree) stands on [the crystal man's] head filling the boundless realms of the world. On the leafy branches of that tree Buddhas are seen preaching the dharma*. Colorful rains of jewels, flowers, and lotuses coming out of their [=the Buddhas'] mouths are scattered over the world. The hollow roots of the tree shining like beryl are seen to be based on the golden circle together with (?) the soles of the feet of the practitioner.

The basic topic is unmistakably the traditional practice of inhalation and exhalation. Nevertheless, the atmosphere differs greatly from that of the *Kāyagatāsati Sutta*. In this case, the image of a gigantic tree on whose branches Buddhas are perching may well reflect an Indian belief that various deities reside in various parts of a tree. Nevertheless, the significance of these unusual images is in most cases not explained by the texts themselves and thus quite enigmatic.

Intriguingly, one finds a similar mysterious image in a Chinese visualization text, the *Guanfo sanmei hai jing* ("Sūtra on the Ocean-Like Samādhi of the Visualization of the Buddha," hereafter *Ocean Sūtra*). For example, concerning the gigantic cosmic tree on which Buddhas are teaching the Dharma, compare the following passage from the *Ocean Sūtra* (T15:663c16–19):

> The pores of the body [of the emanation Buddha] are like flower trees. *Each tree reaches upward to the world of Brahmās. Among the flowers and leaves there are tens of hundreds of billions of śrāvaka monks*. Each monk wears one thousand monastic robes. The thousand robes are in a thousand colors, and in each color are hundreds or thousands of emanation Buddhas, all in a pure golden color.

This quotation from the *Ocean Sūtra* is not from a discussion of *ānāpānasmṛti*. Nevertheless, the similarity between the image in the *Yogalehrbuch* and the *Ocean Sūtra* is clear. Since the *Ocean Sūtra* may well have been compiled in Central Asia (see Yamabe, 1999a), and since the *Yogalehrbuch* was also definitely known in that area (based on the existence of plural manuscripts there), the image of gigantic trees appears to have been well known there. These kinds of somewhat mystifying visual images are seen in a few other Chinese meditation texts from the fifth century and show the tendencies of visualization practiced in that period.

Visualization of a Buddha or Bodhisattva

Another representative method of visualization in Buddhism is that of a Buddha or bodhisattva (hereafter, simply "Buddha visualization"). This method is not found in early Buddhist scriptures and seems to be a new development in Mahāyāna Buddhism.[24] How exactly this method originated is a complicated issue, and a detailed discussion of its historical background is beyond the scope of this chapter.[25] Nevertheless, the natural yearning among Buddhist followers to see the Buddha after his demise must have been the basic motif for introducing a method for visualizing the Buddha (see Yamabe, 1999a, pp. 158–161; McMahan, 2002, pp. 155–157). Passionate devotion (*bhakti*) to deities, visible in Buddhist and non-Buddhist Indian religious traditions ("Hinduism"), might also have promoted this type of practice. The use of visual representations (statues) of Buddhas or bodhisattvas as visual aids may have been another significant element, as will be discussed later. In early Mahāyāna sutras, one can find stories of mystical encounters with Buddhas. When a one's religious zeal reaches its apex, sometimes one sees a vision of countless Buddhas. For example, in the *Aṣṭasāhasrikā prajñāpāramitā* ("The Perfection of Wisdom in Eight Thousand Lines"), an ardent bodhisattva, Sadāprarudita by name, was anxious to hear the Perfection of Wisdom (Wogihara, 1936, 932.10–12):

> A form of Tathāgata (one of the epithets of the Buddha) stood in front of the thus-stressed Sadāprarudita Bodhisattva, the great one, and praised him.

That appearance of Tathāgata told Sadāprarudita to go to the distant city of Gandhavatī to hear the Perfection of Wisdom from Dharmodgata Bodhisattva. Then, without traveling to Gandhavatī, he heard the teaching of Dharmodgata right at the spot, in the following way (Wogihara, 1936, 940.17–942.8):

> Then Sadāprarudita Bodhisattva, the great one, staying in the same place, heard Dharmodgata Bodhisattva, the great one, teaching the Perfection of Wisdom. Hearing [him], he gave rise to the thought that all dharmas are not based [on solid foundations]. Many gates of concentration emerged to him, such as, the concentration called observation of the nature of all the dharmas; . . . *the concentration called seeing Tathāgatas*; and *the concentration called seeing all Tathāgatas*.

24 Although *buddhānussati*, "calling the Buddha to mind," is already mentioned in early scriptures, there the objects of meditation seem to be the Buddha's merits represented in his ten epithets. See the *Aṅguttara Nikāya* 5:336 (Anussati-Vagga); Woodward 1936/2006, p. 214.

25 McMahan (2002) writes about the development of visionary imagery in Mahāyāna Buddhism. A concise but helpful survey of this issue is found in Greene, 2012, p. 141.

While staying in these concentrations, *he saw boundless and numberless Buddhas in the worlds in the ten directions* teaching this Perfection of Wisdom to bodhisattvas, the great people.

This, clearly, is a sudden and unexpected experience and not a result of systematized effort to construct visual images. In other words, this is a "vision" and cannot be called "visualization" (regarding the distinction between "vision" and "visualization," see also Greene, 2012, pp. 141–144). Nevertheless, it is certain that Sadāprarudita was believed to have seen all Buddhas in the ten directions in his meditative concentration (*samādhi*).

In the *Pratyutpanna-buddha-sammukhāvasthita-samādhi-sūtra* ("The Samādhi of Direct Encounter with the Buddhas of the Present," ca. first century[?], hereafter, "*Direct Encounter Sūtra*"), a famous early Mahāyāna scripture[26] that teaches how to see Buddhas in concentration, one can find more conscious effort to see Buddhas (Harrison 1978a, 31.10–31 [§3F]; I have referred to and partly made use of the English translation in Harrison, 1990, pp. 37–38 [§3F]).

Son of a good family, what then is this "calling the Buddha to mind"? It is the meditation on the Tathāgata in the following way:

(1) He is the Tathāgata, arhat, correctly awakened one, endowed with wisdom and action, well-gone, one who knows the world, charioteer who tames people, supreme teacher of human beings and deities, the Buddha, the Blessed One.

(2) [He is] the one who has the *thirty-two marks of a great person* and *a body with a color like gold.* [It is] like a shining, resplendent, and well-set golden image, well-decorated like a jewel pillar.

(3) [He] *preaches the Dharma* in the community of auditors. Namely, he preaches this way: Nothing perishes. What does not perish? Earth does not perish. Water, fire, wind, beings, god, Brahmā, Prajāpati do not perish. Form does not perish. Sensation, ideation, volition, and consciousness do not perish.[27]

One does not reflect on the Tathāgata, does not cognize, cling to, does not realize, does not conceptualize, does not analyze, or does not observe [the Tathāgata]. By thus meditating on the Tathāgata without cognizing him, one obtains *the concentration of emptiness*; it is called calling the Buddha to mind.

The meditation, seen in this passage, on the ten epithets (i.e., merits) of the Buddha (paragraph [1] above) is a traditional method already found in early scriptures. Here, in addition to the traditional method, a meditation on the Buddha's physical characteristics and on his act (preaching) is added, which leads one to the realization of emptiness. This is a significant development.

[26] There is a partial Chinese translation of this sutra, *Bapo pusa jing* 拔陂菩薩經 (T. No. 419), from a very early period (the second or early third century), which suggests an early date of composition of this sutra in India. See Harrison, 1990, pp. xvi, 219.

[27] As Harrison notes (1990, pp. 37–38, n.11), "do not perish" should probably be understood in non-substantialist rather than eternalist sense.

See also the following passage from the same sutra (Harrison, 1978a, 68.3–18 [§8A]; an English translation in Harrison, 1990, pp. 68–69 [§8A]; quoted in Harrison, 1978b, p. 45):

> Bhadrapāla, how should the samādhi of a bodhisattva, a great one, be practiced? Bhadrapāla, just as I am preaching the Dharma right now in front of you, Bhadrapāla, *so should a bodhisattva meditate on the Tathāgatas, arhats, correctly awakened ones as seated on the Buddhas' seats and preaching the Dharma.* He should meditate on the Tathāgatas as endowed with the supreme of all features, having a beautiful form, agreeable, good looking, and endowed with perfect bodies. Each *mark of a great person* of a Tathāgata, *arhat*, correctly awakened one should be seen as generated from one hundred merits. *The images also should be grasped.* The invisible crest should also be inquired about. After they have been inquired about, the marks of a great person should also be grasped. Having been grasped, they should be thus learned.

It is notable that the method of "grasping images" is mentioned here. It suggests that the method used for the visualization of a corpse and *kasiṇa* is influencing the Buddha visualization. The use of a visual aid, however, is not mentioned clearly in the *Direct Encounter Sūtra*. It says that bodhisattvas should make an image or paint a picture out of desire for *pratyutpanna-samādhi* (§4D; Harrison, 1978a, p. 40; 1990, p. 46). Nevertheless, it is not clear whether these were used as visual aids for practice or prepared for merit-making.

Express reference to Buddha statues as visual aids for practice must wait until the fifth-century Chinese meditation texts. Following is an example from the *Sitting Meditation Sūtra* (T15:276a9–14; an English translation in Yamabe & Sueki, 2009, pp. 33–34):

> If the practitioner is at the elementary level, [the master] should lead him to a *statue of the Buddha* or teach him to go there by himself and [make him] clearly observe the major and minor bodily marks of the statue. *When each mark has become clear [in his mind], he should single-mindedly retain [that mental image] and return to a silent place.* [There] he observes the statue of the Buddha with his mental eye and does not let his mind turn away. He fixes his mind on the statue without letting his mind be distracted by other objects. If his mind is distracted, he should concentrate it, so that it is always fixed on the statue.

Similar instructions are also found in the *Wumen chanjing yaoyong fa* ("The Essence of the Meditation Manual Consisting of Five Gates"), compiled in the fifth century (T15:325c18–29; for textual problems with this text, see Yamabe, 2010):

> When one observes the Buddha, one should earnestly observe *the major and minor bodily marks of the Buddha. Having observed them very clearly, one should shut one's eyes and contemplate them in one's mind.* If [the image] is not clear, one should open

> one's eyes and make [it] extremely clear [in one's] mind. Afterwards, *one returns to one's own seat*, with correct bodily posture and mind, makes one's mindfulness present in front [and meditate on the images] as if one were facing the real Buddha. [The image] is extremely clear, no different from [seeing the Buddha oneself]. Then one rises up from the seat, kneels down, and says to the master: "I concentrate on [the Buddha] in my chamber as if seeing the Buddha [in person]." The master says: "Return to your own seat. Fix your mind on the forehead and meditate on the Buddha in one mind." ... They make the ground golden, and these Buddhas all enter the ground. The ground is as plain as a palm and as pure as a mirror. One observes one's own body luminous like the ground. This is called the attainment of the *meditative object of the concentration on calling the Buddha to mind.*

The text simply says, "the Buddha," but in this context it clearly means a statue of the Buddha. Thus, here also one is relying on a human-made object as a visual aid. Seen this way, the structural similarity between this method and the aforementioned *kasiṇa* practice is obvious. In both cases, one first observes an external object and impresses its image on one's mind. Once the image is established in one's mind, one leaves the object and meditates on the mental image in the privacy of one's own residence. Attainment of a truly clear image is associated with some type of concentration in both texts.[28] The overall similarity of these two paragraphs is beyond any doubt.

Note further that a well-known passage from the *Amitāyus Visualization Sūtra* (T12:341c29–42a5) shares essentially the same structure:

> All sentient beings, inasmuch as they are not born blind and have [healthy] eyes, should all look at the setting sun. They should make the mindfulness present, be seated facing the west, and *look at the sun*.[29] They should make their mind stay firm, make their mind concentrated [on the sun] and not let it move away. They see the sun, which is about to set, looking like a hanging drum. *Having seen the sun, they make [the image] clear whether their eyes are open or closed.* This is the visualization of the sun, which is called the first visualization. If they visualize this way, it is a correct visualization. Otherwise, it is a wrong visualization.

In this case, the meditator does not start with a statue but with the setting sun. Nevertheless, the only difference between this and the aforementioned method of using a statue is the object used as a visual aid. Other than that, the structure is exactly the same. Though the *Amitāyus Visualization Sūtra* is extant only in Chinese and it may well have been compiled in Central Asia, the Sanskrit text of the *Śrāvakabhūmi* (Taishō Daigaku Shōmonji Kenkyūkai, 2018, [128]) also mentions a sun's disk and a moon's disk as objects of which images should be grasped in. Thus, this method of "grasping an

[28] Such a structure is also observed in the *Siwei lüeyao fa* 思惟略要法 ("The Abridged Essence of Meditation," T15:299a [No.617]). For an English translation, see Willemen, 2012, pp. 31–33.

[29] Further, note that in the *Chan miyaofa jing* 禪秘要法經 ("Secret Essentials of Meditation," T15:248a5–23 [No.613]), the construction of the mental images of the sun and the moon culminates in the visualization of the Buddha.

image" must have been well established and well known in India, Central Asia, and China by the fifth century.

The method of Buddha visualization was inherited by full-fledged Tantric or Esoteric Buddhism. Detailed discussion of Tantric/Esoteric visualization is beyond the scope of this chapter, but I would just like to point out that today the tradition of Buddhist visualization is maintained primarily in Esoteric traditions (see chapter about Buddhist Meditation in Tibet). In Japan, for example, the visualization of the Siddhan (Sanskrit) letter *a* (*ajikan*), which is still practiced as a first step for Esoteric visualization, uses a scroll painting of the letter *a* on a lotus seat in the moon's disk as a visual aid. In that respect, it clearly follows the tradition of Buddha visualization.

In modern Western countries, popular methods of Buddhist meditation include Zen (Chan in Chinese/Seon in Korean) from East Asia, mindfulness (*satipaṭṭhāna*) from the Theravāda tradition from South and Southeast Asia, and Tantric visualization from Tibet. These methods can be linked to or classified as either mindfulness or visualization, and thus they inherit the long traditions of meditation that have their roots in early Buddhism.[30]

Conclusion

In this chapter I have outlined the development of Buddhist meditation from its early phase in India to the later forms in Central and East Asia. The system of the "applications of mindfulness" itself may have been a composite of elements taken from different sources. Nevertheless, in the received version of the *Satipaṭṭhāna Sutta* and the *Kāyagatāsati Sutta*, both the "mindfulness-per-se" types of meditation, like mindful breathing, and more reflective or visual types of meditation, like the meditation on impurity, are already included.

The "mindfulness-per-se" approach, centering on the mindful breathing method, was transmitted to East Asia and exerted significant influence over such traditions as Tiantai and Chan (Zen). The close similarities between the mindfulness meditation and Japanese Sōtō practice is an indication of such strong influence.

On the other hand, the more visual style of meditation, typically the meditation on the decomposition of a corpse, depicted in early scriptures, involved observation of a dead body in its stages of decomposition. Later texts came to teach a more elaborate method of "grasping the images" of a corpse. Practitioners also started to use human-made objects as an aid to visualization. At this stage, the method can be regarded as

[30] As I said in the beginning of this chapter, Buddhist meditation is manifold, and the discussion in this chapter is selective. Important methods I could not cover in this chapter include *vipassanā*, "introspection" (common English translation: "insight meditation"), and *mettā*, "friendliness" (often translated as "loving-kindness" meditation).

full-fledged visualization. A notable development in visualization is that the images seen by the practitioner came to include more enigmatic images.

In later Buddhism, the method of visualization developed further, and Buddhas and bodhisattvas became important objects of visualization. An undeveloped form is found in early Mahāyāna sutras, but a fully developed version is found in later meditation texts from the fifth century onward. This method of meditation used statues as the object of visualization. This type of visualization was inherited by Tantric/Esoteric Buddhism and is still practiced today. Advanced practice in Esoteric Buddhism is naturally reserved for initiated monks and not open to the public, though some elementary practices like the visualization of the Siddhan letter *a* is open to the public (see Yamazaki, 1974), and there are lay people who practice this method in Japan.

References

Primary Sources

Harrison, P. M. (Ed.). (1978a). *The Tibetan text of the Pratyutpanna-buddha-sammukhavasthita-samādhi-sūtra, Studia Phiologica Buddhica Monograph Series*. Tokyo: The Reiyukai Library.

Mizuno, K. 水野弘元. (2004). *Shōjōdō ron* 清淨道論: *Vol. 2. Nanden daizōkyō* 南伝大蔵経 (Edited by T. Junjijō 高楠順次郎). Tokyo: Daizō Shuppan 大蔵出版.

Ōkubo, D. 大久保道舟 (Ed.). (1989). *Dōgen zenji zenshū* 道元禪師全集 [The complete works of Dōgen]. (Vol. 1). Kyoto: Rinsen Shoten 臨川書店. (Original work published 1969).

Ōkubo, D. (Ed.). (1989). *Dōgen zenji zenshū* 道元禪師全集 [*The Complete Works of Dōgen*]. (Vol. 2). Kyoto: Rinsen Shoten 臨川書店. (Original work published 1970).

Pradhan, P. (Ed.). (1967). *Abhidharm-koshabhāṣya of Vasubandhu* [*Abhidharmakośabhāṣya*], *Tibetan Sanskrit Works Series*, vol. 8. Patna: K. P. Jayaswal Research Institute.

Schlingloff, D. (2006). *Ein buddhistisches Yogalehrbuch: Unveränderter Nachdruck der Ausgabe von 1964 unter Beigabe aller seither bekannt gewordenen Fragmente*. Munich: IUDICIUM. (Original work published 1964).

Stuart, D. M. (2015). *A less traveled path: Saddharmasmṛtyupasthānasūtra chapter 2 critically edited with a study on its structure and significance for the development of Buddhist meditation, Sanskrit Texts from the Tibetan Autonomous Region*. (Vols. 1–2). Beijing: China Tibetology Research Center/Vienna: Austrian Academy of Sciences.

Taishō Daigaku Sōgō Bukkyō Kenkyujo Shōmonji Kenkyūkai 大正大学綜合佛教研究所 声聞地研究会 (Śrāvakabhūmi Study Group, The Institute for Comprehensive Studies of Buddhism, Taishō University). (Ed.). (2007). *Yugaron Shōmonji Daini yugasho fu Hi samakita ji, Mon shojō ji, Shi shojō ji—Sansukurittogo tekisuto to wayaku*—瑜伽論声聞地 第二瑜伽処 付 非三摩呬多地・聞所成地・思所成地—サンスクリット語テキストと和訳— [*Śrāvakabhūmi:* The second chapter with *Asamāhitā bhūmiḥ, Śrutamayī bhūmiḥ, Cintāmayī bhūmiḥ*, revised Sanskrit text and Japanese translation], *Taishō Daigaku Sōgōbukkyō Kenkyūjo sōsho* 大正大学綜合佛教研究所叢書 (Vol. 18). Tokyo: Sankibō Busshorin 山喜房佛書林.

Taishō Daigaku Sōgō Bukkyō Kenkyujo Shōmonji Kenkyūkai 大正大学綜合佛教研究所 声聞地研究会 (Śrāvakabhūmi Study Group, The Institute for Comprehensive Studies of Buddhism, Taishō University). (Ed.). (2018). *Yugaron Shōmonji Daisan yugasho—Sansukurittogo tekisuto to wayaku*—瑜伽論 声聞地 第三瑜伽処—サンスクリット語テキストと和訳—[*Śrāvakabhūmi the third chapter, revised Sanskrit text and Japanese translation*]. *Taishō Daigaku sōgōbukkyō Kenkyūjo Kenkyū sōsho* 大正大学綜合佛教研究所研究叢書 (Vol. 32). Tokyo: Sankibō Busshorin 山喜房佛書林.

Warren, H. C., & Kosambi, Dh. (Eds.). (1989). *Visuddhimagga of Buddhaghosâcariya* (reprint ed.). Delhi: Motilal Banarsidass. (Original work published 1950).

Wogihara, U. (Ed.). (1936). *Abhisamayālaṃkār'ālokā Prajñāpāramitāvyākhyā (commentary on Aṣṭasāhasrikā-Prajñāpāramitā) by Haribhadra, together with the text commented on* (Vol. 2). Tokyo: The Toyo Bunko.

Secondary Sources and Translations

Anālayo, Bhikkhu. (2003). *Satipaṭṭhāna: The direct path to realization*. Cambridge, UK: Windhorse Publications.

Anālayo, Bhikkhu. (2013). *Perspectives on satipaṭṭhāna*. Cambridge, UK: Windhorse Publications.

Anālayo, Bhikkhu. (2014). *The dawn of abhidharma*. Hamburg: Hamburg University Press.

Anālayo, Bhikkhu. (2017). *Early Buddhist meditation studies*. Barre, MA: Barre Center for Buddhist Studies.

Bielefeldt, C. (1988). *Dōgen's manuals of Zen meditation*. Berkeley: University of California Press.

Deleanu, F. (2003). The newly found text of the *An ban shou yi jing* translated by An Shigao. *Kokusai Bukkyōgaku Daigakuin Daigaku kenkyū kiyō* 国際仏教学大学院大学研究紀要 [Journal of the International College for Postgraduate Buddhist Studies] *6*, 63–133.

Deleanu, F. (2006). *The chapter on the mundane path (laukikamārga) in the Śrāvakabhūmi: A trilingual edition (Sanskrit, Tibetan, Chinese), annotated translation, and introductory study* (Vols. 1–2), *Studia Philologica Buddhica Monograph Series*. Tokyo: The International Institute for Buddhist Studies.

Demiéville, P. (1954). La *Yogācārabhūmi* de Saṅgharakṣa. *Bulletin de l'École Française d'Extrême-Orient 44*(2), 339–436.

Dumoulin, H. (1991). Aspects of Buddhist meditation: Satipatthāna and Zen. In V. N. Jha (Ed.), *Kalyāna-mitra: Professor Hajime Nakamura felicitation volume* (pp. 107–116). Delhi: Sri Satguru Publications.

Greene, E. (2012). *Meditation, repentance, and visionary experience in early medieval Chinese Buddhism* (Doctoral dissertation). University of California, Berkeley.

Harrison, P. (1978b). *Buddhānusmṛti* in the *Pratyutpanna-buddha-saṃmukhavasthita-samādhi-sūtra*. *Journal of Indian Philosophy 6*(1), 35–57.

Harrison, P. (1990). *The samādhi of direct encounter with the Buddhas of the present: An annotated English translation of the Tibetan version of the Pratyutpanna-buddha-saṃmukhāvasthita-samādhi-sūtra*, *Studia philologica buddhica monograph series*. Tokyo: The International Institute for Buddhist Studies.

Harvey, P. (2013). *An introduction to Buddhism: Teachings, history and practices* (2nd ed.). New York: Cambridge University Press. (Original work published 1990).

Hattori, M. (1968). *Dignāga, On Perception, being the Praryakṣapariccheda of Dignāga's Pramāṇasamuccaya from the Sanskrit fragments and the Tibetan versions*. Cambridge, MA: Harvard University Press.

Horner, I. B. (2004). *The collection of the middle length sayings (Majjhima-Nikāya)* (Vol. 1). Delhi: Motilal Banarsidass. (Original work published 1954).

Horner, I. B. (2004). *The collection of the middle length sayings (Majjhima-Nikāya)* (Vol. 3). Delhi: Motilal Banarsidass. (Original work published 1959).

Leighton, T. D., & Okumura, S. (Trans.). (1996). *Dōgen's pure standards for the Zen community: A translation of Eihei shingi.* Albany: State University of New York Press.

Matsuda, Kazunobu 松田和信. (2021). Fujōkan o toku Chūagon 139 kyō — *Sankeishū* kara kaishū sareta bonbun tekisuto to wayaku 不浄観を説く中阿含139経——三啓集から回収された梵文テキストと和訳—— (Sanskrit text and Japanese translation of the *Madhyama-āgama* 139 [**Śivapathikā-sūtra]* based on the *Tridaṇḍamālā* manuscript). *Bukkyōdaigaku Bukkyō Gakkai kiyō* 佛教大学 仏教学会紀要 (The Bulletin of the Association of Buddhist Studies, Bukkyō University) 26:63–81.

McMahan, D. L. (2002). *Empty vision: Metaphor and visionary imagery in Mahāyāna Buddhism.* London: RoutledgeCurzon.

Ñāṇamoli, Bhikkhu. (Trans.). (1999). *The path of purification (Visuddhimagga) by Bhadantacariya Buddhaghosa.* Seattle: BPS Pariyatti Editions. (Original work published 1975).

Ñāṇamoli, Bhikkhu, & Bhikkhu Bodhi. (Trans.). (1995). *The middle length discourses of the Buddha: A new translation of the Majjihma Nikāya, The Teachings of the Buddha.* Boston: Wisdom Publications.

Nyanaponika Thera. (1983). *The heart of Buddhist meditation (satipaṭṭhāna): A handbook of mental training based on the Buddha's way of mindfulness, with an anthology of relevant texts translated from the Pali and Sanskrit.* London: Rider. (Original work published 1962).

Rhys Davids, T. W. (Trans.). (2000). *Dialogues of the Buddha: Translated from the Pali of the Dīgha Nikāya* (Vol. 2). Delhi: Motilal Banarsidass. (Original work published 1910).

Schmithausen, L. (1982). Versenkungspraxis und Erlösende Erfahrung in der Śrāvakabhūmi. In G. Oberhammer (Ed.), *Epiphanie des Heils zur Heilsgegenwart in indischer und christlicher Religion* (pp. 59–85). Vienna: Gerold.

Schmithausen, L. (2007). Aspects of spiritual practice in early Yogācāra. *Kokusai Bukkyōgaku Daigakuin Daigaku kenkyū kiyō* 国際仏教学大学院大学研究紀要 [Journal of the International College for Postgraduate Buddhist Studies] *11*, 213–244.

Schmithausen, L. (2016). Die Vier Konzentrationen der Aufmerksamkeit: Zur geschichtlichen Entwicklung einer spirituellen Praxis des Buddhismus. In F. Deleanu, S. Hori, M. Maithrimurthi, & A. von Rospatt (Eds.), *Lambert Schmithausen collected papers: Vol. 1. 1963–1977* (pp. 365–391). Tokyo: The International Institute for Buddhist Studies. (Original work published 1976).

Takakusu, J., & Watanabe, K. (Eds.). 1924–1932. *Taishō shinshū daizōkyō* 大正新脩大藏經. Tokyo: Taishō Shinshū Daizōkyō Kankōkai 大正新脩大藏經刊行會.

Walshe, M. (Trans.). (1995). *The long discourses of the Buddha: A translation of the Dīgha Nikāya.* Boston: Wisdom Publications. (Original work published 1987).

Willemen, C. (2012). *Outlining the way to reflect (T. XV 617) Siwei lüeyao fa* 思惟略要法, *Buddhist Studies Series.* Mumbai: Somaiya Publications.

Woodward, F. L. (2001). *The book of the gradual sayings (Aṅguttara-Nikāya) or more-numbered Suttas* (Vol. 2). Delhi: Motilal Banarsidass. (Original work published 1933).

Woodward, F. L. (2006). *The book of the gradual sayings (Aṅguttara-Nikāya) or more-numbered Suttas* (Vol. 5). Delhi: Motilal Banarsidass. (Original work published 1936).

Yamabe, N. (1999a). *The sūtra on the ocean-like samādhi of the visualization of the Buddha: The interfusion of the Chinese and Indian cultures in Central Asia as reflected in a fifth century apocryphal sūtra* (Doctoral dissertation). Department of Religious Studies, Yale University.

Yamabe, N. (1999b). The significance of the "*Yogalehrbuch*" for the investigation into the origin of Chinese meditation texts. *Bukkyō bunka* 佛教文化 [Buddhist culture] *9*, 1–74.

Yamabe, N. (2003). On the school affiliation of Aśvaghoṣa: "Sautrāntika" or "Yogācāra"? *Journal of the International Association of Buddhist Studies 26*(2), 225–249.

Yamabe, N. (2006). Fragments of the "*Yogalehrbuch*" in the Pelliot Collection. In J-U. Hartmann & H-J. Röllicke (Eds.), *Ein buddhistisches Yogalehrbuch: Unveränderter Nachdruck der Ausgabe von 1964 unter Beigabe aller seither bekannt gewordenen Fragmente* (pp. 325–341). Munich: IUDICIUM.

Yamabe, N. (2009). The paths of śrāvakas and bodhisattvas in meditative practices. *Acta Asiatica 96*, 47–75.

Yamabe, N. (2010). Two Chinese meditation manuals in conjunction with Pozdneyev's Mongolian manual. In E. Franco & M. Zin, *From Turfan to Ajanta: Festschrift for Dieter Schlingloff on the occasion of his eightieth birthday* (pp. 1045–1057). Lumbini, India: Lumbini International Research Institute.

Yamabe, N. (2013). Parallel passages between the *Manobhūmi* and the **Yogācārabhūmi* of Saṃgharakṣa. In U. T. Kragh (Ed.), *The foundation for yoga practitioners: The Buddhist Yogācārabhūmi treatise and its adaptation in India, East Asia, and Tibet* (pp. 596–737). Cambridge, MA: The Department of South Asian Studies, Harvard University.

Yamabe, N., & Sueki, F. (2009). *The sutra on the concentration of sitting meditation: Translated from the Chinese of Kumārajīva*. Berkeley, CA: Numata Center for Buddhist Translation and Research.

Yamazaki, T. (1974). *Mikkyō meisōhō: Mikkyō yoga, ajikan*. Kyoto: Nagata Bunshōdō.

Supplementary Note

Just before the publication of the printed version of this handbook, Matsuda (2021) was published. This article reports the discovery of a Sanskrit manuscript of a canonical sūtra (*Madhyamāgama* no. 139) that mentions the method of "grasping an image" (*nimittam ud-grah-*). This sūtra must be taken into consideration in future discussions of Buddhist visualization. I thank Kazunobu Matsuda for drawing my attention to this important finding.

CHAPTER 17

THE PHENOMENOLOGY OF MEDITATION

Commonalities and Divergences between Christian Meditatio *and Hindu* Dhyāna

CARLOS HENRIQUE DO CARMO SILVA

Introduction

The word meditation derives from the Latin *meditare* and *mediare* (Ernout-Meillet, 1967). These suggest different meanings. On the one hand, it is an action: to "put in the middle" (*medius ire*); on the other hand, particularly in Christianity, it means *mind* (*mens*). Meditation as a practice, *meditatio*, can be understood as an action of *mental concentration*, which inevitably entails a form of *interiorization* that aims to transform one's psychic dynamics (Merton, 1991; Robertson, 2011).

Although meditation has become synonymous in modern culture with a path to personal healing or spirituality, the most rigorous concept of *meditatio* emphasizes a focus on the mind and *reason* (*logos*), a reflexive capacity that is typical of the Axial Age when major systems of philosophy and religions emerged across different parts of the world, from Greece to China (Eisenstadt, 1986; Humphreys, 1986; Jaspers, 1953). There are, of course, many other forms of spiritual practices, but these should not indiscriminately be put under the umbrella of the term "meditation"; from a phenomenological perspective meditation refers strictly to the practices of *meditatio* derived from *reason* or reflexive thinking. One can give plenty of examples of concepts and practices that should not be confused with *meditatio*, such as *qi* circulation in the Daoist tradition (Lai Kuen, 2000; K'uan Yü, 1970; Schipper, 1982) or the Islamic *tafakur*, referred by al-Gazhali as a repetitive mode of prayer (Boutaleb, 2006). One can also mention the ecstasies of union, such as in the metaphysics of Plotinus, or the mental "absolution" of *samādhi* in Advaita Vedanta (Lacombe, 1979; Gardet & Lacombe, 1981). These are sometimes considered to be identical or similar to *meditatio*, but they're not: the variety of mind-altering techniques rather reveals, at the phenomenological level, a plurality of ways in experiencing time, space, self-awareness, and bodily sensations.

A note of caution is necessary about the adoption of a phenomenological perspective on the varieties of meditation, particularly the limits of this approach. The phenomenological methodology focuses on experience, in this case the experience of meditation, with the aim of finding its essence or universal elements. However, in the case of meditation what we propose to consider here is precisely what is *essentially different* across techniques and traditions: a *differential* perspective that, while allowing us to compare the experience of meditation across techniques and traditions, doesn't lose sight of their experiential plurality.

Hindu *Dhyāna*

This chapter will compare two broad meditation traditions: the Western Christian tradition, with its Hellenic background; and the Hindu tradition, particularly the synthesis between Yoga and Vedanta (McEvilley, 2002; Pinchard, 2009). Although these traditions share some philosophical and linguistic affinities, they also present a number of striking contrasts, which will be described later in this chapter (see section 'A comparison of the Christian and Yoga traditions).

In philosophy, the word meditation can be understood as a "conversion unto oneself" (Husserl, 1977), going back to the ancient Greek aphorism *gnothì sautón* ("Know thyself"). *Dhyāna*, on the other hand, in its Sanskrit etymology, points to a state of "enlightenment" referred to as a "light" or "vision"—from the root word *dhya-*, which means "to think, to consider"—activities concerning mental and reflexive processes, particularly of discernment and differentiation (Turner, 1989; Degrâces, 2004, p. 310; Angot, 2008, pp. 115–118).

In its pre-Vedic origin, which precedes the *Yoga Sūtras* (YS) of Patañjali, as well as in other commentaries and treatises (Varenne, 1989; Larson & Battacharya, 2016), the Yoga tradition was formed by a set of techniques that aimed to unify dispersed "body-energies" (Éliade, 1948; 1954). Two strategies were historically developed: one was the search for cosmic unity that had *samādhi* as its goal, a state without self-differentiation (*samādhi nirbījaḥ*, "conjunction without seed of consciousness" or "*samādhi* without an object"; YS 1.18). The second strategy was the search for the path of insight or discernment (*vivekaja marga*), which entailed a liberation from all physical and psychological constraints and obtaining the state of *kaivalya* ("aloneness"). There is a clear phenomenological difference between *samādhi* as a state of mystical union, and this second state of uniqueness that is also named *samādhi sabīja* ("conjunction with seed of consciousness") or *saṃprajñāta* ("entirely aware"; YS 1.17; see also YS 1.41; Chaudhuri, 1965; Leggett, 1992; Lacrosse, 2005).

While the first state of *samādhi* corresponds to a mystic union of absolute fusion, comparable to that of Plotinus's *henosis*, this second *samādhi sabīja* is characterized by a type of reflective consciousness. If we were to use an image to illustrate this difference: while *samādhi* is a state of union similar to the drop of water finding itself merged with the ocean, *kaivalya* conveys the ability to recognize the ocean in a single drop. Some suggest that this second state is comparable to the Christian "vision in God." The key idea is that from the singularity (*kaivalya*) of the spirit (*puruṣa*) the *yogi* contemplates all reality with a kind of supra-mental intelligence and universal understanding (YS 4.23). This is equally reflected in the *Yoga Sūtras*' first definition of Yoga as: "*yogaś citta vṛtti nirodhaḥ*" ("Yoga consists in the suppression of mental vortices)" (YS 1.2)[1].

In the classical philosophy of Yoga, there are various bodily and moral exercises to be undertaken before moving upward in the hierarchy of more advanced states. These include restrictions and observances (*yama* and *niyama*), physical postures (*āsanas*), and breathing (*prāṇāyāma*). These are followed by various degrees of psychic and mental transformation (*antaraṅga*)—psychic refers to sensorial and emotional qualities, and mental to logical and rational thought. This transformation occurs via *dhāraṇā* ("concentration") and *pratyāhāra* ("internalization"), before culminating in *dhyāna*. Within this hierarchy of states, *dhyāna* is placed just before *samādhi*, the end goal of undifferentiated consciousness. *Dhyāna* may then rightly be understood as meditation, not in the sense of a "stopping the wandering of the mind," but of freeing oneself from mental mechanisms of reasoning with which one identifies (Feuerstein, 1971).

Dhyāna is characterised by *nirodha* or "ending"; *ekāgratā* or "one-pointedness of mind"; and *samādhi pariṇāma* or "integration." The type of concentration described as *ekāgratā* is particularly important as a transition technique that allows one to arrive at *dhyāna*. When we speak of "concentration," we tend to think of it as a psychological process where the focus of attention is taken to a single point, sensation, or image. This is not the case with *ekāgratā*, which is better understood as an unconstrained or holistic form of attention. Its aim is rather to strengthen a kind of *universal* attention—an image taken from Christian spiritual experience might be of assistance here; *ekāgratā* can be understood as a process of attention that allows the perception of a reality "whose centre is everywhere, and whose periphery is nowhere" (Alanus of Lille, quoted in St. Bonaventure, *Itin.* 5.8, 2002).

[1] Another possible translation is "yoga is the cessation of mental fluctuation" or "yoga is the stilling of the changing states of mind." The aim here is not a simple process of annihilation but of transformation. In the process of meditation, one finds an initial strategy of *stopping* (*nirodha pariṇāma*) which abolishes "karmic" effects. But note that the energetic work of the *Yoga Sūtras* includes insights from several categories (*tattvas*) and the way they are practiced, based on *darśana* from Sāṃkhya-Yoga (Larson & Bhattacharya, 1987; Reymond, 1984). It is in this underlying structure that one can "map" the human—or even cosmic (Chenet, 1998)—possibilities described in Patañjali's teachings.

Although it is not the aim of this chapter to move deeper into an explanation of this meditative mechanism, it is important to highlight that *dhyāna* is intended as an exercise that develops a very particular *quality* of attention ("self-observation" or *svādhyāya*). This quality allows one to ponder on the "original essence of the self," which then leads to perceiving what "shines in itself" (*nirbhāsa*)—that which is completely free, formless, and contentless, as revealed in *samādhi* (YS 3.3) (Silburn, 1990; Dürkheim, 2004).

Christian *Meditatio*

Let us now consider the Western Christian tradition of *meditatio*. As well as developing different forms of personal and collective prayer with a devotional character, in Christianity we find various mental techniques of meditation, such as silent prayer or prayer of the heart (e.g., hesychasm). There is one Christian method that bears interesting parallels to the hierarchy of states associated with *dhyāna*—this is called *recollection* (from the Spanish *recogimiento*). This practice, originating from sixteenth-century Iberian spirituality, includes a hierarchy of several levels (Osuna, *Tercer Abecedario*, Tr. 6, cs. 1 (1972), pp. 233–244) which aims to quiet or calm the soul, in order to arrive at a state where our process of thinking about the world becomes silent and one prays into that silence (Osuna, *Tercer Abecedario*, Tr. 21, c. 1).

This is the form of *meditatio* that the great mystic Teresa of Ávila advocates. Although Saint Teresa also refers to this as *mental prayer* (*Life*, 8.5, trans. by E. Allison Peers, 2002, *The Complete Works*, Vol. 1, p. 51; Fabre, 1992), her experience of *recollection* anticipates a stage of interiorization characterized by a new form of sensing. She says:

> The first kind of prayer I experienced which seems to me supernatural I should describe as one which, despite all our efforts, cannot be acquired by industry or diligence, though we can certainly prepare for it, and it must be a great help if we do. This prayer is an interior recollection felt in the soul, which seems to have acquired new senses, corresponding to its exterior senses, and appears desirous of withdrawing from outward tumult. (*Spiritual Relations*, V, trans. by Peers, 2002, Vol. 1, p. 327)

It is the very action of allowing oneself to be free from distractions of the senses that, through an internal *loving* dialogue with the soul, allows a special attention to God. In her words, "the possibility of speaking with God alone" (*Life*, 8.5, trans. by Peers, 2002, Vol. 1, p. 51) In other works, Theresa insists that *recollection* is not forced, nor it is only a form of mental suppression. She summarizes this in a famous passage from the *Interior Castle*: "…the important thing is not to think much, but to love much…"(*Moradas del castillo interior*, IV, 1, 13, *[=Interior Castle]*, trans. by Peers, 2002, Vol. II, p. 233) Love here should not be understood in a sentimental way but as an essential quality of God. Thus, *recollection* can be best understood not as an active state of the mind, but as a *passive* one in which the Holy Spirit transforms the mind and effects a deep spiritual realization. Here we are moving away from *meditatio* as an active exercise and into an *enlightening experience* that one has no control over, this being understood in Christian terms as a free gift from God (Silva, 1986).

This type of spiritual exercise is a unique development of Christian spirituality and one which has been compared to Yoga (Siddheswarananda, 1998). But it has deep historical roots, both in Christian monastic doctrine—particularly the *scala coeli* (the scale up to heaven or steps of prayer)—and also in the Eastern Christian tradition of the hesychasm (Hausherr, 1927; Lossky, 1990).

If we travel back a further four hundred years from St. Teresa's age, we find in the method of *lectio divina* another important development of Christian *meditatio*. One of the major exponents of this method, Hugh of St. Victor, defines meditation in his *Didascalion* as "the frequent planned thought that investigates the cause and the origin, the manner and the use of each thing."[2] (Hugh of Saint-Victor, *Didascalion*, 3.10, trans. in C. H. Buttimer (1939); also 1991, trans. M. Lemoine, *L'art de lire* Didascalion, Paris: Cerf, pp. 142–143; trans. in Hugh of Saint-Victor, 1961). This method emphasizes meditation as "*cogitation*," a process of moving from the usual state of dispersed awareness to one of understanding causality and purpose—this prepares the mind for the following stages of contemplation. Hugh of St. Victor sees a moral purpose in meditation, which is complementary to the insight (*scrutinium*) of principles, and of divine purposes (see *Didascalion* 3.10).

The *lectio divina* method works in the following way: we start by reading a sacred text passively, we then meditate actively on the text in order to understand it, and, finally, we contemplate it by the light of God. The method is expected to lead an individual from an attentive reading, which is repeated some times, through to an understanding of the text that comes from God—in Christian terms, to move from a reading *by the letter* to a reading *by the spirit* (*Did* 3.8). It is then an active process of searching for knowledge that eventually moves into a contemplative level, where the individual lets God provide the understanding (Cayré, 1954; Carruters, 1998; Robertson, 2011).

We find this gradation of contemplative degrees in other forms within the Christian tradition. In St. Bonaventure, for example, the meditative process is understood as an intermediary process between the lower faculties of the senses and imagination, and the higher *intelligentia* which has at its apex the *synderesis scintilla* (the summit of divine sight). These degrees are also symbolized in hierarchies of angels, particularly in the six wings of the Seraphim (*Itinerarium mentis in Deum* [*Itin.*] or *The Journey of the Mind into God*, Prol. 3, in Bonaventure, 2002).

Meditation, in this case, has a deep moral and rational character, not as a rationalization of what lies outside, but as a reflection and contemplation of truth which Bonaventure calls *dijudicatio* (abstraction). He says: "Moreover by a more excellent and immediate manner *dijudicatio* leads us to gaze (*in speculandam*) upon eternal truth with more certainty" (*Itin.* 2.9, in Bonaventure, 2002). So in a first step, the mind ascends through the faculty of reflection; then reason is illuminated by Faith, Hope, and Charity

[2] Original Latin text: "*Meditatio est cogitatio frequens cum consilio, quae causam et originem, modum et utilitatem uniuscuiusque rei prudenter investigat.*"

(*Itin.* 4.2, in Bonaventure, 2002)—this meditative state of *speculatio* remains "nocturnal" or apophatic (*Itin.* 5.4, in Bonaventure, 2002, remembering the "blindness by excess of light" of Aristotle, *Metaph.*, a, 1, 993b 5; Silva, 2017), in opposition to the higher—diurnal—state of enlightenment. In the final step, one reaches a contemplative ecstasy in which the mind becomes transparent in the light of Truth like a burning love (*incendium amoris*), so that that it is formed "by Truth Itself" (*Itin.* 7.6 and 5.1, in Bonaventure, 2002). Thus the soul reaches a state of loving recollection of itself:

> Enter therefore yourself and see, that your mind most fervently loves itself...; and from this you advert, that your soul has a threefold power, not in the eye of the flesh, but in the eye of the mind. (*Itin.* 3, 1)

Finally, it is important to note that that within this Christian *meditatio* framework the mind has not yet reached a degree of perfect stillness, which is why the medieval name for meditation is that of *ruminatio* (rumination). This is very different from the negative rumination associated with depressive states; it simply consists of a meditative repetition of words or a sentence with the aim of interiorizing the deeper, spiritual reality of these words.[3]

A Comparison of the Christian and Yoga Traditions

Let us now focus on a comparison between the Christian and the Yoga traditions. Table 16.1 compares the main degrees of Christian *meditatio* with the steps (*aṅga*) in Yoga. This comparative structure is sketched in order to show that each of these traditions describes different practices and corresponding states of being that can be hierarchically placed against each other—at the bottom we find the first stages of the hierarchy. Note that this is a schematic presentation and does not suggest that an individual must, in practice, follow it to move across these states of consciousness.

Although there is no clear parallelism between the particular degrees or steps of these two traditions, there is one major commonality: their sense of hierarchy and differentiation, moving from the sensorial and corporal levels, through emotional and mental forms of consciousness, up to their spiritual apex. But the idiosyncrasies of each tradition cannot be underestimated.

Another commonality in the meditative process of these traditions is that both can be broken into two distinct stages: one corresponding to an interiorization of psychic and mental components (sensorial, affective, and imaginative), and a second one where spiritual fulfillment takes center stage—in *dhyāna* and in *consideratio*—where individual feelings and thoughts are of no significance. Here, however, we are again faced with a difference between these traditions. In Christianity, it is not enough to be

[3] This technique is already present in St. Augustine: *Conf* X, 16, 24; *De Trin.* X, 11, 17; also Moreau, 1955; Cayré, 1954; Cilleruelo, 1973; O'Connell, 1987).

Table 17.1 Main degrees of Christian *meditatio* and steps (*aṅga*) in Yoga

Degrees of Christian Prayer and Meditation	Steps (aṅga) in Yoga
Contemplatio/unio: a mystical state where one attains a perfect vision of God; also described as a *unified* participation in God's inner love, or as a spiritual wedding (*matrimonium*)	*Samādhi*: a non-dual state that consists in the merging of the subject and object of consciousness: a *unio mystica*. (e.g., YS 1.20, 1.46, 1.51, etc.)
Consideratio/illuminatio: a gratuitous (God-given) state of peace and spiritual vision, but not definitive as one's vision is still imperfect—as in a mirror (*speculum*)	*Dhyāna*: a unified state of the entire field of consciousness with an enlightened or lucid awareness (YS 3.2)
Meditatio: a state of *silent prayer* consisting of deep concentration on the gifts of God	*Dhārāṇa*: a fixed state of attention or *concentration* (YS 2.53, 3.1)
Recollection: a non-thinking state of withdrawal from of the senses, where one becomes passive in order to receive spiritual graces	*Pratyāhāra*: a state of withdrawal of the senses from external objects (YS 3.54)
Mental Prayer: an analytical method of prayer using discursive reason in order to achieve a deeper understanding; often used in combination with a mental image of a devotional object	*Prāṇayāma*: controlling the breath in such way as to develop an "interior rhythm" of vital energies (*prāṇa*) (YS 2.49)
Lectio Divina: a form of prayer described as *spiritual reading*, which is accompanied by a sense of stillness and calm	*Āsana postures* or body positions that are associated with feelings of inner calm and serenity (YS 2.29, 2.46)
Affective prayer: *devotional prayer* associated with feelings of reverence and love	*Niyama*: preliminary ascetic exercises or *observances* (YS 2.29, 2.32)
Vocalic Prayer: *liturgical* discipline, including the verbalization of petitions and prayers	*Yama*: techniques of *self-restraint*, including moral discipline (YS 2.29, 2.30)

enlightened by God—what truly matters is to respond to God. This means that the process at stake here is not that of allowing oneself to join in some kind of *pantheistic* unit, but rather to form a *dialogical* union (Pasqua, 2004). This contrasts with Yoga where one supposedly reaches a state no longer enclosed in object or subject; in other words, there no longer is a consciousness of who might be conscious, as pure contemplative consciousness need not be conscious of itself (Lacombe, 1981).

From a Western perspective, the ideal of yogic union strikes us as particularly impersonal. There seems to be a dissolution of the individual into the Absolute, which is opposed to the *individuation* of the Jewish-Christian worldview. This characteristic of individuation is also reflected in Western philosophy, particularly since Descartes, as meditation is understood to be a form of self-reflection whose aim is self-knowledge (Brunschvicg, 1931; Carr, 1999). Undoubtedly, in a general sense, meditation is an individual exercise even when practiced collectively. However, its practice challenges that first-person identification with the "I," either transforming it into a different self or undoing it. Thus, in Yoga, we find a description of an impersonal or supra-personal consciousness that belongs to the highest step of *samādhi* (YS 3.3). Meditation in the Christian tradition does, of course, involve purification and mortification of the self (*purgatio* and *mortificatio*). These are based in the teachings that without the death of selfishness, resurrection will not be possible (as in the Gospel image of the seed that must perish to bear fruit; John 12:24). In Christianity, the end of individuation is not demanded, but it rather involves a process of finding oneself as a person, through an inner dialogue with God that becomes a remembrance of one's real self.

This process of remembrance has deep historical roots, both in the Platonic ("know thyself") and Stoic philosophies (Hadot, 2002, p. 27; Rönnegard, 2013), as well as in the Jewish tradition of recollection of their history (Idel, 1989). It is within this context that the exercise of repetitive remembrance of one's sins in Christian spirituality should be understood; it is this exercise that leads to the purgation of the self and eventually the so-called "fruits of spiritual grace," where the individual enjoys closeness to God. The process of individuation, understood against the background of the eternal destiny of the soul, gives meditation a privileged role in the Christian tradition as an indispensable tool for inner contrition and purging. This comes particularly alive in the dramatic image of the *via crucis* (the agonizing way of the cross that Jesus undertook to save humanity), which symbolizes the contemplation of our mortality and weakness faced with the endless divine mercy of God (Kierkegaard, 2006). As an aside, it is interesting to note that the Christian conscious examination of the self, of bringing into one's attention in a repetitive way all of one's actions, bears similarities to Buddhist forms of mindfulness meditation, which aims to fulfill an equivalent "purification" of the self.

With Yoga, though, we are looking at an altogether different process. Although the first steps of Yoga include a phase of recollection, where all sensorial, emotional, and mental contents are as if held against the illusory character of the universe of limited phenomena (*saṃskāra*), *dhyāna* is not concerned with a knowing of the self, or an undoing of the self (as in Buddhism), but with an objective consciousness of one's own ignorance (Jones, 1993; Hulin, 2001). In this sense, meditation in the Yoga tradition is not an ascetic exercise whose aim is to allow one to remember one's true self or soul, as in Christianity, or a strategy to realize self-emptiness, as in Buddhism. Instead, *dhyāna* envisages the liberating vision of an "I" that is reached through realizing one's own ignorance (*avidyā*) (Hulin, 1978; 1994a). This ignorance is not simply a lack of knowledge, but a knowledge about one's ignorance (*Brahmasûtra*, 1.1.1 (2000), pp. 3–5), perhaps similar to what in the Socratic tradition was understood as *docta ignorantia* (learned ignorance). In other words, the contemplative observation of ignorance is in itself transforming, for it allows enlightened conscience to become aware of its own illusion. It is as if the power of the illusion of the phenomenal universe (*māyā*) becomes a way of deceiving that same illusion, working like a mirror and thus allowing the clearest and purest consciousness. The Yoga tradition sometimes uses the idea of a "game" played between illusion and reality, or a dance, to characterize this process (Hulin, 1994b; Chaudhuri, 1965, pp. 97–99).

The understanding of the self in these two traditions is clearly different. In *dhyāna* any sense of self is still some kind of projection of the phenomenal reality, which is strikingly at odds with the idea of the development of a unique self in the Christian context. We must acknowledge, though, a more nuanced perspective: the exercise of purgation and inner death in Christian meditation presents a kind of hesitation about ascertaining what or who the self is—is the self the one who meditates, or is it the one who is born out of meditation from God's grace? This nuanced or multiple sense of self is also reflected in Western literature and poetry[4] (Pessoa, 1982; Crabtree, 1985; Braude, 1995).

An Intermediate Dimension

To make a full comparison between these two traditions, one must attend to what may be called an *intermediate dimension*, which connects the highest and lowest stages of meditation. It can be argued that in order to reach the highest stage of the hierarchy, it is not enough to engage in a deliberate effort of attention and withdrawal from the senses and imagination (Yoga), or to allow oneself to receive the gratuitous presence of God (Christianity). Something else is required. In Yoga, this is referred to as an energetic dimension (*prāṇa*), sometimes understood almost as a material element (e.g., in the doctrine of *spaṇḍa* or "vibration" of reality). The idea being that one develops certain energies through a number of exercises, such as spiritual breathing (*prāṇāyāma*) (Dyczowski, 1989; Silburn, 1988). In the Christian tradition, this intermediate dimension of meditation can be found in the imitation of Christ, as well as in the spiritual exercises of St Ignatius of Loyola (Fabre, 1992), and in hesychasm (see Eastern Christianity and Meditation), particularly the virtues of voluntary suffering or self-offering love, which can be understood as an *abandonment* of oneself.

It is within this intermediate dimension that we can understand a variety of exercises and symbolisms. Take for example, the technical teachings mentioned by Vijñânabhiksu (*Yogasârasamgraha*, Larson & Bhattacharya, 2016) which revolves around the timing of mental vibrations (*citta*) according to a numerological system of twelve *pratyāhāra*, thereby linking *dhyāna* to twelve moments of concentration. (Silburn, 1990; Silva, 2006). Similarly, in the Christian tradition there are references to a numerological wisdom going back to St. Augustine (*De ordine; De Musica*). St. Bonaventure, for example, acknowledges the existence of numbers in bodies, sounds and words, as well as in the soul as "exemplary principles" (*Itin.* 2.10; in Bonaventure, 2002); these can be understood as underlying structures of the soul without which meditation could never work as a spiritual exercise: "Moreover all these sciences have certain and infallible rules as lights and rays descending from the eternal law in our mind" (*Itin.* 3.7; in Bonaventure, 2002).

[4] See also Pessoa's (1981, p. 132) poetical self-queries:

> Whose stare is
> Glancing through my eyes?
> When I think I see
> Who keeps on seeing
> While I am thinking?

For all its technical details—and embodiment of silence, stillness, and restraint—meditation exercises are understood in both Christian and Hindu traditions as momentary methods that allow one to focus on what is essential. But even as a kind of provisional scaffolding for the "soul to ascend," meditation is expressed as a spiritual art (Govinda, 1977), which lives on after it is no longer needed to enter or reach a certain state of consciousness.

The Impossibility of Doing Meditation

It is important to oppose a popular idea that all spiritual paths converge into the same mountain peak. Contrary to this, our suggestion is that the experience of meditation may be a kind of crossroads where the path widens at the top—potentially leading to a new path that is "individually universal." Let us clarify this apparent paradox. Within Yoga there are paths within paths that occur within a sequence of time (Phan-chon-tôn, 2000; Degrâces, 2004; Grinshpon, 2002). But rather than Yoga necessarily entailing a unit of all things within a whole, there can be what one might call a creative discontinuity—a potential wholeness that is not a unit but something always different and singular. This sense of discontinuity also appears in Christian meditation, as an extremely personal and unique dialogue with God. And the variable character of Christian meditation exercises also provides for a varied and personal dialogue with God. This challenges our usual understanding of God: here one envisages God not as a unit but a *unicity* of being. This includes both the God of monotheistic unity and the God of pagan plurality but, more importantly, the God that is *unique* and *exclusive*, never repeatable, always and ever present and new (Silva, 2001).[5]

But despite the discontinuous, unpredictable—and in Christian terms, gratuitous—end goal of meditation, there is something about its practice that demands some stability (of time, for example) in order for an *experience* to arise (Merton, 2004; Brabant, 2004). There is much interest today in discussing the experiences of meditation, but there is something peculiar in this, as if we are trying to speak about an experience that lies beyond experience (Wittgenstein, 1921; Tyler, 2011). Such is the case of so-called spiritual experiences, where one usually speaks of experiencing a "feeling" that goes far and beyond what language can empirically communicate. If such "experiences" are still described within the discursive meditation in Christian prayer—through indirect symbolism, parables, and analogies—in *dhyāna*, on the other hand, there is nothing that meets the criteria of a communicable and intelligible experience. The meditative state would be best described as ecstatic,[6] a kind of feeling without any thinking, or a pure

[5] See also Guénon's (1932/1984) argument about God as different from multiplicity and unity: if multiplicity is contained in the unity of being, unity is already Being manifested; therefore, there is a vaster Reality that precedes the very manifestation of being as unity and multiplicity.

[6] Or *enstasis*, on which see Éliade, 1948, p. 93.

intuition that surpasses what the mental apparatus of our minds can apprehend or assimilate as experience.

It is precisely for this reason that one finds in these traditions, particularly in Yoga, statements on the *impossibility of doing meditation*, understood as an intentional action leading to a certain experience. Likewise, in the Christian tradition there is a constant reminder about the need to adopt an attitude of radical humility, for everything one receives from God is a free gift and our individual agency and experience do not matter. The principle underlying this is clear: all special knowledge, or gnosis, can only be redemptive if accepted in a state where we realize our "nothingness" (Eckhart, *Sermon 7*, "we have to come to the state of being *nothing* in order to enter into the same nature that He is"; in Eckhart, 1979, trans. Walshe, p. 66).[7]

Conclusions

To be meditative is different from talking and thinking about meditation and the "experiences of meditation," even attempting to classify them in a table of altered states of consciousness, or in illustrations of psychophysiological and neuronal meditative states (Fischer, 1981). But the modern popular interest in meditation goes well beyond the attempt to understand it; we now seek to use meditation as a domesticated or standardized strategy to heal stress or psychological problems of various kinds. This attempt is completely at odds with the traditions described above, where meditation is not meant to be used in any materialistic or spiritual materialistic way (Trungpa, 1973), not even as a form of improving or enhancing our normal functioning. What today is called meditation is generally nothing more than a self-hypnotic state or a sort of mental numbness, radically different from the exercise of unlearning and of inner stripping of Christian asceticism, or of the enlightenment of Yoga.

What gives credit to the ancient traditions of *meditatio* and *dhyāna* cannot be confused with seeing meditation as a kind of panacea, as New Age spirituality and some modern psychologists propose (Raschke, 1996). The value of these traditions rests in technical indications and observations that are only the basis of a teaching, which can best be understood as *Socratic*. It's certainly not the kind of teaching we find in universities, but it's neither a set of prescriptive rituals or restrictions; it's rather a "teaching how to learn" (Krishnamurti, 1972; 1973a; 1973b, pp. 344–353) that seeks to arouse a true metamorphosis of the self, something like moving from sleep to an awakened state (Moore, 1984).

[7] One also finds in Yoga the idea that all forms of action are merely an illusory show and all meditation stages are perhaps nothing more than a moment of waiting—as a delay in thought (Libet, 2004)—for, after all, what is trying to be achieved at the last stage has always been present. This, of course, does not deny the gradation in consciousness from *meditatio* to contemplation (particularly in the *unio mystica*) or the transition from *dhyāna* to *samādhi* (see also Williams, 1998).

The diverse phenomenology of meditation in the Christian and Hindu traditions suggests that these techniques were developed as exercises of *a mental kind*; in other words, exercises that aimed to have certain effects on a *mental* dimension, such in provoking an alteration or intensification of one's perception, memory, imagery, or affect (Corbin, 1976; Chodorow, 1997)—including the use of alternative and paradoxical ways of reasoning about reality. All these *mental* exercises aimed to transform the very process of thinking, envisaging a hierarchy where one moves upward until God, or pure consciousness, is reached (Kühlewind, 1984).[8] As one moves upward in this hierarchy, one finds a kind of aversion to thinking, not just everyday trivial thoughts, but all thoughts. This is why we find descriptions of states with "no-thought" in both traditions, as one aims to become *pure being*. In a way, both traditions consider that to think is to deny being, even if that thinking refers to the affirmation of a metaphysical ontology; thus the meditator becomes the mystic who is no longer interested in the scaffolding of rational elaborations, including the reasons for meditation. So the fruitfulness of meditation, if one can describe it in such a way, is precisely in the opening of a gate where *thought* is transformed into a state of awareness that overcomes the usual categories of thinking, such as singular-universal, cause-consequences, subject-object, and human-divine.

This is very different from the processes of self-knowledge and self-reference that we find in Western philosophy since Descartes' *cogito* (Sorabji, 2006). The process of awareness that meditation engages with cannot be confused with a mere *attentive* state aiming at self-knowledge. But we can use Descartes' *cogitation* to aid us in understanding better the state of consciousness meditation may bring about: if we translate *cogitation* literally as a "thinking agitation," where we feel stirred into attributing a "yes" or "no" to all kinds of propositions and taking this *cogitation* further, and further on; the mental vibration of this positive/negative template of the mind is the very stuff that creates a vortex in which a superior spiritual energy arises, with its own autonomy, and recreates the individual—who no longer is an agent in the way we conceive of someone who has intentions and desires. Consider that in *meditatio* one gives oneself to the ascetic meditative process so that this process becomes the agent, not the individual; the aim here is to create a state of passivity that allows a different autonomy, such as St. Teresa of Ávila notes when she writes that knowledge is then observed "as a windmill that grinds without stopping" independently of our will (St. Theresa of Ávila, *Moradas del castillo interior* [*Interior Castle*], IV, 1, 13; trans. by Peers, 2002, Vol. II, p. 235). Thus, to keep using the windmill analogy of St. Teresa, our *cogitant* minds are no longer in control, but they are the ferment, the energy that allows meditation to operate on the individual.

There is no doubt that these traditions agree on the existence of a state of consciousness that is entirely free and autonomous. The creativity of meditation exercises also addresses

[8] Note that there may be a Christian meditation experience culminating on mystical contemplation that does not go through a comparable *dhyāna* enlightenment. One can also find an enlightened state that is so crystallized in its own gnosis that it constitutes in itself an impediment to the *unio mystica*. The bottom line is that the various meditation practices (*abhyāsa*) always have to be weighed and exercised in relation to life's varying and unique circumstances.

the various ways in which such autonomy can be conceived of and arrived at. For example, within Christian *meditatio*, one can find an exercise of repetition as in the monastic *ruminatio*, the repetition of the sacred text until the text gains a life of its own, allowing a particular kind of spiritual insight (Ruiz Jurado, 1994; McIntosh, 2004). Now this seems like a slow process, and when we speak of meditation we usually picture a quiet stillness, a slow inner dialogue—but it needn't be so. Precisely because we have, on the one hand, the polarized state of our mind with its "thinking agitation," and, on the other, this state of being that has its own agency, so it may very well happen that there are abrupt, frenetic processes, more similar to Dionysian fervor than an Apollonian calm (Dodds, 1951; Padel, 1992). Life's unique circumstances will always weigh and will need to find a balance that moves beyond detailed and universal prescriptions of meditation exercises.

References

Angot, M. (Trans.). (2008). *Le Yoga-Sûtra de Patañjali; Le Yoga-Bhâsya de Vyâsa, avec des extraits du* Yoga-Vârttika *de Vijñâna-Bhiksu*. Paris: Belles Lettres.

Aristotle (Ed.), *Metaph.* a, 1, 993b 5, & Tredennick, H. (Trans.). 1968. *The Metaphysics*. London/ Cambridge, MA: W. Heinemann/Harvard University Press.

Augustine, St. (1947). De musica. In G. Finaert and F.-J. Thonnard (Eds.), *Œuvres de saint Augustin: Dialogues philosophiques, VII (La musique)*. Paris : Desclée de Brouwer.

Augustine, St. (1948). De ordine. In R. Jolivet (Ed.), *Oeuvres de saint Augustin : Dialogues philosophiques, I, (Contra academicos; De beata vita ; De ordine)* (pp. 302–458). Paris: Desclée de Brouwer.

Augustin, St. (1956). *De Trinitate*. In Fr. Luis Arias (Ed. & Trans.), *Tratado sobre la Santísima Trinidad (in: Obras de San Agustín, t. V)*. Madrid: Biblioteca de Autores Cristianos.

Augustin, St. (1977). *Confessiones*. In P. de Labriolle, *Saint Augustin, Confessions* (Vols. 1–2). Paris: Les Belles Lettres.

Bonaventure, St. (2002). *The journey of the mind into God*. Grand Rapids, MI: Christian Classic Ethereal Library.

Boutaleb, H. (Trans. & Intro.). (2006). *Abû Hamid al-Ghazâlî, Le livre de la méditation (Kitâb al-tafakkur)*. Paris: Les Éditions Albouraq.

Brabant, C. (2004). The truth narrated: Ricoeur on religious experience. In L. Boeve & L. P. Hemming (Eds.), *Divinising experience. Essays in the history of religious experience from Origen to Ricoeur* (pp. 246–270). Leuven: Peeters.

Braude, S. E. (1995). *First person plural: Multiple personality and the philosophy of mind*. Boston: Rowman & Littlefield.

Brunschvicg, L. (1931). *De la connaissance de soi*. Paris: Librairie Félix Alcan.

Carr, D. (1999). *The paradox of subjectivity: The self in the transcendental tradition*. New York: Oxford University Press.

Carruthers, M. (1998). *The craft of thought: Meditation, rhetoric, and the making of images, 400–1200*. Cambridge: Cambridge University Press.

Cayré, P. F. (1954). *La contemplation augustinienne: Principes de Spiritualité et de Théologie*. Paris: Desclée de Brouwer.

Chaudhuri, H. (1965). *Integral Yoga: The concept of harmonious and creative living*. London: George Allen & Unwin.

Chenet, F. (1998). *Psychogenèse et cosmogonie selon le* Yoga-Vâsistha, « *Le monde est dans l'âme* » (Vols. 1–2). Paris: Publications de l'Institut de Civilisation Indienne.
Chodorow, J. (Ed.). (1997). *Encoutering Jung: On active imagination*. Princeton, NJ: Princeton University Press.
Cilleruelo, L. (1973). La mística de la «Memoria Dei» en san Agustín. *Estudio Agustiniano 81*, 401–448.
Corbin, H. (1976). *L'imagination créatrice dans le soufisme d'Ibn 'Arabi*. Paris: Flammarion.
Crabtree, A. (1985). *Multiple man: Explorations in possession and multiple personality*. London: Holt, Rinehart & Winston.
Degrâces, A. (Trans.). (2004). *Les Yogasutra de Patañjali: Des chemins au fin chemin*. Paris: Fayard.
Dodds, E. R. (1951). *The Greeks and the irrational*. Cambridge: Cambridge University Press.
Dürkheim, K. G. (2004). *Hara: The vital center of man*. Rochester, VT: Inner Traditions, Bear.
Dyczowski, M. S. G. (1989). *The doctrine of vibration: An analysis of the doctrines and practices of Kashmir Shaivism*. Delhi: Motilal Banarsidass.
Eckhart, M. ("1321", 1979). Walshe (Trans.). *Sermons and Treatises* (Vol. 1). Longmead/ Shaftesbury: Element Books.
Eisenstadt, S. N. (Ed.). (1986). *The origins and diversity of axial age civilizations*. Albany: State University of New York Press.
Éliade, M. (1948). *Techniques du Yoga*. Paris: Gallimard.
Éliade, M. (1954). *Le Yoga. Immortalité et liberté*. Paris: Payot.
Ernout, A., & Meillet, A. (1967). *Dictionnaire étymologique de la langue latine. Histoire des mots*. Paris: Klincksieck.
Fabre, P-A. (1992). *Ignace de Loyola, le lieu de l'image: Le problème de la composition de lieu dans les pratiques spirituelles et artistiques jésuites de la seconde moitié du XVI*[e] *siècle*. Paris: Vrin.
Feuerstein, G. (1971). The essence of Yoga. In G. Feuerstein & J. Miller, *A Reappraisal of Yoga: Essays in Indian philosophy* (pp. 1–47). London: Rider & Co.
Fischer, R. (1981). A cartography of the ecstatic and meditative states. In R. Woods (Ed.), *Understanding mysticism* (pp. 286–305). London: Athlone Press.
Gardet, L., & Lacombe, O. (1981). *L'expérience du soi: Étude de mystique compare*. Paris: Desclée de Brouwer.
Govinda, Lama A. (1977). *Creative meditation and multidimensional consciousness*. London: George Allen & Unwin.
Grinshpon, Y. (2002). *Silence unheard: Deathly otherness in Pâtañjala-Yoga*. Albany: State University of New York Press.
Guénon, R. (1984). *The multiple states of being*. New York: Larson. (Original work published 1932).
Hadot, P. (2002). *Exercices spirituels et philosophie antique*. Paris: Albin Michel.
Hausherr, I., S.I. (1927). *Orientalia Christiana: Vol. IX-2, no. 36. La méthode d'oraison hésychaste*. Roma: Pontificium Institutum Orientalium Studiorum.
Hugh of Saint-Victor. (1939). *Hugonis de Sancto Victore Didascalicon: De studio legendi. A critical text* (C. H. Buttimer, Ed.). Washington, DC: The Catholic University Press.
Hugh of Saint-Victor. (1961). *The Didascalicon of Hugh of Saint-Victor: A medieval guide to the arts* (J. Taylor, Trans.). New York: Columbia University Press.
Hulin, M. (1978). *Le principe de l'ego dans la pensée classique: La notion d'ahamkâra, Publications de l'Institut de Civilisation indienne*. Paris: Collège de France.

Hulin, M. (1994a). *Qu'est-ce que l'ignorance métaphysique (dans la pensée hindoue)? Śaṅkara.* Paris: Vrin.

Hulin, M. (1994b). Vertige et lucidité: Objectivation des affects et détachement selon la doctrine Sâmkhya. In R. Imbach, A. de Libera, M. Hulin, et al., *Le dépassement de soi dans la pensée philosophique: Actes du colloque des 19 et 20 octobre 1990 pour les soixante-dix ans de Fernand Brunner, professeur honoraire de l'Université de Neuchâtel* (pp. 55–67). Neuchâtel: À La Baconnière.

Hulin, M. (2001). *Śaṅkara et la non-dualité.* Paris: Bayard.

Humphreys, S. C. (1986). Dynamics of the Greek breakthrough: The dialogue between philosophy and religion. In S. N. Eisenstadt (Ed.), *The origins and diversity of axial age civilizations* (pp. 92–110). Albany: State University of New York Press.

Husserl, E. (1977). *Cartesianische Meditationen. Eine Einleitung in die Phänomenologie* (E. Ströker, Ed.). Hamburg: Felix Meiner.

Idel, M. (1989). *Hitbodedut* as concentration in ecstatic Kabbalah. In A. Green (Ed.), *World spirituality: An encyclopedic history of the religious quest: Vol. 13. Jewish spirituality: From the Bible through the Middle Ages* (pp. 405–438). New York: Crossroad.

Jaspers, K. (Trans.). (1953). *The origin and goal of history.* London: Routledge.

Jones, R. H. (1993). Knowledge and unknowing in the Îsa Upanisad. In *Mysticism examined: Philosophical inquiries into mysticism* (pp. 47–55.). Albany: State University of New York Press.

Kevala, G. (Trans.). (2000). *Brahmasûtra con il commento di ´Sankara.* Roma: Ed. Âsram Vidyâ.

Kierkegaard, S. (2006). *Exercice en christianisme* (V. Delecroix, Trans.). Paris: Félin.

Krishnamurti, J. (1972). *Freedom from the known.* London: Victor Gollancz.

Krishnamurti, J. (1973a). *Education and the significance of life.* London: Victor Gollancz.

Krishnamurti, J. (1973b). *The awakening of intelligence.* London: Victor Gollancz Ltd.; pp. 344–353.

K'uan Yü, L. [C. Luk]. (1970). *Taoist Yoga: Alchemy and immortality.* London: Rider.

Kühlewind, G. (1984). *Stages of consciousness: Meditations on the boundaries of the soul* (M. St. Goar, Trans.; C. Bamford & F. Paddock, Eds.). West Stockbridge, MA: Inner Traditions/ Lindisfarne Press.

Lacombe, O. (1979). *Indianité: Études historiques et comparatives sur la pensée indienne.* Paris: Belles Lettres.

Lacombe, O. (1981). Le Yoga. In L. Gardet & O. Lacombe, *L'expérience du soi: Étude de mystique comparée* (pp. 115–152). Paris: Desclée de Brouwer.

Lacrosse, J. (2005). De la commensurabilité des discours mystiques en Orient et en Occident: Une comparaison entre Plotin et Çankara. In A. Dierkens and & B. De Ryke (Eds.), *Mystique: la passion de l'Un, de l'Antiquité à nos jours* (pp. 215–223), *Problèmes d'Histoire des religions* (Vol. 15). Bruxelles: Édition de l'Université de Bruxelles.

Lai Kuen, K. (2000). *Qi chinois et anthropologie chrétienne.* Paris: L'Harmattan.

Larson, G. J., and Bhattacharya, R. S. (Eds.). (1987). *Encyclopedia of Indian philosophies: Vol. IV. Sâmkhya: A dualist tradition in Indian philosophy.* Princeton, NJ: Princeton University Press.

Larson, G. J., and Bhattacharya, R. S. (Eds.). (2016). *Encyclopedia of Indian philosophies: Vol. XII. Yoga: India's philosophy of meditation.* Delhi: Motilal Banarsidass.

Leggett, T. (Trans.). (1992). *Śaṅkara on the Yoga Sûtra-s: A full translation of the newly discovered text.* Delhi: Motilal Banarsidass.

Libet, B. (2004). *Mind time: The temporal factor in consciousness.* Cambridge, MA: Harvard University Press.

Lossky, V. (1990). *Essai sur la théologie mystique de l'Église d'Orient*. Paris: Cerf.
McEvilley, T. (2002). *The shape of ancient thought: Comparative studies in Greek and Indian philosophies*. New York: Allworth Press.
McIntosh, M. A. (2004). *Discernment and truth: The spirituality and theology of knowledge*. New York: Herder & Herder/Crossroad.
Merton, T. (1991). *No man is an island*. Turnbridge Wells: Burns & Oates.
Merton, T. (2004). *The inner experience*. New York: Harper Collins.
Moore, J. (1984). *Being in your right mind: The fourfold nature of selfhood*. Salisbury: Element Books.
Moreau, M. (1955). Mémoire et Durée. *Revue des Études Augustiniennes 1*, 239–250.
O'Connell, R. J., S.J. (1987). *The origin of the soul in St. Augustine's later works*. New York: Fordham University Press.
Osuna, F. de. [1527] ed. Melquíades Andres. (1972). *Tercer Abecedario spiritual*. Madrid: Biblioteca de Autores Cristianos.
Padel, R. (1992). *In and out of the mind: Greek images of the tragic self*. Princeton, NJ: Princeton University Press.
Pasqua, H. (2004). La Déité comme unité pure et nue. In A. Dierkens & B. B. de Ryke (Eds.), *Maître Eckhart et Jan van Ruusbroec: Études sur la mystique « rhéno-flamande », XIIIe–XIVe siècle* (pp. 41–51), *Problèmes d'Histoire des Religions* (Vol. 14). Bruxelles: Éditions de l'Université de Bruxelles.
Peers, E. A. (Trans.) (2002). *The complete works of Teresa of Avila* (Vols. 1–3). London: Burns & Oates.
Pessoa, F. (1981). *Obra Poética* (M. Galhoz, Ed.). Rio de Janeiro: Nova Aguilar.
Pessoa, F. (1982). Génese e justificação da heteronímia. In C. Berardinelli (Ed.), *Obras em Prosa*. Rio de Janeiro: Nova Aguilar.
Phan-chon-tôn. (2000). *Le Yoga de Patañjali: La voie de la dés-union*. Paris: Adyar.
Pinchard, A. (2009). *Les langues de sagesse dans la Grèce et l'Inde anciennes*. Genève: Droz.
Raschke, C. A. (Gen. Ed.) (1996). New Age spirituality. In P. H. Van Ness (Vol. Ed.), *World spirituality: An encyclopedic history of the religious quest: Vol. 22. Spirituality and the secular quest* (pp. 203–226). New York: Crossroad.
Reymond, L. (1984). *La vie dans la vie: Pratique de la philosophie du Sâmkhya d'après l'enseignement de Shrî Anirvân*. Paris: Albin Michel.
Robertson, D. (2011). *Lectio Divina: The medieval experience of reading*. Collegeville, MN: Cistercian Publications.
Rönnegard, P. (2013). Meléte in Early Christian Ascetic Texts. In H. Eifring (Ed.), *Meditation in Judaism, Christianity and Islam-Cultural Histories*. London, New Delhi, New York, Sydney: Bloomsbury.
Ruiz Jurado, M., S.I. (1994). *El discernimiento espiritual. Teología, historia, práctica*. Madrid: Biblioteca de Autores Cristianos.
Schipper, K. (1982). *Le corps taoïste: Corps physique—corps social*. Paris: Fayard.
Siddheswarananda, Swami. (1998). *Hindu thought and Carmelite mysticism*. Delhi: Motilal Banarsidass.
Silburn, L. (1988). *Kundalinî: The energy of the depths. A comprehensive study based on the scriptures of nondualistic Kashmir Śaivism* (J. Gontier, Trans.). Albany: State University of New York Press.
Silburn, L. (Intro. & Trans.). (1990). *Spandakârikâ. Stances sur la vibration de Vasugupta et leurs gloses*. Paris: Publications de l'Institut de Civilisation Indienne.

Silva, C. H. d. C. (1986). *Experiência orante em Santa Teresa de Jesus*. Lisboa: Didaskalia.

Silva, C. H. d. C. (2001). Monoteísmo e sedução do múltiplo. [Monotheism and the seduction of multiplicity]. *Cadernos ISTA, Instituto São Tomás de Aquino, 11, Ano IV* (pp. 5–34). Lisbon: Convento de S. Domingos.

Silva, C. H. d. C. (2006). De kâla a ksana ou da recorrência à instantaneidade-nota sobre a temporalidade no pensamento hindu. *Cultura-Revista de História e Teoria das Ideias 23*, 131–178.

Silva, C. H. d. C. (2017). Phantasía segundo Aristóteles: da retórica do senso comum ao exercício (yôguico) da imaginação. In J.-J. Wunenburger, A. F. Araújo, & R. de Almeida (Eds.), *Os trabalhos da imaginação–Abordagens teóricas e modelizações* (pp. 275–324). João Pessoa: Editora da UFPB.

Sorabji, R. (2006). Infallibility of self-knowledge: Cogito and flying man. In *Self: Ancient and modern insights about individuality, life, and death* (pp. 212–229)). Oxford: Clarendon Press.

Trungpa, C. (1972). *Méditation et action: Causeries au Centre tibétain Samyê-Ling*. Paris: Fayard.

Trungpa, C. (1973). *Cutting through spiritual materialism*. Berkeley, CA: Shambhala.

Turner, R. L. (1989). *A comparative dictionary of the Indo-Aryan languages*. London: Oxford University Press.

Tyler, P. (2011). *The return to the mystical: Ludwig Wittgenstein, Teresa of Avila and the Christian mystical tradition*. London: Continuum.

Varenne, J. (1989). *Aux sources du Yoga*. Paris: Éditions Jacqueline Renard.

Vijñânabhiksu. 2016. *Yogasârasamgraha*. In Larson & Bhattacharya, 2016, pp. 320–333.

Walshe, M. O'C. (Ed. & Trans.). (1979) *Meister Eckhart: Sermons and treatises* (Vol. 1). Shaftesbury: Element Books.

Williams, P. (1998). *The reflexive nature of awareness. A Tibetan Madhyamaka defence*. Richmond, Surrey: Curzon Press.

Wittgenstein, L. (1921). *Tractatus Logico-Philosophicus*. London: Routledge & Kegan Paul.

CHAPTER 18

THE SELF IN MEDITATION

The Art of Self-Transformation

JESSICA FRAZIER

INTRODUCTION

> So is the name of spiritual exercises given to any means of preparing and disposing our soul to rid itself of all its disordered affections.
>
> —Ignatius Loyola (*Spiritual Exercises*, no. 1)

> ...technologies of the self...permit individuals to effect by their own means or with the help of others a certain number of operations on their own bodies and souls, thoughts, conduct, and way of being, so as to transform themselves in order to attain a certain state of happiness, purity, wisdom, perfection, or immortality.
>
> —Michel Foucault (1998, p. 18)

In early ninth century Sūs, the Iraqi Sufi mystic al-Hallaj declared that his deepening absorption in God had led him to union with the divine; this controversial claim later contributed to his execution as a heretic and rebel against the local authorities. At the same time in the narrow limestone caves of Thailand, Buddhist anchorites crawled deep into the dark to devote motionless hours to cleansing their consciousness. Meanwhile, further west, Christian monks sat in their cells reciting the scripture in a Hesychastic practice of letting the divine light sink ever deeper into their hearts. These and many other types of "meditation" through history go far beyond the widespread focus on mindfulness, attesting to a widespread desire to curb and craft the self through mental practices. It is on this model of meditation as art of self-transformation that this chapter will focus.

Meditation as Self-Shaping

Meditation raises powerful questions about the nature of conscious life: what if there were a way to control and shape the "self," that mysterious bundle of perceptions, reflections, feelings and actions that we *are*, but which seems to be forever running away with us? What forms of practice might we adopt to change our own thoughts and desires? What is the nature of our agency over ourselves, and what might we want to do if we could transform the very experience of which our lives consist?[1] Meditation traditions help individuals to circumscribe their mental life within a particular habitus; there it can be understood, reshaped, and harnessed to more discriminating goals. In this sense it opens up a whole new resource for living that is hidden from those who must passively receive their mind's content as it comes to them.

The nebulous modern notion of "meditation" is a synthesis of European and Asian ideas such as *meditari*, *theoria*, *contemplatio*, *yoga*, *dhyāna* and its correlates *chan* or *zen*. What this cluster of terms shares is reference to a prolonged constructive engagement of the mind aimed at transforming some facet of experience. The *Yoga Sūtras* (YS; ca. 300 BCE–300 CE) are probably the earliest existing manual of meditation, in the sense that they outline a disciplined program (*sādhana*, or "regular" practice) aimed at cultivation of an extra-ordinary state of experience (*samādhi*, or "absorption") that in turn can help one to achieve a spiritually or psychologically beneficial transformation of the self (*kaivalya*, or "pure isolation"). This text begins by defining yogic meditation as "the stilling of the movements of the mind" (YS 1.2), and it prescribes meditation as a way of harnessing the mind to valuable human goals ("yoga" comes from the Sanskrit root "*yuj*," which is cognate with "yoke," link or join). Thus yoga epitomizes the function of meditation that we will examine in this chapter: it serves as a tool to transform the self in some important way. Like so many other traditions of meditation, classical yogic practice is rooted in a *theory* of what the mind is, resulting in a *map* of how it functions, and a kind of inner "engineering" of how it can be manipulated and reshaped. The world's varied cultures of meditation rely on different mappings of the structure of the self and different practices for achieving change—but what they share is that each helps individuals to take some creative control of their inner world.

Despite extensive theorizing about the self during the last century and a growing seriousness about meditation in the human and natural sciences, relatively little scholarly work has been done at the intersection of meditation and selfhood.[2] This chapter lays some foundations of a theory of meditation by emphasizing the centrality of mental

[1] This chapter has drawn on suggestions from Jonathan Young, Queen Mary's College, University of London, regarding mechanisms underpinning cognition, selfhood, and self-change. Thanks also go to Lee Ritger and Douglas Frazier.

[2] Approaches tend to divide into either cognitive science–based approaches (see for example the studies in West, 2016), or historical/phenomenological studies such as Shulman & Stroumsa, 2002).

plasticity and meditation's efficacy as a tool for self-shaping. First, we will consider modern views of meditation as a medicine for healing the malaise of modernity by bringing the mind "back" to its natural functioning. By contrast, we will then look at the way older traditions have used meditation not to restore our everyday self, but to *change* it in some crucial way. Given the diversity of meditative traditions, the notion of creative self-shaping provides an interpretive framework; in particular, the notion of "attention" in cognitive processing and the making of our mental structures reveals the fundamental plasticity of the self and its potential for change.

Modern Meditation: From Creativity to Healing

Traditional goals of meditation vary widely across cultures: they include trained visionary journeys in Kabbalistic Merkavah mysticism, visualized sacred-sexual encounters in tantric Tibetan Buddhism, rational analysis of one's motivations in Christian moral self-examination, patient logical ascents into the conceptual realm in Plato, and the attempt to purify one's whole consciousness in Patañjali's classical yogic meditation. Such traditional approaches effect "structured transitions in the inner world of the living subject" (Shulman & Stroumsa, 2002, p. 1). In doing so, they serve as what Michel Foucault called "technologies of the self," practices by which individuals "effect... operations on their own bodies and souls, thoughts, conduct and ways of being" (Foucault, 1998, p. 18). In his analysis of classical spiritual practices, Foucault emphasized the complex, versatile self-"governmentality" that classical practices bestow on individuals who are normally the passive recipient of their own thoughts. With the help of meditative "technologies" one can begin to curate one's own inner world, craft one of the "different forms of self" recommended by different cultures, and shape the way it expresses itself as a "principle of activity" (Foucault, 1998, pp. 22, 25).[3]

The possibility of recrafting our basic mental material has become a powerful idea in the modern world, where Freudian narratives about the splitting of the personality into fragmented selves (the rational "Ego," the wayward inner "Id," and the socially constructed "Superego") have become commonplace (Freud, 1961. This pathology of the modern psyche is paralleled in the traditions of existential reflection proceeding from

[3] Foucault interprets Greek thought (extending through Epicurus, Socrates, Philo, and others into early Christian practice) in this way, showing how practical "care" for the self was correlated with the more familiar traditions of "knowledge" of the self (Foucault, 1998, p. 19). Foucault's analysis agreed in certain respects with Pierre Hadot's (1996) analysis of Greek philosophy as a "way of life," and it has been selectively applied to meditative practices beyond the Greek and Christian traditions (e.g., Konik [2016] on Foucault's interest in Zen Buddhism; Horujy [2015] on Eastern Orthodox Christian hesychasm; Hattam & Baker [2015] on Buddhist compassion meditations).

Friedrich Nietzsche's portrait of godless modern man, such as Martin Heidegger's 1927 *Being and Time* (Heidegger, 2010), Jean-Paul Sartre's 1943 *Being and Nothingness* (Sartre, 2003), and Paul Tillich's 1952 *The Courage To Be* (Tillich, 2014). These sources were echoed in later classics of psychology like Carl Jung's 1933 *Modern Man in Search of a Soul* (Jung, 1933/2001), Erich Fromm's 1941 *Escape from Freedom* (Fromm, 2011), or R. D. Laing's 1967 *The Politics of Experience* (Laing, 1990), all of which found Western styles of civilization to have a uniquely repressive effect on the self.

Such views grew partly from philosophical roots in Descartes' definition of the mind as a thing of pure reflective self-awareness. He saw it as being similar to the clockwork automata of the period insofar as it provided motion and life to the body. But it was distinguished from them by its inner phenomenon of luminous reflexivity. For him, then, the self was

> a substance the whole essence or nature of which is to think, and that for its existence [has] no need of any place, nor does it depend on any material thing; so that this 'me,' that is to say, the soul by which I am what I am, is entirely distinct from the body, and is even more easy to know than the latter. from the *Discourse on the Method* part 4: 33 (Descartes 1997, p. 92)

The self that Descartes arrived at via his unique phenomenological method of inner "meditation" replaced the Christian "soul" substance with the rational self-reflective self of the "I-think" or *cogito*. The self was no longer the reflection of the spiritual nature of God as in Augustine, but was now a mechanical agent with rational cogitation as its own inner "spring." Yet Descartes' philosophy still relied on methods of inner reflection that retained the introspective character of Christian contemplation, and his philosophy retained essentially religious goals.

This continuity with religious meditation would be forgotten as the Enlightenment advanced. A century later, in his *Treatise on Human Nature* (1.4.6) David Hume would counter Descartes' conclusions by arguing that his own introspection revealed not a single substance, but a "bundle or collection of different perceptions which succeed one another with an inconceivable rapidity and are in perpetual flux and movement" (Hume, 2011, p. 222). Hume's disassembling of the self paved the way for modern "bundle theories" of mind and the view that selfhood is merely a "convenient fiction" providing a "centre of narrative gravity" to the complex processes that we are (Dennett, 1992). Modern philosophers like Gilbert Ryle, Elizabeth Anscombe, Derek Parfit, Daniel Dennett, Thomas Metzinger have helped to build this view of the self as a "bundle" bound together by the bodily locus, misattributed macro-processes, or mere conventions of language. In the Humanities, this model is echoed in contexts such as Charles Taylor's *Sources of the Self* (1989), Michel Foucault's studies of modern "dividing practices" (1982) by which the self is objectified and controlled, and Paul Ricoeur's account of a "wounded" post-Cartesian self that must continually re-constitute itself through community (1992). The result of these discourses is that scholarly interest in selfhood has largely become a problem-solving exercise aimed at healing the complex of difficulties that Freud saw as an expression of "Civilisation and its Discontents"

(1930/2002). Consequently, much Western theorizing has looked nostalgically to the classical "self" of the past as a more authentic, healthy center of identity, disposition, and agency. In this light, contemporary narratives of "meditation" often recount a nostalgic mythos about how lost techniques for better living can be rediscovered and ultimately restored to modernity. It has become part of a portfolio of "spiritual" practices in the modern Westernized media and marketplaces, providing a "claimed panacea for the angst of modern living" (Carrette & King, 2004, p. 1; see also Wilson, 2014; Purser, 2019; Illouz, 2007; Schmidt, 2002).

Thus meditation has seemed to offer a solution to tensions within the self. For Jung in 1933 (see Jung, 1933/2001, p. 35) it suggested a way to reintegrate the shadowy unknown regions of the unconscious with the conscious mind. In 1960 the psychologist Erich Fromm welcomed Zen meditation as something that seeks "to save us from going crazy or being crippled...giving free play to all the creative and benevolent impulses inherently lying in our hearts" (Fromm, 1960/1974, p. 122). One of the pioneers of the formal integration of meditation into psychotherapy was Jon Kabat-Zinn (himself a student of Thich Nhat Hanh, the influential expositor of Buddhist thought to the West). Kabat-Zinn used his medical expertise to develop an interpretation of Buddhist meditation that emphasized its capacity to overcome trauma and unhappiness. Like R. D. Laing's brand of psychiatry, Kabat-Zinn's "Mindfulness-based Stress Reduction Technique" sought to reclaim autonomy from the whirlwind of external pressures. It deconstructed the social identity, arguing that

> we lock ourselves into a personal fiction that we already known who we are, that we know where we are and where we are going, that we know what is happening—all the while remaining enshrouded in thoughts...which spin out continuously, veiling our direction and the very ground we are standing on. (Kabat-Zinn, 1994, p. viii)

For Kabat-Zinn, meditation is "simply about being yourself and knowing something about who that is" (1994, p. xiv). Such accounts aimed at the secular goals of well-being have maintained the image of meditation as a practice that resolves inner conflict. On the one hand, this has provided a platform for the trans-cultural resurgence of meditation as a semi-medical technique for restoring the integrity of a "core" self. But on the other hand, it has elided a prior, wider use of meditation as a form of creative reshaping of the self into new forms.

Self-Creativity: Mapping the Architecture of Attention

One of the most fundamental characteristics of meditative practices is that they take "ownership" of one's sensations, feelings, and thoughts in such a way that they can be altered.

Pathologies such as schizophrenia, and temporary cognitive dysfunctions such as the "rubber hand" experiment, reveal that it is possible for the mind to lose a sense of what is its own bodily or mental reality and what is not.[4] In radical cases we may experience our thoughts and sensations as distinctly divorced from ourselves, lacking a sense that they have emerged from our own reasons and action. But meditation reminds us that, conversely, we have the ability to lay claim to our thoughts and make them more completely our own.

Recent developments in our understanding of the mind as a neural mechanism can help to provide new "ontologies" of selfhood that map out the lines of influence, showing how our thoughts shape us and how we can turn the tables and learn to consciously shape them. The cognitive sciences retain a tendency to emphasize the kinds of observable, easily testable phenomena that are open to laboratory study.[5] One result is that more complicated, higher-order aspects of mind tend to be emphasized less than basic physiologically evident reactions to physical, verbal, or other sensory stimulus. Yet recent models of cognition give fresh insight into the kinds of higher-order mental causality that makes it possible to consciously alter one's own mental constitution. In particular, a number of key processes can be identified as necessary for meditation's transformation of the self in various ways:

(a) the filtering process of *selective attention* by which our mental processes are focused on a selection of filtered data, which thus shape the contents of the mind and the ways it builds upon them;
(b) the *plasticity* of the attention-based mind, based on variation in focus, variation in scale and intensity, degrees of stability and change, and the constant mutual influence between the more basic sensory stimuli on one hand, and the broader conceptual functions that are built up from them;
(c) the *control* that can be cultivated through focus on the overspanning forms of attention, boosted by *introspective* practices that turn attention toward inner experience, and enhanced by *volitional agency* over one's own experiences.
(d) the underlying cosmology, usually containing some model of the self, that determines the *goals* of such transformation.

We will look at these aspects, outlining a provisional ontology of the self as layers of selective attention in a constant dynamic loop of feedback between the higher and lower

[4] There is a wide-ranging body of literature on ownership or first-person perspectival attribution of bodily and mental life. Approaches to failed bodily ownership or "proprioception" can be found in Jeannerod, 2003; Blanke & Metzinger, 2009; Gallagher 2004; Campbell, 1999, and associated literature, and there is also extensive discussion of the role of misplaced ownership in illusions of body-swapping, virtual bodies, out-of-body experiences, multiple personalities, and the "disordered" selfhood found in schizophrenia (Stanghellini & Rosfort, 2015).

[5] There have been moves to find ways of applying cognitive scientific methods such as brain imaging to subtler "internal" mental phenomena, e.g., Lieberman, 1979; Jack & Shallice, 2001; Jack & Roepstorff, 2002.

parts, exploring the way it underpins different cognitive practices of self-shaping within meditation traditions.

Attention and Plasticity

Work in cognitive science suggests that one of the defining features of consciousness—and one of our most important tools for altering the self—is the capacity of "selective attention."[6] This is the filter that the mind—and to some extent every living thing—applies to the wide field of stimuli that affect it at every moment. In essence, it is the function of data-sorting determining "directivity and selectivity" of response. As one of the first proponents of the idea put it in 1973:

> Of the many stimuli which reach us, we respond only to those few which are particularly strong or which appear particularly important and correspond to our interests, intentions or immediate tasks... the circle of possible sensations, movements, or memory traces is narrowed, the probability of appearance of certain impressions, movements or memory traces becomes unequal and selective: some of them (essential or necessary) begin to dominate, while others (inessential or unnecessary) are inhibited. (Luria, 1973, p. 256)

In many respects, this selective shaping of the human person works on the same model that shapes all organisms: stimuli are detected in the environment, and processed into a response of some kind. In this sense, the development of conscious life has been formed by the same principles that we see at work in the emergence of biological beings from simple systems of selective chemical reaction: the patterns of filtered chemical response that we see in very simple organisms are the earliest "antecedents of the sense of self" (Damasio, 2000, p. 136). The data-stream of external stimuli is filtered by an "attention spotlight" (Sperling & Weichselgartner, 1995). It is attention that allows a fish to note temperature changes in the ocean and turn toward food; in more complex forms of minds it is attention that lets us bracket out distracting noise and focus on a song in the background or the memories and emotions that it has inspired.

In consciousness, this spotlight of attention has a unique ability to vary its own direction, scope, and intensity, focusing on different things, to different degrees, in different contexts. "Focused" attention helps us hone in on one kind of input, "sustained" attention lets us maintain that focus, "executive" attention helps direct our attentional control

[6] Attention has become a focus of much research into cognitive structures since the popularization of the idea by Aleksandr Luria (1973) in his analysis of attention, memory, and activation as major pillars of neural functioning. Since then it has been used to map brain networks in neuroscience, as a tool in psychopathology, and as a way of explaining the ontology of the self and charting its cognition (see Posner & Petersen, 1990, and its review, Posner & Petersen, 2012, for a summary of this approach; also Posner, 1980; Desimone & Duncan, 1995; Styles, 1997; Wright & Ward, 2008). It has also been linked to Indian meditation-informed ideas about of the constitution of selfhood in Buddhism (Ganeri, 2017).

and orchestrate the functions of the complex psyche.[7] One can see this by comparing different cognitive processes: a hunter may hone in her senses on the precise tension and spatial awareness needed to string a bow, then turn her attention back "outward" to survey the surroundings as a whole for visual signs of movement, then perhaps turn the mind "inward" to mentally review the abstract "map" of the landscape in her imagination. Each activity involves a different object, scale, and kind of attention, and together they constitute "massively parallel, highly connected and interactive" systems of focus and response (Styles, 1997, pp. 117–118). The changing flow of thoughts and impressions constantly feed into the self, and are processed by the more stable "neural patterns" (Damasio, 2000, p. 154), thus generating ever-higher filters until the inner world of the mind builds up, layer after layer.

In more complex creatures, the wider and more complex systems of data-filtering gradually achieve increasing levels of conceptual abstraction. This "large-scale neural integration" operates at every moment in daily life in the processes of event perception, "which can unify a blur of millions of individual sensations of sight, sound, touch, taste, smell and emotions into unitary event-percepts" (Donald, 2006, p. 4; see also Donald, 2001). In cognitively complex species it can also integrate subtler data like memory, mental models of the self, and the world, yielding the kind of abstract inner world that we experience "within." We are also able to share indicators that both describe and prescribe this inner world through culture. But the growth of the abstract mind is not a one-way street: once formed, the "higher" systems of selection such as memories, identity, values, and so on proceed to exert their own influence over the "lower" levels of selective attention to data that shaped them, creating a constantly transforming loop. The variability of the attention spotlight, and the dynamic loop of influence between "higher" and "lower" responses, mean that attention is an essentially *variable* building block of consciousness that underpins the malleability of the mind.

Introspection and Agency

While much of the mental world's plasticity is involuntary, it also has a volitional capacity for self-control. Early advocates of attention as a broad explanatory theory noted a "gap . . . between elementary, involuntary forms of attention, on the one hand, and the higher, voluntary forms of attention on the other" (Luria, 1973, p. 258; see also Schneider & Shiffrin, 1977 on "automatic" and "controlled" systems of consciousness). The more complex, overspanning filters such as concepts, memories, or culturally embedded beliefs—many of which help to constitute the network of mental dispositions that we think of as personality—possess a degree of control over the more basic, local filters such as perceptions and motor responses. In this way attention builds a tiered causal structure of summative and subsidiary systems of attention. In this sense, self-

[7] The parsing out of different forms of attention has often been based on analysis of the role that attention plays in various cognitive pathologies; e.g., Mateer & Sohlberg, 2001.

reflexive control over our own attention is really a higher order "metacognitive" function (Styles, 1997, p. 59), shaped by our conceptual map of the world and the intentional practices that we adopt to train our attention. Developing new "habits of attention" (Claxton, 2016, p. 56) can yield substantial changes in the self.

But one of the most sophisticated and powerful forms of attention is the process of introspectively surveying, filtering, and voluntarily shaping one's thoughts. Introspection has been a controversial area for cognitive modeling because its study relies on subjective linguistic reports from the person him or herself (see Lyons, 1983; Varela & Shear, 1999 for surveys of this issue). Yet it seems to be analogous to mechanisms of *interoception* (direct awareness of our own bodily feelings),[8] and *proprioception* ("ownership" of our thoughts and sensations). In interoception, the human somatic experience of "interior" sensations sets up a contrast between the "inner" and "outer" worlds, and lends us a spatio-temporal anchor for our thoughts: we feel that we can "locate" the very processes that constitute us. The concurrent unity of visual, auditory, and gustatory senses in the head confirms this locatedness, and the difficulty of verbally expressing sensations, emotions, and other qualia only adds to this sense that there is a wall between the outside world and what the Stoics called "inner citadel."

Thus meditation implicitly always activates of our self-reflexive agency, and inserts it between the "core and contingent" layers of personhood (Frazier, 2017, p. 69), prying apart what Damasio calls the "core consciousness" (Damasio, 2000). Volition draws upon ownership of certain of these features as self rather than other, the recognition of initiative-related experiences analogous to motor-control, and consciousness of high-order process of deliberation—multiple aspects that, when combined, we experience as "self-agency" over our own minds (see Gallagher, 2007; Jeannerod, 2003 on physical agency). Like a person at a loud party who focuses on attending to a conversation, the meditative practitioner "blinds" herself to certain phenomena (distractions or unwanted thoughts and desires) and selectively attends to what is culturally, philosophically, or emotionally relevant. The selective data can then be processed more richly, and through repetition it becomes enshrined in the stable, long-term parts of the memory, where it will further inform our judgments and shape our attention. Self-reflective introspection, strengthened through meditative attention, interposes a heightened awareness and causal control over our directing of attention; in this way our existential experience of life can be changed at its phenomenological roots, along with our sense of who we are and what we seek.

[8] Moves to recognize the importance of interoception of our physical sensations, and coenesthetic awareness of our total bodily feelings as the sense of being in a "body" for constituting key features of selfhood include Ceunen, Vlaeyen, & Van Diest, 2016; Craig, 2002; Mehling, 2016, and studies that show the significance of interoception particularly for emotions, our own metacognitive sense of them, and the way this relates to our reflexive self-conception include Barrett, Quigley, Bliss-Moreau, & Aronson, 2004; Seth, 2013; Singer, Critchley, & Preuschoff, 2009; Dunn et al., 2010. Studies specifically exploring the relation of interoception and meditative practice include Dahl, Lutz, & Davidson, 2015; Price & Hooven 2018; Farb et al., 2007; Farb et al., 2015; Garland, Farb, Goldin, & Frederickson 2015.

The Art of Self: Practices for Crafting Experience

Meditation thus serves as a tool with which we consciously explore the resources of those systems that define us; it "retrains attention" (Goleman, 1988, p. 107) in a way that increases our ability for "self-regulative mind-control." It is thus concerned with a particular kind of "inner agency" that the mind has over itself—potentially altering the usual human parameters of the will by reflectively attending to its motives, constraints and possibilities (Repetti, 2018). This open-ended changefulness is usually constrained by cultural ideas that "form a subjectivity" and "encode" the self in "tradition-specific and text-specific ways" (Flood, 2006, p. 13).

In addition to giving the practitioner an opportunity to become someone new, meditative practice also opens up a new territory for discovery: it turns human attention away from the treasures that can be gained by exploration of the outer world, toward an equally laborious, skilled search for corresponding treasures "within." Many traditions highlight the importance of consciously prioritizing interiority. The depiction of the self as a little-visited place waiting to be explored, often using the metaphor of a room or cave into which we can enter, is found widely in traditions of Asian origin and has a distinctive place in Christian contemplative religion. Texts exhort us to enter into our "inner space" with clear vision and full volition: Jesus advises his followers to "go into your room, close the door, and pray to your Father, who is unseen" (Matthew 6:6), and this biblical image is mirrored in Anselm's Benedictine instruction in the opening of the *Proslogion* to "escape for a little while from the tumult of your thoughts ... enter into the inner chamber of your soul" (Anselm 1998, p. 84). Such spatializing images set up the goal of introspection in concrete, comprehensible terms. In their use as the first stage of a journey toward the divine, they further imply that

> the inner memory [is] like a vast inner landscape ... a great chamber containing not only images of the past, but the forms of knowledge; a place where all images are stored and, above all, the place where God is found—the ultimate meaning of human life. (Flood, 2013, p. 84)

The self is thus a resource in which the spotlight of attention may find valuable ideas and motivations, and also aims at a transcendence of restriction in the face of the external pressures of society (Flood, 2013, p. 193).

Ascetic practices have a special role. They loosen the ties of the automatic forces in the body and mind, bracketing them sufficiently for the "higher" filters of selection to trigger a more considered kind of action. For instance, impulses may be bracketed in favor of longer-term plans, and scattered, distracting perceptions condensed into focused attention on a single object, idea, or emotion. This liberating feature is widely acknowledged within religions with strong meditative traditions: when the Russian Orthodox thinker Nicolas Berdyaev described asceticism as "the liberation of the human person" through "a concentration of inner forces and command of oneself," he captured the notion that human freedom actually requires a refined form of self-control—an interpretation that has also been given to Indian yoga (Berdyaev in Ware, 1998, p. 3; see Eliade, 1958/2009 on yoga as "freedom"). Thus while the "asceticism of the mind" found in many forms of meditation can be interpreted as a denigration of worldly and bodily life, it can also be taken as a tool for escaping the perceived "demons" of automatic, obsessional attention to things like food, pleasure, anxiety (Graiver, 2018, p. 182). The biographical accounts of ascetics sometimes recount this process: in *The Seal of the Saints*, the ninth-century Uzbek Sufi mystic al-Tirmidhi described his journey toward the spiritual life as being grounded in the adoption of repeated practices of solitary meditative prayer, memorization, and trained desire:

> I pursued my fasting and prayer, until at last [I]...was thus guided to some knowledge of the discipline of the soul. I took up this practice and God helped me. Inspired to deny myself my desires, I found that I could train myself to do one thing after another, even to the point of denying myself cool water.
>
> (al-Tirmidhi, 2015, p. 396)

Here al-Tirmidhi describes a life in which continuous prayer, reading, memorization, and solitude allow him to train his basic impulses—even of thirst. Later he writes that social castigation was the last ascetic experience that allowed him to "purify the heart," "mortify the soul," and "push aside" his desires, so that he "discovered strength and awareness" in himself, and his soul "was humbled, and obeyed" through the course of rigorous self-training (al-Tirmidhi, 2015, pp. 397–398).

Al-Tirmidhi's subjective account of inner transformation through assiduous "internal work" is typical of many such autobiographical records of meditative practice. Yet the techniques and philosophies of such work differ widely across the globe. It is beyond the scope of this chapter to discuss all, or even a representatively wide range of them; instead we look at key themes in the operation of selective attention and consider its relation to absorptive sensory, rational, and emotional meditation, and to deconstructive and narrative techniques.

Absorptive Meditation: Sensory, Rational, and Emotional Techniques

One important theme in meditation is the focusing of attention on something so that the mind is filled with a particular phenomenon. This might be a mandala or crucifix, the sound of a bell or chant, a sensation such as breathing, an emotion of love or even a concept of permanence, balance, compassion, or perfection. Viewing an image is common as a way of encountering deities or remembering some historical event or theological idea; but the *meditative* viewing of it cultivates a more intense focus so that the whole subjective experience becomes oriented to and *absorbed by* it. This meaning is expressed in the Sanskrit term *dhyāna* (the source of the term "zen" in Japanese Buddhism), which refers to the intentional absorption of consciousness in some object of focus. It is also reflected in the early Christian medieval use of "meditation" to mean complete attention to, and assimilation of, a reading "gone over with concentrated intensity... with the goal of absorbing the complete meaning of the text, implanting it in the memory for future use" (Bestul, 2012, p. 158). In other cases, the same idea is applied to intensely visual images that were available through the arts of the church and illuminated manuscripts; for mystics like Julian of Norwich "her practice of meditation trained her eye and focused her powers of visualisation" (Baker, 1994, p. 44). These practices all imprint an object on the self, using attention to transform its fabric.

One of the most intense forms of absorption in Western traditions is the Eastern Orthodox practice of hesychasm, a threefold meditation on the Divine Nature believed to "simplify the mind, bringing it from fragmentation to unity" (Ware, 2014/2017), and ultimately to produce "changes in human nature" (Flory, 2015, p. 2). Formalized in the writings of Evagrius of Ponticus and Macarius the Great, this practice united the biblical idea of prayer as a process of entering the "inner room" within, with the Greek idea of *theoria* as the interior vision of an idea. This synthesis resulted in a form of meditation that purged distractions through relentless watchful care of one's thoughts (*catharsis*), pure contemplation of the divine nature through repetition of the "Jesus Prayer" (*theoria*), and the unceasing direction of the mind toward the divine—understood as pure light. Through stages of ascent the mind was believed to take on the form of what it contemplated (*theosis*)—in this case the divine light of God. Just as Plato's practice of rationally "seeing ideas" such as Goodness aimed at guiding the soul to assimilation of the idea, so *theosis* applied a similar method. It was only one example of a broader wave of visionary inner disciplines that spanned the Jewish, Christian, and Muslim worlds. They became a central meditative tool for Western traditions, although the ontological implications—that humans could change the subjective fabric of the self, identified in religious thought as the *soul*, perhaps reshaping it as the divine—were controversial. While self-shaping was exciting for the practitioners, it could also be destabilizing for accepted ideas about the place of humans in society and the cosmos. Indeed, Hesychastic practice has found a place in the modern Western secular practices for psychological well-being, much like yoga and mindfulness (Johnson, 2010).

While this tradition of trained attentional absorption could elevate the self into what it observed, it could also take a more radical form in kenotic traditions of "emptying" out the self in favor of the intended object. One can see the extreme devotion of the Islamic Sufi practice of *fana* or annihilation as a willing "submission" of one's whole mental content. This idea not of *forming* the personality, but of *emptying* it in order for it to be replaced with new content, heightened the controversial ontological elements of self-transformation. It was through this approach that the tenth century Sufi mystic Mansur al-Hallaj attracted censure by identifying himself with God (Mansur al-

Hallaj, 2009, p. 20). He described his meditative practice in poetic terms that emphasized the role of the mental "eye" in harnessing the heart's desire in order to give intentional direction to his movement through "the waves of thought":

I guide my sight with the eye of knowledge
Unadulterated by doubt...
I ride on the waves of thought
Like an arrow undeterred;
My heart flies with the wings of desire
Carried by the wind of my intent... (Mansur al-Hallaj, 2009, p. 20)

Al-Hallaj is famous for his execution: he was considered to have arrogantly claimed to have "become" one with the divine—and thereby lent authority to political powers of revolution. In a sense he illustrates the radical implications of absorptive self-formation. In contrast to society's mediators between the realms of reality, absorptive meditation offered a direct ontological bridge between the individual person and any reality it could imagine.

Rational Meditation

Implicit in many such practices of immersive attention is the idea that the mind uses a kind of inner "sight" to "envision" things when it holds them intentionally in its gaze. In "rational" forms of meditation the objects of the mental gaze may also be abstract concepts (e.g., of goodness or a logical form). Plato's account of *eros* in the *Symposium* treats our perception of virtue in this way. By directing the mind to a particular instance of value and leading us to focus ever more upon it, the self thereby acquires that value until no further external instance is necessary. It is in a similar way that philosophy's logical debates are seen to cultivate the immortality of the soul (see Plato's most explicitly "salvific" text, the *Phaedo*).

Where Plato favored the training of attention onto values of goodness and beauty, some traditions of "rational" meditation trained attention onto wider cosmological-metaphysical ideas. In the centuries predating the composition of the *Yoga Sūtras*, the earlier Upaniṣads, core texts of classical Indian philosophy, develop an idea that the person who internalizes a comprehensive understanding of the world as a whole is himself expanded by that understanding. The *Bṛhadāraṇyaka Upaniṣad* speaks of a knowledge by which one can "become the whole" (1.4.9), and *Chāndogya Upaniṣad* chapter six describes a pedagogical process of training the self to identify with the being, essence, or overall unity of the universe (see Frazier, 2019, pp. 85–135). Here the scope of the self is dilated so that it sees, feels and makes decisions from the perspective of reality as a whole—rather than merely in terms of the individual personality. The practitioner thereby eludes the particular concerns of individual life, rising instead to an unprecedented freedom and largesse of selfhood. Pierre Hadot has famously made the argument that philosophy in ancient Greece and Rome originally functioned in this way, providing a prolonged "lived" practice of seeing the world according to the "view from above," and this enabled the philosopher to achieve a mental "conquest of space" superior even to the conquering emperors of the day (Hadot, 1996, p. 243). Hadot interprets the Stoic meditations of Marcus Aurelius as just such a constant rational practice, reading his *Meditations* as the diary of his efforts in the "inner citadel" of the mind; some scholars have taken contemporary cognitive behavioral therapy to entail a similar process of rational self-shaping (e.g., Robertson, 2010; Murguia & Diaz, 2015).

These are kinds of conceptual meditation that activate our cognitive capacity to orient toward overarching ideas, thereby "expanding" the scope of the mind and lending it the capacity to choose from a range of sub-ideas, identities, and desires (Frazier, 2017, pp. 135–138). While the cognitive study of meditation tends to prioritize sensory perceptions because their effects are easier to test empirically, some have argued that "we perceive through our sensory organs, to be sure, but no less through our concepts; in other words, we perceive not just physiologically but also intellectually" (Hofstadter & Sandler, 2013, p. 171). In such cases of classical Indian and Greek *rational* absorption, meditation recognizes the therapeutic potential of philosophy for elevating the self and bypassing the sources of anxiety that haunt mortal individuals. Agency remains, but rather than struggling with limited goals, it redirects its attention in the knowledge that "humanity as *mind* is free, mutable and empowered... to transform itself into anything it comprehends, however vast and however abstract" (Frazier, 2017, p. 129).

Emotional Meditation

One of the most pervasive forms of absorptive meditation is that which emphasizes *emotional* immersion. Emotions are interesting contents of experience because many kinds seem to function less as objects of awareness and more as somato-sensory colorings of the whole of experience, directing what we perceive and think (Damasio, 2000, p. 80),[9] and affecting our interpretations of it. In short, they function much like intellectual filters but in an even more visceral, responsive, holistic, and energetic way—often undercutting or operating separately of conscious processing (Jonides, 1981). Emotion has its own *intensifying* power over our experiences, and affective focus is a kind of selective attention that gives drastically increased weight to particular sensations, ideas, activities, memories, concerns, or goals. One effect is that intentional objects may be absorbed more immediately and wholly into the self, becoming associated with our wider range of memories, beliefs, motivations, and values.

[9] There is a well-established literature on the relationship between emotion and attention, largely suggest that attention prioritizes the emotions and whatever is relevant to them (Lang & Davis, 2006; Lang & Bradley, 2009; Fox, Russo, Bowles, & Dutton, 2001, etc.), and may be drawn away from other information by the urgency of negative emotions (Vuilleumier, 2005), or extended more liberally to information that is relevant to positive emotions (Frederikson & Branigan, 2005).

This is a very widespread tool of meditation; as David Haberman put it in his study of disciplined Hindu devotional practice, one sees affective meditative at work in any cultivated tradition

> that greatly values the tremendous power of emotions. Intense emotions, such as passion, produce an intense concentration on the object of the emotions, drawing subject and object together... Passion, therefore, is held to be a highly valuable instrument for spiritual endeavours. (Haberman, 1988, p. 70)

In devotional meditation, emotions are often directed toward some item of great value, and the self is thus enabled to be guided by, identify with, or become that thing. But the emotions involved need not exclusively be pleasant ones; the classic Indian range of cultivatable emotions or *rasa*s include anger, fear, disgust, and awe, as well as vigor, humor, compassion, and love. Anxiety and fear have been shown to be some of the emotions with the greatest cognitive power, diverting attention in a particularly urgent way. Elevated into awe, earnestness, care, compassion, and flight from danger into higher concerns, negative emotions have the power to effect uniquely powerful transformations. Indeed, fear and suffering, when *chosen* in pursuit of affirmative goals in self-sacrificial ascetic practices, can form part of a process by which we "bestow value" in life (see Frazier, 2013).

Western tradition tends to conceive of emotions on the model of the passions—as unruly and uncontrolled forces that "enter" the self from without and overpower its will. This is a model with roots in Plato's image of the person as a chariot carried away by wild horses against the intentions of the charioteer. This notion is similar to the classical Indian idea of emotion as craving or "thirst" (*tṛṣṇa*), a kind of mental phenomenon that threatens the discriminating mind with its power. But many Indian traditions of devotion are influenced by aesthetic theories that explore the way that certain kinds of cultivated emotions or *rasa*s can be built up with care out of a complex combination of factors. They span and elevate sub-affects into higher emergent ones: as a delicious curry may incorporate seasonings such as fiery chili, bitter ginger, sour lime, and sweet sugar, so one's overall happiness may incorporate elements such as delight, courage, gratitude, pleasure, admiration, novelty, comfort, and so on. The analogy between *rasa* emotions and spices ready to be combined into complex flavors is found in the Indian dramaturgical manual, *Nāṭyaśāstra* (ca. 300 BCE–300 CE). Subsequent Hindu religious guidebooks advised on the application of "*rasa*-theory" to mental exercises of focused attention. The arts served as a kind of spice cabinet for judicious recipes of image, poetry, song, and story. This dedicated technology of affective mood has been likened to the "affectivity of the actor's art" in the Stanislavski technique used by professional modern actors; it is effectively a "ritual process formulated in terms of aesthetic experience" and involving identity transformation (Haberman, 1988, pp. 67–69).

In such traditions, the "passivity" of the passions is replaced by a craft of subtly blending attention to different affective objects in order to reshape the moods of the self. Emotional meditation thus serves to draw attention away from local, particular concerns and to widen attention to broader truths and values. This process correlates with studies indicating that where negative emotions decrease the attention we give to other concerns, the positive emotions "broaden and build" our capacity for attention, expanding the base of consciousness and allowing it to integrate our experiences into a total affective response (Frederickson, 1998, 2001).

Deconstructive and Narrative Meditation

The absorptive practices above allow the material of the self to be transmuted into something new. But in some of its most radical forms, meditation seeks to disrupt or destroy the structure of selfhood. Having done so, it can even restructure the ideas and patterns that lend coherence to the self, creating a new structure of personality or mind. The style of Indian meditation found in the *Yoga Sūtras* is one case of this—rather than cultivating devotion or knowledge, the goal is to still, focus, and purify consciousness of *all* content so that it becomes wholly condensed and divested of the processes that shape personhood and the most basic nature of thought. As Larson notes, the development of a yogic ideal of wholly stilled consciousness idealized a state in which "one dwells in pure translucent consciousness... radically emptied of all content" (Larson, 1969, p. 208). Here yoga is a form of mental discrimination that can still the fast and unwieldy movement of thought, turning awareness into a single undifferentiated mass. It is

> the stilling of the turnings of consciousness, so that the seer dwells in its own nature. Otherwise it will take the form of those turnings... (YS1.2; in Patañjali, 2009)

Here the bipartite structure of agency—hierarchically divided between the decision-making self and the subsidiary mental phenomena it controls—is pried apart so that the "higher" self becomes free from the sway of body and emotion. Attention is focused on no object but the pure qualia of awareness itself, thus "breaking the 'bonds' that unite the spirit to the world" in order "to do away with the dispersion and automatism that characterize profane consciousness" (Eliade, 1958/2009, p. 5). Understood in terms of the mind's attention systems, classical yoga is a higher form of self-reflexive attention to one's own inner activity. But it aims to empty out the usual stream of data from our subsidiary systems of perception and calculation, so that one can attend primarily to cognitive attention itself, that is, to the basic structures of "consciousness."

The resulting still, one-pointed, awareness is very far from any of the normal characteristics of the self that we routinely experience. Radical Tibetan Buddhist practices cultivating the " 'clarity' and 'stability' of awareness" (Thompson, 2015, p. 76) similarly seek to minimize personhood, reversing the cohering functions of reason and systematically deconstructing the apparent unities of apperception, conceptualization, self-reflexive mental ownership, memory and personal narrative—so that no centralized structure of selfhood will be left. In such cases, Buddhist meditation aims at a kind of non-self that is neither a "person," nor "conscious," in any way that we would normally recognize. Johannes Bronkhorst has argued that these goals of creating a clear, still form of consciousness are linked to a little-acknowledged cognitive capacity to achieve "more or less dense" forms of consciousness (Bronkhorst, 2017, p. 6) that may seem alarming when we are invested in the narratives of quotidian selfhood, but possess their own qualitative appeal once the processes of consciousness are freed from expectations about the "self."

Some meditative traditions teach practitioners to inhibit agency itself as much as possible, minimizing the top-down control of the mind in ongoing everyday life. Daoist texts, for instance, speak of the sage who "keeps to the deed that consists in taking no action," allowing the natural influence of the environment to work through him in a way that is unimpeded by the analytical mind and the volitions that it generates (*Daode jing* 2–3). Here, to "weaken the mind" yet "strengthen the belly" is to reduce our resistance and discontent in relation to the world. So too, the "no-mind" of Zen, for instance, is not a selfless state so much as a dissolving of differentiating boundaries:

> no-mind or no-thought is a state of consciousness in which the dichotomy between subject and object, experiencer and experienced is overcome... the function of no-mind is to respond immediately to present experiential data... it is an active, responsive awareness of the contents of experience as directly experienced (before the intervention of complex intellectual activity). (Kasulis, 1981, pp. 47–48)

Agency in this Japanese Zen-Daoist context is a kind of automatic raw action: "the Zen ideal is to act spontaneously in the situation without first objectifying it. The person is not something that *has* meaning or *has* relationships: rather, one achieves meaning through relationships" (Kasulis, 1981, p. 132). The goal of this tradition is that natural action in the world should come to constitute the self, and agency's job is to control itself enough to "step aside." Yet even this requires a very refined form of meditation in which the self *weakens* itself, and gives rein to the natural processes around and in us.

Yet some approaches aim not only to "deconstruct" the self, but also to creatively "re-construct" it into a new person or *persons*. On the "ownership" and "attention" models there is nothing to stop one re-claiming other new and different identities, since selfhood simply involves claiming ownership of particular streams of experience (see Smith, 2006; White, 2006; Frazier, 2016). An attentive model alerts us to the way that in focusing on particular dispositions and desires, memories and kinds of event, we can construct a narrative of "one-self" as a particular personality, experiencing a particular sort of world. This identification with a narrative of the self is implied in much affective meditation: adopting the identity of Majnun, the mad Sufi lover of God, or a servant of the Hindu deity Kṛṣṇa, or of Christ himself as he struggles to exemplify good and sacrifice for others, involves empathetically letting another imagined narrative of experience replace one's "own."

In certain Hindu traditions, devotees are encouraged to construct a new "spiritual identity" within the history attributed to their chosen deity. Followers of Kṛṣṇa, for instance, draw on emotionally intense narratives about being a "lover" of god, aided by affective practices such as listening, singing, reading, visualizing, or otherwise "remembering" (*smaraṇa*) the intensity of other lives (Haberman, 1988, p. 128). Imaginal journeys are also a staple of narrative traditions, constructing experiential templates by which diligent readers could re-orient their own personalities. Jewish hermeneutic tradition transformed the nostalgic histories of an exiled community into a "Merkavah" practice of intensely imagined spatial journeys often patterned on the voyage of the prophet Ezekiel from Jerusalem to Babylon and thence to the foot of the divine throne. Undertaken in painstaking detail as a regular and protracted mental practice, the self was changed by these virtual reality experiences. The new self thereby constructed was frequently capable of more dramatic and satisfying achievements than that previously constructed in the physical world.

Possession traditions place narrative shifts in identity at center stage. Frederick Smith's (2006) study of South Asian deity and spirit possession demonstrated the magnetic appeal of adopting alternative or multiple selves. Where possession in Western literatures was typically seen as a sudden hostile takeover by an unwelcome mind, Indian literature often speaks of possessions that are positively welcomed. To use Ganeri's terminology, it is by "performing" other life stories, that ownership of a new self is claimed, and one's ties to the *merely bodily* streams of experience are loosened (Ganeri, 2007, p. 128). The familiar identity to which we awaken daily, and to which we feel irrevocably tied, is revealed to be contingent: meditation brings into reach new selves, limited only by our resources for planning who we would like to be. In this respect all protracted stories in which we are invited to identify repeatedly with a character's inner life are forms of self-transformative "meditation."

The Ontology of the Meditative Self

In these varied examples, the disciplines of meditation allow their practitioners to sculpt specific aspects of mind. As tools of self-reshaping, they include a*bsorptive* meditations that use selective attention to direct our experience toward specific content and alter our mental content accordingly; these may be *sensory* meditation that use image or sound, *rational* meditation that alters our conceptualization of the inner and outer worlds, systematically putting the operations of "reason" to work on them so that their significance for us are also changed at the phenomenal level, or *affective* meditation that intensifies the emotional intensity and scope with which we process the products of our attention. We also see practices of structural change, including *deconstructive* meditation by which we disengage cognitive structures in order to selectively deconstruct features of consciousness or "selfhood" as a whole, and *narrative* meditation that shifts the data that we normally "own" as part of our identity, to an alternative personality reconstructed anew on fresh patterns. This list is by no means exhaustive, and other operations of cognition and kinds of meditation are also found within the wide range of the world's cultures.

But what we learn by applying the attentional model to these cases is that the mind is capable of more forms than daily life and conventional psychology seem to suggest. It is an intrinsically malleable complex of dynamic and intra-causal processes, shaped both by local filters of attention to particular things, and also by overspanning filters that watch and regulate the subsidiary ones. These are colored throughout by wide-reaching concepts and values, all of which continuously shape the self's fabric. Meditation's value is that it activates a structure of agency within this cloud of mental processes and enhances its ability to reflect on and alter itself. But this can never be a fully objective process; meditation is rather like "riding the rapids" of experience since agency is being constituted by the very mental processes that it shapes. Indeed, there is a double dynamism at work in the meditative self as it constantly shapes itself into something new, and thus constantly revises what it wants to become. In contrast to the centralized, stable, and coherent *cogito* implied in Descartes, the ontology of the meditative self is self-creatively dynamic—it is less like a "lamp" that looks out onto a changing world, and more like a weather system that is constantly interacting with itself.

But in the original cultures of meditation, there was a further dimension of this ontology: meditative traditions typically "share a notion of the truth within that is connected to the cosmos without: the macrocosm is recapitulated in the microcosm" (Flood, 2013, p. 28). Meditative selves were often seen as being "open bodies" (Böhler, 2009), intrinsically embedded and participating in the surrounding environment of physical forces, other minds, abstract concepts—and in many cases, spirits, energies, or divine powers. In light of this view of the self as a point of transition into different dimensions of the wider cosmos, meditation usually aimed "outward" at some larger goal than merely the autonomous satisfaction of the self. It was only the first stage in a larger project of accessing some broader truth, for example of alignment with the will of God, or opening to supernatural forces or spirit worlds, or immersing the self in its fundamental material of consciousness, or deconstructing itself altogether in order to make space for other truths. This stands in contrast to purely "secular" modern uses of meditation, styling themselves as a practice with the professional neutrality and universality of medicine. There is a striking contrast between medieval mystics' theological projects, and William James's modern account of mysticism as subjective, psychological, separate from cosmological assumptions (Harmless, 2008, pp. 14–16). Recognising this shift in modern emphasis on currently popular "Eastern" models, a Vatican letter sought to clarify that Catholic practice must always remain focused on divine relationship, and on God rather than self. Proper Christian meditation is

> a flight from "self" to the "You" of God. Thus Christian prayer is at the same time always authentically personal and communitarian. It flees from impersonal techniques or from concentrating on oneself, which can create a kind of rut,

> imprisoning the person praying in a spiritual privatism which is incapable of a free openness to the transcendental God.
>
> (Congregation for the Doctrine of the Faith, 1989)

As Taylor notes, the modern excision of metaphysics from our ideas of self can result in "a drive to make ourselves the centre of our world" (1989, p. 138). Most early meditative innovators themselves typically took not the Self but the reality beyond it to be the end-goal. This direction of outward meditative gaze is exemplified by Rabia of Basra, a ninth century female Muslim mystic who expressed eloquently the open and outward dissolving character formerly attributed to our private inner space of the self:

> In
> my soul
> there is a temple, a shrine, a mosque, a church
> where I kneel.
> Prayer should bring us to an altar where no walls or names exist...
> In
> my soul
> there is a temple, a shrine, a mosque,
> a church
> that dissolve, that
> dissolve in
> God. (Rabia al-Basri, 2009, p. 12)

Rabia al-Basri's words highlight shifting conceptions of meditation and its goals. If the *attentional self* is a "climate" of filtering processes governed by macro-filters of concept, affect, and volition, then the *meditative self* is like a structured "weather system" in which the stratospheric upper tiers have enhanced power to guide the system as a whole. Where the modern meditative self follows more self-contained patterns, the classical meditative self typically contained a drive not only to regulate itself, but also to open *outward* toward some larger force—of values, truths, communities, or beings—with which it sought to become aligned.

References

Anselm, (1998). B. Davies and G.R. Evans (Eds), *The Major Works*. Oxford: Oxford University Press.

Baker, D. (1994). *Julian of Norwich's Showings: From vision to book*. Princeton, NJ: Princeton University Press.

Barrett, L. F., Quigley, K., Bliss-Moreau, E., & Aronson, K. (2004). Interoceptive sensitivity and self-reports of emotional experience. *Journal of Personality Social Psychology 87*, 684–697. doi:10.1037/0022-3514.87.5.684.

Bestul, T. (2012). Meditatio/meditation. In Amy Hollywood & Patricia Beckman (Eds.), *The Cambridge companion to Christian mysticism* (pp. 157–166). Cambridge: Cambridge University Press.

Blanke, O., & Metzinger, T. (2009). Full-body illusions and minimal phenomenal selfhood. *Trends in Cognitive Sciences 13*, 7–13.

Böhler, A. (2009). Open bodies. *Paragrana, Internazionale Zeitschrift für Historische Anthropologie 18*, 119–131.

Bronkhorst, J. (2017). Can religion be explained? *Method and Theory in the Study of Religion 29*, 1–30.

Campbell, J. (1999). Schizophrenia, the space of reasons, and thinking as a motor process. *Monist 82*(4), 609–625.

Carrette, J., & King, R. (2004). *Selling spirituality: The silent takeover of religion*. Abingdon: Routledge.

Ceunen, E., Vlaeyen, J. W. S., & Van Diest, I. (2016). On the origin of interoception. *Frontiers in Psychology 7*, 743. doi:10.3389/fpsyg.2016.00743.

Claxton, G. (2016). How conscious experience comes about, and why meditation is helpful. In M. West (Ed.), *The psychology of meditation* (pp. 49–72). Oxford: Oxford University Press.

Congregation for the doctrine of the faith. (1989). Letter to the bishops of the Catholic Church on some aspects of Christian meditation. Retrieved from http://www.vatican.va/roman_curia/congregations/cfaith/documents/rc_con_cfaith_doc_19891015_meditazione-cristiana_en.html

Craig, A. D. (2002). How do you feel? Interoception: The sense of the physical condition of the body. *Nature Reviews: Neuroscience* 3(8), 655–666.

Dahl, C. J., Lutz, A., & Davidson, R. (2015). Reconstructing and deconstructing the self: Cognitive mechanisms in meditation practice. *Trends in Cognitive Science 19*, 515–523. doi:10.1016/j.tics.2015.07.001.

Damasio, A. (2000). *The feeling of what happens: Body, emotion and the making of consciousness*. London: Vintage.

Dennett, D. (1992). The self as a centre of narrative gravity. In F. Kessel, P. Cole, & D. Johnson (Eds.), *Self and self-consciousness: Multiple perspectives* (pp. 103–115). Hillsdale: Erlbaum.

Descartes, R. (1997). *Key philosophical writings*. Ware, UK: Wordsworth Editions.

Desimone, R., & Duncan, J. (1995). Neural mechanisms of selective visual attention. *Annual Review of Neuroscience 18*, 193–222.

Donald, M. (2006). Art and cognitive evolution. In M. Turner (Ed.), *The artful mind: Cognitive science and the riddle of human creativity* (pp. 3–20). Oxford: Oxford University Press.

Donald, M. (2001). *A mind so rare: The evolution of human consciousness*. New York: W.W. Norton.

Dunn, B. D., Galton, H. C. Morgan, R., Evans, D., Oliver, C., Meyer, M., . . . Dalgleish, T. (2010). Listening to your heart: How interoception shapes emotion experience and intuitive decision making. *Psychological Science 21*(12), 1835–1844.

Eliade, M. (2009). *Yoga: Immortality and freedom* (W. Trask, Trans.). Princeton, NJ: Princeton University Press. (Original work published 1958).

Farb, N., Segal, Z., Mayberg, H., Bean, J., McKeown, D., Zainab, F., & Anderson, A. (2007). Attending to the present: Mindfulness meditation reveals distinct neural modes and self-reference. *Social Cognitive and Affective Neuroscience* 2(4), 313–322.

Farb, N., Daubenmier, J., Price, C., Gard, T., Kerr, C., Dunn, B. D., . . . Mehling, W. (2015). Interoception, contemplative practice, and health. *Frontiers in Psychology 6*, 763. doi:10.3389/fpsyg.2015.00763.

Flood, G. (2006). *The tantric body: The secret tradition of Hindu religion*. London: I. B. Tauris.

Flood, G. (2013). *The truth within: A history of inwardness in Christianity, Hinduism, and Buddhism*. Oxford: Oxford University Press.
Flory, M. (2015). *Transforming practices: Hesychastic correctives to postmodern apophatic theology* (Doctoral dissertation). University of Denver.
Foucault. M. (1982). The subject and power. *Critical Inquiry 8*(2), 777–795.
Foucault, M. (1998). Technologies of the self. In L. Martin, H. Gutman, & P. Hutton (Eds.), *Technologies of the self: A seminar with Michel Foucault* (pp. 16–49). Amherst: University of Massachusetts Press.
Fox, E., Russo, R., Bowles, R., & Dutton, K. (2001). Do threatening stimuli draw or hold attention in subclinical anxiety? *Journal of Experimental Psychology; General 130*, 681–700.
Frazier, J. (2013). Sacrifice as value-bestowal: From sacrificial lambs to dedicated lives. In J. Zacchuber & J. Meszaros (Eds.), *Sacrifice in modern thought* (pp. 100–114). Oxford: Oxford University Press.
Frazier, J. (2016). The overflowing self: The phenomenology of possession in biblical and Indian mysticism. In L. Nelstrop & B. Onishi (Eds.), *Mysticism in the French tradition: Eruptions from France* (pp. 81–100). London: Ashgate.
Frazier, J. (2017). *Hindu worldviews: Theories of self, ritual and reality*. London: Bloomsbury.
Frazier, J. (2019). "Become this whole world": The phenomenology of metaphysical religion in Chāndogya Upaniṣad 6–8. *Religions 10*(6), 368. https://doi.org/10.3390/rel10060368
Frederickson, B. (1998). What good are positive emotions? *Review of General Psychology 2*, 300–319.
Frederickson, B. (2001). The role of positive emotions in positive psychology: The Broaden and Build theory of positive emotions. *American Psychologist 56*, 218–226.
Frederickson, B., & Branigan, C. (2005). Positive emotions broaden the scope of attention and thought-action repertoires. *Cognition and Emotion 19*(3), 313–332.
Freud, S. (1961). The ego and the id. In J. Strachey (Ed.), *The ego and the id and other works: The standard edition*. London: Hogarth Press.
Freud, S. (2002). *Civilisation and its discontents*. London: Penguin. (Original work published 1930).
Fromm, E. (1974). Psychoanalysis and Zen Buddhism. In E. Fromm, D. T. Suzuki, & R. De Martino (Eds.), *Zen Buddhism and psychoanalysis* (pp. 77–141). London: Souvenir Press. (Original work published 1960).
Fromm, E. (2011). *Escape from freedom*. New York: Ishi Press.
Gallagher, S. (2004). Agency, ownership and alien control in schizophrenia. In D. Zahavi, T. Grunbaum, & J. Parnas (Eds.), *The structure and development of self-consciousness: Interdisciplinary perspectives* (pp. 89–104). Philadelphia, PA: John Benjamins.
Gallagher, S. (2007). The natural philosophy of agency. *Philosophy Compass 2*, 347–357.
Ganeri, J. (2012). *The concealed art of the self: Theories of self and practices of truth in Indian ethics and epistemology*. Oxford: Oxford University Press. (Original work published 2007).
Ganeri, J. (2017). *Attention, not self*. Oxford: Oxford University Press.
Garland, E. L., Farb, N., Goldin, P., & Fredrickson, B. (2015). Mindfulness broadens awareness and builds eudaimonic meaning: A process model of mindful positive emotion regulation. *Psychological Inquiry 26*, 293–314. doi:10.1080/1047840X.2015.1064294.
Goleman, D. (1988). *The meditative mind: The varieties of meditative experience*. New York: Tarcher.
Graiver, I. (2018). *Asceticism of the mind: Forms of attention and self-transformation in late antique monasticism*. Toronto: Pontifical Institute of Medieval Studies.

Haberman, D. (1988). *Acting as a way of salvation: A study of rāgānuga bhakti sādhana*. Oxford: Oxford University Press.

Hadot, P. (1996). *Philosophy as a way of life: Spiritual exercises from Socrates to Foucault* (A. Davidson, Ed., M. Chase, Trans.). Oxford: Blackwell.

Hakim al-Tirmidhi, M. (2015). The seal of the prophets (D. Reynolds, K. Brustad, et al., Trans.). In J. Miles (Gen. Ed.) & J. D. McAuliffe (Vol. Ed.), *Norton anthology of world religions: Islam* (pp. 395–405). London: W.W. Norton.

Harmless, W. (2008). *Mystics*. Oxford: Oxford University Press.

Hattam, R., & Baker, B. (2015). Technologies of self and the cultivation of virtues. *Journal of Philosophy of Education* 49(2), 255–273.

Heidegger, M. (2010). *Being and Time* (J. Stambough, Trans.). Albany: State University of New York Press.

Hofstadter, D., & Sander, E. (2013). *Surfaces and essences: Analogy as the fuel and fire of thinking*. New York: Basic Books.

Horujy, S. (2015). *Practices of the self and spiritual practices: Michel Foucault and the Eastern Christian discourse* (K. Stoeckl, Ed., B. Jakim, Trans.). Grand Rapids, MI: Eerdmans.

Hume, D. (2011). A Treatise of Human Nature. In *The Essential Philosophical Works*. Ware: Wordsworth Editions.

Illouz, E. (2007). *Saving the modern soul: Therapy, emotions, and the culture of self-help*. Berkeley: University of California Press.

Jack, A., & Roepstorff, A. (2002). Introspection and cognitive brain mapping: From stimulus report to script report. *Trends in Cognitive Sciences* 6(8), 333–339.

Jack, A., & Shallice, T. (2001). Introspective physicalism as an approach to the science of consciousness. *Cognition* 79, 161–196.

Jeannerod, M. (2003). The mechanism of self-recognition in humans. *Behavioural Brain Research* 142, 1–15.

Johnson, C. (2010). *The globalisation of hesychasm and the Jesus Prayer: Contesting contemplation*. London: Continuum.

Jonides, J. (1981). Voluntary versus automatic control over the mind's eye's movement. In J. B. Long & A. D. Baddeley (Eds.), *Attention and performance IX* (pp. 187–203). Hillsdale, NJ: Erlbaum.

Jung, C. G. (2001). *Modern man in search of a soul* (W. S. Dell & C. Baynes, Trans.). Abingdon: Routledge. (Original work published 1933).

Kabat-Zinn, J. (1994). *Wherever you go, there you are: Mindfulness meditation for everyday life*. London: Piatkus Books.

Kasulis, T. P. (1981). *Zen action, Zen person*. Honolulu: University of Hawai'i Press.

Konik, A. (2016). Reconsidering Foucault's dialogue with Buddhism. *South African Journal of Philosophy* 35, 37–53.

Laing, R. D. (1990). *The politics of experience and the bird of paradise*. London: Penguin.

Lang, P., & Bradley, M. (2009). Emotion and the motivational brain. *Biological Psychology* 84, 437–450.

Lang, P., & Davis, M. (2006). Emotion, motivation, and the brain: Reflex foundations in animal and human research. *Progress in Brain Research* 156, 3–29.

Larson, J. G. (1969). *Classical Sāṃkhya: an interpretation of its history and meaning*. Delhi: Motilal Banarsidass.

Lieberman, D. (1979). Behaviourism and the mind: A (limited) call for a return to introspection. *American Psychologist* 34, 319–333.

Ignatius Loyola (*Spiritual Exercises*, 1).
Luria, A. (1973). *The working brain: An introduction to neuropsychology*. London: Penguin Books.
Lyons, W. (1983). The transformation of introspection. *British Journal of Social Psychology 22*, 327–342.
Mansur al-Hallaj. (2009). I Guide My Sight with the Eye of Knowledge (Mahmood Jamal, Trans.). In M. Jamal (Ed.), *Islamic mystical poetry: Sufi verse from the early mystics to Rumi* (p. 20). London: Penguin Books.
Mateer, C., & Sohlberg, M. (2001). *Cognitive rehabilitation: An integrative neuropsychological approach*. New York: Guilford Press.
Mehling, W. (2016). Differentiating attention styles and regulatory aspects of self-reported interoceptive sensibility. *Philosophical Transactions of the Royal Society of London: Series B, Biological Sciences 19*(371), 1708. doi: 10.1098/rstb.2016.0013.
Murguia, E., & Diaz, K. (2015). The philosophical foundations of cognitive behavioral therapy: Stoicism, Buddhism, Taoism, and Existentialism. *Journal of Evidence-Based Psychotherapies 15*(1), 37–50.
Patañjali. (2009). Yoga Sūtras. In Edwin Bryant (Ed.) *The Yoga Sūtras of Patañjali*. New York: North Point Press.
Posner, M. I. (1980). Orienting of attention. *Quarterly journal of experimental psychology 32*, pp. 3–25.
Posner, M., & Petersen, S. (1990). The attention system of the human brain. *Annual Review of Neuroscience 13*, 25–42.v
Posner, M., & Petersen, S. (2012). The attention system of the human brain: 20 years after. *Annual Review of Neuroscience 35*, 73–89.
Price, C. J., & Hooven, C. (2018). Interoceptive awareness skills for emotion regulation: Theory and approach of mindful awareness in body-oriented therapy (MABT). *Frontiers in Psychology 9*, 798. doi:10.3389/fpsyg.2018.00798.
Purser, R. (2019). *McMindfulness: How mindfulness became the new capitalist spirituality*. London: Repeater Books.
Rabia al-Basri. (2009). In My Soul (Daniel Ladinsky, Trans.). In M. Jamal (Ed.), *Islamic mystical poetry: Sufi verse from the early mystics to Rumi* (p. 12). London: Penguin Books.
Repetti, R. (2018). *Buddhism, meditation, and freewill: A theory of mental freedom*. London: Routledge.
Ricoeur, P. (1992). *Oneself as another* (K. Blamey, Trans.). Chicago: University of Chicago Press.
Robertson, D. (2010). *The philosophy of cognitive behavioural therapy: Stoic philosophy as rational and cognitive psychotherapy*. Abingdon: Routledge.
Sartre, J, (2003). *Being and Nothingness: An Essay in Phenomenological Ontology* (H. E. Barnes, Trans.). Abingdon: Routledge.
Schmidt, L. (2002). *Restless souls: The making of American spirituality*. Berkeley: University of California Press.
Schneider, W., & Shiffrin, R. M. (1977). Controlled and automatic human information processing I: Detection, search and attention. *Psychological Review 84*, 1–66.
Seth, A. (2013). Interoceptive inference, emotion, and the embodied self. *Trends in Cognitive Sciences 17*(11), 565–573.
Shulman, D., & Stroumsa, G. (Eds.). (2002). *Self and self-transformation in the history of religions*. Oxford: Oxford University Press.
Singer, P., Critchley, H. D., & Preuschoff. K. (2009). A common role of insula in feelings, empathy and uncertainty. *Trends in Cognitive Sciences 13*(8), 334–340.

Smith, F. (2006). *The self possessed: Deity and spirit possession in South Asian literature and civilization*. New York: Columbia University Press.

Sperling, G., & Weichselgartner, E. (1995). Episodic theory of the dynamics of spatial attention. *Psychological Review 102*, 503–532.

Stanghellini, G., & Rosfort, R. (2015). Disordered selves or persons with schizophrenia? *Current Opinions in Psychiatry 28*(3), 256–263.

Styles, E. (1997). *The psychology of attention*. Hove: Psychology Press.

Taylor, C. (1989). *Sources of the self: The making of the modern identity*. Cambridge: Cambridge University Press.

Thompson, E. (2015). *Waking, dreaming, sleeping: Self and consciousness in neuroscience, meditation, and philosophy*. New York: Columbia University Press.

Tillich, P. (2014). *The courage to be*. Newhaven: Yale University Press.

Varela, F., & Shear, J. (Eds.). (1999). *The view from within; Special issue of the Journal of Consciousness Studies 6*(2–3).

Vuilleumier, P. (2005). How brains beware: Neural mechanisms of emotional attention. *Trends in Cognitive Science 9*(12), 585–594.

Ware, K. (1998). The way of the ascetics: Negative or affirmative. In Vincent Wimbush & Richard Valantasis (Eds.), *Asceticism* (pp. 3–15). Oxford: Oxford University Press.

Ware, K. (2017). *The Jesus Prayer* (Kindle ed.). London: Catholic Truth Society. (Original work published 2014).

West, M. A. (Ed.). (2016). *The Psychology of Meditation: Research and Practice*. Oxford: Oxford University Press.

White, D. G. (2006). "Open" and "closed" models of the human body in Indian medical and yogic traditions. *Asian medicine 2*(1), 1–13.

Wilson, J. (2014). *Mindful America: The mutual transformation of Buddhist meditation and American culture*. Oxford: Oxford University Press.

Wright, R. D., & Ward, L. M. (2008). *Orienting of attention*. New York: Oxford University Press.

Zohar, A., & Ben David, A. (2009). Paving a clear path in a thick forest: A conceptual analysis of a metacognitive component. *Metacognition and Learning 4*(3), 177–195.

PART IV

APPROACHES TO THE STUDY OF MEDITATION

BIOLOGY AND NEUROSCIENCE

CHAPTER 19

MEDITATION AND THE BRAIN IN HEALTH AND DISEASE

KIERAN C. R. FOX AND B. RAEL CAHN

INTRODUCTION

MEDITATION—THE mysterious capacity of the human mind to turn back upon and contemplate itself—has been developed, debated, practiced, and persecuted for thousands of years. Like music, language, and art, it seems to be a uniquely human quality, and likewise, its origins are lost in legend (Eliade, 1964; Johnson, 1982; Wynne, 2007). Despite being part of our ancient human heritage, serious investigation of meditation's neural basis began only a few decades ago. The nascent fields now being referred to as "contemplative science" and "contemplative neuroscience" (Thompson, 2009) are very much phenomena of the twenty-first century, with an unprecedented acceleration in meditation research in recent years (Van Dam, van Vugt, Vago, Schmalzl, Saron, Olendzki, Meissner, Lazar, Kerr, et al., 2018a)—in contrast to the slow and haphazard accrual of knowledge throughout the twentieth century (Cahn & Polich, 2006).

A truly rigorous neuroscience of meditation still lies in the future (Cahn & Polich, 2006; Fox, et al., 2016; Fox et al., 2014; Van Dam, van Vugt, Vago, Schmalzl, Saron, Olendzki, Meissner, Lazar, Gorchov, et al., 2018b; Van Dam, van Vugt, Vago, Schmalzl, Saron, Olendzki, Meissner, Lazar, Kerr, et al., 2018a), but nonetheless, enormous strides have been taken since scientists first patched electrodes onto the heads of people practicing various forms of meditation in the 1950s and 1960s (Bagchi & Wenger, 1957; Das & Gastaut, 1955; Kasamatsu & Hirai, 1966; Kasamatsu et al., 1957). Since these early studies, virtually every tool available for investigating the structure and function of the human brain has been employed at one time or another to shed some light on the neural correlates of long-term practice of, and short-term training in, meditation.

Meditation is one of those terms that it seems necessary, yet impossible, to properly define; meditation has meant, and continues to mean, so many things to so many groups that any definition is bound to be selective and of only limited generalizability. Here we define meditation as a family of mental training practices aimed at monitoring and regulating attention, perception, emotion, and physiology (e.g., respiration or level of arousal). This relatively bland definition, used before by us (Cahn & Polich, 2006; Fox, Dixon, et al., 2016; Fox et al., 2014) and by other researchers (A. Lutz, Slagter, Dunne, & Davidson, 2008; Tang, Hölzel, & Posner, 2015), has the merits of being *non-sectarian* (it encompasses practices from many different religious and ethnic groups) and of emphasizing aspects of meditation that are *measurable* (i.e., those that can be investigated with contemporary neuroscientific and physiological methods and are therefore admissible in the court of scientific study). On the other hand, such a definition leaves out components that are considered crucial by virtually every contemplative tradition, especially their metaphysical goals and claims (most practices proffer some central insight(s) into the nature of reality and/or the self), and their soteriological aspects (most practices are explicitly aimed at enlightenment [nirvana], liberation [moksha], or some related state or transformation). Defining meditation as mental training therefore encompasses most of the qualities measurable by, and currently of interest to, scientists, but leaves aside those aspects neuroscientists are unable, or at least not yet able, to investigate (although see Davis & Vago, 2013).

Most scientific research to date has focused on Buddhist-derived meditation and mindfulness practices (Tang et al., 2015; Van Dam, van Vugt, Vago, Schmalzl, Saron, Olendzki, Meissner, Lazar, Kerr, et al., 2018a). Although there is growing neuroscientific work on Christian prayer (Neubauer, 2014; Newberg, Pourdehnad, Alavi, & d'Aquili, 2003; Schjødt, Stødkilde-Jørgensen, Geertz, & Roepstorff, 2008), yogic and Hindu meditation practices (Kakigi et al., 2005; Kalyani et al., 2011; Kjaer et al., 2002), and even related ecstatic shamanic techniques (Hove et al., 2015), here we also focus largely on Buddhist-derived techniques, including secular mindfulness practices, because they are by far the most often studied, therefore offering the firmest ground on which to base conclusions and inferences.

The goal of this chapter is to provide a succinct overview of what we have learned to date about the multifaceted relationship between meditation and the brain in both health and disease. The subsequent sections offer a variety of perspectives on these relationships.

First, we review studies examining the relationship between meditation and alterations in the structure of the brain's grey and white matter (so-called morphometric neuroimaging). Next, we discuss findings from functional neuroimaging methods, such as functional magnetic resonance imaging (fMRI) and positron emission tomography (PET) scans, and what they have taught us about the brain's patterns of activity during different forms of meditation, how meditation alters the brain's response to various tasks and experiences, and how the expertise of long-term meditators might be harnessed to help us explore subtle aspects of human cognition. Third, we review electrophysiological methods of measuring brain activity during meditation, such as electroencephalography (EEG), and how these findings relate to what we have learned from morphometric and functional neuroimaging. Finally, we discuss the implications of this research and of meditation more generally for brain health and psychological well-being. Specifically, we focus on how meditation might ameliorate the deficits related to cognitive aging, as well as help ameliorate the symptoms and underlying neural abnormalities associated with neurodegenerative and psychiatric disease.

Meditation and Brain Structure

That the practice of new skills and learning of new information effects changes in the fine-scale structure of the brain is no longer controversial (Caroni, Chowdhury, & Lahr, 2014). This learning-dependent *neuroplasticity* is generally agreed to provide the substratum for retaining new knowledge, memories, and skills. By employing animal models and in vitro investigations of brain tissue, neuroscientists have been able to develop an increasingly refined model of the synaptic and molecular changes underlying neuroplastic changes, and how they relate to learning (Caroni et al., 2014; Marx & Gilon, 2012). In humans, however, studies of these microscale changes generally are not feasible, so research has instead relied upon an ever-expanding suite of methods that can assess the shape, density, and composition of the brain's structure in vivo—tools collectively known as *morphometric neuroimaging* (May & Gaser, 2006; Zatorre, Fields, & Johansen-Berg, 2012).

Early studies using these methods showed that people with high levels of expertise, for instance highly trained or professional musicians, showed greater grey matter volume (compared to non-musician control subjects) in parts of the brain crucial for fine motor control and auditory processing (Gaser & Schlaug, 2003; Schneider et al., 2002). This research suggested that training had induced the changes, but a major limitation was that the musicians had not been investigated *longitudinally*—in other words, the researchers had not studied their brains both before and after musical training, to establish that training itself had been the cause. A glaring and plausible alternative explanation was that people with greater manual dexterity and sensitivity—perhaps instantiated in the brain in measurable differences in grey matter in these motor regions—were likewise those who excelled at, and therefore persisted in, their musical endeavors. In this case, differential grey matter density in motor cortices would be the cause, not the consequence, of long-term musical practice. As we shall see, this same concern remains a major issue in studies of the brains of long-term meditation practitioners. This section explores (i) whether meditation is indeed associated with altered brain structure; (ii) whether different findings have been reported from the study of long-term practitioners as compared to those undergoing short-term meditation training; and (iii) some of the methodological concerns related to this research.

Is Meditation Associated with Altered Brain Structure?

Dozens of studies have now used morphometric neuroimaging to examine whether long-term practice of, or short-term training in, meditation is associated with altered brain structure (Fox et al., 2014). Because of the diversity of methods used and the hundreds of individual findings reported to date, it is difficult to interpret this rapidly growing body of work and understand whether or not there are consistent trends among all these findings. In an effort to synthesize this research, Fox and colleagues (2014) conducted a systematic review and meta-analysis of all morphometric neuroimaging studies of meditation (a *meta-analysis* of neuroimaging studies concatenates data from many independent investigations, seeking for consistency and replicability among the results [Wager, Lindquist, & Kaplan, 2007; Wager, Lindquist, Nichols, Kober, & Van Snellenberg, 2009; Yarkoni, Poldrack, Van Essen, & Wager, 2010]). Collating more than one hundred morphological differences reported in twenty-one studies that recruited more than three hundred meditation practitioners, consistent changes were found in several regions of the brain (Figure. 19.1). For the sake of brevity, we discuss just a few of the most intriguing findings here.

One region found to be altered in practitioners from a variety of contemplative backgrounds was the *insula*, a brain region key to *interoceptive* awareness of the body (e.g., awareness of respiration, heartbeat, abdominal sensations, and so on; Craig, 2002, 2004, 2009; Critchley, Wiens, Rotshtein, Öhman, & Dolan, 2004; Farb, Segal, & Anderson, 2013). Also consistently altered was the somatosensory cortex, the key region for *exteroceptive* awareness of the body (e.g., the sense of touch, pain, and so on; Kaas, 1983; Penfield & Boldrey, 1937). Together, these changes in the insula and somatosensory cortex suggest that meditation practitioners have altered (perhaps heightened) awareness of their body, both inside and out—a hunch supported by evidence that meditators exhibit significantly more sensitive and objective reports of subtle bodily sensations (Fox et al., 2012; Sze, Gyurak, Yuan, & Levenson, 2010), and further

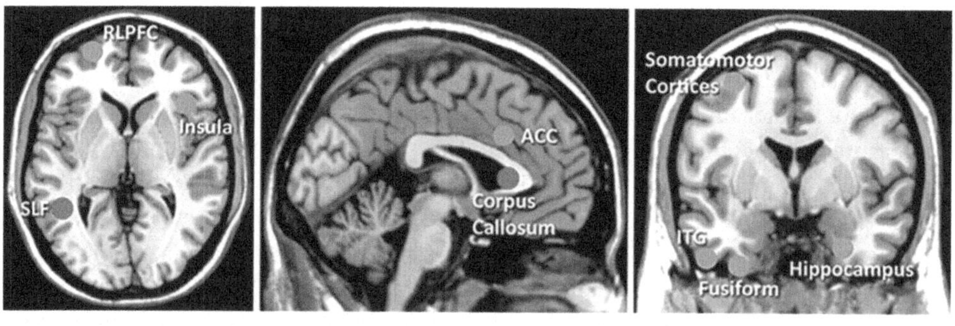

FIGURE 19.1 Putative consistent changes in the brain structure associated with the practice of meditation, from morphometric neuroimaging of meditation practitioners. Grey matter differences are indicated by blue circles, differences in white matter by red circles. ACC: anterior cingulate cortex; ITG: inferior temporal gyrus; RLPFC: rostrolateral prefrontal cortex; SLF: superior longitudinal fasciculus. Reproduced, with permission, from Fox et al. (2014).

corroborated in a recent longitudinal study demonstrating enhanced heartbeat detection over time in practitioners learning mindfulness meditation (Bornemann & Singer, 2017). Contemplative traditions often stress awareness of the body as a means of maintaining attention in the "now" of the present moment, but as will be discussed in the next section, a heightened awareness of the body could also have important benefits when encountering emotional distress (Farb et al., 2010) and pain (Grant, Courtemanche, Duerden, Duncan, & Rainville, 2010; Grant, Courtemanche, & Rainville, 2011).

Another region consistently altered in practitioners from a variety of contemplative traditions is the rostrolateral prefrontal cortex (RLPFC), also known as frontopolar cortex. Although implicated in a wide variety of "higher" cognitive tasks, such as probabilistic reasoning or integrating abstract information stored in working memory (Christoff & Gabrieli, 2000; Ramnani & Owen, 2004), perhaps most intriguing for our purposes is the apparent link between the RLPFC and introspective ability (Fleming, Ryu, Golfinos, & Blackmon, 2014; Fleming, Weil, Nagy, Dolan, & Rees, 2010). Given that most meditation practitioners spend significant time engaging in self-reflective, introspective practices, consistently altered structure in a brain region key to introspective ability suggests that such capacities might be enhanced with meditation training (Fox & Christoff, 2014; Lutz & Thompson, 2003)—a hypothesis supported by some preliminary research (Bornemann & Singer, 2017; Fox et al., 2012; Jo, Hinterberger, Wittmann, & Schmidt, 2015; Sze et al., 2010). As with body awareness, heightened introspective awareness might not only facilitate the goals of meditation practice itself, but might also have ancillary benefits. For instance, accurate introspection is thought to be crucial for facilitating insights into one's behavior in a manner that may play a key role in mitigating psychiatric disorders, such as relapse in major depression (Teasdale, 1999; Teasdale et al., 2002). Furthermore, long-term practitioners with heightened introspective awareness could help neuroscientists explore subtle cognitive phenomena that untrained participants are unable to notice or accurately report on (see next section).

Morphometric Neuroimaging of Long-Term Practitioners vs. Short-Term Meditation Training

The majority of the research discussed in the preceding section was based on comparing meditation-naïve control subjects to long-term practitioners with thousands of hours of meditation experience. As noted earlier (in our discussion of the brains of expert musicians), although such *cross-sectional* studies can reveal differences between groups, they cannot tell us if training induced these changes in the brain, or whether pre-existing differences in neuroanatomy might predispose certain people to persist in long-term training (in either music or meditation). Of course, both factors could also be at play, further complicating the situation. *Longitudinal* studies have helped to resolve this problem by examining the brains of people beginning to practice meditation both before and after a period of meditation training. By comparing any changes to a control group of subjects scanned at the same two time-points but undergoing no meditation training, we can make much better inferences as to whether meditation itself has *caused* the observed differences in brain structure. Several studies have employed this kind of pre-post-longitudinal study to investigate meditation's effects on brain morphometry (Farb et al., 2013; Holzel et al., 2010; Holzel et al., 2011; Tang, Lu, Fan, Yang, & Posner, 2012; Tang et al., 2010). Intriguingly, the effects putatively induced by meditation training overlap considerably with those observed in long-term practitioners (Fig. 19.1), including consistent observations in regions related to emotional awareness and regulation (the anterior cingulate cortex), body awareness (the anterior insula), memory (hippocampus), and integration of information between the two cerebral hemispheres (corpus callosum) (Fox et al., 2014). Although these findings suggest that meditation training can indeed effect changes in brain structure, like other forms of skill learning (Draganski & May, 2008), these results are based on only a handful of studies and need to be replicated and expanded in further work.

Methodological Concerns for the Morphometric Neuroimaging of Meditation

Despite all these apparent consistencies, the verdict is not yet in as to whether or not meditation is truly associated with altered brain structure, much less causes these alterations. Among many other methodological issues (Fox et al., 2014), one of the central concerns is *publication bias* or the "file-drawer problem"—the tendency for researchers to publish only findings that show significant differences, and to refrain from publishing their findings when these show no differences between groups and abandon them in the proverbial file-drawer (Rosenthal, 1979). Under these conditions, which are rampant throughout academia (not just in meditation research), despite the fact that dozens of studies have now shown differences between meditation practitioners and controls (Fox et al., 2014), it could be that many studies have shown no differences, too—only no one has ever seen these "null" results (besides the researchers who conducted the studies), because they have not been published. Statistical methods exist for estimating the degree of publication bias in a given field of study (Egger, Smith, Schneider, & Minder, 1997), and without dwelling on the details, suffice to say that there is evidence for considerable publication bias in morphometric neuroimaging of meditation (Fox et al., 2014). For this reason (as well as others; Thomas & Baker, 2013), findings from morphometric neuroimaging of meditation need to be interpreted with caution.

Functional Neuroimaging of Meditation

Starting in 1999, neuroscientists began to apply methods of *functional neuroimaging* to the investigation of meditation (Lou et al., 1999). In contrast to the morphometric neuroimaging techniques discussed in the previous section, which interrogate various aspects of brain *structure*, functional neuroimaging methods measure the brain at work. Functional magnetic resonance imaging (fMRI) and positron emission tomography (PET) are typically used to measure various aspects of changes of blood flow in the brain (a highly useful correlate of the averaged activity of the brain's neurons, despite being many steps removed from actual neuroelectric activity [Logothetis, Pauls, Augath, Trinath, & Oeltermann, 2001; Mukamel et al., 2005]). Examining changes in blood flow throughout the brain can provide a proxy measure of how different brain regions are recruited during essentially any cognitive task a person can engage in while lying down in a brain scanner—including meditation.

There are at least three ways in which meditation can be investigated with functional neuroimaging. The first and most basic is to simply examine the neural correlates of engaging in a particular form of meditation (for instance, have practitioners engage in a breath awareness meditation and look at brain activity compared to some baseline). Many studies have taken such an approach in an effort to better understand the fundamental neural basis of various meditation techniques (Fox, Dixon, et al., 2016). A second approach is to employ long-term practitioners, or novices after brief meditation training, and explore whether meditation alters the brain's response to a variety of tasks and experiences (for instance, having untrained people vs. trained meditation practitioners view distressing videos [Farb et al., 2010]). A third and more experimental method is to harness the putatively enhanced introspective abilities of long-term meditation practitioners (Fox et al., 2012; Sze et al., 2010) to investigate subtle and difficult-to-study cognitive phenomena (Berman & Stevens, 2015; Ellamil et al., 2016). Examples of each type of approach are discussed in the following subsections.

Neural Correlates of Meditation Practices

Meditation comprises hundreds of different techniques, but many of these can be grouped into a few broad categories. One scheme uses three basic categories: focused attention, open monitoring, and loving-kindness/compassion (Fox, Dixon, et al., 2016; Lutz, Jha, Dunne, & Saron, 2015; Lutz et al., 2008). *Focused attention* meditation involves focalizing and sustaining attention on a single object, often the sensations of respiration or a visual point of fixation. A related practice, sometimes grouped with focused attention but that we consider separately for the purposes of this chapter, is *mantra* meditation, a focused attention practice wherein the single focus of attention is a phrase repeated by the practitioner (we treat mantra meditation as a distinct category because of its distinctive motor/verbalization component). *Open monitoring* (sometimes referred to as "open awareness") is a broad category encompassing many forms of meditation that involve a non-judgmental, non-attached, broad attention to everything arising in one's experience, be it visions, sounds, somatic sensations, and one's own thoughts. Finally, *loving-kindness and compassion* forms of meditation involve cultivating specific positive emotional and relational states of mind characterized by love and the intention to relieve suffering in self and/or others.

Each of these four categories of meditation has been explored with functional neuro imaging in some detail over the past two decades. The most salient finding from this considerable body of work is that *psychologically distinct meditation practices show correspondingly diverse neural correlates*. For instance, focused attention meditation has been shown to recruit several regions of the brain canonically involved in top-down control of attention and other executive processes, including the right dorsolateral prefrontal cortex, the dorsal anterior cingulate cortex, and the premotor cortex (Figure. 19.2). In contrast, mantra meditation (a subtype of focused attention practice), in which practitioners repeatedly recite a specific phrase or word (either out loud or, more often, subvocally), involves a notable recruitment of motor regions, including the supplementary motor area and Broca's area, which is key to speech production (Figure. 19.2). Similar to focused attention, open-monitoring meditation yielded marked recruitment of prefrontal brain areas involved in the top-down control of attention, but also displayed recruitment of the insula (a region involved in awareness of inner body states) on both sides of the brain—a finding suggesting that this form of meditation focuses attention on the present-moment experiences of the body (Farb et al., 2007). Finally, loving-kindness and compassion forms of meditation yielded a variety of brain activations consistent with

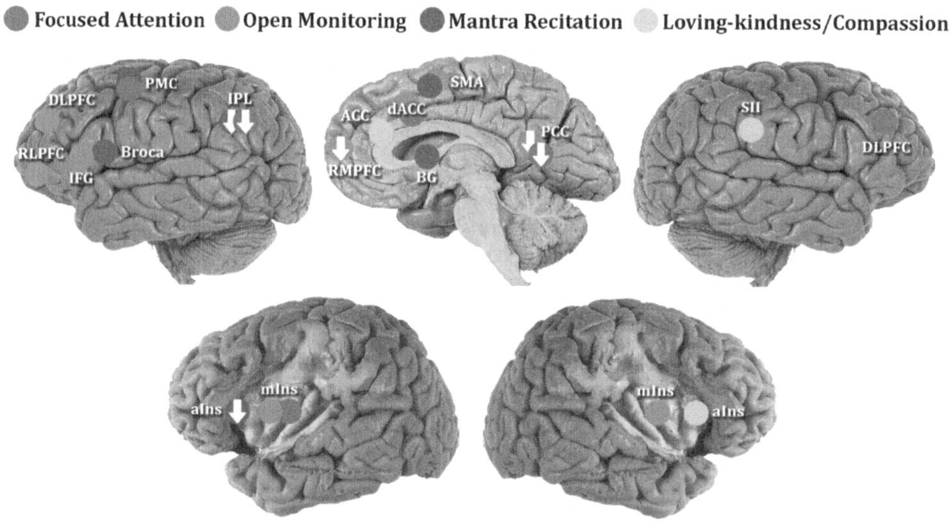

FIGURE 19.2 Meta-analytic activations and deactivations for four categories of meditation. Activations are represented by filled circles, deactivations by circles containing downward arrows. Regional labels are approximate and are shown for illustrative purposes only. For details, see tables of results, main figures, and supplementary figures in Fox et al. (2016). ACC: anterior cingulate cortex; aIns: anterior insula; BG: basal ganglia; Broca: Broca's area; dACC: dorsal anterior cingulate cortex; DLPFC: dorsolateral prefrontal cortex; IFG: inferior frontal gyrus; IPL: inferior parietal lobule; mIns: mid-insula; PCC: posterior cingulate cortex; PMC: premotor cortex; RLPFC: rostrolateral prefrontal cortex; RMPFC: rostromedial prefrontal cortex; SII: secondary somatosensory cortices; SMA: supplementary motor area.

Reproduced, with permission, from Fox et al. (2016).

other neuroimaging studies of non-meditating people generating or expressing emotions like compassion and empathy (Fig. 19.2).

Other types of meditation that do not fit easily within these four categories have only rarely been investigated with functional neuroimaging, but the results of some preliminary investigations are nonetheless intriguing (Josipovic, Dinstein, Weber, & Heeger, 2011; Kakigi et al., 2005; Kjaer et al., 2002; Lou et al., 1999). For instance, an early study of the neural correlates of visualization meditation (where practitioners imagine visual scenes and figures in vivid detail) found widespread activation of visual brain regions (Lou et al., 1999)—a finding not observed during any other form of meditation (Fox, Dixon, et al., 2016). A recent study of non-dual awareness practice—which can be conceived as an advanced open-awareness practice wherein the experience of an observer relating to observed phenomena of experience dissolves into an all-encompassing unity of experience—found decreases in the normally anti-correlated activations of the major circuits of the brain such as the default mode network and the central executive network (Josipovic, 2014; Josipovic et al., 2011).

Differences aside, some similarities are also telling. As noted above, one of the most reliable findings from morphometric neuroimaging of meditation practitioners is structural alteration of the insula (Fox et al., 2014), a brain region key to interoceptive awareness of the body (Craig, 2002, 2004, 2009; Critchley et al., 2004; Farb et al., 2013). Consistent with this finding, Fox et al. (2016) found that all four broad categories of meditation consistently modulated activity in the insula (Fig. 19.2). Although these effects included a mix of activations (for focused-attention, open-monitoring, and compassion meditations) and deactivations (mantra recitation), suggesting that not every form of meditation modulates the insula in the same way, the results nonetheless point to this region's importance across an array of contemplative practices (Fig. 19.2). Given the insula's role in interoceptive awareness, and considering that awareness and regulation of breathing and other aspects of the body are central to most forms of meditation, consistent structural (Fox et al., 2014) and functional (Fox, Dixon, et al., 2016) alterations in the insula are not especially surprising. The unique finding of deactivation of the insula during mantra meditation might be related to this practice's focus on generating verbalizations, and regulating respiration accordingly, in a top-down manner, rather than paying attention to the natural fluctuations of breathing in a bottom-up way, as in most other forms of contemplative practice. It may also point to a decreased tendency of mantra practice to enhance bodily awareness relative to focused attention on bodily processes, open monitoring, and loving-kindness/compassion practices.

How Meditation Changes the Brain's Response to Tasks and Experiences

Another approach is to examine not just the neural correlates of meditation in and of itself, but how meditation practice alters the brain's responses to specific tasks and emotional experiences. For instance, viewing distressing (sadness- or fear-provoking) images and videos is known to have widespread effects on brain activity. Farb and colleagues (2010) investigated whether engaging in an eight-week mindfulness meditation course would alter these patterns of brain activity when viewing sadness-provoking videos. In control subjects that had not undergone any meditation training, they found that watching sad (compared to neutral) videos elicited recruitment in multiple midline default network regions associated with self-referential processing, memory retrieval, mind-wandering, and rumination (Christoff, Irving, Fox, Spreng, & Andrews-Hanna, 2016; Fox et al., 2018; Fox, Foster, Kucyi, Daitch, & Parvizi, 2018; Fox, Spreng, Ellamil, Andrews-Hanna, & Christoff, 2015; Northoff et al., 2006). In contrast, those who had undergone mindfulness training showed increased activation in the insula (as noted above, a region key to interoception) and executive brain regions in the lateral prefrontal cortex. Both groups reported that the videos elicited comparable levels of sadness; however, in the mindfulness group an increased recruitment of body awareness–related brain regions, rather than default network regions involved in mind-wandering and conceptual thinking, suggested that the response was perhaps more present-centered and detached from narrative processing in those who had undergone mindfulness training (Farb et al., 2010).

Functional neuroimaging has also shown that meditation can alter the neural correlates of the experience of pain in a similar fashion. Beyond the purely sensory aspects of pain, the experience of pain ("nociception") tends to also involve thoughts that relate the pain to the self, as well as distress and various other negative emotional valuations of the sensory experience (Grant, 2014; Grant et al., 2011; Rainville, Duncan, Price, Carrier, & Bushnell, 1997). These cognitive-affective elaborations appear to be dissociable from, and temporally subsequent to, the purely sensory aspects of pain—and what's more, they may contribute significantly to the subjectively experienced unpleasantness of nociceptive experience (Rainville et al., 1997). A recent study using fMRI explored whether mindfulness meditation might reduce the habitual affective-elaborative component of pain, by exploring differences in brain activity between long-term Zen practitioners and meditation-naïve controls (Grant et al., 2011). Earlier studies demonstrated that the same group of Zen practitioners exhibited higher self-reported pain thresholds (Grant & Rainville, 2009) and increased cortical thickness in sensory pain areas (Grant et al., 2010). Elaborating on these behavioral findings for pain thresholds, the researchers found that pain elicited greater brain activations in sensory pain areas in the meditators, including the thalamus, insula, and dorsal anterior cingulate cortex—suggesting that the meditators elaborated less on their pain, and instead focused more on its immediate sensory components (Grant et al., 2011). Further support for this interpretation came from the finding that functional connectivity between primary sensory pain areas and secondary affective-elaborative areas was increased in controls and decreased in the long-term Zen practitioners (Grant et al., 2011), again supporting the idea that novices dwelled on their pain with emotional and cognitive associations, whereas the meditators tended to remain focused on its more purely sensory aspects. Intriguingly, the degree of this decoupling in meditation practitioners significantly predicted their lower pain sensitivity—offering perhaps the most persuasive evidence for the aforementioned interpretation. Further work by others has reinforced this general understanding of the effects of mindfulness on the brain processing of pain, revealing that short-term training in mindfulness results in similar changes in the neural underpinnings of pain processing (Zeidan et al., 2016; Zeidan et al., 2015; Zeidan, Grant, Brown, McHaffie, & Coghill, 2012; Zeidan et al., 2011).

Harnessing Meditation to Explore Subtle Neurocognitive Phenomena

Researchers have long suggested that the putatively enhanced attentional (MacLean et al., 2010) and introspective (Fox et al., 2012) abilities of long-term meditation practitioners might be harnessed to help neuroscientists explore subtle cognitive phenomena not easily investigated with untrained participants—an approach falling within the purview of the field of *neurophenomenology* (Fazelpour & Thompson, 2015; Lutz & Thompson, 2003; Varela, 1996). For instance, very little is understood from a neuroscientific perspective about how new thoughts spontaneously arise in our minds (Christoff, 2012; Christoff, Ream, & Gabrieli, 2004), yet this phenomenon is key to an understanding of creative thinking, scientific discovery, and even some forms of mental illness, such as depression (Christoff, Gordon, & Smith, 2011; Christoff et al., 2016; Fox, Andrews-Hanna, & Christoff, 2016; Fox & Christoff, 2018). A general picture of brain regions involved in these forms of internally oriented thinking is emerging (K.C.R. Fox et al., 2015), but the functional role of each region, and which areas are involved specifically in generating thoughts, remains unknown. At the same time, certain meditation traditions, for instance Vipassana or "insight" practices, focus very specifically and intensively on detecting and observing the arising of thoughts (Goenka, 2000). In a recent study, Ellamil and colleagues (2016) therefore recruited highly experienced Vipassana practitioners (with an average of 8,339 hours of practice) to meditate in an MRI scanner and indicate with a button-press the exact moment they noticed thought(s) arising. Working backward from this button-press, the investigators examined which brain areas were most active just *prior* to conscious awareness of a thought arising. They found that the medial temporal lobe and certain regions belonging to the default network were most active as a thought was arising, whereas other regions thought to be involved in spontaneous forms of thought showed peak activity several seconds later, suggesting that they are involved in the elaboration or evaluation of these thoughts (rather than their generation) (Ellamil et al., 2016). This study provides a good example of how the specific expertise of highly experienced meditation practitioners was able to help shed light on the brain dynamics of a subtle yet important cognitive process that may have been difficult to investigate in any other way. Further work could shed light on the neural basis of more unusual experiences in long-term meditators, for instance prolonged states of narrative-free awareness.

THE ELECTROPHYSIOLOGY OF MEDITATION

Electroencephalography (EEG) involves the application of electrodes to the scalp in order to measure the electrical fields produced by the brain. While EEG can detect very fast fluctuations in brain activity (on the millisecond scale), because the signal is filtered through the skull and skin, spatial resolution tends to be poor. Therefore EEG is an excellent tool for determining *when* changes in brain activity take place but tells us much less about *where* in the brain they are happening. Functional MRI generally has the opposite profile—poor temporal but good spatial resolution—making the two methods good complements to one another.

Crucial to understanding EEG studies is an appreciation that the human brain establishes natural rhythms that synchronize electrical activity from its 100 billion neurons (Buzsaki, 2006). These synchronized oscillations can be detected as "brainwaves" with characteristic frequencies (i.e., cycles per second, measured in Hertz, or Hz), and different frequencies, when dominant, broadly correspond to different states of consciousness and alertness (Figure. 19.3). For instance, the slowest brainwaves (0.5–4 Hz) are known as "delta" waves and are characteristic of deep sleep and, in most people, a lack of conscious awareness (Figure. 19.3). In contrast, normal wakeful alertness tends to be associated with a mix of alpha, beta (13–32 Hz), and gamma (≥30 Hz) waves, whereas restful waking with eyes closed results in enhanced brainwaves in the alpha range and is associated with feelings of relaxation (8–13 Hz).

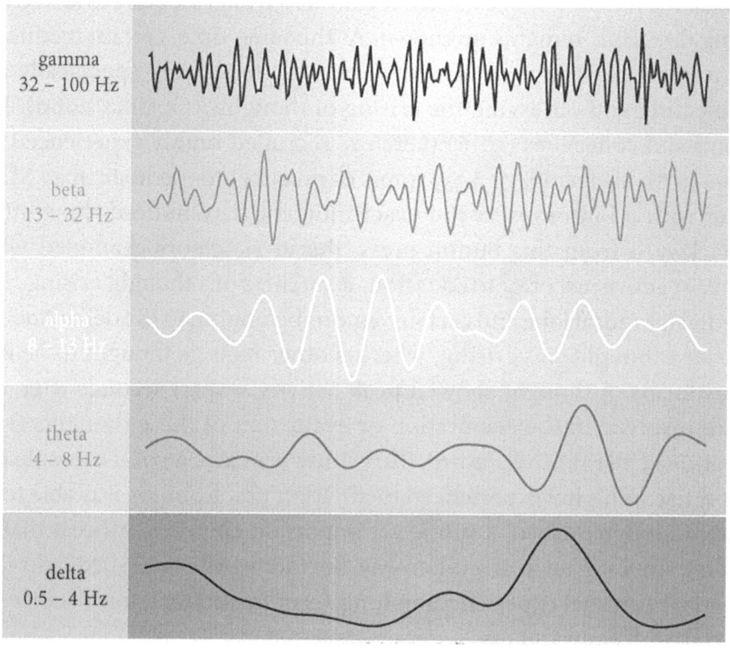

FIGURE 19.3 The standard human brain rhythm frequencies.

This basic rubric is well validated and agreed upon, if grossly simplified. In reality, the brain is generating a mix of frequencies across the delta, theta, alpha, beta, and gamma ranges in every given state of awareness, and the relative strength of each frequency in each brain area is constantly changing. Overall, our understanding of how brain rhythms are affected by experience and mental training remains relatively poor, although some progress with regards to meditation and the EEG has been made. The EEG studies of meditation have been conducted for over fifty years (Cahn & Polich, 2006), with two general approaches: (i) investigation of meditation *states*, that is, the brain's electrical activity during a given meditation practice; or (ii) investigation of meditation *traits*, namely, persisting differences in the electrical activity of the brains of long-term meditation practitioners compared to meditation-naïve control subjects. Because research results are complex and far from wholly consistent, in the following sections we first present an overview of what has been found and then subsequently attempt to integrate and interpret the many disparate findings.

General Electrophysiological Correlates of Meditation

Although the neuroelectric correlates of meditative states and traits of consciousness are not yet firmly established, the primary findings have implicated increases in theta (4–7 Hz) and alpha band (8–12 Hz) power (Andresen, 2000; Cahn & Polich, 2006; Davidson, 1976; Fenwick, 1987; Schuman, 1980; Shapiro & Walsh, 1984; West, 1980). The large number of studies showing enhanced theta and/or alpha power in both novices and experts suggests that enhancements of these electrocortical rhythms are somehow meaningfully related to meditative practices.

A number of the more recent studies showing specific state-related changes during meditation in more advanced practitioners have found alterations in faster beta (~12–30 Hz) and gamma (>30 Hz) frequency ranges. These findings suggest that as meditative expertise develops there may be trait-like alterations in theta and alpha early on, and later-developing alterations in faster beta and gamma frequencies in association with experiencing more and more refined states of meditative awareness.

For instance, numerous recent studies of meditation have demonstrated effects on beta activity (Dor-Ziderman, Berkovich-Ohana, Glicksohn, & Goldstein, 2013; Faber et al., 2015; Hauswald, Übelacker, Leske, & Weisz, 2015; Saggar et al., 2012; Tanaka et al., 2015). Specific examples of such findings include an assessment of experienced Zen meditators demonstrating a state-related decrease in posterior beta power in combination with increased right frontotemporal alpha power (Faber et al., 2015). Another study of Zen meditators similarly found a decrease in beta power in combination with a decrease in delta power (Hauswald et al., 2015). Perhaps the most reliable finding to date was demonstrated in a well-controlled longitudinal study with a cohort of practitioners randomized to an intensive three-month retreat, including assessments before versus after in both the meditation practitioners and control participants (Saggar et al., 2012). This study found only one major effect on band power across any of the assessed frequencies from delta to gamma—decreases in centroparietal beta power (Saggar et al., 2012). In this context it is important to note that one major interpretation of decreases in beta power is that both alpha and beta EEG power have been found to be inversely related to cortical excitability and target detection accuracy; conversely, then, decreases in beta power may be related to *enhanced* cortical excitability and sensory acuity.

Recent studies of meditation have focused also on the gamma band (30–80 Hz), which is known to be associated with the current contents of awareness and perceptual binding (Fries, 2009; Scheeringa et al., 2011). Because the gamma range is subject to potential large-amplitude muscle- and eye-movement-related artifacts, it is difficult to measure with absolute confidence, although methods have been developed to address this issue and are actively being assessed for reliability in dissociating cortical gamma activity from scalp and extraocular muscle gamma activity. The first modern quantitative study demonstrating specific gamma-frequency effects in meditation assessed highly experienced Tibetan Buddhist meditators versus novices while engaged in three separate techniques: one-pointed concentration on an object, open attention without an object, and a state of non-referential love and compassion (Lutz, Greischar, Ricard, Converse, & Davidson, 2003). Large increases in ~40 Hz gamma power were observed in the meditators as both a state effect of meditation and a trait elevation relative to non-meditator controls. A number of further studies over the past ten years have found gamma power increases associated with meditative practice during waking meditation practice (Berkovich-Ohana, Glicksohn, & Goldstein, 2012; Braboszcz, Cahn, Levy, Fernandez, & Delorme, 2017; Cahn, Delorme, & Polich, 2010; Dentico et al., 2016; Ferrarelli et al., 2013).

Understanding and Interpreting Electrophysiological Findings in Meditation Research

Detecting and measuring the electrophysiological effects of meditation is one thing; understanding the functional significance of such differences is another. There are two basic approaches to an understanding and interpretation of electrophysiological findings in meditation research. The first, detailed in this section, is to relate observed changes to the broader field of EEG research. An understanding of what various EEG rhythms are generally thought to represent can shed light on what functional role such changes might have in the specific context of meditation. A second approach, explored in the next section, is to collect detailed first-person reports from meditation practitioners and explore the electrophysiological correlates of particular subjective states.

Recent basic neurophysiological investigations of the functional significance of cortical rhythms in the theta, alpha, beta, and gamma frequency ranges indicate that both alpha and beta are important in top-down attentional control, that is, voluntarily orienting attention toward an object of one's own choosing; gamma, instead, appears to be more significantly related to bottom-up stimulus processing, that is, allowing sensory stimuli to capture attention and then binding them together into unified perceptual experiences (Richter, Thompson, Bosman, & Fries, 2017). But because of the difficulties in localizing the specific spatial source of EEG signals, aligning specific EEG findings with the spatially specific findings from fMRI (discussed in the previous section) remains challenging. Attaining better spatial resolution with EEG might someday provide a much more thorough understanding of the meaning of electrocortical findings.

Nonetheless, in relating investigations of the general functional significance of EEG band power to specific findings from electrophysiological studies of meditation, some meaningful trends emerge. For instance, enhanced frontal theta power is often correlated with decreased default network activation in simultaneous EEG/fMRI studies (Meltzer, Negishi, Mayes, & Constable, 2007; Murta, Leite, Carmichael, Figueiredo, & Lemieux, 2015; Scheeringa et al., 2008). The enhancement of frontal theta often observed in relation to meditative practice could therefore be related to the meditative capacity to decrease default network activation, as has been observed in fMRI studies (cf. Fig. 19.2). Because default network *activation* has been consistently linked to mind-wandering and other forms of internally directed and self-referential thought (Christoff, Gordon, Smallwood, Smith, & Schooler, 2009; Christoff et al., 2016; Dixon, Fox, & Christoff, 2014; Ellamil et al., 2016; Fox et al., 2015), default network *deactivation* might be related to the fact that meditation training is associated with a lower frequency of mind-wandering (Brandmeyer & Delorme, 2016; Mrazek, Franklin, Phillips, Baird, & Schooler, 2013; Rahl, Lindsay, Pacilio, Brown, & Creswell, 2017; Zanesco et al., 2016). Overall, then, research suggests that meditation may be associated with decreased quantity of mind-wandering in conjunction with increased periods of higher theta-alpha power during periods of greater meditative quietude.

With respect to enhanced alpha power, the functional significance of 8–12 Hz alpha activity in the human cortex is still far from clear, although some recent insights are instructive. For instance, *increased* alpha power is observed in sensory areas responsible for processing that is being purposefully ignored, and *decreased* alpha power in areas responsible for sensory processing that *is* being attended to. This implies that at least one functional role for increased alpha power observed is enhanced inhibition of elaborative processing in the cortex from which alpha emanates; in other words, increased alpha power over a given part of the brain might be a marker that this region is functionally inhibited and thus less actively processing information. It therefore seems reasonable to interpret the frequent finding of enhancements of frontal theta as a proxy for enhanced attentional absorption in a non-conceptual domain and resultant decrease in default network activation, and the enhanced alpha power related to functional inhibition of specific brain circuitry depending on where the alpha enhancements are seen.

With respect to beta activity, the canonical understanding has been that beta activity is related to active processing, but there is now growing evidence that, as with alpha, beta activity too is related to decreased metabolic demand and may serve an inhibitory processing function (Murta et al., 2015; Scheeringa et al., 2011; Scheeringa, Koopmans, van Mourik, Jensen, & Norris, 2016), and at least in the somatosensory domain serves as a top-down mediator of decreased cortical excitability, much like alpha (van Ede, de

Lange, Jensen, & Maris, 2011). The relative decreases in beta power that a number of recent studies have demonstrated may therefore be related to enhancements in cortical excitability and sensory acuity.

Neurophenomenological Approaches to the Electrophysiology of Meditation

Beyond speculations based on the general significance of various EEG rhythms, a more targeted approach can be taken by gathering detailed first-person reports from meditation practitioners and exploring how these subjective states are related to specific electrophysiological markers. Such an approach often falls under the umbrella of the method of *neurophenomenology*, as discussed earlier (Fazelpour & Thompson, 2015; Lutz & Thompson, 2003; Varela, 1996). Early efforts to apply neurophenomenological techniques to meditative states were undertaken by researchers of Transcendental Meditation. In these early studies, periods of breath suspension, as well as increased alpha power and alpha inter-channel coherence, were found to characterize periods of self-described "inner silence" (Badawi, Wallace, Orme-Johnson, & Rouzere, 1984; Farrow & Hebert, 1982; Travis, 2001; Travis & Pearson, 2000). More recent investigations with expert meditators in other traditions have attempted to probe specific refined states of meditative awareness using a neurophenomenological approach. These include investigation of the *jhānas* (a sequence of meditative absorptions described in traditional Buddhist teachings) (DeLosAngeles et al., 2016; Hagerty et al., 2013); non-dual states of awareness (Berman & Stevens, 2015; Schoenberg, Ruf, Churchill, Brown, & Brewer, 2018); thoughtless emptiness (Hinterberger, Schmidt, Kamei, & Walach, 2014); and the experiential dimensions of selflessness, timelessness, and spacelessness (Berkovich-Ohana, Dor-Ziderman, Glicksohn, & Goldstein, 2013; Dor-Ziderman, Ataria, Fulder, Goldstein, & Berkovich-Ohana, 2016; Dor-Ziderman et al., 2013).

For instance, exploration of *jhānic* absorptions yielded findings of increased theta, alpha, and gamma power in one case-report (Hagerty et al., 2013), and increased frontal theta and alpha power combined with decreased central beta and gamma power in a study of twelve long-term meditators (DeLosAngeles et al., 2016). In contrast to such focused absorption states, guided non-dual awareness meditation states have been found to be characterized by large broadband decreases in alpha, beta, and gamma power, with subsequent increases in beta and gamma power in successively more refined states of awareness (Schoenberg et al., 2018). In another study, wherein experienced practitioners were instructed to cultivate a state of "thoughtless emptiness," this experience was found to be correlated with reduced delta, theta, and beta power relative to the resting state; in contrast, focused attention and mindful presence states were associated with greater gamma power relative to thoughtless emptiness states (Hinterberger et al., 2014). A recent study using magnetoencephalography (MEG), a method that, like EEG, also measures the brain's electromagnetic potentials, investigated states of "selflessness" in long-term meditators. When the practitioners indicated that they were transitioning from a narrative style of self-awareness to a more minimal self-awareness, the researchers observed a decrease in frontal gamma power; the further transition from a minimal self-awareness to total "selflessness" was accompanied by a decrease in centroparietal beta power (Dor-Ziderman et al., 2016; Dor-Ziderman et al., 2013). In contrast, the transition to an experience of timelessness and spacelessness in the same group of subjects was associated with an increase in frontal theta power (Berkovich-Ohana et al., 2013).

A second type of neurophenomenological approach has been to probe participants or ask them to self-report regarding specific epochs of experience during their meditation sessions while undergoing electrophysiological recording. One such study assessed self-reported "non-thought" or "non-dual" states and found that greater delta, theta, and alpha power, in combination with lower beta and gamma power, were observed when comparing such short periods with the average activity over the long meditation session (Berman & Stevens, 2015). In another study of long-term practitioners, intermittent probes during the meditation session asked the meditators about their meditative depth and incidence of mind-wandering; increased theta and alpha power were demonstrated in epochs of greater self-reported meditative absorption relative to periods higher self-reported mind-wandering (Brandmeyer & Delorme, 2016).

Summary of the Electrophysiology of Meditation

In sum, while electrophysiological studies of meditation have been extensive, many questions remain. The most frequently demonstrated findings include enhanced theta and alpha power as both state and trait effects of meditation, but more recent studies point toward beta and gamma effects, especially in longer-term practitioners. The application of neurophenomenological methods to meditative states alongside EEG recordings has begun in earnest over the past five years, but findings are as yet somewhat inconsistent. One apparent trend from this work, however, is that more concentrative states of meditation tend to demonstrate increases in theta-alpha power, whereas open-awareness types of meditative states appear to demonstrate some consistent decreases in power for both slower and faster frequencies.

Unlike fMRI signals, EEG signals are temporally specific and spatially diffuse; part of the explanation for the great variety of findings reported to date may therefore be the lack of consensus on methods of localizing observed effects. Another source of confusion could be the potentially diverse state-trait changes associated with the many different set points that individuals start at before engaging in meditation (cf. Mascaro, Rilling, Negi, & Raison, 2013) and extensive discussion in Fox, Dixon, et al., 2016). Further advances in signal processing will likely help resolve some of the outstanding questions regarding which frequency bands are related to specific meditative states and traits.

Meditation and Brain Health

Recent years have seen increasing efforts to understand how the long- and short-term practice of meditation relates to brain health. Although investigation of the relationship between meditation and brain health in neurodegenerative and psychiatric disease remains in its infancy, given the increasing popularity of meditation interventions in clinical settings we expect a rapid proliferation of such investigations in the near future. Here we discuss just two avenues of inquiry that have already shown promise. One line of research has investigated how meditation might mitigate age-related cognitive decline, and potentially, more serious conditions such as dementia and Alzheimer's disease, which are associated with progressive atrophy of brain tissue. Another line of research has also examined how meditation might alter brain activity in specific psychiatric conditions like depression, attention-deficit hyperactivity disorder (ADHD), social anxiety disorder, and bipolar disorder.

Meditation and Age-Related Brain Atrophy and Cognitive Decline

Both the structure and functioning of the brain are negatively impacted by normal aging, which progressively reduces the amount and density of grey matter, as well as reducing the metabolic rate of the brain (Chételat et al., 2013; Fjell & Walhovd, 2010), and these structural and functional changes are associated with cognitive impairments such as memory loss, poor attentional focus, and impaired executive function (i.e., voluntary control and flexible shifting of attention) (Fox, Scahill, Crum, & Rossor, 1999; Rusinek et al., 2003). There is evidence that various lifestyle interventions (such as exercise) might help mitigate these cognitive problems (Christie et al., 2017; Norton, Matthews, Barnes, Yaffe, & Brayne, 2014). Preliminary findings suggest that long-term meditation practice, too, might be beneficial (Gard, Hölzel, & Lazar, 2014), raising the question of whether these putative benefits might be mediated by corresponding differences in brain structure and function.

Although firm conclusions are unwarranted at this early stage, several pilot studies have addressed this question in recent years. For instance, Pagnoni & Cekic (2007) investigated brain grey matter volume in thirteen long-term Zen meditation practitioners and thirteen age- and sex-matched controls between the ages of twenty-five and fifty. They found that whereas the control subjects exhibited a sizable negative correlation ($r = -.56$) between age and total grey matter volume (as expected based on trends in the general population), the meditation practitioners showed no such relationship ($r = .006$). That is, the brains of fifty-year-old Zen practitioners showed no overall grey matter differences from those of their much younger counterparts, whereas among control subjects, age significantly predicted less grey matter volume. Intriguingly, a similar trend was observed for a demanding sustained attention task administered to all participants: whereas older control subjects made considerably more errors on the task, performance remained high among nearly all Zen practitioners, and showed no significant relationship with age (Pagnoni & Cekic, 2007).

A related study by Lazar and colleagues (2005) similarly found that grey matter density in the rostrolateral prefrontal cortex, an area of the brain linked to higher cognitive abilities like introspection (Fleming & Dolan, 2012), differed significantly between long-term practitioners and controls. Whereas control subjects showed the anticipated negative correlation between grey matter density and age in this region ($r = -.76$), the meditation practitioners again showed no decline in grey matter with age ($r = 0.05$) (Lazar et al., 2005).

A handful of more recent studies have reported broadly congruent findings, providing some further support for these claims (Chételat et al., 2017; Kurth, Cherbuin, & Luders, 2015; Luders, Cherbuin, & Gaser, 2016; Luders, Cherbuin, Kurth, & Lauche, 2015; Wells et al., 2013). So far, none of these studies has established a *causal* link between meditation practice and these brain structural differences over the lifespan: for instance, people who naturally experience less cognitive decline and brain aging might also be more motivated, and better able, to consistently engage in a meditation practice. Alternatively or additionally, non-specific effects of a meditation practice, such as reduced stress or a more vegetarian diet, could explain the observed correlations. Nonetheless, these intriguing relationships should be pursued further in future research.

We are aware of two studies that have further investigated meditation and aging with functional, rather than morphometric, neuroimaging (Chételat et al., 2017; Wells et al., 2013). Wells and colleagues (2013) investigated the neural effects of mindfulness meditation on adults with mild cognitive impairment (MCI), often a precursor to dementia and Alzheimer's disease. Although the researchers did not measure whether mindfulness meditation actually affected the symptoms of MCI, they did find changes in neural markers that suggest it might be beneficial. These promising indicators included less atrophy in the hippocampus (known to degenerate in dementia and Alzheimer's patients [Buckner et al., 2005; Kaye et al., 1997]) as well as increased functional connectivity (i.e., correlated activity) between various brain regions critical to memory and especially susceptible to degeneration with aging (Wells et al., 2013).

Like age-related grey matter atrophy (Fjell & Walhovd, 2010), glucose metabolism tends to decrease with aging throughout the brain (Chételat et al., 2013). Chételat and colleagues (2017) recently used PET to examine whether glucose metabolism (a proxy for how active a brain area is) differed in elderly meditation practitioners (average age = 65 years, minimum of 10,000 hours of meditation experience) compared to control subjects without meditation experience. Reminiscent of the results from brain structure and aging in meditation practitioners, they found that glucose metabolism was significantly increased in several brain regions in the elderly meditation practitioners, again suggesting some protective effects against normal aging processes. Again, however, other differences in people who tend to consistently practice meditation, such as lower stress or particular diets, are generally not measured or accounted for, and could conceivably play a large role in the observed differences.

Meditation and the Neural Basis of Addiction and Mental Illness

Beyond cognitive decline and brain atrophy associated with aging, a handful of studies have investigated the neural basis of how meditation might ameliorate the symptoms of psychiatric conditions like depression (Bostanov, Keune, Kotchoubey, & Hautzinger, 2012; Chen et al., 2015; Schoenberg & Speckens, 2015), ADHD (Schoenberg et al., 2014), social anxiety disorder (Goldin & Gross, 2010; Goldin, Ziv, Jazaieri, & Gross, 2012; Goldin, Ziv, Jazaieri, Hahn, & Gross, 2013), and bipolar disorder (Ives-Deliperi, Howells, Stein, Meintjes, & Horn, 2013), as well as facilitate abstinence from substance use, for example in tobacco addiction (Westbrook et al., 2013).

For instance, to explore how mindfulness might mitigate addiction and craving, Westbrook and colleagues (2013) trained forty-seven smokers in mindfulness meditation and then had them view smoking-related images designed to induce craving for tobacco. The smokers were instructed to either view the images as they normally would or to practice mindfulness (i.e., maintain a non-judgmental and present-focused attitude) while watching the images, and brain activity during the two conditions was compared. They found that during the mindfulness condition, smokers reported reduced cravings for tobacco, as well as reduced activation in the subgenual anterior cingulate cortex, a brain region widely implicated in craving and addiction for many substances. Functional connectivity between the subgenual anterior cingulate cortex and other brain regions was also reduced in the mindfulness condition, suggesting that meditation practice can have widespread effects on the interactions among multiple brain systems (Westbrook et al., 2013). Clearly, further research into the brain basis of meditation in these and other clinical conditions will be an increasingly important area of study in the future (see further discussion below, in the concluding section).

Conclusions and Future Directions

The growing interest in meditation as both a topic of scientific investigation as well as a means of clinical intervention is long overdue. Nonetheless, this new excitement has to be tempered by the recognition that the research conducted to date has many limitations, as well as the acknowledgment that clinical benefit is far from an established fact, but largely remains to be demonstrated in future, more rigorous research. In this final section, we highlight what the neuroscience of meditation has achieved so far; the caveats that should accompany any interpretation of research to date; and the challenges on the horizon for future studies in both ailing and healthy brains.

What Have We Learned?

Cognitive and clinical neuroscientists have mapped out a preliminary understanding of how meditation relates to altered brain structure and function over the past two decades (Figs. 19.1 and 19.2). We can say with some confidence that meditation training might alter brain structure (Fox et al., 2014), providing some of the first compelling evidence that purely mental practices can alter brain structure in the same way that cognitive and motor practice appear to (Zatorre et al., 2012). Functional neuroimaging and EEG are providing mounting evidence that meditation alters perceptual, cognitive, and emotional reactions to stimuli and tasks; that different styles of meditation can be differentiated at the neural level (Fig. 19.2); and that long-term practitioners' attentional stability and introspective aptitude can be harnessed to explore subtle neurocognitive phenomena, such as the arising of spontaneous thoughts (Ellamil et al., 2016).

Although considerable progress has been made, much remains to be done, particularly in the realm of applied clinical interventions. Researchers are now moving toward understanding the neural mechanisms of meditation's effects on neuropsychiatric conditions as well as natural aging and cognitive decline, but the effectiveness of such interventions, as well as how best to target specific styles of practice to specific clinical conditions, remain challenging but exciting tasks for future research.

Recognizing the Limitations of Present Research

As should be clear by now, the neuroscience of meditation is a nascent field and agreement among studies and researchers is still the exception rather than the rule. It is risky to generalize findings based on studies with few participants and assume that this holds for anyone and everyone practicing meditation. Very few studies have even acknowledged, much less controlled for, the many factors that might differ between meditation practitioners and control participants, such as diet, stress, sleep patterns, and so on. It also seems clear that pre-existing differences in personality and temperament will predispose certain individuals toward persisting in, and benefitting from, contemplative practices, and there is already tentative evidence that these predispositions might have a brain basis (Mascaro et al., 2013). Publication bias (the preferential publication of only positive results) does not appear to be much of a problem in studies of the psychological and emotional effects of meditation (Sedlmeier et al., 2012), but seems to be a serious issue in morphometric neuroimaging of meditation (Fox et al., 2014). Finally, even when a certain finding is repeatedly replicated, this does not mean that all researchers agree on the interpretation of that result's meaning. For instance, structural and functional changes in the insula have now been reported in dozens of studies of the brain basis of meditation (Figs. 19.1 and 19.2); the standard interpretation is that these alterations are somehow related to changes in body awareness, but the insula is a highly variable structure implicated in countless other processes besides simply interoception (Butti & Hof, 2010; Menon & Uddin, 2010). If and when neuroscientists and clinicians do arrive at a consensus about how meditation interacts with and alters structure and function in both healthy and diseased brains, the *meaning* of these alterations will still be open to interpretation and, no doubt, fiercely debated.

Clinical Horizons

The use of meditation as an intervention or preventive measure is growing rapidly in many medical fields (Ludwig & Kabat-Zinn, 2008), and so developing a better understanding of the brain basis of any putative benefits is an important task on the immediate horizon. Neuropsychiatric diseases often show widely differing abnormalities in brain structure and function (Etkin & Wager, 2007; Hamilton et al., 2012; Valera, Faraone, Murray, & Seidman, 2007), yet can also share broad impairments that cross diagnostic boundaries, such as dysfunctions of prefrontal brain regions and cognitive control (Etkin, Gyurak, & O'Hara, 2013). Similarly, while the various methods of meditation also differ widely in their goals and their neural correlates, there are certain commonalities in both psychological experience and neural recruitment across techniques (Fig. 19.2). With the growing recognition by the scientific and clinical community that there are many techniques beyond the well-known mindfulness meditation, increasing opportunities are opening up for targeting specific styles of meditation for specific neuropsychiatric conditions. Early efforts have already been made, for instance using focused-attention mantra meditation to treat attention-deficit/hyperactivity disorder (Travis, Sarina, & Stixrud, 2011) or mindfulness (open monitoring) practices for anxiety (Goldin, Ramel, & Gross, 2009; Hölzel et al., 2013), but this will likely prove to be a long process of trial and error. Much more effort needs to be dedicated to exploring how various forms of meditation can differentially impact particular neuropsychiatric disorders (Fox et al., 2016; Hofmann, Grossman, & Hinton, 2011).

Conclusion

Meditation, practiced in many different forms for thousands of years around the world, has recently given rise to a burgeoning field of scientific study. Neuroscientific methods are teaching us an enormous amount about how the brain generates and sustains contemplative states; in the long-term, understanding of neural correlates should help us better understand who will adhere to, and benefit most from, meditation practice (Mascaro et al., 2013), as well as aid us in targeting specific contemplative practices for particular neuropsychiatric conditions. But this is not a one-way street: experienced practitioners are already being employed to help neuroscientists understand subtle perceptual and cognitive phenomena that ordinary people rarely notice (Ellamil et al., 2016; Fox et al., 2012), and long-term meditators continue to stretch scientists' conceptions of the brain's limitations when it comes to both unusual cognitive abilities like visualization (Kozhevnikov, Louchakova, Josipovic, & Motes, 2009) and voluntary control over the peripheral nervous system (Amihai & Kozhevnikov, 2015; Kox et al., 2012; Kox et al., 2014; Kozhevnikov, Elliott, Shephard, & Gramann, 2013). Ultimately, the neuroscience of meditation promises to shed light on the highest capabilities of the human nervous system and the biological basis of the farther reaches of human spiritual experience (Davis & Vago, 2013). The past few decades of work have set the stage for future research to develop a rigorous and thorough understanding of how the brain instantiates and is altered by this uniquely human practice.

References

Amihai, I., & Kozhevnikov, M. (2015). The influence of Buddhist meditation traditions on the autonomic system and attention. *BioMed Research International 2015*, Article ID 731579, 13.

Andresen, J. (2000). Meditation meets behavioural medicine: The story of experimental research on meditation. *Journal of Consciousness Studies 7*(11–12), 17–74.

Badawi, K., Wallace, R., Orme-Johnson, D., & Rouzere, A. (1984). Electrophysiologic characteristics of respiratory suspension periods occurring during the practice of the Transcendental Meditation program. *Psychosomatic Medicine 46*(3), 267–276.

Bagchi, B., & Wenger, M. (1957). Electrophysiological correlates of some yogi exercises. *Electroencephalography and Clinical Neurophysiology 7*, 132–149.

Berkovich-Ohana, A., Dor-Ziderman, Y., Glicksohn, J., & Goldstein, A. (2013). Alterations in the sense of time, space, and body in the mindfulness-trained brain: A neurophenomenologically-guided MEG study. *Frontiers in Psychology 4*, 1–19.

Berkovich-Ohana, A., Glicksohn, J., & Goldstein, A. (2012). Mindfulness-induced changes in gamma band activity—implications for the default mode network, self-reference and attention. *Clinical Neurophysiology 123*(4), 700–710.

Berman, A. E., & Stevens, L. (2015). EEG manifestations of nondual experiences in meditators. *Conscious Cognition 31*, 1–11.

Bornemann, B., & Singer, T. (2017). Taking time to feel our body: Steady increases in heartbeat perception accuracy and decreases in alexithymia over 9 months of contemplative mental training. *Psychophysiology 54*(3), 469–482.

Bostanov, V., Keune, P. M., Kotchoubey, B., & Hautzinger, M. (2012). Event-related brain potentials reflect increased concentration ability after mindfulness-based cognitive therapy for depression: A randomized clinical trial. *Psychiatry Research 199*(3), 174–180.

Braboszcz, C., Cahn, B. R., Levy, J., Fernandez, M., & Delorme, A. (2017). Increased gamma brainwave amplitude compared to control in three different meditation traditions. *PLoS ONE 12*(1), e0170647.

Brandmeyer, T., & Delorme, A. (2016). Reduced mind wandering in experienced meditators and associated EEG correlates. *Experimental Brain Research 236*, 2519–2528.

Buckner, R. L., Snyder, A. Z., Shannon, B. J., LaRossa, G., Sachs, R., Fotenos, A. F., . . . Morris, J. C. (2005). Molecular, structural, and functional characterization of Alzheimer's disease: Evidence for a relationship between default activity, amyloid, and memory. *Journal of Neuroscience 25*(34), 7709–7717.

Butti, C., & Hof, P. R. (2010). The insular cortex: A comparative perspective. *Brain Structure and Function 214*(5–6), 477–493. https://doi.org/10.1007/s00429-010-0264-y

Buzsaki, G. (2006). *Rhythms of the brain*. New York: Oxford University Press.
Cahn, B. R., Delorme, A., & Polich, J. (2010). Occipital gamma activation during Vipassana meditation. *Cognitive Processing 11*(1), 39–56.
Cahn, B. R., & Polich, J. (2006). Meditation states and traits: EEG, ERP, and neuroimaging studies. *Psychological Bulletin 132*(2), 180–211. https://doi.org/10.1037/0033-2909.132.2.180
Caroni, P., Chowdhury, A., & Lahr, M. (2014). Synapse rearrangements upon learning: From divergent–sparse connectivity to dedicated sub-circuits. *Trends in Neurosciences 37*(10), 604–614.
Chen, F., Lv, X., Fang, J., Yu, S., Sui, J., Fan, L., ... Wang, W. (2015). The effect of body-mind relaxation meditation induction on major depressive disorder: A resting-state fMRI study. *Journal of Affective Disorders 183*, 75–82.
Chételat, G., Landeau, B., Salmon, E., Yakushev, I., Bahri, M. A., Mézenge, F., ... Scheurich, A. (2013). Relationships between brain metabolism decrease in normal aging and changes in structural and functional connectivity. *Neuroimage 76*, 167–177.
Chételat, G., Mézenge, F., Tomadesso, C., Landeau, B., Arenaza-Urquijo, E., Rauchs, G., ... Gonneaud, J. (2017). Reduced age-associated brain changes in expert meditators: A multimodal neuroimaging pilot study. *Scientific Reports 7*(1), 10160.
Christie, G. J., Hamilton, T., Manor, B. D., Farb, N. A., Farzan, F., Sixsmith, A., ... Moreno, S. (2017). Do lifestyle activities protect against cognitive decline in aging? A review. *Frontiers in Aging Neuroscience 9*, 381.
Christoff, K. (2012). Undirected thought: Neural determinants and correlates. *Brain Research 1428*, 51–59. https://doi.org/10.1016/j.brainres.2011.09.060
Christoff, K., & Gabrieli, J. D. E. (2000). The frontopolar cortex and human cognition: Evidence for a rostrocaudal hierarchical organization within the human prefrontal cortex. *Psychobiology 28*(2), 168–186.
Christoff, K., Gordon, A. M., Smallwood, J., Smith, R., & Schooler, J. W. (2009). Experience sampling during fMRI reveals default network and executive system contributions to mind wandering. *Proceedings of the National Academy of Sciences USA 106*(21), 8719–8724. https://doi.org/10.1073/pnas.0900234106
Christoff, K., Gordon, A. M., & Smith, R. (2011). The role of spontaneous thought in human cognition. In O. Vartanian & D. R. Mandel (Eds.), *Neuroscience of Decision Making* (pp. 259–284). New York: Psychology Press.
Christoff, K., Irving, Z. C., Fox, K. C. R., Spreng, R. N., & Andrews-Hanna, J. R. (2016). Mind-wandering as spontaneous thought: A dynamic framework. *Nature Reviews Neuroscience 17*, 718–731.
Christoff, K., Ream, J. M., & Gabrieli, J. D. E. (2004). Neural basis of spontaneous thought processes. *Cortex 40*, 623–630.
Craig, A. (2002). How do you feel? Interoception: The sense of the physiological condition of the body. *Nature Reviews Neuroscience* 3(8), 655–666.
Craig, A. (2004). Human feelings: Why are some more aware than others? *Trends in Cognitive Sciences 8*(6), 239–241.
Craig, A. (2009). How do you feel—now? The anterior insula and human awareness. *Nature Reviews Neuroscience 10*(1), 59–70.
Critchley, H. D., Wiens, S., Rotshtein, P., Öhman, A., & Dolan, R. J. (2004). Neural systems supporting interoceptive awareness. *Nature Neuroscience 7*(2), 189–195.
Das, N., & Gastaut, H. (1955). Variations de l'activite electrique du cerveau, du coeur et des muscles squelettiques au cours de la meditation et de l'extase yogique. *Electroencephalogrophy and Clinical Neurophysiology. Supplement 6*, 211–219.

Davidson, J. M. (1976). The physiology of meditation and mystical states of consciousness. *Perspectives in Biology and Medicine 19*(3), 345–380.

Davis, J. H., & Vago, D. R. (2013). Can enlightenment be traced to specific neural correlates, cognition, or behavior? No, and (a qualified) yes. *Frontiers in Psychology 4*, 1–4.

DeLosAngeles, D., Williams, G., Burston, J., Fitzgibbon, S. P., Lewis, T. W., Grummett, T. S., ... Willoughby, J. O. (2016). Electroencephalographic correlates of states of concentrative meditation. *International Journal of Psychophysiology 110*, 27–39.

Dentico, D., Ferrarelli, F., Riedner, B. A., Smith, R., Zennig, C., Lutz, A., ... Davidson, R. J. (2016). Short meditation trainings enhance non-REM sleep low-frequency oscillations. *PLoS ONE 11*(2), e0148961.

Dixon, M. L., Fox, K. C. R., & Christoff, K. (2014). A framework for understanding the relationship between externally and internally directed cognition. *Neuropsychologia 62*, 321–330.

Dor-Ziderman, Y., Ataria, Y., Fulder, S., Goldstein, A., & Berkovich-Ohana, A. (2016). Self-specific processing in the meditating brain: A MEG neurophenomenology study. *Neuroscience of Consciousness 2016*(1), niw019.

Dor-Ziderman, Y., Berkovich-Ohana, A., Glicksohn, J., & Goldstein, A. (2013). Mindfulness-induced selflessness: A MEG neurophenomenological study. *Frontiers in Human Neuroscience 7*, 582.

Draganski, B., & May, A. (2008). Training-induced structural changes in the adult human brain. *Behavioural Brain Research 192*(1), 137–142. https://doi.org/10.1016/j.bbr.2008.02.015

Egger, M., Smith, G. D., Schneider, M., & Minder, C. (1997). Bias in meta-analysis detected by a simple, graphical test. *BMJ 315*(7109), 629–634.

Eliade, M. (1964). *Shamanism: Archaic techniques of ecstasy*. London: Routledge & Kegan Paul.

Ellamil, M., Fox, K. C. R., Dixon, M. L., Pritchard, S., Todd, R. M., Thompson, E., & Christoff, K. (2016). Dynamics of neural recruitment surrounding the spontaneous arising of thoughts in experienced mindfulness practitioners. *Neuroimage 136*, 186–196.

Etkin, A., Gyurak, A., & O'Hara, R. (2013). A neurobiological approach to the cognitive deficits of psychiatric disorders. *Dialogues in Clinical Neuroscience 15*(4), 419.

Etkin, A., & Wager, T. D. (2007). Functional neuroimaging of anxiety: A meta-analysis of emotional processing in PTSD, social anxiety disorder, and specific phobia. *American Journal of Psychiatry 164*(10), 1476–1488.

Faber, P. L., Lehmann, D., Gianotti, L. R., Milz, P., Pascual-Marqui, R. D., Held, M., & Kochi, K. (2015). Zazen meditation and no-task resting EEG compared with LORETA intracortical source localization. *Cognitive Processing 16*(1), 87–96.

Farb, N. A. S., Anderson, A. K., Mayberg, H., Bean, J., McKeon, D., & Segal, Z. V. (2010). Minding one's emotions: Mindfulness training alters the neural expression of sadness. *Emotion 10*(1), 25.

Farb, N. A. S., Segal, Z. V., & Anderson, A. K. (2013). Mindfulness meditation training alters cortical representations of interoceptive attention. *Social Cognitive and Affective Neuroscience 8*(1), 15–26. https://doi.org/10.1093/scan/nss066

Farb, N. A. S., Segal, Z. V., Mayberg, H., Bean, J., McKeon, D., Fatima, Z., & Anderson, A. K. (2007). Attending to the present: Mindfulness meditation reveals distinct neural modes of self-reference. *Social Cognitive and Affective Neuroscience 2*(4), 313–322. https://doi.org/10.1093/scan/nsm030

Farrow, J. T., & Hebert, R. J. (1982). Breath suspension during the Transcendental Meditation technique. *Psychosomatic Medicine 44*(2), 133–153.

Fazelpour, S., & Thompson, E. (2015). The Kantian brain: Brain dynamics from a neurophenomenological perspective. *Current Opinion in Neurobiology 31*, 223–229.

Fenwick, P. (1987). Meditation and the EEG. In M. A. West (Ed.), *The Psychology of Meditation*. Oxford: Clarendon, 104–117.

Ferrarelli, F., Smith, R., Dentico, D., Riedner, B. A., Zennig, C., Benca, R. M.,... Tononi, G. (2013). Experienced mindfulness meditators exhibit higher parietal-occipital EEG gamma activity during NREM sleep. *PLoS ONE 8*(8), e73417.

Fjell, A. M., & Walhovd, K. B. (2010). Structural brain changes in aging: Courses, causes and cognitive consequences. *Reviews in the Neurosciences 21*(3), 187–222.

Fleming, S. M., & Dolan, R. J. (2012). The neural basis of metacognitive ability. *Philosophical Transactions of the Royal Society of London B: Biological Sciences 367*(1594), 1338–1349. https://doi.org/10.1098/rstb.2011.0417

Fleming, S. M., Ryu, J., Golfinos, J. G., & Blackmon, K. E. (2014). Domain-specific impairment in metacognitive accuracy following anterior prefrontal lesions. *Brain 137*(10), 2811–2822.

Fleming, S. M., Weil, R. S., Nagy, Z., Dolan, R. J., & Rees, G. (2010). Relating introspective accuracy to individual differences in brain structure. *Science 329*(5998), 1541–1543. https://doi.org/10.1126/science.1191883

Fox, K. C. R., Andrews-Hanna, J. R., & Christoff, K. (2016). The neurobiology of self-generated thought from cells to systems: Integrating evidence from lesion studies, human intracranial electrophysiology, neurochemistry, and neuroendocrinology. *Neuroscience 335*, 134–150.

Fox, K. C. R., Andrews-Hanna, J. R., Mills, C., Dixon, M. L., Markovic, J., Thompson, E., & Christoff, K. (2018). Affective neuroscience of self-generated thought. *Annals of the New York Academy of Sciences, Special Issue: The Year in Cognitive Neuroscience 1426*(1), 25–51.

Fox, K. C. R., & Christoff, K. (2014). Metacognitive facilitation of spontaneous thought processes: When metacognition helps the wandering mind find its way. In S. M. Fleming & C. D. Firth (Eds.), *The Cognitive Neuroscience of Metacognition* (pp. 293–319). Berlin: Springer.

Fox, K. C. R., & Christoff, K. (2018). *The Oxford handbook of spontaneous thought: Mind-wandering, creativity, and dreaming*. New York: Oxford University Press.

Fox, K. C. R., Dixon, M. L., Nijeboer, S., Girn, M., Floman, J. L., Lifshitz, M.,... Christoff, K. (2016). Functional neuroanatomy of meditation: A review and meta-analysis of 78 functional neuroimaging investigations. *Neuroscientific Biobehavioral Review 65*, 208–228.

Fox, K. C. R., Foster, B. L., Kucyi, A., Daitch, A. L., & Parvizi, J. (2018). Intracranial electrophysiology of the human default network. *Trends in Cognitive Sciences 22*(4), 307–324.

Fox, K. C. R., Nijeboer, S., Dixon, M. L., Floman, J. L., Ellamil, M., Rumak, S. P.,... Christoff, K. (2014). Is meditation associated with altered brain structure? A systematic review and meta-analysis of morphometric neuroimaging in meditation practitioners. *Neuroscience & Biobehavioral Reviews 43*, 48–73.

Fox, K. C. R., Spreng, R. N., Ellamil, M., Andrews-Hanna, J. R., & Christoff, K. (2015). The wandering brain: Meta-analysis of functional neuroimaging studies of mind-wandering and related spontaneous thought processes. *Neuroimage 111*, 611–621.

Fox, K. C. R., Zakarauskas, P., Dixon, M. L., Ellamil, M., Thompson, E., & Christoff, K. (2012). Meditation experience predicts introspective accuracy. *PLoS ONE 7*(9), e45370. https://doi.org/10.1371/journal.pone.0045370.t001

Fox, N., Scahill, R., Crum, W., & Rossor, M. (1999). Correlation between rates of brain atrophy and cognitive decline in AD. *Neurology 52*(8), 1687–1689.

Fries, P. (2009). Neuronal gamma-band synchronization as a fundamental process in cortical computation. *Annual Review of Neuroscience 32*, 209–224.

Gard, T., Hölzel, B. K., & Lazar, S. W. (2014). The potential effects of meditation on age-related cognitive decline: A systematic review. *Annals of the New York Academy of Sciences 1307*(1), 89–103.

Gaser, C., & Schlaug, G. (2003). Gray matter differences between musicians and nonmusicians. *Annals of the New York Academy of Sciences 999*(1), 514–517.

Goenka, S. N. (2000). *The discourse summaries*. Pariyatti, Vipassana Research Publications, Onalaska, WA, USA.

Goldin, P. R., & Gross, J. J. (2010). Effects of mindfulness-based stress reduction (MBSR) on emotion regulation in social anxiety disorder. *Emotion 10*(1), 83–91. https://doi.org/10.1037/a0018441

Goldin, P. R., Ramel, W., & Gross, J. (2009). Mindfulness meditation training and self-referential processing in social anxiety disorder: Behavioral and neural effects. *Journal of Cognitive Psychotherapy 23*(3), 242.

Goldin, P. R., Ziv, M., Jazaieri, H., & Gross, J. J. (2012). Randomized controlled trial of mindfulness-based stress reduction versus aerobic exercise: Effects on the self-referential brain network in social anxiety disorder. *Frontiers in Human Neuroscience 6*, 295.

Goldin, P. R., Ziv, M., Jazaieri, H., Hahn, K., & Gross, J. J. (2013). MBSR vs aerobic exercise in social anxiety: fMRI of emotion regulation of negative self-beliefs. *Social Cognitive and Affective Neuroscience 8*(1), 65–72. https://doi.org/10.1093/scan/nss054

Grant, J. A. (2014). Meditative analgesia: The current state of the field. *Annals of the New York Academy of Sciences 1307*(1), 55–63.

Grant, J. A., Courtemanche, J., Duerden, E. G., Duncan, G. H., & Rainville, P. (2010). Cortical thickness and pain sensitivity in Zen meditators. *Emotion 10*(1), 43–53. https://doi.org/10.1037/a0018334

Grant, J. A., Courtemanche, J., & Rainville, P. (2011). A non-elaborative mental stance and decoupling of executive and pain-related cortices predicts low pain sensitivity in Zen meditators. *Pain 152*(1), 150–156. https://doi.org/10.1016/j.pain.2010.10.006

Grant, J. A., & Rainville, P. (2009). Pain sensitivity and analgesic effects of mindful states in Zen meditators: A cross-sectional study. *Psychosomatic Medicine 71*(1), 106–114.

Hagerty, M. R., Isaacs, J., Brasington, L., Shupe, L., Fetz, E. E., & Cramer, S. C. (2013). Case study of ecstatic meditation: fMRI and EEG evidence of self-stimulating a reward system. *Neural Plasticity*, 653572, 1–12.

Hamilton, J. P., Etkin, A., Furman, D. J., Lemus, M. G., Johnson, R. F., & Gotlib, I. H. (2012). Functional neuroimaging of major depressive disorder: A meta-analysis and new integration of baseline activation and neural response data. *American Journal of Psychiatry 169*(7), 693–703.

Hauswald, A., Übelacker, T., Leske, S., & Weisz, N. (2015). What it means to be Zen: Marked modulations of local and interareal synchronization during open monitoring meditation. *Neuroimage 108*, 265–273.

Hinterberger, T., Schmidt, S., Kamei, T., & Walach, H. (2014). Decreased electrophysiological activity represents the conscious state of emptiness in meditation. *Frontiers in Psychology 5*, 1–14.

Hofmann, S. G., Grossman, P., & Hinton, D. E. (2011). Loving-kindness and compassion meditation: Potential for psychological interventions. *Clinical Psychology Review 31*(7), 1126–1132.

Holzel, B. K., Carmody, J., Evans, K. C., Hoge, E. A., Dusek, J. A., Morgan, L., . . . Lazar, S. W. (2010). Stress reduction correlates with structural changes in the amygdala. *Social Cognitive and Affective Neuroscience 5*(1), 11–17. https://doi.org/10.1093/scan/nsp034

Holzel, B. K., Carmody, J., Vangel, M., Congleton, C., Yerramsetti, S. M., Gard, T., & Lazar, S. W. (2011). Mindfulness practice leads to increases in regional brain gray matter density. *Psychiatry Research 191*(1), 36–43. https://doi.org/10.1016/j.pscychresns.2010.08.006

Hölzel, B. K., Hoge, E. A., Greve, D. N., Gard, T., Creswell, J. D., Brown, K. W.,... Lazar, S. W. (2013). Neural mechanisms of symptom improvements in generalized anxiety disorder following mindfulness training. *NeuroImage: Clinical 2*, 448–458.

Hove, M. J., Stelzer, J., Nierhaus, T., Thiel, S. D., Gundlach, C., Margulies, D. S.,... Merker, B. (2015). Brain network reconfiguration and perceptual decoupling during an absorptive state of consciousness. *Cerebral Cortex 26*(7), 3116–3124.

Ives-Deliperi, V. L., Howells, F., Stein, D. J., Meintjes, E. M., & Horn, N. (2013). The effects of mindfulness-based cognitive therapy in patients with bipolar disorder: A controlled functional MRI investigation. *Journal of Affective Disorders 150*(3), 1152–1157.

Jo, H.-G., Hinterberger, T., Wittmann, M., & Schmidt, S. (2015). Do meditators have higher awareness of their intentions to act? *Cortex 65*, 149–158.

Johnson, W. L. (1982). *Riding the ox home: A history of meditation from shamanism to science.* London: Rider.

Josipovic, Z. (2014). Neural correlates of nondual awareness in meditation. *Annals of the New York Academy of Sciences 1307*(1), 9–18.

Josipovic, Z., Dinstein, I., Weber, J., & Heeger, D. J. (2011). Influence of meditation on anti-correlated networks in the brain. *Frontiers in Human Neuroscience 5*, 183. https://doi.org/10.3389/fnhum.2011.00183

Kaas, J. H. (1983). What, if anything, is SI? Organization of first somatosensory area of cortex. *Physiological Reviews 63*(1), 206–231.

Kakigi, R., Nakata, H., Inui, K., Hiroe, N., Nagata, O., Honda, M.,... Kawakami, M. (2005). Intracerebral pain processing in a yoga master who claims not to feel pain during meditation. *European Journal of Pain 9*(5), 581–589. https://doi.org/10.1016/j.ejpain.2004.12.006

Kalyani, B. G., Venkatasubramanian, G., Arasappa, R., Rao, N. P., Kalmady, S. V., Behere, R. V.,... Gangadhar, B. N. (2011). Neurohemodynamic correlates of "OM" chanting: A pilot functional magnetic resonance imaging study. *International Journal of Yoga 4*(1), 3–6. https://doi.org/10.4103/0973-6131.78171

Kasamatsu, A., & Hirai, T. (1966). An electroencephalographic study on the Zen meditation (Zazen). *Psychiatry and Clinical Neurosciences 20*(4), 315–336.

Kasamatsu, A., Okuma, T., Takenaka, S., Koga, E., Ikada, K., & Sugiyama, H. (1957). The EEG of "Zen" and "Yoga" practitioners. *Electroencephalography and Clinical Neurophysiology 9*, 51–52.

Kaye, J. A., Swihart, T., Howieson, D., Dame, A., Moore, M., Karnos, T.,... Sexton, G. (1997). Volume loss of the hippocampus and temporal lobe in healthy elderly persons destined to develop dementia. *Neurology 48*(5), 1297–1304.

Kjaer, T. W., Bertelsen, C., Piccini, P., Brooks, D., Alving, J., & Lou, H. C. (2002). Increased dopamine tone during meditation-induced change of consciousness. *Cognitive Brain Research 13*(2), 255–259.

Kox, M., Stoffels, M., Smeekens, S. P., Van Alfen, N., Gomes, M., Eijsvogels, T. M.,... Pickkers, P. (2012). The influence of concentration/meditation on autonomic nervous system activity and the innate immune response: A case study. *Psychosomatic Medicine 74*(5), 489–494.

Kox, M., van Eijk, L. T., Zwaag, J., van den Wildenberg, J., Sweep, F. C., van der Hoeven, J. G., & Pickkers, P. (2014). Voluntary activation of the sympathetic nervous system and attenuation

of the innate immune response in humans. *Proceedings of the National Academy of Sciences 111*(20), 7379–7384.
Kozhevnikov, M., Elliott, J., Shephard, J., & Gramann, K. (2013). Neurocognitive and somatic components of temperature increases during g-Tummo meditation: Legend and reality. *PLoS ONE 8*(3), e58244.
Kozhevnikov, M., Louchakova, O., Josipovic, Z., & Motes, M. A. (2009). The enhancement of visuospatial processing efficiency through Buddhist deity meditation. *Psychological Science 20*(5), 645–653.
Kurth, F., Cherbuin, N., & Luders, E. (2015). Reduced age-related degeneration of the hippocampal subiculum in long-term meditators. *Psychiatry Research: Neuroimaging 232*(3), 214–218.
Lazar, S. W., Kerr, C. E., Wasserman, R. H., Gray, J. R., Greve, D. N., Treadway, M. T., ... Benson, H. (2005). Meditation experience is associated with increased cortical thickness. *Neuroreport 16*(17), 1893–1897.
Logothetis, N. K., Pauls, J., Augath, M., Trinath, T., & Oeltermann, A. (2001). Neurophysiological investigation of the basis of the fMRI signal. *Nature 412*(6843), 150–157.
Lou, H. C., Kjaer, T. W., Friberg, L., Wildschlodtz, G., Holm, S., & Nowak, M. (1999). A 15O-H2o PET study of meditation and the resting state of normal consciousness. *Human Brain Mapping 7*, 98–105.
Luders, E., Cherbuin, N., & Gaser, C. (2016). Estimating brain age using high-resolution pattern recognition: Younger brains in long-term meditation practitioners. *Neuroimage 134*, 508–513.
Luders, E., Cherbuin, N., Kurth, F., & Lauche, R. (2015). Forever Young(er): Potential age-defying effects of long-term meditation on gray matter atrophy. *Frontiers in Psychology 5*, 1–17.
Ludwig, D. S., & Kabat-Zinn, J. (2008). Mindfulness in medicine. *JAMA 300*(11), 1350–1352.
Lutz, A., Greischar, L., Ricard, M., Converse, A., & Davidson, R. (2003). Comparative study of synchrony patterns during three meditative states: Preliminary data. *Abstract Viewer and Itinerary Planner: Abstract 86.*
Lutz, A., Jha, A. P., Dunne, J. D., & Saron, C. D. (2015). Investigating the phenomenological matrix of mindfulness-related practices from a neurocognitive perspective. *American Psychologist 70*(7), 632.
Lutz, A., Slagter, H. A., Dunne, J. D., & Davidson, R. J. (2008). Attention regulation and monitoring in meditation. *Trends in Cognitive Science 12*(4), 163–169. https://doi.org/10.1016/j.tics.2008.01.005
Lutz, A., & Thompson, E. (2003). Neurophenomenology: Integrating subjective experience and brain dynamics in the neuroscience of consciousness. *Journal of Consciousness Studies 10*(9–10), 31–52.
MacLean, K. A., Ferrer, E., Aichele, S. R., Bridwell, D. A., Zanesco, A. P., Jacobs, T. L., ... Shaver, P. R. (2010). Intensive meditation training improves perceptual discrimination and sustained attention. *Psychological Science 21*(6), 829–839.
Marx, G., & Gilon, C. (2012). The molecular basis of memory. *ACS Chemical Neuroscience 3*(8), 633–642.
Mascaro, J. S., Rilling, J. K., Negi, L. T., & Raison, C. L. (2013). Pre-existing brain function predicts subsequent practice of mindfulness and compassion meditation. *Neuroimage 69*, 35–42. https://doi.org/10.1016/j.neuroimage.2012.12.021

May, A., & Gaser, C. (2006). Magnetic resonance-based morphometry: A window into structural plasticity of the brain. *Current Opinion in Neurology 19*(4), 407–411.

Meltzer, J. A., Negishi, M., Mayes, L. C., & Constable, R. T. (2007). Individual differences in EEG theta and alpha dynamics during working memory correlate with fMRI responses across subjects. *Clinical Neurophysiology 118*(11), 2419–2436.

Menon, V., & Uddin, L. Q. (2010). Saliency, switching, attention and control: A network model of insula function. *Brain Structure and Function 214*(5–6), 655–667.

Mrazek, M. D., Franklin, M. S., Phillips, D. T., Baird, B., & Schooler, J. W. (2013). Mindfulness training improves working memory capacity and GRE performance while reducing mind wandering. *Psychological Science 24*(5), 776–781. https://doi.org/10.1177/0956797612459659

Mukamel, R., Gelbard, H., Arieli, A., Hasson, U., Fried, I., & Malach, R. (2005). Coupling between neuronal firing, field potentials, and FMRI in human auditory cortex. *Science 309*(5736), 951–954.

Murta, T., Leite, M., Carmichael, D. W., Figueiredo, P., & Lemieux, L. (2015). Electrophysiological correlates of the BOLD signal for EEG-informed fMRI. *Human Brain Mapping 36*(1), 391–414.

Neubauer, R. L. (2014). Prayer as an interpersonal relationship: A neuroimaging study. *Religion, Brain & Behavior 4*(2), 92–103.

Newberg, A., Pourdehnad, M., Alavi, A., & d'Aquili, E. G. (2003). Cerebral blood flow during meditative prayer: Preliminary findings and methodological issues. *Perceptual and Motor Skills 97*(2), 625–630.

Northoff, G., Heinzel, A., de Greck, M., Bermpohl, F., Dobrowolny, H., & Panksepp, J. (2006). Self-referential processing in our brain—a meta-analysis of imaging studies on the self. *Neuroimage 31*(1), 440–457.

Norton, S., Matthews, F. E., Barnes, D. E., Yaffe, K., & Brayne, C. (2014). Potential for primary prevention of Alzheimer's disease: An analysis of population-based data. *The Lancet Neurology 13*(8), 788–794.

Pagnoni, G., & Cekic, M. (2007). Age effects on gray matter volume and attentional performance in Zen meditation. *Neurobiological Aging 28*(10), 1623–1627. https://doi.org/10.1016/j.neurobiolaging.2007.06.008

Penfield, W., & Boldrey, E. (1937). Somatic motor and sensory representation in the cerebral cortex of man as studied by electrical stimulation. *Brain 60*, 389–443.

Rahl, H. A., Lindsay, E. K., Pacilio, L. E., Brown, K. W., & Creswell, J. D. (2017). Brief mindfulness meditation training reduces mind wandering: The critical role of acceptance. *Emotion 17*(2), 224.

Rainville, P., Duncan, G. H., Price, D. D., Carrier, B., & Bushnell, M. C. (1997). Pain affect encoded in human anterior cingulate but not somatosensory cortex. *Science 277*(5328), 968–971.

Ramnani, N., & Owen, A. M. (2004). Anterior prefrontal cortex: Insights into function from anatomy and neuroimaging. *Nauret Reviews Neuroscience 5*(3), 184–194. https://doi.org/10.1038/nrn1343

Richter, C. G., Thompson, W. H., Bosman, C. A., & Fries, P. (2017). Top-down beta enhances bottom-up gamma. *Journal of Neuroscience 37*(28), 3771–3786.

Rosenthal, R. (1979). The file drawer problem and tolerance for null results. *Psychological Bulletin 86*(3), 638.

Rusinek, H., De Santi, S., Frid, D., Tsui, W.-H., Tarshish, C. Y., Convit, A., & de Leon, M. J. (2003). Regional brain atrophy rate predicts future cognitive decline: 6-year longitudinal MR imaging study of normal aging. *Radiology 229*(3), 691–696.

Saggar, M., King, B. G., Zanesco, A. P., MacLean, K. A., Aichele, S. R., Jacobs, T. L., . . . Sahdra, B. K. (2012). Intensive training induces longitudinal changes in meditation state-related EEG oscillatory activity. *Frontiers in Human Neuroscience 6*, 1–14.

Scheeringa, R., Bastiaansen, M. C., Petersson, K. M., Oostenveld, R., Norris, D. G., & Hagoort, P. (2008). Frontal theta EEG activity correlates negatively with the default mode network in resting state. *International Journal of Psychophysiology 67*(3), 242–251.

Scheeringa, R., Fries, P., Petersson, K.-M., Oostenveld, R., Grothe, I., Norris, D. G., . . . Bastiaansen, M. C. (2011). Neuronal dynamics underlying high- and low-frequency EEG oscillations contribute independently to the human BOLD signal. *Neuron 69*(3), 572–583.

Scheeringa, R., Koopmans, P. J., van Mourik, T., Jensen, O., & Norris, D. G. (2016). The relationship between oscillatory EEG activity and the laminar-specific BOLD signal. *Proceedings of the National Academy of Sciences 113*(24), 6761–6766.

Schjødt, U., Stødkilde-Jørgensen, H., Geertz, A. W., & Roepstorff, A. (2008). Rewarding prayers. *Neuroscience Letters 443*(3), 165–168.

Schneider, P., Scherg, M., Dosch, H. G., Specht, H. J., Gutschalk, A., & Rupp, A. (2002). Morphology of Heschl's gyrus reflects enhanced activation in the auditory cortex of musicians. *Nature Neuroscience* 5(7), 688–694.

Schoenberg, P. L., Hepark, S., Kan, C. C., Barendregt, H. P., Buitelaar, J. K., & Speckens, A. E. (2014). Effects of mindfulness-based cognitive therapy on neurophysiological correlates of performance monitoring in adult attention-deficit/hyperactivity disorder. *Clinical Neurophysiology 125*(7), 1407–1416.

Schoenberg, P. L., Ruf, A., Churchill, J., Brown, D. P., & Brewer, J. A. (2018). Mapping complex mind states: EEG neural substrates of meditative unified compassionate awareness. *Conscious Cognition 57*, 41–53.

Schoenberg, P. L., & Speckens, A. E. (2015). Multi-dimensional modulations of α and γ cortical dynamics following mindfulness-based cognitive therapy in Major Depressive Disorder. *Cognitive Neurodynamics 9*(1), 13–29.

Schuman, M. (1980). The psychophysiological model of meditation and altered states of consciousness: A critical review. In J. M. Davidson (Ed.), *The Psychobiology of Consciousness* (pp. 333–378). Boston: Springer.

Sedlmeier, P., Eberth, J., Schwarz, M., Zimmermann, D., Haarig, F., Jaeger, S., & Kunze, S. (2012). The psychological effects of meditation: A meta-analysis. *Psychological Bulletin 138*(6), 1139–1171. https://doi.org10.1037/a0028168.supp

Shapiro, D. H., & Walsh, R. N. (1984). *Meditation: Classic and contemporary perspectives.* New Brunswick: Aldine Transaction.

Sze, J. A., Gyurak, A., Yuan, J. W., & Levenson, R. W. (2010). Coherence between emotional experience and physiology: Does body awareness training have an impact? *Emotion 10*(6), 803–814. https://doi.org/10.1037/a0020146

Tanaka, G. K., Maslahati, T., Gongora, M., Bittencourt, J., Lopez, L. C. S., Demarzo, M. M. P., . . . Campayo, J. G. (2015). Effortless attention as a biomarker for experienced mindfulness practitioners. *PLoS ONE 10*(10), e0138561.

Tang, Y.-Y., Hölzel, B. K., & Posner, M. I. (2015). The neuroscience of mindfulness meditation. *Nature Reviews Neuroscience 16*(4), 213–225.

Tang, Y.-Y., Lu, Q., Fan, M., Yang, Y., & Posner, M. I. (2012). Mechanisms of white matter changes induced by meditation. *Proceedings of the National Academy of Sciences 109*(26), 10570–10574.

Tang, Y.-Y., Lu, Q., Geng, X., Stein, E. A., Yang, Y., & Posner, M. I. (2010). Short-term meditation induces white matter changes in the anterior cingulate. *Proceedings of the National Academy of Sciences of the United States of America* *107*(35), 15649–15652. https://doi.org/10.1073/pnas.1011043107

Teasdale, J. (1999). Metacognition, mindfulness and the modification of mood disorders. *Clinical Psychology & Psychotherapy* *6*(2), 146–155.

Teasdale, J., Moore, R. G., Hayhurst, H., Pope, M., Williams, S., & Segal, Z. V. (2002). Metacognitive awareness and prevention of relapse in depression: Empirical evidence. *Journal of Consulting and Clinical Psychology* *70*(2), 275–287. https://doi.org/10.1037//0022-006x.70.2.275

Thomas, C., & Baker, C. I. (2013). Teaching an adult brain new tricks: A critical review of evidence for training-dependent structural plasticity in humans. *Neuroimage* *73*, 225–236. https://doi.org/10.1016/j.neuroimage.2012.03.069

Thompson, E. (2009). Contemplative neuroscience as an approach to volitional consciousness. In N. Murphy, G. F. R. Ellis, & T. O'Connor (Eds.), *Downward causation and the neurobiology of free will* (pp. 187–197). Berlin: Springer.

Travis, F. (2001). Autonomic and EEG patterns distinguish transcending from other experiences during Transcendental Meditation practice. *International Journal of Psychophysiology* *42*(1), 1–9.

Travis, F., & Pearson, C. (2000). Pure consciousness: Distinct phenomenological and physiological correlates of "consciousness itself." *International Journal of Neuroscience* *100*(1–4), 77–89.

Travis, F., Sarina, G., & Stixrud, W. (2011). ADHD, brain functioning, and Transcendental Meditation practice. *Mind & Brain* *2*(1), 73-81.

Valera, E. M., Faraone, S. V., Murray, K. E., & Seidman, L. J. (2007). Meta-analysis of structural imaging findings in attention-deficit/hyperactivity disorder. *Biological psychiatry* *61*(12), 1361–1369.

Van Dam, N. T., van Vugt, M. K., Vago, D. R., Schmalzl, L., Saron, C. D., Olendzki, A., . . . Meyer, D. E. (2018a). Mind the hype: A critical evaluation and prescriptive agenda for research on mindfulness and meditation. *Perspectives on Psychological Science* *13*(1), 36–61.

Van Dam, N. T., van Vugt, M. K., Vago, D. R., Schmalzl, L., Saron, C. D., Olendzki, A., . . . Meyer, D. E. (2018b). Reiterated concerns and further challenges for mindfulness and meditation research: A reply to Davidson and Dahl. *Perspectives on Psychological Science* *13*(1), 66–69.

van Ede, F., de Lange, F., Jensen, O., & Maris, E. (2011). Orienting attention to an upcoming tactile event involves a spatially and temporally specific modulation of sensorimotor alpha- and beta-band oscillations. *Journal of Neuroscience* *31*(6), 2016–2024.

Varela, F. J. (1996). Neurophenomenology: A methodological remedy for the hard problem. *Journal of Consciousness Studies* *3*(4), 330–349.

Wager, T. D., Lindquist, M., & Kaplan, L. (2007). Meta-analysis of functional neuroimaging data: Current and future directions. *Social Cognitive and Affective Neuroscience* *2*(2), 150–158. https://doi.org/10.1093/scan/nsm015

Wager, T. D., Lindquist, M. A., Nichols, T. E., Kober, H., & Van Snellenberg, J. X. (2009). Evaluating the consistency and specificity of neuroimaging data using meta-analysis. *Neuroimage* *45*(1 Suppl), S210–S221. https://doi.org/10.1016/j.neuroimage.2008.10.061

Wells, R. E., Yeh, G. Y., Kerr, C. E., Wolkin, J., Davis, R. B., Tan, Y., . . . Kaptchuk, T. J. (2013). Meditation's impact on default mode network and hippocampus in mild cognitive impairment: A pilot study. *Neuroscience Letters* *556*, 15–19.

West, M. A. (1980). Meditation and the EEG. *Psychological Medicine 10*(2), 369–375.

Westbrook, C., Creswell, J. D., Tabibnia, G., Julson, E., Kober, H., & Tindle, H. A. (2013). Mindful attention reduces neural and self-reported cue-induced craving in smokers. *Social Cognitive & Affective Neuroscience 8*(1), 73–84. https://doi.org/10.1093/scan/nsr076

Wynne, A. (2007). *The origin of Buddhist meditation*. London: Routledge.

Yarkoni, T., Poldrack, R. A., Van Essen, D. C., & Wager, T. D. (2010). Cognitive neuroscience 2.0: Building a cumulative science of human brain function. *Trends in Cognitive Science 14*(11), 489–496. https://doi.org/10.1016/j.tics.2010.08.004

Zanesco, A. P., King, B. G., MacLean, K. A., Jacobs, T. L., Aichele, S. R., Wallace, B. A., ... Saron, C. D. (2016). Meditation training influences mind wandering and mindless reading. *Psychology of Consciousness: Theory, Research, and Practice 3*(1), 12.

Zatorre, R. J., Fields, R. D., & Johansen-Berg, H. (2012). Plasticity in gray and white: Neuroimaging changes in brain structure during learning. *Nature Reviews Neuroscience 15*(4), 528–536. https://doi.org/10.1038/nn.3045

Zeidan, F., Adler-Neal, A. L., Wells, R. E., Stagnaro, E., May, L. M., Eisenach, J. C., ... Coghill, R. C. (2016). Mindfulness-meditation-based pain relief is not mediated by endogenous opioids. *Journal of Neuroscience 36*(11), 3391–3397.

Zeidan, F., Emerson, N. M., Farris, S. R., Ray, J. N., Jung, Y., McHaffie, J. G., & Coghill, R. C. (2015). Mindfulness meditation-based pain relief employs different neural mechanisms than placebo and sham mindfulness meditation-induced analgesia. *Journal of Neuroscience 35*(46), 15307–15325.

Zeidan, F., Grant, J. A., Brown, C. A., McHaffie, J. G., & Coghill, R. C. (2012). Mindfulness meditation-related pain relief: Evidence for unique brain mechanisms in the regulation of pain. *Neuroscience Letters 520*(2), 165–173. https://doi.org/10.1016/j.neulet.2012.03.082

Zeidan, F., Martucci, K. T., Kraft, R. A., Gordon, N. S., McHaffie, J. G., & Coghill, R. C. (2011). Brain mechanisms supporting the modulation of pain by mindfulness meditation. *Journal of Neuroscience 31*(14), 5540–5548. https://doi.org/10.1523/JNEUROSCI.5791-10.2011

CHAPTER 20

PSYCHOPHYSIOLOGY OF MEDITATION

DUSANA DORJEE

Introduction

Psychophysiology can be described as the science of bodily functioning in relation to psychological processes. Such a broad definition of psychophysiology encompasses a wide range of research methods investigating the relationship between mental processing and brain functioning, sweat response, hormonal stress response, heart rate and related markers, facial muscle activity, et cetera. The psychophysiological brain measures used in this field traditionally include electroencephalography (EEG) derived indexes, such as prefrontal alpha asymmetry and event-related brain potentials (ERPs). More recent brain imaging methods could also be considered under the label of psychophysiology, but in this chapter, we will focus on meditation studies employing the historically most typical psychophysiological indexes including ERPs, heart-rate variability measures, and galvanic skin response (see chapter by Fox & Cahn in this volume for magnetic resonance imaging and related EEG frequency research on meditation).

Before we consider the specifics of the different psychophysiological markers and their associations with, or modulations by, meditation, it might be helpful to consider a few general methodological points. The first one relates to the participant samples in current psychophysiological meditation research—most of the participants in these studies have been adults with different levels of meditation proficiency compared to meditation novices. Accordingly, very few studies using psychophysiological methods involved children and adolescents (e.g., Sanger, Thierry, & Dorjee, 2018) or older adults (e.g., Malinowski, Moore, Mead, & Gruber, 2017). Similarly, most participants in the studies were healthy, and there is very little research on the effects of meditation in clinical samples (for an exception see Bostanov, Keune, Kotchoubey, & Hautzinger, 2012).

Therefore, in this review we will be mostly focusing on the psychophysiology of meditation in adults but will also consider initial research evidence from research with children, adolescents, older adults, and clinical samples, where relevant, to encourage further research.

The second methodological point is applicable across different methodologies in meditation research and relates to types of study designs—within research on psychophysiology of meditation some (dispositional) studies investigated links between self-reported trait mindfulness and psychophysiological indexes (e.g., Brown, Goodman & Inzlicht, 2013) and other (cross-sectional) studies examined differences in psychophysiological markers between meditators and non-meditators at one point in time (e.g., Teper & Inzlicht, 2013). Dispositional studies typically include participants without prior training in meditation and rely on natural variation in the mindfulness trait. In contrast, cross-sectional studies compare participants who underwent meditation training and those without meditation training on various psychophysiological markers and sometimes also on the mindfulness trait. The methodologically most rigorous category of psychophysiological studies on meditation focused either on pre-post effects of brief one-session meditation practices in comparison to a control group (e.g., Eddy, Brunyé, Tower-Richardi, Mahoney, & Taylor, 2015) or on pre-post effects resulting from more extensive meditation training over days or weeks compared to a control group (e.g., Davidson et al., 2003). In this chapter we will primarily focus on the longitudinal "several-session" studies since these provide the strongest evidence of the causal impact meditation can have on psychophysiological changes.

The final methodological point pertains to systematic and comprehensive theory-driven considerations about the mechanisms of meditation. Most current research on the psychophysiology of meditation, just like research on the neuroscience of meditation and cognitive effects of meditation, has so far mostly focused on associations and changes in attention- and emotion-related indexes. These two areas have been repeatedly highlighted as being central in previous considerations about key mechanisms underlying meditation (e.g., Lutz, Slagter, Dunne, & Davidson, 2008; Tang, Hölzel, & Posner, 2015). However, some recent theoretical models outlined more comprehensive mechanisms of mindfulness (Hölzel et al., 2011) and meditation (Dorjee, 2016). In what follows we will apply a proposal by Dorjee (2016, 2017) considering changes in the metacognitive self-regulatory capacity (MSRC) of the mind and modes of existential awareness (MEA) as the two core mechanisms modulated by meditation. The MSRC includes self-reflective metacognition and attention control, emotion regulation, and relevant language processes involved in understanding and conveying meaning. Self-reflective metacognition refers to the ability to notice and monitor processes of the mind and use this information in guiding attention control, which in turn enables us to decide where we place attention and for how long. Flexible and adaptive self-reflective metacognition and attention control facilitate effective management of emotions and rumination, such as noticing early when emotions or arise and increasing or decreasing their intensity in line with our goals. A sentence from the manuscript is missing here: 'Language processes interact and get modified by the self-reflective metacognition, attention control and emotion regulation processes – for example, one can notice negative rumination arising and shift attention to some neutral activity or content (such as breath), then with practice activation of negative meanings decreases.'

The MEA refer to phenomenological experiential shifts in the construal of self and reality gradually progressing from immersion in mental phenomena through decentering from them (perceiving them more as fleeting phenomena rather than facts) and toward a more "de-constructed" phenomenological sense of self and reality (states sometimes described as "emptiness of self" or states of "non-dual awareness"). Importantly, the model proposes direct reciprocal links between changes in the MSRC and the MEA with further reciprocal connections to the autonomic nervous system. While some psychophysiological methods (such as ERPs) are particularly suitable for assessing changes in the MSRC and MEA with meditation, others (e.g., heart-rate variability measures) can uniquely enhance our understanding of the links between MSRC/MEA and the autonomic nervous system.

Prefrontal EEG Alpha Asymmetry and Meditation

The EEG signal is recorded from the surface of the scalp and measures cumulative electrical activity (on the scale of microvolts) of the brain. The electrical signal relates to neurotransmitter activity at the level of neuronal synapses. The EEG signal can be used to derive a variety of psychophysiological markers indexing brain activity. One of the simplest and historically oldest of these markers is the division of brain activity based on the frequency of the EEG signal into delta, theta, alpha, beta, and gamma frequency bands. Prefrontal alpha asymmetry is a derivative index of the raw frequency band signal in the alpha band range (7 or 8 to 13 Hz). It compares (by subtracting logarithmic transformations of the signal) alpha band signal over the left brain hemisphere to the same alpha band measure over the right hemisphere, with higher values suggesting increased left-sided activation (Sutton & Davidson, 1997; Towers & Allen, 2009).

The prefrontal alpha asymmetry is typically recorded during a several-minute long alternating sequence of resting with eyes open and closed. It has been used as an index of approach-oriented behavior or positive emotions linked to higher left-sided prefrontal alpha activity versus avoidance-oriented behavior or negative emotions associated with higher right-sided prefrontal alpha activity. A relatively extensive body of research suggests that increased right-sided prefrontal alpha asymmetry, particularly during emotionally challenging situations, is associated with depression (Stewart, Coan, Towers, & Allen, 2014), and prefrontal alpha asymmetry has been proposed as a psychophysiological marker of depression vulnerability (Allen & Reznik, 2015).

Within the framework of mechanisms underlying contemplative practice (Dorjee, 2016) the prefrontal alpha asymmetry can be considered as a marker of emotion regulation.

However, the processes of emotion regulation inevitably also entail the contribution of metacognitive attention control involving noticing and monitoring of mental processes and associated shifts in attention focus. In addition, emotion regulation overlaps with regulation of ruminative conceptual processing, such as management of repetitive negative thinking to decrease its frequency and associated intensity of emotions. It is also possible that prefrontal alpha asymmetry could be sensitive to changes in MEA, particularly since decentering—the ability to "step back" and disidentify with one's own thoughts and emotions—has been proposed as the main therapeutic mechanism underlying positive effects of mindfulness-based approaches in depression (Bieling et al., 2012).

In meditation research, a prefrontal alpha asymmetry study by Davidson et al. (2003) that examined changes resulting from attending an eight-week mindfulness-based stress reduction (MBSR) course was the first psychophysiological investigation of a standardized secular meditation-based course. The study examined whether mindfulness training could result in a shift toward increased left-sided prefrontal activity associated with positive emotions and approach-oriented behavior (i.e., a tendency to seek social contact rather than withdraw from others). This randomized controlled study with healthy adults in a workplace context had a very good sample size for standards in psychophysiological research and included assessments before the MBSR course, after its completion, and also a follow-up assessment after four months.

The predicted significant shift toward left anterior activity in the MBSR group in comparison to the control group was present at the post-test and at the follow-up whilst the groups didn't differ at the pre-test (Davidson et al., 2003). In addition, the study reported significant increases in antibodies in response to a flu vaccine in the MBSR group, and the antibody increase was positively related to the shift toward left-sided anterior activity indexed by the change in prefrontal alpha asymmetry.

Other studies on mindfulness-based interventions tried to replicate and extend the findings of Davidson et al. (2003) using prefrontal alpha asymmetry as the main measure. To date the largest-sample longitudinal study on the effects of meditation examining changes in resting prefrontal alpha asymmetry was a randomized-controlled trial with healthy older adults (Moynihan et al., 2013). The effects of an eight-week MBSR course in comparison to treatment as usual were assessed from before to after the course and at twenty-four weeks as a follow-up. Basic statistical tests showed only marginal effects from baseline to post-test, but between-group comparisons at post-test revealed a significant group difference, due to reductions in left-sided anterior activity in the control group. There were no significant differences in prefrontal alpha asymmetry between the two groups at follow-up. Given the strong design of this study, the findings cast doubts on the modifiability of prefrontal alpha asymmetry by secular meditation training and the sustainability of any initial gains.

The evidence of meditation effects in clinical populations assessed using the prefrontal alpha asymmetry is also mixed. One small-scale study investigated changes in prefrontal alpha asymmetry with participants that had a previous history of suicidal depression (Barnhofer et al., 2007). Participants were randomized to either an eight-week mindfulness-based cognitive therapy (MBCT) or a treatment as usual control group, and assessed before and after the eight weeks. The results revealed no change in the MBCT group while the control group showed significant reductions in left-sided anterior activation, suggesting decreases in positive affect/approach-oriented behavior. However, this differential effect was not confirmed in a larger scale randomized-controlled study with recurrently depressed patients in remission, where one group underwent MBCT training and was compared to a waitlist control group (Keune, Bostanov, Hautzinger, & Kotchoubey, 2011). While the MBCT group reported significant reductions in residual depressive symptoms and rumination, both groups showed shifts toward right-sided prefrontal activity with no significant MBCT training effects.

Some studies suggested that meditation can produce more stable short-term modulations of prefrontal alpha asymmetry, rather than lasting longer-term trait changes in this index. For example, one study evaluated the effects of mindfulness in recurrently depressed female participants following negative mood induction during and after brief meditation sessions, in comparison to effects of rumination challenge sessions in which participants heard sentences encouraging them to analyze their feelings (Keune, Bostanov, Hautzinger, & Kotchoubey, 2013). The findings showed significant shifts toward left-sided prefrontal activation during meditation only, suggesting more transient effects of meditation training on prefrontal alpha asymmetry.

Cumulatively the findings across the studies raise questions about the sensitivity and modifiability of prefrontal alpha asymmetry by meditation. It is possible that more intensive long-term meditation training would be needed to produce lasting "trait" shifts in this psychophysiological index. Given the established nature of prefrontal alpha asymmetry as a marker of depression and depression vulnerability, further investigation of such long-term effects seems important for providing insights into the questions about long-term impact of meditation on health and well-being.

Event-Related Potentials and Meditation

Event-related potentials (ERPs) are produced by averaging the EEG signal arising in response to particular stimuli such as emotional images or sounds (Luck, 2012). The ERP components are typically characterized by the polarity of their peak (based on positive or negative voltage), timing of the peak (latency), and its scalp distribution (e.g., frontal, parietal, central, etc.). The main advantage of ERPs is their functional specificity; some event-related potentials, for example, primarily index the ability to inhibit processing of irrelevant stimuli (the N2 ERP component) and other emotion regulation as the ability to modify an emotion response (the LPP component). While many questions about the functional specificity of ERP components remain, several decades of basic research underpin our current understanding of ERPs providing strong foundations for the utilization of ERP indexes in meditation research.

The majority of ERP research on meditation has, thus far, focused on investigating changes in attention with meditation training. For example, one study examined the impact of intensive meditation training in a retreat setting on the P300 ERP component as an index of attention efficiency (Slagter et al. 2007). The P300 is usually defined as a positive peak with latency between 250-500 milliseconds after stimulus onset (Polich, 2007). The study particularly focused on a subtype of the P300 called the P3b, which has parietal distribution and signals detection of a target stimulus. Participants in the study were meditators, and their P3b responses were compared to matched controls; both groups were tested before and after three months during which time the meditators engaged in a Vipassana retreat. This meditation retreat focused on paying attention to the present moment, as well as cultivating feelings of loving-kindness and compassion. The experimental task involved the attention blink paradigm, in which a stream of letters and numbers is presented to participants in a fast succession, and participants are asked to identify certain types of visual stimuli. The term "attention blink" refers to the difficulty in identifying a visual stimulus (such as a number) appearing within five hundred milliseconds after correct detection of another visual stimulus (such as a letter). The researchers in this study wanted to examine whether meditation training could result in a reduction of the attention blink and corresponding modulations of the P3b.

The findings revealed that, after the retreat, the meditators but not the control group showed a better detection of the stimuli appearing within the brief "attention blink" interval. Importantly, they also found a reduction in the P3 component peaks (their amplitude) to the first stimuli preceding the attention blink intervals. This suggested that, after the retreat, meditators used less attention resources to correctly detect the first stimulus; this allowed for sufficient attention resources to be allocated to the detection of the second stimulus appearing within the attention blink interval. However, the results also opened the question about the amount of meditation training needed for such modulations in the P3b to arise, given that the meditation training was intensive, involving ten to twelve hours of meditation per day for three months.

This question was partially answered in a randomized-controlled study, which assessed the effects of a less intensive meditation training, consisting of an initial two-hour introductory session (breath focus with an accepting attitude), followed by regular practice of ten minutes per day during sixteen weeks (Moore, Gruber, Derose, & Malinowski, 2012). The experimental task used was the Stroop test, which requires participants to suppress automatic responses to incongruous stimuli—these were words where the meaning of a word mismatched with the color of the ink in which the word was written (e.g., the word 'RED' written in blue ink). The participants' task was to name the color of the ink and they had to suppress the automatic reading of the word for the incongruous stimuli. The ERP responses were recorded to both congruous (such as the word 'RED' written in red ink) and incongruous stimuli. The focus of the ERP investigations in the study was again on the P300 component as a marker of attentional efficiency—the use of minimum cognitive resources needed to perform correctly on the task. The authors found reduced P300 amplitudes to incongruent stimuli after sixteen weeks of meditation training; no changes were observed eight weeks into the training.

These findings indicate that even less intensive meditation training may result in significant modulations of ERP markers that are sensitive to attention efficiency.

While the findings in these two studies are likely to reflect changes in attention efficiency related to attention control, other studies examined whether meditation training could impact meditators' distractibility. Cahn and Polich (2009) presented long-term meditators in the Goenka Vipassana tradition with a simple auditory oddball paradigm. The task consisted of frequent sounds (80 percent of stimuli), distractor white noise sounds (10 percent of stimuli), and oddball sounds (10 percent)—infrequent higher pitch sounds—during meditation and during a control thinking state. The meditation state involved focusing on sensations in the body, whereas the control thinking state consisted of thinking about emotionally neutral events. The P3a, an ERP component indexing automatic responding to infrequent stimuli, was derived from EEG responses to the sounds. As expected, P3a amplitudes were reduced to the distractor sounds in the meditative state in comparison to the control thinking state, suggesting less automatic reactivity to the distractors during meditation. Interestingly, this effect was only found for meditators not reporting drowsiness during the meditation state. In addition, meditators with more time spent in daily meditation showed greater reductions in the P3a to distractors, providing stronger support for the effect being related to meditation practice.

There are also studies with adolescents and older adults that reported changes in ERP markers of attention processing resulting from meditation. For example, a school-based study with adolescents who participated in an eight-week mindfulness training delivered by their schoolteachers showed improvements in the adolescents' abilities to inhibit irrelevant stimuli (Sanger & Dorjee, 2016). Furthermore, a study with older adults suggested improvements in attention based on a significant shift in an ERP component indexing the ability to inhibit irrelevant stimuli (more negative N2) after eight weeks of regular brief (ten minutes, five times per week) mindfulness training (Malinowski, Moore, Mead, & Gruber, 2017). Overall, the studies reviewed are indicative of the broader pattern of evidence on meditation effects assessed using ERPs, which suggests improvements in control-related facets of attention with meditation.

Attention control strongly contributes to our ability to manage emotions (Ochsner & Gross, 2005). Given the evidence suggesting improvements in attention control (including attention efficiency and inhibition) and the fact that various meditation practices often invite meditators to engage with emotional contents non-judgmentally and without reactivity, it is expected that meditation training would result in emotion regulation improvements (Teper Segal & Inzlicht, 2013). An ERP marker sensitive to different types of emotion regulation is the late positive potential (LPP) (Hajcak, MacNamara, & Olvet, 2010). Previous studies showed that more adaptive forms of emotion regulation, such as cognitive reappraisal involving an adaptive change in thinking about an emotional experience, are associated with less positive LPP mean amplitudes (Hajcak & Nieuwenhuis, 2006). Thus it can be predicted that meditation would improve emotion regulation skills, and accordingly, some ERP studies assessed if meditators would show reduced LPP amplitudes to emotional stimuli.

One study compared the LPP responses to negative, neutral, and positive stimuli during passive viewing between a group of Buddhist meditators and a matched control group (Sobolewski, Holt, Kublik & Wróbel, 2011). The findings revealed significantly reduced LPP mean amplitudes in meditators compared to controls for the negative pictures only—possibly suggesting less emotional reactivity in meditators in response to negative stimuli. The lack of group differences for the positive stimuli in this study may be explained by the fact that these stimuli had lower arousal (emotional intensity) ratings than the negative stimuli. Indeed, a dispositional mindfulness study found that participants with higher trait mindfulness (mindfulness disposition), compared to those with lower trait mindfulness, showed reduced LPP amplitudes to both highly arousing negative stimuli and highly arousing positive stimuli (Brown, Goodman & Inzlicht, 2013). This suggests that higher trait mindfulness may be linked to more effective management of emotional responses by reducing reactivity to emotionally intense experiences.

Another cross-sectional ERP study comparing meditators and non-meditators found that meditators showed less emotional reactivity when they noticed making an error (Teper & Inzlicht, 2013). In a Stroop task the study measured an ERP component called the error-related negativity (ERN); this component measures how one monitors one's performance in response to an error. The meditators made fewer errors than controls and showed more negative ERN on error trials; this likely reflects their better metacognitive monitoring skills. Importantly, the more negative ERN was explained by increased self-reported acceptance scores (non-reactivity to experience) in meditators, who also showed significantly higher acceptance scores when compared to controls. These findings point to the intertwined nature of improvements in emotion regulation and attention control in meditators; their enhanced attention skills likely enable better emotion regulation resulting in improved performance, and in turn, attention control is supported by increased acceptance (Teper, Segal & Inzlicht, 2013).

In addition to the LPP and ERN components, the P300 can also index emotion processing. One study examined the impact of an eight-week mindfulness program delivered by schoolteachers as part of regular school curricula on emotion processing in adolescents (Sanger et al., 2018). The emotional oddball task involved happy- and sad-face target oddballs (10 percent of stimuli each) embedded in a stream of neutral faces. The results indicated no changes in P300 amplitudes across the different stimuli types in the training group, whereas the control group showed reductions in the P300. This pattern of findings was interpreted as suggesting that the mindfulness-trained adolescents were able to sustain focus on socially relevant stimuli in comparison to controls. Since reduced P300 amplitudes have been associated with depression in previous studies (e.g., Cavanagh & Geisler, 2006), the finding of maintained P300 might be indicative of possible protective effects of meditation on depression vulnerability.

The effects of meditation on attention control and emotion regulation potentially have an indirect effect on well-being through the meditator's ability to manage negative rumination—higher negative rumination has been associated with development and maintenance of anxiety and depression (Watkins, 2008). Yet ERP evidence on possible reductions of negative rumination due to meditation is virtually absent. Only one ERP study has so far investigated possible associations between meditation and language processing linked to rumination (Dorjee et al., 2015). This study assessed associations between trait mindfulness and ERP indexes of semantic integration (N400) and semantic reanalysis (P600). Participants were presented with pairs of negative or positive words matching in meaning, in addition to mismatching meaning pairs consisting of positive-negative and negative-positive word pairs. The findings indicated increased N400 differences to negative word targets in comparison to positive word targets in high trait mindfulness participants only. This suggests less frequent access to negative word meanings in those with higher trait mindfulness, which reflects a lower tendency toward negative rumination. The study also reported reductions in the P600 for those higher in trait mindfulness, suggesting an association between higher mindfulness and less re-analysis involving repeated thinking about the words presented, which might be linked to less rumination.

As for language processing, ERP evidence on the effects of mediation on decentering and other modes of existential awareness is very limited. The only relevant study so far (Eddy et al., 2015) assessed the effects of a brief fifteen-minute mindfulness session involving breath focus instructions on P300 and LPP components elicited by viewing positive, negative, and neutral images. While the brief mindfulness session did not result in any ERP changes, the participants who reported higher state decentering during the session also showed less positive P300 responses to negative images. The effect was specific to decentering, not mindfulness. The authors interpreted the findings in terms of a change in the way participants attended to the images due to decentering—this involved disidentification with the emotions the stimuli induced, viewing the emotions as transient rather than identifying with them. This in turn led to reduced reactivity to the negative images indexed by less positive P300. This again highlights the interconnected and overlapping nature of various mechanisms—attention, emotion regulation, rumination, and decentering (as a mode of existential awareness)—which underly meditation.

Overall, the pattern of ERP findings on meditation suggests that meditation practice modulates attention control (including attention efficiency, improved inhibition, and reduced distractibility) and emotion regulation linked to reactivity to high intensity stimuli. The evidence on how meditation might impact language processing is currently very limited, as is our understanding of how decentering and other modes of existential awareness may modify ERPs. Most studies investigated the different mechanisms of the metacognitive self-regulatory capacity in isolation; only one of the studies linked attention control (indexed by the ERN) to emotion regulation (acceptance) (Teper & Inzlicht, 2013). This highlights the need of investigating currently neglected aspects of mechanisms of meditation using ERPs, as well as the importance of examining the links between the different mechanisms to provide a more systemic understanding of how meditation works from a psychophysiological perspective. In addition, future research needs to meaningfully relate variations in these mechanisms to changes in the autonomic nervous system. In this way we will be able to bridge current gaps in the literature on the associations between mind/brain psychophysiological indexes and bodily sympathetic/parasympathetic activation measures.

Psychophysiological Indexes of Autonomic System Activation and Meditation

The largest body of research on meditation using psychophysiological measures of autonomic system activation involves heart-rate variability (HRV) and derived measures. The HRV refers to the beat-to-beat variability (time gaps between heart beats), which has been linked to regulation of the sympathetic/parasympathetic system balance as the basic mechanism of the stress response (Thayer, Åhs, Fredrikson, Sollers, & Wager, 2012). While increases in sympathetic activation are associated with the fight-flight response, the parasympathetic system dominates during the rest-digest activities. Importantly, sympathetic activation can be induced not only by a real threat (e.g., a fast-approaching car when we are crossing the road), but also by a threat such as thinking of a stressful situation. Low frequency (LF) HRV (0.01–0.15 Hz) reflects sympathetic effects associated with neurotransmitter norepinephrine whereas high frequency (HF) HRV (0.15–0.40 Hz) is linked to parasympathetic activation mediated by acetylcholine changes. Importantly, low frequency HRV has been associated with disease, and high frequency HRV has been liked to better emotion regulation (Appelhans & Luecken, 2006).

One interesting meditation study assessed changes in high frequency heart rate variability (HF HRV) in meditators who underwent meditation training over three months (daily guided meditation practice of twenty minutes plus two-hour sessions each week) in three types of meditation: breathing meditation, loving-kindness meditation, and observing-thoughts meditation (Lumma, Kok, & Singer, 2015). The study investigated if all types of meditation resulted in increased HF HRV reflecting possible relaxing effects of meditation. Interestingly, the findings were contrary to this prediction and showed reductions in HF HRV over time, with these reductions being most pronounced for the loving-kindness meditation and least for the breathing meditation. These results indicate that different meditation types may modulate heart rate variability differently depending on the arousal and mental effort required.

An earlier cross-sectional study compared high frequency and low frequency heart rate variability in Theravāda and Tibetan Buddhist meditators during different types of meditation (Amihai & Kozhevnikov, 2014). They found that Theravāda meditators practicing Vipassana showed increases in HF HRV. However, Tibetan Buddhist meditators practicing deity visualization meditation and *rigpa* (abiding in the most advanced non-dual state of awareness) meditations showed decreases in HF HRV.

Yet, a study on integrative mind-body training (IMBT) with Chinese undergraduate students showed increases in HF HRV after only five days of 20-minute long daily sessions in comparison to a relaxation training of the same duration (Tang et al., 2009). Interestingly, mindful breath focus is one of the key elements of the IMBT training. This further supports the proposal that different meditation types are associated with different modulations in the HRV.

There are other heart rate variability derived metrics that have been used to study meditation (Allen, Chambers & Towers, 2007). The two most common ones are the respiratory sinus arrhythmia (RSA) and the cardiac sympathetic index (CSI). The RSA indexes the change in interbeat intervals in relation to the inbreath and outbreath phases of respiration. It reflects the parasympathetic control with higher values indexing better emotion regulation. In contrast, the CSI (Toichi, Sugiura, Murai & Sengoku, 1997) measures sympathetic influence. A higher CSI has been linked to psychopathology and higher stress (Weinberg, Klonsky, & Hajcak, 2009). The RSA and CSI are dissociable antagonist indexes, higher RSA is typically associated with low CSI.

The RSA and CSI indexes have been rarely used in research on meditation. In, so far, the most comprehensive study, Ditto, Eclache & Goldman (2006) compared the effects of body-scan meditation, progressive muscular relaxation or wait-list control group after four weeks of daily practice. The results revealed increases in the RSA only during the meditation sessions after the four weeks. With regards to CSI, a study that recorded changes in CSI during Zen meditation (involving sustain breath focus) in comparison to a control rest condition reported increased CSI during meditation (Kubota et al., 2001). Just like the pattern of findings for the HF and LF HRV, the results from these two studies again demonstrate that changes in RSA and CSI as indexes of parasympathetic and sympathetic activation respectively may depend on the meditation type.

In addition to measures described above, galvanic skin response (GSR) has been traditionally considered an index of sympathetic activation, because it measures sweat gland secretions innervated by sympathetic autonomic neurons. In terms of emotion processing, the magnitude of the GSR is positively correlated with subjective reports of intensity of emotions (Greenwald, Cook, & Lang, 1989).

Decreases in GSR indicate reduced sympathetic activation and have been reported in a few meditation studies. In a study with meditation novices, they found a significant decrease in GSR during twenty minutes of meditation (Mohan, Sharma & Bijlani, 2011). An earlier study comparing the first and last three minutes of a twenty-minute meditation session with control conditions also found reductions in GSR (Wenk-Sormaz, 2005). A similar pattern of findings has been reported with longer-term meditation (one month of daily practice) (Singh & Talwar, 2012). However, the overall evidence base on the effects of meditation on GSR is currently very limited, precluding any firm conclusion.

In summary, the emerging pattern of modulations in psychophysiological indexes of autonomic system activity is currently mixed and limited by an insufficient number of longitudinal studies. The evidence so far suggests that changes in heart rate variability, as well as its derivative indexes, resulting from meditation depend on the type of meditation. While breath-focus meditation tends to result in increased parasympathetic activity, other kinds of meditation, such as loving-kindness practices, may decrease parasympathetic activation. Available evidence on changes in GSR suggest that reductions in this marker are associated with increased parasympathetic activity, but all of the studies seem to have involved basic breath-focus-style meditation practices. The pattern of modulations in the GSR might be different with other meditation types. Further research is needed to elucidate these complex findings and to assess longer term state and trait effects of meditation on these indexes.

Limitations and Future Directions

The general methodological limitations of meditation research (e.g., Davidson & Kaszniak, 2015; Van Dam et al., 2018) are applicable to the psychophysiology of meditation. This includes the need for larger sample sizes, randomization of participants, and active control-group studies. There is also the need for clear specification of meditation experience/training of participants and the experience of meditation teachers delivering the interventions. Nonetheless, there are some methodological issues that are specific to research in the psychophysiology of meditation.

While the psychophysiological markers used in meditation research, such as the P300 and N400 components, or HRV and RSA, are some of the most established indexes in the field of psychophysiology with decades of underpinning research, their application in intervention research, such as meditation training studies, is much more recent. Consequently, the interpretation of changes in these indexes within an intervention study can often be ambiguous and purely reliant on self-report measures. For example, in two studies discussed earlier in this chapter, the P300 has been found to decrease with meditation training in attention blink (Slagter et al., 2007) and a Stroop task (Moore et al., 2012). This decrease has been interpreted as an indicator of improved attention efficiency. However, in studies of mind-wandering, which is a state inversely correlated with mindfulness, reduced P300 was associated with self-reported mind wandering. This is at odds with what one would expect, as mind-wandering reflects lack of attentiveness (more distraction) to the target stimuli.

Another concern is that changes in psychophysiological indexes of autonomic system activation vary greatly based on the type of meditation participants are performing. Increased parasympathetic activity has been mostly associated with breath-focus meditation styles whereas increased sympathetic activity seems linked to "more effortful" kinds of meditation such as loving-kindness or visualization-based meditation. How such differences translate into long-term effects on health and well-being is currently unknown. Overall, the predicted changes in psychophysiological markers often seem to depend on particular experimental tasks and meditation types.

Further issues to be considered pertain to replicability of findings, the context of meditation training, and the long-term effects of meditation. The replicability of findings is a particularly important topic in psychophysiological and neuroscience research, since psychophysiological markers are more subject to variability depending on experimental conditions, participant sample types, data collection and analysis methods than standardized self-report methods. It is very rare to see replications of findings within the same labs and replications across labs are virtually absent. This obviously relates to a broader problem of replication studies being "less valued" than original new findings; however, this seems to be more the case in psychophysiological and neuroscience research than in questionnaire-based intervention research. For example, in clinical intervention studies the replications of randomized controlled trials are often required and funded to inform implementation efforts, as in the case of MBCT for recurrent depression (Kuyken et al., 2008; Kuyken et al., 2015).

The context of meditation practice and associated motivations for engaging in meditation are two factors that very likely impact changes in the mechanisms of underlying meditation (Dorjee, 2016). For example, the psychophysiological effects of meditation might be different for somebody who is practicing meditation to relieve back pain in comparison to another person who meditates in order to reach spiritual insight. The context of meditation practice and motivation training has so far not been explicitly assessed as a possible modulator of findings in psychophysiological studies. These factors need to be considered in the future as possible modulators, particularly since we already know that different meditation types (including Buddhist meditation styles from different schools) may differentially impact psychophysiological markers (Amihai & Kozhevnikov, 2014).

Finally, while there are a few studies using self-reports that investigated longer-term effects of meditation (three-to-five-year follow-ups), psychophysiological studies with a follow-up of any length are virtually absent. This is to a large extent the result of the cost and logistical challenges associated with repeated psychophysiological measures. Yet, to advance our understanding of meditation, it is essential that psychophysiological longitudinal studies include follow-up assessments to evaluate the sustainability or reversibility of the initial changes by the amount (or lack) of further meditation practice, as well as long-term trajectories of changes with practice.

Conclusion

While psychophysiological research holds considerable promise for providing unique insights into the modulations in the brain and body physiology resulting from meditation, and their possible implications for health and well-being, much of this potential remains untapped. Most of the available evidence in this area, including research on prefrontal alpha asymmetry and psychophysiological indexes of autonomic system activation, portrays a picture of mixed findings with a strong need for further rigorous investigation. Research on modulations in ERP indexes with meditation, particularly with regards to changes in attention, provides the most consistent evidence for improvements in attention control and associated attention efficiency with meditation. In contrast, psychophysiological studies about the impact of meditation on relevant language processes linked to rumination and modes of existential awareness, such as decentering, are extremely limited, yet they are much needed in order to provide a more comprehensive understanding of the mechanisms underlying meditation. Future research on the psychophysiology of meditation also needs to address the pitfalls of ambiguous interpretations of findings, include more replication studies and assessments of context and motivation for meditation as well as evaluate the long-term effects of meditation.

References

Allen, J. J., Chambers, A. S., & Towers, D. N. (2007). The many metrics of cardiac chronotropy: A pragmatic primer and a brief comparison of metrics. *Biological Psychology 74*(2), 243–262.

Allen, J. J., & Reznik, S. J. (2015). Frontal EEG asymmetry as a promising marker of depression vulnerability: Summary and methodological considerations. *Current Opinion in Psychology 4*, 93–97.

Amihai, I., & Kozhevnikov, M. (2014). Arousal vs. relaxation: A comparison of the neurophysiological and cognitive correlates of Vajrayana and Theravada meditative practices. *PLoS One 9*(7), e102990.

Appelhans, B. M., & Luecken, L. J. (2006). Heart rate variability as an index of regulated emotional responding. *Review of General Psychology 10*(3), 229–240.

Barnhofer, T., Duggan, D., Crane, C., Hepburn, S., Fennell, M. J., & Williams, J. M. G. (2007). Effects of meditation on frontal α-asymmetry in previously suicidal individuals. *Neuroreport 18*(7), 709–712.

Bieling, P. J., Hawley, L. L., Bloch, R. T., Corcoran, K. M., Levitan, R. D., Young, L. T., ... & Segal, Z. V. (2012). Treatment-specific changes in decentering following mindfulness-based cognitive therapy versus antidepressant medication or placebo for prevention of depressive relapse. *Journal of Consulting and Clinical Psychology 80*(3), 365–372.

Bostanov, V., Keune, P. M., Kotchoubey, B., & Hautzinger, M. (2012). Event-related brain potentials reflect increased concentration ability after mindfulness-based cognitive therapy for depression: A randomized clinical trial. *Psychiatry Research 199*(3), 174–180.

Brown, K. W., Goodman, R. J., & Inzlicht, M. (2013). Dispositional mindfulness and the attenuation of neural responses to emotional stimuli. *Social Cognitive and Affective Neuroscience 8*(1), 93–99.

Cahn, B. R., & Polich, J. (2009). Meditation (Vipassana) and the P3a event-related brain potential. *International Journal of Psychophysiology 72*(1), 51–60.

Cavanagh, J., & Geisler, M. W. (2006). Mood effects on the ERP processing of emotional intensity in faces: A P3 investigation with depressed students. *International Journal of Psychophysiology 60*(1), 27–33.

Davidson, R. J., Kabat-Zinn, J., Schumacher, J., Rosenkranz, M., Muller, D., Santorelli, S. F., ... & Sheridan, J. F. (2003). Alterations in brain and immune function produced by mindfulness meditation. *Psychosomatic Medicine 65*(4), 564–570.

Davidson, R. J., & Kaszniak, A. W. (2015). Conceptual and methodological issues in research on mindfulness and meditation. *American Psychologist 70*(7), 581.

Ditto, B., Eclache, M., & Goldman, N. (2006). Short-term autonomic and cardiovascular effects of mindfulness body scan meditation. *Annals of Behavioral Medicine 32*(3), 227–234.

Dorjee, D. (2016). Defining contemplative science: the metacognitive self-regulatory capacity of the mind, context of meditation practice and modes of existential awareness. *Frontiers in Psychology 7*, 1788.

Dorjee, D. (2017). *Neuroscience and psychology of meditation in everyday life: Searching for the essence of mind*. London: Routledge.

Dorjee, D., Lally, N., Darrall-Rew, J., & Thierry, G. (2015). Dispositional mindfulness and semantic integration of emotional words: Evidence from event-related brain potentials. *Neuroscience Research 97*, 45–51.

Eddy, M. D., Brunyé, T. T., Tower-Richardi, S., Mahoney, C. R., & Taylor, H. A. (2015). The effect of a brief mindfulness induction on processing of emotional images: An ERP study. *Frontiers in Psychology 6*, 1391.

Greenwald, M. K., Cook, E. W., & Lang, P. J. (1989). Affective judgment and psychophysiological response: Dimensional covariation in the evaluation of pictorial stimuli. *Journal of Psychophysiology 3*(1), 51–64.

Hajcak, G., MacNamara, A., & Olvet, D. M. (2010). Event-related potentials, emotion, and emotion regulation: An integrative review. *Developmental Neuropsychology 35*(2), 129–155.

Hajcak, G., & Nieuwenhuis, S. (2006). Reappraisal modulates the electrocortical response to unpleasant pictures. *Cognitive, Affective, & Behavioral Neuroscience 6*(4), 291–297.

Hölzel, B. K., Lazar, S. W., Gard, T., Schuman-Olivier, Z., Vago, D. R., & Ott, U. (2011). How does mindfulness meditation work? Proposing mechanisms of action from a conceptual and neural perspective. *Perspectives on Psychological Science 6*(6), 537–559.

Keune, P. M., Bostanov, V., Hautzinger, M., & Kotchoubey, B. (2011). Mindfulness-based cognitive therapy (MBCT), cognitive style, and the temporal dynamics of frontal EEG alpha asymmetry in recurrently depressed patients. *Biological Psychology 88*(2–3), 243–252.

Keune, P. M., Bostanov, V., Hautzinger, M., & Kotchoubey, B. (2013). Approaching dysphoric mood: State-effects of mindfulness meditation on frontal brain asymmetry. *Biological Psychology 93*(1), 105–113.

Krygier, J. R., Heathers, J. A. J., Shahrestani, S., Abbott, M., Gross, J. J., & Kemp, A. H. (2013). Mindfulness meditation, well-being, and heart rate variability: A preliminary investigation into the impact of intensive Vipassana meditation. *International Journal of Psychophysiology 89*(3), 305–313.

Kubota, Y., Sato, W., Toichi, M., Murai, T., Okada, T., Hayashi, A., & Sengoku, A. (2001). Frontal midline theta rhythm is correlated with cardiac autonomic activities during the performance of an attention demanding meditation procedure. *Cognitive Brain Research 11*(2), 281–287.

Kuyken, W., Byford, S., Taylor, R. S., Watkins, E., Holden, E., White, K.,... & Teasdale, J. D. (2008). Mindfulness-based cognitive therapy to prevent relapse in recurrent depression. *Journal of Consulting and Clinical Psychology 76*(6), 966–978.

Kuyken, W., Hayes, R., Barrett, B., Byng, R., Dalgleish, T., Kessler, D.,... & Causley, A. (2015). Effectiveness and cost-effectiveness of mindfulness-based cognitive therapy compared with maintenance antidepressant treatment in the prevention of depressive relapse or recurrence (PREVENT): A randomised controlled trial. *The Lancet 386*(9988), 63–73.

Luck, S. J. (2012). *Event-related potentials*. Cambridge, MA: MIT Press.

Lumma, A. L., Kok, B. E., & Singer, T. (2015). Is meditation always relaxing? Investigating heart rate, heart rate variability, experienced effort and likeability during training of three types of meditation. *International Journal of Psychophysiology 97*(1), 38–45.

Lutz, A., Slagter, H. A., Dunne, J. D., & Davidson, R. J. (2008). Attention regulation and monitoring in meditation. *Trends in Cognitive Sciences 12*(4), 163–169.

Malinowski, P., Moore, A. W., Mead, B. R., & Gruber, T. (2017). Mindful aging: the effects of regular brief mindfulness practice on electrophysiological markers of cognitive and affective processing in older adults. *Mindfulness 8*(1), 78–94.

Mohan, A., Sharma, R., & Bijlani, R. L. (2011). Effect of meditation on stress-induced changes in cognitive functions. *Journal of Alternative and Complementary Medicine 17*(3), 207–212.

Moore, A. W., Gruber, T., Derose, J., & Malinowski, P. (2012). Regular, brief mindfulness meditation practice improves electrophysiological markers of attentional control. *Frontiers in Human Neuroscience 6*, 18.

Moynihan, J. A., Chapman, B. P., Klorman, R., Krasner, M. S., Duberstein, P. R., Brown, K. W., & Talbot, N. L. (2013). Mindfulness-based stress reduction for older adults: Effects on executive function, frontal alpha asymmetry and immune function. *Neuropsychobiology 68*(1), 34–43.

Ochsner, K. N., & Gross, J. J. (2005). The cognitive control of emotion. *Trends in Cognitive Sciences 9*(5), 242–249.

Polich, J. (2007). Updating P300: An integrative theory of P3a and P3b. *Clinical Neurophysiology 118*(10), 2128–2148.

Sanger, K. L., & Dorjee, D. (2016). Mindfulness training with adolescents enhances metacognition and the inhibition of irrelevant stimuli: Evidence from event-related brain potentials. *Trends in Neuroscience and Education 5*(1), 1–11.

Sanger, K. L., Thierry, G., & Dorjee, D. (2018). Effects of school-based mindfulness training on emotion processing and well-being in adolescents: evidence from event-related potentials. *Developmental Science 21*(5), e12646.

Singh, Y., & Talwar, A. (2012). Immediate and long-term effects of meditation on acute stress reactivity, cognitive functions, and intelligence. *Alternative Therapies in Health and Medicine 18*(6), 46.

Slagter, H. A., Lutz, A., Greischar, L. L., Francis, A. D., Nieuwenhuis, S., Davis, J. M., & Davidson, R. J., 2007. Mental training affects distribution of limited brain resources. *PLoS Biology 5*(6), e138.

Sobolewski, A., Holt, E., Kublik, E., & Wróbel, A. (2011). Impact of meditation on emotional processing—A visual ERP study. *Neuroscience Research 71*(1), 44–48.

Stewart, J. L., Coan, J. A., Towers, D. N., & Allen, J. J. (2014). Resting and task-elicited prefrontal EEG alpha asymmetry in depression: Support for the capability model. *Psychophysiology 51*(5), 446–455.

Sutton, S. K., & Davidson, R. J. (1997). Prefrontal brain asymmetry: A biological substrate of the behavioral approach and inhibition systems. *Psychological Science 8*(3), 204–210.

Tang, Y. Y., Hölzel, B. K., & Posner, M. I. (2015). The neuroscience of mindfulness meditation. *Nature Reviews Neuroscience 16*(4), 213.

Tang, Y. Y., Ma, Y., Fan, Y., Feng, H., Wang, J., Feng, S., . . . & Zhang, Y. (2009). Central and autonomic nervous system interaction is altered by short-term meditation. *Proceedings of the National Academy of Sciences 106*(22), 8865–8870.

Teper, R., & Inzlicht, M. (2013). Meditation, mindfulness and executive control: the importance of emotional acceptance and brain-based performance monitoring. *Social Cognitive and Affective Neuroscience 8*(1), 85–92.

Teper, R., Segal, Z. V., & Inzlicht, M. (2013). Inside the mindful mind: How mindfulness enhances emotion regulation through improvements in executive control. *Current Directions in Psychological Science* 22(6), 449–454.

Thayer, J. F., Åhs, F., Fredrikson, M., Sollers III, J. J., & Wager, T. D. (2012). A meta-analysis of heart rate variability and neuroimaging studies: Implications for heart rate variability as a marker of stress and health. *Neuroscience & Biobehavioral Reviews* 36(2), 747–756.

Toichi, M., Sugiura, T., Murai, T., & Sengoku, A. (1997). A new method of assessing cardiac autonomic function and its comparison with spectral analysis and coefficient of variation of R–R interval. *Journal of the Autonomic Nervous System* 62(1), 79–84.

Towers, D. N., & Allen, J. J. (2009). A better estimate of the internal consistency reliability of frontal EEG asymmetry scores. *Psychophysiology* 46(1), 132–142.

Van Dam, N. T., van Vugt, M. K., Vago, D. R., Schmalzl, L., Saron, C. D., Olendzki, A., . . . & Fox, K. C. (2018). Mind the hype: A critical evaluation and prescriptive agenda for research on mindfulness and meditation. *Perspectives on Psychological Science* 13(1), 36–61.

Watkins, E. R. (2008). Constructive and unconstructive repetitive thought. *Psychological Bulletin* 134(2), 163–206.

Weinberg, A., Klonsky, E. D., & Hajcak, G. (2009). Autonomic impairment in borderline personality disorder: A laboratory investigation. *Brain and Cognition* 71(3), 279–286.

Wenk-Sormaz, H. (2005). Meditation can reduce habitual responding. *Alternative Therapies in Health and Medicine* 11(2), 42.

PSYCHOLOGY

CHAPTER 21

MEDITATION AND EMOTION

TIM LOMAS

Introduction

This chapter examines the relationship between meditation and emotion, in two main parts. The first section explores direct interactions, in which meditative practices specifically focus upon emotional processes. There I consider four main clusters of emotions: dysphoric; compassionate; reverential; and ambivalent. The second section then delves into indirect interactions, where the emotional effects of meditation are more a byproduct of other processes. There I explore three broad classes of process: physiology; cognition; and self-transcendence. First, though, I'll begin by looking at what is meant by meditation and emotion.

Meditation

As this handbook as a whole shows, the term meditation covers a wide range of meanings and practices. Given that one purpose of this handbook is to highlight exactly this range, an exhaustive analysis of meditation per se is not necessary in this chapter. Nevertheless, it will be helpful to introduce a framework that will be useful in the following discussion.

The term meditation derives from the Latin *meditatio*, meaning to engage in reflection. The term was originally deployed in the West to refer to all types of intellectual exercise. However, it began to be employed more specifically as a synonym of contemplation. For instance, in philosophy, one would find "meditations" on particular themes, such as Descartes' (1641/2008) reflections on the mind. In more recent decades, meditation has tended to be more commonly used specifically in relation to contemplative practices in Eastern traditions. Such has been this narrowing in usage that meditation is sometimes assumed to be exclusively a preserve of such traditions. However, viewed functionally in psychological terms, most cultures and traditions have developed activities that could be construed as forms of meditation.

Although there is great diversity among forms of meditation, there are also commonalities. For many scholars, what ultimately defines and unites these disparate forms is the skilled and trained deployment of attention. For instance, Goleman (1988, p. 107) suggests that "[t]he need for the meditator to retrain his attention, whether through concentration or mindfulness, is the single invariant ingredient...in every meditation system." Similarly, Walsh and Shapiro (2006, pp. 228–229) define meditation as "a family of self-regulation practices that focus on training attention and awareness in order to bring mental processes under greater voluntary control and thereby foster general mental well-being and development and/or specific capacities such as calm, clarity, and concentration."

Beneath this broad-brush conceptualization, frameworks have been developed to bring order to the diversity of activities that fall within the overarching umbrella of meditation. One particularly useful schema is provided by Mikulas (1990), who suggest that meditative practices can be understood and differentiated according to four main parameters: (1) behaviors of mind (i.e., types of attention); (2) object (the focus of attention); (3) attitude (the emotional quality with which attention is imbued); and (4) form (the physical nature of the practices). Let's briefly touch upon these parameters in turn.

The first parameter, behaviors of mind, pertains to the idea that practices differ in their deployment of cognitive resources. Buddhism, for instance, differentiates between *samatha* (*śamatha*) and *vipassanā* (*vipaśyanā*) modes of contemplation. (When discussing Buddhism here, I shall generally use Pali terms, accompanied on first usage by their Sanskrit cognates – if different – in parentheses.) The former, which literally means pacification or rest, denotes a form of intense "one-pointed" attention, in which practitioners focus on a specific stimulus for extended durations (e.g., as a means toward calming the mind). This mode has been operationalized in contemporary psychology as a form of "focused attention" (Lutz, Slagter, Dunne, & Davidson, 2008). By contrast, the latter is often translated as awareness, insight, or "clear seeing," implying a process of becoming cognizant of the nature of the mind and of reality more broadly. This mode is sometimes conceptualized in psychology as a form of "open-monitoring." In contrast to the selective attentional focus of *samatha*, this involves "an open field capacity to detect arising sensory, feeling and thought events within an unrestricted 'background' of awareness, without a grasping of these events in an explicitly selected foreground or focus" (Raffone & Srinivasan, 2010, p. 2). However, many practices actually harness both modes of activity. For instance, mindfulness sittings often begin with a period of focused attention (e.g., on the breath) in order to stabilize practitioners' awareness before the more expansive phase of open monitoring (Chiesa, 2010).

The second parameter, object, pertains to the phenomena upon which meditators can direct their attention. These can be very diverse; as the Dalai Lama puts it, meditation is "a deliberate mental activity that involves cultivating familiarity, be it with a chosen object, a fact, a theme, a habit, an outlook or a way of being" (Gyatso, 2006, p. 98). One could focus internally on one's "qualia" (a philosophical term for all subjective events, including emotions, sensations, thoughts, and so on). Such objects—particularly affective qualia (emotions and feelings)—will feature prominently in the first main section. One could also reflect on spiritually significant ideas, such as death, for example, an object of contemplation across cultures, from *memento mori* in Western traditions (an injunction to "remember mortality"), to *maraṇa sati* (*marana smṛti*) in Buddhism (roughly meaning "awareness of death") (Giustarini, 2012). Similarly, people may focus on meaningful phrases or sounds, known as a *mantra*, as found in Transcendental Meditation (Delmonte, 1983). Relatedly, Zen has its system of *koan*, which usually involve unanswerable questions designed to disrupt conventional logical and discursive thought, thereby prompting awakening (Suzuki, 2011). Practitioners might also direct their attention outward, for instance toward religious icons or shrines, and to associated olfactory (e.g., incense) and auditory stimuli (e.g., bells, chanting).

The third parameter, attitude, pertains to the idea that people can imbue their contemplative activities with various emotional qualities. As with the second parameter, this will also feature strongly in the chapter's analysis. For instance, mindfulness has been influentially defined by Kabat-Zinn (2003, p. 145) as "the awareness that arises through paying attention on purpose, in the present moment, and nonjudgmentally to the unfolding of experience moment by moment." However, teachers and scholars have stressed how important the adjective "nonjudgmentally" is here. There is a risk that practitioners may fall into modes of awareness that are relatively cold, clinical, and critical, to the detriment of their well-being (Lomas, Cartwright, Edginton, & Ridge, 2015). As such, practitioners are encouraged to imbue mindful modes of attention with emotional qualities such as compassion and kindness. To that end, practices have been developed to help people cultivate these qualities, such as the *mettā bhāvana* (*maitrī bhāvana*) translated and operationalized in psychology as "loving-kindness meditation" (Fredrickson, Cohn, Coffey, Pek, & Finkel, 2008). As we shall see, meditative practices can encourage a spectrum of emotional qualities, from relatively neutral stances of detachment, to warmer states of compassion and loving-kindness, to more intense stances of devotion and reverence (Lomas, 2019).

The final parameter is form, highlighting the idea that the physical way in which meditation is practiced is a key aspect of the process. Even just with seated forms of meditation, there may be subtle variations in practice. These range from whether one's legs are arrayed in a full- or half-lotus, to the issue of whether one's eyes should be closed (which is more common) or open (as found in some Zen traditions, for instance) (Austin, 1998). But meditative practice does not have to involve sedentary sitting, with a wealth of dynamic forms found cross-culturally. An exemplar is yoga, and specifically Hatha yoga, the branch most commonly practiced in the West (where it is often mistaken for the *only* branch) (Quilty, Saper, Goldstein, & Khalsa, 2013). This involves sequences of *āsana* (postures) and *vinyāsa* (dynamic transitions between postures)—the selection, duration, and speed of which vary by tradition—accompanied by meditative processes (such as breathing and focusing techniques). Other prominent forms of active contemplative range from Tai chi (Wang et al., 2010)—which involves slow deliberative movements, with particular attention paid to shifts in balance and posture—to the multitude of practices assembled under the banner of martial arts (Hyams, 2010).

This framework will be useful in exploring the interaction between meditation and emotion. Before exploring this interaction though, let's clarify what is meant by emotion.

Emotion

Emotion is a much-contested concept. Even in the early 1980s, Kleinginna and Kleinginna (1981) found ninety-two different definitions, and the conceptual confusion has not improved much since then (Reisenzein, 2007). The issue is partly that emotion serves as an overarching term for a complex psychological and physiological process that involves multiple components and dimensions. For instance, Scherer (2001) identified several components—each with their own function and involving different physiological and psychological processes—including cognitive (appraisal of a stimulus), neurophysiological (biological substrates and expressions), motivational (action tendencies), motor-expression (facial and vocal expression), and subjective components (affective experience). As it is beyond the scope of this chapter to offer a detailed theoretical analysis of emotions per se, Scherer's elucidation will suffice as a basic outline of what is meant by emotion.

In addition, this chapter is interested in the broader category of "affective phenomena" (AP), which also includes moods, emotional dispositions, and feelings (Mulligan & Scherer, 2012). Moods and emotional dispositions are differentiated temporally from emotions "proper"—which usually refers specifically to transient and brief emotional states or episodes—by their longer-lasting duration (where moods can last hours or even longer, while dispositions can endure over many years). Finally, feelings could be regarded as constituting qualia more broadly, encompassing everything that falls within the question, what does it *feel* like to be a given person at a particular moment (Nagel, 1974). As articulated by Jackson (1982, p. 127), qualia constitutes all phenomenal experience, covering subjective events such as "the hurtfulness of pains, the itchiness of itches, pangs of jealousy," and so on.

Beyond the issue of defining emotions, there are diverse theoretical perspectives regarding their nature. The psychological literature features two main perspectives (themselves heterogeneous): naturalistic and constructivist. The former treats emotions in an essentialist way as relatively universal affective responses. Within this perspective are two dominant theories: the circumplex model of affect (Russell, 1980) and the paradigm of "basic emotions" (Ekman, 1999). The circumplex model holds that affective states are generated by the interaction of two independent neurophysiological systems: valence (pleasant-unpleasant) and arousal (active-passive). Meanwhile, the basic emotions model holds that a "discrete and independent neural system subserves every emotion," and that these differ in factors such as antecedent events, physiology, appraisal, and probable behavioral responses (Posner, Russell, & Peterson, 2005, p. 715). In that respect, Ekman has suggested that there are five basic emotions: anger, disgust, fear, sadness, and enjoyment (with surprise also sometimes included by scholars as a sixth). Conversely, constructivist theories argue that emotions are not universally available inner states, but are a function of the dynamics of social interaction, and of the broader cultural context in which this occurs (Harré, 1986). From this perspective there is great variation in the way emotions are experienced, interpreted, and understood.

There is also a middle ground between the naturalistic and constructivist perspectives, with scholars incorporating elements of both positions. For instance, Barrett's (2006) conceptual-act model posits that emotions emerge from a conceptual analysis of a "momentary state of core affect" (p. 49). The notion of core affect aligns with the naturalistic theories. However, its "ebb and flow" is filtered through a person's linguistic-conceptual schemas, an idea that aligns with constructivist theories. I personally tend to align with this kind of integrative model. However, this chapter does not require one to endorse any particular theory or perspective, with the analysis being compatible with naturalistic, constructivist, and integrative approaches.

Having offered a brief summary of emotions, we can now turn to the main objective of this chapter: their interaction with meditation. As intimated earlier in the chapter, I will explore both direct and indirect forms of interaction. Direct forms are when meditation specifically targets or encourages a particular emotion, per the second and third parameters. Indirect forms are when meditative practices impinge upon emotions through some intermediary process, with the emotional outcomes a byproduct of the main focus of the practice. As a final point, there is an implicit concern here with viewing emotions through the prism of well-being-related considerations. One rarely finds emotions discussed—in any literature—from a neutral perspective, but rather categorized from a well-being-perspective as desirable or undesirable. Relatedly, in the case of meditation, scholars usually have the value-laden assumption that the central question is the extent to which meditation promotes emotions associated with well-being and ameliorates harmful ones. That assumption applies here too, with an overarching interest in how meditation, via its impact on emotions, might enhance well-being. With that in mind, the first main section considers direct forms of interaction.

Direct Interaction

Across the diversity of meditation practices, many directly "work with" emotions. This might either mean taking these as their object (per the second parameter), or encouraging people to imbue their attention with particular emotional qualities (per the third parameter). One way of organizing the material here is in terms of various emotional clusters, grouping together emotions that share similarities with respect to valence and intensity. We'll briefly touch upon four clusters that can be found in the literature (although one should note that this schema is not exhaustive, and other clusters could no doubt be located): dysphoric, compassionate, reverential, and ambivalent emotions.

Dysphoric Emotions

Some meditation practices focus directly on dysphoric emotions (e.g., anxiety) and qualia more generally (e.g., pain). Not all, of course: many practices involve amplifying positively valenced qualia, or indirectly attenuating negatively valenced ones. With respect to the latter, this often occurs indirectly by the meditator attending to other processes, as I explore in the second main section below. For instance, in the various mindfulness-based interventions (MBIs) that have flourished in recent years (Kabat-Zinn, 2003), participants might concentrate on their breathing as a way of attenuating negative emotions like anxiety. At other points, though, participants may be encouraged to actually *focus* on their dysphoric qualia, but crucially, though, in a careful and specific way. In particular, MBIs may encourage people to attend to the way the dysphoria is manifesting viscerally, focusing on its sensations in an accepting and non-reactive way. As Finucane and Mercer (2006) put it, participants are encouraged to "simply remain open to what is there—to experience it fully, without aversion or attachment."

This approach is central to Kabat-Zinn's (1982) prototypical Mindfulness-Based Stress Reduction (MBSR) program, created initially for patients with chronic pain. Participants learned to be mindful of their pain, which perhaps counterintuitively served to reduce their dysphoric experience of it, with similar results found in relation to Mindfulness-Based Cognitive Therapy (MBCT) (de Jong et al., 2016). This process also applies to emotions specifically. For instance, Finucane and Mercer (2006) offered MBCT to people with depression and anxiety, who were instructed to focus mindfully on their somatic experiences (a very challenging task for some people, it should be noted). The main rationale is that doing so can help people stop dwelling on the *cognitive* dimensions of the dysphoria. The broader context here is the cognitive approach to mental disorder, where disorders are viewed as caused, at least in part, by maladaptive cognitive processes. For instance, in Beck's (1979) theory of depression, the disorder stems from a triad of "automatic negative thoughts" (pertaining to the self, the world, and the future). The negative impact of these thoughts is exacerbated by processes such as rumination, which is implicated in the onset of depressive episodes (Papageorgiou & Wells, 2003). Hence the value of focusing on somatic aspects of the dysphoria: it gets practitioners out of their "head," thereby dampening down processes of rumination.

When attending to dysphoric qualia in this way, an important consideration is the emotional quality of one's attention (per the third parameter). Mindfulness teachers, for instance, emphasize the importance of a kind, compassionate tone (Shapiro & Carlson, 2009). To that end, there are practices designed to cultivate these qualities, as we see next.

Compassionate Emotions

Many spiritual traditions valorize compassion and related prosocial emotions (such as empathy and kindness). For instance, Buddhism is often described as a "religion of compassion" (Price, 2010). Indeed, within the Theravada tradition, compassionate emotions are celebrated as three of the four *brahma-vihārās* (*brahma-vihārāḥs*) (Hofmann, Grossman, & Hinton, 2011). Translated as "abodes of Brahma"—Brahma being a creator god in Hindu theology—these are qualities that practitioners are encouraged to cultivate as means toward psychospiritual development and ultimately liberation. These are (in Pali): *karuṇā* (compassion); *mettā* (loving-kindness); *muditā* (sympathetic or vicarious happiness); and *upekkha* (equanimity). There are many reasons why such emotions are so valorized in such traditions, including being: conducive to the common good (Condon, 2017); associated with positive mental states through causal psychological dynamics (sometimes referred to as *kamma* [karma]) (Kang, 2009); and a pathway to overcoming the self-other duality, thereby facilitating self-transcendence (Lomas, 2015).

Importantly, traditions like Buddhism do not only valorize compassionate emotions, but also have developed practices to help people cultivate these. A prominent example is the aforementioned *mettā bhāvana*, a Pali term denoting the cultivation (*bhāvana*) of *mettā*. This is an imaginative introspective exercise in which people identify, dwell on, and build feelings of *mettā* for various people, usually in five stages. Practitioners often begin by attempting to feel *mettā* for themselves, reflecting work by Neff (2003) on the importance of self-compassion (and the difficulties people can have in generating this). This act of self-care is often aided by gentle prayer-like vocalizations, such as "May I be happy. May I be well. May I be free from suffering. May I be free." After this, the object of well-wishing is usually a friend—with the vocalizations adapted accordingly—followed by a neutral acquaintance, someone whom the person finds difficult, and finally increasingly wide circles of people in general (e.g., everyone in the room, then the community, and outward to all sentient beings in the universe).

Thus, the practice centers on *mettā* both as: (a) an object of practice (per parameter 2), in that practitioners focus on and amplify any latent feelings of *mettā*; and (b) an attitude (per parameter 3), in that they will also call to mind various people (as meditative objects), and imbue their reflections with *mettā*. In that latter sense, the *mettā bhāvana* is treated as complementary to mindfulness, in that it may allow practitioners to transfer these attitudinal qualities into mindfulness practice itself, thus endowing it with the recommended compassion and kindness. For that reason, Buddhist movements like Triratna—one of the most popular in the United Kingdom—offer mindfulness and the *mettā bhāvana* to beginners as their two foundational practices (Lomas, Cartwright, Edginton, & Ridge, 2014). The *mettā bhāvana* is effective in promoting well-being, as shown in a raft of studies (which operationalize it as loving-kindness meditation) (see Galante, Galante, Bekkers, & Gallacher, 2014, and Shonin, Van Gordon, Compare, Zangeneh, & Griffiths, 2015, for reviews). Purported benefits range from reducing anxiety (Weibel, McClintock, & Anderson, 2017) and racial prejudice (Stell & Farsides, 2016), to enhancing altruism (Galante, Bekkers, Mitchell, & Gallacher, 2016) and gratitude (Rao & Kemper, 2016).

Many variants of this kind of practice exist. For instance, Tibetan Buddhism features *tonglen* (Pagliaro et al., 2016). Literally meaning "giving and taking," practitioners imagine taking in the sufferings of others (as if breathing in noxious smoke), transmuting it in their heart through their altruistic love, and emanating goodwill back to the person (Chodren, 2014). Somewhat similarly, most traditions have precepts around acts of compassion and kindness, which can involve meditative (i.e., reflective) aspects, such as the Judaic activity of *gemilut hasadim*, the "bestowal" of loving-kindness (Harvey, 2009). Added to these historical practices are meditation-based interventions developed more recently, including Compassion Meditation (Lutz, Brefczynski-Lewis, Johnstone, & Davidson, 2008), Compassion Cultivating Training (Jazaieri et al., 2013), Compassion Meditation Training (Ruchelli et al., 2014), and Cognitively Based Compassion Training (Ozawa-de Silva & Negi, 2013).

Reverential Emotions

Meditative practices can also involve emotions that could be labelled broadly as reverential. This takes us into rather different affective territory. The previous section covered emotions that pertain to relationships between people of roughly equal standing (e.g., evoking *mettā* for friends). However, another branch of practices involves reflections on beings (and associated phenomena) that are appraised as divine, such as deities. Such dyads have a near-infinite power asymmetry, in that the reverenced being would generally be perceived as incomprehensibly greater than the person in all respects. As such, these practices not only involve feelings like gratitude and devotion—which might also be present in relations between people—but more complex states such as awe, which has been described as a "spiritual emotion" that exists in a powerful, rarefied zone "in the upper reaches of pleasure and on the boundary of fear" (Keltner & Haidt, 2003, p. 297). As with the previous theme, there may still be love present, but one of a different sort. These differences tend to be obscured by the word love, which is "polysemous in the extreme," that is, semantically covering a vast range of feelings (Berscheid, 2010, p. 6). However, other languages have greater granularity in that regard, which helps us better appreciate the distinctions (Lomas, 2018a). For instance, in Greek, compassionate love tends to be known as *agápē*, whereas *sébomai* depicts acts or feelings of devotional love, worship, and "reverential homage" (Ross, 2006, p. 51). This form of love possibly also includes elements of "fear and trembling"—in Kierkegaard's (1843) words—reflecting the power asymmetry of the relationship.

Meditative practices involving such emotions are common across traditions. For instance, Kabbalistic Judaism features visualization prayers that can include imagining the name of God written in letters that are "infinitely large" (Kaplan, 1989, p. 142). Such practices are even found in traditions not conventionally regarded as theistic, such as Buddhism. This has an array of deity meditations, known in Sanskrit as *iṣṭadevatā*, a compound of *iṣṭa* (liked, desired, reverenced) and *devatā* (divine being). These practices are particularly prevalent in Tibet, home to an esoteric school of Buddhism that flowered from the eighth Century BCE onward, known as *Vajrayāna* in Sanskrit—the way of the diamond or thunderbolt—or alternatively as Tantra. These deity practices—*lha'i rnal 'byor* in Tibetan—constitute a form of gnosis, being usually reserved for advanced practitioners or select initiates (Wayman, 2013). While their details are somewhat guarded, they generally involve the practitioner, in a skilled act of imaginative introspection, interacting with divinities of the Tibetan pantheon. The ontological status of such beings is a matter of debate; for instance, rather than viewing these as externally existing divinities, some practitioners might construe them as inner psychological potentials, symbolizing their highest selves (Vessantara, 2002). Whatever their nature, these figures are powerful objects of contemplation, evoking a range of highly charged emotions.

Ambivalent Emotions

There remains one class of emotions to consider, the intriguing phenomenon of ambivalent emotions—also known as mixed emotions—that is, emotional experiences that combine positive *and* negative valence (Lomas, 2018b). A classic example is longing, which is a "blend of the primary emotions of happiness and sadness" (Holm, Greaker, & Strömberg, 2002, p. 608). These are intriguing since well-being—the prism through which emotions tend to be appraised, as noted already—is usually associated simply with positively valenced emotions. However, scholars are increasingly recognizing the value of ambivalent emotions (Lomas & Ivtzan, 2016). For instance, Larsen and colleagues (2003) suggest that these can enhance resilience, since they enable negative emotions and memories to be assimilated with meaningful narratives, thereby ameliorating their impact.

The value of ambivalent emotions has been appreciated within spiritual traditions, particularly Eastern ones. Indeed, while remaining wary of engaging in Orientalism—Said's (1995) pejorative term for the way "The East" as a construct is used to homogenize people in Asian, Middle Eastern, and North African cultures as the "Other"—it has been argued that Eastern cultures are more attuned to dialectical modes of cognition relative to Western ones (Nisbett, Peng, Choi, & Norenzayan, 2001). Appreciation of ambivalent emotions is particularly prominent within Zen. This is the branch of Buddhism that first emerged in China around the fifth century—as Buddhism interacted with the indigenous philosophy of Taoism, whose dialectical sensitivity is embodied in the *yīn-yáng* symbol—and then flowered in Japan from the twelfth century onward (Suzuki, 1959). There are of course many aspects to Zen. But most relevant here is the contention, articulated by the likes of Watts (1957), that it aims to evoke certain ambivalent "perceptual-emotional moods," such as *wabi-sabi* and *mono no aware*.

Wabi-sabi is perhaps the best known of these moods. It captures the strange charm of aged or imperfect phenomena, "a crude or often faded beauty that correlates with a dark, desolate sublimity" (Prusinski, 2013, p. 25). *Wabi* and *sabi* each bring subtly different qualities to the compound, roughly denoting rustic and aged beauty respectively. *Mono no aware* is similarly concerned with the passage of time, albeit slightly differently. The quality was identified by the eighteenth-century scholar Motoori Norinaga, although it predates this identification, being evident in the fourteenth-century epic *The Tale of the Heike*, for instance (Tyler, 2012). The term combines *aware*, which denotes sensitivity or sadness, and *mono*, which means "things." It thus refers to pathos, to the capacity to be "touched or moved by the world," especially its ephemerality and impermanence (Woolfolk, 2002, p. 23). The ambivalent awareness of the passage of time captured in *wabi-sabi* and *mono no aware* is central to Buddhism. For this regards impermanence—*annica* (*anitya*)—as being one of the three *lakshanas* (*lakṣaṇas*), that is, defining attributes of existence (Panpothong & Phakdeephasook, 2014). The second is *anattā* (*anātman*), roughly translatable as "no self," reflecting the idea that all phenomena lack an intrinsic or fixed identity, but instead are brought into being through their dynamic interconnections with other phenomena. The third is *dukkha* (*duḥkha*), namely dissatisfaction or suffering. Buddhism holds that people are usually in denial or ignorance about *anicca* and *anattā*, and so crave and attach to phenomena that are intrinsically subject to change, leading inexorably to *dukkha*. However, liberation can be found through a deep understanding and appreciation of *anitya* and *anattā*.

Hence the importance in Zen of ambivalent sensibilities like *wabi-sabi* and *mono no aware*. As such, these emotions are greatly cherished by Zen and accordingly are the focus of meditative practices designed to engender them (Lomas, 2016). These take a range of forms (per the fourth parameter), with a particular focus on cultural, artistic, or sporting activities, from poetry and painting to flower arrangement and swordsmanship. Zen seeks to overcome the limitations of conceptual thought, and to point directly into the "suchness" (i.e., nature) of reality (Chung-yuan, 1977), and such activities are seen as a potent way of doing so, communicating and engendering spiritual truths in a more effective manner than discursive prose (Lomas, Etcoff, Gordon, & Shonin, 2017). A good example is *chadō*, the Japanese tea ceremony. Hammitzsch (1979) describes how this is designed to induce a sense of *wabi-sabi* (among other qualities), for instance in the way it is ideally taken in a secluded, time-worn tea house, with aged, antique utensils. As Prusinski (2013, p. 32) explains, these elements strengthen "one's consciousness of space and time"—including the relative impermanence and unimportance of the participants themselves—thereby creating a "heightened spirituality." Such activities help to round out our appreciation of the various emotions directly targeted by meditative activities.

Indirect Interaction

So far I have considered direct forms of interaction between meditation and emotion. That meant focusing on instances where emotions have been the direct object of meditation (per parameter 2), and/or emphasized as the quality with which attention should be imbued (per parameter 3). The focus in the remainder of the chapter is on *indirect* pathways connecting meditation and emotion. I'm referring to instances where meditative practices are not concerned with emotion per se, but rather with other biological or psychological processes, which nevertheless influence emotion. I'll briefly touch upon three such processes: physiology, cognition, and self-transcendence. As with the discussion of emotions in the first main part of the chapter, this list is not exhaustive, and other processes could doubtless be identified. However, it is sufficient for showing a range of associations that can mediate the relationship between meditation and emotions.

Physiology

Much could be said about how meditation impacts upon physiological processes, which themselves affect emotion. I'll briefly consider three such processes here: neurophysiology, respiratory functions, and physical movement. To begin with, an extensive body of research has explored how meditative practices engender certain brain states. Then, per the neural correlates of consciousness paradigm (Fell, 2004), these brain states are linked to emotional states of various hues. As one might expect, this is a complex area of research, and moreover one that intersects with the other processes considered here. For instance, as we shall see with respect to cognition—and has been foreshadowed already—meditative practices are linked to the development of attention faculties. Such faculties are in turn associated with specific physiological substrates and processes, as indexed by various empirical paradigms. For instance, fMRI technology indicates that meditative processes supervene on brain regions associated with executive function, such as the prefrontal cortex and the anterior cingulate cortex (Fox et al., 2014). In turn, these brain regions play key roles in emotional processing, including regulating brain areas associated with affect, such as the amygdala, thereby attenuating dysphoric emotions (Etkin, Egner, & Kalisch, 2011). Similarly, EEG assessment has connected meditation to brain wave patterns associated with cognitive functioning, such as elevated theta amplitude, and to patterns implicated in relaxation—and associated qualia such as calmness and tranquillity—particularly elevated alpha amplitude, the combination of which indicates a meditative signature of "relaxed alertness" (Lomas, Ivtzan, & Fu, 2015).

A second prominent process that mediates between meditation and emotion is respiration. Many practices focus on the breath, in sophisticated and subtle ways. For instance, the mindfulness of breathing often features four main stages: counting on the end of the out-breath; counting at the start of the in-breath; attending to the entire influx and efflux; and focusing on specific visceral areas (such as the movement of the diaphragm). Among the benefits of this kind of activity is the "relaxation response" (Lazar et al., 2000), a state of repose associated with activation of the parasympathetic nervous system (Benson, Beary, & Carol, 1974). Consideration of respiratory activity also links to the third physiological process I'll mention here: physical activity. As noted with respect to the fourth parameter, some practices promote physical movement, such as yoga and

Tai chi. These can be analyzed within the broader context of the impact of physical exercise—behaviors that elevate respiration rate and cardiovascular activity (Garber et al., 2011)—upon emotions. For instance, exercise may ameliorate the impact of conditions like depression (Hoffman et al., 2011) and anxiety (Herring, O'Connor, & Dishman, 2010), and promote positive affect (Reed & Ones, 2006), doing so via mechanisms such as endorphin release (Boecker et al., 2008).

Cognition

I have already highlighted the notion that meditative practices are associated with enhanced cognitive functioning, such as the skillful deployment of attention. It should be noted that this contention is not unequivocally accepted; for instance, a systematic review of 18 MBSR and MBCT interventions by Lao, Kissane, and Meadows (2016) found that, contrary to expectation, the studies overall did not improve attention or executive function. However, the literature more broadly does generally endorse an association between mindfulness and enhanced cognitive functioning (even if it is acknowledged that further research and theorizing are required in light of findings such as Lao et al.) (see Alsubaie et al., 2017, for a recent summary). These cognitive processes can of course be considered part of the psychological architecture that makes possible the kind of direct connection between meditation and emotion covered earlier. However, it is also worth noting the indirect role that such processes may play in connecting meditation to AP. For instance, by enhancing attention and executive function, meditative practices like mindfulness have been associated with the development of "metacognition," the ability to monitor and control one's own mental processes (Teasdale, 1999; Bishop et al., 2004).

One prominent model in this area is that of Shapiro, Carlson, Astin, and Freedman (2006), who offer a theoretical elucidation of Kabat-Zinn's definition (cited earlier). They deconstructed this into three key axioms or components: intention (i.e., motivation for engaging in practice, such as commitment to psychological development); attention (i.e., cognitive processes through which one attends to experience); and attitude (i.e., emotional qualities with which one imbues one's attention). Together, these combine to generate an overarching "meta-mechanism" that Shapiro and colleagues refer to as "reperceiving." This is described as a "fundamental shift in perspective," in which "rather than being immersed in the personal drama or narrative of our life story, we are able to stand back and witness it" (p. 377). This shift has also been conceptualized as decentering, defined as "the ability to observe one's thoughts and feelings as temporary, objective events in the mind, as opposed to reflections of the self that are necessarily true" (Fresco et al., 2007, p. 234). Thus, in reperceiving/decentering, people are able to enter into a different *relationship* with their subjectivity, viewing their thoughts and feelings as transient phenomena passing though their internal world, rather than identifying with and attaching to—or alternatively becoming averse to—such qualia (Bishop et al., 2004).

As one can imagine, these metacognitive skills have implications for emotions. For example, as noted earlier, disorders such as depression are associated with maladaptive cognitive schemas, for example negative self-referential thoughts (Beck, 1979). In MBCT, participants are taught to decenter from their negative cognitions, thus helping prevent a "downward spiral" of negative thoughts and worsening negative affect which could otherwise trigger a depressive episode (Segal, Williams, & Teasdale, 2002). The positive impact of retraining awareness in this way is not limited to depression, but extends to mental health generally. Inability to tolerate distressing qualia is seen as a factor underlying diverse psychopathologies (Aldao, Nolen-Hoeksema, & Schweizer, 2010). For example, in substance abuse, it can lead to people attempting to suppress dysphoria through self-medication (Garland, Gaylord, Boettiger, & Howard, 2010). Thus, tolerance of dysphoria engendered through mindfulness can lessen the likelihood of that occurring. Similarly, MBIs for eating disorders can help people to become aware of triggers for their behavior and to stay mindful in the presence of these triggers, rather than reacting in maladaptive ways (Dalen et al., 2010). Through such meta-cognitive mechanisms, meditative practices like mindfulness are able to exert a positive impact on emotional experiences and outcomes.

Self-Transcendence

Finally, cross-cultural surveys of spiritual traditions indicate that most encourage some form of self-transcendence, which can have a profound emotional impact (Lomas, 2015, 2019). While self-transcendence is a complex and contested construct, a common interpretation is that it involves a significant shift in the experience of the self. The "conventional" sense of self—who one commonly understands oneself to be—is perceived as illusory or partial in some way. In its place is an experience of being part of, or identified with, some larger context, with concomitant feelings of liberation and release (Epstein, 1988). As such, traditions have developed meditative practices to help practitioners toward such experiences. By way of example, I'll focus on Buddhism. Even within this one tradition are numerous such practices, so I shall just outline one theory and practice to gain an appreciation of the potential dynamics of self-transcendence. The practice in question centers on the five *khandas* (*skandhas*), a Sanskrit term denoting the corporeal elements which constitute the person (Du Pre, 1993). By meditating upon these elements, the practitioner is thought able to "deconstruct" their conventional notion of self. This means coming to appreciate that the *lakshanas*—*anattā* (no-self) and *anicca* (impermanence)—apply also to *oneself*, therefore rendering the notion of a fixed, immutable self as an illusion.

If practitioners attain a deep experiential understanding of the *kandhas*, Buddhism holds that they will "see through" their self-construct and be liberated. A pivotal exposition of this possibility is found in the Heart Sutra, widely regarded as one of the most important Buddhist texts (Conze, 1948). The sutra advances the idea that a full appreciation of the *khandas* engenders a realization of *suññatā* (*sūnyatā*). Although usually translated as "emptiness," this can misleadingly imply a form of nihilism (Richards, 1978). Rather, *suññatā* captures the ideas of *anattā* and *anicca*: all phenomena, including the self, are not self-subsistent, but come into being dependent upon conditions (a law referred to as *paṭicca-samuppāda* [*pratītya-samutpāda*], i.e., dependent origination or co-arising). Therefore, the Heart Sutra explains that these phenomena are in fact no different from *suññatā*, memorably stating that "form is emptiness and the very emptiness is form."

Realization of *suññatā* is thought to precipitate *moksha* (*mokṣa*), emancipation or liberation, and subsequently the psychospiritual peak of *nibbāna* (*nirvāṇa*), a "permanent" cessation of suffering. The ultimate nature of *nibbāna*—for example, its ontological, spiritual, and/or metaphysical implications—is a matter of much debate. But whatever its nature, although one would not describe it as an emotion per se, it appears to be an experiential event suffused with important and desirable affective qualities, such as feelings of utmost peace and calm, and possibly even a form of "total" imperturbability (where one is completely unmoved or unaffected by negative qualia) (Lee, Lin, Huang, & Fredrickson, 2013). Thus, it perhaps constitutes a zenith of sorts in terms of the way that meditation can—via processes such as self-transcendence—lead to profound emotional experiences.

Conclusion

This chapter has shone a light on the intricate connections between meditation and emotion. I began by exploring a helpful framework for understanding meditation, whereby practices can be organized according to four key parameters: behaviors of mind; object; attitude; and form. Emotions (and affective mental states more generally) are most directly connected to the second and third parameters. First, emotions can be the *object* of one's meditative focus. We saw this, for instance, with dysphoric emotions, whereby participants in MBIs are encouraged to consciously attend—in an accepting, non-judgmental spirit—to somatic feelings relating to experiences such as pain or anxiety. The rationale is that doing so reduces the likelihood of people becoming absorbed in maladaptive *cognitive* patterns relating to such experiences (e.g., rumination). Then, per the third parameter of attitude, the meditators' attention can be imbued with emotional qualities, such as *mettā*. Doing so is regarded by meditation teachers and theorists as important, as otherwise practitioners may fall into relatively cold and critical modes of awareness, which can hinder well-being.

Having established a framework for understanding meditation and having situated emotions within that schema, the chapter then looked at some of the principal connections between meditation and emotion. These were separated into direct and indirect connections. With the former, we examined four clusters of emotions (dysphoric, compassionate, reverential, and ambivalent), whereas with the latter we considered other processes that mediate the emotional effects of meditation (including physiology,

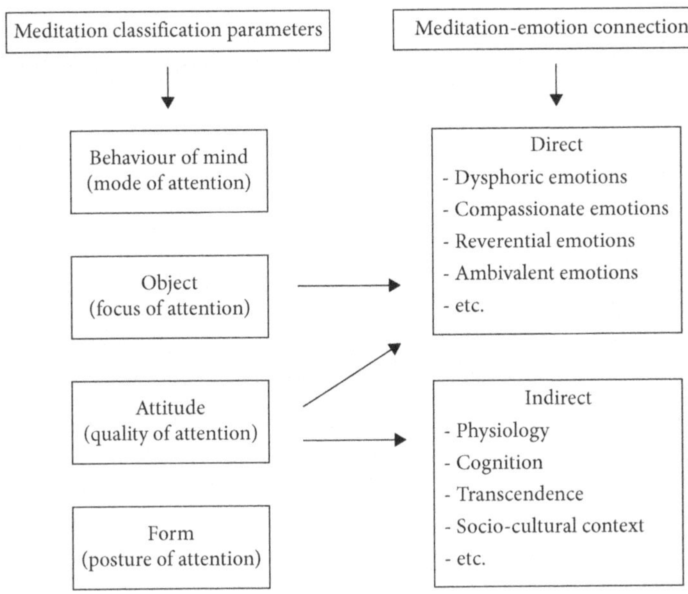

FIGURE 21.1 Direct and indirect connections between meditation and emotions.

cognition, and self-transcendence). These taxonomies of direct and indirect connections are not exhaustive, but are simply some of the more prominent connections one can find analyzed in the literature. For instance, another likely source of indirect connection—which has not yet received the empirical attention it merits—is the sociocultural contexts in which meditators practice, which can powerfully influence people's emotional experience (Lomas, Cartwright, Edginton, & Ridge, 2016). It should also be noted that direct connections relate to the second parameter (i.e., where an emotion is the object of meditation), whereas indirect connections are unrelated to it. Conversely, both types of indirect connection relate to the third parameter, where imbuing attention with particular emotional qualities may be done either directly or indirectly. The meditation framework, the meditation-emotion connections, and the relationships between them, are illustrated in Figure 21.1.

The analysis presented in the paper—as summarized in this figure—is a snapshot of the empirical literature in relation to meditation and emotion as it stands. This research base is stronger in some areas than others, particularly with respect to dysphoric and compassionate emotions (compared to reverential and ambivalent ones), and physiology and cognition (compared to self-transcendence). These trends perhaps reflect the consideration that the bulk of the empirical research into meditation—particularly around mindfulness—appears to have taken place in clinical contexts, where it has been applied and studied in relation to physical and mental health conditions. In those contexts, dysphoric and compassionate emotions are perhaps more relevant and applicable, as are physiological and cognitive mechanisms. They are perhaps also more accepted and less contentious, being more aligned with the theorizing one usually finds in such contexts. Conversely, reverential and ambivalent emotions, and mechanisms such as self-transcendence, have less direct relevance to these clinical contexts, and similarly, can also appear more esoteric and unconventional.

With respect to these latter topics (e.g., reverence or self-transcendence), one can discern a gap between the scientific literature on meditation, and the religious and philosophical contexts in which meditation practices have historically developed, where such topics are significant and central (Epstein, 1988). These haven't been totally neglected by contemporary researchers, of course. For instance, extensive empirical and theoretical work on self-transcendence—often in relation to Transcendental Meditation—has been done by Frederick Travis and colleagues (e.g., Travis & Shear, 2010). Overall, though, researchers have tended to operationalize and study meditation through the prism of conventional scientific models and paradigms—such as cognitive theories of attention—and to steer clear of topics and interpretations more closely associated with religion and philosophy. This has perhaps been understandable and necessary: without this process of "decontextualization"—that is, extricating meditation from the religious/philosophical contexts in which it originally developed—it is possible that meditation would not have been taken seriously within certain areas of academia as a topic of study. But now that it *has* been established as a credible and "appropriate" topic, it is conceivable that researchers will be emboldened and empowered to *re*-contextualize it (Lomas, 2017). This means examining the significance of the wider nexus of teachings and practices in which meditation was embedded—such as phenomena like self-transcendence—thereby fully examining the full potential of this remarkable area of human activity.

References

Aldao, A., Nolen-Hoeksema, S., & Schweizer, S. (2010). Emotion-regulation strategies across psychopathology: A meta-analytic review. *Clinical Psychology Review 30*(2), 217–237. doi:10.1016/j.cpr.2009.11.004

Alsubaie, M., Abbott, R., Dunn, B., Dickens, C., Keil, T. F., Henley, W., & Kuyken, W. (2017). Mechanisms of action in mindfulness-based cognitive therapy (MBCT) and mindfulness-based stress reduction (MBSR) in people with physical and/or psychological conditions: A systematic review. *Clinical Psychology Review* 55, 74–91. doi:10.1016/j.cpr.2017.04.008

Austin, J. H. (1998). *Zen and the brain: Toward an understanding of meditation and consciousness*. Cambridge, MA: MIT Press.

Barrett, L. F. (2006). Are emotions natural kinds? *Perspectives on Psychological Science 1*(1), 28–58. doi:10.1111/j.1745-6916.2006.00003.x

Beck, A. T. (1979). *Cognitive therapy and the emotional disorders*. New York: Penguin.

Benson, H., Beary, J. F., & Carol, M. P. (1974). The relaxation response. *Psychiatry 37*(1), 37–46.

Berscheid, E. (2010). Love in the fourth dimension. *Annual Review of Psychology 61*, 1–25.

Bishop, S. R., Lau, M., Shapiro, S., Carlson, L., Anderson, N. D., Carmody, J., ... Devins, G. (2004). Mindfulness: A proposed operational definition. *Clinical Psychology: Science and Practice 11*(3), 230–241. doi:10.1093/clipsy.bph077

Boecker, H., Sprenger, T., Spilker, M. E., Henriksen, G., Koppenhoefer, M., Wagner, K. J., … Tolle, T. R. (2008). The runner's high: Opioidergic mechanisms in the human brain. *Cerebral Cortex 18*(11), 2523–2531. doi:10.1093/cercor/bhn013

Borton, J. L. S., Markowitz, L. J., & Dieterich, J. (2005). Effects of suppressing negative self-referent thoughts on mood and self-esteem. *Journal of Social and Clinical Psychology 24*(2), 172–190. doi:10.1521/jscp.24.2.172.62269

Chiesa, A. (2010). Vipassana meditation: Systematic review of current evidence. *The Journal of Alternative and Complementary Medicine 16*(1), 37–46.

Chodren, P. (2014). The practice of Tonglen. Retrieved March 9, 2014.

Chung-yuan, C. (1977). *Tao: A new way of thinking. A translation of the Tao Te Ching, with introduction and commentaries*. New York: Harper and Row.

Condon, P. (2017). Mindfulness, compassion, and prosocial behaviour. In J. C. Karremans & E. K. Papies (Eds.), *Mindfulness in social psychology* (pp. 124–138). London: Routledge.

Conze, E. (1948). Text, sources, and bibliography of the Prajñāpāramitā-hṛdaya. *Journal of the Royal Asiatic Society 80*(1–2), 33–51. doi:10.1017/S0035869X00101686

Dalen, J., Smith, B. W., Shelley, B. M., Sloan, A. L., Leahigh, L., & Begay, D. (2010). Pilot study: Mindful eating and living (MEAL): Weight, eating behavior, and psychological outcomes associated with a mindfulness-based intervention for people with obesity. *Complementary Therapies in Medicine 18*(6), 260–264. doi:10.1016/j.ctim.2010.09.008

de Jong, M., Lazar, S. W., Hug, K., Mehling, W. E., Hölzel, B. K., Sack, A. T., … Gard, T. (2016). Effects of mindfulness-based cognitive therapy on body awareness in patients with chronic pain and comorbid depression. *Frontiers in Psychology 7*(967). doi:10.3389/fpsyg.2016.00967

Delmonte, M. (1983). Mantras and meditation: A literature review. *Perceptual and Motor Skills 57*(1), 64–66.

Descartes, R. (1641/2008). *Meditations on first philosophy: With selections from the objections and replies* (M. Moriarty, Trans.). Oxford: Oxford University Press.

Du Pre, G. (1993). Science and the skandhas. In B. P. Kirthisinghe (Ed.), *Buddhism and science* (pp. 119–127). Delhi: Motilal Banarsidass Publisher.

Ekman, P. (1999). Basic emotions. In T. Dalgleish & T. Power (Eds.), *The handbook of cognition and emotion* (pp. 45–60). Sussex, UK: John Wiley & Sons, Ltd.

Epstein, M. (1988). The deconstruction of the self: Ego and "egolessness" in Buddhist insight meditation. *Journal of Transpersonal Psychology 20*(1), 61–69.

Etkin, A., Egner, T., & Kalisch, R. (2011). Emotional processing in anterior cingulate and medial prefrontal cortex. *Trends in Cognitive Sciences 15*(2), 85–93. doi:10.1016/j.tics.2010.11.004

Fell, J. (2004). Identifying neural correlates of consciousness: The state space approach. *Consciousness and Cognition 13*(4), 709–729. doi:10.1016/j.concog.2004.07.001

Finucane, A., & Mercer, S. W. (2006). An exploratory mixed methods study of the acceptability and effectiveness of mindfulness-based cognitive therapy for patients with active depression and anxiety in primary care. *BMC Psychiatry 6*(1), 14. doi:10.1186/1471-244x-6-14

Fox, K. C. R., Nijeboer, S., Dixon, M. L., Floman, J. L., Ellamil, M., Rumak, S. P., … Christoff, K. (2014). Is meditation associated with altered brain structure? A systematic review and meta-analysis of morphometric neuroimaging in meditation practitioners. *Neuroscience & Biobehavioral Reviews 43*, 48–73. doi:10.1016/j.neubiorev.2014.03.016

Fredrickson, B. L., Cohn, M. A., Coffey, K. A., Pek, J., & Finkel, S. M. (2008). Open hearts build lives: Positive emotions, induced through loving-kindness meditation, build consequential personal resources. *Journal of Personality and Social Psychology 95*(5), 1045–1062. doi:10.1037/a0013262

Fresco, D. M., Moore, M. T., van Dulmen, M. H. M., Segal, Z. V., Ma, S. H., Teasdale, J. D., & Williams, J. M. G. (2007). Initial psychometric properties of the experiences questionnaire: Validation of a self-report measure of decentering. *Behavior Therapy 38*(3), 234–246. doi:10.1016/j.beth.2006.08.003

Galante, J., Bekkers, M.-J., Mitchell, C., & Gallacher, J. (2016). Loving-kindness meditation effects on well-being and altruism: A mixed-methods online RCT. *Applied Psychology: Health and Well-Being 8*(3), 322–350. doi:10.1111/aphw.12074

Galante, J., Galante, I., Bekkers, M.-J., & Gallacher, J. (2014). Effect of kindness-based meditation on health and well-being: A systematic review and meta-analysis. *Journal of Consulting and Clinical Psychology 82*(6), 1101–1114. doi:10.1037/a0037249

Garber, C. E., Blissmer, B., Deschenes, M. R., Franklin, B., Lamonte, M. J., Lee, I.-M., . . . Swain, D. P. (2011). American College of Sports Medicine position stand. Quantity and quality of exercise for developing and maintaining cardiorespiratory, musculoskeletal, and neuromotor fitness in apparently healthy adults: Guidance for prescribing exercise. *Medicine and Science in Sports and Exercise 43*(7), 1334–1359.

Garland, E. L., Gaylord, S. A., Boettiger, C. A., & Howard, M. O. (2010). Mindfulness training modifies cognitive, affective, and physiological mechanisms implicated in alcohol dependence: Results of a randomized controlled pilot trial. *Journal of Psychoactive Drugs 42*(2), 177–192. doi:10.1080/02791072.2010.10400690

Giustarini, G. (2012). The role of fear (bhaya) in the Nikāyas and in the Abhidhamma. *Journal of Indian Philosophy 40*(5), 511–531.

Goleman, D. (1988). *The meditative mind: The varieties of meditative experience*. New York: Tarcher.

Gyatso, T. (2006). Science at the crossroads. *EXPLORE: The Journal of Science and Healing 2*(2), 97–99.

Hammitzsch, H. (1979). *Zen in the art of the tea ceremony* (P. Lemesurier, Trans.). New York: Arkana.

Harré, R. (1986). *The social construction of emotions*. Oxford: Basil Blackwell.

Harvey, W. Z. (2009). Grace or loving-kindness. In A. A. Cohen & P. Mendes-Flohr (Eds.), *20th century Jewish religious thought* (pp. 299–303). Philadelphia: Jewish Publication Society.

Herring, M. P., O'Connor, P. J., & Dishman, R. K. (2010). The effect of exercise training on anxiety symptoms among patients: A systematic review. *Archives of Internal Medicine 170*(4), 321–331.

Hoffman, B. M., Babyak, M. A., Craighead, W. E., Sherwood, A., Doraiswamy, P. M., Coons, M. J., & Blumenthal, J. A. (2011). Exercise and pharmacotherapy in patients with major depression: One-year follow-up of the SMILE study. *Psychosomatic Medicine 73*(2), 127–133.

Hofmann, S. G., Grossman, P., & Hinton, D. E. (2011). Loving-kindness and compassion meditation: Potential for psychological interventions. *Clinical Psychology Review 31*(7), 1126–1132. doi:10.1016/j.cpr.2011.07.003

Holm, O., Greaker, E., & Strömberg, A. (2002). Experiences of longing in Norwegian and Swedish 4- and 5-year-old children. *The Journal of Psychology, 136*(6), 608-612. doi:10.1080/00223980209604822

Hyams, J. (2010). *Zen in the martial arts*. New York: Bantam.

Jackson, F. (1982). Epiphenomenal qualia. *The Philosophical Quarterly 32*(127), 127–136.

Jazaieri, H., Jinpa, G. T., McGonigal, K., Rosenberg, E. L., Finkelstein, J., Simon-Thomas, E., . . . Goldin, P. R. (2013). Enhancing compassion: A randomized controlled trial of a compassion cultivation training program. *Journal of Happiness Studies 14*(4), 1113–1126.

Kabat-Zinn, J. (1982). An outpatient program in behavioral medicine for chronic pain patients based on the practice of mindfulness meditation: Theoretical considerations and preliminary results. *General Hospital Psychiatry 4*(1), 33–47. doi:10.1016/0163-8343(82)90026-3

Kabat-Zinn, J. (2003). Mindfulness-based interventions in context: Past, present, and future. *Clinical Psychology: Science and Practice 10*(2), 144–156. doi:10.1093/clipsy.bpg016

Kang, C. (2009). Buddhist and Tantric perspectives on causality and society. *Journal of Buddhist Ethics 16*, 69–103.

Kaplan, A. (1989). *Meditation and Kabbalah*. Boston: Weiser Books.

Keltner, D., & Haidt, J. (2003). Approaching awe, a moral, spiritual, and aesthetic emotion. *Cognition & Emotion 17*(2), 297–314.

Kierkegaard, S. (1843). *Fear and trembling and the sickness unto death* (M. Lowrie, Trans.). Princeton, NJ: Princeton University Press.

Kleinginna, P. R., & Kleinginna, A. M. (1981). A categorized list of emotion definitions, with suggestions for a consensual definition. *Motivation and Emotion 5*(4), 345–379.

Lao, S.-A., Kissane, D., & Meadows, G. (2016). Cognitive effects of MBSR/MBCT: A systematic review of neuropsychological outcomes. *Consciousness and Cognition 45*, 109–123. doi:10.1016/j.concog.2016.08.017

Larsen, J. T., Hemenover, S. H., Norris, C. J., & Cacioppo, J. T. (2003). Turning adversity to advantage: On the virtues of the coactivation of positive and negative emotions. In L. G. Aspinwall & U. M. Staudinger (Eds.), *A psychology of human strengths* (pp. 211–225). Washington, DC: American Psychological Association.

Lazar, S. W., Bush, G., Gollub, R. L., Fricchione, G. L., Khalsa, G., & Benson, H. (2000). Functional brain mapping of the relaxation response and meditation. *NeuroReport 11*(7), 1581–1585.

Lee, Y.-C., Lin, Y.-C., Huang, C.-L., & Fredrickson, B. L. (2013). The construct and measurement of peace of mind. *Journal of Happiness Studies 14*(2), 571–590. doi:10.1007/s10902-012-9343-5

Lomas, T. (2015). Self-transcendence through shared suffering: A transpersonal theory of compassion. *Journal of Transpersonal Psychology 27*(2), 168–187.

Lomas, T. (2016). The art of second wave positive psychology: Harnessing Zen aesthetics to explore the dialectics of flourishing. *International Journal of Wellbeing 6*(2), 14–29. doi:10.5502/ijw.v6i2.2

Lomas, T. (2017). Recontextualising mindfulness: Theravada Buddhist perspectives on the ethical and spiritual dimensions of awareness. *Psychology of Religion and Spirituality 9*(2), 209–219. doi:10.1037/rel0000080

Lomas, T. (2018a). The flavours of love: A cross-cultural lexical analysis. *Journal for the Theory of Social Behaviour 48*(1), 134–152. doi:10.1111/jtsb.12158

Lomas, T. (2018b). The value of ambivalent emotions: A cross-cultural lexical analysis. *Qualitative Research in Psychology*. doi:10.1080/14780887.2017.1400143

Lomas, T. (2019). The dynamics of spirituality: A cross-cultural lexical analysis. *Psychology of Religion and Spirituality, 11*(2), 131-140. doi:10.1037/rel0000163

Lomas, T., Cartwright, T., Edginton, T., & Ridge, D. (2014). A religion of wellbeing? The appeal of Buddhism to men in London, UK. *Psychology of Religion and Spirituality 6*(3), 198–207. doi:10.1037/a0036420

Lomas, T., Cartwright, T., Edginton, T., & Ridge, D. (2015). A qualitative analysis of experiential challenges associated with meditation practice. *Mindfulness 6*(4), 848–860. doi:10.1007/s12671-014-0329-8

Lomas, T., Cartwright, T., Edginton, T., & Ridge, D. (2016). New ways of being a man: "Positive" hegemonic masculinity in meditation-based communities of practice. *Men and Masculinities* *19*(3), 289–310. doi:10.1177/1097184X15578531

Lomas, T., Etcoff, N., Gordon, W. V., & Shonin, E. (2017). Zen and the art of living mindfully: The health-enhancing potential of Zen aesthetics. *Journal of Religion and Health* *56*(5), 1720–1739. doi:10.1007/s10943-017-0446-5

Lomas, T., & Ivtzan, I. (2016). Second wave positive psychology: Exploring the positive-negative dialectics of wellbeing. *Journal of Happiness Studies* *17*(4), 1753–1768. doi:10.1007/s10902-015-9668-y

Lomas, T., Ivtzan, I., & Fu, C. (2015). A systematic review of the neurophysiology of mindfulness on EEG oscillations. *Neuroscience & Biobehavioral Reviews* *57*, 401–410. doi:10.1016/j.neubiorev.2015.09.018

Lutz, A., Brefczynski-Lewis, J., Johnstone, T., & Davidson, R. J. (2008). Regulation of the neural circuitry of emotion by compassion meditation: Effects of meditative expertise. *PLoS One* *3*(3), e1897.

Lutz, A., Slagter, H. A., Dunne, J. D., & Davidson, R. J. (2008). Attention regulation and monitoring in meditation. *Trends in Cognitive Sciences* *12*(4), 163–169. doi:10.1016/j.tics.2008.01.005

Mikulas WL (1990) Mindfulness, self-control, and personal growth. In M. G. T. Kwee (Ed.), Psychotherapy, Meditation, and Health. London: East-West Publications, pp. 151–164.

Mulligan, K., & Scherer, K. R. (2012). Toward a working definition of emotion. *Emotion Review* *4*(4), 345–357.

Nagel, T. (1974). What is it like to be a bat? *The Philosophical Review* *83*(4), 435–450.

Neff, K. D. (2003). Self-compassion: An alternative conceptualization of a healthy attitude toward oneself. *Self and Identity* *2*(2), 85–101. doi:10.1080/15298860309032

Nisbett, R. E., Peng, K., Choi, I., & Norenzayan, A. (2001). Culture and systems of thought: Holistic versus analytic cognition. *Psychological Review, 108*(2), 291–310. doi:10.1037/0033-295X.108.2.291

Ozawa-de Silva, B., & Negi, L. T. (2013). Cognitively-based compassion training: Protocol and key concepts. *Compassion: Bridging Theory and Practice*, 416–437.

Pagliaro, G., Pandolfi, P., Collina, N., Frezza, G., Brandes, A., Galli, M.,... Marconi, L. (2016). A randomized controlled trial of tong len meditation practice in cancer patients: Evaluation of a distant psychological healing effect. *EXPLORE: The Journal of Science and Healing* *12*(1), 42–49. doi:10.1016/j.explore.2015.10.001

Panpothong, N., & Phakdeephasook, S. (2014). The wide use of mai-pen-rai "It's not substantial" in Thai interactions and its relationship to the Buddhist concept of Tri Laksana. *Journal of Pragmatics* *69*, 99–107. doi:10.1016/j.pragma.2012.03.006

Papageorgiou, C., & Wells, A. (2003). An empirical test of a clinical metacognitive model of rumination and depression. *Cognitive Therapy and Research* *27*(3), 261–273. doi:10.1023/A:1023962332399

Posner, J., Russell, J. A., & Peterson, B. S. (2005). The circumplex model of affect: An integrative approach to affective neuroscience, cognitive development, and psychopathology. *Development and Psychopathology* *17*(3), 715–734. doi:10.1017/S0954579405050340

Price, J. (2010). *Sacred scriptures of the world religions: An introduction*. New York: Continuum Books.

Prusinski, L. (2013). Wabi-sabi, mono no aware, and ma: Tracing traditional Japanese aesthetics through Japanese history. *Studies on Asia* *2*(1), 21–45.

Quilty, M. T., Saper, R. B., Goldstein, R., & Khalsa, S. B. S. (2013). Yoga in the real world: Perceptions, motivators, barriers, and patterns of use. *Global Advances in Health and Medicine* 2(1), 44–49.

Raffone, A., & Srinivasan, N. (2010). The exploration of meditation in the neuroscience of attention and consciousness. *Cognitive Processing* 11(1), 1–7. doi:10.1007/s10339-009-0354-z

Rao, N., & Kemper, K. J. (2016). Online training in specific meditation practices improves gratitude, well-being, self-compassion, and confidence in providing compassionate care among health professionals. *Evidence-Based Complementary and Alternative Medicine* 22(2), 237–241. doi:10.1177/2156587216642102

Reed, J., & Ones, D. S. (2006). The effect of acute aerobic exercise on positive activated affect: A meta-analysis. *Psychology of Sport and Exercise* 7(5), 477–514. doi:10.1016/j.psychsport.2005.11.003

Reisenzein, R. (2007). What is a definition of emotion? And are emotions mental-behavioral processes? *Social Science Information* 46(3), 424–428.

Richards, G. (1978). Śūnyatā: objective referent or via negativa? *Religious Studies* 14(2), 251–260.

Ross, A. P. (2006). *Recalling the hope of glory: Biblical worship from the Garden to the New Creation*. Grand Rapids, MI: Kregel Academic.

Ruchelli, G., Chapin, H., Darnall, B., Seppala, E., Doty, J., & Mackey, S. (2014). Compassion meditation training for people living with chronic pain and their significant others: A pilot study and mixed-methods analysis. *Journal of Pain* 15(4), S117.

Russell, J. A. (1980). A circumplex model of affect. *Journal of Personality and Social Psychology* 39, 1161–1178.

Said, E. W. (1995). *Orientalism: Western conceptions of the Orient*. London: Penguin.

Scherer, K. R. (2001). Appraisal considered as a process of multilevel sequential checking. In K. R. Scherer, A. Schorr, & T. Johnstone (Eds.), *Appraisal processes in emotion: Theory, methods, research* (pp. 92–120). New York: Oxford University Press.

Segal, Z. V., Williams, J. M. G., & Teasdale, J. D. (2002). *Mindfulness-based cognitive therapy for depression: A new approach to preventing relapse*. New York: Guilford Press.

Shapiro, S. L., & Carlson, L. E. (2009). *The art and science of mindfulness: Integrating mindfulness into psychology and the helping professions*. Washington, DC: American Psychological Association.

Shapiro, S. L., Carlson, L. E., Astin, J. A., & Freedman, B. (2006). Mechanisms of mindfulness. *Journal of Clinical Psychology* 62(3), 373–386. doi:10.1002/jclp.20237

Shonin, E., Van Gordon, W., Compare, A., Zangeneh, M., & Griffiths, M. D. (2015). Buddhist-derived loving-kindness and compassion meditation for the treatment of psychopathology: A systematic review. *Mindfulness* 6(5), 1161–1180.

Stell, A. J., & Farsides, T. (2016). Brief loving-kindness meditation reduces racial bias, mediated by positive other-regarding emotions. *Motivation and Emotion* 40(1), 140–147. doi:10.1007/s11031-015-9514-x

Suzuki, D. T. (1959/1973). *Zen and Japanese culture*. Princeton, NJ: Princeton University Press.

Suzuki, D. T. (2011). *Zen koan as a means of attaining enlightenment*. Vermont: Tuttle Publishing.

Teasdale, J. D. (1999). Metacognition, mindfulness and the modification of mood disorders. *Clinical Psychology & Psychotherapy* 6(2), 146–155.

Travis, F., & Shear, J. (2010). Focused attention, open monitoring and automatic self-transcending: Categories to organize meditations from Vedic, Buddhist and Chinese traditions. *Conscious Cognition* 19(4), 1110–1118. doi:10.1016/j.concog.2010.01.007

Tyler, R. (Trans.) (2012). *The tale of the Heike*. London: Penguin.

Vessantara. (2002). *Meeting the Buddhas: A Guide to Buddhas, Bodhisattvas, and Tantric Deities*. Birmingham: Windhorse Publications.

Walsh, R., & Shapiro, S. L. (2006). The meeting of meditative disciplines and western psychology: A mutually enriching dialogue. *American Psychologist 61*(3), 227–239. doi:10.1037/0003-066X.61.3.227

Wang, C., Bannuru, R., Ramel, J., Kupelnick, B., Scott, T., & Schmid, C. H. (2010). Tai Chi on psychological well-being: Systematic review and meta-analysis. *BMC complementary and alternative medicine 10*(1), 1.

Watts, A. W. (1957). *The way of Zen*. London: Penguin Books.

Wayman, A. (2013). *The Buddhist Tantras: Light on Indo-Tibetan esotericism*. London: Routledge.

Weibel, D. T., McClintock, A. S., & Anderson, T. (2017). Does loving-kindness meditation reduce anxiety? Results from a randomized controlled trial. *Mindfulness 8*(3), 565–571. doi:10.1007/s12671-016-0630-9

Woolfolk, R. L. (2002). The power of negative thinking: Truth, melancholia, and the tragic sense of life. *Journal of Theoretical and Philosophical Psychology 22*(1), 19–27. doi:10.1037/h0091192

CHAPTER 22

INDIVIDUAL DIFFERENCES IN MEDITATION OUTCOMES

IVANA BURIC, INTI BRAZIL, AND VALERIE VAN MULUKOM

Introduction

Over the past five decades, hundreds of scientific studies have accumulated evidence highlighting the positive effects of meditation (for a review see Goyal et al., 2014; Sedlmeier et al., 2012). As a consequence, meditation has gained popularity and is increasingly used as a tool to cultivate health, happiness, and general well-being. However, little attention has been paid to individual differences in responses to mediation.

As with any other kind of intervention, there is a spectrum of possible responses to meditation, from extremely positive responses at one end to adverse effects at the other. However, it is not clear what factors (e.g., personality traits) cause variation in response to meditation. By calculating the average of the responses, variation in how individual participants are affected by meditation is masked. In each study, there will be individuals who respond to meditation better or worse than the average of a group. Therefore, the individual scores illustrate the variability in responses to meditation, while the average group score masks the fact that for some people a certain meditation program was extremely beneficial, while for others it may not have been beneficial, or may even have been detrimental. Surprisingly, there is no comprehensive study on this topic and only a limited number of studies have directly tested individual differences in responsiveness to meditation. To elucidate the relationship between differences in participant characteristics and meditation outcomes, we need to identify the predictors, moderators, interactions, and correlates of the effects of meditation.

As we do not know what kind of people experience adverse effects or simply show no effects following meditation interventions, we cannot predict or improve people's responses to meditation. In other areas of health-related research, there is a shift occurring in which choices for treatment and diagnosis are tailored to the genetic, biological, and cognitive characteristics of people (Cuthbert & Insel, 2013; Insel, 2014; Jackson & Chester, 2015). For instance, the treatment for many types of cancer is no longer based on the tissue type or anatomical site of origin; instead, the analysis of biomarkers can predict what treatment will be optimal (Jackson & Chester, 2015). The notion that there should be individualized treatment based on patient characteristics is often called "precision medicine" or personalized medicine. The central idea is to create new knowledge that can aid in selecting treatments that will work best for a certain person, unlike most current treatments that are designed based on the one-size-fits-all principle and benefit some individuals, while others show no improvements or even have adverse responses. The same personalized approach could be applied in meditation but, in order to get there, many years of rigorous scientific work are required to understand many participant-related factors that could influence the response to meditation. The current goal is not to provide clinical suggestions at this early stage, but rather to lay groundwork that can foster continual developments in research and inform future strategies for personalized applications of meditation. If we would be able to distinguish positive responders from null and negative responders based on their individual characteristics, then those who would benefit the most could be targeted, while a different evidence-based technique could be applied to those for whom meditation would be contra-indicated. This personalized approach would not only save resources, but also help prevent harm.

The main goal of this chapter is to examine possible sources of individual differences in the current literature and discuss the factors that have been shown to have an impact on the effects of different types of meditation. The central focus is on twenty-six intervention studies obtained through PubMed search, a well-known biomedical publication archive, that explored the effects of learning meditation on people who previously had no experience in meditation. We also consider relevant meta-analyses in addition to controlled and non-controlled interventional studies. We cover four sources of variability in individual responses to meditation that were previously identified in meditation research: (i) psychological variables; (ii) biological variables; (iii) illness severity; and (iv) demographics.

Individual Differences Due to Psychological Variables

The majority of studies that have explored individual differences in responsiveness to meditation have focused on psychological variables. These studies used standardized psychological measures—most commonly questionnaires—through which data can be obtained quickly and efficiently. Out of many possible psychological factors that could have an impact upon the effects of meditation training, personality, stress, and mood are the most researched sources of inter-individual differences.

Stable Psychological Factors

The "Big Five"

Personality traits are linked to characteristic patterns of behavior and, as such, have been a major area of interest in psychology. Personality used to be considered as stable over time and fixed after the age of thirty (McCrae & Costa, 1994), while more recently it has become accepted that personality changes across lifespan (Roberts, Walton & Viechtbauer, 2006). It has been proposed that meditation is also one of the environmental factors that can help shape personality in later life (Crescentini & Capurso, 2015). In psychology, personality is commonly described using the Big Five model that divides personality into five dimensions: extraversion, neuroticism, conscientiousness, agreeableness, and openness to experience (John & Srivastava, 1999).

It is plausible to assume that individuals high in certain personality traits, such as openness to experience, might be more inclined to try meditation. However, it is not clear how different constellations of personality traits are related to how people respond to meditation. Most studies on the topic have focused on individual personality traits, rather than using a holistic person-centered approach that captures the pattern of relationships with multiple traits. For instance, Lane, Seskevich, and Pieper (2007) showed that participants scoring high on neuroticism experienced particularly pronounced effects of reduced perceived stress and less negative emotions after three months of mantra-based meditation practice. However, this study did not explore any other personality trait besides neuroticism. Similar results were found in a study of Mindfulness-Based Stress Reduction (MBSR) in students, which showed that those who scored high on neuroticism benefited more from MBSR than others (de Vibe et al., 2015). Individuals scoring high on neuroticism reported lower levels of mental distress and higher levels of subjective well-being as a result of the training. Notably, this study also explored if conscientiousness and extraversion moderated the response to MBSR, and found that, indeed, students who scored higher on conscientiousness experienced the greatest effect of the intervention on reducing study-related stress, but there were no effects of extraversion (de Vibe et al., 2015). A study of an integrative body-mind raining (IBMT), which is based on mindfulness, compared a one-week IBMT to an equally long relaxation program in terms of improving creativity (Ding, Tang, Deng, Tang, & Posner, 2015). This study showed that creativity improved after the IBMT training, and while the control group (who completed the relaxation training) also improved on creativity, the IBMT group outperformed them significantly. With regard to individual differences in personality, they found that psychoticism did not influence creative performance after IBMT or after relaxation. Furthermore, introversion was associated with a greater increase in creativity after the trainings in both groups, while neuroticism was associated with increases only in the meditation group. Ding and colleagues (2015) interpreted these results as an indication that introverted individuals are overall readier to engage in meditation and relaxation programs. This interpretation is in conflict with the findings of Delmonte (1988), who found that introverted outpatients with psychosomatic and neurotic symptoms were less likely to continue practicing Transcendental Meditation (TM) regularly three, six, twelve, and twenty-four months after learning the technique, suggesting they may be less likely to reap the long-term benefits of meditation. One possibility is that introverts respond more favorably to mindfulness-based programs such as IBMT than to those that are mantra based such as TM. Another explanation is that introverts may show more engagement only during the first eight weeks of learning meditation, which is the length of the IBMT program, and Ding and colleagues' (2015) study did not track long-term effects. Delmonte's (1988) study additionally looked at neuroticism, repression (i.e., being prone to extreme avoidance strategies such as denial), suggestibility, and locus of control (i.e., believing that events in one's own life are under personal control as opposed to external forces that are beyond control). Other than introverts, participants who scored low on repression were also less likely to practice meditation regularly at all follow-ups. Participants who scored high on neuroticism and suggestibility were less likely to practice meditation regularly at three-month follow-up only, whereas no effect was found for locus of control at any follow-up. Further understanding of neuroticism and the response to meditation can stem from examining discomfort with emotions, which is present in people who score high in neuroticism (Bono & Vey, 2007). Distressed adults who reported more discomfort with emotion before a mindfulness intervention had less reduction in distress following the intervention (Sass, Berenbaum, & Abrams, 2013). This was interpreted as them avoiding the exploration of current emotional experiences, which is an important part of mindfulness practice.

Individual differences in trait anxiety, which conceptually largely overlaps with neuroticism (Jorm, 1989), have also been a prominent topic of investigation in meditation research. However, it is important to distinguish trait anxiety/neuroticism from anxiety disorders; trait anxiety is a risk factor for developing anxiety disorders. Both seem to be linked to the effects of meditation, but there are some conflicting findings. An early meta-analysis showed that practicing different types of meditation and relaxation techniques can reduce levels of trait anxiety, and TM reduces trait anxiety the most (Eppley, Abrams, & Shear, 1989). A more recent meta-analysis of sixteen randomized controlled trials of TM tested if baseline trait anxiety was reduced following meditation (Orme-Johnson & Barnes, 2014). It was found that the improvements were the largest for people with high trait anxiety levels (80th to 100th percentile), who responded better to TM than to mindfulness-based therapy. When baseline anxiety is within the normal range, then TM and mindfulness-based intervention appear to be equally effective in reducing anxiety. However, it is not known if these participants had symptoms of anxiety that satisfied the criteria for anxiety disorders.

Two other meta-analyses of studies involving participants diagnosed with anxiety disorders who attended mindfulness-based interventions have found conflicting results. One of these meta-analyses found that following meditation, anxiety was reduced in people with anxiety disorders just as strongly as depression was reduced in those with mood disorders (Hofmann, Sawyer, Witt, & Oh, 2010). The other meta-analysis found that mindfulness interventions are not helpful for individuals with a current episode of anxiety disorder, but they seem to help those with a current episode of depression (Strauss, Cavanagh, Oliver, & Pettman, 2014). Differences between the results of these meta-analyses are likely due to the fact that one only included studies where participants were randomly allocated to groups and that had a control group (Strauss, Cavanagh, Oliver & Pettman, 2014), whereas the other also included pre-post designs, and included (for more than half of the eligible studies) studies without a control group (Hofmann et al., 2010).

In summary, most of the studies that explored how personality relates to meditation response are related to the Big Five personality model, especially to neuroticism and anxiety. People who score high in neuroticism or trait anxiety seem to respond better to meditation, unless they are currently experiencing an episode of anxiety disorder. Conscientious people also seem to respond better, but it is currently unknown if this is only because they are consistent with their practice. The findings for extraversion are mixed; it seems to be associated with the frequency of meditation practice, but not with any other meditation outcomes. However, these conclusions are based on just a handful of studies, and not all of them had a control group or used the same type of meditation or population. Thus, there is still a need for more studies targeting the link between personality and meditation response.

Other Personality Factors

While most of the studies discussed so far were embedded in the Big Five model of personality, others have focused on alternative factors that influence personality. One such factor is *temperament*, which has been defined as "early emerging basic dispositions in the domains of activity, affectivity, attention, and self-regulation, and these dispositions are the product of complex interactions among genetic, biological, and environmental factors across time" (Shiner, Buss, McClowry, Putnam, Saudino, & Zentner, 2012, p. 2). There is a general agreement that temperament remains more stable over the lifespan than personality, and that it is evident from birth because it seems to have detectable biological correlates (Kagan, 2005).

Takahashi and colleagues (2005) explored the effects of temperament on brain activity and heart-rate variability during Zen meditation (based on counting exhales) in people who had never meditated. This study employed a psychobiological model of temperament that regards novelty seeking, harm avoidance, reward dependence, and persistence as components of temperament (Cloninger, Svrakic & Brzybek, 1993). While participants were meditating, the researchers recorded brain activity through electroencephalography (EEG) and assessed heart rate variability. During Zen meditation, individuals with high levels of harm avoidance showed larger changes in power in oscillatory brain activity that range from 4 to 7 Hz, which has been associated with being mindful (e.g., Baijal & Srinivasa, 2010). Individuals with high levels of novelty seeking had larger changes in EEG power in frequencies that range from 10 to 12 Hz, which is associated with top-down attention (Klimesch, Doppelmayr, Russegger, Pachinger, & Schwaiger, 1998). Novelty seeking was also negatively related to changes in heart rate variability, indicating deactivation of sympathetic nervous system (i.e., a part of the autonomic nervous system that prepares the body for action). Taken together, the findings support the view that there is a relationship between facets of temperament, Zen meditation, and bodily changes. However, this study focused on EEG and heart rate variability, while no psychological measures of mindfulness or cognitive measures of attention were included. Thus, it is unclear whether individuals with high levels of harm avoidance were more mindful, and if those with high levels of novelty seeking actually had a better modulation of top-down attention and higher levels of relaxation.

Mindfulness itself can also be defined as a personality trait rather than a transient state measured during meditation practice (Lau et al., 2006). From this perspective, trait mindfulness is considered to reflect the extent to which a person is oriented to the present experience in their daily life and aware of their own thoughts, emotions, and bodily sensations, without judging them or trying to change them (Baer, Smith, Hopkins, Krietemeyer, & Toney, 2006). Trait mindfulness has been found to vary within populations and seems to remain relatively stable when a person has not learned how to practice mindfulness techniques (Brown & Ryan, 2003). It can be assumed that people with "naturally" higher levels of trait mindfulness respond better to mindfulness meditation, because they find it easier to achieve a meditative state, and it may be more pleasant for them. On the other hand, it is also plausible for people who start with low levels of mindfulness to have more space for progress and to be less likely to experience a ceiling effect. The former hypothesis has been confirmed in a study that found that people who score high on mindfulness before they learn how to meditate have better long-term outcomes (following meditation) in terms of increases in mindfulness, hope, empathy, and well-being, with concurrent decreases in perceived stress and rumination (Shapiro, Brown, Tohresen, & Plante, 2011). Another study found that people who are low in trait mindfulness produce more stress hormone cortisol in response to a laboratory-induced stressful situation than other participants after a three-day mindfulness intervention, even though they report perceiving less stress (Creswell, Pacilio, Lindsay, & Brown, 2014). The researchers suggested that a brief mindfulness intervention initially fosters greater coping efforts in people who are low in trait mindfulness, which in turn appears to increase cortisol and reduce stress appraisals. Another possibility is that mindfulness intervention does not actually reduce perceived stress in people who are low in trait mindfulness, but only their responses to questionnaires that measure perceived stress (i.e., this could be an example of a response bias).

Not all studies found that trait mindfulness influenced responses to meditation. Irrespective of initial levels of trait mindfulness, students gained similar benefits from MBSR in a previously mentioned study that measured well-being and distress as outcomes (de Vibe et al., 2015). Similarly, a small uncontrolled study of distressed adults who received mindfulness training found no moderating effects of trait mindfulness on distress (Sass, Berenbaum, & Abrams, 2013). Another study, by Jacobs et al. (2011), examined the influence of trait mindfulness on the response to meditation in experienced meditators. Their focus was on psychological functioning, which consisted of purpose in life, perceived ability to control one's own life, and neuroticism. After three months of intensive meditation, individuals who initially had worse psychological functioning showed the most improvement on these measures compared to other experienced meditators. This group also showed the greatest increase in telomerase activity (i.e., an enzyme associated with longevity), which suggests that meditation reduces the risk for diseases by preventing the shortening of the ends of chromosomes that commonly occurs as we age. These findings overlap with those from studies on neuroticism and anxiety and suggest that people who are initially more mentally unwell, such as the highly neurotic, anxious, and insecurely attached, benefit more from meditation.

Another personality-related construct that influences the response to meditation is attachment style. This is formed in early childhood based on the relationship with the primary caregiver and is thought to influence interpersonal relationships throughout life (Bowlby, 1982). There are considered to be four main attachment styles: secure attachment, insecure anxious-avoidant, insecure anxious-resistant, and disorganized attachment (Ainsworth, Blehar, Waters, & Wall, 2015), although the main distinction that is often made is between secure and insecure attachment. An insecure attachment style is likely to be formed in cases where the caregiver does not respond consistently to the child's needs or is unavailable (Thompson & Raikes, 2003). Attachment style has been explored in the context of MBSR, where those with insecure attachment had higher baseline stress levels, and their stress levels declined dramatically in comparison to participants with secure attachment (Cordon, Brown, & Gibson, 2009). Although insecurely attached individuals were twice as likely to drop out of meditation programs, those that completed them consequently had significantly lower levels of perceived stress than securely attached individuals (Cordon et al., 2009). This finding converges with a study showing that introverted and neurotic people were less likely to adhere to regular meditation practice (Delmonte, 1988). It may be beneficial for teachers to recognize these traits in people who attend meditation programs, so that an effort could be put in to keep them motivated to continue with meditation as these subgroups of individuals might also be more likely to experience benefits.

To summarize, other than the Big Five model of personality, there are some personality-related traits or temperaments that can influence the response to meditation, such as trait mindfulness and type of attachment. Studies suggest that each of these could potentially be a predictor of the response to meditation, but at this point there are not enough studies to draw firm conclusions about any of them specifically. More studies are needed to replicate and extend these findings because of mixed results for trait mindfulness, and in the case of attachment and temperament, respectively, only one study is available. Current inconsistencies in the literature might be due to differences in population types, meditation types, or the choice of outcome measures. Importantly, personality traits are not the only factors that cause individual variability in responses to meditation. Transient factors, such as mood and stress, also seem to have some explanatory value.

Transient Psychological Factors

Mood and Stress

Mood is one of the few transient psychological factors studied in relation to meditation. In a previously mentioned study that found a link between IBMT, personality, and creativity, the researchers also explored how initial mood influences creative performance following this meditation program (Ding et al., 2015). They found that improvement in creativity after one week of meditation was predicted by higher anger/hostile mood states, and lower depression/dejection and fatigue/inertia mood states at baseline, before starting the meditation. Moreover, mood interacted with personality factors and helped explain individual variability; mood and personality explained 57 percent of inter-individual variability in the improvement in creativity, which suggests that initial mood is an important aspect of individual differences in meditation. Another study employed a one-off ten-minute kindness-based meditation and showed that not being in a positive mood prior to meditation leads to less relaxation, less positivity toward self, and lower stress-buffering effects after meditation (i.e., the reduction in heart rate after exposure to social stressors was slower), especially among socially anxious participants (Law, 2011). In a group of cancer patients, those with a heightened negative mood at baseline benefited the most from a mindfulness program in terms of mood improvement and stress reduction, an effect that remained present even at a six-month follow-up measurement (Carlson, Ursuliak, Goodey, Angen, & Speca, 2001). Finally, one study with healthy adults found that initial mood disturbance does not influence how much people will practice compassion meditation over their six-week course, but it was not examined if the initial mood disturbance influences the response to meditation (Pace et al., 2010).

Thus, mood seems to influence the response to meditation, but it is difficult to draw a general conclusion about mood and meditation after only four studies, especially as results vary based on the type of population and assessed outcomes. Following that initial mood seems to influence how a person responds to meditation, one would predict that initial levels of stress would affect the response to meditation in a similar manner, as mood and stress normally have similar effects on behavior (e.g., binge eating, pain, or mother-child interactions). However, this appears to not be the case in response to meditation. What has been found, instead, in a study on cancer patients who underwent MBSR, is that baseline perceived stress (i.e., levels of perceived stress before MBSR training) did not influence mood or stress levels after intervention (Carlson et al., 2001). This could be due to adverse effects experienced during meditation by stressed individuals, who may then lose motivation to practice frequently.

Based on the currently available studies, it seems that initial mood largely influences the response to meditation, while initial stress levels do not have a predictive value. However, it is possible that stress, together with mood, can influence the response to meditation indirectly; when a person is deciding whether to try meditation, current mood and stress may contribute to the generation of expectations. It is well established in health psychology that expectations about outcomes of different kinds of rehabilitations programs influence the recovery, although the underlying mechanisms are not fully understood (Mondloch, Cole, & Frank, 2001). In the next section, we will explore if positive expectations about meditation can influence the response to meditation and lead to more benefits.

Expectations and Emotions

The possible impact that expectations may have on meditation outcomes is a topic that has been neglected in meditation research. One exception is Delmonte (1981, 1985, 1988) who conducted a set of meditation studies showing that positive expectations affect regularity of practice and reported benefits. Furthermore, he showed that expectations concerning the effects of meditation were not stable but varied over time with experience. Positive expectations at baseline were predictive only of practice frequency at a one-month follow-up, but not of long-term practice frequency (Delmonte, 1981). Generally, those who ended up practicing more frequently had reported higher expectations about the positive effects of meditation at baseline. In a later study, Delmonte (1985) manipulated expectations in naïve meditators by presenting meditation as either beneficial or non-beneficial before they began a meditation course. This study demonstrated that fostering positive expectations led to better physiological outcomes, such as lower blood pressure, lower heart rate, and lower skin conductance level. However, none of Delmonte's studies included a control group, and, therefore, it cannot be ruled out that expectations could have had the same physiological effect in a non-meditation intervention. To account for this, Creswell et al. (2014) controlled for the possibility that merely having positive expectations about the outcomes of mindfulness led to perceiving more benefits in its practice. Briefly, in this study, half of the participants were randomly assigned to a brief three-day poem-analysis course, and the other half to a mindfulness course of the same length. Positive expectations about efficacy and relevance of both a poem analysis and a mindfulness course were measured. During the first two days, participants in both groups had equally positive expectations that the courses were improving their cognition. On the third day however, the mindfulness group had significantly more positive expectations than the poem-analysis group, demonstrating the need to take fluctuations of expectations into account in the analyses.

In addition to individual differences in expectations, emotions may be another psychological variable that may have an influence on the effects of meditation. More specifically, emotions experienced during meditation training can predict long-term continuation of meditation practice. In Cohn and Fredrickson's (2010) study, positive emotions (amusement, awe, contentment, gratitude, hope, joy, interest, love) and negative emotions (anger, contempt, disgust, embarrassment, guilt, sadness, shame, fear) were recorded daily during eight weeks of loving-kindness meditation training. Participants who experienced a greater amount of positive emotions during the first few weeks of training were more likely to meditate at a one-year follow-up. Even though other participants practiced just as much during the training, if they did not have an increase in positive emotions before the fifth week, they were less likely to maintain a long-term meditation practice. Interestingly, at baseline, people who became long-term meditators were no different from those who did not continue to practice meditation after the training, in terms of demographic variables, measures of mindfulness, well-being, hope, ego-resilience, savoring, self-other overlap, or symptoms of illness and life satisfaction. The only difference between those who continued to practice meditation and those who did not—aside from early positive emotions—was that continuing meditators gave and received more social support. However, it should be noted in cases like this where there are multiple comparisons (i.e., ten variables were tested as potential differences between meditators and non-meditators), the probability of getting a false positive result is increased. Therefore, the result regarding the influence of social support on continuation of meditation practice might have occurred by chance, which can only be confirmed if future studies attempt to replicate the results. The only other study that explored the effects of emotions was done in individuals with hypertension, and it was found that the greatest reduction in blood pressure was in people who found the practice easy and reported feeling better during meditation, and fresher and more relaxed after the practice (Seer & Raeburn, 1980).

In summary, the evidence suggests that both expectations and experienced emotions account for some of the individual differences in response to meditation. Beginning to learn and practice meditation while having positive expectations leads to more experienced benefits of meditation. Similarly, experiencing positive emotions during and after meditation appears to be important in maintaining long-term practice. The underlying mechanisms are not understood. It is possible that positive expectations foster positive emotions during meditation, although this has not been tested directly. It is crucial that researchers continue to obtain baseline measures in order to better understand the complex dynamics of the interactions between psychological variables and meditation.

Individual Differences Due to Biological Variables

Many have suggested that meditation, as well other mind-body interventions such as yoga or Tai chi, should be associated with changes that extend beyond psychology (Black & Slavich, 2016; Bower & Irwin, 2016; Buric, Farias, Jong, Mee, & Brazil, 2017). This notion that meditation impacts our biology is receiving an increasing amount of attention. Several studies have explored the possibility that a blood test or a brain scan could help to assign a person to the most suitable type of meditation (Jung et al., 2012; Mascaro, Riling, Negi, & Raison, 2013). The core tenet here is that, while employing this approach in practice would be expensive, if it works, it would be more objective than self-report measures commonly used in psychology research.

As our biology is constantly changing in response to the environment, the simplest method to explore whom meditation would benefit the most would be to examine the structure of our genes, which never changes. The only study that explored the relationship between genes and responsiveness to meditation compared experienced meditators with non-meditators of similar demographic characteristics (Jung et al., 2012). The meditation they investigated is called Brain Wave Vibration and includes repetitive movements and a focus on bodily sensations. This study analyzed two genes: brain-derived neurotrophic factor (BDNF), which is associated with neuroplasticity and dopamine regulation; and catechol O-methyl transferase (COMT), which is associated with regulation of dopamine, norepinephrine, and epinephrine. Surprisingly, experienced meditators who had a certain variant of the BDNF gene (Val66Val) showed the same levels of perceived stress levels as non-meditators with the same gene variant. This implies that people with BDNF Val66Val gene polymorphism may not respond to meditation, at least not in terms of stress reduction. On the other hand, meditators with the COMT Val158Val gene variant had lower plasma norepinephrine levels than meditators with the COMT Val158Met or COMT Met158Met variants. This finding suggests that among people with the same amount of meditation experience, there will be differences in how their bodies respond to stress biologically—those with COMT Val158Val will produce lower levels of hormones associated with stress response. Moreover, experienced meditators with the COMT Met158Met gene variant had even higher norepinephrine levels relative to non-meditators with the same gene variant, which suggests that this gene variant provides a disadvantage, because even if you meditate regularly your stress response will not be any better than that of people with other variants of the COMT gene who have never meditated before.

One must take care when considering these results and other studies on genetic variants. First, this study based its conclusions on the analysis of gene variants in only eighty meditators and fifty-seven non-meditators, which is far from a necessary sample size in the studies of gene variants, especially if potential confounding variables are not controlled for (Moonesinghe, Khoury, Liu, & Ioannidis, 2008). Studies on genetics often require much larger sample sizes (Hong & Park, 2012), thus these findings should merely be considered exploratory or hypothesis-generating. Second, even in the case when the sample size is large enough, exploring correlations of just one or a few genes with a certain outcome does not provide a full picture as many features are coded by multiple genes. Even simple characteristics, like our height, are regulated by hundreds of genes (Wood et al., 2014). Finally, genes that we inherited do not fully determine our characteristics because every gene can change its activity in response to the environment. While the genes themselves remain unchanged, the degree to which a gene is expressed (i.e., produces its own proteins) varies over time. A gene can get completely turned off (i.e., stop producing its own proteins) and will then not have an effect on the phenotype. Thus, even if a person has inherited genetic vulnerabilities, these vulnerabilities may not be expressed. Therefore, measuring gene variants and neglecting the measurement of the activity of those genes is not a reliable method for determining the influence of genetics. Even though gene activity can be determined from blood just as easily as gene variants, it is a relatively new field, and at this point there are no studies that have explored individual differences in meditation with this approach.

There are several other biological variables that can be measured from blood samples to explore individual differences, such as interleukins. Interleukins are a set of proteins considered to be the markers of the immune system's activity. An especially relevant interleukin in this context is interleukin-6 (IL-6), which shows increased concentrations in individuals with chronic stress (Carpenter, Gawuga, Tyrka, Lee, Anderson, & Price, 2010). Also, reducing IL-6 concentration has been linked to protective effects on health (Nemeth et al., 2004). One study found that compassion meditation training decreased the levels IL-6 in response to laboratory-induced stress, but only in individuals whose practice frequency was above the median (Pace et al., 2009). However, neither baseline levels of IL-6 nor baseline levels of the hormone cortisol predicted the amount of subsequent meditation practice in this study, thus questioning the robustness of the relationship between IL-6 and meditation.

Reich et al. (2014) identified several biomarkers that can be measured in blood and predicted symptoms that were reduced the most in breast cancer patients following MBSR. More specifically, they found that reductions in gastrointestinal symptoms (dry mouth, nausea, vomiting, and lack of appetite) following MBSR could be predicted by measuring the amount of one type of white blood cells (B lymphocytes) and a protein involved in immunity against infections (interferon-γ). Moreover, psychological improvement in memory, distress, and sadness following MBSR were predicted by another type of white blood cells that fights against infection (CD4 and CD8 cells), while fatigue was predicted by a protein involved in the regulation of the immune system (interleukin IL-4) and the total amount of white blood cells. Generally, participants with increased immune activity at baseline, as measured by interleukins and interferon-γ, had fewer adverse symptoms after meditation training (Reich et al., 2014).

The biological approach to individual differences does not have to stop at the analysis of various markers from blood samples. With the advances in technology, it is now possible to get access to the brain, which provides us with an additional level of explanation for understanding individual differences in meditation outcomes. Since it is known that meditation can affect the structure of the brain and its activity (see chapter in this volume by Fox & Cahn on Meditation and the Brain), we can assume that it might be possible to predict a person's response to meditation based on the structure or activity of their brain. This hypothesis was tested in a study that aimed to determine which type of meditation a person will prefer to practice based on their baseline brain activity (Mascaro et al., 2013). In this study, participants were taught mindfulness meditation (during the first two weeks) and compassion meditation (during the last two weeks) as a part of eight-week cognitively based compassion training (CBCT). Their brain activity was recorded with fMRI before and after intervention, during two conditions: while receiving a painful electrical stimulation, and while watching another person receive a similar type of pain. It was found that frequent practice of compassion meditation during eight weeks of CBCT was related to increased activity in a part of the brain that is mainly associated with empathy while observing others in pain (i.e., anterior insula). On the other hand, frequent practice of mindfulness meditation during CBCT was related to decreased activity in a part of the brain that is mainly associated with emotions while receiving pain (i.e., left amygdala). Unexpectedly, activity in the insula and amygdala while receiving or observing pain was not correlated with self-reported empathy or pain aversion, thus it cannot be concluded that these self-reported psychological constructs predicted the preference for meditation type. Additionally, all participants reported to have practiced the mindfulness meditation technique less often than the compassion meditation technique, which points to the possibility of biased program delivery.

In summary, BDNF and COMT gene variants, at least to some degree, seem to influence the amount of stress reduction that occurs in practitioners of Brain Wave Vibration meditation (Jung et al., 2012). However, no genes were tested besides BDNF and COMT, leaving us with a very large number of candidate genes that could help explain individual differences in meditation. Moreover, Brain Wave Vibration meditation is a rare form of meditation based on repetitive head movements; it does not overlap with common and well-researched meditation programs such as Transcendental Meditation or those based on mindfulness. There are also indications that immune markers may have some predictive value, but a study that tested one of them (interleukin-6) found that it is not related to practice frequency of compassion meditation (Pace et al., 2010). Another study discovered that several immune markers measured from blood were associated with improvements in breast cancer patients after MBSR (Reich et al., 2014). Finally, some suggest that brain scans could be sufficient for predicting what type of meditation would be preferable for a given person, as a study found that amygdala and insula activity during pain experience and observation are indicative of practice frequency of mindfulness and compassion meditation (Mascaro et al., 2013). However, this belief needs to be grounded in a much larger body of empirical evidence.

While biological measures may be alluring because they are not prone to response bias like questionnaires, currently there is only a limited amount of studies on biological measures that have been related to responsiveness to meditation. Generally, collaborations between biology and psychology in meditation research are still quite rare, but the biological approach to meditation holds the promise of opening new avenues for the future. This could be particularly useful for determining the mechanisms through which meditation could influence health and well-being in heterogeneous patient populations. Next, we will briefly review the current evidence on the usefulness of meditation in such populations.

Individual Differences Due to Illness Severity

Some of the most important biological and psychological findings are suggestive that the more severe the patient's condition is, the better they respond to meditation (e.g., Seer & Raeburn, 1980, or for a meta-analysis, Piet & Hougaard, 2011). However, it is unknown whether this effect is due to the possibility that particularly troubled people may have more positive expectations about meditation in the hope of finding alleviation for their symptoms. The relationship between illness severity and responding to meditation is especially evident in people with depression. A meta-analysis found that people who have had three or more episodes of major depression responded better to mindfulness-based cognitive therapy (MBCT) than those that experienced one or two episodes (Piet & Hougaard, 2011). Another study found that MBCT works better than usual treatment or active control only in depressed individuals who were victims of childhood abuse (Williams et al., 2014). The influence of the severity of conditions on the response to meditation has been examined in a non-psychiatric context as well. For instance, individuals with longer hypertension history and higher blood pressure responded better to Transcendental Meditation (TM) than those with shorter hypertension history or lower blood pressure (Seer & Raeburn, 1980). The only two studies that did not find a relationship between illness severity and response to meditation involved cancer patients. Disease stage and disease duration were not significant predictors of responsiveness to MBSR in this study (Carlson et al., 2001). The same was seen in individuals with hypertension, whose length of hypertension history or baseline levels of blood pressure did not influence how much their blood pressure reduced after TM (Hager & Surwit, 1978). Current research does not offer explanations as to why these two studies are so different in their outcomes.

It is clearly of great importance to conduct further research into the link between individual differences, meditation, and severity of illness. This is especially relevant for patient populations, so that the most suitable meditation practices with the best outcomes become available.

Individual Differences Due to Demographic Factors

Many researchers have explored whether age, gender, or education level can account for individual differences in the responses to meditation. Just as is the case with psychological variables, the effects of demographic variables vary depending on the population targeted, meditation type, and measured outcomes. A study that examined the effects of mantra-based meditation on hypertensions found that blood pressure was reduced regardless of gender or marital status (Seer & Raeburn, 1980). Similarly, a study using a mantra-based meditation and relaxation program found that the program reduced blood pressure and that the effects did not differ due to variability in age or sex (Hager & Surwit, 1978). On the other hand, some studies have found that demographic factors do influence the response to meditation. A large-scale study consisting of almost six hundred participants who attended an eight-week mindfulness and yoga program similar to MBSR explored associations between the likelihood that a person will attend all sessions of the program and individual differences in demographic factors (Kabat-Zinn & Chapman-Waldrop, 1988). In this study, participants were divided into two categories: one cohort included people suffering from various chronic pain conditions (the pain cohort), while the other cohort included people with cardiovascular and gastrointestinal conditions, sleep or anxiety disorders, diabetes, or cancer (the stress cohort). It was found that in the pain cohort, women were more likely than men to complete the whole program, showing an effect of gender. In the stress cohort of the same study, only the level of obsessive-compulsive tendencies was a significant predictor of program completion—those with higher scores were more likely to complete the program. Age, length of pain history, medical symptoms, and other subdimensions of distress (besides the obsessive-compulsive score) were not significant predictors of completing the program, either in the pain or in the stress cohort (Kabat-Zinn & Chapman-Waldrop, 1988). In a study with cancer patients who underwent MBSR, women and highly educated individuals showed the greatest improvements in mood and perceived stress, while age had no predictive value (Carlson et al., 2001). Finally, in a study where college students learned mindfulness meditation, women had greater reductions in negative affect and greater improvements in trait mindfulness and self-compassion than men (Rojiani, Santoyo, Rahrig, Roth, & Britton, 2017).

In summary, age and level of education do not seem to influence people's responses to meditation in a consistent way. In contrast, gender does seem to be one factor for which differences have been found across studies. Note, however, that studies on how demographic factors are associated with meditation outcomes are relatively scarce. There are still other factors that need to be examined, such as ethnicity and socio-economic status, which may be explored in future studies.

Conclusions

In this chapter we have provided an overview of the current state of research concerning the potential of psychological, biological, and other factors in accounting for individual differences in the effects of meditation. The majority of studies were related to psychological individual differences that may influence responses to meditation. Psychological factors that were investigated include neuroticism, anxiety, conscientiousness, mindfulness, attachment style, mood, emotions, and expectations.

Of these, trait anxiety/neuroticism and expectations have shown consistent effects over several studies. People high in anxiety generally show more positive effects of meditation, as do people who expect positive outcomes. Important biological factors seem to be related to BDNF and COMT gene polymorphisms, and biomarkers of immune activity such as IL-6. Other than psychological and biological factors, there is some evidence that illness severity, particularly in individuals with recurrent depression and hypertension, is associated with better meditation outcomes. Finally, the findings concerning demographic factors suggest that age and level of education do not seem to have an effect on meditation outcomes, while gender does seem to have an impact.

The paucity of work in the area needs to be underlined. This review is based on twenty-six studies obtained by doing a database search using relevant keywords, and it is possible that some important studies were unintentionally missed. The heterogeneity of the outcome measures that have been used in the area also makes comparability across studies difficult. Overall caution needs to be exercised about the conclusions that can be drawn from this work.

In the majority of the studies examined in this chapter, researchers have assessed their target population using group-comparison designs (i.e., experimental group, active and passive control groups). In these cases, within-group variation has been treated as statistical nuisance: noise or error that needs to be separated from the actual effect. However, as we have seen throughout this chapter, meditation may not just show an effect at the group level, but may also have an effect on the individual level. One way of measuring individual differences (such as within-group variation) is through multilevel modeling, which also allows for the examination of condition-based or group differences (Hoffman, 2007). Such models are also known as hierarchical linear models. The central tenet of this type of modeling is that in cross-sectional studies, individuals (i.e., level-1 measurements) are nested within groups (i.e., level-2 measurements), and in longitudinal studies, measurements on given occasions (level 1) are nested within individuals (level 2). These models allow for individual variance to be taken into account as well as group variance. Moreover, individual differences in within-person variation and within-person covariation over time can be examined simultaneously (Hoffman, 2007), making this approach very useful in longitudinal setups. Several meditation studies have already used multilevel modeling to assess, for example, if the day of measurement influenced the effect of loving-kindness meditation (Carson et al., 2005), or whether the duration of meditation practice and positive emotions differed within persons and between persons (Fredrickson et al., 2017). In one study using Zen meditation, multilevel modeling revealed that individual differences had a significant effect on the meditation outcomes (Christian, Beaujean, & Wright, 2016). Thus, we recommend this statistical method for future studies investigating individual differences in meditation.

In this chapter, we have discussed meta-analyses that tested individual differences through moderator analysis or meta-regressions of meditation outcomes (e.g., Orme-Johnson & Barnes, 2014, which included sixteen studies testing if baseline anxiety influences meditation outcomes). This is because a meta-analysis uses pooled estimates of several studies, which is more precise than a single estimate obtained from an individual study. However, the results that are based on study level (i.e., group-average data) are not optimal to answer questions about individual differences, due to heterogeneity between the results of the studies. The common sources of heterogeneity across studies include differences in the participant inclusion and exclusion criteria between studies, differences in how meditation is taught, or the presence of different types of control group. Meta-regression is a technique that can be used to address such questions, but its downside is that it may not be representative of the true relationship in the data at the individual level because it is calculated using summary values from each study. For instance, imagine that a meta-analysis of sixty studies examined the effects of mindfulness on working memory, and that it has already been established that working memory capacity is affected by age. The effect of participant age on outcomes of meditation may be investigated with a meta-regression by including the mean age of the patients in each study, but this estimate would be biased because it is based on the average age of the sample included in each study, thus neglecting variability within each study. The solution to this problem is to obtain data for each participant of every included study and to use these data as a starting point instead of the group average of every study. This kind of meta-analysis is called *individual patient data meta-analysis* (Lau, Ioannidis, & Schmid, 1998; Stewart & Clarke, 1995), and it is considered to be the gold standard given its superior statistical power relative to meta-regression (Stewart & Clarke, 1995; Lambert, Sutton, Abrams, & Jones, 2002). In summary, meta-analysis can be a valuable tool when the goal is to investigate intervention effects, such as the effects of meditation on stress. However, individual patient data meta-analysis is optimal when the goal is to investigate which individual differences modify the effects of an intervention, such as when determining whether older people experience less stress reduction following meditation. Therefore, we invite researchers to conduct individual patient data meta-analysis, as the effect of participant characteristics on outcomes of meditation may otherwise not be detected.

Whilst the majority of studies discussed in this chapter investigated psychological variables, this does not necessarily mean that these factors are the most important ones or that they will have the biggest explanatory value. Also, if the impact of individual differences on meditation outcomes can be examined at multiple levels (e.g., biological and psychological), then interactions among these levels could be explored. We propose that researchers should shift their central focus from group averages to individual differences, because much of the variance that would otherwise go unnoticed (or indeed be treated as error) can be examined that way.

We would like to end with a suggestion that may be useful for meditation teachers or therapists using meditation interventions. As shown above, individual expectations help to improve meditation outcomes, which leads us to suggest the use of motivation-enhancing procedures, such as giving clear examples of the positive effects of meditation based on the available scientific literature. Similar procedures have already been applied in the context of psychotherapy. For instance, there is a stronger effect of cognitive therapy for depression when it aims to enhance people's expectations of its positive effects—this has been shown to improve retention and engagement in therapy (Constantino, Ametrano, & Greenberg, 2012). We further suggest that it would be useful to monitor individual expectations either informally through dialogue or, ideally, systematically with a questionnaire before starting the meditation teaching. One such questionnaire that can be applied in the context of meditation is the Credibility/ Expectancy Questionnaire (CEQ; Devilly & Borkovec, 2000), which only takes a few minutes to complete. The statements applied to meditation would read like this (meditation students would rate each statement from 0 to 100 percent): (1) At this point, how successful do you think this meditation course will be in raising the quality of your functioning? (2) How confident would you be in recommending this meditation course to a friend who experiences similar problems? (3) By the end of the meditation course, how much improvement in your functioning do you think will occur? (4) At this point, how much do you really feel that the meditation course will help you to improve your functioning? (5) By the end of the mediation course, how much improvement in your functioning do you really feel will occur?

These suggestions are only a starting point, as more research needs to be done in order to develop refined recommendations. Further research on this topic is valuable to meditation teachers and clinicians alike, because it could be used to adapt meditation sessions to make them more effective and reduce the risk for adverse effects. Furthermore, taking sources of individual differences into account could reduce attrition rates in clinical treatments and research projects that are testing the long-term effects of meditation. Meditation is a promising technique for both clinical and non-clinical populations, with potentially large implications for some individuals. Therefore efforts should be made to shed light on individual differences so that we may be able to more accurately predict whom meditation may benefit the most.

References

Ainsworth, M. D. S., Blehar, M. C., Waters, E., & Wall, S. N. (2015). *Patterns of attachment: A psychological study of the strange situation*. East Sussex: Psychology Press.

Baer, R. A., Smith, G. T., Hopkins, J., Krietemeyer, J., & Toney, L. (2006). Using self-report assessment methods to explore facets of mindfulness. *Assessment 13*(1), 27–45.

Baijal, S., & Srinivasan, N. (2010). Theta activity and meditative states: Spectral changes during concentrative meditation. *Cognitive Processing 11*(1), 31–38.

Black, D. S., & Slavich, G. M. (2016). Mindfulness meditation and the immune system: A systematic review of randomized controlled trials. *Annals of the New York Academy of Sciences 1373*(1), 13–24.

Bower, J. E., & Irwin, M. R. (2016). Mind–body therapies and control of inflammatory biology: A descriptive review. *Brain, Behavior, and Immunity 51*, 1–11.

Bowlby, J. (1982). *Attachment and loss: Vol. 1. Attachment* (2nd ed.). New York: Basic Books.

Brown, K. W., & Ryan, R. M. (2003). The benefits of being present: Mindfulness and its role in psychological well-being. *Journal of Personality and Social Psychology 84*(4), 822–848.

Buric, I., Farias, M., Jong, J., Mee, C., & Brazil, I. A. (2017). What is the molecular signature of mind–body interventions? A systematic review of gene expression changes induced by meditation and related practices. *Frontiers in Immunology 8*, 670.

Bono, J. E., & Vey, M. A. (2007). Personality and emotional performance: Extraversion, neuroticism, and self-monitoring. *Journal of Occupational Health Psychology 12*(2), 177–192.
Carlson, L. E., Ursuliak, Z., Goodey, E., Angen, M., & Speca, M. (2001). The effects of a mindfulness meditation-based stress reduction program on mood and symptoms of stress in cancer outpatients: 6-month follow-up. *Supportive Care in Cancer 9*(2), 112–123.
Carpenter, L. L., Gawuga, C. E., Tyrka, A. R., Lee, J. K., Anderson, G. M., & Price, L. H. (2010). Association between plasma IL-6 response to acute stress and early-life adversity in healthy adults. *Neuropsychopharmacology 35*(13), 2617–2623.
Carson, J. W., Keefe, F. J., Lynch, T. R., Carson, K. M., Goli, V., Fras, A. M., & Thorp, S. R. (2005). Loving-kindness meditation for chronic low back pain: Results from a pilot trial. *Journal of Holistic Nursing 23*(3), 287–304.
Christian, T., Beaujean, A. A., & Wright, W. (2016). Individual differences in affective states during meditation. *International Journal for the Psychology of Religion 26*(3), 268–282.
Cloninger, C. R., Svrakic, D. M., & Przybeck, T. R. (1993). A psychobiological model of temperament and character. *Archives of General Psychiatry 50*(12), 975–990.
Cohn, M. A., & Fredrickson, B. L. (2010). In search of durable positive psychology interventions: Predictors and consequences of long-term positive behavior change. *Journal of Positive Psychology 5*(5), 355–366.
Constantino, M. J., Ametrano, R. M., & Greenberg, R. P. (2012). Clinician interventions and participant characteristics that foster adaptive patient expectations for psychotherapy and psychotherapeutic change. *Psychotherapy 49*(4), 557–569.
Cordon, S. L., Brown, K. W., & Gibson, P. R. (2009). The role of mindfulness-based stress reduction on perceived stress: Preliminary evidence for the moderating role of attachment style. *Journal of Cognitive Psychotherapy 23*(3), 258–269.
Crescentini, C., & Capurso, V. (2015). Mindfulness meditation and explicit and implicit indicators of personality and self-concept changes. *Frontiers in Psychology 6*. doi:10.3389/fpsyg.2015.00044.
Creswell, J. D., Pacilio, L. E., Lindsay, E. K., & Brown, K. W. (2014). Brief mindfulness meditation training alters psychological and neuroendocrine responses to social evaluative stress. *Psychoneuroendocrinology 44*, 1–12.
Cuthbert, B. N., & Insel, T. R. (2013). Toward the future of psychiatric diagnosis: The seven pillars of RDoC. *BMC Medicine 11*(1). doi:10.1186/1741-7015-11-126
Delmonte, M. M. (1988). Personality correlates of meditation practice frequency and dropout in an outpatient population. *Journal of Behavioral Medicine 11*(6), 593–597.
Delmonte, M. M. (1985). Effects of expectancy on physiological responsivity in novice meditators. *Biological Psychology 21*(2), 107–121.
Delmonte, M. M. (1981). Expectation and meditation. *Psychological Reports 49*(3), 699–709.
de Vibe, M., Solhaug, I., Tyssen, R., Friborg, O., Rosenvinge, J. H., Sørlie, T., Halland, E., & Bjørndal, A. (2015). Does personality moderate the effects of mindfulness training for medical and psychology students? *Mindfulness 6*(2), 281–289.
Devilly, G. J., & Borkovec, T. D. (2000). Psychometric properties of the credibility/expectancy questionnaire. *Journal of Behavior Therapy and Experimental Psychiatry 31*(2), 73–86.
Ding, X., Tang, Y. Y., Deng, Y., Tang, R., & Posner, M. I. (2015). Mood and personality predict improvement in creativity due to meditation training. *Learning and Individual Differences, 37*, 217–221.
Eppley, K. R., Abrams, A. I., & Shear, J. (1989). Differential effects of relaxation techniques on trait anxiety: A meta-analysis. *Journal of Clinical Psychology 45*(6), 957–974.
Fredrickson, B. L., Boulton, A. J., Firestine, A. M., Van Cappellen, P., Algoe, S. B., Brantley, M. M., Kim, S. L., Brantley, J., & Salzberg, S. (2017). Positive emotion correlates of meditation

practice: A comparison of mindfulness meditation and loving-kindness meditation. *Mindfulness 8*(6), 1623–1633.

Goyal, M., Singh, S., Sibinga, E. M., Gould, N. F., Rowland-Seymour, A., Sharma, R., Berger, Z., Sleicher, D., Maron, D. D., Shihab, H. M., & Ranasinghe, P. D. (2014). Meditation programs for psychological stress and well-being: A systematic review and meta-analysis. *JAMA Internal Medicine 174*(3), 357–368.

Hager, J. L., & Surwit, R. S. (1978). Hypertension self-control with a portable feedback unit or meditation-relaxation. *Applied Psychophysiology and Biofeedback 3*(3), 269–276.

Hoffman, L. (2007). Multilevel models for examining individual differences in within-person variation and covariation over time. *Multivariate Behavioral Research 42*(4), 609–629.

Hofmann, S. G., Sawyer, A. T., Witt, A. A., & Oh, D. (2010). The effect of mindfulness-based therapy on anxiety and depression: A meta-analytic review. *Journal of Consulting and Clinical Psychology 78*(2), 169–183.

Hong, E. P., & Park, J. W. (2012). Sample size and statistical power calculation in genetic association studies. *Genomics & Informatics 10*(2), 117–122.

Insel, T. R. (2014). The NIMH research domain criteria (RDoC) project: Precision medicine for psychiatry. *American Journal of Psychiatry 171*(4), 395–397.

Jackson, S. E., & Chester, J. D. (2015). Personalised cancer medicine. *International Journal of Cancer 137*(2), 262–266.

Jacobs, T. L., Epel, E. S., Lin, J., Blackburn, E. H., Wolkowitz, O. M., Bridwell, D. A., Zanesco, A. P., Aichele, S. R., Sahdra, B. K., MacLean, K. A., & King, B. G. (2011). Intensive meditation training, immune cell telomerase activity, and psychological mediators. *Psychoneuroendocrinology 36*(5), 664–681.

John, O. P., & Srivastava, S. (1999). The Big Five trait taxonomy: History, measurement, and theoretical perspectives. *Handbook of Personality: Theory and Research*, 2, 102–138.

Jorm, A. F. (1989). Modifiability of trait anxiety and neuroticism: A meta-analysis of the literature. *Australian & New Zealand Journal of Psychiatry 23*(1), 21–29.

Jung, Y. H., Kang, D. H., Byun, M. S., Shim, G., Kwon, S. J., Jang, G. E., Lee, U. S., An, S. C., Jang, J. H., & Kwon, J. S. (2012). Influence of brain-derived neurotrophic factor and catechol O-methyl transferase polymorphisms on effects of meditation on plasma catecholamines and stress. *Stress 15*(1), 97–104.

Kabat-Zinn, J., & Chapman-Waldrop, A. (1988). Compliance with an outpatient stress reduction program: Rates and predictors of program completion. *Journal of Behavioral Medicine 11*(4), 333–352.

Kagan, J. (2005). Temperament. *Encyclopedia on early childhood development [online]*. Montreal, Quebec: Centre of Excellence for Early Childhood Development.

Klimesch, W., Doppelmayr, M., Russegger, H., Pachinger, T., & Schwaiger, J. (1998). Induced alpha band power changes in the human EEG and attention. *Neuroscience Letters 244*(2), 73–76.

Lambert, P. C., Sutton, A. J., Abrams, K. R., & Jones, D. R. (2002). A comparison of summary patient-level covariates in meta-regression with individual patient data meta-analysis. *Journal of Clinical Epidemiology 55*(1), 86–94.

Lane, J. D., Seskevich, J. E., & Pieper, C. F. (2007). Brief meditation training can improve perceived stress and negative mood. *Alternative Therapies in Health and Medicine 13*(1), 38–44.

Lau, J., Ioannidis, J. P., & Schmid, C. H. (1998). Summing up evidence: One answer is not always enough. *The Lancet 351*(9096), 123–127.

Lau, M. A., Bishop, S. R., Segal, Z. V., Buis, T., Anderson, N. D., Carlson, L., Shapiro, S., Carmody, J., Abbey, S., & Devins, G. (2006). The Toronto mindfulness scale: Development and validation. *Journal of Clinical Psychology 62*(12), 1445–1467.

Law, R. W. (2011). *An analogue study of loving-kindness meditation as a buffer against social stress.* (Doctoral dissertation) The University of Arizona.

Mascaro, J. S., Rilling, J. K., Negi, L. T., & Raison, C. L. (2013). Pre-existing brain function predicts subsequent practice of mindfulness and compassion meditation. *NeuroImage* 69, 35–42.

McCrae, R. R., & Costa Jr, P. T. (1994). The stability of personality: Observations and evaluations. *Current Directions in Psychological Science 3*(6), 173–175.

Mondloch, M. V., Cole, D. C., & Frank, J. W. (2001). Does how you do depend on how you think you'll do? A systematic review of the evidence for a relation between patients' recovery expectations and health outcomes. *Canadian Medical Association Journal 165*(2), 174–179.

Moonesinghe, R., Khoury, M. J., Liu, T., & Ioannidis, J. P. (2008). Required sample size and nonreplicability thresholds for heterogeneous genetic associations. *Proceedings of the National Academy of Sciences 105*(2), 617–622.

Nemeth, E., Rivera, S., Gabayan, V., Keller, C., Taudorf, S., Pedersen, B. K., & Ganz, T. (2004). IL-6 mediates hypoferremia of inflammation by inducing the synthesis of the iron regulatory hormone hepcidin. *Journal of Clinical Investigation 113*(9), 1271–1276.

Orme-Johnson, D. W., & Barnes, V. A. (2014). Effects of the Transcendental Meditation technique on trait anxiety: A meta-analysis of randomized controlled trials. *Journal of Alternative and Complementary Medicine 20*(5), 330–341.

Pace, T. W., Negi, L. T., Sivilli, T. I., Issa, M. J., Cole, S. P., Adame, D. D., & Raison, C. L. (2010). Innate immune, neuroendocrine and behavioral responses to psychosocial stress do not predict subsequent compassion meditation practice time. *Psychoneuroendocrinology 35*(2), 310–315.

Pace, T. W., Negi, L. T., Adame, D. D., Cole, S. P., Sivilli, T. I., Brown, T. D., Issa, M. J., & Raison, C. L. (2009). Effect of compassion meditation on neuroendocrine, innate immune and behavioral responses to psychosocial stress. *Psychoneuroendocrinology 34*(1), 87–98.

Piet, J., & Hougaard, E. (2011). The effect of mindfulness-based cognitive therapy for prevention of relapse in recurrent major depressive disorder: A systematic review and meta-analysis. *Clinical Psychology Review 31*(6), 1032–1040.

Reich, R. R., Lengacher, C. A., Kip, K. E., Shivers, S. C., Schell, M. J., Shelton, M. M., Widen, R. H., Newton, C., Barta, M. K., Paterson, C. L., & Farias, J. R. (2014). Baseline immune biomarkers as predictors of MBSR (BC) treatment success in off-treatment breast cancer patients. *Biological Research for Nursing 16*(4), 429–437.

Roberts, B., Walton, K., & Viechtbauer, W. (2006). Patterns of mean-level change in personality traits across the life course: A meta-analysis of longitudinal studies. *Psychological Bulletin 132*(1), 1–25.

Rojiani, R., Santoyo, J. F., Rahrig, H., Roth, H. D., & Britton, W. B. (2017). Women benefit more than men in response to college-based meditation training. *Frontiers in Psychology 8*, 551.

Sass, S. M., Berenbaum, H., & Abrams, E. M. (2013). Discomfort with emotion moderates distress reduction in a brief mindfulness intervention. *International Journal of Behavioral Consultation and Therapy 7*(4), 24–27.

Sedlmeier, P., Eberth, J., Schwarz, M., Zimmermann, D., Haarig, F., Jaeger, S., & Kunze, S. (2012). The psychological effects of meditation: A meta-analysis. *Psychological Bulletin 138*(6), 1139–1171.

Seer, P., & Raeburn, J. M. (1980). Meditation training and essential hypertension: A methodological study. *Journal of Behavioral Medicine* 3(1), 59–71.

Shapiro, S. L., Brown, K. W., Thoresen, C., & Plante, T. G. (2011). The moderation of mindfulness-based stress reduction effects by trait mindfulness: Results from a randomized controlled trial. *Journal of Clinical Psychology* 67(3), 267–277.

Shiner, R. L., Buss, K. A., McClowry, S. G., Putnam, S. P., Saudino, K. J., & Zentner, M. (2012). What is temperament now? Assessing progress in temperament research on the twenty-fifth anniversary of Goldsmith et al. *Child Development Perspectives* 6(4), 436–444.

Stewart, L. A., & Clarke, M. J. (1995). Practical methodology of meta-analyses (overviews) using updated individual patient data. Cochrane Working Group. *Statistics in medicine* 14(19), 2057–2079.

Strauss, C., Cavanagh, K., Oliver, A., & Pettman, D. (2014). Mindfulness-based interventions for people diagnosed with a current episode of an anxiety or depressive disorder: a meta-analysis of randomized controlled trials. *PLoS One* 9(4), 1–13.

Takahashi, T., Murata, T., Hamada, T., Omori, M., Kosaka, H., Kikuchi, M., Yoshida, H., & Wada, Y. (2005). Changes in EEG and autonomic nervous activity during meditation and their association with personality traits. *International Journal of Psychophysiology* 55(2), 199–207.

Thompson, R. A., & Raikes, H. A. (2003). Toward the next quarter-century: Conceptual and methodological challenges for attachment theory. *Development and Psychopathology* 15(3), 691–718.

Williams, J. M. G., Crane, C., Barnhofer, T., Brennan, K., Duggan, D. S., Fennell, M. J., Hackmann, A., Krusche, A., Muse, K., Von Rohr, I. R., & Shah, D. (2014). Mindfulness-based cognitive therapy for preventing relapse in recurrent depression: A randomized dismantling trial. *Journal of Consulting and Clinical Psychology* 82(2), 275–286.

Wood, A. R., Esko, T., Yang, J., Vedantam, S., Pers, T. H., Gustafsson, S., …and Buchkovich, M. L. (2014). Defining the role of common variation in the genomic and biological architecture of adult human height. *Nature Genetics* 46(11), 1173–1186.

CHAPTER 23

REFLECTIONS ON THE ROLE OF CONTROL IN MEDITATION

DEANE H. SHAPIRO, JR.

Introduction: Understanding Control

A disturbed mind is forever active, jumping hither and thither, and is hard to control; but a tranquil mind is peaceful; therefore it is wise to keep the mind under control.

—Buddha, *Dhammapada* (Fronsdal, 2006, Chapter 3, p. 11)

The most excellent Jihad (Holy War, struggle) is the conquest of the self.[1]

—Mohammed, Ahadith (Meri, 2005)

But, as often as the heart
Breaks—wild and wavering—from control, so oft
Let him recurb it, let him reign it back/to the soul's governance; for perfect bliss
Grows only in the bosom tranquilized.

—*Bhagavad Gītā*, Chapter 4, verse 1

He who is slow to anger is better than the strong man and a master of his passions is better than the conqueror of a city.

—Rabbi Tarfon, the *Pirke Avot* (cf. Proverbs 16:32)

No drives, no needs, no compulsions, no attractions, then your affairs are under control.
You are a free person

—Zhuangzi (Chuang Tzu, 1996)

[1] The word *jihad* appears frequently in the Quran with and without military connotations, often in the idiomatic expression "striving in the path of God" *(al-jihad fi sabil Allah)*.

In every spiritual tradition the role of control is involved in some way. The above quotations suggest the importance of learning to gain control over one's thoughts, emotions, and behavior. Meditation is one means to achieve that control. All spiritual traditions can be understood as having a varying continuum of "self" power and "other/Other" power (e.g., control by a benevolent Other) (Smith, 1983). Non-theistically we can see this range in self and other control in the "will" of Zen *shikantaza* (nothing but sit) to the Amida prayer, and similar prayers of taking refuge in the *saṅgha*, in the Buddha. Theistically, we can see this continuum in self and Other control in Paramahansa Yogananda's "Strengthen your will power so that you will not be controlled by circumstances but will control them. O Divine Sculptor, chisel Thou my life according to Thy Design (Yogananda, 1946)." And in Jesus's, "not my will but Thy will be done. (Luke 22:42).

Assessing Control

The notion of control has been extensively studied in psychology for several decades. Rotter (1966) developed a scale that measured a generalized expectancy for internal or external control. Here expectations of internal and external control are seen as a single dimension, so the more internal control a person believes they have, the less control they attribute to external factors. A second generation of measures of control, focusing on health (Wallston Wallston, & DeVellis, 1978) allowed for both self-agency (e.g., I can help keep myself healthy) and other-agency (e.g., the doctor is in control of my health) as separate dimensions. It also included a "chance" dimension (e.g., no matter how much I do, or my doctors do, sometimes we just get sick). Several control-related concepts have been developed since, including Bandura's (1977) notion of self-efficacy, Seligman's (1975) learned helplessness, and Burger and Cooper's (Burger & Cooper, 1979) motivational variable—the need for control. Research supported the general idea that a sense of control was important for effective psychological functioning.

To address these refinements, a third generation, more comprehensive measure of control was developed—the SCI (Shapiro Control Inventory) (Shapiro, 1983, Shapiro, 1994).[2] This incorporated the ideas of perceived control ("the ability to cause an influence in the intended direction"; see Rodin, 1986) as well as a motivational variable—the desire for control and fear of loss of control.

[2] Through several factor analytic studies and test, re-test reliability studies, we have identified and refined these four modes of control, seeking to have them gender and culturally sensitive (Shapiro, 1982; cf. Soucar, 2005). Further, there were over a dozen studies looking at reliability and validity of the SCI (see Shapiro, 1994) including looking at the relationship between having control and losing control to functional neuroanatomy, using Positron Emission Tomography (Shapiro, et al., 1995). For additional studies on the SCI and control therapy with different clinical populations, readers are invited to controlresearch.net: see writings under "What Is Control Therapy" and additional networking articles. Other investigators have also used a combination of meditation with behavioral self-control skills: e.g., mindfulness-based cognitive therapy (Seagel, Williams, & Teasdale, 2013); acceptance and commitment therapy (Hayes, Strosahl, & Wilson, 2016); dialectical behavior therapy (Linehan, Comtois, & Murray, 2006).

Table 23.1 A Four-Quadrant Model of Control.

Quadrant 1	Quadrant 2
Active control Positive assertive	Letting-go control Positive yielding Accepting
Quadrant 3	**Quadrant 4**
Over-control Negative assertive	Too little control Negative yielding

This inventory measured two modes of control: assertive/change; and yielding/accepting. Each of these can be positive or negative providing four modes of control shown in Table 23.1.

One can seek to gain a sense of control through causing an effect in oneself and the world by changing a situation, behavior, feeling (assertive/change mode of control). This has been the predominant view of control in Western psychology, though its culture-bound features and limitations have received increasing scrutiny (e.g., Evans, Shapiro, & Lewis, 1993; Shapiro, Evans, & Shapiro, 1987). One can also gain a sense of control by learning to yield to and accept what is—in one's thoughts, feelings, behavior, the world. The positive mode is like Laozi's (Lao-Tzu) stream, flowing around the rock—not seeking to actively control that which cannot (or should not) be actively controlled. The negative mode of this yielding/accepting mode is when there is a helpless resignation, a giving up in situations in which a helpful, wise, or positive assertive response is possible.[3]

These four modes of control can be understood as an effort to operationalize and help create a model of the Reinhold Niebuhr prayer: the courage to change (positive assertive), the serenity to accept (positive yielding). Note that there is a relationship between the quadrants and the various spiritual traditions: theistic, non-theistic, and secular. For example, the Niebuhr (1987) prayer begins with "God grant me," thus there is an asking for guidance from an "Other" in terms of both assertive and yielding modes. The line "God helps those who help themselves" represents a way in which self and Other are integrated on the assertive/change mode; and both theistic and non-theistic traditions invoke the help of other or Other in the yielding mode: taking refuge in the Buddha (non-theistic) or "Thy will, not my will be done" (theistic). Further, secular existential views (e.g., Malraux, 1953; Frankl, 1962/1980) point out the need to "stand forth" against an indifferent universe and create our meaning.

[3] Meditation (and views of control) also occurs within a cultural context, and research needs to be sensitive to these variations. For example, Weisz, Rothbaum, & Blackburn (1984) discussed control in Japan and the United States in terms of primary control (similar to our assertive, change mode of control) and secondary control (fitting in), similar to our yielding, accepting mode of control.

Research on Modes of Control; Meditation and Control

Research shows that reducing the endorsement of the negative quadrants (3 and 4, over control and too little control) and increasing and developing a situationally appropriate balance between the two positive modes of control can have a positive effect on health and well-being. In one study, individuals with cardiovascular disease were given a two year intervention of cognitive/behavioral treatment, compared to a group that was only given cardiac counseling (Shapiro, Freidman, & Piaget, 1991). After two years, their congruence between real and ideal self on the four quadrants was significantly higher than the group without the cognitive/behavioral intervention. Further, on each of the four quadrants, the intervention group had a healthier profile than the other group (i.e., higher positive assertive and positive yielding, lower negative assertive and lower negative yielding scores).

In a study on sense of control and cancer morbidity and mortality, a twenty-year follow-up showed that a greater sense of control at eight months was associated with less cancer recurrence, while higher desire for control at both four and eight months was associated with greater likelihood of recurrence (Astin, Shapiro, & Shapiro, 2013). Utilization of an accepting mode of control appeared to mitigate the negative effects of desire for control on recurrence.

Meditation can facilitate an increase in quadrant two: positive acceptance (Easterline, 1992; Astin, 1997; Shapiro, 1992; Shapiro, Bootzin, Figueredo, Lopez, & Schwartz, 2003). Below is a brief summary of several studies comparing the control profiles of beginning, intermediate, long-term and very-long-term meditators (over 20 years).

The very-long-term meditators had a significantly less negative sense of control. There was a significant association between the length of practice and higher scores on the positive sense of control scale; the very-long-term meditators had a higher positive assertive and positive yielding, and a significantly lower negative yielding; and there were significant differences in desire for control associated with long-term practice. The very-long-term meditators were also significantly more "satisfied" with their "mode of control" style. Finally, the sense of control from both self and Other/other was positively associated with length of practice.

Overall, while the importance of assertive change has been recognized in the psychological literature, the research outlined here shows the importance of positive acceptance and the role of meditation in achieving this.

Control in Context

In order to utilize meditation as a technique for helping improve people's lives, a wide range of factors need to be taken into account. These include the type of meditation as well as the goals of the individual and the relationship between the client/pupil and the "teacher." To help explore these issues a systems model was created in which these questions could be addressed as part of the therapeutic process. "Therapy" is viewed within an educational model, so these components can be applied in any setting where meditation might be taught (e.g., within a religious, spiritual tradition, an educational setting (e.g. Shapiro, Kruse & Astin, 2017) or a therapeutic one).

This systems model (Figure 23.1) can be applied when used specifically in evaluating the technique of meditation within therapy or teaching. This is a complex system composed of several parts, notably the therapist, the client (student), and the relationship between them. The client and therapist each bring their own emphasis, perspective, and worldview to the therapeutic encounter, and these views in turn exert influences on assessment, intervention, evaluation, and termination.

There are different views of the client–therapist relationship, and a wide range of "relational" models have been described, such as the detached observer, the warm non-judgmental reflective guide, the "coach/teacher"; the fellow journeyer (Shapiro & Astin, 1998; Shapiro, Soucar, Shapiro, & Astin, 2010; Soucar, 2005). So which "therapeutic approach" would work best for a particular person with a particular set of goals? One way to explore the question of the value and benefit of the guru/teacher exercising full control might be to look at a continuum of self-learning. From the teacher or therapist side, questions that might be helpful to explore include: How much desire for control in general do you have? Have you had experience with others in which there are potential "power struggles" and control issues—for example, transference, countertransference? What is your goal in these situations and how do you try to address them?

From the client/student side, one question for some might be: What is it in me that makes it so hard to yield to another and fully trust another? For others, it may be important to look at why they seek to let go of control and give up personal responsibility to another.

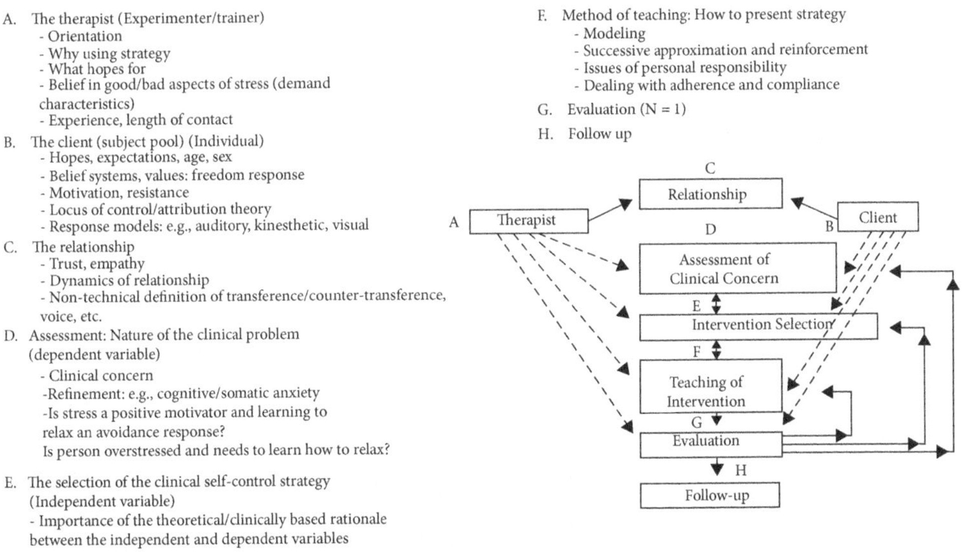

FIGURE 23.1 An Interactive Systems Theory Model for Utilizing Meditation as a Self-Control Technique in the Management of a Clinical Problem, such as Stress.

Reproduced from Shapiro, 1980, p. 255, Figure 10.1 Copyright© 1980, Deane H. Shapiro, Jr.

The therapist/teacher and the client/pupil bring different perspectives to the relationship. The systems model was developed to help us understand these various components and their interactions, and to provide feedback loops for evaluating when progress is not going smoothly. The systems model can be used as a framework to deal with "challenges" in learning, as well as to evaluate the process of the therapy/teaching, such as setbacks, compliance issues, resistances, and when client and therapist disagree.

The Content of a Self-Control Strategy

In order to understand different control-enhancing strategies, it is important to deconstruct the techniques into their building blocks to see where there are similarities and differences. Clinically, this can also be helpful in that by performing a content analysis of different self-control techniques, it allows us to examine and clarify within each technique which building blocks are being utilized in the construction of an intervention technique. As an example of this process, Table 23.2 provides a comparison of two self-control techniques, meditation and behavioral self-control. Meditation is examined both as "formal meditation" (structured at regular times during the day) and as informal meditation, which many traditions discuss as a type of mindfulness awareness throughout the day (Rahula, 1959). Three dimensions are compared: (1) what has been called "environmental planning"—where the technique occurs; (2) what stimulus cues are used, that is, what cues in the internal and external environment are used to remind one to practice the technique, or are used in the practice of the technique; and (3) the nature of the images and thoughts that are used in the technique (e.g., how thoughts are viewed, and, if appropriate, stopped, changed, or "just allowed to be.")

Through this analysis, it is possible to compare similarities and differences in the techniques and thereby clarify the different variables involved. Comparing the strategies at a reductionistic level can help suggest ways that could be used to complement each other, as well as combined and integrated (e.g., contingent informal meditation; see Tloczynski, Malinowski, & Lamorte, 1997).

Attentional and Cognitive Self-Regulation Building Blocks and Skills: Dealing with Negative Thoughts

Let us now look at how variations in meditation strategies alone, and when combined with behavioral self-control strategies, might be utilized in dealing with "negative thoughts."

Building blocks, such as attention and cognitions, can be used as part of a variety of skill-building techniques for either positive assertive/change or the positive yielding/accepting mode of control interventions to help address multiple problematic "mind domain" concerns. Here we explore one example: in what ways do different "techniques

Table 23.2 Comparison of Behavioral Self-Control Strategies with Formal and Informal Meditation.[4]

Topics	Formal Meditation	Behavioral Self-Management	Informal Meditation	Contingent Informal Meditation
Environmental Planning where intervention strategy occurs	specified setting (e.g., room or in nature); reduced external stimuli to initially help individual focus on object of meditation	*in natural environment where problem behavior occurs; or symbolically in neutral environment*	occurs in natural environment	*same as behavioral self-management*
if stimulus cues are used	stimulus cues (control): e.g., incense; or, in case of concentrative meditation, the object of meditation as stimulus cue	*specified cues in natural environment (programming antecedent or initiating stimuli) self-regulated stimulus exposure*	everything is a stimulus cue for "awareness"	same as behavioral self-management
cognitive statements and images; thought stopping	observation without comment (no self-statements); and without evaluation (no thinking); covert images are allowed to "flow down the river of consciousness" and are not dwelled on; focusing on competing response of breathing helps remove thoughts (step 4)	*covert images and self-instruction used extensively: e.g., covert sensitization (images as punishment); cover rehearsal (images and self-instructions as successive approximation): self-modeling; covert self-reinforcement; covert behavior modification; either alter self-statements or emit relaxing instructional self-statements; to stop thoughts, covert yelling of the word "stop!"*	no cognitive statements or images involved in the performance of actions.	use of covert images, self-modeling; and self-instruction: e.g., "I am breath," "I am relaxed, in control, I can handle this"

Adapted from Shapiro, 1978, p. 290, Appendix 3: East-West Techniques, Copyright© 1978 by Prentice-Hall, Inc.

[4] A comparison and contrast of these techniques on several other dimensions is discussed elsewhere (Shapiro, 1978). For example, there can be physical/behavioral building blocks, such as nature of physical posture; the type of breath regulation; other mental building blocks include the nature of cognitive statements and instructions, nature and type of attentional focusing and observation; content of what is observed; nature and type of self-evaluation and goal setting; images used; decisional choices (e.g., the use of preprogrammed punishments and reinforcers).

and traditions" label and address negative thoughts and feelings, in order to enhance a person's positive sense of control?

Skills in this area involve some use of the body building blocks, such as finding a comfortable posture; where to focus one's eyes; relaxed, effortless breathing; but, primarily, they use attentional and cognitive building blocks to deal with negative thoughts and affect.

Below are five different gradations of skills. Notice that they go from the most accepting (just letting go) to more assertive (stopping and replacing thoughts) (Shapiro, 2014). These are adapted from both meditative and cognitive/behavioral self-control schools:

i) letting go of thoughts and stories so one is not so caught up in them;
ii) not taking thoughts so seriously ("I am not my thoughts");
iii) keeping a larger attentional "mind" noticing thoughts;
iv) stopping thoughts;
v) replacing thoughts with more positive ones.

These mental building blocks, which can involve a continuum of accepting to change skills, can be implemented as a way to develop interventions that can be used for goals of either the assertive change mode—to help the client *let go of* or *change* negative thoughts—or as part of interventions directed to the yielding/accepting mode of control: to *let go of* negative thoughts and learn to accept "what is" better; or to *change* negative thoughts to accept what is better. Just to repeat: *both* positive assertive and positive yielding *techniques* can be used to facilitate positive assertive or positive yielding goals.

Let us now look in a bit more detail at these strategies, symbolically going from the most yin, to most yang.

As you read this gradation of strategies below, let me ask you to consider how your meditation practice helps you address negative thoughts (however you define them). Based on our previous research on self-control, there are six dimensions that may be relevant: awareness, choice, responsibility, effort, goal, and skill (Shapiro, 1983):

How do you recognize a "negative thought?" (*awareness*)
How do you "evaluate" it for its helpfulness, accuracy, wisdom? (*goal*)
If you decide the thought is not helpful (*choice*), how do you address it (what level of *effort* is needed; what *skills* do you need)?
Do you use some aspect of the cognitive/attentional meditative/self-control strategies above?
What role does control by a benevolent other or Other play (e.g., friend, doctor, or God, Allah, Brahman)?

Notice Only

The most accepting skill is that which is practiced in the meditation technique of "just noticing the thoughts" without judgment. Thoughts are viewed as "content" stories, and simply observed, allowing whatever is to be. In watching the thoughts, one doesn't "catastrophize" and embellish; one doesn't minimize and dismiss, one doesn't dwell on and ruminate about them. "Don't run toward, don't run away from the thoughts." Again, just observe. Also, if you want to run away, and minimize, or start to embellish and create a story, just notice that, too. Just observing whatever is might be thought of as the ultimate "acceptance" of thoughts (cf. Shapiro & Carlson, 2017).

This "observing and noticing" of thoughts can also be applied to feelings, body sensations, and so on. For example, one useful practice is to just observe mindfully the stories, thoughts, and feelings you have in each of the "negative" quadrants—for example, negative assertive, negative yielding. Just observe from a quiet, centered place what those quadrants are like, without running toward them or away from them. Just sit and observe "with curiosity" and get to know the stories, thoughts, and feelings in those quadrants.

Notice and Let Go

Additional instructions in some schools can include "notice the thoughts as if you were under a bridge and cars are passing over the bridge—just notice the cars, *then let them go* (don't get into the car and drive away in it) and return to breathing." This approach is a bit more "assertive" in terms of changing the "mind's thoughts—using thought (self-instructions) to work toward ceasing thoughts and creating a more "open" mind.

Notice, Let Go, Return to a Competing Response

Whereas one school of meditation says notice and another says notice and "let go" of negative or unproductive thoughts, still another approach involves practicing a competing response: for instance, a mantra, or series of sounds and phrases to stop negative thoughts and replace them with neutral/positive sounds and statements. When a person notices a negative thought, they merely let it go and return to the pre-planned word (e.g., *Oṃ*, peace, gratitude).

This has been referred to as concentrative meditation in which, for example, a specific auditory, visual, or kinesthetic/tactile object becomes the focus of attention. Table 23.3 gives examples of each of these (internal and external) (Shapiro, 1978).

Notice, Stop, "Dialogue," Replace

A cognitive-behavioral approach to dealing with negative thoughts involves various steps: the first is to notice the negative thoughts, and the second is to "stop them." This

Table 23.3 Examples of Concentrative Meditation.

	Auditory	Visual	Tactile
overt, external environment	Verbal–Sufi dervish call mantra	*kasiṇa* maṇḍala cross vase abdomen	Touching thumb to each finger
internal environment	verbal–mantra koan	third eye vault of skull symbol of guru (image)	Heartbeat breathing

Adapted from Shapiro, 1978, p. 39, Copyright© 1978 by Prentice-Hall, Inc.

can include using stimulus cues to remind oneself to check in on one's thoughts, and "catch" and interrupt maladaptive ones, to more vigorous efforts, including a loud covert or overt "STOP!" and even the behavioral use of a real "rubber band" to punish and reduce negative thoughts, and break into a cognitive sequence. When applying this to meditation, its use can range from the gentle instructions to "notice and let go" to more vigorous efforts such as the Zen "*kwat*," which is an internal harsh image of a monk bowing and then using a board to hit one's shoulder in order to interrupt thoughts.

The third step is to explain to oneself about why those thoughts are negative and not helpful: for instance, "I'm catastrophizing, overreacting"; "I've been through this over and over, and am just rehashing old news"; "this is not going anywhere, and it's not worth going there." The final step in the sequence is to replace the negative, unhelpful thoughts with positive, less destructive thoughts, and ones which more accurately reflect how you'd like to think and feel. For example, on one side of an index card, you could have the client write down a negative statement about their body and, on the other side, self-accepting statements to be used as substitutions.

It is helpful to have the clients write down any self-sabotaging or negative thought related to their self-management project or area of concern. Then have them explore what would their wiser, higher self respond to this thought? It's been said that the one who controls the narrative wins. It is useful to anticipate negative thoughts and to plan how one intends to wisely address them.

Affirmations: For the Yielding, Accepting Mode of Control

Below are cognitive statements—affirmations or self-instructions—that can be used to help us accept where and who we are. Skillful use of these can be helpful. As a generic affirmation, the following can be helpful to practice:

- I'm doing the best I can. There's nothing more to be done; I'm coping (solving) what's facing me as best I am able. (Acceptance with gentleness toward self)
- Rather than focusing on what is lacking or missing in my life, I choose to count my blessings, and find things I can be thankful for in my life as it is. (Acceptance with gratitude)
- I will seek to focus on and appreciate those parts of my body/life/relationships that are working, and to develop conscious appreciation for what is.
- I can love and accept myself just as I am.
- My self-worth is not based on "doing" alone.
- Every out breath I take, I am learning to practice consciously by letting go, trusting, and accepting.
- I am increasingly able to be peaceful and accepting, and not rise to every trivial annoyance.
- Good morning, I love you (Shapiro, 2017, 2020).

Finally, accepting beliefs can also be facilitated by one's worldview. For example, affirmations can incorporate a theistic view, such as "I trust in a higher power and that this makes sense. I accept what God gives. It is God's will." or "Everything happens for reason; I choose to trust that this makes sense."

For those with a non-theistic view such as Daoism or Buddhism, affirmations can involve a belief and trust "in the way," such as: "You can't push the river," or "It is what it is," or "Trust the Dao (the way)."

Matching Meditative Strategy to Person

We've seen that there are multiple meditative strategies, including visual, auditory, tactile, concentrative strategies, as well as opening up meditative strategies (*shikantaza*, mindfulness) and combinations. There are two initial questions with which we are now faced:

1) Is there one "right" meditation strategy for all people?
2) If not, then how to explore the best matching (for ourselves and others) of the meditation "technique" to the person (situation, developmental place in life, belief system)?

I have spent the past few decades exploring ways to help individuals gain a positive sense of control in their lives, and meditation has been an important part of that approach (Shapiro & Astin, 1998). This has involved efforts to match "self-control" strategies to an individual's personality, concerns, and goals. Meditation was viewed as one promising technique to help with a positive, yielding, accepting mode of control, as well as a "centering" technique that might be helpful to complement more assertive/change strategies for goal attainment.

To help refine and match a client/person to therapeutic control-enhancing techniques, we have used the SCI. The idea was to try to "match" the most effective techniques, one of which might be meditation, to the specific person. As an example, note the control profiles of two individuals, both at high cardiovascular risk (Fig. 23.2).

While both have a low sense of control, Participant One has a high desire for control, is high in negative assertive and low in "other" as a sense of control. Participant Two is high in negative yielding, and low in self as a source of sense of control. Therefore no "one size fits all" treatment would be appropriate, and it is important to "match" the self-control strategy to the person.

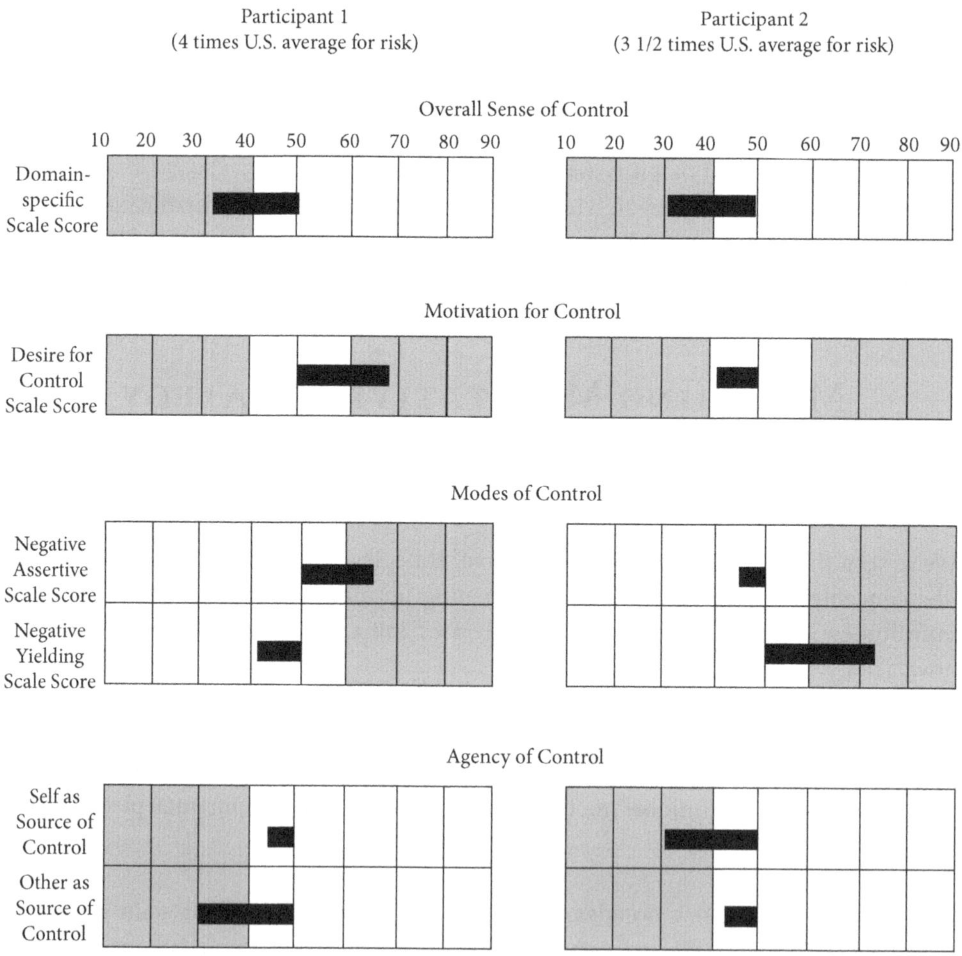

FIGURE 23.2 Control Profile of Two Patients at High Cardiovascular Risk.

Reproduced from Shapiro, Schwartz, & Astin, (1996), copyright© 1996, American Psychological Association.

The important point for this chapter is that meditation as a self-control strategy, when utilized in therapeutic and health care settings, must be evaluated and explored as one possible treatment option, and matched to the individual, the area being addressed, and the goal. The treatment approach for Participant One involves meditation to help lower a desire for control, decrease negative assertive mode, and learning more "trust" from "others" as a sense of control. The treatment approach for Participant Two involves primarily learning to decrease yielding mode of control through the assertiveness/change mode of control and developing a stronger sense of self as agency (here meditation plays a less central role in the therapeutic intervention). Therefore, "matching" self-control strategies to the person is critical, and meditation can be an important part of that effort (Shapiro, 1990b, 2001).

A person's control profile and their sensory orientation and preferences are only two of the range of factors that will have to be taken into account when deciding which methods are most suitable for which individual. Among the other factors, due attention should be paid to the person's own orientation (spiritual, religious, secular), and how a particular method resonates and coheres with such an orientation. In this way, it may be possible to more effectively "match" a person's "Control Profile," clinical concern, personal style, goal, and belief system to the "meditative therapeutic intervention" (see Shapiro, Schwartz, & Astin, 1996 for a biopsychosocial model of this matching).

A Personal Journey through Meditation and Control

The following section is a more autobiographical one where I give an account of how my interests in meditation and control emerged and, eventually, merged. I share this because I believe that those who "work" in the field of meditation have an opportunity to be personal scientists and explore how our own beliefs, experiences, and values influence our research and teaching. Behind the chapters of this book are the lives—the individuals—which have led each of us to become involved in some way with the teaching, study, and practice of meditation. And to those reading, there is some "story" that brought you to this book. All of us have a story about why we became involved in meditation.[5]

My beginning meditation practice began nearly a year and a half after the beginning of my spiritual search. That search involved first going "in and through" my understanding of what I called "my Judeo-Christian" heritage, travel to Israel, living on a kibbutz near Tiberias, and tracing Jesus's path through the Holy Land. It was there I decided that

[5] In a previous version of this chapter, I invited the reader to reflect on their "origin" story involving meditation, their views of control, and how meditation and control are involved in their view of human personality and the nature of the universe. Because of space limitations, those topics were edited out, but if the reader is interested in further exploring them, they may be found at https://deanehshapirojr.org/meditative-reflections/.

I wanted to be a novelist and wrote my first (and only) novel. The novel was a psychological journey in which the "existentially lost" protagonist is writing at a café in Israel, wondering where his life had gone astray, and determined to reflect back and see if he could re-find a thread to reconnect with and begin again. The novel ended with the protagonist evolving through different permutations and challenges of self, family, nation, to finally confronting God: how could an all loving, omnipotent, all knowing God allow the suffering and death of even one innocent child? At the time, through that character, I answered that this was not a God he could believe in.

My experiences in Israel led to a thirteen-month journey to Asia in search of the "miraculous," now with my wife Johanna. Our goal was to reach Sri Aurobindo's ashram in Pondicherry. Meditation became one very important way to gain a positive sense of control. I admired the story of Hakuin, who when faced with lies and distortions about him, was able to keep his equanimity, act caring and lovingly, and non-reactively, and say: "Is that so." I wanted to be like the Zen master, who when threatened by a samurai warrior saying "Don't you know who I am, I could run my sword through you without blinking," replied "Don't you know who I am. I could watch you run your sword through me without blinking." I wanted to be that fearless, that courageous, in responding to all that life might throw at me. I felt meditation could give me that discipline to focus on and to transform "darkness" into soft white.

In many ways, during that time in Asia, I felt whole and complete. Johanna and I were living an "idyllic life" in Penang, where the boat was to set sail for Pondicherry and Sri Aurobindo's ashram. We meditated, wrote poetry, swam. Each day we "lived in the moment" and asked ourselves "why go to seek the miraculous in India in an ashram when we can live here each day, 'every moment Zen?'" And then one day, after about six months, we realized that we weren't going to go to Pondicherry but wanted to return to America to "share" what we had learned.

When we returned to America, we had only our backpacks as possessions. I found a home in graduate school in an interdisciplinary doctoral program I created at Stanford called "Personality and Psychotherapy." I was like a kid in a candy shop: an opportunity to learn about behavioral self-control and the experimental analysis of behavior—and "data"—as a way to complement the Zen. I felt like the precision and data, cause-and-effect learning complimented meditative awareness.

The next phase saw a continued commitment to daily meditation, within an existential/non-theistic worldview, and also one that fit with social learning theory. Our life flourished in what Freud called the areas of "love and work"—we both earned our doctorates—and were able to begin to teach what we had learned. We had three children and were able to teach them meditation from an early age. I continued to write in my journal. But now one journal wasn't enough. I had a personal, meditative journal; a professional journal; a "relational" beloved journal; a journal about being a father with each of my children. And I realized I needed a journal of journals just to keep track of my reflections. Johanna had gotten a job in Southern California at UC Irvine; I was still in Northern California, commuting a thousand miles each week round-trip. We had two homes, two cars, three kids, a dog, and I wondered what happened to voluntary simplicity.

I felt like a "juggler" with something always in the air. I could sense my vaunted "self-control" (meditation and behavioral self-control, East and West) and my mantra from Hesse's Siddhartha "I can think, I can wait, I can fast" was slipping.

At that point I was fortunate to receive a Kellogg Leadership fellowship, designed to "buy our time" so that the fellowship could open doors for us we never dreamed possible. I had started reading about Gauguin's life and then chose a beautiful south seas island—Bali—for part of my fellowship. The stated reason was to study trance as a stress management tool, but I also felt a had a lot of inner work to do, to look at what had happened to me since returning from Asia, and to society.

Professionally, I felt divided, like Ram Dass once quipped at speaking at a conference: "As Ram Dass I feel and espouse love. As Richard Alpert, I count how many people are there at my talks and are revenue." During my thirteen years since returning from Asia, I had met and exceeded every professional dream I might have had for myself. Yet, I was aware during the time in Bali how much egoic dust had accumulated from "success"—for example, first and second authorship, number of book sales, earning "merit" increases.

The people of Bali have it's a worldview of a trusting, benevolent universe (Shapiro, 1989b). During my time there I had several experiences of that world view, which became the impetus for what I later described as my shift from an existential, non-theistic universe, to a belief in a benevolent, theistic universe. Further, as a way to raise our children, and after talking with Huston Smith about the importance of teaching a "particular" path to the universal, we began a return to Judaism.[6] In the Shema meditation in Judaism, we are invited to "Hear, listen, wake up" (*Shema*). "We who struggle with and toward God" (*Israel)*. "This God is both impersonal and distant-- though the universe is trustworthy (*Adonai*). "This God is also close and personal" (*Eloheinu*). And the Shema ends with "One. '*Echad*." All of this journey, the waking up, the struggle with and toward God, the impersonal God, the personal God, is "One." (Cf. Shapiro, 1989a, 1993).

I let myself be cradled in God's arms... much like when our children were young and I would put a magic blanket around them when I put them to bed. I slowly learned to ask for guidance from God—in how to balance all the activities of my life, to help me find my deepest "piece of the cosmic puzzle." I felt myself surrounded by that magic blanket of "God who provides for my every need, God who guides my steps" (part of the Jewish morning prayer of gratefulness). I enlarged my theory of control to include "agency" both from self-control, and control by a benevolent other (other/Other). This other, as research was showing, could give us a sense of control, for example, a feeling of a competent doctor when we are sick; and for me, increasingly, a feeling that I could choose to trust in the essential benevolence of the universe.

[6] When I told him we wanted to raise our children in the "essence" of all religions, he said, "It is as impossible to teach the essence of religion without teaching a particular religion as it is to teach the essence of language without teaching a particular language" (Personal Communication, 1983; cf. also, Smith, 1983).

In my professional writings, I decided that I wanted to enlarge my theory of control. I felt that each of us has a desire to have a positive sense of control in our lives. I wanted to explore how we do that—from "making sense, meaning, purpose" out of our understanding of the universe, and our place in it; to self-regulation of our bodies and minds; to the role of interpersonal belonging and intimacy.

I also decided to look again at the context of meditation. My meditation practice continued with "bare awareness" (Vipassana's mindfulness) and *shikantaza* (nothing but sit). But these practices became surrounded by a very specific theistic context: the morning prayer of gratefulness; the afternoon prayer of thankfulness; the evening prayer of forgiveness (all from Judaism). In addition to the daily activities, I started to live within the weekly cycle of Shabbat singing and going from the "doing" of the week" to "just being" during the Sabbath: to imagine and seek to live a day of heaven on earth. As well, the festival cycles of Judaism became increasingly important as retreat times to explore spiritual themes.

In my sixties I created a wall of elder wisdom. Yes, there is still Gandhi's life as experiment; yes, there is still some seeking to increase "skillful habits." Toward the end of life, though, that effort at self-improvement is really more connected toward service and sharing, motivated by Gandhi's words (1987) "If we could change ourselves, the tendencies in the world would also change." Or as Rumi (1997) wrote, "Wherever you are, be the soul of the place." As my garden grows smaller, I still wish to tend it in a way that "serves water" to all who are thirsty. I also try to remember to balance my efforts at making the world a better place (positive assertive actions) with some acceptance of my limits and abilities.

Meditation is also an important part of addressing "*my ending story*"—including issues of impermanence and mortality. In my late forties, I was living in Safed, a mystical city in Israel where it is claimed that it is difficult to sleep because of the noise of angel wings. One evening, I hiked to the grave site of the noted mystic Rabbi Luria. I began meditating, accompanied by Ram Dass's tapes on death and dying (1992). As I sat, I had an experience, similar in many ways to a previous one I had in Daitoju-ji monastery, in Kyoto, when I was twenty-three. Both of them created a profound sense of peace with each of the three messengers. In the early one, a haiku emerged: (Shapiro & Shapiro, 1971)

The puddle mirrors
Rain drops dissolving in the
Image they contain.

I used that haiku in a novella, *The Last Harbor* (Shapiro, 1971, p. 56) about an old professor preparing his last lecture and reflecting on his unitive experience:

All was still in the zendo, meditation hall, except for the sound of raindrops striking the roof. Before my closed eyes I saw the white sand of the rock garden which lay outside the zendo. The sands were carefully raked to appear like the ocean. The rain mixed with the ocean of sand and out of the union of the two bodies of water, an embryo was formed.

He sits back in his chair. It was all once so clear. The new beginning.
The unity. Such peace in the moment, such hope for that little baby embryo.

The experience in Safed was of ultimate letting go into a benevolent universe. I was reminded of when I was a child, my parents would tuck me into bed, and my mom would sing "Now I lay me down to sleep... if I should die before I wake, I pray the Lord my soul to take."

Why control? I was once asked by a colleague—and fellow meditator—Maurits Kwee, "Why, with such a short time of life on earth, did I decide to devote my entire life with such passion to the issue of human control." When I search the "roots" of my interest in control, certainly one pivotal event was when I became completely deaf in my left ear at age three (due to the side effects of an antibiotic). Once in second grade I was slapped by a teacher, who thought I was being rude and ignoring her. She later apologized when she took me to the principal's office and he told her I wasn't being rude, but couldn't hear her because she was standing by my left (deaf) ear. I had to learn to adjust my environment, making sure in classrooms and in conversations that I had my right ear facing the person so I could hear them.

In addition to realizing that I had to "control" my physical environment, my search for how to gain a positive sense of control emotionally began when at thirteen my parents divorced, the "lovely castle-like environment" I grew up in---one in which my mom had been president of the Parent Teacher Association and my dad the little league baseball coach—began to fall apart.

We were forced to move from our comfortable, safe home, and my world seemed to spiral out of control. I was also told for the first time that I had had a baby brother before me who died a few days after birth. Although I didn't put it together in these terms, two pillars of Buddha—illness, and death—became known to me.

I also became increasingly aware over the next several years of habits within me that were not "helpful" or "kind." It became important to me to learn how (and if) I could best gain a positive sense of control over these unskillful (emotional, attentional, and behavioral ways of being). In looking back, what I was seeking to learn was how to develop an inner peace, and to bring that peace to bear in my interactions with others in the most healing way possible. I sought what Jou (2001) has called a "tai chi" dance a way to interact with others which minimized power struggles, acontrol battles, "unhelpful egoic challenges" and involved careful listening, and sought bridge building and enhanced mutual dialogue and cooperation.

For me, "control" involves conscious reflection and non-defensive self-awareness, going "in and through," nuance, self-regulation, calmness under pressure, sensitive listening, and care in speech and action. Attention to these various processes, in my view, provides us with the best means to achieve wisdom and compassion personally, interpersonally, and for planetary well-being. And that's the gist of why I've devoted my life personally and professionally to studying control, including meditation as one very important aspect of that study and practice.[7]

I'm often amused about the irony (the Universe's cosmic sense of humor?) that I believe one of my "gifts" as a psychologist (and as a human!) is that I, a one eared person, am very good at being able to hear and listen carefully and deeply to whomever I am dialoguing with. And it's through this listening, that I have sought and continue to seek to understand and "hear" myself, my beloved family, my friends and colleagues, and to build bridges with different political, religious and spiritual traditions.

Final Thoughts

> Breathing in, I relax my body and mind
> Breathing out, I smile,
> What a wonderful moment
>
> —Thich Nhat Hanh (1991, p. 25)

Breathing out, let us smile as we come to the end of our journey in this *Oxford Handbook of Meditation*. Let us give thanks to the editors who have gathered together the thoughtful, scholarly, wise, compassionate chapters that have contributed to this book. Taken as a whole, the writings in this book show an extraordinary maturity in the field of meditation scholarship and exploration. Nearly fifty years ago, when Charles Tart edited his seminal book on *Altered States of Consciousness* (1969), he noted that there were only two research studies on meditation available. In 1984, Roger Walsh and I edited the first handbook of meditation, focusing on psychology, psychophysiology, and mental health (Shapiro & Walsh, 1984). More than thirty-five years after that, reflected in the current volume, we see an explosion of research on the scientific content of meditation and its effects, from psychophysiological processes, therapeutic effects for mental and physical health, to altered state experiences.

[7] Because of space limitations, three sections were not included in this chapter

- An invitation to the reader to explore your relationship with meditation, including 1a) your "origin" story of meditation: what brought you to meditation and what it means to you in the context of your life; 1b) your views of control, and how meditation and control are involved in your view of human personality and the nature of the universe.
- "Matching" meditative strategy to the person, including 2a) further discussion of sensory preference; 2b) particular orientation and belief system; 2c) and the possibility of creating a larger "map" for addressing these issues.
- Meditation, control and your ending story, including issues of generativity, impermanence and mortality. (I also discuss my own views further there)

These sections may be found at https://deanehshapirojr.org/category/professional-writings/meditation/.

This edited book makes a major contribution to once again expanding our understanding of meditation's context. In the early days of meditation research, there was often a removal of a religious/spiritual context and its replacement with a secular, therapeutic one in order to facilitate scientific research and acceptance within health care and therapeutic practices (Kutz, Borsenko, & Benson, 1985). Removing the religious/spiritual context helped facilitate a plethora of research on the "content" of meditation, looking at its components, mediating mechanisms, and the ability to compare meditation with other self-regulation strategies (Shapiro & Zifferblatt, 1976).The field has matured sufficiently that this book now adds back the spiritual and particularistic context in several chapters—Hinduism, Judaism, Christianity, Islam, Buddhism, and Daoism. I would like to end this chapter on a personal note, with an expression of gratitude. I would like to give thanks to the editors and fellow contributors in this volume, each trying to share part of their journey, their effort to understand meditation. I also give thanks to my teachers and students from whom I have received so much. This chapter is intended to be my final writing about meditation. I see it as a metaphoric message in a bottle—and as a let it go, I can only bow to the wisdom and compassion of the next generation of messengers. Let us hope (and pray, or affirm), that our efforts and time will become part of the sound of the temple bell to help heal suffering and increase joy of those who follow.

References

Astin, J. (1997). An eight week program in stress reduction based on mindfulness meditation: Effects on psychological symptomatology, sense of control, and spiritual experiences. *Psychotherapy and psychosomatics* 66(2), 97–106.

Astin, J., Shapiro, J., & Shapiro, D. (2013). Psychological control and breast cancer morbidity and mortality: A twenty-year follow-up study. *Journal of Behavioral Medicine* 39, 7–10.

Arnold, E., Sir (Trans.). Bhagavad Gita (Dover Thrift Editions), Paperback–October 12, 1993.

Bandura, A. (1977). Self-efficacy: Toward a unifying theory of behaviour change. *Psychological Reviews 84*, 191–215.

Burger, J. M., & Cooper, H. M. (1979). The desirability of control. *Motivation and Emotion* 3, 381–393.

Dass, R. (1992). *Conscious aging: On the nature of change and facing death* [Audio tapes]. Boulder, CO: Sounds True.

Dass, R. (1994). Talk at International Transpersonal Conference, Santa Clara, CA.

Easterline, B. L. (1992). Buddhist Vipassana meditation and daily living: Effect on cognitive style, awareness affect, and acceptance. (Doctoral dissertation). Retrieved from http://controlresearch.net/support-files/Buddist-Vipassana-Meditation-and-Daily-Living-Dissertation.pdf

Evans, G., Shapiro, D. H., & Lewis, M. (1993). Dysfunctional control: Negative consequences of seeking and maintaining control. *British Journal of Psychology 84*, 255–273.

Frankl, V. (1980). *Man's search for meaning: An introduction to logotherapy*. New York: Simon & Schuster. (Original work published 1962).

Fronsdal, G. (Trans.). (2006). *Dhammapada: A new translation of the Buddhist classic with annotations*. Boulder, CO: Shambala.

Gandhi, M. (1987). *Autobiography: The story of my experiments with truth* (M. Desai, Trans.). London: Penguin. (Original work published 1948).
Hanh, T. N. (1991). *Peace is every step.* New York: Bantam.
Hayes, S. C., Strosahl, K. D., & Wilson, K. G. (2016). *Acceptance and commitment therapy: The process and practice of mindful change* (2nd ed.). New York: Guilford Press.
Jou, T. H. (2001). *The Tao of Taijiquan* (89th printing). Scottsdale, AZ: Tai Chi Foundation.
Kutz, I., Borsenky, J., & Benson, H. (1985). Meditation and psychotherapy: A rationale for the integration of dynamic psychotherapy, the relaxation response, and mindfulness meditation. *American Journal of Psychiatry 14*(1), 1–8.
Linehan, M. M., Comtois, K. A., Murray, A. M., Brown, M. Z., Gallop, R. J., Heard, H. L., . . . Lindenboim, N. (2006). Two-year randomized controlled trial and follow-up of dialectical behavior therapy vs therapy by experts for suicidal behaviors and borderline personality disorder. *Archives of General Psychiatry 63*(7), 757–766.
Malraux, A. (1953). *The voices of silence.* Garden City, NY: Doubleday.
Meri, J. W. (Ed.). (2005). Jihad. In *Medieval Islamic civilization: An encyclopedia* (p. 419). Abingdon-on-Thames: Routledge.
Niebuhr, R. (1987). *The essential Reinhold Niebuhr: Selected essays and addresses* (R. McAfee Brown (Ed.)). New Haven, CT: Yale University Press.
Paul, G. (1966). *Insight vs desensitization in psychotherapy: An experiment in anxiety reduction.* Palo Alto, CA: Stanford University Press.
Rahula, W. (1959). *What the Buddha taught.* New York: Grove Press.
Rodin, J. (1986). Aging and health: Effects of the sense of control. *Science* 233(4770): 1271–1276.
Rotter, J. B. (1966). Generalized expectancies for internal versus external control of reinforcement. *Psychological Monographs: General and Applied 80*(1), 1–28.
Rumi, Jalāl ad-Dīn Muhammad. (1997). *The illustrated Rumi* (C. Barks & M. Green, Trans. & Ed.). New York: Bantam Doubleday.
Scherman, Meir Zlotowitz Nosson. Pirkei Avos (Ethics of the fathers with and interlinear translation) (The Schottenstein edition, art (Hardcover) Hardcover–January 1, 1995.
Seagel, Z. V., Williams, J. M. G., & Teasdale, J. D. (2013). *Mindfulness-based cognitive therapy for depression* (2nd ed.). New York: Guilford Press.
Seligman, M. E. P. (1975). *Learned helplessness.* San Francisco: Freeman.
Shapiro, D. (1971). *The last harbor.* Retrieved from http://deanehshapirojr.org/the-last-harbor/
Shapiro, D. (1978). *Precision Nirvana.* Englewood Cliffs, NJ: Prentice-Hall.
Shapiro, D. (1980). *Meditation: Self-regulation strategy and altered states of consciousness.* New York: Aldine. Retrieved from http://deanehshapirojr.org/meditation-self-regulation-strategy-altered-state-of-consciousness-a-scientificpersonal-exploration/
Shapiro, D. (1982). Reliability of four quadrant model of self-control: Ratings by experts in type A behavior/health psychology; East-West psychology, and sex role psychology. *Psychologia 25*(3), 149–154.
Shapiro, D. (1983). A content analysis of Eastern and Western, traditional and New Age approaches to health, and healing. In R. Walsh and D. Shapiro (Eds.), *Beyond health and normality: Explorations of exceptional psychological well-being* (pp. 432–491). New York: Van Nostrand Reinhold. Retrieved from http://deanehshapirojr.org/a-content-analysis-of-eastern-and-western-traditional-and-new-age-approaches-to-health-and-healing/
Shapiro, D. (1989a). Exploring our most deeply held belief about ultimate reality. *Revision: The Journal of Consciousness and Change 12*(1), 15–28. Retrieved from http://deanehshapirojr.org/exploring-our-most-deeply-held-belief-about-ultimate-reality/

Shapiro, D. (1989b). Self-control and other control in cross-cultural perspective: Balinese trance and religious beliefs. *ReVision: The Journal of Consciousness and Change 12*(2), 33–46.

Shapiro, D. (1990a). Maintaining a sense of control in addressing perennial issues of a personal, interpersonal, and cosmic nature: Reflections on Bali. *International Journal of Psychosomatics 37*(1–4), 40–49.

Shapiro, D. (1990b). Clinical applications of a control model of psychological health: Two case studies of stress-related disorders. *Psychotherapy Patient 7*(1–2), 169–198.

Shapiro, D. (1992). A mode of control and self-control profile for long term meditators: A retrospective and prospective assessment. *Psychologia 35*(1), 1–11.

Shapiro, D. (1993). *One reality, many paths: Exploring the universal/particular relationship.* Sausalito, CA: Institute of Noetic Sciences. Retrieved from http://deanehshapirojr.org/one-reality-many-paths-exploring-the-universalparticular-relationship/

Shapiro, D. (1994). *Manual for the Shapiro Control Inventory (SCI).* Palo Alto, CA: Behavirodata. Retrieved from http://controlresearch.net/shapiro-control-inventory-manual.html

Shapiro, D. (2001). Meditation and psychotherapy: A case study. In D. Wedding & R. J. Corsini (Eds.), *Case studies in psychotherapy* (3rd ed., pp. 225–242). Itasca, IL: FE Peacock Publishers.

Shapiro, D. (2014). *Control therapy: Helping individuals gain a positive sense of control in their lives—The last lecture.* Retrieved from http://controlresearch.net/control-therapy-last-lecture.html

Shapiro, D., & Astin, J. (1998). *Control therapy: An integrated approach to psychotherapy, health, and healing.* New York: John Wiley. Retrieved from http://controlresearch.net/

Shapiro, D., Evans, G., & Shapiro, J. (1987). Human control. *Science 238*, 260.

Shapiro, D., Friedman, M., & Piaget, G. (1991). Changes in mode of control and self-control for post myocardial infarction patients evidencing Type A behavior: The effects of a cognitive/behavioral intervention and/or cardiac counseling. *International Journal of Psychosomatic Medicine 38*(1–4), 4–12.

Shapiro, D., Kruse, J., & Astin, J. A. (2017). Gaining a positive sense of control: Teaching the principles and practice of control therapy in an educational setting. *Psychologia 60*, 147–166. Retrieved from http://controlresearch.net/support-files/Gaining-a-Positive-Sense-of-Control-to-Psychologia.pdf

Shapiro, D., Potkin, S., Jin, Y., Brown, B., & Carreon, D. (1993). Measuring the psychological construct of control: Discriminant, divergent, and incremental validity of the Shapiro Control Inventory and Rotter's and Wallston's Locus of Control Scales. *International Journal of Psychosomatics 40*(1–4), 35–46.

Shapiro, D., Jr., Schwartz, C. E., & Astin, J. A. (1996). Controlling ourselves, controlling our world: Psychology's role in understanding positive and negative consequences of seeking and gaining control. *American Psychologist 51*(12), 1213–1230. Retrieved from https://doi.org/10.1037/0003-066X.51.12.1213

Shapiro, D., & Shapiro, J. (1971). A daily musing: A collection of haiku. Retrieved from http://deanehshapirojr.org/a-daily-musing/

Shapiro, D., Soucar, B., Shapiro, S. L, & Astin, J. A. (2010). Control therapy training manual. Retrieved from controlresearch.net

Shapiro, D., & Walsh, R. (1984). *Meditation: Classic and contemporary perspectives.* New York: Aldine/Walter de Gruyter. Reprinted (2017).

Shapiro, D., Wu, J., Hong, C., Buchsbaum, M., Elderkin-Thompson, V., Hillard, D., Hetu, M., & Friedman, G. (1995). Exploring the relationship between having control and losing control to functional neuroanatomy within the sleeping state. *Psychologia 38*(3), 133–145.

Shapiro, D., & Zifferblatt, S. (1976). Zen meditation and behavioral self-control: Similarities, differences, clinical applications. *American Psychologist 31*, 519–532.
Shapiro, S. (2017). The power of mindfulness: What you practice grows stronger [TED Talk]. Retrieved from https://www.youtube.com/watch?v=IeblJdB2-Vo
Shapiro, S. (2020). *Good morning, I love you: Mindfulness and self-compassion practices.* Louisville, CO: Sounds True Publishing.
Shapiro, S., & Carlson, L. (2017). *The art and science of mindfulness: Integrating mindfulness into psychology and the helping professions* (2nd ed.). Washington, DC: American Psychological Association.
Shapiro, S. L., Bootzin, R. R., Figueredo, A. J., Lopez, A. M., Schwartz, G. E. (2003). The efficacy of mindfulness-based stress reduction in the treatment of sleep disturbance in women with breast cancer: An exploratory study. *Journal of Psychosomatic Research 54*(1), 85–91.
Smith, H. (1983). The sacred unconscious. In R. Walsh and D. Shapiro (Eds.), *Beyond health and normality: Explorations of exceptional psychological wellbeing* (pp. 265–272). New York: Van Nostrand Reinhold.
Soucar, E. A. (2005). *Establishing culturally competent practice: Effects of control-enhancing psychotherapy on depression and anxiety for African American outpatients* (Dissertation, Philadelphia, PA: Temple University). Retrieved from http://controlresearch.net/support-files/Establishing-Culturally-Competent-Practice.pdf
Tart, C. (1969). Altered states of consciousness. New York: John Wiley.
Tloczynski, J., Malinowski, A., & Lamorte, R. (1997). Rediscovering and reapplying contingent informal meditation. *Psychologia* 40, 14–21.
Wallston, K. A., Wallston, B. S., & DeVellis, R. (1978). Development of the Multidimensional Health Locus of Control (MHLC) scales. *Health Education Monographs 6*(2), 160–170.
Watson, B., (Trans.). (1996). *Chuang Tzu: Basic writings.* New York: Columbia University Press.
Weisz, J. R., Rothbaum, F. M., & Blackburn, T. C. (1984). Standing out and standing in: The psychology of control in America and Japan. *American Psychologist 39*, 955–969.
Yogananda, Paramahansa. (1946). *Autobiography of a yogi.* Public Domain version.

CHAPTER 24

PSYCHOLOGICAL THEORIES OF MEDITATION IN EARLY BUDDHISM AND SĀṂKHYA/YOGA

PETER SEDLMEIER AND KUNCHAPUDI SRINIVAS

Introduction

Several meta-analyses indicate that meditation has numerous positive effects, both for healthy practitioners (e.g., Sedlmeier, Loße, & Quasten, 2018; Sedlmeier et al., 2012) as well as patients (e.g., Gotink et al., 2015; Goyal et al., 2014). However, theories about why and how these effects arise are still in their infancy (Sedlmeier, Eberth, & Puta, 2016; Sedlmeier, Eberth, & Schwarz, 2014). In this chapter, we use early Buddhism and the Hindu thought systems of Sāṃkhya/Yoga as representative examples to argue that ancient Indian theoretical approaches that extensively dealt with the topic of meditation could play an important role in eventually arriving at a comprehensive theory (or even several different theories) of meditation. Originally, these approaches have not been developed as psychological theories but as paths to salvation, and the way their contents are described is far from an exposition of a theory one would find in a contemporary textbook. Therefore, it is necessary to first disentangle religious and philosophical contents from psychological ones, and to disambiguate the often cryptic original texts and "translate" them into Western cognitive psychology. Basically, this means teasing out claims that are in principle empirically testable. We will occasionally use the original terms (Pali for early Buddhism and Sanskrit for Sāṃkhya/Yoga) to give the interested reader the opportunity to connect to the extensive background literature.

This chapter is not a further piece of the already innumerable exegeses of the ancient texts, and we also do not aim to give a picture all Buddhist or classical Hindu scholars would be satisfied with. That would be impossible anyway because there exist quite some inconsistencies, and sometimes even contradictions, concerning translations and interpretations of the ancient texts (the Buddha himself seems to have changed his way of teaching over time; see, e.g., Frauwallner, 2003; Gombrich, 2013). Instead, we regard our necessarily subjective rendering of the ancient theories as a building block for arriving at a contemporary theory of meditation that is open to empirical scrutiny.

Traditional Indian Explanatory Systems

Meditation techniques are already mentioned in the most ancient Indian scriptures, the Vedas (see chapter 4 in Feuerstein, 1998). There is some disagreement about when exactly the origin of the Vedas (there are four, consisting of four parts each) should be dated, but estimates for the earliest Veda (the *Ṛgveda Saṃhitā*) range between 3500 BCE and 1200 BCE (e.g., Frawley, 2001; Hiriyanna, 2000; Klostermaier, 2006; Sharma, 2003). However, meditation as well as presumed underlying processes and hypothesized effects were treated in more detail only later in the different schools of interpretations of the Vedas, usually termed "philosophical systems" or just "systems." There are two classes of such systems: ones that strictly adhere to the Vedic texts and ones that are regarded by most scholars as (critical) reactions to these texts. The former are usually summarized as "orthodox systems" and the latter as "heterodox systems" (for details see Dasgupta, 1930; Hiriyanna, 2000; Sedlmeier, 2006; see also Flood, this volume, and Wernicke-Olesen, this volume).

We decided to focus on the heterodox system of Buddhism as well as a combination of two orthodox systems, Sāṃkhya/Yoga, because apart from containing quite elaborate psychological theories that are relevant for explaining the effects of meditation, all other (later) Indian thought systems refer to them (e.g., Flood, 2004; Frauwallner, 2003; Puligandla, 1997; Whiteman, 1993; see also Wernicke-Olesen, this volume).

The Early Buddhist Theory of Meditation

We begin with Buddhism because, although it was certainly influenced by Hindu thought, the first systematic treatises of the orthodox systems, that is, those of Sāṃkhya (Īśvarakṛṣṇa's *Sāṃkhyakārikā*) and Yoga, were probably compiled after the introduction of Buddhism (Raju, 1985, p. 304), and early Buddhism can be shown to have strongly influenced later Hindu thinking (Frauwallner, 2010, p. 1; Upadhaya, 1968). Moreover, conflict with the Buddhists has largely stimulated philosophic enquiry in most of the systems of Hindu thought (Dasgupta, 1997, p. 78). The origin of Buddhism can be traced back to the sixth/fifth century BCE. The Buddha never put down his teachings in writing. It was in the first council held in Rajagriha around 543 BCE that the main Buddhist canon was compiled. This canon consists of "three baskets" (*Tipiṭaka*), namely, the basket of discipline (*Vinaya Piṭaka*), mostly containing rules for monks and nuns, the basket of aphorisms (*Sutta Piṭaka*), containing the sermons of the Buddha, and the basket of higher teaching (*Abhidhamma Piṭaka*), which was added about two hundred years after the first two baskets. The earliest available source of the canon was committed to writing in the Pali language in the first century BCE (de Silva, 1990). Therefore, the *Tipiṭaka* is also known as the Pali Canon. We used the Pali Canon as our main basis. However, as the present work is not a scriptural analysis but an attempt to construct building blocks for a valid theory of meditation, we also freely refer to later sources, for instance commentaries on the Pali Canon (such as Buddhaghosa's famous medieval *Visuddhimagga*) or contemporary commentaries, if we considered them helpful for our purpose. There are many different schools of Buddhism that rely on different authoritative texts, but all seem to agree on the assumptions on human nature in the early forms of Buddhism on which we will concentrate here (for the following see, for instance, Bodhi, 2013; de Silva, 2005; Frauwallner, 2010; Gombrich, 2013; Hamilton, 2000; Kalupahana, 1992; Olendzki, 2003; 2010; and Rahula, 1959).

What Is Meditation in Early Buddhism?

In early as well as later Buddhism, meditation is not a single technique but two or even three collections of techniques that are embedded in a spiritual and moral context. Meditation techniques and their context are summarized in the Noble Eightfold Path, which in its entirety is regarded as the way to attain liberation, the aim of the Buddhist soteriology (for sequences of development toward enlightenment that do not fully coincide with the Noble Eightfold Path, see Johansson, 1970, chapter 15). This Noble Eightfold Path is often depicted not in ascending order but in the form of a spiral or in circular form (Fig. 24.1) to indicate that the eight parts of the path do not have to be progressed through in a definite order (e.g., Harvey, 2004, p. 71). Indeed, what the right order should be is still open to discussion (Gombrich, 2013, p. 109).

Traditionally the two last limbs of the path refer to meditation: right mindfulness (*sammā-sati*) and right concentration (*sammā-samādhi*), but many scholars also count right effort (*sammā-vāyāma*) as part of the "meditation group" (upper left part of Fig. 24.1). Let us begin with right effort. It deals with what to do with "unwholesome mental states," especially any form of aversion including hatred, anger, and resentment toward anything or anyone. If these states have not yet arisen, right effort creates a psychological environment that should impede them from arising. If they are already

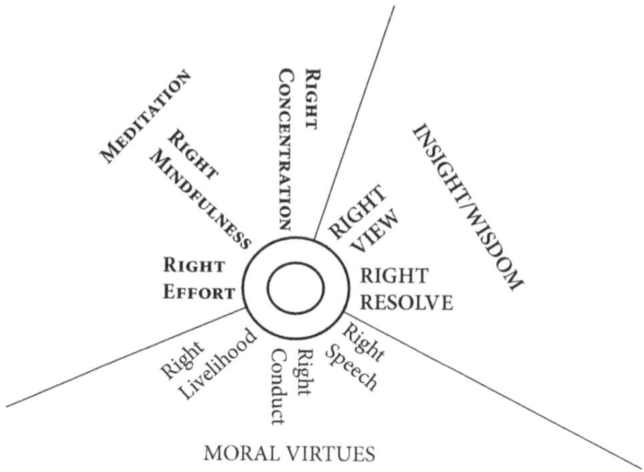

FIGURE 24.1 The Buddhist Noble Eightfold Path.

there, right effort should be used to appease them, and finally, to prevent these unwholesome states from arising at all. On the other hand, wholesome states such as generosity, kindness, and wisdom should be cultivated or applied as antidotes. Therefore, one could argue that what is nowadays known as loving-kindness meditation or compassion meditation (e.g., Salzberg, 1995) corresponds to this limb of the Eightfold Path.

The second collection of meditation techniques in the Eightfold Path refers to mindfulness. The most important original source for describing the practice of mindfulness is the *Satipaṭṭhāna Sutta* (see Anālayo, 2003, for an excellent exposition). According to this *sutta*, practicing mindfulness means to be continuously aware of the "four foundations of mindfulness" (*satipaṭṭhānas*), that is, the body, basic feelings (pleasant, unpleasant, neutral), the mind, and the objects of the mind (*dhammas*). Awareness practices that refer to one or more of the four *satipaṭṭhānas* are central ingredients in all current forms of "*vipassanā* meditation" that can be traced back to the meditation techniques included in the Noble Eightfold Path (Anālayo, 2012). Awareness is also practiced in the many varieties of what nowadays runs under the banner of "mindfulness meditation." However, it should be noted that the use of the term "mindfulness" in the contemporary literature does not always correspond closely to the original concept; and the term "mindfulness meditation" as used in the research literature can refer to many different practices that are sometimes only loosely connected to "right mindfulness" (Amaro, 2015; Anālayo,2019; Belzer et al., 2013; Brazier, 2013; Dreyfus, 2011; Grossman & van Dam, 2011; Lutz, Jha, Dunne, & Saron, 2015; Sharf, 2014; Shonin, van Gordon, & Singh, 2015).

Finally, right concentration means moving toward a state of complete concentration, with the aim of "cessation of apperception and feeling" (*saññā-vedayita-nirodha*). Meditators can achieve this aim by continually concentrating on a given object such as the breath, a visual object, a mantra, and a multitude of other kinds of objects (Shaw, 2006; see also this volume on Theravada Buddhism). The objects of concentration may follow a general order (e.g., Gunaratana, 1980; Johansson, 1970) or may be chosen according to the personality structures of meditators (Buddhaghosa, 2010; Kornfield, 2009). This type of concentrative meditation is known as *samatha* (calming) meditation.

The moral virtues part of the Eightfold Path (bottom part in Fig. 24.1), that is, right speech, right conduct, and right livelihood (for detailed descriptions of the contents of all eight limbs, see Rahula, 1959) do not entail meditation techniques, contrary to the insight/wisdom part (upper right part of Fig. 24.1). Right resolve (*sammā-saṅkappa*) includes the practice of non-greed and non-hatred and the cultivation of the attitude of not expecting anything for one's deeds. Moreover, it contains the cultivation of thoughts of loving-kindness and compassion for all living creatures. As already mentioned, such practices are part of several contemporary kinds of mindfulness meditation. And right view (*sammā-diṭṭhi*), includes the cultivation of insight into the true nature of the world (*yathā-bhūta-ñāṇa-dassana*), including the Four Noble Truths, which will be discussed shortly.

A widespread consensus seems to be that *samatha* practice alone does not lead to the final aim of the Eightfold Path but must be complemented by mindfulness practice, although this view is not universal (for critical discussions, see Griffith, 1981; Gunaratana, 1980). In contrast, insight (mindfulness) meditation alone is sometimes considered sufficient to reach the aim (e.g., Anālayo, 2003; Gombrich, 2006, pp. 123–127). The practice of concentrative methods is generally seen as a beneficial first step in meditation, though (e.g., Batchelor, 2016; Gunaratana, 2015; Lutz, Slagter, Dunne, & Davidson, 2008). Sometimes, the cultivation of loving-kindness and compassion alone is regarded as sufficient to arrive at the goals of the Buddhist path (Gombrich, 1998, 2013, p. 85; Maithrimurthi, 1999, p. 34).

It turns out that the majority of the limbs of the Eightfold Path deal with techniques that are included in contemporary approaches to *vipassanā* meditation, which currently is probably the most widely practiced application of the Eightfold Path. However, these approaches are not identical. There are, for instance, orientations, all from Burmese teachers, that allegedly do without *samatha* (calming) practice, such as that of Mahasi Sayadaw (1904–1982; see Mahasi, 1991), while others present a balance of mindfulness and *samatha* practice, such as the method of U Ba Khin (1899–1971) popularized by his Indian student S. N. Goenka (1924–2013; see Hart, 1987), and again others, such as the approach of Pa Auk Sayadaw (born 1934) emphasize *samatha* practice (Pa Auk, 2003).

What Is the Aim of Meditation in Early Buddhism, and How Does it Work?

Meditation, together with its ethical and moral context, is the solution, but what is the problem? The problem, stated in the Buddha's *first noble truth*, is that everyone is faced with the suffering or unsatisfactory nature of our lives. This unsatisfaction is upheld by the "fires" of greed/passion, hatred/aversion, and ignorance/delusion: we want to have pleasant or attractive things or want someone to love us; we want to get rid of unpleasant or ugly things, or we hate someone; and we often face problems of understanding what things mean and what life is about. Wanting and disliking creates a bond between us and the world, which supports a sense that the world is stable, as is the self; however, because all pleasant things go away after some time and nothing lasts forever, we cannot but feel dissatisfied with our lives, again and again. The Buddha seems to have taken the idea of the three fires, as expressed in the "Fire Sermon" (*Vinaya Piṭaka*, I, 34–35) from the Vedas (Gombrich, 2013, p. 112). Note, however, that in the later Mahayana tradition, the reference to the Vedas seems to have been lost and the "three fires" are often called the "three poisons" (Gombrich, 2013, p. 113) or the "three defiling impulses" (De Silva, 2005, p. 29). Anyway, as long as the three fires burn, there is no liberation. Only if they are extinguished, one experiences *nibbāna* (Sanskrit *nirvāṇa*), that is, the "going out" of the fires (Olendzki, 2010, p. 24). Reaching that state—by means of meditation as the central part of the Noble Eightfold Path—allows one to see how the world really is. And this, according to Buddhist theory, means to have an intuitive insight (*vipassanā*) and understand fully the "three hallmarks" or "characteristics" (*ti-lakkhaṇa*) of life (e.g., Anālayo, 2003, p. 102–106; Premasiri, 2008, p. 97): the transient nature or impermanence of all phenomena, material or mental (*anicca*), the tendency of transient objects to produce a feeling of unsatisfaction or suffering when there are strong attachments to such objects (*dukkha*), and the lack of any substantial reality in them, especially the lack of an independent self (*anattā*).

Two of the characteristics of life, *anicca* and *anattā*, can be seen as a direct consequence of the Buddhist model of the five *khaṇḍas* (usually translated as "aggregates") that together constitute our lives (see Fig. 24.2). The five *khaṇḍas* are ever-changing processes (Hamilton, 2000) that produce the "fuel" that keeps the fires of greed, hatred and delusion burning and thereby are the basis for the unsatisfaction of our lives, as expressed in the Buddha's first noble truth: "in brief, the five aggregates subject to clinging are suffering" (Bodhi, 2005, p. 76).

According to the *Abhidhamma Piṭaka* (see Bodhi, 2013), we experience a continuous stream of consciousness (consciousness is one of the five *khaṇḍas*) that consists of a very rapid succession of extremely short "consciousnesses," one at a time, and one for each sense organ (note that in Buddhist theory, the mind is also considered a sense organ). Each moment of consciousness, which could also be seen as an act of perception of a material or mental object, is accompanied by other bodily and mental activities that take place in the other four *khaṇḍas*. Hereby, the *khaṇḍa* of *form* includes both the external physical world and internally the material body and the physical sense organs (lower right part of Fig. 24.2). Any given moment of consciousness is accompanied by a feeling that can be pleasant, neutral, or unpleasant (*khaṇḍa* of *feeling*), and by some kind of apperception that involves memories of sense impressions, images, ideas, or concepts, related to the current moment of consciousness (*khaṇḍa* of *apperception*). Consciousness, feeling, and apperception work together to answer the question "What is going on here?" The last, and psychologically most interesting, *khaṇḍa*, *saṅkhāra*, usually translated as *mental formations* with volition as the central ingredient (see Gombrich, 2013, p. 135) can be regarded as providing the basis for answering the question

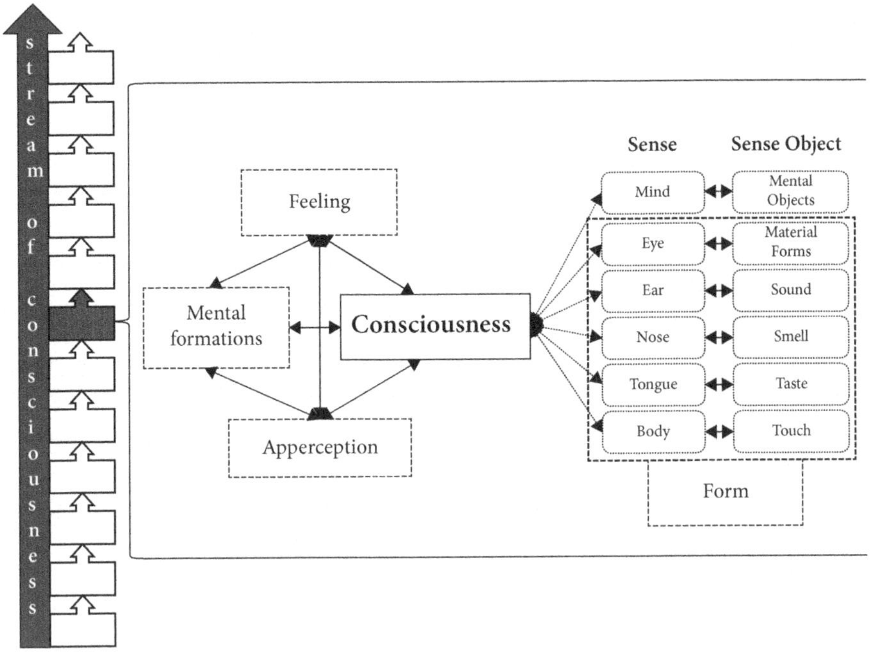

FIGURE 24.2 The five *khaṇḍas* (form, feeling, apperception, mental formations, and consciousness) and the stream of consciousness.

"How do I respond to this?" Apart from volition, this *khaṇḍa* contains mental constituents such as emotions, actions, underlying tendencies (which might be called "habits" in contemporary psychology), and conditioned responses. In all kinds of cognition, all five aggregates potentially take part. For each moment of consciousness, the combination of activities in the aggregates is dependent on prior combinations: According to the law of *dependent origination*, postulated by the Buddha, all physical and mental phenomena arise and pass away in dependence upon multiple causes and conditions. There is no "central processor" in this stream of consciousness and nothing stable, ·just *anattā* and *anicca*.

For some of these causes and conditions that determine the processes taking place in the five *khaṇḍas*, we ourselves (figuratively speaking) are "responsible" because they are the product of our volitions (in the formations *khaṇḍa*). However, it seems to us that this part of the theory, concerning the arising of volitions, is underspecified and potentially problematic. The theory of early Buddhism apparently does not specify when, why, and how volitions arise that yield unfavorable *kamma*. But such *kamma* can only be produced if somebody or some process is responsible for it—only then Buddhist ethics seems to make sense. Anyway, when our volitions are "unwholesome," that is, accompanied by greed, hatred and ignorance, they produce, via the processes of the *khaṇḍas*, negative effects that are accumulated in our *kamma* (Sanskrit *karma*). Note that Buddhists claim that the stream of consciousness does not completely end at death but goes on to a new birth. The *Abhidhamma* describes the respective subtle kind of consciousness as a process consisting of a stream of so-called *bhavaṅgas*, which can be regarded as the life continuum (see Bodhi, 2013). This stream of *bhavaṅgas* is a kind of ongoing default process that is always active if no conscious cognition takes place, and it does not stop at the end of an individual life. So the *kamma* accumulated in the previous life can be seen as the link to the next life, as the principle of continuity, together with the five *khaṇḍas* (Gombrich, 2013). As long as the fire burns, that is, as long as our actions are fed by greed, hatred, and ignorance, the unsatisfaction of our present and future lives does not come to an end.

Here meditation and the rest of the Noble Eightfold Path become relevant. Meditation yields a deep insight into the working of the five *khaṇḍas*, thereby reducing and finally extinguishing the fires of greed, hatred, and ignorance that sustain our "thirst" (*taṇhā*) described in the second noble truth as the basis for the unsatisfaction we encounter in our lives: "It is the thirst leading to rebirth, which, accompanied by delight and passion, finds enjoyment here and there, namely, thirst for desire, thirst for becoming, thirst for annihilation" (cited after Frauwallner, 2010, p. 14). In later sermons, the thirst for annihilation seems to have lost its importance—but note the similarities between the Buddha's account and Sigmund Freud's Eros and Thanatos as the assumed basis of our behavior. Instead, the concept of ignorance has gained much importance as a step in the chain of dependent origination (Frauwallner, 2003, 2010; Gombrich, 2013).

If the three fires are extinguished and replaced by their positive counterparts, that is, by contentment, kindness, and wisdom, no more unfavorable *kamma* is produced and the cycle of rebirths comes to its end (Kalupahana, 2009, p. 139). Such a view of reality might, after all, not sound so tempting to achieve, but although the Buddha mostly used the negative term of *nibbāna* to refer to this state, he mentioned several times in the Pali Canon that the extinguishing of the fires also yields experiences of bliss (*nibbuti*, see Gombrich, 2013, p. 113). According to Buddhist scriptures and according to accounts of people who seem to have attained enlightenment in the Buddhist sense, the experience of *nibbāna* is the most satisfying and happiest experience in life (e.g., Anālayo, 2003, p. 264).

Walpola Rahula, a Theravada Buddhist monk and scholar, has compiled a description of an enlightened person from the suttas (Rahula, 1959, p. 43), which is closely mirrored by the following more contemporary account: "People who have been through it tend to be described by others as simple, natural, genuine and straightforward; serene and peaceful yet alert and full of life and vitality; wise in their words and economical and effective in their actions; kind, friendly, gentle and considerate in their dealings with people; perceptive and intelligent; at ease in their bodies and at home in the world. They seem to have shed the neurotic baggage that the rest of us reluctantly carry about: anxiety, irritation, resentment, regret, guilt, meanness, greed, jealousy, possessiveness, worry, confusion and the rest of the familiar catalogue" (Claxton, 1986, p. 9).

What Can Be Predicted from the Meditation Theory of Early Buddhism?

The Buddha has not laid down his theory in a textbook-like fashion. Instead, he has delivered his insights in several sermons, and he has used different ways to illustrate them over the years of his teaching. For instance, instead of the "fire metaphor," which we have extensively drawn upon, he also used a "burden metaphor" for describing the effects of the five *khaṇḍas* (e.g., Frauwallner, 2010, p. 28), or, to take another example, the chain of dependent origination exists in the scriptures in several versions, with different numbers of links and different orders of the links (Gombrich, 2013, p. 109). Nonetheless a common structure is visible across all his teachings. We are faced with a fundamental problem that arises because of the nature of the world: everything is transient, there are no eternal things (not even the soul), and this causes an ongoing unsatisfaction or, to take Stephen Batchelor's (1997) translation of *dukkha*, anguish, in our lives. The solution to this problem, and the general prediction of the theory is this: Meditation, practiced in the context of the other limbs of the Noble Eightfold Path, eventually leads to an intuitive insight into the "nature" of our life, that is, the working of the five *khaṇḍas* (Fig. 24.2) and thus to *nibbāna*, the appeasement of all anguish.

From the claims described above, predictions can also be made for what happens on the way to this final aim. Here, one has to differentiate between the two main strands of meditation, mindfulness meditation and concentrative meditation. The practice of mindfulness can be expected to produce insight, which will dampen the reactivity toward the affective states of greed and hatred, and appease the suffering of the impermanent, interdependent self (Batchelor, 2016; Hamilton, 2000). Moreover, the *Brahmavihāras*, that is, loving-kindness, compassion, sympathetic joy, and equanimity can be expected to flourish. These four "sublime states" should become more spontaneous with increasing meditation practice, and as the mind is increasingly governed by these sublime states, it will get less resentful, and have less tension and irritability (Nyanaponika, 1999, p. 11). Therefore, with increasing meditation practice, one would expect increasing abilities of emotion regulation, less negative and more positive emotions, increasingly clear thinking and wiser decisions. Mindfulness practice should also increase basic awareness in everyday life, and the practice of loving-kindness and compassion should have a positive effect on the cultivation of positive emotions.

It is also plausible to expect direct positive effects of *samatha* practice on attention and concentration. After mastering the first four stages (*jhānas*) of the *samatha* practice, one could also expect some sorts of higher knowledges (see Sedlmeier, 2018) and after going through all stages, even *nibbāna*, according to some sources (see Harvey, 2004; see *this volume* on meditation in the various Buddhist traditions).

Unfortunately, there are no specific predictions for isolated parts of the Noble Eightfold Path, so it is unclear whether and how, for instance, meditation alone or even mindfulness (*sati*) meditation alone works without the help of the other limbs, although this question is open to empirical scrutiny. However, Buddhist monks were always aware of the fact that different adepts might need different techniques from the Buddhist "meditation toolbox." This has been most prominently expressed in the *Visuddhimagga*, or "Path of Purification," a medieval interpretation of the Pali Canon (see Buddhaghosa, 2010, for a translation from the Pali text). The *Visuddhimagga* suggests different spiritual tasks for the three types of monks who can be distinguished in respect to how strongly the fires of greed, hatred, and ignorance burn in them. Greedy types should, for instance, contemplate old age, sickness, and death in their meditation practice to recognize the inherent transience of all objects and experiences. Hateful types might be advised to learn to relax or notice joy (and not only suffering) and practice loving-kindness meditation to redirect their critical abilities into analytical ones. And finally, deluded types should increase their awareness by, for instance, labeling experiences and practicing single-pointed concentration such as simple breath meditation. Contemporary research strongly suggests that individual differences can also play an important role in whether a certain practice of meditation is effective or whether people are attracted to meditative practices at all (Farias, Claridge, & Lalljee, 2005; Farias & Wikholm, 2016; see also Buric et al., this volume).

The Sāṃkhya/Yoga Theory of Meditation

Sāṃkhya and Yoga are traditionally seen as strongly related, with Sāṃkhya focusing more on the philosophical and Yoga more on the practical aspects of a theory of meditation that can be derived from these systems (for more background information and the relationship between Sāṃkhya/Yoga and Western research, see Rao & Paranjpe, 2008; Sedlmeier & Srinivas, 2016). The *Sāṃkhyakārikā* by Īśvarakṛṣṇa, written about 200 CE (e.g., Dasgupta, 1997, p. 212) is regarded as the first representative source for Sāṃkhya (Raju, 1985, p. 305), although the origins of the system can be traced back to shortly after the death of the Buddha (Frauwallner, 2003, p. 182). Sāṃkhya is the oldest orthodox Indian system that directly goes back to the Vedas and has strongly influenced all later philosophical and religious systems (Frauwallner, 2003, p. 183; Puligandla, 1997, p. 119), most strongly the system of Yoga. The main source of that system are the *Yoga Sūtras* (see Whiteman, 1993; Woods, 1998, for translations). These are usually attributed to one Patañjali but more likely have been written by several authors in between the second century BCE to the fifth century CE (Dasgupta, 1997; Flood, 2004). There are many other sources referred to by practitioners of yoga (for overview see Feuerstein, 1998; Phillips, 2009), but the *Yoga Sūtras* are central to all of these.

What Is Meditation in Sāṃkhya/Yoga?

The meditation techniques mentioned in the four books of the *Yoga Sūtras* (YS) are quite similar to some techniques suggested in early Buddhism, especially the *samatha* part.

The most important ones are, again, parts of an eightfold path, described below. But the *Yoga Sūtras* also contain additional advice on how to meditate. As in Buddhism, "One should cultivate friendship with the joyful, compassion for the sorrowful, gladness for those who are virtuous, and equanimity in regard to the nonvirtuous; through this, the mind is pacified." (YS 1.33, translation from Chapple, 1990, p. 64). This verse, referring to the four so-called *Brahmavihāras* (loving-kindness/friendship, compassion, empathetic joy, and equanimity), already contains a central aim of all yoga techniques: to pacify the mind. This aim, prominently expressed in verse 2 of the first book of the *Yoga Sūtras*, can be achieved by training one's mind appropriately, for example by devotion to a personal god (Īśvara) (YS 1.23), or by practicing dispassion, faith, energy, mindfulness, concentration, and wisdom (YS 1.12–16). Similar to the Buddhist concentration techniques, there are also many possible objects of meditation in the Yoga path (see Sivananda, 1945; Vishnu-Devananda, 1995). Let us now have a closer look at the eightfold path (see Fig. 24.3).

The first four steps in the path of Yoga are usually seen as helping the yogi prepare for his or her meditation practice. The first two of these, ethics (*yama*) and inner spiritual discipline (*niyama*) are similar to the moral virtues contained in the Buddhist Noble Eightfold Path (Fig. 24.1) and the next two, *āsana* and *prāṇāyāma*, are collections of body postures and breathing exercises that prepare for and help with the yogi's meditation practice. The fifth limb, control of the senses (*pratyāhāra*), can be seen as the bridge between the first four (preparatory) limbs and meditation proper, that is, the last three limbs, which are usually summarized as *saṃyama* (holding together, integration).

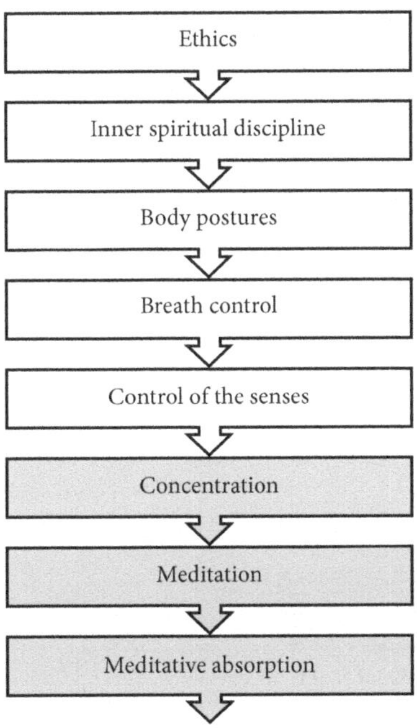

FIGURE 24.3 The limbs of the eightfold Yoga path.

There are different techniques, often relying on *prāṇāyāma*, to prevent sensory information from entering the mind. A mind empty (or less full) of sensations from the senses of taste, touch, sight, hearing, and smell is a good prerequisite for practicing *dhāraṇā*, that is, permanently holding concentration on a given object while avoiding all other thoughts. The next step, *dhyāna*, is usually translated as "meditation" or "contemplation" and the last, *samādhi* as "meditative absorption." Whereas in *dhāraṇā*, the meditator is aware of the act of meditating, of him- or herself doing it, and of the object of meditation, the awareness of the act of meditating disappears in *dhyāna*, and finally, in *samādhi*, also the awareness of oneself dissolves and the meditator becomes one with the object of meditation.

What Is the Aim of Meditation in Sāṃkhya/Yoga, and How Does It Work?

To see the aim of meditation and the role of the meditation techniques in Yoga, one has to have a look at the psychological theory of Sāṃkhya (Fig. 24.4). In Sāṃkhya (and Yoga), a person consists of two components, *prakṛti*, usually translated as nature, and *puruṣa*, sometimes translated as true self or true person but, especially in texts written by Indian academics, as pure consciousness.

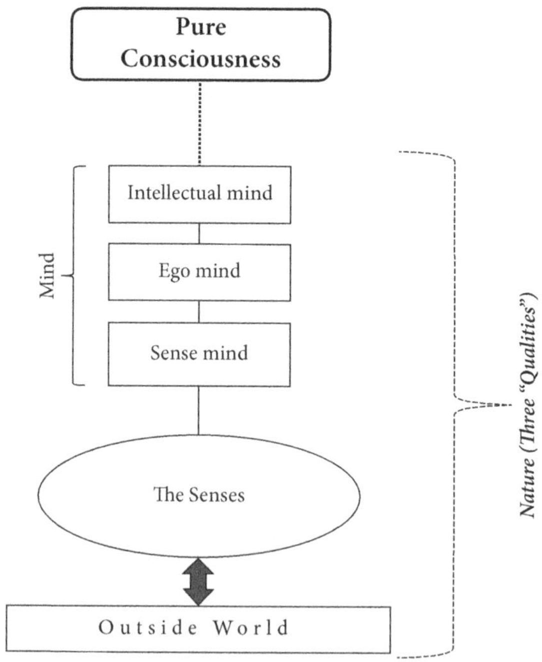

FIGURE 24.4 The Sāṃkhya psychological theory.

Prakṛti, that is, everything material, is regarded as composed of three "qualities," the three *guṇas*. They are *sattva* (purity), *rajas* (energy), and *tamas* (inertia), and their mixture determines the personality of a given person, including their mind (see Puta & Sedlmeier, 2014). Indeed, one should say their *minds*, because in Sāṃkhya/Yoga, the mind is divided up into three different compartments (Fig. 24.4) that differ in their "coarseness." The sense mind (*manas*) reacts to the information provided from the inside and outside, the ego mind (*ahaṃkāra*) appropriates what is provided by the sense mind as its own, and finally, the intellectual mind (*buddhi*), the most subtle part of the three, reacts to the information provided. For instance, if the senses are presented an apple, the sense mind receives information about shape, color, smell, taste, and so on, combines these pieces of information, and separates the ensuing object from other objects, arriving at "this is an apple." Then the ego mind appropriates the perception of the apple and thinks "*I* see an apple." Finally, the intellectual mind might deliberate "What do I do with this apple?"

However, all this would not work without the nonmaterial part of a person, *puruṣa*. As all of *prakṛti* is material and therefore unconscious, the mind only becomes conscious by connecting with *puruṣa*. In ordinary persons, *puruṣa* uses the mind, but the intellectual mind does not notice the presence of pure consciousness. And this causes the problem to be solved by the eightfold path of Yoga with meditation as its central ingredient. Similar to early Buddhism, Sāṃkhya/Yoga argues that life is full of suffering but explains its origin differently: suffering arises due to the ignorance about pure consciousness (*puruṣa*), which makes life be solely driven by sensory inputs and ego cravings. To arrive at the state of pure consciousness is equivalent to liberation from the burdens of life, or to seeing one's true nature, or to seeing the world as it really is. This final goal cannot be achieved until the fluctuations of the mind are brought to a standstill: only then can the intellectual mind (*buddhi*) gain access to pure consciousness (*puruṣa*). However, there are five obstacles or hindrances (*kleśas*) that prevent the access to pure consciousness (see second book of the *Yoga Sūtras*). The first and most prominent one is ignorance, the inability to discriminate between good and evil, the true and the false, the permanent and the impermanent, and so forth (*avidyā*). The others are greed and craving for enjoyment (*rāga*), hate and aversion against anything unpleasurable (*dveṣa*), the erroneous identification of the self with the mind (*asmitā*), and the fear of death or the clinging to life (*abhiniveśa*). Note that the first three of these hindrances are quite similar to the three fires in early Buddhism (delusion, greed, and hatred).

Let us now come back to how meditation deals with this problem. Remember that the intellectual mind can only gain access to *puruṣa* if all fluctuations of the mind are brought to a standstill. For this aim, first the sense mind and then the ego mind have to be "stilled," which is effected by making *sattva* (purity) more and more dominant. Persons with a high degree of *sattva* are expected to be calm, disciplined, and relaxed, to have a well-meaning attitude toward others, and a positive view of the world. A general help for pursuing an increasing "sattvification" of the personality consists in practicing the first four limbs of the eightfold path (e.g., Frawley & Summerfield Kozak, 2001). For persons with a high degree of *sattva*, meditation should work better and more easily, but also meditation itself engenders sattvification. Let us now connect the meditation practices to the Sāṃkhya theory (Fig. 24.4). The impact of meditation can be regarded as successively "cutting off" (shutting down the connections) to parts of the mind. Practicing the fifth limb of the eightfold path (*pratyāhāra*) weakens or cuts the connections of the senses to the outside world. In the next steps, the meditator cuts off the senses (*dhāraṇā*), the sense mind (*dhyāna*), and finally the ego mind (*samādhi*). If there are no more fluctuations of the mind, the intellectual mind can gain access to *puruṣa* and the meditator experiences the true reality.

What Can Be Predicted from the Meditation Theory of Sāṃkhya/Yoga?

The main prediction of the Sāṃkhya/Yoga theory is: If you follow the eightfold yoga path you may eventually gain access to pure consciousness. Reaching that state and staying in it is variously called enlightenment, liberation, or seeing the world as it really is. But predictions are also possible for practitioners who are still moving on the eightfold path. We have already mentioned one: yoga practice should increase the proportion of the *sattva* part in the practitioner's personality and thereby lead to an increase of positive and a decrease of negative aspects of personality, as well as to less fluctuations of the mind or less mind wandering. There are first indications that meditation indeed increases sattvic personality aspects (Puta, 2016) and that it decreases mind wandering (Hasenkamp, Wilson-Mendenhall, Duncan, & Barsalou, 2011; Mrazek, Franklin, Phillips, Baird, & Schooler, 2013). Another prediction is that the five hindrances should weaken with meditation practice. This means, for instance, that suffering should decrease or, to state it positively, meditators should be more satisfied with their lives and experience happier moments than non-meditators. If greed and hatred diminish, well-being should increase and if fear of death becomes less prominent, meditators should become more equanimous. As the main meditation techniques in the yoga practice are concentrative ones, one should also expect positive effects on attention and concentration. Moreover, higher attentional abilities combined with less emotional distraction should yield higher cognitive abilities. In sum, and similar to the predictions that can be derived from early Buddhism, the Sāṃkhya/Yoga theory predicts positive effects on a wide variety of aspects of life.

Commonalities and Differences among the Two Theories

One could argue that the central prediction about the effects of meditation in both theories is quite similar: If you practice the respective paths, you will gain insights that reach far beyond everyday knowledge, and you will eventually experience liberation from all anguish and sorrows and see the world as it really is. This promise holds for following the complete path in both theories, but because meditation is the central part in both, it seems to be a plausible assumption that all the predictions should also apply, at least in a large part, for meditation alone. However, the fundamental intuitive insight of how the world really is might be quite different in the two approaches. In early Buddhism, the fundamental insight is about anguish, impermanence, and non-self, whereas in Sāṃkhya/Yoga an eternal self or pure consciousness is intuitively perceived. Now one could argue that *nibbāna* and *puruṣa*, the terms for the respective goals, might just be two imperfect ways to describe a state (the same one) that is ineffable. But another possibility is that dwelling in *nibbāna* and *puruṣa* are indeed different states, brought about by different meditation techniques. Although Buddhist concentrative techniques (*samatha*) and Yoga meditation can be seen as quite similar, Buddhist mindfulness (*sati*) techniques, that is, the practice of the four foundations of mindfulness, are not explicitly mentioned in the *Yoga Sūtras*. The latter techniques are central to early Buddhism and seem to be ideally suited to gain insight into the working of our body, sensations, consciousness, and the objects of consciousness. Simplified even further, one could say that Yoga meditation and Buddhist meditation as described above could be seen as two extremes: to narrow down consciousness maximally (Yoga meditation) or to enlarge it maximally (meditation establishing the four foundations of mindfulness). Both extremes might have the potential to heighten our awareness drastically and free the mind for *the* fundamental insight about life.

We have seen that the predictions for what happens on the path are quite similar for the two approaches and are generally positive. This general hypothesis has indeed been tested with confirming results in many studies, obviously without much theoretical concern (for meta-analyses with healthy practitioners see Sedlmeier et al., 2012, 2018). In both approaches, meditation is embedded within a moral and ethical context. It is still unclear how important this context is for the effects of meditation to come to fruition. It also differs to some extent: Whereas in the Yoga path breathing exercises and body postures play an important role, such exercises are not explicitly mentioned in the Buddhist path. There are some indications that the inclusion of body exercises might have beneficial effects on some commonly studied dependent variables such as well-being, and the reduction of negative emotions and anxiety (e.g., Eberth & Sedlmeier, 2012), but this effect does not seem to occur generally (Sedlmeier et al., 2018). One should also mention that in both approaches, negative side effects are predicted (e.g., Buddhaghosa, 2010; Hofmann, 2013; Nanamoli, 1997; Ott, 2013; this volume, chapter by Lindahl, Britton, Cooper, & Kirmayer), often in the context of losing one's sense of self.

There are also other predictions specific to each approach that, so far, have only been rudimentarily examined. For instance, early Buddhism predicts that meditation practice should have positive effects especially on the reduction of greed, hatred, and ignorance and on the cultivation of the *Brahmavihāras*, loving-kindness, compassion, empathetic joy and equanimity. Interestingly, it seems that directly training in the

Brahmavihāras may be less efficient than practicing basic meditation techniques. For instance, two meta-analyses have summarized the effects of loving-kindness meditation and found that practitioners experienced more positive emotions than control-group participants (Galante, Galante, Bekkers, & Gallacher, 2014; Zeng, Chiu, Wang, Oei, & Leung, 2015). However, it also seems that less specific meditation training may yield even stronger effects on the same variables (Sedlmeier, 2016). As yet, most of the specific predictions have not been systematically tested. This is probably in part due to the mostly a-theoretical way previous meditation research has been conducted, but it is also impeded by still-missing valid measurement devices. Such measurement devices could also be used to test the hypothesis advanced in the *Visuddhimagga* that practitioners with a preponderance of one of the three fires advance more easily if they practice specific techniques. An example for a specific prediction from Sāṃkhya/Yoga is that the mix of the three *guṇa*s changes over meditation practice: the sattvic proportion should increase, whereas rajasic and tamasic aspects of the personality should decrease. Although there exist quite a number of *guṇa* questionnaires (summarized in Puta & Sedlmeier 2014), it seems that, to date, there are only two systematic studies that examined the impact of meditation on the *guṇa*s (Puta, 2016; Wolf & Abell, 2003).

Conclusion

Our coverage of the two ancient Indian systems is of course incomplete, and other authors might have chosen different aspects to study. However, we think that our presentation represents central ideas that can also be derived from related later Buddhist and Hindu approaches to explaining the effects of meditation. Both theories have been developed more than two millennia ago and therefore one cannot expect them to be fully correct or to cover all relevant aspects. However, we think it plausible to assume that they ultimately stem from successively refined interpretations of repeatedly sampled empirical data, that is, meditators' experiences (for similar opinions, see Aurobindo, 2001; Jayatilleke, 1963; Jitatmananda, 2004; for opposing views, see Lopez, 2009; McMahan, 2008).

Both theories contain two issues that are problematic for many contemporary scholars. One is the claim that life does not end with death, but that instead the cycles of life continue until liberation is attained: the *rebirth hypothesis*. Meanwhile, there exists a large collection of anecdotal evidence, mostly collected by Ian Stevenson and colleagues (e.g., Mills, Haraldsson, & Keil, 1994; Pasricha, Keil, Tucker, & Stevenson, 2005; Stevenson, 2006) that can be construed as supporting the rebirth hypothesis. However, as yet, all attempts to examine the issue systematically seem to have failed. Leaving open the possibility that the rebirth hypothesis might be true, it could be seen as an attempt to explain the obvious fact that already newborn children differ very much in many aspects. In ancient times, nobody knew about genes, and the genetic factors, of course, also stem from previous lives.

The other potentially problematic issue might be called the *siddhi hypothesis*. Both the Buddhist and the Hindu theories claim that a side effect of meditation practice can be the attainment of supernatural abilities. It seems fair to say that also this hypothesis needs more evidence and a better theoretical model to make it acceptable to the scientific community (see also Cardeña, this volume; Sedlmeier, 2018). Anyway, the matter of *siddhis* is only peripheral for the theories and meditators are usually discouraged to stay with them (e.g., Braud, 2008; De Silva, 2005; YS 2.37).

Even without the above two potentially problematic issues, the meditation theories contained in early Buddhism and Yoga/Sāṃkhya still need to be elaborated and made more precise. Attempts to arrive at a more precise specification of processes that might be triggered by practicing meditation techniques can be found in Western theoretical approaches (e.g., Dahl, Lutz, & Davidson, 2015; Hölzel et al., 2011). However, as seen in the versions presented above, the traditional theories contain potential explanations and predictions that go beyond contemporary Western explanations. For instance, although sometimes changes in terms of the perspective on the self are mentioned (e.g., Hölzel, et al., 2011), the final goal in Western theoretical approaches is "well-being" (e.g., Dahl, Lutz, & Davidson, 2015; Lutz, Slagter, Dunne, & Davidson, 2008). Concentrating on well-being is an a priori limitation of the potential effects of meditation. It is understandable in the light of scientific skepticism, especially as far as issues such as the rebirth or the siddhi hypotheses are concerned. However, this restriction is not necessary and could be unnecessarily severe. To date, Western theories also do not deal in a systematic way with the negative side effects of meditation. This issue could be quite important because, in contrast to the traditional landscape in which meditation was practiced, most of Western meditation research is heavily entrenched in issues of psychotherapy. In this context, several problems have been experienced, and additional ones can be expected (e.g., Farias & Wikholm, 2015; Lindahl, Fisher, Cooper, Rosen, & Britton, 2017; Tremmel & Ott, 2016). That theories of meditation have to be adapted to psychotherapy is also indicated by the fact that the effects of meditation for patients are consistently smaller than those for healthy practitioners (Sedlmeier, 2016). Moreover, traditional theories acknowledge the relevance of differences in personality (e.g., the three *guṇas* and the Buddhist "temperaments") whereas this issue seems to have played basically no role in Western theorizing, so far. And finally, ethical and moral issues are not represented in contemporary Western theories, whereas they are an integral part in the traditional ones.

These differences hint at some of the questions that have to be answered in order to arrive at either one comprehensive theory or a compendium of theories of meditation. The answers given in the traditional theoretical approaches outlined above are potentially very useful starting points in that respect. In any case, the main aim of meditation research should not be to remain beholden to some tradition, spiritual or otherwise, but to find out more about why, how, and under which circumstances meditation works.

Acknowledgements

We like to thank Karin Matko, Ulrich Ott, Isabell Winkler, and especially Ritesh Mariadas for their valuable feedback on a previous version of the chapter.

References

Amaro, A. (2015). A holistic mindfulness. *Mindfulness 6*, 63–73.

Anālayo, Bhikkhu. (2003). *Satipaṭṭhāna: The direct path to realization*. Chiang Mai, Thailand: Silkworm Books.

Anālayo, Bhikkhu. (2012). In K.-p. Chuang (Ed.), *Buddhist meditation traditions: An international symposium* (pp. 23–56). Taiwan: Dharma Drum Publishing Corporation.

Anālayo, Bhikkhu. (2019). The emphasis on the present moment in the cultivation of mindfulness. *Mindfulness 10*, 571–581.

Aurobindo, Sri. (2001). *Record of yoga*. Pondicherry, India: Sri Aurobindo Ashram Press.

Batchelor, M. (2016). Meditation: Practice and experience. In M. West (Ed.), *The psychology of meditation: Research & practice* (pp. 27–47). Oxford: Oxford University Press.

Batchelor, S. (1997). *Buddhism without beliefs*. New York: Riverhead Books.

Belzer, F., Schmidt, S., Lucius-Hoene, G., Schneider, J. F., Orellana-Rios, C. L., & Sauer, S. (2013). Challenging the construct validity of mindfulness assessment—A cognitive interview study of the Freiburg Mindfulness Inventory. *Mindfulness 4*, 33–44.

Bodhi, Bhikkhu (Ed.). (2005). *In the Buddha's words: An anthology of discourses from the Pali Canon*. Boston: Wisdom Publications.

Bodhi, Bhikkhu. (2013). *A comprehensive manual of Abhidhamma: The Abhidhammattha Sangaha of Ācariya Anuruddha*. Onalaska, WI: BPS Pariyatti Editions.

Braud, W. G. (2008). Patañjali Yoga and siddhis: Their relevance to parapsychological theory and research. In K. R. Rao, A. C. Paranjpe, & A. K. Dalal (Eds.), *Handbook of Indian psychology* (pp. 217–243). Delhi: Cambridge University Press.

Brazier, D. (2013). Mindfulness reconsidered. *European Journal of Psychotherapy & Counselling 15*, 116–126.

Buddhaghosa, Bhadantácariya. (2010). *The path of purification (Visuddhimagga)*. (B. Ñāñamoli, Thera, trans.). Kandy, Sri Lanka: Buddhist Publication Society.

Chapple, C. (1990). The unseen seer and the filed: Consciousness in Samkhya and Yoga. In R. K. C. Forman (Ed.), *The problem of pure consciousness: Mysticism and philosophy*. (pp. 53–70). New York: Oxford University Press.

Claxton, G. (1986). Editor's introduction. In G. Claxton (Ed.), *Beyond therapy: The impact of Eastern religions on psychological theory and practice*. London: Wisdom Publications.

Dahl, C. J., Lutz, A., & Davidson, R. J. (2015). Reconstructing and deconstructing the self: Cognitive mechanisms in meditation practice. *Trends in Cognitive Sciences 19*, 515–523.

Dasgupta, S. (1930). *Yoga philosophy in relation to other systems of Indian thought*. Calcutta: University of Calcutta.

Dasgupta, S. (1997). *A history of Indian philosophy* (Vol. 1). Delhi: Motilal Banarsidass. (Original work published 1922).

De Silva, P. (1990). Buddhist psychology: A review of theory and practice. *Current Psychology 9*, 236–254.

De Silva, P. (2005). *An introduction to Buddhist psychology* (4th ed.). Houndmills, England: Palgrave/Macmillan.

Dreyfus, G. (2011). Is mindfulness present-centred and non-judgmental? A discussion of the cognitive dimensions of mindfulness. *Contemporary Buddhism 12*, 41–54.

Eberth, J., & Sedlmeier, P. (2012). The effects of mindfulness meditation: a meta-analysis. *Mindfulness* 3, 174–189.

Farias, M., Claridge, G., & Lalljee, M. (2005). Personality and cognitive predictors of New Age practices and beliefs. *Personality and Individual Differences* 39, 979–989.

Farias, M., & Wikholm, C. (2015). *The Buddha pill: Can meditation change you*? London: Watkins Publishing.

Farias, M., & Wikholm, C. (2016). Has the science of mindfulness lost its mind? *BJPsych Bulletin*, *40*, 329–332.

Feuerstein, G. (1998). *The yoga tradition: Its history, literature, philosophy and practice*. Prescott, AZ: Hohm Press.

Flood, G. (2004). *An introduction to Hinduism*. New Delhi: Oxford University Press.

Frauwallner, E. (2003). *Geschichte der indischen Philosophie, I. Band*. [*History of Indian philosophy, Vol. I*]. Aachen: Shaker Verlag. (Original work published 1953).

Frauwallner, E. (2010). *The philosophy of Buddhism*. Delhi: Motilal Banarsidass. (Original work published 1956 in German: *Die Philosophie des Buddhismus*. Berlin: Akademie-Verlag.)

Frawley, D. (2001). *The Rig Veda and the history of India*. New Delhi: Aditya Prakashan.

Frawley, D., & Summerfield Kozak, S. (2001). *Yoga for your type*. Twin Lakes, WI: Lotus Press.

Galante, J., Galante, I., Bekkers, M. J., & Gallacher, J. (2014). Effect of kindness-based meditation on health and well-being: a systematic review and meta-analysis. *Journal of Consulting and Clinical Psychology 82*, 1101–1114.

Gombrich, R. (1998). Kindness and compassion as means to nirvana. *Fifth Gonda lecture*. Royal Netherlands Academy of Arts and Sciences, Amsterdam (pp. 5–27).

Gombrich, R. (2006). *How Buddhism began: The conditional genesis of the early teachings* (2nd ed). London: Routledge.

Gombrich, R. (2013). *What the Buddha thought* (corrected edition). Sheffield: Equinox.

Gotink, R. A., Chu, P., Busschbach, J. J. V., Benson, H., Fricchione, G. L., & Hunink, M. G. M. (2015). Standardised mindfulness-based interventions in healthcare: An overview of systematic reviews and meta-analyses of RCTs. *PLoS ONE 10*(4): e0124344. doi:10.1371/journal.pone.0124344

Goyal, M., Singh, S., Sibinga, E. M., Gould, N. F., Rowland-Seymour, A., Sharma, R.,... & Ranasinghe, P. D. (2014). Meditation programs for psychological stress and wellbeing: A systematic review and meta-analysis. *JAMA Internal Medicine 174*, 357–368.

Griffith, P. (1981). Concentration or insight: the problematic of Theravāda Buddhist meditation-theory. *Journal of the American Academy of Religion* 49, 605–624.

Grossman, P., & Van Dam, N. T. (2011). Mindfulness, by any other name... trials and tribulations of sati in western psychology and science. *Contemporary Buddhism 12*, 219–239.

Gunaratana, H. (1980). *A critical analysis of the jhānas in Theravāda Buddhist meditation*. (Doctoral dissertation). The American University, Washington, D. C.

Gunaratana, H. (2015). *Mindfulness in plain English*. Somerville, MA: Wisdom Publications.

Hamilton, S. (2000). *Early Buddhism: A new approach*. Richmond, Surrey: Curzon.

Hart, William (1987). *The Art of Living: Vipassana Meditation: As Taught by S. N. Goenka*. New York: HarperOne.

Harvey, P. (2004). *An introduction to Buddhism: Teachings, history, and practices*. New Delhi: Cambridge University Press.

Hasenkamp, W., Wilson-Mendenhall, C. D., Duncan, E., & Barsalou, L. W. (2011). Mind wandering and attention during focused meditation: A fine-grained temporal analysis of fluctuating cognitive states. *NeuroImage* 59, 750–760.

Hiriyanna, M. (2000). *Outlines of Indian philosophy*. Delhi: Motilal Banarsidass. (Original work published 1932)

Hölzel, B. K., Lazar, S. W., Gard, T., Schuman-Olivier, Z., Vago, D. R., & Ott, U. (2011). How does mindfulness meditation work? Proposing mechanisms of action from a conceptual and neural perspective. *Perspectives on Psychological Science* 6(6), 537–559.

Hofmann, L. (2013). The impact of Kundalini Yoga on concepts and diagnostic practices in psychology and psychotherapy. In B. Hauser (Ed.), *Yoga traveling—bodily practice in transcultural perspective* (pp. 81–106). Cham: Springer.

Jayatilleke, K. N. (1963). *Early Buddhist theory of knowledge*. London: George Allen and Unwin.

Jitatmananda, Swami, (2004). Spiritual experiences of Ramakrishna–Vivekananda. In K. Joshi & M. Cornelissen (Eds.), *Consciousness, Indian psychology and yoga* (pp. 145–176). New Delhi: Centre for Studies in Civilizations.

Johansson, R. E. A. (1970). *The psychology of nirvana*. London: Garden City: Anchor Books.

Kalupahana, D. J. (1992). *The principles of Buddhist psychology*. Delhi: Sri Satguru Publications.

Kalupahana, D. J. (2009). *Karma and rebirth: Foundations of the Buddha's moral philosophy*. Dehiwala, Sri Lanka: Buddhist Cultural Centre.

Klostermaier, K. K. (2006). *Hinduism: A short history*. Oxford, England: Oneworld.

Kornfield, J. (2009). *The wise heart: A guide to the universal teachings of Buddhist psychology*. New York: Bantam Books.

Lindahl, J. R., Fisher, N. E., Cooper, D. J., Rosen, R. K., & Britton, W. B. (2017). The varieties of contemplative experience: A mixed-methods study of meditation-related challenges in Western Buddhists. *Plos ONE*. doi:10.1371/journal.pone.0176239.

Lopez, D. S., Jr. (2009). *Buddhism and science: A guide for the perplexed*. Chicago: University of Chicago Press.

Lutz, A., Jha, A. P., Dunne, J. D., & Saron, C. D. (2015). Investigating the phenomenological matrix of mindfulness-related practices from a neurocognitive perspective. *American Psychologist* 70, 632–658.

Lutz, A., Slagter, H. A., Dunne, J. D., & Davidson, R. J. (2008). Attention regulation and monitoring in meditation. *Trends in Cognitive Sciences* 12, 163–169.

Mahasi, Sayadew (1991). *Practical vipassana exercises*. Kandy, Sri Lanka: Buddhist Publication Society.

Maithrimurthi, M. (1999). *Wohlwollen, Mitleid, Freude und Gleichmut: Eine ideengeschichtliche Untersuchung der vier apramāṇas in der buddhistischen Ethik und Spiritualiät von den Anfängen bis hin zum frühen Yogācāra* [Benevolence, compassion, joyousness and equanimity: An analysis, from the point of view of a history of ideas, of the four *apramāṇas* in Buddhist ethics and spirituality from the beginnings up to early Yogācāra]. Alt-und Neu—Indische Studien 50: Universität Hamburg, Stuttgart.

McMahan, D. L. (2008). *The making of Buddhist modernism*. Oxford: Oxford University Press.

Mills, A., Haraldsson, E., & Keil, H. H. J. (1994). Replication studies of cases suggestive of reincarnation by three independent investigators. *Journal of the American Society for Psychical Research* 88, 207–219.

Mrazek, M. D., Franklin, M. S., Phillips, D. T., Baird, B., & Schooler, J. W. (2013). Mindfulness training improves working memory capacity and GRE performance while reducing mind wandering. *Psychological Science* 24, 776–781.

Nanamoli, B. (Trans.) (1997). *The path of discrimination*. Bristol: Pali Text Society.

Nyanaponika, Thera (1999). *The four sublime states*. Penang: Inward Path. (Original work published 1958).

Olendzki, A. (2003). Buddhist psychology. In S. Segall (Ed.), *Encountering Buddhism: western psychology and Buddhist teachings*. New York: State University of New York Press.

Olendzki, A. (2010). *Unlimiting mind*. Somerville, MA: Wisdom Publications.

Ott, U., (2013). *Yoga für Skeptiker: Ein Neurowissenschaftler erklärt die uralte Weisheitslehre*. [Yoga for skeptics: A neuroscientist explains ancient wisdom]. München: O. W. Barth.

Pa Auk, Sayādaw (2003). *Knowing and seeing* (Rev. ed.). Kuala Lumpur: Wave Publications.

Pasricha, S. K., Keil, J., Tucker, J. B., & Stevenson, I. (2005). Some bodily malformations attributed to previous lives. *Journal of Scientific Exploration 19*, 359–383.

Phillips, S. (2009). *Yoga, karma, and rebirth: A brief history and philosophy*. New York: Columbia University Press.

Premasiri, P. D. (2008). Varieties of cognition in early Buddhism. In K. R. Rao, A. C. Paranjpe, & A. K. Dalal (Eds.), *Handbook of Indian psychology* (pp. 85–104). Delhi: Cambridge University Press.

Puligandla, R. (1997). *Fundamentals of Indian philosophy*. New Delhi: D.K. Printworld.

Puta, M. (2016). *Promoting health by Sattva-Guna* (Doctoral dissertation). Chemnitz University of Technology. http://nbn-resolving.de/urn:nbn:de:bsz:ch1-qucosa-224078

Puta, M., & Sedlmeier, P. (2014). The concept of tri-guna: A working model. In S. Schmidt & H. Walach (Eds.), *Meditation: Neuroscientific approaches and philosophical implications* (pp. 317–364). Berlin: Springer.

Rahula, W. (1959). *What the Buddha taught*. New York: Grove Press.

Raju, P. T. (1985). *Structural depths of Indian thought*. New Delhi: South Asian.

Rao, K. R., & Paranjpe, A. C. (2008). Yoga psychology: Theory and application. In K. R. Rao, A. C. Paranjpe, & A. K. Dalal (Eds.), *Handbook of Indian psychology* (pp. 186–216). Delhi: Cambridge University Press.

Salzberg, S. (1995). *Loving-kindness: The revolutionary art of happiness*. Boston: Shambhala.

Sedlmeier, P. (2006). Ancient Indian psychology: Can it offer anything to academic psychology? In R. Rapp, P. Sedlmeier, P. & G. Zunker-Rapp (Eds.), *Perspectives on cognition: A Festschrift in honor of Manfred Wettler* (pp. 199–214). Lengerich, Germany: Pabst.

Sedlmeier, P. (2016). *Die Kraft der Meditation: Was die Wissenschaft darüber weiß*. [The power of meditation: What science knows about it]. Reinbek, Germany: Rowohlt Polaris.

Sedlmeier, P. (2018). Meditation and altered states of consciousness. *Journal of Consciousness Studies 25*, 73–191.

Sedlmeier, P. & Eberth, J., & Puta, M. (2016). Meditation: Future research and theory. In M. A. West (Ed.), *The psychology of meditation: Research and practice* (2nd ed., pp. 285–310). Oxford: Oxford University Press.

Sedlmeier, P., Eberth, J., & Schwarz, M. (2014). Meta-analyses and other methodological issues in meditation research: Reply to Orme-Johnson and Dillbeck (2014). *Psychological Bulletin 140*, 617–622.

Sedlmeier, P., Eberth, J., Schwarz, M., Zimmermann, D., Haarig, F., Jaeger, S., & Kunze, S. (2012). The psychological effects of meditation: A meta-analysis. *Psychological Bulletin 138*, 1139–1171.

Sedlmeier, P., Loße, C., & Quasten, L. C. (2018). Psychological effects of meditation for healthy practitioners: An update. *Mindfulness*, 9, 371–387.

Sedlmeier, P., & Srinivas, K. (2016). How do theories of cognition and consciousness in ancient Indian thought systems relate to current Western theorizing and research? *Frontiers in Psychology 7*, 343. doi:10.3389/fpsyg.2016.00343

Sharf, R. (2014). Mindfulness and mindlessness in early Chan. *Philosophy East & West 64*, 933–964.

Sharma, C. (2003). *A critical survey of Indian philosophy*. Delhi: Motilal Banarsidass. (Original work published 1960).

Shaw, S. (2006). *Buddhist meditation: An anthology of texts from the Pali Canon*. London: Routledge.

Shonin, E., Van Gordon, W., & Singh, N. N. (Eds.). (2015). *Buddhist foundations of mindfulness*. Cham: Springer Verlag.

Sivananda, Swami (1945). *Concentration & meditation*. Uttarakhand, India: The Divine Life Society.

Stevenson, I. (2006). Half a career with the paranormal. *Journal of Scientific Exploration 20*, 13–21.

Tremmel, M., & Ott, U. (2016). Negative Wirkungen von Meditation. In L. Hofmann & P. Heise (Eds.), *Spiritualität und spirituelle Krisen. Handbuch zu Theorie, Forschung und Praxis* (pp. 233–243). Stuttgart: Schattauer.

Upadhaya, K. N. (1968). The impact of early Buddhism on Hindu thought (with special reference to the Bhagavadgita). *Philosophy East and West 18*, 163–173.

Vishnu-Devananda, Swami (1995). *Meditation and mantras*. Delhi: Motilal Banarsidass.

Whiteman, J. H. M. (1993). *Aphorisms on spiritual method: The "Yoga Sutras of Patanjali" in the light of mystical experience*. Gerrards Cross, UK: Colin Smythe.

Wolf, D. B., & Abell, N. (2003). Examining the effects of meditation techniques on psychosocial functioning. *Research on Social Work Practice 13*, 27–42.

Woods, J. H. (1998). *The Yoga-system of Patañjali*. Delhi: Motilal Banarsidass. (Original work published 1914).

Zeng, X., Chiu, C. P., Wang, R., Oei, T. P., & Leung, F. Y. (2015). The effect of loving-kindness meditation on positive emotions: A meta-analytic review. *Frontiers in Psychology 6*, 1693. doi:10.3389/fpsyg.2015.01693

SOCIOLOGY

CHAPTER 25

THE SOCIOLOGY OF MEDITATION

MICHAL PAGIS

Introduction

Sociologists have been interested in the societal dimension of meditation practice, including macro-social structures, mezzo-level social institutions and movements, and micro-social relations. Early sociological studies on meditation were conducted mainly by sociologists of religion and were a part of the more general interest in Buddhist groups or new religious movements. As meditation practice spread, it attracted the attention of sociologists from multiple fields, including social movements, health, work, and microsociology. The large majority of sociological studies on meditation have focused on practices that are connected to Eastern traditions (mainly Hinduism and Buddhism) and were adapted to a Western audience. These studies tend to focus on meditation practice in English-speaking countries, with an emphasis on the United States and the United Kingdom.

Sociologists study meditation as a social phenomenon, exploring the connections between contemporary interest in meditation practice and the late-modern social world, including processes of individualization, secularization, and capitalism. From a sociological point of view, the contemporary practice of meditation serves as a window to larger questions about social life and organization in the contemporary world. The studies introduced in this chapter can be grouped according to three central themes:

- Meditation practice as a religious and spiritual phenomenon: this sheds light on transformations in religious practice in the contemporary world and indicates tendencies toward individualization, secularization, and religious syncretism.

- The popularization of meditation as a social movement: this focuses on processes of social change, the emergence of new social networks in a globalized world, and on strategies through which key actors adapt cultural practices to new social contexts and institutions.
- The micro-social world of meditation practice: this includes the social structures of meditation spaces and institutions, the social relations that meditation practice is embedded in or promotes, and how meditation practice relates to the social self.

In what follows, I first introduce the relevance of classical sociological perspectives to the study of meditation and the methodologies used by sociologists in their meditation-focused research. I then turn to each of the above themes and elaborate on the central questions and findings. I end with a conclusion on what the sociological study of meditation can teach us about contemporary social structures and relations.

Classical Sociological Perspectives

While early sociologists did not study meditation practice per se, their perspectives on religion, modernization, and individualization processes remain relevant and central in current sociological studies on meditation.

The most influential classical perspective is Weber's (1946a, 1946b) work on religion and the promise of salvation. Weber categorized contemplative practices, specifically Buddhist meditations, as "other-worldly" mysticism. Since historically contemplative practices were limited to monks and religious virtuosi, Weber saw in meditation a salvation strategy that includes both a negation of this world and a flight from this world. Thus, meditation was understood as part of a larger set of practices that helped the monk to reach enlightenment, practiced only by the chosen religious virtuosi and understood as the "personal act of the single individual" (Weber, 1958a, p. 206). Contemporary sociologists, who study meditation in the context of its popularization outside of the monastic context, frame their studies in reference to Weber's (1946a) "other-worldly mysticism" ideal type. Studies on contemporary meditation practice in the West understand it as a monastic practice that shifted from being "other-worldly" to being "this-worldly." These studies track the shift in the kind of "salvation" that contemporary meditation offers practitioners (McMahan, 2008; Wilson, 2014; Kucinskas, 2018; Pagis, 2019).

Another important Weberian idea central to the study of meditation is the notion of the "disenchantment" of the world (Weber, 1958b). On the one hand, the sociological study of meditation challenges secularization theories by locating meditation practice as part of what has been called the spiritual revolution, illustrating the persistence and even flourishing of mystical and religious traditions in late modernity (Heelas & Woodhead, 2005). On the other hand, studies of meditation practice (and spirituality in general) understand its popularization in the light of processes of rationalization and secularization common to modern society, as in some contexts meditation has been stripped from its religious context and turned into a therapeutic tool (Wilson, 2014; Kucinskas, 2018).

A second influential sociological perspective used in meditation-related studies can be tracked back to Durkheim's (2008/1912) work on the elementary forms of religious life. While Durkheim did not write specifically on meditation, his work on ritual and the affective effervescence that characterizes collective rituals is used by sociologists in order to ask questions regarding solitary and collective meditation practice, especially in the light of processes of secularization and individualization in which the power of religious traditions seems to be declining (Giddens, 1991; Heelas, 1996).

Two developments of Durkheimian thought are particularly relevant to the study of contemporary meditation practice. First, Victor Turner (2017/1966) suggested the notion of "anti-structure" to capture the spaces where the social structure is bracketed and people are stripped of their "regular" social identities. He argued that in complex societies, where traditional rituals are of less importance, we find new spaces where such "anti-structure" can be produced, including alternative models of living or leisure time (Turner, 1974). While Turner did not study meditation practice per se, we can think of the meditation center, and daily meditation practice, as representing a space where individuals withdraw from their everyday social roles and identities, a place outside of "normative" social structure.

Second, Randell Collins's (2004) work on Interaction Ritual Chains combined Durkheim's ideas on affective effervescence with Goffman's micro-sociological insights regarding everyday "natural" interaction rituals and Mead's model of the social self. In his theoretical work on the micro-sociology of religion, Collins (2011) suggested that meditation can be analyzed as an internal interaction ritual, where affective effervescence takes place between two parts of the social self—the "Me," the part that represents the internalization of social attitudes, and the "I," the spontaneous, active part that responds to these attitudes. As he writes, "successful meditation is the high point of self-integration, carrying out an intense Durkheimian ritual but inside the self rather than in an external social assembly" (Collins, 2011, p. 15).

Methodologies: How Do Sociologists Study Meditation?

In contrast to psychological approaches, sociologists do not study the effect of meditation on personal well-being. The sociological study of meditation focuses on contemporary meditation practice as a social phenomenon. Empirically, sociologists have focused on the following questions, each with its specific methodology:

Who Practices Meditation?

Sociologists have been interested in the socio-demographic characteristics of the population that practices meditation. This includes race and ethnicity, gender, religious background, and economic, social, and cultural capital of practitioners. Data is collected through both qualitative and quantitative methods, starting first with national surveys that are based on representative samples. These studies do not usually focus on meditation per se, but offer information on meditation alongside other religious, spiritual practices, or use of alternative medicine (see Conrad Hackett in this volume). Second, we have studies in spaces where meditation is practiced (such as centers and temples), including interviews with participants.

What Are the Justifications and Accounts People Use in Order to Explain Their Meditation Practice?

Sociologists study the justifications and accounts that people give when explaining why they meditate. In order to study this topic, sociologists use in-depth interviews that track the religious, spiritual, moral, and therapeutic justifications practitioners offer in order to explain their choice to meditate. These accounts are compared across populations, for example, by comparing the justifications given by self-defined Buddhists to those given by meditators who do not identify as Buddhists.

Who Are the Social Agents and Networks that Advocate and Adapt Meditation to New Social Contexts?

Sociologists define the spread of meditation practice as a social movement, exploring its diffusion and popularization. These studies have mainly utilized qualitative research including historical and ethnographic methods that locate key agents, their social positions in networks, their connection to social institutions (e.g., science, medicine, economic corporations) and their place and cosmopolitan identifications. In addition, content analysis of the discourses used in books, magazines, scientific publications, and advertisements is used in order to study the adaptation of meditation practice to its contemporary Western audience.

Where Do People Practice Meditation and with Whom?

Sociologists are interested in the social spheres and institutions that are established as meditation practice spreads. Research is based on in-depth interviews and participant observation, which document meditation centers, as well as collective and solitary practice, including new social spheres and institutions that incorporate meditation practice (e.g., hospitals, the army, prison). In addition, the recent novel method of experience sampling based on smartphone applications enable the tracking of individuals along the day with self-reports about spiritual experiences in their everyday life, including where these happened, when, and with whom.

What Is the Connection between Meditation Practice and Social Relationships?

Sociologists study the social relationships that surround meditation practice—either in communities of meditators, or between meditators and their non-meditating significant others. In order to examine such relationships, sociologists utilize qualitative research: observations of relations between practitioners in different spheres (including both the meditation center and daily life), interviews with practitioners, and interviews with non-meditating significant others (either family or close friends).

Current Sociological Study of Meditation Practice

Sociological studies understand meditation as part of larger social phenomena. These can be divided into three key areas: religion and spirituality in late modernity; social movements and institutions; and social relations/social self. An underlying theme that crosses these three themes is the resonance between meditation practice and contemporary late-modern, Western affluent societies.

Religion and Spirituality in Late Modernity

Traditionally those who practiced meditation were monks or a religious elite. The recent popularization of meditation with lay people (who are not ordained as monks or nuns) and with those who are not religiously committed can teach us about religion and spirituality in late modernity. Under this theme, we find three bodies of literature:

1. Studies that regard meditation practice as a small fraction of the larger popularization of New Age spirituality;
2. Studies focusing on Buddhist groups and practice in Western locations;
3. Studies interested in religious syncretism and the integration of Asian types of meditations into non-Buddhist/Hinduist religious practice, specifically Christianity and Judaism.

Meditation as Part of New Age Spirituality

The contemporary rise of interest in spirituality is understood by some as a challenge to Weber's (1958b) theory of "disenchantment" of the world. While the classical secularization thesis pointed to the decline of the importance of religion in the modern world, the visible growing interest in spirituality illustrates that religion is not disappearing—instead, it is transforming. Studies on New Age spiritualty and new religious movements examine types of religious and spiritual practices that became popular from the 1960s onward. These studies examine meditation as one type of practice among others, including yoga, reiki, channeling, or Kabbalah teachings.

Early studies, conducted in the 1970s, depicted meditation groups such as Transcendental Meditation (TM) and Zen as new religious movements, sometimes characterized as cults (Campbell, 1978; Bainbridge & Stark, 1980; Bainbridge & Jackson, 1981). They found that people who were attracted to spirituality were searching for esoteric, mystical, or unusual experiences and resisted mainstream religious institutions (Volinn, 1985). As New Age spiritualties became more mainstream, studies shifted from a focus on cults and esoteric-alternative groups, to a focus on "individualization" or "personalization" of religious practices (Bellah, 1986). With the continuous decline in religious commitments, people can choose or even invent their own religious or spiritual practices. Meditation practice offers an appealing example of such personalization of religion, since it involves a turn inward and emphasizes personal experience.

One of the findings of spirituality studies is that participants in such groups tend to mix different practices and are not necessarily committed to one practice or tradition over the other. They can practice Buddhist meditation, take Kabbalah classes, and visit the church on Sunday with their family (e.g., Heelas & Woodhead, 2005; Bender, 2010). This propensity to mix practices led sociologists and religious scholars to coin the term "spiritual market." This market has become a flourishing industry that involves choosing among a variety of spiritual traditions and practices, many of which involve paying for services; there has also been a growth in nonprofit organizations that offer meditation classes and retreats based on volunteering and free of charge. This marks a break from former religious practice, and points to the influence of capitalism and neoliberalism over the sphere of religion (Redden, 2002; Irizarry, 2015).

Meditation and Western Buddhism

Although early sociological studies on Buddhism and Buddhist practice reference meditation practice, until recently this was of secondary interest. As meditation became more popular, sociologists interested in Buddhism began to pay attention specifically to practitioners of Buddhist meditation. In contrast to the above "spirituality" themed studies, this literature focuses on institutions, groups, and communities and thus does not emphasize the individualization of religion. Instead, the theme that cuts through contemporary studies of Buddhist practice is whether the spread of meditation practice beyond Buddhist communities represents a secularization of meditation.

As part of the secularization question, research on Western Buddhism frequently differentiates between two types of meditation practitioners, especially in the US context. The first are Asian (or cradle) Buddhists, either immigrants or second generation, and the second are non-Asian—usually White—practitioners, some of whom may self-identify as convert Buddhists, while others may be categorized as "sympathizers" of Buddhism (Tweed, 2002; for a review see Numrich, 2003). The first group is considered more religiously oriented, while the second group is viewed as meditation secularizers. Both groups are characterized by a relatively privileged economic and educational status (Wuthnow & Cadge, 2004). According to Numrich (2000), in Chicago these two groups coexisted side by side with almost no interaction. However, more recent studies challenge the separation of these groups, identifying joint networks that are connected to meditation practice (Cadge, 2005).

In her pioneering ethnography on Theravāda Buddhism in the United States, Cadge (2005) compared the two groups in order to understand whether these are indeed two distinct forms of practice. She focused on a Thai temple and the non-Asian Insight Meditation center in the area of Massachusetts. She found that meditation practice is important to both groups. However, "where" and "how" people meditated, and their justification for their practice, were quite different. Thai Buddhists took meditation classes in the temple, taught by a monk, and these classes were part of many other activities—including lessons on the teachings of the Buddha and Buddhist rituals and celebrations. In contrast, the White converts learned meditation in a meditation center, where all lessons and retreats were devoted to meditation-related activity (i.e., no rituals or celebrations), and they were taught by White American meditation teachers. In addition, lay Asian practitioners did not practice to achieve nirvana, as this was understood to only be accessible to monks. In contrast, Cadge found that many White practitioners believed that through the practice of meditation they could reach nirvana, even if they were not celibate and had not renounced family life.

In a more recent ethnographic study on Vipassana practice in the United States and in Israel, which focused on the teaching school of S. N. Goenka, I found that most practitioners were interested in meditation as a way to answer their concerns regarding daily life—emotional and stress management or the search for peacefulness and happiness (see also Goenka's Vipassana meditation retreats, in this volume). Only a minority of serious practitioners showed deep interest in Buddhism or in enlightenment (Pagis, 2010a). In Weberian terms, the salvation that most practitioners of meditation are seeking has changed dramatically from being "other-worldly" and mystical-related (i.e., nirvana) to being "this-worldly" and related to subjective well-being, therapy, and mental health (see also McMahan, 2008; Wilson, 2014). Even though Vipassana retreats introduced the teachings of the Buddha (i.e., Dharma), neither meditation teachers nor practitioners identified as Buddhists. However, I also found that while relatively "secularized," the teachings of Vipassana meditation in this group were based on a cultivation of detachment from this-worldly concerns and achievements, thus sometimes producing tensions with surrounding social relations and structures (Pagis, 2019).

Another study focused on the development of mindfulness meditation in the United States as the ultimate secularization of a Buddhist practice, which is now taught in organizations such as schools, business corporations, and the army, and include little or no reference to the Buddha (Kucinskas, 2014, 2018). Using interviews with the leaders of what she entitles "the contemplative movement," Kucinskas illustrates the existing tensions between the desire to spread meditation to larger audiences that are not necessarily interested in Buddhism, and the spiritual and religious beliefs of the leaders that are much more connected to the teachings of the Buddha. While meditation teachers and supporters used secularization as a deliberate strategy to spread mindfulness practice, many of them also expressed concern that this strategy might be stripping the practice from its core Buddhist values and ethics (e.g., Purser & Loy, 2013).

Religious Syncretism

As interest in meditation crossed boundaries into other religions, sociologists became interested in such new forms of religious pluralism and syncretism. Studies generally focus on two religious groups—Judaism and Christianity—and illustrate how these groups produce new hybrids between contemporary Asian secularized meditation practices and the particular tradition of Jewish or Christian contemplative practices. While these groups are distinct from the Buddhist groups described above, studies show that similarly to the Buddhist-based groups, participants are relatively affluent and educated. In addition, like non-Asian Buddhist converts described above, practitioners of Jewish and Christian meditation are disproportionately White (Mermis-Cava, 2007; Sigalow, 2019).

Incorporating secularized meditation practice into Christian practice is considered relatively marginal, and as Bender (2010, p. 36) showed, is still troubling for many congregations in the United States. Still, some liberal and relatively pluralistic Christian groups have begun to incorporate mantra or mindfulness meditations in their practice, both in the United States (Mermis-Cava, 2007) and in Europe (e.g., Versteeg, 2006). The most institutionalized example of Christian meditation is the World Community of Christian Meditation, whose international center is located in London and includes over twenty-five centers around the world. The meditation practice was founded by John Main, who himself had experience in Asian meditation before becoming a Benedictine monk. The meditation practiced in these centers draws on the Christian tradition of contemplation while adopting the structure and social order of silent contemporary Buddhist meditation retreats. In an ethnographic study of this group, Mermis-Cava (2009) found that, on the one hand, Christian Meditation practitioners adopt a pluralist identity and belief "in the fundamental value of all religious faiths" (p. 440), yet, on the other hand, they anchor their meditation practice in the Christian tradition of contemplative practice, reject any notions of Asian influence or syncretism, and remain active in their specific Christian denominations.

In contrast to Christianity, the incorporation of Buddhist meditations into Jewish practice is more prominent, especially in the American liberal Jewish denominations. In the United States, the percentage of Jews who participate in Buddhist-related groups is disproportionate to their number in the population. In Coleman's (2002) sample of Buddhist groups in the United States, 16.5 percent of practitioners had Jewish background (versus 2–3 percent of all Americans). Many of the key leaders and teachers of Buddhist-based meditations in the United States have a Jewish background, including Joseph Goldstein and Sharon Salzberg who founded of the Insight Meditation Society; Jon Kabat-Zinn, the founder of the popular mindfulness-based stress reduction program; as well as a number of meditation scientists and writers, like Richard Davidson and Daniel Goleman (Cadge, 2005; Sigalow, 2019).

The high interest in meditation among Jews in the United States led to the creation of Jewish meditation, a "new syncretic religious practice that has roots in both the Jewish and Buddhist traditions." (Sigalow, 2019, p. 126; see also Niculescu, 2015). As Sigalow's ethnographic study shows, in these groups the connection between Jewish meditation and Buddhism is acknowledged, but at the same time pushed to the background. The founders of Jewish meditation had significant experience in Buddhist-based meditation practice. Some of them were teachers of Vipassana meditation. The practice of Jewish meditation includes reciting a Hebrew-based mantra, mindfulness sessions, and compassion meditation (*metta*). All these meditation practices are interpreted as having deep roots in Judaism, thus producing cultural linkages to the Jewish tradition. In some cases, the classes are delivered in synagogues, and the meditation classes are followed by discussions of the weekly Torah texts. Jewish meditation centers present traditional Jewish symbols that are sometimes woven into more Eastern ones, such as a Buddhist cushion inscribed with the star of David (Sigalow, 2019; for meditation syncretism in Israel see also Loss, 2010).

While these are only two examples of the incorporation of Eastern types of meditation into Western religions, the practice of Jewish and Christian meditation carries some similarities. Both the Christian and Jewish meditation practitioners are relatively liberal and are open to inter-religious dialogue. In both groups, leaders were influenced by an encounter with Hindu or Buddhist meditations, an experience that led them to revitalize contemplative practice in their specific traditions. Both encourage their members to strengthen their identification with a particular religion while at the same time understanding meditation as a universal practice. (For a history of meditation in Jewish and Christian traditions, see Persico, this volume, Laird, this volume, and Hovorun, this volume).

Social Movement and Diffusion into New Institutions

The popularization of meditation practice presents an interesting puzzle to sociologists of social movements, due to its decentralized and uncoordinated nature, as to the fact that the leaders of this movement lack a shared collective identity (Kucinskas, 2018). Sociologists working on this topic use meditation as a case study in order to learn about the diffusion of cultural practices, the mechanisms through which these practices enter new institutions, and the processes of social change. The study of meditation practice as a social movement focuses on three interrelated themes: the social actors that are involved in the practice and spread of meditation; the strategies used by leaders to facilitate this spread; and the adaptations and outcomes when meditation enters new, secular institutions.

Meditation practitioners in the West are relatively privileged with respect to education and income. For example, in the United States, a national representative survey conducted in 2012 found that greater education is associated with meditation practices and that Blacks and Hispanics are less likely to meditate (Olano et al., 2015; Cramer et al., 2016). There were similar findings based on qualitative research for Christian and Jewish meditation as described earlier in this chapter (e.g., for data in Brazil, see Rocha, 2006). Recent qualitative studies illustrate how meditation practice has begun to expand to new audiences—including studies of mindfulness in prisons (Paulle, 2017). However, this phenomenon is still relatively marginal and under-studied.

Another important finding is that, at least in the United States, there is a higher percentage of women involved in meditation practice than men. According to the 2017 US National Health Interview Survey, 16.3 percent of the women who participated in the survey reported to have used meditation in the previous twelve months compared with 11.8 percent of the men (Clarke et al., 2018). However, while women are highly involved as practitioners, men remain the majority among leaders and teachers. In Asian American groups, this bias may be connected to the traditional gendered role divisions that characterizes South East and East Asia. However, as Cadge (2004) shows, even in groups of American-born White meditation practitioners, who view themselves as completely egalitarian and "gender-blind," men hold a higher proportion of authority roles in the organization.

When focusing on the leaders that advocate for meditation, studies show that these are individuals with a high social status, privileged by education, gender, and race. These include scientists, psychiatrists, and businessmen, who are globally connected to elites in other locations, including economic and religious elites in Asian Buddhist locations (Finney, 1991; Cadge, 2005; Rocha, 2006). In a recent study of the leaders of the meditation movement in the United States, two-thirds of the 101 interviewees were men, 85 percent were White, 96 percent had a college degree or higher, and many of them held prestigious jobs (Kucinskas, 2018). The spread of meditation is thus driven by an elite. In the context of the United States, many of these leaders first encountered meditation practice during the counter-culture period as young students and grew to hold prestigious social positions that helped them to mainstream meditation.

In regard to mechanisms of diffusion and adaptation, an early study on the spread of Transcendental Meditation (TM) analyzed its strategies and coined the term "marketed social movement" (Johnston, 1980). Focusing on marketization strategies, Johnston showed how TM targeted different populations and used different recruitment messages for each of them. Based on ideas of stress or tension reduction, self-improvement, rehabilitation, and spirituality, TM entered mainstream institutions, including business corporations, local governments, drug-treatment agencies, and prisons. More recent studies on TM focus on legitimation mechanisms such as the grounding of meditation practice in scientific explanations (Humes, 2010; see also Williamson, 2010).

The recent popularity of mindfulness meditation offers a fascinating case study for understanding the mechanisms through which cultural practices are diffused. Focusing on what she calls "the contemplative movement," Kucinskas (2018) illustrates how the study of meditation as a social movement can teach us how "previously marginalized, stigmatized cultures can be brought into mainstream, everyday life by an elite to initiate broader cultural and political change." She further suggests that while during the 1980s meditation was considered a counter-cultural practice with negative connotations, a group of elite individuals worked in order to change this reputation. The spread of meditation is thus an example of a social change that was not advocated by people that questioned the status quo, but instead by an "affluent educated elite who work across varied professional fields such as science, healthcare, education and the military."

Based on interviews with key actors of the meditation movement, Kucinskas (2014) identifies the use of non-confrontational tactics that do not threaten the secular character of the institutions. She illustrates how advocates of meditation blended into prestigious and dominant institutions. This meant framing their meditation programs as secular solutions to the problems of each specific institution. For example, in the military meditation was advocated as a tool that helps to maintain performance in violent and stressful situations. Thus, meditation programs in the army omitted any reference to Buddhist concepts of non-violence. After entering the institutions, meditation leaders were hoping to gradually expose practitioners to the values connected to the Buddhist Dharma (Kucinskas, 2018).

Maybe the most successful strategy for the diffusion of meditation practice is the use of the body-mind therapeutic framework. This framework, which challenges the traditional Western body-mind dualism, represents a hybrid of Western therapeutic ideas (including self-help culture) and Eastern bodily-based practices, from yoga to acupuncture to meditation. Paradoxically, the same practice that in the monastic Buddhist context was supposed to lead to the realization of not-self (a central Buddhist tenet) is now used to achieve self-healing and self-integration (Wilson, 2014; Pagis, 2019).

Sociologists that study the diffusion of meditation from the perspective of social movements debate its social and cultural influence on Western institutions. Some argue that the popularity of meditation is a part of the "Easternization of the West" (Campbell, 2015) while others see it as another manifestation of Americanization dubbed by critics as McMindfulness (Purser & Loy, 2013). Likewise, leaders and activists within the movement debate whether the strategies to popularize Buddhist meditation had the detrimental effect of diluting mindfulness practice and stripping it of its moral anchors. Thus, the blending and assimilating may have led to a takeover by the secular institutions, thereby closing the door for institutional change that promoted a Buddhist ethic or spirituality (Kucinskas, 2018).

Empirical studies that examine the adaptation of meditation to specific secular institutions confirm that such institutional takeover is indeed taking place. For example, Barker's (2014) analysis of MBSR (mindfulness-based stress reduction) programs points to the problematic use of medical concepts in the attempt to spread meditation. She illustrates how the framing of mindfulness as "healing" leads to an expansion of the definition of "disease" and to a never-ending therapy-disease cycle. In other words, the entrance of meditation into the medical sphere strengthens the already existing increased medicalization of everyday life, leaving little room for institutional change. Likewise, Islam and colleagues (2017) point to the possibility of "takeover" by an institution, in this case the business corporation. Based on interviews and participant observation in mindfulness programs in the workplace, this study illustrates how mindfulness in the workplace reaffirms the dominant managerial perspective regarding profit and productivity, thus questioning the liberating potential that mindfulness may hold.

Studies that do emphasize the transformative power of meditation focus on the micro-level of self and social relations within the institution. For example, Paulle's (2017) ethnography of mindfulness in rehabilitation programs in the California state prison system illustrates how meditation has turned into a secular rehabilitation technique. While prisoners mainly join the programs in order to improve their application to the parole board, they sometimes end up "stumbling on the gold," as joint meditation produces an alternative social world and a new brotherhood that leads them away from the brotherhood of violence. These programs also introduce mindfulness to a population different from the privileged population discussed already. The large majority of participants are under-privileged in terms of education and economic status, and half of the participants in the programs examined were Black men.

Micro-sociology: Social Interactions and the Self

The practice of meditation has attracted the attention of micro-sociologists interested in social interactions, relationships, and the social self. Since meditation practice is an inward-looking practice, it raises questions regarding the social spheres in which such inward looking is enacted (usually silent spheres), the experiences of selfhood that meditation evokes (non-verbal and embodied), and the social order that meditation practice advocates (compassion, detachment).

Even though meditation is considered an "individualistic" practice, meditation training takes place in social, collective spaces. Meditation is learned in a group, where people sit in close proximity to one another. Reports from practitioners indicate that even after they have learned the practice and can meditate alone at home, they still feel a need to return to the group. When asked to compare their individual and collective meditation experiences, practitioners state that collective meditation leads to deeper and stronger experiences (e.g., Preston, 1988; Pagis, 2010b, Pagis, 2015). These findings are in line with the recent sociological experience-sampling study that found that people report higher experiences of spirituality when in the presence of others (Kucinskas et al., 2017; note that this study did not focus exclusively on meditation, which was reported as one practice among others, such as prayer).

Sociologists analyze the interactive social order of meditation spaces and how this social order supports the achievement of meditative states. Based on participant observation and interviews in two Zen groups in Southern California conducted in the early 1980s, Preston (1988) looked at collective meditation as a joint ritual that is based on non-verbal interaction and results in emotional rewards that do not necessary involve a change in belief. He found that Zen practitioners have limited social interaction, but are still subjected to the social control of the group. The most visible element of this social control is in keeping the right posture and not moving during meditation sessions. Since the posture in Zen meditation is not comfortable, and observation of pain and discomfort without initiating a change is a key to this practice, the social control of the group supports a meditative state of mind.

A key element of the interactive order of meditative spheres is silence. Studies of meditation retreats and group sittings in different traditions, including Zen (Fennell, 2012), Vipassana (Pagis, 2010b), and Christian meditation (Mermis-Cava, 2007), reveal the centrality of silence in the production of what I have called "collective solitude" (Pagis, 2019). These studies illustrate that in contrast to the common sociological view, which conceptualizes silence as alienating and breaking social bonds, the silence of meditation is constructive and, in fact, key to the production of a community of meditators. In my research on Vipassana retreats I found that even though practitioners do not communicate, they keep a subtle awareness of others. I found that within group meditation sittings, movement and non-movement are rhythmically coordinated, and that participants report to experience affective effervescence. I illustrate how the sharing of silence, and, with it, the relief from the need to openly verbalize or communicate, produces an ideal social sphere in which a group of individuals, often strangers to one another, can turn their gaze inward—each observing his or her own interiority together (Pagis, 2010b).

These findings can be extended to solitary meditation practice. Even though meditation can be practiced in solitude, it still depends on an imagined community. Mechanisms that invoke this community include ritualistic elements such as a fixed posture, recordings of meditation instructions, or chanting. These mechanisms help to maintain the community even in its absence. The recent popularity of meditation applications indicates the search for such a community even in solitary meditation. These applications offer an external social frame, which includes instructions, chanting, reminders, and even information about the number of people who are currently meditating with the application around the world, thus producing an awareness of a global community of meditators (Pagis, 2019).

A second "micro" venue that interests sociologists is the relation between meditation practice and the social self. In sociological theory, the dominant model of self and identity is based on G. H. Mead's (1934) claim that the self is a social contrast that emerges through interactions with others. In everyday life, we are constantly responding to the "ME" that is reflected to us from others, thus maintaining social orders in which we hold specific roles and identities. Once we perceive ourselves as others perceive us (i.e., by taking their perspectives and attitudes), we can turn ourselves into an object without the need for others by engaging in internal dialogues.

Meditation retreats and practice can be analyzed as "bracketing" the normative social structure, providing a space outside of our everyday selves. Such a space outside of normative social structure resonates with Turner's definition of a "liminoid" space, a space where the practitioners take a break from the gaze of others and from the tensions induced by daily social interaction. In my ethnographic study of Vipassana meditation, practitioners described meditation as a "pause" from their hectic lives, a place to "recharge the batteries," or a place where "I do not have the need to be in a form" as one practitioner put it (Pagis, 2019, p.82). Thus, while meditation is a social phenomenon, the collective sphere it offers is experienced by meditators as "anti-structure" when compared to their daily social life, a life characterized by hyper-connectivity and increased social complexity. This "bracketing" characteristic of meditation practice led some sociologists to advocate meditation as a tool in sociological research and teaching that helps to distance oneself from the taken-for-granted social reality (McGrane, 1994; González-López, 2011; Song & Muschert, 2014; Lee, 2015).

Sociologists have suggested models for the place of the social self in meditation. In his study of Zen meditation practice, Preston (1982, p. 262) claimed that meditation involves a "reduced role of the speaking self." Extending this view, Boyle (1985) relied on his own meditation experiences to modify Mead's model of the social self, suggesting that meditation enables practitioners to reduce awareness to the "Me" part of the self (i.e., the self as an object, which is perceived by and responded to by others), and enables a direct contact with the "I" part of the self (i.e., the spontaneous, subjective dimension of the self).

Drawing and extending these ideas, I coined the notion "embodied self-reflexivity" in order to capture the process that takes place in Vipassana meditation (Pagis, 2009). I argue that previous models of the social self emphasize language as the main channel through which self-awareness arises and neglect the place of the body as a medium through which people turn to themselves in order to gain self-knowledge and self-control. I illustrate how practitioners of Vipassana use meditation in everyday life as a tool to manage emotions, control social interactions, or create biographical-therapeutic narratives that are anchored in bodily experience.

How is this meditative form of self-awareness connected to social others? In his application of interaction-ritual theory to religious practice, Collins (2011) suggests that meditation can be analyzed as an "internal interaction ritual" taking place within one individual mind. Extending this idea I examined the relation between external interaction rituals and internal interaction rituals during Vipassana meditation retreats

(Pagis, 2015). In the early stages of the retreat there is a resonance between the relatively embarrassing and uncomfortable external interactions and the scattered and disquiet internal dialogue. In successful meditation retreats, however, as the retreat progresses participants experience a change in both internal and external interactions—as they become comfortable with the silence and physical proximity of others, they enter strong experiences of peacefulness (for Collins see also Van der Zeeuw et al., 2017; for more see on Vipassana meditation retreats, in this volume).

A third interest of micro-sociologists is the question of how meditation, a previously monastic practice that, using Weber's terms, enters everyday social life, and how meditators and their significant others understand the influence of meditation on their intimate relationships. This question extends also to the relatively popular compassion meditation, as compassion can be categorized using Weber's ideal type of brotherly love—oriented toward universal humanity at large while negating the social order of natural kin (1946a, p. 330).

In order to understand this under-investigated side of meditation practice, I interviewed both meditators and their family members or friends who do not meditate (Pagis, 2019). The findings reveal both resonance and tension within intimate social relations. Meditators report that their relationships are characterized by increased harmony, as they use meditation to decrease anger and increase compassion. At the same time, they also report that they feel less dependent on their significant others, feel quite comfortable when alone, some even mentioning a need for daily solitary time. While family members report noticing a decrease in conflictual interactions, they also report experiencing a level of social withdrawal, indicated by less engagement in the emotional togetherness of the family. For those living alone, meditation was reported as helpful in coping with loneliness, thus providing an explanation for why meditation practitioners in the United States are 25 percent less likely to be involved in a relationship when compared to non-practitioners (Cramer et al., 2016). These findings illustrate how contemporary meditation practice is used as a tool for achieving modern ideals of personal autonomy (Giddens 1991) and for coping with the growing individualization and solo-living (Klinenberg 2012).

Conclusion: Meditation and contemporary social structures and relations

What can we learn from the rising interest in meditation practice on contemporary social structures and social relations? While the above studies focus on different themes, they all emphasize the changing relationships between the individual and the surrounding social world in a globalized, post-industrial, secularized, affluent society, and how the interest in meditation resonates with these changes. These include: individualization processes that promote personal choice; new types of social relations and communities (including living alone and new forms of collective spaces); and secularization processes that change the practice of religion as the decline in commitment to a specific religious tradition leads to religious syncretism and mobility. Lastly, capitalist and neo-liberal culture of subjective well-being and therapy are pushing meditation practice into new contexts and institutions, a process that might change these institutions, but might also end in an institutional take-over, when, for example, meditation becomes a tool for increasing employees' productivity.

On the micro- and mezzo-social levels, meditation serves as a new institution and social sphere that, on the one hand, embraces the rising individualization and secularization, yet, on the other hand, is based on collective, joint circles, where affective effervescence and emotional energy are produced and where people search for experiences that can be categorized as mystical, transformative, or therapeutic. The fact that the people who are attracted to this institution are relatively privileged in terms of education, race, and economic status, teaches us about the kind of equilibrium between the "secular" and "mystical" and between "being together" and "being alone," that the affluent part of developed-world society is seeking. Future research will tell if meditation crosses boundaries into the less privileged population, and the kind of meditation-related social institutions and circles that will emerge in this process.

References

Bainbridge, W. S., & Jackson, D. H. (1981).The rise and decline of transcendental meditation. In B. Wilson & D. Martin (Eds.), *The social impact of new religious movements* (pp. 135–158). New York: Rose and Sharon Press.

Bainbridge, W. S., & Stark, R. (1980). Client and audience cults in America. *Sociological Analysis 41*(3), 199–214.

Barker, K. K. (2014). Mindfulness meditation: Do-it-yourself medicalization of every moment. *Social Science & Medicine 106*, 168–176.

Bellah, R. N., et al. (1986). *Habits of the heart: Individualism and commitment in American life*. Berkeley: University of California Press.

Bender, C. (2010). *The new metaphysicals: Spirituality and the American religious imagination*. Chicago: University of Chicago Press.

Boyle, R. P. (1985). The dark side of Mead: Neuropsychological foundations for immediate experience and mystical consciousness. *Studies in Symbolic Interaction 6*, 59–78.

Cadge, W. (2004). Gendered religious organizations: The case of Theravada Buddhism in America. *Gender & Society 18*(6), 777–793.

Cadge, W. (2005). *Heartwood: The first generation of Theravada Buddhism in America*. Chicago: University of Chicago Press.

Campbell, B. (1978). A typology of cults. *Sociological Analysis 39*(3), 228–240.

Campbell, C. (2015). *Easternization of the West: A thematic account of cultural change in the modern era*. Boulder, Co & London: Routledge.

Clarke, T. C., Barnes, P. M., Black, L. I., Stussman, B. J., & Nahin, R. L. (2018). Use of yoga, meditation, and chiropractors among U.S. adults aged 18 and over. *NCHS Data Brief*, no 325. Hyattsville, MD: National Center for Health Statistics.

Coleman, J. W. (2002). *The new Buddhism: The Western transformation of an ancient tradition.* New York: Oxford University Press.

Collins, R. (2004). *Interaction ritual chains.* Princeton, NJ: Princeton University Press.

Collins, R. (2011). The micro-sociology of religion: Religious practices, collective and individual. *The Association of Religion Data Archives Guiding Paper Series. Retrieved from* http://www.thearda.com/rrh/papers/guidingpapers.asp

Cramer, H., Hall, H., Leach, M., Frawley, J., Zhang, Y., Leung, B., Adams, J., & Lauche, R. (2016). Prevalence, patterns, and predictors of meditation use among US adults: A nationally representative survey. *Scientific Reports 6*, 36760.

Durkheim, E. (2008/1912). *The Elementary Forms of the Religious Life.* New York: Courier Corporation.

Fennell, D. (2012). Explorations of silence in the religious rituals of Buddhists and Quakers. *Religion 42*(4), 549–574.

Finney, H. C. (1991). American Zen's "Japan connection": A critical case study of Zen Buddhism's diffusion to the West. *Sociological Analysis* 52(4), 379–396.

Giddens, A. (1991). *Modernity and self-identity.* Cambridge: Polity Press.

González-López, G. (2011). Mindful ethics: Comments on informant-centered practices in sociological research. *Qualitative Sociology 34*(3), 447

Heelas, P. (1996). Detraditionalization and its rivals. In P. Heelas, S. Lash, & P. Morris (Eds.), *Detraditionalization: Critical reflections on authority and identity* (pp. 1–20). Oxford: Blackwell.

Heelas, P. & Woodhead L. (2005). *The spiritual revolution: Why religion is giving way to spirituality.* Malden: Blackwell.

Humes, C. A. (2010). The Transcendental Meditation organization and its encounter with science. In J. R. Lewis & O. Hammer (Eds.), *Handbook of Religion and the Authority of Science* (pp. 345–369). Leiden: Brill.

Irizarry, J. A. (2015). Putting a price on Zen: The business of redefining religion for global consumption. *Journal of Global Buddhism 16*, 51–69.

Islam, G., Holm, M., & Karjalainen, M. (2017). Sign of the times, workplace mindfulness as an empty signifier. *Organization.* Online at https://doi.org/10.1177/1350508417740643

Johnston, H. (1980). The marketed social movement: A case study of the rapid growth of TM. *Pacific Sociological Review* 23(3), 333–354.

Klinenberg, E. (2012). *Going solo: The extraordinary rise and surprising appeal of living alone.* New York: Penguin.

Kucinskas, J. (2014). The unobtrusive tactics of religious movements. *Sociology of Religion 75*, 537–550.

Kucinskas, J. (2018). *The mindful elite: Mobilizing from the inside out.* New York: Oxford University Press.

Kucinskas, J., et al. (2017). States of spiritual awareness by time, activity, and social interaction. *Journal for the Scientific Study of Religion 56*(2), 418–437.

Lee, M. T. (2015). North Central Sociological Association presidential address. The mindful society: Contemplative sociology, meta-mindfulness, and human flourishing. *Sociological Focus 48*(4), 271–299.

Loss, J. (2010). Buddha-Dhamma in Israel: Explicit non-religious and implicit non-secular localization of religion. *Nova Religio: The Journal of Alternative and Emergent Religions 13*(4), 84–105.

McGrane, B. (1994). *The un-TV and the 10 mph car experiments in personal freedom and everyday life.* Fort Bragg, CA: The Small Press.

McMahan, D. L. (2008). *The making of Buddhist modernism*. New York: Oxford University Press.
Mead, G. H. (1934). *Mind, self and society*. Chicago: University of Chicago Press.
Mermis-Cava, J. (2009). An anchor and a sail: Christian meditation as the mechanism for a pluralist religious identity. *Sociology of Religion 70*(4), 432–453.
Mermis-Cava, J. M. (2007). *Relating with silence: Christian meditation and the production of roles, relationships, and culture* (Doctoral dissertation). University of California, Davis.
Niculescu, M. (2015). Going online and taking the plane. From San Francisco to Jerusalem. The physical and electronic networks of "Jewish mindfulness." *Heidelberg Journal of Religions on the Internet 8*, 98–114.
Numrich, P. D. (2000). How the swans came to Lake Michigan: The social organizations of Buddhist Chicago. *Journal for the Scientific Study of Religion 39*(2), 189–203
Numrich, P. D. (2003). Two Buddhisms further considered. *Contemporary Buddhism 4*(1), 55–78.
Olano, H. A., et al. (2015). Engagement in mindfulness practices by US adults: Sociodemographic barriers. *Journal of Alternative and Complementary Medicine 21*(2), 100–102.
Pagis, M. (2009). Embodied self-reflexivity. *Social Psychology Quarterly 72*, 265–283.
Pagis, M. (2010a). From abstract concepts to experiential knowledge: Embodying enlightenment in a meditation center. *Qualitative Sociology 33*(4), 469–489.
Pagis, M. (2010b). Producing intersubjectivity in silence: An ethnographic study of meditation practice. *Ethnography 11*(2), 309–328.
Pagis, M. (2015). Evoking equanimity: Silent interaction rituals in Vipassana meditation retreats. *Qualitative Sociology 38*(1), 39–56.
Pagis, M. (2019). *Inward: Vipassana meditation and the embodiment of the self*. Chicago: University of Chicago Press.
Paulle, B. (2017). Stumbling on the rehabilitation gold? Foucault vs. Foucault in San Quentin and Beyond. *Ethnography 18*(4), 471–492.
Preston, D. L. (1982). Meditative ritual practice and spiritual conversion-commitment: Theoretical implications based on the case of Zen. *Sociological Analysis 43*(3), 257–270.
Preston, D. L. (1988). *The social organization of Zen practice: Constructing transcultural reality*. New York: Cambridge University Press.
Purser, R., & Loy, D. (2013). Beyond McMindfulness. *Huffington Post 1*(7), 13.
Redden, G. (2002). The new agents: Personal transfiguration and radical privatization in New Age self-help. *Journal of Consumer Culture 2*(1), 33–52.
Rocha, C. (2006). *Zen in Brazil: The quest for cosmopolitan modernity*. Honolulu: University of Hawai'i Press.
Sigalow, E. (2019). *American JuBu: Jews, Buddhists, and religious change in the United States*. Princeton, NJ: Princeton University Press.
Song, K. Y., & Muschert, G. W. (2014). Opening the contemplative mind in the sociology classroom. *Humanity & Society 38*(3), 314–338.
Turner, V. (1974). Liminal to liminoid, in play, flow, and ritual: An essay in comparative symbology. *Rice Institute Pamphlet-Rice University Studies 60*(3).
Turner, V. (2017/1966). *The ritual process: Structure and anti-structure*. London: Routledge.
Tweed, T. A. (2002). Who is a Buddhist? Night-stand Buddhists and other creatures. In C. S. Prebish & M. Baumann (Eds.), *Westward Dharma: Buddhism beyond Asia* (pp. 17–33). Berkeley: University of California Press
Van der Zeeuw, A., Keesman, L., & Weenink, D. (2017). Sociologizing with Randall Collins: An interview about emotions, violence, attention space and sociology. *European Journal of Social Theory*, doi:10.31857/S013216250003746-3.

Versteeg, P. G. A.(2006) Marginal Christian spirituality: An example from a Dutch meditation group. *Journal of Contemporary Religion 21*(1), 83–97

Volinn, E. (1985). Eastern meditation groups: Why join? *Sociological Analysis 46*(2), 147–156.

Weber, M. (1946a). Religious rejections of the world and their directions. In H. H. Gerth and C. Wright Mills (Eds.), *From Max Weber: Essays in Sociology* (pp. 323–359). New York: Oxford University Press.

Weber, M. (1946b). The social psychology of the world religions. In H. H. Gerth and C. Wright Mills (Eds.), *From Max Weber: Essays in Sociology* (pp. 267–301). New York: Oxford University Press.

Weber, M. (1958a). *The religion of India: The sociology of Hinduism and Buddhism*. Glencoe, IL: Free Press.

Weber, M. (1958b). Science as a vocation. *Daedalus 87*(1), 111–134.

Williamson, L. (2010). *Transcendent in America: Hindu-inspired meditation movements as new religion*. New York: New York University Press.

Wilson, J. (2014). Mindful America: Meditation and the mutual transformation of Buddhism and American culture. New York: Oxford University Press.

Wuthnow, R. & Cadge, W. (2004). Buddhists and Buddhism in the United States: The scope of influence. *Journal for the Scientific Study of Religion 43*(3), 363–380.

CHAPTER 26

THE DEMOGRAPHICS OF MEDITATION IN THE UNITED STATES

CONRAD HACKETT

Survey Measures of Meditation

Good global data exist for many measures of religion. For example, more than 40 percent of the world's population lives in a country where religious identity is measured in a census. In other countries, identity can be measured using large-scale demographic surveys or general population surveys (Hackett et al., 2015). Additionally, cross-national surveys measure other aspects of religion, such as attendance at worship services, frequency of prayer, and the importance of religion.

Unfortunately, it is difficult to analyze the global demography of meditation because meditation is not measured in censuses or demographic surveys. Even cross-national surveys do not ask about meditation specifically. The World Values Survey comes close, but its question is problematic for our purposes. It asks, "Do you take some moments of prayer, meditation or contemplation or something like that?" This question does not differentiate between prayer, meditation, contemplation, or "something like that." Furthermore, it records only "yes" or "no" responses. For those who say "yes," no data are gathered about the frequency with which respondents engage in these acts.

Fortunately, there are country-specific surveys that have asked about meditation specifically. The largest studies that measure meditation are the 2007 and 2014 waves of Pew Research Center's Religious Landscape Study (RLS), which surveyed more than 35,000 Americans in each wave (Pew Research Center, 2015).[1] Respondents in these surveys

[1] More information about the Religious Landscape Study is available at http://www.pewforum.org/religious-landscape-study/. Other country-specific studies that have measures of meditation include the Spiritual Life Study of Chinese Residents (http://www.thearda.com/archive/files/descriptions/sprtchna.asp)

were asked many questions about their religious practices, including, "How often do you meditate? Would you say at least once a week, once or twice a month, several times a year, seldom, or never?" Because the RLS surveys have very large samples, they permit analysis of meditation patterns among groups too small to be measured reliably in typical surveys of 1,000 to 2,000 respondents.

This short chapter describes the demography of meditation in the United States, as measured in the 2014 RLS (Pew Research Center, 2015). Readers may be surprised to learn that the Americans most likely to meditate regularly include Jehovah's Witnesses, older Americans, Black Americans, poorer Americans, and political conservatives.

Frequency of Meditation

Americans tend to say they meditate regularly (40 percent do so at least weekly) or rarely, if at all (45 percent seldom or never do). There's not much middle ground—only 8 percent say they meditate once or twice a month and only 4 percent say they do so several times a year. The discussion below explores which Americans are most likely to report meditating at least weekly.

Religion

Most people in four religious groups report meditating weekly (see Figure 26.1): Jehovah's Witnesses (77 percent), Buddhists (66 percent), Mormons (60 percent), and members of Historically Black Protestant denominations (55 percent). Evangelical Protestants (49 percent) are more likely than average Americans to meditate weekly while Catholics (40 percent) match the general public average. Groups less likely to meditate frequently include mainline Protestants (36 percent), Muslims (35 percent), and Hindus (33 percent). Atheists (19 percent), agnostics (24 percent), those with no religion in particular (28 percent), and Jews (28 percent) are least likely to meditate regularly.

Meditation is widely associated with Asian spirituality and its secular offshoots, such as mindfulness. However, among the general public, it is probably not associated with Jehovah's Witnesses and Mormons, though members of these groups report meditating frequently. While the RLS survey did not ask respondents about their understanding of meditation, online material sheds light on how meditation may be understood in these faiths. An article on the official website of the Jehovah's Witnesses explains, "The Bible

the Taiwan Social Change Survey (http://www.ios.sinica.edu.tw/sc/en/home2.php), the Baylor Religion Survey (https://www.baylor.edu/baylorreligionsurvey/), and the complementary health questionnaire administered every five years in the U.S. National Health Interview Survey (see https://www.cdc.gov/nchs/data/databriefs/db325-h.pdf).

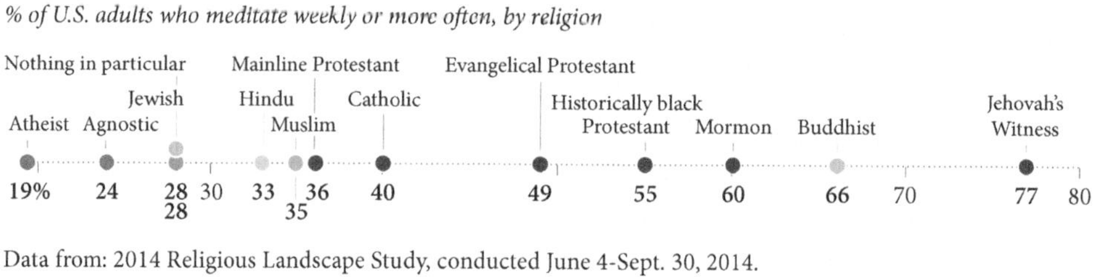

FIGURE 26.1 © Bill Webster, 2020.

puts a high value on meditation. The kind of meditation it encourages, however, does not entail emptying the mind or repeating a certain word or phrase, sometimes called a mantra. Rather, Biblical meditation involves purposeful thinking on wholesome topics, such as God's qualities, standards, and creations" (Jehovah's Witnesses, n.d.-a). Another article asks why meditation is so important and answers, "Meditating on Jehovah and Jesus can help a person become a mature Christian and maintain strong faith" (Jehovah's Witnesses, n.d.-b). Mormons also encourage meditation. David O. McKay, the former president of the Church of Jesus Christ of Latter-Day Saints, said that "[m]editation is the language of the soul. It is defined as 'a form of private devotion, or spiritual exercise, consisting in deep, continued reflection on some religious theme'" (Church of Jesus Christ of Latter-Day Saints. (n.d.)).

Some Christians and others may think of meditation as a form of prayer, given that there can be some overlap between the two practices. In addition to the question about meditation, the survey asked separately about prayer, finding that the more often someone prays, the more likely they are to say they meditate. Among those who say they pray at least weekly, for instance, 50 percent say they meditate regularly. By contrast, among those who rarely pray (less than a few times a month or never), only 17 percent say they meditate.

Other Demographic Characteristics and Meditation

The likelihood of reporting frequent meditation varies little across some demographic characteristics (see Table 26.1). For example, men (37 percent) and women (43 percent) report fairly similar frequencies of weekly meditation. And there is little variation by education categories.

There is considerable variation across other demographic categories, such as age and marital status. The likelihood of weekly meditation increases monotonically across age categories from 29 percent among those aged eighteen to twenty-nine to 53 percent among those sixty-five and older. In terms of marital status, frequent meditation is least

Table 26.1 Share of Americans who report meditating at least weekly

All adults	40%
Gender	
Men	37
Women	43
Age	
18–29	29
30–49	38
50–64	44
65+	53
Marital status	
Never married	32
Living with a partner	35
Married	41
Divorced or separated	47
Widowed	57
Race/ethnicity	
White	36
Black	52
Latino	49
Asian	31
Education	
High school or less	40
Some college	41
College	39
Post-graduate degree	42
Household income	
<$30,000	45
$30,000–$49,000	41
$50,000–$99,000	37
$100,000 or more	34
Political ideology	
Conservative	45
Moderate	37
Liberal	38

Data from: 2014 Religious Landscape Study
(Pew Research Center, 2015)

common among the never married (32 percent) and most common among the widowed (57 percent).

While some people associate meditation with Asia, Asian-Americans are less likely to meditate weekly (31 percent) than Whites (36 percent), Latinos (49 percent) or Blacks (52 percent). Meditation may also be associated in popular imagination with liberalism, but self-reported political liberals are less likely to meditate weekly (38 percent) than political conservatives (45 percent).

Lower household income is associated with greater likelihood of reporting weekly meditation. Those living in households with income below $30,000 are most likely to meditate weekly (45 percent) and those in households with income of $100,000 or more are least likely to report weekly meditation (34 percent).

Social Views

While 47 percent of those who say abortion should be illegal in all or most cases meditate regularly, 35 percent who favor legal abortion meditate regularly. Similarly, frequent meditation is more common among those who say that homosexuality should be discouraged (51 percent) than among those who say it should be accepted (35 percent). Meditation is also more common among Americans who believe humans have always existed in their present form (49 percent) than among those who affirm that humans have evolved due to natural processes (29 percent).

Conclusion

Although there is limited data and prior research on demographic characteristics associated with meditation, this brief analysis of data from the United States demonstrates the characteristics of survey respondents most likely to report frequent meditation often diverge from popular stereotypes about practitioners of meditation.

References

Hackett, C., Connor, P., Stonawski, M., Skirbekk, V., Potančoková, M., & Abel, G. (2015). The future of world religions: Population growth projections, 2010–2050. Washington, DC: Pew Research Center.

Jehovah's Witnesses. (n.d.-a). The Bible's viewpoint: Meditation. Retrieved from https://www.jw.org/en/publications/magazines/g201405/meditation/

Jehovah's Witnesses. (n.d.-b). Keep meditating on spiritual things. Retrieved from https://www.jw.org/en/publications/magazines/ws20151015/keep-meditating-on-spiritual-things/

Church of Jesus Christ of Latter-Day Saints. (n.d.). Elements of worship. *Teachings of presidents of the church: David O. McKay*. Retrieved from https://www.lds.org/manual/teachings-david-o-mckay/chapter-4?lang=eng

Pew Research Center. (2015, May 12). America's changing religious landscape. [Report on the 2014 Religious Landscape Study]. Retrieved from https://www.pewforum.org/2015/05/12/americas-changing-religious-landscape/

ANTHROPOLOGY

CHAPTER 27

MEDITATION AND THE POST-SECULAR CONDITION

MANU BAZZANO

Introduction

As a relatively new phenomenon, the post-secular turn (Braidotti, 2008; Braeckman, 2009; McLennan, 2010; Habermas, 2010; Staudigl & Alvis, 2017) generally denotes a variety of theories that explore the reappearance of religious ideas in a cultural milieu that has been dominated, particularly in the West, by secularism. Its emergence is partly due to the increasing recognition that there is something missing in the secular societies many of us live in and, more generally, that there is something missing within the secularist worldview (Habermas, 2010). Yet there is more to the post-secular turn than a pure and simple return to religion. Among the various theories that attempt to define the post-secular, this chapter will focus on one perspective that presents interesting and potentially innovative implications for the practice of meditation. Often overlooked, this perspective has itself a long and intricate genealogy. Its name is *immanence* (Deleuze, 1990; Barber, 2014), a term stepped in theology and whose Latin origin means *remaining within*, that is, within this world, denoting the presence of God in all things. Immanence is opposed to *transcendence*, whose meaning is to climb (*scandere*) over (*trans*), denoting in theology a "creator" standing outside this world. For transcendental thinkers like Thomas Aquinas, in whose reflections Aristotle, Plato, and Christianity all converged, the world is good and true not in essence, but only *indirectly*, by "analogical participation" (Barber, 2010, p. 431) in a transcendent God. For transcendentalists of all persuasions, this world is not good enough: too imperfect and samsaric; an unfair world of blood, sweat, and tears.

When applied to the practice of meditation, the immanentist stance discussed in this chapter can potentially circumvent the limitations of both religious and secularist understandings of meditation, while at the same time fully respecting the deep insights generated by both "traditions." The immanentist perspective builds on the critique of secularism implicit in the post-secular turn, delving into some of the more dubious aspects of secularist meditation that have been recently popularized and applied to areas whose associations present ethical challenges and concerns. Inspired by a pivotal figure in the history of Zen Buddhism—the thirteenth century Japanese monk and founder of the Soto school, Dōgen Zenji—as well as on a phenomenological understanding of meditation, the chapter attempts to spell out a new perspective.

Skin, Flesh, Bone, and Marrow

Before leaving China for his native India and wanting to nominate a successor, the legendary Buddhist monk Bodhidharma assembled four of his disciples. He asked them to convey their understanding of the Dharma. Each of them gave a different answer.

> Dao-fu said: "One should not cling to words and letters nor abandon words and letters." Bodhidharma said: "You conveyed my skin." Then Nun Zongchi said: "To me, the Dharma is the joy of seeing the land of Akshobhya Buddha once and never again." Bodhidharma said: "You conveyed my flesh." Daoyu said: "At their origin, air, earth, water and fire are empty. The five aggregates do not exist. Thus, there is nothing to attain." Bodhidharma said: "You conveyed my bones." Finally, Huike came forward, bowed deeply, and went back to his seat. Bodhidharma said: "You conveyed my marrow." Then he transmitted the Dharma, the bowl, and the robe to Huike. (Bazzano, 2017a, p. 116)

Until a commentary by Dōgen appeared, several centuries later, it was a given that only the fourth disciple, Huike, "got it." Dōgen points at something more subtle. In his commentary to a famous passage in Zen literature, commonly known as *Bodhidharma's Skin, Flesh, Bone, and Marrow* (Heine, 2008), he debunks the notion that there is a set of hierarchical values in relation to the depth of meditative absorption.

For Dōgen, the four disciples' responses were *equally valid*. If one takes them as superior or inferior to each other, one fails to see Bodhidharma's objective. Each student, in his or her own way, contains the teacher's all being. Evading hierarchical notions of depth and surface, Dōgen provided a welcome antidote to status-centered notions of spiritual awakening and accomplishment.

Like a language learned, a habit acquired over years, a set of deeds that over time makes and unmakes us, Zen is a kind of sickness, a blissful thorn used to dislodge the aching thorn, the poison that reveals the nectar deep in the heart of our existential affliction. To say that the Dharma is not learned academically through memorizing or imbibing this or that doctrine but through incarnate, somatic practice, is probably a truism: it is a given in Zen that meditation practice has to be inhabited in one's body, that one has to translate the doctrine into skin, bone, flesh, and marrow. The tradition is inherited only when it becomes alive in this body. This body finds in turns a speech that reason alone is unable to articulate or fathom. Incarnate practice retrieves a voice or a host of voices, according to one's power to receive. And all voices are but the voices of Śākyamuni Buddha.

This is arguably the heart of "meditation." How can anyone seriously claim that by simply assuming the zazen or sitting meditation posture, a flawed human being will host within his/her body the very essence of the Dharma? How can a tormented, stumbling sentient being retrieve in his/her own flesh the voice and presence of the great ancestors? Yet this is precisely what Dōgen's commentary seems to be saying.

There is more: this seeming emphasis on incarnate expression of the Dharma through zazen does not entail preference for an instinctual, wordless realm of communion with living things in a hierarchy that places intellect on the lowest rung, followed, on the way up, by feelings and then "pure silence" on the snowy peaks.

It may be useful to note how, by sitting in zazen, one enters a living stream and instinctively inherits the skin or flesh or bone or marrow of the great ancestors. Beginners too are already endowed with the fundamental prerequisite for becoming a Buddha, that is, we are alive, sentient, and manifest an intention to look for something that that has already found us.

On Mainstream Secular Meditation

It is now the norm to speak of meditation without referring to its enduring and inextricable links to ethics, anthropology, spirituality, and religion. We have come to ascribe to meditation the functional role of technique and performance, as means to an end: altered states or relaxation, or as device for decreasing the pressure of modern living. While it is true that both religious and secular approaches to meditation are, to a certain extent, functional, their functions differ greatly. In my understanding, secular approaches to meditation by and large try to formulate a response to modernity; in so doing, they roughly reproduce classical modernity's customary focus on (a) *rationalization* in relation to culture, (b) *individualization* in relation to human societies, and (c) *subordination* (to the discontents of civilization) in relation to "nature" and "instinct."

In critiquing the pervasive *rationalization* typical of Western societies influenced by Protestantism, Max Weber (2004) noted how rationalism was heavily applied not only to economics, scientific research, technology, administration, law, and military training but peculiarly extended to spiritual and religious contemplation, divesting the latter from formerly magical and mysteric elements (e.g., transubstantiation in the Catholic mass), in favor of a more utilitarian as well as more ascetic stance centered on work and personal salvation. For Weber, "the man who, *par excellence*, lived a rational life in the religious sense was, and remained, alone the monk" (2004, p. 74). Thus rationalization fostered *individualization*, a personal route to salvation that, emphasized by Luther, was later perfected in Calvinism and transmuted into the emphasis on productivity and work, introducing, as it were, a double-entry bookkeeping attitude to the religious and spiritual life. This stance may be implicit but rather pervasive and akin to what David Smail called *magic voluntarism* (Smail, 2015): decontextualized individuals alone are held responsible for their stress and anguish, regardless of the social and economic milieu in which their lives are embedded. This particular facet is important: we now tend to speak, for instance, of mindfulness in isolation, and not only in terms of something that an isolated individual can perform in order to cope with the challenges of modernity.

The third element, *subordination*, partly refers to the historical dependence of "national or religious minorities... in relation to a group of rulers" (Weber, 2004, p. 6) and could be extended in our times to the general subordination of meditative practices to the dominant scientific and cultural views—something evident, as we shall see in a moment, in relation to the coveted domain called "mainstream."

As a consequence of this threefold focus I have sketched, the complex culture(s) out of which Buddhist meditation emerged—with its animistic, shamanic, existential, and theistic components—becomes, in secularist approaches, thoroughly rationalized and expediently downsized to a string of techniques aimed at achieving "happiness," reducing cholesterol levels, or soothing work-related strain. Equally, the existential burden of societal malaise, ethico-political unfairness, and injustice is transferred onto the shoulder of isolated individuals who, divested of their dignity as citizens, are explicitly or subliminally deemed responsible for their fate.

Improvement of our lot (whether facing illness or redundancy) will come about, according to this cheerfully coercive narrative, through meditation, positive thinking, and smiling more often (Ehrenreich, 2010). Finally, by chastising the instinctual and sensuous life and looking down on the "ruminative," naturally meandering aspects of the psyche, secularist approaches to meditation (e.g., mindfulness programs) echo more or less the "civilizing" work of modernity, endorsing human types able to rise above "the passions" and the inherently creative contradictions of their condition with the aim of becoming efficient employees, keen consumers, and, some would say, "excellent sheep" (Deresiewicz, 2014). A winning subordination of the allegedly unruly life of the affects often goes hand in hand with conformity, whose complementary flipside is an unbridled, equally conformist, and desublimated hedonism (Marcuse, 1964).

Mindfulness and Acceleration

The threefold process outlined above draws largely from Max Weber's take on some of the effects of modernity (Weber, 2004). With the advent of post-modernity, a new feature has become central: technical acceleration. It is not a coincidence that avowedly secular approaches to meditation are hugely popular in our age of post-modernity characterized by the "self-propelling circular process" (Rosa, 2013, p. 23) of *social acceleration* that is at the heart of current collective permutations. The "mindfulness app" is one of many gadgets now available that promise to take the user "to a more relaxed and healthier state of mind" (Apple Inc., 2017, Internet file). I have met people who use it before going to bed: it helps them fall asleep after a long working day. Increased technical acceleration requires continuous technological innovation, the creation of new gadgets that help lighten the pressures of a faster tempo and the time shortage it engenders and renew the cycle of acceleration. It is hardly controversial to suggest that the mindfulness app constitutes one of the smartest outcomes of a secular approach to meditation. The trend described above has been developed for some time and has on the whole succeeded in bringing the once marginal practice of meditation into the *mainstream*, a term praised by Jon Kabat-Zinn (2015) as a desirable goal for the mindfulness movement. The problem with "going mainstream" is that dominant practices are no longer critiqued but taken at face value. Some of the ethical implications of this are far-reaching and worrisome. Mainstream applications of secular meditation include mindfulness in the military as well as corporate mindfulness. The hybrid of positive psychology and mindfulness in the US military and the CIA gave birth to obnoxious reinterpretations of *resilience* as well as the gruesome promotion of *adaptive killing* and torture (Shaw, 2016). Moments of difficulty and crisis arguably require a threefold movement of (a) recognition of human fragility, (b) attending to the problem at hand, and (c) moving forward. But the increasingly popular notion of resilience (from the Latin *resilire*), to rebound, only describes the third movement, the bouncing back and moving forward; there is no recognition or attending. There is more to this than semantic inaccuracy, and the question may be asked whether what looks like shorthand may in fact be avoidance, plain and simple: avoidance of our inherent vulnerability as human beings (often revealed to us by a crisis) and of the need to attend compassionately to the difficulties we experience. Has "resilience" in other words been hijacked, its meaning distorted by an altogether different worldview that regards vulnerability as weakness?

Resilience as a New Psychological Fetish

Positive psychology has been at the forefront of the popularisation of the concept of resilience. The mission of its founder and chief protagonist, US psychologist Martin Seligman, is to put an end to what he calls "victimology"—the "passive view of the human being" that has, he argues, contaminated the social sciences (Seligman, 1999). Another of Positive Psychology's leitmotifs is "learned helplessness." This is based on Seligman's finding that dogs can be brought to a state of passivity when subjected to repeated, painful electric shocks. From this he deduced that humans, when faced with unmanageable situations, "experience disruptions in motivation, emotion, and learning that amount to a sense of helplessness" (Seligman, 1999). He applied this theory to depression in relation to social problems, which he represented in terms of "helpless cognitions" among "demoralized women on welfare" and Asian Americans, and as "defeatism" among Black Americans (Shaw, 2016, p. 39). It is a stance that disregards the socio-political context that discourages and humiliates those women, Asian American, and Black Americans in the first place.

The rhetoric of resilience is echoed by Linley, founding director of the Centre of Applied Positive Psychology (CAPP) in the United Kingdom, who spoke enthusiastically of Martin Seligman's Comprehensive Soldier Fitness program in the United States "[as a] superb example of how you can take some of the principles of positive psychology and apply those in a way that makes a real and lasting difference to people's lives" (Jarden, 2012, p. 83).

The Comprehensive Soldier Fitness program, established in 2009, was aimed at "creating more resilient soldiers by helping them with the necessary psychological adjustments" (Shaw, 2016, p. 40). To this purpose, Seligman devised a method for measuring resilience, the Global Assessment Tool. The notion of resilience was met with great enthusiasm by other psychologists who came up with creative variations on the theme. Professor Michael Matthews promptly supplied the notion of "adaptive killing": a set of cognitive and behavioral techniques "focus[ed] on eliminating irrational thoughts and beliefs... on changing a soldier's belief structure regarding killing." As he sees it, "these interventions could be integrated into immersive simulations to promote the conviction that adaptive killing is permissible" (Matthews, 2014, p. 187).

Resilience has effectively become a new fetish in contemporary psychology, useful in fostering the neoliberal agenda at a time of heightened security and financial austerity. Unsurprisingly, it has found applications in several areas. The International Monetary Fund (IMF)'s website has over two thousand documents discussing the topic, and similar emphasis is found within the World Bank (which has created a "Social Resilience" group) and the World Economic Forum with its focus on "systemic financial resilience." A newly founded academic journal, *Resilience*, is entirely dedicated to the topic (Neocleous, 2013).

The above examples illustrate how psychology, a complex science designed to help human beings and alleviate suffering, can be made to serve agendas that oppose its original ethos. Something similar is beginning to take place with mindfulness when the latter is reduced to a mere set of techniques divested of the ethical context.

Corporate mindfulness is equally representative of this generalized tendency to capsize the Buddha's teachings of spiritual awakening for purposes that are uncoupled from the former's fundamental ethical context, as Ron Purser and Edwin Ng (2015) explain:

> Instead of cultivating awareness of the contingencies of present reality that cause suffering, and thereby developing the capacity to intervene in those conditions of suffering, corporate mindfulness goes no further than encouraging individuals to manage stress so as to optimize performance within existing conditions of precarity. (Internet File)

It is still "business as usual," the authors argue: political corruption, the underfunding of education, the concentration of wealth, and an overall sociopathic work culture all go on undeterred. What is also overlooked is that the Buddha's mention of mindfulness was invariably contextual: mindfulness *of*, and in particular mindfulness of impermanence. Rather than the trumpeted "stress reduction," paying heed to the Buddha's prompting may in fact bring about stress *induction*—an altogether natural response for anyone who wakes up to the stark reality of our certain demise and the uncertain hour of its occurrence. As many practitioners will attest, this voluntarily sought form of stress-induction often does not result in discouragement but works as antidote against complacency. It makes us cherish our being in the world; it engenders compassion and self-compassion for our common predicament; it affords greater meaning to our existence.

Existentialist Secular Meditation

A secular understanding of meditation is not limited to the examples highlighted above. There are arguably deeper manifestations trying to link practice to a more generalized, *existential* human anguish that goes beyond the circumstantial concerns associated with modern living. Rather than offering consolation to a self buffeted by stress, so that it can eventually step back into the ring rejuvenated, these existential accounts of secular meditation are thoroughgoing; their modes of enquiry do address our intrinsic human dread of impermanence. They invite us to face with greater honesty the anxiety of uncertainty latent within our agitated striving. It remains to be seen whether this process is genuinely liberating or whether it in fact engenders its own "Protestant" congregations of secular meditators with their own secular preachers and hierarchical systems that replicate all aspects of religious Buddhism with only a few doctrinal differences. It remains to be seen whether this approach to meditation still provides valid responses to the challenges of the post-secular turn.

In order to proceed on our investigation, it will be useful to refine our understanding of the post-secular.

What Is the Post-Secular?

The practice of "just sitting" has its origins within the Hindu and later Buddhist religious practice of *dhyāna*. Opinions may differ on how to correctly translate this Sanskrit term—whether as deep concentration of the mind, refined state of absorption, or, in theistic versions, communion with the divine. But one thing *dhyāna* is *not*—at least in the anthropological and mythico-religious context in which it originally emerged. It is not a technique or a skillful ruse one learns in order to *achieve* a coveted state of mind. It appears to belong instead to the sphere of the *sacred*. Secular meditation has arguably discarded the domain of the *sacred*, a sphere normally but not exclusively associated with religion and closely linked to spirituality.

But what is the sacred? Does it coincide with the religious? Does it coincide with spirituality? Can it be equated with the religious dimension even when the latter reifies a specific goal (e.g., enlightenment, spiritual awakening) for its practice? Asking these types of questions places us already within a mode of thinking that is at the threshold of what some will inevitably describe as "post-modern." The term is ambiguous yet it has largely come to mean a stance of detached irony with regards to "grand narratives," whether metaphysical or not, that provide an explanation of reality. Despite the wide difference among cultural artifacts or modes of thinking that get labeled as "post-modern," the latter could be safely assumed to be almost unanimously *post-metaphysical*. That is, they question religious or scientific systems alike (e.g., Christianity and Darwinism) because they are seen as providing ready-made answers to reality and presenting the latter as truths. The very notion of a pre-established truth is questioned in most post-modern stances in favor of a situational version of truth, one that has to be constructed every step of the way. The post-metaphysical and post-modern stance has, however, thrown away the baby with the bath water: it has discarded religion without truly understanding its depth and breadth. In so doing, it has left a void. The human thirst for the sacred did not find satisfaction in the fragmentary self-reference of post-modern culture.

The longing for the sacred in all its forms gave rise to the *post-secular turn* (Braidotti, 2008; Braeckman, 2009; McLennan, 2010; Staudigl & Alvis, 2017). This "post-secular" has itself created its own set of doctrines and, more importantly, has not responded adequately to the human thirst for the sacred. We have reached a point where the rational and empirical tenets of secularism, useful at first in freeing us from the shackles of superstitious beliefs, are no longer enough, no longer satisfying. This dissatisfaction manifests itself as a new feeling of restlessness that prompts some to go back to the tenets of religion, while others find new avenues for the sacred, a practice of meditation that values religious teachings but re-interprets them in a new immanent form—that is, in a form that is deeply connected to the world rather than resorting to a transcendental explanation of reality.

At its most superficial level, the term post-secularism simply describes a return to religion and religious values. This is partly an understandable backlash against fundamentalist forms of secularism whose adherents speak of liberty, but in actual fact hate otherness and, moreover, regard religious beliefs, especially those of foreigners, with suspicion and a good degree of prejudice (Riemer, 2016; Hasan, 2016). This version of post-secularism as return to religion would also describe, more generally, the search for certainties in an era of "post-truths" and increasing levels of manipulation in civic life. A religious approach to meditation would in this case provide a map as well as a grand narrative that can be comforting at times of personal and societal uncertainty.

To know that one's meditation practice is not just sitting, but that it belongs to a purposeful spiritual and religious program variously aimed at raising one's level of consciousness, improving oneself morally, communicating with the divine, and so forth, will provide some with a rationale and a sense of direction. This point is crucial in our discussion of post-secularism, and it will help redress the conventional opposition between the secular and the religious in a fundamental way.

Immanence and Transcendence

From a post-secular perspective, the real antithesis is not secularism versus religion but *immanence* versus *transcendence*—"remaining within" versus "climbing over," as the Latin etymology of the two terms suggests: either remaining within our everyday, imperfect world or climbing over it. Religion (as well as theology and spirituality in general) has long been associated with transcendence: God (or the divine, enlightened and awakened beings) has long been linked with otherworldliness, a dimension beyond the everyday, separate from the impermanent world of phenomena. This categorization (Weber, 2004), however, does not allow for a religious discourse uncoupled from transcendence. It also assumes that a secular worldview—at times characterized, for instance, by excessive trust in science—would be automatically free of metaphysics.

Above all, a simplistic polarization of secular versus religious summarily excludes the existence of *immanent spirituality*—that is, of a thoroughly *mundane* (this-worldly) rather than otherworldly form of spirituality.

Immanence and Spiritual Transformation

A philosopher of immanence par excellence is Gilles Deleuze. In re-visioning the work of Spinoza, Deleuze (1990) helped problematize the conventional opposition of *immanence versus transcendence*, enunciating in the process three fundamental levels of investigation: (a) Can one speak of God and of immanence in the same breath? (b) Is spiritual or existential transformation thinkable without a transcendent dimension? and (c) Can we speak of a new—more compassionate society—without positing an otherworldly ideal?

Can One Speak of God and of Immanence in the Same Breath?

Could, for instance, meditation practice embrace the secular *and* the religious, and in so doing leave aside this obsolete division? Adapting Deleuze's stance to the domain of meditation, two other questions arise:

Is Spiritual or Existential Transformation Thinkable without a Transcendent Dimension?

Do we need to imagine and believe in a divine, eternal, blissful, and enlightened realm to pit against our world of delusion, impermanence, and suffering? Doesn't a merely secular understanding of meditation encourage the status quo, our complacent, self-congratulatory belief that we are fine as we are and all is well with the world? And could a process of transformation be ignited within an immanent dimension?

Can We Speak of a New—More Compassionate Society—without Positing an Otherworldly Ideal?

In putting forward a new, "post-secular" understanding of meditation, our challenge is to move away from notions of temporality and of a new model of humanity. It has been and still is tempting to link the practice of meditation—particularly communal meditation—to the creation of a new society based on wisdom, compassion, and so forth.

Perhaps meditation may bring the practitioner closer to a threshold where the immanent "outside" (rather than the "new") is perceived. It is this experience, rather than belief in an otherworldly dimension, that brings about transformation and a break with the "given form of the present" (Barber, 2014, pp. 9–10). This experience is immanent: it is *of this world* and can bring about a sense of mystery, of an outside that enriches one's experience while at the same time making one aware of the inherent limitations of subjectivity. Immanent spirituality does not imply passive acceptance of the world: transformation is possible without having to resort to transcendence. Transformation in this context occurs not solely via transcendental representations, but from a worldly concrete perception of an *outside* that challenges and disrupts what Deleuze calls *diagram*, our "fixed set of relations that determine the world" (Barber, 2014, p. 47): our bounded self-concept or self-construct.

Inherent in the secular sensibility is the rationalist belief that reality can be fully apprehended, measured, and quantified. Similarly, conventional religiosity provides us a set of ready-made metaphysical remedies to the vagaries and vicissitudes of experience. To speak of immanence may then be a way of addressing more effectively a point of ambivalence, a crossroads from which an entry into a new landscape may be found.

Within the Sensory

When meditating, I may be focusing on the breath, on something closely linked with being alive. I attempt to stay with a simple but wondrous activity, one that is so easy to forget. My eyes are half-closed, gazing softly. I listen to my breath, just the way it is this moment. Inevitably, I get sidetracked. I accept it; I follow for a while the mind's trajectory before deciding to go back to the breath, renewing my intent and also noticing the body posture: an act of remembrance—of the task at hand, of the facticity of living. I begin to notice more clearly thoughts, sensations, feelings, and emotions. At times there is a sense of spaciousness and freedom. There are sounds all around: I try not to label them or speculate about them. They emerge, dwell for a while, and then fade. There are sounds in the room, sounds in the street, even in the sky above and far away. When it's really quiet, early in the morning, say, or late at night, I think I can hear the blood murmuring in my veins. I am inside a vast phenomenal world whose wide contours I can only imagine. There are sounds and subtle movements I know nothing about—the shift in the Earth's tectonic plates; I can read about them and know that they are pieces of the Earth's crust, sixty-two miles long, made up of oceanic crust and continental crust. Their activities are imperceptible to me as I sit here, a participant in the very same place of immanence—not a being who is "having" sensations but a situated being, a being within the sensory. This seemingly simple, straightforward moment in time has such richness and complexity that to call it the present moment does not do it justice in the least. I don't know what it is, yet welcome the experience. It is sumptuous and I'm tempted to call it *chaos*. It is also rhythmic and wave-like; it has an order, a word whose ancient name was *cosmos*. It is then, to borrow Joyce's famous coinage, a *chaosmos*. Being alive at this moment—something I usually take for granted—can be as mystifying, as wonderful and unbearable as any unresolved mystery.

The experience described above can be aligned with religion. For all intents and purposes, I have given an account of me "practicing Buddhist meditation." Buddhism is, after all, a religion. So why is it that I don't feel satisfied with the label? Because "religion" normally gestured toward certainty, and the meditative experience described above is rooted in *uncertainty*. Because religion commonly deals with transcendental claims while meditation as I understand it is wholly embedded within a *plateau* or plane of immanence. Unless of course one begins to accept that there can be a religion and a spirituality that appreciate the mystery of immanence. This is an example of the "post-secular *condition*": not a mere revival of religion but a seismic shift that compels us to problematize our understanding of secularism and religion altogether.

Are We All Christians?

I called the above shift "seismic," and I cannot stress enough how sweeping a break from the past this truly represents. A post-secular, immanentist perspective suspends and interrupts transcendental narratives. On the other hand, Western secularism's historic preoccupation has always been to *preserve* and *develop* what it sees as the great theological and religious tradition. In his introduction to Rorty and Vattimo's stimulating dialogue published as *The Future of Religion*, Santiago Zabala writes:

The rebirth of religion in the third millennium is to be located in the secularization of the sacred that has been at the center of the process by which the civilization of the western world developed (2005, p. 2). Zabala sees secularization as a suitable way to bear witness to the "attachment of modern European civilization to its own religious past," a relationship that would consist "not of surpassing and emancipation alone, but *conservation*, too" (Zabala, 2005, p. 2, my emphasis). The context here is Europe and the religion in question is Christianity, but a similar argument can be applied to the Dharma and Buddhist meditation. Secularization then "becomes a way of inheriting and working through Christianity [which is] the very process of 'western civilization's development'" (Barber, 2014, p. 24). What is possibly happening here is, a process of *decolonization* from transcendental narratives.

The implications of the above stance are momentous, particularly for Western practitioners of the Dharma. A meditation practice that draws on Buddhism without *cutting through* both religious and secularist frames of reference is, strictly speaking, Christian. The very fabric of Western being, thinking, and feeling is steeped in Christian transcendence, and that is true for avowed secularists as well. No matter how thorough and assiduous our meditation practice may be, it is bound to be shaped by two thousand years of Christian psychic encrustation. To move away from this frame and favor a philosophy of immanence is a mighty task. For those of us who feel the urgency of the task, great encouragement comes from realizing that Western culture has long harbored in its midst a thoroughgoing heretical counter-tradition that has consistently articulated and treasured immanence.

Like Water in Water: Sketches of Modern Immanence

Since antiquity, both the philosophical and the religious counter-tradition wove several threads leading to immanence. Their proponents have often been considered either "obscure" (Heraclitus), or exiled and excommunicated (Spinoza), or burned at the stake (Bruno). It appears that upholding immanence over transcendence in various ways (whether as privileging becoming over being or speaking of the existence of a God within nature rather than outside of it) and suggesting that God is another name for nature are statements that far exceed both religious and secularist claims. Leaving antiquity aside, it may be useful at this juncture to cast a cursory glance at how one key twentieth-century thinker regarded immanence. At the start of *The Theory of Religion*, Bataille (1989) gives so stark an account of immanence to offset any bucolic image one might harbour. He writes of the "immanence of the eater and the eaten" (p. 17), of the animal that devours and the one who is being devoured. Fierce poetry is found in this harsh terrain: "every animal is *in the world like water in water*" (p. 19). For Bataille, this world of pure immanence is mostly closed to humans, except for those moments of tears and ecstasy, intense joy or sorrow—detours and derailments from the linear, all-too-neat path of logical reason. Rather than an appeal to un-reason, this can be understood to be a powerful indicator of the limits of reason, of the dangers of human hubris and as an invitation to explore the wholly uncharted terrain of experience.

Conclusion

To speak of immanence does not imply enclosure—least of all foreclosure of change and transformation. This is often an argument posed by transcendentalists: without the positing of a transcendent world, no spiritual transformation is possible at either a personal or societal level. We must be able to transcend this imperfect, samsaric, unjust world of blood, sweat, and tears. We must be able to hold a spiritual vision, they say, in our hearts and minds. This position certainly has appeal. In some exceptional cases, the spindrift gaze toward heaven comes with formidable flights of the imagination: many a great poet endorsed it, from Dante to Milton to William Blake. Moreover, I also believe, with Levinas (2003), in the profound human need for escape. What is objectionable is not the flight per se but the looking down on the world from on high, its categorization as *evil*. For a transcendental thinker like Thomas Aquinas the world is good and true not in essence, but only *indirectly*, by "analogical participation" (Barber, 2010, p. 431) in a transcendent God. The equivalent in meditation practice is to posit a wide gap between delusion and enlightenment, the world of samsara populated by ordinary sentient beings and the "pure land" of the Buddhas. The person who can see the world as good and true only indirectly, as an *emanation* of a transcendental and eternal reality, effectively steps aside the living stream of living-and-dying in which he or she cannot but participate and plays at being arbitrator and judge.

> The world, because it has not rendered itself amenable to the truth, is evil—it must be judged by the truthful man. (Deleuze, 1989, p. 431)

This stance is often motivated by an understandable need for consolation, and by the very real sense that the world is too much for us: "too powerful, or too unjust, but sometimes also too beautiful" (Deleuze, 1989, p. 18). But to look away, step aside from the living stream and, at times, deliberately minimize our level of experiencing is also a doorway to great mental distress (Goldstein, 1995) and incongruence.

There is a concrete alternative to this impasse: embracing *immanent spirituality* through a meditation practice that, rather than averting its gaze from the unbearable suffering and excruciating beauty of the world and seeking inspiration in a transcendent realm, intensifies instead our inherent connection to the world. True, the world is intolerable, immeasurable, and unassimilable. Its sheer intensity gives us anguish. But in averting this intensity, we deny ourselves the possibility for healing. It is here that

Dharma teachings, several other spiritual traditions and the counter-traditional philosophy of immanence find common ground.

The first noble truth taught by the historical Buddha invites us to consider deeply and take to heart the suffering that is inherent in all living things. This is what often arises when just sitting in zazen: the beauty and anguish of the world seizes us unaware and affects us deeply.

A post-secular philosophy of immanence equally invites us to go beyond divisions of religious versus secular. It invites us to take an important spiritual decision whose implications are primarily *affective*. Rather than averting our gaze from the world in the name of either rationalist or secular explanations or metaphysical or transcendental justifications, it dares us to deepen our affective involvement with immanent reality.

References

Adorno, T. (1997). *Aesthetic theory*. (R. Hullot-Kentor, Trans.). Minneapolis: University of Minnesota Press.

Apple Inc. (2017). The mindfulness app. Retrieved from https://itunes.apple.com/us/app/the-mindfulness-app-meditation-for-everyone/id417071430?mt=8

Barber, D. C. (2010). Immanence and the re-expression of the world. *SubStance* 39(121), 38–48.

Barber, D. C. (2014). *Deleuze and the naming of God: Post-secularism and the future of immanence*. Edinburgh: Edinburgh University Press.

Bataille, G. (1989). *The theory of religion*. New York: Zone Books.

Bazzano, M. (2017a). *Zen and therapy: Heretical perspectives*. Abingdon, OX: Routledge.

Braeckman, A. (2009). Habermas and Gauchet on religion in postsecular society: A critical assessment. *Continental Philosophy Review* 42(3): 279–296.

Braidotti, R. (2008). In spite of the times: The postsecular turn in feminism. *Theory, Culture & Society* 25(1): 1–24.

Deresiewicz, W. (2014). *Excellent sheep: The miseducation of the American elite and the way to a meaningful life*. New York: Simon & Schuster.

Deleuze, G. (1989). *Cinema 2: The time image*. (H. Tomlinson & R. Galeta, Trans.). Minneapolis: University of Minnesota Press.

Deleuze, G. (1990). *Expressionism in philosophy: Spinoza*. (M. Joughin, Trans.). New York: Zone Books.

Ehrenreich, B. (2010). *Smile or die: How positive thinking fooled America and the world*. London: Granta.

Goldstein, K. (1995). *The organism*. New York: Zone Books/MIT Press.

Habermas, J. (2010). An awareness of what is missing. In J. Habermas, et al., *An awareness of what is missing: Faith and reason in a post-secular age* (C. Cronin, Trans., pp. 1–14). Cambridge: Polity.

Hasan, M. (2016). Islam and the myth of French secularism. *Al Jazeera*. Retrieved from http://www.aljazeera.com/programmes/upfront/2016/10/islam-myth-french-secularism-161007131555990.html

Heine, S. (2008). *Zen skin, Zen marrow: Will the real Zen Buddhism please stand up?* New York: Oxford University Press.

Jarden, A. (2012). Positive psychologists on positive psychology: Alex Linley. *International Journal of Wellbeing* 2(2), 83–87. doi:10.5502/ijw.v2i2.4

Kabat-Zinn, J. (2015). The deeper dimensions of mindfulness. The mindfulness summit. Retrieved from http://themindfulnesssummit.com/sessions/jon-kabat-zinn

Levinas, E. (2003). *On escape*. Stanford, CA: Stanford University Press.

Marcuse, H. (1964). *One dimensional man*. London: Routledge & Kegan Paul.

Matthews, M. D. (2014). *Head strong: How psychology is revolutionizing war*. New York: Oxford University Press.

McLennan, G. (2010). The postsecular turn. *Theory, Culture and Society 27*(4), 3–20.

Neocleous, M. (2013). Resisting resilience. *Radical Philosophy 178*(March/April), Retrieved from https://www.radicalphilosophy.com/commentary/resisting-resilience

Purser, R., & Ng, E. (2015). Corporate mindfulness is bullsh*t: Zen or no Zen, you are working harder and being paid less. *Salon*, September 27, http://www.salon.com/2015/09/27/corporate_mindfulness_is_bullsht_zen_or_no_zen_youre_working_harder_and_being_paid:less

Riemer, N. (2016). The roots of Islamophobia in France. *Jacobin*. Retrieved from https://www.jacobinmag.com/2016/08/burkini-ban-islamophobia-valls-france-secularism-islam

Rorty, R., & Vattimo, G. (2005). *The future of religion*. (Santiago Zabala, Ed.). New York: Columbia University Press.

Rosa, H. (2013). *Social acceleration: A new theory of modernity*. New York: Columbia University Press.

Seligman M. (1999). Seligman speech at Lincoln Summit. [Online.] Penn Positive Psychology Center; 1999. www.sas.upenn.edu/psych/seligman/lincspeech.htm

Shaw. T. (2016). The psychologists take power. *New York Review of Books 63*(3), February 25, 38–41.

Smail, D. (2015). *The origins of unhappiness: A new understanding of personal distress*. London: Karnac.

Staudigl, M., & Alvis, J. W. (2017). Phenomenology and the post-secular: Reconsidering the "return of the religious. *International Journal of Philosophical Studies 24*(5), 589–599.

Weber, M. (2004). *The Protestant ethic and the spirit of capitalism*. London: Penguin.

Zabala, S. (2005). Introduction. In R. Rorty & G. Vattimo (Eds.), *The future of religion*. New York: Columbia University Press.

CHAPTER 28

CHRISTIAN CONTEMPLATIVE THOUGHT AND PRACTICE IN THE CONTEMPORARY WORLD

DOUGLAS E. CHRISTIE

INTRODUCTION

"SIT in your cell and your cell will teach you everything." So claimed one of the desert elders from the ancient Christian monastic tradition. This teaching from *The Sayings of the Desert* Fathers reflects the fundamental importance of silence and stillness within Christian spiritual practice born of the desert: its essentially contemplative character. Nor is it an isolated or unusual expression. In the writings that emerged from the early Christian monastic world, one finds intense and persistent interest in questions about how to cultivate a simple, deep awareness of God's presence in one's life; about how practices born of silence and stillness could reshape one's entire orientation to existence; and about how such transformed awareness could contribute to the creation of communities rooted in humility and love. Such questions have had a long afterlife in the Christian spiritual tradition, especially within monastic and mystical traditions; and they continue to shape attitudes toward Christian spiritual practice in the contemporary moment. The resurgent interest among Christians in contemplative thought and practice is in fact one of the most striking features of Christian spirituality in the late twentieth and early twenty-first centuries.

Within contemporary Christianity, a variety of terms are employed to describe such practice: Christian meditation, centering prayer, and contemplation among others.

So too are the locations of such practice diverse: one finds renewed attention to contemplative and meditative practice at the heart of Catholic, Protestant, and Orthodox Christian communities as well as in experimental forms of Christian life that often exist on the margins of these communities. One thinks here, for example, of the communities of Taizé and Jerusalem in France; of Bose in Italy; of the Center for Action and Contemplation in Albuquerque, New Mexico; of Gravity: A Center for Contemplative Activism in Omaha, Nebraska; and of the varied expressions in Europe, North America, and elsewhere of what has come to be known as the "new monasticism." Also important here are the Christian Meditation and Centering Prayer movements, both of which draw deeply upon Christian monastic traditions while also extending them in creative ways. The story of the renewal of contemplative thought and practice within contemporary Christianity is not simple and cannot be understood in terms of easy dichotomies (Catholic or Protestant; cloistered or non-cloistered; single-gender or mixed-gender). Nor is it possible to understand it apart from the complex and increasingly eclectic patterns of spiritual practice so much in evidence in the contemporary moment (McGuire, 2008; Drescher, 2016), or the shifting social-political-cultural ground that shaped the earliest attitudes toward Christian contemplative practice and continues to influence them now. It is fundamentally the story of a complex, dynamic, and varied effort to reimagine ancient contemplative ideas and practices in terms that can have meaning in the current historical moment. Still, it is an immensely challenging task to describe much less map this effort. I want to begin then by posing some questions, not with the intention of addressing them all in depth, but rather as a way of suggesting some of the tensions and ambiguities inherent in the contemporary renewal of Christian contemplative practice.

Contemporary Christian Contemplative Practice: Questions and Context

What does Christian contemplative practice look like in the present moment? Who engages in such practice and why? And what can one say about the meaning and significance of such practice, both in terms of its meaning to those who engage in it and in terms of its wider ecclesial and social meaning? These fundamental questions in turn provoke others. How, for example, can we best situate the growing interest in meditative and contemplative practice within Christianity in relation to the larger social, political, and religious and ecclesial shifts of the past fifty or so years? In particular, is there a relationship between the growing disaffection many people profess with organized religion and the rise of interest in forms of prayer that can be practiced in solitude or in small communities and that draw upon stillness and silence for their meaning? And how can we best understand the relationship (and possible tensions) between this distinctive form of spiritual practice and others long practiced by members of the

Christian community? That is, is contemplative practice simply one among many choices available to Christians? Or does it, with its commitment toward creating the conditions for a deeper and more encompassing awareness of the divine, make claims to be a universal and utterly fundamental dimension of Christian experience? Also, even as Christians struggle to understand the place of contemplative practice within their own spiritual identity, there is the question of how or whether to incorporate contemplative teachings and practices from other spiritual traditions. Should the spiritual hybridity and eclecticism that one so often encounters in contemporary Christian practice be understood as creative and meaningful, a sign of the openness of Christianity to expressions of spiritual thought and practice found in other traditions? Or is such hybridizing problematic, even dangerous (Congregation for the Doctrine of Faith, 1989)?

It is also important to consider how dimensions of social location—class, race, ethnicity, gender, and age—shape and are shaped by contemplative forms of spiritual practice. A recurring and significant question relating to the meaning of Christian spiritual thought and practice is: Does it lead to greater concern for social justice? (Ruffing, 2001; Wolfteich, 2006). If so, how does such concern manifest itself? And how do the commitments informed by this concern enliven the work of cultivating a deeper, more encompassing awareness of the divine? It should be noted that responses to these questions are often mixed or ambiguous, with greater value sometimes being placed on silence, stillness, and refuge, and other times on the importance of sustained social and even political commitment. So too, one often encounters a struggle to balance or integrate these different dimensions of spiritual practice in a way that honors the whole reality of Christian identity and the ethical commitments that flow from it. Yes, there is withdrawal into silence and solitude, fundamental to the work of cultivating a deep awareness of God; but also a return to shared communal life, and a commitment to live out this awareness in relation to others in love. In the Christian tradition, this tension has often been described in terms of the dynamic relationship between contemplation and action. Or, as one of the early followers of St. Ignatius of Loyola, Jerome Nadal, described it: learning to become *simul in actione contemplivus*, a "contemplative *in* action." That is: living in silence and stillness, suffused with a deep awareness of the divine, while simultaneously responding to one's ethical obligations toward others, toward the world, arising from that deepening awareness. Increasingly this question has come to shape much thought about what it means to live contemplatively in the world, especially in response to suffering and injustice (Gutiérrez, 1984; Ashley, 2006).

These ethical questions often have theological meaning. This might seem paradoxical or even contradictory. Why, within a practice oriented toward helping one cultivate a simple awareness of God's loving presence, should theological questions arise at all? Isn't the point to dispense with discursive thought and let oneself simply dwell in the presence of God? Yes. The Christian tradition testifies to this continuously. Still, it often happens that, within contemplative practice, questions arise. Who or what is one seeking in such practice? How does deepening and transformation of awareness happen? Through assiduous labor? Or grace? Or by some mysterious convergence of effort and grace? What to make of the alternating experiences of joy and consolation, on the one hand,

and suffering and loss on the other that course through contemplative thought and practice? Where is God in all of this, and how can God in fact be at the center of such divergent and even contradictory experiences? For Christians, contemplative practice is always at its root a search to know and live more deeply in God. Because of this, the vagaries of experience, the confrontation with one's own psychic and spiritual ambiguity, the seemingly endless suffering one encounters in one's own existence and in the lives of others, the sudden, unexpected surfacing of unbidden joy: these all become, at least potentially, theological questions. They are not abstract intellectual exercises. Rather, they are lived existential questions touching on the depth and meaning of experience. It may be true that in the stillness of contemplative practice, there is no thought or thinking in the sense that we normally use these terms, but only an open, receptive awareness; still, contemplative practice often provokes thought, even requires it. Here one confronts all the most difficult and challenging and exhilarating questions of one's existence. Above all else: one encounters the question of whether God is the center. Paul Ricoeur once remarked "the symbol gives rise to thought." Something similar could be said of contemplative practice: even as it stills and simplifies thought in one sense, it opens it up in other ways, creating new paths to travel. Hence, in these pages, contemplative thought and practice are bound together as elements of a whole fabric.

A brief word about terminology: for the purposes of this chapter, I employ the term "contemplative practice" to refer to the broad range of spiritual practices under consideration. In a volume dedicated to meditation, this choice calls for some explanation. Within the ancient Christian spiritual tradition, meditation and contemplation are often used almost as synonyms, each connoting spiritual practices oriented toward helping the spiritual practitioner open himself or herself more fully to spacious, purposeless awareness of God's presence. Within such practices, thinking, at least discursive thinking, recedes in importance and something more capacious and mysterious unfolds in its place: simple awareness of oneself in relation to God (Laird, 2006; Stewart, 1999; Burton-Christie, 1993). Or, as the Christian mystics often suggest: an unmediated awareness of oneself as alive *in* God.

Still, it is also true that meditation is often used in the Christian tradition to refer to a discursive process in which one considers the meaning of something (a sacred text or image for example) as a means of cultivating this deeper awareness. In historical terms, meditation is a somewhat narrower and more particular term, often referring to this or that spiritual practice, while contemplation is the wider, more capacious and encompassing term, referring to the fundamental aim of cultivating awareness of the divine. Even so, contemporary usage is fluid, flexible, and not always consistent. Some writers prefer the term meditation, in no small part because of its strong association with practice (Finley, 2005). And while such language does often refer to the specific practices employed in meditation, it sometimes opens out onto the same spacious horizon to which the term contemplation points. Others prefer "contemplation" or "contemplative practice," not least because of the consistent use of these expressions in the tradition to refer to our deepest capacity for awareness of God, but also because of their longstanding association with the life of prayer, a term with rich and enduring meaning in Christian spiritual practice (Merton, 1969). In examining contemporary Christian contemplative practice, then, one must be prepared to move among and between an array of different terms and ideas used to describe the fundamental work of cultivating a deeper awareness of the presence of God. This diversity of expression is itself a reflection on the evolving and still-emerging practice of Christian contemplative practice in the contemporary moment.

The Growth and Development of Contemporary Christian Contemplative Thought and Practice

Any account of the growth and development of Christian contemplative thought and practice in the twentieth and twenty-first centuries should include not only a descriptive account of key moments and figures, but also some analysis of the root causes of this phenomenon as well as its meaning and significance. This is not easy to do, certainly not in any exhaustive way. Still, in what follows, I first will provide a broad, descriptive account of the growth and development of Christian contemplative practice in the contemporary period, which includes an analysis of some of the key figures who have shaped its growth; and, second, will offer some thoughts about the meaning and significance of its continued emergence as a force for spiritual vitality and renewal within and beyond the Christian community.

One of the most striking things about the deepening attention to contemplation and meditation among contemporary Christians is how much it owes to the past. This is hardly surprising, given how often the Christian tradition has drawn on ancient ideas and practices to reimagine its life at a later historical moment. The mid-twentieth-century Catholic theological renewal movement known as *ressourcement*, rooted in a desire to reimagine Catholic life and thought by drawing deeply on writings from the early Christian community, offers one compelling example from recent history (Flynn & Murray, 2014). But something analogous has occurred in relation to the writings of Christian spirituality in general and to Christian contemplative writings more particularly. The increased accessibility of classic Christian spiritual texts in good translations—for example, Paulist Press's *The Classics of Western Spirituality* series and the Cistercian Publications translations of ancient and medieval monastic texts—has made a significant impact on the ability of contemporary Christians to read and absorb ancient Christian spiritual thought and practice. So too has the renewed commitment to serious scholarship in Christian spirituality contributed to the ability of contemporary readers of ancient texts to engage them critically and with serious attention to their linguistic, historical, and cultural particularity (Schneiders, 1989; Sheldrake, 1991/1998; McGinn, 2002).

The contemporary renewal of Christian contemplative thought and practice owes much to this broader, deeper work of retrieval. Certainly this is true of the work of the central figures who helped lead this revival—Thomas Merton, John Main, and Thomas Keating being three of the most important figures. The latter two helped bring into being something akin to a movement rooted in the retrieval of ancient contemplative traditions of thought and practice for contemporary life. In Merton's case, the retrieval was first of all part of an effort to call his own Cistercian monastic community toward greater faithfulness to the sources of monastic life and thought arising out of the ancient and medieval monastic traditions. Later it opened out onto something more wide ranging: an argument that contemplative thought and practice ought to be central to the life of all Christians, and that it ought to have a social and political meaning. In each one of these cases, something important and unexpected happened: spiritual practices once understood as belonging primarily (even exclusively) to cloistered contemplative communities became available to ordinary Christians. The Second Vatican Council would signal its own interest in these questions by articulating what it referred to as the "universal call to holiness." This was part of the Catholic tradition's effort to recover, theologically, spiritually, and pastorally, the ancient understanding of baptism as an initiation of *all* Christians into a deep and mature spiritual practice aimed at facilitating intimacy with and awareness of God. This more inclusive, expansive spiritual vision can be seen manifested in the increasing practice of contemplation among Christians outside the cloister. This has been one of the most significant impacts of this renewal of contemplative practice among Christians in the contemporary era.

How did this happen? To address this question, at least within the Roman Catholic context, it is important to recognize the challenge facing many vowed religious communities during the past century, especially those with a distinctively contemplative dimension to their ethos—Benedictines, Cistercians, Dominicans, Carmelites, and others—as they sought to renew their own lives. The "return to the sources" has been a key part of the renewal of many of these communities, with the revision of constitutions and the publication of critical editions of classic texts playing an important role in this process. In the case of orders such as the Benedictines and Cistercians, there have been assiduous efforts to recover the spirit of "primitive monasticism," whether in relation to the ancient desert monastic tradition or the Rule of St. Benedict or the writings of St. Bernard of Clairvaux and other early Cistercian figures. This intra-monastic work of *ressourcement* was significant not only for the renewal of monastic contemplative thought and practice; but it also helped create the conditions for contemplative thought and practice to move beyond the relatively narrow confines of the monastic world into wider usage among ordinary Christians.

It is doubtful whether anyone played a more important role in this process during the twentieth century—at least within the context of Roman Catholicism—than the American Trappist monk and writer Thomas Merton (1915–1968). The publication of Merton's best-selling autobiography, *The Seven Storey Mountain* in 1948 signaled the arrival of something new, both in literary terms and as a contribution to the Roman Catholic faith community: a thoughtful, imaginatively engaging account of a life devoted to

Christian contemplative thought and practice. In retrospect, one can say that the theological and spiritual vision of *The Seven Storey Mountain* was somewhat narrow, exclusive, and theologically conservative; still, it had a significant impact on contemporary readers and helped inspire a renewal of Christian monastic vocations both in the United States and elsewhere. It marked the beginning of what would prove to be, for Merton, a sustained, ever-evolving, and increasingly expansive and inclusive analysis of the meaning of contemplative thought and practice in the contemporary world. Much of Merton's subsequent writing and thinking, at least in relation to the Cistercian monastic community, was oriented toward deepening its own spiritual practice, especially by recovering its kinship with the tradition of the desert fathers and mothers and with the writings of the early Cistercian tradition. Some of this work consisted of advocating for greater solitude and silence within Cistercian life, including the idea that more eremitical (or solitary) *forms of life*—something that had been part of the earliest monastic traditions but which had fallen out of practice in later generations—should be included within Cistercian monastic practice, But he also advocated consistently for a renewal of monastic *thought*, drawing upon the work of the early desert monks, the writings of John Cassian, the hesychastic monks of the Christian East, and other ancient writers to argue for the fundamentally mystical-contemplative character of Christian thought and practice. His writing on these subjects was lucid and compelling, drawing upon the best scholarly work on ancient sources that was emerging during the mid-twentieth century, and benefiting from dialogue with scholars such as Jean Leclerq, Jean Danielou, and others. Merton became convinced that a renewal of contemplative thought was critical to any sustained renewal of contemplative practice, both within Christian monasticism and beyond.

In his classic work *Contemplative Prayer*, Merton offers a subtle and perceptive account of the Christian approach to the practice of contemplative prayer. Drawing deeply upon the historical sources that so informed his own Cistercian tradition, he notes the fluidity and organic wholeness that characterizes both the vocabulary of Christian contemplative prayer and its practice. For the ancient monastic writers, he notes: "*Meditatio* must be seen in its close relation to *psalmodia*, *lectio*, *oratio* and *contemplatio*. It is part of a continuous whole, the entire unified life of the monk" (Merton, 1969, p. 4). It is this sense of wholeness and simplicity to which he returns again and again. Yes, there are distinctive practices and modes of consciousness that characterize Christian contemplative practice. But ultimately these all flow together in a practice that is fundamentally simple: "Meditation and contemplative prayer is not so much a way to find God as a way of resting in him whom we have *found*, who loves us, who is near to us, who comes to us to draw us to himself." All the distinctive practices undertaken by one who sets out along this path lead ultimately to "a prayer of silence, simplicity, contemplative and meditative unity, a deep personal integration in an attentive, watchful listening of 'the heart'" (Merton, 1969, pp. 32–33). Here one senses the depth of integration that characterized Merton's mature thought on Christian contemplative thought and practice. What begins as a reflection on a particular dimension of the Christian monastic tradition gradually opens out to encompass something more universal.

And with it comes the conviction that such practice is available and possible for all who seek to live out their faith more deeply.

That his dialogue on the meaning of contemplative thought eventually transcended not only the Christian monastic world but also the world of Christian thought itself, drawing upon a lively engagement with key Jewish, Muslim, Buddhist, and Hindu thinkers, is suggestive of the fecundity of his work for the larger expansion of contemplative thought and practice in the twentieth and twenty-first centuries. Later works such as *Zen and the Birds of Appetite* (1968) reveal a contemplative thinker utterly at home in his own Christian spiritual tradition, but also open to the way contemplative awareness could be experienced and cultivated through an extraordinary range of modes, places and traditions. So too does one encounter in his later works, such as *Conjectures of a Guilty Bystander* (1966), a conviction that Christian contemplative thought and practice must always lead to a greater awareness of the realities of war, violence, racism, and other social injustices that afflict the world, and to our ethical obligation not to stand aloof from these realities. Here was a vision of contemplative practice that was at once deeply traditional and utterly open, expansive, and critical.

Still, Thomas Merton was not the only monastic figure thinking about these questions during the twentieth century. Others, including John Main, OSB (1926–1982), Laurence Freeman, OSB, Thomas Keating, OCSO (1923–2018), William Menninger, OCSO, and Basil Pennington, OCSO (1931–2005), developed their own approaches to Christian contemplative practice and worked to ensure that such practice would transcend the cloister and become accessible to ordinary Christians and others seeking to deepen their spiritual practice. Main's and Freeman's work eventually came to be associated with the term "Christian meditation." The work initiated by Keating, Menninger, and Pennington helped create a movement devoted to "centering prayer." While each of these initiatives have developed in their own distinctive ways, both draw deeply on the teachings of ancient Christian monasticism and share the common goal of making contemplative thought and practice available to contemporary men and women seeking to live a deeper, fuller spiritual life.

John Main first learned about the practice of meditation from Swami Satyandanda while serving as a British civil servant in Kuala Lumpur in the 1950s. Later, after entering the Benedictines, he undertook a serious study of the writings of desert father John Cassian and in the 1970s began teaching Christian meditation groups at Ealing Abbey in west London together with Laurence Freeman. Later, he and Freeman moved to Montreal where they founded a new monastic community and continued teaching Christian meditation. After Main's death in 1982, Freeman continued this work, teaching Christian meditation to an expanding network of small communities around the world. In 1991, this network constituted itself formally as The World Community for Christian Meditation (WCCM), an ecumenical group that exists to promote and deepen Christian meditation based on the teachings of John Main and the ancient desert monastic tradition. At the heart of this work, Main suggests, is a simple, profound vision of spiritual practice:

> Meditation is learning to be sensitive to and aware of [God's] presence within us. It is this presence that teaches us that each of us is made a real person by the power of his love. If we can make contact with those depths within us we discover that we are not just autonomous, isolated persons. Each of us, in this mystery of Christ dwelling within our hearts, is called to love and to be loved beyond all division.
>
> (Main, 2013, p. 8)

The WCCM, an embodiment of John Main's aim of creating a "monastery without walls," exists to promote and deepen this vision among practitioners of Christian meditation. It is currently active in over 120 countries around the world, convening group meetings in homes, parishes, schools, offices, hospitals, prisons, and universities. It also promotes the value of continued intellectual reflection on the contemplative spiritual traditions, especially through the annual gathering of the John Main Seminar. A new permanent center for the group is currently under development on the site of an ancient monastic community in Bonnevaux, France.

Centering prayer is the spiritual practice most closely associated with the teaching of three Cistercian monks from St. Joseph's Abbey in Spencer, Massachusetts, Frs. Keating, Menninger, and Pennington. The idea arose in response to an invitation from Pope Paul VI during a meeting in Rome in 1971 to members of the clergy, asking them to help revive traditions of ancient contemplative thought and practice for contemporary use among laypersons. Thomas Keating attended that meeting and took the invitation to heart. Upon his return to St. Joseph's Abbey, he initiated a process that eventually led him, Menninger, and Pennington to begin developing a simple method of silent prayer that could be shared beyond the monastery in workshops and retreats with clergy and laypersons. It drew its inspiration from classic works of Christian spirituality, such as the fourteenth-century *Cloud of Unknowing* and the writings of John Cassian, Francis de Sales, John of the Cross, and Teresa of Avila. Menninger found the teaching of *The Cloud of Unknowing* especially helpful and developed a simple method of silent prayer that he called "the prayer of the cloud." Eventually, as this teaching on contemplative practice matured, it became known as centering prayer, which is the most common name for it today. Shortly after the first intensive Centering Prayer retreat in 1983 at the Lama Foundation in San Cristobal, New Mexico, Contemplative Outreach was formed as a network of centering-prayer practitioners. Today Contemplative Outreach facilitates retreats and workshops and offers a range of online programs for those seeking to deepen their understanding of contemplative thought and practice. At the heart of this work is a vision of contemplative practice that points to the potential for healing and transformation that, according to Fr. Keating, has significance not only for persons but for society and the world. In his 1997 Harold M. Wit lecture at Harvard Divinity School, he articulates his healing vision this way:

> If we don't allow the Spirit of God to address the deep levels of attachment to ourselves and to our programs for happiness, we will pour into the world the negative elements of our self-centeredness, adding to the conflicts and social disasters that

> come from identifying with the biases and prejudices of our particular culture and upbringing. This is becoming more important as we move into a global culture and into the increasing pluralism of religious beliefs. (Keating, 1999, p. 36)

Such work requires the kind of radical self-honesty that is one of the characteristic features of the earliest monastic traditions and retains its significance for us now (Stewart, 1991). Fr. Keating's writings consistently advocate for such honesty. And it has become one of the hallmarks of the contemplative practice undertaken by members of the Contemplative Outreach network.

This brief sketch tells part of the story of how contemplative thought and practice has grown and developed within the Christian community during the past fifty years or so. But it is hardly the whole story. The work of the WCCM and Contemplative Outreach suggests the significant role Christian monastic traditions have played in the revival of contemplative thought and practice among non-monastics in the contemporary period. But it is noteworthy that this story unfolds almost solely within a Roman Catholic context and that its principal protagonists are almost all men. There is a larger story to be told, which includes the contributions of women, persons of color, persons whose thought has been influenced by non-monastic contemplative traditions (e.g., the Ignatian spiritual tradition), members of other Christian denominations, as well as writers and thinkers and practitioners from places outside of North America.

New Directions in Christian Contemplative Thought and Practice

This larger story can be told in different ways. In what follows, I call attention to several key elements of the story that, taken altogether, suggest how Christian contemplative thought and practice is growing and developing in the current moment. First, I note the contributions of some of the emerging writers and thinkers who are helping to shape our perception of Christian contemplative practice. Martin Laird's books *Into the Silent Land* (2006), *A Sunlit Absence* (2011), and *An Ocean of Light* (2018) have helped to set a new standard for lyrical, theologically informed writing about Christian contemplative practice; one of the noteworthy features of Laird's work is his careful attention to both Western and Eastern Christian thought. James Finley has also made an important contribution with his book *Christian Meditation* (2005), an eloquent and discerning primer on the subject that is notable for its psychological and theological acuity and its success at locating meditation at the very heart of Christian spiritual practice. So too, one can point to the ongoing impact of Franciscan writer Richard Rohr's deeply integrating thinking on contemplative practice—for example, *Everything Belongs: The Gift of Contemplative Prayer* (2003), and his teaching at The Center for Action and

Contemplation in New Mexico. The work of Episcopal priest and teacher Cynthia Bourgeault, which arises from close dialogue with the work of Thomas Keating, Bruno Barnhart, and Richard Rohr, among others, offers its own creative and synthetic vision of the continuing power of centering prayer (Bourgeault, 2004, 2016). In a slightly different vein, Kathleen Norris's work—*Dakota*, *The Cloister Walk* and others—has drawn deeply on Christian monastic thought and practice to give beautiful literary expression to the idea of contemplative living while also offering astute cultural criticism rooted in ancient contemplative wisdom (Norris, 1993, 1997).

A work that provides an important corrective to the perception that Christian contemplative practice is fundamentally monocultural, Barbara Holmes's *Joy Unspeakable: Contemplative Practices of the Black Churches* offers a creative and groundbreaking interpretation of African American spiritual practices as deeply contemplative in their origins and diverse expressions (Holmes, 2004/2017). And the work of French Orthodox writer Jean-Yves Leloup—*Being Still: Reflections on an Ancient Mystical Tradition* (2003), and *Compassion and Meditation: The Spiritual Dynamic Between Buddhism and Christianity* (2009)—offers important insight regarding the creative contributions being made by Orthodox Christianity to the work of reimagining contemplative thought and practice and concerning the possible rapprochement between Christian and Buddhist approaches to contemplation. One sees evidence of this same orientation among Christian thinkers and writers who incorporate mindfulness into their reflections on contemplative thought and practice. Although some Christians continue to express reservations regarding the idea that Christian prayer and non-Christian practices of mindfulness can be usefully integrated, there is increasing evidence that the language and vocabulary of mindfulness is entering into the Christian understanding of contemplation (Oden, 2017; Reynolds, 2017; Stead, 2017; Bottaro, 2018).

One should also include here work arising from the diverse and variegated movement known as "new monasticism." This movement has made clear the continuing allure of contemplative thought and practice among those—often laypersons rather than vowed religious, persons drawn from diverse Christian denominations and sometimes no denominations at all, and an increasingly younger generation of spiritual practitioners—wishing to create new forms of life grafted onto the rootstock of the ancient monastic forms (Bucko & McEntee, 2015). The Christians undertaking these emerging experiments in intentional Christian living, while varied in their spirit and aims, share a commitment to root themselves in ancient forms of Christian contemplative practice, while also seeking to live out lives of solidarity in response to social injustice (Heuertz, 2017).

This is far from a complete account of significant contemporary writers on Christian contemplative thought and practice. But it suggests the creative work being done in this area at the moment and the vitality of thought that is emerging in response to the question of how or whether ancient Christian contemplative traditions can be retrieved and reinterpreted in light of contemporary concerns. It also signals the growing diversity of voices entering into the conversation: Catholic, Protestant, and Orthodox Christians; vowed religious and laypersons; women and men; and at least some ethnic and racial diversity (a question to which I shall return shortly). Another common feature of this emerging work is its shared concern to understand the relationship between contemplative practice and the ethical commitments flowing from such practice, in particular the commitment to justice. So, too, one can discern an openness in this work to other traditions of spiritual practice, a commitment to engage in contemplative practice that is fundamentally dialogical or, as Wayne Teasdale has described it, "interspiritual" (Teasdale, 2001). Finally, there is a recognition in such work that voices from the margins have something distinctive and essential to contribute to the future of Christian contemplative practice. In the final part of this chapter, I want to draw attention to the importance of this question for the continued growth and development of Christian spirituality in general and Christian contemplative practice in particular.

Earlier, I noted the centrality of the dialectical tension between "contemplation and action" in the history of Christian spiritual practice. The importance of this idea has become, if anything, even more pronounced in the current historical moment. Learning to integrate serious contemplative practice as part of a sustained commitment to justice has emerged as a crucial and necessary task within contemporary Christianity. Nor can one hope to understand the moral significance of this question without considering the significance of social location and the imbalance of power within social and political structures upon the understanding and practice of spirituality. French scholar Michel de Certeau has long advocated for such a view, arguing that emerging movements of spiritual or mystical renewal often arise from conditions of acute social and political dislocation (1986). Our sense of the meaning and significance of spiritual practice changes profoundly when we view it from the perspective of what Peruvian liberation theologian Gustavo Gutiérrez has called "the underside of history."

The life and work of the great African American theologian and pastor Howard Thurman (1899–1991) offers important insight into this question. The grandson of a slave, Thurman became one of the most significant theological writers and thinkers of the twentieth century, not least because of his sustained attention to what he referred to simply as "the inward journey" (Thurman, 1961). He wrote compellingly about religious experience and understood commitment to spiritual practice to be fundamental to any hope of seeking racial and social justice in the United States. His thinking about contemplative practice was profoundly influenced by, among others, the great Quaker philosopher and mystic Rufus Jones (1863–1948), with whom he studied for a brief period of time during the late 1920s; throughout his work, one can find traces of this influence in his allusions to silence, stillness, quietness, and emptiness as standing at the heart of spiritual practice. But it is his distinctive effort to integrate this contemplative practice with social justice that sets his work apart. In his book *Jesus and the Disinherited* (Thurman, 1949), Thurman argued that Jesus taught the oppressed a faith-based unconditional love that would enable them to endure their oppression. He was intensely interested in understanding what spiritual resources could help those with their "backs against the wall" resist and overcome the oppression they faced every day in a country so deeply infected with racism. His encounter in India with Mahatma Gandhi in 1935 contributed to his ability to articulate unconditional love as embodied in non-violent resistance, something that made his work particularly compelling to Dr. Martin Luther

King, Jr. (who is said to have carried a copy of *Jesus and the Disinherited* with him during the 1955–1956 Montgomery Bus Boycott). Some criticized Thurman for remaining too much on the sidelines during the civil rights movement. But he maintained a steady focus on the necessity of cultivating a rich inner life and spiritual disciplines as a means of resisting and responding to the chronic and debilitating effects of racism and other forms of social injustice. In his 1962 collection of sermons, *Temptations of Jesus*, he articulated his sense of the importance of spiritual disciplines this way:

> In the total religious experience we learn how to wait; we learn how to ready the mind and the spirit. It is in the waiting, brooding, lingering, tarrying timeless moments that the essence of the religious experience becomes most fruitful. It is here that I learn to listen, to swing wide the very doors of my being, to clean out the corners and crevices of my life—so that when His Presence invades, I am free to enjoy His coming to Himself in me. (Thurman, 1962, pp. 14–15)

Nothing in this passage explicitly reflects Thurman's awareness of or concern for the intense suffering and struggling among African Americans in mid-twentieth-century America. But seen within the larger context of his thought and work, in which such concerns are central, we can understand the ideas expressed here as being reflective of Thurman's conviction that only through an assiduous cultivation of a sense of Presence will persons and communities be able to respond meaningfully to the intense challenges they face daily, including the challenges of structural racism. There are echoes here of a long and ancient Christian contemplative teaching, reinterpreted and recast to address the needs of a particular community facing the harsh reality of racism during the middle of the twentieth century. Thurman's vision of Christian contemplative life remains one of the enduring treasures of contemporary Christian thought and continues to exert influence in the lives and work of African American writers and thinkers (Holmes, 2017).

One can see a similar set of concerns present in the work of Gustavo Gutiérrez, Jon Sobrino, Ivone Gebara, Segundo Galilea, Maria Clara Bingemer, and other Latin American writers who have worked hard to situate spiritual practice and renewal at the heart of the struggle for social and political liberation. Gutiérrez's ground-breaking 1968 book *A Theology of Liberation* hinted at the importance of spirituality for those struggling against oppressive social and political realities. Still, it was only many years later, in his book *We Drink from Our Own Wells* (1984), that he gave full attention to spiritual thought and practice, drawing upon elements of the Christian mystical tradition to articulate a deeply contemplative vision of spiritual practice at once intensely personal and oriented toward the rekindling of community life. The "Dark Night" of John of the Cross is recast here to address the sense of impasse and suffering endured by so many contemporary persons and communities living under unjust social and political structures. Spiritual life and practice in this context is not an escape to a disembodied realm or a call to place all one's hopes in a future life, but instead a serious way of engaging the whole of one's life and reality in light of lived faith. This is a spiritual practice rooted in what Jon Sobrino has articulated simply as "fidelity to the real" (Sobrino,

1988, p. 17). Understood in a liberationist context, such fidelity often brings with it intense suffering. There is a reason that the images of the dark night (Gutiérrez) and the cross (Sobrino) figure so prominently here. Sobrino even speaks of the silence of the cross, in recognition of all that we cannot know or say either about the experience of suffering and loss or about God's place in such realities. There is no attempt to evade or ignore these harsh realities, or to explain them, theologically or otherwise. Rather there is daily commitment to remain faithful, to respond to the call of love, to allow oneself to be swept along by what Sobrino describes as the "more" of reality. It is precisely when the struggle against the structures of injustice feels intractable and the way forward appears shrouded in darkness that contemplative traditions of thought and practice become so significant and impactful (Eggemeier, 2012).

It is perhaps not surprising that insight about such experience is emerging increasingly from those bearing witness from the margins. This also helps to account for the growing significance of the voices of women to this discussion. Historians of Christian spirituality have long recognized the extent to which women's voices have been excluded, often systematically, from the historical record. The emergence of women's voices in the present moment stands in stark contrast to that earlier silence; increasingly, we are coming to recognize that contemplative practice involves attending to that silence and asking how we might recover and respond to the presence of those who are slowly emerging from the shadows and finding their voices. I think here of significant work that has been done by Constance Fitzgerald (1984), Beverly Lanzetta (2005), Sarah Coakley (2015), Bernadette Flanagan (2014), and others to open up and advocate for new ways thinking about and understanding contemplative practice in light of this silencing. A deepening sense of the corrosive and destructive effects of patriarchy and other unjust social structures must become part of what it is to deepen one's awareness of who one is in prayer. So too, at times anyway, it will mean summoning the courage to face the darkness and acknowledge one's own helplessness and vulnerability in the face of it. Here one discovers what it is to open oneself to the suffering, helplessness, and vulnerability of others.

Constance Fitzgerald's now classic essay "Impasse and Dark Night" articulates with uncommon insight the complexity and ambiguity of this experience and gives voice to a recurring question facing many contemporary Christians who have opened themselves to the path of contemplative practice (Fitzgerald, 1984). It is the question of how one can proceed (with spiritual practice or with any sense of hope at all) when all ways appear blocked. Fitzgerald takes seriously the socially and historically constituted character of all spiritual thought and practice and wants to understand how the integration of contemplation and social commitment can be deepened in the face of such impasse. But she is also acutely sensitive to how the social and historical realities that stand at the root of so much human suffering can make prayer (and the presence of God) seem impossible. There is not only the dark night of the soul, but also the dark night of the world. And they are deeply intertwined. For Fitzgerald, the sense of impasse (akin to but not precisely the same as what St. John of the Cross refers to as darkness) is fundamental to contemporary Christian contemplative practice. She provides an uncommonly honest and delicate examination of spiritual lostness, allowing the sense of darkness and bewilderment that so often emerges in contemplative practice to stand on its own terms. Still, she is also sensitive to the mysterious transformations born of love that sometimes occur in the night—one of the great insights of apophatic mystics such as John of the Cross. Such transformations, making possible a greater awareness of the presence of God and oneself as beloved of God, are hardly inevitable. But Fitzgerald helps us to understand how sustained contemplative practice can make it possible to gaze courageously into the night and navigate it with grace and hope.

Conclusion

The sense of being lost in the darkness or of wandering through a desert without a clear sense of the way forward is increasingly common in the writings of Christian contemplatives. Here one finds a growing conviction that to practice contemplation is to open oneself to a continuous deepening of awareness that transforms one's relationship to everyone and everything. In his recent encyclical on the environment, *Laudato Si*, Pope Francisco makes a plea for just this kind of deepening awareness as a key to our common work. "Our goal," he says, "is... to become *painfully aware*, to dare to turn what is happening to the world into our own personal suffering and thus to discover what each of us can do about it" (Pope Francis, 2015, p. 19). There is a clear reminder here that to engage in such practice is to open oneself to an awareness of one's participation in the life, suffering, and joy of others, not as an occasional feeling, but as part of everyday practice and living. This is what it means to become a "contemplative in action": to dwell deeply in the desert, ever mindful of the sustaining presence of God, while also remaining mindful in every moment of one's responsibility to love and care for others.

References

Ashley, J. M. (2006). Contemplation in the action of justice: Ignacio Ellacuría and Ignatian spirituality. In K. Burke (Ed.), *Love that produces hope: The thought of Ignacio Ellacuría*. Collegeville, MN: Liturgical Press, 144–165.

Bottaro. G. (2018). *The mindful Catholic: Finding God one moment at a time*. Boston: Beacon.

Bourgeault. C. (2004). *Centering prayer and inner awakening*. Lanham, MD: Rowman and Littlefield.

Bourgeault, C. (2016). *The heart of centering prayer: Nondual Christianity in theory and practice*. Boulder, CO: Shambala.

Bucko, A., & McEntee, R. (2015). *The new monasticism: An interspiritual manifesto for contemplative living*. New York: Orbis.

Burton-Christie, D. (1993). *The Word in the desert: Scripture and the quest for holiness in early Christian monasticism*. New York: Oxford.

Certeau, M. de. (1986). *Heterologies: Discourse on the other*. Minneapolis: University of Minnesota Press.

Coakely, S. (2015). *The new asceticism: Sexuality, gender and the quest for God*. London: Bloombury.
Congregation for the Doctrine of Faith. (1989). Letter to the bishops of the United States on some aspects of Christian meditation. Retrieved from http://www.vatican.va/roman_curia/congregations/cfaith/documents/rc_con_cfaith_doc_19891015_meditazione-cristiana_en.html.
Drescher, E. (2016). *Choosing our religion: The spiritual lives of America's nones*. New York: Oxford.
Eggemeier, M. T. (2012). A mysticism of open eyes: Compassion for a suffering world and the *askesis* of contemplative prayer. *Spiritus 12*(1), 43–62.
Finley, J. (2005). *Christian meditation: Experiencing the presence of God*. New York: Harperone.
Fitzgerald, C. (1984). Impasse and dark night. In *Living with apocalypse: Spiritual resources for social compassion*. San Francisco: Harper & Row. Reprinted in Joann Conn (Ed.), (2005). *Women's spirituality: Resources for Christian development* (pp. 410–435). Eugene, OR: Wipf & Stock.
Flanagan, B. (2014). *Embracing solitude: Women and the new monasticism*. Eugene, OR: Wifpf & Stock.
Flynn, G., & Murray, P. (2014). *Ressourcement: A movement for renewal in twentieth century Catholic theology*. New York: Oxford.
Galiliea, S. (1988). *The way of living faith: A spirituality of liberation*. New York: Harper & Row.
Gutiérrez, G. (1988). *A theology of liberation*. (Rev. ed.). New York: Orbis. (Original work published 1971).
Gutiérrez, G. (1984). *We drink from our own wells*. New York: Orbis.
Heuertz, P. (2017). *Pilgrimage of a soul: Contemplative spirituality for the active life*. Intervarsity Press.
Holmes, B. A. (2017). *Joy unspeakable: Contemplative practices of the Black Church* (Rev. ed.). Minneapolis: Augsburg Fortress. (Original work published 2004).
Keating, T. (1999). *The human condition: Contemplation and transformation*. New York/Mahwah, NJ: Paulist.
Laird, M. (2006). *Into the silent land: A guide to the Christian practice of contemplation*. New York: Oxford.
Laird, M. (2011). *A sunlit absence: Silence, awareness, and contemplation*. New York: Oxford.
Laird, M. (2018). *An ocean of light: contemplation, transformation, and liberation*. New York: Oxford.
Lanzetta, B. (2005). *Radical wisdom: A feminist mystical theology*. Minneapolis: Augsburg Fortress.
Leloup, J-Y. (2003). *Being still: Reflections on an ancient mystical tradition*. Mahwah, NJ: Paulist.
Leloup, J-Y. (2009). *Compassion and meditation: The spiritual dynamic between Buddhism and Christianity*. Rochester, Vermont: Inner Traditions.
Main, John (2013). *Fully alive*. Norwich: Canterbury.
McGinn, B. (2002). *The foundations of mysticism: Origins to the fifth century*. New York: Crossroad.
McGuire, M. (2008). *Lived religion: Faith and practice in everyday life*. New York: Oxford.
Merton, T. (1966). *Conjectures of a guilty bystander*. New York: Doubleday.
Merton, T. (1968). *Zen and the Birds of Appetite*. New York: New Directions.
Merton, T. (1969). *Contemplative Prayer*. New York: Herder & Herder.

Merton, T. (1979). *Love and living*. London: Sheldon
Merton, T. (1948/1998). *The Seven Storey Mountain*. New York: Harcourt.
Norris, K. (1997). *Cloister walk*. New York: Riverhead.
Norris, K. (1993). *Dakota: a spiritual biography*. Boston: Houghton Mifflin.
Oden, A. (2017). *Right here right now: The practice of Christian mindfulness*. Nashville: Abingdon.
Pope Francis. (2015). *Laudato Si': Care for our Common Home*. [Encyclical letter].
Reynolds, S. (2017). *Living with the mind of Christ: Mindfulness and Christian spirituality*. London: Darton, Longman & Todd.
Rohr, R. (2003). *Everything belongs: The gift of contemplative prayer*. New York: Crossroad.
Ruffing, J. (Ed.). (2001). *Mysticism and social transformation*. Syracuse: Syracuse University Press.
Schneiders, S (1989). Spirituality in the academy. *Theological Studies* 50, 676–697.
Sheldrake, P. (1998). *Spirituality and history: Questions of interpretation and method*. (Rev. ed.) New York: Orbis. (Original work published 1991).
Sobrino, J. (1988). *Spirituality of liberation*. New York: Orbis.
Stead, T. (2017). *Mindfulness and Christian spirituality: Making space for God*. Louisville, KY: Westminster John Knox.
Stewart, C. (1991). The desert Fathers on radical self-honesty. *Vox Benedictina* 8, 7–53.
Stewart, C. (1999). *Cassian the monk*. New York: Oxford.
Teasdale, W. (2001). *The mystic heart: Discovering a universal spirituality in the worlds' religions*. Novato: New World Library.
Thurman, H. (1949). Jesus and the disinherited. Nashville, TN: Abingdon.
Thurman, H. (1961). *The inward journey*. New York: Harper & Row.
Thurman, H. (1962). *Temptations of Jesus*. San Francisco: Lawton Kennedy.
Wolfteich, C. (2006). *Lord have mercy: Praying for justice with conviction and humility*. San Francisco: Jossey-Bass.

CHAPTER 29

GOENKA'S VIPASSANA MOVEMENT

From Conversion to Disaffiliation

MASOUMEH RAHMANI

Introduction

Many contemporary Buddhist meditation masters present their teachings as "universal" and as scientific "tools" for observing reality as it is, arguing that the Buddha did not promote a "religion" (Buddhism) or any doctrine; that the "pure teachings of the Buddha," the Dhamma, are non-sectarian and reflect the law of nature. They might also claim that, upon discovering the true nature of mind and matter through self-exploration, the Buddha encouraged others to also experientially discover this truth for themselves.

Such discourses, which seek to depict Buddhism as a rational tradition compatible with empirical science, are rooted in the Buddhist reform movements, known as Buddhist Modernism, that developed as a resistance to nineteenth-century imperialism and missionization of Southeast Asian counties by European nations.

Satya Narayan Goenka (1924–2013) was one of the famous teachers whose representation of Vipassana meditation as a freestanding secular practice has helped to establish and promote these Buddhist modernist trends globally. Goenka achieved an international popularity by refashioning his teachings in a pseudo-scientific and world-affirming language. His movement is best known for its ten-day silent meditation retreats and a consistent refusal to identify itself as religious/Buddhist, even though its teachings and practices are directly and blatantly derived from Theravada Buddhism.

The unique environment of Goenka's Vipassana course—where people are asked to disconnect from the external world, commit to a strict code of conduct, and meditate for ten hours per day—are attractive to many individuals who desire fulfilment through self-transformation. While some people are contented to experience this novelty once and move on, others become committed members, advance to longer courses, and shape a life around this practice. However, both groups commonly conceptualize their commitment in non-religious terms and reject the notion of conversion.

Here, I explore the implication of Goenka's discourse on shaping unique patterns of religious conversion and disengagement. My arguments are based on ethnographic fieldwork and in-depth interviews with twenty-six current and former Vipassana meditators in New Zealand (Rahmani, 2017). Seeing conversion as a process that is constituted in language, I argue that conversion to Goenka's movement paradoxically results in the member's rejection of religious labels and categories including conversion, and, ironically, can even adopt atheist identities (Loss, 2010). This is a process I refer to as "tacit conversion" (Rahmani, 2017, 2020). Goenka's rhetoric disassociates his movement from "organised religion" and so rejects such terms as "conversion."

> Dhamma is not Hindu, Buddhist, Jain, Christian or Muslim. It has nothing to do with organised religion. It has nothing to do with any particular tradition. Conversion can happen only from one "organised religion" to another, which is not the case here.
> (Goenka cited in Melnikova, 2014, p. 59)

In this chapter I highlight linguistic, sociocultural, and institutional structures undergirding tacit conversion. I show how, in rejecting conversion and religious categories, committed members *identically* draw from the same set of rhetorical strategies that Goenka himself offers to distinguish his movement from religion. In the later part of this chapter I explore patterns of disengagement in a context where the concept of conversion was taken-for-granted in the first place.

Religious Conversion

In the matter of conversion, we can usefully distinguish: (a) "experiences of personal transformation" and (b) "change in religious affiliation" (Stromberg, 2014, p. 118). While affiliating with, or disaffiliating from, a religious organization may certainly bring about personal transformation, the association is not guaranteed. Thus, a person may formally change religious affiliation to fulfill other goals such as marriage, yet this does not necessarily mean that they also undergo a profound transformation in the way they understand the world and their place within it. Here, I use the terms "affiliation" and "disaffiliation" to refer to the formal processes and narratives of joining and leaving an organization. Hence, "disaffiliation narratives" are a cluster of stories about leaving Goenka's Vipassana movement and its community—it does *not* mean that the participant has rejected the movement's teachings and truth claims.

I use the terms "conversion" and "deconversion" to refer to the personal transformations prompted by one's acceptance or rejection of a system of meaning, or "universe of discourse" that provides the individual with the linguistic resources to create a new self-concept and to change the basic interpretive framework within which events, experiences, and actions of self and others are understood (Buckser & Glazier, 2003, p. xi; Heirich, 1977; Snow & Machalek, 1983). From this perspective, conversion is a *process*, not a singular event, and converts are viewed as active agents who draw upon and manipulate linguistic resourses to bring about their desired self-transformation (Stromberg, 2014).

From a linguistic perspective, the personal transformation associated with conversion and deconversion is achieved through narration and is observable in the forms of language and the patterns of reasoning used. Thus, when individuals convert, they tend to interpret their *previous* motives, evaluations, and understandings of self, and their relationships with others, as a "misunderstanding." Following the formula of "then I thought, now I know" (Berger & Luckmann, 1967, p. 160), converts actively reconstruct their biography and their view of others and of the world from the perspective of the enlightened presence and in according to the "new universe of discourse and its amended grammar" (Snow & Mackalek, 1983, Staples & Mauss, 1987, p. 143).

Correspondingly, deconversion is the mirror image of conversion: when an individual no longer interprets the world from the vantage point of that particular system of meaning. Finally, I use "disengagement" and "exit" as umbrella terms to address a variety of pathways outlined in this chapter.

S. N. Goenka's Vipassana Movement

Satya Narayan Goenka (1924–2013), a former businessman of Indian descent, was the most recent leader of the international Vipassana Movement, best known for its ten-day silent meditation retreats. To date, Goenka's network is the largest donor-funded Vipassana organization, with over 170 official (and over 130 non-official) centers worldwide that offer meditation courses free of charge. From teachers to administrators, all involved in Goenka's organization are "dhamma service" volunteers and receive no salary. All tasks including cooking, cleaning, and maintenance of the center are done by the dhamma servers. Any individual who has completed a ten-day course can offer their services to the movement, provide that they adhere to the organization's moral code and commit to regular practice. The organization also receives donations from "old students" (see the final paragraph in this section).

Similar to most contemporary Vipassana meditation teachers, Goenka was an advocate of a non-monastic[1] approach to meditation known as "the householder

[1] The modern lineage of Goenka's Vipassana meditation is traced to the famous Burmese monk, Ledi Sayadaw (1846–1923), who established meditation centers across Burma (Braun, 2013), and was among the first to authorize a non-monastic person, Saya Thetgyi (1873–1945) as his successor in 1915. Saya Thetgyi in turn passed the tradition to U Ba Khin, a Burmese government official who taught many householders and international students in his lifetime, including Mother Sayamagyi (Sayamagyi Daw Mya Thwin), Ruth Denison, John Coleman, Robert Hover, and S. N. Goenka (Rawlinson, 1997, p. 593).

tradition" (Pagis, 2008, p. 94). After the death of his teacher, U Ba Khin (1899–1971), Goenka took the role of supreme authority within this organization and did not appoint a successor prior to his own demise. Instead, in an attempt to standardize his teachings and prevent deviations, in 1982 Goenka recorded all of his teachings and instructions and appointed assistant teachers to conduct courses on his behalf. All Goenka centers follow a set of guidelines, which prohibits them from altering his teachings, instructions, recordings, and the structure of the courses. Around the world, Goenka's ten-day Vipassana courses are conducted more or less identically. Thus, if students returns to attend a second ten-day course, they will be listening to the same instructions. Practitioners in non-English-speaking countries are provided with a translated version of Goenka's instructions. According to a Vipassana teacher I interviewed in New Zealand, these tapes will be used until the English language has changed to such an extent that people are no longer able to comprehend Goenka's language.

Goenka's organization offers a diverse range of courses (from three-day to sixty-day ones). The ten-day courses are the required introduction into the movement and therefore are the most frequently held and best attended. On successful completion of the standard ten-day course, first-time course attendees or "new students" are granted the title of "old students" and will henceforth be eligible to attend other shorter/longer courses and give dhamma service, provided they adhere to the organization's code of conduct and maintain a regular practice. They will also gain access to the movement's online resources (text, audio, and video material) that are otherwise inaccessible to the public.

The Ten-Day Vipassana Course

Contrary to its name, a standard ten-day Vipassana course consists of twelve days, starting on day zero and ending on day eleven. During the course, students follow a strict timetable with ten to twelve hours of meditation from 4:30 to 21:00 each day. The course officially commences on the evening of day zero when all students take the Three Refuges (Buddha, Dhamma, and Saṅgha), surrender to the teacher, and formally request to be taught instructions to *Anapana* meditation. The Three Refuges are a cornerstone of Buddhism (Gombrich, 2006), yet many who take part are not aware that they are participating in the standard initiation into Buddhism. There is an obvious tension between propagating a supposedly non-religious, non-sectarian practice and encouraging students to take the Three Refuges, to the point that both Goenka and his insider scholars feel compelled to justify this inconsistency time after time (Goldberg & Décary, 2013; Melnikova, 2014).

A similar request is made by students to be taught Vipassana meditation on day four. Students take a vow of "Noble Silence," which prohibits all communication with one another whether by speech, eye contact, gesture, sign language, or written notes. Gender segregation and restrictions on contact with the world outside of the center, possession of religious objects, practice of religious rituals, listening to music, reading, or writing are also imposed to limit external stimuli during the course (Pagis, 2010b).

Additionally, all students must adhere to a strict code of conduct (*sīla*): the five precepts for new students and eight precepts for old students, to abstain from: (1) killing, (2) stealing, (3) all sexual activity, (4) telling lies, and (5) intoxicants, (6) eating after midday, (7) sensual entertainment and bodily decorations, and (8) sleeping on high luxurious beds.

Each day commences with thirty minutes of pre-recorded audiotapes in which Goenka chants passages from the *Tipiṭaka* in Pali for the purpose of enhancing the environment with "good vibrations," and ends with an hour of his evening "discourses" in which relevant Buddhist theories and doctrines are explained in a language replete with humorous analogies (such as the story of The Doctor's Prescription mentioned later in this chapter).

The teachings that Goenka offers at this course rest on a selective interpretation of the *Satipaṭṭhāna Sutta* in light of the *Abhidhamma* and Buddhaghosa's *The Path of Purification.* While the *Satipaṭṭhāna Sutta* offers four objects for the practice of mindfulness—body, sensations, mind, and mental objects—Goenka's teachings (following his teacher U Ba Khin) are focused predominantly on sensations. Goenka's Vipassana technique is theoretically underpinned by the basic Buddhist doctrines of the Four Noble Truths, and his courses are meticulously structured to practice the three stages of the Noble Eightfold Path: morality (*sīla*), concentration (*samādhi*), and wisdom (*paññā*). Goenka thus closely follows the Buddhist premise that all physical and mental phenomena (including our human existence) are marked by suffering (*dukkha*), impermanence (*anicca*), and not-self (*anattā*). From the Theravada perspective, enlightenment (*nibbāna*) consists of realizing this reality in the fullest sense.

In order to practice morality, the first component of the Noble Eightfold Path, all students must take a vow to keep the five precepts for the duration of the course. The second component of the path, *concentration*, is practiced from day one to day three, during which students learn the *Anapana* meditation, which is a breath observation technique aimed at increasing the students' concentration. The *Anapana* meditation consists of focusing one's attention to a limited area under the nostrils—between the tip of the nose and the upper lip—and observing the sensations that arise from the uncontrolled breath as air moves in and out of the nostrils. In order to practice wisdom, the final component of the Eightfold Path, from the fourth day onward students learn the practice of Vipassana meditation. Once again, students must officially request to be taught instructions to this practice. Vipassana instructions are provided in phases and involve systematically extending the concentration gained during the first three days to other areas of the body.

In Goenka's Vipassana tradition, biographical reconstruction generally echoes the Four Noble Truths and involves the acknowledgement/acceptance of an "unbalanced" and "conditioned" self whose suffering in life is the result of one's "ignorance" toward the true source of suffering. All past events and incidents that culminated in suffering are now interpreted as the result of one's own ignorance and/or mind conditioning. The reconstruction of the self in this paradigm is entangled with a newfound sense of responsibility for one's actions. However, as far as the acknowledgement of the cause and nature of suffering (i.e., ignorance) is concerned, biographical reconstruction in the Vipassana movement runs parallel to general markers of conversion to Buddhism (Brekke, 2003, p. 181; Yü, 2014, p. 466). In order to distinguish biographies that were reconstructed in the light of Goenka's teachings from those that vaguely echoed Buddhist worldviews I have attended to the *vocabulary*, *grammar*, and *language* of the participants and only considered accounts where there was clear overlap with the movement's universe of discourse (Rahmani, 2017).

Goenka's Vipassana courses aim to give an experiential understanding of the Four Noble Truths. Goenka (1997, p. 12) constantly reminds his students that a merely intellectual understanding of these concepts does not produce "real wisdom," and therefore cannot lead one to liberation from suffering. Instead, one must understand the true source of this suffering at the *experiential* level. Students are advised to invest time in meditation rather than reading or engaging in "useless" intellectual endeavours (Goenka, 2005, p. 99, cited in VRI Dhamma, 2014).

This epistemic strategy—which considers embodied experience and not intellectual understanding as the true source of knowledge—is implicit in much of Goenka's enterprise including his efforts to abstract his movement from religion and claim that the movement and its teachings are non-sectarian. For instance, despite teaching various Buddhist doctrines (including *dukkha*, *anicca*, *anattā*, *saṅkhāra*, *kamma*, etc.), Goenka discourages his students from accepting them "blindly" and advises them to only accept these insights as "truths" once they have experienced them for themselves. As Goenka (1997, cited in VRI Dhamma, 2014) conveys:

> Beliefs are always sectarian. Dhamma has no belief. In Dhamma you experience, and then you believe. There is no blind belief in Dhamma. You must experience and then only believe whatever you have experienced.

This rationalization enables Goenka and (by extension) his followers to disassociate the movement from religion in a twofold manner: first, by adopting a limited Protestant notion of religion as being primarily about beliefs and second, by distinguishing (1) a belief that is uncritically accepted from (2) a belief that is acquired through experience. Yet, given that course attendees are introduced to the doctrines of *dukkha*, *anicca*, *anattā*, and *saṅkhāra* on day three and prior to any Vipassana instructions, the question remains whether they are preconditioned with a series of expectations that are to be internalized and later "re-discovered." (Deleanu, 2010, p. 616). For example, Goenka's constant repetition of the term impermanence (almost as a mantra: *anicca*, *anicca*, *anicca*), does not allow the student to independently develop this insight (Singh, 2007, p. 19).

Another element of ambiguity is Goenka's vacillation between promoting (1) Vipassana meditation as a "practical" practice attuned to the demands of the conventional life (Medini Dhamma, 2017) and (2) promoting it as a transformative path leading to *nibbāna* or enlightenment. While this vacillation commonly leads new students to be confused about the purpose of the technique, there is often no such ambivalence in the mind of committed meditators who unequivocally pursued the ultimate goal of enlightenment. As becomes clear in the following pages, these rhetorical strategies have significant implications for both conversion (i.e., rendering it tacit) and disengagement (e.g., instigating self-doubt).

Introducing the Research Participants

The fifteen male and eleven female participants in this research belonged to the middle and upper-middle class. Most had university education. They included postgraduate students, freelance artists, builders, and accountants—a wide range. All were of European descent, between the ages of twenty-four and seventy-six.

Some participants indicated an exclusive commitment to the practice, with several years or even decades of involvement and had typically attended above three ten-day courses, lived near the Vipassana center, and, following Goenka's guidelines, observed *sīla* in their private life, meditated at least two hours a day, and participated in at least one ten-day course each year. Henceforth, I use the term "committed" meditators or practitioners to refer to this group.

Others adopted a more selective approach and conveyed a commitment to different aspects of the movement such as the practice itself without following *sīla*, or some of the concepts that left a lasting impression with them. These individuals had typically attended between one to three ten-day courses and their involvement with the movement was relatively short-lived. In scrutinizing disengagement narratives, a qualitative distinction is drawn between "disaffiliation narratives" (accounts of those who disengaged *after* years of intense participation) and the narratives of "Pragmatic Leavers" (accounts of those who disengaged *before* developing an exclusive commitment).

Despite this diversity, all actively emphasized that their participation at a ten-day Vipassana course had resulted in a dramatic change in their sense of self and perspective on the world: "I walked in one person and walked out another," "I came out of that first course thinking... I've sort of unlocked the key to the universe."

They rejected conversion for the religious overtones of the term; for its association with "cult brainwashing"; and because from their perspective, a convert is a passive subject undergoing a radical and sudden change in beliefs due to external forces.

The majority of the participants were born into Christian households, and all had distinct reasons for arriving at Vipassana. Leslie was craving silence; Carole wanted to be happy; and Damian was searching for a spiritual discipline that would give him a "boot up the bum."[2] In spite of this diversity, all participants represented themselves (in explicit or implicit terms) as the unconventional segment of society, conveyed in

[2] Pseudonyms are used to ensure the anonymity of those who requested it. I have also respected the decision of other participants who desired to be named.

attitudes toward Western medicine, critique of consumerist culture, and yet more commonly, manifested in stories of teenage rebellion against their parental religion.

Generally speaking, Vipassana meditators understood themselves as "autonomous spiritual seekers," who rebelled against their parental religion (predominantly Christianity) due to personal dissatisfactions with the behavior of Church members (e.g., hypocrisy, dogmatism, narrow-mindedness) and a perceived inadequacy of the tradition to meet their needs. This, according to their narratives, often occurred in conjunction with leaving home and/or exposure to other traditions.

In general, most of the narratives corresponded with, and confirmed, Peter Berger's (1999) refined ideas about pluralism and its effect on modes of religiosity. For instance, they spoke about how encountering others who live by different values and hold onto other truths fractured their taken-for-granted certainties in the tradition they were raised within, and eventually providing them with the opportunity to seek out and explore other practices/traditions and piece together a new worldview. I should stress that in spite of their dissatisfaction with Christianity, these individuals did *not* dwell on, discuss, or explicitly reject the ontological realities of the tradition; rather they expressed disapproval with its institutional, authoritarian, fanatical, and hierarchical modes of religiosity. Their religious background hence colored their understanding of religion and supported their rationale for abstracting Goenka's movement from this category.

Thematic analysis of the interviews showed that Vipassana meditators commonly conceptualized religion and spirituality in opposition to each other as in Table 29.1.[3] More importantly, they situated Goenka's movement under the spiritual canopy because, for them, the practice involved a direct experience with the self and hence alluded to a sense of autonomous exploration corresponding with their desire to feel "authentic" on their spiritual "journey." To put it bluntly, the weight that Vipassana meditators ascribed to these values (e.g., seekership, autonomy, authenticity, individualism, self-exploration) permitted them to overlook those characteristics that they themselves associated with "religion" (e.g., structure, required belonging, dogma).

Another important disposition undergirding tacit conversion involved the Vipassana meditators' *commitment* to a modernist conceptualization of Buddhism, which, in line with Goenka's representation of pure Dhamma, emphasized and valued the "detraditionalization, demythologization and psychologization" (McMahan, 2008, p. 42) of this tradition. From this perspective, (1) Buddhism is not a religion, but a philosophy; (2) true Buddhism is devoid of dogma and rituals; (3) meditation can/should be practiced divorced from its Buddhist foundations; and (4) Buddhism is categorically

[3] This table was produced from my thematic analysis of the interview segments in which participants described what they mean by "religion" and "spirituality." In most instances, they were asked to provide their definitions as a follow-up question, once each term was brought up in the conversation. At other times, this took place in the context of questions such as, "do you think Vipassana is a religion?" All paragraphs containing references to each term were coded, their underlying themes were abstracted, compared, and summarized into this table. Note that they were not asked to contrast these terms; rather, they were asked to provide explanations if and when they rejected one term (e.g., religion) and emphasized the other (e.g., spirituality).

Table 29.1 Participants' definition of religion and spirituality

Religion	Spirituality
External Path	Internal Path
Structured, Organized	Intuitive, Organic, Authentic
Dogmatic	Experimental
Passive Recipient	Active Agent
Conventional	Idiosyncratic
Authoritarian and Controlling	Autonomous and Fluid
Absolutism	Relativism
Does not allow Subjective Interpretations	Encourages Subjective Interpretations
Requires Exclusive Belonging	Open and Inclusive
Empty Rituals	Pragmatic, Transformative Tool
Anthropomorphized Deities	Impersonal Entities
Source of Conflict and War	Source of Connectedness

different from other religions. These four characteristics define a position that can be referred to as "Buddhist modernism" (McMahan, 2008; Sharf, 1995), or "Protestant Buddhism" (Gombrich & Obeyesekere, 1988), which is not unique to Goenka, but rather captures the contemporary imagination of Buddhism in many non-Buddhist contexts (McMahan, 2008; Sharf, 1995, 2015; Wallace, 2002; Yü, 2014). Many of the people who arrive at Goenka's centers already hold these views and attend because the movement represents itself in this light.

Not all the twenty-six participants rejected a Buddhist identity as a result of a lack of association between Goenka's teachings and the Buddhist tradition. A close reading of their narratives indicates the presence of a strong sense of ambivalence over the links the participants perceived between Vipassana and Buddhism. The heart of this ambivalence was anchored on a disturbance to their modernist conceptions of Buddhism, typically as a result of traveling to Buddhist countries. This was indeed the premise upon which those participants with lesser degrees of involvement in Goenka's movement rejected the Buddhist identity. For example, drawing upon his experience of living in Thailand, Ian argued, "I think the reason why I would never say I'm a Buddhist even though I have adopted a lot of practices in my life... [is that] most of the people I know who identify as Buddhist don't actually practice Buddhism or meditation. They go to temples and give money and they pray." Many other participants drew similar comparisons between Vipassana and Buddhism in Asian contexts (Japan, China, and Korea). These participants' arguments were generally value-laden, trivialized the category of ritual, and indicated that they viewed themselves from a superior position in relation to traditional forms of Buddhism as practiced Asia. Thus:

> Ross: Look at the Buddhism in Japan, I lived in Japan, it's got nothing to do with the original teaching...... it's not what the Buddha was teaching... monks officiate and perform ceremonies at funerals... they will chant some prayers so that the soul of the person will get a good rebirth. Ah and you can pay money for that. What's

> that got to do with it . . . An "ism" becomes when you, it's not, say all the Buddha's teachings is "Buddhism." It's when it's moved away from the [pause] the fundamental teaching of the Buddha.

Adoption of Goenka's Rhetorics

Second, and more significant in terms of support of the concept of tacit conversion, committed meditators utilized an additional set of rhetorical strategies—identical to the arguments Goenka puts forth in his discourses—to support their non-Buddhist, non-religious identities, reject conversion, and to resolve any tension that came up during the interviews regarding the links between Vipassana and religion. At a linguistic level, these rhetorics functioned to conceal the religious elements of the movement. They include rhetoric of: (1) experience, (2) meditation as a "tool," (3) pure teachings of the Buddha, and (4) "here and now." In the following passage Carole responds to my question whether she conceives Vipassana meditation as a religious practice. Carole is a serious Vipassana meditator of over twenty years and has attended countless courses including a number of forty-five-day courses for which she had to travel abroad. Carole meditates regularly and observes the five precepts.

> Carole: Before you can even answer a question like that you have to sort of say "what do you mean by religious"? Religious to me means longing for some religion which is some kind of organized, to me, is some kind of organized [pause] or some sort of, kind of, organization that um, [pause] believes in certain things [pause] and [pause] um [long pause] so you could say I belong to an organization and I do believe in certain things although I believe in very little, because I understand so little that actually what I believe in is very little, because I only believe in what I've experienced myself. And I've experienced very little [loud inhale] so it's very little that I believe in . . . so I wouldn't say I was religious [giggle].

As this passage demonstrates, Carole feels somewhat compelled to justify the contradiction arising from her definition of "religious" (as belonging to an organization and believing in certain things) and her desire to frame her involvement with the movement in non-religious terms (as she does in the end). To resolve this tension, she draws upon the rhetoric of experience, which ironically leads her to argue that she has had little experience despite years of intense practice. It is not that committed Vipassana meditators are unaware of these links; rather, they draw upon an identical pattern of reasoning to resolve these ambivalences during the interviews.

Framing Vipassana meditation as a "tool" (following Goenka) for personal development and transformation was another common rhetorical strategy that the committed meditators used (following Goenka) to distance the movement from religious categories. This pattern of reasoning is largely influenced by the secular and scientifically oriented vocabulary (e.g., self-exploratory technique, scientific laws) in which Goenka delivers his teachings. Moreover, in his discourses, Goenka represents Vipassana meditation in *constant* juxtaposition to traditional forms of religious practices (e.g., prayers, chanting, and worship), which he devalues by labeling them "empty rituals."

To adequately explain this, I will refer to one of Goenka's well-known analogies, The Doctor's Prescription. This story resonates strongly with many participants (as evidenced by the fact that they commonly incorporate this analogy in their narratives) and strikes laughter among the students in the meditation hall. This analogy depicts a sick man with "great faith" in his doctor, who instead of "taking the medicine" prescribed, sets up a shrine in his house, bows to the doctor's statue, offers flowers, and starts reciting "Two pills in the morning! Two pills in the afternoon! Two pills in the evening!" The moral of the story is that "without actually taking the medicine, one cannot be cured of the disease" (Goenka, cited in Hart, 1987, pp. 65–66).

Much like this analogy, this rhetorical strategy—Vipassana as "tool"—involves two intrinsically linked ideas: autonomy and practicality. On the one hand, the movement's emphasis on individual responsibility (you must take the medicine yourself) and self-exploration alludes to a sense of spiritual autonomy that, as noted before, was the basis upon which many meditators distinguish Vipassana from traditional religions. On the other hand, because the pragmatic aspect of the practice is depicted in contrast to prayer and worship, it provokes an image of a rational and effective practice, and thus marginalizes Vipassana's religious elements in the practitioners' mind (such as chanting in Pali for "good vibrations," the strict code of conduct, gender segregations). The committed meditators I spoke with used this rhetorical strategy to reject religious categories, resolve their ambivalences, or to abruptly *end* any discussion that disconfirmed their positions (i.e., their context-dependent identities).

The following passage is from Elijah, who had one year of experience within the movement:

AUTHOR: Do you think Vipassana is a religion?

ELIJAH: What defines a religion?

AUTHOR: Exactly! But how do you understand religion yourself?

ELIJAH: Something that's organized. That has, I was gonna say restrictions and boundaries. Which in some way, there is that, there is a lot of that here. But I can understand why, that, they keep these spaces like this. To keep that purity. Which is, is, he, Goenka says there's a lot of people that continue to do Vipassana but have their own ways of doing it, which are relaxed ways. Not in its pure form. So I can understand why there are those limitations. but I don't know if I see it as much of a religion... I don't know what my definition of religion is. But I don't see Vipassana as a religion.

AUTHOR: Ok.

ELIJAH: For me, Vipassana is a tool.

AUTHOR: It's a tool?

ELIJAH: Yeah.

This passage also illustrates the third rhetorical strategy, "pure teachings of the Buddha" or "pure Dhamma," anchored in Goenka's claim that at once (1) authenticates his teaching and lineage as directly connected to the historical Buddha, (2) emphasizes the *universality* of the teaching, and (3) justifies the movement's strict regulations.

On the movement's official website (Medini Dhamma, 2017) and during his courses, Goenka asserts that the Vipassana technique was "rediscovered" 2,500 years ago by the Buddha and it has been handed down in its "pristine purity" through an unbroken chain of teachers. He says that five centuries after Buddha, people started to add elements of other traditions (rituals, dogmas, rules, etc.) and the pure Dhamma was lost in its birthplace, India (Goenka, 1999, p. 156, cited in VRI Dhamma, 2014). This rhetoric therefore has entanglements with the previous rhetoric (meditation as tool) for it implicitly downplays rituals. In fact, Goenka explicitly notes, "Every rite, ritual or ceremony is nothing but a corrupt form of pure Dhamma" (Goenka, 1989, cited in VRI Dhamma, 2014). Accordingly, any alterations to the movement's fixed set of instructions, teachings, and guidelines are perceived as threats to the purity of the technique. Preserving purity thus functions as a rhetorical justification for guidelines for committed meditators, such as following the *sīla* (particularly abstinence from sexual misconduct) and hard restrictions on "mixing" the technique with other practices/ philosophies.

Lastly, the concept of "here and now" or "living in the present moment" was also rhetorically drawn upon to ward off discussions about the religious elements of the practice including the Buddhist doctrines that underpin it. This pattern of reasoning predominantly emerged as a substitute for the rhetoric of experience in the context of concepts such as reincarnation and *nibbāna*. For instance, in response to whether he believes in reincarnation, Elijah noted, "in the past I think I have because of random fluffy things... but now I feel like because I'm experiencing so much stuff that feels um [pause] real to me that [pause] I'm much more open to what is being said in the same arena. Yeah so I'm far more open to what I'm being told now, to be correct." Similarly, I was occasionally told, "for me the goal is not some sort of theoretical understanding or some idea. For me, the goal is to try not to develop impurity in the present moment."

Ross is a celibate Vipassana teacher who has been involved with this movement for over forty years. He explained to me the four stages leading to *nibbāna* and how, by purifying the mind, Vipassana meditation leads one to this end. I asked him about the Buddhist identity and religious aspects of Goenka's Vipassana organization. This was followed by a discussion in which Ross explained to me the four stages leading to *nibbāna* and how, by purifying the mind, Vipassana meditation leads one to this end.

> ROSS: I felt very strong, feeling that this was gonna to lead to the purification of the mind.
>
> AUTHOR: Do you ever doubt it?
>
> ROSS: Well I think there's gonna be doubt, a little doubt till one has reached the first stages of *nibbāna*. Cause, you know what I mean, one can only know the path absolutely,

when one has had the absolute experience of it.... So the whole practice should be experiential based. Your level of confidence will be depending on the level of experience.

AUTHOR: But—

ROSS: But each, as you perhaps get a little deeper in each course, and as your confidence grows that this. Um [pause] and it's and it's having the benefit in daily lives. I don't mind it, I'm living in the present and I want to improve myself in the here and now... So, yes this path will lead to full liberation but, [pause] I like to feel the reality [pause] of, our goal [long pause] is the present moment... So I, I have confidence, there is such an experience of nibbana, but it doesn't concern me that I haven't experienced it. Cause I, I do have the confidence that, [pause] if one has awareness, and the equanimity, of the present moment, [pause] as it is, [pause] then one is purifying the mind [pause] and we let nature take its course that's all and I don't call that Buddhism.

The extent to which committed Vipassana meditators were able to operationalize these rhetorical strategies depended on their level of exposure to Goenka's universe of discourse. Thus, Elijah's use of these rhetorical strategies is less developed than Carole's, which demonstrates a gradual learning process of assimilation. This provides a linguistic marker of commitment. Carole shows a stronger emphasis on the experiential approach to "belief" and her rhetorical strategy is relatively more integrated and coherent, whereas Elijah seems unable to articulate how the movement is distinct from religion and effectively puts an end to discussion by stating that regardless of definition, he does not perceive Vipassana as religion and uses the rhetoric of "tool" to abruptly end the conversation. This observation becomes far more evident once we compare these two with the excerpt from Ross, who eloquently chained several themes so as to convince the listener of his particular line of reasoning. These passages illustrate that conversion and commitment to this tradition entails a change in the way a person *expresses* a particular belief through language. The themes of experience, meditation as tool, pure teaching of Buddha, and here and now, emerged in my conversations with all except one of the participants.

Religious Disengagement

Religious disengagement is a gradual and multidimensional process (Bromley, 2006). Some may leave a religious group due to the deterioration of their interpersonal relationships with other members. Others begin to question the teachings, values, and truth claims of a group. The disengagement literature suggests that exit is often negotiated by the member (or jointly with the organization) when doubts and conflicts become irresolvable. Doubt does not necessarily immediately result in disengagement. Commonly, members (or believers) adopt coping strategies such as denial in order to defer exit until an alternative identity or social network becomes available (Healy, 2011; Coates, 2013; Wright, 1984). In other cases, members continue to reconcile doubts until avoidance strategies become ineffective and conflicts culminate in a "crisis" event

(Bromley, 2004; Wright, 1991). Doubt is, therefore, an integral element of religious disengagement. The sources of doubt could fall within the two categories of "intellectual" or "interpersonal":

- Intellectual or cognitive doubt: skepticism about the truth of a system of belief (Barbour, 1994, p. 2; Streib, Silver, Csöff, Keller, & Hood, 2011);
- Interpersonal doubt: feelings of alienation from or perceived hypocrisy among members of the religious community (Brinkerhoff & Mackie, 1993; Bromley, 2006).[4]

Vipassana Disaffiliation Narratives

While disaffiliation from Goenka's movement parallels many contours of religious exit from other traditions, "intellectual doubt" was rare in the narratives of formerly committed Vipassana meditators. Instead, they predominantly relied on moral criticism to vindicate their exit.

They often depicted their disengagement as a gradual, lengthy, and emotionally painful process, instigated by events that disturbed their assumptions about the *institutional* aspect of the movement. Some morally criticized its hierarchical structure or the discrepancy between how the movement first represented itself as being "open" and compatible with conventional life, yet *gradually* revealed and increased its demands from advanced meditators such as expectations of exclusive commitment and complete celibacy from single students. They rarely harbor doubts about the movement's ideologies and often actively distinguished the institutional and discursive facets of the teachings from what they considered as the core of the technique (i.e., Four Noble Truths, observing sensations in a non-judgmental manner, etc.). They praised the latter component as an "indisputable," "compelling," "elegantly simple," "universal," and "incredibly on the ball" for "understanding reality."

The narratives were characterized by an ambivalent language that implied the individual's conviction of the movement's truth claims, coupled with a strong sense of *self-doubt*. In saying this, I do not claim that self-doubt is unique to Vipassana disaffiliation narratives; nor do I intend to suggest that self-doubt and doubt in a theory or interpersonal relationships are watertight categories. Rather my intention is to stress that self-doubt in the context of Vipassana disaffiliation narratives stems from an ongoing commitment to a particular form of language:

> Damian: I had doubts about the teachings, not that it didn't work, but that there was a propaganda element within the teaching of retreats that made you believe you

[4] That said, not all scholars discern these two facets of doubt in religious disengagement. In fact, there seems to be a considerable bias toward coalescing all forms of doubt under the banner of "intellectual doubt" (Streib et al., 2011), which may be related to the theological features of the traditions in which these studies were commonly grounded.

> were near to a break through... and you thought... "I'm gonna get there, I'm gonna like um get enlightened"... and then on the last day he [Goenka] says "well it is a long path... maybe a lifetime path"... So I had doubt about my progress... In fact the first two years I was terribly wracked with doubt... I felt that in fact I was going backwards. I was becoming more mentally unstable and more unhappy [*In a follow-up interview he added*] In my current life, there's an element of resignation... feeling that not much can change for me in the rest of my life... what Vipassana showed me was that the process of transformation is very, very slow... and the karmic history of each consciousness in general is quite vast... so I feel a bit resigned to the shit parts of me.

As this passage demonstrates, on the one hand, Damian is determined to show his approval of the technique (e.g., "not that it didn't work") and, on the other, he indicates certain skepticism about the efficacy of it through utterances such as "going backwards" and "becoming more mentally unstable." Yet, the weight of his conviction and commitment to the movement's language takes precedence over his experience:

> Damian: I believed some elements of it [Vipassana] are non-sectarian, are not religious, they are not biased, according to um [pause] just the, the historical, fancies of, of, of, you know, some god creator in that story, um [pause] according to a certain cultural background they seemed to be [pause] um universal!... So, that, apparent universality, um makes me feel like, those elements are worth hanging on to.

Goenka's teachings on progress are ambiguous, which ultimately leads many to self-doubt (Rahmani, 2019). On a standard ten-day course, students are discouraged from developing expectations, yet constantly reassured that "results are bound to come" and that they will experience some sort of transformation if they practice the technique "properly" (Goenka, 1997, p. 33) and that progress cannot be measured by the types of sensations they experience, but only in terms of "equanimity," which is difficult to measure (Pagis, 2008, p. 174). However, Goenka's instructions include descriptions of meditative states that are taken by the practitioners as indicators of progress. Students are told that by maintaining equanimity, "gross, solidified and unpleasant sensations begin to dissolve into subtle vibrations. One starts to experience a very pleasant *flow* of energy throughout the body" (Goenka, 1997, p. 35). Similar descriptions are provided for the experience of *bhanga* (dissolution) in both standard and advanced courses. Yet at the same time, the instructions also remind the practitioners that it is normal to experience gross sensations after one has experienced a free flow. According to Goenka (1997, pp. 35–36), this is *not* to be interpreted as a sign of regression, but rather as a sign of progress.

Beyond these ambiguous remarks, the Vipassana teachers provide no detailed feedback other than encouraging meditators to *observe* their experiences in an "equanimous" way. Such vague responses by the teachers can be seen as an attempt to detach the meditator from external measurements and to anchor their self-knowledge in their embodied experiences (Pagis, 2008, p. 175). In practice, however, the lack of a clear-cut response from the teachers often leads the meditators into uncertainty so that they turn to one another in order to assess their progress and validate their experiences. As one participant (Kevin) noted, "I've heard people talking about it, you know, 'oh I've experienced the *bhanga* or dissolution.' Not me! [hah] plus, you know, I was never really going for that, I knew I was a plonker."

Doubt about progress figures centrally in disaffiliation narratives. Post-exit this can generate a search for resolution of doubts. In a few instances, these endeavors led participants to *retrospectively* adopt a Buddhist identity after disaffiliation. For instance, Kevin enrolled in an introductory course in Buddhism:

> Kevin: When I was doing Vipassana, I probably didn't think of it as Buddhism [giggle] I thought of it as Vipassana... and therefore to call myself a Buddhist would be a bit silly, cause the Buddhists were doing it wrong!... Now I call myself a Buddhist and think that Vipassana is just one small part of Buddhism.

Examining the disaffiliation narratives one can discern three trajectories (Rahmani, 2019):

1. Drifters in Samsara, who idealized a traditional Theravada approach with strict morality and belief in enlightenment as a transcendental reality *beyond* their reach and agenda for this life.
2. Pursuers of the Gateless Gate, who abandoned the pursuit of enlightenment as transcendental and sought meaning in the concrete experiences of the everyday such as eating, walking, and parenting, as found in interpretations set forth by modernist Zen (i.e., D. T. Suzuki's legacy) and west coast American interpretations of Vipassana (i.e., views pioneered by Jack Kornfield).
3. Deconversion into Secularism, where they leave the universe of Buddhist discourse completely. This only related to one participant in this study.

The first two trajectories retain enduring traces of the movement's language, while giving up a preoccupation with enlightenment.

Narratives of Pragmatic Leavers

Ambivalence in the narrative of Pragmatic Leavers—individuals who disengaged *prior* to developing a commitment—hinged on a dissonance between their experience and their culturally informed expectations of meditation: that happiness is a worthy goal; each person is responsible for their own well-being; self-discovery and self-development are necessary; and meditation *is* an effective technique to deal with these concerns. Participants referenced various scientific literature that promotes secular forms of Buddhist meditation as increasing mental and physical well-being and/or to productivity. Thus:

> Ian: I think the real draw for me came from, um, reading about some of the scientific literature that come back from um, studies done in America with interesting

> findings of just how meditation, um, restructure[s] your brain and that's and the other, lot of other studies just showing how it increases well-being and attention.

Such values shape meditators' imaginations, expectations, and experiences of meditation, and also influence how they experience, rationalize, and negotiate disengagement.

However, ambivalence and even *impatience* could result from the deep-seated dichotomies in the movement's discourse on progress and its marketing strategies, which portray Vipassana as a "universal remedy"; an "easy" and straightforward path to "real happiness"; a "practical" practice attuned to the demands of the conventional life; or simply as an "art of living" (Medini Dhamma, 2017). In reality, as noted before, the purpose of the practice shifts toward other-worldly concerns and enlightenment for individuals within the movement, while the path to real happiness is gradually stretched to demand higher levels of commitment.

Pragmatic Leavers are particularly interested in the experiences they have during meditation. Positive experiences reinforce their enthusiasm, while negative ones generate reflection and interrogation. While all Vipassana meditators valued experience for the sake of the insights and knowledge they gained about themselves, others, and the world, the Pragmatic Leavers wanted to experience something different, extraordinary, and transcendental. In other words, Pragmatic Leavers were to some extent *experience seekers*. Most Pragmatic Leavers framed their first course participation as partly motivated by "curiosity" (e.g., "go and do it and have the full experience"). This perhaps explains why their narratives involved some of the most colorful and detailed depictions of meditative experiences and the fact that all Pragmatic Leavers exhibited a sense of accomplishment for successfully completing a ten-day course, for example, "it was self-confidence boost in that you sort of think 'wow I did that,' I'm silent for ten-days and you know I kept to the rules" and "Vipassana was like running a marathon, now I know I can do it."

Some Pragmatic Leavers who had experienced depersonalization, depression, suicidal ideation, or other negative psychological states understandably used pragmatic language to rationalize their disengagement and make sense of their inactivity. For example, Leslie argued that sitting meditation may be most useful for people who are "body oriented," but that physical activities such as walking in nature or Tai Chi were more relevant for people like themselves who are "head-oriented":

> Leslie: So I found the meditation made me...it almost made me a little depressed more than anything...it doesn't necessarily bring me to a quiet happy peaceful place...and that a lot of that [pause] wasn't interesting enough. Um so, I wasn't finding [pause] hugely useful things about myself, to pay attention to, or to work on, or, great insight...I don't know if that's terrible, [I'm] probably a failed meditator...I think I find I get, nourish by the natural world so much...that [pause] yeah putting in, so much in my own world, does feel like it's cutting off, a big part of the bigger world that we inhabit.

Meditators who reported negative experiences tended to be skeptical of the movement's claims of practicality and usefulness for conventional life. For instance, Andrew's meditative experiences (depersonalization) led him to conclude that ten-day Vipassana courses and the state of mind that arises from them are impractical for a person leading a "daily life" and belong to "monks" with "very little responsibility outside [who] got the space to be crazy." For those who thought meditation to be an undemanding, painless relaxation technique that calms the mind and takes the practitioner to a "quiet, happy, peaceful place" such experience was a shock. These people tended to revert to less demanding physical activities.

Ambivalences regarding the efficacy of meditation tended to come from those who had difficulty in doing it, due to inability to concentrate or otherwise. However, many of these people, despite having arrived at the movement thinking about their spiritual search—"search for truth," "finding answers to life's big questions," and so on—now reverted to a more pragmatic, secular assessment—"time restrictions," "not seeing results." This enabled them to rationalize disengagement through a cost-benefit logic *without explicitly* having to question the *efficacy* of the practice or considering their own spiritual progress. Many felt guilt, remorse, and even anger in response to the expectations that they had taken upon themselves, such as keeping a regular practice of two hours of meditation each day for the sake of one's happiness, well-being, and progress, and/or expectations of experiencing extraordinary meditative states (such as dissolution).

> Katrin: I guess that's probably not the right attitude when you do meditation, but I kind of wanted to see outcomes... but I couldn't really see outcomes... I guess the reason why I kept doing it was I've been reading so much about it for my research in my PhD that always told me meditation is great for you and um very beneficial and hundreds of reasons why I should do it and I thought alright!... now that I reflect back on the last year, I don't know if my life has changed, maybe because I'm pregnant [giggle] I'm just happy in general, but I feel that I've got a good life, and I guess, I'm less desperate than I was maybe a year before, so I think that meditation must have had, an impact on my life, a good one.

As this passage demonstrates, Katrin harbors ambivalence about the efficacy of meditation. On the one hand, showing some self-deprecation, Katrin suggests that she had stopped meditation because she could not "see outcomes"; on the other, she concludes that meditation "must have had an impact" because she now feels content with herself (self-acceptance) and her life. After disengagement from Vipassana, Pragmatic Leavers who felt frustrated and impatient often gravitated toward practices with more easily accomplished goals and tangible outcomes.

Finally, ambivalence was also present in the narratives of those Pragmatic Leavers who passionately reported positive meditative experiences, which they construed as "glimpses of enlightenment," "entering nirvana," or "transcending the self." However, in these cases, the ambivalence is mainly anchored on conflict between (1) mundane and spiritual motives, aims, and desires, and (2) the idea that the practice is unsuitable for the conventional, everyday environment and its "distractions." Their doubts were about *practicality* rather than efficacy. They commonly fantasized about deferring spiritual development to a later phase in life, when they have fulfilled their conventional responsibilities, being unable to recreate their unique experiences in the everyday environment. Put simply, participants with positive extraordinary experiences presented narratives of conflicted selves torn between the inescapable mundane and the irresistible transcendent. Take, for instance, the following statements in which Matilda, who reported experiencing "glimpses of enlightenment" during meditation, explains why she is unable to fully commit to Vipassana:

> Matilda: I agree with the, what they do at the course, not eating meat, I have this funny thing where I kind of belie[ve] that for a spiritual journey that definitely no meat, is a really good idea but then... So I have this total conflict in my head where my body wants one thing [giggle] my mind wants the other... I feel like I would be, sacrificing other things in my life, for example my, relationship, so my husband, um, my relationship with my daughter, so my role as a parent to a certain degree. um and also sort of like, my, my passions, so in art practice my painting... you know I might hit sixty or eighty or who knows and be like, yeah! now I'm ready. Bye to my daughter, I'll see you once a year I'm gonna be in the Vipassana. Bless. See you later!

Matilda's statement raises serious questions about the relevance of this laicized version of Vipassana meditation marketed for individuals living a conventionally domestic life in an increasingly secularized society. Matilda prioritizes her roles as mother, wife, and artist over the idea of a spiritually oriented self. Finally, Pragmatic Leavers who reported positive meditative experience did not emphasize a need to actively search for another tradition/practice after their disengagement. Instead, they considered the possibility that they may someday return to the Vipassana center, which they perceived as a spiritual haven. However, similar to other Pragmatic Leavers, most tended to integrate the insights gained from Vipassana (e.g., awareness) with other practices, most typically yoga.

Conclusion

This chapter explored the role of Goenka's modernist Buddhist language in shaping unique patterns of conversion and disengagement. I introduced the concept of tacit conversion as a framework for conceptualizing the commitment of individuals to groups in which the denial of conversion is inherent to its universe of discourse. I examined four often-interrelated rhetorical strategies used by Goenka—experience, tool, pure teachings of the Buddha, and here and now—and demonstrated how they functioned to conceal the religious elements of the movement for its committed followers. Yet, while the emphasis on experience was an effective rhetoric for rendering conversion tacit, it also failed to sustain membership in the long run and caused significant self-doubt for many practitioners who had no external resource to measure their progress. This was particularly relevant to the disaffiliates, who left after years of intense involvement. The analyses of their narratives indicated that in the vast majority of cases (with the exception of one deconversion narrative), disaffiliation did not result in *total* rejection of the movement's system of meaning and that they also sustained an intellectual commitment to the above mentioned rhetoric; nor did it result in complete migration outside of the Buddhist universe of discourse. Rather it involved a reorientation toward the concept of enlightenment, which could be imagined on a continuum between traditional Theravada and modernist Zen conceptions of enlightenment.

Another reason that Goenka's approach resonates with many (committed or non-committed) Vipassana practitioners is that his discourse taps into a certain anxiety they had about religion due to their experiences with their parents' religion (Christianity) and that it accommodates their values (see Table 29.1). Indeed, the analysis of disengagement narratives demonstrates that as the result of the harmony between, on the one hand, the movement's linguistic strategies and ideologies, namely claims of rationality, universality, and instrumentality, their dispute of religious labels, and emphasis on experience, scientific rhetoric, individual responsibility, self-development, and, on the other, the dominant cultural dispositions in New Zealand (which itself values these ideas), which limits the ability of current and former members to question the efficacy of the practice, even when their personal experiences suggest otherwise. This, in addition to the vast array of positive discourse surrounding meditation authored by psychologists and others in contemporary scientific publications can leave little room for former meditators to articulate their dissatisfactions in any other terms than doubting their own abilities.

Socio-cultural trends shape effective language, and the use of such language leads to the popularity of meditation groups molding the public's expectations and imagination of what can be achieved by these practices. As shown, the Pragmatic Leavers' commitment to these ideas steered the ways in which they negotiated their disengagement: by utilizing specific forms of language (pragmatic and dualistic) that enabled them to avoid questioning the efficacy, practicality, or universal applicability of meditation, or in fact, to avoid jeopardizing the value of their spiritual seekership by rendering its growth stalled.

Finally, the four rhetorics explored in this chapter are by no means an exhaustive list, nor exclusively unique to Goenka's movement. Similar patterns of reasoning can be traced in the discourse of other contemporary meditation groups such as the Mindfulness movement that have drawn inspirations from Goenka's approach. The ideas presented here may inspire a more careful examination of the language that meditation groups tactfully use to maintain a blurred boundary between the religious and the secular and hold a fast-and-loose association with Buddhism in order to relish the positive image of the tradition (peacefulness, direct link to the Buddha, etc.) and discard its other connotations.

References

Barbour, J. D. (1994). *Versions of deconversion: Autobiography and the loss of faith*. Charlottesville: University of Virginia Press.

Berger, P. L. (1999).The desecularization of the world: A global overview. In P. L. Berger (Ed.), *The desecularization of the world: Resurgent religion and world politics* (pp. 1–18). Grand Rapids, MI: Wm. B. Eerdmans.

Berger, P. L., & Luckmann, T. (1967). *The social construction of reality*. Garden City: Doubleday-Anchor.

Braun, E. (2013). *The birth of insight: meditation, modern Buddhism, and the Burmese monk Ledi Sayadaw*. Chicago: University of Chicago Press.

Brekke, T. (2003). Conversion in Buddhism? In R. Robinson & S. Clarke (Eds.), *Religious conversion in India: Modes, motivations, and meanings* (pp. 181–191). Delhi: Oxford University Press, USA.

Brinkerhoff, M. B., & Mackie, M. M. (1993). Casting off the bonds of organized religion: A religious-careers approach to the study of apostasy. *Review of Religious Research 4*(3), 235–258.

Bromley, D. G. (2004). Leaving the fold: Disaffiliating from new religious movements. In J. R. Lewis (Ed.), *The Oxford handbook of new religious movements* (pp. 298–314). Oxford: Oxford University Press.

Bromley, D. G. (2006). Affiliation and disaffiliation careers in new religious movements. In E. V. Gallagher & W. M. Ashcraft (Eds.), *Introduction to new and alternative religions in America: Vol. 1. History and controversies* (pp. 42–64). Westport, CT: Greenwood.

Buckser, A., & Glazier, S. D. (2003). *The anthropology of religious conversion*. Lanham: Rowman & Littlefield.

Coates, D. (2013). Disaffiliation from a new religious movement: The importance of self and others in exit. *Symbolic Interaction 36*(3), 314–334.

Deleanu, F. (2010). Agnostic meditations on Buddhist meditation. *Zygon: Journal of Religion & Science 45*(3), 605–626.

Goenka, S. N. (1997). *Discourse summaries*. Onalaska, WA: Vipassana Research Institute.

Goldberg, K., & Décary, M. (2013). *Along the path: The meditator's companion to the Buddha's land*. 2nd ed. Onalaska, WA: Pariyatti.

Gombrich, R. F. (2006). *Theravada Buddhism: A social history from ancient Benares to modern Colombo*. London: Routledge.

Gombrich, R. F., & Obeyesekere, G. (1988). *Buddhism transformed: Religious change in Sri Lanka*. Delhi: Motilal Banarsidass.

Hart, W. (1987). *The art of living: Vipassana meditation as taught by S. N. Goenka*. Onalaska, WA: Pariyatti.

Healy, J. P. (2011). Involvement in a new religious movement: From discovery to disenchantment. *Journal of Spirituality in Mental Health 13*(1), 2–21.

Heirich, M. (1977). Change of heart: A test of some widely held theories about religious conversion. *American Journal of Sociology* 83(3), 653–680.

Loss, J. (2010). Buddha-Dhamma in Israel: Explicit non-religious and implicit non-secular localization of religion. *Nova Religio: The Journal of Alternative and Emergent Religions 13*(4), 84–105.

McMahan, D. L. (2008). *The making of Buddhist modernism*. Oxford: Oxford University Press.

Medini Dhamma. (2017). *Vipassana Meditation Center*. Retrieved from http://medini.dhamma.org/center-2/

Medini Dhamma. (2017). *Vipassana: The technique.* Retrieved from http://medini.dhamma.org/vipassana/vipassana-technique/

Melnikova, N. (2014). *The modern school of Vipassana—A Buddhist tradition?* (Doctoral dissertation). Masaryk University, Brno.

Pagis, M. (2008). *Cultivating selves: Vipassana meditation and the microsociology of experience* (Doctoral dissertation). University of Chicago.

Pagis, M. (2010b). From abstract concepts to experiential knowledge: Embodying enlightenment in a meditation center. *Qualitative Sociology 33*(4), 469–489.

Rahmani, M. (2017). *Tacit conversion and disengagement in Goenka's Vipassana movement in New Zealand* (Doctoral dissertation). University of Otago, Dunedin.

Rahmani, M. (2019). Leaving Vipassana meditation. In D. Enstedt, G. Larsson, & T. Mantsinen (Eds.), *Handbook of leaving religion* (pp. 130–141). Leiden: Brill.

Rahmani, M. (2020). Tacit conversion: A linguistic analysis of a Vipassana meditator's narrative of self-transformation. In S. Sremac & I. W. Jindra (Eds.), *Lived religion, conversion and recovery: Negotiating of self, the social, and the sacred* (pp. 121–146). Cham: Palgrave Macmillan.

Rawlinson, A. (1997). *The book of enlightened masters: Western teachers in Eastern traditions.* Chicago: Open Court.

Sharf, R. H. (1995). Buddhist modernism and the rhetoric of meditative experience. *Numen 42*(3), 228–283.

Sharf, R. H. (2015). Is mindfulness Buddhist? (and why it matters). *Transcultural Psychiatry 52*(4), 470–484.

Singh, H. (2007). *A critique of Vipassana meditation as taught by Mr S N Goenka.* Retrieved from https://eldar.cz/kangaroo/mirror/vipassana-critique.pdf

Snow, D. A., & Machalek, R. (1983). The convert as a social type. *Sociological Theory 1*, 259–289.

Staples, C. L., & Mauss, A. L. (1987). Conversion or commitment? A reassessment of the Snow and Machalek approach to the study of conversion. *Journal for the Scientific Study of Religion 26*(2), 133–147.

Streib, H., Silver, C. F., Csöff, R. M., Keller, B., & Hood, R. W. (2011). *Deconversion: Qualitative and quantitative results from cross-cultural research in Germany and the United States of America.* Göttingen: Vandenhoeck & Ruprecht.

Stromberg, P. G. (2014). The role of language in religious conversion. In L. R. Rambo & C. E. Farhadian (Eds.), *The Oxford handbook of religious conversion* (pp. 117–139). Oxford: Oxford University Press.

VRI Dhamma (2014). *Talks and answers to questions from Vipassana students, 1983–2000.* Retrieved from http://www.vridhamma.org/uploadedfiles/BenefitofMany.pdf

Wallace, B. A. (2002). The spectrum of Buddhist practice in the West. In C. S. Prebish & M. Baumann (Eds.), *Westward Dharma: Buddhism beyond Asia* (pp. 34–50). Berkeley: University of California Press.

Wright, S. A. (1984). Post-involvement attitudes of voluntary defectors from controversial new religious movements. *Journal for the Scientific Study of Religion 23*(2), 172–182.

Wright, S. A. (1991). Reconceptualizing cult coercion and withdrawal: A comparative analysis of divorce and apostasy. *Social Forces 70*(1), 125–147.

Yü, D. S. (2014). Buddhist conversion in the contemporary world. In L. R. Rambo & C. E. Farhadian (Eds.), *The Oxford handbook of religious conversion* (pp. 465–487). Oxford: Oxford University Press.

CHAPTER 30

MEDITATION IN CONTEMPORARY MONASTIC LIFE

CAROLINE STARKEY

Introduction

The image of the solitary Buddhist monk with his shaven head and saffron robes, deep in silent meditation, has come to represent the epitome of otherworldly concentration. There is an almost timeless quality to this image, at least in the Western imagination, and a sense that through meditation and monastic vows the Buddhist monk and his spiritual practice are completely set apart from the mundane, the temporal, and the communal. However, as Eifring (2015, p. 3) states, "even when seeking to reach a dimension beyond all phenomena, [meditation] is clearly situated within the social, cultural, and historical context in which it is practiced."

In this chapter, I take this proposition seriously and examine closely the role of meditation in one particular social and cultural context: that of contemporary British Buddhism. More specifically, I focus my analysis on the diverse experiences of convert monastic women. This heterogeneous group has received relatively little academic attention, despite Buddhism's recent growth in popularity in Britain and the steady increase in numbers of people wanting to make formal commitments to Buddhist practices and monastic communities.

According to the 2011 census, there are 238,626 Buddhists in England and Wales, an increase of 100,000 from the previous census in 2001 (O.N.S, 2012). Approximately 35 percent of these are from White British backgrounds and it is likely that these are converts or from convert families. Data about monastic Buddhist women is not collected in such a systematic way, however I estimate that there are likely to be around 500 monastic women connected formally or informally to various Buddhist groups in

Britain. There are currently more male than female monastics on the basis that there are a greater number of monastic communities in Britain that cater to men. While the numbers of Buddhist monastics in the British context are still relatively small, attention to their experiences can help us think carefully about the ways in which meditation (both in idea and practice) has crossed geographic and temporal boundaries and is shaped by the particular local contexts and individual communities within which it is translated and adapted.

To explore this, I draw on detailed ethnographic research conducted between 2010 and 2014 with seventeen Buddhist convert monastic women in the British context who were connected to six different Buddhist traditions and schools (Tibetan Karma Kagyu, Nyingma, Gelug, Pure Land, Theravada, and Sōtō Zen). This research forms part of a monograph (Starkey, 2020) exploring the experiences of women (both monastic and non-monastic) in contemporary British Buddhism. The meaning of the term "monastic" and the adoption of particular religious practices and lifestyle restrictions differs between the Buddhist groups in this study and I discuss these differences further as the chapter progresses. It is important to note that not all of the groups considered here follow the traditional Buddhist monastic code known as the *vinaya*, as specific adaptations to monastic regulations have occurred as Buddhism migrated across Asia and, later, to the West (see Holt, 1995). For the purposes of this chapter, I have classified someone as a monastic if they have made a specific and (typically) institutionally sanctioned commitment to Buddhist practice that is likely to involve some form of renunciation (for example, of work, money, family, food, and associated changes to physical appearance such as robes or tonsure); if they also refer to themselves as "monastic," "monk," or "nun"; and if this was envisaged at the time to be a life-long commitment (see also Starkey, 2014). For some scholars and practitioners, the categories "monastic" or "ordained" should be reserved for those who had taken full *bhikkhu* or *bhikkhunī* ordination; however this does not reflect how the terms are used in a UK context and correspondingly, I adopt a more inclusive definition here (Salgado, 2004).

All of the women discussed in this chapter were British nationals or had spent a significant amount of time connected to British Buddhist monastic communities. They lived in temples and monasteries, small Buddhist centers or communities, or independently across the British Isles. Each had converted to Buddhism in adulthood, the majority while they were living in Britain. Their experiences of meditation will be explored using two principal foci. The first is an analysis of the ways that meditation functions in women's early connections with Buddhism and their later desire to make formal, monastic commitments. The second is a critical discussion about the way in which meditation is woven into their daily lives. Through both lenses, I conduct a close analysis of original interview data and ethnographic observation and, at key points, compare and contrast these experiences with those of renunciant Buddhist women outside Britain. In doing this, I draw attention to the impact of temporal and geographic location in shaping monastic engagement with Buddhist meditation practices.

Providing descriptive detail about specific meditation practices or rituals is not the primary aim of this chapter, nor will I conduct a comprehensive overview of the histories of meditation and Buddhist monasticism in different countries. One could turn to Cook (2010) as an excellent example of an anthropological analysis of meditation in contemporary Thai monastic life, for example, or to scholarship that investigates meditation within early Buddhist texts such as that provided by Shaw (2006). What I explore (after providing a contextual overview) is the multi-faceted role that meditation plays in the lives of contemporary Buddhist monastic women and, in doing so, enable a more holistic picture of its value in a lived sense. Specifically, I argue that even though private silent meditation practice is often lauded as the sine qua non of contemporary Western Buddhism (Coleman, 2001, pp. 197–199) meditation should not be seen as something entirely set apart from communal daily living or other ritual and devotional practices, nor should its collective role in bringing and binding Buddhist groups together be underestimated.

Meditation and Buddhist (Monastic) Life

The renunciant monastic tradition that is now associated with many forms of contemporary Buddhism was initiated by the historical Buddha, Siddhartha Gautama (ca. sixth century BCE). It is said that following his enlightenment at the age of thirty-five, the Buddha offered his initial teachings to five former ascetic men who, with modest ritual initiation, became his first official renunciant followers (Gethin, 1998, p. 87; Prebish, 2007, p. 653). This community of male renunciants or monks (*bhikkhu*) grew and, sometime later, an order of female renunciants or nuns (*bhikkhunī*) was also established (for a detailed history, see Wijayaratna, 1990, 2010). For the early *saṅgha* (Buddhist community), relinquishing marriage and sexual relationships, ceasing working for money, being reliant on alms donated by lay supporters, and participating in a mendicant lifestyle owning few possessions is represented as an ideal way of life (Tsomo, 1999, p. 5). Although, as Silber (1981) highlights, the initial model for monastic Buddhist life was that of the "wandering mendicant" (only resting in one place during the annual rains retreat, or *vassa*), this changed later as more stable monastic communities developed.

The Buddha did not construct all the rules and regulations for his new followers in one sitting. The practices that were adopted by the *saṅgha* developed in response to problems or concerns arising within the early communities (Lopez, 2001, p. 140). Regulations and guidance were initially given orally by the Buddha, and then later compiled into written form (according to Schopen [2004, p. 329], in the first four to five hundred years of the Common Era) within the *Vinaya Piṭaka* scriptures, which include a list of rules (*pāṭimokkha/prātimokṣa*) for monks and nuns to follow (Harvey, 1990, p. 224). After the Buddha's death, and as his teachings spread beyond their Indian homeland, monastic practice changed as different Buddhist schools were established and as local need arose, although the routine of ordination continues to be shaped in various ways by translations of the *vinaya* (Gethin, 1998, p. 88). As Harvey (1990, p. 224) states, "*vinaya*" means "that by which one is led out (from suffering)," and, as I will show, "suffering" remains a significant concept for contemporary Buddhist practitioners in Britain (Starkey, 2020). Following a religious and philosophical path which recognizes the universality of suffering, dissatisfaction, or stress (*dukkha/duḥkha*) leading toward its cessation is the purpose of Buddhist spiritual life and is central to the Four Noble Truths as expounded by the Buddha. According to Conze (1982, p. 20), "the purpose of the *vinaya* rules was to provide the ideal conditions for meditation and renunciation." Although achieving Buddhism's soteriological goals as a lay person is certainly possible, for many Buddhist traditions the monastic way of life is seen as more conducive to spiritual attainment (Cantwell & Kawanami, 2002, p. 45). This is principally because monasticism is deemed to enable more time to focus on the *Buddha-dhamma* (the teachings of the Buddha), away from the daily distraction of marriage, work, and children, including more regular and intense periods of meditation. The Buddha's advice on meditation contained within the Pali texts is directed at monks, despite evidence that the laity were also engaged in practice (Shaw, 2006, p. 12).

The purpose of meditation in Buddhism is exemplified in the Buddha's experiences under the Bodhi tree, where he vowed not to relinquish his meditative state until he understood the true nature of reality, despite being tormented by Māra, the personification of death (Harvey, 1990, pp. 20–21). Throughout one night, the Buddha was said to have been able to recollect his past lives and understand the ways to end suffering and rebirth through his attainment of various meditative states (Harvey, 1990, pp. 21–22). Although the word "meditation" in English has no direct Buddhist equivalent, and Shaw (2006, p. 3) suggests that the Pali *bhāvanā* (which she translates as "production or cultivation") is the most appropriate comparable term, the practice of focused awareness and absorption (*samadhi*) is a central facet of a Buddhist way of life, in conjunction with wisdom or insight (*paññā*) and ethics (*sīla*) (Shaw, 2006, p. 3). Although its individual impact can be difficult to articulate, arguably the overall purpose of Buddhist meditation is to objectively recognize the vacillations of our own minds and temperaments in order to enable a "transformative waking up" to the true nature of reality and existence (Harvey, 2013, p. 318). Buddhist meditation practice is commonly divided into calm (*samatha/śamatha*) and insight (*vipassanā/vipaśyanā*) (Shaw, 2006, p. 18). In practice one encounters many different techniques and approaches, which are variously adopted by different monastic (and lay) practitioners across Buddhist communities. These include seated meditation focusing on the breath or other objects of attention such as *koans* (thought-provoking statements) or images of enlightened beings, the development of loving-kindness (*mettā*), walking meditation, and practices such as prostrations, chanting mantras, and *pūjā* (ritual devotion), and writing or copying Buddhist scriptures and texts. Observances such as chanting or prostrations might not always be considered "meditation." However, as I show in this chapter, rigid distinctions between "meditation" and "devotional practice" are blurred by my participants, as are the divisions between silent seated meditation and paying close and careful attention to tasks in daily life, such as cleaning, washing, or cooking. What I aim to do here is to question the assumed boundaries of "meditation" and how this relates to contemporary Buddhist monastics in their everyday lives.

In terms of Buddhism in Britain (and the West more broadly), silent meditation is generally considered to be a (if not *the*) central practice, especially among convert Buddhists (Bluck, 2006, p. 192; McMahan, 2008, p. 183). Although writing over two decades ago, Bell (1991, p. 155) argues that meditation "defines a person as a Buddhist in Britain" and both she and Waterhouse (1997, p. 54) highlight that an interest in learning to meditate (as a form of self-improvement) attracts British people to Buddhism. The emphasis on meditation among convert Buddhists is deemed by Bell (2000) to be given greater priority in British Buddhism than the practice of *dāna* or *puñña* (merit making), although this may be changing. A wide range of meditation techniques are regularly taught at British Buddhist centers and groups, typically on a donation basis, and include weekly classes and longer residential and non-residential retreats. On any one given evening, Buddhist meditation groups (either as introductory classes or gatherings for more experienced meditators) are meeting all across the country in dedicated Buddhist temples and centers, hired spaces, and private homes, and the number of groups continues to grow (Starkey & Tomalin, 2016).

While a key feature of British Buddhism is the dominant role given to lay Buddhists, Bluck (2006, p. 182) found that in terms of meditation, the practices that have now become established on British shores strongly mirror the approaches of "parent traditions" (often based outside the UK) with little formal adaptation, including for those groups who predominantly engage converts or members of convert families. Yet Buddhism in Britain encompasses more than just the groups catering for "White British converts," even though academic attention has typically focused on these Buddhist groups and experiences (Bluck, 2006, p. 16). More recent work, such as Thanissaro (2014), Smith, Munt, and Yip (2016), Starkey and Tomalin (2016), and Page and Yip (2017) have given more attention to "heritage" experiences of Buddhism in the British context, although it is clear that more work is necessary to fully understand the diverse ways in which Buddhism generally, and meditation specifically, is practiced in Britain.

Buddhist Monasticism in Britain

Although monastic practice is certainly not as dominant either numerically or culturally as lay Buddhist practice in Britain, the endeavor to establish sustainable monastic communities is a key part of British Buddhist history. There were notable early attempts to bring Buddhist monasticism to Britain, for example by Ananda Metteyya (born Henry Alan Bennett), who was ordained in Burma in 1902, returning to Britain as a monk in 1908 but who eventually disrobed following difficulties maintaining the monastic lifestyle in the British climate (Batchelor, 1994, p. 40). There were also British and Irish nationals who took Buddhist monastic ordination outside of the United Kingdom, for example U Dhammaloka (Turner, Cox, & Bocking, 2010). Slightly later, in 1926, the London Buddhist *vihara* was opened as "the first missionary *vihara* to be founded outside the Asian continent" by Anagarika Dharmapala, and this housed a small group of Sinhalese monks until the Second World War, but was later re-opened in 1955 in Knightsbridge (Scott, 1981).

It was, however, post-1950s, following wide-scale social changes in religious affiliation and increased interest in global travel and alternative spiritual forms (particularly those from the East) that more successful Buddhist monastic communities began to appear, particularly in the 1960s and 1970s (Bluck, 2006, pp. 11–12). Alongside a pattern of visiting monastics and lay teachers from different Buddhist traditions and countries, prominent examples of monastery establishment include Samye Ling in Scotland, the first Tibetan Buddhist center in the West, founded by Chogyam Trungpa Rinpoche and Akong Tulku Rinpoche, and Throssel Hole, the Northumberland Sōtō Zen monastery established by Reverend Master Jiyu Kennett (born Peggy Kennett) in 1972. The first Thai temple, also supporting a small group of Thai missionary monks, Wat Buddhapadipa, was established in 1966, moving to their current premises in Wimbledon in 1976. In addition, the English Sangha Trust (EST), who had been struggling for some time to launch a sustainable Theravada *sangha* in Britain, invited American monk Ajahn Sumedho, ordained in Thailand in the lineage of Ajahn Chah, to live at the Hampstead Buddhist *vihara* in 1977 with three other *bhikkhus* (Batchelor, 1994, p. 42). In 1979, the EST bought a larger property in Sussex, which became Cittaviveka monastery and, in the early 1980s, purchased another property in Hertfordshire—a former school and summer camp—which became Amaravati monastery: two examples of the successful transplantation of Buddhist monasticism outside Asia. Buddhist monastic communities in Britain are now found connected to purpose-built temples, in adapted listed buildings in both urban and rural locations, and in small semi-detached houses, typically in suburban areas. In a recent study, funded by Historic England, Tomalin and Starkey (2016) identified that in England alone, there are approximately ninety different Buddhist buildings that are public-facing and provide accommodation for monastics, and this number does not include monks and nuns living alone in private houses nor those monks visiting different venues across the United Kingdom on a temporary basis to give teachings. Taken together, this is evidence of a small, yet thriving monastic element to British Buddhist practice (see also, Starkey & Tomalin, 2016).

Women have played an important, although certainly less charted, role in the development of British Buddhist monastic communities. From high-profile figures founding monastic orders (such as the aforementioned Jiyu Kennett), to pioneers of innovative renunciant practice such as the Thai Forest Sangha *sīladharā* (Angell, 2006), to less publicly prominent, although no less significant, female monastics, women have helped to build and maintain Buddhism in Britain (Starkey, 2020).There is diversity in monastic practice, living situation, and approach adopted by Buddhist women in Britain, and this partly is reflective of the differences between different traditions, including in their attitude to female ordination. Not all Buddhist groups authorize women to take an equivalent monastic ordination to men, although the reasons for this are beyond the scope of this chapter to explore (see, for example, Mohr & Tsedroen, 2010; Tsomo, 1988). The women who were part of my research had each taken a varied number of vows or precepts to guide their daily lives, ranging from five to over three hundred. These vows typically incorporate the "Five Precepts," which are held in common with many lay Buddhists across the world: not to kill, steal, talk falsely, take intoxicating substances, or practice sexual misconduct. Monastic vows characteristically regulate the intricacies of daily life in great detail, including structuring the time of day one might eat a meal, what is worn and owned, proper deportment in public and private, and the ways that one must behave toward other monastics and the laity. Those connected to Mahāyāna Buddhist traditions also take variations on *bodhisattva* vows, which prioritize the liberation of all sentient beings on the route to enlightenment. For some of the women (for example, those in the Tibetan traditions), the vows that they had taken mirrored exactly the vows taken by nuns outside of the United Kingdom in the same tradition. However, others (for example, those associated with the Pureland Amida Trust, or the Sōtō Zen Order of Buddhist Contemplatives) take precepts written and adapted specifically for a UK or Western context, albeit based closely on Buddhist monastic vows of their respective schools. Although comparing monastic vows and the ways that they are currently implemented across the Buddhist world would be an extensive exercise, beyond the scope of this chapter, what is most helpful for our purposes here is to examine the different ways in which monastic daily living might differ for women across the Buddhist schools and groups in Britain, a theme that will be revisited as this chapter progresses.

Of the seventeen monastic women interviewed, eight lived in communal monastic settings and nine lived independently or as the sole monastic connected to a lay Buddhist community. In some monastic settings, men and women live together in the same buildings (for example, Throssel Hole Buddhist Abbey in Northumberland), but in others (such as Samye Ling in Eskdalemuir, Scotland), male and female monastics live in adjacent properties. Of those women living independently, three lived with partners and families and had to hold down jobs and maintain familial responsibilities alongside their monastic vows, including, for some, looking after their children (see also, Starkey, 2014). However, it is important to note here that being able to take monastic ordination and still maintain a direct responsibility for children or live with a partner is unusual and only occurred among certain Tibetan practitioners in this context. All of the monastic women I interviewed wore monastic robes of different colors and types, and many shaved their heads to reflect the commitments they had made on ordination, including celibacy. Those in the Forest Sangha relinquished money and the ownership of property, but again this was not a practice adopted by every Buddhist monastic across the board. This begins to highlight the significant diversity of lifestyle between monastic Buddhist women in the British context, and as I will later discuss, these differences have an impact on women's relationships to, and practice of, meditation.

Meditation and the Attraction of Buddhism

For the majority of women involved in my research, meditation was in some way formative both in their initial introduction to Buddhism and in their later decision to follow a monastic or renunciant path. It is meditation that attracted many of them to Buddhist groups and teachers initially, and it is shared meditation practice that continues to connect them over decades. None of the women had Buddhist family backgrounds, and each of them made their commitment to Buddhism in adulthood, most in their twenties or thirties. In fact, perhaps unusually in the arguably post-Christian context of contemporary Britain, the majority had strongly Christian backgrounds (Gilbert, 1980). For most, this was either within the Church of England or the Roman Catholic Church. Although for a small number this engagement was nominal, many narrated a powerful sense of religious dedication and commitment even from a young age. This may be a partial explanation as to why they eventually made the commitment to live as full time *religieuses*.

For a few women, the desire to learn how to meditate precipitated a concerted search, mostly in their local area, for a Buddhist group or teacher. In some cases, this was because they had experienced anxiety or depression and they felt that meditation would be one way to assist them to cope with this. This motivation is a reflection of the fact that in the past twenty years, meditation, particularly in secular, but also in Buddhist forms, has come to public prominence in Britain as a way to improve mental health (Cook, 2016). This has had an impact on British Buddhist groups, giving them increasing prominence in the public sphere, arguably bolstering their legitimacy and acceptability in the eyes of the wider non-Buddhist public and the state. Although this has yet to be understood fully, this move has increased the traffic to certain British Buddhist centers. Those women who became involved with Buddhist groups after the millennium were more likely to have been attracted to Buddhism as a result of hearing about the efficacy of meditation in the promotion of health and well-being. They were attracted to the perceived therapeutic benefits of meditation, particularly as emphasized in *samatha* practices and those that focus on the breath, as these are seen as having a noticeable impact on levels of anxiety, depression, and general well-being. However, those connecting with Buddhism in the decades before the millennium described a more ineffable feeling of being compelled to try new spiritual practices because of a perceived past-life connection or some more transcendent feeling of being drawn to iconography or ideas with a cosmological and soteriological slant, for example about *karma, nirvana*, or *bodhicitta* (compassion for all sentient beings). With the growing prominence of mindfulness and the popular association between meditation and positive mental well-being, it is perhaps not surprising that a therapeutic interest in meditation is increasingly shaping the initial trajectory of British monastic women's early engagements with Buddhism, and this is likely to continue.

Yet a deliberate and conscientious search for meditation instruction wasn't the most common introductory trajectory found among the women in this study (see also, Starkey, 2020). In the majority of cases, women learnt about Buddhist practices and teachings in more accidental ways—either being introduced to teachers and groups through friends or partners, coming across Buddhist temples while traveling outside of the United Kingdom, or hearing Buddhist monastic teachers speak and wanting to find out more. Meditation does feature in this more organic connection to Buddhism as, after these initial introductions, it is the experience of meditation practice that is described as particularly captivating. Meditation instruction is equally available for lay men and women in Britain, and none of the monastic women indicated any early difficulty accessing particular teachings on the grounds of their gender, or any overt assumptions made about their abilities to practice meditation as lay women. For one Theravada nun, the techniques that she was introduced to were "immediately accessible" and this was mirrored by a Sōtō Zen female monk ("monk" is the title given to both male and female monastics in this particular tradition). She said: "the meditation just made total sense to me... [I had] found the most meaningful thing in my life". One Tibetan Gelug nun, who had only visited a Buddhist monastery when she fell ill while travelling around Asia, described how she went along to a meditation session, which "blew me away," and her continued practice in just one week "started to open up channels and thoughts and feelings that I didn't know existed." It was as a direct result of this experience that she made a formal commitment to Buddhism as a lay practitioner, and began a thirty-year journey that would later see her ordain as a nun and participate in a number of long meditation retreats, sometimes for extended periods in complete solitude. For others, meditation might not have been the first thing they were attracted to, but they describe a slowly deepening affiliation with the practice over a number of years, narrating this more along the lines of a "gradual growing of my practice and engagement with it." In each of these journeys, however, it is meditation that is a common thread.

This common thread endures when we investigate women's motivations to follow a monastic path. Wanting more time and space to focus on meditation was cited as a reason to consider monasticism in a significant number of cases. A Thai Forest Sangha *sīladharā* explained that, although she had "put a lot of energy into... attending meditation groups" as a lay person, the pull of monastic renunciant life was the ability to "make a whole-hearted commitment to one thing," namely meditation and Buddhist practice. One nun in the Tibetan Karma Kagyu school felt that in lay life she wasn't able to "come to grips with practice," only "dipping here, dipping there." Through making a monastic commitment, the theory was that she would be able to focus more successfully. As I will discuss in the next section, this isn't always the experience in practice in the modern world, particularly in a cultural context where Buddhist monasticism has only a very recent history and is not promoted by the state. However, the impression of monastic life that women typically hold is one that is pared back, streamlined, and ultimately dedicated to a thorough investigation of the Buddha's teaching through meditation. This perception of renunciant life was also highlighted in an earlier study of the Thai Forest Sangha in Britain in the 1980s (Goswell, 1988) and remains significant now and across Buddhist traditions (Starkey, 2020). This also reflects similar motivations for monastic ordination given in first-person accounts by other Western Buddhist nuns in the United States and Europe (for example, Chodron, 1999; Tsedroen, 1988).

The connection between motivations for renunciation and meditation are not always presented as so sharply defined in scholarship on Buddhist women in Asian contexts. In her study of a Northern Thai monastery, Cook (2010, p. 67) identifies that for both men and women there were a range of motivations for renunciation, which included a desire to focus on meditation practice but also those which appear somewhat more social in nature, such as furthering educational aspirations and upholding promises made to family members during times of ill-health. In a study of Taiwanese Buddhist nuns, Crane (2004) also calls attention to social as well as spiritual motivations for renunciation, as ordination was seen as a way to avoid unwanted marriage, a concern also raised in Gutschow's (2004, p. 136) study of Zangskari nuns.

These types of social motivation are never mentioned in the narratives of Western Buddhist nuns in Britain, who give clear priority to the focus on spiritual practice, including meditation, as their rationale for ordination. This is certainly not because they are somehow inherently more spiritually orientated than monastics in other contexts. It is more likely to reflect their different social and economic status prior to ordination, the social circumstances of the countries within which they live, and the culturally conditioned ways in which they are expected to narrate their religious journeys. In Britain, monastic women, particularly in "convert" focused groups, are likely to be middle class, highly educated, and economically self-sufficient, turning to Buddhism after successful careers and, quite often, marriages and parenthood. There is, arguably, less stigma associated with being unmarried in contemporary Britain and less pressure on young women to conform to particular ways of being and living than in the settings described by Crane (2004) or Gutschow (2004). There is little need to turn to Buddhist ordination to avoid marriage in the British context; indeed, becoming a Buddhist nun is a far more unusual choice than remaining single. Furthermore, with the typical emphasis given by British convert Buddhist communities on the importance of individual meditation practice and personal experience of the Buddha's teachings (Waterhouse, 1999), it is likely that these types of experiences will be prioritized in the narration of one's spiritual journey, as this is what is deemed socially desirable. This is not to say that individual life histories are somehow fabricated in retrospect, only that certain aspects may be given greater emphasis and furnished with particular language that is more acceptable to the social group in question (Beckford, 1978).

What both Kawanami (2013) and Cheng (2007) note, and I echo with comparative evidence from Britain, is the need to avoid homogenizing the experiences and rationales for renunciation given by Buddhist nuns, either in cross-cultural comparison or within one cultural and geographic location. Each of the aforementioned studies of renunciant women outside the West clearly indicate that spiritual motivations for ordination are present, if not predominant, in women's narratives, including the desire to give more attention to meditation and other Buddhist practices. These are intertwined with motivations that seem more mundane. Furthermore, while individual meditation practice features strongly in the narratives of many British Buddhist women, not all of these women begin their engagement with Buddhism or decide to ask for monastic ordination as a result of interest in silent meditation. There were those who were involved in groups with strong meditation traditions but who honestly explained that they had never been particularly interested in meditation, preferring either study or devotional practices. There were also those who were committed to Buddhist traditions that did not prioritize silent meditation as the primary practice, for example two nuns affiliated with a Pure Land group. These women describe being attracted to chanting practices and forms of ethical engagement in social welfare projects. While silent meditation has a dominant place in the narrative life histories of British Buddhist convert monastic women, it is not the only practice that is worthy of scholarly attention. Beyond a focus on personal and individual practice, a strong theme throughout many of the British monastic women's narratives is the desire to connect with, build, and be part of Buddhist *communities*. Among British Buddhist communities, meditation is practiced both alone and with other people (and this pattern mirrors many Buddhist communities outside the UK). The communal role that meditation plays in the development and maintenance of British Buddhist monasticism will be discussed in the next section.

Meditation at the Kitchen Sink

While recognizing the potential variety in monastic experience and motivation is vital, it is striking that among Buddhist monastic women in the British context, all had a silent meditation practice. This may not have been a sole priority (for example, amongst the Pure Land monastics) but it remained a feature of their lives, and an important part of what they taught to others. Experience of meditation and also the ability to teach accessibly is accorded a particular status in British Buddhism. As Waterhouse (1999) discovered, authentic and direct knowledge of Buddhist practices are at least equal to the authority of lineage in this context. Although the Western image of Buddhism may well be intrinsically tied up with silent meditation perhaps as a reflection of modernist tendencies, not all Buddhist monastics across the globe prioritize it in the same way (McMahan, 2008, p. 183). As Crosby (2014, p. 147) notes, while Western monastics are more likely to regularly meditate, among mainstream Theravada communities meditation is seen as "more often a specialist vocation or undertaken for a special period," although certain groups and individuals prioritize meditation more strongly than others. It is necessary to allow space to consider the varied role that meditation might play in the daily lives of Buddhist monastics, even in the British context where silent meditation may well be held in common across most Buddhist groups.

In practical terms, meditation provides a routine for the monastic day, both for those living in a communal environment and those living alone. This is not to say that meditation is always practiced communally for monastics living in monasteries and, indeed, practicing meditation alone is also a feature of monastery life. However, having one, two, or more set times for practice that may be taken alone or in a communal meditation hall provides helpful daily structure, particularly when one first takes vows, but also beyond this. For British Buddhist monastic women, meditation is seen as an important tool with which one might investigate and realize the Buddha's teachings, particularly around suffering and the way to end suffering—the cornerstone of the *dhamma*. This prominence given to narratives of suffering and the work to end it is present in ethnographies of Buddhist female renunciants outside of the West, for example in Tibet (Havnevik, 1989), Myanmar (Kawanami, 2013) and Sri Lanka (Salgado, 2013). This is perhaps no surprise, given that an understanding of suffering and stress (*dukkha*) is the foundation of the Buddha's Four Noble Truths and the motivation for monastic life more generally. Yet, as one Sōtō Zen female monk explains, it is important not to over-romanticize the experience of meditation:

> When you meditate you begin to see how you are and frequently it's not pretty… You are not meditating to find peace and to be calm and all of that, you are sitting down and saying I'm willing to see all the icky stuff, basically, because you have to go through that before you are going to get anywhere… it can be quite painful.

As a result of this, what is important is the availability of a teacher or guide. For some, having teachers living in Britain was vital and why they chose to associate with a particular Buddhist group. For those with principal teachers based outside of Britain, in India or Myanmar for example, it was sometimes difficult to receive the level of support and guidance in meditation they needed on a regular basis. For example, one might have a particular (negative or positive) experience during a meditation session and want to talk about it, or want some additional support with learning different techniques. If the principal teacher is based outside of the United Kingdom, it can be difficult to secure time with them on a one-to-one basis in order to have a productive discussion about spiritual practice. Some women from this study, particularly those in Tibetan traditions who did not live in monasteries, might only see their principal teacher annually (for some, even less than this), which does not necessarily provide an adequate support or mentoring. This is not solely an issue for contemporary Buddhists, as Shaw (2006:10) identifies the significance of a teacher as meditation guide in the early Pali literature. It is, however, a feature of life in British Buddhist communities where teachers, home monasteries, and communities of practice may be located in other countries. Therefore, when teachers visit Britain to give meditation instruction or *dhamma* talks, these are significant events in the annual calendar both for monastic and lay practitioners.

The daily routine of monastic life, and the place for focused meditation periods within it, differs across Buddhist traditions. It is tempting to want to envision a typical day for a Buddhist nun in Britain and then to try to compare this across different Buddhist contexts, highlighting the points of similarity and difference. However, this runs the risk of being overly reductive of very heterogeneous lives and experiences. It is less problematic, perhaps, to consider the daily lives of female monastics in established monasteries as opposed to those living alone or in smaller groups. Certainly, in the British context, this difference affects women's engagement with Buddhist teachings and practices, including meditation. In most British Buddhist monasteries, the typical picture is two to three communal meditation periods per day, at least in the early morning and evening, although in certain traditions, following the novitiate period these can sometimes be optional or undertaken alone. These regularly scheduled periods can include walking and sitting meditation, chanting *pūjā*, and ceremonial ritual activity. There are changes to this broad schedule at different times, for example, for some Theravada monastics on *uposatha* (lunar observance days) the evening meditation period, including both silent meditation and chanting *pūjā*, is extended to midnight to mark particular dedication to the *dhamma*. For many Buddhist monastics, including in Britain, there are times in the year that are more intensely focused on meditation and contemplative practice, for example during the *vassa* (rains retreat) or winter retreats where, typically, monastics will remain in one place with perhaps more limited administrative duties. As a result, the structure provided by meditation in most British Buddhist monasteries isn't entirely static and changes over the course of the annual calendar. In addition, some groups have a particular emphasis on meditation and long retreats, such as the Tibetan Karma Kagyu school, which offers the option to be cloistered for three to four years, with intense schedules for meditation and ritual practice. However, this is far from the majority approach in contemporary Britain and, of the women I interviewed, only two of them had undertaken extended retreats of over six months, and only one of these had taken a four-year retreat. For most, more secluded retreat periods might last for two to three months, or sometimes less. Secluded or solitary retreat isn't always part of Buddhist monastic life, and some participants narrated their monastic schedule through their engagement in community welfare projects and charitable social work.

In monastic communities, individuals might have specific administrative roles, such as working in the kitchen, supporting novices, facilitating lay people's retreats, teaching and one-to-one support for lay practitioners and, at times, these administrative and pastoral duties are given priority. One participant described this as trying to find the balance between "meditation and Hotel Management." This is the reality of life in a contemporary monastic community, particularly one in the West that might cater to large numbers of lay visitors on retreat. Living alone, or in a smaller monastic community, also has an impact on the place that meditation has in daily life. As I have discussed, roughly half of the women I spoke to lived alone in their own privately owned or rented homes, or as a monastic in sole charge of a communally owned Buddhist center. This relates both to personal choice, but also to a lack of monastery settings that might cater to women who have taken particular monastic vows in Britain (Starkey, 2014, 2020). While for those living in smaller centers or temples, although being in sole charge of such places has an impact on their responsibilities as a monastic, the daily pattern of meditation and ceremonial periods typically mirrors that of the mother-monastery. However, unlike in some parts of Asia, for example, Western women have been given Buddhist monastic ordination while still holding familial or householder responsibilities such as a need to earn money or look after children, particularly in some Tibetan traditions. While these women do work hard to integrate monastic practices, including meditation, into their daily lives, it isn't always easy and necessitated increased discipline. It may involve getting up very early to complete the required ritual practices prior to going to work, and then staying up late into the night to meditate. This sometimes led to feelings of tension and a personal worry that monastic vows and practices were not being upheld as they might initially have been intended. As one nun described: "To fully devote yourself to full time practice and meditation and all of those things as a monastic, you need to not have to worry about where money is going to come from".

However, both for those women living alone and for those living communally, when examining the ways in which they narrate their relationship with meditation, it is clear that dividing "meditation" and "daily life" is artificial. What is important is the integration of meditation, mindfulness, and concentration into daily tasks and interactions with others. Here, then, it should be difficult to ascertain where meditation stops and daily life begins and vice versa. As one Sōtō Zen female monk illustrates: "Meditation [is] not about going off for an hour a day and sitting on your backside, it [is] . . . how do you operate at the kitchen sink, how do you deal with people?" This also applies to any analysis of the role of devotional or ritual practice. For the monastics in this study, any attempt to draw firm boundaries between meditation and other practices such as chanting or *pūjā* was questioned, for these are all typically viewed as functioning in similar ways: to encourage concentration, to show respect and reverence, and to build and maintain community cohesion.

Beyond the impact on the individual, meditation in this context also works to construct and maintain communities and communal identity. In one Thai monastic setting, Cook (2010, p. 7) argues that meditation helps to nurture a particular type of monastic identity and, as a result, its social nature is significant. McMahan (2008, p. 191) argues that Buddhist practice "including meditation, has always been a communal as well as individual endeavor." In a similar way, these social aspects should not be overlooked in British monastic communities, although the contextual specificities may be different than monasteries in Asia. Due to the growing prominence of meditation in contemporary Britain, offering meditation instruction to the general public helps to support and financially sustain Buddhist monastic communities and individuals, particularly in the situation where monasteries are not directly funded or endorsed by the state, as they may be where Buddhism is the national religious tradition. In terms of the Buddhist monastic groups that were the focus of my research, none of them received direct state funding for religious activities, either from the United Kingdom or elsewhere. However, all of the principal monasteries are either registered as charities and are subsequently regulated by the Charity Commission of England and Wales or are connected closely to charitable trusts designed to provide ongoing support. Therefore they receive certain tax exemptions as a result. The *dāna* or donations provided by lay communities in return for monastic teaching, whether in an evening class or a longer retreat, provides funds to build and maintain Buddhist centers and temples (including supporting necessary renovations on monastic buildings) and gives them a social purpose—to teach others and spread the *dhamma*. Teaching meditation is also a way in which certain Buddhist monasteries uphold their UK charitable status, and thus this enables relationships to be built between Buddhist organizations and the British state, with concomitant responsibilities arising as a result. Furthermore, some Buddhist groups in Britain, including those connected to monastic traditions, have more recently begun to provide "secular" mindfulness meditation (such as Mindfulness Based Stress Reduction) to non-Buddhists, sometimes in conjunction with statutory bodies such as the National Health Service. Whilst they may do this through a separate charitable trust, they have forged new relationships (including financial ones) with the British state through the provision of such meditation courses (Starkey, 2020).

For monastic women living alone, teaching meditation may also contribute to sustaining their monastic practice. Offering a regular *dhamma* class and meditation retreats helps to build supportive surrounding communities of lay people that can provide financial assistance, which is particularly important for those who have vowed not to work for money, but also offers elements of emotional and spiritual friendship they might need while living outside of a traditional monastery environment or away from their teacher. While it is not always as easy as this, particularly when living alone with little institutional support, meditation is thus woven into the social fabric of monastic living in Britain. It is a tool to help an individual realize the Buddhist path, but it is equally significant in enabling the collective to develop and thrive.

Conclusion

As I have demonstrated, through the ethnographic evidence analyzed in this chapter, meditation is a key component of Buddhist monastic life in contemporary Britain. For monastic women, "meditation" includes silent seated practice, which has a particular resonance in the contemporary British imagination; walking meditation; and other observances that sometimes come under the rubric of "devotion," such as chanting or prostrations. These are blended together in different ways and at different times with other responsibilities to contribute to an overall structure for monastic life. Meditation is seen as a way to help in the realization of the Buddha's teachings, and is something that initially attracts women to Buddhist groups in Britain, as well as providing a motivation for monastic ordination. Yet, importantly, meditation has a dual function and it operates on an individual and a social level, binding communities together and helping to sustain them. In taking a closer look at the contextually specific detail of contemporary monastic life, we can more easily articulate the ways in which Buddhism and Buddhist meditation are integrated into differing social and cultural contexts and how they, in turn, are shaped by them.

A question I have returned to throughout this chapter is how the experiences of Buddhist monastic women in Britain might be different from monastic or renunciant women in majority-Buddhist or non-Western contexts in terms of their relationship with Buddhism generally, and meditation practices specifically. I have been keen to avoid an overly reductive analysis that makes homogenizing statements about "Western Buddhist women" or "Asian Buddhist women" without recognizing that different institutions, practices, approaches, personalities, and backgrounds shape both individual choices and patterns of collective daily living. Buddhist women, including monastic practitioners, are a diverse group and any one-dimensional comparison risks simplifying their varied experiences. Yet even with this caveat in mind, in this chapter I have indicated several points of similarity and difference that enable us to better articulate the ways in which the experience of meditation among female Buddhist monastics in Britain might be molded by context.

Chief among these differences are the social and economic backgrounds and circumstances of Buddhist monastic women. The majority of monastic women referred to in this chapter had all received a level of tertiary education, many had high-profile careers and had been economically self-sufficient prior to ordination, including living independently, often as home-owners. None of the women in this study ordained as teenagers or very young adults, and most waited until their thirties or forties or even later before becoming monastics, bringing with them life experiences and particular ways of envisioning monastic practice. None mentioned a desire to ask for ordination in order to avoid marriage, poverty, or to improve their social status. This is not always the picture presented in studies of female renunciation outside of the United Kingdom. In different Buddhist Asian contexts, such as Myanmar, younger women are also taking ordination alongside those who are older, and some do not have the same levels of education and social or financial background that many Western Buddhist women have. Some are less concerned with silent meditation as a primary practice. As I have shown, this is likely to have a bearing on the ways in which women articulate their motivations for monastic life and the journeys that they subsequently take. Yet Buddhist nuns outside the West are not all cut from the same cloth. Ethnographic work tells us that, across different Asian contexts, there are highly educated women with substantial social and economic status who are choosing a renunciant path in order to focus on meditation and spiritual goals, in very similar ways to the women described in this chapter. It is clear that there are differences within Buddhist Asian contexts, as well as differences between women in Asia and the West and, indeed, among women within Western cultural settings. As I have articulated in this chapter, one of the ways to examine these differences is to look at the different living situations of Buddhist renunciant women and consider how these affect meditation and the daily concerns of monastic life.

Although Buddhist monastic women in Britain adopt different approaches to spiritual practice and live in vastly different settings, many put an emphasis on silent meditation. The importance of having personal experiences of the Buddha's teachings is, in general terms, prioritized in the United Kingdom in monastic as well as lay circles, although this is not to say that studying the *dhamma*, for example, isn't also highly valued (Waterhouse, 1999). Yet silent meditation has an increasingly well-established place in contemporary British popular and health culture, and this has impacted on the spiritual trajectories of monastic women in Britain. One example of this is the initial articulation of the therapeutic benefits of meditation by women who became involved with Buddhism in Britain within the last two decades. Yet understanding the significance of silent meditation in the lives of many Western Buddhists should not obscure the variation of practices that are adopted by monastics, including other devotion and ritual, ethical and communal observances, and a dedication to social engagement and social work projects for Buddhists and the wider British public.

One of the key issues facing Buddhist monastic women in Britain is support, both practical and emotional. While in Asia there are a number of monastic communities, including nunneries, that provide structured homes and localized networks for renunciant practitioners, this is not universally the case elsewhere. While there are British monasteries that have been established now for decades and that have a community of lay supporters, such as Samye Ling, Throssel Hole, or Amaravati, there are some traditions, such as the Tibetan Gelug or Nyingma, who do not have monasteries for women in Britain. As a result, some women struggle to balance their monastic vows and their meditative and ritual practices with the realities and responsibilities of daily life and financial survival (Starkey, 2014, 2020). The impact on their meditation practice is twofold and includes the potential for lack of time and dedicated space for meditation and ritual practice, and the challenges that come from not being in close proximity to other practitioners and teachers in a communal setting in order to foster spiritual progression. There are similar concerns that have been raised in terms of support for Buddhist nuns in Asian contexts also (see, for example, Tsomo, 2002); however, the high cost of living coupled with the relative infancy of Buddhist monasticism in Britain can lead to a lack of understanding and support for renunciant lifestyles, all of which has a particular effect on women and their religious practice.

Notwithstanding this, what is clear from the testimonies of monastic women, both in Britain but also beyond, is their dedication to the spiritual life and Buddhist teachings, and their willingness to work toward realizing them regardless of any individual or institutional opportunities and constraints. The women involved in my research often acknowledge the difficulties that they face as Buddhist monastics in a new environment, whether they live in monasteries or alone, following a path that isn't easy or culturally familiar. What meditation provides, therefore, is routine, shape, and structure to British Buddhist monastic life and a sense of ongoing connection to Buddhist traditions, teachers, and communities. Buddhist meditation has both individual and collective value and is likely to continue to play a central role in the development of Buddhist monastic culture in Britain.

Acknowledgements

This research was funded by the Arts and Humanities Research Council, UK and the Spalding Trust.

References

Angell, J. (2006). Women in brown: A short history of the order of *siladhara*, nuns of the English Forest Sangha, part one. *Buddhist Studies Review* 23, 93–112.

Batchelor, S. (1994). *The awakening of the West: The encounter of Buddhism and Western culture*. Berkeley: Parallax Press

Beckford, J. A. (1978). Accounting for conversion. *British Journal of Sociology* 29(2), 249–262.

Bell, S. (1991). *Buddhism in Britain—development and adaptation*. (Doctoral dissertation). University of Durham.

Bell, S. (2000). Being creative with tradition: Rooting Theravada Buddhism in Britain. *Journal of Global Buddhism* 1, 1–23.

Bluck, R. (2006). *British Buddhism: Teachings, practice and development*. New York: Routledge.

Cantwell, C., & Kawanami, H. (2002). Buddhism. In L. Woodhead, P. Fletcher, H. Kawanami, & D. Smith (Eds.), *Religions in the modern world* (pp. 47–81). London: Routledge.

Cheng, W.-Y. (2007). *Buddhist nuns in Taiwan and Sri Lanka: A critique of the feminist perspective*. London and New York: Routledge.

Chodron, T. (1999). Introduction. In T. Chodron (Ed.), *Blossoms of the Dharma: Living as a Buddhist nun* (pp. xxv–xxxvi). Berkeley, CA: North Atlantic Books.

Coleman, J. W. (2001). *The new Buddhism: The Western transformation of an ancient tradition*. Oxford: Oxford University Press.

Conze, E. (1982). *A short history of Buddhism*. London: Unwin.

Cook, J. (2010). *Meditation in modern Buddhism: Renunciation and change in Thai monastic life*. Cambridge: Cambridge University Press.

Cook, J. (2016). Mindful in Westminster: The politics of meditation and the limits of neoliberal critique. *HAU: Journal of Ethnographic Theory* 6, 141–161.

Crane, H. (2004). Resisting marriage and renouncing womanhood: The choice of Taiwanese Buddhist nuns. *Critical Asian Studies* 36, 265–284.

Crosby, K. (2014). *Theravada Buddhism: Continuity, diversity and identity*. Chichester: Wiley Blackwell.

Eifring, H. (2015). Meditative practice and cultural context. In H. Eifring (Ed.), *Meditation and culture* (pp. 3–8). London and New York: Bloomsbury.

Gethin, R. (1998). *The foundations of Buddhism*. Oxford: Oxford University Press.

Gilbert, A. (1980). *The making of post-Christian Britain*. London: Longman.

Goswell, M. (1988). *Motivational factors in the life of a religious community and related changes in the experience of self* (Doctoral dissertation). University of Bath.

Gutschow, K. (2004). *Being a Buddhist nun: The struggle for enlightenment in the Himalayas*. Cambridge, MA: Harvard University Press.

Harvey, P. (1990). *An introduction to Buddhism: Teachings, history and practices*. Cambridge: Cambridge University Press.

Harvey, P. (2013). *An introduction to Buddhism: Teachings, history and practices* (2nd ed.). Cambridge: Cambridge University Press.

Havnevik, H. (1989). *Tibetan Buddhist nuns: History, cultural norms and social reality*. Oslo: Norwegian University Press.

Holt, J. C. (1995). *Discipline: The canonical Buddhism of the Vinayapitaka*. Delhi: Motilal Banarsidass.

Kawanami, H. (2013). *Renunciation and empowerment of Buddhist nuns in Myanmar-Burma: Building a community of female faithful*. Leiden: Brill.

Lopez, D. S. (2001). *The story of Buddhism: A concise guide to its history and teachings.* New York: Harper Collins/Harper One.
McMahan, D. L. (2008). *The making of Buddhist modernism.* Oxford: Oxford University Press.
Mohr, T., & Tsedroen, J. (Eds.). (2010). *Dignity and discipline: Reviving full ordination for Buddhist nuns.* Somerville, MA: Wisdom.
O.N.S. (2012). *Religion in England and Wales 2011* [Online]. ONS. Retrieved from http://www.ons.gov.uk/ons/rel/census/2011-census/key-statistics-for-local-authorities-in-england-and-wales/rpt-religion.html
Page, S.-J. & Yip, A. K.-T. (2017). *Understanding young Buddhists: Living out ethical journeys.* Leiden: Brill.
Prebish, C. S. (2007). Sangha. In D. Keown & C. S. Prebish (Eds.), *Encyclopedia of Buddhism* (pp. 653–661). London and New York: Routledge.
Salgado, N. S. (2004). Religious identities of Buddhist nuns: Training precepts, renunciant attire and nomenclature in Theravada Buddhism. *Journal of the American Academy of Religion 72*, 935–953.
Salgado, N. S. (2013). *Buddhist nuns and gendered practice: In search of the female renunciant.* Oxford: Oxford University Press.
Schopen, G. (2004). *Buddhist monks and business matters: Still more papers on monastic Buddhism in India.* Honolulu: University of Hawai'i Press.
Scott, A. (1981). *Anagarika Dharmapala: The founder of the London Buddhist Vihara and Maha Bodhi Society* [Online]. Retrieved from http://www.londonbuddhistvihara.org/Dharmapala.htm
Shaw, S. (2006). *Buddhist meditation: An anthology of texts from the Pali Canon.* London and New York: Routledge.
Silber, I. F. (1981). Dissent through holiness: The case of the radical renouncer in Theravada Buddhist countries. *Numen 28*, 164–193.
Smith, S., Munt, S. & Yip, A. K.-T. (2016). *Cosmopolitan Dharma: Race, sexuality, and gender in British Buddhism.* Leiden: Brill.
Starkey, C. (2014). Experiencing the liminal: Understanding separation and transition amongst Buddhist monastic women in contemporary Britain. In I. Jonveaux, E. Pace, & S. Palmisano (Eds.), *Sociology and monasticism: Between innovation and tradition* (pp. 206–226). Leiden: Brill.
Starkey, C. (2020) *Women in contemporary British Buddhism: Ordination, community, connection.* London: Routledge.
Starkey, C., & Tomalin, E. (2016). Building Buddhism in England: The flourishing of a minority faith heritage. *Contemporary Buddhism 17*, 326–356.
Thanissaro, P. N. (2014). Almost a proper Buddhist: The post-secular complexity of heritage Buddhist teen identity in Britain. *Journal of Global Buddhism 15*, 1–14.
Tsedroen, J. B. (1988). Living by the Vinaya in the West. In K. L. Tsomo (Ed.), *Sakyadhita: Daughters of the Buddha* (pp. 202–213). Ithaca, NY: Snow Lion.
Tsomo, K. L. (1988). Nuns of the Buddhist traditions. In K. L. Tsomo, (Ed.), *Sakyadhita: Daughters of the Buddha* (pp. 103–108). Ithaca, NY: Snow Lion.
Tomalin, E., & Starkey, C. (2016). A survey of Buddhist Buildings in England. *Historic England,* Project 6749. Retrieved from https://historicengland.org.uk/images-books/publications/survey-of-buddhist-buildings-in-england/
Tsomo, K. L. (1999). History of Buddhist monasticism and its Western adaptation. In T. Chodron (Ed.), *Blossoms of the Dharma: Living as a Buddhist nun* (pp. 3–16). Berkeley, CA: North Atlantic Books.

Tsomo, K. L. (2002). Buddhist nuns: Changes and challenges. In C. S. Prebish and M. Baumann (Ed.), *Westward Dharma: Buddhism beyond Asia* (pp. 255–274). Berkeley, CA: University of California Press.

Turner, A., Cox, L., & Bocking, B. (2010). Beachcombing, going native and freethinking: Rewriting the history of early Western Buddhist monastics. *Contemporary Buddhism 11*, 125–147.

Waterhouse, H. (1997). *Buddhism in Bath: Adaptation and authority*. Leeds: University of Leeds (Department of Theology and Religious Studies).

Waterhouse, H. (1999). Who says so? Legitimacy and authenticity in British Buddhism. *Scottish Journal of Religious Studies 20*, 19–36.

Wijayaratna, M. (1990). *Buddhist monastic life according to the texts of the Theravada tradition*. Cambridge: Cambridge University Press.

Wijayaratna, M. (2010). *Buddhist nuns: Birth and development of a women's Buddhist order*. Kandy, Sri Lanka: Buddhist Publication Society.

PART V

INDIVIDUAL AND SOCIAL CHANGE THROUGH MEDITATION

THERAPEUTIC APPLICATIONS

CHAPTER 31

MENTAL ILLNESS THROUGH THE LENS OF MINDFULNESS

PATRICIA LYNN DOBKIN AND KAVEH MONSHAT

Introduction: Modern Psychological and Psychiatric Views

The paradigms we use to understand mental illness have shifted over time and varied across cultures; they have included viewpoints from different disciplines (e.g., psychiatry, psychology, neuroscience) as well as interest groups, such as feminists, social reformers, and industry (i.e., pharmaceutics). For the past decade or so, the neuroscientific perspective has overshadowed other important developments in psychiatry such as multidisciplinary, community-based care. The biomedical approach has gained prominence based on the assumption that mental health problems arise from "faulty mechanisms" within the person. The editorial of a special issue of the *British Journal of Psychiatry*, composed by twenty-nine eminent psychiatrists, highlights the importance of "non-technical aspects" of care: the nonspecific therapy factors such as the therapeutic alliance and patients' hopes and expectations (Bracken et al., 2012). In the case of depression, for example, the evidence fails to support the common assertion that medications work by correcting a pre-existing "chemical imbalance." Instead, the editorial authors advocate a "recovery approach" that takes into consideration the complex interplay of biopsychosocial forces underlying patients' conditions. This argument can be taken further by envisaging a psychosocial model of mental illness that integrates factors such as poverty and domestic violence alongside social and community services (Kinderman, 2014).

Until recently, modern psychotherapy mirrored the medical model where the patient or client is considered to have *internal* emotional conflicts, irrational thoughts, and maladaptive behaviors that require "fixing." In some cases, existential issues such as identity, meaning, and mortality may be addressed, but predominantly the focus is squarely upon the individual seeking care (except for couple or family systems therapy). Little to no attention is paid to the person's context, culture, and religious or spiritual orientation.

Diagnostic Labels

Psychiatry has a history of categorizing people who suffer. This is intended to help but may inadvertently inflict harm. As Tsou (2016) points out in his review of the *Diagnostic and Statistical Manual of Mental Disorders* (*DSM*) (American Psychiatric Association, 1980), the third version was stripped down to a descriptive approach to *facilitate communication between researchers and clinicians*. It signaled a shift toward a "neo-Kraepelinian" outlook—a biological approach to psychiatry. The *DSM-V* goes further in its claim to be informed by genetics and neuroscience. Tsou offers the alternative term "natural," referring to mental disorders (e.g., schizophrenia, major depression, bipolar) that share similar biological causation. Others disagree. Lakeman and Cutcliffe (2016) contend that the *DSM-V* is "merely the latest in a long line of failed, misplaced nosological attempts" that has contributed to the "unwarranted medicalization of everyday life" (p. 125).

Frances (2016), an editor of the *DSM-IV*, concurs, noting that the pharmaceutical industry has played a role in pathologizing and over medication. The diagnostic categories fail to acknowledge the heterogeneity of experience within all those labeled with a certain disorder. Jureidini (2012) states that psychiatric diagnoses are mostly "unexplanatory." He underlines the breadth of "reasons to be sick" that see the whole person living within a community. For instance, he notes that in our society we are collectively intolerant of common emotions including sadness, anger, and fear. We hold being distressed as being "not myself." Subsequently the label "depression" engages health care systems that locate the problem within the person, deflecting attention away from the social context that may be contributing to the individual's experiences (see Neitzke, 2016).

Broadening the View: Mindfulness and Its Spiritual Background

Mindfulness within a secular context can be mistakenly perceived as a psychological technique meant to smooth the rough edges of life rather than transform the person living it. Kabat-Zinn (2003, p. 145) encourages clinicians and researchers to recognize "the unique qualities and characteristics of mindfulness as a meditative practice, with all that implies, so that mindfulness is not simply seized upon as the next promising cognitive behavioral technique or exercise, decontextualized, and 'plugged' into a behaviorist paradigm with the aim of driving desirable change, or of fixing what is broken."

When authentic, mindfulness informs values, ethics, and the way one lives. To learn how best to meet needs, we begin by observing ourselves and those around us. If this exercise of observation generates judgmental guilt or anger, we remind ourselves that we are doing it because we care about ourselves—in other words, out of and with compassion.

Modern secular mindfulness has been influenced by Buddhism. The classical Buddhist scriptural text on the foundations of mindfulness asks the practitioner on twenty-nine occasions to observe phenomena "internally, externally and both internally and externally" (Ñāṇamoli & Bodhi, 1995, S10:43). This is often taken to mean being aware not just of oneself but of others as well. Although the lonely meditator may develop certain helpful qualities, the breadth of Buddhist practice recognizes mindfulness as being socially grounded. This reflects the principle of "inter-being," an acknowledgement of our necessarily interdependent natures (Nhat Hanh, 1999).

The first aspect of mindfulness practice the Buddha highlighted was ethical conduct, particularly a non-harming orientation toward oneself and others born of compassionate awareness and the clarity of mind and wisdom it generates. Skillful actions, that is, those that a clear and compassionate mind sees as promoting mental and physical health in ourselves and others, calm the mind, which, in turn, promotes greater awareness and wisdom, thus forming a virtuous circle (Keown, 2013). As a basis for healing oneself and promoting healing in others, this view concurs with current psychology and psychiatry, which emphasize objectivity and empirical evidence but extend it by highlighting compassion and felt understanding.

Mental Illness through a Spiritual Lens

Cultural and religious mythologies have occasionally provided misguided or stigmatizing explanations of depressive or psychotic symptoms (e.g., as possession by unearthly beings). Although we have largely adopted the secular view of mindfulness advanced by authors like Kabat-Zinn (2003) and Batchelor (2015), we wish, nonetheless, and as they themselves encourage, to put mindfulness in its spiritual, rather than a religious context. By "spiritual" we refer to the sense of an underlying and self-transcendent reality. It is broader than religious beliefs and also differs from existential matters—the latter usually referring to suffering that is not relieved by treatment for physical symptoms, or that occurs in the absence of such symptoms. Examples of spiritual distress are the need to reconcile with "God," or others, or oneself; or perceptions of being distant from one's spiritual community. In contrast, sources of existential distress may be feelings of alienation, loss of sense of dignity, loss of meaning, or loneliness.

In contrast to a normative diagnostic model where a person tends be considered as either ill or healthy, a humane awareness of emotional suffering advocates a spectrum model. At one end there are extreme experiences (e.g., schizophrenic psychosis) in which biological disturbances are evident and where biological treatments are usually necessary and sometimes lifesaving. Milder forms of disturbance (e.g., non-melancholic depression) lend themselves to a complementary mix of psychotherapeutic and biological treatments. At the other end of the spectrum is what is typically diagnosed as a psychiatric disorder, but may also be seen as an expression of distress born of psychosocial or spiritual challenge or deprivation. An example would be the difference between depression and burnout—burnout being the likely outcome of psychosocial or existential problems.

Spiritual needs, such as finding purpose in life, a sense of belonging to a community, or experiencing inner peace, are worthy of clinical attention across this spectrum of distress. Although mental health professionals are encouraged to apply a biopsychosocial model of care, patients with psychotic disorders tend to receive little more than antipsychotic medications and social support. At best, psychological techniques to deal with the distress associated with hallucinations may be introduced. Often no attention is paid to how the person's sense of meaning or identity is affected by their altered perceptions of reality.

At times, the intense emotions and permeability of perceptual boundaries that arise in psychosis can allow patients access to spiritual experiences and insights that might have genuine value, but are usually dismissed as psychotic symptoms.

A Psychosis Case Study

Fred[1] *is a man in his forties living with his frail, elderly parents and his twenty-year-old son. He receives a monthly injection of antipsychotic medication, which allows him relief from auditory hallucinations and religious delusions. He has become obese, lacks energy, and has blurred vision since commencing medication. Due to a chronic shortage of permanent medical staff in his rural public mental health service, psychiatric input tends to be intermittent and brief.*

He feels devalued by psychiatrists who associate the spiritual experiences he reports with his illness. When explored in detail, two categories of experience emerge. He has at times felt that although he is a separate entity in some ways (in terms of physical boundaries), he is also intimately connected with and somehow one with all of existence. This pleasant experience is associated with a calming awareness of a benevolent unifying principle or force. At other times he has formed the belief, which he finds unpleasant, that he is called to a religious mission. In preparation for this he has felt compelled to cleanse himself through burning the palms of his hands with candle flames.

Once the first set of experiences is acknowledged as spiritually meaningful, he is able to more readily distinguish the second as destructive and a product of a mental disturbance. He expresses gratitude for being heard and respected. A more collaborative and less patronizing approach to managing his antipsychotic medications becomes possible, which

[1] Clinical vignettes represent actual patients treated by Kaveh Monshat or Patricia Lynn Dobkin. Names have been changed to preserve confidentiality.

eventually results in a significant reduction of side-effects, and in turn greater motivation to take medication.

Buddhism: A Clinical Reading

Most Buddhist scholars agree that Buddhist scriptures have been influenced by local cultures and politico-religious institutions over the past 2,500 years (Batchelor, 2015; Nhat Hanh, 1999). As Nhat Hanh states, "we have to use our own intelligence" and take "an overall view of the teachings" (Nhat Hanh, 1999, p. 24) to apply what has been handed down to our modern, present circumstances. This is the stance we adopt in this chapter.

The Buddha maintained a pragmatic approach. He aimed to instill a felt sense of principles to help practitioners independently discern how to deal with any set of given circumstances and shunned proclaiming religious rules that told people how to live (Batchelor, 2015). This applies equally to the choice between different ways of cultivating compassionate awareness (i.e., mindfulness "practices"), where the practitioner is guided to develop and rely on her individual judgment in finding what best serves her and others' well-being.

How can the vast Buddhist canon and its various interpretations, bodies of commentaries, and practices guide clinicians? They may be informed by the overall aims of the teachings, which are to diminish suffering and nurture well-being. Rather than equating mindfulness with sitting meditation or a scriptural view of the human condition, they encourage individuals to continually ask themselves: "What is kind and conducive to happiness?" (Fulton, 2009). In this way, patients can discover what is healing in each phase of life given their socio-cultural context and developmental strengths and vulnerabilities.

Let us take the cultivation of pleasant emotions, such as gratitude and joy, as examples. Western psychotherapy and certain traditional interpretations of mindfulness practice, particularly in Theravada schools, tend to focus on a pure observation of whatever is present. Other Buddhist traditions (e.g., Tibetan and Vietnamese) highlight the need for a compassionate, relaxed, and even playful attitude while witnessing what arises. Greater emphasis is placed on practices such as *mettā* (loving-kindness) and being in touch with joyous elements of moment-to-moment experience (Ricard, 2007; Nhat Hanh, 2009).

Buddhism and Western Psychology in Dialogue

The view of suffering in Buddhism has been likened to a clinician's approach (Norman, 2003). In the exposition of the Four Noble Truths we progress from becoming aware of ill-being (symptoms); to identifying a discernable cause (underlying pathology); to a recognition that relief and well-being are possible; and an outline of the path towards health the(cure or healing). One is guided to bring a curious, caring awareness to suffering, which generates a felt understanding (i.e., not simply an intellectual or speculative one) of its causes. One is encouraged, in parallel, to notice, understand, and nurture moments of wholeness. Thus, one learns to be with suffering on the one hand (e.g., not drink to escape), and nurture peace of mind and joy on the other (Batchelor, 2015; Nhat Hanh, 1999).

Kelly (2008) summarizes Buddhist psychology and its pertinence to psychiatry and psychotherapy by introducing a distinctive view of distress and mental illness. For example, "conditionality" ("dependent arising") describes how emotional and cognitive states are dependent on a limitless, inter-dependent, inter-generational range of causes and conditions. People are not singled out as individually disordered; instead, Buddhist psychology aims to address the human condition as a whole. Actions that harm us or others tend to naturally trigger unpleasant feelings. Meditation practice that incorporates ethical living protects us against unhelpful internal states taking hold.

Mindfulness practice emphasizes grounding awareness in the body as a way to heal emotional difficulties. For example, two basic emotions, fear and anger, can manifest as bodily tensions. These may be physical correlates of psychological pain. When chronic, and sometimes following acute severe trauma, a vicious circle of mind-body discomfort can develop. Mindfulness encourages exploring and letting go of tensions lodged in the body, which even if initially protective, have become maladaptive. Although there are several schools of Western body-oriented psychotherapy (Röhricht, 2009), the majority of evidence-supported interventions are based on psychodynamic or cognitive-behavioral paradigms. This is beginning to change with the popularity of Mindfulness-Based Interventions (MBIs) that introduce therapists to a more integrative view of the body-mind relationship. These interventions use mindfulness meditation, as well as ideas from Buddhist mindfulness regarding observing events and oneself in a neutral, non-judgmental way, in order to stimulate self-detachment from thoughts and emotions.

A Complementary View of the Self

In many spiritual traditions, especially in Buddhism, individuals are encouraged to let go of their attachment to the self. Western psychology and Buddhism may be viewed as having opposing aims: one aims to strengthen the self and the other to arrive at "no-self" or "emptiness" (Meadows, 2003). Here we propose that the two approaches may overlap and be complementary.

Like in psychotherapy, non-judgmental awareness in meditation strengthens the integrative function of the ego (e.g., to accept oneself in the presence of both wanted and unwanted feelings). This may be helpful, for instance, for people who have suffered neglect or emotional or physical abuse in early life. In addition, the sense of calm and connectedness often associated with concentration-oriented meditative practices can "provide a stabilizing force in the mind... with a sense of ontological security" (Epstein, 2007, p. 129).

It is a mistake to think that the aim of mindfulness practice is to annihilate the ego, even if ego*ism* may lessen (Epstein, 2007). Rather, the objective is to see through the usual representations of the self. By sensing how one habitually constructs an image of the self out of a stream of experiences, we reduce identification with feelings ("I *am* angry"), which allows for greater freedom of action (what is usually referred to in the psychoanalytic literature as "mature defences" such as humor or sublimation). "No-self is the whole self functioning in a non-self-centered way" (Magid, 2002, p. 82). In other words, "The self is still present—but it is not self-preoccupied. It washes the dishes and puts them away" (Magid, 2002, p. 95; quoting Aitken Roshi, 1991).

"Emptiness" is specifically used in Buddhism to mean "devoid of an inherent, independent existence," rather than not *at all* extant. It is to be differentiated from the sense of emptiness that plagues those suffering from borderline or narcissistic personality structures. Here a pathologic feeling of inner hollowness or "deadness" exists, due to a failure to develop or sustain a stable, cohesive self (Magid, 2002).

For mindfulness practitioners to develop "a more fluid ego able to constantly integrate potentially destabilizing experiences of insubstantiality and impermanence" (Epstein, 2007, p. 52), they need to be able to "let their mind rest in its natural state" (Epstein, 2007, p. 146). Also, to dismantle old structures during meditation, one must have the basic skills of affect regulation, that is, to be able to tolerate, endure, and organize in a meaningful way one's experiences so as not to be overwhelmed by anxiety, pain, uncertainty, or other reactions as one sheds the light of awareness onto difficulties.

For some individuals, concentration-oriented practices quiet the mind, although they can be overused as defensive avoidance in relation to inner conflict or strong emotions (Magid, 2002). In addition, even in long-term practitioners of mindfulness meditation, core psychodynamic conflicts and deficits can remain intact. Nonetheless, the practitioner can become aware and less reactive to them and, as a result, suffer less frustration or narcissistic injury (Rosenbaum, 1999).

While psychotherapy can help a person discover the roots of an emotion, such as anger, understand how it is fueled in the present, as well as provide means to cope better, it may not offer a reason to let go of it. Insights gained through mindfulness practice (e.g., seeing through a rigid self-construct to be defended at all costs) can facilitate acceptance and allow thoughts and emotions to dissipate.

But we must also take into account that for many people struggling with mental illness, intense feelings of anxiety, rage, or despair serve as barriers to developing meditative insight; these can become even more overwhelming during sitting meditation practice, especially in silent retreat settings. For such individuals, psychotherapeutic methods, used in a long-term therapeutic relationship, are essential to help them regulate affect and arrive at a healthy sense of self.

Healing Versus Curing

Eradicating symptoms through a pharmacological or psychotherapeutic "cure" is perhaps the key aim in orthodox mental health care. A mindfulness perspective, in contrast, emphasizes coming to terms with symptoms or to exercise the capacity for healing as being central to well-being. In some cases, mental illness may be curable, but healing is possible in all cases.

Healing can be defined as "a shift in our quality of life away from anguish and suffering, toward an experience of integrity, wholeness, and inner peace" (Mount, 2006, p. 50). Healing involves openness, trust, hope, and acceptance. When a person lives according to what makes life meaningful, then he or she is less likely to suffer. Schmidt (2004) notes that self-awareness and compassion promote healing in both the therapist and patient. The non-specific elements of the healing environment, such as when the therapist acts as a healer within a safe space that allows patients' novel understanding of the nature of their illness to arise, enables them to "re-perceive" their illness. Then life can be viewed as coherent and meaningful. This motivates patients to take responsibility for their well-being, not in a sense that blames them for their illness but by allowing them to understand how distress and mental illness have their origins in how people view themselves and their predicament, and how these perceptions impact the social aspects of their life.

Diagnostic Labels Revisited

Classification systems were originally conceived to *aid* or expedite rather than replace professional communication. To explain how and why a person is suffering, clinicians arrive at and communicate a "formulation" that even in concise form requires several paragraphs. Collapsing the myriad aspects of a patient's suffering and its causes into a diagnosis stated in a few words is a necessary simplification.

Despite controversies surrounding both the Diagnostic and Statistical Manual of Mental Disorders (DSM) and the International Classification of Diseases classification systems, it is possible to use them skillfully. When the clinician is conscious of the benefits and limitations of using a specific diagnostic label, it is possible to maintain an open and flexible attitude to take into consideration the complexities underlying both the label and the person given the diagnosis. If, in addition, we bring into awareness of principles such as "conditionality" and "non-self," then a diagnosis may serve to guide treatment decisions while considering the interconnected network of factors affecting the individual (Kelly, 2016).

For patients and their caregivers, diagnostic labels *can* be helpful especially in some cases (e.g., severe schizophrenia). Here the experience of "disease" is arguably comparable to diabetes or dementia. The label itself can then have a relieving explanatory power and reduce existential distress and confusion associated with a painful, bewildering experience.

However, when explaining less severe distress and dysfunction, diagnostic labels are a double-edged sword. The patient may be left with the notion that she is inherently disabled or incomplete as a human being. For example, when using the word "depression" a clinician reifies a vast network of interrelated phenomena from poor sleep to social rejection. Moreover, the word "intervention" itself reinforces this newly constructed identity of being inherently and personally damaged or disordered, and requiring to be fixed.

A Whole-Person Perspective on Selected Illnesses

Depression

Depression and anxiety are by far the most common diagnoses in mental health care. In a unified model of depression it is suggested that "depression represents an adaptation to the perceived loss of a vital resource investment that exceeds the individual's competencies and capacities (e.g., resourcefulness, problem-solving, support), to mitigate the impact of the loss" (Beck & Bredemeier, 2016, p. 507). "Vital resources" are above all social relationships in which one has heavily invested and bear on the person's identity and access to basic needs. This parallels the emphasis in Buddhism on healthy social relationships for both well-being and as a support for mindfulness practice (Batchelor, 2015).

Beck and Bredemeier review the cognitive triad (self-image, images of the world, and expectations for the future) that simultaneously operate to determine the meaning and value of life events and generate responses accordingly. Early traumatic experiences (e.g., child abuse, parental loss) as well as predisposing genetic factors put an individual at risk for depression. Acute (e.g., death of a child) and chronic stressors (e.g., unemployment) may precipitate a depressive episode mediated and maintained by psychological (e.g., undermining of supportive attitudes and beliefs) and biological (e.g., elevated levels of cortisol) reactions to stress. Once depressed, individuals selectively attend to negative information. Biases in information processing mediate the effects of genetic and environmental risk factors that bear on serotonergic neurotransmission.

How a person appraises and gives personal meaning to an event is critical to how it is dealt with. If there is great investment in a lost "vital resource" and it is perceived to be out of the person's control, then the reaction is likely to be more pronounced. This becomes entrenched with repeated episodes of depression. "Depressogenic beliefs" (e.g., "I am a loser"; "Life will never get better") are key mediators of recurrence.

Reversing these processes align well with Cognitive Behavior Therapy (CBT) and Mindfulness-Based Cognitive Therapy (MBCT). Engagement with the therapist is viewed as powerful in itself to help the patient alter distorted self and worldviews, and as a form of social support. Finally, the use of antidepressant medications can be effective in more severe cases.

Marchand (2016) provides a comprehensive examination of how mindfulness practices, such as those learned in MBCT, may be helpful for people with depression. As in CBT, "stimulus-independent thoughts" that arise spontaneously and contribute to depressive symptoms are recognized. Such thoughts are typically oriented toward the past or future, and are based on negative self-schemas. Moreover, they involve stories about the self that do not match reality and have an unhelpful impact on functioning and may trigger distress. Much like physical pain, resistance to emotional pain exacerbates it.

While both have been shown to be beneficial, MBCT differs from CBT in many ways. First, rather than attempt to challenge or change thoughts, one's relationship with them is altered. Second, motivation for practice may shift over time from relief of symptoms to a felt self-understanding and spiritual development. Both approaches promote healthier choices when responding to stressful situations by coping better with difficulties. In addition, MBCT fosters a sense of common humanity and connection. With the regular practice of meditation, the individual begins to "re-perceive," that is, to be awakened to and accept how life really is in the present moment. Importantly, the concept of self may be altered when it becomes clear that stories about one's life are selective reconstructions of memories.

While numerous studies provide evidence for the efficacy of MBCT comparable to other forms of therapy (Chiesa et al., 2015; Kuyken et al., 2015), here, we focus on the processes that appear to underlie positive changes. Lemmens, Müller, Arntz, and Huibers (2016) reviewed thirty-five studies (including MBCT and CBT, among others) that identified thirty-nine potential candidates for mechanisms of positive change. For the MBCT studies these mechanisms included rumination, mindfulness, and worry. While not specifying which type of therapy was responsible for improvements per se, studies of CBT and MBCT showed decreases in dysfunctional attitudes, negative (automatic) thoughts, rumination, and worry, and increases in mindfulness (defined as non-judgmental acceptance) were associated with decreased intensity or risk of depression relapse across studies. However, the methodology made it difficult to determine what came first and *how* variables impacted outcomes.

Van der Velden and colleagues (2015) reviewed twelve MBCT studies focusing on mechanisms underlying positive changes in depressed patients. Changes in mindfulness, worry, self-compassion, and decentering were associated with, predicted, or mediated the effect of MBCT on treatment outcomes. Kuyken and colleagues (2015) have noted that MBCT provided significant protection against relapse and recurrence for patients with increased risk due to childhood abuse. Why this happens is unclear. One possibility is that because mindfulness practice encourages one to stay in the present moment rather than the past, with body awareness being used as an anchor, one's sense of self may change so that feelings of self-blame resulting from childhood abuse are released (Marchand, 2016).

Dobkin, Zhao, and Monshat (2017) examined a mixed group of patients with chronic illness, some of whom remained depressed post-MBSR. These patients were unable to perceive stressors in another light (as reflected by high stress post-MBSR), engaged in more often in emotional coping strategies (e.g., overreacting), and had less of a sense that life was manageable and comprehensible. Palliative coping (e.g., engaging in actions to alleviate the unpleasantness of a situation), which may be an expression of self-compassion, lessened from pre- to post-MBSR. This finding is noteworthy as it has been suggested that self-compassion partially mediates the relationship between mindfulness and well-being.

It is difficult to define the boundary between "true illness" and healthy distress or painful adjustments to socio-cultural contexts that may be unhealthy or spiritually unfulfilling (Hassed, 2000). There are qualitative and biologically demonstrable differences (Rothermundt et al., 2001; Baumeister, 2012) between severe, melancholic, or psychotic depressive illness and the variety of helpless, resigned, or withdrawn expressions of inner distress that also fulfill the DSM criteria for "major depressive disorder."

At the more severe end of the spectrum it may be judicious to limit a mindfulness "intervention." At the other end, depending on the phase of distress, what may be called for is not only meditation training, but also gradually engaging with the deeper spiritual underpinnings of mindfulness practice, which may lead to inner peace and contentment that surpass mere symptom alleviation.

Depression Case Study

Josephine is an intelligent woman in her fifties who has suffered with a variety of vague physical symptoms, anxiety, and low mood for many years. She has begun and given up a number of career paths over the years, despite her considerable talents. Not knowing her own mind has been a barrier to finding a long-term partner, which has robbed her of the chance to have children. When she was a child, her parents showed extreme favoritism toward her much older brother, who was an international sports star. Not only were Josephine's needs and aspirations not taken into account, but she was often asked to help her brother fulfill his relentless training requirements.

In the past few years, she has been in a committed relationship with a man she loves and respects, she's now financially secure, and she has the chance to work part-time and invest in her singing hobby. Nonetheless she has been suffering from depression and started therapy following a trial of antidepressants and training in breath-focus meditation—which only partially helped her.

Ongoing therapy has been informed by mindfulness principles, including the primacy of self-compassion; her inherent value; her non-separateness from others; as well as her past and future selves. She is able to experience these principles through mindfulness practices such as loving-kindness/compassion meditation, and establishing a caring connection with her sense of self as a young child.

Anxiety

Vøllestad (2016) describes anxiety disorders as a set of clinical conditions characterized by excessive fear, worry, and anxious apprehension. Mindfulness-based interventions appear to alleviate suffering across diagnoses through similar effects in cognitive, behavioral, and emotional domains. This is consistent with the "transdiagnostic" approach to anxiety disorders suggested by the overlap between symptoms, physiological disturbances, temperamental underpinnings, as well as by the efficacy of treatments across diagnostic categories (Barlow & Kennedy, 2016).

Not only do anxiety disorders overlap, but emotional dysregulation manifests in other ways as well, such as depression, either concurrently or sequentially. Barlow and Kennedy (2016) propose a formulation for anxiety along seven dimensions: (1) depressed mood; (2) autonomic arousal; (3) somatic anxiety; (4) social anxiety; (5) intrusive cognitions; (6) traumatic re-experiences and dissociation; and (7) avoidance. As cornerstones of a treatment approach informed by this model, they suggest training in objective, present-focused, non-judgmental awareness of emotions and recognition, and letting go of emotion avoidance and emotion-driven behaviors.

These are, of course, core mindfulness practices. Rather than avoid situations one learns to be in touch with discomfort and allow exposure to alter conditioned responses. Rumination is reduced when attending to the present moment, and the perpetuation of fear and worrying thoughts can be disrupted. Rather than being hypervigilant (associated with sensations such as a racing heart), one notices the transiency of negative feelings and thoughts. Ultimately, one's perception shifts from thinking "*I* am anxious" to "I notice anxiety."

Mindfulness of anxiety enables people to loosen their grip on the object of anxiety (i.e., what they are worrying *about*) and to accept the feeling of fear itself. In addition, insight regarding what lies underneath the emotion may arise. This can promote healing of long-ignored wounds and point the way to meaningful actions and the opportunity to live more fully.

Anxiety Case Study

Luke is a twenty-five-year-old man living with his sister who began feeling intensely anxious and worrying substantially about everyday matters a year ago. His difficulties arose soon after a year-long travel, which culminated in his coming out as gay to his family and friends, and finding a decent job. He feels bewildered and ashamed about his anxiety after such a successful and happy year.

He was brought up in a loving family and has had a passion for drama from an early age. Throughout his schooling in a religious institution, he was severely bullied and often felt depressed. This all changed at university where he completed a business degree, and felt that he had "got over" his school experience.

He came to therapy after having gained only limited relief from psychiatric medications. His stated goal was simply to feel less anxious so that he could get on with his life. He was instructed to pay caring attention to feelings of fear and recognize rumination and worry as expressions of avoidance that fuelled further anxiety. This was balanced with an awareness of neutral and pleasant sensations, such as the breath.

While attending in this way, he was invited to be curious as to what may underlie his anxiety, without resorting to analytical thought. This helped him recognize the deep wounds and the deficit in self-confidence due to bullying. Additionally, he came to see that he had chosen a business career to appear productive and successful to his now-internalized tormentors. In his heart he lived with an unfulfilled longing for the creative expression that he had only allowed himself to experience in drama classes. Having understood the roots of his anxiety, as well as following the mindfulness strategies he learned, led to an alleviation of anxiety.

Being able to experience anxiety with a caring curiosity about its nature is markedly different from being caught in the thoughts it triggers: "Why do I feel this way? I don't want to feel this way? What can I do to not feel this way?" When overwhelmed by strong painful feelings, the mind may be caught in endless self-analysis. At first this seems to offer some relief as it allows distancing from unpleasant feelings, but in the long term it reinforces the negative feelings. A caring non-analytical curiosity, by contrast, allows understanding, healing, and lasting relief.

Obsessive Compulsive Disorder

Obsessive compulsive disorder (OCD) is characterized by persistent ego dystonic thoughts and associated anxiety, leading to behaviors that seek to reduce the latter. From a behavioral viewpoint, this condition is maintained through negative reinforcement. For example, if one fears contamination and washes one's hands in reaction to that threat, anxiety may be momentarily reduced. Behavior therapy was therefore designed to decondition the person with OCD via exposure and response prevention. Cognitive therapy aims to identify and challenge intrusive, inaccurate appraisals in order to reduce the urge to engage in compulsive behaviors.

Mindfulness-Based Interventions (MBIs) invite people with OCD to pay attention to their thoughts and urges with curiosity and non-judgment. Thoughts are not seen as facts, allowing for dis-identification. Hale, Strauss, and Taylor (2013) compared outcomes between Cognitive Behavior Therapy (CBT) and MBIs, while examining the processes that might have contributed to these changes. Both approaches were helpful. Preliminary results for the MBIs suggest that thought-action "defusion" (i.e., bearing witness to thoughts; not acting upon them as if they are true) was a potential mechanism of change, but the sample sizes were small and further studies are needed to replicate this finding.

In a qualitative study, twelve patients with OCD were interviewed after taking a tailored Mindfulness Based Cognitive Therapy (MBCT) program. Seven patients found the course helpful and reported an increased ability to let unpleasant emotions surface, a willingness to entertain insights into the nature of the mind, and living more consciously in the present moment (Hertenstein et al., 2012). These changes were accompanied by the ability to refrain from compulsive behaviors and increased self-acceptance, improved mood, and sleep. In another qualitative study of MBCT for residual symptoms of OCD, 60 percent of thirty-two patients indicated improved cognition and acceptance of negative thoughts, as well as resorting less to automatic reactivity patterns (Sguazzin, Key, Rowa, Bieling, & McCabe, 2017).

If we examine these findings from a Buddhist-psychology perspective, we see that patients become more impartial observers of their thoughts, feelings, and actions.

Rather than reason with or resist the obsessions, much like pulling on the strings of a knot to untangle it, one simply notices them with a non-judgmental attitude. This allows space for other—positive and helpful— thoughts to arise. Osborne and Bhugra (2003) point out that most people ruminate regularly and what distinguishes individuals without OCD from those with OCD is that the latter act upon their thoughts. The emphasis on noticing the impermanence of all perceived phenomena in mindfulness practice can help a person with OCD realize that thoughts are transient and insubstantial events, which are allowed to come and go.

Obsessive compulsive disorder points to how a mindfulness approach can be beneficial beyond a cognitive-behavioral paradigm. On the one hand, MBIs may offer specific cognitive or behavioral skills that are particularly suited to altering maladaptive patterns in OCD. On the other, if a patient adopts mindfulness as a way of being and a path of spiritual development, some of the psychodynamic, existential, or spiritual conflicts that may underlie the OCD may be understood and resolved.

Obsessive Compulsive Disorder Case Study

Walter is a man approaching mid-life. He is in good physical condition and sought a "mindful therapist" to deal with his long-standing OCD. He had been treated by a psychiatrist, but discontinued medication prescribed as he believed mindfulness meditation and yoga had the potential to cure him. He has read extensively on the topic while using audio tapes to learn how to meditate. He was living on social assistance, had not worked as an artist for several years, and had some support from his ageing parents. Walter had a series of roommates that were "challenging" to live with for various reasons. He regretted and ruminated extensively about a failed romantic relationship.

He attended several years of psychotherapy. Progress was slow in part because his daily meditation and yoga practice had become compulsive behaviors that failed to relieve his anxiety. Shame and disgust regarding his violent sexual fantasies contributed to his self-loathing. Rituals surrounding sleep contributed to insomnia and exhaustion.

The first phase of therapy was based on Acceptance and Commitment Therapy, which aimed to help him define how he intended to live his life (e.g., work part-time, sleep normal hours) and identify his values (e.g., honesty, integrity). Since he was practicing yoga, we integrated body-wisdom into his repertoire. For example, when he felt overwhelmed by obsessions, he stood up and dropped his attention into his feet. The therapeutic relationship enabled him, slowly, to face and accept his emotions.

Rather than focus on the content of his obsessions, he worked on becoming aware of them as events of the mind; then he examined how he related to to them. Instead of feeling ashamed by his OCD, he was able to understand how it affected him.

Psychosis

Various psychotherapeutic approaches have been found to be useful adjuncts to psychotropic medications for people with psychotic disorders (Dickerson, 2000; Lysaker,

Glynn, Wilkniss, & Silverstein, 2010). A recent review and meta-analysis of MBIs found moderate short- and long-term effects on positive outcomes and duration of hospitalization, while negative symptoms and affect appeared unchanged (Cramer, Lauche, Haller, Langhorst, & Dobos, 2016).

Chadwick, Newman-Taylor, and Abba (2005) pioneered this field with a pilot study in which eleven patients with unremitting psychotic experiences attended a weekly ninety-minute group MBI intervention for six weeks. This consisted of ten-minute guided mindfulness exercises (e.g., brief body scan, mindful breathing), along with psychoeducation. Improvements found in this group were replicated in a small randomized clinical trial with twenty-two patients in another intervention lasting ten weeks. In both studies they found that patients were able to respond better to distressing thoughts and images.

In a longer, larger randomized clinical trial with 107 outpatients in China, Chien and Thompson (2014) compared three groups: six-month mindfulness-based psychoeducation (including elements of CBT), conventional psychoeducation, and routine care. The mindfulness group reported significantly greater improvements in psychiatric symptoms, psychosocial functioning, insight into illness/treatment, and duration (albeit not frequency) of hospital readmissions over a two-year period. Cultural factors seemed to facilitate understanding of Buddhist psychology principles: self-compassion was used as a way to resolve self-identity threats (i.e., shame among extended family and the need to save face; self-blame for having a mental illness); and inviting more communal support among group members served as a positive expression of interdependence.

Langer, Carmona-Torres, van Gordon, and Shonin (2016) reviewed the qualitative literature on MBIs for people with schizophrenia and other forms of psychosis, shedding light into what was perceived as most helpful. Like MBCT for depression, patients' relationship with symptoms changed as a function of metacognitive awareness. Voices, images, and thoughts were viewed as transitory. Self-acceptance emerged and patients found working in groups safe and supportive, allowing for the creation of "shared meanings."

It is important to highlight that these programs were designed so that meditations were brief and carefully guided; therapists were experienced with psychosis and capable of establishing a strong therapeutic alliance; patients continued to take their medications; groups were relatively small; and sessions were shorter than in other MBIs. Modifications were crucial for feasibility and acceptability of mindfulness training with this population (Chadwick, 2014).

Being at the extreme end of the spectrum of mental disorders, psychosis is an excellent illustration of how mindfulness may be helpful or ill-advised for certain populations. As with patients who suffer with dissociative phenomena (e.g., post-traumatic stress disorder), the "inner space" accessed during formal sitting meditation may give rise to distressing images or sounds. It may, therefore, be preferable to emphasize movement practices (e.g., walking meditation or yoga) or awareness of external auditory (e.g., birds singing) or visual stimuli to help patients feel more grounded in concrete aspects of their experience.

Psychosis Case Study

Claire is a personable twenty-two-year-old woman with a diagnosis of schizophrenia who lives with her parents. For a number of years, she has suffered from a perception that the skin of her face and her hair look dreadful. She uses various creams and shampoos with little perceived effect and needs to be talked out of more invasive dermatological interventions. A related fear is that others look at her in an intrusive way, judge her unfavorably, and may have malign intentions toward her. She tries to maintain various courses of study and part-time work, but finds it difficult to see it through, given her fears. She occasionally experiences a vague sense of a shadow out of the corner of her eye along with hearing her name being called. She appears to have no inherent difficulty organizing her thoughts, save for the distractions that her symptoms evoke.

Since receiving a low dose of antipsychotic medication, the frequency and intensity of her unusual experiences have lessened, and she can better tolerate being out of the house and interacting with others. However, she continues to doubt whether she is actually ill and is reluctant to make changes to the type and dose of medication. She is deemed suitable for adjunctive mindfulness-informed psychotherapy.

The importance of her relationship with her symptoms (examining whether they are "true") is discussed and following a trial of various techniques she settles on taking her dog for daily walks in the park as her mindfulness "practice." She is guided to notice pleasant body sensations and cultivate appreciation and gratitude for the ways in which her body is functioning well and is aesthetically pleasing. When she sees others, she is instructed to pay a kind attention to the body sensations associated with her fears. In this way, she is able to gradually place her fears in greater perspective and able to live better in spite of their continuing presence.

Conclusion

A Middle Way Toward Integration

Mindfulness practice rests on a dynamic balance of polarities and can be described as a "Middle Way" between the perspectives offered by modern science and Buddhist psychology. Spiritual traditions help us to understand our common humanity and interconnectedness, as well as the existential malaise that we may *all* suffer from—to a greater or lesser degree. In contrast, psychology and psychiatry have historically focused on the sickness of the *few*, and they have generated a body of knowledge oriented toward understanding and treating mental illness. Contemplative practices emphasize the subjective and personal, while the Western medical approach focuses on what is objective, generalizable, and verifiable using the scientific method. The biopsychosocial-spiritual formulation highlighted here aims to integrate these perspectives.

The relationship between the perceived phenomenon of mind and the physical nervous system reflects this complementarity. When both patient and clinician view the subjective and the objective as inseparable phenomena, they will not fall prey to a false mind-body dichotomy. When oriented toward the whole person, the search for physical causes and the underlying psychodynamic conflicts is no longer an either/or exercise. Instead, the symptoms work as a starting point for understanding and caring for all aspects of the person.

For instance, an integrative view can help the clinician detect and treat thyroid hypofunction in a patient with depression, while concurrently honoring her feelings of dejection and despair. In this way, the strain on the patient's emotional equilibrium brought about by a physical illness is acknowledged, instead of it being rejected as meaningless or of little relevance.

Intentions and Methods

The *intention* in mindfulness practice is to cultivate qualities of the mind that promote greater well-being. The ability to regulate emotions, have a balanced relationship with one's self-concept, and be embedded within a social network has been highlighted as central to well-being in this chapter. Mindfulness, conceived of as an aspiration to live with greater compassionate awareness, may be supportive for most people in this regard. However, each particular *method* is not to be confused with or over-valued at the expense of these qualities themselves.

Formal mindfulness meditation is by no means a panacea. For some individuals, alternatives to sitting with breath awareness meditation promote inner calm more effectively (e.g., yoga in those with a tendency to dissociate). For a subset of people, an inflexible emphasis on a particular approach may be harmful. Adverse outcomes such as psychotic episodes in schizophrenia and bipolar disorder, suicidal ideation in depression, or re-traumatization in post-traumatic stress disorder have been documented, particularly during long meditation retreats (Lindahl, Fisher, Cooper, Rosen, & Britton, 2017; Magid, 2002).

As Magid (2002, p. 102) states, "For the dismantling of old structures of subjectivity to result in a breakthrough rather than a breakdown, the student must have basic skills of affect regulation at his or her disposal... In the absence of this capacity, a student may panic, feel pointlessly or sadistically tortured by painful sitting, or evolve quasi-delusional grandiose fantasies of enlightenment as a way of making sense of what's happening." Furthermore, meditators whose core neurotic conflicts and deficits have not been adequately addressed may find that the practice of meditation reinforces defensive patterns.

Medication and psychotherapy treatments may serve overlapping and complementary roles in relation to mindfulness practice. The long-term psychotherapeutic relationship and the illness-specific knowledge base are essential for many patients, as is presenting a context for mindfulness practice. Concurrently, skills and perspectives gained by mindfulness practitioners can enrich psychotherapy experiences (Epstein, 2007).

Broadly speaking, mindfulness practice includes *techniques* to support emotion regulation, as well as a *perspective* and a *way of being* that allows for a different relationship with oneself and the difficulties experienced. Kabat-Zinn (2015) calls these the *instrumental* and *non-instrumental* aspects of the practice. These mirror psychotherapy models like Cognitive Behavior Therapy where one is asked to do a certain exercise or learn a skill, or the interpretive work offered by long-term interventions such as psychodynamic or analytic therapy. Here the individual senses a way of being that opens them to a deep, felt understanding of their situation and its origins.

The Buddha is said to have lauded spiritual friendship as containing within it the entire path of spiritual development (Batchelor, 2015). A sense of well-being results when mindfulness practice is embedded in one's connection with others; this is similar to emphasis on social factors for mental health, mentioned earlier. The presence of like-hearted individuals who share similarly salubrious aspirations can be healing, whatever formal practices one engages in. Thus, secular-trained clinicians can recommend patients seek companionship on the path of healing and growth. In this way, the focus in formal therapy or medication treatment for symptoms of illness can be balanced by an explicit emphasis on positive emotions and connectedness.

References

Aitkin, R. (1919). *The gateless barrier*. San Francisco: North Point.

American Psychiatric Association. (1980). *The diagnostic and statistical manual of mental disorders* (3rd ed.). Washington, DC: APA. https://ajp.psychiatryonline.org/doi/abs/10.1176/ajp.145.10.1301

Barlow, D. H, & Kennedy, K. A. (2016). New approaches to diagnosis and treatment in anxiety and related emotional disorders: A focus on temperament. *Canadian Psychology* 57(1), 8–20.

Batchelor, S. (2015). *After Buddhism: Rethinking the dharma for a secular age*. New Haven, CT: Yale University Press.

Baumeister, H., & Parker, G. (2012). Meta-review of depressive subtyping models. *Journal of Affective Disorders* 139(2), 126–140.

Beck, A. T., & Bredemeier, K. (2016). A unified model of depression: Integrating clinical, cognitive, biological and evolutional perspectives. *Clinical Psychological Science* 4(4), 596–619.

Bolier, L., Haverman, M., Westerhof, G. J., Riper, H., Smit, F., & Bohlmeijer, E. (2013). Positive psychology interventions: A meta-analysis of randomized controlled studies. *BMC Public Health* 13(1), 119.

Bracken, O., Thomas, P., Timimi, S., et al. (2012). Psychiatry beyond the current paradigm. *British Journal of Psychiatry* 201(6), 430–434. https://doi.org/10.1192/bjp.bp.112.109447

Chadwick, P. (2014). Mindfulness for psychosis. *British Journal of Psychiatry* 204(5), 333–334.

Chadwick, P., Hughes, S., Russell, D., et al. (2009). Mindfulness groups for distressing voices and paranoia: A replication and randomised feasibility trial. *Behavioural and Cognitive Psychotherapy* 37, 403–412.

Chadwick, P., Newman-Taylor, K., & Abba, N. J. (2005). Mindfulness groups for people with psychosis. *Behavioural and Cognitive Psychotherapy* 33, 351–359.

Chien, W. T., & Thompson, D. R. (2014). Effects of a mindfulness-based psychoeducation programme for Chinese patients with schizophrenia: 2-year follow-up. *British Journal of Psychiatry* 205(1), 52–59. https://doi.org.10.1192/bjp.bp.113.134635

Chiesa, A., Anselmi, R., & Serretti, A. (2014). Psychological mechanisms of mindfulness-based interventions. *Holistic Nursing Practice* 28(2), 24–148.

Chiesa, A., Castagner, V., Andrisand, C., et al. (2015). Mindfulness-Based Cognitive Therapy vs. psycho-education for patients with major depression who did not achieve remission following antidepressant treatment. *Psychiatry Research* 226, 474–483.

Cramer, H., Lauche, R., Haller, H., Langhorst, J., & Dobos, G. (2016). Mindfulness- and acceptance-based interventions for psychosis: A systematic review and meta-analysis. *Global Advances in Health and Medicine* 5(1), 30–43. https://doi.org/10.7453/gahmj.2015.083

Crowe, K., & McKay, D. (2016). Mindfulness, obsessive-compulsive symptoms and executive dysfunction. *Cognitive Therapy and Research* 40, 627–644.

Dickerson, F. B. (2000). Cognitive behavioral psychotherapy for schizophrenia: A review of recent empirical studies. *Schizophrenia Research* 43(2), 71–90.

Dobkin, P. L., Zhao, Q., & Monshat, K. (2017). Who experiences depressive symptoms following Mindfulness-Based Stress Reduction and why? *International Journal of Whole Person Care* 4(1), 13–31.

Epstein, M. (2007). *Psychotherapy without the self: A Buddhist perspective.* New Haven, CT: Yale University Press.

Frances, A. (2016). A report card on the utility of psychiatric diagnosis. *World Psychiatry* 15(1), 32–33.

Fulton, P. R. (2009). Mindfulness-based intervention in an individual clinical setting: What difference mindfulness makes behind closed doors. In F. Didonna (Ed.), *Clinical handbook of mindfulness* (pp. 407–416). New York: Springer.

Grossman P. (2010). Mindfulness for psychologists: Paying kind attention to the perceptible. *Mindfulness* 1(2), 87–97.

Hale, L., Strauss, C., & Taylor, B. L. (2013). The effectiveness and acceptability of mindfulness-based therapy for OCD: A review of the literature. *Mindfulness* 4, 375–382.

Hassed, C. S. (2000). Depression: Dispirited or spiritually deprived? *Medical Journal of Australia* 173(10), 545.

Hertenstein, E., Rose, N., Voderholzer, U., Nissen, C., Thiel, N., Herbst, N., & Külz, A. K. (2012). Mindfulness-Based Cognitive Therapy in obsessive-compulsive disorder: A qualitative study on patients' experiences. *BMC Psychiatry* 12, 1–10. https://doi.org/10.1186/1471-244X-12-185

Jureidini, J. (2012). Explanations and unexplanations: Restoring meaning to psychiatry. *Australian & New Zealand Journal of Psychiatry* 46(3), 188–191. https://doi.org/10.1177/0004867412437347

Kabat-Zinn, J. (2003). Mindfulness-based interventions in context: Past, present, and future. *Clinical Psychology: Science and Practice* 10(2), 144–56.

Kabat-Zinn, J. (2015). Two ways to think about meditation: The instrumental and the non-instrumental. *Mindfulness* 6, 396–397.

Kearns, N. P., Shawyer, F., Brooker, J. E. et al. (2016). Does rumination mediate the relationship between mindfulness and depressive relapse? *Psych and Psychotherapy Theory, Research and Practice* 89, 33–49.

Kelly, B. (2008). Buddhist psychology, psychotherapy and the brain: A critical introduction. *Transcultural Psychiatry* 45(1), 5–30. https://doi.org/10.1177/1363461507087996

Kelly, B. (2016). Compassion, cognition and the illusion of self: Buddhist notes towards more skillful engagement with diagnostic classification systems in psychiatry. In E. Shonin et al. (Eds.), *Mindfulness and Buddhist-derived approaches in mental health and addiction* (pp. 9–28). Cham, Switzerland: Springer International Publishing

Keown, D. (2013). *Contemporary Buddhist ethics*. London: Routledge.

Kinderman, P. (2014). *A prescription for psychiatry: Why we need a whole new approach to mental health and wellbeing*. London: Palgrave and Macmillan.

Kuyken, W., Hayes, R., Barrett, B., et al. (2015). Effectiveness and cost-effectiveness of MBCT compared with maintenance antidepressant treatment in the prevention of depressive relapse or recurrence (the PREVENT study): A RCT. *Lancet 386*, 63–73.

Lakeman, R., & Cutcliffe, J. (2016). Diagnostic sedition: Re-considering the ascension and hegemony of contemporary psychiatric diagnosis. *Issues in Mental Health Nursing 37*, 125–130. https://doi.org/10.3109/01612840.2015.1103341

Langer, A. I., Carmona-Torres, J. A., van Gordon, W., & Shonin, E. (2016). Mindfulness for the treatment of psychosis: Start of the art and future developments. In E. Shonin et al. (Eds.), *Mindfulness and Buddhist-derived approaches to mental health and addiction* (pp. 211–224). Cham: Springer International Publishing. https://doi.org/10.1007/978-3-319-22255-4_10

Lemmens, H. J. M., Müller, V., Arntz, A., & Huibers, M. (2016). Mechanisms of change in psychotherapy for depression: An empirical update and evaluation of research aimed at identifying the psychological mediators. *Clinical Psychology Review 50*, 95–107.

Lindahl, J. R., Fisher, N. E., Cooper, D. J., Rosen, R. K., & Britton, W. B. (2017). The varieties of contemplative experience: A mixed-methods study of meditation-related challenges in Western Buddhists. *PLoS One 12*(5), e0176239.

Lysaker, P. H., Glynn, S. M., Wilkniss, S. M., & Silverstein, S. M. (2010). Psychotherapy and recovery from schizophrenia: A review of potential applications and need for future study. *Psychological Services 7*(2), 75.

Magid, B. (2002). *Ordinary mind: Exploring the common ground of Zen and psychotherapy*. Boston: Wisdom Publications.

Marchand, W. R. (2016). Mindfulness in the treatment of depression. In E. Shonin et al. (Eds.), *Mindfulness and Buddhist-derived approaches in mental health and addiction* (pp. 139–164). Cham, Switzerland: Springer International Publishing.

Meadows, G. (2003). Buddhism and psychiatry: Confluence and conflict. *Australasian Psychiatry 11*, 16–20.

Mount, B. (2006). The 10 commandments of healing. *Journal of Cancer Education 21*(1), 50–51.

Ñāṇamoli, Bhikkhu, & Bodhi, Bhikkhu. (1995). *The middle-length discourses of the Buddha: A translation of the Majjhima Nikāya*. Boston: Wisdom.

National Center for Health Statistics. (2016). *International Statistical Classification of Diseases and Related Health Problems* (10th rev.). Retrieved from http://apps.who.int/classifications/icd10/browse/2016/en

Neitzke, A. B. (2016). An illness of power: Gender and the social causes of depression. *Culture, Medicine and Psychiatry 40*, 59–73. https://doi.org/10.1007/s11013-015-9466-3

Nhat Hanh, Thich. (1999). *The heart of the Buddha's teachings*. Berkeley, CA: Parallax.

Nhat Hanh, Thich. (2009). *Happiness: Essential mindfulness practices*. Berkeley, CA: Parallax.

Norman, K. R. (2003). The Four Noble Truths. In *Collected Papers II* (pp. 210–223). Oxford: Pali Text Society.

Osborne, T. R., & Bhugra, D. (2003). Spiritual thoughts in psychiatry. *Indian Journal of Psychiatry 45*, 142–146.

Plante, T. G. (2008). What do the spiritual and religious traditions offer the practicing psychologist? *Pastoral Psychology* 56(4), 429–444.

Ricard, M. (2007). *Happiness: A guide to developing life's most important skill*. New York: Little Brown.

Röhricht, F. (2009). Body oriented psychotherapy. The state of the art in empirical research and evidence-based practice: A clinical perspective. *Body, Movement and Dance in Psychotherapy* 4(2), 135–156.

Rosenbaum, R. (1999). *Zen and the heart of psychotherapy*. Philadelphia: Brunner/Mazel.

Rothermundt, M., Arolt, V., Fenker, J., Gutbrodt, H., Peters, M., & Kirchner, H. (2001). Different immune patterns in melancholic and non-melancholic major depression. *European Archives of Psychiatry and Clinical Neuroscience* 251(2), 90–97.

Schmidt, S. (2004). Mindfulness and healing intentions: Concepts, practice and research evaluation. *Journal of Alternative and Complementary Medicine* 10(1), S7–S14.

Sguazzin, C. M. G., Key, B. L., Rowa, K., Bieling, P. J., & McCabe, R. E. (2017). Mindfulness-Based Cognitive Therapy for residual symptoms of obsessive-compulsive disorder: A qualitative analyses. *Mindfulness* 8(1),190–203.

Tsou, J. Y. (2016). Natural kinds, psychiatric classification and the history of the DSM. *History of Psychiatry* 27(4), 406–424. https://doi.org/10.1177/0957154X16656580

Van der Velden, A. M., Kuyken, W. K., Waar, U., et al. (2015). A systematic review of mechanisms of change in MBCT in the treatment of recurrent major depressive disorder. *Clinical Psychology Review* 37, 26–39.

Vøllestad, J. (2016). Mindfulness and acceptance-based interventions in the treatment of anxiety disorders. In E. Shonin et al. (Eds.) *Mindfulness and Buddhist-derived approaches to mental health and addiction* (pp. 97–137). Cham, Switzerland: Springer International Publishing.

CHAPTER 32

MINDFULNESS-BASED INTERVENTIONS IN THE TREATMENT OF PHYSICAL CONDITIONS

MADHAV GOYAL AND HEATHER L. RUSCH

Introduction

Mindfulness meditation is a style of meditation stemming from a Buddhist practice called Vipassana. The Buddhist Four Noble Truths and Noble Eightfold Path posit that humans are subject to existential delusions, which result in suffering—namely that all perceived things are impermanent (*anicca*), unsatisfactory (*dukkha*), and none represent an actual permanent self (*anatta*).(Müller, 1881). The dissolution of these delusions is believed to result in the end of suffering, and with increased awareness one begins to see things as they really are.

The mindfulness-based interventions that have been tested in clinical trials primarily revolve around mindfulness-based stress reduction (MBSR), an eight-week course involving about 2.5 hours per week of class with daily homework exercises. In the evolution of clinical trials using mindfulness interventions, modified courses have been created, such as mindfulness-based cognitive therapy (MBCT), a hybrid of MBSR and cognitive behavioral therapy (CBT). Other modifications include shorter or, rarely, longer versions of MBSR. Still others modify the MBSR course to target a particular condition, such as substance abuse issues for people with tobacco, alcohol, or other addictions.

Mindfulness-based interventions have been tested in numerous health conditions, ranging from anxiety to HIV and cancer. We've focused mainly on results from randomized controlled trials in this chapter. One challenge to understanding research investigating mindfulness-based interventions on physical conditions is the use of different control groups, which results in a different interpretation of the conclusions. It is no longer a question of whether mindfulness has an effect, but rather of the magnitude of effect it has compared with a particular type of control.

Understanding Control Groups

In a typical research study involving drugs, researchers will use a placebo control. For example, to test whether a particular drug reduces blood pressure, researchers will create a placebo pill that looks and tastes identical to the actual blood pressure pill so that the person taking the pill can't tell if they are taking the actual medicine or the placebo. Since placebos can have biological effects on the body, the design of the research study using placebos allows us to tell how much more effect the drug has than a placebo. If it isn't much different from the effect of the placebo, then we say that the drug doesn't have an effect. Another way of thinking about this is to say that the drug doesn't have an effect that is larger than the effect that our minds can convince ourselves of having (i.e., the placebo effect) when the mind believes that something will help it.

Studies of mindfulness are more complicated since mindfulness is a behavioral intervention, and one can't simply give a placebo pill to compare it to. Researchers can get around this by creating comparison groups that would act like placebos. These placebo groups are often support groups or involve educational training on the condition of interest without teaching the main skills taught in the meditation group. They also match the time and attention given by an instructor in the meditation group to make the two groups feel similar. However, such studies are expensive and more difficult to carry out. Thus, researchers have conducted studies of mindfulness interventions using three basic types of control groups. The first type is a "usual care" or "wait-list" control group. In these control groups, the participants don't meditate and don't get any special treatment the way the mindfulness group does. Everyone continues to get the usual care they get from their doctors, and if they are wait-listed they are also allowed to attend the mindfulness course after the study is completed. This design does not measure how effective mindfulness is compared with a placebo, but rather against a group of people who are getting usual medical care. This design is often meaningful when comparisons to usual medical care are desired. However, if scientists are interested in knowing more about the specificity and mechanisms of how mindfulness works, they may want an actual placebo comparison group, which is the second type of control group. The third type of comparison is against a known therapy or something that is already known to improve the outcome. For example, regular exercise has been shown to boost immunity and reduce respiratory infections. If we wanted to test how well mindfulness reduces colds, and we compared mindfulness practitioners to people who exercised daily, we would be asking ourselves whether a mindfulness intervention was better than another known therapy. In this third comparison, we are typically asking for much more than a placebo comparison. This is called comparative effectiveness research since we are comparing the effectiveness of a mindfulness intervention against something already shown to have an effect.

Strengths of Evidence

Since it can be onerous to make sense of the numerous randomized trials of mindfulness on the various clinical conditions, individual reviews have been conducted to synthesize the results of relevant clinical trials on a given condition or topic. These "systematic reviews" usually find a mix of good quality and poor quality studies, along with some studies finding an improvement while other studies didn't. In summarizing the different clinical trials, systematic reviews will often rate the overall evidence as insufficient, low, moderate, or high. These ratings combine different measurements such as quality of trials, consistency of the evidence, and other criteria to convey the scientists' confidence of how strong the evidence for or against a particular therapy is. A high strength of evidence indicates that future trials on the same subject are unlikely to change the conclusions, and are therefore unnecessary.

Most of the studies reviewed in this chapter will focus on usual care/wait-list controls or placebo controls for physical health conditions. While there is some overlap between mental and physical conditions, a comprehensive review of mental health conditions found that mindfulness has moderate strength of evidence to improve symptoms of anxiety, depression, and pain (Goyal et al., 2014b). Since one or two trials on a particular outcome generally provide limited preliminary information, and are often small pilot studies, we've mainly focused on the conditions for which a systematic review has already been undertaken. This chapter reviews the more salient conditions for which there is a body of evidence, citing individual trials where relevant. Some are known medical conditions such as hypertension, diabetes, and heart or lung disease. Others studies focus on symptoms common to many medical conditions such as symptoms associated with cancer, various pain syndromes, and insomnia.

Conditions and Symptoms

Pain

Pain is one of the most common and troubling symptoms that people present with to the doctor's office. It is also a particularly relevant condition to target given the number of opioid-related deaths that have occurred recently. A number of trials have evaluated the effects of mindfulness-based interventions on different types of pain. A comprehensive review conducted in 2014 of the effects of meditation programs on mental health, attention, substance use, sleep, eating, pain, and weight looked specifically for trials that used a placebo control in order to assess whether meditation programs had an effect above and beyond a placebo (Goyal et al., 2014a). It found only 36 clinical trials of mindfulness interventions that used a placebo control, and of those, eight trials evaluated pain as an outcome. Of these eight trials, four used a known therapy such as massage or yoga as a control and found no difference between MBSR and the control. The remaining four used a placebo control. One trial assessed pain in 122 organ transplant recipients, another assessed pain in 109 patients with fibromyalgia, a third assessed pain in 35 patients with chronic low back pain, and the fourth assessed it in 75 women with irritable bowel syndrome. In the first three trials mild improvements in pain of 5–8 percent were seen in the MBSR groups relative to the placebo one, but the trial among women with irritable bowel syndrome showed very significant 30 percent improvements in pain. These four trials were all of good to excellent quality, and the review rated mindfulness meditation as having moderate strength of evidence for small improvements in pain severity. Since few trials were conducted with a placebo control, the authors were not able to conclude whether mindfulness was better for one type of pain or another, but the magnitude of improvement in the irritable bowel syndrome group certainly raised this question.

Another systematic review evaluated randomized trials of patients with any chronic pain condition that used any kind of a control group (Hilton et al., 2017). They found thirty-eight trials involving patients with a wide range of pain conditions. They also included some studies that used internet-based mindfulness courses rather than in-person courses. Compared with the prior review, this one found overall low strength of evidence that mindfulness meditation can improve pain. However, similar to the prior review, the magnitude of effect that the authors felt mindfulness had on pain was small. The review also investigated whether higher quality studies showed different results from poor quality studies. When excluding poor quality studies, they found that mindfulness had an even smaller effect.

Irritable Bowel Syndrome

There has been one other trial on irritable bowel syndrome that was conducted in Canada (Zernicke et al., 2013). They randomized ninety participants to MBSR or a wait-list control group. Ninety percent of participants were women. This study had a large dropout rate limiting its findings, but also found similarly large (24 percent) reductions in pain.

Fibromyalgia

Few trials have been conducted on fibromyalgia. A systematic review in 2013 found six randomized and non-randomized trials (Lauche, Cramer, Dobos, Langhorst, & Schmidt, 2013). They found a small effect on pain, but the overall strength of evidence was low. Online mindfulness interventions have also been tried with similar results (Davis & Zautra, 2013).

Low Back Pain

Some of the largest trials of mindfulness meditation are on those suffering from chronic low back pain, as it is a significant public health concern. About 20 percent of the population suffers from it annually, and about 75 percent of us will suffer from it over our lifetimes (Anheyer et al., 2017). The overall magnitude of effect remains small, but the American College of Physicians recently published a guideline recommending mindfulness meditation in the treatment of chronic low back pain with moderate strength of evidence (Chou et al., 2017). Two large trials are worthy of comment. The first trial randomized 342 patients with chronic low back pain to MBSR, cognitive behavioral therapy (an established mind-body intervention recommended in chronic low back pain guidelines), or usual care (Cherkin et al., 2016). At six months, the percentage of patients with clinically meaningful improvements in disability and pain bothersomeness was similar for both MBSR and cognitive behavioral therapy, but significantly more than those receiving usual medical care. The differences remained significant up to one year after the eight-week course, indicating a considerable number of people experienced clinically important relief of pain and disability. However, the results did not hold at two years for the MBSR group, but did for the cognitive behavioral therapy group. The second trial randomized 282 elderly patients suffering from chronic low back pain to MBSR or a placebo control (Morone et al., 2016). This trial found improvements in disability and severe pain in the short term, but not at six months. The two trials were different in that the first one did not focus exclusively on elderly patients, a group that may be more difficult to treat. It also compared MBSR with usual care rather than an active placebo group.

Other Pain Conditions

Few randomized trials have been conducted on other forms of pain. A study on headaches randomized thirty-six people with headaches to mindfulness-based cognitive therapy or wait-list control. This trial found no evidence of any effect on pain intensity or frequency (Day et al., 2014). A study of fifty-five Gulf War I veterans who were randomized to MBSR or usual care found significant reductions in pain, fatigue, cognitive failures, and depression at six months (Kearney et al., 2016). A variant of MBSR called mindfulness-oriented recovery enhancement (MORE) unites mindfulness training with cognitive behavioral therapy and principles from positive psychology. This therapy was tested in a clinical trial of 115 chronic pain patients to evaluate whether it could reduce chronic pain as well as opioid misuse (Garland et al., 2014). After randomizing to MORE or a placebo control group, this trial found that MORE participants had significantly lower pain severity and pain interference up to three months after the training. Immediately after the eight-week training, there was also a significant reduction in opioid misuse, but that effect dissipated with time.

None of the systematic reviews stratified their analysis by type of pain to evaluate whether one form of pain was more responsive to mindfulness training than another. In the review by Goyal and colleagues, it appeared that musculoskeletal pain had less of a response to MBSR than visceral pain such as occurs in irritable bowel syndrome. The improvements in pain are generally also accompanied by improvements in mood, which can be important to the changes seen in pain. There may be some gender-specific responses to the mindfulness training that could account for the differences we see. The studies of irritable bowel syndrome were largely conducted in women. The training of CBT could also be more effective than what is accomplished in an eight-week course of mindfulness. These are questions still and will hopefully be clarified with future studies.

Cancer

While cancer survivors suffer from physical and psychological symptoms, most of the outcomes studied of mindfulness interventions in cancer have focused on psychological health. A few systematic reviews have been conducted and the most recent included ten trials of MBSR or MBCT that were tested on women with breast cancer (Haller et al., 2017). All the studies used wait-list controls and the systematic review found short-term improvements in quality of life, fatigue, sleep, stress, anxiety, and depression among women who had been treated for breast cancer. However, the review questioned whether the small improvements were clinically meaningful for any of the outcomes.

Although breast cancer appears to have been the most widely studied cancer with a mindfulness intervention, other trials have been conducted. Cachexia is a wasting syndrome characterized by loss of weight, fatigue, and weakness. It is often seen in cancer patients. A trial in Belgium randomized fifty-three cachectic cancer patients to either usual care or a mindfulness intervention that also incorporated a dietary workshop emphasizing that food had to be appreciated through the five senses (Focan et al., 2015). This trial found a statistically significant increase of 2.8 kg in the mindfulness eating group compared with the usual medical care group, as well as an increase in physical functioning. The usual care group actually lost weight in this trial. This is unusual to find in a mindfulness trial, and it is unclear how much of the effect was due to the mindfulness versus dietary portion, or whether it is was a combination of these that produced this effect. However, treating cachexia in cancer patients is a challenge, and the positive findings deserve further investigation.

Fatigue is a significant disabling symptom in cancer treatment. A small trial in Indiana randomized thirty-five patients with cancer-related fatigue to a seven-week mindfulness course or wait-list control (Johns et al., 2015). Most of the patients had breast cancer, but a few had hematologic malignancies. They found large improvements in the degree to which fatigue interfered with their daily lives among those who underwent the MBSR course. Various other studies have found similar results on fatigue (van der Lee & Garssen, 2012).

Sexual Function

Sexual function is becoming a greater societal concern in the west with the advent of medicines to improve it and is certainly a concern among those with gynecologic malignancies. Thirty-one women who had completed treatment for endometrial or cervical cancer and who reported significantly diminished sexual desire or arousability were randomized to MBCT or a wait-list control (Brotto et al., 2012). Mindfulness-based cognitive therapy was administered in individual sessions lasting ninety minutes once a month for three months by a registered psychologist or sex therapist. Significant improvements in desire, arousal, lubrication, orgasm, and satisfaction were observed. Sexual distress also improved. These improvements lasted at least six months. A systematic review of mindfulness-based interventions for female sexual dysfunction found eleven trials (Stephenson & Kerth, 2017). This review concluded that all aspects of sexual function and subjective sexual well-being improved significantly with moderately large effects. However, there were several limitations to the studies in that most of them were conducted by one research group, the number of studies were few, and the number of women in each study quite small. The mindfulness program incorporated many aspects of CBT, and it was unclear to what degree the mindfulness aspect was responsible for the effects. As this is a nascent area of research, further trials with greater number of participants and improvements in research design are needed.

Blood Pressure

Very few studies have been conducted evaluating the effects of mindfulness meditation on blood pressure. A Canadian study randomized 101 adults with prehypertension and stage I hypertension who were not on blood pressure medication to MBSR or wait-list control (Blom et al., 2014). It found no difference between the groups that were treated or untreated. Another much smaller trial randomized twenty African Americans living in a low-income senior residence to eight weeks of MBSR or placebo control group (Palta et al., 2012). They found a twenty-two-point drop in systolic blood pressure in the MBSR group compared with the placebo group and a seventeen-point drop in diastolic blood pressure. These are incredibly large improvements that have not been borne out in other studies. The authors of the Canadian study conducted a review of the effects of numerous mind-body treatments on blood pressure. They compared those trials that found a blood-pressure-lowering effect with those trials that did not find an effect. It appeared that all of the trials that found an effect also had a large number of patients on antihypertensive medication, whereas the patients that were in the trials that did not find an effect were not taking blood pressure medications. They surmised that the mind-body treatments may be making patients more adherent with their medications, thus lowering the blood pressure (Blom et al., 2014).

Heart Disease

Very few randomized trials of mindfulness have been conducted on patients with heart disease. Most of the meditation studies involving heart patients have been conducted with transcendental meditation. One relevant mindfulness study was conducted in the Netherlands in which 324 patients with heart disease were randomized to an online twelve-week mindfulness course or usual care (Younge et al., 2015). Approximately 40 percent of the patients had congenital heart disease, 40 percent had cardiomyopathy, and another 20 percent had valvular heart disease. The primary outcome of the study was a six-minute walk test in which patients are asked to walk a long corridor to see how far they can go in six minutes. This study showed that at the end of the twelve-week online training, patients in the mindfulness group were able to walk 13.2 meters farther on average than those receiving usual care. Their heart rates were also lower by about three beats per minute, and although this is a small reduction it was statistically significant. This trial found no reductions in blood pressure, respiratory rate, nor any improvement in any of the psychological outcomes.

Diabetes

Diabetes has many adverse effects on the body, damaging multiple organ systems including the heart, brain, and kidneys. We often measure how well it is controlled by a blood test called hemoglobin A1c (HbA1c). This test measures the average glucose levels in the blood over the past three months. A non-diabetic will have a value of less than 5.7 percent while a diabetic is defined as someone with a HbA1c level of 6.5 percent or higher.

A recent systematic review identified eleven trials evaluating mindfulness-based interventions among patients with diabetes (Noordali, Cumming, & Thompson, 2017). This review found that there were a significant number of studies showing positive psychological benefits in terms of reductions in symptoms of depression, anxiety, and distress among diabetics. However, only five trials measured biological outcomes, and they did not see any changes.

Three trials were conducted in Europe. A Netherlands trial randomized 139 patients with either type 1 or type 2 diabetes who also had low levels of emotional well-being to MBCT or a wait-list control group (van Son et al., 2012). Negative mood symptoms affect a large percentage of diabetics and are associated with suboptimal self-care behaviors. Their hypothesis was that if negative mood could be addressed through mindfulness therapy, this may improve diabetic outcomes such as hyperglycemia.

They found significant improvements in anxiety and depression, but not in the HbA1c at three or six months; moreover, this trial suffered from a high drop-out rate. A second trial from the Netherlands randomized ninety-four diabetic patients with depressive symptoms to MBCT, CBT, or a wait-list control (Tovote et al., 2014). At three months this trial found large improvements in depression, anxiety, and well-being among those randomized to MBCT or CBT as compared with those in the wait-list group. However, there were no improvements in HbA1c. At the nine-month follow-up, they continued to see large improvements in depression, anxiety, and well-being in both MBCT and CBT groups, but saw no improvements in HbA1c (Tovote et al., 2015). A group in Germany initiated a five-year study of the effects of MBSR among diabetics with albuminuria, an excessive leakage of albumin through the kidneys (Hartmann et al., 2012). Albuminuria is one of the main outcomes doctors test for in diabetics due to the damaging effects of diabetes on the kidneys. Similar to the previous studies, preliminary results at one year show improvements in depressive symptoms, but no change in albuminuria, HbA1c, or blood pressure.

A study in Korea randomized fifty-six diabetics to MBSR, a walking group, or a placebo group (Jung, Lee, & Park, 2015). It found no differences in psychological stress, fasting glucose, or vascular inflammation. A study in the USA randomized fifty-two patients with type 2 diabetes and a body-mass index (BMI) of twenty-seven or more to a three-month mindful-eating class or a diabetes self-management education class called Smart Choices (Miller, Kristeller, Headings, Nagaraja, & Miser, 2012). A BMI of twenty to twenty-five is considered normal, while BMIs higher than twenty-five are considered overweight or obese. At the three-month follow-up there were no differences between the two groups in weight, waist circumference, or HbA1c. However, all of these outcomes improved within each group from baseline. The HbA1c improved by 0.8 percent in the mindful eating group, and by 0.7 percent in the Smart Choices group. These are small improvements but still clinically meaningful. This is also the only study to show improvements in the HbA1c from baseline for a mindfulness intervention.

Substance Use

Smoking

More people are addicted to nicotine than to any other drug. Quitting smoking often requires several attempts, and those who stop often start again due to withdrawal symptoms, stress, and weight gain (CDC, 2017). Several randomized trials have been conducted to assess the effects of a mindfulness-based intervention on smoking cessation. Initial results from these trials suggested that adaptations of MBSR such as MBCT, mindfulness-based relapse prevention (MBRP), and mindfulness-based addiction treatment (MBAT) may be useful in helping people quit smoking. However, the earlier trials were limited in scope and small in size. A recent systematic review identified ten trials of mindfulness meditation on smoking (Maglione et al., 2017). Only one trial was deemed of good quality. When synthesizing the results, the authors found no overall evidence that mindfulness-based interventions help a person to quit smoking.

The good-quality trial identified in the review is also the largest trial conducted to date of a mindfulness program on smoking cessation (Vidrine et al., 2016). This trial randomized 412 smokers who on average smoked twenty cigarettes per day (one pack per day). These smokers were randomized to three different arms: MBAT, CBT, and usual care. Seven-day point prevalence abstinence from smoking was assessed at four and twenty-six weeks following the quit day. Self-reported abstinence was biochemically confirmed using exhaled carbon monoxide measurements. Over the twenty-six weeks, there were no differences in smoking abstinence between the three groups, and smoking abstinence remained at about 10–15 percent for the entire cohort.

Alcohol and Other Drugs

There are a number of trials that have been conducted of mindfulness-based interventions on alcohol and other drugs. Two systematic reviews were identified. One focused on the effects of mindfulness-based relapse prevention (MBRP) on any addiction (Grant et al., 2017). It found nine trials, most of which enrolled people with a mix of alcohol and other substance-use issues. This review found that there was no evidence that MBRP had any effect on relapse, frequency of drug use, treatment drop-out, anxiety, or depression. It did find that MBRP reduced the amount of withdrawal symptoms and cravings, but gave this a low strength of evidence grade. A second review sought to find any mindfulness program that used a quasi-randomized or a fully randomized trial design, and targeted any kind of drug use (Li, Howard, Garland, McGovern, & Lazar, 2017). This review identified twenty-eight randomized trials. These trials used a range of outcomes, had a diversity of control groups, and were of varying quality. Due to these various issues, the synthesis was not straightforward and did not lend itself to a clear conclusion of whether any form of mindfulness intervention has an effect on any particular drug habit. For example, of the twenty-eight trials they identified, they found that only six had information on continued substance use after their intervention. While they did conduct a meta-analysis to assess the effect of these six trials, with twenty-two trials missing from the analysis, this does not provide a convincing picture of whether mindfulness-based interventions have an effect. Finally, this review did not synthesize the overall strength of evidence to give a sense of their confidence in the estimates they obtained, making the review less useful.

Lung Disease

Few studies have been conducted among people with respiratory conditions. One systematic review of mindfulness for respiratory illness only found four trials (Harrison, Lee, Janaudis-Ferreira, Goldstein, & Brooks, 2016). It concluded that no overall effects were seen on health-related quality of life or stress levels, and could not see any effectiveness of mindfulness for these outcomes. One trial randomized eighty-three patients with asthma to MBSR or placebo (Pbert et al., 2012). This trial measured outcomes at twelve months and found improvements in asthma quality of life and perceived stress. However, it did not find any improvements in lung function or in the percentage of patients with well-controlled asthma. Another trial randomized eighty-six patients with chronic obstructive pulmonary disease (COPD) to eight weeks of mindfulness-based breathing therapy and compared them to placebo (Mularski et al., 2009). Most of the patients were elderly men with moderate to severe COPD. The trial measured breathing ability by the six minute walk test. This trial found no difference in breathing ability, breathing symptoms, or stress, and moreover suffered from a high drop-out rate.

Insomnia

It is estimated that more than 10 percent of adults in the United States have chronic insomnia, with higher rates among women, older adults, military personnel, and clinical populations (Ohayon, 2002). Insomnia is characterized by difficulties in initiating and/or maintaining sleep, and is accompanied with significant daytime impairments. Although pharmacotherapy can help, many people prefer non-pharmacological approaches due to concerns regarding drug dependency, drug tolerance, and side effects.

Participants with chronic insomnia are thought to be hyperaroused and often experience ruminations when trying to fall asleep. Mindfulness-based interventions are hypothesized to reduce rumination and thus potentially improve insomnia. In addition, accepting one's current sleep state, letting go of the need to stay in bed, and nonstriving for a certain sleep outcomes are possible benefits from both Cognitive Behavioral Therapy for Insomnia (CBT-I) and mindfulness meditation. In contrast to CBT-I, however, which emphasizes changing maladaptive patterns to improve sleep quality, mindfulness encourages observing thoughts and emotions with objectivity, compassion, and curiosity (Shapiro, Bootzin, Figueredo, Lopez, & Schwartz, 2003).

Although sleep has many ways to be measured, we simplify it to four ways:

(1) Time to fall asleep (Sleep onset latency)
(2) Total wake time—total time a person is awake from the moment they fall asleep to when they finally get up and stop trying to go back to sleep
(3) Total sleep time—the total number of hours a person sleeps from the time they get into bed and finally get up
(4) Overall sleep quality

For people with insomnia—whether they have difficulty falling asleep, maintaining sleep, getting enough sleep time, or achieving sufficient sleep quality—finding an intervention that improves any of these outcomes compared with how they slept before would be appreciated. Such a person may not feel they need the therapy to be compared with a placebo if it helps them sleep better than they slept before.

Mindfulness therapies have been evaluating their effects on treating insomnia and sleep disturbance on a variety of clinical populations including patients who have cancer, recieved an organ transplant, have anxiety, PTSD, fibromyalgia, are on antidepressants, are of older age, or are care givers of disabled children. However, systematic reviews have shown conflicting results for its effectiveness in helping people sleep. A recent systematic review identified only two trials that used a wait-list or usual medical care control. These trials recruited people with insomnia and found that while total sleep time did not improve, people were taking less time to fall asleep and overall sleep quality did improve with a moderate-sized effect (Gong et al., 2016). When this review looked at comparisons with placebo or known therapies such as sleep medications, they did not find any benefit in any of the other outcomes. Another review that identified six trials using a placebo control found that although there were two studies that showed mildly positive benefits to mindfulness, there was no overall effect of mindfulness therapies on sleep quality (Goyal et al., 2014a).

One possible explanation for these findings is that mindfulness-based therapies may result in a decreased need for sleep without compromising sleep quality or daytime functioning. In a study comparing experienced meditators to novice mediators, the experienced meditators had total sleep time below the control population and had substantial periods of meditation each day approximately equal to the "lost" sleep (Kaul, Passafiume, Sargent, & O'Hara, 2010). An alternative explanation might be that meditators have deeper sleep, and thus may be able to achieve the restorative benefits of sleep in less time. However, a few studies have found that although the sleep of meditators may qualitatively appear deeper, polysomnographic evidence points toward lighter sleep and more awakenings (Britton, Haynes, Fridel, & Bootzin, 2010; Ferrarelli et al., 2013). These findings are not well-understood.

In the only randomized controlled clinical trial exploring the efficacy of MBSR as a treatment for insomnia compared to a drug, thirty adults with primary chronic insomnia were randomized to either MBSR or nightly pharmacotherapy with eszopiclone (Gross et al., 2011). While there were no significant differences between the groups, people in the mindfulness group improved from baseline. There were no significant improvements at eight weeks, but at the five-month follow-up total sleep time increased by over thirty minutes and time to fall asleep was reduced by over twenty minutes. Sleep quality also improved significantly. Participants in the pharmacotherapy group had similar results, but had lower treatment satisfaction scores and reported adverse events.

Immune Function

The research supporting the effectiveness of mindfulness-based therapies relies heavily on participants' self-reports of their own health status, which can be prone to bias. Markers of immune system activity are particularly relevant to evaluate how mindfulness-based therapies influence biological processes that are involved in disease pathogenesis. A comprehensive review that included 20 randomized controlled trials and data from 1,602 participants revealed tentative evidence that mindfulness meditation is associated with changes in select biomarkers of immune system activity

(Black & Slavich, 2016). Using the criteria of three or more randomized trials with a positive effect, the authors identified that mindfulness meditation has at least a trend-level or dosage-dependent effect on the following four immune outcomes: reductions in circulating C-Reactive Protein (CRP) levels, increases in CD4+ T cell count (in HIV-diagnosed participants), increases in telomerase activity, and reductions in cellular transcription factor NF-κB activity. In contrast, null findings or a lack of replicated effects were found for interleukins (IL-1, IL-6, IL-8, IL-10), IFN-γ, antibodies (IgA, IgG, influenza), tumor necrosis factor (TNF-α), and various measures of cell count (Black & Slavich, 2016).

Circulating and Stimulated Inflammatory Proteins

A number of inflammatory proteins are produced by the immune system and serve as markers of inflammation. Interleukin 6 (IL-6) is produced by white blood cells and mediates fever and the acute phase response to infection. It is also found to be elevated in many chronic stressful conditions including depression, diabetes, atherosclerosis, Alzheimer's, systemic lupus erythematosis, multiple myeloma, some cancers, and rheumatoid arthritis.

Interleukin 6 is one of the signals that cause the liver to produce CRP, an important inflammatory protein. This protein binds to dying cells to activate their removal from the body by the immune system. It rises within a couple hours in response to infections or other inflammation. Chronic elevations of CRP are associated with many diseases (Allin & Nordestgaard, 2011). Interleukin 8 is produced by white blood cells and other cells and induces the immune system to focus on the site of an infection. Interleukin 10 is an anti-inflammatory protein that reduces other inflammatory proteins.

White blood cells produce TNF-α, which causes fever, cell death, cachexia, and physical signs of inflammation (Kalliolias & Ivashkiv, 2016). Elevated production of this protein has been linked to many diseases including rheumatoid arthritis, inflammatory bowel disease, psoriasis, and ankylosing spondylitis. It is also found to increase our feelings of pain during inflammation. There are currently five drugs that inhibit TNF and are used widely for the treatment of Crohn's disease, ulcerative colitis, rheumatoid arthritis, psoriasis, psoriatic arthritis, ankylosing spondylitis, and hidradenitis suppurativa.

At least ten randomized trials have been conducted that measured the effects of mindfulness-based interventions on these and other inflammatory proteins. These studies were carried out in a variety of patient populations including breast cancer, HIV, ulcerative colitis, rheumatoid arthritis, and community residents without a specific diagnosis. Thus far, there is no clear signal that mindfulness reliably affects or improves any of the above mentioned inflammatory proteins. A few studies suggested that it may reduce CRP and TNF, but an equal number showed no change. The overall evidence for an effect is fairly weak for either.

Another systematic review that focused on mindfulness-based trials in healthy people as well as in people with cancer was also not able to find any beneficial effect of mindfulness for either group for any specific inflammatory marker (Sanada et al., 2017).

Immune Cell Count

When challenged by an infection, many different types of immune cells are activated to protect the body against the infection and promote recovery. The cell count is used as a diagnostic marker in the evaluation of various diseases. Only a handful of mindfulness studies have evaluated the cell count, and the only positive outcomes reported are for HIV. The CD4 count is one of the most important markers of disease progression in HIV-infected patients. Three studies have been conducted but the findings are somewhat mixed. The first randomized trial had forty-eight HIV patients and the MBSR group found no change in CD4 count after eight weeks; however, the control group had a drop in their CD4 count by 185 (Creswell, Myers, Cole, & Irwin, 2009). It isn't clear why the control group dropped so much after eight weeks, but this drop was not seen in the other two trials. A second trial involving forty HIV patients found that both groups increased their CD4 count at eight weeks, the mindfulness group by about 60 and the control by about 20 (Gonzalez-Garcia et al., 2014). A change of 50 is roughly within the margin of error for CD4 counts; thus changes greater than 50 more strongly suggest clinically significant effects. At twenty weeks, the mindfulness group had increased by about 130 while the control dropped by about 50. In both these trials patients were already taking antiretroviral medications. The largest study was conducted in Iran, and involved 173 patients with HIV who were not on any antiretroviral medication (SeyedAlinaghi et al., 2012). They reported no change at all in the control group (579–582 cells/μL) from baseline to three months or at twelve months. It was unclear why there was so much stability in the cell count in this group as we would normally expect some fluctuation. The mindfulness group had a minor initial increase in CD4 that did not persist to the end of the trial. Overall the findings are weak that mindfulness has an effect on CD4 count among HIV-infected individuals, but larger and more rigorous studies would help elucidate its effects more accurately.

Antibody Response

Antibodies are immunoglobulins (e.g., IgA) or molecules secreted by immune cells to recognize and neutralize invading pathogens such as viruses and bacteria. Of the twenty studies reviewed by Black and Slavich (2016), two studies examined antibody response to an influenza vaccination; one revealed a significantly greater rise in influenza antibody titers from the MBSR group compared with controls while the second study did not show any changes. The first study was done among corporate employees, while the second study was done among a geriatric population. Overall, there is no clear evidence of an effect of mindfulness on antibody titers to flu vaccine, and further studies are needed to clarify whether it does or does not have an effect.

Susceptibility to Colds

A well-done trial in 2012 showed that mindfulness can help reduce susceptibility to colds (Barrett et al., 2012). About 150 adults that were fifty years old and older who had a susceptibility to colds (participants reported two or more colds in the last twelve

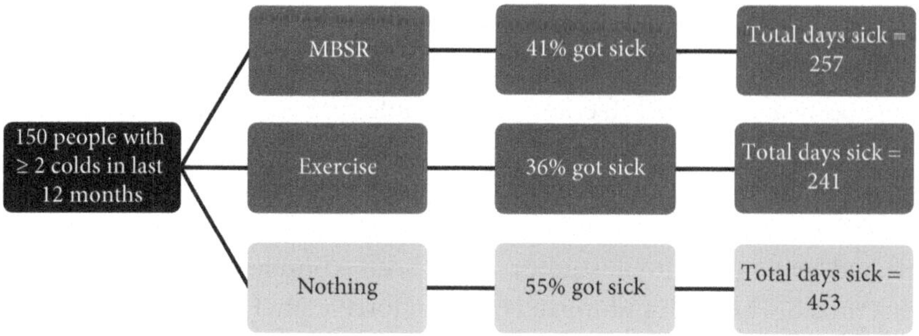

FIGURE 32.1 Does MBSR reduce our susceptibility to colds over 3–6 months?

months) and did not do much exercise were randomized to one of three groups: (1) eight weeks of MBSR; (2) eight weeks of moderate-intensity exercise, or (3) observation only. These people were followed for three to six months, and the study found that the group that was only observed had a total of 453 sick days (Figure 32.1). The exercise and mindfulness groups had just a little over half those number of sick days (53 percent and 57 percent, respectively). The main outcome measure for this study was a global severity index that accounted for the number of sick days as well as the severity of symptoms such as fever, body aches, congestion, and other bothersome symptoms. The mindfulness group had less than half of the global symptoms that the control had, while there wasn't a measurable difference between the exercise group and control in terms of the global severity index. This is a provocative trial that deserves further study.

Cellular Aging

We can tell how much a person has aged by knowing when they were born. However, chronologic age only gives us partial information on the biologic deterioration that occurs in a person's body that leads to unwanted symptoms and eventually death. Assessing how "old" a cell is can be difficult, since cells are dividing all the time and it is not easy to tell how old a certain set of cells is by just looking at them. One way to tell, however, is through the length of their telomeres, as well as through the activity of an enzyme called telomerase, which helps keep telomeres longer.

Telomeres are complexes that cap the ends of chromosomes, and serve to protect the chromosomes. Telomeres tend to shorten with cell division, and cells in older people have on average shorter telomeres than cells in younger people (Epel, Daubenmier, Moskowitz, Folkman, & Blackburn, 2009). Telomerase is an enzyme that adds telomeric DNA to shortened telomeres, thereby helping to protect the chromosome during any further replication. Telomeres shorten with age, predict risk factors for various diseases independent of age, and are shortened in individuals with premature death and age-related diseases (Epel et al., 2009). Conversely, longer telomeres are related to a healthier diet, including greater intake of antioxidants (Richards et al., 2007; Xu et al., 2009); limited consumption of processed meat (Nettleton, Diez-Roux, Jenny, Fitzpatrick, &

Jacobs, 2008) and a healthy lifestyle consisting of increased consumption of fruits and vegetables, less cigarette smoking, and greater exercise (Mirabello et al., 2009).

Only two studies using mindfulness have measured telomere length. Both studies were among breast cancer survivors and showed no effect. However, there have been four studies that measured telomerase activity, and a meta-analysis that combined the results for these studies found that mindfulness meditation leads to increased telomerase activity in circulating white blood cells (Schutte & Malouff, 2014). While the studies were conducted among a diverse group of people, the results need much further study. However, these results are exciting in that they suggest a possible means to understand physical aging and how changing our mental activities might be able to affect it.

Transcription Factors and Gene Expression

Certain molecules, called transcription factors, work on activating or deactivating parts of the DNA to control an immune response. Nuclear factor-kappa B (NF-κB) is a transcription factor that has been found to play a role in inflammatory responses, cellular growth, cell death, as well as mediating diseases such as cancer, arthritis, and asthma (Dolcet Llobet, Pallares, & Matias-Guiu, 2005). While it has many functions, some of which are anti-inflammatory, it is generally thought of as a factor that promotes inflammation (Lawrence, 2009). A few systematic reviews have examined a variety of mind-body interventions, including mindfulness, on gene expression changes (Buric et al., 2017; Black & Slavich, 2016; Bower & Irwin, 2016). The results of these reviews indicate that although there are very few studies of mindfulness interventions, they all show a decrease in NF-κB. There also appears to be a consistency that other mind-body interventions such as Tai chi have similar effects.

Cortisol

Cortisol is a steroid hormone that is released in response to stress. Severe stress or chronic stress can chronically elevate this hormone, generally leading to adverse health (Gill, Vythilingam, & Page, 2008; Miller, Chen, & Zhou, 2007). Dysregulated cortisol output is associated with stress-induced diseases; therefore normalized cortisol may translate to better health outcomes. A systematic review of six studies examining mindfulness intervention effects on cortisol found inconsistent results (O'Leary, O'Neill, & Dockray, 2016). Significant changes in serum cortisol levels have not been observed in randomized controlled trials.

Conclusion

Research in mindfulness has come a long way over the past few decades. It used to comprise mostly small poorly designed studies, but over the years these studies have become more rigorous and with larger numbers of participants. The number of outcomes studied has multiplied and given us a sense that a relatively brief intervention involving training the mind can help people to feel better. It helps common symptoms such as pain, anxiety, and depression. It might even help reduce our susceptibility to colds, something that has eluded the pharmaceutical industry. These conclusions are not based on hype, but rather on the same type of scientific evidence we base any other medical therapy on. The field of research in mindfulness is still nascent, however, and needs far more study.

While mindfulness has gained much attention in recent years, it is not a cure-all for anything, and its effects are limited. Of the hundreds of studies done on mindfulness-based interventions on a variety of physical and mental health outcomes, in general, mindfulness has not been found to be superior to any known therapy such as cognitive behavioral therapy or exercise. Most of the studies reviewed in this chapter focused on usual care/wait-list controls, or placebo controls. When reviews find that mindfulness-based interventions do improve a health outcome, the magnitude of the effect is usually low and sometimes moderate. Mindfulness-based interventions have not been found to be effective as a single therapy to drastically mitigate or cure any health problems. However, they are useful to lessen symptoms or can be used together with other therapies to improve symptoms. When found to be effective for a particular health outcome, the reviews thus far have rated the overall strength of evidence as low to medium, indicating that our confidence of its effectiveness for a particular condition needs to be tempered until further studies are done to give greater clarity to its true effects. Mindfulness has not yet found a high strength of evidence for any mental or physical health condition. This does not preclude its use in clinical medicine, as many therapies are used with a moderate strength of evidence. Mindfulness-based interventions also give patients the opportunity to choose a therapy that does not come with the typical side effect concerns that they have with drugs. A summary of the findings is presented in Table 32.1.

These findings are somewhat at odds with the popular view that mindfulness strongly and consistently reduces stress, and therefore should have a major impact on stress-related conditions. While "stress" is something that everyone can relate to and on occasion identify, it is a difficult concept to quantify scientifically. Several attempts have been made, but none of them completely captures a person's experience of stress. A comprehensive review of the effects of meditation on psychological stress found only low confidence of a positive effect on stress levels when compared with placebo controls (Goyal et al., 2014a). While a few small studies found positive effects of mindfulness on perceived stress, the largest study which was also rated as high quality found null results. There are many biologic measures of stress such as cortisol and blood pressure, but in general if we see a signal in these measures, it is minor.

Conceptually, the idea of pausing, reflecting on what our minds are doing, how our bodies are feeling, and learning skills to help us deal with negative mental activities should help us lead healthier and happier lives. Why aren't we seeing greater improvements in the numerous symptoms and conditions we've studied? It could be that mastering particular aspects of our minds requires much more training than a typical eight-week course of MBSR provides. The Indian traditions from which

Table 32.1 Summary of findings for mindfulness-based therapies

	Effect[1]	Confidence in effect[2]	comments
Pain in general	+	moderate	
Irritable Bowel Syndrome	++	low	
Fibromyalgia	+/–	low	
Chronic low back pain	+	moderate	
Cancer-associated symptoms	+/–	moderate	
Sexual function	+	low	
Blood pressure	0	low	
Heart disease	+	low	
Diabetes	0	moderate	+ improvements in psychological outcomes associated with DM, such as anxiety and depression
Substance use			
Smoking	0	low	
Alcohol & other drugs	0	low	
Lung disease	0	low	
Insomnia	+/–	low	
Immune function			
Circulating & stimulated inflammatory proteins (IL-6, IL-8, IL-10, TNF-α, CRP)	0	moderate	
Immune cell count (CD4)	+/–	low	
Antibody response	+/–	low	
Susceptibility to colds	+	low	
Cellular aging	+/–	low	
Transcription factors/gene expression (NF-κB)	+	low	
Cortisol	0	low	there may be an effect on salivary cortisol, but unclear clinical significance

1 effect: 0 = no effect +/- = possible or mild effect + = moderate effect ++= large effect

2 Qualitative summary of the overall confidence of the reported effect based on number/quality of trials and consistency of findings: low, moderate, high

mindfulness derives were never conceptualized as an expedient therapy for health problems. Rather, meditation was a skill or state one learned and practiced over time to increase one's awareness, and through this awareness gain insight and understanding into the various subtleties of one's existence. Training the mind in awareness, non-reactive states, control of thoughts—these are daunting accomplishments that an eight-week course can only scratch the surface of. However, if one were to be able to do all these things, we still don't know what kinds of effects they would have. It could also be that we just don't understand enough about how our mental and physical activities contribute to these conditions in the first place. While we've learned much over the past three decades, there is still considerable work to do in the pursuit of understanding how our minds contribute to our health.

References

Allin, K. H., & Nordestgaard, B. G. (2011). Elevated C-reactive protein in the diagnosis, prognosis, and cause of cancer. *Critical Reviews in Clinical Laboratory Sciences 48*, 155–170.

Anheyer, D., Haller, H., Barth, J., Lauche, R., Dobos, G., & Cramer, H. (2017). Mindfulness-based stress reduction for treating low back pain: A systematic review and meta-analysis. *Annals of Internal Medicine 166*, 799–807.

Barrett, B., Hayney, M. S., Muller, D., Rakel, D., Ward, A., Obasi, C. N., Brown, R., Zhang, Z., Zgierska, A., Gern, J., West, R., Ewers, T., Barlow, S., Gassman, M., & Coe, C. L. (2012). Meditation or exercise for preventing acute respiratory infection: A randomized controlled trial. *The Annals of Family Medicine 10*, 337–346.

Black, D. S., & Slavich, G. M. (2016). Mindfulness meditation and the immune system: A systematic review of randomized controlled trials. *Annals of the New York Academy of Sciences 1373*, 13–24.

Blom, K., Baker, B., How, M., Dai, M., Irvine, J., Abbey, S., Abramson, B. L., Myers, M. G., Kiss, A., Perkins, N. J., & Tobe, S. W. (2014). Hypertension analysis of stress reduction using mindfulness meditation and yoga: Results from the HARMONY randomized controlled trial. *American Journal of Hypertension 27*, 122–129.

Bower, J. E., & Irwin, M. R. (2016). Mind-body therapies and control of inflammatory biology: A descriptive review. *Brain, Behavior, and Immunity 51*, 1–11.

Britton, W. B., Haynes, P. L., Fridel, K. W., & Bootzin, R. R. (2010). Polysomnographic and subjective profiles of sleep continuity before and after mindfulness-based cognitive therapy in partially remitted depression. *Psychosomatic Medicine 72*, 539–548.

Brotto, L. A., Erskine, Y., Carey, M., Ehlen, T., Finlayson, S., Heywood, M., Kwon, J., McAlpine, J., Stuart, G., Thomson, S., & Miller, D. (2012). A brief mindfulness-based cognitive behavioral intervention improves sexual functioning versus wait-list control in women treated for gynecologic cancer. *Gynecologic Oncology 125*, 320–325.

Buric, I., Farias, M., Jong, J., Mee, C., & Brazil, I. A. (2017). What is the molecular signature of mind-body interventions? A systematic review of gene expression changes induced by meditation and related practices. *Frontiers in Immunology 8*, 670.

CDC. (2017). *Smoking & tobacco use* [Online]. Retrieved from https://www.cdc.gov/tobacco/data_statistics/fact_sheets/cessation/quitting/index.htm.

Cherkin, D. C., Sherman, K. J., Balderson, B. H., Cook, A. J., Anderson, M. L., Hawkes, R. J., Hansen, K. E., & Turner, J. A. (2016). Effects of mindfulness-based stress reduction vs cognitive-behavioral therapy and usual care on back pain and functional limitations among adults with chronic low back pain: A randomized clinical trial. *JAMA* 315(12), 1240–1249.

Chou, R., Deyo, R., Friedly, J., Skelly, A., Hashimoto, R., Weimer, M., Fu, R., Dana, T., Kraegel, P., Griffin, J., Grusing, S., & Brodt, E. D. (2017). Nonpharmacologic therapies for low back pain: A systematic review for an American College of Physicians clinical practice guideline. *Annals of Internal Medicine* 166, 493–505.

Creswell, J. D., Myers, H. F., Cole, S. W., & Irwin, M. R. (2009). Mindfulness meditation training effects on CD4+ T lymphocytes in HIV-1 infected adults: A small randomized controlled trial. *Brain, Behavior, and Immunity* 23, 184–188.

Davis, M. C., & Zautra, A. J. (2013). An online mindfulness intervention targeting socioemotional regulation in fibromyalgia: Results of a randomized controlled trial. *Annals of Behavioral Medicine* 46, 273–284.

Day, M. A., Thorn, B. E., Ward, L. C., Rubin, N., Hickman, S. D., Scogin, F., & Kilgo, G. R. (2014). Mindfulness-based cognitive therapy for the treatment of headache pain: A pilot study. *The Clinical Journal of Pain* 30, 152–161.

Dolcet, X., Llobet, D., Pallares, J., & Matias-Guiu, X. (2005). NF-kB in development and progression of human cancer. *Virchows Archiv* 446, 475–482.

Epel, E., Daubenmier, J., Moskowitz, J. T., Folkman, S., & Blackburn, E. (2009). Can meditation slow rate of cellular aging? Cognitive stress, mindfulness, and telomeres. *Annals of the New York Academy of Sciences* 1172, 34–53.

Ferrarelli, F., Smith, R., Dentico, D., Riedner, B. A., Zennig, C., Benca, R. M., Lutz, A., Davidson, R. J., & Tononi, G. (2013). Experienced mindfulness meditators exhibit higher parietal-occipital EEG gamma activity during NREM sleep. *PLoS One* 8, e73417.

Focan, C., Houbiers, G., Gilles, L., Van Steeland, T., Georges, N., Maniglia, A., Lobelle, J. P., Baro, V., & Graas, M. P. (2015). Dietetic and psychological mindfulness workshops for the management of cachectic cancer patients: A randomized study. *Anticancer Research* 35, 6311–6315.

Garland, E. L., Manusov, E. G., Froeliger, B., Kelly, A., Williams, J. M., & Howard, M. O. (2014). Mindfulness-oriented recovery enhancement for chronic pain and prescription opioid misuse: Results from an early-stage randomized controlled trial. *Journal of Consulting and Clinical Psychology* 82, 448–459.

Gill, J., Vythilingam, M., & Page, G. G. (2008). Low cortisol, high DHEA, and high levels of stimulated TNF-alpha, and IL-6 in women with PTSD. *Journal of Traumatic Stress* 21, 530–539.

Gong, H., Ni, C. X., Liu, Y. Z., Zhang, Y., Su, W. J., Lian, Y. J., Peng, W., & Jiang, C. L. (2016). Mindfulness meditation for insomnia: A meta-analysis of randomized controlled trials. *Journal of Psychosomatic Research* 89, 1–6.

Gonzalez-Garcia, M., Ferrer, M. J., Borras, X., Munoz-Moreno, J. A., Miranda, C., Puig, J., Perez-Alvarez, N., Soler, J., Feliu-Soler, A., Clotet, B., & Fumaz, C. R. (2014). Effectiveness of mindfulness-based cognitive therapy on the quality of life, emotional status, and CD4 cell count of patients aging with HIV infection. *AIDS and Behavior* 18, 676–685.

Goyal, M., Singh, S., Sibinga, E. M., Gould, N. F., Rowland-Seymour, A., Sharma, R., Berger, Z., Sleicher, D., Maron, D. D., Shihab, H. M., Ranasinghe, P. D., Linn, S., Saha, S., Bass, E. B., & Haythornthwaite, J. A. 2014a. Meditation programs for psychological stress and well-being: A systematic review and meta-analysis. *JAMA Internal Medicine* 174, 357–368.

Goyal, M., Singh, S., Sibinga, E. M. S., Gould, N. F., Rowland-Seymour, A., Sharma, R., Berger, Z., Sleicher, D., Maron, D. D., Shihab, H. M., Ranasinghe, P. D., Linn, S., Saha, S., Bass, E. B.,

& Haythornthwaite, J. A. 2014b. *Meditation programs for psychological stress and well-being*. U.S. National Library of Medicine: Rockville, MD.

Grant, S., Colaiaco, B., Motala, A., Shanman, R., Booth, M., Sorbero, M., & Hempel, S. (2017). Mindfulness-based relapse prevention for substance use disorders: A systematic review and meta-analysis. *Journal of Addiction Medicine*, 11(5), 386–396.

Gross, C. R., Kreitzer, M. J., Reilly-Spong, M., Wall, M., Winbush, N. Y., Patterson, R., Mahowald, M., & Cramer-Bornemann, M. (2011). Mindfulness-based stress reduction versus pharmacotherapy for chronic primary insomnia: A randomized controlled clinical trial. *Explore (NY) 7*, 76–87.

Haller, H., Winkler, M. M., Klose, P., Dobos, G., Kummel, S., & Cramer, H. (2017). Mindfulness-based interventions for women with breast cancer: An updated systematic review and meta-analysis. *Acta Oncologica, 56*(12), 1–12.

Harrison, S. L., Lee, A., Janaudis-Ferreira, T., Goldstein, R. S., & Brooks, D. (2016). Mindfulness in people with a respiratory diagnosis: A systematic review. *Patient Education and Counseling 99*, 348–355.

Hartmann, M., Kopf, S., Kircher, C., Faude-Lang, V., Djuric, Z., Augstein, F., Friederich, H. C., Kieser, M., Bierhaus, A., Humpert, P. M., Herzog, W., & Nawroth, P. P. (2012). Sustained effects of a mindfulness-based stress-reduction intervention in type 2 diabetic patients: Design and first results of a randomized controlled trial (the Heidelberger diabetes and stress-study). *Diabetes Care 35*, 945–947.

Hilton, L., Hempel, S., Ewing, B. A., Apaydin, E., Xenakis, L., Newberry, S., Colaiaco, B., Maher, A. R., Shanman, R. M., Sorbero, M. E., & Maglione, M. A. (2017). Mindfulness meditation for chronic pain: Systematic review and meta-analysis. *Annals of Behavioral Medicine 51*, 199–213.

Johns, S. A., Brown, L. F., Beck Coon, K., Monahan, P. O., Tong, Y., & Kroenke, K. (2015). Randomized controlled pilot study of mindfulness-based stress reduction for persistently fatigued cancer survivors. *Psychooncology 24*, 885–893.

Jung, H. Y., Lee, H., & Park, J. (2015). Comparison of the effects of Korean mindfulness-based stress reduction, walking, and patient education in diabetes mellitus. *Nursing & Health Sciences 17*, 516–525.

Kalliolias, G. D., & Ivashkiv, L. B. (2016). TNF biology, pathogenic mechanisms and emerging therapeutic strategies. *Nature Reviews Rheumatology 12*, 49–62.

Kaul, P., Passafiume, J., Sargent, C. R., & O'Hara, B. F. (2010). Meditation acutely improves psychomotor vigilance, and may decrease sleep need. *Behavioral and Brain Functions 6*, 47.

Kearney, D. J., Simpson, T. L., Malte, C. A., Felleman, B., Martinez, M. E., & Hunt, S. C. (2016). Mindfulness-based stress reduction in addition to usual care is associated with improvements in pain, fatigue, and cognitive failures among veterans with Gulf War illness. *The American Journal of Medicine 129*, 204–214.

Lauche, R., Cramer, H., Dobos, G., Langhorst, J., & Schmidt, S. (2013). A systematic review and meta-analysis of mindfulness-based stress reduction for the fibromyalgia syndrome. *Journal of Psychosomatic Research 75*, 500–510.

Lawrence, T. (2009). The nuclear factor NF-kappaB pathway in inflammation. *Cold Spring Harbor Perspectives in Biology 1*, a001651.

Li, W., Howard, M. O., Garland, E. L., McGovern, P., & Lazar, M. (2017). Mindfulness treatment for substance misuse: A systematic review and meta-analysis. *Journal of Substance Abuse Treatment 75*, 62–96.

Maglione, M. A., Maher, A. R., Ewing, B., Colaiaco, B., Newberry, S., Kandrack, R., Shanman, R. M., Sorbero, M. E., & Hempel, S. (2017). Efficacy of mindfulness meditation for smoking cessation: A systematic review and meta-analysis. *Addictive Behaviors 69*, 27–34.

Miller, C. K., Kristeller, J. L., Headings, A., Nagaraja, H., & Miser, W. F. (2012). Comparative effectiveness of a mindful eating intervention to a diabetes self-management intervention among adults with type 2 diabetes: A pilot study. *Journal of the Academy of Nutrition and Dietetics 112*, 1835–1842.

Miller, G. E., Chen, E., & Zhou, E. S. (2007). If it goes up, must it come down? Chronic stress and the hypothalamic-pituitary-adrenocortical axis in humans. *Psychological Bulletin 133*, 25–45.

Mirabello, L., Huang, W. Y., Wong, J. Y., Chatterjee, N., Reding, D., Crawford, E. D., De Vivo, I., Hayes, R. B., & Savage, S. A. (2009). The association between leukocyte telomere length and cigarette smoking, dietary and physical variables, and risk of prostate cancer. *Aging Cell 8*, 405–413.

Morone, N. E., Greco, C. M., Moore, C. G., Rollman, B. L., Lane, B., Morrow, L. A., Glynn, N. W., & Weiner, D. K. (2016). A mind-body program for older adults with chronic low back pain: A randomized clinical trial. *JAMA Internal Medicine 176*, 329–337.

Mularski, R. A., Munjas, B. A., Lorenz, K. A., Sun, S., Robertson, S. J., Schmelzer, W., Kim, A. C., & Shekelle, P. G. (2009). Randomized controlled trial of mindfulness-based therapy for dyspnea in chronic obstructive lung disease. *Journal of Alternative and Complementary Medicine 15*, 1083–1090.

Müller, F. M. (Trans.) (1881). *The Dhammapada* [Online]. Retrieved from http://www.sacred-texts.com/bud/sbe10/index.htm.

Nettleton, J. A., Diez-Roux, A., Jenny, N. S., Fitzpatrick, A. L., & Jacobs, D. R., Jr. (2008). Dietary patterns, food groups, and telomere length in the Multi-Ethnic Study of Atherosclerosis (MESA). *The American Journal of Clinical Nutrition 88*, 1405–1412.

Noordali, F., Cumming, J., & Thompson, J. L. (2017). Effectiveness of mindfulness-based interventions on physiological and psychological complications in adults with diabetes: A systematic review. *Journal of Health Psychology 22*, 965–983.

O'Leary, K., O'Neill, S., & Dockray, S. (2016). A systematic review of the effects of mindfulness interventions on cortisol. *Journal of Health Psychology 21*, 2108–2121.

Ohayon, M. M. (2002). Epidemiology of insomnia: What we know and what we still need to learn. *Sleep Medicine Reviews 6*, 97–111.

Palta, P., Page, G., Piferi, R. L., Gill, J. M., Hayat, M. J., Connolly, A. B., & Szanton, S. L. (2012). Evaluation of a mindfulness-based intervention program to decrease blood pressure in low-income African-American older adults. *Journal of Urban Health 89*, 308–316.

Pbert, L., Madison, J. M., Druker, S., Olendzki, N., Magner, R., Reed, G., Allison, J., & Carmody, J. (2012). Effect of mindfulness training on asthma quality of life and lung function: A randomised controlled trial. *Thorax 67*, 769–776.

Richards, J. B., Valdes, A. M., Gardner, J. P., Paximadas, D., Kimura, M., Nessa, A., Lu, X., Surdulescu, G. L., Swaminathan, R., Spector, T. D., & Aviv, A. (2007). Higher serum vitamin D concentrations are associated with longer leukocyte telomere length in women. *The American Journal of Clinical Nutrition 86*, 1420–1425.

Sanada, K., Alda Diez, M., Salas Valero, M., Perez-Yus, M. C., Demarzo, M. M., Montero-Marin, J., Garcia-Toro, M., & Garcia-Campayo, J. (2017). Effects of mindfulness-based interventions on biomarkers in healthy and cancer populations: A systematic review. *BMC Complementary and Alternative Medicine 17*, 125.

Schutte, N. S., & Malouff, J. M. (2014). A meta-analytic review of the effects of mindfulness meditation on telomerase activity. *Psychoneuroendocrinology 42*, 45–48.

SeyedAlinaghi, S., Jam, S., Foroughi, M., Imani, A., Mohraz, M., Djavid, G. E., & Black, D. S. (2012). Randomized controlled trial of mindfulness-based stress reduction delivered to human immunodeficiency virus-positive patients in Iran: Effects on CD4(+) T lymphocyte count and medical and psychological symptoms. *Psychosomatic Medicine 74*, 620–627.

Shapiro, S. L., Bootzin, R. R., Figueredo, A. J., Lopez, A. M., & Schwartz, G. E. (2003). The efficacy of mindfulness-based stress reduction in the treatment of sleep disturbance in women with breast cancer: An exploratory study. *Journal of Psychosomatic Research 54*, 85–91.

Stephenson, K. R., & Kerth, J. (2017). Effects of mindfulness-based therapies for female sexual dysfunction: A meta-analytic review. *Journal of Sex Research 54*, 832–849.

Tovote, K. A., Fleer, J., Snippe, E., Peeters, A. C., Emmelkamp, P. M., Sanderman, R., Links, T. P., & Schroevers, M. J. (2014). Individual mindfulness-based cognitive therapy and cognitive behavior therapy for treating depressive symptoms in patients with diabetes: Results of a randomized controlled trial. *Diabetes Care 37*, 2427–2434.

Tovote, K. A., Schroevers, M. J., Snippe, E., Sanderman, R., Links, T. P., Emmelkamp, P. M., & Fleer, J. (2015). Long-term effects of individual mindfulness-based cognitive therapy and cognitive behavior therapy for depressive symptoms in patients with diabetes: A randomized trial. *Psychotherapy and Psychosomatics 84*, 186–187.

van der Lee, M. L., & Garssen, B. (2012). Mindfulness-based cognitive therapy reduces chronic cancer-related fatigue: A treatment study. *Psychooncology 21*, 264–272.

van Son, J., Nyklicek, I., Pop, V. J., Blonk, M. C., Erdtsieck, R. J., Spooren, P. F., Toorians, A. W., & Pouwer, F. (2012). The effects of a mindfulness-based intervention on emotional distress, quality-of-life, and HbA1c in outpatients with diabetes (DiaMind): A randomized controlled trial. *Diabetes Care, 36*(4), 823–830.

Vidrine, J. I., Spears, C. A., Heppner, W. L., Reitzel, L. R., Marcus, M. T., Cinciripini, P. M., Waters, A. J., Li, Y., Nguyen, N. T., Cao, Y., Tindle, H. A., Fine, M., Safranek, L. V., & Wetter, D. W. (2016). Efficacy of mindfulness-based addiction treatment (MBAT) for smoking cessation and lapse recovery: A randomized clinical trial. *Journal of Consulting and Clinical Psychology 84*, 824–838.

Vipassana meditation: As taught by S.N. Goenka in the tradition of Sayagyi U Ba Khin [Online]. (n.d.) Retrieved from dhamma.org. (Accessed February 27, 2018).

Xu, Q., Parks, C. G., Deroo, L. A., Cawthon, R. M., Sandler, D. P., & Chen, H. (2009). Multivitamin use and telomere length in women. *The American Journal of Clinical Nutrition 89*, 1857–1863.

Younge, J. O., Wery, M. F., Gotink, R. A., Utens, E. M., Michels, M., Rizopoulos, D., Van Rossum, E. F., Hunink, M. G., & Roos-Hesselink, J. W. (2015). Web-based mindfulness intervention in heart disease: A randomized controlled trial. *PLoS One 10*, e0143843.

Zernicke, K. A., Campbell, T. S., Blustein, P. K., Fung, T. S., Johnson, J. A., Bacon, S. L., & Carlson, L. E. (2013). Mindfulness-based stress reduction for the treatment of irritable bowel syndrome symptoms: A randomized wait-list controlled trial. *International Journal of Behavioral Medicine 20*, 385–396.

CHAPTER 33

TRANSCENDENTAL MEDITATION IN THE TREATMENT OF MENTAL AND PHYSICAL CONDITIONS

DAVID W. ORME-JOHNSON

Introduction

THE Transcendental Meditation (TM) technique has its roots in the ancient Vedic tradition of India and was introduced to the West in the 1950s by Maharishi Mahesh Yogi (Maharishi Mahesh Yogi, 1963, 1969). It has been taught in a standardized way worldwide since then, and there are now about ten million practitioners (Forem, 2012; Roth, 2018). The standardization of TM has facilitated research on it, and there are currently over 675 studies on it conducted at over 250 universities and research centers in thirty countries and published in over two hundred peer-reviewed journals. This body of research has been anthologized in seven volumes of collected papers on TM (Orme-Johnson & Farrow, 1977; Chalmers, Clements, Schenkluhn, & Weinless, 1989; Wallace, Orme-Johnson, & Dillbeck, 1990; Dillbeck, 2011; Dillbeck, Barnes, Schneider, Travis, & Walton, 2013; Dillbeck, Barnes, Schneider, & Travis, 2020).

This chapter reviews work on the effects of TM in major areas of human functioning such as physical and psychological health, considers its impact on behavior, and examines some of the processes through which TM has its effects. However, it also has some omissions. Discussion of work on the "Maharishi effect," where it has been shown that groups of people meditating together can have marked influences on various societal indices including infant mortality and violent crime (Cavanaugh & Dillbeck, 2017a, 2017b; Dillbeck & Cavanaugh, 2016, 2017; Hagelin et al., 1999), is beyond the scope of the chapter. So also is work by Alexander and colleagues integrating Maharishi's descriptions of the stages of enlightenment from the ancient Vedic tradition of India with concepts of higher levels of mental health and cognitive development as conceptualized in contemporary psychology (Alexander, Druker, & Langer, 1990; Alexander, Davies, et al., 1990; Alexander, Heaton, & Chandler, 1994; Orme-Johnson, Zimmerman, & Hawkins, 1997; Orme-Johnson, 2000; Dillbeck, 1983, 1990).

What Is the Transcendental Meditation Technique?

There are many definitions of the word "meditation." For TM practitioners, meditation means transcending or going beyond the thinking level of the mind, hence the name "Transcendental" Meditation. During TM, one sits comfortably for about twenty minutes and silently repeats a mantra or sound as taught by the teacher, which allows the mind to settle down to quieter levels. The TM mantras are ancient traditional sounds from the Vedic tradition of India, which are said to have beneficial effects on all levels of the mind. They were handed down by Maharishi on behalf of the tradition to the TM teachers who, also on behalf of the tradition, pass them on to the TM students.

Whereas other types of mantra meditations focus on the meaning of the mantras, an important feature of TM is that the mantras do not have a meaning. They are not Sanskrit words; they are just sounds. Their purpose is to keep the mind lively but undirected, because in that condition attention is effortlessly drawn to inner silent levels of the mind. Maharishi explains: "The manner in which Transcendental Meditation takes the mind from the gross to the subtle is very simple and based upon the innate tendency of all human minds to seek happiness. The very nature of the mind is to go to a field of greater happiness. The happiness referred to is not pleasure, nor sensual gratification, nor excitement, but a tranquil and confident state of knowing—of knowing that '*I am*,' of knowing that '*I*' exist and that it is permanent and unchanging" (Maharishi Mahesh Yogi, 2013).

The Transcendental Meditation technique can only be learned from a certified teacher and not from a book or on the internet because learning it requires an interaction between the teacher and the student and instruction proceeds according to what the student experiences. Teachers of Transcendental Meditation are highly trained and certified, guaranteeing that instruction is standardized worldwide, which has protected its effectiveness and facilitated research on it. It is taught in a standard seven-step course, typically over four consecutive days (Forem, 2012).

This technique can be practiced anywhere, even on a bus or in a noisy airport, but a quiet place is preferable. One only needs a comfortable chair. It does not require any faith or belief in it for it to work. It works even for skeptics. In fact, it is better to approach it innocently, with no preconceptions about what is supposed to happen. As the mind settles down, the body settles down, and the person typically reports experiencing deep relaxation. Exactly what happens during meditation depends on the condition of the

FIGURE 33.1 Photo taken in Fiuggi Fonte, Italy, June 1972. From left to right are Peggy and Dr. Vincent Snell, national directors of the TM organization in the United Kingdom, Dr. David Orme-Johnson, and Dr. Keith Wallace, who had recently published his research on the physiological effects of TM in *Science* (Wallace, 1970a). I was explaining to Maharishi about my research showing TM increases stability of the autonomic nervous system, which regulates emotional and motivational responses.

body. If one is fatigued, one might fall asleep. Thoughts inevitably arise, and the meditator is taught how to deal with them, and not to struggle against them or against noise. There is no concentration or control of the mind involved in TM, which distinguishes it from most other meditation techniques.

Cultural Background

In the Vedic literature from which TM is derived, the state of deep inner peace has been variously called pure consciousness, transcendental consciousness, the Self, *samādhi*, *atman*. In the Vedic literature, Patañjali's *Yoga Sūtras* described pure consciousness as yoga, the union of the individual mind with the cosmic mind. It describes how this union is achieved as:

> *Yogaś citta-vṛtti-nirodhaḥ*
>
> *yogaḥ* union, transcendental consciousness, *citta* mind. *vrtti* activity, *nirodhaḥ* complete settling, cessation
>
> Yoga is the complete settling of the activity of the mind. (2)
>
> TM is seen as a means to achieve this end (Egenes, 2010).

According to the Vedic tradition, pure consciousness is the fourth major state of consciousness, different from waking, dreaming, and sleeping. For example, the *Māṇḍūkya Upaniṣad* 7 states: "The fourth condition is Atman in his own pure state. It is neither outer nor inner consciousness, neither semi consciousness, nor sleeping consciousness. It cannot be seen or touched. It is above all distinctions, beyond thought, ineffable. In the union with him is the supreme proof of his identity. It is peace and love" (Mascaro, 1965; see also Katz & Egenes, 2015).

Differences between Meditation Techniques

Scientifically, TM is called automatic self-transcending because it is an effortless, automatic process by which the mind transcends or goes beyond the technique itself. That is, it goes from effortless thinking of the mantra to silence. This process is associated with a brain wave (EEG) frequency of 8–10 cycles per second (Hz), called Alpha1, which is seen during *restful alertness*, the state when the mind is resting but wide awake inside (Travis & Shear, 2010). Studies have shown that during specific periods of pure consciousness the breath markedly slows and the brain becomes globally coherent, as indicated by increased EEG coherence among all cortical areas in all frequency bands (Badawi, Wallace, Orme-Johnson, & Rouzeré, 1984; Farrow & Hebert, 1982; Travis, 2001, 2004), which suggests a high level of global integration in the brain.

Meditation techniques that require focused mental activity have different physiological effects. Non-reactive monitoring of one's thoughts, as in some mindfulness (Open Monitoring) techniques, are associated with theta EEG (2–7 Hz), characteristic of that kind of mental activity. Focused Attention meditation, voluntarily focusing attention on a chosen object, is associated with gamma EEG (20–50 Hz), a frequency band generally known to correlate with focusing attention (Travis & Shear, 2010).

Areas of TM Research Not Reviewed in This Chapter

The reader may be interested to know that Alexander and colleagues have integrated Maharishi's descriptions of the stages of enlightenment from the ancient Vedic tradition of India with concepts of higher levels of mental health and cognitive development as conceptualized in contemporary psychology (Alexander, Druker, & Langer, 1990; Alexander, Davies, et al., 1990; Alexander, Heaton, & Chandler, 1994; Orme-Johnson et al., 1997; Orme-Johnson, 2000; Dillbeck, 1983, 1990). Maharishi described the growth of enlightenment in terms of seven states of consciousness, of which waking, dreaming, and sleeping are the first three, the four others being a sequence of higher states of consciousness (Maharishi Mahesh Yogi, 1963, 1969). This is the general theoretical framework from which specific research hypotheses for TM research were derived.

Another body of research studies beyond the scope of the present chapter is on collective consciousness. According to the Vedic tradition, everyone and everything is interconnected by a common universal field of consciousness. Consequently, when we directly experience pure consciousness, a positive influence on others is radiated throughout the field. There have been over fifty studies showing that when the TM technique and its advanced program, the TM-Sidhis, including Yogic Flying, are practiced in a group of at least the $\sqrt{1}$ percent of a population, they produce beneficial changes in the larger society. For example, four recent studies in the United States have shown that when such a group was formed in Iowa, there were simultaneous reductions in national rates of violent crime, motor vehicle fatalities, other accidental deaths, infant mortality, and drug-related deaths, which could not be explained by other events at the time (Cavanaugh & Dillbeck, 2017a, 2017b; Dillbeck & Cavanaugh, 2016, 2017; Hagelin et al., 1999). Other studies have reported reductions of armed conflict and terrorism, as well as improved cooperation among nations acting as a whole when the requisite size groups are created (Orme-Johnson, Alexander, Davies, Chandler, & Larimore, 1988; Orme-Johnson, Dillbeck, & Alexander, 2003; Davies & Alexander, 2005; Orme-Johnson, 2016). It has been pointed out that these studies are not random assignment, which would be ideal (Kreplin, Farias, & Brazil, 2018). However, to put it in context, there have never been any random assignment studies in the entire history of social science on the level of cities, states, nations, and the world like the TM research. Moreover, this is the only body of experimental research on conflict resolution that has created groups in conflict areas to successfully reduce armed conflict, with changes in objective, publicly available social indicators (Orme-Johnson, Alexander, & Davies, 1990; Hagelin et al., 1999). In the tradition of naming scientific discoveries after their founder (e.g., the Meissner Effect, the Doppler Effect), this discovery was named the Maharishi Effect after Maharishi Mahesh Yogi.

The Transcendental Meditation Technique and Physical Health

The basic rationale for TM's effects on health is that stress adversely affects virtually all areas of health, and TM reduces stress, as measured by many physiological and neurohormonal parameters. During TM the body gains deep rest like sleep, but the mind maintains inner awareness. Thus, the TM state is called *restful alertness* (Wallace, 1970b, 1972; Wallace, Benson, & Wilson, 1971). Compared to just sitting with eyes closed resting, TM produces greater reductions of physiological stress markers, suggesting that it may have additional healing properties not afforded by ordinary forms of rest (Dillbeck & Orme-Johnson, 1987). A recent neuroimaging study reinforces earlier findings that TM produces restful alertness (Mahone, Travis, Gevirtz, & Hubbard, 2018; see Table 33.1).

Table 33.1 Decreased Physiological Indices of Stress

Authors	Study Design	Results
Wallace, 1970a, 1972; Jevning, Wallace, & Biedebach, 1992; Wallace et al., 1971	**Physiological changes** during TM compared to eyes closed baseline in the same subjects.	Significant decreases in oxygen consumption, CO_2 elimination, minute ventilation, respiratory rate, heart rate, plasma lactate, with no change in PO_2 or pCO_2. Increased basal skin resistance and increased alpha1 (8–9 Hz) EEG power, indicating a state of restful alertness.
Dillbeck & Orme-Johnson, 1987	**Meta-analysis of physiological changes** during TM compared to sitting resting eyes closed, 32 studies.	During TM, strong to moderate effects on decreasing basal skin resistance, respiratory rate, and plasma lactate. Outside of TM, moderately lower stress indicators: spontaneous GSR, heart rate, plasma lactate, and respiratory rate.
Mahone et al., 2018	**Functional Magnetic Resonance Imaging (fMRI) study:** Changes during TM compared to ordinary resting eyes closed in long-term TM meditators.	Increased blood flow in areas associated with awareness and attention (anterior cingulate and dorsolateral prefrontal) and reduced blood flow in areas associated with somatic arousal (pons and cerebellum).

Cardiovascular Health

By far the most extensive TM research using the gold standard of randomized controlled trials (RCTs) has been on cardiovascular disease, spearheaded by Robert Schneider and Charles N. Alexander (Alexander, Langer, Newman, Chandler, & Davies, 1989; Schneider et al., 1995; Alexander et al., 1996). Cardiovascular disease is the leading cause of death in the United States and the world (Mackay, Mensah, Mendis, & Greenland, 2004). One of the principle risk factors for it is psychosocial stress, which is directly addressed by TM.

Most of the studies on heart disease have compared TM with health education (HE) classes as a control treatment. Like TM, HE subjects were presented with research on the health benefits of diet, exercise, and other health recommendations so that their expectations were similar to the TM group. The studies also typically have made the TM and HE groups equivalent on the amount of attention given to the subjects by the therapists, the teaching environments, and by the course schedule and contact time with the instructors. To further ensure that the studies were as objective as possible, the attending physicians and the personnel collecting the data did not know which group the subjects were in. In all studies, TM was an adjunct to standard treatment, with all participants continuing with their usual medical care.

Blood Pressure

There are nine randomized controlled trials using TM as a treatment for blood pressure, with subjects ranging from adolescents to eighty-one-year-olds (Anderson, Liu, & Kryscio, 2008). Thirty percent of American adults have high blood pressure, and 45 percent of coronary heart disease deaths and 51 percent of stroke deaths are attributable to it (Stevens, Mascarenhas, & Mathers, 2009). The mechanism for how TM affects blood pressure is by reducing stress. One of the potential biological mechanisms through which TM lowers stress is by reducing beta-adrenergic receptor sensitivity (Mills, Schneider, Hill, Walton, & Wallace, 1990) and levels of vanillylmandelic acid, indicating reduced turnover of the major stress hormones norepinephrine and epinephrine. This may contribute to decreased contractility of the vascular smooth muscles, thus allowing blood to flow more freely at lower pressures and reducing the risk of heart disease (Walton & Pugh, 1995). In support of this hypothesis, studies have shown that both total resistance to blood flow in the body and blood pressure decrease during TM, suggesting an underlying hemodynamic mechanism for TM's protective effects on the heart (Barnes, Treiber, Turner, Davis, & Strong, 1999).

A systematic review and meta-analysis of the effects of stress reduction programs on hypertensive patients evaluated high-quality studies that used active controls, adequate baseline measurement, and blood pressure assessment by professionals who didn't know which group the patients were in. The Transcendental Meditation technique significantly lowered systolic/diastolic blood pressure, while the blood pressure decreases associated with biofeedback, relaxation-assisted biofeedback, progressive muscle relaxation, and stress management training were not statistically significant (Rainforth et al., 2007; see Table 33.2). Significant reductions of blood pressure by TM have been corroborated by other systematic reviews and meta-analyses, and its results are clinically meaningful (Anderson et al., 2008; Bai et al., 2015). One study, which needs to be replicated, found that TM also reduced the use of blood pressure medication (Schneider, Alexander, Staggers, Orme-Johnson et al., 2005a). A scientific review by the American Heart Association found the Transcendental Meditation technique to be the only meditation practice that has been shown to lower blood pressure and concluded that physicians could recommend TM in treatment plans for all individuals with blood pressure higher than 120/80 mm Hg (Brook et al., 2013).

A series of studies by Barnes and colleagues have explored the potential of TM for prevention by offering it to adolescents at risk for heart disease (Barnes, Bauza, & Treiber, 2003; Barnes, Treiber, & Davis, 2001; Barnes, 2004; Barnes, Johnson, & Treiber, 2009; Barnes, Kapuku, & Treiber, 2012; Barnes & Orme-Johnson, 2006). A study of adolescents found that two months of TM practice improved their blood pressure, heart rate and cardiac output responses to stress tests (Barnes et al., 2001). These findings suggest that TM practice may help protect from the detrimental effects of exaggerated cardiovascular stress reactivity. Other well-controlled studies on heart disease shown in Table 33.2 indicate that TM shows promise for helping to unblock arteries (carotid atherosclerosis), reducing or preventing enlargement of the heart (left ventricular

Table 33.2 Cardiovascular Health

Authors	Study Design	Results
Rainforth et al., 2007	Blood Pressure systematic review and meta-analysis of RCTs on five stress reduction programs on hypertensive patients evaluating high-quality studies using active controls, adequate BP baseline measurement, and blinded BP assessment.	Seventeen trials with twenty-three treatment comparisons and 960 participants with elevated BP met the study criteria, with six TM studies. TM significantly lowered SBP/DBP by 5.0/2.8 mm Hg. No BP decreases were associated with biofeedback, relaxation-assisted biofeedback, progressive muscle relaxation, or stress management training.
Barnes et al., 2001	Cardiovascular Reactivity: RCT of cardiac function during stress tests of adolescents at risk for heart disease, mean age 16, TM vs. HE controls, two-month intervention	TM subjects exhibited significantly greater decreases from pre- to post-intervention in SBP, heart rate and cardiac output reactivity to a simulated car-driving stressor, and reduced SBP reactivity to a social stressor interview compared to the control group.
Castillo-Richmond et al., 2000	Carotid Atherosclerosis: RCT on hypertensive patients (mean age 55), TM vs. HE, six-to-nine-month intervention.	Significant decrease in carotid artery blockage in TM subjects compared to controls, indicating TM reduces carotid atherosclerosis.
Kondwani et al., 2005; Salerno et al., 2004	Left Ventricular Hypertrophy: RCTs on hypertensive patients (mean age 53), TM vs. HE. one year and seven months intervention.	In one study, the TM group showed decreases in their enlarged hearts, whereas the controls subjects did not decrease. In the second study, the TM subjects' hearts did not change while the control subjects' hearts continued to enlarge over the same period of time.
Paul-Labrador et al., 2006	Metabolic Syndrome: RCT on stable coronary heart disease (CHD) inpatients (mean age 67), TM vs. HE, sixteen-week intervention.	Use of TM for sixteen weeks in CHD patients found improved blood pressure and insulin resistance and other components of the metabolic syndrome, as well as improved cardiac autonomic nervous system tone compared with controls.
Jayadevappa et al., 2007	Congestive Heart Failure (CHF): RCT of CHF patients, (mean age 64), TM vs. HE, six-month intervention.	The TM group significantly improved on functional capacity on a six-minute walk test compared with control subjects who received only HE. TM subjects also had reduced depression.
(Zamarra et al., 1996)	Myocardial Ischemia: Controlled trial of patients with coronary artery disease and symptoms of angina, mean age 55, TM vs. WLC, 7.6-month intervention.	The cardiac response during a standard exercise protocol for TM subjects compared to controls showed reduced workload of the heart, as measured by reduced oxygen demand, increased maximum workload the patient could tolerate before angina symptoms occurred, and delayed appearance of electrocardiographic abnormalities.

Continued

Table 33.2 (Continued)

Authors	Study Design	Results
Barnes et al., 2005; Schneider Schneider, Alexander, Staggers, Rainforth, et al., 2005	Mortality: A pooled analysis of the results from two randomized trials of TM in subjects with high blood pressure used meta-analysis of individual patient data (N = 202) to compute mortality risk.	At a mean follow-up of 7.6 ± 3.5 years, the TM group showed a 30 percent decrease in the rate of cardiovascular mortality and 23 percent risk reduction for all-cause mortality compared to HE and relaxation controls. The relative risk for cardiovascular disease (risk of the experimental group divided by risk of the control group) was 0.70, and the relative risk of all-cause mortality was 0.77.
Schneider et al., 2012	Heart Attacks, Strokes, and Death: RCT of patients with coronary artery disease (mean age 59), TM vs. HE, 5.4 year mean follow-up.	Compared to controls, for all subjects the TM technique had 48 percent lower rates of a combined endpoint of all-cause mortality, nonfatal heart attacks, and nonfatal strokes. Mean regularity of TM practice was 61 percent, a little over once a day.

BP = Blood Pressure, SBP = Systolic Blood Pressure, DBP = Diastolic Blood Pressure, RCT = Randomized Controlled Trial, Hg = Mercury, TM = Transcendental Meditation technique, HE = Health Education, WLC = Waitlist Control, CHF = Congestive Heart Failure

hypertrophy), reducing insulin resistance and other parameters of metabolic syndrome, and restoring functionality to people whose hearts do not supply enough blood to their bodies (congestive heart failure).

Attention-Deficit/Hyperactivity Disorder and Human Immunodeficiency Viruses

Table 33.3 shows pilot studies indicating that TM may be effective for treating attention-deficit/hyperactivity disorder (ADHD), a chronic condition marked by persistent inattention, hyperactivity, and sometimes impulsivity that plagues so many of our children and adults. Another promising area in research indicates that TM increases mental and physical health in patients with human immunodeficiency virus (HIV), a virus that attacks the body's immune system, which can lead to acquired immunodeficiency syndrome (AIDS), the most severe phase of HIV infection that weakens the body's ability to fight infection (see Table 33.3).

Health Insurance Statistics

Studies of health insurance data have their advantages and disadvantages. The main disadvantage is self-selection, as the subjects have chosen to learn meditation, and this

Table 33.3 Other Health Conditions

Authors	Study Design	Results
Grosswald, Stixrud, Travis, & Bateh, 2008; Travis, Grosswald, & Stixrud, 2011	ADHD: Pilot study followed by pilot RCT on ADHD students, 11–14 years, TM vs. delayed-start controls, three and six month post-test. Controls learned TM after three months and were tested at six months.	The pilot study found significant reductions in stress, anxiety, and improvements in ADHD symptoms and executive function. The RCT found three months' TM practice resulted in improvements in brain measures of ADHA (theta/beta ratios, increased theta coherence) and increased letter fluency. The delayed-start group similarly had changes at the six-month post-test, after they practiced TM for three months.
Chhatre et al., 2013	HIV: RCT on persons with HIV, age ≥ 18 years, TM vs. HE, six-month intervention.	Vitality, mental health, depression, social function, physical well-being and general health showed improvement in the TM group compared to controls. Evidence suggests immune activation stabilization.

ADHD = Attention-Deficit/Hyperactivity Disorder, HIV = Human Immunodeficiency Viruses

opens the possibility that such people may already be healthier than the general population or different on some other parameters that may confound the outcomes. The advantage of randomized controlled studies is that out of a pool of all people who are willing to try meditation, some are randomly assigned to a control group to either delay starting or to receive some other program, such as health education, that they perceive may be beneficial to them.

An advantage of studies on health insurance statistics is that they are blinded. That is, neither the people who learn to meditate, the people who collect the data, nor even the researchers know that the information collected is part of a study until after the data is all in. These data are likely to be accurate as they are part of financial accounting, and the data are available from independent agencies—the health insurance businesses. Such studies also have the advantage of being inexpensive to do on large numbers of people over many years, as they behave in their natural environment, choosing to meditate, organizing to learn it, paying for it themselves, and practicing it in their homes.

Table 33.4 shows a series of large studies of TM's effects on health insurance statistics. Herron and colleagues conducted a series of longitudinal studies on data on physician's payments collected from the government health insurance agency for Quebec, Canada. Fourteen years of data were collected for 1,418 people who had learned TM compared to a random sample of 1,418 people of the same age and habitation, half men and half women in each group. The data went back eight years before the TM group learned to meditate so that the TM group and controls could be compared *before* TM began. In addition, there were six years of data after the TM practice began, so TM and controls could be compared *after* TM commenced. The results showed that before learning TM, the TM and control groups were similar, indicating that before they learn to meditate, people who learn TM are not different from other people on how much they spend on

Table 33.4 Medical Care Utilization

Authors	Study Design	Results
Herron & Hillis, 2000; Herron & Cavanaugh, 2005; Herron, 2011	Medical Care Expenses: fourteen-year study of Quebec statistics of the general population for 1,418 TM and 1,418 matched controls for eight years before the TM group learned TM and six years after.	For all subjects, the medical expenditures of the TM and control groups were increasing at a similar rate during the 8 years before TM began. After TM began, the expenditures for the TM group began to decrease by 14 percent per year relative to controls. Similar findings were found for the subgroup of elders over sixty-five and for high-medical-cost people.
Orme-Johnson, 1987	Medical Care Utilization: A five-year study comparing Blue Cross insurance statistics for a TM group (average over 5 years, 1,468) with normative data (N ≈ 600,000) and controls matched for age, profession (N = 22,440).	The TM group compared to the norm and controls had reduced rates of hospitalization across all disease categories and age groups. The largest decreases were for TM participants over forty, who had 69 percent less hospitalization than the norm, compared to younger people, who had only 50 percent less. Similarly, outpatient visits were 74 percent less than the norm for TM participants over forty compared to 55 percent less for younger TM.
Orme-Johnson & Herron, 1997	Medical Care Utilization: An eleven-year study of Blue Cross insurance statistics on a group of 695 practicing TM plus other Maharishi Ayurveda modalities compared with normative data and controls matched for age, profession, and geographic region (N = 4,148).	This study replicated the results of the previous study of TM on medical care utilization, finding reduced hospitalization across all disease categories and age groups, with the largest decreases in hospitalization for the older subjects (−88 percent) relative to the norm and controls. Over all nine years of the study the TM group consistently showed reduced hospitalization by 74 percent, reduced outpatient visits by 55 percent, and reduced medical expenditures by 63 percent. TM had the strongest effects on more serious health issues that required hospitalization.

health, suggesting that they have equivalent sickness rates. However, *after* learning TM, the medical expenses of the TM group began to decrease relative to controls every year by 14 percent per year. Subgroup analyses of 142 high-cost people and 163 elders over sixty-five years old show very similar results, approximately 14 percent reductions per year through TM practice compared to controls.

Table 33.4 also gives the results of a five-year study of Blue Cross insurance statistics showing that TM participants had reduced rates of hospitalization compared to normative data or matched controls across all disease categories and age groups, with the largest reductions for the older age group, who showed 69 percent fewer hospitalizations and 74 percent fewer doctor visits. Hospital admission rates for the TM group for diseases of the cardiovascular system, which include hypertensive disease, ischemic heart disease, coronary heart disease, angina, atherosclerosis, congestive heart failure, heart attacks, stroke, and aneurysm, were a mean of 87.3 percent lower than the norm over the five years. Other notable statistics were that hospitalization rates for the TM group were 55 percent less for cancer, 87 percent less for diseases of the nervous system, and 65 percent lower for metabolic diseases (Orme-Johnson, 1987).

A second study of Blue Cross data in Table 33.4 shows the results of medical utilization rates for the employees of an academic institution in Iowa (Maharishi International University, 693 members) who practiced TM and other Maharishi Ayurveda (MAV) natural health care modalities. Controls were equivalent on profession, age distribution, gender (about half males and half females in each group), climate, and geographic location. All three groups had similar insurance factors that could influence utilization (Orme-Johnson & Herron, 1997). Reductions in utilization were even greater than the previous study of TM alone, showing an 80 percent lower overall rate of hospitalization, with 66 percent less for benign and malignant tumors, 92 percent less for cardiovascular disease, 93 percent less for all infectious diseases, 92 percent less for all mental disorders, and 76 percent less for diseases of the nervous system. This suggests that the additional Ayurvedic modalities added health protective value to TM. Nine years of data were available for this study, which showed average reductions of 55 percent less for outpatient visits, 74 percent less for hospitalization, and 63 percent less for medical expenditures in the TM plus MAV group compared to the norm.

The conclusion from these long-term health insurance studies and the 5.4 year study on heart attacks, strokes, and death is that TM reduces sickness rates and medical expenses by 10 percent to 14 percent per year, with the caveat that more large well-designed randomized controlled studies are needed to replicate these results.

The Transcendental Meditation technique and Psychological Health

Beginning in 1971, a series of promising studies were published on the effects of the TM technique on psychiatric patients, which were conducted at the Institute of Living, a leading residential psychiatric facility in Hartford, Connecticut (Glueck & Stroebel, 1975a, 1975b, 1984; Stroebel & Glueck, 1978). Stroebel & Glueck, 1978 wrote: "Clinical outcome data comparing TM patients and their matched controls receiving just the usual hospital treatment plan overwhelmingly favoured the TM group by whatever measure has been evaluated (condition on discharge, MMPI admission-discharge difference scores, daily automated nursing-note evaluation of psychopathology, decrease in medication for insomnia, etc., with TM versus matched control group p values ranging from .05 to .001 using t tests and chi-square tests of significance, as appropriate)." p. 413.

Also in the 1970s, an epidemiological study by the Swedish government found that the rate of mental health problems among the 35,000 people in the country who practiced the Transcendental Meditation technique was one hundred to two hundred times lower than the general population. Questionnaires were sent to 182 psychiatric care units in Sweden, including 133 hospitals and forty-nine policlinics. It was found that whereas the total incidence of psychiatric hospital care was 1:20 for the whole population of Sweden, the incidence for the subpopulation of 35,000 TM meditators in Sweden was 1:3,500. This government-sponsored study provided strong evidence that the TM program is beneficial to mental health (Ottoson, 1977; Suurkula, 1977).

Similarly, our large health insurance studies in the United States have found 30 percent lower rates than the norm of hospitalization for the category of all mental disorders for TM subjects (Orme-Johnson, 1987) and 92 percent lower for the study where the subjects practiced other Ayurvedic modalities in addition to TM (Orme-Johnson & Herron, 1997). A major systematic review and meta-analysis reported that no safety concerns were raised in a report examining 813 studies of meditation practices for health, including the TM technique (Ospina et al., 2008). Similarly, other systematic reviews and meta-analyses have found no adverse effects of meditation reported in the studies they reviewed (Brook et al., 2013; Orme-Johnson & Barnes, 2013; Ospina et al., 2008; Sedlmeier, Eberth, Schwarz, Zimmermann, & Haarig, 2012). These findings support the safety and the potential efficacy of TM and other meditation practices for treating physical and mental problems.

Trait Anxiety

"Trait" anxiety means how anxious a person generally is, whereas "state" anxiety refers to how anxious a person is at a particular time, such as at this specific moment. A meta-analysis of trait anxiety on 146 independent outcomes for various meditation and relaxation techniques found that the TM program had moderate to strong effects on reducing anxiety in a wide variety of populations. This conclusion was upheld in subgroup analyses that controlled for potential confounding variables, including mental health status of the population, age, gender, strength of experimental design, attrition, treatment duration and hours of treatment, pretest anxiety, and expectation effects. It is noteworthy that studies comparing TM with alternate treatments published by authors with neutral or negative attitudes toward TM had strong effects (Eppley, Abrams, & Shear, 1989). Two other meta-analyses have also reported that the size of the effects for TM are no larger in studies conducted by researchers who practice TM and/or who are affiliated with any Maharishi organization than studies by independent researchers and institutions (Orme-Johnson & Barnes, 2013; Orme-Johnson & Dillbeck, 2014). This suggests there is no author or institutional bias in the TM research.

It is noteworthy that one review of sixteen randomized studies on TM found that its effects on anxiety ranged widely, from no effect to strong effects. This heterogeneity was found to be due to how anxious the subjects were initially. For people who are not anxious to begin with, meditation does not reduce their anxiety, which would be expected. However, for highly anxious populations, such as veterans suffering from PTSD or prison inmates, TM produced large reductions in anxiety, which could not be accounted for by regression toward the mean (Orme-Johnson & Barnes, 2013).

A meta-analysis of randomized controlled trials with active or attention controls on clinical or "stressed" adult populations located only two studies on TM and trait anxiety and reported it had nil effects (Goyal et al., 2014). A rebuttal article located six randomized controlled trials comprising 308 subjects meeting the study's criteria, which, like other meta-analyses, found that TM significantly reduces anxiety. Of the two nil-effect studies, one was on patients with below-average initial anxiety, so no reduction would be expected, and in the other both TM and the active control were highly effective in reducing anxiety compared to a wait-list control (Orme-Johnson & Barnes, 2017).

A "trait," by definition, is a relatively stable aspect of the personality, so one may question how TM could change a chronically anxious person into a calm one. As noted earlier, the physiology of TM is the opposite of anxiety. The repeated experience of this low-anxiety "state" during TM, alternated with regular daily activity outside of TM, habituates the function in low-stress style as a "trait" outside of meditation. Studies supporting this hypothesis show that outside of meditation TM subjects have lower levels of stress hormones, plasma lactate, heart rate, and spontaneous skin responses than controls (Dillbeck & Orme-Johnson, 1987; Infante et al., 2001; Walton, Pugh, Gelderloos, & Macrae, 1995).

Another example of the physiology being transformed through repeated meditation is that of EEG coherence. It is inversely correlated with anxiety: the higher the coherence, the lower the anxiety. Practice of TM increases EEG coherence longitudinally over a year, providing further indirect evidence for TM's physiological effects on lowering trait anxiety (Travis & Arenander, 2006).

Numerous other studies also support the hypothesis that regular TM practice habituates the physiology to function in a more coherent, efficient, low-stress style by showing that the long-term benefits gained from practicing TM are proportional to how regularly one practices it. People who practiced once a day instead of the recommended twice daily get approximately half the benefit in stress reduction (Orme-Johnson & Moore, 2003), reduced PTSD symptoms (Herron & Rees, 2017), reduced heart attacks, strokes, and death (Schneider et al., 2012), increased resilience (Wendt et al., 2015), and increased intelligence (Tjoa, 1975).

Depression

Randomized controlled trials on patient populations have found that the TM program reduces depression in patients who have chronic heart failure (Jayadevappa et al., 2007), enlarged hearts (ventricular hypertrophy) (Kondwani et al., 2005), HIV (Chhatre et al., 2013), and PTSD (Brooks & Scarano, 1985; Nidich et al., 2018); are prison inmates (Nidich et al., 2016); and in pre-hypertensive young adults (Nidich et al., 2009).

Controlled trials of the general population have found that TM practice reduces depression in business managers (Sheppard, Staggers, & Johns, 1997), industrial workers in Japan (Haratani & Hemmi, 1990b), ninth grade students (Wendt et al., 2015), and in school teachers suffering from burnout (Elder, Nidich, Moriarty, & Nidich, 2014). Subgroup analyses of the randomized controlled trial on cardiovascular events demonstrated that the high-stress subgroup had significant reductions in psychosocial stress, which is a composite index of hostility, depression, and anger (Schneider et al., 2012).

Insomnia

Nearly 30 percent of Americans complain about insomnia (Roth, 2007). Insomnia causes unclear thinking, poor motor performance, and impaired quality of life. It increases healthcare utilization, absenteeism, and accidents, and presents a substantial financial burden on society (Szentkirály, Madarász, & Novák, 2009). Research has shown that TM reduces insomnia in a variety of populations. A three-month randomized controlled trial found TM improved sleep in war vets with PTSD compared to psychotherapy (Brooks & Scarano, 1985). A controlled longitudinal study reported improved sleep as well as reduced hostility and decreased neuroticism in incarcerated offenders (Abrams & Siegel, 1978). A five-month controlled study of 735 Japanese industrial workers found that TM reduced the number of people who took twenty minutes or more to fall asleep by 30 percent and reduced the number of people who woke up during night sleep by 26 percent (Haratani & Hemmi, 1990a).

A physiological mechanism by which TM could be expected to reduce insomnia is that it reduces cortisol. Elevated cortisol, particularly in the first part of nighttime sleep, is associated with chronic insomnia (Bush & Hudson, 2010). Practice of TM reduces cortisol throughout the twenty-four-hour daily cycle, during the night as well as during the day (MacLean et al., 1997; Walton et al., 1995).

Post-Traumatic Stress Disorder

Post-traumatic stress disorder (PTSD) is a mental health condition resulting from experiencing or witnessing terrifying and life-threatening events. Symptoms of PTSD are classified into four clusters: *intrusions*, such as flashbacks and nightmares; *persistent avoidance* of stimuli and memories associated with the trauma; *negative alterations in cognition and mood*, such as uncontrollable thoughts and mood swings; and *marked alterations in arousal* such as panic attacks, depression, and insomnia (American Psychiatric Association, 2013).

The WHO World Mental Health Survey of 68,894 people in twenty-four countries found that 70.4 percent of respondents had experienced lifetime trauma. Post-traumatic stress disorder was most likely to develop from persistent interpersonal traumas. The trauma types with the highest PTSD burden were rape, other sexual assaults, being stalked, and the unexpected death of a loved one (Kessler et al., 2017). Similarly, in the United States, 70 percent of adults have experienced some type of traumatic event at least once in their lives (223.4 million people). Of those 20 percent go on to develop PTSD (44.7 million). At any one time 8 percent of Americans have PTSD (24.4 million). An estimated one in nine women develops PTSD, making them twice as likely as men; 17 percent of combat troops are women and 71 percent of them develop PTSD due to sexual assault within the ranks (PTSD United, 2018).

The gold standard for treating PTSD is prolonged exposure (PE), which requires the patient to repeatedly reexperience memories and stimuli associated with the trauma until their conditioned responses to them are extinguished. Because PE and other trauma-focused interventions are not emotionally tolerable for many patients, non-trauma-focused interventions such as meditation have been studied by the military and other agencies (Gallegos, Crean, Pigeon, & Heffner, 2017; Hilton et al., 2017).

The TM technique has consistently been found to be effective for treating veterans of the wars in Vietnam, Iraq, and Afghanistan (Brooks & Scarano, 1985; Heffner et al., 2014; Herron & Rees, 2017; Kang et al., 2018; Rosenthal, Grosswald, Ross, & Rosenthal, 2011; Heffner, Crean, & Kemp, 2016; Nidich et al., 2018). A high-quality randomized controlled trial of veterans with PTSD funded by the U.S. Department of Defense found that TM was not inferior to PE in reducing PTSD symptoms severity and co-morbid depression. Overall, 61 percent of those receiving TM, 42 percent of those receiving PE, and 32 percent of those receiving health education showed clinically significant improvements in PTSD symptoms severity over twelve weeks (Nidich et al., 2018).

Two studies have been conducted on refugees in the Congo who had been exposed to combat, sexual assault, torture, and/or forced to witness the abuse or killing of loved ones (Rees, Travis, Shapiro, & Chant, 2013, 2014). Within one month of TM practice the refugees went from highly traumatized to non-symptomatic levels of PTSD.

Two of the civilian populations in the United States with the highest levels of PTSD are incarcerated women and men, who typically have a history persistent abuse. Studies show that TM significantly reduces PTSD symptoms in prison inmates of both genders (Nidich et al., 2017; Nidich et al., 2016).

Self-Actualization

Self-actualization is a term that expresses the quest for and attainment of higher levels of mental health in which one fully actualizes one's potential and creativity. Abraham Maslow and others considered self-actualization to be a basic biological need. Maslow devoted his studies to the healthiest, most creative people and observed that the characteristics of self-actualized people include the ability to judge situations correctly and honestly, and to comfortably accept oneself, others, and nature. They are independent, not reliant on culture and environment to form opinions and views. They are spontaneous and natural, autonomous, with constantly renewed appreciation of life's basic goods. They tend to form profound interpersonal relationships, yet be comfortable with solitude, to have a non-hostile sense of humor, to be socially compassionate, and to frequently have peak experiences, which are feelings of ecstasy, harmony, and deep meaning (Maslow, 1968, 1977).

A meta-analysis of forty-two independent outcomes on the effects of various meditation and relaxation techniques found that TM has a strong effect on increasing self-actualization (Alexander, Rainforth, & Gelderloos, 1991). Over an average three-month intervention period, TM subjects became more open to their own feelings and more capable of warm interpersonal relations, with emotional expressions guided more by an internal gyroscope than by fleeting circumstances, indicating emotional maturity. They gained a more positive view of self and humanity, were better able to integrate dichotomies, and increasingly embraced higher values such as nurturance of the good in oneself and others (integrative perspective on self and world). Their awareness became more stabilized in the "here and now," and they responded more adaptively to both internal and external challenges, indicating a more resilient sense of self (Alexander et al., 1991).

In a related series of studies, Alexander and colleagues explored the effects of TM on ego development, the maturation of the human mind over the life span to more self-actualizing values (Alexander, Davies, et al., 1990). In his doctoral dissertation at Harvard, Alexander found that maximum security prisoners grew more in cognitive complexity, character, and social development in one year of TM practice than is typically found in college students over a four-year period (Alexander & Orme-Johnson, 2003; Alexander, Walton, & Goodman, 2003). The inmates grew from the "conformist" stage (a dominance of concrete thinking) to the "self-aware" stage (a dominance of reflective thinking integrative of self and others).

A randomized study of TM's effects on institutionalized elderly in their eighties found it improved their memory and cognitive flexibility, it decreased their blood pressure, they felt "less old," they lived longer, and they loved their TM practice (Alexander et al., 1989). A ten-year longitudinal study of college graduates practicing TM found an unprecedented continued increase in ego development and moral reasoning, with 87 percent reaching above the highest level typically reached by adults. The matched control group showed the typical finding of little change on these measures after college (Chandler, Alexander, Heaton, & Grant, 2005).

Learning and Creativity

Great scientific and artistic discoveries have been documented to occur in flashes of insight, the Eureka Effect, when the mind is relaxed, such as during a vacation, while jogging, or some other time when the mind is not engaged in focused activity. The mechanism by which TM could be expected to affect cognitive abilities is that it produces an integrated state of silence in which information gets consolidated and creativity takes place.

Studies show that TM increases alpha1 *coherence* and *synchrony* between the left and right hemispheres and anterior and posterior cortical areas (Wallace, 1970b; Banquet, 1973;

Dillbeck & Bronson, 1981; Travis & Arenander, 2006; Travis et al., 2009; Cahn & Polich, 2006) and that alpha1 EEG coherence is correlated with increased creativity (Orme-Johnson & Haynes, 1981), concept learning, (Dillbeck, Orme-Johnson, & Wallace, 1981), and moral reasoning (Nidich, Ryncarz, Abrams, Orme-Johnson, & Wallace, 1983). There is wide agreement that alpha and theta EEG coherence functionally bind distal cortical areas for perception, motor performance, task switching, and memory (Sauseng & Klimesch, 2008; Palva & Palva, 2007)

Moreover, TM increases EEG coherence within the default network, a network of frontal and parietal brain areas that operates during states of rest to integrate memories and thoughts through largely unconscious processes (Raichle & Snyder, 2007; Cabane & Pollack, 2017). Three randomized experiments on 362 high-school students compared TM either to napping, to a Taoist meditation technique, or to no-treatment wait-list controls. Various cognitive variables, as well as state and trait anxiety, were measured over a period of six months in two studies and of one year in a third study (So & Orme-Johnson, 2001). Students did not know they were in a study and thought the battery of tests were part of the regular school testing program. Strong effects of TM were seen across all three studies on creativity, practical intelligence, and field independence. The creativity test (Test for Creative Thinking-Drawing Production) is said to evaluate convergent and divergent thinking processes and to reflect affective and volitional domains, such as sensitivity, passion, humor, unconventionality, boundary-breaking, and willingness to take chances. Practical intelligence (Constructive Thinking Inventory) centers around non-intellective factors such as optimism and a positive outlook on life necessary for success in work, love, social relationships, and maintaining emotional and physical well-being. Field independence indexes executive functioning in working memory, sustained attention, and visual spatial organization, which is especially important in the management and interpretation of complex cognitive tasks.

The TM technique also had moderate effects on measures of fluid intelligence. Improved fluid intelligence and choice reaction time were also found in a two-year study of college students practicing TM compared to matched controls (Cranson et al., 1991). These choice reaction time measures have been interpreted as indicating reduced noise in the nervous system and as stability of attention. Practice of TM has also been found to improve cognitive flexibility and signal detection (Alexander et al., 1989; Dillbeck, 1982).

In other school settings, TM has been found to be effective in reducing psychological distress and improving academic achievement (Nidich et al., 2009; Nidich et al., 2011), in improving basic language and math skills in one year in Maharishi School children (Nidich, Nidich, & Rainforth, 1986; Nidich & Nidich, 1989), as well as in at-risk urban middle school students (Nidich et al., 2011; Nidich & Nidich, 1989; Nidich, Nidich, & Rainforth, 1986). The TM program is now being implemented in Quiet Time programs in schools with impressive results throughout Latin America, India, and in major US cities such as San Francisco, Chicago, and New York (see https://www.davidlynchfoundation.org/schools.html).

Limitations of TM Research on Psychological Health

Despite Bernard Glueck and Charles Stroebel's promising research in the 1970s on the effectiveness of TM as an adjunct therapy for serious mental health problems (Glueck & Stroebel, 1975a, 1975b, 1984; Stroebel & Glueck, 1978) over the ensuing forty-five years there have been few high-quality large studies on TM and mental health. More research is needed on clinical populations with different types of depression, anxiety, and other specific diagnostic categories. Perhaps even more urgent are good large-scale longitudinal studies on teaching TM in schools to evaluate if it can *prevent* psychological problems.

The Transcendental Meditation technique and Behavior

Like physical and mental health, problems of social behavior are exacerbated by stress. Research shows that social problems such as violent crime, diseases, alcoholism, and drug abuse are linked to social stressors, such as the prevalence of unemployment, bankruptcies, divorces, and high school students dropping out of school (Linsky & Strauss, 1986). Since TM reduces stress at the individual level, it can be considered to be a grass-roots approach to behavioral problems in society.

School Behavior

The impact of TM practice on school behavior was studied in the context of a randomized study of ambulatory blood pressure in forty-five African American adolescents (ages 15–18 years). After four months, the TM group exhibited significantly fewer suspension days due to behavior-related problems, less absenteeism, and fewer rule infractions (Barnes et al., 2003). Practice of TM has also been shown to reduce the dropout rate, increase graduation rate, and increase acceptance to college and post-secondary school in inner city high school students, with the largest improvements found in students with low grades (Colbert & Nidich, 2013).

Alcohol, Drug, and Cigarette Use

Evidence suggests that the restorative rest produced by TM practice normalizes the neurochemical imbalances motivating substance abuse, eliminating the physiological basis for craving to take drugs (Walton & Levitsky, 1994). A meta-analysis of 198 studies on behavioral techniques for reducing tobacco, alcohol, and drug consumption found that TM practice had substantially larger effect sizes in reducing harmful substance consumption than other techniques (Alexander, Robinson, & Rainforth, 1994). Practice of TM has moderate effects on reducing alcohol consumption. The average effect size for TM in the ten studies reporting illicit drug consumption relative to controls was strong. For reduction of smoking cigarettes, the average effect size for the six randomized and six longitudinal controlled trials on the TM technique was very strong.

The pattern of change produced by TM across substances is a gradual decline in abstinence over the course of a year. In contrast, other programs typically show 100 percent abstinence at the start of the program due to inspiration to quit, which falls off to only 10 percent by the end of the year. By contrast, the gradual change produced by TM apparently reflects the progressive normalization of physiological stresses, which reduces the desire to self-medicate in a mal-adaptive attempt to achieve a more ideal psychophysiological state (Alexander, Robinson, & Rainforth, 1994).

Prison Rehabilitation

There have been roughly one hundred prison projects using TM worldwide, with twenty empirical studies (Hawkins, Orme-Johnson, & Durchholz, 2005). Incarcerated offenders show rapid positive changes in risk factors associated with criminal behavior, including reduced aggression, hostility, anxiety, and substance abuse, and increased moral judgment. Behavioral indications include reduced in-prison rule infractions in maximum security prisons (Anklesaria & King, 2003; Hawkins et al., 2005). A fifteen-year follow-up showed over 40 percent reduction in recidivism, defined as new incarcerations in inmates who learned TM while in prison compared to matched controls who participated in other rehabilitation programs (Rainforth, Bleick, Alexander, & Cavanaugh, 2003).

The studies on TM and behavior generally confirm the hypotheses that reducing stress in the individual improves their social behavior.

Conclusion and Future Directions

Even after fifty years of research on TM, most governmental agencies and policy makers would maintain that there still need to be large-scale randomized trials in all areas of physical and mental health before public policy can be implemented to include it in national health care and educational systems. In this regard, I propose three directions for future research: (1) basic research using state-of-the-art technologies, such as neuroimaging, to study the meditation process and higher states of consciousness; (2) large-scale well-controlled research applications in medicine, education, and conflict resolution, etc.; and (3) theoretical research integrating the emerging empirical evidence on meditation and the traditional knowledge about it with the larger body of scientific knowledge.

But even given the body of research as it stands today, TM clearly is a valuable life-skill tool for most to consider, and it may well be an effective adjunct therapy for many physical and mental ailments.

References

Abrams, A., & Siegel, L. (1978). The Transcendental Meditation program and rehabilitation at Folsom State Prison: A cross-validation study. *Criminal Justice and Behavior* 5, 3–20.

Alexander, C. N., Davies, J. L., Dixon, C. A., Dillbeck, M. C., Druker, S. M., Oetzel, R. M.,... Orme-Johnson, D. W. (1990). Growth of higher stages of consciousness: Maharishi's Vedic psychology of human development. In C. N. Alexander & E. J. Langer (Eds.), *Higher stages of human development: Perspectives on adult growth* (pp. 286–341). New York: Oxford University Press.

Alexander, C. N., Druker, S. M., & Langer, E. J. (1990). Major issues in the exploration of adult growth. In C. N. Alexander & E. J. Langer (Eds.), *Higher stages of human development: Perspectives on adult growth* (pp. 3–32). New York: Oxford University Press.

Alexander, C. N., Heaton, D. P., & Chandler, H. N. (1994). Advanced human development in the Vedic psychology of Maharishi Mahesh Yogi: Theory and research. In M. Miller & S. Cook-Greuter (Eds.), *Transcendence and mature thought in adulthood* (pp. 39–70). Savage, MD: Rowman and Littlefield.

Alexander, C. N., Langer, E. J., Newman, R. I., Chandler, H. M., & Davies, J. L. (1989). Transcendental Meditation, mindfulness, and longevity: An experimental study with the elderly. *Journal of Personality and Social Psychology* 57, 950–964.

Alexander, C. N., & Orme-Johnson, D. W. (2003). Walpole study of the TM program in maximum security prisoners II: Longitudinal study of development and psychopathology. *Journal of Offender Rehabilitation* 36, 127–160.

Alexander, C. N., Rainforth, M. V., & Gelderloos, P. (1991). Transcendental Meditation, self-actualization and psychological health: A conceptual overview and statistical meta-analysis. *Journal of Social Behavior and Personality* 6, 189–247.

Alexander, C. N., Robinson, P., & Rainforth, M. V. (1994). Treating alcohol, nicotine and drug abuse through Transcendental Meditation: A review and statistical meta-analysis. *Alcohol Treatment Quarterly* 11, 13–87.

Alexander, C. N., Schneider, R. H., Staggers, F., Sheppard, W., Clayborne, M., Rainforth,... Egan, B. (1996). A trial of stress reduction for hypertension in older African Americans (Part II): Sex and risk factor subgroup analysis. *Hypertension* 28, 228–237.

Alexander, C. N., Walton, K. G., & Goodman, R. S. (2003). Walpole study of the TM program in maximum security prisoners I: Cross-sectional differences in development and psychopathology. *Journal of Offender Rehabilitation* 36, 97–125.

American Psychiatric Association. (2013). *Diagnostic and statistical manual of mental disorders* (5th ed.). Washington, DC: Author.

Anderson, J. W., Liu, C. H., & Kryscio, R. J. (2008). Blood pressure response to Transcendental Meditation: A meta-analysis. *American Journal of Hypertension* 21, 310–316.

Anklesaria, F. K., & King, M. S. (2003). The Transcendental Meditation program in the Senegalese penitentiary system. *Journal of Offender Rehabilitation* 36, 303–318.

Badawi, K., Wallace, R. K., Orme-Johnson, D. W., & Rouzeré, A.-M. (1984). Electrophysiologic characteristics of respiratory suspension periods occurring during the practice of the Transcendental Meditation program. *Psychosomatic Medicine* 46, 267–276.

Bai, Z., Chang, J., Chen, C., Li, P., Yang, K., & Chi, I. (2015). Investigating the effect of Transcendental Meditation on blood pressure: A systematic review and meta-analysis. *Journal of Human Hypertension* 29(11), 653–662.

Banquet, J. P. (1973). Spectral analysis of EEG in meditation. *Electroencephalography and Clinical Neurophysiology 35*, 143–151.
Barnes, V., Schneider, R., Alexander, C., Rainforth, M., Salerno, J., Kondwani, K., & Staggers, F. (2005). Impact of Transcendental Meditation on mortality in older African Americans with hypertension—Eight-year follow-up. *Journal of Social Behavior and Personality 17*, 201–216.
Barnes, V. A. (2004). Impact of meditation on resting and ambulatory blood pressure and heart rate in youth. *Psychosomatic Medicine 66*, 909–914.
Barnes, V. A., Bauza, L. B., & Treiber, F. A. (2003). Impact of stress reduction on negative school behavior in adolescents. *Health and Quality of Life Outcomes 1*, 10.
Barnes, V. A., Johnson, M. H., & Treiber, F. A. (2009, November 19–20). Transcendental Meditation® Lowers body mass index in African American adolescents. Childhood Obesity Research Conference, Atlanta, GA.
Barnes, V. A., Kapuku, G. K., & Treiber, F. A. (2012). Impact of Transcendental Meditation® on left ventricular mass in African American adolescents. *Evidence-Based Complementary and Alternative Medicine 2012*, 1–6.
Barnes, V. A., & Orme-Johnson, D. W. (2006). Clinical and pre-clinical applications of the Transcendental Meditation program in the prevention and treatment of essential hypertension and cardiovascular disease in youth and adults. *Current Hypertension Reviews 2*, 207–218.
Barnes, V. A., Treiber, F. A., & Davis, H. (2001). Impact of Transcendental Meditation on cardiovascular function at rest and during acute stress in adolescents with high normal blood pressure. *Journal of Psychosomatic Research 51*, 597–605.
Barnes, V. A., Treiber, F. A., Turner, J. R., Davis, H., & Strong, W. B. (1999). Acute effects of Transcendental Meditation on hemodynamic functioning in middle-aged adults. *Psychosomatic Medicine 61*, 525–531.
Brook, R. D., Appel, L. J., Rubenfire, M., Ogedegbe, G., Bisognano, J. D., Elliott, W. J., . . . Rajagopalan, S. (2013). Beyond medications and diet: Alternative approaches to lowering blood pressure: A scientific statement from the American Heart Association. *Hypertension: Journal of the American Heart Association 61*, 1360–1383.
Brooks, J. S., & Scarano, T. (1985). Transcendental Meditation and the treatment of post-Vietnam adjustment. *Journal of Counseling and Development 64*, 212–215.
Bush, B., & Hudson, T. (2010). The role of cortisol in sleep. *Natural Medicine Journal, 2*(6).
Cabane, O. F., & Pollack, J. (2017). *The net and the butterfly: The art and practice of breakthrough thinking*. New York: Penguin Random House.
Cahn, B. R., & Polich, J. (2006). Meditation states and traits: EEG, ERP, and neuroimaging studies. *Psychological Bulletin 132*(2), 180–211.
Castillo-Richmond, A., Schneider, R. H., Alexander, C. N., Cook, R., Myers, H., Nidich, S. I., . . . Salerno, J. W. (2000). Effects of stress reduction on carotid atherosclerosis in hypertensive African Americans. *Stroke 31*, 568–573.
Cavanaugh, K. L., & Dillbeck, M. C. (2017a). The contribution of proposed field effects of consciousness to the prevention of U.S. accidental fatalities: Theory and empirical tests. *Journal of Consciousness Studies 24*, 53–86.
Cavanaugh, K. L., & Dillbeck, M. C. (2017b). Field effects of consciousness and reduction in U.S. urban murder rates: Evaluation of a prospective quasi-experiment. *Journal of Health and Environmental Research 3*, 32–43.

Chalmers, R., Clements, G., Schenkluhn, H., & Weinless, M. (Eds.). (1989). *Scientific research on Maharishi's Transcendental Meditation and TM-Sidhi program: Collected papers* (Vols. 2–4). Vlodrop, Netherlands: Maharishi Vedic University Press.

Chandler, H., Alexander, C., Heaton, D., & Grant, J. (2005). Transcendental Meditation and postconventional self-development: A 10-year longitudinal study. *Journal of Social Behavior and Personality 17*, 93–122.

Chhatre, S., Metzger, D. S., Frank, I., Boyer, J., Thompson, E., Nidich, S., ... Jayadevappa, R. (2013). Effects of behavioral stress reduction Transcendental Meditation intervention in persons with HIV. *AIDS Care 25*, 1291–1297.

Colbert, R. D., & Nidich, S. (2013). Effect of the Transcendental Meditation program on graduation, college acceptance and dropout rates for students attending an urban public high school. *Education 133*, 495–501.

Cranson, R. W., Orme-Johnson, D. W., Gackenbach, J., Dillbeck, M. C., Jones, C. H., & Alexander, C. N. (1991). Transcendental Meditation and improved performance on intelligence-related measures: A longitudinal study. *Personality and Individual Differences 12*, 1105–1116.

Davies, J. L., & Alexander, C. N. 2005. Alleviating political violence through reducing collective tension: Impact assessment analysis of the Lebanon war. *Journal of Social Behavior and Personality 17*, 285–338.

Dillbeck, M. C. (1982). Meditation and flexibility of visual perception and verbal problem solving. *Memory and Cognition 10*, 207–215.

Dillbeck, M. C. (1983). Testing the Vedic psychology of the Bhagavad-Gita. *Psychologia—An International Journal of Psychology in the Orient 26*, 232–240.

Dillbeck, M. C. (1990). The concept of self in the Bhagavad-Gita and in the Vedic psychology of Maharishi Mahesh Yogi: A further note on testability. *Psychologia—An International Journal of Psychology in the Orient 33*, 50–56.

Dillbeck, M. C. (Ed.). (2011). *Scientific research on Maharishi's Transcendental Meditation and TM-Sidhi program: Collected papers* (Vol. 6). Vlodrop, Netherlands: Maharishi Vedic University Press.

Dillbeck, M. C., Barnes, V. A., Schneider, R. H., & Travis, F. T. (Eds.). (2020). *Scientific Research on the Transcendental Meditation and TM-Sidhi Programme: Collected Papers* (Vol. 8). Vlodrop, Netherlands: Maharishi Vedic University Press.

Dillbeck, M. C., Barnes, V. A., Schneider, R. H., Travis, F. T., & Walton, K. G. (Eds.). (2013). *Scientific research on the Transcendental Meditation and TM-Sidhi program: Collected papers* (Vol. 7). Vlodrop, Netherlands: Maharishi Vedic University Press.

Dillbeck, M. C., & Bronson, E. C. (1981). Short-term longitudinal effects of the Transcendental Meditation technique on EEG power and coherence. *International Journal of Neuroscience 14*, 147–151.

Dillbeck, M. C., & Cavanaugh, K. L. (2016, April–June). Societal violence and collective consciousness: Reduction of U.S. homicide and urban violent crime rates. *SAGE Open*, pp. 1–16.

Dillbeck, M. C., & Cavanaugh, K. L. (2017, January–March). Group practice of the Transcendental Meditation® and TM-Sidhi® program and reductions in infant mortality and drug-related death: A quasi-experimental analysis. *SAGE Open*, pp. 1–15.

Dillbeck, M. C., & Orme-Johnson, D. W. (1987). Physiological differences between Transcendental Meditation and rest. *American Psychologist 42*, 879–881.

Dillbeck, M. C., Orme-Johnson, D. W., & Wallace, R. K. (1981). Frontal EEG coherence, H-reflex recovery, concept learning, and the TM-Sidhi program. *International Journal of Neuroscience 15*, 151–7.

Egenes, T. (2010). *Maharishi Patañjali Yoga Sūtra*. Fairfield, IA: 1st World Publishing.

Elder, C., Nidich, S., Moriarty, F., & Nidich, R. (2014). Effect of Transcendental Meditation on employee stress, depression, and burnout: A randomized controlled study. *Permanente Journal 18*, 19–23.

Eppley, K., Abrams, A. I., & Shear, J. (1989). Differential effects of relaxation techniques on trait anxiety: A meta-analysis. *Journal of Clinical Psychology 45*, 957–974.

Farrow, J. T., & Hebert, J. R. (1982). Breath suspension during the Transcendental Meditation technique. *Psychosomatic Medicine 44*, 133–153.

Forem, J. (2012). *Transcendental Meditation: The essential teachings of Maharishi Mahesh Yogi*. New York: Hay House.

Gallegos, A. M., Crean, H. F., Pigeon, W. R., & Heffner, K. L. (2017). Meditation and yoga for posttraumatic stress disorder: A meta-analytic review of randomized controlled trials. *Clinical Psychology Review 58*, 115–124.

Glueck, B. C., & Stroebel, C. F. (1975a). Biofeedback and meditation and the treatment of psychiatric illness. *Current Psychiatric Therapies 15*, 109–115.

Glueck, B. C., & Stroebel, C. F. (1975b). Biofeedback and meditation in the treatment of psychiatric illnesses. *Comprehensive Psychiatry 16*, 303–321.

Glueck, B. C., & Stroebel, C. F. (1984). Meditation in the treatment of psychiatric illness. In D. H. Shapiro & R. N. Walsh (Eds.), *Meditation: Classic and contemporary perspectives* (pp. 143–151). New York: Alden Publications.

Goyal, M., Singh, S., Sibinga, E. M. S., Gould, N. F., Rowland-Seymour, A., Sharma, R., ... Haythornthwaite, J. A. (2014). Meditation programs for psychological stress and well-being. *JAMA Internal Medicine 174*, 357–368.

Grosswald, S. J., Stixrud, W. R., Travis, F., & Bateh, M. A. (2008). Use of the Transcendental Meditation technique to reduce symptoms of Attention Deficit Hyperactivity Disorder (ADHD) by reducing stress and anxiety: An exploratory study. *Current Issues in Education 10*(2). Retrieved from http://cie.asu.edu/ojs/index.php/cieatasu/article/view/1569

Hagelin, J. S., Rainforth, M. V., Orme-Johnson, D. W., Cavanaugh, K. L., Alexander, C. N., Shatkin, S. F., ... Ross, E. (1999). Effects of group practice of the Transcendental Meditation program on preventing violent crime in Washington DC: Results of the National Demonstration Project, June–July, 1993. *Social Indicators Research 47*, 153–201.

Haratani, T., & Hemmi, T. (1990a). Effects of Transcendental Meditation on health behavior of industrial workers. *Japanese Journal of Public Health 37*, 729.

Haratani, T., & Hemmi, T. (1990b). Effects of Transcendental Meditation on the mental health of industrial workers. *Japanese Journal of Industrial Health 32*, 656.

Hawkins, M. A., Orme-Johnson, D. W., & Durchholz, C. F. (2005). Fulfilling the rehabilitative ideal through the Transcendental Meditation and TM-Sidhi programs: Primary, secondary, and tertiary prevention. *Journal of Social Behavior and Personality 17*, 443–488.

Heffner, K. L., Caine, E. D., Crean, H., Franus, N., Moynihan, J. A., & Talbot, N. (2014). Meditation for PTSD demonstration project: Final report to Mental Health Services, Department of Veteran Affairs. Rochester, NY: Department of Psychiatry at the University of Rochester.

Heffner, K. L., Crean, H. F., & Kemp, J. E. (2016). Meditation programs for veterans with posttraumatic stress disorder: Aggregate findings from a multi-site evaluation. *Psychological Trauma 8*(3), 365–374.

Herron, R., & Cavanaugh, K. (2005). Can the Transcendental Meditation program reduce the medical expenditures of older people? A longitudinal cost reduction study in Canada. *Journal of Social Behavior and Personality 17*, 415–442.

Herron, R., & Hillis, S. (2000). The impact of the Transcendental Meditation program on government payments to physicians in Quebec: An update. *American Journal of Health Promotion 14*, 284–293.

Herron, R. E. (2011). Changes in physician costs among high-cost Transcendental Meditation practitioners compared with high-cost nonpractitioners over 5 years. *American Journal of Health Promotion 26*, 56–60.

Herron, R. E., & Rees, B. (2017). The Transcendental Meditation program's impact on the symptoms of post-traumatic stress disorder of veterans: An uncontrolled pilot study. *Military Medicine 183*, e144–e150.

Hilton, L., Maher, A. R., Colaiaco, B., Apaydin, E., Sorbero, M. E., Booth, M., . . . Hempel, S. (2017). Meditation for posttraumatic stress: Systematic review and meta-analysis. *Psychological Trauma 9*, 453–460.

Infante, J. R., Torres-Avisbal, M., Pinel, P., Vallejo, J. A., Peran, F., Gonzalez, F., . . . Latre, J. M. (2001). Catecholamine levels in practitioners of the Transcendental Meditation technique. *Physiology & Behavior 72*, 141–146.

Jayadevappa, R., Johnson, J. C., Bloom, B. S., Nidich, S. I., Desai, S., Chhatre, S., . . . Schneider, R. H. (2007). Effectiveness of Transcendental Meditation on functional capacity and quality of life of African Americans with congestive heart failure: A randomized control study. *Ethnicity and Disease 17*, 72–77.

Jevning, R., Wallace, R. K., & Biedebach, M. (1992). The physiology of meditation, a review: A wakeful hypometabolic integrated response. *Neuroscience and Biobehavioral Reviews 16*, 415–424.

Kang, S. S., Erbes, C. R., Lamberty, G. J., Thuras, P., Sponheim, S. R., Polusny, M. A., . . . Lim, K. O. (2018). Transcendental Meditation for veterans with post-traumatic stress disorder. *Psychological Trauma 10*, 675–680.

Katz, V., & Egenes, T. (2015). *The Upanishads: With an introduction by the translators.* New York: Penguin Random House.

Kessler, R. C., Aguilar-Gaxiola, S., Alonso, J., Benjet, C., Bromet, E. J., Cardoso, G., . . . Koenen, K. C. (2017). Trauma and PTSD in the WHO world mental health surveys. *European Journal of Psychotraumatology 8*(sup5).

Kondwani, K., Schneider, R. H., Alexander, C. N., Sledge, C., Staggers, F., Clayborne, B. M., . . . Orme-Johnson, D. (2005). Left ventricular mass regression with the Transcendental Meditation technique and a health education program in hypertensive African Americans. *Journal of Social Behavior and Personality 17*, 181–200.

Kreplin, U., Farias, M., & Brazil, I. A. (2018). The limited prosocial effects of meditation: A systematic review and meta-analysis. *Nature.* Retrieved from 10.1038/s41598-018-20299-z

Linsky, A. S., & Strauss, M. A. (1986). *Social stress in the United Sates: Links to regional patterns of crime and illness.* Dover, MA: Auburn House.

MacKay, J., Mensah, G. A., Mendis, S., & Greenland, K. (2004). *The atlas of heart disease and stroke, world health statistics.* Geneva, Switzerland: World Health Organization. Retrieved from https://apps.who.int/iris/handle/10665/43007

MacLean, C. R. K., Walton, K. G., Wenneberg, S. R., Levitsky, D. K., Mandarino, J. V., Waziri, R., . . . Schneider, R. H. (1997). Effects of the Transcendental Meditation program on adaptive mechanisms: Changes in hormone levels and responses to stress after 4 months of practice. *Psychoneuroendocrinology 22*, 277–295.

Maharishi Mahesh Yogi. (1963). *The science of being and the art of living.* New York: New American Library.

Maharishi Mahesh Yogi. (2013). *Transcendental Meditation with questions and answers*. Vlodrop, Netherlands: Maharishi Foundation International, Maharishi Vedic University. (Original work published 1967).

Maharishi Mahesh Yogi. (1969). *On the Bhagavad-Gita: A new translation and commentary: Chapters 1–6*. Baltimore, MD: Penguin Books.

Mahone, M. C., Travis, F., Gevirtz, R., & Hubbard, D. (2018). fMRI during Transcendental Meditation practice. *Brain and Cognition June*, 30–33.

Mascaro, J. (1965). *The Upanishads: Translations from the Sanskrit with introduction*. London: Penguin Books.

Maslow, A. H. (1968). *Toward a psychology of being* (2nd ed.). New York: Van Nostrand Reinhold.

Maslow, A. H. (1977). *Farther reaches of human nature*. New York: Penguin.

Mills, P. J., Schneider, R. H., Hill, D., Walton, K. G., & Wallace, R. K. (1990). Beta-adrenergic receptor sensitivity in subjects practicing Transcendental Meditation. *Journal of Psychosomatic Research 34*, 29–33.

Nidich, S., Mills, P. J., Rainforth, M., Heppner, P., Schneider, R. H., Rosenthal, N. E., ... Rutledge, T. (2018). Non-trauma-focused meditation versus exposure therapy in veterans with post-traumatic stress disorder: A randomised controlled trial. *Lancet Psychiatry*, Online First.

Nidich, S., Mjasiri, S., Nidich, N., Rainforth, M., Grant, J., Valosek, L., ... Zigler, R. L. (2011). Academic achievement and Transcendental Meditation: A study with at-risk urban middle school students. *Education 131*, 556–564.

Nidich, S., & Nidich, R. (1989). Increased academic achievement at Maharishi School of the Age of Enlightenment: A replication study. *Education 109*, 302–304.

Nidich, S., O'Connor, T., Rutledge, T., Duncan, J., Compton, B., Seng, A., & Nidich, R. (2016). Reduced trauma symptoms and perceived stress in male prison inmates through the Transcendental Meditation program: A randomized controlled trial. *Permanente Journal 20*, 16-007.

Nidich, S., Rainforth, M., Haaga, D., Hagelin, J., Salerno, J., Travis, F. T., ... Schneider, R. (2009). A randomized controlled trial on effects of the Transcendental Meditation program on blood pressure, psychological distress, and coping in young adults. *American Journal of Hypertension 22*, 1326–1331.

Nidich, S., Seng, A., Compton, B., O'Connor, T., Salerno, J. W., & Nidich, R. (2017). Transcendental Meditation and reduced trauma symptoms in female inmates: A randomized controlled study. *Permanente Journal 21*, 39–43.

Nidich, S. I., Nidich, R. J., Rainforth, M. (1986). School effectiveness: Achievement gains at Maharishi School of the Age of Enlightenment. *Education 107*, 49–54.

Nidich, S. I., Ryncarz, R. A., Abrams, A. I., Orme-Johnson, D. W., & Wallace, R. K. (1983). Kohlbergian moral perspective responses, EEG coherence, and the Transcendental Meditation and TM-Sidhi program. *Journal of Moral Education 12*, 166–173.

Orme-Johnson, D. W. (1987). Medical care utilization and the Transcendental Meditation program. *Psychosomatic Medicine 49*, 493–507.

Orme-Johnson, D. W. (2000). Charles N. (Skip) Alexander's contribution to psychology. *Journal of Adult Development 7*, 199–215.

Orme-Johnson, D. W. (2016). Factor analysis of social indicators in the Middle East: Effects of cultural, military, political, and climatic events and group practice of the Transcendental Meditation and TM-Sidhi programs. *Journal of Maharishi Vedic Research Institute 1*, 5–39.

Orme-Johnson, D. W., Alexander, C. N., & Davies, J. L. (1990). The effects of the Maharishi technology of the unified field: Reply to a methodological critique. *Journal of Conflict Resolution 34*, 756–768.

Orme-Johnson, D. W., Alexander, C. N., Davies, J. L., Chandler, H. M., & Larimore, W. E. (1988). International Peace Project: The effects of the Maharishi technology of the unified field. *Journal of Conflict Resolution 32*, 776–812.

Orme-Johnson, D. W., & Barnes, V. A. (2013). Effects of the Transcendental Meditation technique on trait anxiety: A meta-analysis of randomized controlled trials. *Journal of Alternative and Complementary Medicine 20*, 330–341.

Orme-Johnson, D. W., & Barnes, V. A. (2017). Comment on "Review of meditation programs for psychological stress and well-being." *Journal of Complementary and Alternative Medicine, Jan*, 75–78.

Orme-Johnson, D. W., & Dillbeck, M. C. (2014). Methodological concerns for meta-analyses of meditation: Comment on Sedlmeier et al. (2012). *Psychological Bulletin 140*, 610–616.

Orme-Johnson, D. W., Dillbeck, M. C., & Alexander, C. N. (2003). Preventing terrorism and international conflict: Effects of large assemblies of participants in the Transcendental Meditation and TM-Sidhi programs. *Journal of Offender Rehabilitation 36*, 283–302.

Orme-Johnson, D. W., & Farrow, J. T. (Eds.). (1977). *Scientific research on Maharishi's Transcendental Meditation and TM-Sidhi program: Collected papers* (Vol. 1). Livingston Manor, NY: Maharishi International University Press.

Orme-Johnson, D. W., & Haynes, C. T. (1981). EEG phase coherence, pure consciousness, creativity and TM-Sidhi experiences. *International Journal of Neuroscience 13*, 211–217.

Orme-Johnson, D. W., & Herron, R. E. (1997). An innovative approach to reducing medical care utilization and expenditures. *American Journal of Managed Care 3*, 135–144.

Orme-Johnson, D. W., & Moore, R. M. (2003). First prison study using the Transcendental Meditation program: La Tuna Federal Penitentiary. *Journal of Offender Rehabilitation 36*, 89–96.

Orme-Johnson, D. W., Zimmerman, E., & Hawkins, M. A. (1997). Maharishi's Vedic psychology: The science of the cosmic psyche. In H. S. R. Kao & D. Sinha (Eds.), *Asian Perspectives on Psychology* (pp. 282–308). *New Delhi*: Sage Publications.

Ospina, M. B., Bond, K., Karkhaneh, M., Buscemi, N., Dryden, D. M., Barnes, V. A., . . . Shannahoff-Khalsa, D. (2008). Clinical trials of meditation practices in health care: Characteristics and quality. *Journal of Alternative and Complementary Medicine 14*, 1199–1213.

Ottoson, J. O. (1977). Swedish National Health Board Report on Transcendental Meditation: Report No. D: nr SN 3-9-1194/73. Stockholm: Socialstyrelsen (Swedish National Health Board). (Summarized in English by Suurkala J. (1989), see reference below).

Palva, S., & Palva, J. M. (2007). New vistas for α-frequency band oscillations. *Trends in Neurosciences 30*, 150–158.

Paul-Labrador, M., Polk, D., Dwyer, J. H., Velasquez, I., Nidich, S. I., Rainforth, M. V., . . . Bairey-Merz, C. N. (2006). Effects of a randomized controlled trial of Transcendental Meditation on components of the metabolic syndrome in subjects with coronary heart disease. *Archives of Internal Medicine 166*, 1218–1224.

PTSD United. (2018). *PTSD statistics* [online]. Retrieved from http://www.ptsdunited.org/ptsd-statistics-2/

Raichle, M. E., & Snyder, A. Z. (2007). A default mode of brain function: A brief history of an evolving idea. *Neuroimage 37*, 1083–1090.

Rainforth, M. V., Bleick, C., Alexander, C. N., & Cavanaugh, K. L. (2003). The Transcendental Meditation program and criminal recidivism in Folsom State prisoners: A 15-year follow-up study. *Journal of Offender Rehabilitation 36*, 181–204.

Rainforth, M. V., Schneider, R. H., Nidich, S. I., Gaylord-King, C., Salerno, J. W., & Anderson, J. W. (2007). Stress reduction programs in patients with elevated blood pressure: A systematic review and meta-analysis. *Current Hypertension Report 9*, 520–528.

Rees, B., Travis, F., Shapiro, D., & Chant, R. (2013). Reduction in post-traumatic stress symptoms in Congolese refugees practicing Transcendental Meditation. *Journal of Traumatic Stress 26*, 295–298.

Rees, B., Travis, F., Shapiro, D., & Chant, R. (2014). Significant reductions in posttraumatic stress symptoms in Congolese refugees within 10 days of Transcendental Meditation practice. *Journal of Traumatic Stress 27*, 112–115.

Rosenthal, J., Grosswald, S., Ross, R., & Rosenthal, N. (2011). Effects of Transcendental Meditation (TM) in veterans of Operation Enduring Freedom (OEF) and Operation Iraqi Freedom (OIF) with posttraumatic stress disorder (PTSD): A pilot study. *Military Medicine 176*, 626.

Roth, B. (2018). *Strength in stillness: The power of Transcendental Meditation*. New York: Simon and Schuster.

Roth, T. (2007). Insomnia: Definition, prevalence, etiology, and consequences. *Journal of Clinical Sleep Medicine 3*, S7–S10.

Salerno, J. W., Schneider, R. H., Alexander, C. N., Orme-Johnson, D. W., Castillo-Richmond, A., Rainforth, M., & Nidich, S. (2004). A controlled trial of effects of stress reduction on left ventricular mass in hypertensive African Americans. *Ethnicity & Disease 14*(Autumn), S2–S54.

Sauseng, P., & Klimesch, W. (2008). What does phase information of oscillatory brain activity tell us about cognitive processes? *Neuroscience & Biobehavioral Reviews 32*, 1001–1013.

Schneider, R. H., Alexander, C. N., Staggers, F., Orme-Johnson, D. W., Rainforth, M. V., Salerno, J. W., . . . Nidich, S. I. (2005). A randomized controlled trial of stress reduction in African Americans treated for hypertension for over one year. *American Journal of Hypertension 18*, 88–98.

Schneider, R. H., Alexander, C. N., Staggers, F., Rainforth, M. V., Salerno, J. W., Hartz, A., . . . Nidich, S. I. (2005). Long-term effects of stress reduction on mortality in persons ≥ 55 years of age with systemic hypertension. *American Journal of Cardiology 95*, 1060–1064.

Schneider, R. H., Grim, C. E., Rainforth, M. A., Kotchen, T. A., Nidich, S. I., Gaylord-King, C., . . . Alexander, C. N. (2012). Stress reduction in the secondary prevention of cardiovascular disease: Randomized controlled trial of Transcendental Meditation and health education in Blacks. *Circulation: Cardiovascular Quality Outcomes 5*, 750–758.

Schneider, R. H., Staggers, F., Alexander, C. N., Sheppard, W., Rainforth, M. V., Kondwani, K., . . . Gaylord-King, C. (1995). A randomized controlled trial of stress reduction for hypertension in older African Americans. *Hypertension 26*, 820–827.

Sedlmeier, P., Eberth, J., Schwarz, M., Zimmermann, D., & Haarig, F. (2012). The psychological effects of meditation: A meta-analysis. *Psychological Bulletin 138*, 1139–1171.

Sheppard, W. D., Staggers, F., & Johns, L. (1997). The effects of a stress management program in a high security government agency. *Anxiety, Stress, and Coping 10*, 341–350.

So, K. T., & Orme-Johnson, D. W. (2001). Three randomized experiments on the holistic longitudinal effects of the Transcendental Meditation technique on cognition. *Intelligence 29*, 419–440.

Stevens, G., Mascarenhas, M., & Mathers, C. (2009). Global health risks: Progress and challenges. *Bulletin of the World Health Organization 87,* 646. doi: 10.2471/BLT.09.070565

Stroebel, C. F., & Glueck, B. C. (1978). Passive meditation: Subjective, clinical, and electrographic comparison with biofeedback. In G. E. Schwartz & D. Shapiro (Eds.), *Consciousness and self-regulation* (pp. 401–429). New York: Plenum Press.

Suurkula, J. (1977). The Transcendental Meditation technique and the prevention of psychiatric illness. In R. Chalmers, G. Clements, H. Schenkluhn, & M. Weinless (Eds.), *Scientific research on the Transcendental Meditation program: Collected papers* (Vol. 2, pp. 896–897). Vlodrop, Netherlands: Maharishi Vedic University Press.

Szentkirály, A., Madarász, C. Z., & Novák, M. (2009). Sleep disorders: Impact on daytime functioning and quality of life. *Expert Review of Pharmacoeconomics & Outcomes Research,* 9(1), 49–64.

Tjoa, A. (1975). Increased intelligence and reduced neuroticism through the Transcendental Meditation program. *Gedrag: Tijdschrift voor Psychologie (Behavior: Journal of Psychology)* 3, 167–182.

Travis, F. T. (2001). Autonomic and EEG patterns distinguish transcending from other experiences during Transcendental Meditation practice. *International Journal of Psychophysiology 42,* 1–9.

Travis, F. T. (2004). Psychological and physiological characteristics of a proposed object-referral/self-referral continuum of self-awareness. *Consciousness and Cognition 13,* 401–420.

Travis, F. T., & Arenander, A. (2006). Cross-sectional and longitudinal study of effects of Transcendental Meditation practice on interhemispheric frontal asymmetry and frontal coherence. *International Journal of Neuroscience 116,* 1519–1538.

Travis, F. T., Grosswald, S., & Stixrud, W. (2011). ADHD, brain functioning, and Transcendental Meditation practice. *Mind & Brain, the Journal of Psychiatry 2,* 73–81.

Travis, F. T., Haaga, D., Hagelin, J. S., Tanner, M., Nidich, S. I., King, C. G., . . . Schneider, R. H. (2009). Effects of Transcendental Meditation practice on brain functioning and stress reactivity in college students. *International Journal of Psychophysiology 71*(2), 170–176.

Travis, F. T., & Shear, J. (2010). Focused attention, open monitoring and automatic self-transcending: Categories to organize meditations from Vedic, Buddhist and Chinese traditions. *Consciousness and Cognition 19,* 1110–1118.

Wallace, R. K. (1970a). The physiological effects of Transcendental Meditation: A proposed fourth major state of consciousness. In D. W. Orme-Johnson & J. T. Farrow (Eds.), Scientific *research on the Transcendental Meditation program: Collected papers* (2nd ed., Vol 1, pp. 43–78). Livingston Manor, NY: Maharishi International University Press.

Wallace, R. K. (1970b). Physiological effects of Transcendental Meditation. *Science 167,* 1751–1754.

Wallace, R. K. (1972). The physiology of meditation. *Scientific American 226,* 84–90.

Wallace, R. K., Benson, H., & Wilson, A. F. (1971). A wakeful hypometabolic physiologic state. *American Journal of Physiology 221,* 795–799.

Wallace, R. K., Orme-Johnson, D. W., & Dillbeck, M. C. (Eds.). (1990). *Scientific research on Maharishi's Transcendental Meditation and TM-Sidhi program: Collected papers* (Vol. 5). Fairfield, IA: Maharishi International University Press.

Walton, K., & Pugh, N. (1995). Stress, steroids and ojas: Neuroendocrine mechanisms and current promise of ancient approaches to disease prevention. *Indian Journal of Physiology and Pharmacology 39,* 3–36.

Walton, K. G., & Levitsky, D. (1994). A neuroendocrine mechanism for the reduction of drug use and addictions by Transcendental Meditation. In D. F. O'Connell & C. N. Alexander (Eds.), *Self recovery—Treating addictions using Transcendental Meditation and Maharishi Ayur-Veda*. Binghamton, NY: Harrington Park Press.

Walton, K. G., Pugh, N., Gelderloos, P., & Macrae, P. (1995). Stress reduction and preventing hypertension: Preliminary support for a psychoneuroendocrine mechanism. *Journal of Alternative and Complementary Medicine 1*, 263–283.

Wendt, S., Hipps, J., Abrams, A., Grant, J., Valosek, L., & Nidich, S. (2015). Practicing Transcendental Meditation in high schools: Relationship to well-being and academic achievement among students. *Contemporary School Psychology 19*, 312–319.

Zamarra, J. W., Schneider, R. H., Besseghini, I., Robinson, D. K., & Salerno, J. W. (1996). Usefulness of the Transcendental Meditation program in the treatment of patients with coronary artery disease. *American Journal of Cardiology 78*, 77–80.

CHAPTER 34

ZEN THERAPY

DAVID BRAZIER

Introduction: The Image of the Meditating Buddha

The image that most people associate with Buddhism is Buddha Śākyamuni sitting in meditation. This image has a direct appeal, even to those who have no knowledge of the teachings. It speaks of tranquility and equanimity in the midst of a world gone mad. In many a modern city there are far more Buddha statues than Buddhists. There is a great deal more to Buddhism than just meditation, but this image of inner and outer peace is iconic and a good representation of the essential message. The Buddha appears as tranquil and poised and evidently a good listener, as we see from the outsized ears in Figure 34.1.

Religions have many dimensions and stimulate the emergence of cultural arts and values. Whether in literature, painting, ceramics, flower arranging, or many other domains, Buddhism has inspired harmony, simplicity, and unadorned goodness. This message has an obvious appeal to people anxious to find alternatives to the stress, complexity, double dealing, speed, profit orientation, and consumerism of modern life. Simply to walk in a Zen garden may be a therapy in itself. Such inner tranquility is surely the longed-for goal of many coming to psychotherapy today.

The famous image is of Buddha at the moment of enlightenment, both hands in open gestures, one reposed in his lap, the other touching the earth. The meaning is sensed without words. Zen therapy aims to operate substantially at that level beyond words. Open-handedness is something we respond to, loss of contact with the earth something we regret, the stability of the seated figure something to aspire to. The half smile speaks of deep contentment. And here we see a moment of crucial life transformation, a liberation of heart and mind. Any procedure that brings about such a transformation must be considered a psychotherapy.

FIGURE 34.1 The enlarged ears are one of the traditional thirty-two marks of a Buddha.
Source: mai111/Shutterstock.com

A Psychological Religion

Already in considering the factors that are subliminally active in anybody who glances in the direction of this image, we have broached many of the principles of Buddhist psychology. Psychology is a modern word, yet Buddhism is, arguably, by far the most psychological of the great religions. Its canon has three sections: *Vinaya*, the rationale for the life of religious renunciation; *Sutra*, the dialogues and lectures of the Buddha; and *Abhidharma*, catalogues of mental states and their conditioned origins. These writings are aids to persons following the Buddhist path, both in their formal meditation practice and in the conduct of daily life. The Abhidharma especially is packed with terminology that is clearly psychological, concerned with mental conditioning, mental factors, mental states, traits, and how to change them. It is the result of many introspective studies by meditators seeking better understanding of the mind. It is a gold mine for psychologists. Its principles anticipate by millennia many of the findings of modern psychology, but they also present a refreshingly different perspective from contemporary self psychology. In this Buddhist approach, it is the self that is the obstacle (Gorkom, 1990; Narada, 1969, 1979, 1981).

The Zen Spirit

The term *zen* is the Japanese pronunciation of Sanskrit *dhyāna*, signifying meditation. In the early texts, *dhyāna* is generally described as a stepwise development with four or five stages, commencing with absorption in thought and progressing through states of joy or rapture to highest equanimity. This emphasis on dwelling upon the positive continues in Zen therapy where the aim is not merely to analyze unfortunate states, but also to cultivate positive aspects. Clients are to be seen as already necessarily engaged in a spiritual quest that therapy will accompany and facilitate.

In China and Japan, Zen transmuted with the idea that one can be in a meditative state in the conduct of any activity, hence giving rise to the idea of intensive (formal) practice and extensive (informal) practice. Intensive practice came to be called *zazen*, meaning "sitting meditation." In the Linji-Rinzai tradition, meditation focused on the solving of spiritual problems called koans. A koan is a succinct summary of the story of an encounter between two people in the course of which at least one of them experiences a spiritual awakening. To work with the koan is to attempt to understand, or, more properly, bring to life, this encounter. The koan illustrates a unique individual instance of a universal spiritual problem. It is thus possible to say that everybody has their particular koan and when they transcend it, they will be liberated from their own particular obstacle. Such liberation generally occurs in the course of an interpersonal encounter and is, therefore, by definition, an instance of psychotherapy, even if not necessarily occurring in a consulting room.

In the Sōtō tradition meditation became *shikantaza*, "just sitting," meaning sitting in complete authenticity with "no deliberate thought" (*Fukanzazengi* in Kennett, 1972, p. 232). In this tradition it is said that the koan arises naturally in daily life. The master observes adepts and sees where their spiritual blocks lie and arranges things to bring them to a crisis, the transcendence of which may liberate the adept. In Zen therapy, authenticity and the idea of koan play important roles as it aims to restore spontaneity by cutting through the koan or spiritual obstacle of the individual.

As Zen came West, the writings of D. T. Suzuki, Paul Reps, and Alan Watts established it as a popular genre, not merely a religious sect. To be Zen became "cool." The word simultaneously conjured associations with existentialism, anarchism, iconoclasm, esotericism, minimalism, Japanese aesthetics, and the beatnik phenomenon. It carried a flavor of liberation. However, in a Buddhist context too, "cool" had a venerable history, as Buddha frequently juxtaposed "coolness" to the "fever" of worldly life.

Nowadays, Zen meditation, Zen activities, and forming a relationship with a Zen master are often undertaken to enhance ordinary life or solve personal problems. Consequently the interplay of Buddhist and especially Zen wisdom with psychology has become a widely studied phenomenon well pre-dating the current plethora of studies of mindfulness (Trungpa, 1992; D. Brazier, 1995; Claxton, 1996; Welwood, 2000; Safran, 2003; C. Brazier, 2003).

Definition

Here Zen therapy indicates psychotherapy grounded in Buddhist psychology. It aims to yield liberation from conventional mores and personal inhibitive conditioning by disrupting their internalized causes, conditions, and attachments. Or, more succinctly, by finding a way through the individual koan.

It is not the application of Buddhist-sourced techniques toward Western self-assertiveness goals, or the rewriting of Buddhism within a Western secular paradigm, or a "treatment," or quasi-medical activity. It is not a technique or protocol, but rather an approach: a collective term for the efforts of those who seek to ground psychotherapeutic change in Buddhist principles.

The Zen Relationship

The common idea of Zen as a solitary pursuit is a misperception in two respects: first the importance of community, and second that of the teacher-disciple relationship.

Skill in Living with Others

Many psychotherapy problems are problems in how to live with others in a mass society. There is, therefore, much to be learned from Zen as a style of community living. Zen practitioners established large practice communities in China, Korea, and Japan (Welch, 1967; Buswell, 1992), sometimes housing several thousand people with a developed economic and communal life, with fields to till and small industries. Not everybody was a meditation practitioner, but the "meditation monk" was a unifying icon for the community as a whole. It is not necessary for everybody to meditate in order for everybody to be affected by meditation. In individualistic Western societies it is easy to lose sight of the much stronger communal spirit pervading Eastern life. One way of understanding the aim of Zen is as an eclipse of self, and that eclipse manifests in an attitude to living among others, each gladly accepting his or her lot (D. Brazier, 2019). Meditation is then not a retreat into a personal subjectivity, but an extinction of "self." Such communities necessarily have rules, but the real skill involved must, of necessity, be conveyed largely by example and presence. Thus, in her study of Zen nuns, Robinson Arai (1999) reports on an occasion when the community leader was absent:

> Tension and conflict in the monastery mounted with every whispered conversation and with each set of averted eyes. The air grew thick with insecurity and disharmony. Then at lunch, unannounced, the abbess returned. Upon seeing her, quite by surprise, tears of joy and relief came to the eyes of a number of the novices. Everyone began acting differently. It seemed as if the abbess's mere presence instantly healed the self-inflicted wounds. (p. 94)

One of the nuns comments, "In this place... you even learn to be kind to people who dislike you." Robinson Arai continues, "It is precisely these moments—when people are not acting exactly according to the discipline—that train people to pare down their ego" (Robinson Arai, 1999, p. 95). Clearly being a Zen therapist or guide is not simply a role that one can put on and off. It demands a depth of personal training and character formation in which ego reduction plays a central role.

The Spiritual Guide

Second, the part played by the teacher, therapist, or guide is of vital importance. There are a few people in Zen history who have attained enlightenment unaided, but they are the exception rather than the rule. In the *Denkuroku* (Cleary, 1990), Zen master Keizan's compendium of great masters of the Zen lineage, almost all became enlightened by an interpersonal encounter with a previous master. This, then, is the standard model. Although it is commonly presented that Śākyamuni Buddha became enlightened while meditating and so one must meditate in order to become enlightened, in fact, hardly anybody else seems to have been enlightened *while* meditating. Mostly it happens in an encounter. This, in other words, is not different from psychotherapy in general form.

In the stories of Zen history we usually get only the nub of each encounter. Thus:

> Ananda asked Makakashyo "My dear senior, what did Shakyamuni transmit to you other than his kesa (robe) of gold brocade?" Makakashyo called "Ananda!" Ananda replied "Yes?" Makakashyo said, "Chop down the flagpole." Ananda was enlightened. (Kennett, 1972, p. 4)

Here, "Chop down the flagpole" is roughly equivalent to the English colloquialism "Get off your soap box." Makakashyo challenges Ananda's spiritual cupidity. So here is depicted a crucial moment of encounter. This, however, would have occurred within a relationship between these two men extending over many years.

A fuller account of such a relationship is the Tibetan story of the training of Mila Repa by Marpa. Initially, Mila is eaten up by a craving for vengeance against his wicked uncle. Mila thinks Marpa can give him magical powers with which to inflict torment on the uncle. Marpa sets Mila a series of near impossible tasks which the younger man eventually fulfills. In the course of this long relationship, Mila gradually lets go of hatred and acquires new insights, ultimately becoming a great yogin himself (Lhalungpa, 1992).

It is worth noting here that Marpa does not set Mila to meditation until a late stage. The therapy is not meditation, but what prepares Mila for meditation.

Not only in Japan and Tibet, but throughout Buddhism, the importance of the relationship with the spiritual guide is universally asserted. The sutras mostly record encounters between Buddha and enquirers, in which the enquirers attain profound insights or make a change of direction in their lives. Thus they can be considered as brief case histories of therapeutic encounters wherein the Buddha is revealed as an adaptable therapist, speaking the language of the enquirer as much as delivering a doctrine. His aim is to liberate the mind of the seeker using whatever means are to hand.

Sudden Awakening, Gradual Cultivation

In Zen Buddhism quasi-medical categories such as depression, anxiety, or borderline states do not figure. It is not a matter of diagnosis and treatment. Rather it is a matter of unfolding life potential. When Ananda "chops down the flagpole" the consequences will naturally ramify throughout his life, releasing energies previously tied up in rumination and self-obsession. He will be released into greater wisdom and compassion. The therapeutic effect is sudden, but the consequences unfold over time. For sure, these may include improvements in mood and diminution of obsessions and anxieties, but these are not targeted specifically. This approach, therefore, is more about growth than repair, realisation than remedy. Nor is meditation to be taken as a treatment. To meditate is to reflect upon inspiration received. It, as it were, allows the learning to settle and consolidate. This follows the adage that "gradual cultivation" follows naturally from "sudden awakening," most clearly expressed in the teachings of Zen Master Chinul (Buswell, 2012).

On Being Alone with Others

Both in community and in relating with the guide, the practitioner is challenged to be "alone" (*ekāgratā*). This may seem paradoxical, but liberation is a matter of taking full responsibility. Meditation provides an experience of such aloneness as well as being a contemplation of wholesomeness. This "alone with others" (Batchelor, 1983) condition is a significant dimension of what Zen inculcates.

A key concept of Fujio Tomoda, a pioneer of psychotherapy in Japan, was the psychological vacuum. When there is empathic connection with the therapist, clients can have moments in which they have handed over their internalized others to the therapist. The client then experiences the vacuum or emptiness that is the experience at the heart of Zen. According to Tomoda, this vacuum experience brings healing. "In short, according to Tomoda, the essential meaning of listening lies in the paradoxical relationship where a person becomes 'utterly alone' through another person's empathic understanding. After the experience of 'vacuum,' clients go back to their real relationships and continue to identify the meaning of such experience." (Morotomi, 2010). In this aloneness a person is totally in contact with and responsible for life. Excuses, resentments, cravings, and fears all lose their support and drop away.

All-Accepting Spaciousness

The Zen master should ideally be a model of relating from such *ekāgratā*. She or he provides spaciousness, which offers no leverage for manipulation. Trungpa says, "when we come across somebody who is absolutely mad, our immediate response is to try to do something with them, rather than trying to understand the basic ground. So you have to allow yourself space" (Trungpa, 1992, p. 85). Thus it is often not the positive input of the therapist that proves effective so much as the fact that the client's "games" fall flat because the therapist is not caught up in trying to do something with the client. The good therapist accepts clients profoundly exactly as they each are. Into this space then come tumbling all the internalized others that are haunting the mind of the client. The therapist receives them all in a spirit of deep compassion. Thus Zen therapy is as much a practice of compassion and acceptance toward the other's others—the internalized others of the client—as it is focused upon the client him or herself. There is thus less scope for the therapy to cultivate self-obsession and more possibility of the client experiencing that emptiness in which life becomes real.

We need now to examine this matter of the internalized others. In Tomoda's schema we can think of the mind as being full of "strangers." In the terms of basic Buddhist psychology, these strangers are *rūpa*, the first of the *skandhas*.

Elements of Buddhist Psychology: *Rūpa*

A basic teaching of Śākyamuni Buddha was that of the *skandhas*—the components of ordinary life. They sketch out the steps in how one becomes imprisoned by conditions. Here we must introduce a little more Sanskrit terminology. The five *skandhas* are: *rūpa*, *vedanā*, *saṃjñā*, *saṃskāra*, and *vijñāna*. As common translations vary, I shall use the original terms and explain their meanings and functions as we proceed.

Definition of Rūpa

First, *rūpa*. *Rūpa* is often translated as "form" or "appearance." However, the word has more force than these translations imply. Originally, *rūpa* meant "icon." The statue on an altar is a *rūpa*. *Rūpa* implies objects with iconic power.

Thus, this chapter began with a reference to the powerful effect that merely seeing a Buddha statue or walking in a Zen garden can have (Fig. 34.2). There is power in objects.

FIGURE 34.2 The tranquility of a Zen garden speaks for itself.

Source: cowardlion/Shutterstock.com

Much energy in Zen goes into creating environments that quieten the mind, bring the solace of beauty to the troubled heart, and re-establish contact with a sense of quality, profundity, and eternity, as in the famous phrase of William Blake in "Auguries of Innocence":

To see a World in a Grain of Sand
And a Heaven in a Wild Flower
Hold Infinity in the palm of your hand
And Eternity in an hour

Objects inspire and sustain mind states, for good or ill, both collectively and individually. Social and personal values need continual reanimation, and this is generally achieved by the use of *rūpas*. Such icons as a national anthem and flag are obvious, but more subtle layers concern the way that advertising works, the value attached to setting, as when a politician chooses a meaningful venue to make a notable speech, down to the simple choices that we all make in decorating our houses, choosing models of automobile, or buying toys for our children. Thus we recondition ourselves and others by setting up certain forms—sounds, colors, shapes, materials, and so on—as significant. The culture is sustained by its icons, and the individual mind is then further conditioned by the significant objects of his personal history, from parents through to all that presented itself at key moments in life. All these "objects" are *rūpa*—significant others, "strangers" in Tomoda's language.

The Object Relation

This brings us to a first principle of Buddhist psychology: the mind is object related, it is conditioned by its icons, kidnapped by strangers. The mind is conditioned by all its objects, but some stand out with a magnetic persistent power. We are all vaguely aware of this principle. We see how teenagers imitate their idols. We notice how certain words, like "sex," stand out from a page and how we hear our name mentioned through the noise of many conversations in a crowded room.

We shall define the other *skandhas* in due course, but first let us investigate *rūpa* further through the frame of meditation.

Definition of Meditation and Mindfulness

Meditation can be defined, basically, as the mind held upon a wholesome object (Gyatso, 1990, p. 2). What counts as "wholesome" will be a function of learning. Keeping such learning in mind is what, in Buddhism, is meant by "mindfulness" (*smṛti*). Traditional Buddhist meditation manuals such as the *Visuddhimagga* (Ñanamoli, 1956) provide extensive catalogues of suitable wholesome objects—"recollection of the Buddha," "of the Dharma," "of generosity," "deities," "the body," "breathing," "peace," and so on—all intended to acquaint the mind with virtue. There are also objects such as mindfulness of the physical elements, the stages of decay of the body after death, and moral defilements, which are not immediately evidently "wholesome," but which are intended to acquaint the mind with wisdom.

There are also meditations that are said to be without a specific object, and some would seek to define meditation as a state of empty mind, but this is somewhat removed from the early Buddhist view where even "infinite space" and "infinite consciousness" are objects. "Choiceless awareness" is widely practiced in various modern schools of Buddhism and brings some access to corners of the mind that otherwise remain unswept. However, mind is always cognizing something.

Mapping the Rūpas *of the Mind*

If we let go of the idea of meditation as only an artificial exercise following a protocol, we can see that people are often meditating naturally. The mind tends to dwell upon significant objects. A first step for a Zen therapist will be to discern what it is that constitutes the *rūpa* map in the mind of the client. What does the client naturally and habitually meditate upon? This lends a particular focus to the way to read the presenting problem. The initial story that a client tells is commonly a parade of his significant *rūpa*s. (For convenience, I use the masculine pronouns for the client role and the feminine ones for the therapist role, though these are not intended as gendered statements).

The application of the notion of *rūpa* in psychotherapy can have a marked impact upon therapeutic methodology. Empathy is even more about perception than feelings. It is best achieved by the therapist orienting herself in parallel with the client in imaginatively perceiving the client's *rūpa* constellation. If she regards the same object in the same way she will naturally tend to inhabit the same mental space as he does. This will be a recognizable principle to hypnotists who also seek such a parallelism as a preliminary to exercising influence. Once the existing disposition of significant *rūpa*s is discerned, we can think of the ongoing use of *rūpa* in constructive and reconstructive terms.

Using Rūpa *Constructively*

The introduction of wholesome *rūpa*s into the mental landscape of the client will be growth promoting. A grieving person may be more powerfully helped by going to walk in a place of beauty than by any amount of talking, for instance. The client's attention can be subtly drawn to wholesome objects that may console, strengthen, or simply distract from other less helpful alternatives. Much of the success of modern forms of "mindfulness" may be attributable to their ability to distract the subject's attention from more stress-inducing alternatives (D. Brazier, 2016, p. 67). Mental health is largely a function of what one habitually meditates upon.

Again, the vast literature on transference tells us how very important the therapist herself becomes in the *rūpa* constellation of the client. Much of what happens in therapy is attributable to modeling (D. Brazier, 2009, 1993). If the therapist is empathic, unconditionally positive and congruent, for instance, it will not merely be the case that this releases an inherent actualizing tendency in the client (Rogers, 1965); it will, perhaps even more tellingly, be a process of influence whereby the client, conditioned by his psychological investment in the iconic figure of the therapist, absorbs similar traits into his own life with widespread consequences for improved social functioning and relationships. The therapist is a powerful *rūpa* inserted into the life of the client. Therefore the qualities of the therapist matter.

Using Rūpa *Reconstructively*

Reconstructively, the therapist begins from an alert awareness of the *rūpa* constellation that is already dominating the mind of the client. Thus, typically, a client comes to a therapist and relates a story of woe, embedded in which is a procession of the significant others that are influential in the client's life. The experienced psychotherapist will, naturally, keep track of this information as, indeed, would a sympathetic friend. However, in therapy as commonly practiced, the therapist will fairly soon draw the client's attention away from a direct consideration of these objects onto a focus upon the client's own self, using a remark such as, "And how is this for you?" or "And what are you feeling right now?" However, a person cognizant with Buddhist psychology might well linger longer over the naturally arising objects since these are the true conditioning factors in the client's mentality. They are potential objects of compassion.

She might, therefore, focus attention upon the objects themselves with "Please tell me more about your mother," or "And are you seeing your boss, as it were, standing before you right now? Tell me, how does he look?" By a series of gentle prompts it is usually possible to help the client to investigate the object that so powerfully holds his attention. The first responsibility of a therapist working this way is to keep the *rūpa* vivid in the mind of the client. As long as it is so, the client will live and relive the corresponding mind states. It will generally not be necessary for the therapist to ask, "What are you feeling?" as it will be obvious. Also, the therapist is going with the grain of the client's mind and so is not likely to meet such resistance as when a direct assault is made upon the client's self.

This kind of object-related work (C. Brazier, 2009) can function in many varied modes and situations. As the client examines the iconic other in more detail, it is highly likely that a shift of perception will occur. When a *rūpa* is reconstructed there will be a corresponding shift in the personality of the client. The changed attitude will generalize. For this process to have conviction it is necessary for the therapist to maintain a warm neutrality, encouraging but not biasing the exploration. The client's change of attitude must be of his own generation, albeit resulting from a process supported by the therapist. By deconstructing a stereotyped image of the *rūpa* and reconstructing it more realistically the client attains a degree of freedom.

An Example

Peter has long regarded John as a rival and opponent. One day Peter inadvertently overhears two colleagues talking about a recent meeting, in which several people were criticizing Peter's work and John was the only person who vigorously defended Peter's reputation. Peter, unable to disbelieve the evidence, goes through an immediate emotional episode that continues to work in his mind so that that night he gets hardly any sleep. His turmoil changes him, altering not only his attitude to John, but also the way he relates to other friends and colleagues. It also reduces his self-certainty and makes him a softer, easier colleague.

Another Example

A client had a difficult decision to make. One option involved going abroad, the other staying in his own country. It was evident from the client's eye movements that he imagined one *rūpa* (abroad) to his left and the other to his right. It was tempting to engage the client in a discussion of the pros and cons of the options. However, following the principle of keeping the *rūpa*s vivid the therapist avoided this course and simply indicated the options with gestures to their psychological locations in the room. The client said, "I always make my decisions myself, alone, I don't involve others. I stand on my own feet." The therapist took this cue and had the client stand up. The client arranged himself and the therapist standing side by side facing the "abroad" option. The therapist asked, "Are you more conscious of what is ahead of you or what is behind?" The client said, "Neither. I am most conscious of you beside me." At this point the client had an important insight accompanied by strong emotion, realizing his great suppressed desire for somebody to stand beside him so that he would not have to make decisions alone.

In this second case, we can see there are three *rūpa*s for the client, not just the two that were originally presented. The therapist is also an important *rūpa*. Realizing how important this third *rūpa* is brings about a vital shift, not just in the client's attitude to the presenting problem, but to his whole life. This shift is achieved without enquiry into the client's inner life, without asking about emotions, and with minimal reference to cognitive processes. Simply the juxtaposition of significant *rūpa*s brings about the insight. Also, the insight comes unexpectedly. This is not a case of identifying a syndrome, applying a treatment, and getting an expected or corresponding result. It is rather an open spacious process in which new understandings arrive spontaneously that change life direction. The therapist refrains from problem solving and accepts the client as an unfolding process. There is nothing wrong that needs to be fixed. The client experiences a softening, a fuller appreciation of his own humanity.

Liberating the Others

Earlier we spoke of Tomoda's vacuum as an aloneness of the subject who parts company with his internalized *rūpa*s. It is equally possible to view this as a liberation of the others. Therapy enables the client to let them go. One of the ways this happens is that the client realizes his own frailty, vulnerability, and proneness to error. Realizing one's own humanity in this way enables the client to appreciate the similar state of others. This fellow feeling is the basic ground of compassion. When we see others as being similar to ourselves, we are less inclined to blame, hold resentments, make unreasonable demands or criticize. We let our others off the hook that we have kept them on.

In these case examples, the clients discover their humanity and vulnerability. The therapist accepts this. The client may now drop the pose of rugged independence. This is likely to provide a grounding for a softening of attitude toward others in the client's life.

In the first case, the change is precipitated by indubitable evidence. It illustrates the principle that if the way the *rūpa* is construed changes, the person changes. In the second case, the change of attitude toward third parties is achieved without direct investigation of those relationships and without any diagnosis of relationship problems. The therapist works with whatever spontaneously presents. There is an implicit assumption that a benign process will unfold spontaneously if it is not blocked. The therapist, therefore, does not *treat* the client, but provides conditions of spaciousness in which the power of the *rūpas* can resolve naturally.

Elements of Buddhist Psychology: From *Vedanā* to *Samādhi*

Knowing Before the Fact

There are five *skandhas*. *Rūpa* has been discussed. The other four can be seen as describing the way that one responds to *rūpa* and how a (largely unconscious) mentality is thus formed and sustained.

The term *vedanā*, often rather misleadingly translated as "feeling," refers to one's immediate reaction to the perception of an iconic object. It has three basic valences: attraction, repulsion, and confusion. These are extremely basic visceral characteristics that can be seen in most non-human animals, even of the most primitive kinds.

In humans, what is treated as attractive, repulsive, and confusing is as much a function of learning as of instinct. Experience yields knowledge. *Veda* means "knowledge," just as the Vedas are a collection of holy books—the Knowledge. *Veda-nā* thus means "knowingness." This, however, is not just cognitive. In function, it is precognitive. We react to something before we think about it or even label it. The *veda* is embedded in our very senses, in our familiarity with things bred of experience. Thus, trivially, one's eye might be drawn to the chocolate lying on the table before any conscious thought about it has occurred. In Buddhist psychology the senses *are* minds and (including the mind's eye as a sixth) are referred to as *ṣaḍ-āyatana*, literally, six uncontrollables.

Rūpa alerts us and we are immediately attracted or put on our guard, seduced, or incensed. It gets to us. The general idea in Buddhism is that people rather go through life in a daze and are only roused by those things (*rūpa*) that have salient power. This is in contrast to the enlightened person who is "Buddha" (literally, "awake"). Meditation can, therefore, be regarded as the practice of being awake. This might be understood as awake to the world around one, as alertness, or awake to a transcendent world, as in *dhyāna*, but in any case, a rapture of wakefulness. When attention is rapt in this way the state is called *samādhi*, loosely translated as "concentration." When people are not awakened their lives are effectively controlled by the *rūpas* that prompt them. When they are awakened, such prompts do not stand out: the numinous quality being then found everywhere, not simply in a select range of things, favored or loathed.

One way of summarizing the therapeutic direction of Buddhism is, therefore, as a movement from *vedanā* to *samādhi*. *Sama* has the implication of "whole" and *dhi* is vision. Thus, the awakened person has a more complete vision and greater freedom, not merely a limited stimulus-response repertoire. Another way of understanding this is as a letting go of the attempt to control. In some areas of life we have a modest degree of control, but the big things—birth and death, aging and loss, major changes of fortune—are usually or always out of our control. The person with "whole vision" accepts this as it is. He is able to meet the "slings and arrows" of fortune with equanimity.

An Example

The client had abdominal pains that he connected with his proneness to bouts of "irrational anger." He talked in rapid succession of a series of scenes from his life, any of which could be thought of as sources of his condition: death of father, disputes with brother, unfairness and mistreatment at school, marriage and business problems, and so on. Interspersed were accounts of small successes in life and affection for his mother. Any of these could have been a basis for object-related work as in the previous section, but the quantity and density of presentation did not allow easy selection. Nonetheless, the therapist was able to acknowledge the client's reactions to each of these things that had befallen him, and this global acceptance gradually brought the client to a more philosophical frame, an acknowledgement that, "Yes, life's like that!"

In this case there is a temptation for the therapist to seize upon the material presented and start to think: It's no wonder this client is a mess. This can undermine the therapy. A great quantity of interventions and exercises is possible, but they tend to carry the underlying message that the client is a hopeless case while boosting the therapist's own ego as she shows off her repertoire of interventions. The Zen therapist needs a broad perspective that can encompass the full range of what it is to be human in a world of afflictions.

The Role of Affliction

Buddhism begins with reflection upon *duḥkha*, affliction. Affliction is unwelcome but also an awakener. Fear and dread wake us up. The Buddha realized the critical importance of *duḥkha*. His very first teaching was concerned with it. Buddhism is commonly presented as a way to bring an end to it, a path to untroubled happiness, but this seems wide of the mark (D. Brazier, 1997). The items listed by Buddha as *duḥkha*, which include being born, growing old, getting sick, dying, being conjoined with those we hate or separated from those we love, are existential, and while we might mitigate some, we cannot avoid them. Buddha says that *duḥkha* is a truth for noble ones.

Rūpa provokes *vedanā*. *Rūpa*s that are *duḥkha* provoke *samudaya*. *Duḥkha-samudaya* means "that which comes up with *duḥkha*." In the case of the normal unaware person, the feelings, thoughts, images, and motives that arise with *duḥkha* tend to lead to more *duḥkha*. A bad day at the office may rouse the impulse to get drunk, producing a hangover, which may well mean another bad next day at the office. Thus *duḥkha* and *samudaya* endlessly cycle, each occasioning more of the other. This cycle is called samsara. Therapy aims to break or dissolve this cycle.

Buddha taught that the very energy roused by *duḥkha* can provide the royal road to awakening. This is a basis of Zen therapy. All instances of *rūpa* have similar potential, hence the therapist's all-acceptance. The client is not seen as being damaged and in need of repair, but rather as already engaged in important work toward liberation.

Meditation deepens acceptance. To remain sitting without flight or pursuit as habitual *rūpas* surface is a training in restraint that is not merely the ground of morality, but, therapeutically, the means by which to convert *vedanā* into *samādhi*. In Zen such sitting is called *shikantaza*, *shikan* meaning "just," thus "Just sitting with no deliberate thought is the important aspect of zazen." (Kennett, 1972, p. 232).

Elements of Buddhist Psychology: *Saṃjñā* to *Prajñā*

The Trance of Everyday Life

The third *skandha* is *saṃjñā*, the ordinary, transient floating consciousness of the unenlightened person, tossed about from one *rūpa* to another. It is a species of trance, adventitiously pushed this way or that, like a cork bobbing on waves. In traditional Indian psychology, *saṃjñā* is that part of life that does not carry over into one's next incarnation, since it is just of the moment. So, *saṃjñā* is made up of the ordinary trance routines of daily life, prompted by *rūpa* and triggered by *vedanā*.

RŪPA → VEDANĀ → SAṂJÑĀ

Thus, to take an everyday example, one is dreamily walking along the pavement when the smell of coffee impacts one's nostrils. Before one has even labelled this sensation, one's eyes have turned, seeking the source and, perhaps, one's feet are already turning in the direction of the café door. Of course, one may instantly recover one's composure and decide that one does not have time or does not want to spend the money, but the sequence of *rūpa–vedanā–saṃjñā* has already occurred in the bat of an eye. Without any formal knowledge of Buddhist psychology, coffee shop owners know to install fans near the shop door to waft the odor into the street.

Saṃjñā also operates on a larger scale and time span. Whole societies can be entranced collectively. Provocative incidents may trigger a war, charismatic leadership stir up a movement. In small matters and large, the ordinary person, trivially or consequentially, individually and en mass, passes through this sequence again and again, and does so largely unconsciously, beyond rational judgement.

Meditation can be seen as a training in resisting this enslavement to one's personal and cultural programming. Meditation disrupts the habitual trance. It needs the alertness to not give way to the *vedanā* impulse. In therapy more generally, we are concerned most immediately with those trances that give rise to dysfunctional behavior.

An Example

The client reports frequently getting into fights in bars. The therapist has the client recount a recent incident. The client reports a range of provocative behaviour that readily engages others in conflict. The therapist takes the client back in imagination to earlier the same evening. The client is thinking about going to the bar, chooses what to wear, combs his hair, all the while imagining how he will inevitably get into a fight once he gets to the bar. Thus it becomes clear that the trance does not start when the client enters the bar, but much earlier. Even simply imagining going out, the client can feel his blood temperature rising. If a trance is to be broken or averted, one has to catch its incipient phase, the point of *vedanā–saṃjñā* transition.

Prajñā

Prajñā, wisdom, is a matter of cutting through the flow. The client wanted to give up his aggressiveness but did not know how. He could see the disadvantage but not get leverage on the pattern. We all know how difficult it is to keep New Year's resolutions. While one is conscious, it is possible, but then we slip into the usual trance and before we know it all our resolution has faded away.

Buddhist meditation classically consists of insight and calm. One can have the insight, but can one persist in the calm? At the next session the client reported back. No fight this week. How so? "When I looked in the mirror to comb my hair, I noticed my blood heat and I immediately thought of you. It made me laugh. I was still laughing when I got to the bar." To put this more technically, in Buddhist psychology language, a new *rūpa–vedanā–saṃjñā* format has been implanted.

Elements of Buddhist Psychology: *Saṃskāra* and the Mirror Mind

Confections of the Mind

Saṃskāra, cognate with "confection," is commonly translated less precisely as "mental formations" (e.g., Hanh, 1987, p. 31), the elaboration of thought, image, and emotion that proceeds as we integrate experience. When salient experience occurs, we weave a narrative around it, that it not hurt or excite us excessively in the future. Much of this process happens during sleep. Sleep is reparative and self-protective, which perhaps partly explains why we so readily drift into *saṃjñā* even in the daytime. *Saṃjñā* generates *saṃskāra*.

RŪPA → VEDANĀ → SAṂJÑĀ → SAṂSKĀRA

The Buddha points out that all *saṃskāra*s are *duḥkha, sarva saṃskāra duḥkha*, because they are impermanent. They hold for a while, enmeshing one further in the complications of life, often making them worse. The stories that we tell ourselves often amplify a false position, of personal importance or victimhood, guilt, or self-justification. The ego proceeds like a comic book avatar, narrowly escaping dangers, intrinsically heroic, indulging in distractions and finding excuses whenever necessary (cf. Thurber, 2000).

An Example

The client talked about two dreams: (1) of being in a small room alone, becoming aware of people outside and opening a tiny window; (2) of his father taking a knife to the client's throat. It became apparent that the client had left home ten years earlier and only recently re-established contact. He wanted to be closer to his father, but also feared the father's anger as he had abandoned the family.

Dreams are *saṃskāra*s in the process of coming into being. In this case we can see that the message of the dreams is to advise him to reduce his isolation slowly and carefully since dangers still lurk in wait.

Manas, *the Scheming Mind*

The *saṃskāra*s are, therefore, our internal advisors, for good or ill. They can solidify into scripts (cf. Berne, 1964). They are the work of *manas*, the calculating part of the brain (Suzuki, 1998). To a degree this activity is healthy, rather in line with the principles of personal construct psychology (Kelly, 1955; Bannister & Francella, 1986), which suggests that people are a bit like scientists formulating hypotheses and going through life testing them. However, in the Buddhist view, this "scientist" has an inbuilt bias. His theories are almost always about himself, and this "self" is illusory.

Another Example

In a therapy group, a client presented herself as an intelligent, happy, well-adjusted person who, nonetheless, was currently experiencing serious difficulties in the relationship with her nineteen-year-old son, now away from home for higher education.

The son has no social life and talks of suicide. The son communicates with his mother every day, sometimes at unsocial hours. The mother feels herself essential to her son's well-being, survival even, and believes she has done everything for his good, resulting in his place at a prestigious university. The following day, another client in the group talked about his love-hate relationship with his mother and how her efficient, but not tender, care had given him a head start in society, but made it impossible to love her. The first client fled from the room in tears.

This is a not uncommon situation where the intimate revelations of one group member destabilize the *saṃskāras* of another, provoking insight, contrition, and internal reconfiguration.

Saṃskāras are not passive, not merely information; they have purpose and guide future action. They constitute a mapping of the world with the ego as its putative capital city. The activity of meditation is intended both to give one discernment of the activity taking place (insight) and practice in letting it subside (tranquility). The aim of therapy is to help the client to arrive at a more satisfactory map, and, ultimately, demote the ego.

Mirror Mind

The Buddhist ideal is often presented as the mind being a mirror (D. Brazier, 2019). In the seminal text *Genjōkōan*, Dōgen Zenji (2011), the most important Zen Buddhist author in Japanese history, says that one's relation to the Dharma should be as that of a dewdrop to the moon. The dewdrop is fragile and transitory, but when still and dark it naturally reflects the moon. Though the moon is huge and the dewdrop tiny, still the whole moon, the whole sky, is reflected.

The transition from comic book hero to dewdrop suggests the kind of transformation Zen therapy intends and Buddhist meditation embodies. The hero is larger than life, and everything revolves around him. Only his needs and purposes count. Mayhem is permissible so long as the hero survives and triumphs. The dewdrop is tiny, almost insignificant, yet participates in a glory far vaster than itself.

Buddhist Therapy?

Every therapy has a theory of personality and of the good life. It is not much of an exaggeration to say that much Western psychotherapy is aimed at helping the client be the comic book hero more successfully, whereas Buddhist therapy is concerned with helping the client to realize his dewdrop nature. Lifting methods out of Buddhism and deploying them to serve a Western agenda reverses the intention of the original. If psychotherapy is defined as accommodating people to contemporary materialist society, then there probably cannot be a truly Buddhist psychotherapy, and Buddhism and therapy are opposed. But if we admit completely different ideas of the good life, then Buddhism must surely count as a therapy with profound implications.

ELEMENTS OF BUDDHIST PSYCHOLOGY : FROM *VIJÑĀNA* TO *JÑĀNA*

The Buddhist Unconscious

There are a number of Indian words that get translated as "consciousness." The most common is *vijñāna*. *Vijñāna* is the fifth *skandha* and thus something that Buddha classifies under *duḥkha* and lists specifically as something to eliminate. Is Buddha saying we should eliminate consciousness? (cf. *Majjhima Nikāya* 22: 40 in Ñanamoli & Bodhi, 1995, p. 235). It seems very unlikely. In fact, the structure of the word suggests that something like "the unconscious" or "disconscious" might be a better translation, as *jñāna* indicates liberated consciousness. We can take the term disconscious to refer to a mostly unconscious distortion of the way one perceives the world.

Perhaps there is more commonality between Śākyamuni Buddha and Western notions of the unconscious than generally recognized (Epstein, 1996). Both see the mind as being dominated by wayward passions that interfere with rational thought. The functioning of the *skandhas* is largely unconscious or only on the threshold of awareness. With an effort we can notice what is happening, but generally we do not. Meditation can be a time when we do so. The *skandha* theory offers an analysis of how unconscious mentality forms.

RŪPA → *VEDANĀ* → *SAṂJÑĀ* → *SAṂSKĀRA* → *VIJÑĀNA*

The personal disconscious, *vijñāna*, is a deposit and residue from the four previous *skandhas*. They provide its content and establish its dominance in the unexamined life.

We hang onto a repertoire of programmed responses to foreguard against circumstances that, having arisen once, may befall us again. This has obvious utility. Unfortunately it also reduces us to a machinelike existence, pre-programmed to behave in a stereotyped fashion according to which button is pressed. Freshness of perception is systematically eliminated. Vijñāna manifests in implicit intention. This then shapes and directs attention and disguises reality as *rūpa*. Hence the *skandha* sequence is a complete cycle, which explains its persistence and self-perpetuation.

RŪPA → *VEDANĀ* → *SAṂJÑĀ* → *SAṂSKĀRA* → *VIJÑĀNA* → *RŪPA*

An Example

The client, a nurse, reported feeling differently toward male and female patients, seeing the latter only as individuals. Men were indistinguishably "pathetic." Therapeutic work came to focus upon her disgust at her father's behavior during the divorce of her parents. In further exploration she rediscovered feelings of tenderness for the father earlier in her life. Seeing how the disgust had come to extend to men in general she was freed from this *rūpa* and could see each man as a distinct personality.

This is a not untypical therapy case in which a *vedanā* reaction to an important *rūpa* has generalized (*saṃskāra*) and given rise to a mentality (*vijñāna*) that then colors the perception of whatever associates mentally with the original *rūpa*: in this case, the sight of any man triggering the judgement of "pathetic" that was originally attached to her father. This will be familiar to most therapists. Buddhist psychology provides a clear conceptual framework for analyzing what is happening. Once the *vijñāna* is established, the mind gathers evidence of the pathetic nature of men, and via the *skandha* sequence, the *vijñāna* perpetuates and elaborates on it.

Sudden Awakening

All the examples above illustrate "sudden awakening—gradual cultivation." The crucial therapeutic insight comes all at once, but the working through of consequences and implications takes longer. Most of this gradual work will be done outside of the therapy session, though some will include a working through of the relationship with the therapist herself, in which the crucial element is that she appears human and not overly idealized.

Such awakenings may be precipitated in all manner of ways, and it is impossible and a self-contradiction to offer any kind of protocol. Planned spontaneity is not real. The poet Coleridge expressed a deeply Zen sentiment when he said that the purpose of poetry was:

> awakening the mind's attention from the lethargy of custom and directing it to the loveliness and the wonders of the world before us; an inexhaustible treasure, but for which, in consequence of the film of familiarity and selfish solicitude, we have eyes yet see not, ears that hear not, and hearts that neither feel nor understand.
>
> (Coleridge, 1975, p. 169)

If poetry may be said to be words that touch the heart, therapy often does have such poetic quality. Here we encounter not *vijñāna* but *jñāna*, not unconsciousness and lethargy, but consciousness and vibrancy of life energy.

Conclusion

In this essay I have deployed some of the central concepts of Buddhist teaching to make clear the way in which therapy and meditation are complementary dimensions of the struggle toward liberation; how awakening to a more vibrant spiritual life is in nowise fundamentally dissimilar to bringing a distressed client to a state of greater tranquility, insight, and well-being; and, further, how the Buddhist theory of mental processes, grounded in meditation practice, can guide therapeutic dialogue and yield release from the "film of familiarity and selfish solicitude," to use Coleridge's image.

In an "awakened" life, things appear less "familiar," stereotyping ceases, and all is seen anew. The old phrase is heard afresh. This requires a diminution of knowingness, a ceasing to act and think in purely pre-programmed ways, an acceptance of the limitations of the stories we tell ourselves and thus arrival at a more fluid mentality.

From the examples given, we can see that a frequent result of Zen therapy is a softening of attitude. The client emerges more humble and open-minded. Ego diminishes. This may lead to greater fellow-feeling and compassion for others, releasing the "strangers" and yielding the sense of spaciousness that Zen equates with mental health. This outcome is only incidentally related to eliminating pathological psychological syndromes, yet cultivates a growth of character that many may find praiseworthy.

References

Bannister, D., & Fransella, F. (1986). *Inquiring man: The psychology of personal constructs.* London: Routledge.

Batchelor, S. (1983). *Alone with others.* New York: Grove Press.

Berne, E. (1964). *Games people play: The basic handbook of transactional analysis.* New York: Ballantine Books.

Brazier, C. (2003). *Buddhist psychology: Liberate your mind, embrace life.* London: Constable.

Brazier, C. (2009). *Other-centred therapy: Buddhist psychology in action.* Winchester, UK: John Hunt.

Brazier, D. (1993). The necessary condition is love: Going beyond self in the person-centred approach. In D. Brazier (Ed.), *Beyond Carl Rogers* (pp.72–91). London: Constable.

Brazier, D. (1995). *Zen therapy.* London: Constable.

Brazier, D. (1997). *The feeling Buddha.* London: Constable.

Brazier, D. (2009). *Love and its disappointment: The meaning of life, therapy and art.* Winchester, UK: John Hunt.

Brazier, D. (2016). Mindfulness, traditional and utilitarian. In R. E. Purser, D. Forbes, & A. Burke (Eds.), *Handbook of mindfulness: Culture, context and social engagement* (pp. 63–74). Switzerland: Springer International.

Brazier, D. (2019). *The dark side of the mirror: Forgetting the self in Dogen's Genjo koan.* Cambridge, UK: Windhorse.

Buswell, R. (1992). *The Zen monastic experience.* Princeton, NJ: Princeton University Press.

Buswell, R. (2012). *Chinul: Selected works.* Seoul: Chogye Order.

Claxton, G. (1996). *Beyond therapy: The impact of Eastern religions on psychological theory and practice.* London: Prism Press.

Cleary, T. (1990). *Transmission of light.* San Francisco: North Point Press.

Coleridge, S. T. (1975). *Biographia literaria.* London: J. M. Dent & Sons.

Dogen, E. (2011). *Dogen's Genjokoan: Three commentaries.* Berkeley, CA: Counterpoint.

Epstein, M. (1996). *Thoughts without a thinker.* New York: Basic Books.

Gorkom, N. V. (1990). *Abhidhamma in daily life*. Bangkok: Dharma Study & Propagation Foundation.
Gyatso, K (1990). *A meditation handbook*. London: Tharpa.
Hanh, N. (1987). *Being peace*. London: Rider.
Hanh, N., & Nguyen, A. (2006). *Walking meditation: Peace is every step*. Boulder, CO: Sounds True.
Kelly, G. A. (1955). *The psychology of personal constructs* (Vols. 1–2). New York: Norton.
Kennett, J. (1972). *Selling water by the river: A manual of Zen training*. New York: Pantheon.
Lhalungpa, L. (1992). *The life of Milarepa*. London: Penguin Compass.
Morotomi, Y. (2010). http://www.focusing.org/fot/murasato_theory.html#Morotomi
Ñanamoli, Bhikkhu. (trans) (1956). *The path of purification (Visuddhimagga) by Bhadantācariya Buddhaghosa*. Singapore: Buddhist Meditation Centre, reprinted & distributed by Corporate Body of the Buddha Educational Foundation, Teipei, Taiwan.
Ñanamoli, Bhikkhu, & Bodhi, Bhikkhu. (trans.) (1995). *The middle length discourses of the Buddha*. Boston: Wisdom.
Narada, U. (1969). *Conditional relations* (Vol. 1). London: Pali Text Society.
Narada, U. (1979). *A manual of Abhidhamma*. Taipei: Corporate Body of Buddha Educational Foundation.
Narada, U. (1981). *Conditional relations* (Vol. 2). London: Pali Text Society.
Robinson Arai, P. K. (1999). *Women living Zen: Japanese Soto Buddhist nuns*. Oxford: Oxford University Press.
Rogers, C. R. (1965). *Client-centered therapy*. London: Constable.
Safran, J. D. (2003). *Psychoanalysis and Buddhism: An unfolding dialogue*. Somerville, MA: Wisdom Books.
Suzuki, D. T. (1998). *Studies in the Lankavatara Sutra*. New Delhi: Munshiram Manoharlal.
Thurber, J. (2000). *The secret life of Walter Mitty and other pieces*. London: Penguin.
Trungpa, C. (1992). *Transcending madness*. Boston: Shambhala.
Welch, H. (1967). *The practice of Chinese Buddhism, 1900–1950*. Cambridge, MA: Harvard University Press.
Welwood, J. 2000. *Toward a psychology of awakening: Buddhism, psychotherapy and the path of personal and spiritual transformation*. Boston: Shambhala.

SOCIAL CHANGE

CHAPTER 35

ENACTING SOCIAL CHANGE THROUGH BUDDHIST MEDITATION

ANN GLEIG

INTRODUCTION

IN October 2011, the Interdependence Project, a Buddhist-inspired organization in New York City, organized a mass meditation at Zuccotti Park, the site of the anti-capitalist Occupy Wall Street protests in downtown Manhattan. Photographs of the event show protestors wearing shirts that read "We are the 99%," sitting cross legged among cardboard signs that declared "Being Present." Patrick Groneman, one of the organizers of the event, explained, "By sitting in solidarity with the occupation, we were hoping to help lay a foundation of mindfulness beneath a social movement with far-reaching implications" (Groneman, 2011). Similar images came from other Occupy protests. In Oakland, a solitary protestor meditates with eyes closed as two police officers lean in behind to arrest him, while in London, at the Occupy London Stock Exchange event, the steps of Saint Paul's Cathedral appear to be populated with cross-legged participants dressed casually with brightly dyed hair (Glassman, 2011).

One year later, U.S. Congressman Tim Ryan published his book *The Mindful Nation: How a Simple Practice Can Help Reduce Stress, Improve Performance, and Recapture the American Spirit.* In an accompanying video, Ryan, dressed smartly in a suit and tie and standing next to an American flag with the iconic House of Congress as backdrop, presents mindfulness as a "fundamental skill to pay attention," which offers a "great opportunity for us as a country" to improve individual performance and develop kindness for others. He says that a mindful nation is not "about the 99% versus the 1%, but it's about the 100%, all of us together and when we all move in concert together we have success as a country" (Ryan, 2012). This best-selling text inspired the establishment of "The Mindful Nation Foundation," a non-profit organization begun in 2013 to build a "national grassroots, ambassador-led community," to support mindful living for "veterans, children, teachers, leaders and healthcare professionals" (Mindful Nation Network, 2015). In the United Kingdom, such a project has gone one step further with the establishment in 2014 of a Mindfulness All-Party Parliamentary group (MAPPG) with the purpose of researching evidence and best practices for the implementation of mindfulness in a range of policy issues (Mindfulness Initiative, 2016).

These two snapshots of mindfulness as a tool for street activists and meditation as a tool for politicians signify related but distinct currents in the adoption of meditation as a means to enact social change in the United States and Western Europe. The first illustrates the adoption of meditation as a strategy of self-care and a creative tool of protest for those committed to progressive politics and social justice with the goals of radical structural change and collective liberation. These movements are generally concerned with opposition to patriarchy, racism, capitalism, and colonialism, though most recently, ecological concerns have come to the fore. The second illustrates the assimilation of meditation into established public institutions such as schools and hospitals and as a tool for the political state in nation-building and social stability. Here self-care aims for health, stress reduction, work effectiveness, and social well-being.

This chapter will use these two currents—radical and assimilative—as one useful way to approach the theme of enacting social change through meditation. Historically, both can be traced to a common origin in the reformation of Buddhism that occurred during the period of colonialism in South East Asia. This reformation included the Burmese Buddhist use of meditation as a central component of religious nationalism, yet, ultimately, when transferred to the West, resulted in a de-contextualization of meditation from its original religious matrix and its re-contextualization in various new matrices, including ones primarily geared toward social transformation and justice.

While the differentiations between assimilative and radical meditative currents of social change are useful as heuristic devices, the boundaries between them are fluid and contingent, and there is much crossover as well as mutual critique between the individual actors and communities that constitute them.

From Radicalism to Assimilation: Buddhist Modernism in Asia

The nineteenth-century encounter between traditional Asian Buddhism and Western modernity, which occurred under the oppressive conditions of colonialism, has produced a historically distinct form of Buddhism that has since become commonly identified as "Buddhist modernism." (Bond, 1988; Swearer, 1995; Lopez, 2002; McMahan, 2008). Simultaneously demonstrating both accommodation and resistance to colonialism, the vision of Buddhism that emerged from these reforms selectively privileged aspects of Buddhism that were compatible with modern Western discourses and discarded elements that were incompatible. Common characteristics include:

(1) a claim to return to the "original" and "pure" teachings of the Buddha that had supposedly been distorted by cultural and institutional overlays;
(2) a framing of Buddhism as a rational and scientific religion;
(3) rejection of the traditional Theravada separation of the mundane and supermundane levels and blurring of the roles of the layperson and monk;
(4) a revival of meditation practice and a claim that Nibbana is an attainable goal in this lifetime not only for monastics but also the laity; and
(5) an interest in social reform issues such as gender equality.

Meditation as Resistance to Colonialism

The Theravada meditation revival began in Burma (renamed Myanmar in 1989), as both reaction and resistance to colonialism. Before the nineteenth century, Burmese monastics devoted their time to community life, scholarship or devotional merit-making activities, and interest in meditation practice was rare. The monk Ledi Sayādaw (1846–1923), however, developed a popular meditation movement in order to protect Buddhism (Buddha Dhamma) from the threat of colonialism (Braun, 2013).

Between 1824 and 1885, Burma had come under the control of the British, and this occupation by a Christian power posed a threat to the safety of the Dhamma. With the king no longer able to serve as Dhamma protector, Ledi believed the responsibility fell to the Burmese Buddhist population, including the laity. One of his solutions was to popularize the study of Buddhist doctrine, particularly the Abhidhamma, which is the third part of the Pali Canon, the oldest surviving collection of Buddhist scriptures. Another was to offer an accessible meditation practice for a wide range of people. Drawing on the Abhidhamma and the fifth-century monk Buddhaghosa's influential commentary on it, the *Visuddhimagga* or *Path of Purification*, Ledi made insight meditation (Vipassana) available to the laity in a systematic way that was unprecedented in Buddhist history. This innovation marked the beginnings of popular insight meditation, which would eventually develop into a global movement.

Meditation as Nation Building

When Burma became independent in 1948, meditation practice became associated with nation building as the first prime minister, U Nu, invited the monk Mahāsī Sayādaw (1904–1982) to be the resident teacher at a newly established meditation center in Yangon, which came to be called the Mahāsi Sāsana Yeiktha (MSY). The idea behind this development, drawn from the Pali *sutta*s, is that the purification of the state proceeds from the purification of its citizens.

Mahasi Sāsana Yeiktha differs from the traditional Burmese monastery. In addition to scriptural study, it places a strong focus on meditation and also in the significant role played by the laity. At MSY the model religious figure is not the forest-dwelling monk, but the layperson engaged in full-time pursuit of the soteriological goal of Nibbana in a bureaucratically organized urban center. This mass scale pursuit of enlightenment primarily by laypeople is a new development in Buddhist history (Jordt, 2007).

We can see the movement to resist colonialism as a radical current against the British Empire. As this movement achieved its goal, however it transformed into an assimilative one dedicated to consolidating the new Burmese state.

Meditation and Engaged Buddhism in Asia

The coining of the term Engaged Buddhism (originally "*le bouddhisme engagé*") to describe social justice actions based on Buddhist thought and practice is generally attributed to the Vietnamese Buddhist monk and peace activist Thich Nhat Hanh (b. 1926). Hanh and his close associate, the nun Chân Không (b. 1938), have an extensive history of social work and peace activism in Vietnam and elsewhere and "all of Thich Nhat Hanh's writings on socially engaged Buddhism, emphasize the necessity of meditation and/or mindfulness practice" (Queen and King, 1996, p. 342).

However, other Asian Engaged Buddhist leaders such as Bhimrao Ramji Ambedkar (1891–1956), who spearheaded the Buddhist conversion of millions of members of India's Dalits as part their struggle against the injustices of the Hindu caste system, and A. T. Ariyaratne (b. 1931), the founder of the Sarvodaya Shramadana movement, focused on economic justice in Sri Lanka, have not placed such importance upon meditation.

In the Ambedkarite movement there has been debate about whether meditation is important in a social action context. Proponents of meditation, some of whom have trained at Goenka centers and others in Ambedkar-inspired organizations, such as the Triratna Bauddha Mahāsaṅgha (TBM), see meditation as an indispensable tool in the struggle for social justice. Opponents, however, argue that meditation produces political passivity and a "regression" to a Hindu mindset. Meditation advocates claim that Buddhist mindfulness is different from the more trance-like meditations practiced in Hinduism. Ambedkar did not meditate himself, but his writings do note the centrality of meditation in Buddhism, and his last public speech acknowledged the positive role meditation could play in socially engaged Buddhism (Queen, 2017).

A leading figure in socially engaged Buddhism in Thailand has been Sulak Sivaraksa (b. 1932), one of the founders of the International Network of Engaged Buddhists (INEB). His extensive social activity is based on mindfulness, non-violence, and interconnectedness. When Sivaraksa first visited the West, however, he was dismayed to find that meditators were generally not socially engaged. More recently there has been some convergence between meditation and social engagement in Thailand (Schedneck, 2017) and, inter alia, this has led to greater participation by women. While monks still predominate in teaching roles, female lay practitioners, fully ordained *bhikkhunīs*, and "precept nuns" are "able to enact Buddhist roles in much more diverse ways"

(Schedneck, 2017, p.312). Female leaders have emerged. In Chiangmai, Northern Thailand, for example, Buddhist feminist activist Ouyporn Khuankaew (b. 1963) leads women's retreats and workshops on domestic violence. In 2002 she founded the International Women's Partnership for Peace and Justice, which offers leadership training for Buddhist nuns drawing from Buddhism and feminism as well as programs for women on Buddhist peacebuilding, non-violent resistance, and social change. This organization emphasizes empowerment for women through working with female populations of activists, refugees, and abused women throughout Asia (International Women's Partnership for Peace and Justice, 2015).

Controversy and Development

Meditation is a major component of Buddhism. As is apparent from this brief survey, Buddhism has played a significant part in decolonization, nation building, modernization, and social reform movements. Some of the leaders of these movements have considered meditation to be an essential ingredient, while others have not. On one side, meditation is seen as raising awareness and cultivating the kinds of virtues that are essential to a reformed society. On the other side, some suspect that meditation leads to passivity and undermines social struggle.

Nonetheless, meditation and mindfulness continue to evolve as do their application. In 2006, Melvin McLeod, editor of the popular Buddhist magazine *Lion's Roar*, brought out an edited collection of writings called *Mindful Politics* that raises such questions as whether foundational Buddhist principles like loving-kindness, compassion, sympathetic joy, and equanimity could become a political platform. "Politics is really about how we live together as human beings, and all spiritual practices point to one simple but profound truth about human life—that only love leads to peace, hatred never does. This is as true for nations as it is for individuals" (McLeod, 2006, p. 10). The book offers suggestions on how Buddhist thought and practice can ameliorate racism, sexism, economic oppression and environmental degradation and offers meditations specifically designed to support individual and social transformation. Thus, contemporary spiritual leaders are adapting and designing new methods, loosely connected to traditional Buddhism, to serve modern agendas. One helpful way to organize these activities is by dividing them into assimilative and radical currents.

The Assimilative Current in the West

Mindfulness

While meditation can be used as part of a movement to bring about radical social change, it can also form part of programs to make the existing system of society work better. We can thus speak of a conservative or assimilative current. The most prominent recent example is the increasing popularity of mindfulness as an aid to ordinary life situations, effectiveness at work, and the amelioration of various quasi-medical syndromes. Mindfulness has evolved out of Buddhist meditation practices, yet most practitioners of mindfulness do not see themselves as contemplatives. Nonetheless, mindfulness methods can be seen as part of a wider movement advocating the practice of meditation as beneficial both to the individual and to society.

Mahāsī Sayādaw and Thich Nhat Hanh, who are directly linked to the emergence of meditation as a tool for social change in the United States, also figure in the emergence of mindfulness. Mindfulness practices came to America via the major Asian Buddhist modernist teachers and their American students starting early in the twentieth century.

In the 1970s three major players and institutions dedicated to disseminating mindfulness emerged:

(1) The Insight Meditation Society (IMS) was established on May 19, 1975, to provide a retreat environment for the intensive practice of Theravada Buddhist meditation. The co-founders of IMS, Joseph Goldstein, Jack Kornfield, Sharon Salzberg, and Jacqueline Mandell, had trained in Mahāsī lineages in Asia, and this lineage along with that of Ajahn Chah's Thai forest-meditation tradition are the two main Asian influences in the Insight community.
(2) Thich Nhat Hanh began teaching meditation to Westerners in the 1970s. After being exiled from Vietnam he founded Plum Village monastery in France. A prolific author, Hanh frames all Buddhist practice and meditation as "mindfulness training." A large international network of practitioners, both monastic and lay, have formed around him.
(3) Jon Kabat-Zinn took mindfulness completely out of a Buddhist context by pioneering mindfulness-based stress reduction (MBSR), the most well-known of medical mindfulness models. (Wilson, 2014)

A Secular Religion

Mindfulness transitioned from a popular Buddhist modernist practice to a mainstream secular one, in which it has been applied to a wide range of pragmatic concerns as well as social change (Wilson, 2014). Wilson suggests that mindfulness has been "moralized" and related to certain values aimed at the transformation of American society (Wilson, 2014, pp. 59–185). Mindfulness advocates such as Kabat-Zinn, and Goleman have implicitly, and sometimes explicitly, re-contextualized mindfulness within a value system that aims to bring about dramatic changes on national and international levels as well as within individuals. Here mindfulness becomes a personal virtue to be cultivated by all citizens and applied to all aspects of society. Thus: "The total transformation of all... aspects of society through the adoption of mindfulness is indeed a vision of the good society—the 'Mindful Society'" (Wilson, 2014, p. 162).

In 2011, Barry Boyce, a long-term Tibetan Buddhist practitioner, produced a collection called *The Mindfulness Revolution*. It features reflections on mindfulness practice from popular Western Buddhist teachers, psychologists, and scientists and shows how mindfulness is being adopted in contexts ranging from education to health care, business to law. It contains several essays that claim that mindfulness can generate transformative social change. One of these is Goleman's "A Mindful Consumer Can Change the World," which links consumerism with climate change and argues that the key to preventing environmental destruction is to be mindful when we are making purchases. "Mindful shopping is a potentially important practice, a socially engaged act that could collectively help us save the world from its greatest threat: us" (Goleman, 2011, p. 242).

From this last example, we can see that mindfulness does not mean the same thing to all its advocates. It can mean non-judgmental awareness in the present moment (Kabat-Zinn), or it can refer to being aware of the long-term consequences of one's actions and choices (Goleman). It can also mean keeping in mind important principles, or it can mean paying attention to whatever arises spontaneously in the mind. These usages are not all compatible with one another. Those that concentrate on present-moment awareness are closer to the currently dominant usage, whereas those that involve taking a longer-term view are closer to the original meaning in Buddhist texts and to the meaning that originally attached to the word in the English language.

Both *Mindful Politics* (McLeod, 2006) and *The Mindful Revolution* (Boyce, 2011) point to key areas in which Buddhist-derived meditation practices have been adopted as part of a broad, assimilative agenda toward social change or adaptation extending to education, medicine, business, law, and even the military. These programs have rapidly proliferated, and different forms of certification are being developed to accommodate their rapid growth.

Mindfulness in Education

Examples in education include:

- Peace in Schools, with Transformative Mindfulness Education, was the first organization to bring for-credit mindfulness programs to public schools in the United States. Founded by Caverly Morgan, who has a background in Zen Buddhism, their mission is to "make mindfulness an accepted and valued discipline in secondary education." They also work with at-risk teen populations and offer accredited mindfulness training for teachers, school counselors, and other professionals who work regularly with young people (Peace in Schools, n.d.).
- Inward Bound Mindfulness Education (iBme) is another organization that focuses on teen and young adult populations. Co-founded by Jessica Morey, who has trained intensively in insight meditation, iBme offers meditation retreats and trainings as part of their larger mission "to support future generations of heart-centered diverse leaders" (Inward Bound Mindfulness Education, 2017).
- iBme programs are also taught in the United Kingdom through Youth Mindfulness Education, a U.K. community-interest company that runs in-depth mindfulness

training to guide young people in improving their lives and communities. Jem Shackleford, one of its co-founders, is a registered Mindfulness in Schools training consultant with the U.K. Mindfulness-Based Teachers Network, a group that has developed a set of best practices for teaching mindfulness in schools as well as training teachers to offer meditation in secondary education (Mindfulness Foundation, 2017).

Mindfulness in Business

Google was one of the first major transnational companies to introduce mindfulness programs for employees. Mirabai Bush, a Buddhist and Hindu practitioner who has been long involved in social activism, and Chade-Meng Tan, a high-ranking employee and mindfulness practitioner, designed a training called Search Inside Yourself: A Mindfulness-Based Emotional Program (SIY). As indicated by the title of Tan's best-selling 2012 book *Search Inside Yourself: The Unexpected Path to Achieving Success, Happiness (and World Peace)*, the logic behind such programs is that not only can mindfulness practice produce individual well-being and productivity but through such, individuals can transform business and society. Also, the emphasis on introspection shows the close link between this kind of mindfulness and insight meditation.

The annual Wisdom 2.0 Conferences in San Francisco, begun in 2010, are another well-known venue. Established by tech entrepreneur Soren Gordhamer, the meetings explore the confluence of mindfulness, business, and technology, as tech entrepreneurs, venture capitalists, and various Buddhist and mindfulness luminaries investigate how to work with greater awareness, compassion, and wisdom in the digital age (Wisdom 2.0, 2017).

The mindfulness movement is still growing and adapting. It is being used by people who want to radically change society, and, at the same time, it is being used to make establishment institutions more stable or more effective. It is presented as ethically neutral and non-judgmental, yet is concurrently associated with strongly held values that some regard as progressive. It is coupled with the argument that if each individual changes, society will be transformed, even when deployed by institutions that exist to maintain the status quo. It has roots in Buddhism yet is commonly presented as having nothing to do with those roots, even though some of its main advocates are Buddhist practitioners. Is it a new secular religion? Is it a passing fashion? Are moral values implicit or is it a value-free scientific procedure? These and many other issues remain contentious.

Meditation and Progressive Social Change: CMind

The Center for Contemplative Mind in Society (CMind) traces its origins to two meditation retreats that occurred in 1991–1992: one led by American Hindu guru Ram Dass and IMS co-founders Goldstein and Salzberg, and another led by Hanh. Conversations generated by these retreats led Charlie Halpern to convene an inaugural meeting in 1993 on the role of meditative activities in social transformation. Halpern came from the Nathan Cummings Foundation, an organization rooted in the Jewish tradition of social justice and dedicated to developing a more equitable and sustainable society (Center for Contemplative Mind in Society, 2015).

In 1994, the group stated their goal as "not to isolate meditation, but to reflect on the contemplative traditions as powerful techniques that have potential for beneficial change in American society." Over the following years, they developed a non-profit organization "to integrate contemplative awareness into contemporary life in order to help create a more just, compassionate, and reflective society." It has six major areas of focus: (1) philanthropy and spirituality; (2) academic fellowships; (3) youth program; (4) business retreats; (5) environmental programs; and (6) law.

The CMind organization has grown and now offers programs and fellowships. In particular, it developed in 2008 the Association for Contemplative Mind in Higher Education, the first professional association for contemplation in higher education. In *Meditation and the Classroom: Contemplative Pedagogy for Religious Studies* (2011) Judith Simmer-Brown and Fran Grace gather together twenty-five contributors discussing issues such as why professors teach contemplative studies and the methods they use. The collection includes a review of the history of meditation and contemplative education, showing how professors across the spectrum of academic disciplines have been integrating meditation in the classroom and curriculum since the 1990s.

In recognition that meditation could help social workers deal with the emotional strain of their work, CMind ran a program from 2004–2009 to create a "more sustainable movement for social change." It also produced *The Activist's Ally: Contemplative Tools for Social Change* (2007; 2011) which provides many resources for activists seeking to bridge social justice and contemplative worlds.

While fully engaged with mainstream assimilative areas, CMind has also supported additional social justice endeavors through their alliances with Engaged Buddhists. Engaged Buddhist Maia Duerr, a former director of the Buddhist Peace Fellowship, designed "The Tree of Contemplative Life," for CMind, a diagram that depicts seven major branches of contemplative practice. One of these is activism, including pilgrimages to areas where social justice issues are highlighted, work and volunteering, vigils and marches, and bearing witness.

The Radical Current

Organizations in this section exemplify the radical current in the adoption of meditation for social change. One of the hallmarks of the radical current is that it identifies the mutual reinforcement of the systems of patriarchy, racism, capitalism, and colonialism and employs an intersectional approach to tackle social injustice. Another characteristic of the radical current is that it often frames itself as a progressive critique of the classical liberalism underlaying much of the assimilative current and is linked to demographic shifts from the boomer generation to generation X and the millennials in convert Buddhist and contemplative communities (Gleig, 2019).

Meditation and War Resistance: Buddhist Peace Fellowship

The Buddhist Peace Fellowship (BPF) is an affiliate of the international peace network Fellowship of Reconciliation. It is the largest network of Engaged Buddhists in the United States. The BPF founders included Zen Buddhist Robert Baker Aitken (1917–2010) and Jodo Shin Buddhist Ryo Imamura (1944–). It started in Hawaii in 1978 as a response to the threat of nuclear war and militarism and aimed to develop non-violent forms of social justice advocacy and peacebuilding. In the 1980s, it moved its headquarters to Berkeley, California, and began to produce a journal called *Turning Wheel*. Officially a non-sectarian Buddhist organization, it has historically been heavily populated and influenced by the American Zen and Insight communities, both of which are strongly meditation centered, though the adoption of meditation as an integral part of BPF's social justice initiatives can be traced to Diana Winston, a mindfulness teacher who made meditation a central part of BPF's Buddhist Alliance for Social Engagement (BASE) program of service, scholarship, and meditation. Winston, who trained in the Theravada lineage, had been "frustrated that most Buddhist activists didn't actually practice meditation and that her fellow retreatants showed little interest in social engagement" (Simmer-Brown, 2000, pp. 86–87).

More recently, generation X and millennial co-directors Dawn Haney and Katie Loncke have revitalized the organization through what they call its "radical rebirth." They have urged members to go beyond personal practice and "organize collective expressions of compassion and awakening," to challenge structural systems of oppression such as racism, capitalism, the prison-industrial complex, and U.S. militarism (Loncke, 2013). An example was BPF's meditative sitting blockade on the steps of the Oakland Marriott Hotel to protest its hosting of Urban Shield, a weapons exposition and SWAT training for police to practice militarized techniques. Haney explains that this blockade exemplified BPF's commitment to extend individual meditation practice from the cushion to the streets (Fisher, 2014).

How Are Meditation and Social Change Related?

On January 15, 2016, iconic social justice activist Angela Davis and the "father" of modern mindfulness, Jon Kabat-Zinn, held a public dialogue on mindfulness as a fundraising benefit for the East Bay Meditation Center (EBMC) in Oakland, California. During their conversation, Davis, who practices yoga and mindfulness, asked Kabat-Zinn how mindfulness could support social change. Kabat-Zinn responded that the awareness fostered by mindfulness could gradually overcome the greed, hatred, and delusion at the root of collective suffering. Davis, however, argued that a stronger link needed to be forged between individual and systemic change and that for mindfulness to become a truly revolutionary force, it needed to be combined with an explicit commitment to challenging the oppressive systems of racism, colonialism, and capitalism.

According to Kabat-Zinn, social change was a "natural" outcome of individual meditation practice; for Davis, however, there was no guarantee that individual practice would translate into social change, nor that the types of social change generated by individual mindfulness practice would necessarily benefit diverse populations. Whereas Kabat-Zinn was content with the implicit impact of individual mindfulness practice on dominant institutions and systems, Davis advocated for the need to wed mindfulness with an explicitly radical social agenda (Davis & Kabat-Zinn, 2015). The dialogue between Kabat-Zinn and Davis well illustrates the differences between radical and assimilative currents in the relationship between social change and meditation.

Meditation Alone Is Not Enough, but It Is Finding New Applications

I will now give examples of these modern concerns by presenting some further examples of secular and Buddhist organizations, primarily radical ones, active in social change. Among these there is generally agreement that:

(1) meditation practice alone is not sufficient to overcome structural systems of oppression or the individual internalization of such systems;
(2) social justice work is depleting, and activist communities can unwittingly reproduce the very systems they seek to challenge without sufficient attention to inner transformation;
(3) the integration of meditation and social justice can foster not only individual but collective transformation and awakening.

Thus, meditation is coming to be recognized as a form of consciousness-raising that can transform attitudes. Social change movements are made up of people who were socialized within the systems that they now wish to change. Inevitably, they are not themselves totally free from the attitudes embodied by those systems. Radical movements, and even assimilative ones that have a clear change agenda, have therefore generally incorporated some methodology for consciousness-raising to help their members and supporters overcome this social conditioning. Meditation is now coming to be seen as one methodology that can assist this kind of mental reform.

Meditation to Counter Structures of Injustice: Occupy Wall Street

In the case of the radical protest movement, Occupy Wall Street, meditation practice may have been "integral to its endurance and impact" (Rowe, 2015). One source of meditation came from Meditation Flash Mob, a grassroots network that had organized public meditations as strategies of disruption in the financial district prior to Occupy. Members of MFM joined the Occupy Wall Street camp and offered meditation as self-care for their fellow protestors. Another source was the Interdependence Project (IDP), an organization that offers secular Buddhist practice in order to "awaken the world and support engagement leading to personal, social, and political transformation" (Interdependence Project, n.d.).

Adreanna Limbach, a coordinator for IDP, explained to Rowe that she adopted meditation to disrupt the replications of power dynamics within the camp. "About three weeks into my experience at Occupy, I began to think of meditation practice less as a service, and more a strategy, since we are bound to recreate structures of injustice in our daily interactions if we are not working with internal belief systems, and how they are shaped by power, privilege and positionality" (Rowe, 2015).

This acknowledgement of the danger of the internalization of systems of oppression within social justice activists themselves is leading to an increase in the number of activists who are "hungry for transformation and transformative practices" (Rowe, 2015). Consciousness-raising has been an important element in left-wing political movements ever since Marx, but it is a new development that this is increasingly seen in terms of meditation practice.

Meditation and Internalized Oppression: The Center for Transformative Change

The Center for Transformative Change (CXC), the "first national center entirely dedicated to bridging the inner and outer lives of social change agents, activists and allies to support a more effective and sustainable social justice movement" The Center for Transformative Change, 2017), was founded by Rev. angel Kyodo williams, an ordained Zen priest. It offers practices and programs for individual activists and organizations. Williams has shown leadership in uniting meditation and social justice across Buddhist and secular worlds. Her book *Being Black: Zen and the Art of Living with Fearlessness and Grace* (2002) explored how meditation could be adopted by African Americans to heal the internalization of oppression. She also, in conjunction with Lama Rod Owens and Jasmine Syedullah, co-authored *Radical Dharma: Talking Race, Love and Liberation* (Williams, Owens, & Syedullah, 2016).

Williams is on the leadership board for CTZNWELL, another organization centered around the three principles of personal practice, community building and collective action. It runs a number of programs including "a mindful platform" for voting and "Mindful Monday" guided meditations. In organizations of this kind we see the radical and assimilative currents intermingling. Meditation is offered as a self-care service, but with a longer-term radical reform agenda (CTZNWELL, 2016).

Meditation and Diversity: East Bay Meditation Center

East Bay Meditation Center (EBMC) is a Buddhist organization that since 2007 has served the multicultural population of Oakland, California, presenting Buddhist wisdom teachings in their social justice relevance. It operates using transparent democratic government, gift economics, and environmental sustainability. The center hosts a number of programs and trainings including weekly meditation groups for specific populations such as the People of Color Sangha and the Every Body, Every Mind Sangha for people with disabilities and chronic illnesses (Gleig, 2014).

The EBMC attempts to bring greater social progressiveness into the practice of Buddhism. Just as radical movements can imperceptibly morph into conservative ones, so Buddhism itself, which began as a radical religious reform in India millennia ago, nowadays often adopts a socially conservative stance. Therefore EBMC aims to reinject some of the original radical spirit into American convert Buddhism, which has been critiqued for its overwhelmingly white and upper-middle-class demographic as well as its assimilation into capitalism and neoliberal values.

Mushim Patricia Ikeda, a founding member of EBMC and pioneer in bringing diversity and inclusion to American Buddhist communities, also regularly teaches "Practice in Transformative Action" programs, which offer training in secular mindfulness for social justice activists. This program inspired Kazu Hagu, founder of East Point Peace Academy also in Oakland, to adopt meditation and mindfulness as part of the academy's nonviolent trainings within the lineage of Martin Luther King (Rowe, 2016, p. 214).

Feminist Meditation

Spirituality can be seen in terms of "practices, experiences, and ideas through which people seek to connect with nature, larger communities, their bodies, or an internal sense of wisdom, values or principles" (Doetsch-Kidder, 2012). For many years, Feminists of Color such as bell hooks, Gloria Anzaldua, and Audre Lorde have insisted on the intertwined nature of spiritual and political work (Doetsch-Kidder, 2012, p. 5). A practitioner of Shambhala Buddhism, Doetsch-Kidder presents meditation as a valuable tool to connect with the deepest parts of oneself and to develop an affective sense of connection with other humans and the world. Regular meditation practice can help activists develop understanding and compassion for those who hold opposing beliefs and develop an emotional resilience that can withstand conflict (Doetsch-Kidder, 2012, p. 95).

In the educational field, mindfulness meditation has been integrated into feminist and critical pedagogies. Contemplative practices can be important additions to university courses that focus on uncovering oppression and promoting diversity and inclusion (Berila, 2014). "If students are to really reflect on their roles in these systems, they need to cultivate the tools for recognizing and understanding their internal and external reactions to that realization" (Berila, 2014, p. 56).

An issue that arises here is that reflection upon these issues is often accompanied by difficult and uncomfortable emotions as students recollect their own, often traumatic, experience. Meditation can be a practice that brings such emotions to the surface. It can also be a means to helping students cope with them. Thus, meditation can be used in both consciousness-raising and emotionally calming ways.

Meditation and Racial Justice

The assault upon racial injustice in relation to meditation began with the observation that American Buddhist communities themselves were not free from the imperialism, racism, and patriarchy that afflicted the wider society. Nonetheless, African American feminist and author bell hooks (2006) embraced Engaged Buddhism as a foundational part of her quest "to end the suffering caused by a global politics of domination," seeing that "mindful awareness is the skillful means by which we release the attachment to dominator thinking and practice" (hooks, 2006, p. 57).

Echoing hooks, a number of American Buddhist teachers of color and their white allies came to see meditation within a wider critical perspective to help practitioners heal the wounds of racism and challenge white privilege inside and outside of Buddhist *communities*. These teachers have established annual meditation retreats and sitting groups for people of color as well as developing initiatives to uproot individual and structural racism in Buddhist communities and beyond (Gleig, 2016).

An example is Ruth King, an Insight Meditation teacher and coach, who has developed a training program called "Mindful of Race: A Stimulus for Social Healing and Leadership," which combines mindfulness practice with diversity awareness training (King, 2017).

Another group is White Awake, which offers educational resources and training for people who are socialized as "white" to become conscious and free of their complicity with white supremacy and develop a commitment to a just and equitable society (White Awake, n.d.).

Meditating for the Planet

Many ecological activists and communities have adopted meditation and mindfulness practices in their activism, both as personal self-care and as a creative protest strategy. One Earth Sangha, a Buddhist climate justice group co-founded by Insight practitioners Kristin Barker and Lou Leonard, blends ecology with the Buddhist concept of the bodhisattva to develop an eight-week program of "Ecosattva training," structured around the three Buddhist trainings of wisdom, meditation and ethics (One Earth

Sangha, n.d.). It is delivered by "some of the most powerful voices today on the intersection of mindfulness, Buddhist practice and ecological crisis" and over 1,500 students have taken it. One of the participating teachers is Lindsay Alderton, who is based at the Ecodharma Center in Catalonia, which also promotes the "radical transformation" of individual consciousness and applies Buddhism to socio-economic and cultural structures. It offers meditation retreats, study seminars, and training programs in the context of sustainable low-impact living (Eco Dharma Centre, 2017).

One of the largest environmental protests in the history of the United States was the Dakota Access Pipeline protests, also known by the hashtag #NoDAPL, that began at the start of 2016 at Standing Rock reservation in North Dakota where indigenous groups came together as "water protectors" to stop the construction of an oil pipeline that threatened the ecological balance of the land and the treaty rights and well-being of the Lakota The protests included ceremonies, ritual, healing practices, and meditation. The Lakota tribe approved "Pray for Standing Rock," a global synchronized prayer and meditation action, which was supported by groups around the world.

Another earlier protest had been the reoccupation by the Unist'ot'en clan in Northern British Columbia, which for eight years had successfully returned land to indigenous people and blocked oil and gas companies from building new fossil fuel infrastructure. The affinity between indigenous and Buddhist ritual practices has been an inspiration for many groups advancing meditation as a social action method (Rowe & Simpson, 2017).

Ecological activism is on the rise. In the latter part of 2019, in England, the group Extinction Rebellion brought parts of London to a standstill in protest at government inaction on the climate issue. These protests included mass meditation sessions on Waterloo and Lambeth Bridges amidst a considerable police presence. This action brought together groups from several faith communities, prominent among them XRBuddhists, which brings together Buddhists from many different schools. The Buddhist contingent sees a close connection between traditional Buddhist values and ecological concern. Meditation is a practice that is literally close to the earth. A leading figure in XRBuddhists is Satya Robyn, a member of the Amida Order, itself a Buddhist organization founded in the 1990s around social engagement issues.

Meditation Across Assimilative and Radical Currents

There are a number of different ways in which meditation and social change or stability can be related.

- Meditation practice may lead individuals to adopt new values. This may lead them to initiate or support movements for social change. Such movements may or might not themselves employ meditation as a means.
- Alternatively, meditation practice may enable individuals to feel calmer and at peace so that they are no longer motivated toward social change, or they may

become so engrossed in their own development through meditation that they no longer have the time or inclination to be involved in activism.

- Meditation may be used as a support for people engaged in social activism or, indeed, for those resisting it.
- It is held by many that if a sufficient number of people within a given society regularly practice meditation, this, of itself, will naturally and inevitably bring about social transformation, but not everybody agrees.
- The sight of people meditating is an iconic image. Movements for peace and reconciliation may deploy such imagery, including by conspicuously meditating in situations associated with conflict or suffering. This can also function in a similar manner to the sit-down protests originally organized by Gandhi.
- Alternatively, countries that identify with religious traditions that favor meditation may use the same imagery to promote patriotism and social stability.

Asian and Buddhist Roots

How do assimilative and radical currents relate to classical Buddhism? In Buddhism, meditation is only one part of a larger system of religious philosophy and practice. In particular, mindfulness in Buddhism is underpinned by wisdom teachings and expressed through ethical behavior.

Proponents of the assimilative current have sought Buddhist canonical legitimation for their approach in two main ways, first by framing mindfulness as a form of *upāya* or skillful means, and second by aligning it with the universal truth of Dharma rather than the religious particularity of Buddhism (Boyce, 2011). Radical critics, however, have also turned to canonical Buddhism. Purser and Loy (2013) have targeted the separation of mindfulness from its wider Buddhist ethical and soteriological context, particularly pointing to inconsistency between Buddhist ethics, including non-harm and right livelihood, and the adoption of mindfulness in business and the military.

It has been suggested that while one can find precursors of social action in Buddhist texts, Engaged Buddhist movements in the period since World War II differ in that they are not "a policy of enlightened Buddhist monarchs or governments" but, rather, "popular non-government movements, inspired by ordained and lay leaders who publicly oppose the social, political, military and corporate structures they believe to be the cause of widespread suffering and harm" (Queen,2018. pp, 503). Engaged Buddhism departs from classical Buddhist ethics in highlighting forms of suffering caused by structural or institutional factors and calling for collective responses rather than focusing on individual transformation.

However, while the mindful politician and the mindful street activist may seem to mark a significant departure from the meditative monastic of classical Buddhism, in reality Buddhist monks have traditionally often been social agents, sometimes radical and sometime conservative, and there are plenty of examples of turbulent monks in the history of Buddhist Asia. Socially engaged Buddhism is not a new Western invention. It started with Asian Buddhists such as Sivaraksa and Ariyaratne and drew many of its methods from Gandhi. Few, fortunately, have gone as far as the Vietnamese monks who immolated themselves to protest the Vietnam War.

What, however, is new includes:

- an upsurge of social concern within the Western meditation and mindfulness movements in the last few decades, a change largely stimulated and provoked by Asian forerunners.
- the introduction into the mix of concepts such as justice, democracy, and human rights that derive from Plato, Protestantism, and the French Revolution and do not figure in classic Buddhist texts. Buddhist social action revolved around concepts of compassion, harmony, and karma. It is notable, however, that much of this introduction is also attributable to Asians thinkers such as Ambedkar who, after his Western education, declared liberty, equality, and fraternity to be Buddhist concepts.
- an increasing recognition by social radicals that meditation may have a role in consciousness-raising and in the self-care needed to sustain radical movements.
- new topics of concern. Classically Buddhist radicals such as Kuya (903–972), an early medieval Japanese street activist, were concerned about care of the sick, accessibility of potable water, disposal of corpses, digging wells, and building bridges and were obviously not actively involved in nuclear disarmament, inter-ethnic harmony, climate change, or other modern concerns.

Clashing and Converging Currents

Much of the radical current arises as a critique and alternative to the assimilative claim that individual meditation practice will "naturally" result in wider social transformation. Radicals argue that there is no substantial evidence for this claim beyond anecdotal accounts of personal and group transformation.

In the 2014 Wisdom 2.0 conference, a panel on Google's Search Inside Yourself mindfulness program was just about to begin when three people strode onto the stage and unraveled an "Eviction Free San Francisco" banner whilst chanting "Wisdom means no displacement" and "San Francisco: Not for Sale." One of the organizers of the action, Amanda Ream (2014), an Engaged Buddhist who is a member of the East Bay Meditation Center, declared that social transformation would not come about by "an evolution in consciousness of the wealthiest among us," achieved through mindfulness practices, but rather through "the redistribution of wealth and power."

The debate is sharp. Radicals reject the foundational premise of the assimilative current: that individual mindfulness practice automatically leads to social transformation. They castigate the corporate co-opting of mindfulness, lamenting that rather than transforming business, mindfulness has become a tool of neoliberal ideology (Purser,

Forbes, & Burke, 2016). As we have seen, however, boundaries between the two currents are porous and more recently there are some signs of merger between them as social justice concerns and themes—such as the spiritual bypass, transformative social change, and collective liberation—move from the margins to the mainstream.

Thus, the Mind and Life Institute's 2016 International Symposium for Contemplative Studies (ICSC), included an increased demographic and disciplinary diversity. Three of ICSC's eight keynote speakers were women of color, one of whom was Rhonda Magee, a professor of law at the University of San Francisco concerned with bringing racial justice work to contemplative and mindfulness movements. Magee discussed bringing mindfulness- and compassion-based practices to community racial justice work in order to reduce "identity-based suffering."

Concerns with diversity, inclusion, and equity are increasing within Western Buddhism and in the mindfulness movement that has grown from it. The most popular article in 2017 in **Buddhist** magazine *Lion's Roar* was Mushim Patricia Ikeda's "I vow not to burn out." It identified the Buddhist bodhisattva vow to save all sentient beings with the path of radical social transformation. Here meditation serves to both motivate individuals toward radical social concern and also provide a means for them to take care of themselves while engaged in such struggle.

The debate between radicals and assimilationists will no doubt continue, but the increasing inclusion of radical representatives in mainline forums and the extension of assimilative practices to serve radical social groups is also having a homogenizing effect. Radicals note, however, that there is still much work to be done to "de-colonize" the mainstream contemplative and mindfulness movements (Walsh, 2017).

Conclusion

We have examined here how a reformation of Buddhism provoked by colonialism that began in the nineteenth century resulted in the de-contextualization of Buddhist meditation from its religious context and its re-contextualization into a variety of new applications related to social change in twenty-first-century America. In this essay, I have adopted the categories of radical and assimilative currents as one way to organize and trace the variety of these new applications. While sometimes placed in opposition for their respective emphasis on individual and collective change, these currents are increasingly merging as the need to respond to social and ecological injustices, such as systemic racism and climate change, grows more urgent.

What is most clear from tracing these two currents—both of which depart significantly from classical Buddhist meditation—is the determinative role that context plays in shaping how meditation is understood, practiced, and adopted as a tool for social change. Dependent upon the context, we find the fashioning of meditation as a tool of religious nationalism, social assimilation, social transformation, creative protest, and radical self-care.

References

The Arrow. (2017). *The Arrow: A Journal of Wakeful Society, Culture, and Politics*. Retrieved from http://arrow-journal.org

Berila, B. (2014). Contemplating the effects of oppression: Integrating mindfulness into diversity classrooms. *Journal of Contemplative Inquiry 1*(1), 55–68.

Bond, G. D. (1988). *The Buddhist revival in Sri Lanka: Religious tradition, reinterpretation and response*. Columbia: University of South Carolina Press.

Bond. G. D. (1996). A. T. Ariyaratne and the Sarvodaya Shramadana Movement in Sri Lanka. In C. S. Queen & S. B. King, *Engaged Buddhism: Buddhist liberation movements in Asia* (pp. 121–147). Albany: State University of New York Press.

Boyce, B. (Ed.). (2011). *The mindfulness revolution: Leading psychologists, scientists, artists and meditation teachers on the power of mindfulness in daily life*. Boston: Shambhala.

Braun, E. (2013). *The birth of insight: Meditation, modern Buddhism, and the Burmese monk Ledi Sayadaw*. Chicago: University of Chicago Press.

Center for Contemplative Mind in Society. (2015). *Our history*. Retrieved from http://www.contemplativemind.org/about/history

Center for Contemplative Mind in Society. (2007). *The activist's ally : Contemplative tools for social change*. Retrieved from http://www.contemplativemind.org/admin/wp-content/uploads/2012/09/Ally-sample.pdf

CTZNWELL. (2016). *About us*. Retrieved from http://www.ctznwell.org/#about-us

Davis, A., & Kabat-Zinn, J. (2015, January 15). Mindfulness and the possibility of freedom: Angela Davis and Jon Kabat-Zinn in dialogue. Fundraising benefit for the East Bay Meditation Center, Oakland, CA.

Doetsch-Kidder, S. (2012). *Social change and intersectional activism*. London: Palgrave McMillian.

Eco Dharma Centre. (2017). *Ecodharma: Radical ecology, radical dharma*. Retrieved from http://www.ecodharma.com

Fisher, D. (2014, September). *Interview with Dawn Haney and Katie Loncke* [Audio podcast]. Off the Cushion with Danny Fisher. Retrieved from http://www.buddhistpeacefellowship.org/bpf-goes-off-the-cushion-with-rev-danny-fisher/

Glassman, B. (2011). *Arising to the interconnectedness of life? A Buddhist perspective on the Occupy movement*. Huffington Post. Retrieved from https://www.huffingtonpost.com/bernie-glassman/buddhism-and-occupy-wall-street_b_1136501.html

Gleig, A. (2014). East Bay meditation center. *World Religions and Spirituality*. Retrieved from https://wrldrels.org/2016/10/08/east-bay-meditation-center/

Gleig, A. (2016). The dukkha of racism. *Patheos*. Retrieved from http://www.patheos.com/blogs/americanbuddhist/2016/01/the-dukkha-of-racism-racial-inclusion-and-justice-in-american-convert-buddhism.html

Gleig, A. (2019). *American dharma: Buddhism beyond modernity*. New Haven, CT: Yale University Press.

Goleman, D. (2011). A mindful consumer can help change the world. In Barry Boyle (Ed.), *The mindfulness revolution: Leading psychologists, scientists, artists and meditation teachers on the power of mindfulness in daily life* (pp. 242–247). Boston: Shambhala.

Groneman, P. (2011). Being present: Meditation at Occupy Wall Street. *Shambhala Times*. Retrievedfromhttps://shambhalatimes.org/2011/10/21/being-present-meditation-at-occupy-wall-street/

hooks, b. (2006). Buddhism and the politics of domination. In M. McLeod (Ed.), *Mindful politics: A Buddhist guide to making the world a better place* (pp. 57–62). Somerville, MA: Wisdom Publications.

Ikeda, M. P. (2017). I vow not to burn out. *Lion's Roar*. Retrieved from https://www.lionsroar.com/i-vow-not-to-burn-out/

Interdependence Project (n.d.) *Our mission and vision*. Retrieved from http://theidproject.org/about/mission

International Women's Partnership for Peace and Justice. (2015). *About IWP*. Retrieved from http://womenforpeaceandjustice.org/about-iwp/

Inward Bound Mindfulness Education. (2017). *Mindfulness retreats for teens and young adults*. Retrieved from https://ibme.info

Jordt, I. (2007). *Burma's mass lay meditation movement: Buddhism and the cultural construction of power*. Athens: Ohio University Press.

King, R. (2017). *Mindful of race training: A stimulus for social healing and leadership*. Retrieved from https://ruthking.net/mindful-of-race-2/

Loncke, K. (2013). *10 Principles of our radical rebirth*. Buddhist Peace Fellowship. Retrieved from http://www.buddhistpeacefellowship.org/10-principles-of-our-radical-rebirth/

Lopez, D. S. (2002). *A modern Buddhist bible: Essential readings from East and West*. Boston: Beacon Press.

McLeod, M. (Ed.). (2006). *Mindful politics: A Buddhist guide to making the world a better place*. Somerville, MA: Wisdom Publications.

McMahan, D. (2008). *The making of Buddhist modernism*. Oxford: Oxford University Press.

Mindful Nation Network. (2015). *Mindful nation*. Retrieved from http://mindfulnation-network.com

Mindfulness Foundation. (2017). *UK network for mindfulness-based teacher training organisations*. Retrieved from https://www.mindfulnessfoundation.org.uk/campaigns/databases/mbtt-network/

Mindfulness Initiative. (2016). *Mindfulness all-party parliamentary group*. Retrieved from http://www.themindfulnessinitiative.org.uk/about/mindfulness-appg

One Earth Sangha (n.d.). *One Earth Sangha: Expressing a Buddhist response to climate change and other threats to our one home*. Retrieved from https://oneearthsangha.org

Peace in Schools. (n.d.). *Transformative mindfulness education for educators and youth*. Retrieved from https://www.peaceinschools.org

Purser, R., Forbes, D., & Burke, A. (2016). *Handbook of mindfulness: Culture, context and social engagement*. Cham: Springer.

Purser, R. and Loy, D. (2013). *Beyond McMindfulness*. Huffington Post. Retrieved from https://www.huffingtonpost.com/ron-purser/beyond-mcmindfulness_b_3519289.html

Queen, C. S. (Ed.) (2000a). *Engaged Buddhism in the West*. Boston: Wisdom Publications.

Queen, C. S. (2018). The ethics of Engaged Buddhism in the West. *Oxford handbook of Buddhist ethics* (pp. 501–529). New York: Oxford University Press.

Queen, C. S. (2017, April 28–30). *Ambedkar Buddhists: To meditate or not?* Conference presentation at The Unfinished Legacy of Dr. B. R. Ambedkar: Third Annual International Conference. Brandeis University, Waltham, MA.

Queen, C. S. & King, S. B. (1996). *Engaged Buddhism: Buddhist liberation movements in Asia*. Albany: State University of New York Press.

Ream, A. (2014). Why I disrupted the wisdom conference. *Tricycle*. Retrieved from https://tricycle.org/trikedaily/why-i-disrupted-wisdom-20-conference/

Rowe, J. K. (2016). Micropolitics and collective liberation: Mind/body practices and left social practices. *New Political Science 38*(2), 206–225.

Rowe, J. K. (2015). Zen and the art of social movement maintenance. *Open Democracy*. Retrieved from https://www.opendemocracy.net/transformation/james-k-rowe/zen-and-art-of-social-movement-maintenance

Rowe, J. K. & Simpson M. (2017). Lessons from the front lines of anti-colonial pipeline resistance. *Waging Nonviolence*. Retrieved from https://wagingnonviolence.org/feature/lessons-front-lines-anti-colonial-unistoten-pipeline-resistance/

Ryan, T. (2012). *A mindful nation with Congressman Tim Ryan* [Video]. YouTube. Retrieved from https://www.youtube.com/watch?v=3sZDM93HFGs

Schedneck, B. (2017). The rise of female meditation teachers in Southeast Asia. In Z. Kassam (Ed.), *Women and Asian religions* (pp. 213–328). Santa Barbara, CA: Praeger.

Simmer-Brown, J. (2000). Speaking truth to power: The Buddhist peace fellowship. In C. S., Queen (Ed.), *Engaged Buddhism in the West* (pp. 67–94). Somerville, MA: Wisdom Publications.

Simmer-Brown, J., & Grace, F. (Eds.). (2011). *Meditation and the classroom: Contemplative pedagogy for religious studies*. Albany: State University of New York Press.

Swearer, D. (1995). *The Buddhist world of Southeast Asia*. Albany: State University of New York Press.

Tan, C. M. (2012). *Search inside yourself: The unexpected path to achieving success, happiness (and world peace)*. New York: HarperCollins.

Thanissaro, Bhikkhu. (2015). *Buddhist Romanticism*. Retrieved from https://www.dhammatalks.org/Archive/Writings/BuddhistRomanticism151231.pdf

The Center for Transformative Change. (2017). *Transform*. Retrieved from http://transform.transformativechange.org

Walsh, Z. (2017). Making refuge at Mind & Life's 2016 International symposium: Opportunities for decolonizing contemplative studies. *The Arrow*. Retrieved from http://arrow-journal.org/makingrefuge-at-mind-lifes-2016-international-symposium-opportunities-for-decolonizing-contemplative-studies/

White Awake. (n.d.). *White Awake*. Retrieved from https://whiteawake.org

Williams, A. K. (2002). *Being Black: Zen and the art of living with fearlessness and grace*. New York: Viking Compass.

Williams, A. K., Owens, R., & Syedullah, J. (2016). *Radical dharma: talking race, love and liberation*. Berkeley, CA: North Atlantic Books.

Wilson, J. (2014). *Mindful America: The mutual transformation of Buddhist meditation and American culture*. New York: Oxford University Press.

Wisdom 2.0. (2017). *The power of transformation: Wisdom 2.0*. Retrieved from http://www.wisdom2summit.com

Work That Reconnects Network. (2017). *Deep Times: A Journal of the Work that Reconnects*. Retrieved from http://journal.workthatreconnects.org

CHAPTER 36

MEDITATION AND EDUCATION

CANDY GUNTHER BROWN

Introduction

Meditation has joined math as a subject taught to schoolchildren worldwide. Just two of a proliferating array of school programs, MindUP and Mindful Schools, had by 2020 instructed nine million children, in the United States, United Kingdom, Canada, and across a hundred countries (Hawn Foundation, 2020b; Mindful Schools, 2020). The National Center for Health Statistics tracks an increase in U.S. meditators ages 4–17 from 1.6 percent (927,000 children) to 5.4 percent (3.1 million children) from 2012 to 2017 (Black, Clarke, Barnes, Stussman, & Nahin, 2015, p. 10; Black, Barnes, Clarke, Stussman, & Nahin, 2018, p. 5). In 2019, the U.K. Departments of Education and of Health and Social Care announced plans for a study of mindfulness in 370 schools (Government of the United Kingdom, 2019). This chapter narrates the history of meditation in education, examines representative programs, assesses their impacts, and recommends transparency and voluntarism in program delivery.

Moral Character sans Religion

The educational mainstreaming of meditation is largely a post-1960s development, with accelerating growth since the 1990s. This chapter foregrounds the U.S. context because U.S.-based programs have significantly influenced the global movement. Beginning in the colonial period, American educational leaders envisioned schools as shaping moral character. The Massachusetts Bay Colony passed a school law in 1642 to prevent children from growing "rude, stubborn & unruly" (Shurtleff, 1853–1854, p. 203). Although the First Amendment to the U.S. Constitution (Government of the United States, 1791) stipulates that "Congress shall make no law respecting an establishment of religion, or prohibiting the free exercise thereof," until the mid-twentieth century, U.S. schools commonly used "non-sectarian" Christian prayer and Bible lessons to form "character." The U.S. Supreme Court issued a series of rulings, notably *Engel v. Vitale* (1962) and *School District of Abington Township v. Schempp* (1963), prohibiting public schools from endorsing religious practices such as prayer and devotional Bible reading (Green, 2012, p. 8).

The United States is not unique in such restrictions. The Constitution of India, as amended in 1976, identifies the state as "secular" and prohibits "religious instruction" in state-funded schools (Government of India, 2019, pp. 22, 30). Canada's Constitution Act of 1982 guarantees "freedom of conscience and religion," and provincial laws, for example the British Columbia School Act of 1996, require that government schools "must be conducted on strictly secular and non-sectarian principles" (Government of Canada, 1982, Part I§2; Government of British Columbia, 1996, Chap. 412§76.1). By contrast, the United Kingdom does not prohibit schools from providing religious instruction, but the Human Rights Act of 1998 respects parental rights to ensure that their children's education conforms with "their own religious and philosophical convictions" (Government of the United Kingdom, 1998, part II§2).

Legal prohibitions of state-endorsed religious education in the United States have provoked controversy. Certain Americans criticized court rulings such as *Schempp* for creating a vacuum of moral character (Gordon, 2010, p. 86). For example, Congressman John Saylor of Pennsylvania agreed with a lament by the *Washington Evening Star* that: "God and religion have all but been driven from the public schools" (1963, p. 13936). With religious instruction off the table, educators cast around for alternatives to instill moral and ethical values in constitutionally permissible ways.

Market demand for non-religious meditation in state schools reflects a perception that schools have failed to provide moral grounding for an emotionally healthy, self-controlled, virtuous citizenry. The U.S.-based Pure Edge (aka Jois/Sonima Foundation) school yoga and meditation program identifies the "overarching need" in "public school environments" as "stress management" (2016, p. 3:221). Pure Edge's solution is to cultivate "character," instill "values" of "friendliness, compassion, and equanimity," and develop a sense of "interconnectedness and interdependence" by "sending kindness" through "loving kindness meditation" (2016, pp. 2:50, 3:4, 3:72, 3:220, 3:222). American school psychologist Patricia Broderick's *Learning to Breathe* (2013) curriculum addresses "disruptive behavior in the classroom, poor academic performance, [and] *out-of-control* emotions" that might provoke "*acting out* by taking drugs, displaying violent behavior or *acting in* by becoming more depressed" (Broderick, Kabat-Zinn, & Kabat-Zinn, 2013, italics mine). The raison d'etre for the Calmer Choice program in Massachusetts is prevention of drug-related murders and suicides of pre-college students by teaching "kindness and compassion" (Jensen, 2015, p. 3). The MindUp curriculum helps children with "self-regulation" of "impulses" and reduces "peer-to-peer conflict" by growing "empathy, compassion, patience, and generosity" (Hawn Foundation, 2011, p. 11).

Meditation purportedly calms stress, restores order, and cultivates virtues to renew the moral fabric of American education.

In 2012, U.S. Congressman Tim Ryan of Ohio published a bestseller, the title of which captures the appeal of meditation for many educators: *A Mindful Nation: How a Simple Practice Can Help Us Reduce Stress, Improve Performance, and Recapture the American Spirit*. Ryan's assessment that mindfulness could restore the "American Spirit" persuaded lawmakers to direct $1 million in government funds to teach mindfulness in schools (2012, p. 72). Playing off Ryan's title, in 2015, the United Kingdom's Mindfulness All-Party Parliamentary Group published a report entitled *Mindful Nation*. As evidence of need for mindfulness, the report cites low "academic achievement," a "mental health crisis," and the recent doubling of "conduct disorder[s]" among teenagers. Mindfulness avowedly addresses these problems through "character-building," defined as developing "a wide range of moral and civic virtues" (Mindfulness All-Party Parliamentary Group, 2015, p. 29). The British Mindfulness in Schools Project promotes mindfulness as "enjoyable and *civilizing*, for pupils and staff" (Weare, 2012, italics mine). In 1940, Winston Churchill famously revered "Christian civilization" as being foundational to British life and institutions. Eighty years later, "secular" meditation offers an alternative foundation for civilization. This raises the question of how meditative practices developed in religious contexts came to be regarded by many as "secular" and thus appropriate for schools serving diverse religious populations.

Science versus Religion: Transcendental Meditation

In the wake of U.S. restrictions on school prayer, Transcendental Meditation (TM) was the first meditative practice to be widely integrated into U.S. public schools by framing it as secular science rather than religion. The Indian-born Hindu Mahed Prisad Varma (ca. 1918–2008), who adopted the title "Maharishi" (Great Seer), popularized Transcendental Meditation (TM). By the late 1970s, TM had several million practitioners worldwide (Pair, 1978, p. 506; "Poll," 1976, p. 24).

The Maharishi initially identified TM as religious. He claimed membership in the "blessed" and "holy" Śaṅkarācārya tradition of Advaita Vedānta, a Hindu "direct path to Realization" of the unity of the Self (Ātman) with the Divine (Brahman) (Maharishi Mahesh Yogi, 1968a, p. 106; 1967, pp. 9, 11, 256). Articles of incorporation for the Spiritual Regeneration Movement Foundation in Los Angeles, California, in 1959 designate the Maharishi's corporation as "religious" (Maharishi Mahesh Yogi, 1961). The basic TM practice involves silent repetition of a mantra for fifteen to twenty minutes twice daily. Initiates receive a mantra during a *pūjā* ceremony, which involves bowing, offerings, and Sanskrit chants to venerate deities, including Nārāyaṇa, Brahmā, Viṣṇu, and Śiva (*Malnak v. Yogi*, 1977, at 1306–1307).

Although initiates must promise to keep their mantras secret, disaffected practitioners have disclosed mantras—combinations of Sanskrit root sounds and endings, such as "*aing*," "*kirim*," "*hiring*," "*shama*," "*shirim*"—associated with the deities Sarasvatī, Kālī, Śiva, Kṛṣṇa, and Lakṣmī (Mullen, 1991). Such mantras are not necessarily identical to names of associated deities, explains scholar Sir John Woodruffe, but rather are *bīja* or "seed" mantras that invoke the presence of corresponding deities because "the mantra of a Devata *is* the Devata" although the syllables themselves may lack "meaning according to the ordinary use of language" (1922, pp. 244–245). Scholar Mircea Eliade elaborates that the meditator who repeats a semantically meaningless *bīja* mantra "appropriates its ontological essence, concretely and directly assimilates the god" (1958, p. 215). The Maharishi explained in 1955 that TM avoids selecting "any sound at random" as a mantra because "ordinary sounds can do nothing more than merely sharpening the mind." By contrast, in TM "we select only the suitable mantras of personal Gods," which "fetch the grace of personal Gods," bringing the meditator into contact with "transcendental reality," "almighty creative intelligence," "Brahman which is the supreme ultimate absolute," "omniscient, omnipotent supreme lord of the universe" (Maharishi Mahesh Yogi, 1955, pp. 65–66; Maharishi Mahesh Yogi, 1968b, pp. 21–22, 25, 33, 46, 206).

By the 1970s, the Maharishi began replacing religious with scientific explanations of TM to broaden its appeal, particularly in educational settings. The Maharishi recruited adherents through free introductory courses, often on university campuses. In 1969, Stanford University authorized a course on the "Science of Creative Intelligence" (SCI), a phrase selected as being more "academic" than TM (Forem, 1973, pp. 216, 2, 40). The Maharishi also founded his own university, which opened in Santa Barbara, California, in 1973 as Maharishi International University, relocated to Fairfield, Iowa, in 1974, and was renamed Maharishi University of Management in 1995. Research studies conducted at Maharishi University supported the claim that TM is science rather than religion by reporting—in hundreds of published articles—the beneficial effects of TM on physical and mental health, for instance by reducing stress as indicated by heart and breathing rates (Maharishi University of Management, 2020a; Transcendental Meditation, 2020).

By 2020, Maharishi University had collected $32 million in grants, including $26 million from the U.S. National Institutes of Health and $4 million from the Department of Defense to support TM research (Maharishi University of Management, 2020b). Already in 1972, before the university had formally opened, it won a $20,000 grant from the U.S. government "to study possible applications of SCI and TM in secondary education" (Maharishi University of Management, 1973). In 1975, the U.S. Department of Health, Education, and Welfare awarded five public high schools in New Jersey $40,612 to teach elective courses in TM (Butz, 1998, p. 1). Having bolstered TM's legitimacy with federally funded research, the Maharishi—working through the World Plan Executive Council (established in 1972 as successor to the Spiritual Regeneration Movement)—began offering TM courses at high schools across the United States and Canada (Kleiman, 1977, pp. A1, D13; *Minnesota Law Review*, 1978, p. 925).

Rebranding TM as science did not persuade everyone that the program was secular. New Jersey parents Alan and Edwina Malnak sued World Plan and New Jersey for violating the establishment clause. In *Malnak v. Yogi*, the U.S. District Court and Third Circuit appellate court agreed with the plaintiffs, ruling that TM's religious beliefs and practices "do not shed that religiosity merely because they are presented as philosophy or science" (*Malnak v. Yogi*, 1977, at 1322). The courts voiced concern about devotional language in the Maharishi's textbook—*The Science of Creative Intelligence for Secondary Education* (1975)—and in *pūjā* chants. A concurring opinion by Justice Arlin Adams—which delineated criteria for determining whether contested practices are "religious" for legal purposes—noted "considerable doubt" about the secularity of TM mantras (*Malnak v. Yogi*, 1979, n. 54; *Minnesota Law Review*, 1978, p. 948). In the context of litigation, World Plan described TM mantras as "meaningless sound" (*Malnak v. Yogi*, 1977, at 1288). World Plan did not explain TM's foundational premise that mantras are significant *not* for their semantic meaning but for their presumed equivalence with personal gods and power to bring meditators into contact with the transcendent source of all meaning.

Despite *Malnak*, the David Lynch Foundation for Consciousness-Based Education and World Peace, established in 2005, donates millions of dollars to teach TM in schools on five continents (Goyanes, 2015). The Lynch Foundation distanced its programming from the "SCI/TM" course found unconstitutional in *Malnak* by rebranding it as "TM/Quiet Time." Quiet Time programs dispense with the SCI textbook but are otherwise similar to the New Jersey course, including assignment of secret mantras in *pūjās* that incorporate bowing, offerings, and Sanskrit chants. Students may "opt out" by reading or napping during twice-daily, fifteen-to-twenty-minute periods of quiet, but the only meditative technique taught is TM (Masters, 2014, pp. 280, 288–89). Parents in California, Connecticut, and North Carolina have complained that school programs are unconstitutional in the same ways as programs prohibited by *Malnak* (Street, 2007; Varley, 2006; Bolling, 2004). In 2006, a third-generation TM practitioner with forty years of personal involvement in the Fairfield TM community wrote to a California school board, characterizing the Lynch-funded TM program as "identical" to that originally taught by the Maharishi (Catena, 2007); the Foundation rescinded its $175,000 grant, and the matter was dropped (Wohlsen, 2006). To date, no one has litigated. Public schools are motivated to accept Lynch Foundation grants—although they must replace 150–200 minutes weekly of instructional time with meditation—because research studies report that TM improves academic performance, physical and mental health, and behavior, and because schools need private funding to supplement state support (Siegel, 2020).

Stripping Religious Language: Yoga

Although TM continues to be taught in schools in the United States and globally, the movement's heyday has passed. Meanwhile, other meditative practices—such as yoga—have grown increasingly popular. According to the U.S. National Center for Health

Statistics, the proportion of U.S. children ages 4–17 practicing yoga rose from 2.3 to 8.4 percent (4.9 million children) from 2007 to 2017 (Black et al., 2015, p. 10; Black et al., 2018, p. 5). A 2015 survey identified thirty-six school programs that had trained 5,400 teachers in 940 U.S. schools (Butzer, Ebert, Telles, & Khalsa, 2015, p. 18).

Because many people associate yoga with religion and specifically Hinduism, the introduction of yoga into state-funded schools has been controversial—even in yoga's homeland, India. The Indian Hindu Shri Krishna Pattabhi Jois (1915–2008), reputed developer of modern ashtanga (eight-limbed) yoga, argued as early as 1962 that yoga should be compulsory for all schoolchildren: "Were the government itself to understand their usefulness, and make the practice of *yogasana*, the *Surya Namaskara*, and their traditions *compulsory* for *all students* in all educational institutions, boys and girls alike, which would help to render their lives *pure*, it would be doing a great service to the world" (Jois, 1962/1999, pp. 41–42, emphasis mine). Jois explained *sūrya namaskāra* as "prayer to the sun God," Sūrya (Supreme Light), and defined the eighth limb of ashtanga—*samādhi*—as becoming "one with God" (Jois, 1962/1999, p. 30; Medin, 2004, p. 18). The central purpose of school yoga, according to Jois, is not physical exercise or mental clarity, but spiritual purity.

In 2017, India's Supreme Court dismissed a public interest litigation to make yoga compulsory in schools (Datta, 2017). The Court reasoned that it "cannot force anyone to do yoga" because India is a "secular" state, and state-funded schools cannot require students to participate in "religious instruction" (TNN, 2015). India's Muslim, Sikh, and Christian minorities have resisted compulsory yoga as an imposition of Hinduism. Muslim spokespersons complain that *sūrya namaskāra* "requires a person to bow to the Sun God." A Muslim mother voiced her concern in 2016 that "Islam being a monotheistic religion doesn't allow followers to bow before anyone except Allah" (Lal, 2016). Yoga is widely practiced in schools in India, but it is sufficiently controversial not to have yet been made compulsory.

Efforts to integrate yoga into U.S. education have provoked similar controversies. A 2016 U.S. national survey found that 9 percent of those who had never tried yoga agreed that "the 'spirituality' aspect of the practice bothers me" (p. 41). Enough Americans perceive yoga as spiritual, religious, and/or Hindu, that school-program developers have stripped programs of religious-sounding language. One influential pioneer of U.S. school-based yoga is Tara Guber, wife of movie producer Peter Guber. In 1999, Guber started Yoga Ed. in California. As Guber expanded into other schools, she experienced resistance, particularly from "Fundamentalist Baptists" on a Colorado school board who complained in 2002 that Yoga Ed. is "religious." Guber denied that Yoga Ed. is "religious-, dogma- or faith-based" and decided to "change a few words." She replaced "meditation" with "time in," *samādhi* with "oneness," and *prāṇāyāma* with "bunny breathing" (Associated Press, 2007; Havlen, 2002; Frazier, 2002). Two years later, Guber told *Hinduism Today* that these semantic changes were superficial since, regardless of terminology, the practice of yoga will "go within, shift consciousness and alter beliefs." Thus, getting Yoga Ed. into public schools constituted a "Vedic Victory"

(Guber, 2004). By 2020, Yoga Ed. was in forty countries, 9,600 schools, and 76,000 classrooms globally (Yoga Ed., 2020).

Although Guber overcame religious objections by making semantic changes, other programs provoked more persistent criticisms—in one notable example culminating in litigation. *Sedlock v. Baird* (2013) challenged ashtanga yoga in California's Encinitas Union School District (EUSD). The historical backdrop is that ashtanga yoga developer Pattabhi Jois began visiting Encinitas in 1975, at the invitation of an American disciple. Jois's son, Manju, relocated to Encinitas, and Manju's wife, Nancy, taught kindergarten in EUSD (Williams, 2010, pp. 17, 19; Gray, 2013). In 2011, Jois devotee Sonia Jones, wife of hedge-fund billionaire Paul Tudor Jones, incorporated the K. P. Jois USA Foundation, with its principal office in Encinitas (Jois Foundation, 2011, p. 2). The foundation's "mission" was to "bring the philosophy, teachings, and values of Sri K. Pattabhi Jois" to "youths in underserved communities" (Jois Yoga, 2013). It did so by developing a yoga and meditation curriculum for ages 4–17 and by supporting "changes in public policy" to require "yoga and meditation competency" for "public education credentialing" and "health and wellness best practices (yoga, meditation and nutrition) [as] an essential component of the education system" (Sonima Foundation, 2012, p. O). From 2012–2016, the foundation gave EUSD $4 million to teach yoga and meditation districtwide and co-develop a curriculum transferrable to other districts (Sonima Foundation, 2012, pp. 2, I; Sonima Foundation, 2013, pp. 2, O; Sonima Foundation, 2014, p. I; EUSD, 2015–2016a; EUSD, 2015–2016b).

The Jois-EUSD curriculum taught core ashtanga practices. Every session began with *sūrya namaskāra* (sun salutations)—defined by Jois as prayer to the sun god, and ended with *padmāsana* (lotus position) and *savāsana* ("taking rest" in corpse pose)—postures envisioned by Jois as facilitating "concentration, meditation, and ultimately Samadhi, or enlightenment" (EUSD, 2013; Jois, 1995, 1962/1999, p. 30; Kaivalya & Kooij, 2010, loc. 218). The EUSD children colored mandalas, put their hands in the symbolic gestures *añjali mudrā* (prayer) and *jñāna mudrā* (wisdom), and closed their eyes to meditate while sitting in a lotus posture and chanting *OṂ* (Meyer, 2013, p. 10:23, 11:16–22). The program incorporated "character" lessons based on *yama*s and *niyama*s—moral and ethical teachings from the *Yoga Sūtras* (Brown, 2013).

Christian and Hindu children and parents complained that the program violates the establishment clause (Eady, 2012). One nine-year-old girl told her mother that she was "asked to sit with her hands in a position that felt like a prayer to her, so she refused to do it" (Gray, 2013). Administrators responded by reducing Sanskrit terminology and "cultural references" (Meyer, 2013, p. 11:9) As the case came to trial, EUSD relabeled "ashtanga yoga" as "EUSD yoga" and "lotus" as "criss-cross applesauce"—although the written curriculum never used the phrase "criss-cross applesauce," but did use "lotus" 194 times (Meyer, 2013, pp. 11:15, 9:8-9; EUSD, 2013). Defense lawyers presented "EUSD yoga" as a "perfect example that yoga can be stripped of any religious aspects" (Sleeth, 2014). The judge concluded that "yoga *is* religious," having "religious roots, in Hindu, Buddhist, and other metaphysical" practices, and that ashtanga is the "cornerstone" of "EUSD yoga," since sessions begin and end with sequences "identical" to ashtanga. But the judge allowed the program, reasoning that EUSD yoga had stripped enough religious language, or "trappings," that a "reasonable student" would not perceive it as endorsing or disfavoring religion (Meyer, 2013, pp. 14:19–21, 28:5, 11:16, 24, 26:7). In 2015, an appellate court affirmed (*Sedlock v. Baird*, 2015). By 2016, the foundation (rebranded as Sonima in 2014 and Pure Edge in 2016) had introduced yoga and meditation to 40,000 children in 114 partner schools across the United States and in Kenya, Africa (Sonima Foundation, 2012, 2013, 2014, 2016). Under each brand name, foundation programs taught ashtanga practices, increasingly paired with mindfulness.

Cultivating Virtues: Mindfulness

Mindfulness has grown dramatically in popularity over the past two decades. The U.S. National Center for Health Statistics (NCHS) did not consider the practice sufficiently widespread to ask about it in its 2007 report. In 2012, 0.3 percent—out of 1.6 percent of U.S. children ages 4–17 who practiced some form of meditation—engaged in mindfulness. By 2017, 5.4 percent of this age group was meditating (Black et al., 2015, p. 10; Black et al., 2018, p. 5); although the NCHS did not specify the proportion involved in mindfulness, there is reason to believe that spiking interest in mindfulness accounts for much of this growth. Indeed, news headlines regularly report on the power of school mindfulness to counteract stress, inattention, and unkindness by cultivating compassion (Davis, 2015).

No individual played a more foundational role in the cultural and educational mainstreaming of mindfulness in the United States than Jon Kabat-Zinn (1944–), a European-American molecular biologist "first exposed to the dharma" (teachings and practices of the Buddha) in 1966 while studying at MIT (2011, p. 286). In 1979, Kabat-Zinn attended a Vipassana meditation retreat at the Insight Meditation Society, where he had a flash of insight for how to accomplish "the mainstreaming of dharma practice in society." His insight was to frame mindfulness as a secular stress-reduction method that implicitly communicates the "essence of the Buddha's teachings" about *dukkha*—suffering or stress—and the path to its cessation (2000, p. 227). Kabat-Zinn stopped "identifying myself as a Buddhist" and established the Center for Mindfulness in Medicine, Health Care, and Society (CfM), with its signature Mindfulness-Based Stress Reduction (MBSR) program, at the University of Massachusetts Medical School (2010). By 2017, CfM had enrolled 24,000 patients, certified 1,000 instructors, spawned 740 MBSR programs in medical settings across thirty countries, and become a model for innumerable mindfulness-based programs (MBPs) in hospitals, prisons, government, media, sports, businesses—and public schools (Center for Mindfulness in Medicine, Health Care, and Society, 2017; Wylie, 2015, p. 19; Kabat-Zinn, 2017, p. 1130).

Mindfulness-based stress reduction is premised on the *Satipaṭṭhāna Sutta* ("The Discourse on the Establishing of Mindfulness"), one of the most studied discourses in the Theravada Buddhist canon. *Sammā-sati* (right mindfulness) comprises the seventh aspect of the "Noble Eightfold Path" to liberation from *dukkha*, the fourth of the Buddha's "Four Noble Truths" (Wilson, 2014, p. 16; Stanley, 2015, p. 102; Coleman, 2001, p. 31). According to senior MBSR leaders, the class sequence teaches systematically, though implicitly, the "4 noble truths," "4 foundations of mindfulness," "7 Factors of Awakening," and "3 marks of existence" (no-self, impermanence, suffering), and counteracts the "3 poisons" (grasping, aversion, delusion) with the "4 virtues" (loving-kindness, compassion, sympathetic joy, equanimity) (Stahl & Goldstein, 2010; Stahl, 2015; Cullen, 2011, pp. 188–189, 191; Cullen, 2006, p. 5). Kabat-Zinn conceptualized MBSR as "skillful means" or "launching platforms" for "direct experience of the noumenous, the sacred, the Tao, God, the divine" (Kabat-Zinn, 2003, pp. 147–148; 1994a, p. 4; 2011, p. 281). Kabat-Zinn trainee Trudy Goodman brings mindfulness into "hospitals, and universities, and schools" by offering classes that "aren't that different from our Buddhist classes. They just use a different vocabulary"—a tactic Goodman describes as "Stealth Buddhism" (2014).

Kabat-Zinn popularized a definition of mindfulness that, on its surface, sounds thoroughly secular but is grounded in Buddhist assumptions about causes and remedies for *dukkha*, and value judgments about which states of mind are (un)wholesome. Mindfulness is "paying attention in a particular way: on purpose, in the present moment, and non-judgmentally," "free of grasping, aversion and delusion" (Kabat-Zinn, 1994b, p. 4; Williams & Kabat-Zinn, 2011, p. 10). Amy Saltzman, a pioneer in bringing MBSR to youth through Still Quiet Place, defines mindfulness as "paying attention, here and now, with kindness and curiosity" (Saltzman, 2014, p. 2). Neither definition reduces mindfulness to bare attentional training. They indicate an ethical stance of *how* to pay attention—non-judgmentally, with kindness and curiosity (Dodson-Lavelle, 2015, p. 28). Conversely, one should not grasp or be averse to certain experiences, dwell on the past, or anticipate the future—ideals that reflect MBSR's Buddhist orientation.

Mindfulness-based stress reduction has inspired numerous school MBPs. Mindful Schools Director of Programs Matthew Brensilver identifies MBSR as a "North Star for all of our work here" (2017). Founded in California in 2007, Mindful Schools was by 2020 serving three million children in one hundred countries (Mindful Schools, 2020). Brensilver describes Mindful Schools as a "thoroughly secular articulation of mindfulness," though he learned to meditate in Shambhala and Vipassana Buddhist traditions, and Mindful Schools's co-founders, Richard Shankman and Megan Cowan, have Buddhist credentials (Brensilver, 2016a; Shankman, 2015; Cowan, 2010). Brensilver told Spirit Rock that "Buddhist practices are more widely disseminated through many secular institutions," and his own research in behavioral science mobilizes "particular aspects of science that support the Dharma" (2016b). Program Director Chris McKenna, whose background includes meditation in Zen, Daoist, and Vajrayana traditions (2010), explained to *Tricycle: The Buddhist Review* that Mindful Schools facilitates "transmission of Buddhism to the West" through a "translation process." McKenna is "optimistic" that "young people are going to assimilate the dharma" (2014, p. 21).

Mindful Schools lessons resemble MBSR but add instruction in "heartfulness." This latter term is a translation of *mettā* (loving-kindness), one of four main virtues identified in Buddhist texts, which Mindful School teachers perceive to be lacking in public education (Barnhofer, Chittka, Nightingale, Visser, & Crane, 2010). A film linked from the Mindful Schools website, *Healthy Habits of Mind* (2013), portrays classroom heartfulness. The teacher tells her students: "I want you to first picture Aiden [an absent, presumably sick classmate] in your mind.... And now I want you to say: 'May you be happy. May you be healthy, and may you be peaceful.'... It could be somebody who has already passed [died] too." The teacher explains to an interviewer: "we close our eyes, and we send good thoughts" to those absent due to sickness or death (Bahnsen, 2013). The film depicts the teacher and children with eyes closed, hands in prayer position (*jñāna mudrā*), repeating scripted blessings that mirror language used in Buddhist contexts.

Buddhist influences are present but downplayed in British as well as American MBSR-inspired programs. Richard Burnett at Tonbridge in Kent, England, and Chris Cullen at Hampton in London co-founded the Mindfulness in Schools Project (MiSP), with its ".b" mindfulness curriculum, in 2009. The curriculum is mandatory for students ages 14–15 at Tonbridge and Hampton, both of which are independent, rather than state-run, schools (Simpson, 2017, p. 55.). State schools have also adopted the curriculum; indeed, by 2015, three thousand teachers in twelve countries used .b, and the curriculum had been translated into ten languages (Mindfulness All-Party Parliamentary Group, 2015, p. 32). Although the U.K. government does not regulate religious instruction to the same extent as the U.S. government, programs are still more likely to be adopted when presented as secular, and thus applicable to all, regardless of religious background. The MiSP curriculum is accordingly framed as secular mindfulness, though Burnett acknowledges that "there is a huge degree of overlap in the early stages of mindfulness practice, be it in a secular or a Buddhist context." The goal of MiSP is to "give all students a taste of mindfulness, so they know about it, and can return to it later" (2012). The "job" of .b is "to 'sell' mindfulness" and "spark" participants "into an entirely new way of seeing things." After "brief exposure in a classroom context there are usually a few pupils" whose "appetite" is "whetted" to ask where they can "find out more" (Burnett, 2011, pp. 81, 93, 96, 113). The MiSP website recommends resources, noting that "mindfulness can be presented as an entirely secular practice or as a more 'spiritual' one," and indicating which suggested books are "more 'Buddhist'" (MiSP, 2017b). The website links to the Buddhist Insight Meditation Society and Spirit Rock Insight Meditation Center in the United States as places where students can dive deeper into mindfulness (MiSP, 2017a).

Alongside the United States and United Kingdom, Canada has birthed mindfulness programs with a global reach. Actress and movie producer Goldie Hawn lived in Vancouver, British Columbia, in 2005 when she established the Hawn Foundation to promote her proprietary MindUP program (2011). In 2011, a prominent educational press, Scholastic Books, published *The MindUP Curriculum* for ages 3–14. By 2020, MindUP operated three hubs, in Canada, the United States, and the United Kingdom, from which it had reached 150,000 teachers and six million children in thirteen countries (Hawn Foundation, 2020b). Hawn's stated "mission" is to get programs like MindUP into "every school"—and "absolutely mandated" (2011).

Hawn learned meditation in religious contexts, but she presents MindUP as neuro-science. She was initiated into TM in 1971 and subsequently visited Buddhist monasteries in India, accepted a personalized mantra from the Dalai Lama, and described herself as a "Jew-Bu"—by "tribe" Jewish, "but my philosophy and my practice is really Buddhist" (Elliott, 2015; Hawn, with Holden, 2005, p. 436; Hawn, 2005a; Hawn, 2005b). In speaking to Buddhist sympathizers, Hawn has described MindUP as a "script" that brings Buddhist meditation "into the classroom under a different name," by replacing the terms "Buddhism" and "meditation" with "neuroscience" and "Core Practice" (Hawn, 2013). Hawn hired educators, neuroscientists, and psychologists to work alongside Buddhist meditators in crafting lessons that frame mindfulness as being grounded in brain anatomy. The basic neuroscience lesson is that mindful children resist impulses from their "reflexive, reactive amygdala" and follow their "reflective, thinking prefontal cortex" (Hawn Foundation, 2011, pp. 41, 77, 137, 151).

Instruction in the "MindUP Core Practice" not only teaches children something about their brains, it also communicates Buddhist assumptions about causes and remedies for suffering. Students "prepare" by "sitting cross-legged in a circle on the floor; resting their hands naturally in their laps or palms up on their knees; closing their eyes or looking down at their hands." During "brain breaks" of two to three minutes three times daily, "students are asked to focus their attention on their breath. When their mind wanders, they are asked to return their attention to their breath." Cued by a resonant sound (often a "Tibetan singing bowl" or Zenergy chime) to begin and end "deep belly breathing and attentive listening," students cultivate "non-judgmental awareness." Such "awareness of the mind without judgment... means to free oneself from the agony of what has happened or the dread of what is yet to be." MindUP counteracts the agony (or *dukkha*) caused by grasping or aversion of the past or future by cultivating the same four virtues foregrounded in Buddhist teachings. Children who engage in the Core practice learn "kindness," become "more compassionate," experience "joy" as they "attune to [their] inner voice," and "regulate their emotions and temper their reactivity" (equanimity). The curriculum emphasizes that "to get the full benefit of MindUp lessons, children will need to know a specific vocabulary," principally the term "mindfulness"—a term that points children to extracurricular contexts where they can go deeper in learning about mindfulness (Hawn Foundation, 2011, pp. 12, 40, 41, 42, 46, 54, 57; Calos, 2017; Hawn Foundation, 2020a).

As with TM and yoga, introducing mindfulness into school curricula has provoked complaints that programs are religious. School mindfulness has not yet been litigated, though there have been threats. In 2016, a parent and school board member in Massachusetts retained an attorney to serve a legal memorandum requesting that her school district discontinue its Calmer Choice mindfulness program because of its Buddhist foundations (Broyles, 2016). The challenge did not surprise leaders in the mindfulness-in-education movement. As the founder of Calmer Choice, Fiona Jensen, recounts, one leader after another told her: "We've been waiting for this to happen"

(Jensen, 2016). Senior Editor at *Mindful* Heather Hurlock inferred that "if this [challenge] can happen in Massachusetts," one of the "most liberal, most educated, and most open-minded states," then "it can (and probably will) happen anywhere" (Hurlock, 2016).

The challenged school district did not comply with the request to stop teaching mindfulness, but neither did the parent litigate. By 2020, Calmer Choice had trained 1,000 teachers and 26,000 children in twenty-eight schools (Calmer Choice, 2020a). Jensen's goal is for every student to be "expected to attend" mindfulness classes: "math, science, history, mindfulness, and English . . . just part of what was part of their day" and for mindfulness lessons to overflow formal instructional time to shape "school culture" (Jensen, 2015; Calmer Choice, 2020b). The difficulty of "opting out" of a mindfulness culture is one of the most frequent complaints—raised by Christians, Buddhists, atheists, and committed meditators, among others, in British Columbia, Canada, as well as in several U.S. regions, including not only Massachusetts, but also Indiana, New Mexico, New York, Ohio, and Virginia (Chwartkowski, 2016; Brown, 2014; Thoren, 2013; informant e-mail Jan. 30, 2017; Warsmith, 2013; informant e-mail June 1, 2016). It can be even more difficult for teachers than students to opt out. For example, teachers in British Columbia and California lost their classrooms because they could not in good conscience teach mindfulness (informant e-mail Feb. 10, 2014; Draper, 2017). In 2018, the American Center for Law and Justice publicly contemplated litigating school mindfulness and collected 86,593 signatures on a petition (Stierhoff, 2018)—a development that may yet progress.

Assessment

The educational mainstreaming of meditation has depended upon its classification as science rather than religion. Research on meditation for children ages 4–17 is limited by the number of randomized controlled trials (RCTs) and by quality; studies share methodological weaknesses of research on adults, as discussed in chapters in this volume by Oman, "Studying the Effects of Meditation," and Goyal and Rusch, "Mindfulness-based Interventions in the Treatment of Physical Conditions."

One of the few TM studies *not* conducted by researchers with allegiance to the practice found that TM has no effect on grades and notes that studies reporting grade improvements "failed to isolate effects of TM from other concurrent activities" (Carsello & Creaser, 1978). A 2015 study that reports that TM/Quiet Time helps academically does not differentiate among subjects who, instead of repeating a mantra, read or rested—practices that might also improve grades (Wendt et al., 2015).

There is more research on yoga for children, but there are similar limitations. A 2015 review of RCTs of school yoga from 1980 to 2014 ($N = 9$) concluded from "low"-quality evidence that "the utility of yoga in educational settings is uncertain" (Ferreira-Vorkapic et al., 2015, pp. 1, 3, 15). A 2015 meta-analysis found that aerobic exercise had a "moderate to large effect" on ADHD but detected "less evidence about the benefits of the yoga programmes" (Cerillo-Urbina, 2015). A 2015 systematic review of anxiety research concluded that "large-scale, randomized trials with physiological and psychological measures are still needed" to "determine yoga's effectiveness" (Weaver & Darragh, 2015). A 2016 systematic review of "yoga in school" observed that in most studies ($N = 47$) "methodological quality is low to moderate. . . . Sample sizes are typically small, self-reported subjective measures have been the most common outcome, many of the studies did not incorporate control groups." The review observed that "many of the positive results reported in fact appear as trends (e.g., $P < 0.1$) rather than statistically significant (i.e., $P < 0.05$) changes, suggesting relatively weak outcomes. . . . In the controlled studies, it is not uncommon that very few of the outcomes measured have shown positive changes or, in some cases, no significant improvements at all." Some studies found "*counterintuitive increases in negative mood state and perceived stress with the yoga*" (Khalsa & Butzer, 2016, p. 52, italics mine).

Indeed, some studies report negative effects from school yoga. A 2012 study ($N = 155$) assessed yoga adapted from MBSR for girls ages 9–11 (White, 2012, p. 52). The yoga group did no better than a wait-list control group with self-esteem or self-regulation. Over time the yoga group reported *higher* perceived stress and feeling worse about stressors, although no increase in frequency of stressors was found. A 2013 comparison of yoga with physical exercise for children ages 8–13 found no significant difference for physical fitness or academic performance, but the yoga group exhibited significantly *lower* social self-esteem (Telles, Singh, Bhardwaj, Kumar, & Balkrishna, 2013).

A series of studies on Jois/Sonima Foundation "ashtanga-informed yoga" found that students in yoga did no better than physical education (PE) students on any study measure: self-reported positive affect, global self-worth, aggression indices, parent reports, or stress reactivity. The yoga group reported "*increased negative emotions*" such as "sadness and shame," while the PE group reported a "decrease in these feelings" (Haden, Daly, & Hagins, 2014, pp. 148, 152, 153, italics mine; Hagins, Haden, & Daly, 2013, p. 5). Although focus groups "uniformly expressed an improvement in self-regulation and decreases in mental stress," written surveys showed no difference between participants in yoga versus PE for "self-regulation, executive function, well-being, and mindfulness." Some benefits reported are nonspecific to yoga: "I am sleep deprived and the resting made me feel more energized," "We like the 5 minute nap," and "You get 45 minutes to relax and mellow down." The researchers acknowledged "a trend, although nonsignificant, of yoga assignment being associated with *poorer scores on the psychosocial scales*." Moreover, the study's "primary hypothesis that yoga would improve academic performance was not supported by intent to treat analysis" (Hagins & Rundle, 2016, pp. 108, 113; Wang & Hagins, 2016, pp. 2, 4, 5).

Systematic reviews of mindfulness-based programs (MBPs) for children note similar methodological challenges as those for yoga and MBPs for adults. A 2014 systematic review concluded that school-based MBPs "hold promise" for "improving cognitive performance and resilience to stress," but called for studies with "active controls" (Zenner, Hernleben-Kurz & Walach, 2014, pp. 1, 18). A 2015 meta-analysis concludes that "high-quality evidence on mindfulness-training for youth is relatively sparse" (Black, 2015). A 2016 review of research on school MBPs ($N = 28$) notes that only sixteen studies used any kind of control group; most (10) used nonactive "treatment as usual" comparisons; three used a "semi-active" control of didactic instruction; only three employed an active control of didactic instruction plus role-play activities; just ten randomized group assignment. The "lack of both a comparison condition and random assignment represents the single largest limitation in the existing literature"; most (23) studies relied solely on questionnaires to assess effectiveness, and none considered school-collected academic or behavioral outcome data (Felver, Celis-de Hoyos, Tezanos, & Singh, 2016, p. 41). Self-reports may be particularly unreliable in assessing levels of stress—given that even asking about one's stress levels can affect one's answer. A 2014 study of adults and a 2015 study of elementary-school children both found that although mindfulness participants self-reported decreased stress, biological markers such as cortisol levels indicated *increased* stress (Creswell, Pacilio, Lindsay, & Brown, 2014, "Stress"; Schonert-Reichl et al., 2015). A 2019 systematic review found "insufficient evidence to conclude that educational setting-based interventions," including mindfulness, are "effective for the prevention of anxiety and depression in children" (Caldwell et al., 2019, pp. 1017, 1012). The review recommended against commissioning future trials that lack active controls. A 2019 systematic review of MBPs for ADHD found benefits for ADHD symptoms and executive function but concluded that "due to poor methodological design and significant risk of bias across students, mindfulness approach remains an investigational treatment" (Pozneanscaia, 2019, p. 1).

Research suggests that school-based MBPs may be less effective than alternatives. A 2017 meta-analysis of research on youth ($N = 76$) found that MBPs were "associated with small treatment effects in studies using pre-post ($g = 0.305$, $SE = 0.039$) and controlled designs ($g = 0.322$, $SE = 0.040$)." Of studies analyzed, thirty-five (46.1 percent) were RCTs, fifteen (19.7 percent) used nonrandomized controls, and twenty-six (34.2 percent) were uncontrolled. Analysis showed that publication bias is likely. An inverse association between treatment effect and study quality suggests that effects "may be smaller in more rigorous designs." Systematic reviews of other social and emotional learning (SEL) interventions show moderate-to-large treatment effects across academic, social-emotional, and behavioral outcomes. The authors conclude that the comparatively "rather small effects" for MBPs indicate that "school-based practitioners should prefer these alternative [non-MBP] interventions for targeted purposes (i.e. secondary or intensive interventions)." The authors "recommend a limited-use approach" to MBPs in schools (Klingbeil et al., 2017, pp. 94–95, 96, 97, 99). James Coyne, professor of health psychology at University Medical Center, Groningen, the Netherlands, critically analyzed studies cited by the 2016 U.K. *Mindful Nation* report to support funding mindfulness in education. Coyne concluded that "most students do not show any benefit whatsoever from mindfulness training over being in a reading group" and recommended redirecting resources elsewhere (Coyne, 2016). A 2019 review reported that when non-MBP active controls are included in studies of mindfulness, "often both intervention and active control arms show increases in self-reported mindfulness." The authors found that "regular exercises not considered mind-body practices were associated with increased mindfulness" and that "physical exercise for young adults with elevated stress levels and a group hiking trip for 14-year-old healthy boys were associated with some of the greatest increases in mindfulness among all interventions." The authors conclude that "there are many roads to developing mindfulness" (Xia, Hu, Seritan, & Eisendrath, 2019, pp. 2, 13, 1).

There is even less data for children than adults on risks of adverse effects from MBPs (for the latter, see the chapter by Lindahl et al. in this volume, "The Adverse Effects of Meditation.") Few school-based MBPs have a plan for addressing meditation difficulties. For example, Calmer Choice was, until legally scrutinized in 2016, marketed to schools as a "universal/primary prevention program" designed to reduce risks of "violence, suicide, and self-destructive behaviors in young people." The program was delivered to "entire classrooms" without asking students to "identify any challenges they may be confronting" or listing contraindications (Calmer Choice, 2015, 2014). Yet Calmer Choice contractually obligated each school to "indemnify and hold CALMER CHOICE, its officers, directors and employees harmless from any loss, liability or actions by third parties or government agencies" arising from use of the Calmer Choice curriculum (Broyles, 2016, p. 8). Studies of school-based MBPs do not generally report—or look for—adverse effects.

School-based meditation programs may inadvertently perpetuate cultural stereotypes, pervasive in the United States, of recent immigrants, people of color, and the working classes as particularly lacking virtues cultivated by meditation. Promotional videos from the David Lynch Foundation feature "inner-city" schools with African American and Latinx populations transformed by TM (taught primarily by White, middle-to-upper-class experts) into oases of non-stressful academic achievement, peace, kindness, and optimism (Lynch Foundation, 2010). The Jois/Sonima Foundation prioritized funding schools with a "large underserved population" of "primarily minority youth," such as the Houston Independent School District, where "80 percent of HISD's students were low-income, and 87 percent were black or Hispanic" (Foster, 2016). The Mindful Schools documentary film *Room to Breathe* (2012) portrays a White mindfulness emissary overcoming the purported "defiance" of low-income, urban students of color who failed to share her academic and social goals (Long, 2012).

Certain research studies of U.S. school meditation disproportionately enroll low-income students of color. Psychologist Tamar Mendelson and colleagues target African American, "mixed race," and Latinx children because "youth in underserved, urban communities are at risk for a range of negative outcomes... mindfulness-based approaches may improve adjustment among chronically stressed and disadvantaged youth by enhancing self-regulatory capacities" (2010, p. 985). This language may be interpreted as implying that "disadvantaged" children are "at risk" because they have lower "self-regulatory capacities." Pediatrician Erica Sibinga and colleagues justify enrolling "low-income, minority" middle-school students, "99.7% African American, and 99% eligible for free lunch," since "many urban youth" face "violence, multigenerational poverty, failing educational systems, substance use, limited avenues for success, health risks, and trauma." The authors address none of these structural problems, but instead endorse mindfulness as ameliorating "trauma-associated symptoms among vulnerable urban middle school students" (2016, p. 1). Readers might infer that "vulnerable" students have the most to gain from mindfulness not only because their circumstances have been challenging, but also because they naturally lack moral character to rebound from these challenges.

In contexts where government promotion of religion is illegal, school meditation not only raises ethical concerns but may also violate the law. U.S. Supreme Court rulings prohibit even "voluntary" school prayer programs that allow students to "remain silent or be excused from the room" by opting out. The Court's concern is that the "power, prestige, and financial support of government," coupled with involuntary attendance, teacher authority, and peer pressure, exerts "indirect coercive pressure" to participate (*Engel v. Vitale*, 1962, at 430, 431; *Edwards v. Aguillard*, 1987, at 583–84). The Court has allowed voluntary devotional Bible programs only if offered outside school hours (*Good News Club v. Milford Central School*, 2001). *Malnak* ruled that an elective TM course is unconstitutional when offered during the school day.

As *Malnak* recognized, school meditation may exert similarly coercive pressure as prayer and Bible reading. For example, a Mindful Schools student told an interviewer that she had "initially refused" to meditate to the sound of a "Tibetan meditation bell" during a required English class. Instead, she sat "defiantly while others participated.... Eventually, though, she realized she was alone in her resistance, and she began to go through the motions, largely because she likes and respects" her teacher, and all her peers were compliant (Davis, 2015). This student had little choice but to participate or watch—day after day; repeated encouragements from a beloved teacher, combined with peer pressure, made it difficult to keep resisting. A British Columbia parent whose son wanted to opt out of mindfulness had to supervise his child off school grounds during thrice-daily loudspeaker-led schoolwide mindfulness practice (Chwartkowski, 2016). When meditation is taught as part of a class, scattered throughout the day, or cultivated as a "school culture," opting out takes special effort and may be a practical impossibility, short of withdrawing from school altogether.

Offering meditation on an "opt-in" as opposed to an "opt-out" basis may better facilitate the transparency and voluntarism constitutive of informed consent (Faden, Beauchamp, & King, 1986, p. 125). Opt-out (passive consent) programs have higher participation rates than opt-in (active consent) programs precisely because opting in requires an affirmative decision (Gillin, 2001). Those convinced of the benefits of meditation may resist an opt-in model because they want to maximize participation and distribution of benefits—and assume that those students and parents least likely to opt in most "need" meditation. Automatic enrollment plays on human inertia, herd instincts, respect for authority, and peer pressure. Opt-in programs respect the wishes of children and parents whose priorities, values—and religious commitments—may diverge from those of meditation advocates.

Conclusion

Meditation entered the educational mainstream as program advocates framed Transcendental Meditation, ashtanga yoga, and mindfulness-based stress reduction as scientifically validated techniques that not only benefit academic achievement and health but also develop moral character sans religion. Ongoing religious associations, particularly with Hinduism and Buddhism, have been a source of controversies, including litigation. Studies specific to school-based meditation report benefits, for instance on grades and physical and mental health. The implications of this research are, however, limited by methodological weaknesses and evidence suggesting that alternatives such as aerobic exercise or quiet reading may be at least as beneficial. Programs, and associated research, targeted to low-income students of color may inadvertently imply that these are the populations most in need of meditation because they are the most lacking in moral character. Mandatory, and even opt-out, meditation programs may exert coercive pressures similar to those of Christian prayer and Bible reading. Therefore, upholding legal and ethical standards of secularity and informed consent may best be facilitated by transparent, voluntary programs offered on an opt-in basis.

References

Associated Press. (2007, January 28). Yoga causes controversy in public schools. Retrieved from http://www.nbcnews.com/id/16859368/#.Xj6TSmhKhaQ

Bahnsen, M. (2013). *Healthy habits of mind* [Video file]. Aarhus, Denmark: Persona Film. Retrieved from http://www.mindfulschools.org/resources/healthy-habits-of-mind/

Barnhofer, T., Chittka, T., Nightingale, H., Visser, C., & Crane, C. (2010). State effects of two forms of meditation on prefrontal EEG asymmetry in previously depressed individuals. *Mindfulness 1*(1), 21–27.

Black, D. S. (2015). Mindfulness training for children and adolescents: A state-of-the-science review. In K. Warren Brown, J. D. Creswell, & R. M. Ryan (Eds.), *Handbook of mindfulness: Theory, research, and practice* (pp. 283–310). New York: Guilford.

Black, L. I., Clarke, T. C., Barnes, P. M., Stussman, B. J., & Nahin, R. L. (2015). Use of complementary health approaches among children aged 4–17 years in the United States: National Health Interview Survey, 2007–2012. *National Health Statistics Reports 78*, 1–19.

Black, L. I., Barnes, P. M., Clarke, T. C., Stussman, B. J., & Nahin, R. L. (2018). Use of yoga, meditation, and chiropractors among U.S. children aged 4–17 years. *NCHS Data Brief 324*, 1–8.

Bolling, C. B. (2004, April 9). Board tells future school: Remove religion from lessons or lose charter. *The Charlotte Observer*. Retrieved from http://wwrn.ors/4778/

Brensilver, M. (2016a, September 6). Guidelines for secular teaching of mindfulness. *Mindful Schools*. Retrieved from http://www.mindfulschools.org/foundational-concepts/secularity/

Brensilver, M. (2016b). Interview by Spirit Rock. Honoring a love of the Dharma: A conversation with Matthew Brensilver. *Spirit Rock: An Insight Meditation center*. Retrieved from https://www.spiritrock.org/2016/the-teachings/article-archive/interview-matthew-brensilver

Brensilver, M. (2017, March 23). Essentials of mindfulness-based programs & the qualities of teachers who share mindfulness. *Mindful Schools*. Retrieved from http://www.mindfulschools.org/foundational-concepts/essentials-mindfulness-based-programs-qualities-teachers-share-mindfulness/

Broderick, P. C., Kabat-Zinn, M., & Kabat-Zinn, J. (2013). *Learning to breathe: A mindfulness curriculum for adolescents to cultivate emotion regulation, attention, and performance*. Oakland, CA: New Harbinger. Publisher's description at https://www.amazon.com/Learning-Breathe-Mindfulness-Adolescents-Performance/dp/1608827836

Brown, C. G. (2014, December 16). Guest column: MindUP: Does it put religion in the classroom? *Bloomington Herald-Times*. Retrieved from https://www.hoosiertimes.com/herald_times_online/opinion/guest-column-mindup-does-it-put-religion-in-the-classroom/article_71ae5c70-a4c8-530a-a077-a37976999b5f.html

Brown, J. Declaration, 2:28–3:3. In *Sedlock v. Baird* (2013).

Broyles, D. R. (2016, February 2). *Legal & practical concerns regarding the District's Calmer Choice mindfulness curriculum*. Retrieved from http://www.nclplaw.org/wp-content/uploads/2011/12/DYRSD-Legal-Opinion-Memorandum-2-2-161.pdf

Burnett, R. (2011). Mindfulness in secondary schools: Learning lessons from the adults, secular and Buddhist. *Buddhist Studies Review 28*(1), 79–120.

Butz, M. (1998). Transcendental Meditation. *Watchman Fellowship*. Retrieved from http://www.watchman.org/profiles/pdf/tmprofile.pdf

Butzer, B., Ebert, M., Telles, S., & Khalsa, S. B. S. (2015). School-based yoga programs in the United States: A survey. *Advances in Mind-Body Medicine 29*(4), 18–26.

Caldwell, D. M., Davies, S. R., Hetrick, S. E., Palmer, J. C., Caro, P., López-López, J. A., Gunnell, D., Kidger, J., Thomas, J., French, C., Stockings, E., Campbell, R., & Welton, N. J. (2019). School-based interventions to prevent anxiety and depression in children and young people: A systematic review and network meta-analysis. *Lancet Psychiatry 6*, 1011–1020.

Calmer Choice. (2014, October 2). Cultivating awareness, living mindfulness, enhancing resilience [1440 Foundation profile]. Retrieved from https://web.archive.org/web/20141002024659/http://1440.org:80/who-we-support/calmer-choice/

Calmer Choice. (2015). The Calmer Choice program. Retrieved from https://web.archive.org/web/20171119190037/http://www.calmerchoice.org/new-page/

Calmer Choice. (2020a). Home. Retrieved from http://www.calmerchoice.org/

Calmer Choice (2020b). Learn about our programs. Retrieved from https://calmerchoice.org/what-we-do

Calos, R. (2017, November 27). Social and emotional learning empowers children [Blog post]. *Scientific American: Streams of Consciousness*. Retrieved from http://blogs.scientificamerican.com/streams-of-consciousness/social-and-emotional-learning-empowers-children/

Carsello, C. J., & Creaser, J. W. (1978). Does Transcendental Meditation affect grades? *Journal of Applied Psychology 63*(5), 644–645.

Catena, G. (2007, January 13). Letter to San Rafael School Board . . or . . How TM lures the young and vulnerable [Blog post]. *TM-Free Blog*. Retrieved from http://tmfree.blogspot.com/2007/01/letter-to-san-rafael-school-boardor-how.html

Center for Mindfulness in Medicine, Health Care, and Society. (2017). History of MBSR. Retrieved from http://www.umassmed.edu/cfm/stress-reduction/history-of-mbsr/

Cerillo-Urbina, A. J., García-Hermoso, A., Sánchez-Lopez, M., Pardo-Guijarro, M. J., Santos Gómez, J. L., & Martínez-Vizcaíno, V. (2015). The effects of physical exercise in children with attention deficit hyperactivity disorder. *Child: Care, Health and Development 41*(6), 779–788.

Churchill, W. (1940, June 18). Their finest hour. Speech before the House of Commons. Retrieved from https://winstonchurchill.org/resources/speeches/1940-the-finest-hour/their-finest-hour/

Chwartkowski, R. (2016, July). Please remove mindfulness programs (inc. MindUP) from Canadian public schools [Petition]. Retrieved from https://www.change.org/p/minister-of-education-please-remove-the-mindfulness-program-from-canadian-public-schools

Coleman, J. W. (2001). *The new Buddhism: The Western transformation of an ancient tradition.* New York: Oxford University Press.

Cowan, M. (2010, May 23). Insight Meditation Center profile. Retrieved from http://www.insightmeditationcenter.org/2010/05/a-benefit-for-mindful-schools-with-megan-cowan/

Coyne, J. (2016, November 16). Unintended consequences of universal mindfulness training for schoolchildren? Retrieved from http://www.coyneoftherealm.com/2016/11/16/unintended-consequences-of-universal-mindfulness-training-for-schoolchildren/

Creswell, J.D., Pacilio, L. E., Lindsay, E. K., & Brown, K. W. (2014). Brief mindfulness meditation training alters psychological and neuroendocrine responses to social evaluative stress. *Psychoneuroendocrinology 44*, 1–12.

Cullen, M. (Ed.). (2006). Mindfulness: The heart of Buddhist meditation? A conversation among Jan Chozen Bays, Joseph Goldstein, Jon Kabat-Zinn and Alan Wallace. *Inquiring Mind* 22(2), 4–7.

Cullen, M. (2011). Mindfulness-based interventions: An emerging phenomenon. *Mindfulness* 2(3), 186–193.

Datta, S. (2017, August 8). Supreme Court dismisses PIL to make yoga compulsory in schools. *Bar & Bench: Indian Legal News.* Retrieved from https://barandbench.com/yoga-cannot-compulsory-schools-supreme-court/

Davis, L. C. (2015, August 31). When mindfulness meets the classroom. *Atlantic.* Retrieved fromhttps://www.theatlantic.com/education/archive/2015/08/mindfulness-education-schools-meditation/402469/

Dodson-Lavelle, B. (2015). *Against one method: Toward a critical-constructive approach to the adaptation and implementation of Buddhist-based contemplative programs in the United States* (Doctoral dissertation). Emory University.

Draper, A. (2017). Remove mandatory MindUp/mindfulness from my classroom [Petition]. *Ipetitions.* Retrieved from https://www.ipetitions.com/petition/remove-mindfulness-classroom

Eady, M. (2012). Remove the Ashtanga Yoga Program from EUSD [Petition]. *Ipetitions.* Retrieved from https://web.archive.org/web/20121208134335/http://www.ipetitions.com:80/petition/remove-the-ashtanga-yoga-program-from-eusd/signatures/page/5

Elliott, M. (2015, October 17). Teaching children mindfulness. Retrieved from http://www.gratitudeseeds.com/teaching-children-mindfulness/

Edwards v. Aguillard, 482 U.S. 578 (1987).

Eliade, M. (2009). *Yoga, immortality, and freedom* (2nd ed.). Princeton, NJ: Princeton University Press. (Original work published 1958).

Engel v. Vitale, 370 U.S. 422 (1962).

Encinitas Union School District [EUSD]. (2013, May). *On the Mat.* In *Sedlock v. Baird* (2013).

Encinitas Union School District [EUSD]. (2015–2016a). Memorandum of Understanding between Encinitas Union School District and Regur Development Group Solutions.

Retrieved from http://encinitasparents4truth.com/wp-content/uploads/2016/06/EUSD-RDG-MOU-for-2015-16.pdf

Encinitas Union School District [EUSD]. (2015–2016b). Sonima / EUSD Health and Wellness Program Memorandum of Understanding 2015–2016. Retrieved from http://ww2.eusd.net/board/Documents/Board%2520ATtachments/Sonima%2520MOU%25202015-2016.pdf

Faden, R. R., & Beauchamp, T. L., with King, N. M. P. (1986). *A history and theory of informed consent*. New York: Oxford University Press.

Felver, J. C., Celis-de Hoyos, C. E., Tezanos, K., & Singh, N. N. (2016). A systematic review of mindfulness-based interventions for youth in school settings. *Mindfulness 7*, 34–45.

Ferreira-Vorkapic, C., Feitoza, J. M., Marchioro, M., Simões, J., Kozasa, E., & Telles, S. (2015). Are there benefits from teaching yoga at schools? A systematic review of randomized control trials of yoga-based interventions. *Evidence-Based Complementary and Alternative Medicine 2015*, Article 345835.

Forem, J. (1973). *Transcendental Meditation: Maharishi Mahesh Yogi and the science of creative intelligence*. New York: Dutton.

Foster, D. (2016, January 23). Is mindfulness making us ill? *Guardian*. Retrieved from http://www.theguardian.com/lifeandstyle/2016/jan/23/is-mindfulness-making-us-ill

Frazier, D. (2002, Sept. 2). Religion or exercise? Debate on yoga raises concerns. Retrieved from http://www.beliefnet.com/Faiths/2002/09/Religion-Or-Exercise-Debate-On-Yoga-Raises-Concerns.aspx

Gillin, D. (2001, February 28). The opt-in vs. opt-out debate. *Insights Association*. Retrieved from http://www.insightsassociation.org/article/opt-vs-opt-out-debate

Goodman, T. (2014, August 27). Stealth Buddhism. Interview by V. Horn & E. Horn. *Buddhist Geeks*. Retrieved from https://web.archive.org/web/20160405015832/http://www.buddhistgeeks.com/2014/08/bg-331-stealth-buddhism/

Good News Club v. Milford Central School, 533 U.S. 98 (2001).

Gordon, S. B. (2010). *The spirit of the law: Religious voices and the Constitution in modern America*. Cambridge, MA: Harvard University Press.

Government of British Columbia. (1996). *School Act*. Retrieved from https://www2.gov.bc.ca/assets/gov/education/administration/legislation-policy/legislation/schoollaw/revisedstatutescontents.pdf

Government of Canada. (1982). *Constitution Act*. Retrieved from http://laws-lois.justice.gc.ca/eng/const/page-15.html

Government of India. (2019, April 1). *The Constitution of India*. New Delhi: Government of India Ministry of Law and Justice. Retrieved from http://legislative.gov.in/sites/default/files/COI-updated.pdf

Government of the United Kingdom. (1998). *Human Rights Act*. Retrieved from http://www.legislation.gov.uk/ukpga/1998/42

Government of the United Kingdom. (2019, February 4). One of the largest mental health trials launches in schools. Retrieved from https://www.gov.uk/government/news/one-of-the-largest-mental-health-trials-launches-in-schools

Government of the United States. (1791). *Amendments to the Constitution*. Retrieved from http://constitutionus.com/

Goyanes, C. (2015, October 14). Why kids need quiet time. Retrieved from http://www.sonima.com/meditation/quiet-time/

Gray, C. (2013, May 9). Declaration, 2:11–12. In *Sedlock v. Baird* (2013).

Green, S. K. (2012). *The Bible, the school, and the Constitution: The clash that shaped modern church-state doctrine*. New York: Oxford University Press.
Guber, T. (2004, April/May/June). Interview by *Hinduism Today*. Tara's Yoga for Kids: One noble soul takes on the public school system and wins a Vedic victory. *Hinduism Today*. Retrieved from http://www.hinduismtoday.com/modules/smartsection/item.php?itemid=1328
Haden, S. C., Daly, L., & Hagins, M. (2014). A randomised controlled trial comparing the impact of yoga and physical education on the emotional and behavioural functioning of middle school children. *Focus on Alternative and Complementary Therapies 19*(3), 148–155.
Hagins, M., S. C. Haden, & L. Daly. (2013). A randomized controlled trial on the effects of yoga on stress reactivity in 6th grade students. *Evidence-Based Complementary and Alternative Medicine 2013*, Article 607134.
Hagins, M., & A. Rundle. (2016). Yoga improves academic performance in urban high school students compared to physical education: A randomized controlled trial. *Mind, Brain, and Education 10*(2), 105–116.
Havlen, N. (2002). Yoga in classroom brings out critics and supporters. *Aspen Times*. Retrieved from https://web.archive.org/web/20061121055249/http://yogaed.com/ye_new_site/pdfs/ASPEN/aspentimes2.pdf
Hawn, G. (2005a, April 28). Interview by R. Leung. Goldie Hawn a wallflower? *60 Minutes*. Retrieved from https://www.cbsnews.com/news/goldie-hawn-a-wallflower/
Hawn, G. (2005b, August). Interview by D. Caldwell. Goldie: Buddhist, Jew, Jesus freak. *Beliefnet*. Retrieved from http://www.beliefnet.com/Wellness/2005/08/Goldie-Buddhist-Jew-Jesus-Freak.aspx#
Hawn, G. (2011, April 20). Interview by M. Schnall. Goldie Hawn talks "MindUP" and her mission to bring children happiness. *Huffington Post*. Retrieved from http://www.huffingtonpost.com/marianne-schnall/goldie-hawn-mindup_b_850226.html
Hawn, G. (2013, June 20). How mindfulness helps children thrive. *Heart-Mind 2013, The Dalai Lama Center for Peace-Education*. Retrieved from https://www.youtube.com/watch?v=7pLhwGLYvJU
Hawn, G., with Holden, W. (2005). *A lotus grows in the mud*. New York: Putnam.
Hawn Foundation (2011). *MindUP curriculum: Brain-focused strategies for learning—and living. Vol. 1: Pre-K–2*. New York: Scholastic.
Hawn Foundation. (2020a). About Us. Retrieved from https://mindup.org/about/
Hawn Foundation. (2020b). About Us. Retrieved from https://workforgood.co.uk/about/charities/view/the-goldie-hawn-foundation/
Hurlock, H. (2016, Feb. 11). Rainbows, sunshine, and unicorns: How right-wing Christians are attempting to bring down mindfulness programs in our public schools. *Mindful*. Retrieved from https://www.mindful.org/rainbows-sunshine-and-unicorns/
Jensen, F. (2015). A note from Fiona. Preface to Calmer Choice, *Instructor training manual: Pre-K through grade 2/3*. 2nd Draft.
Jensen, F. (2016, July 29). Facing pushback on mindfulness in schools. *Omega Institute*. Retrieved from https://www.eomega.org/node/17016
Jois Foundation [K. P. Jois USA Foundation, Inc.] (2011). *IRS Form 990-EZ*. Retrieved from http://pdfs.citizenaudit.org/2012_12_EO/45-3182571_990EZ_201112.pdf
Jois, K. P. (1995, June). Wisdom of the masters. *Yoga Journal*. Retrieved from https://web.archive.org/web/20181025045759/http://grimmly2007.blogspot.com/p/old-ashtanga-videos.html

Jois, K. P. (1999). *Yoga Mala* [English]. Maisuru, India: Astangayoganilaya; New York: Eddie Stern/Patanjali Yoga Shala. (Original work published 1962 [Kannada]).

Jois Yoga. (2013, September 15). Story. Retrieved from https://web.archive.org/web/20130915012245/http://joisyoga.com/about/story/

Kabat-Zinn, J. (1994a, September 29–October 2). Catalyzing movement towards a more contemplative / sacred-appreciating / non-dualistic society. *The Contemplative Mind in Society, The Nathan Cummings Foundation & Fetzer Institute*. Retrieved from http://www.contemplativemind.org/admin/wp-content/uploads/2012/09/kabat-zinn.pdf

Kabat-Zinn, J. (1994b). *Wherever you go, there you are: Mindfulness meditation in everyday life*. New York: Hyperion.

Kabat-Zinn, J. (2000). Indra's net at work: The mainstreaming of dharma practice in society. In G. Watson, S. Batchelor, & G. Claxton (Eds.), *The psychology of awakening: Buddhism, science, and our day-to-day lives* (pp. 225–249). York Beach, ME: Weiser.

Kabat-Zinn, J. (2003). Mindfulness-based interventions in context: Past, present, and future. *Clinical Psychology: Science and Practice 10*(2): 144–156.

Kabat-Zinn, J. (2010, October 7). Interview by D. Fisher. Mindfulness and the Cessation of Suffering. *Lion's Roar*. Retrieved from http://www.lionsroar.com/mindfulness-and-the-cessation-of-suffering-an-exclusive-new-interview-with-mindfulness-pioneer-jon-kabat-zinn/

Kabat-Zinn, J. (2011). Some reflections on the origins of MBSR, skillful means and the trouble with maps. *Contemporary Buddhism 12*(1), 281–306.

Kabat-Zinn, J. (2017). Too early to tell: The potential impact and challenges—ethical and otherwise—inherent in the mainstreaming of dharma in an increasingly dystopian world. *Mindfulness 8*, 1125–1135.

Kaivalya, A., & Kooij, A. van der. (2010). *Myths of the asanas: The stories at the heart of the yoga tradition*. San Rafael, CA: Mandala.

Khalsa, S. B. S., & Butzer, B. (2016). Yoga in school settings: A research review. *Annals of the New York Academy of Sciences 1373*, 45–55.

Kleiman, D. (1977, October 21). T. M. study barred in Jersey's schools. *New York Times*, A1, D13.

Klingbeil, D. A., Renshaw, T. L., Willenbrink, J., Copek, R. A., Chan, K. T., Haddock, A., Yassine, J., & Clifton, J. (2017). Mindfulness-based interventions with youth: A comprehensive meta-analysis of group-design studies. *Journal of Psychology 63*, 77–103.

Lal, N. (2016, April 4). The politics of yoga. *The Diplomat*. Retrieved from http://thediplomat.com/2016/04/the-politics-of-yoga/

Long, R. (2012). *Room to breathe*. San Francisco, CA: Video Project.

Lynch Foundation. (2010, October 4). Violence rate down 50% and grades up with TM in AZ school. Retrieved from https://www.youtube.com/watch?v=GUZRIX_SlHU

Maharishi Mahesh Yogi. [Maharshi Bala Brahmachari Mahesh Yogi Maharaj] (1955). *Beacon light of the Himalayas: The dawn of a happy new era in the field of spiritual practices; mind control, peace & atmananda through simple & easy methods of spiritual sadhana*. Ernakulam, Kerala, India: Adhyatmic Vikas Mandal.

Maharishi Mahesh Yogi. (1961). Amended articles of incorporation of the Spiritual Regeneration Movement Foundation. In *TM-EX Newsletter*, spring 1993. Retrieved from http://minet.org/Documents/srm-incorporation

Maharishi Mahesh Yogi. (1967). *On the Bhagavad-Gita: A new translation and commentary with Sanskrit text*. Baltimore, MD: Penguin.

Maharishi Mahesh Yogi. (1968a). *Meditations of Maharishi Mahesh Yogi*. New York: Bantam.

Maharishi Mahesh Yogi. (1968b). *Science of being and art of living: Transcendental Meditation* (Reprint). New York: New American Library. (Original work published 1963).
Maharishi Mahesh Yogi. (1975). *The science of creative intelligence for secondary education first-year course: Dawn of the first year of the age of enlightenment*. Bremen, West Germany: MIU Press.
Maharishi University of Management. (1973, summer). General Information. Quoted in *Minnesota Law Review*, Note, 924.
Maharishi University of Management (2020a). History. Retrieved from https://www.mum.edu/about-mum/inside-story/history/overview/
Maharishi University of Management (2020b). The university at a glance. Retrieved from https://www.mum.edu/university-at-a-glance
Malnak v. Yogi, 440 F. Supp. 1284 (D.N.J. 1977).
Malnak v. Yogi, 592 F.2d 197 (1979).
Masters, B. (2014). The (f)law of karma: In light of *Sedlock v. Baird*, would meditation classes in public schools survive a first amendment establishment clause challenge? *California Legal History* 9, 255–295.
McKenna, C. (2010, October 22). Interview by T. Meissner. Episode 35: Chris McKenna: The Mind Body Awareness Project. *Secular Buddhist Association*. Retrieved from https://web.archive.org/web/20180209093528/http://secularbuddhism.org/2010/10/22/episode-35-chris-mckenna-the-mind-body-awareness-project/
McKenna, C. (2014, spring). Interview by E. Varvaloucas. *Tricycle: The Buddhist Review*, pp. 20–21.
Medin, R. A., (2004, fall). 3 Gurus, 48 Questions: Matching interviews with Sri T. K. V. Desikachar, Sri B. K. S. Iyengar & Sri K. Pattabhi Jois. (D. Summerbell, Ed.). *Namarupa*, pp. 6–18.
Mendelson, T., Greenberg, M. T., Dariotis, J. K., Gould, L. F., Rhoades, B. L., & Leaf, P. J. (2010). Feasibility and preliminary outcomes of a school-based mindfulness intervention for urban youth. *Journal of Abnormal Child Psychology 38*, 985–994.
Meyer, J. S. (2013, July 1). Statement of Decision. In *Sedlock v. Baird* (2013).
Mindful Schools. (2020). Join our community. Retrieved from http://www.mindfulschools.org/
Mindfulness All-Party Parliamentary Group. (2015). *Mindful nation UK*. Retrieved from http://www.themindfulnessinitiative.org.uk/images/reports/Mindfulness-APPG-Report_Mindful-Nation-UK_Oct2015.pdf
Mindfulness in Schools Project [MiSP]. (2012). What is .b? Retrieved from https://holisticed.files.wordpress.com/2012/12/what-is-dotb-2012.pdf
Mindfulness in Schools Project [MiSP]. (2017a). Articles. Retrieved from https://web.archive.org/web/20170313205245/https://mindfulnessinschools.org/mindfulness/articles/
Mindfulness in Schools Project [MiSP]. (2017b). Book List. Retrieved from https://web.archive.org/web/20170314031246/http://mindfulnessinschools.org/mindfulness/book-list/
Minnesota Law Review. (1978). Note: Transcendental Meditation and the meaning of religion under the establishment clause. *Minnesota Law Review 62*(5), 887–948.
Mullen, R. J. (1991, spring). Mantras: Separating fact from fiction. *TM-EX Newsletter*. Retrieved from http://minet.org/Documents/TM-FAQ
Pair, M. W., ed. (1978). *Encyclopedia of associations* (12th ed., Vol. 1). Detroit: Gale.
Poll finds meditation, mysticism and yoga growing in popularity. (1976, November 18). *New York Times*, p. 24. Retrieved from http://www.nytimes.com/1976/11/18/archives/poll-finds-meditation-mysticism-and-yoga-growing-in-popularity.html

Pozneanscaia, C. (2019). *The effects of mindfulness-based interventions on functioning of children and youth with attention deficit hyperactivity disorder: A systematic literature review* (Master's thesis). Jönköping University.

Pure Edge [Stern, E., McDowell, C., Parker, M. J., Reich, C., & Verrochi, B.]. (2016). *POWER curriculum, Vols. 1 (Grades K–2), 2 (3–5), 3 (6–12)*. Palm Beach, FL: Pure Edge.

Ryan, T. (2012). *A mindful nation: How a simple practice can help us reduce stress, improve performance, and recapture the American spirit*. Carlsbad, CA: Hay House.

Saltzman, A. (2014). *A still quiet place: A mindfulness program for teaching children and adolescents to ease stress and difficult emotions*. Oakland, CA: New Harbinger.

Saylor, J. P. "Aid to Education Without Federal Interference: Extension of Remarks of Hon. John P. Saylor of Pennsylvania in the House of Representatives, August 1, 1963." In *Congressional Record: Proceedings and Debates of the 88th Congress*. First Session, Volume 109, Part 10. Washington D.C.: U.S. Government Printing Office, 1963.

Schonert-Reichl, K. A., Oberle, E., Lawlor, M. S., Abbott, D., Thomson, K., Oberlander, T. F., & Diamond, A. (2015). Enhancing cognitive and social-emotional development through a simple-to-administer mindfulness-based school program for elementary school children: A randomized controlled trial. *Developmental Psychology* 5(1), 52–66.

School District of Abington Township v. Schempp, 374 U.S. 203 (1963).

Sedlock v. Baird, Superior Court of San Diego County, No. 37-2013-00035910-CU-MC-CTL (2013).

Sedlock v. Baird, 235 Cal. App. 4th 874 (2015).

Shankman, R. (2015). *The art and skill of Buddhist meditation*. Oakland, CA: New Harbinger.

Shurtleff, N. B. (Ed.). (1853–1854). *Records of the Governor and Company of Massachusetts Bay, 1628–1686. Vol. 2, 1642–1649*. Boston: W. White.

Sibinga, E. M. S., Webb, L., Ghazarian, S. R., & Ellen, J. M. (2016). School-based mindfulness instruction: An RCT. *Pediatrics 137*(1), 1–8.

Siegel, A. (2020, June 24). Exclusive: Why did Chicago public schools just quietly drop Transcendental Meditation? *Religion Dispatches*. Retrieved from https://religiondispatches.org/exclusive-why-did-chicago-public-schools-just-quietly-drop-transcendental-meditation/

Simpson, D. (2017). From me to we: Revolutionising mindfulness in schools. *Contemporary Buddhism 18*(1), 47–71.

Sleeth, J. M., Jr. (2014, Sept. 11). Respondents' brief. In *Sedlock v. Baird* (2015).

Sonima Foundation [Sonima Health and Wellness Foundation, Inc.]. (2012). *IRS Form 990*, 2012. Retrieved from http://pdfs.citizenaudit.org/2013_12_EO/45-3182571_990_201212.pdf

Sonima Foundation. (2013). *IRS Form 990*, 2013. Retrieved from http://pdfs.citizenaudit.org/2014_12_EO/45-3182571_990_201413.pdf

Sonima Foundation. (2014). *IRS Form 990*. Retrieved from http://pdfs.citizenaudit.org/2015_12_EO/45-3182571_990_201412.pdf

Sonima Foundation. (2016). In the community. Retrieved from http://web.archive.org/web/20160918104335/http://www.sonimafoundation.org/community/

Stahl, B. (2015, February 28). MBSR underpinnings. CfM secure online teacher forum.

Stahl, B., & Goldstein, E. (2010). *A mindfulness-based stress reduction workbook*. Oakland, CA: New Harbinger.

Stierhoff, C. (2018). ACLJ challenges Buddhist meditation practices in public schools. Retrieved from https://aclj.org/religious-liberty/aclj-challenges-buddhist-meditation-practices-in-public-schools

Stanley, S. (2015). *Sīla* and *sati*: An exploration of ethics and mindfulness in Pāli Buddhism and their implications for secular mindfulness-based applications. In E. Shonin, W. V. Gordon, & N. N. Singh (Eds.), *Buddhist foundations of mindfulness* (pp. 89–113). Cham, Switzerland: Springer.

Street, N. (2007, July 25). Take a breath. *L.A. Times*. Retrieved from http://articles.latimes.com/2007/jul/25/opinion/oe-street25

Telles, S., Singh, N., Bhardwaj, A. K., Kumar, A., & Balkrishna, A. (2013). Effect of yoga or physical exercise on physical, cognitive and emotional measures in children: A randomized controlled trial. *Child and Adolescent Psychiatry and Mental Health 7*(37), 1–16.

Thoren, L. (2013, Aug. 16). Mother upset over school-wide meditation program. *KOAT 7 ABC Albuquerque*. Retrieved from http://www.koat.com/article/mother-upset-over-school-wide-meditation-program/5049790

TNN. (2015, Dec. 15). We can't force anyone to do yoga: Supreme Court. *The Times of India*. Retrieved from http://timesofindia.indiatimes.com/india/We-cant-force-anyone-to-do-yoga-Supreme-Court/articleshow/50179825.cms

Transcendental Meditation (2020). What's the evidence? Retrieved from https://www.tm.org/research-on-meditation

Varley, R. (2006, June 16). Meditation program challenged in Branford; Mom says plan to teach TM puts religion into classroom. *New Haven Register*. Retrieved from https://web.archive.org/web/20171222210757/https://www.highbeam.com/doc/1P2-12596731.html

Wang, D., & M. Hagins. (2016). Perceived benefits of yoga among urban school students: A qualitative analysis. *Evidence-Based Complementary and Alternative Medicine 2016*, Article 8725654.

Warsmith, S. (2013, April 15). Plain Township school stops "mindfulness" program after some in community raise concerns. *Akron Beacon Journal*. Retrieved from https://www.beaconjournal.com/article/20130414/NEWS/304149442

Weare, K. (2012, April). Evidence for the impact of mindfulness on children and young people. *The Mindfulness in Schools Project*. Retrieved from https://mindfulnessinschools.org/wp-content/uploads/2013/02/MiSP-Research-Summary-2012.pdf

Weaver, L. L., & Darragh, A. R. (2015). Systematic review of yoga interventions for anxiety reduction among children and adolescents. *American Journal of Occupational Therapy* 69(6), 1–7.

Wendt, S., Hipps, J., Abrams, A., Grant, J., Valosek, L., & Nidich, S. (2015). Practicing Transcendental Meditation in high schools: Relationship to well-being and academic achievement among students. *Contemporary School Psychology 19*(4), 312–319.

White, L. S. (2012). Reducing stress in school-age girls through mindful yoga. *Journal of Pediatric Health Care 26*(1), 45–56.

Williams, D. (2010). Interview. In G. Donahaye & E. Stern, *Guruji: A portrait of Sri K. Pattabhi Jois through the eyes of his students* (pp. 17–23). New York: North Point.

Williams, J. M. G., & Kabat-Zinn, J. (2011). Mindfulness: Diverse perspectives on its meaning, origins, and multiple applications at the intersection of science and dharma. *Contemporary Buddhism 12*(1), 1–18.

Wilson, J. (2014). *Mindful America: Meditation and the mutual transformation of Buddhism and American culture*. New York: Oxford University Press.

Wohlsen, M. (2006, October 19). Calif. school site of meditation flap. *Fox News*. Retrieved from http://www.foxnews.com/printer_friendly_wires/2006Oct19/0,4675,MeditationConfrontation,00.html

Woodruffe, S. J. (2008). *The garland of letters* (varnamala)*: Studies in the mantra-sastra* (Reprint). Leeds: Celephais. (Original work published 1922).
Wylie, M. S. (2015). The Mindfulness explosion. *Psychotherapy Networker* 39(1), 19–45.
Xia, T., Hu, H., Seritan, A. L., & Eisendrath, S. (2019). The many roads to mindfulness: A Review of nonmindfulness-based interventions that increase mindfulness. *The Journal of Alternative and Complementary Medicine*, 25(9), 874–889.
Yoga Ed. (2020). Celebrating 20 years. Retrieved from https://yogaed.com/20-year-anniversary
Zenner, C., Hernleben-Kurz, S., & Walach, H. (2014). Mindfulness-based interventions in schools—a systematic review and meta-analysis. *Frontiers in Psychology* 5, Article 603.

CHAPTER 37

MEDITATION IN PRISON

KATHERINE M. AUTY

Introduction

The potential for meditation to help individuals deal with the negative effects of incarceration has been known for some time. A recent meta-analysis found that across a range of outcomes, mindfulness-based initiatives yielded the largest effects for reducing levels of stress and depression (Per, Spinelli, Sadowski, Schmelefske, Anand, & Khoury, 2020). More specifically, the part that meditation can play on a prisoner's pathway toward rehabilitation is of particular interest. Similarities between meditation and desistence from crime are tantalizing; both involve changes to behavior and identity, together with attempts to re-establish oneself among others in a (moral) community (see McNeill & Schinkel, 2016; Settle, Zephaniah, & Morgan, 2017). Yet, so far, this potential has for the most part not been realized.

Official reoffending figures for both England and Wales and the United States are worryingly high. The most recent figures for England and Wales show that rates of proven reoffending within a year of release for adult offenders to be 28.0 percent. For juvenile offenders, this figure is 39.2 percent. (Ministry of Justice, 2020). Figures from the United States tell us that about two-thirds (67.8 percent) of released prisoners were arrested for a new crime within three years (Bureau of Justice Statistics, 2014). These figures strongly suggest that the prison regimes in these two countries are not enabling individuals to lead a crime-free life upon release.

The increasing popularity of mindfulness meditation in criminal justice settings (Black, 2014; Murray, Amann, & Thom, 2018) is justified by various factors. Criminal justice systems in most Western countries are under intensive pressure to reduce budgets, and mindfulness meditation programs have proven attractive in that respect. The upsurge of interest in meditation programs in prison mirrors the growing interest in contemplative practices in society more generally. Furthermore, there is a growing awareness that traditional therapies, such as cognitive behavioral therapy (CBT) may not be as effective as was once thought (Johnsen & Friborg, 2015). Mindfulness programs are rapidly becoming a credible and evidence-based alternative to psychotherapeutic groups, and mindfulness meditation's focus on the present moment means the group is often experienced by participants as less intrusive (Baker, Young, & Wolfe, 2016). Determining the benefits of prison meditation programs is extremely important, yet as Weisburd et al. (2017) point out, program effectiveness is only one of several important concerns when commissioning rehabilitative interventions for prisoners: "Issues of fairness, equity, and public support for the legitimacy of criminal justice must be key concerns in assessing programs and practices" (Weisburd et al., 2017, p. 437).

Until recently, evidence for the positive effects of meditation programs for incarcerated populations was largely anecdotal. It was thought that contemplative programs might appeal to those who did not wish to engage with standard programs, such as cognitive behavioral therapy programs, life skills programs, or vocational work training programs. Research into prison meditation programs has been gathering pace recently mainly due to the increased understanding of *what* prison meditation programs consist of and *how* they might be able to exert a positive influence on incarcerated populations. As this review will show, prison meditation programs often contain elements from more conventional correctional programs, such as substance abuse, psychosocial, or behavioral (e.g., cognitive behavioral) programs. They also often are targeted at specific populations, such as those with mental health problems.

A recent systematic review and meta-analysis of prison yoga and meditation programs (Auty, Cope, & Liebling, 2017) found significant overlap in the use of yoga and meditation in prisons; five of the studies focused primarily on yoga, eighteen focused on meditation (of which, fourteen were Vipassana programs), and five were considered a combination of yoga and meditation. The meta-analysis also found that participants experienced small increases in their psychological well-being and small improvements to their behavioral functioning, for example, their substance misuse, impulse control, executive function, attentional capacity, and their behavioral response inhibition. The review also found that less intensive programs of longer duration had a statistically significant larger effect on the behavioral functioning of prisoners, when compared to the shorter, more intense ones. This difference in effects was also observed for prisoners' psychological well-being but was not found to be statistically significant. Several recent narrative reviews of meditation programs (Fix & Fix, 2013; Himelstein, 2011a; Lyons & Cantrell, 2015; Shonin, Van Gordon, Slade, & Griffiths, 2013) have also identified that the benefits of meditation programs for participants' psychological well-being are complex and only now starting to become more widely understood. It is thought that these programs may be particularly helpful for those with substance misuse problems (Himelstein, 2011b) and may even contribute to reducing reoffending by increasing the chances that offenders will engage positively with other rehabilitation programs (Himelstein, 2011a).

This chapter will explore the current evidence for the benefits of meditation programs for incarcerated populations in three main areas, psychological well-being, substance misuse, and reoffending, with an emphasis on the theoretical mechanisms that may help explain meditation's positive effects in each of these three areas. Priority will be given to studies that employ a high-quality study design. The University of Maryland's Scientific Methods Scale (Farrington, Gottfredson, Sherman, & Welsh, 2002; Sherman, Gottfredson, Mackenzie, Eck, Reuter, & Bushway, 1998) classifies evaluative studies according to five levels from 1 = weakest to 5 = highest level of overall internal validity, according to the following: (1) correlational evidence; (2) no statistical control for selection bias, but some kind of comparison; (3) moderate statistical control; (4) strong statistical control; and (5) randomized experiment (summarized in Welsh & Farrington, 2001). Priority was given to studies rated as equivalent to level three or higher. So, as a minimum, all studies compared the meditation program to a control group, including pre-post and experimental-control comparisons. Promising findings from studies that do not meet these criteria are included where appropriate.

Meditation in the Prison Context

The acceptance and flourishing of prison meditation programs within a prison context has challenged many people's understanding of what the *purpose* of prison is and who prisoners *are*. Some aspects of meditation dovetail with prison experiences, yet others are dramatically at odds with the reality of the day-to-day running of a large institution. Upon first glance, the austere surroundings of a Zen Buddhist monastery may be in keeping with the austere surroundings of prison, yet prisoners are incarcerated against their will and often experience Feelings of guilt and shame over their offences and experiences. Some ex-prisoners who have become meditators have written about how prisons are inherently inhospitable environments to practice meditation in (Maull, 2005).

Prisoners "import" many health-related burdens that make the experience of imprisonment all the more difficult. Prisoners report higher levels of premorbid stress and increased exposure to trauma and violence prior to their incarceration (Gibson, Holt, Fondacaro, Tang, Powell, & Turbitt, 1999; Teplin, 1994). Compared with general population samples from the United States or United Kingdom, prisoners are between two and four times more likely to have a psychotic illness or major depression, and about ten times more likely to have antisocial personality disorder (Fazel & Danesh, 2002). American male prisoners have slightly higher levels of alcohol dependence but are between two and ten times more likely to have drug dependence. Female prisoners are between two and four times more likely to be alcohol dependent and thirteen times more likely to be drug dependent when compared to a general population sample (Fazel, Bains, & Doll, 2006). Rates of infectious diseases, such as HIV, also far exceed those in the general population (see Fazel & Baillargeon, 2011).

There are also several environmental factors particular to prisons that make the practice of meditation challenging in this context. The physical environment of prisons are challenging as they are frequently noisy and often overcrowded and short on quiet spaces appropriate for meditation. Prison meditation programs may struggle to find a place within the roster of prison programming, with their emphasis on measurable outcomes, standardization, and linear approach to progress. It can also happen that meditation programs in prison are considered as too "alternative" or "novel" and incompatible with the identities and expectations of prisoners. This could become compounded by prisoner and staff aversion to change or differences in their daily routines. Last but not least, there are the challenges of coming to terms with one's crime, restricted and infrequent contact with loved ones, and the sense of a loss of agency associated with having to unwillingly give up control over one's day-to-day needs to prison officers and the prison bureaucracy system, which can be frustratingly slow.

Brief History of Meditation in Prison

Prison meditation programs have become increasingly established in recent decades. The prison meditation movement began in the late 1960s, when volunteers began supporting prisoners who were interested in various forms of meditation. Since then, they have continued doing this in two main ways: first, meditation practitioners provide courses on meditation inside prison; and second, they enter into written correspondence with meditators in prison and provide information in the form of books and pamphlets.

In the 1970s two organizations, the Prison-Ashram Project and the SYDA Foundation, started offering meditation and yoga programs to prisoners in the United States. The movement has not always met with acceptance from prison authorities, and in some instances, prison authorities prohibited practices such as Buddhism. This led to a landmark 1972 Supreme Court decision (*Cruz v. Beto*)[1] affirming that a Texan prisoner called Fred Arispe Cruz had his religious rights violated when he was placed in solitary confinement for sharing his Buddhist materials with other prisoners.

As time went on, other groups and organizations started offering meditation programs to prisoners. The 1980s also saw the publication of the influential book, *We're All Doing Time* by Bo Lozoff (1985), co-founder of the Prison-Ashram Project and Human Kindness Foundation. This book, which has been sent to 300,000 prisoners, so far, offers practical guidance and teachings on mediation. It also included some excerpts from the many letters from prisoners that Bo and co-founder Sita Lozoff had received over the years. Prison meditation programs continued to expand throughout the 1980s in number and variety. This decade saw the establishment of a program of Transcendental Meditation (TM) classes at high-security prisons in California and Massachusetts. Zen meditation classes were held in New York State prisons from 1984 onward, and a Buddhist prisoner called Fleet Maull formed the Prison Dharma Network in 1989, which evolved to include other contemplative traditions (Christian Centering Prayer, yoga, TM, and others) in its work with prisoners.

[1] Cruz v. Beto, 405 U.S. 319 (1972).

The 1990s saw further expansion and collaboration between prison meditation pioneers. Jacques Verdun created the Insight Prison Project to deliver mindfulness meditation at the infamous San Quentin, a maximum-security prison in California. He also established the Prison Mindfulness Initiative with James Fox (director of the Prison Yoga Project), which formed a network of volunteers to deliver meditation and yoga programs in prisons across California. From 1997, prisons in Washington and Alabama have hosted ten-day Vipassana meditation retreats, which are offered by the Vipassana Prison Trust.

Mindfulness-based stress reduction (MBSR) has been offered in juvenile facilities in San Francisco and New York State since the late 1990s. From 2000 onward, many smaller organizations combined forces to create more effective organizations, such as the Mind Body Awareness project in California, and the Prison Mindfulness Institute.

Today there are hundreds of organizations or projects spread across most US states providing meditation in prison, either on their own or as an adjunct to a rehabilitation program. Prison authorities in England and Wales are increasingly recognizing the potential of meditation to enhance prisoner well-being through experiential accounts, despite there being (until quite recently) a paucity of evidence for its effectiveness. A notable example of the willingness of prison authorities to work with outside organizations is the Prison Phoenix Trust (PPT) in the England and Wales, which was established in the late 1980s by Ann Weatherall. The PPT has a similar model to many US organizations. It offers weekly yoga classes in over eighty prisons throughout England and Wales. The PPT also have a team of letter writers who correspond with prisoners, offering guidance and support. For more information on the history of prison meditation movements, please see Lyons and Cantrell (2015), and for a global history of Vipassana meditation, please see Vipassana Research Institute (2016).

Types of Meditation

There are three main styles of mediation that the research has primarily focused on: Transcendental Meditation (TM), mindfulness-based stress reduction (MBSR), and Vipassana retreats.

Transcendental Meditation

Transcendental Meditation is defined as a "wakeful condition of alertness... [and] a restful physiological condition" (Ferguson & Gowan, 1976, p. 53). Practitioners of TM recite a given mantra, which they return to when their mind wanders. They aim to practice twice a day for about fifteen to twenty minutes (Himelstein, 2011a). The goal of TM is for the individual to allow the mind to experience the finer levels of the thinking process until the mind transcends and experiences the least excited state of human awareness (Roth, 1994). It was popularized in Western countries by Maharishi Mahesh Yogi in the 1960s and remains one of the most widely researched forms of meditation (Himelstein, 2011a). The TM programs are advantageous given that they have a standardized and reproducible format and curriculum, the instructors are thoroughly certified and widely available, and thus TM provides an established research base in the area of mental health (Nidich, Seng, Compton, O'Connor, Salerno, & Nidich, 2017).

Mindfulness-Based Stress Reduction (MBSR)

Mindfulness is a multi-faceted concept that many have noted is not easy to define (Block-Lerner, Salters-Pednault, & Tull, 2005; Brown & Ryan, 2003). Often mindfulness is taken to mean the mental capacity for being present and aware of one's moment-to-moment thoughts. Mindfulness is also thought to be an inherent human characteristic that everyone possesses to a greater or lesser extent (Kabat-Zinn, 2003), even if they have never practiced mindfulness and have no understanding of the term. Mindfulness meditation aims not to alter a person's thoughts, but rather to facilitate the development of a non-judgmental approach to thoughts as they occur (Teasdale, Segal, & Williams, 1995). "At its core, mindfulness promotes present awareness, acceptance of experience, a quiet mind, and non-judgement" (Malouf, Youman, Stuewig, Witt, & Tangney, 2017, p. 603). In this respect, mindfulness has something in common with several other therapeutic approaches such as dialectical behavior therapy (Linehan, 1993a) and acceptance and commitment therapy (Hayes, Strosahl, & Wilson, 1999).

The principles of mindfulness have been distilled and embedded within a series of innovative and structured programs. Most notably, mindfulness-based stress reduction (MBSR) was developed by Jon Kabat-Zinn in 1979 with the intention of making meditation techniques accessible for a Western audience who may not be seeking any spiritual elements. MBSR comprises three elements: awareness of breathing whilst meditating in the seated position, the body scan whilst lying down, and Hatha yoga postures (Kabat-Zinn & Hanh, 2013). The teaching content of the classes follow a standardized format, reproduced in a manual, led by a teacher, and guided by audio recordings. The classes are typically held over six to eight weeks.

There are two further adaptations that are of note: first, mindfulness-based relapse prevention (MBRP), which was adapted from MBSR by Alan Marlatt and colleagues to treat substance misuse disorders (Bowen, Chawla, & Marlatt, 2010); and second, mindfulness-based cognitive therapy (MBCT; Segal, Williams, & Teasdale, 2002) that was also developed from MBSR to prevent the reoccurrence of depression.

Vipassana Meditation

Vipassana courses are usually offered in a standardized ten-day program. The style of Vipassana meditation most frequently practiced in prison is that of S. N. Goenka (1995).

All participants are required to observe five moral principles: refrain from violence, lying, stealing, sexual misconduct, and drugs and alcohol (as would be expected in any prison regime). Participants are also required to maintain a silence for the duration of the course. They typically spend ten hours a day meditating and watching instructive videos in a quiet group room away from any potential distractions coming from the main prison (for more details see chapter by Sara Rahmani in this volume). Research into the effects of Vipassana meditation retreats in prison has been growing in recent years (Bowen et al., 2006; Chandiramani, Verma, & Dhar, 1995; Simpson et al., 2007).

Effects on Mental Health and Psychological Well-Being

Research into meditation in prison suggests that it can improve a number of psychosocial functions (Chandiramani et al., 1995; Samuelson, Carmody, Kabat-Zinn, & Bratt, 2007). In clinical and forensic samples, evidence is gathering that suggest that meditation programs can assist in reducing depression and anxiety (Banerjee et al., 2007; Michalsen et al., 2005) and improve emotional well-being (Moadel et al., 2007). Prison-based studies have shown that meditation can lower stress (Bilderbeck, Farias, Brazil, Jakobowitz, & Wikholm, 2013) and increase levels of sustained attention (Rangan, Nagendra, & Bhatt, 2009).

Orme-Johnson and Moore (2003) report findings from the first study of TM in prison, which took place in 1971. In La Tuna Federal Penitentiary, El Paso, Texas, they examined the effects of TM on seventeen inmates (twelve participated in the TM program and five served as controls). The prisoners were participating in the Narcotics Rehabilitation Act program. The TM participants were instructed through a four-day course and upon completion they were required to practice TM for twenty minutes twice a day. Only five of the twelve meditators had meditated regularly (at least sixty out of a possible 120 sessions). However, the TM participants showed increased stability of the autonomic nervous system, compared to controls, as indicated by fewer spontaneous skin resistance responses (SSRR), which measures a person's "fight or flight" response, whereby the body prepares itself for the exertion needed to deal with a perceived threat by increasing sweat activity to cool itself. The five that had meditated regularly were found to have even greater reductions on the SSRR test. The Minnesota Multiphasic Personality Inventory (MMPI) was administered to both the program and the control group before the trial and two months later. The MMPI results revealed that the TM group had reduced rigidity, obsessive thoughts, and compulsive behavior.

Nidich et al. (2016) were the first to evaluate the effects of TM on the trauma symptoms of prisoners (anxiety, depression, dissociation, sleep disturbance, and stress) in two male Oregon correctional facilities. They conducted a randomized controlled trial (RCT) whereby seventy-three prisoners were randomized to the TM program and seventy-one to a control group. The TM group participated in a standardized course of five sessions lasting approximately an hour each. After that, they were requested to practice on their own for twenty minutes twice a day. Optional follow-up sessions were also offered. Both groups were assessed at baseline and then four months post-test using a modified Trauma Symptom Checklist (TSC; Briere, 1996), which includes the subscales of dissociation, depression, anxiety, and sleep problems plus the ten-item Perceived Stress Scale (PSS; Cohen, Karmack, & Mermelstein, 1983), which assesses the self-perception of stress. The results revealed significant reductions in total trauma symptoms and each of the subscales of the TSC and in the PSS for the TM group, when comparing them to the controls. Their results also indicated that TM may be particularly suitable for those with high levels of trauma. When explaining their results, the authors refer to previous studies that indicate that practicing TM decreases hyperarousal of the sympathetic nervous system and hypothalamic-pituitary-adrenal axis. This is the "fight-or-flight" set of responses (increased levels of alertness and anxiety and elevated heart rate and respiration), which are classic aspects of post-traumatic stress disorder (PTSD) symptomatology. Nidich et al. (2017) replicated many of the features of the previous trial, this time with a sample of female prisoners. Ten prisoners were randomized to the TM group and ten served as controls. The Post-traumatic Stress Disorder Checklist—Civilian version (PCL-C; Ruggiero, Ben, Scotti, & Rabalais, 2003) includes the subscales of intrusions, avoidance, and hyperarousal. At baseline, most of the women in the sample had clinically significant symptoms of post-traumatic stress. The PCL-C was administered four months later, revealing that those practicing TM had significantly reduced total trauma symptoms, compared to the control group, particularly for the intrusions subscale and the hyperarousal subscale.

Samuelson et al. (2007) report on a large study of 113 MBSR courses involving 1,953 male and female adult prisoners in six Massachusetts correctional facilities that ran between 1992 and 1996. Each weekly session had between twelve and twenty participants; 75 percent were male and all had substance misuse problems. Sixty-nine percent of the participants completed the course (n = 1,350), which lasted between one and one and a half hours and ran for six to eight weeks. The study also had a wait-list control group (n = 180), who attended other programs such as education and exercise. They looked at hostility, self-esteem, and mood disturbance for those who attended the MBSR program. They found changes in the participants' score on the Cook and Medley Hostility Scale (Barefoot, Dodge, Peterson, Dahlstrom, & Williams, 1989), suggesting that participants had reduced hostility. Changes in the Rosenberg Self-Esteem Scale scores (Rosenberg, 1979) showed improvements in self-esteem. Finally, participants had lower scores on the Profile of Mood States (McNair, Lorr, & Droppleman, 1992), showing a reduction in mood disturbance. Notably, the percentage reduction in each of the three outcomes was greatest for the female participants.

Similar improvements in psychological well-being have been observed for incarcerated adolescents by Himelstein, Hastings, Shapiro, and Heery (2012). In a much smaller study, thirty-two participants completed a ten-week mindfulness program. The course was based on the Mind Body Awareness project's mindfulness course, but due to institutional limitations, the course had to be adapted. Each class lasted one hour and included group discussions as well as sitting meditation. Participants were encouraged to practice what they had learned between the classes. They completed self-report questionnaires before and after the course revealing significant decreases in perceived stress, as captured using the Perceived Stress Scale (PSS; Cohen et al., 1983) and a significant increase in healthy self-regulation, as captured using the Healthy Self-Regulation Scale (West, 2008). Despite these findings, they found no significant differences in self-reported mindfulness (as captured using the Mindfulness Attention Awareness Scale, Brown & Ryan, 2003). The authors attributed this to the lack of mindfulness training between the classes or that the curriculum did not cover mindfulness in sufficient detail. However, the study's lack of a control group prevents a real test of the effect of the program on participants, and if differences were detected in their psychometric evaluations, they would be unable to disentangle the effects of the meditation from the effects of the group discussions.

Another study investigated whether a combination of cognitive behavioral therapy and mindfulness training (CBT/MT) would have an impact on the attention task performance of a sample of incarcerated adolescents (aged 16–18; Leonard et al., 2013). Attention is one aspect of the cognitive system necessary for regulating emotions and managing stress, and attention deficits are associated with the development of antisocial behavior in young people (Teplin, Abram, McClelland, Dulcan, & Mericle, 2002). Each dormitory in the prison was randomized to a cognitive-perception intervention or to Power Source (Casarjian & Casarjian, 2003), a group-based program which blends "the social/cognitive change components of CBT with the attentional and response modification elements of mindfulness meditation" (Leonard et al., 2013, p. 3). Using small groups, participants were encouraged to develop a repertoire of behaviors that enabled them to avoid risky behavior in various circumstances. Researchers expected that the mindfulness meditation practice would allow prisoners to reappraise stressful situations by encouraging them to focus on more neutral stimuli, and as a consequence of this stress reduction to increase their prosocial behavioral response. One-hundred and forty-seven male prisoners who participated in the program and 117 who received an evidence-based cognitive-perception intervention (focusing on attitudes and beliefs about substance use and violence) were assessed using the Attention Network Test (a computerized test where participants are asked to press the right or left arrow key in response to a target coming toward them in the computer screen) at baseline and four months later. The results revealed that test performance declined over time for participants in both groups; however, this was less so in the Power Source group. Within this group, performance declined for those who did not practice mindfulness exercises independently outside the structured sessions, but remained stable for those that did. The authors tentatively suggest that the combined cognitive-mindfulness program may have a protective effect on the functional attentional impairments of incarcerated youth, yet concede that motivation levels may have varied between the two groups due to the differing content of the two programs. When speculating as to the mechanisms responsible for their findings, they highlight the importance of the development of metacognitive skills[2] during the reflective elements of the sessions, which could be encouraging participants to re-evaluate their response to stressful situations, as the researchers had anticipated. It is also important to note that the effect could be due primarily, or in part, to the cognitive-behavioral component of the program.

A study by Perelman, Miller, Clements, Rodriguez, Allen, and Cavanaugh (2012) attempted to measure the underlying changes that meditation can produce in a maximum-security prison in Alabama. Vipassana retreats were held for three cohorts of sixty prisoners each. These courses all followed a ten-day intensive program of meditation for around ten hours a day. The course engaged participants in a "strict schedule" during which they must refrain from communicating for the first nine days, encouraging a state of deep reflection. A one-year follow-up found that participants on the Vipassana course had improved levels of mindfulness and emotional intelligence. Further studies of Vipassana courses have found reductions in anxiety and depression, and short-term increases in hopefulness (Chandiramani et al., 1995), as well as improvements on subjective well-being measures (Khurana & Dhar, 2002). However, these two studies were weaker methodologically in that they lacked a control group, and therefore their findings should be interpreted with caution.

There are very few studies on the effects of mindfulness training on prisoners in non-Western countries. One exception is a study by Xu, Jia, Liu, and Hofmann (2016) where they examined the potential benefits to emotional health a six-week mindfulness training program. The sample comprised nineteen long-term prisoners in China (twenty-one prisoners formed a wait-list control group). The training emphasized present-focused and non-judgmental awareness and was adapted to the prison context; lack of privacy meant that group mindfulness sessions replaced individual practice. The program was based on MBCT and also incorporated elements of MBSR. Weekly sessions lasting between two and a half and three hours included a body scan, sitting and walking meditation, yoga, and group discussions. The results showed that after the course was completed, those in the mindfulness training group had improved mindfulness (as measured using the Five-Facet Mindfulness Questionnaire, Deng, Liu, Rodriguez, & Xia, 2011), less anxiety, depression, tension anxiety, depression-dejection, anger-hostility, confusion-bewilderment, and total mood disturbance. The authors conclude that mindfulness training has the potential to enhance emotional health through two mechanisms: by helping to be less sensitive to emotional distress, and by decreasing fatigue or increasing energy levels.

These studies demonstrate that meditation has great potential for enhancing the mental health and psychological well-being of prisoners, including males, females, and juveniles. Positive benefits have been demonstrated in a wide variety of settings and using many different research tools. Perhaps the most notable finding is the positive effect that meditation appears to have on stress levels; this finding has been replicated in several studies.

[2] Knowledge about when and how to use particular strategies for learning or problem solving, e.g., evaluating your progress toward completing a task and then modifying your approach as necessary.

Effects on Substance Misuse

Substance misuse is a pervasive and persistent problem for incarcerated populations and one of the most active areas of research on the potential effectiveness of meditation.

A pilot RCT of a mindfulness-based intervention called REVAMP (Re-Entry Values and Mindfulness Program) was conducted that aimed to reduce post-release risky behavior by targeting the non-judgmental and willingness/acceptance dimension of mindfulness, as well as emotion regulation and self-control (Malouf et al., 2017). Prisoners who were nearing release were randomized to the REVAMP group (n = 21) or a control group (treatment as usual n = 19). REVAMP is a group intervention for prisoners nearing the end of their sentence. It combines elements from several mindfulness-based interventions, such as acceptance and commitment therapy (Hayes, Luoma, Bond, Masuda, & Lillis, 2006), mindfulness-based relapse prevention (MBRP; Bowen, Chawla, & Marlatt, 2010), and dialectical behavioral therapy (Linehan, 1993b). The authors found that although REVAMP participants reported less substance misuse post-release, this was not found to be statistically significant.

Some more promising results were found in a small-scale RCT in Taiwan (Lee, Bowen, & An-Fu, 2011). This study tested the efficacy of MBRP in a sample of ten male prisoners serving short sentences for drug offences (fourteen prisoners were in a "treatment as usual" [TAU] control group). The MBRP was delivered over ten weekly sessions, each lasting 1.5 hours. After completing the program, the MBRP group had significantly less positive attitudes to substance use (as captured by the Drug Use Identification Disorders Test—extended (DUDIT-E; Berman, Palmstierna, Kallmen, & Bergman, 2007), compared to the TAU group. The MBRP group experienced significantly less depressive symptoms (as captured by the Beck Depression Inventory [BDI]; Beck, Steer, & Brown, 1996), and improved drug refusal self-efficacy (as captured using the Drugs Avoidance Self-Efficacy Scale (Martin, Wilkinson, & Poulos, 1995). These modest findings should be interpreted with caution. The study seems to suggest that MBRP are appropriate for this Taiwanese population, yet there were questions as to whether the research instruments were culturally appropriate, as it is possible that some of the constructs in their study (e.g., depression) are culturally invariant. Taken together with the small sample size, this makes the generalizability of the findings somewhat questionable.

Bowen and colleagues (Bowen et al., 2006; Bowen, Witkiewitz, Dillworth, & Marlatt, 2007) have completed a series of studies that illustrate the effects of Vipassana meditation on substance misuse in a minimum-security adult jail in Seattle, housing males and females. In the first study (Bowen et al., 2006), 173 participants completed a post-course assessment (79 percent were male) three months post-release. There was a sizeable attrition rate, but eighty-seven participants remained in the study. They found that Vipassana group participants reported significantly lower alcohol, crack cocaine, and marijuana use three months after their release from prison. In a follow-up study at the same institution, using another ten-day Vipassana course, Sarah Bowen et al. (2007) found that after the course participants reported significant decreases in thought avoidance, but not intrusive thoughts (as measured by the White Bear Suppression Inventory, Wegner & Zanakos, 1994).

The findings from studies that show the potential for meditation to have positive benefits on substance misuse are particularly tantalizing, as it appears that meditation may be able to have a lasting effect on prisoners' lives "through-the-gate." Studies that have not followed-up prisoners post-release have been able to show that meditation has the potential to alter attitudes toward substance misuse. It remains to be shown that reducing pro–substance misuse attitudes is related to a lower likelihood of substance misuse upon release.

Effects on Criminogenic Cognitions and Reoffending Behavior

Those that have participated in prison meditation programs have been shown to have lower rates of reoffending, compared to non-participants. Bleick and Abrams (1987) conducted a study of 259 inmates that had participated in a TM program and had then been released from three Californian prisons (two were maximum and one was high-medium security). They compared their reoffending rates to that of a matched control group. Over a five-year period, the TM participants' rates of reincarceration and long sentences were on average 43 percent lower than the controls. Rainforth, Alexander, and Cavanaugh (2003) repeated Bleick and Abrams (1987) study by following-up the men who had been released from Folsom Prison fifteen years later. They found that for those in the TM group, 46.7 percent had received a conviction for a felony, compared to 66.7 percent of the controls. Their models also suggested that the risk of reoffending for the TM group had decreased by 43.5 percent. In both of these studies, the control group was matched on the ethnicity and seriousness of offence. Their models also take into account a number of sociodemographic variables that would also be related to reoffending.

Some have questioned how mindfulness might be related to criminogenic cognitions (antisocial attitudes that are thought to reinforce and predict involvement with the criminal justice system) and whether it has the potential to reduce recidivism. Tangney, Dobbins, Stuewig, and Schrader (2017) asked a sample of 259 male jail inmates to complete a forty-five-item self-report mindfulness assessment (Harty et al., 2009), which captures six core components of mindfulness—present awareness, metacognition, quiet mind, willingness/acceptance, non-judgment of self, non-judgment of others—and three proximal dimensions that are theoretical outcomes of mindfulness: distress tolerance; (lack of) experiential avoidance; and (lack of) emotion-driven impulsivity. Inmates also completed the twenty-five-item Criminal Cognitions Scale (Tangney et al., 2012), which covers five dimensions: notions of entitlement, failure to accept responsibility, short-term orientation, insensitivity to the impact of crime, and negative attitudes toward authority. They found that individuals higher in the core components of mindfulness were less likely to rationalize, excuse, or justify their criminal behavior. Next they examined whether inmates' emotional regulation mediated the relationship between mindfulness and criminogenic cognitions. When they included emotional regulation in the model they found that there was a *positive* direct link between mindfulness and criminogenic cognitions, suggesting that those higher in mindfulness also show more criminogenic thinking. They discovered that it was the non-judgment of self (defined as an overall acceptance of oneself; not criticizing one's own thoughts and actions) component that was largely responsible for this finding and concluded that some self-judgment may actually be beneficial when engaging with treatment for incarcerated populations.

In the REVAMP study mentioned above (Malouf et al., 2017), they found that three months after the program was completed the REVAMP group showed statistically significant lower scores on the measure of non-judgment of self, when compared to the TAU group. Scores on willingness/acceptance were approaching statistical significance. Increases in scores for shame in the REVAMP group were also observed. Arrests were examined for both groups in the three years following release. The mean arrest rate for the TAU group was almost twice that of the REVAMP group and the TAU group also reoffended sooner, though both of these differences did not quite reach statistical significance. It is likely that the small sample size made it difficult to detect statistically significant results, yet one of the study's main strengths is its randomization; participants did not self-select into either treatment or control group.

The increases in self-judgment and shame for the REVAMP group seem contrary to the intention of mindfulness to stress non-judgment and self-compassion. The authors explain that "this may be the natural ramification of increased willingness/acceptance in a population facing difficult, typically self-imposed circumstances... For REVAMP participants, enhanced willingness/acceptance may have allowed them to overcome this defensiveness in order to openly reflect on past behavior and take a good hard (somewhat negative) look at the self" (Malouf et al., 2017, pp. 611–612). The authors reflect on these somewhat surprising findings, saying that this may be an example of how increases in willingness/acceptance might be used adaptively, to face one's own shortcomings, rather than avoidance, denial, or blaming others. They propose that REVAMP may increase an individual's tolerance for uncomfortable or unpleasant emotions, such as shame and self-judgment, which are likely to be part of an individual's rehabilitation journey. The findings from this study really highlight the complex pathways out of crime.

The results from the two early studies of reoffending rates (Bleick & Abrams, 1987; Rainforth et al., 2003) appear to offer very promising findings for those that attend TM groups. The more recent studies are employing more complex measures to capture the criminogenic thinking of those attending meditation programs and are uncovering some of the mechanisms that may go some way to explain how meditation can help rehabilitate prisoners.

CONCLUSIONS

The variety of studies on meditation in prison has captured the imagination of researchers and practitioners alike. In this chapter I have either focused on the studies with the most rigorous methodological approaches or with the most insightful findings, but this does not encompass many other studies that are less rigorous, yet show the level of enthusiasm and commitment in this area of research.

Prison meditation programs have the potential to offer something unique that distinguishes them from standard prison programs: the chance to take their meditation practice with them "through the gate" when they leave prison; they are much less stigmatizing than other programs as meditation is taught to prisoners in the same way it is taught to any other group of individuals. Meditation's growing popularity in society means that it is increasingly likely that those leaving prison and wishing to continue their practice will find support to carry on this practice.

It is important to bear in mind that some have questioned the underlying ideology of secular meditation practices, arguing that although they might enable individuals to "cope," far more radical changes are required in our unjust society (Purser, 2019). The commercial aspects of the mindfulness movement certainly sometimes seem at odds with the origins of the movement, and although a derivative of Buddhism, much of this is stripped away as it is packaged for a secular audience. Meditation has also been criticized for failing to acknowledge that personal ills (e.g., stress and anxiety) also have societal causes, and this point is especially relevant for (ex-)prisoners, who suffer disproportionate levels of societal disadvantage before, during, and after their sentences (Armour, 2012; Gover, Mackenzie, & Armstrong, 2000).

Prison can be a stressful and dehumanizing place for staff as well as prisoners, and meditation programs should be offered not only to prisoners but to prison staff as well. Currently there are no studies that include staff in their analytical sample. This is a great oversight, and future studies should aim to fill this gap. It would also be interesting to conduct a "through the gates" study to find out how many prison meditators continue their practice when they leave custody. This would also provide us with further information of what the long-term effects of prison meditation might be.

Research on prison meditation programs suffer from the same issues of many intervention programs that take place in prison, that of the lack of sufficient evaluative studies. Future studies can benefit from the knowledge gained so far by employing robust designs and avoiding the pitfalls that have beset researchers in this area so far. I outline the main ones identified in this review below.

Many studies have issues with "unknown" TAU conditions; "Future RCTs should include a comparison condition similar in format and time engaged" by/to the treatment group (Malouf et al., 2017, p. 613). Many of the experimental and quasi-experimental studies typically compare outcomes for prisoners attending a meditation program to TAU. In practice, this can mean experiencing a "no frills" prison regime to attending a mix of work, educational, and rehabilitative programs. This makes it difficult to interpret findings, as they do not represent the effect of the meditation program in isolation, but rather its added value (Wilson, 2016) relative to the regular prison regime. Therefore, "the nature of research in this area likely downwardly biases any estimate of effectiveness" (Wilson, 2016, p. 214).

Furthermore, accumulating evidence that a prison meditation program is effective in producing positive outcomes for a certain incarcerated population is not enough. Attention must be paid to the "dosage" and the size of its relationship to the desired outcome, given there are restrictions on resources in most custodial establishments. The demographics and histories of study participants must be explored and reported in detail, as some findings may not generalize to other populations, for example, female inmates or adolescent offenders (Malouf et al., 2017, p. 613).

Additional research is clearly needed to better understand how to effectively implement meditation programs, given the limitations of a correctional setting (Wilson, 2016). Prison yoga programs are now becoming part of the correctional rehabilitative landscape. They should be seen/examined within this broader context. "We need to better understand what the targets of rehabilitative interventions should be" (Wilson, 2016).

References

Armour, C. (2012). Mental health in prison: A trauma perspective on importation and deprivation. *International Journal of Criminology and Sociological Theory* 5(2), 886–894.

Auty, K. M., Cope, A., & Liebling, A. (2017). A systematic review and meta-analysis of yoga and mindfulness meditation in prison. *International Journal of Offender Therapy and Comparative Criminology 61*(6), 689–710. doi:10.1177/0306624X15602514

Baker, V., Young, K., & Wolfe, S. (2016). Incorporating and adapting shared experience of mindfulness into a service for men who have committed serious offences and who have significant personality difficulties. *Probation Journal* 63(1), 80–87. doi:10.1177/0264550515620693

Banerjee, B., Vadiraj, H. S., Ram, A., Rao, R., Jayapal, M., Gopinath, K. S., . . . Prakash Hande, M. (2007). Effects of an integrated yoga program in modulating psychological stress and radiation-induced genotoxic stress in breast cancer patients undergoing radiotherapy. *Integrative Cancer Therapies* 6(3), 242–250. doi:10.1177/1534735407306214

Barefoot, J. C., Dodge, K. A., Peterson, B. L., Dahlstrom, W. G., & Williams, R. B., Jr. (1989). The Cook-Medley Hostility Scale: Item content and ability to predict survival. *Psychosomatic Medicine* 51(1), 46–57.

Beck, A. T., Steer, R. A., & Brown, G. K. (1996). Beck Depression Inventory-II. *San Antonio 78*(2), 490–498.

Berman, A. H., Palmstierna, T., Kallmen, H., & Bergman, H. (2007). The self-report Drug Use Disorders Identification Test—Extended (DUDIT-E): Reliability, validity, and motivational index. *Journal of Substance Abuse Treatment* 32, 357–369.

Bilderbeck, A. C., Farias, M., Brazil, I. A., Jakobowitz, S., & Wikholm, C. (2013). Participation in a 10-week course of yoga improves behavioural control and decreases psychological distress in a prison population. *Journal of Psychiatric Research 47*(10), 1438–1445. doi:10.1016/j.jpsychires.2013.06.014

Black, D. S. (2014). Mindfulness-based interventions: An antidote to suffering in the context of substance use, misuse, and addiction. *Substance Use & Misuse 49*(5), 487–491.

Bleick, C. R., & Abrams, A. I. (1987). The Transcendental Meditation program and criminal recidivism in California. *Journal of Criminal Justice 15*(3), 211–230. doi:10.1016/0047-2352(87)90045-6

Block-Lerner, J., Salters-Pednault, K., & Tull, M. T. (2005). Assessing mindfulness and experiential acceptance: Attempts to capture inherently elusive phenomena. In S. M. Orsillo & L. Roemer (Eds.), *Acceptance and mindfulness-based approaches to anxiety: Conceptualization and treatment* (pp. 71–100). New York: Springer.

Bowen, S., Chawla, N., & Marlatt, G. A. (2010). *Mindfulness-based relapse prevention for addictive behaviors: A clinician's guide.* New York: Guilford.

Bowen, S., Witkiewitz, K., Dillworth, T. M., Chawla, N., Simpson, T. L., Ostafin, B. D., . . . Marlatt, G. A. (2006). Mindfulness meditation and substance use in an incarcerated population. *Psychology of Addictive Behaviors 20*(3), 343–347. doi:10.1037/0893-164X.20.3.343

Bowen, S., Witkiewitz, K., Dillworth, T. M., & Marlatt, G. A. (2007). The role of thought suppression in the relationship between mindfulness meditation and alcohol use. *Addictive Behaviors 32*(10), 2324–2328. doi:10.1016/j.addbeh.2007.01.025

Briere, J. (1996). Psychometric review of the Trauma Symptom Checklist 40. In B. H. Stamm (Ed.), *Measurement of stress, trauma, and adaptation.* Lutherville, MD: Sidran Press.

Brown, K. W., & Ryan, R. M. (2003). The benefits of being present: mindfulness and its role in psychological well-being. *Journal of Personality and Social Psychology 84*(4), 822–848.

Bureau of Justice Statistics. (2014). Recidivism. Retrieved from https://www.bjs.gov/index.cfm?ty=tp&tid=17

Casarjian, B., & Casarjian, R. (2003). *Power Source: Taking charge of your life.* Boston, MA: Lionhart Press.

Chandiramani, K., Verma, S. K., & Dhar, P. L. (1995). *Psychological effects of Vipassana on Tihar Jail inmates.* Maharashtra, India: Vipassana Research Institute.

Cohen, S., Karmack, T., & Mermelstein, R. (1983). A global measure of perceived stress. *Journal of Health and Social Behavior 24*(4), 385–396.

Deng, Y.-Q., Liu, X.-H., Rodriguez, M. A., & Xia, C.-Y. (2011). The Five Facet Mindfulness Questionnaire: Psychometric properties of the Chinese version. *Mindfulness 2*(2), 123–128. doi:10.1007/s12671-011-0050-9

Farrington, D. P., Gottfredson, D. C., Sherman, L. W., & Welsh, B. C. (2002). The Maryland scientific methods scale. In L. W. Sherman, D. P. Farrington, B. C. Welsh, & D. L. Mackenzie (Eds.), *Evidence-based crime prevention* (pp. 13–21). New York: Routledge.

Fazel, S., & Baillargeon, J. (2011). The health of prisoners. *Lancet 377*(9769), 956–965. doi:10.1016/s0140-6736(10)61053-7

Fazel, S., Bains, P., & Doll, H. (2006). Substance abuse and dependence in prisoners: A systematic review. *Addiction 101*(2), 181–191. doi:10.1111/j.1360–0443.2006.01316.x

Fazel, S., & Danesh, J. (2002). Serious mental disorder in 23,000 prisoners: A systematic review of 62 surveys. *The Lancet 359*(9306), 545–550. doi:10.1016/s0140-6736(02)07740-1

Ferguson, P., & Gowan, J. (1976). TM: Some preliminary findings. *Journal of Humanistic Psychology 16*(3), 51–60. doi:10.1177/002216787601600307

Fix, R. L., & Fix, S. T. (2013). The effects of mindfulness-based treatments for aggression: A critical review. *Aggression and Violent Behavior 18*(2), 219–227. doi:10.1016/j.avb.2012.11.009

Gibson, L. E., Holt, J. C., Fondacaro, K. M., Tang, T. S., Powell, T. A., & Turbitt, E. L. (1999). An examination of antecedent traumas and psychiatric comorbidity among male inmates with PTSD. *Journal of Traumatic Stress 12*(3), 473–484. doi:10.1023/A:1024767020280

Goenka, S. N. (1995). *Excerpts from opening talks, Vipassana: Its relevance to the present world: An international seminar held at the Indian Institute of Technology, Delhi on 15–17 April 1994*. Igatpuri, Maharashtra, India: Vipassana Research Institute.

Gover, A. R., Mackenzie, D. L., & Armstrong, G. S. (2000). Importation and deprivation explanations of juveniles' adjustment to correctional facilities. *International Journal of Offender Therapy and Comparative Criminology 44*(4), 450–467.

Harty, L., Youman, K., Malouf, E. T., Appel, M., Hall, S., Pilafova, A., & Tangney, J. P. (2009). *Mindfulness Inventory: Nine dimensions (MIND)*. Fairfax, VA: George Mason University.

Hayes, S. C., Luoma, J. B., Bond, F. W., Masuda, A., & Lillis, J. (2006). Acceptance and commitment therapy: Model, processes and outcomes. *Behaviour Research and Therapy 44*(1), 1–25. doi:10.1016/j.brat.2005.06.006

Hayes, S. C., Strosahl, K. D., & Wilson, K. G. (1999). *Acceptance and commitment therapy: An experiential approach to behavior change*. New York: Guilford.

Himelstein, S. (2011a). Meditation research: The state of the art in correctional settings. *International Journal of Offender Therapy and Comparative Criminology* 55(4), 646–661. doi:10.1177/0306624x10364485

Himelstein, S. (2011b). Mindfulness-based substance abuse treatment for incarcerated youth: A mixed method pilot study. *International Journal of Transpersonal Studies 30*, 1–10.

Himelstein, S., Hastings, A., Shapiro, S. L., & Heery, M. (2012). Mindfulness training for self-regulation and stress with incarcerated youth: A pilot study. *Probation Journal* 59(2), 151–165. doi:10.1177/0264550512438256

Johnsen, T. J., & Friborg, O. (2015). The effects of cognitive behavioral therapy as an anti-depressive treatment is falling: A meta-analysis. *Psychological Bulletin 141*(4), 747–768. doi:10.1037/bul0000015

Kabat-Zinn, J. (2003). Mindfulness-based interventions in context: Past, present, and future. *Clinical Psychology: Science and Practice 10*(2), 144–156. doi:10.1093/clipsy.bpg016

Kabat-Zinn, J., & Hanh, T. N. (2013). *Full catastrophe living: Using the wisdom of your body and mind to face stress, pain, and illness* (Rev. ed.). Random House.

Khurana, A., & Dhar, P. (2002). *Effect of Vipassana meditation on quality of life, subjective well-being, and criminal propensity among inmates of Tihar Jail, Delhi*. Igatpuri, India: Vipassana Research Institute.

Lee, K. H., Bowen, S., & An-Fu, B. (2011). Psychosocial outcomes of mindfulness-based relapse prevention in incarcerated substance abusers in Taiwan: A preliminary study. *Journal of Substance Use 16*(6), 476–483. doi:10.3109/14659891.2010.505999

Leonard, N., Jha, A., Casarjian, B., Goolsarran, M., Garcia, C., Cleland, C., . . . Massey, Z. (2013). Mindfulness training improves attentional task performance in incarcerated youth: A group randomized controlled intervention trial. *Frontiers in Psychology* 4(792). doi:10.3389/fpsyg.2013.00792

Linehan, M. M. (1993a). *Skills training manual for treating borderline personality disorder* (1st ed.). New York: Guilford.

Linehan, M. M. (1993b). *Cognitive-behavioral treatment of borderline personality*. New York: Guilford.

Lozoff, B. (1985). *We're all doing time: A guide for getting free*. Durham, NC: Human Kindness Foundation.

Lyons, T., & Cantrell, W. D. (2015). Prison meditation movements and mass incarceration. *International Journal of Offender Therapy and Comparative Criminology 60*(12), 1363–1375. doi:10.1177/0306624x15583807

Maull, F. (2005). *Dharma in Hell: The Prison Writings of Fleet Maull.* South Deerfield, MA: Prison Dharma Network.

Malouf, E. T., Youman, K., Stuewig, J., Witt, E. A., & Tangney, J. P. (2017). A pilot RCT of a values-based mindfulness group intervention with jail inmates: Evidence for reduction in post-release risk behavior. *Mindfulness 8*(3), 603–614. doi:10.1007/s12671-016-0636-3

Martin, G. W., Wilkinson, D. A., & Poulos, C. X. (1995). The Drug Avoidance Self-Efficacy scale. *Journal of Substance Abuse 7*(2), 151–163. doi:10.1016/0899-3289(95)90001-2

McNair, D. M., Lorr, M., & Droppleman, L. F. (1992). *EdITS Manual for the Profile of Mood States (POMS).* San Diego, CA: Educational and Industrial Testing Service.

McNeill, F., & Schinkel, M. (2016). Prisons and desistance. In Y. Jewkes, B. Crewe, & J. Bennett (Eds.), *Handbook on prisons* (pp. 607–621). Oxford: Routledge.

Michalsen, A., Grossman, P., Acil, A., Langhorst, J., Ludtke, R., Esch, T., . . . Dobos, G. J. (2005). Rapid stress reduction and anxiolysis among distressed women as a consequence of a three-month intensive yoga program. *Medical Science Monitor 11*(12), Cr555–561.

Ministry of Justice. (2020). *Proven reoffending statistics quarterly bulletin, England and Wales, January 2018 to March 2018.* London: Ministry of Justice.

Moadel, A. B., Shah, C., Wylie-Rosett, J., Harris, M. S., Patel, S. R., Hall, C. B., & Sparano, J. A. (2007). Randomized controlled trial of yoga among a multiethnic sample of breast cancer patients: Effects on quality of life. *Journal of Clinical Oncology25*(28), 4387–4395. doi:10.1200/jco.2006.06.6027

Murray, R., Amann, R., & Thom, K. (2018). Mindfulness-based interventions for youth in the criminal justice system: A review of the research-based literature. *Psychiatry, Psychology and Law 25*(6), 829–838.

Nidich, S., O'Connor, T., Rutledge, T., Duncan, J., Compton, B., Seng, A., & Nidich, R. (2016). Reduced trauma symptoms and perceived stress in male prison inmates through the Transcendental Meditation program: A randomized controlled trial. *The Permanente Journal 20*(4), 43–47. doi:10.7812/tpp/16-007

Nidich, S., Seng, A., Compton, B., O'Connor, T., Salerno, J. W., & Nidich, R. (2017). Transcendental Meditation and reduced trauma symptoms in female inmates: A randomized controlled study. *The Permanente Journal 21*(16-008), 29–43. doi:10.7812/tpp/16-008

Orme-Johnson, D. W., & Moore, R. M. (2003). First prison study using the Transcendental Meditation program. *Journal of Offender Rehabilitation 36*(1–4), 89–95. doi:10.1300/J076v36n01_05

Per, M., Spinelli, C., Sadowski, I., Schmelefske, E., Anand, L, & Khoury, B. (2020). Evaluating the effectiveness of mindfulness-based interventions in incarcerated populations: A meta-analysis. *Criminal Justice and Behavior 47*(3), 310–330. doi:10.1177/0093854819891457

Perelman, A. M., Miller, S. L., Clements, C. B., Rodriguez, A., Allen, K., & Cavanaugh, R. (2012). Meditation in a Deep South prison: A longitudinal study of the effects of Vipassana. *Journal of Offender Rehabilitation 51*(3), 176–198. doi:10.1080/10509674.2011.632814

Purser, R. (2019). *McMindfulness: How mindfulness became the new capitalist spirituality.* London; Watkins Media.

Rainforth, M. V., Alexander, C. N., & Cavanaugh, K. L. (2003). Effects of the Transcendental Meditation program on recidivism among former inmates of Folsom Prison. *Journal of Offender Rehabilitation 36*(1–4), 181–203. doi:10.1300/J076v36n01_09

Rangan, R., Nagendra, H. R., & Bhatt, R. (2009). Effect of yogic education system and modern education system on sustained attention. *International Journal of Yoga* 2(1), 35–38. doi:10.4103/0973-6131.53840

Rosenberg, M. (1979). *Conceiving the self.* New York, NY: Basic Books.

Roth, R. (1994). *Maharishi Maheesh Yohi's Transcendental Meditation.* Washington DC: Primus.

Ruggiero, K. J., Ben, K. D., Scotti, J. R., & Rabalais, A. E. (2003). Psychometric properties of the PTSD checklist—civilian version. *Journal of Traumatic Stress 16*(5), 495–502. doi:10.1023/A:1025714729117

Samuelson, M., Carmody, J., Kabat-Zinn, J., & Bratt, M. A. (2007). Mindfulness-based stress reduction in Massachusetts correctional facilities. *The Prison Journal 87*(2), 254–268. doi:10.1177/0032885507303753

Segal, Z. V., Williams, J. M. G., & Teasdale, J. D. (2002). *Mindfulness-based cognitive therapy for depression: A new approach to preventing relapse* (1st ed.). New York: Guilford.

Settle, S., Zephaniah, B., & Morgan, P. (2017). *Peace inside: A prisoner's guide to meditation.* London, UK: Jessica Kingsley.

Sherman, L. W., Gottfredson, D. C., Mackenzie, D. L., Eck, J., Reuter, P., & Bushway, S. D. (1998). *Preventing crime: What works, what doesn't, what's promising* (Research brief). Washington, DC: US National Institute of Justice.

Shonin, E., Van Gordon, W., Slade, K., & Griffiths, M. D. (2013). Mindfulness and other Buddhist-derived interventions in correctional settings: A systematic review. *Aggression and Violent Behavior 18*(3), 365–372. doi:10.1016/j.avb.2013.01.002

Simpson, T. L., Kaysen, D., Bowen, S., MacPherson, L. M., Chawla, N., Blume, A.,...Larimer, M. (2007). PTSD symptoms, substance use, and Vipassana meditation among incarcerated individuals. *Journal of Traumatic Stress 20*(3), 239–249. doi:10.1002/jts.20209

Tangney, J. P., Dobbins, A. E., Stuewig, J. B., & Schrader, S. W. (2017). Is there a dark side to mindfulness? Relation of mindfulness to criminogenic cognitions. *Personality and Social Psychology Bulletin 43*(10), 1415–1426. doi:10.1177/0146167217717243

Tangney, J. P., Stuewig, J., Furukawa, E., Kopelovich, S., Meyer, P. J., & Cosby, B. (2012). Reliability, validity, and predictive utility of the 25-item Criminogenic Cognitions Scale (CCS). *Criminal Justice and Behavior 39*(10), 1340–1360. doi:10.1177/0093854812451092

Teasdale, J. D., Segal, Z. V., & Williams, J. M. G. (1995). How does cognitive therapy prevent depressive relapse and why should attentional control (mindfulness) training help? *Behaviour Research and Therapy 33*, 25–39.

Teplin, L. A. (1994). Psychiatric and substance abuse disorders among male urban jail detainees. *American Journal of Public Health 84*(2), 290–293. Retrieved from http://www.ncbi.nlm.nih.gov/pmc/articles/PMC1614991/

Teplin, L. A., Abram, K. M., McClelland, G. M., Dulcan, M. K., & Mericle, A. A. (2002). Psychiatric disorders in youth in juvenile detention. *Archives of General Psychiatry 59*(12), 1133–1143. Retrieved from http://www.ncbi.nlm.nih.gov/pmc/articles/PMC2861992/

Vipassana Research Institute. (2016). Vipassana in prisons: History and spread. Retrieved from www.vridhamma.org/Vipassana-in-Prisons-History-and-Spread

Wegner, D. M., & Zanakos, S. (1994). Chronic thought suppression. *Journal of Personality 62*(4), 616–640.

Weisburd, D., Farrington, D. P., Gill, C., With Ajzenstadt, M., Bennett, T., Bowers, K., ...Wooditch, A. (2017). What works in crime prevention and rehabilitation: An assessment of systematic reviews. *Criminology & Public Policy 16*(2), 415–449. doi:10.1111/1745-9133.12298

Welsh, & Farrington, D. P. (2001). Toward an evidence-based approach to preventing crime. *The Annals of the American Academy of Political and Social Science 578*, 158–173. Retrieved from http://www.jstor.org/stable/1049873

West, A. M. (2008). *Mindfulness and well-being in adolescence: An exploration of four mindfulness measures with an adolescent sample* (Doctoral dissertation). Retrieved from ProQuest (304824868).

Wilson, D. B. (2016). Correctional programs. In D. Weisburd, D. P. Farrington, & C. Gill (Eds.), *What works in crime prevention and rehabilitation* (pp. 193–217). New York: Springer-Verlag.

Xu, W., Jia, K., Liu, X., & Hofmann, S. G. (2016). The effects of mindfulness training on emotional health in Chinese long-term male prison inmates. *Mindfulness 7*(5), 1044–1051. doi:10.1007/s12671-016-0540-x

PART VI

DEBATES AND CONTROVERSIES IN MEDITATION

CHAPTER 38

CHALLENGING AND ADVERSE MEDITATION EXPERIENCES

Toward a Person-Centered Approach

JARED R. LINDAHL, WILLOUGHBY B. BRITTON, DAVID J. COOPER, AND LAURENCE J. KIRMAYER

Introduction

LITERATURE from many religious traditions on the theory, practice, and result of meditation tends to emphasize processes of self-transformation that culminate in changes in consciousness or modes of understanding ascribed ultimate value. The contemporary science of meditation has often reframed these practices as a means of attaining physical health or psychological well-being. Although some difficulty or discomfort might be expected in learning to meditate and undergoing a process of self-transformation, these changes are typically described in positive terms. In both religion and science, the notion that extremely challenging and adverse experiences can arise during or as a result of meditation has been downplayed or ignored. Most scientific research does not report adverse effects and generally relies on passive monitoring on the assumption that meditation is safe (Wong et al., 2018). However, a range of meditation-related challenges have been documented in both traditional religious literature and contemporary psychological research. Challenging experiences include perceptual changes such as hypersensitivity to stimuli or hallucinations, and cognitive changes such as impairments in executive functioning or delusions. Affective changes include increased emotional lability and emotional blunting, re-experiencing of traumatic memories, and a wide range of specific emotions such as fear, anxiety, and depression. Somatic or physiological changes also occur, including intense pain, involuntary movements, and disrupted sleep. Changes in motivation and sense of self can also lead to challenges, especially when there is impairment or loss of ordinary functioning. Many of these and other challenging experiences also have deleterious impacts on social and occupational functioning.

How are such experiences to be understood? When are they indications of practice gone wrong? When are they intended effects that signal the undoing of habitual patterns that will ultimately draw a practitioner closer to the intended goal? These questions are of great theoretical and practical importance for meditation practitioners and for those who seek to understand the mechanisms and implications of meditative practices. This chapter introduces the topic of meditation-related challenges and focuses on how certain experiences are appraised within Buddhist conceptions of self-transformation, in clinical psychology and psychiatry, and at the intersection of these domains. Based upon Buddhist textual sources, prior scientific and psychological research, and qualitative data from the authors' study of Buddhist meditators in the West (Lindahl et al., 2017), this chapter will describe specific meditation-related challenges, their impact on the lives of meditation practitioners, and how both appraisals of and responses to meditation-related challenges are situated in cultural contexts. The scope of this chapter is limited to studies and texts concerning Buddhist meditation and will not comment on challenging or adverse effects in the context of other meditation traditions or in contemporary programs such as mindfulness-based interventions.[1]

While research on meditation-related challenges has tended to focus primarily on individual experiences, a small number of qualitative studies have begun to explore how meditation-related challenges are negotiated in broader socio-cultural contexts. The reports offered by meditation practitioners and teachers in these studies call attention to the processes through which teachers appraise and manage meditation-related challenges in their students. These studies have also begun to identify the scope of meditation teachers' authority and expertise, especially in situations where the meaning and nature of meditation-related experiences is contested. There is often a lack of consensus around which types of experiences should be deemed "normative" within the context of a Buddhist framework of self-transformation—that is, experiences that could occur, are expected to occur, or even ought to occur as "part of the path." Moreover, contemporary practitioners in the West regularly have to reconcile Buddhist frameworks with other, sometimes conflicting worldviews. Consequently, meditation practitioners, meditation teachers, and meditation communities, as well as psychologists and psychiatrists can all contribute to determining what constitutes a meditation-related "adverse effect" and what constitutes a "normative" meditation experience, as well as how to best respond to them when they occur.

[1] For adverse effects in the context of Transcendental Meditation (TM) see Kennedy (1976), Otis (1984), and Castillo (1990). For a summary of practice-related challenges in Abrahamic religions, see Fisher, this volume. For more information on meditation-related challenges in Ch'an and Zen Buddhism, see Ahn, this volume.

Types of Meditation-Related Challenges

Buddhist literature provides various characterizations of how to practice meditation and the ideal trajectory of contemplative development. This is often presented in terms of a path structure (Pali *magga*; Skt. *mārga*) in which practices are developed in stages and meditation experiences are also expected to develop sequentially to some extent (Buswell & Gimello, 1992). Sharf (1995) argued that these texts rarely if ever serve as straightforward descriptions of experience, highlighting instead how paths are means of organizing Buddhist ideas in prescriptive and even polemical terms. Gyatso (1999) countered that, at least for Tibetan Buddhism, there is a rich history of describing experiences across various literary genres. Nevertheless, few textual sources provide descriptions of the range of meditative experiences or advice on how to work with specific challenging or adverse experiences.

How different types of meditation experiences are evaluated, interpreted, or appraised depends upon both the type of experience in question as well as the perspective of the teachers, clinicians, or researchers involved in the appraisal. In research contexts, the objectives of the study and the use of interview or self-report methods all impact the degree to which challenging, difficult, or adverse experiences are likely to be reported. Clinical case reports are a common source for descriptions of distressing and functionally impairing meditation experiences; however, these tend to include only those cases brought to clinical attention, and because of that setting are usually associated with psychiatric diagnoses (e.g., Chan-Ob & Boonyanaruthee, 1999; Yorston, 2001). By contrast, studies investigating mystical experiences may catalog a range of changes, but tend to emphasize positively framed experiences (e.g., Chen et al., 2011). While open-ended qualitative research may capture both positive and negative experiences (e.g., Kornfield, 1979; Shapiro, 1992), studies directly inquiring about challenges are the most reliable methods for documenting these experiences (VanderKooi, 1997; Lomas et al., 2015; Lindahl et al., 2017; Kaselionyte & Gumley, 2018).

The most comprehensive study to date to investigate challenging meditation-related experiences is the Varieties of Contemplative Experience (VCE) project (Lindahl et al., 2017). This study employed a mixed-methods research design using outlier or deviant case sampling in order to investigate experiences associated with the practice of different forms of Buddhist meditation that were unexpected, challenging, difficult, distressing, or functionally impairing. The VCE study also investigated how such experiences are interpreted and understood by practitioners and teachers, their impact on the lives of practitioners, and the ways in which both practitioners and teachers respond to meditation-related challenges. In the subsequent sections, we adopt the classificatory scheme of the VCE study to provide an overview of some of the most commonly reported meditation-related challenges in case studies, qualitative and quantitative research, and Buddhist textual sources.

Perceptual Changes

Changes in the perceptual domain range from benign and even expected experiences such as hypersensitivity to light, sound, or body sensations, to more unusual and unexpected experiences such as distortions in space and time, derealization, and visions or visual hallucinations. Reports of visual lights are given varied appraisals across Buddhist traditions ranging from an unimportant side-effect of practice to a sign of progress in concentration that should become a new meditation object (Lindahl et al., 2014). A qualitative study of advanced Burmese meditators documented increased perceptual sensitivity and clarity, which were framed in terms of a valued insight into impermanence (Full et al., 2013). Yet, even a commonly reported change such as perceptual hypersensitivity can be appealing in one context, such as during a retreat, but considered a challenge or unwanted effect in another context, such as when a practitioner leaves the retreat and resumes ordinary life. Shapiro (1992) described how following an intensive Vipassanā retreat, some meditators experienced "societal adverse effects" including feeling "hypersensitive in the city environment" (p. 65). Perceptual hypersensitivity-related challenges following intensive practice were also found in the VCE study.

Other types of perceptual changes are more ambiguous in their significance for the meditator and are often negotiated through interactions with an authority such as a meditation teacher. For example, whether a practitioner reports a visual experience as a "vision" or as a "hallucination" depends in part on their expectations, goals, and feedback from their teachers or their tradition, which illustrates how phenomenology and appraisals are closely related. In addition to being the most commonly reported perceptual change in the VCE study (Lindahl et al., 2017), visions and hallucinations have been documented in many other previous studies of meditation experiences (Kornfield, 1979; Miller, 1993; VanderKooi, 1997; Chan-Ob & Boonyanaruthee, 1999; Chen et al., 2011; Lomas et al., 2015). For example, Chen and colleagues (2011), in a qualitative study of Chinese Buddhists using Hood's mysticism scale, reported a range of perceptual experiences. Visual experiences of seeing light or the Buddha were valued positively by some practitioners but in other cases were rejected as hallucinations (p. 663). In Zen Buddhism, the term *makyō* is used to refer to largely perceptual distortions that indicate some progress in practice; however, *makyō* are also treated as being of little significance or importance lest they become pursued as an end unto themselves (Aitken, 1982; Sogen, 2001). Similar to the Zen term *makyō*, in Tibetan Buddhism *nyam* (Tib. *nyams*) refers to various types of meditation experiences, including visions, that can be signs of progress but which are generally to be regarded as incidental to the purpose of meditation. Tibetan Buddhist practitioners and teachers in the VCE study were more inclined than those of other traditions to offer positive or mixed appraisals of visions, perhaps because of the greater importance of visionary experiences in Tibetan Buddhism (e.g., Gyatso, 1998; Doctor, 2005; Jacoby, 2015).

Teachers from Theravada Buddhist traditions tended to express skepticism or concern over reports of visions or visual hallucinations. Indeed, in some Theravada texts, visual experiences such as lights and images of the Buddha are appraised as one of the "corruptions of insight" (Pali *vipassanā-upakkilesā*) (Buddhaghosa, 1991; Sayadaw, 2016). Like *makyō* and *nyam*, these experiences may be signs of a developing practice, but they are also viewed with caution due to their allure and potential to destabilize practice. Kornfield (1979) reported a wide range of perceptual changes, including alterations in body image and visual phenomena, described alternately as visions and hallucinations. Kornfield concluded that "unusual experiences, visual or auditory aberrations, 'hallucinations,' unusual somatic experiences and so on, are the norm among practiced meditation students" (p. 51).

While isolated and short-lived perceptual changes might be easily negotiated as a part of the path, such experiences tend to be more concerning when they are associated with additional features such as agitation, strong negative emotions, mania, delusions, or disruptive behaviors. For example, VanderKooi (1997) described the case of a woman who re-experienced a traumatic memory that then led to a period of intense fear, insomnia, and visual hallucinations, which resolved when she discontinued practice and took medication. According to a Theravada Buddhist teacher interviewed in the VCE study, if visual experiences are not interfering, the response could be to just continue practicing. However, if they also coincided with not eating and sleeping and being "wound up in an ecstatic way," then the practitioner would "need grounding." Thus, the appraisal of a perceptual experience depends on the context of practice (e.g., in which tradition of Buddhism and in which setting) and also, in some cases, on the occurrence of other changes in functioning that suggest a need for additional support or intervention.

Affective Changes

Within and beyond the VCE study, a wide range of changes in affect or emotion has been associated with meditation. Affective states such as bliss and joy have been reported, and these are generally framed as positive and in relation to stages of the path (Kornfield, 1979; Chen et al., 2011; Berkovich-Ohana et al., 2013); however Buddhist literature also contains cautions concerning positive states (e.g., Sayadaw, 1965; Lingpa, 2015). Positive emotions can also develop into intensely euphoric or manic experiences that practitioners can find frightening or destabilizing (Yorston, 2001; Lomas et al., 2015). Studies have also documented increased emotional sensitivity or reactivity, anxiety, and depression (Kornfield, 1979; Shapiro, 1992; Miller, 1993; Lomas et al., 2015), and in other cases, blunted affect or loss of affective response altogether (Kornfield, 1979).

Experiences of fear or terror were among the more commonly reported intense affective experiences in the VCE and other studies (Kornfield, 1979; Shapiro, 1992; Kutz et al., 1985; VanderKooi, 1997; Chan-Ob & Boonyanaruthee, 1999). The VCE study documented both primary fear, in which fear arose on its own, as well as secondary fear, in which fear was a response to another change such as a hallucination or a loss of sense of self. Both types of experiences can also be found in Buddhist literary sources, which identify fear, terror, panic, and related affective states as possible consequences of meditation practice, although determinations of their cause, importance, and need for intervention vary. In Tibetan traditions, experiences of intense fear are acknowledged as a potential consequence of insight into the selflessness of persons or phenomena, even in some cases arising simply from hearing discourses on the teachings of emptiness (Pabongka, 1991). In his nineteenth-century treatise *The Vajra Essence*, Dudjom Lingpa enumerated a number of *nyam* associated with the practice of *śamatha* meditation. Emotional experiences are the most frequently mentioned, ranging from an "ecstatic, blissful sense [of] mental stillness" to "unbearable misery." Also mentioned among his list of *nyam* are "an inexplicable sense of paranoia" and "fear and terror" concerning a variety of topics "because your mind is filled with a constant stream of anxieties," such that you experience "everything around you leading to all kinds of hopes and fears" (Lingpa, 2015, pp. 23–24). As with *makyō*, these experiences are framed as being transient signs of progress, and practitioners are warned not to become overly concerned about or attached to them. However, modern teachers have also acknowledged that *nyam* may "become so disturbing that psychological counseling or medical intervention may be necessary" (Wallace, 2006, p. 107).

In Theravada Buddhist traditions, certain experiences of fear and terror are also viewed as normative. Buddhaghosa's fifth-century *The Path of Purification* includes as part of the path various "insight knowledges" (*vipassanā-ñāṇa*), two of which are described as "knowledge of appearance as terror" and "knowledge of danger" (Buddhaghosa, 1991). According to modern commentators and teachers of the Southeast Asian Vipassanā tradition, meditators progress through the various insight knowledges in sequence, and these two insights are framed as particularly challenging and difficult stages. In contrast to Buddhaghosa and other earlier sources, for whom these stages are a way of characterizing insights into the impermanence and unreliability of phenomena, the tradition of Mahāsi Sayadaw has tended to place more emphasis on their affective character (Sayadaw, 1965; Namto, 1989; Sayadaw, 2016). Some modern Western interpreters in this tradition have dubbed this trajectory of difficult stages as the "dark night," borrowing the term from the Carmelite mystic St. John of the Cross (Kornfield, 1993; Ingram, 2008). While some research studies on challenging meditation experiences have presented fear and terror as expected parts of the path (Kornfield, 1979) or as experiences from which the practitioner can learn (Shapiro, 1992), others have considered fear a potential warning sign of more serious adverse effects (VanderKooi, 1997).

Another significant and commonly reported affective challenge is the re-experiencing of traumatic memories (Kutz et al., 1985; VanderKooi, 1997; Miller, 1993; Lomas et al., 2015; Lindahl, 2017; Kaselionyte & Gumley, 2018). Miller (1993) reports a case of a woman engaged in a three-month mindfulness meditation retreat who began experiencing pain and pressure in her head and back. Encouraged by her teacher to direct her attention to the sensation of pressure, she experienced strong negative emotions of terror and hatred and began having recurring images of sexual abuse from her early childhood. While for this woman the response was to discontinue meditation and consult with a psychiatrist, another woman in Miller's study was able to continue mindfulness meditation in conjunction with psychotherapy and medication.

Lindahl (2017) described a similar variability in working with traumatic memories among practitioners of Tibetan Buddhism from the VCE project. Many of these practitioners also reported the surfacing of traumatic memories associated with a release of pressure or tension in a specific part of the body. For some practitioners, the container of practice sufficiently enabled them to explore traumatic and other intense emotional experiences in a way that was not destabilizing. These practitioners often framed their experiences as instances of "purification," which is a central aspect of the preliminary practices of Vajrayāna Buddhism among Tibetan lineages. For other practitioners, the re-experiencing of traumatic memories was too destabilizing, and they tended not to describe their experiences as purification but instead discontinued practice and sought additional psychotherapeutic support.

Many teachers in the VCE study acknowledged the difficulties in deciding how to respond to intense affective experiences. Some asserted that having a trauma history can make difficult stages of practice more challenging, and that meditators can become "flooded" by traumatic memories to the extent that they become re-traumatized. And although most teachers considered the presence of suicidal ideation a "red flag" that would be best addressed through psychotherapy and not meditation alone, one teacher thought that transient suicidality could arise during the difficult stages of the "insight knowledges" and could be addressed through practice. The duration of the experience and the degree of functional impairment often served as indicators of whether a meditator should seek additional support.

Somatic Changes

A wide range of somatic or physiological experiences has been documented in research on meditation. In the VCE study, practitioners reported sleep changes, appetitive changes, sensations of pressure or tension, pain, thermal changes, somatic energy, and involuntary movements, and similar experiences have been documented in other studies (Kornfield, 1979; Shapiro, 1992; Miller, 1993; VanderKooi, 1997; Chan-Ob & Boonyanaruthee, 1999; Yorston, 2001; Chen et al., 2011; Lomas et al., 2015). Many somatic changes were described by Buddhist teachers as expected effects of practice, in particular more intensive or long-term practice. Practitioners also reported that somatic energy—"a type of sensation moving throughout the body or throughout a body area described with language of vibration, energy, current, or other related metaphors"—was often distressing and impairing, especially when prolonged and when management strategies were unknown (Lindahl et al., 2017, Appendix S4).

Experiences of somatic energy are associated with a wide range of valences, appraisals, and responses. In their study of Chinese Ch'an and Pure Land monastics, Chen and colleagues (2011) reported a case of "electricity flowing through my body when meditating" (p. 663). The authors classified this experience as corresponding to the "sacredness" facet of Hood's mysticism scale. Kornfield (1979) found that somatic energy was described by meditators as frequently occurring in conjunction with "spontaneous" and "involuntary" movements (p. 45), and was framed by some as part of a process of "unstressing" and "energy release" (p. 52). Kornfield, who is also a Vipassanā teacher, characterized these experiences as "common and normal" results of intensive mindfulness and concentration practice (p. 41). He rejected the tendency within Western psychology to offer "pathological interpretations" of such phenomena, arguing this was based on lack of awareness of the "frequency and variety of unusual experiences" found in meditative practice and that such experiences are better understood as part of a "non-linear process of growth in meditation" (pp. 41, 53). In contrast, Shapiro (1992) documented similar experiences of "energy releasing" occurring along with "shaking" among Vipassanā practitioners, but in the context of other disabling symptoms, he described them not as indications of a process of growth but as "profound adverse effects" (p. 64).

In the VCE study, experiences of somatic energy yielded similarly diverse appraisals. Generally speaking, Tibetan Buddhist teachers and practitioners employed resources within their tradition to interpret and work with these sensations, while Zen and Vipassanā teachers and practitioners often drew upon frameworks from outside their traditions, in particular that of "*kuṇḍalinī* awakening." The Tibetan Buddhist tradition explicitly acknowledges somatic energies, which are understood as connected to the "subtle body" and its system of "channels," and the tradition has models for working with this energy at various stages of practice (Lindahl, 2017, p. 8). Tibetan teachers in the VCE study as well as in VanderKooi (1997) made reference to *lung* or "wind" (Tib. *rlung*), a bodily energy that is cultivated through advanced practices such as "inner heat" as part of the process of purification and self-transformation (Lindahl, 2017, p. 4). However, these and other meditation practices can also cause problems if energy begins to "flow" in an "incorrect" fashion (VanderKooi, 1997, p. 40). These teachers indicated that such difficulties could arise as a result of "an improper use of certain advanced meditation practices" or "excess concentration and overexertion" (VanderKooi, 1997, pp. 40–41), for which they may apply the Tibetan medical diagnosis of *lung* disorder (Tib. *srog rlung*) (Lindahl, 2017, pp. 9–10). Such problems are often not trivial and can include psychosis, which is why teachers referred to these practices as potent tools for awakening, but also as potentially "dangerous" (VanderKooi, 1997, p. 34).

Some Zen and Vipassanā teachers and practitioners indicated that the lack of a clear framework around somatic energy in their traditions proved to be a challenge as they attempted to manage these experiences that nevertheless arose from meditating. For practitioners, the distress associated with their experience could be compounded when teachers were unable to provide practical advice for managing energy. In multiple cases, practitioners from Zen and Vipassanā traditions looked beyond their tradition to teachers familiar with "*kuṇḍalinī*"—a key concept associated with energy in yogic and tantric traditions from South Asia. *Kuṇḍalinī* experiences are also paradigmatic examples of "spiritual emergencies" and, according to Grof and Grof (1989), must be worked with carefully in order to lead to positive transformation. This understanding has been influential in Western conceptions of meditation-related experiences of somatic energy and has thus likely influenced (indirectly or directly) some Buddhist meditation teachers and practitioners as well, especially in cases where emic frameworks for somatic energy are absent.

Changes in Sense of Self

The sense of self is supported through various conceptual, affective, and embodied processes, and meditation can have various impacts on one or more of these processes. This includes changes in the narrative self and extends to changes in the sense of ownership over thoughts, emotions, and body sensations, or to the sense of agency over actions. In addition, changes in one's sense of location relative to one's body and changes in the sense of boundaries between self and world have also been documented. Given the centrality of Buddhist teachings around not-self (Pali. *anattā*) and the selflessness or emptiness of persons (Skt. *pudgala-nairātmya*, *pudgala-śūnyatā*), some of these changes are appraised in relation to normative Buddhist views, values, and conceptions of goals. However, changes in sense of self can also be distressing, destabilizing, involuntary, and enduring, resulting in practitioners seeking alternate clinical diagnoses and support.

Chen and others (2011) reported "out-of-body" experiences, a sense of merging with "being," or becoming "one with the universe" or the natural world. Although some meditators "rejected the legitimacy" of these experiences, none were reported as challenging, distressing, or impairing (pp. 659–662). Similarly, recent studies of Vipassanā practitioners have documented a decreased sense of ownership over body sensations and sense of agency over actions, changes in location of self relative to the body, and diminishment of the sense of boundaries between the body and the world (Dor-Ziderman et al., 2013; Berkovich-Ohana et al., 2013; Ataria et al., 2015; Ataria, 2015). The meditators in these studies were long-term practitioners who could induce these changes at will or were familiar with them from prior meditation experience; however, this research did not comment on the psychological or behavioral impact of these experiences or appraisals of their meaning or value.

A different picture emerges from research specifically aimed at investigating challenging, distressing, or adverse effects of meditation. In a study of long-term Vipassanā practitioners, Shapiro (1992) included the report of a meditator who experienced a "brief but powerful experience of egolessness which brought deep terror and insecurity" (p. 65); the practitioner related to the experience as transitory and did not experience persistent distress. Lomas and others (2015) found that 6 of 30 male Buddhist meditators in their study reported "depersonalization," which they described in "highly negative terms" (p. 857). Summarizing one case study of an "out-of-body" experience reported as "alienating and disturbing," Lomas and colleagues noted that "without guidance from a teacher or a *sangha* to help him interpret his experiences, the deconstruction of the self (which is the goal of the practice) was experienced as a frightening dissolution of identity, rather than as a sense of liberation (which the practice is arguably designed to invoke)" (p. 855). While this suggests that a "challenging" or "adverse" change in sense of self is simply one that is inadequately contextualized or understood, these might not be the only criteria that are important in considering whether or not an experience is deemed normative.

The VCE study documented a wide range of changes in sense of self among meditation practitioners, many of which were associated with significant distress, impairments in functioning, or both. Teachers in the VCE study acknowledged that because of their importance in Buddhist theory and practice, changes in the sense of self posed particular challenges for deciding whether to appraise an experience as a normative part of the path or as a potential problem in need of additional support. Many teachers acknowledged that one of the fundamental components of meditation practice was to "destabilize" or "deconstruct" the sense of self, or to experience a "dissolution of self." However, others identified certain "dissociative experiences," which they differentiated from valid insights and attributed to improper practice. Still others believed that anticipated, normative experiences from meditation practice were akin to the psychiatric understanding of dissociation and depersonalization. These perspectives are further complicated when one considers that from a traditional Buddhist perspective, genuine insights into not-self can themselves be distressing (Buddhaghosa, 1991; Pabongka, 1991).

Cognitive Changes

Cognitive changes associated with meditation include normative meditation experiences of heightened meta-cognition, increased mental stillness, or changes in worldview (Kornfield, 1979; Pagis, 2010; Chen et al., 2011; Full et al., 2013), as well as impairments in executive functioning (Shapiro, 1992; Yorston, 2001) and delusional, irrational, or paranormal thoughts and beliefs (Walsh & Roche, 1979; Miller, 1993; VanderKooi, 1997; Chan-Ob & Boonyanaruthee, 1999; Lomas et al., 2015; Kaselionyte & Gumley, 2018). The issue of appraisal is particularly salient with respect to the phenomenology of delusional, irrational, and paranormal beliefs. Clinical research typically views such experiences as evidence of psychosis, especially when they coincide with other changes such as hallucinations, disordered thinking, mania, or disruptive behaviors (Walsh & Roche, 1979; Miller, 1993; VanderKooi, 1997; Chan-Ob & Boonyanaruthee, 1999; Lomas et al., 2015). Walsh and Roche (1979) and Chan-Ob and Boonyanaruthee (1999) described delusions of persecution and religiously-themed delusions of grandeur, which were accompanied by significant additional phenomenology, including lack of "insight,"[2] "flight of ideas," and "loosening of association" (Chan-Ob &

[2] Lack of insight in this context refers to the individual's lack of awareness that they are ill (Kirmayer et al., 1998).

Boonyanaruthee, 1999, p. 926), as well as hallucinations, insomnia, and bizarre, disruptive, or violent behavior. In many cases, practitioners were directed to psychiatric treatment (including inpatient hospitalization) and medication.

Qualitative studies tended to capture a broader range of appraisals that demonstrated some ambiguity between delusional beliefs that might be concerning to a meditation teacher and paranormal beliefs that could be appraised as normative. VanderKooi (1997) reported experiences where "everything seemed symbolic and had cosmological dimensions" to the extent that one participant believed her teacher "was God" (p. 36), and Lomas and colleagues (2015) described a practitioner who believed he "was going to be the next Buddha," a belief he thought "contributed to his breakdown" (p. 855). Two Buddhist teachers interviewed by Kaselionyte and Gumley (2018) described "powers of the mind" such as supernormal hearing or vision, reading minds, and seeing past lives (p. 6), experiences recognized as normative within the Buddhist tradition (Buddhaghosa, 1991). One of the teachers indicated that there was danger in practitioners getting "caught up" in such experiences due to the risk of developing "delusions about themselves and the nature of things" or believing they had become enlightened (Kaselionyte & Gumley, 2018, p. 8)—a concern also identified in Buddhist literature (Sayadaw, 1965; Hsuan Hua, 2003).

Teachers in the VCE and other studies acknowledged that extreme cognitive changes were sometimes difficult to distinguish from religiously normative experiences. While a Tibetan teacher claimed that "advanced meditators need a qualified teacher...to differentiate between psychotic states and true spiritual visions" (VanderKooi, 1997, p. 42), teachers often acknowledged that they did not have the requisite qualifications to make this assessment. Similarly, Kaselionyte and Gumley (2018) found that teachers varied in their self-assessed ability to differentiate a spiritual experience from a mental health problem. This challenge is not limited to meditation research, however, as there have been various other attempts at establishing differential diagnosis between religious, spiritual, or mystical experiences on the one hand, and delusions or psychopathology on the other.

Approaches to Differentiating Religious Experiences from Psychopathology

This section reviews various previous attempts at differentiating religious, spiritual, or mystical experiences from schizophrenia, psychosis, or psychotic-like symptoms. The criteria offered come from researchers adopting different methodologies, ranging from phenomenology, psychology, and psychiatry (Brett, 2002; Heriot-Maitland, 2008; Parnas & Henriksen, 2016) to proponents of transpersonal psychology (Grof & Grof, 1989; Viggiano & Krippner, 2010; Vieten & Scammel, 2015), and also previous reviews on this topic (Menezes & Moreira-Almeida, 2009, 2010). Despite the intuitive assumption that some experiences would be either "religious" or "psychopathological" simply by virtue of their characteristics, research has generally concluded that the core qualities of an experience are not sufficient for making a differentiation and that other criteria must be taken into consideration. These additional criteria can be summarized as referring to (1) individual factors, such as attributes, traits, or qualities of the person, and the impact of the experience on the person; and/or (2) socio-cultural factors that take into account the person's social situation, cultural background, and current contexts.

Individual Factors

Criteria for differentiating religious experiences from psychopathology based upon the individual undergoing the experience include appraisals of the person's health, their capacities, and their intentions or attitudes, as well as the subsequent impact of the experience on their functioning or well-being. Both Menezes and Moreira-Almeida (2009; 2010) as well as Vieten and Scammel (2015) included the absence of medical or psychiatric comorbidities among their criteria. Other mental health requirements are described in terms of capacities, such as "intact reality testing," a "critical attitude," "psychological maturity," healthy personality or ego structure, or the ability to induce or control the experience (Miller, 1993; Heriot-Maitland, 2008; Menezes & Moreira-Almeida, 2009, 2010; Vieten & Scammel, 2015; Parnas & Henriksen, 2016). Some capacities may be acquired or trainable. These include attributions to the person's "relationship to the meditation practice" (Miller, 1993, pp. 176–177) or concerns over inadequate preparation, particularly prior to undertaking advanced practices (Preece, 2011; Lomas et al., 2015). Individual criteria also extend to include identity and worldview. Brett (2002) argued that it is the presence of an epistemic framework that will allow a person to take the "appropriate perspective" toward an experience (p. 336). Thus, religious experiences could be differentiated by their coherence and meaningfulness (Vieten & Scammel, 2015). As Heriot-Maitland (2008) put it, the mystic will have "a *context* to provide meaning for the experience, thus allowing the development of a *structured* appraisal" (p. 317). Many researchers also considered the impact of the experience on the individual, positing that religious or spiritual experiences do not require additional clinical support, are associated with minimal distress and impairment, and promote a sense of meaning or personal growth over time (Menezes & Moreira-Almeida, 2009, 2010; Viggiano & Krippner, 2010; Dein & Littlewood, 2011; Vieten & Scammel, 2015; Parnas & Henriksen, 2016).

Many of these criteria have exceptions, caveats, or contradictions. In terms of a person's mental health, individuals with no comorbid prior psychiatric or trauma history can still have experiences that they and others do not consider religious or spiritual. Furthermore, a history of psychopathology does not preclude the possibility of having a positive religious experience, as religious experiences and psychopathology can co-occur. In terms of capacities, practitioners could lose their critical attitude regarding the reality of the experience or their control over it and still conclude that it was a religious experience. In terms of impact, experiences appraised as religious could still be associated with considerable distress or suffering, including functional impairment. Conversely, while religious experiences are characterized as transient and non-impairing (Menezes & Moreira-Almeida, 2009, 2010; Vieten & Scammel, 2015), psychiatric problems can also be acute and time-limited, and the impact of experiences appraised as religious can last for many years.

Socio-cultural Factors

On account of these challenges, an increasing number of scholars are acknowledging that differentiating religious experiences from psychopathology is possible only when the cultural embeddedness of the experience itself as well as those appraising it are taken into consideration. In this view, a foundational criterion is whether or not a given experience would be accepted as normative within a religious community or is in some other way compatible with the person's cultural background (Menezes & Moreira-Almeida, 2009, 2010; Dein, 2012; Taylor & Murray, 2012). In some cases, the consideration of cultural background will conflict with other prospective criteria such as distress or functional impairment. In particular, Buddhist meditation traditions complicate the picture considerably by framing various types of challenging and even distressing experiences as normative parts of the path, which means that religious experiences cannot be straightforwardly disambiguated from psychopathology simply on account of being positive in valence or impact.

Similar considerations of cultural background significantly informed the 4th and 5th editions of the *Diagnostic and Statistical Manual of Mental Disorders* (*DSM*), including how the relationship between depersonalization disorder and meditation was characterized. The *DSM* considers depersonalization as non-pathological if it was intentionally induced by meditation, stating: "Volitionally induced experiences of depersonalization/derealization can be part of meditative practices that are prevalent in many religions and cultures and should not be diagnosed as a disorder." Nevertheless, there remain further considerations to be applied to each case: "However, there are individuals who initially induce these states intentionally but over time lose control over them and may develop a fear and aversion for related practices" (*DSM*-5 American Psychiatric Association, 2013, §300.6, p. 304). This acknowledges the potential complexity of experiences of depersonalization and suggests that the clinician should be alert to the possibility that such experiences may become associated with a loss of control and distress. The recommendation here is that diagnosis should not be made based on isolated features of the experience; rather, it depends on whether the experience is persistent, escapes individual control, and causes distress and impairment. Even if the experience does cause distress, if it is normative or expected and can be addressed adequately within the cultural context (in this case a meditation tradition and practice setting), then the key issue is whether the person requires additional (psychiatric, psychological, or biomedical) support. This determination involves assessing local contexts and resources for coping and recovery as much as it does determining the nature of the individual's condition. In either case, assessment includes determining both vulnerability and strengths or resilience factors (Kirmayer et al., 2016b).

Appraisals of meditation experiences are not simple determinations made by a meditation expert in relationship to a straightforward report of an experience. Rather, as with other experiences, appraisal processes are multiple, take place at both intrapersonal and interpersonal levels, and are further embedded in the views and values of the broader society (Kirmayer, 2008, 2015a; Taves, 2009). Meditation teachers, practitioners, and clinicians all contribute to determining which experiences are significant, identifying plausible causal attributions or explanations, and deciding how challenging experiences should be managed. Clarifying the overlapping set of forces that shape meditative experiences is crucial in order to advance an ethically sound and pragmatically effective approach to assessing and responding to challenges.

Situating Meditation-Related Challenges in Context

Decision-making and attributions for meditation-related challenges have tended to overemphasize the characteristics of individual practitioners and often insufficiently attend to embeddedness of both the meditator and other decision-makers in larger social contexts, including relationships to practice communities, authorities, institutions, traditions, and cultures—all of which influence appraisals of experiences and responses to them. With examples from the VCE study and other research, this section illustrates how socio-cultural factors impact appraisals and responses of both meditation practitioners as well as meditation teachers and clinicians. These dynamics also highlight why general or universal recommendations for differential diagnosis are not possible. Rather, the unique situatedness of each meditator must be considered on a case-by-case basis.

Meditator-in-Context

A meditator's social positioning and worldview can impact how they view and respond to their own meditation-related challenges. For example, appraising challenges as part of the path and getting through such challenges without resort to outside help confers the higher social position that comes from spiritual attainment. Such incentives could increase the desire to appraise a challenging experience in spiritual terms and avoid psychological or medical treatment, especially medications, which, by being biologically based, would associate the experience with a biological disease state.

Practitioners in the VCE study held a wide range of attitudes toward supplementing practice with psychotherapy or medication. Some did not believe that their challenges warranted psychological support or intervention; others were concerned that going to a psychologist would not have been helpful because a psychologist would not understand their experiences as part of a religious path and would diagnose them with a mental illness. Some practitioners found talking with a therapist to be helpful when their experiences were normalized or validated. One of the variables that determined how well an encounter went between a meditation practitioner and a psychotherapist was the therapist's ability to understand the worldview and belief system of the practitioner. Some clinicians and many practitioners acknowledged that certain meditation-related problems warranted not only psychotherapy but also medication (cf. Kaselionyte & Gumley, 2018, p. 10). In many cases, medications were reported as helpful in allowing practitioners to stabilize and overcome distress and functional impairments. However, some meditators associated use of medications with a sense of shame, stigma, or loss of status within their meditation community.

These data highlight the tension between social values and medical recommendations, as avoiding medication may confer social status and spiritual attainment, but may also increase the risk of chronic disability from untreated illness (Judd, 1997; Drancourt et al., 2013; Santesteban-Echarri et al., 2017). While there is empirical evidence of poor outcomes when biomedical frameworks are not followed, there is no corresponding empirical evidence for positive outcomes when normative, non-pathologizing frameworks are followed (Menezes & Moreira-Almeida, 2010). More research is needed to provide accurate estimates of both risks and benefits for each choice.

Understanding the Context of the Assessment of Meditation Experiences

The social embeddedness and positioning of those who assess meditation experiences (e.g., meditation teachers, clinicians, or psychiatrists) impacts the decision-making process. For example, a teacher's educational background or training is likely to influence their appraisals. VanderKooi (1997) found that teachers whose own training and approach had been influenced by psychology were more likely to consult with mental health professionals when students encountered severe psychological problems and believed that "pushing students to 'break through' does not facilitate integration of an enlightenment experience and can damage students who are psychologically fragile" (p. 42). Conversely, both the VCE study and Kaselionyte and Gumley (2018) found that some teachers without clinical training acknowledged their limitations in identifying or responding to destabilizing experiences that could be indicative of mental illness. Teachers in the VCE study also reported that experiences that require a great deal of time and attention are likely to be appraised as problematic. Thus, the decision to send a meditator home from a retreat or to a hospital could be based not only on the nature of the experiences of that meditator, but also on the resources available, including time, training, and staff.

The teacher's social position must always be considered as a potential causal influence on their appraisals, particularly on their causal attributions. Two common causes of meditation problems given by teachers in the VCE and other studies were the meditator's "incorrect practice" and "incorrect response or attitude." Although both VanderKooi (1997) and the VCE study found that teachers cited a meditator's "excessive effort and striving" as a common source of problems, there was generally little consensus among meditation teachers regarding which dimensions of practice were problematic. VanderKooi (1997) reported that for Theravada Buddhist teachers, problems arise "when concentration is not balanced with adequate mindfulness," whereas Zen teachers attributed difficulties to "incorrect posture and breathing," and Tibetan teachers attributed energy imbalances in particular to "an improper use of certain advanced meditation practices" (p. 40). These attributions have also been made in clinical case studies. Chan-Ob and Boonyanaruthee (1999) declared that "meditation, regardless of kinds or schools, has never produced psychotic symptoms provided it is practiced in the right way"; however, "wrongly practiced meditation causes more stress," leading to sleep loss, which, in their view, is the real cause of psychosis (pp. 927–928).

Teachers have also attributed the cause of meditation-related challenges to the meditator's "incorrect" attitude or response, which therefore can be remedied by the "correct" response. For example, some teachers thought that extreme experiences, including psychosis, could arise because of "overidentifying with NSC [non-ordinary states of consciousness] and being unable to disidentify and let go" (VanderKooi, 1997, p. 40). Similarly, Kornfield (1979) suggested that "periods of strong fear and insecurity... are usually resolved by surrender, by fully experiencing them" (p. 54). Such attitude-based attributions also imply that any enduring difficulty or distress is a result of insufficient acceptance. While some practitioners in the VCE study reported that an experience became less difficult or distressing when it was accepted, others noted that acceptance resulted in their symptoms being prolonged unnecessarily when some sort of intervention would have been more appropriate. Further, the notion that with the right attitude any adversity will subside creates a situation in which practitioners may be found deficient and blamed for their own suffering (Kirmayer, 1990).

Teacher Social Positioning and Victim-Blaming

The tendency toward victim-blaming—or, more generally, to attribute causes to dispositional traits rather than to external conditions—is a well-documented attribution error (Heider, 1958) and is further influenced by social identity, gender, affective reaction, and personal and financial investments (Bal & van den Bos, 2010; van der Bruggen & Grubb, 2014). This victim-blaming tendency has been well documented in other contexts, and often serves the function of deflecting responsibility away from incumbent power structures. For example, reports of "shell-shock" (later called Post-Traumatic

Stress Disorder or PTSD) were attributed by military doctors to soldiers' preexisting psychological instability or "weak personalities" (Roberts-Pedersen, 2012), and sexual assault is often causally attributed to traits or behaviors of the victim (promiscuity, intoxication) rather than to the perpetrator (Davis et al., 1991; Ullman, 1996).

As described in both the VCE study and in other studies, when teachers were interviewed or when teachers' attributions were mentioned by practitioners, it was frequently the case that they attributed meditation-related difficulties to practitioner-level factors or to vague, difficult-to-quantify, dispositional deficiencies of the meditator (e.g., preexisting psychological vulnerabilities, unstable psyches, trauma histories, perpetuation of ego-structures, inadequate preparation or understanding, incorrect practice, insufficient acceptance of an experience, or insufficient surrendering or letting go). Placing exclusive emphasis on individual attributions can serve to deflect responsibility and blame to the meditators and away from the teachers, practices, or other aspects of the meditation culture. Since such attributions are often made retrospectively, after a positive or negative outcome is known, these attributions allow for negative outcomes to be attributed to the meditators, while positive outcomes can still be claimed as benefits of the meditation practice. This selective attribution process constitutes a "secondary victimization" (Symonds, 1980), which increases trauma-like symptoms and prolongs recovery time (Davis et al., 1991; Ullman, 1996). Victim-blaming also discourages disclosure, which contributes to past, current, and future underreporting of challenging or negative experiences (Ahrens, 2006).

Toward a Person-Centered Approach

Practitioners consistently reported that finding helpers who supported their goals, expectations, and values around meditation was critical for navigating meditation-related challenges. Values-based and person-centered approaches in mental health offer ways to think through the negotiation of meaning in the context of challenging meditation experiences (Jackson & Fulford, 2002). A "person-centered approach" is contrasted with a disease or disorder-centered approach in that it aims to address the needs *of* the person (including the totality of the person's health, both illness- and wellness-related aspects), as engaged *by* the person (with both patients and clinicians extending themselves as full human beings), *for* the person (assisting the fulfillment of the person's aspirations and life project), and *with* the person (in a respectful and empowering relationship with the person who consults) (Mezzich et al., 2010; Cloninger & Cloninger, 2011; Kirmayer et al., 2016b). With respect to meditation, this approach emphasizes the practitioner's agency and autonomy in deciding when meditation-related challenges need additional support through social, psychological, or medical interventions. From this perspective, what constitutes health and well-being, as well as what has ultimate value for the person, is determined through dialogue with them and by consideration of their lifeworld and social context; it is not simply assumed or imposed by others.

Clinically, distinguishing between normative or desirable experiences and psychopathology depends on understanding the individual's social and cultural contexts—an approach central to cultural and person-centered psychiatry (Kirmayer et al., 2016a, 2016b). This cultural context includes identities, roles, values, goals, norms, and expectations, some of which are explicit but many of which may remain tacit or implicit until they are highlighted by a challenge or conflict. Thus, assessing the meaning of unusual or distressing experiences requires not just information about explicit cultural norms and values, but also modes of dialogical engagement that allow the individual and others to explore and negotiate the meaning of experiences (Rashed, 2010). In the mental health literature, the conditions for this are sometimes framed as "cultural safety" and clearly depend on addressing hierarchies of power that may result in the silencing of challenging or divergent perspectives (Kirmayer et al., 2016a).

Increased recognition of the importance of cultural context has also shaped the most recent version of the *Diagnostic and Statistical Manual of Mental Disorders* (*DSM*). In an attempt to provide a more culturally-sensitive and person-centered approach to clinical diagnosis, the *DSM-5* Cultural Formulation Interview gives concrete and detailed methods for exploring the embeddedness of both the client and the provider in multiple overlapping cultural contexts with multiple social identities, values, and priorities, all of which interact with illness experience and treatment trajectories that change over time and circumstance (Lewis-Fernández et al., 2014, Adeponle et al., 2015). This approach has the potential to address some of the problems of differential diagnosis of meditation-related challenges by situating individual experiences in their personal and social contexts (Kirmayer, 2015b).

Instead of focusing exclusively on symptoms, a person-centered approach attempts to contextualize meditation-related challenges by relating them to relevant social and cultural frameworks, including religion and practice setting. Experiences that are not distressing or functionally impairing may be more likely to be framed adequately in terms of a religious worldview. But even distressing or impairing experiences may also be accepted by a community as expected challenges or even as positive indicators of progress along a religious path. This renders the use of local norms for differential diagnosis more complicated. In particular, the fact that a range of challenging, distressing, and impairing experiences can be considered part of the path across Buddhist traditions further complicates attempts to determine when a challenging experience is normative and when it is considered a problem requiring additional support or intervention.

Challenges to a Person-Centered Approach to Meditation in the West

The person-centered approach is one of the dominant paradigms in clinical psychotherapeutic settings. However, this privileging of the individual's experience and values is sometimes at odds with other institutional commitments and authority structures, including those of religions. Given the plurality of discourses concerning meditation—especially in the modern West, where it is presented as scientific, secular, or religious depending on context and intent—these commitments may not always be clear. Some contemporary meditation organizations may imply they are following a person-centered approach, when in fact they share more characteristics with institutionalized religions, where key values and beliefs (such as the purpose of life, definitions of health and well-being, the nature or purpose of human existence, or the causes of suffering and happiness) tend to be predetermined, immutable, and not open to individual interpretation. These religious commitments may often be tacit or presented behind a veneer of secularity, and may lead to conflict for those who assume that meditation is primarily a means to reach their own, preexisting goals, rather than having their goals and values challenged and changed. The individual reporting an adverse experience may then constitute a challenge to the authority of the religious institution and evoke responses that aim not only at managing their distress but also at containing or limiting the threat they represent to the institution. Examining these social and political processes of dealing with challenges to collective norms is an important, but relatively neglected, dimension of understanding meditative practices and traditions.

Conclusion

In this chapter, we have introduced a typology of challenging experiences associated with the practice of meditation. We have also identified some of the ways in which experiences are appraised by practitioners, teachers, clinicians, and researchers. The current data suggest that establishing a clear differential diagnosis between a "normative" meditation experience and "psychopathology" might not be straightforward. As with psychiatric diagnoses, the purpose is to offer guidance or intervention to people faced with difficult or troubling experiences. Recognizing the forms of culturally valid and non-pathological experiences is basic to spiritual and religious competence for clinicians, and it is equally important for meditation teachers to recognize that not all meditation-related experiences have to be viewed as a part of the path and responded to only by means of continued practice. Instead of aiming to establish criteria for differential diagnosis, practitioners, teachers, and clinicians may be better served by focusing on the practical questions: (1) whether the experience warrants additional support or intervention; and (2) what type of support or intervention might be most appropriate.

Among meditation teachers, the most widely agreed upon criteria for pursuing additional support are similar to the criteria for clinical significance: degree of distress and functional impairment, duration, degree of control, and relationship to the client's and the tradition's cultural norms. In addition to these criteria, cultural psychiatry and psychology emphasizes the importance of considering the social contexts, positions, identities, relationships, and power dynamics of the practitioner and others, including any authorities—such as a clinician or meditation teacher—who are involved in the decision-making process. Elaborating this broader contextual view requires further research on the social and cultural contexts of meditation and the looping effects between individual expectations, embodied experiences, and social responses.

References

Adeponle, A. B., Groleau, D., & Kirmayer, L. J. (2015). Clinician reasoning in the use of cultural formulation to resolve uncertainty in the diagnosis of psychosis. *Culture, Medicine, and Psychiatry* 39(1), 16–42.

Ahrens, C. E. (2006). Being silenced: The impact of negative social reactions on the disclosure of rape. *American Journal of Community Psychology 38*, 263–274.

Aitken, R. (1982). *Taking the path of Zen*. San Francisco: North Point Press.

American Psychiatric Association. (2013). *Diagnostic and statistical manual of mental disorders, Fifth edition (DSM-5)*. Arlington, VA: American Psychiatric Association.

Ataria, Y. (2015). Where do we end and where does the world begin? The case of insight meditation. *Philosophical Psychology 28*(8), 1128–1146.

Ataria, Y., Dor-Ziderman, Y., & Berkovich-Ohana, A. (2015). How does it feel to lack a sense of boundaries? A case study of a long-term mindfulness meditator. *Consciousness and Cognition 37*, 133–147.

Bal, M., & van den Bos, K. (2010). The role of perpetrator similarity in reactions toward innocent victims. *European Journal of Social Psychology 40*, 957–969.

Berkovich-Ohana, A., Dor-Ziderman, Y., Glicksohn, J., & Goldstein, A. (2013). Alterations in the sense of time, space, and body in the mindfulness-trained brain: A neurophenomenologically-guided MEG study. *Frontiers in Psychology 4*(912), 1–19.

Brett, C. (2002). Psychotic and mystical states of being: Connections and distinctions. *Philosophy, Psychiatry & Psychology 9*(4), 321–341.

Buddhaghosa, B. (1991). *The path of purification (Visuddhimagga)*. Bhikkhu Ñaṇamoli (Trans.). Onalaska, WA: BPS Pariyatti Editions.

Buswell, R., & Gimello, R. (1992). *Paths to liberation: The mārga and its transformations in Buddhist thought*. Honolulu, HI: Kuroda Institute/University of Hawaii Press.

Castillo, R. J. (1990). Depersonalization and meditation. *Psychiatry 53*(2), 158–168.

Chan-Ob, T., & Boonyanaruthee, V. (1999). Meditation in association with psychosis. *Journal of the Medical Association of Thailand 82*, 925–929.

Chen, Z., Qi, W., Hood, R. W. Jr., & Watson, P. J. (2011). Qualitative and quantitative analysis of mysticism in Chinese Buddhist monks and nuns. *Journal for the Scientific Study of Religion 50*(4), 654–670.

Cloninger, C. R., & Cloninger, K. M. (2011). Person-centered therapeutics. *International Journal of Person-Centered Medicine 1*, 43–52.

Davis, R. C., Brickman, E., & Baker, T. (1991). Supportive and unsupportive responses of others to rape victims: Effects on concurrent victim adjustment. *American Journal of Community Psychology 19*, 443–451.

Dein, S. (2012). Psychosis and religious/spiritual experience: Ethnographic, cognitive, and neurobiological perspectives. In C. Murray (Ed.), *Mental health and anomalous experience* (pp. 179–192). Hauppauge, NY: Nova Science.

Dein, S., & Littlewood, R. (2011). Religion and psychosis: A common evolutionary trajectory? *Transcultural Psychiatry 48*(3), 318–335.

Doctor, T. (2005). *Tibetan treasure literature: Revelation, tradition, and accomplishment in visionary Buddhism*. Boston: Snow Lion Publications.

Dor-Ziderman, Y., Berkovich-Ohana, A., Glicksohn, J., & Goldstein, A. (2013). Mindfulness-induced selflessness: A MEG neurophenomenological study. *Frontiers in Human Neuroscience 7*(582), 1–17.

Drancourt, N., Etain, B., Lajnef, M., Henry, C., Raust, A., Cochet, B., . . . Bellivier, F. (2013). Duration of untreated bipolar disorder: Missed opportunities on the long road to optimal treatment. *Acta Psychiatrica Scandinavica 127*, 136–144.

Full, G. E., Walach, H., & Trautwein, M. (2013). Meditation induced changes in perception: An interview study with expert meditators (*sotapannas*) in Burma. *Mindfulness 4*(1), 55–63.

Grof, C., & Grof, S. (Eds.). (1989). *Spiritual emergency: When personal transformation becomes a crisis*. Los Angeles: Jeremy P. Tarcher.

Gyatso, J. (1998). *Apparitions of the self: The secret autobiographies of a Tibetan visionary*. Princeton, NJ: Princeton University Press.

Gyatso, J. (1999). Healing burns with fire: The facilitations of experience in Tibetan Buddhism. *Journal of the American Academy of Religion 67*(1), 113–147.

Heider, F. (1958). *The psychology of interpersonal relations*. New York: Wiley.

Heriot-Maitland, C. P. (2008). Mysticism and madness: Different aspects of the same human experience? *Mental Health, Religion, and Culture 11*(3), 301–325.

Hsuan Hua, V. M. (2003). *The Shurangama Sutra, Volume 8*. Burlingame, CA: Buddhist Text Translation Society.

Ingram, D. M. (2008). *Mastering the core teachings of the Buddha: An unusually hardcore Dharma book*. London: Aeon Books.

Jackson, M., & Fulford, K. W. M. (2002). Psychosis good and bad: Values-based practice and the distinction between pathological and nonpathological forms of psychotic experience. *Philosophy, Psychiatry, & Psychology 9*(4), 387–394.

Jacoby, S. (2015). *Love and liberation: Autobiographical writings of the Tibetan Buddhist visionary Sera Khandro*. New York: Columbia University Press.

Judd, L. L. (1997). The clinical course of unipolar major depressive disorders. *Archives of General Psychiatry 54*(11), 989–991

Kaselionyte, J., & Gumley, A. (2018). "It's like a charge—either fuses you or burns you out": An interpretative phenomenological analysis of extreme mental states in meditation context. *Mental Health, Religion, and Culture*, doi:10.1080/13674676.2017.1422237.

Kennedy, R. B. (1976). Self-induced depersonalization syndrome. *American Journal of Psychiatry 133*, 1326–1328.

Kirmayer, L. J. (1990). Resistance, reactance, and reluctance to change: A cognitive attributional approach to strategic interventions. *Journal of Cognitive Psychotherapy 4*(2), 83–104.

Kirmayer, L. J. (2008). Culture and the metaphoric mediation of pain. *Transcultural Psychiatry 45*(2), 318–338.

Kirmayer, L. J. (2015a). Re-visioning psychiatry: Toward an ecology of mind in health and illness. In L. J. Kirmayer, R. Lemelson, & C. Cummings (Eds.), *Re-visioning psychiatry:*

Cultural phenomenology, critical neuroscience and global mental health (pp. 622–660). New York: Cambridge University Press.

Kirmayer, L. J. (2015b). The future of cultural formulation. In R. Lewis-Fernández, N. Aggarwal, L. Hinton, D. Hinton & L. J. Kirmayer (Eds.), *DSM-5® Handbook on the Cultural Formulation Interview* (pp. 267–288). Washington, DC: APA Press.

Kirmayer, L. J., Corin, E., & Jarvis, G. E. (1998). Inside knowledge: Cultural constructions of insight in psychosis. In A. David (Ed.), *Insight and psychosis* (pp. 193–220). Oxford: Oxford University Press.

Kirmayer, L. J., Bennegadi, R., & Kastrup, M. C. (2016a). Cultural awareness and responsiveness in person-centered psychiatry. In J. Mezzich et al. (Eds.), *Person Centered Psychiatry* (pp. 77–95). Switzerland: Springer.

Kirmayer, L. J., Mezzich, J. E., & Van Staden, C. W. (2016b). Health experience and values in person-centered assessment and diagnosis. In J. Mezzich et al. (Eds.), *Person Centered Psychiatry* (pp. 179–199). Switzerland: Springer.

Kornfield, J. (1979). Intensive insight meditation: A phenomenological study. *Journal of Transpersonal Psychology 11*(1), 41–58.

Kornfield, J. (1993). *A path with heart: A guide through the perils and promises of spiritual life.* New York: Bantam Books.

Kutz, I., Leserman, J., Dorrington, C., Morrison, C. H., Borysenko, J. Z., & Benson, H. (1985). Meditation as an adjunct to psychotherapy: An outcome study. *Psychotherapy and Psychosomatics 43*, 209–218.

Lomas, T., Cartwright, T., Edington, T., & Ridge, D. (2015). A qualitative analysis of experiential challenges associated with meditation practice. *Mindfulness 6*, 848–860.

Lewis-Fernández, R., Aggarwal, N. K., Bäärnhielm, S., Rohlof, H., Kirmayer, L. J., Weiss, M. G., . . . & Groen, S. (2014). Culture and psychiatric evaluation: Operationalizing cultural formulation for DSM-5. *Psychiatry: Interpersonal and Biological Processes 77*(2), 130–154.

Lindahl, J. (2017). Somatic energies and emotional traumas: A qualitative study of practice-related challenges reported by Vajrayāna Buddhists. *Religion 8*(8), 153, 1–22.

Lindahl, J. R., Fisher, N. E., Cooper, D. J., Rosen, R. K., & Britton, W. B. (2017). The Varieties of contemplative experience: A mixed-methods study of meditation-related challenges in Western Buddhists. *PLoS ONE 12*(5), 1–38.

Lindahl, J. R., Kaplan, C. T., Winget, E. M., & Britton, W. B. (2014). A phenomenology of meditation-induced light experiences: Traditional Buddhist and neurobiological perspectives. *Frontiers in Psychology 4*(973), 1–16.

Lingpa, D. (2015). *Düdjom Lingpa's Visions of the great perfection: Vol. 3: The vajra essence.* B. A. Wallace (Trans.). Boston: Wisdom Publications.

Menezes, A., & Moreira-Almeida, A. (2009). Differential diagnosis between spiritual experiences and mental disorders of religious content. *Revista de Psiquiatria Clínica 36*(2), 69–76.

Menezes, A., & Moreira-Almeida, A. (2010). Religion, spirituality, and psychosis. *Current Psychiatry Reports 12*, 174–179.

Mezzich, J. E., Salloum, I. M., Cloninger, C. R., Salvador-Carulla, L., Kirmayer, L. J., Banzato, C. E., . . . & Botbol, M. (2010). Person-centred integrative diagnosis: Conceptual bases and structural model. *Canadian Journal of Psychiatry 55*(11), 701–708.

Miller, J. J. (1993). The unveiling of traumatic memories and emotions through mindfulness and concentration meditation: Clinical implications and three case reports. *Journal of Transpersonal Psychology 25*, 169–180.

Namto, A. S. S. (1989). *Insight meditation: Practical steps to ultimate truth*. Fawnskin, CA: Vipassanā Dhura Meditation Society.

Otis, L. (1984). Adverse effects of Transcendental Meditation. In D. H. Shapiro & R. Walsh (Eds.), *Meditation: Classic and Contemporary Perspectives* (pp. 201–208). New York: Aldine.

Pabongka Rinpoche. (1991). *Liberation in the palm of your hand: A concise discourse on the path to enlightenment*. Boston: Wisdom Publications.

Pagis, M. (2010). From abstract concepts to experiential knowledge: Embodying enlightenment in a meditation center. *Qualitative Sociology* 33, 469–489.

Parnas, J., & Henriksen, M. G. (2016). Mysticism and schizophrenia: A phenomenological exploration of the structure of consciousness in the schizophrenia spectrum disorders. *Consciousness and Cognition* 43, 75–88.

Preece, R. (2011). *Preparing for tantra: Creating the psychological ground for practice*. Ithaca, NY: Snow Lion Publications.

Rashed, M. A. (2010). Religious experience and psychiatry: Analysis of the conflict and proposal for a way forward. *Philosophy, Psychiatry, & Psychology* 17(3), 185–204.

Roberts-Pedersen, E. (2012), A weak spot in the personality? Conceptualising "war neurosis" in British medical literature of the Second World War. *Australian Journal of Politics and History* 58(3), 408–420.

Santesteban-Echarri, O., Paino, M., Rice, S., Gonzalez-Blanch, C., McGorry, P., Gleeson, J., & Alvarez-Jimenez, M. (2017). Predictors of functional recovery in first-episode psychosis: A systematic review and meta-analysis of longitudinal studies. *Clinical Psychology Review* 58, 59–75.

Sayadaw, M. (1965). *The progress of insight: A treatise on Satipaṭṭhāna meditation*. Nyanaponika Thera (Trans.). Kandy, Sri Lanka: Buddhist Publication Society.

Sayadaw, M. (2016). *Manual of insight*. Somerville, MA: Wisdom Publications.

Shapiro, D. (1992). Adverse effects of meditation: A preliminary investigation of long-term meditators. *International Journal of Psychosomatics* 39, 62–67.

Sharf, R. (1995). Buddhist modernism and the rhetoric of meditative experience. *Numen* 42, 228–283.

Sogen, O. (2001). *An Introduction to Zen training*. Boston: Tuttle Publishing.

Symonds, M. (1980). The "second injury" to victims. *Evaluation and Change*, 36–38.

Taves, A. (2009). *Religious experience reconsidered: A building-block approach to the study of religion and other special things*. Princeton, NJ: Princeton University Press.

Taylor, G., & Murray, C. (2012). The role of understanding, engagement, and meaning in anomalous experience: A narrative review of the evidence from cultural research. In C. Murray (Ed.), *Mental health and anomalous experience* (pp. 1–18). Hauppauge, NY: Nova Science.

Ullman, S. E. (1996). Social reactions, coping strategies, and self-blame attributions in adjustment to sexual assault. *Psychology of Women Quarterly* 20, 505–526.

van der Bruggen, M., & Grubb, A. R. (2014). A review of the literature relating to rape victim blaming: An analysis of the impact of observer and victim characteristics on attribution of blame in rape cases. *Aggression and Violent Behavior* 19(5), 523–531.

VanderKooi, L. (1997). Buddhist teachers' experience with extreme mental states in Western meditators. *Journal of Transpersonal Psychology* 29(1), 31–46.

Vieten, C., & Scammel, S. (2015). *Spiritual and religious competencies in clinical practice: Guidelines for psychotherapists and mental health professionals*. Oakland, CA: New Harbinger.

Viggiano, D. B., & Krippner, S. (2010). The Grof's model of spiritual emergency in retrospect: Has it stood the test of time? *International Journal of Transpersonal Studies* 29(1), 118–127.

Wallace, B. A. (2006). *The attention revolution: Unlocking the power of the focused mind.* Boston: Wisdom Publications.

Walsh, R., & Roche, L. (1979). Precipitation of acute psychotic episodes by intensive meditation in individuals with a history of schizophrenia. *American Journal of Psychiatry* 136(8), 1085–1086.

Wong, S. Y. S., Chan, J. Y. C., Zhang, D., Lee, E. K. P., & Tsoi, K. K. F. (2018). The safety of Mindfulness-Based Interventions: A systematic review of randomized controlled trials. *Mindfulness*, doi:10.1007/s12671-018-0897-0.

Yorston, G. A. (2001). Mania precipitated by meditation: A case report and literature review. *Mental Health, Religion, and Culture* 4(2), 209–213.

CHAPTER 39

THE DARK NIGHTS OF THE SOUL IN ABRAHAMIC MEDITATIVE TRADITIONS

NATHAN FISHER

INTRODUCTION

WHILE unknown even to many of the adherents of Judaism, Christianity, and Islam, all three religions have given rise to rich and sophisticated meditative traditions over the past two millennia. Although manuals with explicit meditation instructions are less prevalent than in some Asian religions, this is partly due to such instruction being intentionally relegated to the realm of oral transmission between teachers and students. More common in the traditional literature of Abrahamic traditions are exoteric and esoteric descriptions of the territory of the contemplative paths for the sake of preparation and guidance of the wayfarers (see Silverstein, Stroumsa, and Blidstein (2015) for category of "Abrahamic" religions). In fact, central mystical texts in all three religions are explicit and forthcoming about the many pitfalls or wrong turns that it is possible to make, as well as the challenging stages that indicate spiritual progress despite the appearance to the contrary.

To investigate if these maps correspond to the experiences of contemplatives today, the Varieties of Contemplative Experience: Abrahamic (VCE-A) project interviewed practitioners and teachers in Western Jewish, Christian, and Islamicate traditions about their positively and negatively valenced experiences and how they interpreted them (Lindahl et al., 2017, p. 30). This chapter will explore some of the religious texts, figures, and ideas that the subjects in this study referenced most often in order to highlight the appraisal processes involved in normalizing distressing and challenging experiences (see Lindahl et al., this volume, for a fuller discussion of normalizing appraisal processes related to meditation-related difficulties). In general, teachers and practitioners interpret such distressing experiences as either "adverse effects" or as "part of the path." In the context of this study, the phrase "adverse effects" refers to difficult or distressing experiences that were appraised as preventative of, or antithetical to, growth and development along an emically significant trajectory and thereby entail unnecessary suffering. Subjects posited causal factors that can lead to such unnecessary suffering, and some of the most common included prematurely engaging in advanced practices and not working closely with a knowledgeable teacher or guide. This is in contrast to distressing experiences that are "part of the path," meaning they are actually indicative of growth and development (despite appearing otherwise) and therefore involve necessary suffering. Since there is still much debate as to what exactly constitutes adverse effects of meditation, this paper will explore emic understandings of necessary difficulties in Abrahamic contemplative traditions to begin to disambiguate the latter from the former and examine what such paths look like today.

Catholic Traditions

The Dark Nights

By far the most common interpretation for necessary difficulties associated with Catholic contemplative practices in the VCE-A study were the "dark nights" (*noches oscuras*) first elucidated by the Carmelite monk John of the Cross (1542–1591). While earlier Christian mystics certainly discussed necessary difficulties one will encounter on the path to union with God, Bernard McGinn argues that St. John's writings on the dark nights are "the best known treatment of mystical dereliction in Christian history" (McGinn, 2017, p. 280). Particularly relevant for our study is what John describes as the two "passive" nights—the night of the senses and the night of the spirit. The passive night of the senses involves a purification of the sensory faculties and is understood as the beginning of the contemplative or "illuminative" stage of the threefold path of purgation, illumination, and union. The passive night of the spirit is a more dramatic and painful purification of one's faculties of intellect, memory, and will—the latter of which is the "spiritual faculty of appetite and affectivity" (McGinn, 2017, p. 257). This dark night signals the beginning of the unitive stage of the path that culminates in a mystical "marriage" to God, also conceived of as the realization of the "center of the soul" (*centro del alma*) (McGinn, 2017, p. 260).

John primarily uses two analogies to describe such necessarily difficult stages of the path, a damp log of wood being burned and a mother weaning her child. The purgative dimension of the log analogy is that just as the heat of a flame pushes all of the moisture of a log to the surface before it can become completely enflamed, so too do the states of contemplation illuminate and bring to the surface all of one's normally unconscious inner conflicts and imperfections before a complete union can be achieved (Payne, 1990, p. 74). He then describes the weaning analogy as follows:

> It should be known, then, that God nurtures and caresses the soul, after it has been resolutely converted to his service, like a loving mother who warms her child with the heat of her bosom, nurses it with good milk and tender food, and carries and caresses it in her arms. But as the child grows older, the mother withholds her caresses and hides her tender love; she rubs bitter aloes on her sweet breast and sets the child down from her arms, letting it walk on its own feet so that it may put aside the habits of childhood and grows accustomed to greater and more important things.
> (Saint John of the Cross, 1991, p. 361)

In relation to the two different challenging stages, in the night of the senses the contemplative is "weaned" off of sensory nourishment and reliance so as to begin experiencing the more refined nourishment of the states of contemplation where the senses are absorbed to various degrees. In the night of the spirit, the contemplative is weaned off even this more spiritual nourishment so as to enter into a more mature and abiding relationship with God symbolized by "marriage."

Sister Constance Fitzgerald, a contemporary Carmelite author and teacher, has written several influential pieces on how she has observed the dark nights manifest for contemplatives today and how to work skillfully with them when such stages arise. She uses the language of "impasse" to describe the dark nights, by which she means "there is no way out of, no way around, no rational escape from, what imprisons one" and that it entails "unavoidable suffering"(Fitzgerald, 1984, p. 94). She describes how these stages entail feelings of despair and rejection (as a child may initially feel when being weaned) by God and perhaps one's peers as well and counsels that in order to see this experience as "the condition for creative growth and transformation" one must first acknowledge and accept the experience of powerlessness (Fitzgerald, 1984, pp. 96–97). Fitzgerald borrows from psychodynamic approaches to psychology when she equates this acceptance of powerlessness with an awareness of the fact that such growth can only come from unconscious processes that will occur mysteriously beyond one's control. In this way she understands the dark night of the senses as a kind of withdrawal from a reliance on "left-brain," conscious processes that thereby activates "right-brain" processes in that it "puts a reverse pressure on imagination . . . that throws the intuitive, unconscious self into gear"(Fitzgerald, 1984, pp. 115, 95). Fitzgerald describes the experience of the purification of the intellect, will, and memory in the dark night of the spirit as the loss of "the very support systems that have structured our lives, given them meaning and value, and provided a source of affirmation and final assurances" (Fitzgerald, 1995, p. 103).

Divine Therapy

One of the most influential contemporary translations of the contemplative path of John of the Cross is the movement known as Centering Prayer, first developed by Trappist monks William Meninger, Basil Pennington, and Thomas Keating. Over the last four decades, Father Keating (1923–2018) has developed a conception of the contemplative path that, drawing on classical Christian mystical sources, acknowledges that some challenging or distressing experiences are necessary and unavoidable. He describes how "through the regular practice of centering prayer the dynamism of interior purification is set in motion" which he calls "a kind of divine psychotherapy, organically designed for each of us, to purify our unconscious and free us from the obstacles to the free flow of grace in our minds, emotions, and bodies" (Keating, 2006, p. 95). He continues:

> Empirical evidence seems to be growing that the consequences of traumatic emotional experiences from earliest childhood are stored in our bodies and nervous systems in the form of tension, anxiety, and various defense mechanisms. Ordinary rest and sleep do not get rid of them. But with interior silence and the profound rest that this brings to the whole organism, these emotional blocks begin to soften up, and the natural capacity of the human organism to throw off things that are harmful starts to evacuate them. (Keating, 2006, p. 95)

Keating elaborates that this charged psychological material may sometimes also have a somatic dimension and may manifest as "emotional knots" that can cause physical pain as they are "unwinding" (Keating, 2006, p. 105). He also notes the conative dimension of this process in that the quieting or withdrawal from one's normal thought patterns exposes our unconscious motivations and value systems that are often rooted in early childhood. Collectively these hidden motivations and unconscious drives constitute the "monumental illusion" of what he termed the "false self," and the unloading of the unconscious is its slow deconstruction (Keating, 2006, p. 15). He advises practitioners not to sift through the material that is arising or being unloaded during the prayer period since the "psychological refuse comes up as a kind of compost. It's like throwing out the garbage. You don't separate the eggshells from the orange peels. You just throw the whole thing out"(Keating, 2006, p. 100). He notes that distressing thoughts, moods, or feelings of depression might last for days as part of this process or even longer if it is particularly "heavy weather" (Keating, 2006, p. 95). In the latter case, he notes that as one goes deeper into the unconscious, one "may hit something like an oil well and up will come a whole stream of stuff," which can result in "a period of several months or years when it is rough going" that he identifies as John of the Cross's dark nights (Keating, 2006, p. 93).

Keating's student, Cynthia Bourgeault, writes how much of Keating's "psycho-spiritual paradigm" was inspired by the first Centering Prayer intensive in 1983 at the Lama Foundation that was modeled on a Zen Buddhist *sesshin* retreat (Bourgeault, 2004, p. 91). She discusses how "no one was prepared for the volume and vibrancy of emotional outpouring that flooded forth from five hours a day of Centering prayer practice" and describes "people going through in ten days what it would have taken them twenty years to go through at a monastery" (Bourgeault, 2004, p. 92). Bourgeault further adds that the work of transpersonal psychologist Michael Washburn influenced Keating's paradigm, specifically his notion of "regression in the service of ego-transcendence," which is seen as "the heart of the divine therapy" (Bourgeault, 2004, p. 108). This model suggests that, contrary to traditional understandings of spiritual transformation as a linear ascent,

> the ascent is inextricably bound to a descent into the ground of our own psyche... Thus, periods of psychological ferment and destabilization are signs that the journey is progressing, not that it is a failure. As a practice of meditational prayer loosens repressed material in the unconscious, the initial fruits of spiritual practice may not be the expected peace and enlightenment, but destabilization and the emergence into consciousness of considerable pain. (Bourgeault, 2004, p. 97)

Keating himself uses a rich variety of metaphors and imagery to describe this oscillatory trajectory and the necessary difficulties and suffering that this path of purification entails. For example, he likens the contemplative to a basketball, in the sense that the harder it is thrown down, the higher it will bounce back up, and likens the contemplative path to the growth of a tree in that its fruit will only emerge and become ripe in the fall after its flowers bloom in spring and then die in the summer (Keating, 2006, p. 114). He also compares the contemplative path to "a spiral staircase" as well as "an eagle rising to the sun" that "keeps returning to the same place on the horizontal plane, but to a higher place on the vertical plane" (Keating, 2006, p. 114; Keating, 2009, p. 50).

The Night of the Self

As we saw above, Keating equates particularly acute or challenging periods of "unloading" with John of the Cross's (passive) dark nights. Elsewhere in his writings he follows John more closely, for example, in describing the process of being "weaned" off sensory rewards and identifying the three signs of the dark night of the senses as "aridity in prayer and daily life," "the fear that we are going backwards and that... we have offended God," and finally, "the inability or disinclination to practice discursive meditation" (Keating, 2012, pp. 79–81). While the night of the senses "immobilizes" the false self, the night of the spirit purifies its roots in the unconscious, a process that may evoke experiences of tremendous fear (Keating, 2012, p. 110).

Once the false self is completely "dismantled," the stage of "transforming union" is automatically entered (Keating, 2012, p. 110). This consists of a "restructuring of consciousness, not an experience or set of experiences" in which "the presence of God becomes a kind of fourth dimension to the three-dimensional world in which we have been living"(Keating, 2012, p. 109). In this abiding stage of the path "emotional swings disappear," though the emotions themselves do not, and "there is no longer a self-centered

'I'"(Keating, 2012, p. 119). He concludes that transforming union "is the goal of the first part of the spiritual journey," intriguingly implying there is a second part of the path aimed at an even more elevated or complete union with God (Keating, 2012, p. 120). In one of his last books, he describes this more ultimate goal as "non-dual consciousness," "unity consciousness," and the "death of the separate-self sense" and adds that the "sense of a separate self is the ultimate cause of all our problems in the first place, even more fundamental than the false self" (Keating, 2014, p. 50). He makes very brief mention of a "night of the self," which precedes this final attainment, though he doesn't elaborate on what it involves (Keating, 2014, p. 144). Fortunately Keating's student David Frenette offers a bit more on the topic:

> Some modern contemplative writers also speak of a third dark night: *the dark night of self.* In the dark night of spirit, God disappears. In the dark night of self, "self disappears—or gradually diminishes until it is finally gone" as you are subsumed in the embrace of the inner life of the Trinity itself, when you lose any fixed point of self-subjectivity in the subjectivity of what is called the Godhead.
>
> (Frenette, 2017, p. 199, emphasis in original)

Frenette describes the considerable fear, dread, and desolation that can arise in this night and refers to the writings of Bernadette Roberts, who has described her own destabilizing experiences and the functional impairment that she encountered in this phase of her own contemplative path (Frenette, 2017, pp. 186–187; Roberts, 2005, pp. 174–182; see Blaschke, 2017, pp. 119–120 for more on the "night of self"). Thus according to this contemporary tradition, necessary difficulties may be encountered in the process of the unloading of the unconscious, which overlaps with what they interpret to be the passive dark nights, or in the more advanced (and theologically novel) night of the self, culminating in a more radical unity with the divine.

Sufi Traditions

Polishing the Heart

One of the most common images that gets used to describe the Sufi path is "polishing the mirror of the heart" based on a Hadith describing "invocation" (*dhikr*) as cleansing the "rust of the heart" (Sviri, 2002, p. 16). In the VCE-A study, those interviewed referred to necessary difficulties of contemplative practices in the context of this broad framework of purification and the "states" (*hal*) and "stages" (*maqamat*) that describe this process in more detail. In early Sufi literature, as Klogge describes more in depth (in this volume), the heart is understood as the organ of personal and transpersonal consciousness. The process of polishing it consists of the painstaking work of ethical, devotional, and contemplative practices as well as the effects of such practices—often conceived of as some kind of experience of divine love (*ishq*). As scholar of Sufi psychology Sara Sviri describes, this kind of love, however, "is not a mild pietistic affection or ideal, nor a dreamy, sentimental, poetic metaphor, nor a refined, philosophic concept. It is a crude, ruthless, and glorious reality which pervades all levels of being, body and soul" (Sviri, 2002, p. 111). As such, this dynamic experience of love is intense enough to purify the heart, to "burn away" its impurities in the metallurgic and alchemical imagery that is employed. The famous Sufi poet Jalal al-Din Rumi (1207–1273) incorporates this imagery throughout the corpus of his poetry and describes this alchemical property of love when he writes,

> Through Love all that is bitter will be sweet.
> Through Love all that is copper will be gold.
> Through Love all dregs will turn to purest wine.
> (Sviri, 2002, p. 206)

Here we find another related metaphor for the purgative effects of contemplative practice—the fermentation process of turning grapes to wine—which is used often in the poetry of Rumi as well as many other Sufi poets before and after him. In the metaphor, the "dregs" (*durd*) of the wine can be identified with necessary suffering, for example, the despair and longing that is left over after the "intoxicating" effects of the contemplative practice subside (Chittick, 1983, p. 317). Summarizing such purification imagery used in early Sufi poetry, Annemarie Schimmel explains that "just as grape juice is purified by constant 'tribulation' of fermenting until it becomes pure wine, and just as wheat is ground and kneaded and apparently mistreated until it becomes bread, thus the human soul can mature only through suffering" (Schimmel, 2011, p. 137).

Contemporary Sufi traditions have continued to make use of such purgative imagery while connecting or translating them into modern psychological terminology. Western Sufi teacher Llewellyn Vaughan-Lee describes the love cultivated in the central meditation practice in his tradition as follows:

> It is a love that burns and purifies, cleansing the heart of many impurities that belong to the ego and *nafs*, the desires and distortions in which the pure soul of the newborn child becomes trapped as it grows into the density of this world. The fire of the heart begins to burn away this dross, often confronting us with our own darkness, our shadow qualities. (Vaughan-Lee, 2011, p. 25)

The framework of purification is related here to an embodied psychological model, specifically the Jungian framework of the "shadow" as one's personal unconscious. Since the psyche is understood to be rooted in the heart in this model, this effect of contemplative practice has both somatic and psychological repercussions, the latter of which will make conscious "patterns of resistance or repressed inner pain," which will then need to be addressed with the assistance of a teacher (Vaughan-Lee, 2011, p. 102).

Sufi Psychology and the Yo-Yo Syndrome

This modern Western tradition in fact understands the blissful and absorptive experiences of love and the challenging psychological material that will be evoked by them to be rooted in classical Sufi psychological literature that details this trajectory in exquisite detail. Sviri describes the trajectory of the classical Sufi path, beginning in the tenth century, as an "ascending road or ladder along which several stations or stages (*maqamat*) are situated," each one designating "a psychological obstacle, related basically to physical and egotistic needs" (Sviri, 1987, p. 338). While different Sufi manuals enumerate different names for, and quantities of, these stations, most also include another "category of psychological events... which is much more ephemeral, intensified and spontaneous, and is regarded as an utterly divine grace" that are called "states" (*hal*) (Sviri, 1987, p. 338). She argues that "the neat portrayal of consecutive *maqamat* does not, in fact, presuppose a straightforward line of ascent" since different emotional states are correlated with different revelations of God, and God will reveal Godself at times as compassionate and loving and at other times as wrathful and judging (Sviri, 1987, p. 338). These dual modes of divine revelation will thus be experienced by the wayfarer as being "constantly thrown between extreme emotional poles," and this dynamism or fluctuation is very often referred to in Sufi literature as "variegation" (*talwin*) (Sviri, 1987, pp. 339–340). As one makes one's way up the ladder, the wayfarer continues to ascend from one polar set of divine qualities/emotions to a more refined pair, and in the intermediate stages of the path will encounter "expansion" (*bast*) and "contraction" (*qabd*), either understood as stations in themselves or dimensions of every station (Sviri, 1987, p. 341; Nurbaksh, 1993, p. 27). Expansion consists of feeling

> intoxicated and elated, life feels vibrant and full of possibilities, there is a sense of purpose and direction, hardships seem manageable, obstacles are easily overcome, synchronicities come in abundance, and one gets insights and revelations—sheer ecstasy.... Then one's inner state changes, sometimes with no apparent reason: a deep depression sets in, apathy and inertia, there is no light, no hope, no comfort, no security, no guidance, no God; an unexplained anxiety blocks the chest and the throat, and everything is dark and gloomy. (Sviri, 1987, p. 341)

Both Sviri and Schimmel identify this state of contraction (*qabd*) with the "dark night of the soul" (Sviri, 2002, p. 30; Schimmel, 2011, p. 129).

While there is often a great range and variety of differences in the maps of the stations of the Sufi path, the oscillation between expansion and contraction is ubiquitous throughout Sufi literature and is reported by Sufi communities to the present day (Sviri, 1994, p. 206). For example, members of Vaughan-Lee's own lineage (the Naqshbandiyya-Mujaddidiyya order) have nicknamed this phenomenon, as they have witnessed its occurrence among members of their community, the "Yo-Yo syndrome" (Sviri, 1994, p. 206). His predecessor, Irina Tweedie, describes how some days,

> on the mystical path—the meditation is easy; all is wonderful. We call God or That, the Beloved. The Beloved is near... The next day I am alone. I can't find the Beloved. God doesn't exist. It is awful. We call it the yo-yo syndrome—up and down, and up and down, and up and down, endlessly... And as you can compare spiritual life to a spiral, the experiences repeat themselves in a higher and higher spiral, or rather higher and higher frequencies. [Simultaneously] the dark night of the soul gets deeper and deeper and deeper. (Tweedie, 1998)

Tweedie clarifies that in the conception of the path in her tradition this oscillation between expansive, blissful, and absorptive states with psychological and emotional suffering causes "a great friction," which catalyzes the "purifying of the mind" necessary to eventually realize an intimate union with God (King, 1992, pp. 295–296).

Bewilderment and Annihilation

In one influential and allegorical map of a Sufi path, Farid ad-Din Attar's (1145–1221) *The Conference of the Birds*, the wayfaring birds must travel across seven valleys symbolizing stations (*maqamat*) of the path before reaching their goal, a mythical bird known as a "Simurgh." The sixth valley is called "the valley of bewilderment" (*wadi-i hayrat*) and in this station one doesn't know "whether he exists or not, whether he's in the middle or on the edge, whether he's visible or hidden, whether he's extinct (*fani*) or permanent (*baqi*), or both of these at the same time" (Ritter, 2003, p. 149). Attar then offers a parable to elucidate this particular predicament:

> The daughter of a king falls in love with the handsome slave of her father. She has ten serving maidens to whom she complains about her suffering in love. The latter promise to bring the slave to her in secret. They give him a sleeping potion and manage to bring him to the princess's room. When he wakes up, he sees himself surrounded by royal splendor and festive arrangements. The young women are playing music, incense is burning, and opposite him sits the most beautiful of all princesses who immediately overwhelms him with caresses. Drunk from abundant enjoyment of wine, in the morning he is taken back to where he has been. He wakes up in a confused state and doesn't know what to answer those who question him about his nocturnal experience, whether he experienced something real or a dream, whether he was drunk or sober... And between this and that he's now bewildered and helpless, and he feels he's at his wits end. (Ritter, 2003, p. 149)

This valley, interesting enough, comes right after the valley of union (*wadi ittihad*), which is not actually the goal of the path in this allegory. Nevertheless, the effect of such an experience was potent enough to have dramatically destabilizing effects, and it brings one to a state of helplessness—a prerequisite for the attainment of the final goal of "poverty and annihilation" (*faqr u fana*) (Stone, 2006, p. 101). This penultimate stage of the path can be described as one in which the mystic is "thrust" back into the phenomenal world of multiplicity and egoic consciousness after a particularly potent experience beyond both (Stone, 2006, p. 98). This can be a very disorienting situation to be in, leading Attar to describe one in this state as being "like a madman" (Stone, 2006, p. 101). Vaughan-Lee again offers a contemporary interpretation of this stage of contemplative development:

> After certain inner experiences you know that your ego is an illusion. It is not real. You have tasted of the truth of who you really are, the center of being that really belongs to you. And yet you have to wear its clothes like everyone else... Initially this can be very confusing for the ego. Before, it was the main actor in your life; now it is just a bit player, mostly repeating old lines. (Vaughan-Lee, 2011, p. 152)

Once again, this stage is not yet the goal, which in this parable would be understood as engagement and marriage to the princess rather than occasionally being deposited in her chambers before returning to one's life (or trying to) as it was previously. This can be a particularly precarious and disorienting time for the contemplative, however, and it is here that some teachers have noted that a strong relationship between a teacher and student is helpful or even necessary, since "without this complete commitment the disciple can easily be left stranded between the worlds, unable to return to a former ego-identity, yet lacking the energy or guidance needed to cross into the deeper reality of the Self" (Vaughan-Lee, 2011, p. 97).

As stated above, the pair of terms *fana* and *baqa* ("annihilation" and "subsistence") are acknowledged as the "highest stage" on the Sufi contemplative path and are rooted in a verse from the Qur'an: "All that is upon it passes away (*fanin*). And there remains (*wa-yabqa*) the Face of thy Lord, Possessed of Majesty and Bounty" (Sura 55:26–27, Nasr 2015). While *fana* "indicates the annihilation of the psychological identification with the lower self, the ego" (*nafs*), *baqa* refers to "the permanence of the higher Self, the soul, man's everlasting core of being" (Sviri, 2002, p. 86). This dual stage refers to a structural change in one's consciousness and identity, beginning with an ecstatic (literally outside one's *self*) experience of undifferentiated unity, which ultimately stabilizes as a sense of self comes back 'on-line,' though in a transformed capacity (Stone, 2006, p. 104). In the Nuriyya-Malamiyya Sufi tradition, the first stage of this attainment is discussed as a kind of psychological death where "the servant temporarily ceases to be, often falling into a state of total intoxication in which the apparent world disappears" (Toussulis, 2010, p. 177). This can also be a challenging stage as one confronts the terror and dread associated with the prospect of one's death, and here a teacher is understood to be helpful or even necessary to help one "die" to his or her old identity and then "act as a midwife" for the birth of a new one (Toussulis, 2010, p. 177). The classic and authoritative formulation of *baqa* after *fana* is attributed to the ninth-century Baghdadi Sufi master Abu al-Qasim al-Junayd (835–910), who made this stage the defining characteristic of his "sober" system of Sufism and describes it as follows:

> He is himself, after he has not been truly himself. He is present in himself and in God after having been present in God and absent in himself. This is because he has

> left the intoxication of God's overwhelming *ghalaba* (victory), and comes to the clarity of sobriety... Once more he assumes his individual attributes, after *fana*.
> (Abdel-Kader, 1962, p. 90)

Baqa is also sometimes referred to as the *fana* of *fana* or "annihilation of annihilation," in that the state of disappearance of one's individuality then itself concludes whereupon a transformed sense of individuality returns. The contemporary Nuriyya-Malamiyya Sufi teacher Mehmet Selim Ozic describes this culminating stage in his own words:

> For me, a fully matured human being has access to the experience of unification and separation in a fluctuating manner in the station we refer to as *jam al-jam*. At the station of *jam*, an individual experiences that nothing exists but God, but this is normally an intoxicating experience of short duration. An individual cannot live in that state for very long as mentally balanced; and as soon as he returns to soberness, he perceives other individual presences as real, though in a manner that is "qualified" by the experience of unity or oneness. (Toussulis, 2010, p. 152)

In this system, the experience of annihilation is also termed "gathering" (*jam*) and is considered so impairing that "one cannot remain in this state for too long, for to do so would be to risk becoming 'mad in Allah'" (*mualla*), so therefore the teacher "immediately coaxes his student into the next stage of *baqa*" (Toussulis, 2010, p. 178). The next stage is the "second separation" from God—the first separation occurring at one's physical birth when one's connection to God is concealed—where a transformed sense of self re-emerges and then "dries out" after the "ravishment of union" (Toussulis, 2010, p. 185). Finally, the previous two stages reach a kind of synthesis or fruition in the "gathering of gathering" (*jam al-jam*), an inherently dynamic stage where the experiences of union and separation oscillate, perhaps even in each moment or with each breath (Toussulis, 2010, p. 180; Sells, 1996, p. 123).

Jewish Traditions

Descent for the Sake of Ascent

Several teachers and practitioners in the VCE-A study interpreted challenging experiences according to the doctrine of "descent for the sake of ascent" (*yeridah tachlit aliyah*). Elliot Wolfson describes how this idea first occurs in the Zohar, the bible of Jewish mysticism, and then was incorporated into later Jewish mystical systems (Wolfson, 1988, p. 76). In one passage of the Zohar, the biblical verse "And Abraham went down to Egypt" (Gen. 12:10) is explained as follows:

> Come and see the secret of the word: If Abram had not gone into Egypt and been refined there first, he could not have partaken of the Blessed Holy One. Similarly

> with his children, when the Blessed Holy One wanted to make them unique, a perfect people, and to draw them near to Him: If they had not gone down to Egypt and been refined there first, they would not have become His special ones.
>
> (Wolfson, 1988, p. 85)

In this passage, the word "went down" (*yored*) is interpreted by the author(s) of the Zohar to refer to a spiritual descent to the realm of the demonic before a corresponding ascent to the higher spiritual level of "partaking of" the divine. Abraham is "refined" (*tzeruf*) while in Egypt and so too were the Israelites after him while they were enslaved in Egypt during the time of Moses (Wolfson, 1988, p. 85). Egypt also represents a place of spiritual constriction in Jewish mysticism due to its narrow physical geography and the related etymological connection between Egypt (*mitzrayim*) and "narrowness" (*tzar*). This metallurgic refinement and purification imagery was later incorporated into some Hasidic traditions that identified contemplative prayer as the crucible that burns the "dross" off one's animal soul to reveal the precious metal of one's divine soul (Jacobs, 2006a, pp. 114–115). Other Hasidic traditions similarly compared the contemplative path to boiling a pot of water where all the impurities first rise to the surface as well as to "cooking" one's heart with the fire of ecstatic experiences cultivated in contemplative prayer (Hoffman, 1981, p. 114; Jacobs, 2006b, p. 157).

For some Jewish contemplatives today, the "animal soul" or "heart" is identified with one's unconscious mind, and therefore these teachings are understood to mean that a descent into the places of constriction in one's psyche is necessary to ascend spiritually. In other words, some distressing effects and experiences associated with contemplative practices are actually signs of progress indicative of the purification and refinement of one's psyche (Ginsburgh, 2002, p. 25). One contemporary scholar and meditation teacher, Rabbi Moshe Krassen, explains that contemplative prayer can "open up regions of the unconscious where negative material is stored and concealed," which can manifest as "intrusions" of "various types of thoughts and impulses that are repressed" (Krassen, 2011, p. xxiii). For Krassen, once these thoughts and impulses arise in the context of contemplative practice, they need to be intentionally "refined" by recognizing them as manifestations of "divine energy" in order that such energy can be integrated into one's consciousness to ultimately realize one's "true nature" (Krassen, 2011, p. xxiii).

Expanded and Constricted Consciousness

A second (though related) way in which Jewish subjects interpreted necessary difficulties was in reference to the Lurianic and Hasidic doctrine of "constricted consciousness" (*mochin d'katnut*) and "expansive consciousness" (*mochin d'gadlut*), which some scholars have even gone so far as to identify with, or connect to, the idea of the "dark night of the soul" in Catholic traditions (Jacobs, 1996, p. 2). In the Kabbalistic system of Rabbi Isaac Luria (1538–1572), these two terms refer to the radical theological conception of God's own conception, pregnancy, birth, and subsequent development, which is then mirrored in the human realm (theomorphism) in terms of both physical and spiritual growth (Scholem, 1995, p. 271; Pachter, 2004, p. 205). *Mochin d'katnut* in the Lurianic system can sometimes refer to a state of gestation (*ibbur*) or nursing (*yenikah*) for an individual, the collective Jewish people, or a dimension of the divine itself, and it is possible for the state of an individual and the collective to mirror each other or to be relatively independent (Pachter, 2004, pp. 190, 223). Hasidic teachers built on and adapted this doctrine and its relevance to contemplative practice, particularly emphasizing *gadlut* and *katnut* as "degrees of contemplative concentration," and it is in this context that Jewish practitioners and teachers today identify necessary meditation-related difficulties with *mochin d'katnut* (Krassen, 1998, pp. 71–72). In fact, this pair of terms and experiences played a prominent role in the teachings attributed to the founder of Hasidism, Rabbi Israel ben Eliezer (1700–1760), also known as the Baal Shem Tov, and the following parable elucidates how they are widely understood:

> A disciple asked the Baal Shem: "Why is it that one who clings to God and knows he is close to him, sometimes experiences a sense of interruption and remoteness?" The Baal Shem explained: "When a father sets out to teach his little son to walk, he stands in front of him and holds his two hands on either side of the child, so that he cannot fall, and the boy goes toward his father between his father's hands. But the moment he is close to his father, he moves away a little, and holds his hands further apart, and he does this over and over, so that the child may learn to walk.
>
> (Buber, 1991, p. 65)

In the parable, the moments of "expansive consciousness" correspond to the times of being close to and held by the (divine) father where all of a sudden the child has a new and elevated perspective on the world and enjoys the thrill of this newfound power. The moments of "constricted consciousness" are the times when the parent retreats and the child falls and feels abandoned, and yet the parable suggests this dialectical movement is in service of the greater developmental goal of the child learning to walk and achieving some level of autonomy. Similarly, the goal of contemplative practice according to the Baal Shem Tov is not to remain in expansive states of consciousness but to reach more lasting developmental goals, and for this, periods where such states are inaccessible are understood to be instrumental and necessary (Kallus, 2011, p. 160).

This kind of oscillatory trajectory later became an important point of emphasis in the life and teachings of the Baal Shem Tov's great-grandson, Rabbi Nachman of Bratslav (1772–1810), who likewise emphasized the larger developmental context in which such rhythms of contemplative practice occur. Tzvi Mark argues that Nachman's depiction of *katnut* and *gadlut* are more aligned with the Lurianic use of these terms than other earlier Hasidic thinkers, particularly with respect to the "regressive quality" of such states where "a person reverts to previous stages of his development," given how central the association with biological development is for Luria (Mark, 2009, pp. 189, 193–194; Garb, 2015, p. 34). He adds that "katnut is not negative regression, but a functional and desirable stage of [the] dynamic expressed by the Hasidic axiom 'descent for sake of ascent'" (Mark, 2009, p. 206). Mark finally compares this dynamic as represented by Nachman to a process of death and re-birth in which one must "pass anew through a second Ibur (gestation), birth, and katnut (childhood)" (Mark, 2009, p. 206).

Today some Jewish contemplatives continue to echo this connection between descent, regression, and constricted consciousness by making the additional connection between *katnut* (smallness) and one's childhood, since a child is also called a *katan* in rabbinic and later texts (Ginsburgh, 2002, p. 25; Starrett, 2008, p. 19). Invoking that same vein in the tradition, some contemporary contemplatives draw inspiration from Rabbi Kalonymous Kalman Shapira (1889–1943), the Piasetzner Rebbe, who writes how negative or distressing emotions conceal divine intent and light, and, playing on two words with a shared root—garment (*beged*) and traitor (*boged*)—argues that the distress of distressing emotions is the garment that betrays the divine life concealed within them (Maisels, 2014, p. 471). Rabbi James Jacobson Maisels argues that to access the divine light within such challenging emotions, there must be "a kind of searching out of the core nature of the emotion, the divine light, and a discarding or letting go of the damaging aspect of the experience, the wicked garment which covers the divine light" (Maisels, 2014, p. 475). Creatively weaving this etymological connection between a child (*katan*) and constricted or immature consciousness (*mohin d'katnut*) into practice instructions, one way that the Piasetzner recommends this can be accomplished is by relating and even speaking to such challenging emotions as if they are crying children (Maisels, 2014, p. 456).

This practice of accessing the divine energy in distressing or afflictive emotions is also relevant (if not identical) to the Hasidic practice of the "uplifting of thoughts"(*ha'alot machshavot*), which consists of an unusual approach to a problem common to all contemplative practices: navigating distractions. While earlier approaches to contemplative prayer and meditation advocated suppression of such distracting thoughts, early Hasidism was novel (and controversial) for introducing the idea that distractions could be part of the practice as well (Krassen, 1998, pp. 48–49). This doctrine is particularly relevant to our topic since some of these foreign thoughts are understood to be uncomfortable or distressing. The key insight behind this practice, however, is that such thoughts are arising as a kind of psychic reflex to allow the energy animating them to be re-incorporated into the soul or psyche (Krassen, 2011, p. xxiv). As one contemporary Kabbalist and meditation teacher, Rabbi Abraham Sutton, explains it:

> On a deeper level, these very thoughts represent parts of our self that need to be redeemed. In a hidden way, they are saying, "Please take us with you too! We also need to be fixed! Don't leave us behind." Thus when we are attacked by such thoughts... this is a sure sign that we are contacting a deeper strata of our psyche, and are thus on the verge of a major breakthrough in our lives. Moreover, this is a sure sign that the spark of holiness and goodness that was trapped in our own negativity is finally being freed. (Sutton, 2010, pp. 30–31)

In practice however, contemporary teachers note that not all distracting thoughts are meant to be elevated and that the discernment is predicated on whether the means of elevating the thought arises at the same moment the thought does (Jacobs, 1989, p. 120; Krassen, 1998, p. 76). This may be a function of how engrossing or overwhelming such a thought is, particularly if it is a distressing memory or psychological state that is arising. Sutton argues that this is a practice should be understood on a "sliding scale": "for a novice, most thoughts should be pushed aside. At more advanced stages, most thoughts should be raised up" (Sutton, 2010, p. 30).

Chaos and Liminality

The Lurianic myth of the creation of the world discusses an event known as the "breaking of the vessels" (*shevirat ha-keilim*) in which the initial light emanated from the light of the Godhead was too unstable and thus shattered the first divine vessels meant to contain it, causing the shards of the vessels with sparks of divine light trapped inside to descend and ultimately give rise to the sensible world of physical reality. Gershom Scholem remarks that for Kabbalists after Luria this creative cataclysm "is connected, like so many other things, with the law of organic life in the theosophical universe. Just as the seed must burst in order to sprout and blossom, so too the first bowls had to be shattered in order that the divine light, the cosmic seed so to speak, might fulfill its function" (Scholem, 1995, p. 268). Once again, what occurs in the sphere of the divine is mirrored in the natural and human realms, and this idea was translated into Hasidic garb by the successor of the Baal Shem Tov, the Maggid of Mezeritch (1704–1772), in his understanding of this dynamic of spiritual growth in an individual:

> Nothing in the world can change from one reality into another, unless it first turns into nothing, that is, into the reality of the between-stage. In that stage it is nothing and no one can grasp it, for it has reached the rung of nothingness, just as before creation. And then it is made into a new creature, from the egg to the chick. The moment when the egg is no more and the chick is not yet, is nothingness... it is called chaos. It is the same with the sprouting seed. It does not begin to sprout until the seed disintegrates in the earth and the quality of seed... is destroyed in order that it may attain to nothingness which is the rung before creation.
>
> (Buber, 1991, p. 104)

This understanding of "chaos" (*tohu*) as a liminal or transitional state has a technical sense in the Lurianic system as referring to the pre-creation world of the shattered vessels, also known as the world of chaos (*olam ha-tohu*) (Toyryla, 2000, p. 18.). One contemporary teacher of Jewish meditation, Zvi Ish-Shalom, draws upon this teaching of the Maggid to appraise the "psychic death" that occurred at a major transition on his own path:

> everything I had known to be who I am and what reality was, went through a process of erasure in a way and dissolution, dissolving. And... on the other side of that experience I found myself in a state in which perception was radically altered and that marked a turning point in my life really because there was a radical shift in terms of literal perception, actual visuals, the way the world looks.... it was like there was a life before that event and then life after. And then life afterward became for me a process of integrating this newfound mode of experiencing and perceiving reality that was not marked by the usual filters of the personal history. So it had felt in a way that my personal history until that point had been erased and I was reborn in a sense into this new life that had no psychic investment in the history that I had lived until that point. So it was like a kind of new life that was born and then there was a process of how to integrate that and figure out how to actually live in the world from that state. (Ish-Shalom, 2018)

Ish-Shalom speaks about this process as a kind of a death of one's identity that can be quite a distressing or challenging experience, as "you can feel like your guts have been ripped out, like there is nothing to substantiate you.... empty, parched, dry, lack, void" (Ish-Shalom, 2017, p. 257). Drawing on the Lurianic and Hasidic descriptions of *katnut* and *gadlut* discussed earlier in this section, he describes how this challenging stage of the path is where experiences of "contraction and expansion interpenetrate and cross fertilize, creating the necessary friction to metabolize our unconscious material" in the same way that salt and sea water creates the friction that refines a pearl (Ish-Shalom, 2017, p. 259). Ultimately the fruition of this process is a kind of death and rebirth, which he identifies with the Hasidic principle of "the nullification of one's somethingness" (*bittul ha-yesh*) that then gives rise to one's "true self" or "essential self" (Ish-Shalom, 2017, pp. 259, 266).

"Non-linear" Paths

Recently a growing cadre of scholars of mysticism have proposed the framework of "paths" (as opposed to just experiences) to discuss and compare religious traditions, and indeed it is a particularly well-suited construct for all three Abrahamic traditions given how central it is within each (Buswell & Gimello, 1992; Wolfson, 1995; Parsons, 1999; Taves, 2011; Idel, 2015). We have seen how, in trying to understand challenging experiences associated with meditation, practitioners and teachers from all three religions (in the West) rely upon conceptions of "the path" that involve oscillations between experiences of ecstasy and despair, euphoria and dysphoria. In all three traditions they are conceived as reflecting various degrees of proximity to, and distance from, some dimension of the divine. In Sufi traditions the oscillation (*talwin*) is between states of expansion (*qabd*) and constriction (*bast*), in Jewish traditions between expansive consciousness (*mochin d'gadlut*) and constricted consciousness (*mochin d'katnut*), and in Catholic traditions typically between states of grace or consolation (*contentos*) and aridity or desolation (*discontentos*). In these spiral conceptions of the contemplative path, "non-linearity" refers to the fact that progress of growth entails challenging, uncomfortable, distressing, or impairing experiences before new baselines of awareness or senses of self in relation to the divine can be reached. The path is non-linear with regard to the *valence* of experiences encountered along the contemplative developmental trajectory.

However scholars as well as teachers and practitioners also refer to paths as non-linear in the sense of *non-sequential*. For example, while Teresa of Avila depicts the stages of the contemplative path as seven concentric castles, she admits that one does not always enter each castle in order (Frohlich, 1993, p. 179). Mary Frohlich refers to this latter conception of the path by Teresa as "non-linear" in that it is not a "step-by-step journey from one place to another" noting that Teresa herself indicates that only the beginner images the seven castles linearly one after the other (Frohlich, 1993, p. 191; see also May, 2004, p. 127). In a similar vein, John of the Cross writes that despite his portrayal of the stages of the contemplative path, "God leads each one along different paths" (*diferentos caminos*), and Thomas Keating argues that despite being presented sequentially by John, individuals may experience the dark nights in reverse order or even at the same time (McGinn, 2017, p. 264; Keating, 2012, p. 116). In Sufi traditions, despite many sequential depictions of the stations that constitute the path, there is also an awareness of individual variability and that the stages may be experienced in different orders as well—perhaps one reason for the great variability of stages across this literature. For example, at the end of a short treatise describing the Sufi path to God as he formulated it, Abu Hamid al-Ghazali (1058–1111) writes that while the order of the stages he elucidated is true for some people, others will experience the advanced stages at the beginning of their path (al-Ghazali, 1988, p. 52). About a hundred years later, the "Great Shaykh" Muhyiddin Ibn al-Arabi (1165–1240) writes in his meditative retreat manual that the "seekers of the Way of Truth are individuals. So although the Way of Truth is one, the aspects it presents vary with the varying conditions of its seekers" (Ibn Arabi, 1989, p. 26). Furthermore, while the "stations" are often presented as a ladder emphasizing a sequential order, the "states" (*hal*), which can manifest within each station, are completely unpredictable and, in fact, are not always clearly differentiated from the stations (Chittick, 1989, p. 279; Sviri, 1987, p. 341).

Both senses of non-linear paths that we have seen so far are certainly not limited to Abrahamic traditions, and indeed this is why this particular construct may prove to be more generally useful. Textual sources in Buddhist traditions discuss similarly structured non-linear paths of contemplative practice involving challenging or distressing stages, and some Buddhist maps are also "not linear" in the sense of non-sequential (Lindahl et al., 2017, p. 3; Lindahl, 2012, p. 260). Some contemporary Buddhist teachers also discuss the effects of concentration practices leading to states of absorption (*jhānas*) using similar psychological terminology of relaxing the mechanisms of repression in the psyche. For example, *Jhāna* meditation teacher Leigh Brasington reports in a recent interview:

> At the start of every retreat I teach, I warn students that if you have unresolved psychological issues, they quite likely will show up... It's a common thing... whatever unresolved psychological issues that you have, they're unresolved because you are using your energy and your distractions to keep them at bay. They will probably show up at some point when you get really quiet because there's no more distractions to keep them at bay and all your energy is going into your focus rather than keeping them at bay. And it can be quite unexpected, it can be stuff that you knew was there... or it can be stuff that you have no idea was there. And it is so common that I have to give this warning at the beginning of every retreat.
>
> (Brasington, 2013)

And finally, already forty years ago Buddhist teacher Jack Kornfield wrote that it "is essential to recognize the non-linear process of growth in meditation," by which he meant "the meditative pattern of periodic regression, re-structuring and reintegration" (Kornfield, 1979, pp. 53–54).

Conclusion

Our brief survey of the traditional literature describing necessary suffering within Abrahamic meditative paths uncovered some patterned similarities in the classical "non-linear" paths of all three mystical traditions and in some of their contemporary manifestations. This is not to collapse the differences between (or within) the three mystical streams nor is it a claim that the paths lead to identical goals—since there are a variety in changes to different senses of self that can be considered normative even in one tradition (Lindahl & Britton, 2019). It is merely an initial effort to bring attention to this topic and explore emic perspectives of challenging experiences associated with meditation, with an emphasis on how contemporary traditions draw upon traditional literature in such appraisals. While the first sense of non-linear paths (valence) emphasizes the idea that some distress and suffering may be considered necessary for the attainment of traditional goals, the second sense (non-sequentiality) highlights the fact that many Abrahamic contemplative traditions have historically acknowledged considerable individual variability and the unpredictable effects of such practices.

While stages-of-the-path literature seeks to map out the territory that may be encountered through meditative practice, many traditions were also aware that people will only experience some states or stages and that they may do so in very different orders. I suggest that this fact is one reason for the stress laid on working closely with a teacher—and relatedly, the relegation of many practical instructions to oral traditions—in these religions, since, if maps corresponded exactly to practitioner's experiences, a teacher would be largely obsolete. Instead, due to the individual variability and unpredictability of these trajectories, working closely with a teacher who has personal familiarity with some swath of these territories has become an inalterable requirement for many of these traditions (Schimmel, 2011, pp. 100–104; Silvers-Alario, 2003). I would also argue that this historical data suggests that in the contemporary dissemination of meditation, teachers, clinicians, and meditation researchers ought to heed calls for more "person-centered" approaches to these practices (Lindahl et al., this volume). While many today highlight the power of meditative practices to reduce suffering and promote human flourishing, it is time to become mindful of the dark nights and non-linear paths that may need to be traversed to bring those goals to fruition.

References

Abdel-Kader, A. H. (1962). *The life, personality and writings of Al-Junayd.* London: Luzac & Company.

al-Ghazali, A. H. (1988). *The niche of lights.* (D. Buchman, Trans.). Provo, UT: Brigham Young University Press.

Blaschke, B. A. (2017). *Consciousness of God as God is: The phenomenology of Christian centering prayer* (Doctoral dissertation). Victoria University of Wellington.

Bourgeault, C. (1999). The egoic system and the nurture of the heart. *Sacred Web 4* (Winter). Retrieved from http://www.sacredweb.com/online_articles/sw4_bourgeault.html

Bourgeault, C. (2004). *Centering prayer and inner awakening.* Plymouth, MA: Cowley Publications.

Brasington, L. (2013). *Cheetah house on-the-road* [Video Interview] (Dr. Willoughby Britton, Interviewer) *Cheetah House* (Winter). Retrieved from https://www.youtube.com/watch?v=qBzA4jeee3g

Buber, M. (1991). *Tales of the Hasidism* (3rd ed). New York: Schocken Books.

Buswell, R. and Gimello, R. (Eds.). (1992) *Paths to liberation: The marga and its transformations in Buddhist thought.* Honolulu: University of Hawaii Press.

Chittick, W. C. (1983). *The Sufi path of love: The spiritual teachings of Rumi.* Albany: State University of New York Press.

Chittick, W. C. (1989). *The Sufi path of knowledge: Ibn al-'Arabi's metaphysics of imagination.* Albany: State University of New York Press.

Fitzgerald, C. (1984). Impasse and dark night. In T. Edwards (Ed.), *Living with apocalypse: Spiritual resources for social compassion* (pp. 93–116). San Francisco: Harper & Row.

Fitzgerald, C. (1995). Desolation as dark night: The transformative influence of wisdom in John of the Cross. *The Way Supplement 82*, 97–108.

Frenette, D. (2017). *The path of centering prayer: Deepening your experience of God* (2nd ed.) Boulder, CO: Sounds True.

Frohlich, M. (1993). *The intersubjectivity of the mystic: A study of Teresa of Avila's Interior Castle.* Atlanta, GA: Scholars Press.

Garb, J. (2015). *Yearnings of the soul: Psychological thought in modern Kabbalah.* Chicago: University of Chicago Press.

Ginsburgh, Y. G. (2002). *Transforming darkness into light.* Kfar Chabad: Gal Einai.

Hoffman, E. (1981). *The way of splendor: Jewish mysticism and modern psychology.* Boulder, CO: Shambhala.

Ibn Arabi, M. (1989). *Journey to the Lord of power: A Sufi manual on retreat* (Rabia Terri Harris, Trans.). Rochester, NY: Inner Traditions International.

Idel, M. (2015). Mysticism in the Abrahamic religions. In A. J. Silverstein, G. G. Stroumsa, & M. Blidstein (Eds.), *The Oxford Handbook of the Abrahamic Religions* (pp. 373–389). Oxford: Oxford University Press.

Ish-Shalom, Z. (2017). *The Kedumah experience: The primordial Torah.* Boulder, CO: Albion-Andalus Books.

Ish-Shalom, Z. (2018, May). *Stories of silence* [Audio podcast]. (T. Rawl, Host). Mind Guides. Retrieved from https://soundcloud.com/storiesofsilence/tracks

Jacobs, L. (1989). The uplifting of sparks in later Jewish mysticism. In A. Green (Ed.), *Jewish spirituality: From the sixteenth-century revival to the present.* (pp.99–126). New York: The Crossroad Publishing Company.

Jacobs, L. (1996). *The Schocken book of Jewish mystical testimonies* (2nd ed.). New York: Schocken Books.

Jacobs, L. (2006a). *Seeker of unity: The life and works of Aaron of Starosselje* (2nd ed.) Portland, OR: Vallentine Mitchell.

Jacobs, L. (2006b). *Tract on ecstasy* (2nd ed.). Portland, OR: Vallentine Mitchell.

Kallus, M. (2011). *Pillar of prayer: Guidance in contemplative prayer, sacred study, and the spiritual life, from the Baal Shem Tov and his circle.* Louisville, KY: Fons Vitae.

Keating, T. (2006). *Open mind, open heart* (2nd ed.). New York: Continuum International.

Keating, T. (2009). *Intimacy with God: An introduction to centering prayer* (2nd ed.). Snowmass, CO: Crossroad Publishing Company.

Keating, T. (2012). *Invitation to love: The way of Christian contemplation* (2nd ed.). London: Bloomsbury Publishing.

Keating, T. (2014). *Reflections on the unknowable.* Brooklyn, NY: Lantern Books.

King, T. (1992). *The spiral path: Explorations into women's spirituality.* Saint Paul, MN: Yes International Publishers.

Kornfield, J. (1979). Intensive insight meditation: A phenomenological study. *Journal of Transpersonal Psychology 11*(1), 41–58.

Krassen, M. (1998). *Uniter of heaven and earth: Rabbi Meshullam Feibush Heller of Zbarazh and the rise of Hasidism in eastern Galicia.* Albany: State University of New York Press.

Krassen, M. A. (2011). Introduction. In *Pillar of Prayer: Guidance in contemplative prayer, sacred study, and the spiritual life, from the Baal Shem Tov and his circle* (M. Kallus, Trans.). Louisville, KY: Fons Vitae.

Lindahl, J. (2012). Self-transformation according to Buddhist stages of the path literature. *Pacific World: Journal of the Institute of Buddhist Studies* 3(14), 231–275.

Lindahl, J. R., & Britton, W. B. (2019). "I have this feeling of not really being here": Buddhist meditation and changes in sense of self. *Journal of Consciousness Studies*, 26 (7–8).

Lindahl, J. R., Fisher, N. E., Cooper, D. J., Rosen, R. K., & Britton, W. B. (2017). The varieties of contemplative experience: A mixed-methods study of meditation-related challenges in Western Buddhists. *PLoS ONE 12*(5): e0176239. Retrieved from https://journals.plos.org/plosone/article?id=10.1371/journal.pone.0176239.

Lindahl, J. R., Britton, W. B., Cooper, D. J., & Kirmayer, L. J. (in press). Challenging and adverse meditation experiences: Toward a person-centered approach. In M. Lalljee, D. Brazier, & M. Farias (Eds.), *The Oxford Handbook of Meditation.* Oxford: Oxford University Press.

Maisels, J. (2014). *The self and self-transformation in the thought and practice of Rabbi Kalonymus Kalmish Shapira* (Doctoral dissertation). The University of Chicago. Proquest (3627853).

Mark, T. (2009). *Mysticism and madness: The religious thought of Rabbi Nachman of Bratslav*. London and New York: Continuum.

May, G. (2004). *The dark night of the soul: A psychiatrist explores the connection between darkness and spiritual growth*. New York: HarperCollins Publishers.

McGinn, B. (2006). *The essential writings of Christian mysticism*. New York: Modern Library.

McGinn, B. (2017). *Mysticism in the Golden Age of Spain (1500–1650)*. New York: Crossroad Publishing Company.

Nasr, H. (2015) *The study Quran: A new translation with notes and commentary*. New York: HarperOne

Nurbaksh, J. (1993). *Sufism II* (William Chittick, Trans., 2nd ed.). New York: Khaniqahi-Nimatullahi Publications.

Pachter, M. (2004). *Roots of faith and devequt: Studies in the history of Kabbalistic ideas*. Los Angeles: Cherub Press.

Parsons, W. (1999). *The enigma of oceanic feeling: Revisioning the psychoanalytic theory of mysticism*. New York: Oxford University Press.

Payne, S. (1990). *John of the Cross and the cognitive value of mysticism*. Dordrecht: Kluwer Academic Publishers.

Ritter, H. (2003). *The ocean of the soul: Man, the world and God in the stories of Farid al-Din 'Attar* (J. O'Kane, Trans.). Leiden: Brill.

Roberts, B. (2005). *What is self? A study of the spiritual journey in terms of consciousness*. Boulder, CO: Sentient Publications.

Saint John of the Cross. (1991). *The collected works of Saint John of the Cross*. (K. Kavanaugh & O. Rodriguez, Trans., rev. ed.). Washington, DC: ICS Publications.

Schimmel, A. (2011). *Mystical Dimensions of Islam* (2nd ed.). Chapel Hill: University of North Carolina Press.

Scholem, G. (1995). *Major trends in Jewish mysticism* (4th ed.). New York: Schocken Books.

Sells, M. (1996). Bewildered tongue: The semantics of mystical union in Islam. In M. Idel & B. McGinn (Eds.), *Mystical union in Judaism, Christianity, and Islam* (pp. 87–124). New York: Bloomsbury Academic.

Silvers-Alario, L. (2003) The teaching relationship in early Sufism: A reassessment of Fritz Meier's definition of the *shaykh al-tarbiya* and the *shaykh al-talim*. *The Muslim World* 93, 69–97.

Silverstein, A. J., Stroumsa, G. G., & Blidstein, M. (Eds.). (2015). *The Oxford Handbook of Abrahamic Religions*. Oxford: Oxford University Press.

Starrett, Y. (2008). *Keser Shem Tov: Mystical teachings on the Torah* (Vol. 1). Cleveland, OH: BST Publishing.

Stone, L. (2006). Blessed perplexity: The topos of *Hayrat* in *'Attar's Mantiq al-tayr*. In L. Lewisohn and C. Shackle (Eds.), *Attar and the Persian Sufi tradition: The art of spiritual flight*. (pp. 95–111). London: I.B. Tauris Publishers.

Sutton, A. (2010). *Purim light: The reality of G-d in our lives*. Brooklyn, NY: Geula Press.

Sviri, S. (1987). Between fear and hope: On the coincidence of opposites in Islamic mysticism. *Jerusalem Studies in Arabic and Islam 9*.

Sviri, S. (1994). The mysterium coniunctionis and the "Yo-Yo Syndrome": From polarity to oneness in Sufi psychology." In J. R. Menuhin (Ed.), *Jung and the Monotheisms: Judaism, Christianity, and Islam*. (pp. 192–213). New York: Routledge.

Sviri, S. (2002). *The taste of hidden things: Images on the Sufi path* (2nd ed.). Inverness, Scotland: The Golden Sufi Center.

Taves, A. (2011). *Religious experience reconsidered: A building block approach to the study of religion and other special things*. Princeton, NJ: Princeton University Press.
Toussulis, Y. (2010). *Sufism and the way of blame: Hidden sources of a sacred psychology*. Wheaton, IL: Quest Books.
Toyryla, H. (2000). Slimy stones and philosophy: Some interpretations of Tohu wa-Bohu. *Nordisk Judaistik/Scandinavian Jewish Studies 21*(1–2), 91–110. doi:10.30752/nj.69569
Tweedie, I. (1998). *Thinking allowed: Conversations on the leading edge of knowledge and discovery*. [TV series] (Dr. J Mishlove, Host) Thinking Allowed Productions.
Vaughan-Lee, L. (2011). *Fragments of a love story: Reflection on the life of a mystic*. Point Reyes, CA: The Golden Sufi Center.
Wolfson, E. (1988) Light through darkness: The ideal of human perfection in the Zohar. *Harvard Theological Review 81*(1), 73–95.
Wolfson, E. (1995). *Along the path: Studies in Kabbalistic myth, symbolism, and hermeneutics*. Albany: State University of New York Press.

CHAPTER 40

MEDITATION SICKNESS

JUHN Y. AHN

Introduction

Buddhism emerged as part of a larger *śramaṇa* ("one who strives") non-Vedic movement in India that charted a distinctively ascetic path toward felicity and salvation. Rather than accept Brahmanical claims about the importance of ritual purity and the household sacrificial fire, the individuals and communities who gave shape to this movement ethicized ritual action (Sanskrit *karman*) by framing it in retributive terms and pursued, as their socio-religious ideal, the homeless life of a wandering ascetic or renouncer (Skt. *saṃnyāsin*). The pursuit of this new ascetic ideal was also accompanied by the development of a variety of new techniques for attaining liberation (Skt. *mokṣa*). The Jains, for instance, strove to attain liberation from karma through the cessation of all mental and physical activity and the continued practice of severe austerities (Skt. *tapas*). In keeping with an example ostensibly set by the historical Buddha himself, Buddhists rejected such extreme forms of asceticism and chose to seek liberation through seated meditation and/or liberating insight instead (Bronkhorst, 2000). It is in this context of experimenting with new theories and techniques of liberation that the issues addressed in Buddhist discourses about meditation sickness began to crystalize.

Two broad categories of meditation sickness became the most common sources of concern for practitioners of Buddhist meditation. These sicknesses were products of the way in which Buddhists structured their path(s) to liberation. Buddhist sources are in general agreement that the cultivation of an extraordinary form of absorption (Skt. *dhyāna*) in a state of perfect concentration (Skt. *samādhi*), the attainment of a supernatural insight into the nature of reality (enlightenment), or the combination thereof, is a necessary condition for attaining liberation (de La Vallée Poussin, 1936–1937; Vetter, 1988). To attain concentration it was generally assumed that one had to calm the mind. Buddhist sources that emphasize concentration therefore tend to voice their concerns about the mind that stays agitated, restless, and unfocused during seated meditation. This was one common form of meditation sickness (Chinese *chanbing* 禪病). In Buddhist sources it is listed as one of the five hindrances (see the following section).

Other sources that emphasize the attainment of supernatural insight tend to voice their concerns about a different kind of problem. They claim that there is the possibility of becoming deludedly attached to the insight that everything is empty and devoid of inherent existence, an insight that is ironically supposed to free one from all attachments. This was another common form of meditation sickness (Ahn, 2007). Unlike the former meditation sickness, the latter was unique to Buddhism. New techniques were developed to tackle this sickness. The Chan/Sŏn/Zen practice of koan meditation is a noteworthy example.

In Buddhism meditation sickness can also refer to the inability to wake from meditation (Griffiths, 1986) or to specific symptoms that trouble meditators such as hallucinations, terror, depression, lethargy, heaviness, dizziness, itchy hands, pain, pride, excessive heat or coldness in the body, and nocturnal emissions (caused by demonic possession), but canonical Buddhist sources do not make frequent references to these forms of meditation sickness. Rather than provide an exhaustive list of all the symptoms and cures mentioned in the various Buddhist discourses about meditation sickness, this chapter focuses on the two kinds of meditation sickness most commonly discussed in canonical sources. It begins with an explanation of how the five hindrances and their remedies are understood in Pali sources associated with Theravada tradition and also fifth-century texts about Buddhist meditation associated with the Sarvāstivāda tradition in Kashmir. The rest of the chapter focuses on the attachment to insight or emptiness, which is a meditation sickness that is mentioned most frequently in canonical sources associated with Mahayana Buddhism and the Chan/Sŏn/Zen traditions. Brief explanations of the sundry symptoms of meditation sickness are provided when necessary.

Hindrances to Concentration

Lists of hindrances (Skt. *nīvaraṇa*) to the attainment of concentration are not difficult to find in Buddhist sources. These lists vary in size and content. But one that does appear with some frequency in Buddhist sources is a list of five hindrances: sensual desire, hatred, sloth, restlessness, and doubt. Doubt, here, can refer to, among other things, an incapacitating wavering, indecisiveness, sense of loss, fear of the unknown, and consequent lack of sustained thought. This list appears in such authoritative and influential sources on Buddhist meditation as the *Foundations of Mindfulness Sutra* (*Satipaṭṭhāna Sutta*, DN II: 301–302), *Path of Purification* (*Visuddhimagga*, Vism IV, pp. 79, 86, and 104), and *Great Calming and Contemplation* (*Mohe zhiguan*; T46.1911.44c6–47a24). The five hindrances are not, however, always presented as issues that pertain only to

Buddhist meditation. The same list of hindrances was also often invoked in contexts where Buddhists were trying to define their meditative system(s) vis-à-vis other non-Buddhist systems (e.g., DN I, p. 246; DN III, pp. 49–51; MN II, p. 203; and MN III, p. 14). In these contexts, the five hindrances were treated not as obstacles peculiar to Buddhist meditation but as generally disturbing psychosomatic conditions (Gethin, 2004, p. 208), which were assumed to be disturbing not only to Buddhists but non-Buddhists as well. In some instances, the five hindrances were invoked specifically for the purpose of ridiculing the rote learning of the Vedas: a brahmin with knowledge of the *Ṛg-*, *Sāma-*, and *Yajurvedas* who claims to know the path leading to union with Brahmā without ever having seen Brahmā himself is, for instance, likened to someone who is entangled in the five hindrances (DN I, p. 246). What these criticisms of Vedic learning assumed was that the five hindrances could be recognized by anyone and so gave an easily grasped sense of the possibility of directly or personally experiencing liberation—a *śramaṇa* movement ideal.

Perhaps for this very reason, Buddhist sources tend not to offer explicit explanations of the relationship between the removal of these hindrances and the attainment of concentration and absorption. The two could be understood as two sides of the same experience, or the former could be regarded the cause or condition of the latter. Either way, sources that speak of the hindrances to concentration are in agreement that overcoming the hindrances is an integral part of the path to absorption and liberation.

According to the *Aṅguttara Nikāya* of the Pali Canon, the Buddha criticized the pursuit of severe austerities—the practices of rival *śramaṇa* groups—and promoted instead the life of a celibate monk (AN II, pp. 205–211). One should, the Buddha explained, maintain good conduct (P. *sīla*), find a secluded place, and begin to practice seated meditation by removing the five hindrances. If the hindrances are removed, then the monk is expected to enter the first absorption (P. *jhāna*). The monk can further remove initial thought (P. *vitakka*), discursive thought (P. *vicāra*), joy (P. *pīti*), and happiness (P. *sukha*) in this state of absorption to eventually reach the fourth absorption, a state of perfect concentration or one-pointedness of mind where he can see the four noble truths and attain liberation. Noting that the *Sāmaññaphala Sutta* of the *Digha Nikāya* (DN I, p. 74) is the first sutra (P. *sutta*) in the Pali Canon to use the above schema to explain the meditative path, Rupert Gethin (2004, p. 202) calls it the "*sāmañña-phala* schema." This schema occurs with considerable frequency throughout the Pali Canon.

In the *sāmañña-phala* schema hindrances to concentration are treated as things that need to be removed. In other contexts, however, they are treated as things that need to be prevented. Again, in the *Aṅguttara Nikāya*, a monk who wishes to attain liberation is advised, for instance, to maintain a balanced approach while practicing seated meditation (AN I, pp. 256–258). He should give equal attention to concentration, exertion (P. *paggaha*), and equanimity (P. *uppekhā*), for attending only to the sign (P. *nimitta*) of concentration can result in sloth, attending only to the sign of exertion can result in restlessness, and attending only to the sign of equanimity can lead to improper concentration. A monk who gives equal attention to concentration, exertion, and equanimity is likened to a goldsmith who from time to time blows on, sprinkles water on, and examines molten gold in a crucible. Just as this goldsmith can make whatever he wants with gold that is prepared with such care, the monk who maintains a balanced approach in seated meditation can also achieve his desired goal, namely the attainment of liberating insight.

So, in these early texts, the five hindrances represent a stage on the path. Gradually, however, they tend to be regarded more and more as being in the nature of pathologies that are to be removed, the path being presented in a quasi-medical model. Discussions of their removal often invoke a set of meditative techniques or methods considered more or less as remedies. These include "the contemplation of the foul," cultivation of loving-kindness, and the practice of awareness of the breath. Each method was often understood to be particularly effective in removing a specific hindrance, thus yielding a system of diagnosis and remedy.

The *Aṅguttara Nikāya* offers a detailed explanation of how to remove hindrances to concentration (AN I, pp. 3–4, cited in Shaw, 2006, pp. 48–49). Here, it is explained, for instance, that an image of the foul (P. *asubhanimittaṃ*)—the image of a decomposing corpse—can remove sensual desire, loving-kindness (P. *mettā*) can remove hatred, strenuous effort (P. *āraddhavīriya* can remove sloth; a calmed mind (P. *cetaso vūpasamo*) can remove restlessness, and careful attention (P. *yonisomanasikāro*) can remove doubt (AN II, pp. 354–358).

A similar account can be found in a sutra about a monk named Meghiya who once experienced sensual, malicious, and cruel thoughts while trying to meditate under a mango tree by himself (AN IV, p. 356). As a remedy, the Buddha recommended, among other things, a good friend (P. *kalyāṇamitta*)—that is, a teacher—and the maintenance of good conduct. After the removal of sensual, malicious, and cruel thoughts, the Buddha also further recommended that Meghiya use an image of the foul to abandon sensual desire, loving-kindness to abandon hatred, mindfulness of breathing (P. *ānāpānasatti*) to cut off restlessness, and the perception of impermanence (P. *aniccasaññā*) to remove the conceit "I am" during seated meditation. If Meghiya could remove these hindrances, then he would, according to the Buddha, experience nirvana in this very life.

Meditation Sicknesses: Five Paths and Five Gates

Early Sources

The Pali Canon is not the only place where relatively early information about meditation sickness in Buddhism can be found. Some of the earliest datable sources on Buddhist meditation are, in fact, extant only in their Chinese translations. These sources place heavy emphasis on the explanation of the various methods for removing hindrances to concentration and the attainment of absorption or *dhyāna*, which in China was better known by its transliteration *chan* 禪. These sources include:

- The *Scripture on Seated Meditation* Samādhi (Zuochan sanmei jing 坐禅三昧經; T15.614; Yamabe & Sueki, 2009)
- *Essential Methods for Practicing the Five Gates of Meditation* (Wumen chan jingyao yongfa 五門禪經要用法; T15.619)
- *Dharmatrāta's Meditation Scripture* (Damoduoluo chan jing 達摩多羅禪經; T15.618)
- *Scripture on the Secret Essential Methods of Meditation* (Chan miyao fa jing 禪秘要法經; T15.242)
- *Secret Methods for Curing Meditation Sicknesses* (*Zhi chanbing miyao fa* 治禪病秘要法; T15.620).

They were translated in the fifth century, when a sustained effort to develop *chan* into a legitimate field of religious training and expertise was made for the first time in China (Greene, 2012, pp. 15–41; for a fourth or fifth-century visual representation of meditation from Hadda, Afghanistan, see figure 40.1).

Prior to this period, access to knowledge about Buddhist theories of *chan* were limited to a handful of sources attributed to the Parthian An Shigao 安世高 (fl. 147–168).

FIGURE 40.1 Hadda, Monastery of Tapa-e-shotor. Source: Niche with the Seated Bodhisattva Shakyamuni Flanked by Devotees and an Elephant, ca. 4th-5th century. Purchase, Walter Burke Gift, and Anonymous Gift, Rogers Fund, and Gift of George D. Pratt, by exchange, 2005. Accession Number:2005.314.

According to scholarly consensus, the texts introduced to China by An were products of a community of meditators or *yogācāras* affiliated with, or at least cognizant of, the Buddhist Sarvāstivāda (and, more specifically, Vaibhāṣika) tradition in Kashmir (Deleanu, 1992). The texts translated by An tend to focus on two preparatory practices for entering the path to the attainment of *dhyāna* and eventually liberation. These, again, are contemplation of the foul and mindfulness of breathing. There is a text called the *Abhidharma mahāvibhāṣa śāstra*—whence the name Vaibhāṣika is derived—which explains that one enters the path with these two practices, which it calls the two "gates of ambrosia" (C. *ganlu men* 甘露門; Skt. *amṛta dvāra*; T27.1545.348b16–17).

The Fivefold Path

Another important Sarvāstivādin source, the *Abhidharmakośabhāṣya*, also presents the same practices as important preparatory steps for cultivating the foundations of mindfulness (Skt. *smṛtyupasthāna*) and entering "the path of seeing" (Skt. *darśana-mārga*). The path of seeing is the third path in a larger path-scheme consisting of a total of five paths (de La Vallée Poussin, 1991, pp. xiv, 916–925). As one would expect of any meditative path-scheme in mainstream Buddhism, the fivefold path begins with (1) the cultivation of good conduct or the path of equipment (Skt. *sambhāra-mārga*). This initial step is followed by (2) the contemplation of the foul for those in whom sensual desire (Skt. *rāga*) is predominant or the mindfulness of breathing for those in whom restlessness (Skt. *vitarka*) is predominant. After concentration is attained through these preparatory practices, one then (3) contemplates the four foundations of mindfulness—body, feeling, mind, and physical and mental processes (Skt. *dharma*)—in order to see that they are impermanent, suffering, empty, and not-self. This is expected to result in (4) the direct seeing of the four truths, the first stage of which is likened to "heat" (Skt. *uṣmagata*). Three more "aids to penetration" (Skt. *nirvedhabhāgīya*) follow heat, namely summit (Skt. *mūrdhan*), acceptance (Skt. *kṣānti*), and the highest ordinary state (Skt. *laukikāgra-dharma*) (Buswell, 1997). These stages of penetrating insight are followed immediately by (5) a direct vision of the four truths in sixteen aspects, that is, the path of seeing (Gethin, 1998, pp. 194–198).

The Importance Attached to Contemplation of the Foul

The explanation of the contemplation of the foul and mindfulness of breathing (most notably the explanation of its "sixteen bases" and "six aspects") provided in the texts translated by An and also later texts such as *Dharmatrāta's Meditation Scripture* and the *Scripture on Seated Meditation* Samādhi is largely consistent with the accounts of these practices found in the *Abhidharmakośabhāṣya*, the Pali Canon, and other mainstream Buddhist literature (Deleanu, 1992). There is, however, an unmistakable tendency in the texts translated by An to grant more significance to the contemplation of the foul.

Although its title implies otherwise, An's *Scripture on Mental Restraint through Breathing* (Anban shouyi jing 安般守意經; Zacchetti, 2008), for instance, devotes as much attention to the contemplation of the foul as it does to the mindfulness of breathing, and the contemplation of the foul is presented in An's scripture as a more advanced practice (Greene, 2014, pp. 155–156). Similarly, An's *Scripture on the Twelve Gates* (Shier men jing 十二門經; Ochiai, 2004, pp. 195–203; Zacchetti, 2003) places greater emphasis on this practice. The scripture explicitly associates the four *dhyānas* with the mindfulness of breathing, which it presents as having six aspects, that is, counting (C. *shu* 數), pursuing (C. *sui* 隨), calming (C. *zhi* 止), contemplating (C. *guan* 觀), turning away (C. *huan* 還), and purifying (C. *jing* 淨) (Deleanu, 1992, pp. 52–53), but its explanation of the cultivation of *dhyāna* actually focuses on the contemplation of the foul (Ochiai, 2004, p. 198; Greene, 2014, p. 157).

The same scripture also explicitly refers to the "three poisons" of sensual desire, hatred, and delusion as "meditation sicknesses" (C. *chanbing* 禪病) and explains that the four *dhyānas* (the first four "gates") can be used to counteract sensual desire, the four *apramāṇas* (i.e., loving kindness, compassion, sympathetic joy, and equanimity) to counteract hatred, and the four formless meditations to counteract delusion (Ochiai, 2004, p. 198; cited in Greene, 2014, 158). As Eric Greene points out, the fact that the four *dhyānas* are being used here to counteract sensual desire seems to imply that the author(s) of our scripture largely equated the cultivation of the four *dhyānas* with the contemplation of the foul. This emphasis on the contemplation of the foul can also be found in many of the fifth-century *chan* texts mentioned above. One of these texts, however, gives equal attention to both preparatory practices.

A Diversity of Meditation Sicknesses

Dharmatrāta's Meditation Scripture, a compendium of meditative practices translated by Buddhabhadra (359–429) from Gandhāra, offers a balanced explanation of the two "gates of ambrosia" in verse form. According to Buddhabhadra's compendium, mindfulness of breathing, if carried out properly, can counteract restlessness, and the contemplation of the foul can counteract sensual desire. But if the mindfulness of breathing is carried out improperly, then the mind can become restless or confused (C. *huoluan* 惑亂) and the meditator can experience headaches and a "whirlwind" (C. *jiaofeng* 絞風) within. Left untreated, the meditator can further experience extreme heat (C. *shaore* 燒熱) and experience even more restlessness (T15.618.302a6–14).

Elsewhere, Buddhabhadra's compendium mentions the following signs (C. *xiang* 相) of backsliding (C. *tui* 退), which also seem to be meditation sicknesses: the mind feels unstable (C. *fu* 浮), floating (C. *piao* 飄), rough (C. *cu* 麁), harsh (C. *se* 澁), or slippery (C. *hua* 滑) (T15.618.302b28; cf. Deleanu, 1992, p. 48). The following signs of backsliding are also mentioned: the meditator feels heavy, confused, dull, sleepy, and sunken (T15.618.302c6). The compendium also explains that extreme views of annihilation and permanence can cause restlessness, resulting in the appearance of signs of "stagnation"

(C. *zhu* 住) and the failure to make "progress" (C. *shengjin* 昇進) such as the lack of bliss, happiness, and the enjoyment of calmness. These signs of stagnation—another meditation sickness—are also attributed to the failure to develop a repulsiveness toward the body (T15.618.304b26–c8).

Buddhabhadra's compendium does not limit its discussion of basic meditative techniques to the two gates of ambrosia. It also mentions the contemplation of the elements or *dhātu-prabheda*, which can counteract pride (C. *woman* 我慢, S. *māna*) (T15.618.318b2). In its prose sections, which seem to bear little or no relation to the verse sections, the compendium also explains how to counteract hatred with the four *apramāṇa*s and ignorance with the contemplation of dependent origination. The prose sections also contain lengthy discussions of the contemplation of the aggregates and the sense bases (Skt. *āyatana*). Like the other meditation techniques, the compendium presents these contemplations as part of the fivefold path but, in this case, not as remedies for specific meditation sicknesses. Buddhabhadra's compendium thus uses the fivefold path to bring together a broad selection of independent *chan* practices that may or may not have always been taught together as a group. This is a strategy that it shares with other *chan* texts transmitted to China in the fifth century, most notably Kumārajīva's (344–409/413) *Scripture on Seated Meditation* Samādhi and *Scripture on the Secret Essential Methods of Meditation*.

Signs and Visions

A distinctive feature of these fifth-century *chan* texts as well as of Buddhabhadra's compendium and Buddhaghosa's *Path of Purification*, is their emphasis on signs or verificatory visions (C. *jingjie* 境界) functioning as evidence of meditative attainment or the lack thereof (Greene, 2012, pp. 48–92). This is something we do not see in earlier *chan*-related texts. The *Secret Methods for Curing Meditation Sicknesses*, a text that exerted a considerable amount of influence in China (Greene, 2012, pp. 77–79), is a good example of a fifth-century *chan* text that emphasizes verificatory visions. Like Buddhabhadra's compendium, the *Secret Methods for Curing Meditation Sicknesses* seems to have originated in northwest India. A monk from Kashmir named Buddhasena is said to have transmitted this "Sanskrit" text through oral recitation to Juqu Jingsheng 沮渠京聲 (d. 464), a royal clan member of the Northern Liang (397–439) kingdom who traveled to Khotan in search of the Dharma (T15.620.42b6–14). Juqu's Chinese translation, dated 454, however, is the only form in which Buddhasena's text survives today.

Buddhasena's text is a collection that consists of two sutras. The first sutra, addressed to the famed disciple Śāriputra, offers a detailed description of various (officially 72 in total) preparatory meditative techniques that wilderness-dwelling (Skt. *āraṇyaka*) monks can use to counteract hindrances to concentration. The sutra first features the Buddha's discourse on the mindfulness of breathing as a remedy for restlessness. According to the Buddha in this sutra, if a wilderness-dwelling meditator practicing the twelve ways of cultivating the mind (presumably referring to the four *dhyāna*s, the four *apramāṇas*, and four formless meditations) is disturbed by loud noises while practicing the preparatory step of the mindfulness of breathing, the 404 channels in his body will restlessly move about, a powerful wind element will cause insanity, and winds will enter the throat and force the meditator to utter inappropriate words. As a cure, the meditator is advised to first construct and focus on the mental image of his reflection in a mirror. He is then instructed to construct a mental image of two large wish-fulfilling jewels in his ears that transform into milk, which moistens the ears and prevents clamor from entering the mind. The meditator is then expected to have the following visions: a vajra-canopy emerging from these jewels and completely enveloping his entire body and, after that, vajra-mountains tightly surrounding him, leaving no gaps for sound to enter. On top of each mountain, the meditator will also see seven Buddhas expounding the four foundations of mindfulness. With these verificatory visions, the meditator can firmly shield his mind from all external disturbances (T15.620.333b5–b23).

As a remedy for internal "wind" or breath-related disturbances that may cause the heart to beat faster and make the meditator want to sing or dance, the meditator is similarly instructed to practice "washing the mind-and-heart contemplation." For this contemplation the monk is instructed to focus on visualizing the heart-mind (C. *xin* 心) as a ball of fire that burns away all thoughts. The monk is then expected to have the following vision: a brahmā king appears with a mirror-like wish-fulfilling jewel and a reflection of the heart-mind as a ball of fire appears in it. From the jewel in the brahmā king's palm a lotus and a youth appear. The youth on the lotus pours drops of milk out of a jar into the practitioner's heart, intestines, bones, and joints. The vision continues with the image of the practitioner sitting on a lotus in the middle of a pond of milk and taking a milk bath. In this vision the brahmā king cleanses the practitioner's mouth with his own milk and covers the practitioner with a parasol full of marvelous visions. With these verificatory visions, the meditator no longer feels confused and restless (T15.620.333b24–c27).

The next few techniques introduced in the sutra teach the practitioner how to control sicknesses caused not by the mindfulness of breathing gone awry, but by the four elements of meditation. This too involves visions. The practitioner is told, for instance, to seek remedies if he sees a vision of his 336 bones turning into various mountains, mountain gods, and rocks while cultivating "earth *samādhi*" (C. *di sanmei* 地三昧). As a remedy, the practitioner is told to construct a mental image of the dissected body (bones, joints, sinews, and skin) being repeatedly lathered, cleansed, and covered with various medicines and butter (Greene, 2017). Other techniques explained in the sutra similarly encourage the contemplation of pleasant and calming mental images to counteract lust, greed, attachment to music, the urge to break monastic rules, and various kinds of discomfort caused by the four elements. These are techniques, in other words, employed to counteract sensual desire.

The relatively short second sutra, which bears no obvious relation to the first sutra, is addressed to Ānanda and explains how to use the recitation of the names of the seven Buddhas of the past and a *dhāraṇī* spell to cure practitioners of the mindfulness of breathing who are disturbed by a succubus-like demon named Buti. The demon causes nocturnal emissions. Those who are disturbed by this demon are said to also experience unwanted hallucinatory visions (T15.620.341c26–27). The second sutra also explains how to use the contemplation of images of Buddhas and legendary healers to counteract physical (e.g., ear aches, itchy hands, pain in the feet) and mental sicknesses (e.g., hallucinatory visions of ghosts) that disturb the practitioner during seated meditation. These contemplations also consist of mental images of medicinal substances being poured onto the practitioner.

A similar interest in visions as verificatory or curative can also be seen in the *Essential Methods for Practicing the Five Gates of Meditation* (Greene, 2012, p. 67). The translation of this text, which is attributed to a Gandhāran monk named Dharmamitra (356–442), appears to consist of a number of independent segments (Greene, 2012, pp. 64–67). The text's interest in visions is most apparent in the segments where an imagined exchange about the recollection of an image of the Buddha (C. *nianfo* 念佛) takes place between master and student. The very first segment of Dharmamitra's text features just such an exchange. After this segment, Dharmamitra's text offers an explanation of how to contemplate, among other things, the foul, white bones, the Buddha (C. *guanfo* 觀佛), and the dharma body (C. *fashen* 法身). These segments are followed by another where master and student engage in a conversation about the verificatory visions that occur during the contemplation of white bones, loving-kindness, and the four elements. If the student fails to see these visions, which presumably means that she is experiencing restlessness, the master again recommends using the recollection of the Buddha.

The Five Gates

But, as its title implies, the *Essential Methods for Practicing the Five Gates of Meditation* actually was meant to serve not as a random collection of texts about meditation but as an introduction to the "five gates." This, in fact, is stated quite explicitly in the opening sentence of the entire text (T15.619.325c11–13). The text, however, mentions the five gates only briefly after the last segment about the four *apramāṇa*s. The opening paragraph of the entire text explains that the five gates should be used to counteract specific meditation sicknesses:

- mindfulness of breathing to counteract restlessness
- contemplation of the foul to counteract sensual desire
- loving-kindness to counteract hatred
- dependent origination to counteract attachment to the conceit "I am"
- the recollection of the Buddha to counteract a "sunken mind-and-heart" (C. *xinmo* 心沒).

This last refers to a lack of concentration or energy, or perhaps even depression (T15.619.325c14–16). But in the last segment, where the five gates are briefly mentioned, a different but familiar list of sicknesses (i.e., five hindrances and three poisons) is cited

(T15.619.332b9–14, 24–26, and 332c7). And, curiously, nowhere in the entire text is an explanation of the mindfulness of breathing or dependent origination actually provided. Moreover, for the conceit "I am," the text actually prescribes not dependent origination but the contemplation of white bones. We can assume, therefore, that some equivalence was assumed between the understanding of dependent origination and the contemplation of white bones, the latter being a graphic and concrete instance of the impermanent and dependent nature of phenomena.

It may be the case that Dharmamitra's *Essential Methods for Practicing the Five Gates of Meditation* simply assumes that the reader knows what the five gates are. Its purpose, in other words, is not to provide a comprehensive overview of the five gates. Rather, the purpose may have been to promote one particular practice, namely the recollection of the Buddha. This promotion was perhaps necessary because this practice had not always been included in the five gates. According to the *Śrāvakabhūmi* preserved in Asaṅga's *Yogācārabhūmi*, the five gates—the contemplation of the foul, loving-kindness, contemplation of dependent origination, contemplation of the elements, and the mindfulness of breathing—can be used to counteract sensual desire, hatred, the conceit "I am," pride, and restlessness (Deleanu, 2006, p. 20). No mention is made of the recollection of the Buddha or a sunken mind. Such reference is, however, made in other fifth-century Chinese *chan* texts such as the *Scripture on Seated Meditation* Samādhi. We shall now deal with this scripture in a little more detail.

Kumārajīva's Scripture

The *Scripture on Seated Meditation* Samādhi was prepared by the famed monk Kumārajīva at the request of a Chinese monk named Sengrui 僧叡 (352–436) in 401 (T25.1509.756c9–18). According to Sengrui's biography in the *Biographies of Eminent Monks* (Gaoseng zhuan 高僧傳) and the short preface that he prepared for the scripture, Kumārajīva assembled the scripture from a variety of different sources (T50.2059.364a22–25). Sengrui attributes the first forty-three verses of the scripture to Kumāralāta (T15.614.269c29–270c27) and the last twenty verses to Aśvaghoṣa (T15.614.285c1–286a11). The verses can in fact be found in Aśvaghoṣa's *Saundarananda* (Matsunami, 1967, cited in Yamabe, 1999, p. 79). Sengrui also states that the five gates in the middle of the scripture were culled from the meditation instructions of Vasumitra, Saṃgharakṣa, Upagupta, Saṃghasena, Pārśva, Aśvaghoṣa, and Kumāralāta, whose names are also mentioned in the preface to *Dharmatrāta's Meditation Scripture* (T15.618.301c7–9). The *Scripture on Seated Meditation* Samādhi relies especially on Saṃgharakṣa's *Yogācārabhūmi*, which served as the basis for the scripture's extensive instructions concerning the treatment of sensual desire, hatred, and delusion (Ōdani, 2000, pp. 198–201). The subsequent section on the mindfulness of breathing, in contrast, is said to be a blend of the theories of various teachers. Kumārajīva's scripture was not, however, a simple pastiche of earlier meditation manuals. Sengrui also claims that the scripture's instructions regarding the bodhisattva's techniques of cultivating *chan* was extracted not from a meditation manual but from a scripture known as the [*Questions of the Bodhisattva*] *Who Holds the World Sutra* (C. Chishi jing 持世經, T14.482).

Following the opening verse attributed to Kumāralāta, Kumārajīva's scripture begins, as one might expect, with the preparatory steps that one must take before actually partaking in seated meditation. One must first seek out a teacher who will ask of him or her to answer a series of important questions such as "have you upheld the precepts," "have you committed any serious crimes," and "which among the three poisons trouble you the most" (T15.614.270c28–271a8 passim)? The bulk of the scripture, however, is devoted to answering the last of these three questions. For instance, for someone with too much sensual desire, the manual recommends the contemplation of the foul and white bones. If absorption is attained in the realm of form (Skt. *rūpadhātu*) by cultivating these contemplations, then one is to expect three effects: a sense of bliss and suppleness in the body, radiance emitted by the white bones, and quiescent stilling of the mind (T15.614.272a20–29).

Following this discussion on the antidote for sensual desire, the scripture goes on to prescribe antidotes for the other two poisons, namely hatred and delusion. Like other texts that explain the five gates, what the scripture recommends are contemplation of compassion for the former (T15.614.272b1–c9) and the analysis of the chain of dependent origination—a causal explanation for the origination and eradication of suffering that traditionally consists of twelve links (ignorance, karmic activities, consciousness…rebirth, old age, and death) (T15.614.272c10–273a11). To these three poisons, or what it calls the "gross sicknesses" (C. *cubing* 麁病), the scripture also adds the "subtle sicknesses" (C. *xibing* 細病) of restlessness and dividedness (C. *dengfen* 等分) (T15.614.273b2). There are, the scripture explains, six kinds of restlessness (i.e., sensual desire, hatred, delusion, [restless thoughts about] relatives, land, and deathless ones), which themselves can be divided further into gross and subtle forms (cf. de La Vallée Poussin, 1991, p. 852). As expected, the scripture recommends using the mindfulness of breathing to counteract these different forms of restlessness. The subtle sickness of dividedness, which appears in place of pride, refers to actions of the conscious faculties and senses that generate karma. The eyes, for instance, perceive form and create corresponding karma (de La Vallée Poussin, 1991, pp. 108–111). For this sickness, the scripture recommends the mindful recollection of the Buddha.

Although this scripture distinguishes between gross and subtle sicknesses, there is no indication that they are to be cured in any sort of sequence. If anything, the antidotes or remedies outlined in the scripture seem to be equally efficient, preparatory techniques for attaining concentration. An explanation of these preparatory techniques in the scripture is followed or accompanied by, among other things, an explanation of the four absorptions, the four formless realms, the four *apramāṇa*s, the five supernatural powers (i.e., the divine eye, divine ear, knowledge of previous lives, knowledge of others' minds, and ability to do anything and go anywhere at will), and the four foundations of mindfulness.

The scripture's explanation of seated meditation is thus largely in keeping with earlier Sarvāstivādin schemes of the path. It does, however, diverge from these earlier schemes in one important way in that it also introduces the meditative techniques of a bodhisattva. However, with the obvious exception of the vow to attain Buddhahood and to save all living beings, the techniques associated with the bodhisattva are for the most part a reworking of earlier techniques. In reference to sensual desire, for instance, the scripture simply reiterates the importance of contemplating the impurities of the body, but also adds that the bodhisattva should not therefore come to espouse hatred toward the world (T15.614.281c17–18). In keeping with this pattern of appropriation, the manual prescribes the cultivation of compassion for those bodhisattvas who harbor too much hatred while underscoring the importance of increasing this compassion until he or she can offer the bliss of the Buddha's Way and nirvana to all people (T15.614.282b10–11).

Bodhisattvas are, however, said to suffer the most from ignorance, which they must counteract with the contemplation of dependent origination (T15.614.282c11–12). Bodhisattvas suffering from restlessness are also encouraged, like their *śrāvaka* counterparts, to mindfully observe their breathing and thereby attain concentration (T15.614.285a6–9). This, the scripture explains, will also allow the bodhisattva to eradicate the five hindrances. But, in order to enter the path of seeing, the scripture insists that the bodhisattva should cultivate what it calls the three endurances. By doing so, the bodhisattva will attain the perfection of wisdom and a meditative state known as *pratyutpanna samādhi* wherein the practitioner finds himself standing face-to-face with the Buddhas of the present.

Meditation Sickness as Sickness of Insight

As particular meditative techniques, such as washing-the-mind-and-heart contemplation, contemplation of the elements, recollection of the Buddha, and so on either gained or lost favor among mainstream Buddhist communities, the kinds of meditation sicknesses that most concerned these communities changed as well. These changes notwithstanding, meditation sicknesses continued to be generally understood as unwanted psychosomatic and spiritual conditions that had to be cured or removed to make progress along an elaborate path toward perfect absorption, a direct vision of the four truths, and eventually arhatship (i.e., enlightenment).

There are, however, Buddhist sources that speak of a very different kind of meditation sickness. Some of these sources—Mahayana sources such as the *Aṣṭasāhasrikā prajñāpāramitā-sūtra* and *Vimalakīrti nirdeśa*—were produced by Buddhist communities whose central concern was less the attainment of absorption or arhatship than the attainment of supernatural insight and Buddhahood. These communities were critical of those who, as a means to reform mainstream Buddhism, favored the ideal of wilderness dwelling (Boucher, 2008, pp. 56–61). But other Mahayana sources that voice their concerns about the same sickness such as the *Kāśyapaparivarta* of the *Mahāratnakūṭa*

(Great Pile of Jewels) speak favorably of this ideal. Regardless, in other words, of their attitude toward wilderness dwelling, Buddhist sources influenced by the development of Mahayana thought shared a common concern about this type of sickness.

This influence can also be seen in the *Scripture on Seated Meditation* Samādhi. In its description of the meditations of a monastic bodhisattva we find what appears to be an intrafraternal debate about the contemplation of impermanence (T15.614.283c13–29). The debate begins with this passage from the *Mahāprajñāpāramitā* (Great Perfection of Wisdom) of the Mahayana: "the various dharmas are unborn and do not perish; they are empty and without existence; [they bear but] the one mark of no mark—this is called right view" (T15.614.283c11–12; cf. T25.1509.222b27–28). If so, why then would the contemplation of impermanence be called right view? Impermanence, the *Scripture on Seated Meditation* Samādhi explains, can be used to destroy the mistaken view of permanence. But impermanence, like permanence, must eventually be destroyed lest it become an object of attachment itself. The scripture here raises an important question: does the contemplation of something necessarily imply attachment to that thing? In lieu of a straightforward answer, the scripture explains the rationale for practicing the contemplation of impermanence, and the argument is made that once the contemplation has fulfilled its intended purpose it has to be abandoned. The scripture likens this to using medicine to eradicate sickness and then also doing away with the medicine. If medicine is not done away with, then later the medicine itself becomes a sickness.

Similar arguments can be seen in other sources influenced by *prajñāpāramitā* or perfection of wisdom literature. For instance, writing sometime in the seventh century, the Indian exegete Candrakīrti offers the following parable in his *Prasannapadā* (Lucid Exposition): If one were to mistake emptiness (Skt. *śūnyatā*)—the absence of views (Skt. *dṛṣṭi*) and of own being (Skt. *svabhāva*)—for a real entity (Skt. *bhāva*), this is "as if a shopkeeper were to say, 'I have nothing to sell you,' and would receive the answer, 'Very well, then just sell me this—your absence of goods for sale'" (La Vallée Poussin, 1992, pp. 247–248; trans. Huntington, 1989, p. 29). Shortly after relating this parable Candrakīrti claims that even "the greatly wise, the tathāgatas, having diagnosed this sickness with their great art of healing, reject it." Candrakīrti was prompted to speak of the parable of the shopkeeper by a specific verse from Nāgārjuna's influential work the *Mūlamadhyamakakārikās* (Verses on the Principles of the Middle), also known as the *Madhyamakaśāstra* (Treatise on the Middle). The verse in question goes as follows: "Emptiness is declared by the victorious ones as the exhaustion of all views; those who take emptiness [itself] as a view are called incurable (*asādhya*)" (La Vallée Poussin, 1992, p. 247). As if to provide scriptural support for this verse and his own reading of it, Candrakīrti also makes reference to an influential passage from the *Kāśyapaparivarta* of the *Mahāratnakūṭa* (Great Pile of Jewels):

> It is not, Kāśyapa, that emptiness leads to the annihilation of personhood; persons themselves are empty and emptiness itself is empty, absolutely empty, empty in the past, empty in the future, and empty in the present. You must rely, Kāśyapa, on emptiness, not on the person. However, those, Kāśyapa, who rely on emptiness with

> an objectification of emptiness I speak of as lost and vanished from this teaching. The speculation on the existence of the person in which one's reliance has been placed, be it as great as Mount Sumeru, is indeed better than the speculation on emptiness into which the conceited have settled. Why? Emptiness is the way out for those who engage in items of wrong speculation on the person, but by what means will they find a way out who hold to the speculations on emptiness? (64)
>
> It is just like this, Kāśyapa. Should some man be sick, and should a physician give medicine to him, and should that medicine, having evacuated all his diseases, not [itself] come to be cleared from his viscera, what do you think, Kāśyapa? Shall that sick man be freed of that sickness if that medicine, having evacuated all the diseases settled in his viscera, would not itself depart his viscera?
>
> Kāśyapa said: "No, Blessed One. The disease of that man would be more serious if that medicine, having evacuated all the diseases, was settled in all his viscera and would not depart."
>
> The Blessed One said: "Just so, Kāśyapa, emptiness is the remedy for all items of wrong speculation, but then, Kāśyapa, one for whom emptiness itself becomes a wrong speculation I speak of as incurable. (Silk, 2004, pp. 353–354)

Emptiness Sickness

Another well-known source that speaks of the attachment to emptiness as sickness is the *Vimalakīrti nirdeśa*. In this sutra, the layman Vimalakīrti claims that "the root of illness" (C. *bingben* 病本) lies in the deluded attachment to the notion of a self (T14.475.545a1–12 passim). To rid oneself of this stubborn attachment one must rid oneself of dualisms. This can be done, Vimalakīrti explains, by treating all things, even such unlikely bedfellows as self and nirvana, as "equal" (C. *pingdeng* 平等). This, he adds, is possible precisely because all dualisms (and discriminations) are empty. However, "Once one has acquired this kind of equal outlook, one will be freed of all other illness and will have only the illness of emptiness, and the illness of emptiness too is empty" (Watson, 1997, p. 69; T14.475.545a12–13; cf. T14.474.526a23–24).

Echoes of these claims about emptiness sickness (C. *kongbing* 空病) found in the *Prasannapadā*, *Kāśyapaparivarta*, and *Vimalakīrti nirdeśa* can also be heard in later Chinese and Japanese sources associated with the Chan and Zen traditions. One particularly noteworthy instance is the work of Chan master Dahui Zonggao 大慧宗杲 (1089–1163). According to Dahui, many Chan students foolishly believed that they could attain a state of calm and relaxation and quite literally have "no mind" (C. *wuxin* 無心) by shunning the objects of the senses and maintaining a state of absolute tranquility. In the absence of mind, these students also believed that they would encounter the radiance of inherent Buddhahood. Dahui was skeptical. In his sermons and letters, Dahui repeatedly urged his students—monks, nuns, and prominent laymen and laywomen—to refrain from seeking such "special states" outside the hustle and bustle of everyday life. Instead, he claimed that one should realize that "the very place where one cannot escape [from the turmoil of everyday life] *is* meditative-work (T47.1998A.923c6–7). To see otherwise and become attached to quietude, Dahui also claimed, was nothing but a grave sickness: "The Buddha cured this [i.e., sickness of attachment] with the medicine of tranquility-*pāramitā*. The sickness is gone but the medicine stayed, and this sickness is even worse" (T47.1998A.926b22–24).

The Koan Method

The notion of meditation sickness sometimes even entered into disputes between different schools of practice. Dahui voiced these concerns about the tendency to seek calm and relaxation as a practice called "silent illumination" (C. *mozhao* 默照) gained popularity, especially among lay practitioners of Chan meditation. This practice is often associated with the Song dynasty Caodong Chan tradition (Schlütter, 2008; Shinohara, 1997, p. 181). These heretics, Dahui complained, teach people to follow objects and "fasten [their mind]" (C. *guandai* 管帶) on them, to forget emotions and silently illuminate, and to illuminate and fasten their minds on objects as they come and go. Students may thus reach a state of no-perception and no-knowing through this form of relaxing, but this state, according to Dahui, was actually a kind of meditation sickness (T47.1998A.918a25–b24 passim).

Often Dahui also used canonical understandings of meditation sickness as sloth and restlessness to explain this sickness to his students: "nowadays not only practitioners of Chan but also the literati, who are intelligent, sharp, and extremely well read—each and every one of them suffer from two general sicknesses. If they aren't [suffering from] attachment to thoughts (C. *zhuoyi* 著意) then they are [suffering from] forgetting feelings (C. *wanghui* 忘懷)." As he explains, "to forget feelings is to fall into the ghost cave underneath a black mountain—in the teachings this is referred to as sloth (C. *hunchen* 昏沈); to be attached to thoughts is to have [your] consciousness whirl around in confusion—one thought continues to another, [but] even before the former thought has come to cease the next thought continues [in its place]—in the teachings this is referred to as restlessness (C. *diaoju* 掉舉)" (T47.1998A.884c17–21). Sloth and restlessness correspond to two of the five hindrances discussed earlier.

Dahui's proposed remedy for the sickness of silent illumination was a practice called "observing the phrase" (C. *kanhua* 看話). He often instructed his students to study the stories of ancient Chan masters—koans—and focus on a single "critical phrase" (C. *huatou* 話頭) from those stories. Dahui was particularly fond of giving his students Chan master Zhaozhou's 趙州 (778–897) famous dog koan: "Does a dog have Buddha nature? Zhaozhou answered, 'no.'" Dahui urged his students to try approach this koan without relying on discursive reasoning and conceptual dichotomies such as existence and non-existence. He also warned against using existing written studies of this koan to make sense of it (Ahn, 2017).

Similar claims about the heresy of silent illumination and the importance of curing this sickness with the practice of observing the critical phrase were also made by the

Japanese Zen master Hakuin Ekaku 白隠慧鶴 (1686–1769), who is most commonly remembered for his efforts to revitalize his own Rinzai Zen sect, and for his popular writings on meditation (or Zen) sickness. Although Hakuin relied heavily on the teachings of Dahui, the unique historical conditions under which the Japanese Zen master wrote about Zen sickness enabled him to advance new theories about the subject (Ahn, 2008). Hakuin wrote about the subject at a time when an ethos of diligence and concomitant concerns about exhaustion swept through the Tokugawa populace and a vibrant Japanese print industry made medical texts imported from China more accessible.

Unlike Dahui, Hakuin used his newly acquired knowledge of traditional Chinese meditation to explore the distinctly physical aspect of meditation (or Zen) sickness in his writings such as the *Yasenkanna* 夜船閑話 (Idle Talk on a Night Boat; Yoshizawa, 2000; Waddell, 2002). Often presenting his thoughts on this subject in the form of an autobiography, Hakuin claimed that the experience of Zen sickness entails the following: a "fire" mounting in the upper body followed by parched lungs, cold feet, fear, depression, ringing in the ears, constant perspiration, and hallucinations. Lest his experience of Zen sickness seem unrelated to tradition, Hakuin made sure to attribute his sickness to the misguided practice of silent illumination. Naturally, he recommended the practice of observing the critical phrase as a cure.

In his *Yasenkanna*, however, Hakuin also claimed that Zen sickness can be cured with something called "inner contemplation" (J. *naikan* 内觀), a teaching he purportedly received from a mysterious recluse named Hakuyū 白幽. Citing classical sources on Chinese medicine, Hakuyū is said to have explained to the young Zen monk that one could cure Zen sickness by bringing the mind down to the lower body and nourishing vital energy (J. *ki* 氣). In addition this method of inner contemplation and the Chan or Zen practice of observing the phrase, Hakuin also recommends using something he calls the soft butter pill (J. *nansogan* 輭酥丸) method, a method that he seems to have devised on the basis of his reading of a similar method described in the *Secret Methods for Curing Meditation Sicknesses* (Greene, 2017).

Conclusion

In sum, although meditation sickness can refer to a variety of different symptoms and psychosomatic conditions in the context of Buddhism, canonical sources tend to speak most frequently of two specific kinds of meditation sickness. Because Buddhists commonly assumed the path to liberation to require perfect concentration, supernatural insight, or the combination of the two, concerns were most often voiced about the inability to attain concentration and the possibility of insight going awry. Various lists of hindrances to the attainment of concentration can be found in canonical Buddhist sources, but no list was invoked more frequently than that of the five hindrances: sensual desire, hatred, sloth, restlessness, and doubt. As for the attachment to insight, this concern was voiced mainly in Mahayana sources.

As Buddhists continued to borrow and develop new meditative techniques, the way they voiced their concerns about meditation sickness, especially its symptoms, changed over time. In order to highlight the continuity that we can see in the various Buddhist discourses about meditation sickness, this chapter has inevitably not been able to cover the whole range of different views, practices, and theories. It would, however, be a mistake to take the continuity of ideas described in this chapter as evidence of Buddhists always sharing a common experience across time and space. As Robert H. Sharf (1995) has shown, the contemporary approach to meditative experience in Buddhism was the invention of twentieth-century Asian reform movements. Things have often changed over the years. Canonical sources, moreover, offer not a descriptive but a prescriptive account of Buddhist meditation and the path to liberation. The legitimacy of the claims made in these sources were sought, in other words, not in the personal experiences of their authors but in their "filiality to the canon" (Sharf, 1995, p. 239).

This, however, is not to say that Buddhist discourses about meditation sickness were fated to be nothing more than reproductions of orthodox texts. As Hakuin's example makes clear, historical contingencies that necessitate innovative reinterpretations of tradition have continued to serve as a powerful motor of change in the history of Buddhism. These contingencies have not only made new experiences of meditation sickness possible, but they also have made the invention of new techniques, such as the practice of observing the critical phrase, possible as well. In both theory and practice Buddhist meditation may at first appear to be resistant to change and innovation, but this, as the present chapter has tried to show, is an assumption that is open to much critical examination.

Abbreviations

AN	Morris & Hardy, 1885–1900
C	*Chinese*
DN	Rhys Davids, Carpenter, & Stede, 1890–1911
MN	Trenckner & Chalmers, 1888–1902
P.	Pali
Skt.	Sanskrit
T	Takakusu & Watanabe, 1924–1932
Vism.	Buddhaghosa, 1991

References

Ahn, J. (2007). *Malady of meditation: A prolegomenon to the study of illness and Zen* (Doctoral dissertation). University of California, Berkeley.

Ahn, J. (2008). Zen and the art of nourishing life: Labor, exhaustion, and the malady of meditation. *Japanese Journal of Religious Studies 35*(2), 177–229.

Ahn, J. (2009). Who has the last word in Chan? Secrecy, transmission, and reading during the Northern Song dynasty. *Journal of Chinese Religions 37*, 1–72.

Ahn, J. (2017). Getting sick over nothing: Hyesim and Hakuin on the maladies of meditation. In P. Salguero (Ed.), *Buddhism and medicine: An anthology of premodern sources* (pp. 390–397). New York: Columbia University Press.

Boucher, D. (2008). *Bodhisattvas of the forest and the formation of the Mahāyāna: A study and translation of the* Rāṣṭrapālaparipṛcchā-sūtra. Honolulu: University of Hawai'i Press.

Bronkhorst, J. (2000). *The Two Traditions of Meditation in Ancient India*. New Delhi, India: Motilal Banarsidass.

Buswell, R. (1997). The "aids to penetration" (*nirvedhabhāgīya*) according to the Vaibhāṣika school. *Journal of Indian Philosophy* 25(6), 589–611.

Buddhaghosa. (1991). *The Path of Purification (Visudhimagga) by Bhadantācariya Buddhaghosa* (Bhikkhu Ñāṇamoli, Trans.). (5th ed.). Kandy, Sri Lanka: Buddhist Publication Society.

de La Vallée Poussin, L. (1936–1937). Mūsila and Nārada: le chemin du nirvāṇa. *Mélanges chinois et bouddhiques* 5, 189–222.

de La Vallée Poussin, L. (1991). *Abhidharmakośabhāṣyam* (L. Pruden, Trans.)(Vol. 3). Berkeley, CA: Asian Humanities Press.

de La Vallée Poussin, L. (1992). *Madhyamakāvatāra*. Bibliotheca Buddhica 9. Delhi: Motilal Banarsidass.

Deleanu, F. (1992). Mindfulness of breathing in the Dhyāna Sūtras. *Transactions of the International Conference of Orientalists in Japan* 37, 42–57.

Deleanu, F. (2006). *The chapter on the mundane path (*laukikamārga*) in the* Śrāvakabhūmi*: A trilingual edition (Sanskrit, Tibetan, Chinese), annotated translation, and introductory study* (Vols. 1 & 2). Tokyo: International Institute for Buddhist Studies.

Gethin, R. (1998). *The foundations of Buddhism*. Oxford: Oxford University Press.

Gethin, R. (2004). On the practice of Buddhist meditation according to the Pāli Nikāyas and exegetical sources. *Buddhismus in Geschichte und Gegenwart* 9, 201–221.

Greene, E. (2012). *Meditation, repentance, and visionary experience in early medieval Chinese Buddhism* (Doctoral dissertation). University of California, Berkeley.

Greene, E. (2014). Healing breaths and rotting bones: On the relationship between Buddhist and Chinese meditation practices during the Eastern Han and Three Kingdoms period. *Journal of Chinese Religions* 42(2), 145–184.

Greene, E. (2017). Healing sicknesses caused by meditation: "The enveloping butter contemplation" from the *Secret Essential Methods for Curing Meditation Sickness*. In P. Salguero (Ed.), *Buddhism and medicine: An anthology of premodern sources* (pp. 373–381). New York: Columbia University Press.

Griffiths, P. J. (1986). *On being mindless: Buddhist meditation and the mind-body problem*. La Salle, IL: Open Court.

Huntington, C. (1989). *The emptiness of emptiness: An introduction to early Indian Mādhyamika*. Honolulu: University of Hawai'i Press.

Matsunami, S. (1967). *Bukkyō ni okeru shin to gyō*. Kyoto: Heirakuji shoten.

Morris, R., & Hardy, E. (Eds.). (1885–1900). *Aṅguttara-nikāya*. London: Pali Text Society.

Ochiai, T. (2004). *Kongōji issaikyō no kisoteki kenkyū to shinshutsu butten no kenkyū: Heisei 16-nen 3-gatsu*. Tokyo: Kokusai Bukkyōgaku Daigakuin Daigaku.

Ōdani, N. (2000). *Hō to gyō no shisō to shite no bukkyō*. Kyoto: Beneidō.

Rhys Davids, T. W., Carpenter, J. E., & Stede, W. (Eds.). (1890–1911). *Digha-nikāya*. London: Pali Text Society.

Schlütter, M. (2008). *How Zen became Zen: The dispute over enlightenment and the formation of Chan Buddhism in Song-dynasty China*. Honolulu: University of Hawai'i Press.

Sharf, R. H. (1995). Buddhist modernism and the rhetoric of meditative experience. *Numen* 42(3), 228–283.
Shaw, S. (2006). *Buddhist meditation: An anthology of texts from the Pāli Canon*. London: Routledge.
Shinohara, K. (1997). Ta-hui's instructions to Tseng K'ai: Buddhist "freedom" in the Neo-Confucian context. In I. Bloom and J. Fogel (Eds.), *Meeting of minds* (pp. 175–208). New York: Columbia University Press.
Silk, J. (2000). The Yogācāra bhikṣu. In J. Silk (Ed.), *Wisdom, compassion, and the search for understanding: The Buddhist Studies legacy of Gadjin Nagao*. Honolulu: University of Hawai'i Press.
Silk, J. (2004). Wisdom and compassion. In D. Lopez (Ed.), *Buddhist scriptures* (pp. 350–360). New York: Penguin.
Takakusu J., & Watanabe K. (Eds.). 1924–1932. *Taishō shinshū daizōkyō shinshū daizōkyō*. Tokyo: Taishō Issaikyō Kankōkai.
Trenckner, V., & Chalmers, R. (Eds.). (1888–1902). *Majjhima-nikāya*. London: Pali Text Society.
Waddell, N. (trans.) (2002). Hakuin's *Yasenkanna*. *Eastern Buddhist (New Series)* *34*(1), 79–119.
Watson, B. (trans.). (1997). *The Vimalakirti Sutra*. New York: Columbia University Press.
Vetter, T. (1988). *The ideas and meditative practices of early Buddhism*. Leiden: E.J. Brill.
Yamabe, N. (1999). *The Sūtra on the Ocean-Like Samādhi of the Visualization of the Buddha: The interfusion of the Chinese and Indian cultures in Central Asia as reflected in a fifth-century apocryphal sūtra* (Doctoral dissertation). Yale University.
Yamabe, N., & Sueki, F. (2009). *The Sutra on the Concentration of Sitting Meditation*. Berkeley: Numata Center for Buddhist Translation and Research.
Yoshizawa, K. (ed.) (2000). *Yasenkanna*. Hakuin zenji hōgo zenshū 4. Kyoto: Zenbunka kenkyūsho.
Zacchetti, S. (2003). The rediscovery of three early Buddhist scriptures on meditation: A preliminary analysis of the *Fo shuo shi'er men jing*, the *Fo shuo jie shi'er men jing* translated by An Shigao and their commentary preserved in the newly found Kongoji manuscript. *Journal of the Internal Research Institute for Advanced Buddhology at Soka University 6*, pp. 251–300.
Zacchetti, S. (2008). The Nature of the *Da anban shouyi jing* 大安般守意經 T602 Reconsidered. *Journal of the International Association of Buddhist Studies* *31*(1–2), 421–484.

CHAPTER 41

MEDITATION TO KILL AND BE KILLED BY

The Use of Samādhi *Power in Imperial Japan*

BRIAN VICTORIA

Introduction

In principle, examining whether meditation could be involved in killing others, let alone being killed by others, would seem to be a fool's errand, or more accurately, an oxymoron. How could sitting silently in one or another meditative posture possibly be linked to killing of any kind? Yet, as those who meditate know, the purpose or goal of meditation is not to remain seated in lifelong meditation. Instead, the insights and understandings realized in meditation are to be applied to, or invested in, all daily activities. For those taking part in warfare, the possibility of killing others, or being killed by others, becomes part of daily life. Thus, the state of mind, or state of being, derived from meditation finds itself applied to this realm.

Although meditation is neither historically, nor today, a practice exclusively connected to Buddhism, many of its forms and methodologies are either derived or closely connected with this faith. Thus, while many branches of "mindfulness meditation," for example, promote themselves as purely secular activities, their roots can often be traced back to one or another form of Buddhism. For this reason, to understand meditation, it is both helpful and necessary to understand the nature of the role meditation plays, and continues to play, within Buddhism. In this context, *Buddhist* meditation *can be*, or *has been*, involved in killing, but in asserting this, however, it is equally important to point out that killing via meditation is certainly not limited to Buddhism alone.

For example, Professor Emeritus M. E. Marty, distinguished scholar of religion at the University of Chicago, described one aspect of religion as follows:

> Positive thinkers and public relations officers for the faiths would repudiate this notion or evade the fact. They want religion to be nothing but gospel, good news.

> Apologists for the faiths usually minimize the distress that can come with religion or that religion can produce. You will not read about the destructive element in religious impulses in the advertisements for the church of your choice. Yet if the pursuit of truth is still to be cherished as a foundational theme in the academy, one must note the feature of religion that keeps it on the front page and on prime time: it kills. Or, if, as the gun lobbies say of weapons—that they do not kill; people do—one must say of religion that if it does not kill, many of its forms and expressions motivate people to kill. Experts on what motivates the scores of wars or, as some would have it, "tribal conflicts," today know that not only do many belligerent partisans wear names like "Protestant" and "Catholic," "Shi'ite" and "Sunni," "Jewish" and "Sikh," but leaders and followers alike fire on the demonized Other, the enemy, in the name of God or the gods. (Marty, 1996, p. 14)

In reflecting on Marty's comments, on the one hand, he primarily states that it is "religion" that kills, but on the other, in his examples, e.g., Protestant and Catholic, etc., Buddhism is not included. Why not?

Buddhists, this author among them, would like to believe this is because Buddhism is the one great exception to the rule that religion kills. That is to say, the very first precept both lay and clerical Buddhists commit themselves to observe is "not to take life." Therefore, the claim is made that Buddhists, no matter the reason, do not engage in killing. Yet, knowledgeable readers recognize that, unfortunately, this is false. Historically speaking, there have been many instances in Asia's long Buddhist history of people calling themselves Buddhists, both lay and cleric, but who have killed, or supported the act of killing. They typically justify their actions as conforming with, if not motivated by, the doctrines of their faith.

This chapter looks at one instance of the use (or abuse) of Buddhist meditation in Japan during and prior to the Asia-Pacific War (1937–1945) in support of Japanese aggression in Asia and beyond. Inasmuch as I have described the general nature of this support in my book, *Zen at War*, I will not repeat that material here. Instead, this chapter focuses on one particular aspect of that use, i.e., the application of meditative *samādhi* power (禅定力) in support of war and violence in modern Japan, most especially, but not exclusively, during the Second World War. This chapter also addresses the question of whether this use of *samādhi* power can in fact be called a "misuse" or "abuse" of that power.

Samādhi Defined

The definition of *samādhi* within Buddhism refers to a state of meditative consciousness. The term *samādhi* derives from the root *sam-a-dha*, which means "to collect" or "bring together," and is often translated as "concentration" or "unification of mind." In early Buddhist texts, *samādhi* is associated with the term *samatha* (calm abiding). In the *suttas* (Sankrit, *sūtras*), *samādhi* is defined as "one-pointedness of mind," a meditative absorption attained by the practice of *dhyāna* (Korean, Seon; Japanese, Zen; Chinese, Chan).

Dhyāna, a core Buddhist practice commonly translated as meditation, is a state of "no mind" referring to a series of cultivated states of mind which lead to a state of perfect equanimity and awareness (Pali, *upekkhii-sati-piirisuddhi*). Upon entrance into *samādhi*, the mind becomes still, yet totally aware of the present moment; a one-pointedness of mind. As such, it is also the last of the eight elements of the Buddhist Noble Eightfold Path.

Note, too, that because "one-pointedness of mind" is an intrinsic and indivisible part of *samādhi*, the *mental* power produced by this concentrated state of mind is a potent force in the hands of the experienced meditator. Given their indivisible nature, this chapter uses the terms *samādhi* and *samādhi* power interchangeably.

Samādhi Power Weaponized

For those who have experienced it, *samādhi* is a luminous experience that seems to transcend time and place. It is, however, definitely not a trance-like experience in which the meditator is transmitted to a supernatural realm. In fact, if anything, the meditator is more fully "present" in the realm of the "here and now" than ever before. Thus, the use of anything related to *samādhi* to harm another sentient being would appear to be utterly impossible.

Nevertheless, prior to and during the Asia-Pacific War, Japanese Zen leaders, D. T. Suzuki included, often wrote about this meditation-derived mental power, emphasizing the effectiveness of *samādhi* power (Japanese, *jōriki*) in battle. Suzuki described the great *samurai* general of sixteenth-century Japan, Uesugi Kenshin (1530–1578), who instructed his retainers as follows:

> Those who cling to life die, and those who defy death live. The essential thing is the mind. Look into this mind and firmly take hold of it and you will understand that there is something in you which is above birth-and-death and which is neither drowned in water nor burned by fire. I have myself gained an insight into this *Samādhi* and know what I am telling you. Those who are reluctant to give up their lives and embrace death are not true warriors (Suzuki, 1938, p. 56).

Here, Suzuki is expressing Kenshin's belief that it was hesitation on the battlefield, stemming from fear of death, that would lead the warrior to lose his life by providing his opponent with an opening to strike him down. *Samādhi* power, on the other hand, supplied fearlessness in battle, i.e., transcendence of "birth and death," thereby leading to victory. Suzuki, like virtually all Zen leaders of wartime Japan, agreed that the Zen practice of seated, cross-legged meditation (Japanese, *zazen*), was the fountainhead of the mental power derived from *samādhi*, a power that was as available to modern Japanese soldiers as it had once been to *samurai* warriors.

Samādhi in the Imperial Army

Lt. Col Sugimoto Gorō (1900–1937), who died on a northern Chinese battlefield, provides an example of *samādhi* power during the Asia-Pacific War (see Figure 41.1). Following Sugimoto's death, his Rinzai Zen Master Yamazaki Ekijū offered the following eulogy:

> A grenade fragment hit him in the left shoulder. He seemed to have fallen down but then got up again. Although he was standing, one could not hear his commands. He was no longer able to issue commands with that husky voice of his .... Yet he was still standing, holding his sword in one hand as a prop. Both legs were slightly bent, and he was facing in an easterly direction [toward the imperial palace]. It appeared that he had saluted though his hand was now lowered to about the level of his mouth. The blood flowing from his mouth covered his watch .... From long ago, the true sign of a Zen priest had been his ability to pass away while doing *zazen*. Those who were completely and thoroughly enlightened, however, ... could die calmly in a standing position .... This was possible due to *samādhi* power. [...]
> Although it can be said that his life of thirty-eight years was all too short, for someone who has truly obtained *samādhi* power, long and short are not important.

FIGURE 41.1 A photo of Imperial Army Lt. Col Sugimoto Gorō (1900–1937)

> The great, true example of Sugimoto Gorō was that of one who had united with emptiness, embodying true loyalty (to the emperor) and service to the state. I am convinced he is one of those who, should he be reborn seven times over, would reverently work to destroy enemies of the emperor (written on the 11th of February of the 2,598th year of the imperial reign) [1938] (Victoria, 2006, p. 125–126).

These descriptions by Yamazaki make it clear just how wide-ranging *samādhi* power was believed to be. In the first instance, it provided Sugimoto with the same power as that of ancient Zen masters, i.e., the power to choose one's posture at the time of death even when mortally wounded. In addition, it facilitated a state of true loyalty to the emperor such that an early death on the battlefield was "not important." In fact, Sugimoto's death was regarded as no more than a prelude to his being reborn and repeatedly killed in loyal service to emperor and state.[1] Needless to say, Rinzai Zen Master Yamazaki Ekijū expressed no concern for the "all too short" lives of slain enemy soldiers.

Note that the application of *samādhi* power to the battlefield did not begin with the Asia-Pacific War. There is record of its use as early as the 1904–1905 Russo-Japanese War. It was Japan's victory in this war that made it possible for Japan to force Korea into protectorate status in November 1905, and subsequently to colonize the entire country in 1910. An Imperial Japanese naval officer in that conflict, Vice Admiral Yamaji Kazuyoshi (1869–1963) wrote *Zen no Ōyō* (The Practical Application of Zen), a book describing how he put his many years of Zen training to practical use during the Russo-Japanese War. He specifically discussed *samādhi* in a section called *The Realm of Samādhi*:

> In Zen, there is something called "*samādhi*." This is a realm where there is neither "self" nor "others," neither mountains nor rivers; the entirety of one's whole mind becomes "the character mu" (*muji*), "[the sound of] one hand" (*sekishu*). If you do not endeavor to sit quietly in this realm you will never realize enlightenment. [...]
>
> At first, I was unable to unify my spirit by becoming the character *mu* or [the sound of] one hand for even three to five minutes. I was attacked by various illusory and worldly thoughts from the front, rear, left and right. However, as I continued to practice, it gradually became easier to enter *samādhi*. And after sitting quietly in the realm of *samādhi* I was finally able to penetrate my assigned *kōan*, achieve great peace of mind (i.e. become enlightened) and experience a feeling of great exultation. It was then I realized the mental state where throughout heaven and earth I alone am honored.[2] [...]

[1] The reference here is to Kusanoki Masashige (1294–1336), a fourteenth-century *samurai* and devout Buddhist, who fought for Emperor Go-Daigo in an attempt to wrest rulership of Japan away from the Kamakura shogunate. In post-Meiji Restoration Japan, the Japanese government promoted Kusanoki as the ideal of samurai loyalty and a model for all Japanese soldiers. According to legend, when his army was completely surrounded, with only fifty of his original seven hundred horsemen still alive, Kusanoki and his brother pledged to be reborn seven times to serve the emperor.

[2] The words, "throughout heaven and earth I alone am honored" are alleged to have first been spoken by Shakyamuni Buddha shortly after his birth. By quoting these words the author is claiming that he became enlightened at that time, i.e., he became a "Buddha" (*lit.* an awakened one).

> In the midst of war, each time I sat quietly and entered *samādhi* a wise plan would suddenly appear. Furthermore, the moment I saw the enemy a countermeasure would emerge. Still further, when faced with various problems in daily life, I found my practice of *zazen* very helpful to their resolution. (Kazuyoshi, 1941, pp. 29–30)

Here, the reader learns further of the wide usage enjoyed by *samādhi* power. Firstly it allowed an Imperial Navy Vice Admiral to devise a "wise plan" even in the midst of war. Moreover, when the enemy appeared, *samādhi* power facilitated "countermeasure(s)," i.e., countermeasures to *more effectively kill the enemy.* And even in "daily life," *samādhi* power was a valuable resource for problem solving. If not precisely a "man for all seasons," *samādhi* is definitely a "power for all seasons" (see Figure 41.2).

Samādhi Power as Terrorism

What is perhaps most surprising about the Japanese use of *samādhi* power is that it even played an important role in Buddhist-related acts of terrorism in 1930s Japan. The Third

FIGURE 41.2 A drawing of Imperial Army officers practicing meditation in their military unit's martial arts hall. The translated caption reads: "All assigned officers gathered in the unit's martial arts hall to practice meditation (zazen)".

Reich's first victims were not foreign nationals or Jews; instead they were Hitler's domestic political enemies, especially, but not exclusively, his enemies on the left, i.e., German communists and socialists, as well as other domestic forces who dared oppose Hitler's rise to power. Sometimes these forces were imprisoned in concentration camps and other times they were murdered in the streets or at their homes in domestic incidents of Nazi-sponsored acts of terror.

Something similar occurred in 1930s Japan. Thus, *samādhi* power was utilized by Buddhist-related terrorists in 1930s Japan in what was popularly known as the "Blood Oath Corps Incident" (*Ketsumeidan Jiken*). For example, Onuma Shō (1911–1978) assassinated Japan's former finance minister, Inoue Junnosuke (1869–1932), on February 9, 1932. At his trial, Onuma stated:

> After starting my practice of *zazen*, I entered a state of *samādhi* the likes of which I had never experienced before. I felt my spirit become unified, really unified, and when I opened my eyes from the half-closed meditative position I noticed the smoke from the incense curling up and touching the ceiling. At this point it suddenly came to me — I would be able to carry out [the assassination] that night.
> (Victoria, 2006, p. 214)

This kind of testimoney raises the question if the employment of *samādhi* power in warfare and killing, including assassination, should be considered a legitimate expression of the Buddha Dharma. Did Shakyamuni Buddha, in his many teachings, fail to address this question?

Theravāda and Mahāyāna Views on Killing

In examining the Theravāda tradition, it is clear that Shakyamuni Buddha was well aware of the multiple possibilities of the misuse of meditation, and he criticized them severely. The following passage from the *Gopaka Moggallana Sutta* (Moggallana the Guardsman) in the *Majjhima Nikaya* [The Middle-length Discourses] proves his awareness:

> Once, Ven. Ananda, Master Gotama was staying near Vesali in the Peaked Roofed Pavilion in the Great Wood. I [Vassakara] went to him at the Peaked Roofed Pavilion in the Great Wood, and there he spoke in a variety of ways on mental absorption. Master Gotama was both endowed with mental absorption & made mental absorption his habit. In fact, he praised mental absorption of every sort. [...]
>
> It wasn't the case, brahman, that the Blessed One praised mental absorption of every sort, nor did he criticize mental absorption of every sort. And what sort of mental absorption did he not praise? There is the case where a certain person dwells

> with his awareness overcome by sensual passion, seized with sensual passion. He does not discern the escape, as it actually is present, from sensual passion once it has arisen. Making that sensual passion the focal point, he absorbs himself with it, besorbs, resorbs, & supersorbs himself with it. [...]
>
> *He dwells with his awareness overcome by ill will...*
>
> He dwells with his awareness overcome by sloth & drowsiness...
>
> He dwells with his awareness overcome by restlessness & anxiety...
>
> He dwells with his awareness overcome by uncertainty, seized with uncertainty. He does not discern the escape, as it actually is present, from uncertainty once it has arisen. Making that uncertainty the focal point, he absorbs himself with it, besorbs, resorbs, & supersorbs himself with it. This is the sort of mental absorption that the Blessed One did not praise (emphasis mine) (See Bhikkhu, 1998).

Inasmuch as becoming "overcome by ill will" is the *sine qua non* for killing another human being, it would appear to be self-evident that, according to this sūtra, Shakyamuni Buddha (aka Master Gotama) proscribed the use of meditation for the purpose of killing, among other misuses. Nevertheless, it is true there are Buddhists who believe it is possible to kill *without ill will.* This belief transforms the act of killing into a permissible act, or at least an act not specifically proscribed. For example, Capt. Somya Malasri, a former Thai monk, is currently one of two active-duty US Army Buddhist chaplains. He explained the Buddhist rationale for warfare, saying:

> A lot of people ask if a Buddhist can be a soldier because the first precept is no killing. The answer is yes. You can protect yourself or sacrifice yourself to do the righteous thing. You can sacrifice yourself to protect your country because if there's no country, there's no freedom and you cannot practice your religion. In Buddhism, if you go to war and kill others, it's your duty, not your intention to kill other people. If a person dies of your intention, and you have anger, that is wrong in Buddhism. *When soldiers go to war, they don't have any intention to kill others and they don't have hatred in their minds* (emphasis mine).[3]

On the one hand, there is doctrinal support for Capt. Malasri's position. Interestingly, however, the clearest expression of this support is to be found in the Mahāyāna school, not in Theravāda. The *Upāyakauśalya Sūtra* (Skillful Means Sūtra) contains a story about Shakyamuni Buddha in a former life, i.e., when he was yet a *bodhisattva* on his way to Buddhahood. As a ship's captain, named "Greatly Compassionate," Shakyamuni discerned that there was a robber onboard whose intent was to rob and kill all five hundred of the passengers who were themselves *bodhisattvas.* Although reluctant to take life, Shakyamuni ultimately decided to kill the robber. He did so, however, not only without ill will but, on the contrary, with compassion for both the would-be victims and

[3] Quotation posted on Friday, August 17, 2007 on the Buddhist Military Sangha website. http://buddhistmilitarysangha.blogspot.jp. (Accessed January 9, 2017).

even for the robber himself—Shakyamuni sought to prevent the latter from being reborn and suffering in hell as karmic retribution for his evil deeds.

Unsurprisingly, Shakyamuni's act of killing is presented in accordance with the view that acts of killing are instances of unwholesome karma, given the latter's universal and inescapable nature. Nevertheless, although the negative karma resulting from his killing of the robber should have accrued even to Shakyamuni, it did not, for, as he explained: "Good man, because I used ingenuity [skillful means] out of great compassion at that time, I was able to avoid the suffering of one hundred thousand *kalpas* of *samsāra* [the ordinary world of form and desire], and that wicked man was reborn in heaven, a good plane of existence, after death" (Chang, 2008, pp. 456–457). In the Mahāyāna school, this sūtra has often been used to support those, like Capt. Malasri, who claim that a good Buddhist may kill if the act is done out without ill will toward the victim.

The Theravāda school, at least doctrinally, takes a strong position against the use of violence and war. As the Ven. Bhikkhu Bodhi notes, "The *suttas,* it must be clearly stated, do not admit any moral justification for war. Thus, if we take the texts as issuing moral absolutes, one would have to conclude that war can never be morally justified" (Bodhi, 2014, p. 5). The *Seyya Jātaka,* for example, conveys a story about yet another of Shakyamuni's former lives as a *bodhisattva.* In this story, Shakyamuni was a king of Benares and ruled well. However, he discovered one of his courtiers was involved in an intrigue in his harem and punished him with banishment. Angered, the banished courtier went to the court of an enemy king and persuaded him to lead an army against the king of Benares. When attacked, Shakyamuni (as the king) offered no resistance and was captured and imprisoned. While in prison Shakyamuni manifested such great compassion towards this enemy king that, as a consequence, the latter's body was filled with great physical pain. Upon realizing the cause of his pain, the conquering king regretted his actions and set Shakyamuni free, returning his kingdom in Benares to him without any loss of life.[4]

In comparing these two stories, it is important to note that both the Theravāda and Mahāyāna schools are united in emphasizing both the intention and goal of the actor in judging the karmic merit (or demerit) of a particular act. Yet, as Rupert Gethin notes, the Theravāda view is that killing can never be based on auspicious, *kuśala*, or neutral, *avyākṛta*, states of mind. He writes:

> In the Theravāda exegetical tradition, the notion that intentionally killing a living being is wrong involves a claim that when certain mental states (such as compassion) are present in the mind, it is simply impossible that one could act in certain ways (such as to intentionally kill) .... The only criterion for judging whether an act is "moral" (*kusala*) or "immoral" (*akusala*) in Indian systematic Buddhist thought is the quality of the intention that motivates it. (Gethin, 2004, p. 167)

[4] For a complete recounting of this *Jātaka* story, see: http://www.sacred-texts.com/bud/j2/j2135.htm.

Therefore, according to Gethin, the Theravāda position is that killing can never truly be based on compassion, nor can it be auspicious. Gethin provides an additional example concerning a laughing king who orders the execution of a criminal. On a subtle level, Buddhist commentaries state that, in doing so, the king's mind is still qualified by aversion. Nevertheless, the Theravāda view does recognize that not all killing is equally inauspicious, e.g., killing a mosquito does not result in the same karmic recompense as killing a human being. Gethin acknowledges the broad range of conditions in Theravāda that serve to qualify the act of killing, including the moral status of the victim (see Gethin, 2004, pp 177–182).

By comparison with the Theravāda school, Mahāyāna appears, at least doctrinally speaking, to have a less stringent attitude toward the act of killing. Yet, as a *practical matter*, is it reasonable, or even possible, to expect participants in warfare, inevitably involving the killing of mass numbers of human beings, both civilians and military, to kill "without ill will" or "compassionately"? As military personnel well know, harboring "ill will" toward an "evil" enemy is an essential element needed in order to morally justify their deadly acts.

Even if the doubtful proposition was acceptable that it is *possible* for a Buddhist soldier to go into battle without ill will toward the enemy, i.e. to kill, compassionately, is it realistic to expect that same soldier to maintain this attitude after he has seen one or more of his fellow soldiers killed by the enemy? And what is a Buddhist soldier to do if he realizes that, for whatever reason, he is unable to kill without ill will? At that point, should the Buddhist soldier report his crisis of conscience to his military superior and ask to be relieved of duty? Or should he nevertheless, filled with ill will, kill the enemy knowing that according to traditional Buddhist doctrine he is heading for one or another of various Buddhist hells for a lengthy stay?

In light of these eminently *practical* questions, it is clear how little of a practical guide the preceding nuanced discussion provides to today's modern Buddhist soldier, whether affiliated with the Theravāda or Mahāyāna schools. Note, too, that despite a lack of doctrinal justification, both lay and clerical Theravāda Buddhists in contemporary Thailand, Myanmar (aka Burma), and Sri Lanka have shown they can also be violent *in practice*.[5]

However, it is vital to recall an exchange contained in the *Yodhājīva Sutta*. When Shakyamuni Buddha was asked whether it is true that soldiers who die on the battlefield are reborn in heaven, Shakyamuni remained silent. A second request elicited the same response. Finally, on being asked a third time, Shakyamuni replied that soldiers dying on the battlefield will not be reborn in heaven. As Daniel Kent notes, "He [Shakyamuni] explained that those who die on the battlefield are *inevitably* overcome with hatred and pain and are born, according to those feelings, in a hell realm" (emphasis mine) (Demiéville & Kent, 2010, pp. 157–158). With this in mind, it is difficult to know how apologists for Buddhist-justified violence, like Capt. Malasri, would respond.

[5] For an introduction to Buddhist-related violence in contemporary Sri Lanka and Thailand, see *Buddhist Warfare*, Chs 7 and 8.

SAMĀDHI POWER IN MAHĀYĀNA TEACHING

Returning to the question of *samādhi* power, this author admits that to date, he has been unable to locate a Mahāyāna scripture explicitly addressing the question of the use of *samādhi* power on the battlefield. At this point, the closest Mahāyāna-related references found are contained in *Dharma* talks given by distinguished Chinese Chan (Zen) masters.

For example, there is a record of questions and answers between Master Ling Yuan and Master Xuyun during a seven-day winter retreat held in 1947. The record is entitled "When the Mind Is at One Point, There Is Nothing That Cannot Be Accomplished" and contains the following passage:

> Grand master (Xuyun) asked me (Ling Yuan): "What method are you using?" I (Ling Yuan) said: "Reciting Buddha's name and investigating Chan. Both Chan and Pure Land are practiced."
>
> Question: "How can you be investigating Chan when you are reciting Buddha's name?" I said: "When I recite the Buddha's name, there is this doubt of who is reciting Buddha's name hidden in my consciousness. So even though I'm reciting Buddha's name, I'm also investigating Chan."
>
> Question: "Are there wandering thoughts or not?" Answer: "When the right thought (method) is brought forth, often wandering thoughts are there along with it. However, when the right thought is put down neither are there wondering thoughts, pure and at ease."
>
> Grand master said: "This pure and at ease state is laziness, (You're already off the method) like a rock soaking in cold water. If one is like this, even if he practices for one thousand years it is still useless. One must bring forth the right thought with a bold and persevering mind investigating till the end and really see through just who is reciting the Buddha's name. Only then can the investigation be shattered. You should really practice with great determination."
>
> Question: "I have heard that grandmaster had entered *samādhi* for eighteen days in Chung Nan Mountain, was there a mind to enter? or no mind to enter?" Answer: "If there is a mind to enter *samādhi* then one cannot be in *samādhi*. If there's no mind to enter *samādhi* then it's like a statue made out of wood or mud. *When the mind is at one point, there's not a thing that cannot be accomplished*."[6]

Needless to say, to claim that when Ven. Ling Yuan said "there's not a thing that cannot be accomplished" he was alleging, let alone promoting, the use of *samādhi* on the battlefield, let alone in acts of terrorism, is ill founded. Yet, in light of the way in which *samādhi* power was clearly used in violent acts in Japan, it can equally be said that in claiming

[6] This is a dialogue between Master Ling Yuan and his grand master, Master Xuyun. It was recorded by Master Ling Yuan as "The elder grand master's dharma discourses" in the Chinese book "The Collection of Master Xuyun's Dharma Talks," pp. 177–178.

anything can be accomplished by virtue of *samādhi*, the *possibility* of misuse or abuse is present.

Additionally, Ven. Ling Yuan's disciple, Chan Master Sheng-Yen (1930–2009) gave a Dharma talk on "Supernormal Power," and said:

> The emphasis of the *Surangama Sūtra* is on *samādhi* and the power of *samādhi*, the concentration of the mind. Through *samādhi*, the Buddha radiates his power, his teaching. Only through personal realization and experience attained through practice can *samādhi* be developed. Otherwise, it is impossible to achieve any real power or strength. Simply being associated with a powerful being or receiving the help of a deity is not enough.... *The practice and experience of samādhi generates mental power. This power does not necessarily have to be supernormal, but it can be. The important point is that samādhi can help increase mental power.* [...]
>
> The practice of *dhyāna* and *samādhi* can clear a scattered mind, and bring it to a state of concentration. The mind can become so concentrated, in fact, that you can keep it on one single thought, *whatever thought you choose*....
>
> What you can do depends on the power of your *samādhi*. If you have enough power, you can hold a piece of iron or steel in your hand and turn it into gold, then you could take it to a jewelry store and exchange it for cash. All of you in business should learn this technique. Of course, *the consequences of trying something like this are that you will probably get yourself killed or end up killing someone else* (emphasis mine).[7]

As the Ven. Sheng-Yen states repeatedly, there can be no doubt of the great mental power acquired through the practice of *samādhi*. In fact, so great is this power that Sheng-Yen asserts it is possible for the meditator to "hold a piece of iron or steel in your hand and turn it into gold...and exchange it for cash." Yet, Ven. Sheng-Yen warns that the consequence of doing so would "get yourself killed or end up killing someone else." In the context of the Venerable's talk, however, his reference to killing is clearly a warning about the misuse of supernormal powers rather than an admonition against using *samādhi* power as an instrument to kill.

Notwithstanding Ven. Shen-Yen's Dharma talk, it is significant that he mentioned the *Surangama Sūtra* as a source for his understanding of *samādhi* and its associated power. Chapter 6 of the sūtra contains the following passage:

> The Buddha told Ananda, "You constantly hear me explain in the *Vinaya* that there are three unalterable aspects to cultivation. That is, collecting one's thoughts constitutes the precepts; from the precepts comes *samādhi*; and out of *samādhi* arises wisdom. *Samādhi* arises from precepts, and wisdom is revealed out of *samādhi*. These are called the Three Non-Outflow Studies." [...]

[7] Master Sheng-Yen, Supernormal Power. http://www.chancenter.org/chanctr/ddp/channews/056-1986.html (Accessed January 3, 2017).

> Ananda, I permit the *Bhikshus* to eat five kinds of pure meat. This meat is actually a transformation brought into being by my spiritual powers. It basically has no life-force. You Brahmans live in a climate so hot and humid, and on such sandy and rocky land, that vegetables will not grow; therefore, I have had to assist you with spiritual powers and compassion. Because of the magnitude of this kindness and compassion, what you eat that tastes like meat is merely said to be meat; in fact, however, it is not. After my extinction, how can those who eat the flesh of living beings be called the disciples of Shakya? [...]
>
> You should know that these people who eat meat may gain some awareness and may seem to be in *samādhi,* but they are all great *rakshasas* [demons]. When their retribution ends, they are bound to sink into the bitter sea of birth and death. They are not disciples of the Buddha. Such people as these, kill and eat one another in a never-ending cycle. How can such people transcend the Triple Realm? [...]
>
> *When you teach people in the world to cultivate samādhi, they must also cut off killing.* This is the second clear and unalterable instruction on purity given by the Thus Come Ones and the Buddhas of the past, World Honored Ones. [...]
>
> Therefore, Ananda, if cultivators of Chan *samādhi* do not cut off killing, they are like one who stops up his ears and calls out in a loud voice, expecting no one to hear him. It is to wish to hide what is completely evident. [...]
>
> *Bodhisattvas* and *Bhikshus* who practice purity will not even step on grass in the pathway; even less will they pull it up with their hand. How can one with great compassion pick up the flesh and blood of living beings and proceed to eat his fill? (emphasis mine).[8]

On the one hand, there is a clear statement in this Mahāyāna sūtra that for those who would "cultivate *samādhi,* they must also cut off killing." However, when read in context, it is clear that the proscription against killing refers, at least in this instance, to the killing and eating of animals. In other words, the passages in question are meant to promote vegetarianism for Buddhist practitioners. However, the strict vegetarianism promoted in this sūtra is one reason it has long been regarded as an apocryphal text, i.e., originating in its present form in China. This is because in China, unlike India, Buddhist clerics and many lay adherents have, for historical reasons, been vegetarians. Be that as it may, while this author cannot claim to have conducted an exhaustive study, it appears there are no passages in the Mahāyāna sūtras that explicitly prohibit, or warn against, the application of *samādhi* power to warfare.

No doubt there are apologists of Mahāyāna Buddhism who would claim that whether discussing the *Suragama Sūtra* or similar sutras, their opposition to all forms of killing is obvious. In principle, I agree with this proposition, but, unfortunately, as revealed in *Zen at War* and other writings, wartime Japan's allegedly fully enlightened Zen masters and their disciples drew semantic distinctions concerning the prohibition against killing.

[8] The English translation of this *sūtra* appears on the Webpage of the *City of Ten Thousand Buddhas.* http://www.cttbusa.org/shurangama/shurangama3.asp (Accessed January 8, 2017).

They demonstrated just how easily Buddhist doctrines prohibiting killing can be invoked in support of killing and destruction, often in the name of "compassion."

For example, Japanese Buddhist terrorist Onuma Shō, who killed Japan's former finance minister Inoue Junnosuke in 1932, testified in court that:

> Our goal was not to harm others but to destroy ourselves. We had no thought of simply killing others while surviving ourselves. We intended to smash ourselves, thereby allowing others to cross over [to a new society] on top of our own bodies. I think this is what our master Inoue meant when he told us that our goal was not to sacrifice personal affections on the altar of justice but to destroy ourselves. In the process of destroying ourselves it couldn't be helped if there were [other] victims. This was the fundamental principle of our revolution. *A mind of great compassion was the fundamental spirit of our revolution* (emphasis mine)
>
> (Hiroaki, 1963, p. 188).

It is not surprising that Onuma testified in this manner, for the head of his terrorist band, lay Zen practitioner Inoue Nisshō (1886–1967), had previously explained the purpose of the violent revolution they intended to carry out, saying:

> Revolution employs compassion on behalf of the society of the nation. Therefore, those who wish to participate in revolution must have a mind of great compassion toward the society of the nation. In light of this there must be no thought of reward for participating in revolution. A revolution that does not encompass a mind of great compassion is not Buddhist. That is to say, revolution itself is the mind of great compassion (Victoria, 2006, p. 212).

Almost unbelievably, one of the Rinzai sect's most highly respected Zen masters, i.e., Yamamoto Gempō (1866–1961), testified in court on behalf of Onuma and his fellow band of terrorists, including Inoue Nisshō, one of Yamamoto's most accomplished lay disciples. Yamamoto's defense was clearly meant to apply to all of the defendants on trial:

> In light of the events that have befallen our nation of late, there is, apart from those who are selfish and evil, no fair and upright person who would criticize the accused for their actions in connection with the Blood Oath Corps and 15 May Incidents.[9] Since agreeing to appear in court on behalf of the defendants, I have received several tens of letters. All of these letters, with but one exception, have expressed support for the defendants, identifying their actions as being at one with the national spirit. Notwithstanding this, however, it is utterly impossible to express by the spoken or

[9] The May 15th Incident refers to the second stage of the Blood Oath Corps Incident, i.e., an attempted *coup d'état* in Japan, launched on May 15, 1932 by reactionary elements of the Imperial Japanese Navy, aided by cadets in the Imperial Japanese Army and civilian remnants of the Blood Oath Corps. The Incident centered on the assassination of Prime Minister Inukai Tsuyoshi (1855–1932) by 11 young naval officers.

> written word the true meaning and intent of either Inoue or those allied with him in these two incidents.
>
> No doubt there are those who would ask why, in light of his devotion to religion, a believer in Buddhism like Inoue would act as he did? This is especially true given that Buddhism attaches primary importance to social harmony as well as repaying the four debts of gratitude owed others and practicing the ten virtues.[10]
>
> It is true that if, motivated by an evil mind, someone should kill so much as a single ant, as many as one hundred and thirty-six hells await that person. This holds true not only in Japan, but for all the countries of the world. Yet, the Buddha, being absolute, has stated that *when there are those who destroy social harmony and injure the polity of the state, then even if they are called good men killing them is not a crime.*
>
> Although all Buddhist statuary manifests the spirit of Buddha, there are no Buddhist statues, other than those of Shakyamuni Buddha and Amitābha Buddha, who do not grasp the sword. Even the guardian Ksitigarbha Bodhisattva holds, in his manifestation as a victor in war, a spear in his hand. Thus Buddhism, which has as its foundation the true perfection of humanity, has *no choice but to cut down even good people in the event they seek to destroy social harmony* (emphasis mine)
>
> (Victoria, 2003, pp. 216–217).

Yamamoto's claim that because the Buddha is "absolute... then even if they are called good men killing them is not a crime" is one of the most chilling statements in Buddhist history. Yamamoto attempted to preserve the precept forbidding killing by assigning those who killed so much as a single ant with an evil mind to "one hundred and thirty-six hells." On the other hand, killing good people who were guilty of destroying social harmony was "not a crime." Today it is difficult to believe that a sane person, let alone an allegedly "fully enlightened" (Japanese, *daigo tettei*) Zen master, could so readily twist Buddhism into a violence-affirming faith in support of domestic terrorists. Yet, not only did Yamamoto do so, he was so highly regarded by his fellow Zen masters that he was chosen to head what was then the unified Japanese Rinzai Zen sect in 1946, in the immediate aftermath of Japan's defeat.

The Historical Background of the Problem in Mahāyāna

As this chapter demonstrates, it is clear that there have been those in the Mahāyāna school, most especially in Japan, who have utilized *samādhi power* as a useful mental/

[10] The four debts of gratitude are: 1) the debt of gratitude to be paid to one's father and mother; 2) the debt of gratitude to be paid to the ruler of the nation; 3) the debt of gratitude to be paid to all living beings; and 4) the debt of gratitude to be paid to the three treasures [the Buddha, the *Dharma*, and the *Sangha*]. The ten virtues are: 1) no killing; 2) no stealing; 3) no improper sexual activity; 4) no lying; 5) no slandering; 6) no harsh words; 7) no gossip; 8) no coveting; 9) no aversion; and 10) no incorrect views.

spiritual aid in killing, especially on the battlefield. Unlike the doctrinal disavowal of this usage in the Theravāda school, the Mahāyāna school appears to have either overlooked or ignored this issue, thus making it possible for the application of *samādhi power* to death and warfare to continue without prohibition or condemnation.

Currently this author believes the origin of the use of *samādhi* power in killing can be traced back to Buddhism's long subservience to the state, in both the Theravāda and Mahāyāna schools. *Zen at War* traces this subservience in the Mahāyāna school back at least as far as the Northern Wei dynasty (386–534 CE) in China. It was then that Buddhist monks offered their services to the state not simply as political and diplomatic advisors but military advisors as well:

> Whatever motives one may ascribe to these northern Buddhist monks, the fact remains they established a pattern that was to characterize Chinese Buddhism down through the ages. That is to say, in return for imperial patronage and protection, Buddhism was expected to protect the interests of the state and its rulers, including the attainment of victory on the battlefield. Thus, the foundation was laid for what came to be known in Japan as "Nation Protecting-Buddhism" (Japanese, *gokoku bukkyō*). It can be argued, of course, that this was but an extension of the *Sangha's* subservience to the state as first observed in India (Victoria, 2003, pp. 200–201).[11]

Exactly when and where *samādhi power* was incorporated, for the first time, into Buddhism's assistance to the state at war, and/or mental preparation for individual warriors, is something the author has not yet been able to ascertain. In Japan, however, it is clear that this incorporation dates back to the introduction of the Zen sect at the beginning of the thirteenth century. D. T. Suzuki relates the story of Hōjō Tokimune (1251–1284), the eighth regent (Japanese, *shikken*) of the Kamakura shogunate (military government). Tokimune, like his father Tokiyori, was a long-time Zen practitioner. In 1279, he invited Mugaku Sogen (Chinese, *Wuxue Zuyuan*, 1226–1286) from the Southern Song Dynasty (1127–1279) to become the abbot of Kenchōji temple in Kamakura.

Not long after Mugaku's arrival in 1281, Kublai Khan ordered his troops to invade Japan a second time, having failed on their first attempt in 1274. Upon receiving word, the Mongol soldiers were on their way; Tokimune went to Mugaku (aka Bukkō Kokushi) and said:

> The greatest event of my life is at last here.
> Bukkō asked, "How do you plan to face it?"

[11] Some of the early examples of Buddhist subservience to the state came during the reign of King Ashoka (ca. 269–232 BCE). For example, King Ashoka is said to have had the power to prescribe passages from the sūtras that Buddhist clerics were required to read as well as receive his permission to become a Buddhist cleric. For additional examples of Indian Buddhism's subservience to the state, see Victoria, *Zen at War*, pp. 195–199.

> Tokimune uttered "*Kwatsu!*" as if he were frightening away all the enemies actually before him.[12]
>
> Bukkō was pleased and said, "Truly, a lion's child roars as a lion!"
>
> (Suzuki, 1938, p. 41).

When Tokimune died, Mugaku eulogized him as a *bodhisattva* whose Zen practice had led to his enlightenment. For his part, Suzuki claimed that Tokimune's life demonstrated that "Zen is for the warrior" (Suzuki, 1938, p. 43).

True, Suzuki didn't specifically attribute Tokimune's fearless attitude to *samādhi* power, but inasmuch as acquisition of this power is an integral part of Zen meditation, there can be no doubt that Tokimune's possession of this power was believed to have contributed to, if not enabled, his fearlessness.

It is noteworthy that Mugaku was a Chinese priest, which suggests the employment of Zen meditation in preparation for battle was not excluded from the Chinese Chan tradition. Mugaku's acceptance, however, may also have been connected to the fact that, while yet in China, Mongol soldiers nearly killed him when they invaded Southern Song.[13] Thus, it would hardly be surprising if he harbored more than a little antipathy toward the Mongols and the prospect of once again coming under their control. After all, had the Mongols succeeded in conquering Japan, where else could Mugaku have fled?

Regardless, the author would be deeply grateful should readers of this chapter know of any earlier incidents in which meditation, specifically *samādhi* power, was utilized as a form of mental preparation for battle.

Conclusion

This chapter has demonstrated there is little doubt that there have been those in the Mahāyāna school, most especially in Japan, who have utilized meditation-derived *samādhi* power as a useful tool to kill, especially on the battlefield. And despite the doc-

[12] *Kwatsu* (aka *Katsu*) is a piecing shout thought to reveal the awakened state (Japanese, *satori*) of the Zen master, and/or to induce the initial awakening experience in a student. It gives concrete form to the Zen belief that "reality" cannot be expressed with words and letters.

[13] In 1275 the Mongols were completing their conquest of China, and enemy soldiers scoured the countryside looking to suppress pockets of resistance. A group of these raided Mugaku's temple, intending to put any monks they found to death as they had elsewhere. Although the other monks fled the temple, Mugaku remained. When a Mongol soldier drew his sword to kill him, Mugaku didn't move an inch. Instead, he recited the following poem in a loud voice: "Throughout heaven and earth there is not a piece of ground where a single stick can be inserted; I am glad all things are empty, including myself and the world; Honored be the sword, three feet long, wielded by the great Mongol swordsmen; For it is like cutting a spring breeze in a flash of lightning." Hearing this, the soldier was touched and sheathed his sword. He expressed his respect for Mugaku and left.

trinal disavowal in the Theravāda school, it has shown that Theravāda adherents have what may be described as a "get out of (karmic) jail free card" that makes killing possible in this school as well, i.e., by killing *without ill will.* In contrast, the Mahāyāna school, both in doctrine as well as practice, appears to have either overlooked or ignored this issue altogether, thus facilitating the application of *samādhi* power to death and warfare without prohibition or condemnation.

Given this, this author concludes with the hope that readers realize that if meditation, and the mental power derived from meditation, can be used to be promote and deepen self-understanding, it can also be used to harm others, either singly or in mass, i.e., applied to warfare. In other words, as liberating and sublime as meditation can *and ought* to be, it is also open to misuse and abuse when applied to almost any endeavor, from making a (self-aggrandizing) killing on Wall Street to killing the enemy on the battlefield. In short, when meditation is removed or disconnected from a humane ethical system, Buddhist or otherwise, it can easily be utilized to accomplish any narrow self-centered purpose.

Given the twofold nature of meditation, it can be either a blessing or a curse. It is ultimately up to the individual to choose which.

References

Bhikkhu, T. (Trans.). (1998). Gopaka Moggallana Sutta: Moggallana the Guardsman (MN 108). In: Majjhima Nikaya [The Middle-length Discourses]. Retrieved from http://www.accesstoinsight.org/tipitaka/mn/mn.108.than.html.

Bodhi, B. (2014). War and Peace: A Buddhist Perspective. *Inquiring Mind*, 30(2), 5–7.

Buddhist Military Sangh. http://buddhistmilitarysangha.blogspot.jp.

Chang, G. C. C. (Ed.). (2008). *A Treasury of Mahāyāna Sutras.* PA: Pennsylvania State University Press.

Gethin, R. (2004). Can killing a living being ever be an act of compassion? The analysis of the act of killing in the *Abhidhamma* and Pali commentaries. *Journal of Buddhist Ethics*, 11, 166–202.

Demiéville, P., & Kent, D. W. (2010). Onward Buddhist soldiers: preaching to the Sri Lankan army. In: M. Jerryson & M Juergensmayer, (Eds.), *Buddhist Warfare*, (pp.157–173). New York: Oxford University Press.

Marty, M. E. (1996). An exuberant adventure: the academic study and teaching of religion. *Academe* 82(6), 14–17.

Hiroaki, O. (1963). *Ketsumeidan Jiken Kōhan Sokki-roku*, vol. 3. Tokyo: Ketsumeidan Jiken Kōhan Sokki-roku Kankō-kai.

Suzuki, D. T. (1938). *Zen Buddhism and Its Influence on Japanese Culture.* Kyoto: The Eastern Buddhist Society.

Kazuyoshi, Y. (1941). *Zen no Ōyō (The Practical Use of Zen).* Tokyo: Shūbunkaku Shobo.

Victoria, B. (2003). *Zen War Stories.* New York: Routledge Curzon.

Victoria, B. (2006) *Zen at War.* Boulder, CO: Rowman & Littlefield.

Yoga Journal, Yoga Alliance, & Ipsos Public Affairs (2016). 2016 yoga in America study conducted by yoga journal and yoga alliance. http://media.yogajournal.com/wp-content/uploads/2016-Yoga-in-America-Study-Comprehensive-RESULTS.pdf (accessed via Internet Archive for Dec. 16, 2016 on 1 Mar. 2021).

CHAPTER 42

NEUROSCIENCE AND MEDITATION

Help or Hindrance?

RONALD E. PURSER AND DAVID J. LEWIS

Introduction

Contemplative neuroscience is "still in its infancy" (Lutz, Slagter, Dunne, & Davidson, 2008; Tang, Hölzel, & Posner, 2015, p. 213). As yet little is definitively known about the neural mechanisms of meditation and its psychological benefits. At the same time, a burgeoning neuroscience research community is putting forward a substantial and influential body of significant claims about its accomplishments and prospects. There is reason to think that such claims are inflated. The spread of these ideas is, nonetheless, an interesting cultural phenomenon.

We begin by examining the influence of this promotion of neuroscience as a "regime of truth." We point out how graphic imagery, especially the proliferation of functional magnetic resonance imaging (fMRIs) of brain scans, has had a powerful effect upon the public imagination. We consider how contemplative neuroscience communications and the popularity of fMRI brain imaging is, perhaps unwittingly, reinforcing and reifying a sense of self-as-brain. As a form of subjectivity, the self-as-brain idea allies itself with the popularity of mindfulness as "brain-hacking," in which there is a loop-back effect and mutual reinforcement between the claims of neuroscience and those of the mindfulness movement (Hacking, 1998, 2004, 2006).

We then explore the influence of self-as-brain on the practice of Buddhism. We first offer a vivid illustration of the impact via an autobiographical anecdote by Stephen Batchelor, a seminal figure in what is sometimes called secular Buddhism, then consider how Madhyamaka Buddhism offers a radically different way of thinking about these issues. The Madhyamaka tradition centers upon meditation on emptiness and thus offers a distinctive perspective upon our sense of the materiality of mind and self. It may be that Buddhism needs to be inoculated from the effects of the neuronal-self regime of truth.

Neuroscience and the Neuromolecular Gaze

The nature of life is an enigma to science, that of the mind no less. In recent years, many have come to believe that neuroscience, under-pinned by molecular biology, may provide some answers. This idea has become a powerful and influential narrative. In such an approach the complex, holistic phenomena of psychic mental life are reduced to manifestations of brain activity. This reductionist approach can be called the "neuromolecular gaze" (Abi-Rached & Rose, 2010). Once this gaze is established, it provides "a common vision of life itself" (Abi-Rached & Rose, 2010, p. 13). It becomes a persuasive mode of language and perception. In identifying the rise of neuroscience as having been a matter of establishing a dominant mode of discourse, Rose and Abi-Rached were following the methodology of the philosopher Michel Foucault. This is called a genealogical approach because it traces how ideas arise and become established over a period of time and according to a historical context. In writing a history of neuroscience, they identified a major break in 1960, leading to shifts in how things were talked about, thought about, and understood, as various scientific discourses became centered on molecular approaches in biology, chemistry, and biophysics. The dominance of this way of thinking then influenced how science was institutionally funded. Out of this matrix emerged the field of neuroscience.

Before the term "neuroscience" took hold, terms such as "mental biophysics" and "biophysics of the mind" were being used in attempts to bring together hybrid disciplines and sub-disciplines (Abi-Rached & Rose, 2010, p. 26). The term "neuroscience" first appeared in 1963 in the Neurosciences Research Program Bulletin. Francis O. Schmitt, who was a biophysicist by training, is considered the father of American neuroscience. He remarked in this report that "It now seems possible to achieve similar revolutionary advances in understanding the human mind.... By making full use of [the approaches of physiology and the behavioral sciences] and by coupling them with the conceptual and technical strengths of physics, chemistry, and molecular biology, great advances are foreseeable" (Abi-Rached & Rose, 2010, pp. 27–28).

Rose and Abi-Rached conclude that even four decades after the birth of the neuromolecular gaze, the quest to unlock the "key to the management of all manner of human activities and experiences, from psychiatric illness to economic behavior, from human sociality to spirituality and ethics" (Abi-Rached & Rose, 2010, p. 32) is still ongoing. However, as they caution, it remains to be seen whether a reductionistic and molecular understanding of human beings can translate into or lead to any comprehensive and ecological understanding of human affairs.

Despite the fact that the project of neuroscience has yet to provide significant or ecological insight into human affairs, the neuromolecular gaze has gained widespread cultural currency. Just by adding the "neuro-" prefix, whole "brain imaging" fields have arisen, such as neuromarketing, neuroeconomics, neuropolitics, neuropsychiatry, neurolaw, and neurotheology, just to name a few. The proliferation of fMRI and PET (positron emission tomography) scan images of brains, whether they depict flaws in conservative Republican brains or the "Happiest Man in the World," serve as powerful rhetorical devices for advancing socio-political interests, the government of conduct, or bolstering existing claims in various disciplines (Burri, 2012, pp. 52–54; Pickersgill, 2013, pp. 326–332).

What Does Neuroscience Know?

Despite discoveries about the *biology of the brain*, neuroscience has learned essentially nothing of scientific or practical value about *mind*, specifically cognition and affect (by contrast with sensory and motor function), and there are no scientifically founded prospects that the situation will improve. The inability of neuroscience to make reliable statements about mind begins with the inherent unidirectional nature of imaging, the technology for the vast majority of brain studies. Researchers have subjects perform mental or behavioral activities and use imaging to observe brain activation patterns in specific regions, each containing millions of neurons. *Forward inference* is simply reporting and generalizing the results of such observations, say that a threat metabolically engages a brain region called the amygdala, which says something about the biology of the brain (LeDoux, 2015). *Reverse inference* would be concluding that any mental process that lights up the amygdala in fMRI imagery perforce involves a threat. If it were true, we might be able to read people's feeling of threat by observing their amygdala activation and use that fact to tell us something about mind, say that certain activities make people feel threatened, and do that purely biologically, without observing behavior or asking for reports. That was actually once a hypothesis, but research soon found that the amygdala also responds to stimuli related to eating, drinking, sex, and addictive drugs (LeDoux, 2015), so the reverse inference is invalid and the deduction about the mind fails.

This multiplicity has turned out to be true of every brain region involved in cognition and affect. Worse, even trying to understand and structure the various precursors for each region has not led to scientific consensus on the cognitive or affective function in human terms of any brain region or subregion, though the regions are clearly different from one another. Various theories are hotly debated for each region, but experiments regularly turn up new observations that entail reconsideration, and there is no trend toward convergence.

A major problem is that there is activity across the entire brain at all times, even at so-called rest. The bright coloring in fMRI images just shows the most metabolically active regions, which may be only a few percent more active than regions colored gray. When forward inference pinpoints the amygdala, for example, it does not mean that only the amygdala is active, but that it ranks high among regions. The images are thus actually statistical patterns of brain-wide metabolic activity, not actual engagement of specific regions as if they were mental organs in any meaningful sense, as much of the public believes. Use of brain regions is thus a simplifying heuristic that makes neuroscientific analysis tractable. More statistically complex methods that do not depend on regions, often augmented with machine learning, have become widely used in the past decade or so, but these have yielded only marginally better results. Even to the extent that these methods do succeed, however, they lack the potential reverse-inference explanatory power of region-based analysis (Barrett & Satpute, 2019, pp. 11–12), providing only correlation without meaning, much the way biological tests for cancer such as PSA (prostrate-specific antigen) called biomarkers, as useful as they are for diagnosis and prognosis, are neither derived from nor cast light on underlying disease mechanisms. It is even more telling that neuroscience (and biomedicine in general) has failed to produce even such purely statistical but medically useful individual biomarkers for any psychiatric disorder, despite the widespread belief that such disorders must somehow be biological brain disorders and thus amenable to biological diagnosis as well as the treatment afforded by psychopharmaceuticals, and decades of intensive efforts toward that end (Arbabshirani, Plis, Sui, & Calhoun, 2017, p. 138; Borsboom, Cramer, & Kalis, 2019, pp. 44–45; Ioannidis, 2019, pp. 23–24; Rose & Abi-Rached, 2013, pp. 137–139).

Despite tens of thousands of studies and widespread optimism, drawing conclusions about the mind using brain-imaging studies has failed to produce any substantial and verifiable insights. Meaningful insight into cognition or emotion, in general or for individuals from their fMRI scans or any biological measurements, even purely correlational, is not possible today nor foreseeable with any known technology, and the field has largely acknowledged that the initial goals of cognitive and affective neuroscience have not only failed, but are nowhere in sight.

Contemplative Neuroscience

Contemplative neuroscience is the use of neuroscience to study meditation, yoga, and other spiritual disciplines, which is, in effect, a subfield or offspring of cognitive/affective neuroscience discussed in the previous section. A key selling and marketing point for secularized mindfulness programs is that science has *proven* meditation "works" based on the "latest neuroscience." However, in the academic literature, contemplative neuroscientists are much more circumspect regarding such claims. Consider the comprehensive review by three prominent neuroscientists (Tang et al., 2015) of the current state of the field of contemplative neuroscience. In an unusually forthright statement (Tang et al., 2015, pp. 213–215) they not only describe contemplative neuroscience as being in its infancy, they characterize as "trivial" our understanding of brain changes due to meditation and how they "are related to the reported improvements in affective, cognitive and social function." They further imply that we have not even begun to unravel this mystery. To back up this judgment, Tang et al. (2015) list numerous shortcomings in studies, such as: lack of replication, low methodological quality, bias toward publishing positive or significant results, absence of elaborated theories, and post-hoc conclusions.

The neuromolecular gaze has influenced the discourse of contemplative neuroscience by fostering the development of the *brain-self* or *cerebral subject* as a particular discursive formation and regime of truth. A discursive formation is a "consistent set of images, texts, metaphors and institutional norms that can be shown to be coherent, despite contradictions and digressions" (McInerney, 2011, p. 3). A *regime of truth* refers to the way discursive formations proliferate under appropriate socio-historical conditions. In other words, this is about how a story takes hold, spreads, and becomes a powerful influence shaping how people think. Such a story typically has no singular traceable source as it maintains a circular relation to systems of power, supporting them as they produce and sustain it. Discursive practices include speech acts, linguistic statements, and written texts (Barad, 2007, p. 63) but also extend to the socio-historical conditions that "define what counts as meaningful statements," both constraining and enabling the constructions and legitimization of "knowledge." The power referred to here is not particularly the central political power, but rather the authority that prevails and is institutionalized within disciplines that then come to be pervasive, naturalized, and internalized (Foucault, 1972, pp. 113–117).

We see a similar pattern in the rise of mindfulness. Mindfulness and contemplative neuroscience have formed a powerful alliance, each supporting and reinforcing the other. Jenny Eklöf (2016) has chronicled how experts in the field of contemplative neuroscience seek to communicate to the public at large the imperative of practicing mindfulness to achieve brain fitness and for the promotion of health, well-being, and happiness. Eklöf (2016, p. 324) makes an astute observation that not only has the scientization of mindfulness coincided with its rise in popularity, "but the cultural and social impact of this field is often taken to be a sign of its prior academic validation."

In contrast to the more conservative and circumspect tone in academic journal publications noted previously, more popular and personalized communications by contemplative neuroscientists often claim that the field is making "cutting-edge discoveries" or that they are on the brink of a revolution in science that could save our culture (Eklöf, 2016, p. 328). A notable example is the article, "Mindfulness Can Literally Change Your Brain" in the *Harvard Business Review*, in which Hölzel appears again as a co-author (Congleton, Hölzel, & Lazar, 2015). It opens with a bold title and claim regarding the science of mindfulness:

> The business world is abuzz with mindfulness. But perhaps you haven't heard that the hype is backed by hard science. Recent research provides strong evidence that practicing non-judgmental, present moment awareness (a.k.a mindfulness) changes

> the brain, and it does so in ways that anyone working in today's complex business environment, and certainly every leader, should know about.
>
> (Congleton et al., 2015, p. 309)

The evangelical zeal and utopian tone of such statements contradicts the more circumspect qualifications that appear in scientific journals. However, even hedged speculation in scientific journals can be considered as a sly form of prophecy. As Eklöf (2016, p. 325) suggests, scientists are often in collusion with journalists. When popular media reports prophesize even more explicitly, ignoring the hedging and the limitations sections of papers, or more generally the manifest weaknesses, contemplative neuroscientists rarely object. Communicating weaknesses and limitations in the popular press simply doesn't sell.

What might account for this Janus-faced stance? Lynda Walsh (2013, p. 2) describes how scientists through history have taken on a prophetic voice to persuade the public, especially in the infancy of some fields. She describes this as a prophetic ethos, which "is a role that a polity—a group of people who must work together to stay together—authorizes to manufacture certainty for them." She goes on to argue that since "uncertainty is our perennial and inescapable political condition certainty...is a chimera." Such prophecies, masquerading as science, create a self-serving illusion of certainty and the dominance of "covenant values," the shared values of a polity that differentiate it from other communities. For scientific communities, covenant values bolster their institutional authority, credibility, and public support. When a polity encounters a crisis or is not yet firmly established, it turns to its prophets for the manufacture of certainty.

John Tresch (2011), in his ethnographic study of the Mind & Life Summer Research Institute (MLSRI), describes first-hand how faculty and organizers instilled covenant values in a kind of a missionary initiation rite for eighty young, aspiring contemplative neuroscientists, enjoining them to "heal a sick culture." Jon Kabat-Zinn, founder of mindfulness-based stress reduction (MBSR), proclaimed "a truly Copernican moment" (Tresch, 2011, p. 55) that would manifest what he has prophesized elsewhere (Kabat-Zinn & Simon, 2011) as "the potential to ignite a universal or global renaissance...that would put even the European and Italian Renaissance into the shade." Adam Engle, a founder and then president of the Mind & Life Institute, declared: "We're making some pretty crazy decisions as a culture, something is wrong with people's minds if they make such wrong interpretations about what will make them happy" (quoted in Tresch, 2011, p. 54). The prophetic declarations that mindfulness and its scientific-credibility companion, contemplative neuroscience, will rescue and change our sick culture are coupled with an intentional effort at institution-building. Tresch quotes Richard Davidson, often called the founder of contemplative neuroscience, in this impassioned plea:

> If we are really going to change the culture...we need the aspiration to have effects as wide and deep as possible...We have to influence the most important and

> powerful and prestigious institutions. The only way to do this is by playing the game as well or as better as they do... this will require a lot of time, money and hard work. [We need to aim for] the very highest level of respectability and to pursue this research at the highest level... The people in this room are poised to do this. They have the credentials, the wherewithal, the resources, and dharmic background. It's going to have to happen on a level we have never seen before on the planet.
>
> (Davidson, quoted in Tresch, 2011, p. 55)

We can see Davidson here playing gatekeeper, ensuring that contemplative neuroscience not be seen as "woo-woo," lacking science's rigor and credibility. Yet, his call for respectability is a prophetic belief that the science of mindfulness, via neuroscientific research, *can* change the world (Eklöf, 2016).

Brain Plasticity

The arrival of the idea of brain plasticity has both leveraged and reinforced the notion that we can change ourselves by changing our brains. It used to be thought that the brain reached its final state at age twenty and could no longer grow, only gradually decay. More recent work has shown that areas of the brain that are much used can grow during adult life, much as muscles that are regularly used add bulk and strength. This implies that we can encourage the brain to keep changing. Essentially, however, this means that we are now holding out hopes in relation to bumps on the brain rather than bumps on the skull. In general, the notion of brain plasticity is both ill-defined and incoherent since any mental activity perforce changes the brain at many levels. Brain plasticity has, however, come to play an explicitly rhetorical role when selling, marketing, and delivering mindfulness programs, namely as an antidote to the pessimism induced by materialism, that things inscribed in matter are inherently permanent, "hard wired," and unchangeable. Can mindfulness and meditation so change the brain as to release us from this?

Brain-Hacking

As the foundation of neuroscience is built upon the idea of a material basis of the mind, the moral imperative since the "Decade of the Brain" has been to change one's brain (Eklöf, 2016). Improving emotional health, facilitating moral development, developing compassion, and cultivating mindfulness, like the treatments of schizophrenia and depression, are simply to be regarded as a matter of brain management—whether it entails meditation or drugs. The self is now a *neuronal self*, rooted in neurobiological views of the mind (Joldersma, 2016, pp. 91–92, 97–100; Malabou, 2008;

Pitts-Taylor, 2010). Sociologists and historians of science have characterized these shifts in the way human beings are coming to understand themselves as amounting to the "neurobiologization of selfhood," the "neurochemical self" (Rose & Abi-Rached, 2013, p. 201), and formation of the "cerebral subject" (Ehrenberg, 2004; Vidal, 2005, 2009).

A few years ago, *Wired* magazine ran a feature article on the popularity of mindfulness in Silicon Valley. Kenneth Folk, a meditation teacher who self-identifies as being "enlightened" is quoted: "All the woo-woo mystical stuff, that's really retrograde... This is about training the brain and stirring up the chemical soup inside" (Shachtman, 2013). Bill Duane, Google's senior mindfulness teacher, makes it clear that "we are into 'brain-hacking' here" (personal communication, January, 2015). Hacking here means improvised alterations to hardware, software, or processes, and applying it to the mind further reinforces the identification of brain and mind. There is even a class at Google called "Neuro Self-Hacking" in which the neuroscience of mindfulness is another tool in the brain-hacker's toolbox, alongside neurofeedback, electrical and transcranial magnetic stimulation, micro-dosing LSD, and "smart drugs." Chade-Meng Tan, Google's former corporate mindfulness advocate, likens mindfulness meditation to exercising a muscle—a form of mental fitness training, not unlike going to a gym (Tan, 2012, p. 34). Brain-hacking is thus a way of working on one's self by working one's brain (Brenninkmeijer, 2010, pp. 109–112). Interestingly, mindfulness works from the mind to the brain, the opposite of the usual direction, but if mind and brain are the same, so what! They all share a common core in being techniques put in the service of the self's desire to work on its own brain and, supposedly, thereby on itself.

Mindfulness as brain-hacking is the manifestation of a loop-back or looping effect (Hacking, 1998, 2004, 2006) from the mass public diffusion of neuroscientific claims. The looping effects of brain-hacking, however, are not limited to hipsters in Silicon Valley or the Buddhist Geeks. Many contemplative neuroscientists, especially those who are actively involved in the Mind & Life Institute, are themselves practitioners of mindfulness and other forms of meditation. A brain-based view of meditation, a view that is very much shaped by the influence of fMRI studies, is a clear example of what Hacking (1998, p. 21) would characterize as an experience of "a human kind." By this, Hacking means that humans are transformed by their own descriptions.

We are being taught to think about ourselves using a new language. For example, mindfulness programs in schools routinely teach students to conceptualize their emotions using a neurological vocabulary. A student will say "my amygdala hijacked me" with the implication to be more mindful. Importing "folk neurology" (Vrecko, 2006) into public and educational discourse illustrates not only how such institutional knowledge is being internalized, but also how such discourses are framing our cognitive and affective life as being confined to, and locatable within the brain. The promissory potential of neurologic narratives have inserted themselves in child development, as well as educational policies and practices (Pickersgill, 2013, p. 239). However, the British Royal Society report on "Neuroscience: Implications for Education and Lifelong Learning" does not provide a reassuring endorsement:

> There is great public interest in neuroscience, yet accessible high quality information is scarce. We urge caution in the rush to apply so-called brain-based methods, many of which do not yet have a sound basis in science. There are inspiring developments in basic science although practical applications are still some way off.
> (The Royal Society, 2011, p. v; quoted in Pickersgill, 2013, p. 330)

Such linguistic programming is a discipline in two senses: first, it indoctrinates the public (and in this example, young children) into a disciplinary language (neuroscience); second, it is a discipline in the sense of requiring a willingness to be subjugated and obedient to that knowledge (McInerney, 2011, pp. 6, 29–30). It tends to make people docile (Foucault, 1977, pp. 135–169).

This disciplining is doubly influential and effective for not being experienced as the result of external surveillance nor as being outward compliance to norms set by authorities, but, rather, as the willing internalization of such norms through self-discipline. "Disciplinary power" thus is productive; mindfulness (conceived as brain-hacking), is considered as a technology of the self that enhances agency, autonomy, and individual freedom. The subjective modality employed is through an identification of the self as what one's brain does.

The increasing influence of the idea that the self is a neuronal phenomenon and that, therefore, the means to bring about hopefully beneficial changes is by "brain-hacking" using, among others, methods such as meditation and mindfulness derived ultimately from Buddhism and other spiritual traditions, stands in sharp contrast to the core teachings of those traditions themselves, wherein there is no indication that spiritual liberation depends upon the induction of changes in the physical structure or anatomical functioning of the brain.

According to philosopher Evan Thompson (2020, pp. 12–19, 64–67, 144, 163–164), the field of contemplative neuroscience has been driven by two misguided ideas that reinforce each other: (1) mindfulness is an inward awareness of one's own private mind; and (2) the best way to understand mindfulness is to conduct neuroscientific studies of the brain of meditators. The result is a popular form of what Thompson calls "Neural Buddhism." Thompson also points out that the legacy of Buddhist modernism is that the West has given Buddhism special treatment by claiming it is really not a religion, but a "science of mind," or that it is "spiritual but not religious." At the same time, Buddhist modernists have appealed to the authority of neuroscience, which has enabled its mass marketing.

The increasingly large number of people engaged with these disciplines are thus now exposed to a clash of cultural paradigms that can have large-scale personal consequences, as is illustrated in the next section.

The Case of Stephen Batchelor

A story from Stephen Batchelor encapsulates several of the themes of this chapter. Batchelor is a key figure in the movement often called secular or agnostic Buddhism

(Gleig, 2018, pp. 4–5; Nourie, 2012), comprising forms of Buddhist practice aiming to be consistent with the prevailing naturalistic zeitgeist that privileges scientific understanding.

At the time of this anecdote, in the late 1970s, Batchelor was a monk in the Tibetan tradition, in his mid-twenties. He describes himself as "smitten" at the age of nineteen with the Dalai Lama and other Tibetan masters, and by this time had become "totally absorbed in the world of Tibetan Buddhism" (Batchelor, 2011, p. 16). At one point, however, he found himself "waking up in the middle of the night in a cold sweat."

> This crisis erupted because, when we finally came to the proof for rebirth, I was not at all convinced by it. Here it is... Being by nature immaterial, mind cannot, in principle, be produced by something material, such as a body or a brain. Therefore, the mind of a newborn baby must have come from a previous continuum of mind; it cannot have emerged out of mindless physical causes alone.
>
> I was skeptical. Given current scientific knowledge of the brain, I did not find it difficult to believe that such an organ was capable of producing thoughts, feelings, and perceptions. That seemed an entirely reasonable hypothesis to explain the origin of mental phenomena. (Batchelor, 2011, pp. 36–37)

After this incident, Batchelor went on to give up not only Tibetan Buddhism, with skepticism of rebirth as a crucial fulcrum, but eventually all traditional forms of Buddhism. He described himself in 2003 as "a meditation teacher who doesn't meditate any more," deeming meditation "a kind of evasion... a cutting off from experience, rather than a full-blooded engagement with all of its ambiguities and messiness" (Horgan, 2017). A major point of a recent book of his (Batchelor, 2015, pp. 9–10) was to answer the question, "how, in the course of Buddhist history, did the concept of emptiness evolve from a way of dwelling on earth unconditioned by reactivity into an ultimate truth to be directly cognized in a nonconceptual state of meditation?" In other words, Batchelor's crisis has grown into a full rejection of the transcendental side of Buddhadharma and the use of meditation to engage it.

Beyond the Physical: Madhyamaka Philosophy

Let us now turn to a consideration of one Buddhist approach on its own terms. Because Buddhadharma is so multifarious, we focus on one tradition, the Madhyamaka (usually translated as Middle Way or Centrist) school of Mahayana Buddhism that reached its apogee in Tibet. Madhyamaka is widely accepted by Tibetan philosophers and practitioners as the most incisive and profound Buddhist system (Duckworth, 2018) and the most efficacious soteriology. Philosophically, Madhyamaka analyzes and contextualizes many other traditions such as the Theravada and is the most thorough in interpreting the fundamental Buddhist insight of dependent arising (Arnold, n.d., secs. 2b, 6). It embodies very sophisticated approaches to Buddhist notions of self, mind, and duality/non-duality, so crucial in the debate with the current neuro-materialist zeitgeist, as exemplified in Batchelor's crisis.

Madhyamaka holds that the self, the mind, and all phenomena without exception lack inherent or intrinsic existence. That is, they have no permanent, unchanging essence; they are said to be *empty of intrinsic existence* or characterized by *emptiness*, usually shortened to say simply that they are *empty*.

But Madhyamaka is not nihilism: the self does exist, but merely by labelling, the collection of primal constituents of experience (the aggregates, Sanskrit *skandhas*): forms, sensations, perceptions, higher level mentation (cognitions, emotions, volitions, etc.), and consciousness itself. The aggregates are roughly what the modern West calls the body-mind complex (K. Gyatso, 2008, pp. 371, 373, 406, 414; Newland, 2009, pp. 91–92).

Likewise, each outer phenomenon is labelled on a base; for example, a chair is imputed on the aggregation of its legs, seat, back, and other parts and their relationships to each other. This way of existing by mere labelling is called *conventional* or *relative existence*; the self and things do exist *conventionally* or *relatively*, that is in dependence on causes, conditions, designations, and parts. In fact, this merely *conditioned existence* is simply the other side of the coin from emptiness, since to exist intrinsically would entail independence of any conditions and vice versa.

Further, the bases for imputation themselves lack intrinsic existence too, so the entirety of the experienced world, according to Madhyamaka, is an indefinitely layered, intertwined complex of countless, mentally imputed relationships, without substantial foundation (MacKenzie, 2011, pp. 242–247). Dependence on causes and conditions and on parts are forms of imputation, so in the final analysis, all dependence is fundamentally mental, according to Madhyamaka (Westerhoff, 2009, pp. 27, 124). Nevertheless, terminology for the full set of dependences is often shortened to "causes and conditions," perhaps in keeping with the earliest Buddhist texts. As should be clear even from this brief description, in Madhyamaka, as in Buddhism in general, the mental takes priority over the physical. While the latter is not denied relevance, it does not have the dominant place that it occupies in our modern materialistic culture.

Madhyamaka distinguishes *conventional reality*, our everyday experience of a world of causes and conditions, from *ultimate reality*, the emptiness of everything. Since emptiness is, however, just the other side of the coin from conditioned existence, conventional and ultimate reality are in fact the same (Newland, 2009, pp. 32–33), a fact called *non-duality* and reflected in other non-dualities such as that of knowing subject and known object, compassion and wisdom, form and emptiness, cause and effect, and so on.

In the Madhyamaka analysis, suffering arises because we *reify* self and phenomena that are actually only labelled on their bases, that is, we project intrinsic existence on them. This is very close to saying that our tendency to look for a physical basis in experience is itself delusion. Reification gives them an illusory unity, solidity, permanence, and independence that we cling to; *precisely this* is the root of suffering. Suffering here includes not only overt pain, but also all forms of dissatisfaction, including the subtle suffering inherent in ordinary pleasure, which is by nature temporary and insubstantial, and even the "existential insecurity at the heart of our being" (Jinpa, 2000, pp. 13–14).

The realm or state of mind of suffering sustains itself in "a perpetual cycle of confusion and dissatisfaction through interlocking chains of causes and conditions" (Jinpa, 2000, pp. 11, 13–14). The aim of Mahayana Buddhist practice, according to Madhyamaka, is to cut that cycle, and decisively and permanently relieve the suffering by realizing emptiness. To do that, one must dispel, through deep, transformative insight, the dysfunctional reification, the misapprehension that the self and phenomena exist intrinsically. That is accomplished through analyzing the fundamental nature of self and phenomena according to Madhyamaka and realizing it in meditation, using highly developed attentional capacity, supported by ethically conducive behavior. The result, enlightenment, is to perceive continuously the ultimate nature of self and phenomena, their emptiness, simultaneously with their conventional, dependent nature (Newland, 2009, p. 18). This not only ends one's personal suffering at all levels, it equips one with the utmost capacity to guide others to the same realizations, thus advancing the Mahayana determination to likewise relieve the suffering of all.

Mind, though part of the body/mind complex and thus also empty of intrinsic existence, plays a special role in Madhyamaka and indeed throughout Buddhadharma. Not only is conventional existence based on mental imputation, the mistaken additional reification at the root of all suffering is fundamentally mental, so the solution is also in the realm of mind. Mind is the subtlest, naturally least reified aspect of conventional reality, and thus the closest to emptiness itself. Meditation on the empty nature of mind is therefore particularly incisive and holds a special place in Tibetan Mahayana, exemplified by traditions such as Dzogchen and Mahāmudrā.

Where Western thought tends to assume that it has located a fundamental when it has found the most gross, material element in a body/mind process, in Madhyamaka the converse is the case: the most subtle is regarded as most primary. Many Buddhist traditions (Fuller, 2004, pp. 50–52, 121; Dalai Lama, 1996, pp. 207–208; K. Gyatso, 2008) conceive that experiences lie along a phenomenological continuum from *gross* to *subtle* according to solidity or fluidity, permanence or impermanence, substantiality or evanescence, and so on (Thompson, 2015, pp. 6–7), which we might call a spectrum of degrees of reification. Material sense objects are at the gross, thoroughly reified end of this spectrum, mental phenomena at the subtler, less reified end.

We may think of progress toward liberation as experiencing ever subtler phenomena, a progressive *dereification* of the mind and its objects (Dorjee, 2016, pp. 7–9; Dunne, 2013, pp. 7–9), aiming at realizing emptiness, a total lack of reification. Meditators may progress in subtlety from the breath as object, to mental events, and finally to awareness itself (Wallace, 2006, pp. 6–7). The latter prepares the way particularly effectively for realization of emptiness, a principle embodied in the Dzogchen and Mahāmudrā practice systems (Dzogchen Ponlop Rinpoche, 2008).

The neuronal self, however, moves in the opposite direction. It assimilates mind, a relatively subtle phenomenon, to body and senses, far grosser ones, going against the desired progression of dereification. Besides implicit bias toward the physical, it thus adds an explicit, vivid layer of conceptual materiality to mind, reinforced by the persuasive force of fMRI imagery. Ideas of this kind, arising during meditation, may obstruct progress toward the experience of emptiness.

Meditation and the Role of Philosophical Doctrines

How does one dispel innate ignorance and attain a liberation that is a radical transformation of one's very being? Intellectual analysis alone, as important as it is, will not suffice (Ñānamoli & Bodhi, 1994, introduction; Cabezón, 1990, p. 154; Suzuki, 1999, p. 94). The answer is meditation.

We can briefly define meditation as: training the mind's attentional capacity to profound heights of stability and clarity and deploying it to observe and investigate phenomena, including the mind's own processes, at a deeper level than is possible with ordinary conceptual analysis. The result of meditation is immediate, experiential insight unmediated by concepts, often called *trans-conceptual* insight (*prajñā*, in Sanskrit) (Keown, 2003, p. 218; R. Walsh, 2011, pp. 109–111, 124–125), and that is what frees one from innate ignorance. No matter how accurate and extensive a practitioner's intellectual grasp of emptiness, until they meditate deeply on it and gain firm trans-conceptual insight, they retain at least some measure of innate, primal ignorance about the self and the world, and continue to think and act from it in ways that lead to suffering.

Any significant intellectual misunderstandings will inevitably impede progress at the deeper level. This is so even in Zen, which is known for its emphasis on intensive meditation practice, as articulated by Shunryu Suzuki, founder of the San Francisco Zen Center:

> Student: Can we practice Buddha's way without knowing Buddha's way intellectually?
>
> Suzuki Roshi: If you can, you are very lucky. But, unfortunately, we cannot practice without intellectual understanding. (Suzuki, 1999, p. 94)

Clearly cultivating an experiential right view is also central to the Theravada school of Buddhism, as explained by two leading scholars ("experiential right view" is what we are calling trans-conceptual insight):

> Such understanding, though conceptual rather than experiential... serves as a critical phase in the development of wisdom (pañña), for it provides the germ out of which experiential right view gradually evolves.
>
> (Ñānamoli & Bodhi, 1994, introduction)

We see here, therefore, that in other forms of Buddhism, as in Madhyamaka, the whole explication of liberation is based in the mind rather than the brain, and the idea that the kinds of transformation that they envisage could be brought about by brain-hacking seems rather far-fetched, and certainly so at the present level of neuroscientific understanding.

The Limits of Neural Buddhism and the Brain-as-Self

Rose and Abi-Rached (2013, p. 219) ask:

> What happens when the quotidian conception that human beings have of themselves is itself shaped in part by the truth claims made in an esoteric language of science? This certainly was the case for psychological conceptions of personhood across the twentieth century. Is it also our contemporary condition in relation to neurobiology?

Neuroscience seems to significantly exceed psychology in this impact. It claims even deeper access to cognition, emotion, and mind itself, by and indeed specifically because of its material means. It promises to forge a direct path to the psyche unmediated by behavior and self-report so central to psychology and often problematic to interpret. Neural Buddhism strengthens the impression of its power by claiming to probe depths of mind reached by profound Buddhist meditation (Brewer & Garrison, 2014; Davis & Vago, 2013; Ingram, 2017). It does all this with the apparent authority not only of science but of the most archetypal of the "hard" sciences, thanks to its use of "magnetic resonance," "electro-encephalography," and other such technology.

These claims, promises, and effects for neuroscience are propagated by a truth regime more pervasive than psychology's. They are conveyed to the general public, not just a cultural elite, in television and print news and features, Facebook posts and videos, supermarket checkout aisles, and the like, with language and imagery from a wide range of sources, not just technical experts in the field, including especially a vast array of popular journalism.

The overall effect is unprecedented conditioning of the general public in the putative physicality of mind and self. This is bolstered and reinforced by the panoply of science and the imagery that accompanies it, portraying the mind as a container of brightly colored, oddly shaped thoughts and emotions in particular locations. This is the source of the exhortations that general public needs to hack into their brains in order to stir its chemical soup. The neuronal-self thus claims to implicitly answer a question formerly of interest mainly to philosophers, theologians, and spiritual seekers in traditions like Buddhism: what is the ultimate nature of the mind and the self? This adds a conceptual dimension to the innate sense of physicality that arises simply from being embodied.

The Neuronal Self and the Practice of Buddhadharma

What does the sense of the mind as a physical phenomenon mean for the practice of meditation? Madhyamaka posits that people's everyday conception of themselves is the ignorance that sees the self as intrinsically existent. For most people, this ignorance is unexamined, primordial, and fully conscious. In contrast, the neuronal self is potentially just such an obstacle because it adds another layer of ignorance as a conceptual view that has no innate counterpart: nobody instinctively knows that the mind is associated with the brain; that is a learned concept that is publicly, consciously, socially reinforced, in a putatively scientific form. In Madhyamaka terms, the neuronal self adds a significant layer of conceptual reification to the reification represented by primordial, innate ignorance. In other words, it makes the existing delusion worse. As with Batchelor, it comes to seem to most people that their mind and hence their self is rooted in their brain, and this induces a sense of materiality and hence intrinsic existence to their self.

To forestall such interference, the practitioner might first work to undermine their conceptual association of mind with brain and related imagery. Of course that entails directly challenging the neuronal truth regime.

In Madhyamaka insight meditation for realizing emptiness there are two steps (Hopkins, 1996, pp. 44–51): first, to vividly experience in meditation the mistakenly reified self at the innate level, so it can become the *object of negation* to be dissolved; second, to use reasoning to challenge the existence of that object of negation until it does dissolve, leaving only emptiness. In this process, one must take care not to negate the valid, conventionally existent self, because dissolving that would be tantamount to nihilism.

In keeping with the general principles of the path to liberation, the practitioner must at least tentatively undermine conceptual natural ignorance by grasping the logic of emptiness via study and analysis, as a prerequisite or co-requisite to meditation on emptiness. Since conceptual natural ignorance is typically private and relatively unformed, as well as inherently continuous with innate natural ignorance, which the practitioner is targeting, there is typically little conscious resistance to the idea. The challenge is comprehending the difficult doctrine, plus subliminal resistance arising from innate clinging to self. As for social resistance, thanks to the trendiness of Buddhism, no-self is *au courant*. Or if a Madhyamaka practitioner is accused of nihilism around the dinner table, they can respond that they are not questioning the self per se, just its reification, its apparent solid, permanent, non-interdependent nature. They can even give examples from everyday psychology where excessive reification leads to clinging and hence suffering, for example, narcissism or rumination on negative emotions.

It seems, therefore, that cultivating doubt that mind is substantially rooted in brain is very likely to assist the practitioner proceeding with emptiness meditation, otherwise many pitfalls loom. For example, at the beginning, believing in the physicality of mind, one might doubt that the self actually *is* empty of intrinsic existence. For another, one might take the neuronal self, with its pervasive, vivid imagery, *as* the object of negation and miss the actual one, which is deeply subliminal and not easy to evoke (Hopkins, 1996, pp. 44–46; Newland, 2009, p. 87). Worse, meditating to dissolve the neuronal self, which has no innate counterpart, risks undermining its conventional validity, that a brain and body are real and necessary for everyday functioning, with many negative consequences of a nihilistic view. For yet another, one way of dissolving innate ignorance is to search for the innately reified self in the body/mind complex and not find it. The neuronal self, unless already dissolved, however, might lead one to believe that *one has* found the self in the body, and thus be blocked from realizing emptiness.

This is only a speculative taste of the obstacles that might arise from the presence of the neuronal self in the Madhyamaka practitioner's phenomenological world. There are countless other practices, many which use the duality of mind and body, or knower and known, in meditation, particularly in Vajrayana, which would likewise be affected. Our analysis therefore suggests that the belief in the equivalence of self with brain is likely to produce the same or related problems in other Buddhist systems as well. In any case, it seems likely that any traditional form of Buddhism would object to declaring "your brain is your self" as an ultimate truth, as the neuronal-self implies.

Even secular Buddhism, in which Batchelor is a seminal figure, and which, like Batchelor himself, typically welcomes the claims of neuroscientific insights into meditation for their credibility (Gleig, 2018, pp.122–126; Nourie, 2012), might not be well-served by the association. The sense of materiality and hence permanence of mental phenomena induced by a neuronal self contradicts the narrative of personal transformation across the spectrum form the transcendental to the psychological (Dorjee, 2016, pp.7–12; Lewis & Rozelle, 2016, pp. 250–262). If one believes one's problems at any level are rooted in the structure of one's brain, one may find it more difficult to believe in the possibility of relief, much less carry out the difficult task of actual change.

Conclusion

Neural Buddhism has propagated a "truth regime" that makes it difficult to challenge the commonly proposed notion that self is an epi-phenomenon of neural activity and that "you are what your brain does." Nonetheless, as science penetrates ever deeper into the murky borderland between mind and matter, nature—or conventional reality—seems to throw up one obstacle after another. The science is nowhere near to engaging with the reality. A prominent Tibetan abbot in a presentation with Richard Davidson (K. Tsultrim Lodro & Davidson, 2016) suggested that the way neuroscience researches mind is like studying fish by measuring the ripples they sometimes make on the surface of the water. Davidson did not object.

Batchelor's crisis occurred well into the age of the neuronal self, but before the current explosion of neuroscience research. At that historical moment, and arguably until the last few years, there was a lack of firm scientific evidence either for or against the ultimate materiality of mind and self. The physical and biological sciences did not even hope, much less claim to get close enough to mind by material means, to cast any significant light on the issue.

We now know enough to understand why the hopes and claims have failed and are unlikely to succeed with any foreseeable method. Perhaps it is time to entertain a different sort of scientific conclusion, that there might be fundamental limits to our ability to ever succeed at this quest, likely due to overwhelming complexity in many guises, much the way there are scientific limits to how fast we can travel or how precisely we can measure the physical world. Sometimes science has to press an idea to its limit to establish that it cannot be sustained. After all, empirically invalidating hypotheses is a basic methodology of science. The same is the case for neuroscience which has thus far reinforced the neuronal-self via a regime of truth. Our critique has pointed out the intractable complexity of the brain deeply enough that we can now conscientiously doubt the neuronal-self.

REFERENCES

Abi-Rached, J.M. & Rose, N. (2010). The birth of the neuromolecular gaze. *History of the Human Sciences* 23(1), 11–36.

Arbabshirani, M. R., Plis, S., Sui, J., & Calhoun, V. D. (2017). Single subject prediction of brain disorders in neuroimaging: Promises and pitfalls. *NeuroImage*, *145*, 137–165. doi:10.1016/j.neuroimage.2016.02.079

Arnold, D. (n.d.). Madhyamaka Buddhist philosophy. *The Internet Encyclopedia of Philosophy*. Retrieved February 10, 2018, from https://www.iep.utm.edu/b-madhya/

Barad, K. (2007). *Meeting the universe halfway: Quantum physics and the entanglement of matter and meaning*. Durham, NC: Duke University Press.

Barrett, L.F., & Satpute, A.B. (2019). Historical pitfalls and new directions in the neuroscience of emotion. *Neuroscience Letters* 693, 9–18. doi:10.1016/j.neulet.2017.07.045

Batchelor, S. (2011). *Confession of a Buddhist atheist*. New York: Spiegel & Grau.

Batchelor, S. (2015). *After Buddhism: Rethinking the Dharma for a secular age*. New Haven, CT: Yale University Press.

Bell, V. (2010, June 7). Neuroplasticity is a dirty word. *Mind Hacks*. https://mindhacks.com/2010/06/07/neuroplasticity-is-a-dirty-word/

Borsboom, D., Cramer, A. O. J., & Kalis, A. (2019). Reductionism in retreat. *Behavioral and Brain Sciences* 42, e32. doi:10.1017/S0140525X18002091

Brenninkmeijer, J. (2010). Taking care of one's brain: How manipulating the brain changes people's selves. *History of the Human Sciences* 23(1), 107–126. doi:10.1177/0952695109352824

Brewer, J. A., & Garrison, K. A. (2014). The posterior cingulate cortex as a plausible mechanistic target of meditation: Findings from neuroimaging. *Annals of the New York Academy of Sciences* 1307(1), 19–27. doi:10.1111/nyas.12246

Burri, R. V. (2012). Visual rationalities: Towards a sociology of images. *Current Sociology* 60(1), 45–60. doi:10.1177/0011392111426647

Cabezón, J. I. (1990). Review of "The emptiness of emptiness: An introduction to early Indian Madhyamika," by C. W. Huntington, Jr., with Geshe Namgyal Wangchen. *The Journal of The International Association of Buddhist Studies 13*(2), 152–161.

Congleton, C., Hölzel, B. K., & Lazar, S. W. (2015). Mindfulness can literally change your brain. *Harvard Business Review*, January, 309–318.

Dalai Lama, H.H. (1996). *Beyond dogma: Dialogues & discourses* (M. Dresser, Ed.; A. Anderson, Trans.). Berkeley, CA: North Atlantic Books.

Davis, J. H., & Vago, D. R. (2013). Can enlightenment be traced to specific neural correlates, cognition, or behavior? No, and (a qualified) yes. *Frontiers in Psychology 4*, 870.

Dorjee, D. (2016). Defining contemplative science: The metacognitive self-regulatory capacity of the mind, context of meditation practice and modes of existential awareness. *Frontiers in Psychology 7*. doi:10.3389/fpsyg.2016.01788

Duckworth, D. (2018, Spring). Gelukpa [dge lugs pa]. In E. N. Zalta (Ed.), *The Stanford encyclopedia of philosophy*. Metaphysics Research Lab, Stanford University. https://plato.stanford.edu/archives/spr2018/entries/gelukpa/

Dunne, J. D. (2013, October). *Dereification: The Main Mechanism of Mindfulness?* 2013 Maitripa College Buddhism and Science Symposium, Maitripa College. https://www.youtube.com/watch?v=H9VwCTjjyF4

Dzogchen Ponlop Rinpoche. (2008, May 1). This very mind, empty and luminous. *Lion's Roar*. https://www.lionsroar.com/this-very-mind-empty-and-luminous/

Ehrenberg, A. (2004, November). *Le sujet cérébral*. Esprit Presse. https://esprit.presse.fr/article/alain-ehrenberg/le-sujet-cerebral-8123

Eklöf, J. (2016). Saving the world: Personalized communication of mindfulness neuroscience. In R. E. Purser, D. Forbes, & A. Burke (Eds.), *Handbook of mindfulness: Culture, context and social engagement* (pp. 323–335). Cham: Springer.

Foucault, M. (1972). *The archaeology of knowledge*. New York: Pantheon Books.

Foucault, M. (1977). *Discipline and punish: The birth of the prison*. New York: Vintage Books.

Fuller, P. (2004). *The notion of ditthi in Theravada Buddhism: The point of view*. London: Routledge.

Gleig, A. (2018, February 3). The shifting landscape of Buddhism in America. *Lion's Roar*. https://www.lionsroar.com/the-shifting-landscape-of-buddhism-in-america/

Gyatso, K. (2008). *Meaningful to behold: Becoming a friend of the world*. Glen Spey, New York: Tharpa Publications.

Hacking, I. (1998). *Rewriting the soul: Multiple personality and the sciences of memory*. Princeton, NJ: Princeton University Press.

Hacking, I. (2004). *Historical ontology*. Cambridge, MA: Harvard University Press.

Hacking, I. (2006, August 17). Making Up People. *London Review of Books 28*(16). https://www.lrb.co.uk/the-paper/v28/n16/ian-hacking/making-up-people

Hopkins, J. D. (1996). *Meditation on emptiness* (Second). Wisdom Publications. http://books.google.com/books/about/Meditation_on_Emptiness.html?id=26FkjziPVfAC

Horgan, J. (2017, October 24). Does Buddhism give us answers or questions? *Scientific American Blog Network*. https://blogs.scientificamerican.com/cross-check/does-buddhism-give-us-answers-or-questions/

Ingram, D. (2017, November). Judson Brewer called out Daniel Ingram? *Dharma Overground*. https://www.dharmaoverground.org/discussion/-/message_boards/message/7047835#_19_message_7045167

Ioannidis, J. P. A. (2019). Therapy and prevention for mental health: What if mental diseases are mostly not brain disorders? *Behavioral and Brain Sciences 42*, e13. doi:10.1017/S0140525X1800105X

Jinpa, T. (2000). The foundations of a Buddhist psychology of awakening. In G. Watson, S. Batchelor, & G. Claxton (Eds.), *The psychology of awakening: Buddhism, science, and our day-to-day lives* (pp. 10–22). York Beach, ME: Samuel Weiser.

Joldersma, C. W. (2016). Neoliberalism and the neuronal self. In C. W. Joldersma (Ed.), *Neuroscience and education: A philosophical appraisal* (pp. 91–107). London: Routledge.

Kabat-Zinn, J. (2011). *Jon Kabat-Zinn: The mindfulness revolution.* Recorded interview by Tami Simon. Sounds True. https://www.resources.soundstrue.com/transcript/jon-kabat-zinn-the-mindfulness-revolution/

Keown, D. (2003). *A dictionary of Buddhism.* Oxford: Oxford University Press.

Khenpo Tsultrim Lodro, & Davidson, R. J. (2016, May 20). *Science of the brain, training of the mind: A conversation between neuroscience and the contemplative tradition of Tibetan Buddhism.*https://asiaevents.harvard.edu/event/science-brain-training-mind-dialogue-between-neuroscience-and-contemplative

LeDoux, J. E. (2015, August 10). The amygdala is NOT the brain's fear center. *Psychology Today.* https://www.psychologytoday.com/blog/i-got-mind-tell-you/201508/the-amygdala-is-not-the-brains-fear-center

Lewis, D. J., & Rozelle, D. (2016). Mindfulness-based interventions: Clinical psychology, Buddhadharma, or both? A wisdom perspective. In R. E. Purser, D. Forbes, & A. Burke (Eds.), *Handbook of Mindfulness* (pp. 243–268). Cham: Springer. doi:10.1007/978-3-319-44019-4_17

Lutz, A., Slagter, H. A., Dunne, J. D., & Davidson, R. J. (2008). Attention regulation and monitoring in meditation. *Trends in Cognitive Sciences 12*(4), 163–169. doi:10.1016/j.tics.2008.01.005

MacKenzie, M. (2011). Enacting the self: Buddhist and enactivist approaches to the emergence of the self. In M. Siderits, E. Thompson, & D. Zahavi (Eds.), *Self, no self? Perspectives from analytical, phenomenological, and Indian traditions* (pp. 239–273). Oxford: Oxford University Press.

Malabou, C. (2008). *What should we do with our brain?* New York: Fordham University Press.

McInerney, R. (2011). *The docile body of the brain: A Foucauldian critical discourse analysis of capacity.* https://www.academia.edu/1033677/The_Docile_Body_of_the_Brain_A_Foucauldian_Critical_Discourse_Analysis_of_Capacity

Ñānamoli, Bhikkhu, & Bodhi, Bhikkhu. (1994). *The discourse on right view: The Sammaditthi Sutta and its commentary.* https://www.accesstoinsight.org/lib/authors/nanamoli/wheel377.html

Newland, G. (2009). *Introduction to emptiness: As taught in Tsong-kha-pa's great treatise on the stages of the path.* Ithaca, NY: Snow Lion Publications.

Nourie, D. (2012, July 9). *What is a Secular Buddhist, and what do they believe?* http://secularbuddhism.org/2012/07/09/what-is-a-secular-buddhist-and-what-do-they-believe/

Pickersgill, M. (2013). The social life of the brain: Neuroscience in society. *Current Sociology 61*(3), 322–340.

Pitts-Taylor, V. (2010). The plastic brain: Neoliberalism and the neuronal self. *Health: An Interdisciplinary Journal for the Social Study of Health, Illness and Medicine 14*(6), 635–652. doi:10.1177/1363459309360796

Rose, N. S., & Abi-Rached, J. M. (2013). *Neuro: The new brain sciences and the management of the mind.* Princeton, NJ: Princeton University Press.

Shachtman, N. (2013). In Silicon Valley, meditation is no fad. It could make your career. *Wired.*

Suzuki, S. (1999). *Branching streams flow in the darkness: Zen talks on the Sandokai.* Berkeley: University of California Press.

Tan, C.-M. (2012). *Search inside yourself: The unexpected path to achieving success, happiness* (1st ed., p. 34). New York: HarperOne.

Tang, Y.-Y., Hölzel, B. K., & Posner, M. I. (2015). The neuroscience of mindfulness meditation. *Nature Reviews Neuroscience 16*(4), 213–225.

Thompson, E. (2015). *Waking, dreaming, being: Self and consciousness in neuroscience, meditation, and philosophy.* New York: Columbia University Press.

Thompson, E. (2020). *Why I am not a Buddhist.* New Haven, CT: Yale University Press.

Tresch, J. (2011). Experimental ethics and the science of the meditating brain. In F. Ortega & F. Vidal (Eds.), *Neurocultures: Glimpses into an expanding universe* (pp. 49–68). New York: Peter Lang.

Vidal, F. (2005). Le sujet cérébral: Une esquisse historique et conceptuelle. *PSN 3*(1), 37–48. doi:10.1007/BF03006830

Vidal, F. (2009). Brainhood, anthropological figure of modernity. *History of the Human Sciences 22*(1), 5–36.

Vrecko, S. (2006). Folk neurology and the remaking of identity. *Molecular Interventions 6*(6), 300–303.

Wallace, B. A. (2006). *The attention revolution: Unlocking the power of the focused mind.* Somerville, MA: Wisdom Publications.

Walsh, L. (2013). *Scientists as prophets: A rhetorical genealogy.* New York: Oxford University Press.

Walsh, R. (2011). The varieties of wisdom: Contemplative, cross-cultural, and integral contributions. *Research in Human Development 8*(2), 109–127. doi:10.1080/15427609.2011.568866

Westerhoff, J. (2009). *Nāgārjuna's Madhyamaka: A philosophical introduction.* New York: Oxford University Press.

CHAPTER 43

MEDITATION, EXCEPTIONAL PSYCHOPHYSIOLOGICAL CONTROL, AND PARAPSYCHOLOGY

ETZEL CARDEÑA

Introduction

Alterations of consciousness, both transient (i.e., "altered *states* of consciousness") and long-term (i.e., "altered *traits* of consciousness") have been related to extraordinary psychological and psychophysiological abilities (Cardeña, 2020). Contemplative traditions have also described exceptional and even seemingly implausible abilities, which may be the result of training or happen spontaneously during the course of long-term practice, yet little research has been conducted on this issue (Vieten et al., 2018). These claims have been often dismissed in the study of religion as symbolic or mere fantasies, but these interpretations have been questioned by serious scholars such as the comparative historian of religion Jeffrey Kripal (2017). The reader of this chapter may be surprised to find out that some of the claims have a decades-long history of controlled research, with some of them having received empirical support.

In this chapter, I first define what I cover under meditation practices and psi phenomena, provide a brief historical review of reports in Asian and Western traditions of exceptional abilities, and then discuss the research on the relation of meditation with exceptional psychophysiological control and with parapsychological (psi) phenomena. The first type, however impressive it may be to an observer, might be explained through conventional mechanisms such as extensive training to control breathing or other parameters. Not so in the case of psi phenomena, which suggest that ordinary explanations are insufficient and that some spatial and temporal limitations may be breachable.

The reader of this volume will very likely have some familiarity with meditation, a complex and fuzzy concept whose boundaries are in contention. Although most authors would include some systematic practice to achieve greater awareness and/or control of attention and other psychological processes, others (e.g., Naranjo & Ornstein, 1971) would also include intense bodily practices and surrendering to impulses, as well as extreme forms of asceticism. Adding surrender practices to more conventional forms of meditation would greatly expand a very complex literature and require adding shamanic and "ecstatic religion" traditions (e.g., de la Garza, 2012; Lewis, 1989). Thus, for the purpose of this chapter I will circumscribe *meditation* to the three main types of practice described by Dahl, Lutz, and Davidson (2015): *attentional* (e.g., breath counting practice), *constructive* (e.g., loving-kindness and compassion meditation), and *deconstructive* (e.g., mindfulness meditation). The distinction between meditation and hypnotic practices depends on which specific variant one is talking about (Cardeña, 2016), so I will only address the literature on hypnosis when it is relevant to some point about meditation. In the brief historical survey below, I have concentrated on classical Greek, Judeo-Christian, and Asian philosophies/religions.

The concept of parapsychological or psi phenomena requires greater clarification, as the non-specialist is likely to have a vague and/or overbroad notion of it. Psi refers to experiences or events that suggest that individual can obtain accurate information not mediated through the senses or reason, known as *anomalous cognition*, receptive psi, "extrasensory perception," or ESP. Anomalous cognition (AC) includes ostensible *telepathy*, or being affected by what is in someone else's mind (e.g., a person suddenly and without any reason thinking of someone s/he had not thought about in years before receiving later in the day an unexpected message from that person). *Clairvoyance* refers to the possibility of learning some distant state of affairs (as when someone describes accurately where a person who has disappeared may be found even though s/he would have had no way to know that information). Finally, *precognition* describes an event in the future seeming to affect someone in the present and unexplainable by mere inference (e.g., someone dreaming about planes crashing against a building the night before the 9/11 attacks). Research on anomalous cognition includes verbal reports and/or physiological measures, such as comparing the ERPs (EEG responses tied to the presentation of stimuli) of arousing versus neutral stimuli *before* they are presented in a random order. When ostensible psi occurs in everyday life, no matter how impressive it may be, it is very difficult if not impossible to rule out conventional explanations such as inaccurate recollection, unconsciously reacting to nonverbal behaviors of someone else (as in muscle reading by some magicians), an incorrect understanding of the probability of unusual events, or mere chance. Laboratory research sets up conditions so that if precise information is acquired it cannot readily be explained by conventional mechanisms. For instance, in an experiment participants may be asked to select an image or film clip out of different choices, before it is randomly selected by a computer out of an unknown large database. Participants' selections can be aggregated and, barring methodological artifacts, subjected to statistical analyses to evaluate whether or not individuals choose the correct item more often than would be expected by chance.

Parapsychology also investigates psychokinesis, or PK, sometimes called in lay terms "mind over matter," namely the possibility that intention or other mental processes can directly affect physical objects, unmediated by mechanical or other known forces. This research evaluates potential small effects on random systems (i.e., micro-PK), such as trying to bias the output of thousands of bits of a random number generator (RNG) that ordinarily does not deviate from randomness. Research on macro-PK investigates whether mental intentions or states can affect large objects, such as the images being produced by a camera without using mechanical or similar mechanisms (Braude, 2015). Controlled research on PK sets up conditions so that, for instance, the performance of a RNG when a person is trying to affect it can be compared with times when the person is not. In the case of macro-PK research controls are implemented to eliminate or at least reduce the possibility of conventional physical explanations, fraud, and so on.

The systematic investigation of psi phenomena using scientific methods took off formally with the formation of the (British) Society for Psychical Research in 1882, which had among its members very eminent scientists, including Nobel prizewinners, and foundational psychologists such as William James. During its history, parapsychology (or psychical research) has continued to attract interest, if not outright support, from many notable scientists including people of the stature of Marie Curie, Albert Einstein and Max Planck (Cardeña, 2015). Psi research has shown throughout its history and in a recent summary of more than ten meta-analyses (cumulative statistical analyses of all studies in an area) of diverse research paradigms, replicable small effects, comparable to those of accepted research in psychology, medicine, and other disciplines (Cardeña, 2018). It is important to mention that, contrary to what is sometimes claimed by uninformed or biased critics, empirical support for these phenomena has continued even after improving research protocols in response to criticisms, and with careful controls and analyses for alternative explanations such as sensory information, biased publication of results, and chance results. Furthermore, contemporary physicists and psychologists have developed theories to explain psi phenomena (for a review of the research, theory, and criticisms, see Cardeña, 2018; Cardeña, Palmer, & Marcusson-Clavertz, 2015; May & Marwaha, 2015).

A Historical Review

Western Tradition

In her authoritative work *Divine Manias*, Yulia Ustinova (2018) provides an overview of alterations of consciousness and ostensible psi and other extraordinary phenomena in classical Greece. Her treatise shows that the relation between some type of contemplative practices and reputed extraordinary abilities is not exclusive to Asian traditions. Among the presocratic philosophers, various sources claim that Pythagoras had paranormal knowledge of the past and the present (there is even a Greek term for divination, *μαντική*), could suppress winds or calm storms, abstain from food and water, and heal people; it was also claimed that he and his followers used breath control, abstinence from nutriment, and sensory isolation to achieve extraordinary deeds. Parmenides and Empedocles, among other Greek philosophers, described experiences that clearly parallel the shamanic "magical flight" of experiencing a phenomenal body detaching from the physical one and traveling to other realms, and having a sense of mystical insight of reality, besides their reputations as being healers and possessing other extraordinary abilities.

The foundational philosopher Socrates was described as psychologically detaching himself from his surroundings and being able to endure hunger, cold, and other hardships to an exceptional degree, besides having precognitive abilities including anticipating danger and choosing a different path than that that took by his fellow soldiers, who were killed by the enemy farther ahead (Cicero, *de Divinatione* 1.54; Ustinova, 2018). Plato, the foremost student of Socrates, provides in his dialogue *Phaedrus* a still resonant classification of alterations of consciousness (or *manias*), including one in which a person is assumed to obtain valid knowledge of the future (prophetic mania). While some Greeks followed ascetic contemplative practice, others employed more physical/emotional means (Ustinova, 2018), exhibiting a similar dichotomy to that of *ecstasy* and *trance* described by Rouget (1985). Broadly, these practices also correspond to the different types of meditation practices proposed by Naranjo (Naranjo & Ornstein, 1971), and to the imaginative versus dissociative types of individuals who are very responsive to hypnosis (Cardeña & Krippner, 2018).

The Judeo-Christian tradition chronicles many figures including prophets and Jesus Christ as having precognitive and other extraordinary abilities. Nevertheless, the accounts were typically written a long time after the events they refer to and although some prophets might have been ascetic it is not certain that all of them practiced something akin to meditation. The Jewish tradition, however, mentions *kavanah* or the intentional deployment of attention while praying, and there are illustrations of eminent figures exhibiting reputed psi abilities, including the founder of Hasidism, the Baal Shem Tov, and the Rabbi Salma of Liady (Murphy, 1992, p. 472). In later Christianity we also encounter accounts of ostensible psi phenomena such as precognition tied to traditions of asceticism, remaining motionless, contemplative and repetitive prayer, and mindful movement and perception, described in the *Philokalia* and the writings of St. Ignatius of Loyola, among others (Murphy, 1992; Murphy, Donovan, & Taylor, 1997). Especially relevant to this chapter are the accounts of Catholic saints, whose process of canonization has required evidence of exceptional abilities that could withstand skeptical evaluation. Rhea White (1981) discussed official Christian documents mentioning psi abilities by 29 percent of those listed in *Butler's Lives of the Saints*, including telepathy, clairvoyance, and prophesizing future events. She remarked that these abilities seemed to have developed after years of contemplative practice. The *New Catholic Encyclopedia* (in Murphy, 1992) considers more than fifteen extraordinary phenomena to be signs, or charisms, of sanctity. They include visions of distant things (i.e., clairvoyance), "reading of hearts" (telepathy), stigmata, bilocation (simultaneous presence in two places), levitation, body elongation or shrinking, inedia (abstinence of nourishment for a long time), bodily incorruptibility, and absence of rigor mortis.

Classical Eastern Traditions

Some accounts of the exceptional abilities of Buddhist practitioners were written centuries after the death of the person they refer to and seem to be more mythical than literal accounts, as in the chronicles of the eighth-century Buddhist saint Vilamitra, portrayed as being able to fly, destroy statues mentally, and live for 313 years before reincarnating later (Gruber, 2017). Sonali Marwaha (2016) reviewed accounts of psi in classical Indian thought, which continue to be discussed by contemporary Eastern researchers (e.g., Rao, 2017). In Jainism, which may involve meditation and asceticism, there are three types of direct knowledge: awareness not limited by time and space, knowledge of events spatially or temporally distant, and direct knowledge of the minds of others. Like Jainism, Buddhism also parted from Hinduism and did not accept its sacred Vedas. Early Buddhism listed various extraordinary abilities, among them: *iddhividhā* (psychokinesis), *dibbasotta* (perception of sounds at a distance), *cetopariyañāna* (telepathy), *pubbenivāsânussati* (retrocognition: the ability to know information about the past), and *dibbacakkhu* (clairvoyance but also knowledge of deceased individuals) (Marwaha, 2016).

The most influential and best-known discussion of exceptional abilities or powers (i.e., *siddhis*) in classical Eastern traditions occurs in the third of four parts of the Hindu *Yoga Sūtras* of Patañjali, compiled before 400 CE. The *siddhis* discussed in the text are an amalgam of abilities, some mundane, others referring to exceptional physiological control, personal development, and ostensible psi phenomena. Knut Jacobsen (2017) provides an excellent discussion of the *siddhis* in the *Yoga Sūtras*, which included knowing the thoughts of others, precognizing deaths, cessation of thirst and hunger, exiting from one's own body, and levitation. However, it was also believed that these powers might derail the task of obtaining ultimate knowledge and avoiding injury to others. Becoming attached to these powers could prevent the ultimate goal of *Yoga*, namely salvific liberation or not being reborn again. Similarly, for the Japanese Zen Buddhist tradition, practice may bring about "side effects," or *makyo*, including psi and other unusual phenomena that should not be pursued for themselves as they might hinder the path to enlightenment when the meditator becomes attached to them (Naranjo & Ornstein, 1971 pp. 92–93).

Late Tantra, an esoteric Indian tradition, follows the *Yoga* conception of *siddhis* but in contrast to other schools its practitioners may purposefully seek to attain extraordinary powers and use them (Marwaha, 2016). Similarly, current Transcendental Meditation has competitions on what is called "yogic flying," which is not levitation but an impressive gymnastic ability to hop from a lotus position (https://www.youtube.com/watch?v=q1U4skQYG3g). The leader of Transcendental Meditation (TM) stated in 2003 that a lack of "coherence in the world consciousness" prevented those practitioners from actually flying (in Radin, 2013, pp. 202–203).

The overlap of reputed exceptional abilities in Eastern and Western meditation traditions is remarkable. They include phenomena studied experimentally by parapsychology (telepathy, clairvoyance, precognition, and PK), the ability to withstand hardships and deprivations, and incorruptibility after death. Some phenomena such as purported body elongation are not listed as often, but they have not been completely unreported in psi research (Beloff, 1977). How might the commonalities between such different traditions be explained? One mechanism could be the cultural diffusion of beliefs, but this solution would still beg the question of the source and maintenance of such beliefs. A plausible explanation, as I will discuss below, is that the subjective experiences (for instance in body sensation changes) arising during meditation practice could have arisen spontaneously among practitioners (Gifford-May & Thompson, 1994; for similar spontaneous experiences in hypnosis see Cardeña, 2005). There is also reason to believe that some of these capacities may reflect observable phenomena and not only subjective experiences. This is what the remaining sections of this chapter will cover.

Exceptional Psychophysiological Abilities

I will follow to an extent in the organization of the remaining sections Radin's (2013) classification of the *Yoga siddhis* into three types: (1) exceptional mind-body control; (2) clairvoyance (or AC or receptive psi, more generally); and (3) psychokinesis or PK. Although the *siddhis* include both exceptional physiological abilities and psi phenomena, there is no necessary link between them. Physiological and/or cognitive training and practice might explain most of the abilities discussed in this section, although they offer a challenge to reductionist materialist positions of mind-brain relations (cf. E. F. Kelly, 2015). Some abilities such as temporary incorruptibility or ostensible levitation seem to cross into the psi territory. The areas reviewed below, for which there is some track record of research, are: perceptual sensitivity, stigmata and controlled bleeding, heart rate control, reduced metabolism, ability to withstand cold temperature, and imperviousness to pain.

Perceptual sensitivity. Michael Murphy (1992) cites reports by athletes and traditional Eastern scriptures of extraordinary sensory abilities after intense focusing activities, including enhanced vision, hearing, tactile experience, smell, taste, and even synesthesia (experiencing a stimulus in more than its typical sensory modality, as in seeing colors tied to specific musical notes; Marks, 2014). Some studies support the possibility of increased sensitivity following intense meditation practice. Participants in a three-month mindfulness meditation retreat increased their visual discrimination sensitivity in two tasks involving light flashes, whereas a control group did not (Brown, Forte, & Dysart, 1984). Similarly, MacLean and colleagues (2010) found that participants in an intensive retreat of focusing meditation evidenced significant increases in perceptual sensitivity/stimuli discrimination, particularly when they practiced more time, as compared to a waiting-list group. Enhanced sensitivity may depend on the specific meditation practiced (Kok & Singer, 2017).

Stigmata and controlled bleeding. Throughout the centuries there have been dozens of reports, some with photographic evidence, of individuals claiming spontaneously appearing wound marks or actual bleedings associated with the (depicted) wounds of Christ (Thurston, 1952/2013). The stigmata of St. Francis of Assisi are the most famous and a model for many later ones. Although stigmata can be produced by deliberate or nonconscious manipulation, some recent investigators have concluded, after systematic evaluations, that there was no reason to assume that the bleeding they studied had been produced by external physical manipulations in the people they studied (e.g., Margnelli, 1999; Fisher & Kollar, 1980). Not all stigmatics have followed a contemplative practice as St. Francis of Assisi did, but some have, and Murphy (1992) proposed that emotionally intense images (e.g., artistic depiction of Christ) and sensations can serve as powerful targets for sustained attentional focus, similar to concentrative meditation. In a similar vein, Emily W. Kelly (2007) reviewed cases suggesting that absorption and high suggestibility may produce related psychophysiological changes such as skin marks, internal bleeding, and bruising when remembering or witnessing very stressful situations.

Although stigmata and similar forms of bleeding seem to occur uncontrollably and/or may be the product of medical conditions (e.g., Maglie & Caproni, 2017), there is also some literature on intentional control of bleeding. With respect to meditation proper, a Western practitioner showed the ability to control the bleeding produced by a sharp rod piercing his arm in a laboratory setting (Green & Green, 1977) and the Indian yogi Sri Ramakrishna was strongly affected by suggestions to begin or stop his bleeding (Murphy, 1992, p. 476). Sufi dervishes have shown little or no bleeding and rapid healing after inflicting severe damage to their skin with razors and glass in a controlled setting (Hall, 2011). Relatedly, T. X. Barber (1984) concluded that highly hypnotizable individuals may be able to control their vascular system, and a more recent study found that the hemodynamics of a hypnotic suggestion to experience a phlebotomy were similar to those of a group actually undergoing the procedure (Casiglia et al., 1997).

In sum, there have been intriguing observations that some meditators (and highly suggestible individuals) may affect their blood flow, but there has been no systematic research on the matter, and even less on the more challenging reports that some individuals may stop the bleeding of humans and non-human animals, described in the Sámi healer Nordic tradition (Sexton & Buljo Stabbursvik, 2010) and also observed in Western technological settings (e.g., Carpenter, 2015).

Heart rate control. A swami who could also alter his palm's skin temperature (see "Ability to withstand cold temperatures") showed the ability to control his heart rate and at one point seemed to induce heart fibrillation, without any pain or negative consequences, in a laboratory setting (Green & Green, 1977). A study with four selected Indian yogis did provide some evidence that they could noticeably slow down their heart rate or momentarily even stop it, and make their pulse very faint (Wenger, Bagchi, & Anand, 1961), changes that may be mediated by breathing control (Raghavendra et al., 2013). A recent literature review found that yoga practice can affect heart rate variability, but the authors warned that this preliminary conclusion was based on many studies with methodological and reporting problems (Tyagi & Cohen, 2016).

The ability to control the heart rate does not seem exclusive to meditators as an individual who just relaxed deeply also showed such ability (Murphy, 1992), as did Alexander Luria's (1968) famous mnemonist and synesthete "S," who could affect his heart rate through imagining sedate or vigorous activities. This ability may not be mediated by interoceptive awareness as experiments comparing meditators with non-meditators on objective measures of interoceptive sensitivity have not found evidence of increased sensitivity (Khalsa et al., 2008; Melloni et al., 2013), although subjective measures of interoceptive awareness do increase (Fischer, Messner, & Pollatos, 2017), particularly after breathing and body-scan meditation (e.g., Kok & Singer, 2017). However, similar research does not seem to have been conducted with meditators who showed evidence of controlling their heart rate.

Reduced metabolic rate. Some meditation practitioners have exhibited the ability to drastically reduce their metabolism, with some of them staying buried in pits for a long time without food or water, and with a limited amount of oxygen, in a state of suspended animation or *samādhi*. Perhaps the most thorough study of this claim was conducted by Kothari, Bordia, and Gupta (1973), who tested a yogi buried in an underground pit for eight days. He showed increased heart rate for the first twenty-nine hours, replaced by what looked like an unchanging electric signal, which restarted half an hour before the yogi was about to be raised, at which point he showed metabolic signs of initial starvation. Another study with a yogi showed a 40 percent decrease of oxygen consumption from resting during a four-hour meditation (Craig Heller, Elsner, & Rao, 1987). Similarly, a group of yoga practitioners showed a 32 percent decrease of oxygen consumption and 18 percent decrease of breath rate following a calming and stimulating (cyclic) type of meditation (Telles, Reddy, & Nagendra, 2000). There is also evidence of changes due to length of practice: long-term mindfulness training, as measured by a history of intensive retreat practice, has been associated with a lower resting respiration rate (Wielgosz, Schuyler, Lutz, & Davidson, 2016). Meditation-related decreases in breathing may not, however, translate into improved exercise performance (Beutler, Beltrami, Boutellier, & Spengler, 2016), although the practitioners' metabolic responses may recover faster from mental stress (arithmetic tasks) than that of non-meditators (Tyagi, Cohen, Reece, & Telles, 2014).

Ability to withstand cold temperatures. Murphy (1992, p. 101) mentions various phenomena such as the *incendium amoris* of the Catholic mystics and the n/um of the

Ju/'hoansi (previously called !Kung; Katz, Biesele, & St. Denis, 1997) that describe experiences of great internal heat. How these experiences might affect physiological responses has received some research attention. With respect to the Tibetan Buddhist *g Tum-mo* practice of generating bodily heat while meditating in very cold environments, Benson and colleagues (1982) reported that three long-term practitioners could raise the temperature of their fingers and toes by more than eight degrees centigrade. A later study with meditator and a non-meditator control groups suggests that the temperature changes may depend on a certain type of controlled breathing and meditative visualization, correlated with EEG alpha power (Kozhevnikov, Elliott, Shephard, & Gramann, 2013).

An Indian swami produced significant differences in skin temperatures between the two sides of his hand in a laboratory setting (Green & Green, 1977), and "S" (Luria, 1968) could increase or decrease hand temperature at will, as could participants trained in hypnosis (Maslach, Marshall, & Zimbardo, 1972). A detailed set of studies was conducted with Wim Hof, who holds world records for enduring cold temperatures, including being immersed in ice for close to two hours. Hof uses conscious hyperventilation and focusing exercises to endure the cold, which may change his heart rate, adrenaline, and blood alkalinity levels. When compared with 112 controls his practice during and after full-body ice immersion resulted in greater cathecolamine/cortisol release, which attenuates the immune response to low temperature (Kox et al., 2012). A group trained in Hof techniques also showed hormonal changes and reduced inflammatory responses when exposed to a bacterial endotoxin (Kox et al., 2014). In sum, the ability to control reactions to cold seems to depend on breathing and higher cognitive processes such as imagination, and has received corroboration from various studies.

Imperviousness to pain. Ascetic religious practices often involve contemplative practices and may also include exposure to painful stimuli, from hooks piercing the skin to self-immolation without expressing much if any pain. Examples are mentioned in the *Lotus Sūtra* and also observed in Christian and Sufi practices (Hall, 2011; Simons, Ervin, & Prince, 1988; Thurston, 1925/2013). The most famous and dramatic case of self-immolation in recent decades was that of the Buddhist monk Thich Quang Duc, who set himself on fire in Vietnam as a political protest. One of the striking aspects of his filmed self-sacrifice was that he did not seem to evidence pain, which should be excruciating at least in the initial stages of being burned alive. There have been many similar cases since (Biggs, 2005). There is also experimental evidence that some meditators may be at least partly impervious to more moderate painful stimuli. Anand, Chhina, and Singh (1961) reported that two yogis could leave their hands in four degrees Celsius water for forty-five to fifty-five minutes without expressing discomfort. In the same study, two other yogis who practiced *samādhi* meditation showed their slow alpha EEG activity turning into faster EEG activity when exposed to various types of photic and other external stimulation *when they were not meditating*, but the same stimuli did not seem to disrupt their alpha activity *when they were meditating*.

Paradoxically, focusing on the pain reaction but treating it as just a sensation may be one way of achieving analgesia. A practitioner of various forms of self-inflicted pain, including hanging himself in the air from hooks in his breasts, explained that the way he dealt with pain was to use it as a focus of single-pointed meditation until he attained a disembodied altered state of consciousness (Cardeña, 1999). More generally, a meta-analysis of mindfulness meditation reported significant but small analgesic effects, and brain imaging has shown consistent changes with those effects (Grant, Courtemanche, & Rainville, 2011; Grant & Rainville, 2009).

Analgesic effects in meditation are probably mediated by individual differences. It is of relevance that those who are responsive to hypnotic suggestions can develop considerable analgesia to experimentally induced pain (e.g., Hilgard & Hilgard, 1975/2013). The hypnotic analgesia effect has had medium to strong effects in both laboratory and clinical samples (Montgomery, DuHamel, & Redd, 2000), but only with those who are at least moderately susceptible (Thompson et al., 2019).

Other. In ascetic traditions, restraint from eating, drinking, and sexual activity are common, but a more extreme claim is that individuals can survive without nutrition for long periods of time (i.e., inedia). Although people die when deprived of food and water for a number of days, there have been reports of meditation practitioners (and other individuals) seemingly able to survive such deprivations without evidencing negative effects (e.g., Rawstorne, 2010), but I did not find scientific studies about this issue. There have also been claims that the bodies of advanced meditators/saints corrupt more slowly or not at all, do not exhibit rigor mortis shortly after dying, and might even emit a pleasant fragrance and/or luminous phenomena, but these reputed effects have not been systematically assessed (e.g., by assessing joint flexibility at predetermined times) and have lacked comparison groups (Murphy, 1992; Thurston, 1952/2013). In 2007, the Thukdam Project was initiated by researcher Richard Davidson to evaluate rates of decay after death of some Tibetan Buddhist practitioners (http://www.phayul.com/news/article.aspx?id=22935&t=1), but I could find no references to papers or presentations about the project in search engines or the researcher's webpage as of the writing of this chapter (March, 2019), nor did his institute respond when I sent an email query.

Other claims found in both the *Yoga Sūtras* and Christian documents include the body becoming taller or smaller and levitating. These reports may reflect the spontaneous *phenomenology* of individuals with the talent to focus on their inner experience, who may experience the body changing in size and floating or flying in meditation (Gifford-May & Thompson, 1994) and hypnosis (Cardeña, 2005). There are however a few cases that question whether in every case these changes refer only to subjective experience. One of them is the seventeenth-century Franciscan friar St. Joseph of Copertino, who was described for years and by hundreds of witnesses, including some originally skeptical ones, as levitating when fully absorbed in prayer or contemplation (Grosso, 2016; Thurston, 1952/2013). In the nineteenth century the psychic D. D. Home was observed levitating in good light by researchers investigating his claims (Beloff, 1977), and he was never unveiled as fraudulent. Nonetheless, ostensible levitation has been reported very few times in the past and there have been no systematic studies closer to our time.

Meditation and Psi Phenomena

Investigation on psi and meditation has included studies with AC and PK psi tasks with (a) individual long-term meditators (e.g., Schmeidler, 1970); (b) groups of long-term meditators alone or in comparison with non-meditators (e.g., Roney-Dougal, 2015); and (c) groups given tests for psi before and after meditation training (e.g., Honorton, 1977).

The first review of more than a dozen controlled studies of receptive and PK psi and meditation was conducted by Charles Honorton (1977) under the umbrella of *internal attention states* (Table 43.1). He reported that nine out of sixteen studies had significant effects, which gave an overall $p = 6 \times 10^{-12}$ against chance, The probability of nine out of sixteen studies being significant at the .05 level gave an exact binomial value of $p = 1.62 \times 10^{-8}$ against chance. To arrive to these figures, Honorton conducted additional analyses in studies without exact probability values, using the "worst case scenario" for reports of nonsignificant results of $p = 0.99$. He concluded that meditation is "an effective means of producing controlled psi interactions" (Honorton, 1977, p. 442). Because in some of the studies there was significant psi missing (i.e., scoring significantly *below* chance) during the premeditation phase, Honorton warned that some of the results could be explained by the motivation and expectation of doing well after meditation, rather than by the meditation practice enhancing psi abilities per se. Interestingly, in one study phenomenological reports of "self-transcendence and openness" related statistically to doing well in the psi task.

In a review of six later AC psi experiments between 1978–1992, Gertrude Schmeidler (1994, pp. 112–113) concluded that four evidenced significant psi performance by meditators and that the two studies with null results were atypical in that one of them used an unusual form of meditation and had mixed/marginal ($p = 0.075$) results, and the other had tested participants who were not motivated to take part in the study (Table 43.1). She concluded that meditation is conducive to psi, but only among those with a positive attitude toward the task. With respect to meditation and PK, William

Table 43.1 Cumulative Analyses of Research on Meditation and Psi

	Type of Psi	Studies	Significance
Honorton, 1977	AC and PK	16	1.62×10^{-8}
Schmeidler, 1994	AC	6	4 significant
Braud, 1990	PK	8	"yes"
Roney-Dougal, 2015	AC and PK	43	27 significant
Schmidt, 2015	Focus facilitation	11	.029

Note: AC = anomalous cognition. PK = psychokinesis.

Braud (1990) wrote a non-quantitative summary of eight studies. The targets for PK influence were different systems including random-event generators and pre-recorded melodic or noise stimuli. He concluded that in studies comparing meditators with non-meditators the former showed consistently higher scoring, with one exception in which meditators significantly disliked the PK task more than non-meditators, and concluded that meditation is PK conducive (Table 43.1).

The most recent review of studies on meditation and AC or PK since the 1990s was carried out by Serena Roney-Dougal (2015). In her summary, she stated that out of forty-three experiments (some of them including multiple studies but analyzed overall), twenty-seven had supportive results in at least one analysis, far more than would be expected by chance, although she did not do a systematic meta-analysis that might have taken into consideration multiple analyses. In twenty-two studies, meditators had been compared with controls or with beginners, and in thirteen of them meditators had significantly better scores than non-meditators, with results exceeding what would be expected by chance (Table 43.1). With respect to PK, a recent set of experiments found that a group of participants engaged in meditation or other mental disciplines had a highly significant but small effect on the output of a quantum double-slit optical system (six experiments reported in Radin et al., 2012, included in Roney-Dougal, 2015; replicated recently by Radin, Michel, & Delorme, 2016).

Another set of studies meta-analyzed by Stefan Schmidt (2015) found significant evidence for attention-focusing facilitation, in which someone at a distance and at random times tries to assist a meditator in maintaining focus (Table 43.1). The distractions during non-assisted times are compared with those during distant assistance, with a research group reporting that the strongest results were obtained with a facilitator with meditation experience (Roney-Dougal, 2015).

Serena Roney-Dougal (2015) also reported on various studies she conducted with collaborators, testing long-term meditators in India, Tibet, and Scotland. In the two studies carried out in India, there was a sizable correlation between yogic attainment, as a proxy measure of long-term practice, and psi scoring ($r = 0.57$, $p = 0.02$), which was in the same direction but not significant in a second study ($r = 0.15$, $p =$ ns). Two studies were also carried out in Tibet and the combined correlation between the psi score and years of meditation was $rho = 0.74$, $p = 0.0005$. In Tibet, those with more than fifteen to twenty years of practice were the most consistent psi scorers, achieving on average a correct guessing of 33 percent (when 25 percent would be expected by chance, or MCE) and some guessed correctly around 50 percent of the times. These results were not replicated, however, in the study in Scotland, which she speculated might be due to cultural differences such as the greater acceptance of psi in India and Tibet. Finally, in a recent experiment in France although participants overall did not score significantly above MCE, the subgroup of experienced meditators had a hit rate of 55% percent (where 50 % was MCE), which was statistically significant, $p = 0.02$ (Varvoglis, Bancel, Ahmed, Boban, & Bailly, 2017).

Mention should also be made of the "Maharishi effect," a purported beneficial field effect on the social, non-immediate environment (e.g., reducing overall criminality in the community) when 1 percent or more of people practice transcendental meditation (for an overview of thirteen published studies see Orme-Johnson, 2003). This line of research has been criticized for not offering a plausible explanation and having been conducted by TM-affiliated researchers, although actual experiments or data re-analyses by the critics are rather sparse. Nonetheless, and consistent with a general notion of a field effect, the Global Consciousness Project, an open data international collaboration, has offered evidence that events with a marked shared emotional impact such as the terrorist attack in 9/11 may significantly alter the variability of RNGs distributed throughout the world (Nelson, 2015).

Overall, cumulative analyses and recent research support a relation between meditation and significant results in controlled psi studies, particularly when the sample consists of motivated, long-term meditators. There are, however, important caveats to consider. First, although Honorton's 1977 meta-analysis was a pioneering study, there have been no recent meta-analyses for subsequent meditation-psi studies. Second, as is true for research on psi in general (and in other areas in psychology, medicine, and other fields), significant effects cannot be replicated on demand. Thus, although more studies than would be expected by chance have had significant results, not all studies have. Ideally, studies should be carried out with strongly motivated, very long-term meditators, but this requirement clashes with the reluctance of some meditators to participate in research, which may be irrelevant to their practice (cf. Goleman & Davidson, 2017), not to mention the issue that putative psi abilities are considered temptations to be avoided by some schools.

Conclusions: Why Might Meditation Be Linked to Exceptional Abilities?

A baseline to consider regarding psychophysiological control is that people in general have some control over their physiology. Anybody can increase or decrease their breathing rate, affect muscle tension, and so on. Furthermore, Miller and collaborators (e.g., Miller, 1969) showed in the 1960s that organisms could achieve control of visceral and glandular responses through instrumental learning. When there is a clear signal that a being can become conscious of, as in biofeedback, exquisite control can be exerted, as evidenced by monkeys who can modulate the activity of single neurons after biofeedback training (Hall, Nazarpour, & Jackson, 2014). Meditators who seem to exhibit great physiological control do not typically have access to biofeedback instrumentation, but they may be able to train themselves to affect their own physiology, whether directly or through other means such as breathing control. Nonetheless, we know very little about how a mental event such as an intention is actualized into a specific physiological response such as warming the body (E. F. Kelly, 2015). The literature reviewed indicates that mediating physiological (such as rapid breathing in *g*

Tum-mo) and higher cognitive processes (such as imagination) may be instrumental in achieving physiological control, and years-long practice in meditation may very well achieve a control that would seem impossible to most people. There is also evidence, mostly from the hypnosis literature, that there are important individual differences in the ability of people to exert psychophysiological control.

With respect to meditation and psi phenomena, it is important to first discuss two general views of psi. One suggests that information not mediated by the senses or reason may affect the person only when it refers to important events, such as unexpected accidents and deaths. This view would need to explain why some ostensible psi phenomena refer to trivial events, such as guessing better than chance when an acquaintance calls (Sheldrake, 2015). The alternative view, and the one favored by current psychological theories of psi (Stanford, 2015), is that psi information is always impinging on the person, who nonetheless is usually unaware of it unless it becomes salient, as in the hunch of the unexpected death of a loved one. This view is compatible with the evidence reviewed in this chapter suggesting that long-term meditators who train themselves to become more aware of their own mental contents generally perform better in psi studies than those without such training. It is also compatible with the view held by some distinguished contemporary physicists about the interconnected, nonlocal, and nontemporal nature of the universe (for a review see Cardeña, 2018), a view shared by some traditions of meditation. There is also research suggesting that a person may react physiologically or behaviorally to an event spatially or temporally distant without being aware of it (Mossbridge, Tressoldi, & Utts, 2012; Palmer, 2015; Radin & Pierce, 2015). Such findings could be accounted for by the idea that psi information is continuously present even though we may not be aware of it.

Adopting the view that psi information is potentially available all the time, an immediate question is why most of us are rarely aware of it, if at all (even people showing such talent in controlled research are far from showing perfect accuracy). An important factor is that in ordinary circumstances there is ongoing competition as to what mental content we will become conscious of among stimuli springing from diverse sources, including sensory information, endogenous stimuli, memory associations, and so on. Generally, the contents of consciousness show that sensory stimuli likely to have survival value are valued over others (Baars, 1997).

So what circumstances make individuals more likely to become conscious of the usually nonconscious psi information? Honorton (1976) proposed these conditions: (a) the influence is detected; (b) it is sufficiently prominent or impactful to distinguish it from competing sources of information; (c) the information is stored and reported; and (d) there is confirmation of a correspondence between the influence and the receiver (i.e., there is feedback of the psi information).

The following procedures or states of consciousness may facilitate these circumstances:

(a) The person is in a naturally occurring state of consciousness, such as REM stage sleep, in which the influence of sensory stimulation is greatly reduced while considerable mental activity remains. In support of this, a meta-analysis of studies revealed evidence that individuals' dreams can be impacted by information spatially or temporally distant (Storm et al., 2017).

(b) The person is awake but exposed to procedures geared to increase physical and psychological relaxation and focus on inner experiences, while reducing competing sensory stimulation, as in hypnosis or artificial homogenization of sensory stimulation (i. e., the technique called ganzfeld, which involves unpatterned colored light and pink or white noise) (Fig. 43.1). Evidence from various meta-analyses show that these procedures can facilitate the presence of psi phenomena compared to the ordinary waking state (Cardeña, Palmer, & Marcusson-Clavertz, 2015; Storm, Tressoldi, & Di Risio, 2010), particularly when the person experiences greater alterations of consciousness (Cardeña, & Marcusson-Clavertz, 2020; Marcusson-Clavertz & Cardeña, 2011).

(c) And/or the psi information may be of such import to the person that it becomes salient enough to reach consciousness.

With respect to meditation, Honorton concluded that it can be seen as a system to reduce external and internal distraction and focus on inner experiences. He also pioneered the ganzfeld method, probably the most consistently successful research paradigm in parapsychology, to reduce mental "noise" while maintaining an active mental set to become receptive to subtle information (Honorton, 1977, p. 438). A supplementary explanation is that alterations of consciousness that elicit a greater sense of interconnectedness may also make a person more likely to believe in and be more receptive to spatially and temporally distant phenomena (Cardeña, 2006; Cardeña & Marcusson-Clavertz, 2015). This hypothesis is consistent with the results of a meta-analysis showing that those who believe in the reality of psi phenomena tend to score significantly higher in psi tasks than those who do not (Zdrenka & Wilson, 2017).

Meditation may enhance receptivity to psi information by the potential ability of meditators to detect subtle mental phenomena and/or maintain focus on them, although the evidence for meditation practice enhancing attention capacities is not completely consistent (e.g., Lao, Kissane, & Meadows, 2016), probably because meditation practices emphasize different techniques and goals. In addition, alterations of consciousness occurring during prolonged/intense meditation may enhance a sense of interconnectedness and atemporality. With respect to PK, Braud (1990, p. 9) speculated that the following predict success in an experiment: (a) generating and maintaining unswerving attention to the target; (b) producing and maintaining a mental representation of the desired goal; (c) attending to potential feedback related to the target; and (d) being unperturbed by distractions. To them we could add that a sense of interconnectedness may also enhance the belief of a participants that they are part of a system including the PK target.

Across studies, there is cumulative evidence that meditators score better than chance in psi research and perform better than non-meditators, and there is also some evidence that experiencing a different state of consciousness than the ordinary one is conducive to performing well in a psi experiment. Unfortunately, very few meditation-psi studies

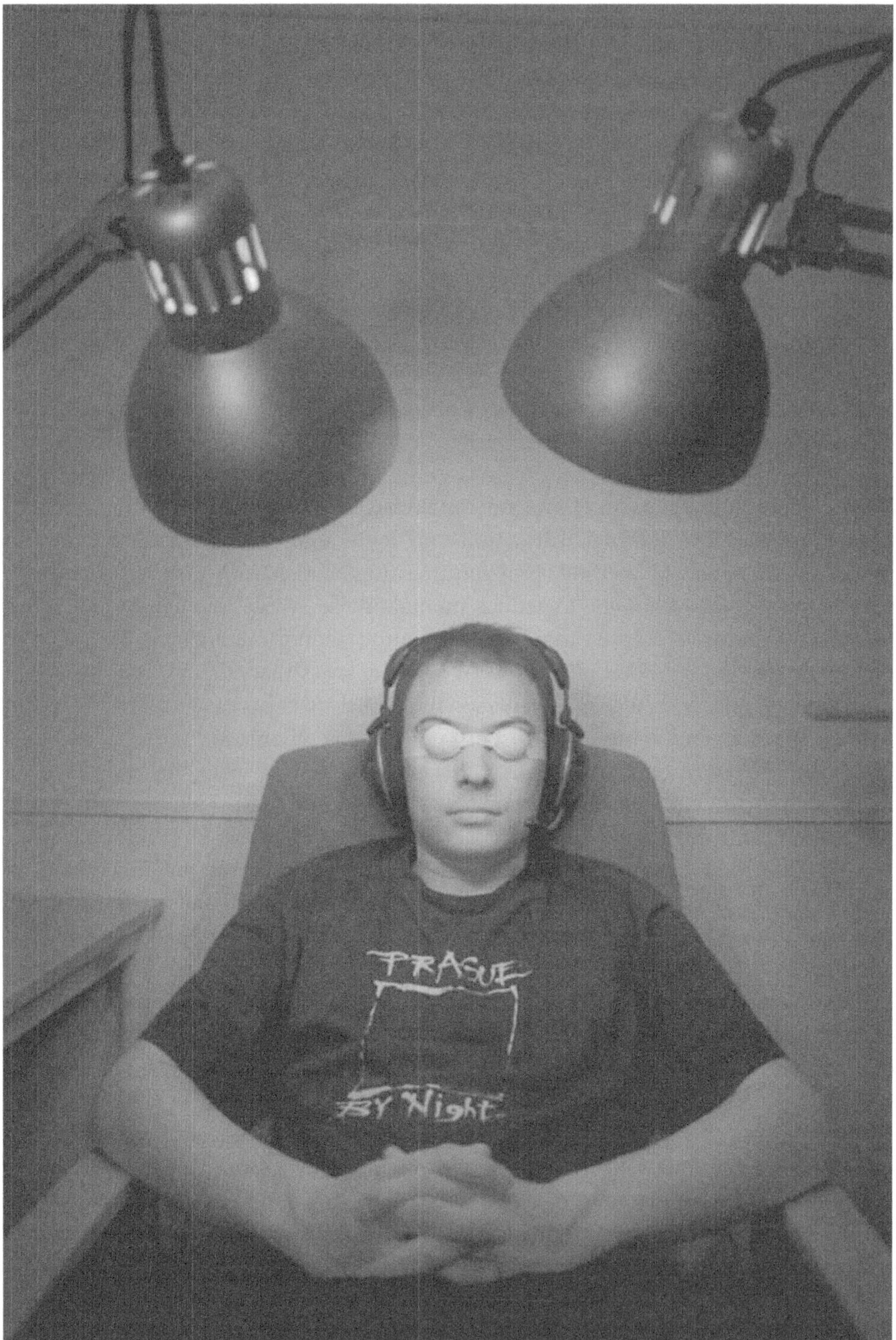

FIGURE 43.1 Researcher in a Ganzfeld Set-up

have evaluated the state of consciousness of the meditators during the experiment (an exception is Palmer, Khamashta, & Israelson, 1979). Without this information, it is impossible to evaluate whether practitioners exhibit significant results because of experiencing an altered state, the ability to maintain focus, the motivation to perform well in the experiment, the belief that they will be successful in the experiment, or an interaction among them. Future research on the area should emphasize *process research*, in which the focus is not to test whether a psi effect occurs, but which variables relate to it. It is also important to evaluate the characteristics of the researcher(s), as there is evidence that the attitude of those conducting experiments may be crucial to the results. For instance, in a joint effort by a psi-supporter and a psi-skeptic, the first had significant supportive results in two out of three studies that she conducted, while the latter did not have significant results in any of the three studies he ran, both using the same procedures (e.g., Schlitz, Wiseman, Watt, & Radin, 2006).

In sum, although there is no scientific evidence for some of the exceptional abilities depicted in traditional texts, such as invisibility or lack of body corruption after death, there is supportive evidence that meditation relates to the manifestation of exceptional psychophysiological control and receptive and expressive forms of psi. The evidence, however, should not be overstated. In the case of psychophysiological control and enhanced sensory sensitivity, there are few studies and some of them have had methodological limitations. In the case of psi and meditation, the various reviews conducted have found an overall significant effect, sometimes with summarizing statistics, but no systematic meta-analysis has been conducted recently. And, as with other areas in psi research (as with other areas in psychology, medicine, and other sciences), studies do not always replicate the overall findings. This lack of "replication on demand" has been used to challenge reported findings, but a counter-argument is that in complex phenomena with small statistical effects (as those in some areas in biology, medicine, and psychology), many variables interact among themselves and with random events, making the kind of replication and prediction seen in the physical sciences unattainable (Barrett, 2015; Lewontin, 1994; Rosenthal, 1990).

There has been scant research on the cognitive and physiological processes that might make meditation psi-conducive (Roney-Dougal, 2015, p. 132), not to mention that different types of meditation have been analyzed jointly even though they may differ substantially (cf. Goleman & Davidson, 2017). A program of research should, if possible, evaluate the characteristics of (one or a few) very long-term meditators who are reliably successful in psi studies with respect to experimental conditions, cognitive strategies, and brain dynamics, using neurophenomenological and other mixed methods that give their due to experiential, cognitive, and biological processes (Cardeña & Pekala, 2014; Cardeña, Jönsson, Terhune, & Marcusson-Clavertz, 2013). The following stage could include manipulating relevant variables deconstructed from this type of research with more general samples, for instance by using preparatory cognitive strategies and EEG biofeedback with motivated participants who may not necessarily be long-term meditators. This plan of research will not be easy to accomplish considering the scarcity of funding and the reluctance of some long-term meditation practitioners to become research participants, but it is a goal worth meditating on.

References

Anand, B. K., Chhina, G. S., & Singh, B. (1961). Some aspects of electroencephalographic studies in yogis. *Electroencephalography and Clinical Neurophysiology, 13*, 452–456.

Baars, B. (1997). *In the theatre of consciousness*. Oxford, UK: Oxford University Press.

Barber, T. X. (1984). Changing "unchangeable" bodily processes by (hypnotic) suggestions: A new look at hypnosis, cognitions, imaging, and the mind-body problem. In A. A. Sheikh (Ed.), *Imagery and healing*. Farmingdale, NY: Baywood.

Barrett, L. F. (2015, September 1). *Psychology is not in crisis*. Retrievable from https://www.nytimes.com/2015/09/01/opinion/psychology-is-not-in-crisis.html?_r=0

Beloff. J. (1977). Historical overview. In B. B. Wolman (Ed.), *Handbook of parapsychology* (pp. 3–24). Jefferson, NC: McFarland.

Benson, H., Lehmann, J. W., Malhotra, M. S., Goldman, R. F., Hopkins, J., & Epstein, M. D. (1982). Body temperature changes during the practice of g Tum-mo yoga. *Nature, 295*, 234–236.

Beutler, E., Beltrami, F. G., Boutellier, U., & Spengler, C. M. (2016). Effect of regular yoga practice on respiratory regulation and exercise performance. *PLoS ONE, 11*(4), e0153159. doi:10.1371/journal.pone.0153159

Biggs, M. (2005). Dying without killing? Self-immolations, 1963–2002. In D. Gambetta (Ed.), *Making sense of suicidal missions* (pp. 173–208). Oxford, UK; Oxford University Press.

Braud, W. G. (1990). Meditation and psychokinesis. *Parapsychology Review, 21*, 9–11.

Braude, S. (2015). Macro-psychokinesis. In E. Cardeña, J. Palmer, & D. Marcusson-Clavertz (Eds.), *Parapsychology: A handbook for the 21st century* (pp. 258–265). Jefferson, NC: McFarland.

Brown, D., Forte, M., & Dysart, M. (1984). Visual sensitivity and mindfulness meditation. *Perceptual and Motor Skills, 58*, 775–784.

Cardeña, E. (1999). "You are not your body." Commentary on the motivation for self-injury in psychiatric patients. *Psychiatry, 62*, 331–333.

Cardeña, E. (2005). The phenomenology of deep hypnosis: Quiescent and physically active. *International Journal of Clinical & Experimental Hypnosis, 53*, 37–59.

Cardeña, E. (2006). T. X. Barber's typology implications for parapsychology. *Proceedings of the 49th Annual Convention of the Parapsychological Association*, 370.

Cardeña, E. (2015). *Eminent people interested in psi*. Retrievable from: https://psi-encyclopedia.spr.ac.uk/articles/eminent-people-interested-psi

Cardeña, E. (2016). Towards a comprehensive neurophenomenological research in hypnosis and meditation. In A. Raz & M. Lifshitz (Eds.), *Hypnosis and meditation: Towards an integrative science of conscious planes* (pp. 281–301). Oxford, UK: Oxford University Press.

Cardeña, E. (2018). The experimental evidence for parapsychological phenomena: A review. *American Psychologist, 73*, 663–677. doi:10.1037/amp0000236

Cardeña, E. (2020). Derangement of the senses or alternate epistemological pathways? Altered consciousness and enhanced functioning. *Psychology of Consciousness: Theory, Research, and Practice*, 7(2), 242–261. dx.doi.org/10.1037/cns0000175

Cardeña, E., Jönsson, P., Terhune, D. B., & Marcusson-Clavertz, D. (2013). The neurophenomenology of neutral hypnosis. *Cortex 49*, 375–385. doi:10.1016/j.cortex.2012.04.001

Cardeña, E., & Krippner, S. (2018). Some needed psychological clarifications on the experience(s) of shamanism. *Behavioral and Brain Sciences 41*. doi:10.1017/S0140525X17002035

Cardeña, E., & Marcusson-Clavertz, D. (2015). States, traits, beliefs, and psi. In E. Cardeña, J. Palmer, & D. Marcusson-Clavertz (Eds.), *Parapsychology: A handbook for the 21st century* (pp. 110–124). Jefferson, NC: McFarland.

Cardeña, E., & Marcusson-Clavertz, D. (2020). Changes in state of consciousness and psi in ganzfeld and hypnosis conditions. *Journal of Parapsychology, 84*, 66–84. doi:10.30891/jopar2020.01.07.

Cardeña, E., Palmer, J., & Marcusson-Clavertz, D. (2015). *Parapsychology: A handbook for the 21st century*. Jefferson, NC: McFarland.

Cardeña, E., & Pekala, R. J. (2014). Methodological issues in the study of altering consciousness and anomalous experience. In E. Cardeña, S. J., Lynn, & S. Krippner (Eds.), *Varieties of anomalous experience: Examining the scientific evidence* (2nd ed., pp. 21–56). Washington, DC: American Psychological Association.

Carpenter, J. (2015). Many thanks. *Mindfield, 7*, 52–58.

Casiglia, E., Mazza, A., Ginocchio, C., Onesto, C., Pessina, A. C., Rossi, A., . . . Marotti, A. (1997). Hemodynamics following real and hypnosis-simulated phlebotomy. *American Journal of Clinical Hypnosis, 40*, 368–375.

Cicero. *De divinatione*, 1.54 http://www.perseus.tufts.edu/hopper/text?doc=Perseus%3Atext%3A2007.01.0043%3Abook%3D1%3Asection%3D123

Craig Heller, H., Elsner, R., & Rao, N. (1987). Voluntary hypometabolism in an Indian yogi. *Journal of Thermal Biology, 12*, 171–173.

Dahl, C. J., Lutz, A., & Davidson, R. J. (2015). Reconstructing and deconstructing the self: Cognitive mechanisms in meditation practice. *Trends in Cognitive Science, 19*, 515–523.

de la Garza, M. (2012). *Sueño y éxtasis. Visión chamánica de los nahuas y los mayas* (Dream and ecstasy: Shamanic vision among the nahuas and mayas). México, DF México: Universidad Nacional Autónoma de México/Fondo de Cultura Económica.

Fischer, D., Messner, M., & Pollatos, O. (2017, September 12). Improvement of interoceptive processes after an 8-week body scan intervention. *Frontiers in Human Neuroscience*, doi:10.3389/fnhum.2017.00452

Fisher, J., & Kollar, E. (1980). Investigation of a stigmatic. *Southern Medical Journal, 73*, 1461–1466.

Gifford-May, D., & Thompson, N. L. (1994). "Deep states" of meditation: Phenomenological reports of experience. *Journal of Transpersonal Psychology, 26*, 117–138.

Goleman, G., & Davidson, R. (2017). *Altered traits: Science reveals how meditation changes your mind, brain, and body*. New York, NY: Avery.

Grant, J. A., Courtemanche, J., & Rainville, P. (2011). A non-elaborative mental stance and decoupling of executive and pain-related cortices predicts low pain sensitivity in Zen meditators. *Pain, 152*, 150–156. doi:10.1016/j.pain.2010.10.006

Grant, J. A., & Rainville, P. (2009). Pain sensitivity and analgesic effects of mindful states in Zen meditators: A cross-sectional study. *Psychosomatic Medicine 71*, 106–114. doi:10.1097/PSY.0b013e31818f52ee

Green, E., & Green, A. (1977). *Beyond biofeedback*. Ft. Wayne, IN: Knoll.

Grosso, M. (2016). *The man who could fly: St. Joseph of Copertino and the mystery of levitation*. Lanham, MD: Rowman & Littlefield.

Gruber, J. (2017). Becoming Vilamitra: Manufacturing the supernatural in Tibetan Buddhism. In J. J. Kripal (Ed.), *Religion: Super religion* (pp. 139–153). Farmington Hills, MI: Macmillan.

Hall, H. (2011). Sufism and healing. In H. Walach & W. G. Jonas (Eds.), *Neuroscience, consciousness and spirituality* (pp. 263–278). New York, NY: Springer. doi:10.1007/978-94-007-2079-4_16

Hall, T. M., Nazarpour, K., & Jackson, A. (2014). Real-time estimation and biofeedback of single-neuron firing rates using local field potentials. *Nature Communications* 5, 5462, doi:10.1038/ncomms6462

Hilgard, E. R., & Hilgard, J. R. (2013). *Hypnosis in the relief of pain* (Rev. ed.). New York, NY: Brunner-Routledge. (Original work published 1975).

Honorton, C. (1976). Has science developed the competence to confront the claims of the paranormal? Presidential Address, Parapsychological Association. In J. D. Morris, W. G. Roll, & R. L. Morris (Eds.), *Research in parapsychology, 1975* (pp. 199–223). Metuchen, NJ: Scarecrow.

Honorton, C. (1977). Psi and attentional internal states. In B. B. Wolman (Ed.), *Handbook of parapsychology* (pp. 435–472). Jefferson, NC: McFarland.

Jacobsen, K. A. (2017). Extraordinary capacities in the religions of South Asia: Yoga power and cosmology. In J. J. Kripal (Ed.), *Religion: Super religion* (pp. 125–138). Farmington Hills, MI: Macmillan.

Katz, R., Biesele, M. St., & Denis, V. (1997). *Healing makes our hearts happy: Spirituality & cultural transformation among the Kalahari Ju/'hoansi*. Rochester, VT: Inner Traditions.

Kelly, E. F. (2015). Parapsychology in context: The big picture. In E. Cardeña, J. Palmer, & D. Marcusson-Clavertz (Eds.), *Parapsychology: A handbook for the 21st century* (pp. 30–41). Jefferson, NC: McFarland.

Kelly, E. W. (2007). Psychophysiological influence. In E. F. Kelly, E. W. Kelly, A. Crabtree, A. Gauld, M. Grosso, & B. Greyson (Eds.), *Irreducible mind: Toward a psychology for the 21st century* (pp. 117–239). Lanham, MD: Rowan & Littlefield.

Khalsa, S. S., Rudrauf, D., Damasio, A. R., Davidson, R. J., Lutz, A., & Tranel, D. (2008). Interoceptive awareness in experienced meditators. *Psychophysiology, 45*, 671–677.

Kok, B. E., & Singer, T. (2017). Phenomenological fingerprints of four meditations: Differential state changes in affect, mind-wandering, meta-cognition, and interoception before and after daily practice across 9 months of training. *Mindfulness, 8*, 218–231.

Kothari, L. K., Bordia, A., & Gupta, O. P. (1973). Studies on a yogi during an eight-day confinement in a sealed underground pit. *Indian Journal of Medical Research 61*, 1645–1650.

Kox, M., Stoffels, M., Smeekens, S. P., Alfen, N. v., Gomes, M., Eusvogels, T. M. H., . . . Pickkers, P. (2012). The influence of concentration/meditation on autonomic nervous system activity and the innate immune response: A case study. *Psychosomatic Medicine 74*, 489–494. 10.1073/pnas.1322174111

Kox, M., van Eijk, L. T. v., Zwaag, J. van den Wildenberg, J. v. d., Sweep, F., van der Hoeven, J. G., & Pickkers, P. (2014). Voluntary activation of the sympathetic nervous system and attenuation of the innate immune response in humans. *Proceedings of the National Academy of Sciences, 111*, 7379-7384. doi:10.1073/pnas.1322174111

Kozhevnikov, M., Elliott, J., Shephard, J., & Gramann, K. (2013). Neurocognitive and somatic components of temperature increases during g-Tummo meditation: Legend and reality. *PLoSONE 8*, e58244. doi:10.1371/journal.pone.0058244

Kripal, J. J. (2017). Introduction: Reimagining the super in the study of religion. In J. J. Kripal (Ed.), *Religion: Super religion* (pp. xv–xlviii). Farmington Hills, MI: Macmillan.

Lao, S-A, Kissane, D., & Meadows, G. (2016). Cognitive effects of MBSR/MBCT: A systematic review of neuropsychological outcomes. *Consciousness and Cognition, 45*, 109–123.

Lewis, I. M. (1989). *Ecstatic religion: A study of shamanism and spirit possession*. London, UK: Routledge.

Lewontin, R. (1994). A rejoinder to William Wimsatt. In J. Chandler, A. I. Davidson, & H. D. Harootunian (Eds.), *Questions of evidence: Proof, practice, and persuasion across the disciplines* (pp. 504–509). Chicago, IL: University of Chicago Press.

Luria, A. R. (1968). *The mind of a mnemonist*. New York, NY: Basic Books.

MacLean, K. A., Ferrer, E., Aichele, S. R., Bridwell, D. A., Zanesco, A. P., Jacobs, T. L., . . . Saron, C. D. (2010). Intensive meditation training improves perceptual discrimination and sustained attention. *Psychological Science, 2*, 829–839.

Maglie, R., & Caproni, M. (2017). A case of blood sweating: Hematohidrosis syndrome. *CMAJ 189*, E1314. doi:10.1503/cmaj.161298

Marcusson-Clavertz, D., & Cardeña, E. (2011). Hypnotizability, alterations in consciousness, and other variables as predictors of performance in a ganzfeld psi task. *Journal of Parapsychology, 75*, 235–259.

Margnelli, M. (1999). An unusual case of stigmatization. *Journal of Scientific Exploration, 13*, 461–482.

Marks, L. E. (2014). Synesthesia: A teeming multiplicity. In E. Cardeña, S. J. Lynn, & S. Krippner (Eds.), *Varieties of anomalous experience: Examining the scientific evidence* (2nd ed., pp. 79–108). Washington, DC: American Psychological Association. doi:10.1037/14258-004

Marwaha, S. B. (2016). Siddhis and psi research: An interdisciplinary analysis. *Confluence. Online Journal of World Philosophies, 4*, 33–58. https://nirc.nanzan-u.ac.jp/en/files/2017/01/Philosophy-on-a-Bridge-2016.pdf

Maslach, C., Marshall, G., & Zimbardo, P. G. (1972). Hypnotic control of peripheral skin temperature: A case report. *Psychophysiology, 9*, 600–605. doi:10.1111/j.1469–8986.1972.tb00769.x

May, E. C., & Marwaha, S. B. (2015). *Extra sensory perception. Support, skepticism, and science*. (2 vols.). Santa Barbara, CA: Praeger.

Melloni, M., Sedeño, L., Couto, B., Reynoso, M., Gelormini, C., Favaloro, R., . . . Ibanez, A. (2013). Preliminary evidence about the effects of meditation on interoceptive sensitivity and social cognition. *Behavioral and Brain Functions, 9*(47). doi:10.1186/1744-9081-9-47

Miller, N. E. (1969). Learning of visceral and glandular responses. *Science, 163*, 434–445.

Montgomery, G. H., DuHamel, K. N., & Redd, W. H. (2000). A meta-analysis of hypnotically induced analgesia: How effective is hypnosis. *International Journal of Clinical and Experimental Hypnosis, 48*,138–153.

Mossbridge, J., Tressoldi, P., & Utts, J. (2012). Predictive physiological anticipation preceding seemingly unpredictable stimuli: A meta-analysis. *Frontiers in Psychology, 3*, 390. doi:10.3389/fpsyg.2012.00390

Murphy, M. (1992). *The future of the body: Explorations into the further evolution of human nature*. Los Angeles, CA: Tarcher.

Murphy, M., Donovan, S., & Taylor, E. (1997). *The physical and psychological effects of meditation: A review of contemporary research with a comprehensive bibliography*. San Francisco, CA: Institute of Noetic Sciences.

Naranjo, C., & Ornstein, R. E. (1971). *On the psychology of meditation*. New York, NY: Viking.

Nelson, R. D. (2015). Implicit physical psi: The global consciousness project. In E. Cardeña, J. Palmer, & D. Marcusson-Clavertz (Eds.), *Parapsychology: A handbook for the 21st century* (pp. 282–292). Jefferson, NC: McFarland.

Orme-Johnson, D. W. (2003). Preventing crime through the Maharishi effect. *Journal of Offender Rehabilitation, 36*, 257–282.
Palmer, J. (2015). Implicit anomalous cognition. In E. Cardeña, J. Palmer, & D. Marcusson-Clavertz (Eds.), *Parapsychology: A handbook for the 21st century* (pp. 215–229). Jefferson, NC: McFarland.
Palmer, J., Khamashta, K. K., & Israelson, K. (1979). An ESP ganzfeld experiment with transcendental meditators. *Journal of the American Society for Psychical Research, 73*, 333–348.
Radin, D. (2013). *Supernormal: Science, yoga, and the evidence for extraordinary psychic abilities.* New York, NY: Deepak Chopra Books.
Radin, D., Michel, K., Galdamez, K., Wendland, P., Rickenbach, R., & Delorme, A. (2012). Consciousness and the double-slit interference pattern: Six experiments. *Physics Essays, 5*, 157–171.
Radin, D., Michel, L., & Delorme, A. (2016). Psychophysical modulation of fringe visibility in a distant double-slit optical system. *Physics Essays, 29*, 14–22.
Radin, D., & Pierce, A. (2015). Psi and psychophysiology. E. Cardeña, J. Palmer, & D. Marcusson-Clavertz (Eds.), *Parapsychology: A handbook for the 21st century* (pp. 230–243). Jefferson, NC: McFarland.
Raghavendra, B., Telles, S., Manjunath, N., Deepak, K., Naveen, K., & Subramanya, P. (2013). Voluntary heart rate reduction following yoga using different strategies. *International Journal of Yoga, 6*, 26–30.
Rao, K. R. (2017). *Foundations of Yoga psychology*. Singapore: Springer.
Rawstorne, T. (2010). The man who says he hasn't eaten or drunk for 70 years: Why are eminent doctors taking him seriously? *The Mail.* Retrieved from http://www.dailymail.co.uk/news/article-1274779/The-man-says-eaten-drunk-70-years-Why-eminent-doctors-taking-seriously.html
Roney-Dougal, S. M. (2015). Ariadne's thread: Meditation and psi. In E. Cardeña, J. Palmer, & D. Marcusson-Clavertz (Eds.), *Parapsychology: A handbook for the 21st century* (pp. 125–138). Jefferson, NC: McFarland.
Rosenthal, R. (1990). Replication in behavioral research. *Journal of Social Behavior and Personality*, 5, 1-30.
Rouget, G. (1985). *Music and trance: A theory of the relations between music and possession.* Chicago, IL: University of Chicago Press.
Schlitz, M., Wiseman, R., Watt, C., & Radin, D. (2006). Of two minds: Skeptic-proponent collaboration within parapsychology. *British Journal of Psychology, 97*, 313–322.
Schmeidler (1970). High ESP scores after a swami's brief instruction in meditation and breathing. *Journal of the American Society for Psychical Research, 64*, 100–103.
Schmeidler, G. (1994). ESP experiments 1978–1992. In S. Krippner (Ed.), *Advances in parapsychological research, Vol. 7* (pp. 104–197). Jefferson, NC: McFarland.
Schmidt, S. (2015). Experimental research on distant intention phenomena. In E. Cardeña, J. Palmer, & D. Marcusson-Clavertz (Eds.), *Parapsychology: A handbook for the 21st century* (pp. 244–257). Jefferson, NC: McFarland.
Sexton, R., & Buljo Stabbursvik, E. A. (2010). Healing in the Sámi North. *Culture, Medicine, and Psychiatry, 34*, 571–589.
Sheldrake, R. (2015). Psi in everyday life: Nonhuman and human. In E. Cardeña, J. Palmer, & D. Marcusson-Clavertz (Eds.), *Parapsychology: A handbook for the 21st century* (pp. 350–363). Jefferson, NC: McFarland.

Simons, E. R., Ervin, F. R., & Prince, R. H. (1988). The psychobiology of trance, I: Training for Thaipusam. *Transcultural Psychiatry, 25*, 249–266. doi:10.1177/136346158802500401

Stanford, R. G. (2015). Psychological concepts of psi function: A review and constructive critique. In E. Cardeña, J. Palmer, & D. Marcusson-Clavertz (Eds.), *Parapsychology: A handbook for the 21st century* (pp. 94–109). Jefferson, NC: McFarland.

Storm, L., Sherwood, S. J., Roe, C. A., Tressoldi, P. E., Rock, A. J., & Di Risio, L. (2017). On the correspondence between dream content and target material under laboratory conditions: A meta-analysis of dream-ESP studies, 1966–2016. *International Journal of Dream Research: Psychological Aspects of Sleep and Dreaming, 10*, 120–140.

Storm, L., Tressoldi, P. E., & Di Risio (2010). Meta-analysis of free-response studies, 1992–2008: Assessing the noise reduction model in parapsychology. *Psychological Bulletin, 136*, 471–485.

Telles, S., Reddy, S. K., & Nagendra, H. R. (2000). Oxygen consumption and respiration following two yoga relaxation techniques. *Applied Psychophysiology and Biofeedback, 25*, 221–227.

Thompson, T., Terhune, D. B., Oram, C., Sharangsparni, J., Rouf, R., Solmi, M., . . . Stubbs, B. (2019). The effectiveness of hypnosis for pain relief: A systematic review and meta-analysis of 85 controlled experimental trials. *Neuroscience and biobehavioral reviews, 99*, 298–310.

Thurston, H. (2013). *The physical phenomena of mysticism*. Hove, UK: White Crow Books. (Original work published 1952).

Tyagi, A., & Cohen, M. (2016). Yoga and heart rate variability: A comprehensive review of the literature. *International Journal of Yoga, 9*, 97–113.

Tyagi, A., Cohen, M., Reece, J., & Telles, S. (2014). An exploratory study of metabolic responses to mental stress and yoga practices in yoga practitioners, non-yoga practitioners and individuals with metabolic syndrome. *BMC Complementary and Alternative Medicine 14*, doi:10.1186/1472-6882-14-445

Ustinova, Y. (2018). *Divine mania. Alterations of consciousness in ancient Greece*. New York, NY: Routledge.

Varvoglis, M., Bancel, P., Ahmed, D. si, Boban, J., & Bailly, J-P (2017). The Selfield: A precognition study using an immersive display system [Abstract]. *Journal of Parapsychology, 81*, 120–121.

Vieten, C., Wahbeh, H., Cahn, B. R., MacLean, K., Estrada, M., Mills, P., . . . Delorme, A. (2018). Future directions in meditation research: Recommendation for expanding the field of contemplative science. *PLoS ONE 13*(11), e0205740. doi:10.1371/journal.pone.0205740

Wenger, M. A., Bagchi, B. K., & Anand, B. K. (1961). Experiments in India on "voluntary" control of the heart and pulse. *Circulation, 24*, 1319–1325.

White, R. (1981). Saintly psi. *Journal of Religion and Psychical Research 98*, 156–167.

Wielgosz, J., Schuyler, B. S., Lutz, A., & Davidson, R. (2016). Long-term mindfulness training is associated with reliable differences in resting respiration rate. *Scientific Reports, 6*, doi:10.1038/srep27533

Young, S. (2006). *Break through pain*. Louisville, CO: Sounds true.

Zdrenka, M., & Wilson, M. S. (2017). Individual difference correlates of psi performance in forced-choice precognition experiments (1945–2016). *Journal of Parapsychology, 81*, 9–32.

Index

For the benefit of digital users, indexed terms that span two pages (e.g., 52–53) may, on occasion, appear on only one of those pages.

B

C

I

K

L

O

S

T

W

The manufacturer's authorised representative in the EU for product safety is Oxford University Press España S.A. of El Parque Empresarial San Fernando de Henares, Avenida de Castilla, 2 - 28830 Madrid (www.oup.es/en or product.safety@oup.com). OUP España S.A. also acts as importer into Spain of products made by the manufacturer.
Printed and bound by CPI Group (UK) Ltd, Croydon, CR0 4YY
22/09/2025
01960245-0013